MCAD/MCSD

Developing and Implementing Windows-Based Applications with Microsoft Visual Basic® .NET and Microsoft Visual Studio® .NET

Exam 70-306

Mike Gunderloy

Training Guide

MCAD/MCSD TRAINING GUIDE EXAM (70-306): DEVELOPING AND IMPLEMENTING WINDOWS-BASED APPLICATIONS WITH MICROSOFT VISUAL BASIC® .NET AND MICROSOFT VISUAL STUDIO® .NET

International Standard Book Number: 0-7897-2819-2

Library of Congress Catalog Card Number: 2002110897

Printed in the United States of America

First Printing: December 2002

05   04   03   02   4   3   2   1

Trademarks

All terms mentioned in this book that are known to be trademarks or service marks have been appropriately capitalized. Que Publishing cannot attest to the accuracy of this information. Use of a term in this book should not be regarded as affecting the validity of any trademark or service mark.

Microsoft is a registered trademark of Microsoft Corporation.

Visual Basic is a registered trademark of Microsoft Corporation.

Visual Studio is a registered trademark of Microsoft Corporation.

Warning and Disclaimer

Every effort has been made to make this book as complete and as accurate as possible, but no warranty or fitness is implied. The information provided is on an "as is" basis. The author and the publisher shall have neither liability nor responsibility to any person or entity with respect to any loss or damages arising from the information contained in this book or from the use of the CD or programs accompanying it.

EXECUTIVE EDITOR
Jeff Riley

DEVELOPMENT EDITOR
Steve Rowe

MANAGING EDITOR
Thomas F. Hayes

PROJECT EDITOR
Tonya Simpson

COPY EDITORS
Jennifer Lewis
Kitty Jarrett

INDEXER
Kelly Castell

PROOFREADER
Linda Seifert

TECHNICAL EDITORS
Kourosh Ardestani
Emmett Dulaney

TEAM COORDINATORS
Rosemary Lewis
Kimberly Herbert

MULTIMEDIA DEVELOPER
Michael Hunter

INTERIOR DESIGNER
Louisa Klucznik

COVER DESIGNER
Charis Ann Santillie

PAGE LAYOUT
Cheryl Lynch

Que Certification • 201 West 103rd Street • Indianapolis, Indiana 46290

A Note from Series Editor Ed Tittel

Congratulations on your purchase of the 70-306 Training Guide, the finest exam preparation book in the marketplace!

As Series Editor of the highly regarded Training Guide series, I can assure you that you won't be disappointed. You've taken your first step toward passing the 70-306 exam, and we value this opportunity to help you on your way!

As a "Favorite Study Guide Author" finalist in a 2002 poll of CertCities readers, I know the importance of delivering good books. You'll be impressed with Que Certification's stringent review process, which ensures the books are high-quality, relevant, and technically accurate. Rest assured that at least a dozen industry experts—including the panel of certification experts at CramSession—have reviewed this material, helping us deliver an excellent solution to your exam preparation needs.

Favorite Study Guide Author

We've also added a preview edition of PrepLogic's powerful, full-featured test engine, which is trusted by certification students throughout the world.

As a 20-year-plus veteran of the computing industry and the original creator and editor of the Exam Cram series, I've brought my IT experience to bear on these books. During my tenure at Novell from 1989 to 1994, I worked with and around its excellent education and certification department. At Novell, I witnessed the growth and development of the first really big, successful IT certification program—one that was to shape the industry forever afterward. This experience helped push my writing and teaching activities heavily in the certification direction. Since then, I've worked on more than 70 certification related books, and I write about certification topics for numerous Web sites and for *Certification* magazine.

In 1997 when Exam Cram was introduced, it quickly became the best-selling computer book series since "...*For Dummies*," and the best-selling certification book series ever. By maintaining an intense focus on the subject matter, tracking errata and updates quickly, and following the certification market closely, Exam Cram was able to establish the dominant position in cert prep books.

You will not be disappointed in your decision to purchase this book. If you are, please contact me at etittel@jump.net. All suggestions, ideas, input, or constructive criticism are welcome!

Ed Tittel

Contents at a Glance

PART III Appendixes

Table of Contents

PART I: Exam Preparation

11 Printing   691

Part II: Final Review

PART III: Appendixes

About the Author

Mike Gunderloy pursued his first Microsoft certification the year the program was introduced, and he has earned the MCP, MCT, MCSE, MCDBA, and MCSD credentials in the decade since. As lead developer for Lark Group, Inc., Mike has worked with small businesses and Fortune 500 corporations, and he has trained many other developers in the use of Microsoft products. He got hooked on computers when you still had to build your own out of parts, and he is still passionately interested in cutting-edge software technology. As a long-time member of the editorial staff of *MCP Magazine*, Mike has remained in close touch with the certification community.

Mike lives on a farm in eastern Washington state, along with his wife and children and an ever-changing array of horses, sheep, llamas, geese, turkeys, chickens, ducks, peacocks, cats, dogs, and guinea fowl. When he's not busy testing and writing about software, Mike can usually be found in his garden or greenhouse, trying to persuade recalcitrant vegetables to grow.

You can reach Mike at MikeG1@larkfarm.com or www.larkware.com.

Dedication

This one's for Kayla.

Acknowledgments

It's never possible to thank everyone who contributed to a book in some way, but it's always fun to try. I'd like to start with Robert Shimonski, who first put me in touch with Que when this project was still being hatched. From there, it's been a treat to work with the editorial staff at Que, including Jeff Riley, Steve Rowe, and Tonya Simpson, who helped turn a mass of manuscript into a book. Technical editors Emmett Dulaney and Kourosh Ardestani deserve special mention for wading through this entire book and pointing out the things that I missed.

Of course, no book ever happens without a production staff. I'm happy that Jennifer Lewis, Kitty Jarrett, Kelly Castell, Linda Seifert, and Cheryl Lynch were working behind the scenes to take the final manuscript and put it between covers and on the shelf.

I've benefited over the years from many people in the wider development community. The editorial staff at *MCP Magazine*, including Dian Schaffhauser, Keith Ward, Michael Domingo, Becky Nagel, and Kris McCarthy, have helped me stay in touch with certification issues, and they were very understanding when I trimmed my magazine duties to be able to tackle this project. Many people helped me develop some of my

.NET skills; of these, Ken Getz, Mary Chipman, and Steve White deserve special mention. Let's tackle some development projects together again in the future, folks!

Although his name isn't on the cover, in many ways Amit Kalani is a co-author of the book you're holding now. Amit wrote the C# version of this book, and generously shared chapter drafts with me as both projects moved forward. This book benefited immensely from his insights into .NET. An added bonus for me was the chance to see step-by-step how C# handles some of the same topics tackled in this book.

Finally, and as always, I'd like to thank my family for supporting me through another book. My wonderful wife Dana was always patient and understanding when I got up early or stayed up late to poke the Visual Basic .NET compiler for just a few minutes longer. And of course, it's her encouragement that keeps me going, even when the deadlines are stacked higher than my head. Adam was always around when I needed a time-out to play, often when I didn't even know it. And thanks to Kayla, who gestated at the same time as this book, for the constant reminder that there's more to life than coding!

We Want to Hear from You!

As the reader of this book, *you* are our most important critic and commentator. We value your opinion and want to know what we're doing right, what we could do better, what areas you'd like to see us publish in, and any other words of wisdom you're willing to pass our way.

As a publisher for Que, I welcome your comments. You can email or write me directly to let me know what you did or didn't like about this book—as well as what we can do to make our books better.

Please note that I cannot help you with technical problems related to the *topic* of this book. We do have a User Services group, however, where I will forward specific technical questions related to the book.

When you write, please be sure to include this book's title and author as well as your name, email address, and phone number. I will carefully review your comments and share them with the author and editors who worked on the book.

Email: feedback@quepublishing.com

Mail: Jeff Riley
              Que Publishing
              201 West 103rd Street
              Indianapolis, IN 46290 USA

For more information about this book or another Que title, visit our Web site at www.quepublishing.com. Type the ISBN (excluding hyphens) or the title of a book in the Search field to find the page you're looking for.

How to Use This Book

Que Certification has made an effort in its Training Guide series to make the information as accessible as possible for the purposes of learning the certification material. Here, you have an opportunity to view the many instructional features that have been incorporated into the books to achieve that goal.

CHAPTER OPENER

Each chapter begins with a set of features designed to allow you to maximize study time for that material.

List of Objectives: Each chapter begins with a list of the objectives as stated by the exam's vendor.

Objective Explanations: Immediately following each objective is an explanation of it, providing context that defines it more meaningfully in relation to the exam. Because vendors can sometimes be vague in their objectives list, the objective explanations are designed to clarify any vagueness by relying on the authors' test-taking experience.

OBJECTIVES

This chapter covers the following Microsoft-specified objectives for the "Creating User Services" section of the Visual Basic .NET Windows-Based Applications exam.

Create a Windows Form by using the Windows Forms Designer.

- **Add and set properties on a Windows Form.**
- **Create a Windows Form by using Visual Inheritance.**
- **Build graphical interface elements by using the System.Drawing namespace.**

▶ Windows Forms are the basic user interface element of a Windows application. The exam objectives addressed in this chapter cover the basics of designing a Windows Form using the Windows Form Designer. Specifically, the exam objective addresses the following topics:

▶ How to create a Windows Form and change its behavior and appearance through its built-in properties and through custom-added properties.

▶ How to use Visual Inheritance to rapidly design a Windows Form by inheriting it from an existing Windows Form.

▶ How to build various graphical interface elements using System.Drawing namespace.

Create, implement, and handle events.

- **Handle events**

▶ Event handling is the core part of programming a user interface. In this chapter I'll cover a part of this exam objective that will teach you:

▶ How to make a Windows Form respond to user actions. You'll find further coverage of this exam objective (Create, implement, and handle events), in Chapter 2.

CHAPTER 1

Introducing Windows Forms

Chapter Outline: Learning always gets a boost when you can see both the forest and the trees. To give you a visual image of how the topics in a chapter fit together, you will find a chapter outline at the beginning of each chapter. You will also be able to use this for easy reference when looking for a particular topic.

STUDY STRATEGIES

▶ You should understand how to construct and interpret simple Transact SQL statements including SELECT, INSERT, UPDATE, and DELETE, as well as SQL Server stored procedures. Spend some time practicing with the Visual Data Tools inside .NET or with another query front end such as SQL Server Query Analyzer. Be sure to work with the raw T-SQL, not just the graphical tools.

▶ For file-based access, understand the difference between a stream and a backing store. Practice reading and writing data with FileStream, StreamReader, and StreamWriter objects.

▶ Sometimes you'll come across the claim that ADO.NET is just an evolutionary improvement on classic ADO, and that your knowledge of classic ADO will help you learn ADO.NET. This is not true! ADO.NET is an entirely new model for working with data. Pay attention to the uses and functions of the ADO.NET objects, and don't get confused by the similarity of names between these objects and classic ADO objects.

▶ Know which objects are part of the System.Data namespace (and so shared by all data providers) and which are part of specific data provider namespaces such as System.Data.SqlClient and System.Data.OleDb.

▶ You'll need to know the classes contained within a DataSet and the methods available to manipulate them. Be sure you understand when to use a strongly typed DataSet and how this affects the syntax of DataSet operations.

▶ You should also know how to read and write XML data using the classes from the System.Xml namespace. Understand how to synchronize an XML document with a DataSet and some of the reasons that you might want to do this.

Study Strategies: Each topic presents its own learning challenge. To support you through this, Que Certification has included strategies for how to best approach studying in order to retain the material in the chapter, particularly as it is addressed on the exam.

INSTRUCTIONAL FEATURES WITHIN THE CHAPTER

These books include a large amount and different kinds of information. The many different elements are designed to help you identify information by its purpose and importance to the exam and also to provide you with varied ways to learn the material. You will be able to determine how much attention to devote to certain elements, depending on what your goals are. By becoming familiar with the different presentations of information, you will know what information will be important to you as a test-taker and which information will be important to you as a practitioner.

EXAM TIP

MsgBox Versus MessageBox   The MsgBox keyword from Visual Basic 6.0 is still supported by Visual Basic .NET, but its use has been deprecated. You should choose the MessageBox class for new projects and use MsgBox only when upgrading existing Visual Basic 6.0 projects.

Exam Tip: Exam Tips appear in the margins to provide specific exam-related advice. Such tips may address what material is covered (or not covered) on the exam, how it is covered, mnemonic devices, or particular quirks of that exam.

Note: Notes appear in the margins and contain various kinds of useful information, such as tips on the technology or administrative practices, historical background on terms and technologies, or side commentary on industry issues.

NOTE

Visually Displaying an Ampersand in the Text Property   What if you would like to display an ampersand (&) in a control's text property rather than to have it function as an access key? If the control is a Label control, you can set its UseMnemonic property to False. When UseMnemonic is False, the control will not interpret the ampersand as an access key modifier. But only the Label and LinkLabel controls have a UseMnemonic property. What about other controls, such as a Button? You can use a double ampersand (&&) in the Text property to represent a single ampersand. This trick will work with any standard control.

Some controls, such as a Label control, cannot receive the focus. If you assign a keyboard access key for such a control, the focus will instead go to a control with the next higher TabIndex value. You can use this behavior to your advantage: To identify controls like a TextBox, a RichTextBox, a TreeView, or a ListView, you can place a Label beside them. You can then associate an access key with the Label control and keep the TabIndex property of the Label and the corresponding control in immediate succession. This way when the user presses the access key for the Label, it will transfer focus to the control with the next higher TabIndex value, and the corresponding control will receive the focus.

Visible

The Visible property determines whether a control will actually be displayed. The Visible property is a Boolean value, set to True by default. When you set it to False, you still see the control in the Form designer, but users of the application won't see the control at runtime. Setting the Visible property to False does not remove the control from its container's Controls collection. (You'll learn more about the Controls collection later in this chapter.)

NOTE

Control Transparency   No property directly allows you to set the transparency value for a control. But you can use the BackColor property of a control and set a color using the Color.FromArgb method. The Color.FromArgb method lets you specify an alpha component that controls transparency.

Configuring the Order of Tabs

Implement navigation for the user interface (UI)

• **Configure the order of tabs.**

Many people use the keyboard for navigating between the various controls on a form. A Windows user expects to move from one control to another in a logical order by using the Tab key. The Visual Studio .NET Forms designer provides a Tab Order Wizard to allow you to conveniently set the order in which the controls will receive focus when the Tab key is pressed. See Step By Step 2.3 for an exercise in configuring tab order.

Objective Coverage Text: In the text before an exam objective is specifically addressed, you will notice the objective is listed to help call your attention to that particular material.

Warning: In using sophisticated information technology, there is always potential for mistakes or even catastrophes that can occur through improper application of the technology. Warnings appear in the margins to alert you to such potential problems.

WARNING

Data Loss Danger!   Be careful when testing this program. It doesn't check for the existence of the backup file, so it will overwrite any existing file without warning.

STEP BY STEP

2.3 Configuring the Order of Tabs

1. Add a Windows Form to your Visual Basic .NET application.

In Step By Step 1.8 you will see how to inherit from an existing form using Visual Inheritance

STEP BY STEP

1.8 Using Visual Inheritance

1. Open the project 306C01. In the Solution Explorer right-click on the project name and select Add, Add Inherited Form from the context menu. Name the new form StepByStep1-8 and click the Open button.

2. From the Inheritance Picker dialog box (see Figure 1.14), select the component named StepByStep1-7 and click OK.

3. Open the Properties window. Click the Categorized icon on its toolbar. Look for the Custom category. The FormState property within this category will be set to Processing, as shown in Figure 1.15. Change the FormState property to Idle.

4. In the Solution Explorer, right-click the project name and select Properties from the context menu. In the Project Property page, select StepByStep1_8 as the startup object. Click OK to close the Project Property page.

5. Select Run from the Debug menu. Since you have set the FormState property to Idle, the form will be displayed

FIGURE 1.14
The Inheritance Picker dialog box.

Figure: To improve readability, the figures have been placed in the margins wherever possible so they do not interrupt the main flow of text.

Step by Step: Step by Steps are hands-on tutorial instructions that walk you through a particular task or function relevant to the exam objectives.

---

4. Set the form as the program's startup object and execute the program.

If you had difficulty following this exercise, review the sections, "Designing a Windows Form Using the Windows Forms Designer" and "Using Visual Inheritance." Make sure you do Guided Practice Exercise 1.1 before attempting this one. The text and examples presented in these sections should help you in relearning this material. After review, try this exercise again.

REVIEW BREAK

► Form inheritance allows you to create a new form by inheriting it from a base form. This allows you to reuse and to extend the coding you've already finished.

► The Windows Forms Designer lets you inherit a form visually from an existing form through the Inheritance picker. You can also visually manipulate the inherited properties through the Properties window.

EVENT HANDLING

When you perform an action with an object, the object in turn raises *events* in your application. When you drag the title bar of the form and move it around, the object generates an event; when you resize the form it generates another event. A large portion of code for any typical Windows application is responsible for handling various events the application responds to. Events are at the heart of GUI-based programming.

Not all events are triggered by user actions. Events can be triggered by changes in the environment, like arrival of an email, modifications done to a file, change in time, completion of a program execution, and so on.

Review Break: Crucial information is summarized at various points in the book in lists or tables. At the end of a particularly long section, you might come across a Review Break that is there just to wrap up one long objective and reinforce the key points before you shift your focus to the next section.

CHAPTER SUMMARY   *continued*

- Field
- Framework Class Library
- Garbage collection
- GDI+
- Inheritance
- Intermediate language
- JIT compilation
- Managed code

In this chapter you learned how to manipulate a form's properties and how to add a custom property to a form. You also learned how to derive from an existing form and extend the functionality of an existing form by adding your own properties and methods.

Event handling plays a key role in user-interface–based programming; through event handling you respond to various events fired a a result of user actions and make the programs interactive. I discussed various ways to handle events in this chapter. In the next chapter you will see how to define your own events.

You also learned how to use the classes from the .NET Framework that implement graphic functionality. You saw how to draw text,

Key Terms: A list of key terms appears at the end of each chapter. These are terms that you should be sure you know and are comfortable defining and understanding when you go in to take the exam.

Chapter Summary: Before the Apply Your Knowledge section, you will find a chapter summary that wraps up the chapter and reviews what you should have learned.

APPLY YOUR KNOWLEDGE

Exercises

2.1   Adding ToolTips to Controls

Some Windows Forms controls, such as the TabControl, ToolBarButton, and StatusBarPanel controls, have a ToolTipText property to show ToolTips. But other commonly used controls do not have any built-in property to contain ToolTip text. That's the job of the ToolTip component.

In this exercise you will learn how to set ToolTips for a form.

Estimated Time: 25 minutes.

1. Create a new Visual Basic .NET Windows Application in the Visual Studio .NET IDE.

2. Add a new form to your Visual Basic .NET application. Change the Text property of the form to Find, the FormBorderStyle property to Fixed3D, and the TopMost property to True. Set the MaximizeBox, MimimizeBox, and ShowInTaskBar properties to False.

3. Place a ToolTip component on the form to add to the component tray. Name the component tTip.

4. Place a Label control, one TextBox control (txtTextToFind), two button controls (btnFind and btnCancel), one CheckBox control (chkMatchCase), and a group box with two RadioButton controls (rbUp and rbDown) on the form. Arrange the controls as shown in Figure 2.46.

5. You will find a property named ToolTip on tTip in the Properties window for each control. Enter an appropriate ToolTip message for each control in the ToolTip on tTip property.

6. Set the form as the startup object of the project.

7. Run the project. The ToolTip message will be displayed when you hover over the control, as shown in Figure 2.46.

FIGURE 2.46
ToolTips on a form.

2.2   Dynamically Creating Menu Items

While creating menus in Windows applications, you might be required to add menu items dynamically. The following exercise shows how to create menu items dynamically. The exercise shows a list of the recent files opened by application.

Estimated Time: 40 minutes.

1. Add a new form to your Visual Basic .NET project.

Review Questions

1. Where can controls be placed in a form? What are the two ways to add controls?

2. What is the shortcut way to create an event handler for the default event of a control?

3. When should you choose a combo box instead of a list box in your application?

4. What different modes of selection are possible in a list box control?

5. What are the roles of the TabIndex and TabStop properties?

Exercises: These activities provide an opportunity for you to master specific hands-on tasks. Our goal is to increase your proficiency with the product or technology. You must be able to conduct these tasks in order to pass the exam.

Review Questions: These open-ended, short-answer questions allow you to quickly assess your comprehension of what you just read in the chapter. Instead of asking you to choose from a list of options, these questions require you to state the correct answers in your own words. Although you will not experience these kinds of questions on the exam, these questions will indeed test your level of comprehension of key concepts.

Exam Questions: These questions reflect the kinds of questions that appear on the actual vendor exam. Use them to become familiar with the exam question formats and to help you determine what you know and what you need to review or study more.

APPLY YOUR KNOWLEDGE

Exam Questions

1. You are creating a data import utility for a personal information system that you designed recently. When the record in the source data file is not in the required format, your application needs to throw a custom exception. You will create an exception class with the name InvalidRecordStructureException. Which of the following classes would you choose as the base class for your custom exception class?

   A. ApplicationException

   B. Exception

   C. SystemException

   D. InvalidFilterCriteriaException

2. You are assisting your colleague in solving the compiler error that his code is throwing. The problematic portion of his code is

```
Try
    Dim success As Boolean = GenerateNewton-
Series(500, 0)
    ' more code here
Catch dbze As DivideByZeroException
    ' exception handling code
Catch nfne As NotFiniteNumberException
    ' exception handling code
Catch ae As ArithmeticException
    ' exception handling code
Catch e As OverflowException
    ' exception handling code
End Try
```

To remove the compilation error, which of the following ways would you modify the code?

   A.
   Try

Answers to Review Questions

1. The .NET framework terminates the application after displaying an error message when an exception is raised.

2. The Exception class is the base class that provides common functionality for exception handling. The two main types of exceptions derived from Exception class are SystemException and ApplicationException. SystemException represents the exceptions thrown by the common language runtime, whereas ApplicationException represents the exceptions thrown by user code.

3. The Message property describes the current exception. The InnerException property represents an exception object associated with the exception object; this property is helpful when a series of exceptions are involved. Each new exception can preserve information about a previous exception by storing it in InnerException property.

4. The Try block encloses code that might raise an exception. The Catch block handles any exception raised by the code in the Try block.

5. Zero or more Catch blocks can be associated with a single Try block. If no Catch block is associated with a Try block, a Finally block should follow the Try block; otherwise a compile-time error occurs. The Catch blocks should be arranged from specific to general exception types to avoid a compile-time error.

6. The code contained by the Finally block always executes regardless of any exception in the application. Therefore, you can use the Finally block

Answers and Explanations: For each of the Review and Exam questions, you will find thorough explanations located at the end of the section.

Suggested Readings and Resources: The very last element in every chapter is a list of additional resources you can use if you want to go above and beyond certification-level material or if you need to spend more time on a particular subject that you are having trouble understanding.

Suggested Readings and Resources

1. Ritcher, Jeffery. *Applied Microsoft .NET Framework Programming*. Microsoft Press, 2001.

2. Siler, Brian and Jeff Spotts. *Special Edition Using Visual Basic .NET*. Que, 2002.

3. Visual Studio .NET Combined Help Collection
   - Best Practices for Exception Handling
   - Exception Handling Statements
   - Exception Management in .NET

Introduction

MCAD/MCSD Training Guide Exam (70-306): Developing and Implementing Windows-Based Applications with Microsoft Visual Basic .NET and Microsoft Visual Studio .NET is designed for developers who are pursuing the Microsoft Certified Application Developer (MCAD) or Microsoft Certified Solution Developer (MCSD) certifications from Microsoft. This book covers the exam "Developing and Implementing Windows-Based Applications with Microsoft Visual Basic .NET and Microsoft Visual Studio .NET" (exam 70-306), which is a core exam for both MCAD and MCSD certifications. The exam is designed to measure your skill in developing Windows-based applications using Windows Forms and the other tools in the Microsoft .NET Framework, with Visual Basic .NET as your programming language.

This book is designed to cover all of Microsoft's objectives for this exam. It doesn't offer end-to-end coverage of the Visual Basic .NET language or the .NET Framework; rather, it helps you develop the specific core competencies that Microsoft says Visual Basic .NET–based Windows application developers need to master. You can pass the exam by learning the material in this book, without taking a class. Of course, depending on your own personal study habits and learning style, you might benefit from studying this book *and* taking a class.

Even if you're not planning to take the exam, you might find this book useful. In particular, experienced Visual Basic developers looking for a reference on the new features of Visual Basic .NET should appreciate the coverage of topics here.

HOW THIS BOOK HELPS YOU

This book gives you a self-guided tour of all the areas that are covered by the Visual Basic .NET Windows-Based Applications exam. The goal is to teach you the specific skills you need to achieve your MCAD or MCSD certification. You'll also find helpful hints, tips, examples, exercises, and references to additional study materials.

Organization

This book is organized around the individual objectives from Microsoft's preparation guide for the Visual Basic .NET Windows-Based Applications exam. Every objective is covered in this book. The objectives are not covered in exactly the same order in which you'll find them in the official preparation guide (which you can download from www.microsoft.com/traincert/exams/70-306.asp); rather, they are reorganized for more logical teaching. I've also tried to make the information more accessible in several ways:

◆ This introduction includes the full list of exam topics and objectives.

◆ Read the "Study and Exam Preps Tips" chapter early on. It will help you develop study strategies, and it provides you with valuable exam-day tips and information.

◆ Each chapter starts with a list of objectives that are covered in that chapter.

◆ Each chapter also begins with an outline that provides an overview of the material for that chapter as well as the page numbers where specific topics can be found.

- Each objective is repeated in the text where it is covered in detail.

- The tear card in the front of the book provides a handy cross-reference between test objectives and page numbers in the book.

Instructional Features

This book is designed to provide you with multiple ways to learn and reinforce the exam material. Here are some of the instructional features you'll find inside:

- **Objective explanations**—As mentioned previously, each chapter begins with a list of the objectives covered in the chapter. In addition, immediately following each objective is a more detailed explanation that puts the objective in the context of the product.

- **Study strategies**—Each chapter offers a selected list of study strategies: exercises to try or additional material to read that will help you learn and retain the material in the chapter.

- **Exam tips**—Exam tips appear in the margin and provide specific exam-related advice. Such tips might address what material is likely to be covered (or not covered) on the exam, how to remember the information, or particular exam quirks.

- **Review breaks and chapter summaries**—Crucial information is summarized at various points in the book, in lists of key points you need to remember. Each chapter ends with an overall summary of the material covered in that chapter as well.

- **Guided Practice Exercises**—These exercises offer you additional opportunities to practice the material within a chapter and to learn additional facets of the topic at hand.

- **Key terms**—A list of key terms appears at the end of each chapter.

- **Notes**—Notes appear in the margin and contain various kinds of useful information such as tips on technology, historical background, side commentary, or where to go for more detailed coverage of a particular topic.

- **Warnings**—When you use sophisticated computing technology, there is always the possibility of mistakes or even catastrophes. Warnings appear in the margin and alert you of such potential problems, whether they're related to following along with the text or implementing Visual Basic .NET in a production environment.

- **Step By Steps**—These are hands-on, tutorial instructions that lead you through a particular task or function related to the exam objectives.

- **Exercises**—Found at the end of each chapter in the "Apply Your Knowledge" section, the exercises include additional tutorial material and more chances to practice the skills that you learned in the chapter.

Extensive Practice Test Options

This book provides numerous opportunities for you to assess your knowledge and practice for the exam. The practice options include the following:

- **Review questions**—These open-ended questions appear in the "Apply Your Knowledge" section at the end of each chapter. They allow you to quickly assess your comprehension of what you just read in the chapter. The answers are provided later in the section.

◆ **Exam questions**—These questions appear in the "Apply Your Knowledge" section. They reflect the kinds of multiple-choice questions that appear on the Microsoft exams. You should use them to practice for the exam and to help determine what you know and what you might need to review or study further. Answers and explanations are provided later in the section.

◆ **Practice exam**—The Final Review section of this book includes a complete practice exam. The Final Review section and the Practice Exam are discussed in more detail later in this introduction.

◆ **PrepLogic**—The PrepLogic software included on the CD-ROM that accompanies this book provides further practice questions.

Final Review

This part of the book provides two valuable tools for preparing for the exam:

◆ **Fast Facts**—This condensed version of the information contained in the book is extremely useful for last-minute review.

◆ **Practice Exam**—A full practice test for the exam is included in this book. Questions are written in the style and format used on the actual exams. You should use the Practice Exam to assess your readiness for the real thing.

This book includes several valuable appendixes as well, including a glossary (Appendix A), an overview of the Microsoft certification program (Appendix B), and a description of what is on the CD-ROM (Appendix C). Appendix D covers the use of the PrepLogic software. Finally, Appendix E provides a list of suggested readings and resources that contain useful information on Visual Basic .NET and the .NET Framework.

These and all the other book features mentioned previously will provide you with thorough preparation for the exam.

For more information about the exam or the certification process, you should contact Microsoft directly:

◆ By email: MCPHelp@microsoft.com

◆ By regular mail, telephone, or fax, contact the Microsoft Regional Education Service Center (RESC) nearest you. You can find lists of Regional Education Service Centers at www.microsoft.com/traincert/support/ northamerica.asp (for North America) and www.microsoft.com/traincert/support/ worldsites.asp (worldwide).

◆ On the Internet: www.microsoft.com/traincert

WHAT THE "DEVELOPING AND IMPLEMENTING WINDOWS-BASED APPLICATIONS WITH MICROSOFT VISUAL BASIC .NET AND MICROSOFT VISUAL STUDIO .NET" EXAM (70-306) COVERS

The "Developing and Implementing Windows-Based Applications with Microsoft Visual Basic .NET and Microsoft Visual Studio .NET" exam covers several major topic areas: "Creating User Services," "Creating and Managing Components and .NET Assemblies," "Consuming and Manipulating Data," "Testing and Debugging," "Deploying a Windows-Based Application," "Maintaining and Supporting a Windows-Based Application," and "Configuring and Securing a Windows-Based Application."

The exam objectives are listed by topic area in the following sections.

Creating User Services

Create a Windows Form by using the Windows Forms Designer.

- ◆ Add and set properties on a Windows Form.
- ◆ Create a Windows Form by using visual inheritance.
- ◆ Build graphical interface elements by using the System.Drawing namespace.

Add controls to a Windows Form.

- ◆ Set properties on controls.
- ◆ Load controls dynamically.
- ◆ Write code to handle control events and add the code to a control.
- ◆ Instantiate and invoke an ActiveX control.
- ◆ Configure control licensing.
- ◆ Create menus and menu items.

Implement navigation for the user interface (UI).

- ◆ Configure the order of tabs.

Validate user input.

- ◆ Validate non-Latin user input.

Implement error handling in the UI.

- ◆ Create and implement custom error messages.
- ◆ Create and implement custom error handlers.
- ◆ Raise and handle errors.

Implement online user assistance.

Incorporate existing code into a Microsoft Windows-based application.

Display and update data.

- ◆ Transform and filter data.
- ◆ Bind data to the UI.

Instantiate and invoke a Web service or component.

- ◆ Instantiate and invoke a Web service.
- ◆ Instantiate and invoke a COM or COM+ component.
- ◆ Instantiate and invoke a .NET component.
- ◆ Call native functions by using platform invoke.

Implement globalization.

- ◆ Implement localizability for the UI.
- ◆ Convert existing encodings.
- ◆ Implement right-to-left and left-to-right mirroring.
- ◆ Prepare culture-specific formatting.

Create, implement, and handle events.

Implement print capability.

Implement accessibility features.

Creating and Managing Components and .NET Assemblies

Create and modify a .NET assembly.

- ◆ Create and implement satellite assemblies.
- ◆ Create resource-only assemblies.

Create a Windows control.

 ◆ Create a Windows control by using visual inheritance.

 ◆ Host a Windows control inside Microsoft Internet Explorer.

Consuming and Manipulating Data

Access and manipulate data from a Microsoft SQL Server database by creating and using ad hoc queries and stored procedures.

Access and manipulate data from a data store. Data stores include relational databases, XML documents, and flat files. Methods include XML techniques and ADO.NET.

Handle data errors.

Testing and Debugging

Create a unit test plan.

Implement tracing.

 ◆ Add trace listeners and trace switches to an application.

 ◆ Display trace output.

Debug, rework, and resolve defects in code.

 ◆ Configure the debugging environment.

 ◆ Create and apply debugging code to components and applications.

 ◆ Provide multicultural test data to components and applications.

 ◆ Execute tests.

 ◆ Resolve errors and rework code.

Deploying a Windows-Based Application

Plan the deployment of a Windows-based application.

 ◆ Plan a deployment that uses removable media.

 ◆ Plan a Web-based deployment.

 ◆ Plan a network-based deployment.

 ◆ Ensure that the application conforms to Windows Installer requirements and Windows Logo Program requirements.

Create a setup program that installs an application and allows for the application to be uninstalled.

 ◆ Register components and assemblies.

 ◆ Perform an install-time compilation of a Windows-based application.

Deploy a Windows-based application.

 ◆ Use setup and deployment projects.

Add assemblies to the Global Assembly Cache.

Verify security policies for a deployed application.

 ◆ Launch a remote application (URL remoting).

Maintaining and Supporting a Windows-Based Application

Optimize the performance of a Windows-based application.

Diagnose and resolve errors and issues.

Configuring and Securing a Windows-Based Application

Configure a Windows-based application.

Configure security for a Windows-based application.

◆ Select and configure authentication type. Authentication types include Windows Authentication, None, forms-based, Microsoft Passport, and custom authentication.

◆ Specify the security level for an application.

◆ Use custom attributes to configure security.

Configure authorization.

◆ Configure role-based authorization.

◆ Implement identity management.

WHAT YOU SHOULD KNOW BEFORE READING THIS BOOK

The Microsoft Visual Basic .NET exams assume that you're familiar with the Visual Basic language and the use of Visual Studio .NET to create applications, even though there are no objectives that pertain directly to this knowledge.

NOTE

If You're Just Getting Started with the Visual Basic .NET Language   In this book, I'll show you tasks that are directly related to exam objectives, but this book *does not* include a tutorial in Visual Basic .NET itself. Check out some of the references in Appendix E for the information that you'll need to get you started. For beginners, I particularly recommend these references:

· The samples and QuickStart Tutorials, which are installed as part of the .NET Framework SDK (which is a component of a full Visual Studio .NET installation) are an excellent starting point for information on Windows Forms and common tasks.

· *Special Edition Using Microsoft Visual Basic .NET*, by Brian Siler and Jeff Spotts (Que Publishing, 2002)

· *Visual Basic .NET: The Complete Reference*, by Jeffrey R. Shapiro (McGraw-Hill/Osborne, 2002)

· *Programming Visual Basic .NET*, by Dave Grundgeiger (O'Reilly, 2002)

· *VB .NET Language in a Nutshell*, by Steven Roman, Ron Petrusha, and Paul Lomax (O'Reilly, 2002)

HARDWARE AND SOFTWARE YOU'LL NEED

Although you can build Visual Basic .NET applications by using nothing more than the tools provided in the free .NET Framework SDK, to pass the exam you need to have access to a copy of Visual Studio .NET. Visual Studio .NET includes many tools and features not found in the free command-line tools. There are three editions of Visual Studio .NET:

◆ **Professional**—Visual Studio .NET Professional is the entry-level product in the product line. This edition allows you to build Windows, ASP.NET, and Web services applications. It includes visual design tools, Crystal Reports, and the MSDE version of SQL Server 2000.

◆ **Enterprise Developer**—Building on the Professional edition, the Enterprise Developer edition adds the full versions of SQL Server 2000, Visual SourceSafe, Application Center Test, and Visual Studio Analyzer, as well as developer licenses for Exchange Server, Host Integration Server, and Commerce Server. It also contains additional samples and templates.

◆ **Enterprise Architect**—The high-end Enterprise Architect edition adds Visio Enterprise Architect, a development license for SQL Server, and high-end enterprise templates.

You should be able to complete all the exercises in this book with any of the three editions of Visual Studio .NET. Your computer should meet the minimum criteria required for a Visual Studio .NET installation:

◆ A Pentium II or better CPU running at 450MHz or faster.

◆ Windows NT 4.0 or later.

◆ The following memory, depending on the operating system you have installed: 64MB for Windows NT 4.0 Workstation, 96MB for Windows 2000 Professional, 160MB for Windows NT 4.0 Server or Windows XP Professional, or 192MB for Windows 2000 Server.

◆ 3.5GB of disk space for a full installation.

◆ A CD-ROM or DVD drive.

◆ A video card running at 800×600 with at least 256 colors.

◆ A Microsoft or compatible mouse.

Of course, those are *minimum* requirements. I recommend the following more realistic requirements:

◆ A Pentium III or better CPU running at 800MHz or faster.

◆ Windows 2000.

◆ At least 256MB of RAM, and as much more as you can afford.

◆ 5GB of disk space for a full installation.

◆ A CD-ROM or DVD drive.

◆ A video card running at 1280×1024 or higher with at least 65,000 colors.

◆ A Microsoft or compatible mouse.

You might find it easiest to obtain access to the necessary computer hardware and software in a corporate environment. It can be difficult, however, to allocate enough time within a busy workday to complete a self-study program. Most of your study time will probably need to occur outside normal working hours, away from the everyday interruptions and pressures of your job.

ADVICE ON TAKING THE EXAM

You'll find more extensive tips in the "Study and Exam Prep Tips," but keep this advice in mind as you study:

◆ Read all the material in this book. Microsoft has been known to include in its exams material not expressly specified in the objectives for an exam. This book includes additional information that is not reflected in the objectives, in an effort to give you the best possible preparation for the examination—and for the real-world experiences to come.

◆ Do the Step By Steps and complete the exercises and Guided Practice Exercises in each chapter. They will help you gain experience with Visual Basic .NET. All Microsoft exams are task- and experience-based and require you to have experience using the Microsoft products, not just reading about them.

◆ Use the review and exam questions to assess your knowledge. Don't just read the chapter content; use the review and exam questions to find out what you know and what you don't. Study some more, review, and then assess your knowledge again.

◆ Review the exam objectives. Develop your own questions and examples for each topic listed. If you can develop and answer several questions for each topic, you should not find it difficult to pass the exam.

Remember, the primary objective is not to pass the exam: It is to understand the material. When you understand the material, passing the exam should be simple. To really work with Visual Basic .NET, you need a solid foundation in practical skills. This book and the Microsoft Certified Professional program are designed to ensure that you have that solid foundation.

Good luck!

> **EXAM TIP**
>
> **No Substitute for Experience** The single best study tip that anyone can give you is to actually work with the product that you're learning! Even if you could become a "paper MCAD" simply by reading books, you wouldn't get the real-world skills that you need to be a Visual Basic .NET success.

This section of the book provides you with some general guidelines for preparing for the exam "Developing and Implementing Windows-Based Applications with Microsoft Visual Basic .NET and Microsoft Visual Studio .NET" (exam 70-306). It is organized into three parts. The first part addresses your pre-exam preparation activities and covers general study tips. This is followed by an extended look at the Microsoft Certification exams, including a number of specific tips that apply to the Microsoft exam formats. Finally, changes in Microsoft's testing policies and how they might affect you are discussed.

To better understand the nature of preparation for the test, it is important to understand learning as a process. You probably are aware of how you best learn new material. You might find that outlining works best for you, or you might need to see things, as a visual learner. Whatever your learning style, test preparation takes place over time. Obviously, you can't start studying for this exam the night before you take it; it is very important to understand that learning is a developmental process. Understanding it as a process helps you focus on what you know and what you have yet to learn.

Thinking about how you learn should help you recognize that learning takes place when you are able to match new information to old. You have some previous experience with computers and software development, and now you are preparing for this certification exam. Using this book, software, and supplementary materials will not just add incrementally to what you know; as you study, you actually change the organization of your knowledge and integrate this new information into your existing knowledge base. This leads you to a more comprehensive understanding of the tasks and concepts outlined in the objectives and of computing in general. Again, this happens as a repetitive process rather than as a single event. Keep this model of learning in mind as you prepare for the exam, and you will make good decisions concerning what to study and how much more studying you need to do.

Study and Exam Prep Tips

STUDY TIPS

There are many ways to approach studying, just as there are many different types of material to study. However, the tips that follow should work well for the type of material covered on this certification exam.

Study Strategies

Although individuals vary in the ways they learn information, some basic principles of learning apply to everyone. You should adopt some study strategies that take advantage of these principles. One of these principles is that learning can be broken into various depths. Recognition (of terms, for example) exemplifies a surface level of learning in which you rely on a prompt of some sort to elicit recall. Comprehension, or understanding (of the concepts behind the terms, for example), represents a deeper level of learning. The ability to analyze a concept and apply your understanding of it in a new way represents a further depth of learning.

Your learning strategy should enable you to know the material at a level or two deeper than mere recognition. This will help you do well on the exams. You will know the material so thoroughly that you can easily handle the recognition-level types of questions used in multiple-choice testing. You will also be able to apply your knowledge to solve new problems.

Macro and Micro Study Strategies

One strategy that can lead to deep learning includes preparing an outline that covers all the objectives and subobjectives for the exam you are working on. Then you should delve a bit further into the material and include a level or two of detail beyond the stated objectives and subobjectives for the exam. Then you should expand the outline by coming up with a statement of definition or a summary for each point in the outline.

An outline provides two approaches to studying. First, you can study the outline by focusing on the organization of the material. Work your way through the points and subpoints of your outline, with the goal of learning how they relate to one another. For example, be sure you understand how each of the main objective areas is similar to and different from the others. Then do the same thing with the subobjectives; be sure you know which subobjectives pertain to each objective area and how they relate to one another.

Next, you can work through the outline, focusing on learning the details. You should memorize and understand terms and their definitions, facts, rules and strategies, advantages and disadvantages, and so on. In this pass through the outline, you should attempt to learn detail rather than the big picture (the organizational information that you worked on in the first pass through the outline).

Research has shown that attempting to assimilate both types of information at the same time seems to interfere with the overall learning process. Separate your studying into these two approaches, and you will perform better on the exam.

Active Study Strategies

The process of writing down and defining objectives, subobjectives, terms, facts, and definitions promotes a more active learning strategy than merely reading the material. In human information-processing terms, writing forces you to engage in more active encoding of the information. Simply reading over the information exemplifies more passive processing.

Next, you should determine whether you can apply the information you have learned by attempting to create examples and scenarios on your own. You should think about how or where you could apply the concepts you are learning. Again, you should write down this information so you can process the facts and concepts in a more active fashion.

The hands-on nature of the Step By Step tutorials, the Guided Practice Exercises, and the exercises at the ends of the chapters provide further active learning opportunities that will reinforce concepts as well.

Common-Sense Strategies

Finally, you should also follow common-sense practices when studying. You should study when you are alert, reduce or eliminate distractions, take breaks when you become fatigued, and so on.

Pretesting Yourself

Pretesting enables you to assess how well you are learning. One of the most important aspects of learning is what has been called meta-learning. *Meta-learning* has to do with realizing when you know something well or when you need to study some more. In other words, you recognize how well or how poorly you have learned the material you are studying.

For most people, this can be difficult to assess objectively. Practice tests are useful because they objectively reveal what you have learned and what you have not learned. You should use this information to guide review and further study. Developmental learning takes place as you cycle through studying, assessing how well you have learned, reviewing, and assessing again until you feel you are ready to take the exam.

You might have noticed the practice exam included in this book. You should use it as part of the learning process. The PrepLogic software on the CD-ROM also provides a variety of ways to test yourself before you take the actual exam. By using the practice exams in the book and on the CD-ROM, you can take an entire practice test and gauge from your performance on each practice exam what areas you have mastered and what areas you still need to work on. As you complete the practice exams, one effective study method is to take notes on the items you missed as you move through the explanations of the answers.

This is active learning on your part, and with it you are more likely to learn and remember correct answers.

You should set a goal for your pretesting. A reasonable goal would be to score consistently in the 90% range.

See Appendix D, "Using the *PrepLogic, Preview Edition* Software," for a more detailed explanation of the test engine.

EXAM PREP TIPS

Having mastered the subject matter, the final preparatory step is to understand how the exam will be presented. Make no mistake: A Microsoft Certified Professional (MCP) exam will challenge both your knowledge and test-taking skills. This section starts with the basics of exam design, reviews a new type of exam format, and concludes with hints targeted to each of the exam formats.

The MCP Exam

Every MCP exam is released in one of two basic formats. What is called *exam format* here is really little more than a combination of the overall exam structure and the presentation method for exam questions.

Each exam format uses the same types of questions. These types or styles of questions include multiple-rating (or scenario-based) questions, traditional multiple-choice questions, and simulation-based questions. You may also see visual question types such as select-and-place questions (which require you to drag and drop elements onscreen) and hot-area questions (which require you to click an appropriate item onscreen). It's important to understand the types of questions you will be asked and the actions required to properly answer them.

Understanding the exam formats is key to good preparation because the format determines the number of questions presented, the difficulty of those questions, and the amount of time allowed to complete the exam.

Exam Forms

There are two basic formats for the MCP exams: the traditional fixed-form exam and the adaptive form. As its name implies, the fixed-form exam presents a fixed set of questions during the exam session. The adaptive form, however, uses only a subset of questions drawn from a larger pool during any given exam session.

Fixed-Form Exams

A fixed-form computerized exam is based on a fixed set of exam questions. The individual questions are presented in random order during a test session. If you take the same exam more than once, you won't necessarily see exactly the same questions because two or three final forms are typically assembled for every fixed-form exam Microsoft releases. These are usually labeled Forms A, B, and C.

The final forms of a fixed-form exam are identical in terms of content coverage, number of questions, and allotted time, but the questions are different. You might notice, however, that some of the same questions appear on, or are shared among, different final forms. When questions are shared among multiple final forms of an exam, the percentage of sharing is generally small. Many final forms share no questions, but some older exams may have a 10% to 15% duplication of exam questions on the final exam forms.

A fixed-form exam also has a fixed time limit in which you must complete the exam. The *PrepLogic, Preview Edition* software on the CD-ROM that accompanies this book carries fixed-form exams.

The score you achieve on a fixed-form exam, which is always reported for MCP exams as either Pass or Fail, is based on the number of questions you answer correctly. Internally, Microsoft tracks exam scores on a scale of 0 to 1,000, but the actual score is no longer shared with the certification candidate. The exam's passing score is the same for all final forms of a given fixed-form exam.

The typical format for the fixed-form exam is as follows:

◆ The exam contains 50 to 60 questions.

◆ You are allowed 75 to 90 minutes of testing time.

◆ Question review is allowed, and you have the opportunity to change your answers.

Adaptive Exams

An adaptive-form exam has the same appearance as a fixed-form exam, but its questions differ in quantity and process of selection. Although the statistics of adaptive testing are fairly complex, the process is concerned with determining your level of skill or ability with the exam subject matter. This ability assessment begins by presenting questions of varying levels of difficulty and ascertaining at what difficulty level you can reliably answer them. Finally, the ability assessment determines whether that ability level is above or below the level required to pass that exam.

Examinees at different levels of ability see quite different sets of questions. Examinees who demonstrate little expertise with the subject matter continue to be presented with relatively easy questions. Examinees who demonstrate a high level of expertise are presented progressively more difficult questions. Individuals with both levels of expertise might answer the same number of questions correctly, but because the higher-expertise examinee can correctly answer more difficult questions, he or she receives a higher score and is more likely to pass the exam.

The typical design for the adaptive form exam is as follows:

◆ The exam contains 20 to 25 questions.

◆ You are allowed 90 minutes of testing time, although this is likely to be reduced to 45 to 60 minutes in the near future.

◆ Question review is not allowed, providing no opportunity to change your answers.

The Adaptive-Exam Process

Your first adaptive exam will be unlike any other testing experience you have had. In fact, many examinees have difficulty accepting the adaptive testing process because they feel that they are not provided the opportunity to adequately demonstrate their full expertise.

You can take consolation in the fact that adaptive exams are painstakingly put together after months of data gathering and analysis and are just as valid as fixed-form exams. The rigor introduced through the adaptive testing methodology means that there is nothing arbitrary about what you see. It is also a more efficient means of testing, requiring less time to conduct and complete than the traditional fixed-form methodology.

As you can see in Figure 1, a number of statistical measures drive the adaptive examination process. The measure that is most immediately relevant to you is the ability to estimate. Accompanying this test statistic are the standard error of measurement, the item characteristic curve, and the test information curve.

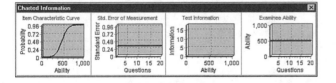

FIGURE 1
Microsoft's adaptive testing demonstration program.

The standard error, which is the key factor in determining when an adaptive exam will terminate, reflects the degree of error in the exam ability estimate. The item characteristic curve reflects the probability of a correct response relative to examinee ability. Finally, the test information statistic provides a measure of the information contained in the set of questions the examinee has answered, again relative to the ability level of the individual examinee.

When you begin an adaptive exam, the standard error has already been assigned a target value below which it must drop below in order for the exam to conclude. This target value reflects a particular level of statistical confidence in the process. The examinee's ability is initially set to the mean possible exam score (which is 500 for MCP exams).

As the adaptive exam progresses, questions of varying difficulty are presented. Based on your pattern of responses to these questions, the ability estimate is recalculated. Simultaneously, the standard error estimate is refined from its first estimated value, toward the target value. When the standard error reaches the target value, the exam terminates. Thus, the more consistently you answer questions of the same degree of difficulty, the more quickly the standard error estimate drops and the fewer questions you end up seeing during the exam session. This situation is depicted in Figure 2.

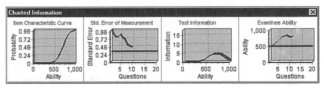

FIGURE 2
The changing statistics in an adaptive exam.

As you might suspect, one good piece of advice for taking an adaptive exam is to treat every exam question as if it is the most important. The adaptive scoring algorithm attempts to discover a pattern of responses that reflects a level of proficiency with the subject matter.

Incorrect responses almost guarantee that additional questions must be answered (unless, of course, you get every question wrong). This is because the scoring algorithm must adjust to information that is not consistent with the emerging pattern.

New Question Types

A variety of question types can appear on MCP exams. Examples of multiple-choice questions and scenario-based questions appear throughout this book and the *PrepLogic, Preview Edition* software on the accompanying CD. Simulation-based questions are new to the MCP exam series.

Simulation Questions

Simulation-based questions reproduce the look and feel of key Microsoft product features for the purpose of testing. The simulation software used in MCP exams has been designed to look and act, as much as possible, just like the actual product. Consequently, answering simulation questions in an MCP exam entails completing one or more tasks just as if you were using the product itself.

The format of a typical Microsoft simulation question consists of a brief scenario or problem statement, along with one or more tasks that must be completed to solve the problem.

A Typical Simulation Question

It sounds obvious, but your first step when you encounter a simulation is to carefully read the question. Do not go straight to the simulation application! You must assess the problem being presented and identify the conditions that make up the problem scenario. Note the tasks that must be performed or outcomes that must be achieved to answer the question and review any instructions on how to proceed.

The next step is to launch the simulator by using the button provided. After clicking the Show Simulation button, you see a feature of the product, presented in a dialog box. The simulation application is likely to partially cover the question text. Feel free to reposition the simulation or move between the question text screen and the simulation by using hotkeys, by using point-and-click navigation, or by clicking the simulation launch button again.

It is important to understand that your answer to the simulation question will not be recorded until you move on to the next exam question. This gives you the added capability to close and reopen the simulation application (by using the launch button) on the same question without losing any partial answer you may have made.

The third step is to use the simulator as you would the actual product, to solve the problem or perform the defined tasks. Again, the simulation software is designed to function, within reason, just as the product does. But don't expect the simulation to reproduce product behavior perfectly. Most importantly, do not allow yourself to become flustered if the simulation does not look or act exactly like the product.

Two final points will help you tackle simulation questions. First, respond only to what is being asked in the question; do not solve problems that you are not asked to solve. Second, accept what is being asked of you. You may not entirely agree with conditions in the problem statement, the quality of the desired solution, or the sufficiency of defined tasks to adequately solve the problem. Always remember that you are being tested on your ability to solve the problem as it is presented. If you make any changes beyond those required by the question, the item will be scored as wrong on an MCP exam.

Putting It All Together

Given all these different pieces of information, we now present a set of tips that will help you successfully tackle the exam.

More Pre-Exam Preparation Tips

Generic exam-preparation advice is always useful. Tips include the following:

◆ Become familiar with the product. Hands-on experience is one of the keys to success on any MCP exam. Review the exercises, the Guided Practice Exercises, and the Step By Steps in the book.

◆ Review the current exam-preparation guide on the Microsoft MCP Web site. The documentation Microsoft makes available over the Web identifies the skills every exam is intended to test.

◆ Memorize foundational technical detail, but remember that MCP exams are generally heavy on problem solving and application of knowledge rather than just questions that require only rote memorization.

◆ Take any of the available practice tests. We recommend the one included in this book and the ones you can create by using the *PrepLogic, Preview Edition* software on the CD-ROM. Although these are fixed-form exams, they provide preparation that is just as valuable for taking an adaptive exam. Because of the nature of adaptive testing, these practice exams cannot be taken in the adaptive form. However, fixed-form exams use the same types of questions as adaptive exams and are the most effective way to prepare for either type.

◆ Look on the Microsoft MCP Web site (www.microsoft.com/traincert) for samples and demonstration items. These tend to be particularly valuable for one significant reason: They help you become familiar with any new testing technologies before you encounter them on an MCP exam.

Tips for During the Exam Session

The following generic exam-taking advice you've heard for years applies when taking an MCP exam:

◆ Take a deep breath and try to relax when you first sit down for your exam session. It is very important to control the pressure you might (naturally) feel when taking exams.

◆ You will be provided with scratch paper. Take a moment to write down any factual information and technical detail that you have committed to short-term memory.

◆ Carefully read all information and instruction screens. These displays have been put together to give you information relevant to the exam you are taking.

◆ Accept the nondisclosure agreement and preliminary survey as part of the examination process. Complete them accurately and quickly move on.

◆ Read the exam questions carefully. Reread each question to identify all relevant detail.

◆ On a standard exam, tackle the questions in the order in which they are presented. Skipping around won't build your confidence; the clock is always counting down. On an adaptive exam, of course, you don't have any choice.

◆ Don't rush, but also don't linger on difficult questions. The questions vary in degree of difficulty. Don't let yourself be flustered by a particularly difficult or verbose question.

Tips for Fixed-Form Exams

Building from this basic preparation and test-taking advice, you also need to consider the challenges presented by the different exam designs. Because a fixed-form exam is composed of a fixed, finite set of questions, add these tips to your strategy for taking a fixed-form exam:

◆ Note the time allotted and the number of questions appearing on the exam you are taking. Make a rough calculation of how many minutes you can spend on each question and use this to pace yourself through the exam.

◆ Take advantage of the fact that you can return to and review skipped or previously answered questions. Record the questions you can't answer confidently, noting the relative difficulty of each question, on the scratch paper provided. When you have made it to the end of the exam, return to the more difficult questions.

◆ If there is session time remaining after you have completed all questions (and if you aren't too fatigued!), review your answers. Pay particular attention to questions that seem to have a lot of detail or that require graphics.

◆ As for changing your answers, the general rule of thumb here is don't! If you read the question carefully and completely and you felt like you knew the right answer, you probably did. Don't second-guess yourself. If, as you check your answers, one clearly stands out as incorrectly marked, however, of course you should change it. If you are at all unsure, go with your first instinct.

Tips for Adaptive Exams

If you are planning to take an adaptive exam, keep these additional tips in mind:

◆ Read and answer every question with great care. When reading a question, identify every relevant detail, requirement, or task that must be performed and double-check your answer to be sure you have addressed every one of them.

◆ If you cannot answer a question, use the process of elimination to reduce the set of potential answers, and then take your best guess. Careless mistakes invariably mean additional questions will be presented.

◆ You cannot review questions and change your answers. When you leave a question, whether you've answered it or not, you cannot return to it. Do not skip any questions either; if you do, the item is counted as incorrect.

Simulation Questions

You might encounter simulation questions on either the fixed-form or adaptive-form exam. If you do, keep these tips in mind:

◆ Avoid changing any simulation settings that don't pertain directly to the problem solution. Solve the problem you are being asked to solve and nothing more.

◆ Assume default settings when related information has not been provided. If something has not been mentioned or defined, it is a noncritical detail that does not factor into the correct solution.

◆ Be sure your entries are syntactically correct, paying particular attention to your spelling. Enter relevant information just as the product would require it.

◆ Close all simulation application windows after completing the simulation tasks. The testing system software is designed to trap errors that could result when using the simulation application, but you should trust yourself over the testing software.

◆ If simulations are part of a fixed-form exam, you can return to skipped or previously answered questions and change your answers. However, if you choose to change an answer to a simulation question or even attempt to review the settings you've made in the simulation application, your previous response to that simulation question is deleted. If simulations are part of an adaptive exam, you cannot return to previous questions.

Select-and-Place Questions

You might encounter select-and-place questions on either a fixed-form or an adaptive-form exam. If you do, keep these tips in mind:

◆ You must always drag your answers from the answer objects section to the answer field section. If you drag an answer object from one answer field directly to another answer field, it will not count as a correct answer.

◆ Although you can review a select-and-place question, the answers will be cleared if you do so and you'll need to answer the question over again.

Hot-Area Questions

You might encounter hot-area questions on either a fixed-form or an adaptive-form exam. If you do, keep these tips in mind:

◆ Remember, it's your final mouse click that counts on a hot-area question. Be sure to click your answer area immediately before moving to the next question.

◆ Although you can review a hot-area question, the answers will be cleared if you do so and you'll need to answer the question over again.

FINAL CONSIDERATIONS

Finally, a number of changes in the MCP program affect how frequently you can repeat an exam and what you see when you do:

◆ Microsoft's policy on retaking exams is simple. You can attempt any exam twice, with no restrictions on the time between attempts; your second try can follow the first on the very next day if you like. But after the second attempt, you must wait two weeks before you can attempt that exam again. After that, you are required to wait two weeks between subsequent attempts. Plan to pass the exam in two attempts or plan to increase your time horizon for receiving an MCP credential.

◆ New questions are being seeded into the MCP exams. After performance data is gathered on new questions, the examiners replace older questions on all exam forms. This means that the questions that appear on exams regularly change.

◆ Many of the current MCP exams will be republished in adaptive form in the coming months. Prepare yourself for this significant change in testing as it is entirely likely that this will become the preferred MCP exam format.

These changes mean that the brute-force strategies for passing MCP exams are much less viable than they once were. So if you don't pass an exam on the first or second attempt, it is entirely possible that the exam's form will change significantly before the next time you take it. It could be updated to adaptive form from fixed form or it could have a different set of questions or question types.

The intention of Microsoft is clearly not to make the exams more difficult by introducing unwanted change, but to create and maintain valid measures of the technical skills and knowledge associated with the different MCP credentials. Preparing for an MCP exam has always involved not only studying the subject matter, but also planning for the testing experience itself. With the recent changes, this is now truer than ever.

EXAM PREPARATION

This chapter covers the following Microsoft-specified objectives for the "Creating User Services" section of the Visual Basic .NET Windows-Based Applications exam.

Create a Windows Form by using the Windows Forms Designer.

- **Add and set properties on a Windows Form.**

- **Create a Windows Form by using Visual Inheritance.**

- **Build graphical interface elements by using the System.Drawing namespace.**

▶ Windows Forms are the basic user interface element of a Windows application. The exam objectives addressed in this chapter cover the basics of designing a Windows Form using the Windows Form Designer. Specifically, the exam objective addresses the following topics:

▶ How to create a Windows Form and change its behavior and appearance through its built-in properties and through custom added properties.

▶ How to use Visual Inheritance to rapidly design a Windows Form by inheriting it from an existing Windows Form.

▶ How to build various graphical interface elements using System.Drawing namespace.

Create, implement, and handle events.

- **Handle events**

▶ Event handling is the core part of programming a user interface. In this chapter I'll cover a part of this exam objective that will teach you:

▶ How to make a Windows Form respond to user actions. You'll find further coverage of this exam objective (Create, implement, and handle events), in Chapter 2.

CHAPTER 1

Introducing Windows Forms

▶ Make yourself comfortable with the major properties of Windows Forms. This chapter's examples and exercises introduce the most important form properties.

▶ Invest time to look at and understand the code that was automatically generated by Visual Studio .NET for you.

▶ Ensure that you fully understand event handling. This will give you access to writing interactive Windows applications.

▶ Experiment with the classes in the System.Drawing namespace. In addition to the examples and exercises covered in this chapter, it would be a good idea to create a small sample program to test the behavior of a class or a property whenever you are in doubt.

▶ If you are new to object-oriented programming, consider reading all or some of recommended material in the reading list at the end of this chapter.

INTRODUCTION

It's time to start your journey to passing Exam 70-306. In your first step toward this goal you will do lot of groundwork to build the foundation for the rest of the book.

This chapter starts with an overview of the .NET Framework and Visual Studio .NET (VS .NET). This overview will be enough to get you started; I'll cover advanced features as they become important for meeting exam objectives.

After the overview of .NET Framework and Visual Studio .NET, I'll talk about designing Web forms, both by using a visual designer and by manually writing the code. The visual designer inside Visual Studio .NET helps with rapid development of forms. As you design forms, you will also learn about many useful classes available in the System.Windows.Forms namespace. You'll also learn how to visually inherit a Window form from an existing form.

A Windows application generally interacts with the user. Responding to actions the user takes is the job of event handling. You will learn how to make your programs interactive using event handling.

Finally, I'll talk about the various classes in the System.Drawing namespace. These classes allow you to add typography, 2D graphics, and imaging features to your applications.

OVERVIEW OF THE .NET FRAMEWORK AND VISUAL STUDIO .NET

The Microsoft .NET Framework provides a new paradigm for developing Windows applications. It has three major components:

◆ The .NET Framework Class Library

◆ Language compilers

◆ The Common Language Runtime

The .NET Framework Class Library (FCL) is an extensive collection of reusable types that allows you to program databases, strings, Extensible Markup Language (XML), network, security, Windows applications, Web applications, and Web Services, to name just a few of its purposes. The classes in this library are organized in hierarchical namespaces, so they are logically grouped and easy to identify. You'll learn about several of these namespaces and the classes they contain in this book as you develop Windows-based applications.

The FCL itself is designed to be language neutral. The .NET Framework Software Development Kit (SDK) provides four language compilers: C# (pronounced "see-sharp"), Visual Basic .NET, Managed C++ .NET, and JScript .NET. In addition, you can obtain .NET compilers for languages such as Java, COBOL, Eiffel, Perl, Python, and Haskell. These language compilers translate code to a common intermediate language called the *Microsoft intermediate language (MSIL)*. The use of MSIL as a common target format for all code in .NET allows you to create components in one programming language and use them transparently in other programming languages.

The Common Language Runtime (CLR) executes the code and provides it with runtime services like memory management, automatic garbage collection, thread management, security, and remoting. The Common Language Runtime uses just-in-time (JIT) compilation to convert the MSIL to native code that can be understood by the target machine.

In addition to the .NET Framework, the introduction of Visual Studio .Net is a significant change for Windows application developers. It provides developers with a full service integrated development environment for developing applications based on the Microsoft .NET Framework. Some of the important features of Visual Studio .NET are the following:

◆ **Integrated development environment (IDE)**—Supports development, compilation, debugging, and deployment from within the development environment.

◆ **Editing tools**—Supports language syntaxes for multiple languages. IntelliSense provides help with syntax. The editing tools also support editing of XML, HTML, and cascading style sheets (CSS) documents, among other types.

NOTE

Running .NET Applications Applications developed using Visual Studio .NET or the .NET Framework SDK require the Common Language Runtime on each machine they are deployed on. The Common Language Runtime is installed as part of .NET Framework redistributable, available as a free download (approximately 21MB) from Microsoft's Web site at http://msdn.microsoft.com/ downloads/default.asp?url=/ downloads/sample.asp?url=/ msdn-files/027/001/829/ msdncompositedoc.xml.

EXAM TIP

Visual Studio .NET Is Nice, But Not Necessary Visual Studio .NET is not a required tool to develop .NET applications. It's possible to develop your programs using just a text editor and the command-line compilers provided by the .NET Framework SDK. However, the rapid application development (RAD) features of Visual Studio .NET make it an extremely productive development environment.

Use the IDE   The 70-306 exam requires you to know Visual Studio .NET and the Visual Basic .NET programming language for Windows-based application development. You might be asked questions on specific Visual Studio .NET features. So even if you learn how to write applications in a text editor, ensure you can work with the IDE as well.

◆ **Integrated debugging**—Supports cross-language debugging, including debugging SQL Server-stored procedures. It can seamlessly debug applications running locally or running on the remote server.

◆ **Deployment tools**—Supports Windows Installer and provides graphical deployment editors that allow you to visually control various deployment settings for a Visual Studio .NET project.

◆ **Automation**—Provides tools for extending, customizing, and automating the Visual Studio .NET integrated development environment.

I'll cover all these features in the course of this book.

CREATING A WINDOWS APPLICATION

The .NET Framework is designed to be object-oriented from the ground up. I'll cover the different elements of object-oriented programming as they come up, but you should be familiar with some terms right from the start. You need to understand how .NET discusses classes, namespaces, inheritance, and other object-oriented concepts.

Understanding Classes, Inheritance, and Namespaces

Visual Basic .NET (VB .NET) is an object-oriented programming language. One of the tasks of a VB .NET developer is to create user-defined types of data called *classes*. A class encapsulates data (such as constants and fields) and behavior (including methods, properties, constructors, and events) for your user-defined type. A class represents an abstract idea that you want to include in your application. For example, the .NET Framework includes a Form class. The Form class includes data fields for such information as the size of the form, its location, its background color, the title bar text, and so on. These data fields contain enough information to draw a form onscreen. The Form class also contains a set of methods that defines how a form behaves, such as a Show method to show the form onscreen and an Activate method to activate the form by giving it the focus.

A class functions as the blueprint of a concept. When you want to work with a class in your program, you create instances of the class called *objects*. Objects are created from the blueprint defined by class, but they physically exist in the sense that they have memory locations allocated to them and will respond to your messages. When you want to create an actual form in your program, you create an instance of the Form class, or a Form object. Once you have this instance available, you can actually work on it: You can set its properties and call its methods.

Each object maintains its own copy of the data defined by the class. This allows different instances of a class to have different data values. The members of an object are accessed using the ObjectName.MemberName syntax, where ObjectName is name of the class instance, and MemberName can be a field, property, method, or an event. When an object is created, it creates its members in a special area in memory called the *heap* and just stores a pointer to that memory itself. Because they use pointers to refer to their data, classes are sometimes also called *reference types*.

In contrast to what you just covered, Visual Basic .NET also defines a *structure type* using the Structure keyword. Structure types are almost like classes, but rather than storing a pointer to the memory location, they use the memory location directly to store their members. A structure type is also referred to as a *value type*.

Among the members of a class, properties deserve special attention. A *property* provides access to the characteristics of a class or of an instance of that class (an object). Examples of properties include the caption of a window, the name of an item, the font of a string, and so on.

To the programs using a class, the property looks like a field; in other words, a storage location. Properties and fields have the same usage syntax, but their implementation is different. In a class, a property is not a storage location but rather a set of accessors that contain code to be executed when property value is read or written. This piece of code allows properties to preprocess the data before it is read or written to ensure integrity of a class. Properties are the preferred way to expose attributes or characteristics of a class, and you will see them used extensively by various classes in this chapter.

NOTE

Static Members   A class can have static members (fields, methods, and so forth), which belong to the class itself rather than to a particular instance. No instance of a class is required to access its static members. To access a static member of a class prefix its name with the name of the class (ClassName. StaticMemberName).

Access Modifiers   A class can define the accessibility of its members by including an access modifier in their declarations. There are four different access modifiers in VB. NET:

- Public—Allows the member to be globally accessible.

- Private—Limits access to its containing type only.

- Protected—Limits access to the containing type and all classes derived from the containing type.

- Friend—Limits access to classes within the current project.

Object-oriented programming languages such as VB .NET provide another feature called *inheritance*. Inheritance allows you to create new types based on existing types. The original type is called a *base class*, and the new type is called a *derived class*. When one class inherits from another class, the derived class gets all the functionality of the base class. The derived class can also choose to extend the base class by introducing new data and behavioral elements. In Windows Form development, you will frequently inherit from the Form class to create your own custom forms; these custom forms will be at least as functional as an object of the Form class even without your writing any new code in the derived class. Value types (such as types defined with the Structure keyword) cannot be used for inheritance.

Every single type (other than the Object type itself) that you create or that is already defined in the framework is implicitly derived from the Object class of the System namespace to ensure that all classes provide a common minimum functionality. Also note that a VB .NET type can only inherit from a single parent class at a time.

Inheritance is widely used in the FCL, and you will come across classes (for example, Form) that get their functionality from other classes (for example, Control) as a result of a chain of inheritances.

Several hundred classes are already available to you in the FCL. In addition, an increasingly large number of classes are available through third-party component vendors. These are all in addition to the classes you develop on your own. Having many classes not only makes organization difficult but can also create naming conflicts between various vendors. The .NET Framework provides a feature called a *namespace* to allow you to hierarchically organize classes in logical groups based on what they do and where they originate. Using namespaces organizes your classes, but it also avoids naming conflicts between vendors because each class name is required to be unique only within its namespace. A general convention is to create a namespace like this:

```
CompanyName.ApplicationName
```

Here `CompanyName` is your company name, and `ApplicationName` is a unique application name within your company. All classes related to this application will belong to this namespace. A class is then identified as, for example, `QueCertifications.Exam70306.ExamQuestions`, where `QueCertifications` is the unique name for a company;

Exam70306 is a unique application within the company; and ExamQuestions is the name of actual class. QueCertifications could have another class with the same name, ExamQuestions, as long as it belongs to a different application, such as QueCertifications.Exam70316. The whole objective is to keep the complete naming hierarchy unique to avoid naming conflicts.

A namespace is just a string in which a dot helps to create a hierarchy. In the namespace QueCertifications.Exam70306, Exam70306 is called *a child namespace* of the QueCertifications namespace. You could organize your classes at two levels here: at the level of QueCertifications and also at the level of Exam70306. You can create as deep a hierarchy as you want.

The System namespace in the FCL acts as the root namespace for all the fundamental and base classes defined inside the library. One of the fundamental classes defined in the System namespace is the Object class (uniquely identified as System.Object). This class acts as the ultimate base class for all other types in the .NET Framework.

The System.Windows.Forms namespace organizes classes for working with Windows Forms. The System.Drawing namespace organizes classes for creating graphical elements. You will use many classes from these two namespaces in this chapter.

> **NOTE**
>
> **Two Hierarchies** A namespace hierarchy has nothing to do with inheritance hierarchy. When one class inherits from another, the base class and derived class can belong to different and unrelated namespaces.

Using the System.Windows.Forms.Form Class

A Windows application generally consists of one or more Windows Forms. A Windows Form is a (usually) rectangular area on the screen over which you will design the user interface of your Windows application. This area acts as a placeholder for various user interface elements such as textboxes, buttons, lists, grids, menus, scroll bars, and so forth.

Programmatically speaking, a Windows Form is an instance of the Form class of the System.Windows.Forms namespace. The form class derives from the inheritance hierarchy shown in Figure 1.1.

FIGURE 1.1
Inheritance hierarchy of a form.

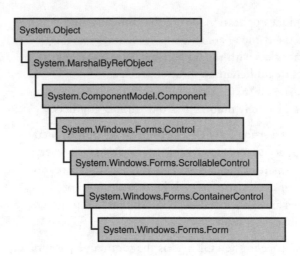

You should know the following from this hierarchy:

◆ The Form class inherits from the ContainerControl class. By the virtue of this inheritance, the Form class becomes capable of acting as a placeholder for various user interface elements or controls such as the TextBox, Label, Button, and ToolBar controls.

◆ A Form is also a Control, but a special type of control that is scrollable as well as capable of acting as a container control. This is because the Form class inherits from the Control class via the ScrollableControl and ContainerControl classes.

◆ The Form class is ultimately derived from the Object class of the System namespace just like any other class. As a result of this inheritance you can also say that a form is of type Object.

◆ As a result of the inheritance chain, the Form class has access to several members (methods, properties, events etc.) that are available to it through its parent classes. The Form class also adds a set of new members for its specific functionality. This is typical of the way that inheritance hierarchies work.

You can use the properties of a Form object (such as Size, BackColor, Opacity, and so on) to modify the way the form appears on the screen.

Methods of a Form object can be used to perform actions on the form like Show, Hide, etc. You can also attach your custom code as event handlers to the form; this will enable form to respond to different actions performed on the form.

Designing a Windows Form Using the Windows Forms Designer

Visual Studio .NET provides a Windows Forms Designer (sometimes also called the *designer* or *visual designer*) for designing Windows Forms. To get started with the designer you can use it to create a simple Windows Form. Step By Step 1.1 will help you in making yourself familiar with different pieces of the development environment that you will use to create Windows Forms.

STEP BY STEP

1.1 Creating a Windows Form

1. Launch Visual Studio .NET. On the Start page, click the New Project button (alternatively, you can select New, Project from the File menu). In the New Project dialog box, select Visual Basic Projects as the Project Type and Windows Application as the Template. Name the project 306C01 and save it in a convenient location, as shown in Figure 1.2

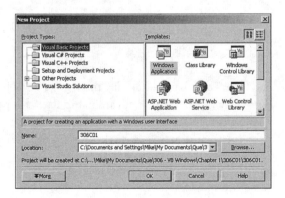

FIGURE 1.2
Creating a new Visual Basic .NET Windows application.

continues

continued

2. The development environment will be in Design mode (see Figure 1.3). You will be shown an empty form. The Solution Explorer window, shown in Figure 1.4, allows you to see all files included in your project by Visual Studio .NET. If the Solution Explorer window is not visible, select Solution Explorer from the View menu to invoke it. Form1.vb is the file that stores the VB .NET code for the default Windows Form created as part of a new project. Right-click on Form1.vb in Solution Explorer and select Rename from the context menu. Rename the file as StepByStep1-1.vb.

FIGURE 1.3▶
The Windows Forms designer environment.

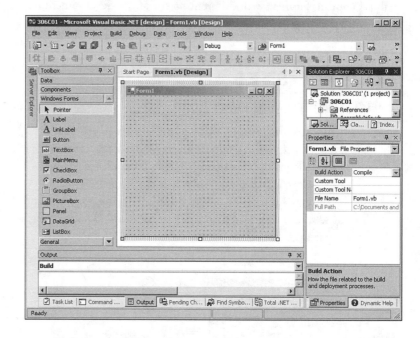

FIGURE 1.4▲
You can use the Solution Explorer to manage files within your Visual Studio .NET Solution.

3. The form's title bar will display the text Form1. This title is a property of the form. You can manipulate this property through the Properties window. Click on the form to give it the focus. and press F4 or select Properties Window from the View menu. Change the Text property of the form in the Properties window to StepByStep1-1, as shown in Figure 1.5

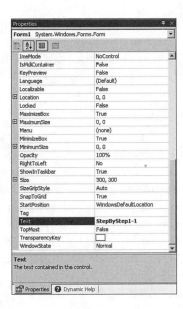

FIGURE 1.5 ◄
The Properties window shows the properties of an object.

4. Select Start from the Debug menu or click F5 to execute the project, which will display your very first Windows Form. You should see something similar to Figure 1.6. Try positioning this form anywhere on screen by dragging its title bar. You can increase or decrease the form size by dragging its border.

5. Click the close box of the form to end the execution of this application and return to Design view.

6. Right-click anywhere on the form and select View Code from the context menu to open a new window in the Visual Studio .NET environment, showing the code corresponding to your Windows Form. Click on the + sign next to the Windows Forms Designer Generated Code section and observe all the code that designer generated automatically for you.

FIGURE 1.6▲
A simple Windows Form in execution.

In this Step By Step you created a Windows application to instruct Visual Studio .NET to generate code that enables a form to launch itself when you execute the code in the project. When you create a new Windows application, Visual Studio will automatically include a Windows Form inside it.

Projects and Solutions   A *solution* groups one or more projects. In a typical application you will first create a solution and then add projects to it. If you directly create a project, Visual Studio .NET will automatically create a solution for it. In this case the name of the solution defaults to the name of project.

Each Windows Form resides in a code file where the file extension depends on the language you are using (.vb for Visual Basic .NET). Visual Studio .NET originally assigned the name Form1.vb to the code file, but you changed it to StepByStep1-1.vb through the Solution Explorer. This code file contains the definition of the Windows Form that you saw when you executed the project.

The Visual Studio .NET designer provides two views of a Windows Form: the Design view and the Code view (see Figure 1.7). What you see in the Design view is nothing but a visual representation of the code. When you manipulate the form using the designer, this code is automatically generated or modified based on your actions. If you wish you can also write the complete code yourself in the Code window. When you switch back to the Design view, the designer will read the code to draw the corresponding form onscreen.

FIGURE 1.7
Exploring the code using the Code view.

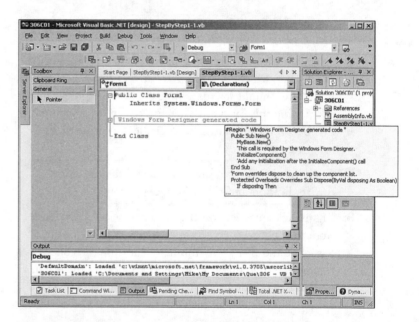

Exploring the Forms Designer Generated Code

While exploring the code in the previous exercise, you probably noticed that Visual Studio .NET groups code into blocks. This feature is called *code outlining*. You can expand and collapse these code blocks using the (+) and (–) signs near the left margin of the window in Code view.

This feature is especially helpful when working with large code files. You can collapse areas of code that you don't want to focus on at that time and continue editing the expanded sections you are interested in. If you hover over a collapsed block, you can see the start of the code that's contained in that block.

In the previous Step By Step you also might have noticed a rectangular block marked Windows Form Designer code. This is a block of collapsed code with a name. When you expand this block, you will see a set of statements included between #Region and #End Region directives. These directives mark the beginning and end of a named code block. You can specify a name after the #Region directive to identify your code block with a name. When you collapse this region, you can easily figure out what the collapsed code block does by looking at the name associated with region. These directives are only useful for the visual designers such as Visual Studio .NET for effective presentation of your code. When your code is compiled, these directives are not present in the executable code.

When you create a Windows Form using Visual Studio .NET, VS .NET will define a class for you that inherits its functionality from the standard Form class in the System.Windows.Forms namespace. In the exercise, although you changed the name of code file containing the class from Form1.vb to StepByStep1-1.vb, the name of the class itself was not changed. Here's the class definition that the designer created:

```
Public Class Form1
    Inherits System.Windows.Forms.Form
```

Form1 is the class name automatically generated by Visual Studio .NET when you create a Windows application. If you want to change it, either change it in the code or modify the Name property of the form in Form Design mode.

The Inherits System.Windows.Forms.Form part in the code specifies that the Form1 class inherits from the Form class that belongs to the System.Windows.Forms namespace. All of the basic functionality of the Form1 class that you experienced (such as moving and resizing) comes from the base Form class.

Any class can have a constructor definition. A *constructor* is a special method to create new instances of a class. A constructor can be easily recognized because it always has the special name New.

NOTE

Static Constructor   A class can also have a *static constructor*, which is called automatically before any of the members of the class are accessed. A common use of static constructors is to initialize static fields and properties of the class.

Here's the constructor that the designer created for the Form1 class:

```
Public Sub New()
    MyBase.New()

    'This call is required by the Windows Form
    ➥Designer.
    InitializeComponent()

    'Add any initialization after the
    ➥InitializeComponent() call

End Sub
```

Ignoring the lines starting with ' (which are comments and do not generate any code), Visual Studio .NET puts just two lines of code inside the default Form1 constructor. The first is a call to the constructor of the form's base class, here represented by the special name MyBase. This ensures that the Form1 class will properly inherit the constructor behavior of its base class. The other line of code is a call to the InitializeComponent() method of the class. The Windows Forms Designer uses the InitializeComponent method to store the customizations to the form through the Design view. In this case the InitializeComponent method is pretty simple:

```
'NOTE: The following procedure is required by the
➥Windows Form Designer
'It can be modified using the Windows Form Designer.
'Do not modify it using the code editor.
<System.Diagnostics.DebuggerStepThrough()>
➥Private Sub InitializeComponent()
    '
    'Form1
    '
    Me.AutoScaleBaseSize = New System.Drawing.Size(5, 13)
    Me.ClientSize = New System.Drawing.Size(292, 273)
    Me.Name = "Form1"
    Me.Text = "StepByStep1-1"

End Sub
```

You can see here that the Text property of Form1, which you manipulated using the Properties window, has been inserted as a code statement. The Me keyword qualifies the property names and refers to the current instance of the class for which the method is called. The designer also automatically adds some initializations without your intervention.

The generated code also includes the Dispose method. In its simple form it looks like this:

```
'Form overrides dispose to clean up the component list.
Protected Overloads Overrides Sub Dispose(ByVal disposing
➥As Boolean)
    If disposing Then
        If Not (components Is Nothing) Then
            components.Dispose()
        End If
    End If
    MyBase.Dispose(disposing)
End Sub
```

The Dispose method is an ideal place to put any cleanup code that you want to be executed when you're done with the class. This method is automatically called as part of the cleanup process for the form.

Running the Windows Form

When you instruct Visual Studio .NET to run the form, it will first compile the form's code using an appropriate language compiler (VB .NET in this case for a VB .NET Windows application). If the compiler does not find any errors, it generates an executable file with the name of the project and extension .EXE (306C01.exe). The default location of this file is in the bin\debug directory within the project's directory. Where is this file located in the project? You can explore that through Solution Explorer by following Step By Step 1.2.

STEP BY STEP

1.2 Using Solution Explorer to See Hidden Files

1. Open the Solution Explorer window if it is not already open by selecting View, Solution Explorer.

2. Click the project name 306C01 to select it. From the toolbar in the Solution Explorer click Show All Files.

continues

> **NOTE**
>
> **Calling Dispose**—The Common Language Runtime features automatic garbage collection for all memory resources no longer required. Dispose isn't necessary for the managed code, but it's a good place to place cleanup code for any of the nonmanaged or nonmemory resources you created in the program.

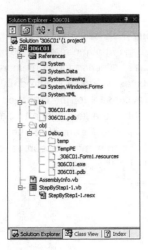

FIGURE 1.8
Showing all files in Solution Explorer.

NOTE

Don't Confuse Library Names with Namespaces   Sometimes the name of a library looks similar to the name of a namespace. For example, I talked about a namespace System.Windows.Forms, and a library by the same name exists as System.Windows.Forms.dll. Don't be mistaken: They are totally different concepts. A library exists as a file and can contain code for one or more classes. These classes can belong to different namespaces. A namespace is logical organization of classes and has no physical form, whereas a library is physical unit that stores classes as a single deployment unit. I'll discuss this in more depth in Chapter 4, "Creating and Managing Components and .NET Assemblies."

---

continued

3. You will see a dimmed folder icon named `bin`, visible in your project's file hierarchy. Expand this folder fully by clicking on the + signs (see Figure 1.8). You will see a file named `306C01.exe`. This is the project's executable file. The other file named `306C01.pdb` (pdb stands for program database) stores debugging and project information.

4. Click the project name again to select it. From the toolbar in the Solution Explorer window, click Show All Files. The `bin` folder will be hidden now.

You might be wondering whether the little code you see in the form is enough for all its functionality. Where is the code to actually draw the form on the screen? Where is the code that responds to dragging or resizing the form? The answer is that this form is inheriting its functionality from other classes.

Well, where is the code for those classes? Code for various classes in the FCL is packaged as *library files* (.dll files), and Visual Studio .NET is smart enough to automatically include their reference in your project. It will select a few common libraries, depending on the project type, and leave including references to other libraries to you. You can see what libraries are included with your project by opening Solution Explorer and navigating to the References hierarchy within your project, as was shown in Figure 1.8.

Using the Application Class

The Application class is responsible for *managing* a Windows application and provides a set of properties for you to get information about the current application (see Table 1.1). It also provides methods to start an application, end an application, and process messages waiting for an application (see Table 1.2). It is important that all methods and properties of Application class are static. Because they're static, you need not create an instance of Application class to use them.

You can directly call these methods by prefixing them with the name of the class. As a matter of fact, creating an instance of Application class is not possible. The class designers assigned the Private access modifier to the constructor of Application class to prevent you from creating instances of this class. If a constructor is not accessible for a class, it cannot be instantiated. See Step By Step 1.3 for more experience using Application class properties.

TABLE 1.1

SOME IMPORTANT STATIC PROPERTIES OF THE APPLICATION CLASS

Property Name	Description
CompanyName	Company name associated with the application. This information will be available in the properties of the executable file in Windows Explorer.
CurrentCulture	Culture information for the current thread.
CurrentInputLanguage	Current input language for the current thread.
ExecutablePath	Path of the executable file that started the application.
ProductName	Product name for current application.
ProductVersion	Product version for current application.

TABLE 1.2

SOME IMPORTANT STATIC METHODS FROM THE APPLICATION CLASS

Method Name	Description
DoEvents	Processes all Windows messages currently in the message queue.
Exit	Terminates the application.
ExitThread	Exits the message loop on the current thread and closes all windows on the thread.
Run	Begins a standard application message loop on the current thread.

STEP BY STEP

1.3 Using Application Class Properties

1. Launch Visual Studio .NET. From the File menu select Open, Project. Navigate to and open the existing project `306C01`.

2. In the Solution Explorer, right-click the project name and select Add, Add Windows Form. (Alternatively, you can select Add Windows Form from the Project menu.) Name the new form `StepByStep1-3.vb`.

3. Switch to the Code view, and just after the Windows Forms Designer generated code block insert the following procedure:

```
Private Sub StepByStep1_3_Load(ByVal sender As Object, _
 ByVal e As System.EventArgs) Handles MyBase.Load
    'Display a MessageBox
    MessageBox.Show(Application.ExecutablePath,
    ➥"Location of Executable", _
    MessageBoxButtons.OK, MessageBoxIcon.Information)
End Sub
```

4. In the Solution Explorer, right-click the project name and select Properties from the context menu. In the Project Property page, set the startup object to `StepByStep1_3`, as shown in Figure 1.9. Click OK to close the Project Property page.

FIGURE 1.9

Changing the startup object by using the Project Property page.

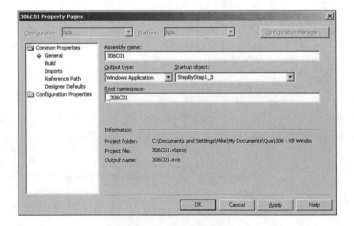

5. Select Run from the Debug menu. The application will display a message box showing the application's executable path (see Figure 1.10). When you close the message box, the application will display the new form.

FIGURE 1.10
A message box displaying the executable's path.

This code uses the Show method of the MessageBox class to display a message box to the user. The message box displays the value of the ExecutablePath property of Application class.

You can guess that since you're calling the Show method prefixed by the name of the class (MessageBox), Show must be a static method. You will also note that as you type the code, Visual Studio .NET will help you with syntaxes, methods, and properties of various code items. This feature is called *IntelliSense* (see Figure 1.11).

```
Public Class StepByStep1_3
    Inherits System.Windows.Forms.Form

    Windows Form Designer generated code

    Private Sub StepByStep1_3_Load(ByVal sender As Object, _
      ByVal e As System.EventArgs) Handles MyBase.Load
        'Display a MessageBox
        MessageBox.s
    End Sub           Show    Displays a message box with the specified text, caption, buttons, icon, default button, and options.
End Class
```

FIGURE 1.11
IntelliSense lets you easily complete statements.

As a small exercise, try placing the MessageBox.Show method in a different procedure and note the difference in execution:

```
Private Sub StepByStep1_3_Closed(ByVal sender As Object, _
  ByVal e As System.EventArgs) Handles MyBase.Closed
    'Display a MessageBox
    MessageBox.Show(Application.ExecutablePath,
    ➥"Location of Executable", _
    MessageBoxButtons.OK, MessageBoxIcon.Information)

End Sub
```

Using the `MessageBox` Class

The MessageBox class belongs to System.Windows.Forms namespace and inherits from the Object class. In addition to the methods it inherits from Object, it provides a Show method in 12 different variations to display different kinds of message boxes to the user. Some of the arguments of the Show methods are values of *enumerated types* such as MessageBoxButtons and MessageBoxIcon. Enumerated types provide a set of named constants. You will see extensive usage of enumerators in .NET Framework class libraries. They are the preferred, type-safe, and object-oriented way of referring to a list of constant values. For example, the MessageBoxButtons enumeration provides a list of named values. Each of these values specifies a set of buttons that can be displayed in a message box. Table 1.3 lists the values of this enumeration and their meanings.

N O T E

Using Message Boxes Message boxes can also help in debugging code quickly. For example, you can use a message box to display the values of variables, fields, and properties at different stages in program execution. When the user clicks a button in the message box, an enumerated value is returned to your code. That way you can tell which button was clicked and take the appropriate action.

E X A M   T I P

MsgBox Versus MessageBox The MsgBox keyword from Visual Basic 6.0 is still supported by Visual Basic .NET, but its use has been deprecated. You should choose the MessageBox class for new projects and use MsgBox only when upgrading existing Visual Basic 6.0 projects.

TABLE 1.3

MessageBoxButtons ENUMERATION LIST

Member Name	The Message Box Shows the Following Buttons
AbortRetryIgnore	Abort, Retry, and Ignore
OK	OK
OKCancel	OK and Cancel
RetryCancel	Retry and Cancel
YesNo	Yes and No
YesNoCancel	Yes, No, and Cancel

The MessageBoxIcon enumeration type provides a value used to determine what icon will be shown on a message box. Table 1.4 lists the values and their meanings for this enumeration (note that some of the names have identical meanings).

TABLE 1.4

MESSAGEBOXICON ENUMERATION LIST

Member Name	The Message Box Contains This Symbol
Asterisk	A lowercase letter *i* in a circle.
Error	A white *X* in a circle with a red background.

Member Name	The Message Box Contains This Symbol
Exclamation	An exclamation point in a triangle with a yellow background.
Hand	A white *X* in a circle with a red background.
Information	A lowercase letter *i* in a circle.
None	No symbol
Question	A question mark in a circle.
Stop	A white *X* in a circle with a red background.
Warning	An exclamation point in a triangle with a yellow background.

REVIEW BREAK

- ▶ Each form definition is contained in a class. Forms generally derive their functionality from the standard `System.Windows.Forms.Form` class.

- ▶ The Solution Explorer window allows you to manage all the files in your project.

- ▶ The `Application` class provides methods and properties that apply to your program as a whole.

- ▶ The `MessageBox` class can be used to display various types of messages to the user.

SETTING AND ADDING PROPERTIES TO A WINDOWS FORM

The properties of an object provide a mechanism through which objects can expose their characteristics to the external world. In this section you will first learn how to customize a form's appearance using its properties. Later in this section you will see how to add your own properties to a form.

Using the Visual Designer to Set Windows Form Properties

A Windows Form derives from several other classes like Object, Control, and so on through a chain of inheritances. As a result it will inherit the properties of its parent classes in addition to its own specific properties. You can manipulate all these properties via the Properties window of Visual Studio .NET to change the behavior of a form. See Step By Step 1.4 to manipulate form properties and behavior.

STEP BY STEP

1.4 Working with Windows Forms Properties

1. Open the project `306C01`. In the Solution Explorer right-click on the project name and select Add, Add Windows Form from the context menu. Name the new form `StepByStep1-4`.

2. Right-click on the form and select Properties from the context menu. Find the `BackColor` property and click the down arrow of the drop-down list to invoke a tabbed list of colors. Three categories of colors are available: Custom, Web, and System. Click of the tab titled Web and select `AntiqueWhite` from the list. Note that the form's surface will immediately change color to reflect this property.

3. In the Property sheet, locate the property named `FormBorderStyle` and change its value from `Sizable` to `FixedSingle`.

4. Next, in the Properties window look for the property named `Size`. Expand this property by clicking on the + sign next to it. Change the `Width` subproperty to 400 and the `Height` subproperty to 200.

5. Next go to the `StartPosition` property and change its value to `CenterScreen`.

6. Change the `MinimizeBox` property to False.

7. In the Solution Explorer, right-click the project name and select Properties from the context menu. In the Project Property page, select StepByStep1_4 as the startup object. Click OK to close the Project Property page.

8. Select Run from the Debug menu. The application will display the form, showing the effects of the property settings you made. The output looks similar to Figure 1.12.

FIGURE 1.12
A form with customized appearance.

In the preceding exercise, you manipulated various properties of a form to change its visual appearance. When you invoked the Properties window for the form, you saw a big list of properties available to you. These properties provide significant control over the characteristics of the form. Table 1.5 includes a partial list of important properties of a Windows Form.

TABLE 1.5

IMPORTANT PROPERTIES OF FORM CLASS

Property Name	Description
BackColor	Background color of the form.
BackgroundImage	Background image displayed in the form.
ClientSize	Size of the Client area of the form.
ControlBox	Indicates whether a control box must be displayed in the caption bar of the form.
DesktopLocation	Location of the form on the Windows desktop.
Enabled	Indicates whether a control can respond to user interaction.
FormBorderStyle	Border style of the form.
Handle	Gets the window handle (hWnd) of the form.
HelpButton	Indicates whether a Help button will be displayed on the caption bar of the form.
Icon	Specifies the icon for the form.
MaximizeBox	Indicates whether a maximize button will be displayed on the caption bar of the form.
MaximumSize	Maximum size to which this form can be resized.

continues

TABLE 1.5	*continued*

IMPORTANT PROPERTIES OF FORM CLASS

Property Name	Description
MinimizeBox	Indicates whether a minimize button will be displayed in the caption bar of the form
MinimumSize	Minimum size to which this form can be resized.
Modal	Indicates whether this form will be displayed modally. If a form is displayed modally, you cannot interact with any other part of the application until the form is closed.
Name	Name of the form.
Opacity	Opacity level of the form.
ShowInTaskbar	Indicates whether this form will be displayed in the Windows taskbar.
Size	Size of the form.
StartPosition	Starting position of the form at runtime.
TopMost	Indicates whether this form should be displayed as the top-most form of the application.

These properties have various data types. You will find that some properties, like FormBorderStyle, are enumerated types; some properties, like Size, are of a type structure whose value is made up of the value of its contained members (x and y in this case); and other properties, like MinimizeBox, accept a simple Boolean value. The Properties window provides a nice user interface for working with these values.

It's a good idea to switch to the Code view, expand the Windows Form Generated Code section, and analyze the generated code.

Setting Windows Form Properties Programmatically

The Windows Forms Designer is a quick and easy way to manipulate form and control properties, but the designer can only set the properties at design time. What if you want to change the appearance of a form at runtime? This is possible by writing your own code in the Code view. In complex projects, as you need more functionality in your application you will switch frequently to the Code view.

Sometimes you can learn more about the Framework using Code view, as it gives an opportunity to directly play with .NET Framework data structures.

In the Step By Step 1.5 you will explore more properties of a Windows Form, in addition to programmatically coding properties you used in Step By Step 1.4. You will also see how to create a form programmatically and how to show more than one form at runtime.

STEP BY STEP

1.5 Setting Windows Form Properties Programmatically

1. Open the project 306C01. In the Solution Explorer right-click on the project name and select Add, Add Windows Form from the context menu. Name the new form StepByStep1-5.

2. Right-click anywhere on the form and select View Code from the context menu. In the Code window insert the following code just after the Windows Forms Designer Generated Code section.

```
Private Sub StepByStep1_5_Load( _
 ByVal sender As System.Object, _
 ByVal e As System.EventArgs) Handles MyBase.Load
    Me.BackColor = Color.AntiqueWhite
    Me.FormBorderStyle = FormBorderStyle.FixedSingle
    Me.Size = New Size(400, 200)
    Me.StartPosition = FormStartPosition.CenterScreen
    Me.MinimizeBox = False
End Sub
```

3. In the Solution Explorer, right-click the project name and select Properties from the context menu. In the Project Property page, select StepByStep1_5 as the startup object. Click OK to close the Project Property page.

4. Select Run from the Debug menu. The form displayed looks similar to the form that you created in the previous exercise (refer to Figure 1.12).

In Step By Step 1.5, when you added a new Windows Form to your project, a new class representing this form was created. When you run the project with this form as the startup object, the form is automatically loaded. This fires the Load event of the form. I'll discuss events in more detail later in the chapter. The important thing for now is that the procedure you entered is declared in such a fashion that it's automatically run in response to the Load event.

In Step By Step 1.5, when you added a new Windows Form to your project, a new class representing this form was created. When you run the project with this form as the startup object, the form is automatically loaded. This fires the Load event of the form. I'll discuss events in more detail later in the chapter. The important thing for now is that the procedure you entered is declared in such a fashion that it's automatically run in response to the Load event.

While typing the code in the Code view, you will see Visual Studio helping with the properties and syntaxes through IntelliSense. Values for properties like BackColor, FormBorderStyle, and so forth are encapsulated in enumerated types. You can find out what enumerated type to use for a property by hovering over a property name in the Code view. This will display a ToolTip to help identify the type of a property.

If you compare the code you wrote manually with the code generated by the Windows Forms designer in Step By Step 1.4, the most significant difference is that the designer included all of its code to set form properties in the InitializeComponent method.

You can alternatively place the code inside the form's constructor. Including the code in the constructor will ensure that the code is executed every time an instance of this form is created. The effect in this case would be to the same as placing the code in the InitializeComponent method.

So far you've seen how to get and set properties for a Windows Form. The Form class also provides a set of methods, and Step By Step 1.6 demonstrates how to use them.

NOTE

Leave the Autogenerated Code Alone The Windows Forms Designer manages the InitializeComponent method. Putting your own code within this method can interfere with the designer's working, so avoid modifying the code contained in this method.

STEP BY STEP

1.6 Invoking Methods of Windows Forms

1. Open the project 306C01. In the Solution Explorer right-click on the project name and select Add, Add Windows Form from the context menu. Name the new form StepByStep1-6.

2. Right-click on the form anywhere and select View Code from the context menu, or press F7. In the Code window insert the following code just after the Windows Form Designer Generated Code section.

```
Private Sub StepByStep1_6_Load _
 (ByVal sender As System.Object, _
 ByVal e As System.EventArgs) Handles MyBase.Load
    ' Set properties for this form
    Me.BackColor = Color.AntiqueWhite
    Me.FormBorderStyle = FormBorderStyle.FixedSingle
    Me.Size = New Size(400, 200)
    Me.StartPosition = FormStartPosition.CenterScreen
    Me.MinimizeBox = False

    ' Create a new form and set its
    ' properties to stay on top
    Dim frmOnTop As Form = New Form()
    frmOnTop.TopMost = True
    frmOnTop.Opacity = 0.7
    frmOnTop.Show()
End Sub
```

3. In the Solution Explorer, right-click the project name and select Properties from the context menu. In the Project Property page, select StepByStep1_6 as the startup Object. Click OK to close the Project Property page.

4. Select Run from the Debug menu. The application will display two forms. The top form is transparent and stays on the top even when you click on the other form, as shown in Figure 1.13.

In the preceding exercise you created a new form by creating an instance of the Form class. You set the properties of the new form to be the topmost form in your application and then reduced its opacity to make it slightly transparent. You finally invoked the Show method of the form to actually display the form onscreen. (Guided Practice Exercise 1.1 offers another opportunity to develop your skills.)

That raises an obvious question. Two forms are in the previous Step By Step exercise, but you are calling the Show method for only one of them. When we run the program you actually see both the forms onscreen. How? The bottom form is the startup object for the project and is launched by the .NET Framework when you run the project. In the running program if you close the top form it will just close itself, but if you close bottom form, it will close all open forms and quit the application.

NOTE

Opacity Property Transparent forms are only supported on operating systems that can display layered windows, including Windows 2000 and higher versions of Windows. This property will have no effect when you run the program on older operating systems, such as Windows 98. On those systems, the topmost form in this example will be opaque.

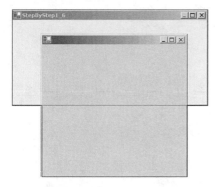

FIGURE 1.13
Calling the Show method on a form.

EXAM TIP

Form.Close() Versus Form.Hide() When you close a form using its Close method, all resources related to form are released. You cannot call the Show method to make the form visible again, as the form itself does not exist anymore. If you want to temporarily hide a form and show it at a later time, use the form's Hide method. Using the Hide method is equivalent to setting the form's Visible property to False. The form still exists in memory and can be made visible any time by calling the Show method of the form or by setting its Visible property to True.

GUIDED PRACTICE EXERCISE 1.1

You are a Windows developer for SpiderWare Inc. In one of your applications you are required to create a form that enables users to set various options of your application. You want the form to have the following characteristics:

▶ The form should have a thin title bar with the text Options and a close button. It should not be possible to resize, minimize, or maximize this form.

▶ The form should always appear on the top of other forms in the application.

▶ The form should always be displayed in the center of the screen.

How would you create such a form?

Try doing this on your own first. If you get stuck or would like to see one possible solution, take a look at the following the steps:

1. Open the project 306C01. Add a Windows Form by the name GuidedPracticeExercise1-1 to this project.

2. Open the Properties window for this form. Change the value of the Text property to Options.

3. Change the FormBorderStyle property to FixedToolWindow.

4. Change the StartPosition property to CenterScreen.

5. Change the TopMost property to True.

6. Set the form as the startup object and execute the program.

If you had difficulty following this exercise, review the section, "Designing a Windows Form Using the Windows Forms Designer." Also spend some time looking at various properties available for a form in the Properties window. Experimenting with them in addition to the text and examples should help you in relearning this material. After review, try this exercise again.

Adding New Properties to a Windows Form

You can add custom properties to a Windows Form in addition to using the existing properties (see Step By Step 1.7). A custom property can be used to store application specific data.

STEP BY STEP

1.7 Adding New Properties to a Windows Form

1. Open the project `306C01`. In the Solution Explorer right-click on the project name and select Add, Add Windows Form from the context menu. Name the new form `StepByStep1-7`.

2. Right-click the form anywhere and select View Code from the context menu. Add one line of code at the very top of the code:

```
Imports System.ComponentModel
```

3. In the Code window insert the following code just after the Windows Forms Designer Generated Code section.

```
' define constant values for State
Public Enum State
    Idle
    Connecting
    Processing
End Enum

' use this field as storage location for FormState property
Private mFormState As State

' set attributes for FormState property
<Browsable(True), _
 EditorBrowsable(EditorBrowsableState.Never), _
 Description("Sets the custom Form state"), _
 Category("Custom")> _
Public Property FormState() As State
    Get
        FormState = mFormState
    End Get
```

continues

continued

```
Set(ByVal Value As State)
    mFormState = Value
    Select Case mFormState
        Case State.Idle
            Me.BackColor = Color.Red
            Me.Text = "Idle"
        Case State.Connecting
            Me.BackColor = Color.Orange
            Me.Text = "Connecting..."
        Case State.Processing
            Me.BackColor = Color.Green
            Me.Text = "Processing"
    End Select
End Set
End Property
```

4. Expand the Windows Form Designer Generated Code section. Change the form's constructor so that it looks like this:

```
Public Sub New()
    MyBase.New()

    'This call is required by the Windows Form Designer.
    InitializeComponent()

    'Add any initialization after the
    ➥InitializeComponent() call
    'set the FormState property of this form
    Me.FormState = State.Processing

End Sub
```

5. In the Solution Explorer, right-click the project name and select Properties from the context menu. In the Project Property page, select StepByStep1_7 as the startup object. Click OK to close the Project Property page.

6. Select Run from the Debug menu. The project will show a green form onscreen with the title text Processing....

Most important to note from the above exercise is that you added a custom property named FormState to a form. The property you created was even visible in the IntelliSense list when you tried to access the members of this form object by typing a dot (.) after the Me keyword in the form's constructor code.

To a program that uses the properties, these properties will look just like a data field, but properties by themselves do not have any storage location, and their definitions look almost like function definitions. Properties provide two accessors (`Get` and `Set`) that are called respectively when a program wants to read from or write to this property. In Step By Step 1.6 you used a private field `mFormState` that works as a storage location for the `FormState` property; since `mFormState` is private, the rest of the world can only access it through the `FormState` public property. The data type of `FormState` is an enumerated type `State` defined with a limited set of named constant values at the beginning of the code segment.

If you go to the Design view and inspect the properties of the form, you won't find the new property. Although in the Code view the FormState property works like any other property, it is not visible in the Properties window because the Properties window only shows the properties of the base class. You can think of it like this: the Properties window helps you design a new class (StepByStep1-7) in terms of an already existing class (System.Windows.Forms.Form). So while designing the StepByStep1-7 class, the Properties window shows the properties of the base Form class. If it showed the properties of the StepByStep1-7 class, that would be like defining a class in terms of itself.

If somehow you could define a form in terms of StepByStep1-7, it would make sense to have these properties available to the derived form through the Properties window. In fact, you can do this with Visual Inheritance, which I'll talk about later in this chapter.

Also note that the new property has a big list of attributes. This isn't required to create a property but helps specify the runtime behavior of the property. Table 1.6 tells what each of these attributes does for the new property.

EXAM TIP

Read-only and Write-only Properties   The Get and Set accessors allow you both read and write access to a property. If you would rather make a property read-only, don't include a Set accessor in its property definition. On the other hand, if you just want a write-only property, don't include a Get accessor in the property definition.

NOTE

Using Accessors   Properties let you encapsulate additional logic through Get and Set accessors. These accessors let you preprocess the data before allowing the programs to store them or read them from the original field storing the data.

TABLE 1.6

ATTRIBUTES THAT CONTROL BEHAVIOR OF A PROPERTY

Attribute Name	Description
Browsable	Indicates whether the property is displayed in the Properties window. Its default value is True.

continues

TABLE 1.6	*continued*

ATTRIBUTES THAT CONTROL BEHAVIOR OF A PROPERTY

Attribute Name	*Description*
EditorBrowsable	Indicates whether the property should appear in the IntelliSense list of an object in the Code view. Its value is of type EditorBrowsableState enumeration with three possible values: Advanced, Always, or Never. Its default value is Always, meaning "always list this property." If you change it to Never, Visual Studio .NET will hide this property from the IntelliSense feature.
Description	Description string for the property. When specified it is displayed in the description area of the Properties window when the property is selected.
Category	Specifies the category of the property. The category is used by the Properties window to categorize the property list.

You won't be able to see the effect of these attributes in this form but can when you inherit a form from it. You'll see how to do this in the next section of this chapter.

REVIEW BREAK

▶ Properties let you customize the appearance and behavior of a Windows Form.

▶ The Windows Forms Designer lets you define a form based on the properties available in its base class (that is, usually the Form class).

▶ You can add custom properties to a form.

▶ Attributes let you define the runtime behavior of a property.

USING VISUAL INHERITANCE

In the earlier discussion on inheritance you learned that when a class inherits from its base class, it derives a basic set of functionality from the base class. No additional programming needs to be done in the derived class for this functionality. You are free to add extra functionality to the derived class to make it more functional.

Because a Windows Form is also a class, inheritance applies to it. In some projects you will create a new form almost like the one you had previously created, only this time you want an additional functionality. In this case, rather than creating a new form from the scratch, you can start by inheriting it from a form with similar functionality and customize the inherited form to add extra functionality.

Inheritance, when applied to a Windows Form, is known as *Visual Inheritance* because you inherit the visual characteristics of a form, like its size, color, any component placed on the form, and so forth. You can also visually manipulate the properties you inherit from the base class.

In Step By Step 1.8 you will see how to inherit from an existing form using Visual Inheritance

STEP BY STEP

1.8 Using Visual Inheritance

1. Open the project 306C01. In the Solution Explorer right-click on the project name and select Add, Add Inherited Form from the context menu. Name the new form StepByStep1-8 and click the Open button.

2. From the Inheritance Picker dialog box (see Figure 1.14), select the component named StepByStep1-7 and click OK.

3. Open the Properties window. Click the Categorized icon on its toolbar. Look for the Custom category. The FormState property within this category will be set to Processing, as shown in Figure 1.15. Change the FormState property to Idle.

4. In the Solution Explorer, right-click the project name and select Properties from the context menu. In the Project Property page, select StepByStep1_8 as the startup object. Click OK to close the Project Property page.

5. Select Run from the Debug menu. Since you have set the FormState property to Idle, the form will be displayed in red.

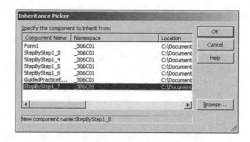

FIGURE 1.14
The Inheritance Picker dialog box.

FIGURE 1.15
The custom property is now available in the Properties window in the specified category along with proper description.

Inheriting Private Members   When you inherit from a class you inherit everything from it. But to the derived class, only the public and protected members of class are accessible. The .NET Framework hides the private members of the base class from the derived class. Even though those members are still there, they cannot be accessed.

When you run the form in this exercise you will note that the newly created form has the same behavior as the form created in StepByStep1-7. The new form inherited its behavior from the already existing form. In other words, the form named StepByStep1-8 is based on the form named StepByStep1-7. You have access to all browsable properties of the base form through the Properties window. When you selected FormState property of this form, you had access to its possible values in a drop-down list. Because of the run-time attribute applied to FormState properties in the base class, it was filed in the Custom category. You were also able to see the description of this property at the bottom of the Properties window when the property was selected.

After you inherit the form, you are free to add extra functionality to your form. This functionality will be available only in the newly created class and the classes that you derive from it; it will not affect any of the base classes. Guided Practice Exercise 1.2 offers another opportunity to develop your skills.

GUIDED PRACTICE EXERCISE 1.2

You are a Windows developer for SpiderWare Inc. In one of your applications you recently created a form to set various options of your application (see Guided Practice Exercise 1.1). Your application now requires another form like the one you designed earlier. The only difference is that this form should always have its color the same as the user's desktop color.

How would you create such a form?

Try this on your own first. If you get stuck or would like to see one possible solution, take a look at the following steps:

1. Open the project 306C01. Add an inherited form by the name GuidedPracticeExercise1-2 to this project.

2. From the Inheritance picker select the component named GuidedPracticeExercise1_1 and click OK.

3. Open the Properties window for this form and change its BackColor property to Desktop.

4. Set the form as the program's startup object and execute the program.

If you had difficulty following this exercise, review the sections, "Designing a Windows Form Using the Windows Forms Designer" and "Using Visual Inheritance." Make sure you do Guided Practice Exercise 1.1 before attempting this one. The text and examples presented in these sections should help you in relearning this material. After review, try this exercise again.

▶ Form inheritance allows you to create a new form by inheriting it from a base form. This allows you to reuse and to extend the coding you've already finished.

▶ The Windows Forms Designer lets you inherit a form visually from an existing form through the Inheritance picker. You can also visually manipulate the inherited properties through the Properties window.

EVENT HANDLING

When you perform an action with an object, the object in turn raises *events* in your application. When you drag the title bar of the form and move it around, the object generates an event; when you resize the form it generates another event. A large portion of code for any typical Windows application is responsible for handling various events the application responds to. Events are at the heart of GUI-based programming.

Not all events are triggered by user actions. Events can be triggered by changes in the environment, like arrival of an email, modifications done to a file, change in time, completion of a program execution, and so on.

With Visual Basic .NET, you can also define your own custom events that your class is interested in listening to. (You'll see how to do that in the next chapter.) You can also handle an event by executing custom code when the event is fired. I'll show you two different ways to handle events in this section:

◆ Handling events by overriding a protected method of the base class

◆ Handling events by attaching a delegate

Handling Events by Overriding a Protected Method of the Base Class

When you create a Windows Form, it inherits from the base Form class. The Form class has a set of events already defined (accessible through the Code window). If your program is interested in taking actions when one of those events is fired, it must define an appropriate *event handler*, a method executed as a response to an event. The event handler must be registered with the event source so that when the event occurs, the handler will be invoked (also referred to as *event-wiring*). It is possible to have multiple event handlers interested in responding to an event. It is also possible to have a single event handler responding to multiple events. Follow steps to handle the MouseDown event in Step By Step 1.9.

Overriding the base class methods is the visual designer's approach for event handling, so for most of the book this will be the preferred approach.

STEP BY STEP

1.9 Handling the MouseDown Event

1. Open the project 306C01. In the Solution Explorer right-click the project name and select Add, Add Windows Form from the context menu. Name the new form StepByStep1-9 and click the Open button.

2. Open the Properties window of this form. Change the form's Text property to Event Handling Form.

3. Right-click anywhere on the form and select View Code from the context menu.

4. In the left combo box at the top of the Code window, select Base Class Events. In the right combo box at the top of the Code window select MouseDown. This will insert a template for the `MouseDown` event handler, as shown in Figure 1.16. Add code to the event handler so that it looks like this:

```
Private Sub StepByStep1_9_MouseDown( _
 ByVal sender As Object, _
 ByVal e As System.Windows.Forms.MouseEventArgs) _
 Handles MyBase.MouseDown
    MessageBox.Show(String.Format( _
    "X ={0}, Y={1}", e.X, e.Y), _
    String.Format("The {0} mouse button hit me at:", _
    e.Button.ToString()))
End Sub
```

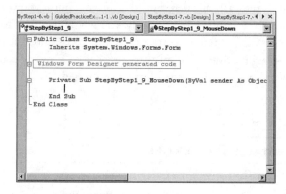

FIGURE 1.16 ◀
The combo boxes in Code view let you insert empty event handlers.

5. Set this form as the startup object. Run the project. You will observe that whenever you click on the form area, it invokes a message box displaying the position of the click and which mouse button was clicked (see Figure 1.17).

FIGURE 1.17 ▲
The event handler displays a message box showing event-related data.

In Step By Step 1.9, you were interested in responding to the `MouseDown` event of the form. The form inherits this event (and many others) from its base class form. The Code window let you see all of the events available for a control or other object. You chose `MouseDown` from that list. When you clicked the event name, the designer inserted a template for the `MouseDown` event handler.

You inserted a line of code that generated a message box showing the coordinates of the point at which mouse button was clicked. You get this information from the `MouseEventArgs` parameter passed to the event handling method.

The name of the event handler is `StepByStep1_9_MouseDown`; that is of the form `ClassName_Eventname`. That's the general naming convention followed by Visual Studio .NET for naming event handlers. Event handlers will normally have a void return type and will accept two arguments. The first is the object on which the event occurred, and the second argument is of type `EventArgs` (or a type derived from it such as `MouseEventArgs`), which contains event-related data. In the `StepByStep1_9_MouseDown` event handler, the second argument is of type `MouseEventArgs`, which contains data specific to mouse events (such as position where the button was pressed). See Table 1.7 to see what kind of information can be retrieved from the `MouseEventArgs` object. The type of second argument will depend on the nature of the event. Visual Studio .NET automatically determined it for you, but if you would have written the event handler manually, you would have had to look in the documentation to find its correct type. The code inside the event handler is straightforward; it displays a message box showing coordinates of the location and which mouse button was pressed.

TABLE 1.7

`MouseEventArgs` PROPERTIES

Member	*Description*
`Button`	Returns a value of type `MouseButtons` that specifies which mouse button was pressed.
`Clicks`	Returns number of times the mouse button was pressed and released.
`Delta`	Delta is a signed count of the number of detents the mouse wheel has rotated. A *detent* is one notch of the mouse wheel.
`X`	The x coordinate of a mouse click.
`Y`	The y coordinate of a mouse click.

How did this event handler get wired up with the actual event? The designer did it for you when you selected the name of the event from the combo box. The Handles clause of the event declaration tells the .NET runtime which event this event handler should be wired to.

In this case, by telling the event handler to handle the MyBase.MouseDown event, you're telling the .NET runtime that this code will respond whenever the MouseDown event is raised in the base class.

What makes this event code work? The above code works because a MouseDown event is the core method that is invoked when the mouse button is pressed. If you like, you can locate this event by using the Class View window.

Open the Class View window by selecting Class View from the View menu (or by using the keyboard shortcut Ctrl+Shift+C). Navigate to the StepByStep1_9 node. Expand the Bases and Interfaces node. You will see a node corresponding to the base class form. Keep on expanding until you see the members of the Control class (see Figure 1.18). Scroll down in this list and find the original definition of the MouseDown event.

Recall from the discussion of inheritance that the derived class inherits all members from its base classes in the inheritance tree. Step By Step 1.11 gets the MouseDown event from the Control class. By registering a handler for this event, Step By Step 1.11 becomes the class that handles the event.

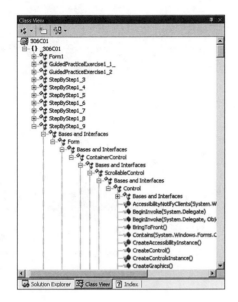

FIGURE 1.18
Class view lets you explore the complete inheritance hierarchy.

Handling Events by Attaching a Delegate

There's a second way to handle events with Visual Basic .NET. The alternative to handling the event from the base class is to use a special function called a *delegate*. A delegate is a function whose job it is to respond to an event. Step By Step 1.10 demonstrates how to do this.

STEP BY STEP

1.10 Handling Events by Using a Delegate

1. Open the project 306C01. In the Solution Explorer right-click on the project name and select Add, Add Windows Form from the context menu. Name the new form StepByStep1_10 and click the Open button.

---

continues

continued

2. Open the Properties window of this form. Change the
Text property of the form to Events Handling Through a
Delegate.

3. Right-click on the form and select View Code from the
context menu. Enter this code after the Windows Form
Designer Generated Code section:

```
' Delegate to handle the MouseDown event
Sub StepByStep_1_10_Mousedown(ByVal sender As Object, _
 ByVal e As MouseEventArgs)
    MessageBox.Show(String.Format( _
    "X ={0}, Y={1}", e.X, e.Y), _
    String.Format("The {0} mouse button hit me at:", _
    e.Button.ToString()))
End Sub
```

4. Expand the Windows Form Designer Generated Code
section and modify the form's constructor to look like
this:

```
Public Sub New()
    MyBase.New()

    'This call is required by the Windows Form Designer.
    InitializeComponent()

    'Add any initialization after the
    ➥InitializeComponent() call

    ' Add an event handler for the form's MouseDown event
    AddHandler Me.MouseDown, _
     AddressOf Me.StepByStep_1_10_MouseDown

End Sub
```

5. Set this form as the startup object. Run the project and
click on the form surface with left and right mouse buttons. You will see the form responding to MouseDown event
by displaying a message box.

The result of this exercise is similar to that of Step By Step 1.9, in
which you handled the event by attaching a delegate to the event.
Only the implementation is different. The key line of code is the
one that adds the delegate to the event:

```
AddHandler Me.MouseDown, _
  AddressOf Me.StepByStep_1_10_MouseDown
```

This statement has three parts:

1. `AddHandler` is a Visual Basic .NET keyword.

2. `Me.MouseDown` is the name of the event.

3. `Me.StepByStep_1_10_MouseDown` is the name of a delegate to handle the event.

The effect of executing this statement is to wire the delegate to actually handle the event. After this statement is executed, every time the `MouseDown` event is raised the `StepByStep_1_10_MouseDown` delegate will be executed.

I mentioned earlier that it is possible to attach multiple event handlers with an event. In the following Step By Step you'll attach a second event handler to the same MouseDown event. When you execute the code and press the mouse button on the form, both event handlers will get executed.

> **NOTE**
>
> **Detaching an Event Handler** You can detach an event handler from an event using the RemoveHandler keyword. Its syntax is similar to AddHandler. You might like to detach an event if at run time you are no longer interested in responding to a particular event.

STEP BY STEP

1.11 Attaching Multiple Event Handlers to the MouseDown Event

1. Open the project `306C01`. In the Solution Explorer right-click on the project name and select Add, Add Windows Form from the context menu. Name the new form `StepByStep1_11` and click the Open button.

2. Open the Properties window for this form. Change the form's `Text` property to Multiple Events Handling Form.

3. Right-click on the form and select View Code from the context menu. Enter this code after the Windows Form Designer Generated Code section:

```
' Delegate to handle the MouseDown event
Sub StepByStep_1_11_MouseDown(ByVal sender As Object, _
 ByVal e As MouseEventArgs)
    MessageBox.Show(String.Format( _
    "X ={0}, Y={1}", e.X, e.Y), _
    String.Format("The {0} mouse button hit me at:", _
    e.Button.ToString()))
End Sub
```

continues

continued

```
' Delegate to handle the MouseDown event
Sub StepByStep_1_11_MouseDown2( _
 ByVal sender As Object, ByVal e As MouseEventArgs)
    Dim frm1_11 As Form = CType(sender, Form)
    If frm1_11.BackColor.ToArgb = _
     Color.AntiqueWhite.ToArgb Then
        frm1_11.BackColor = Color.LightCoral
    Else
        frm1_11.BackColor = Color.AntiqueWhite
    End If
End Sub
```

4. Expand the Windows Form Designer Generated Code section and modify the form's constructor to look like this:

```
Public Sub New()
    MyBase.New()

    'This call is required by the Windows Form Designer.
    InitializeComponent()

    'Add any initialization after the
    ➥InitializeComponent() call

    ' Add two event handlers for the form's MouseDown event
    AddHandler Me.MouseDown, _
     AddressOf Me.StepByStep_1_11_MouseDown
    AddHandler Me.MouseDown, _
     AddressOf Me.StepByStep_1_11_MouseDown2

End Sub
```

5. In the left-hand combo box at the top of the Code window, select Base Class Events. In the right-hand combo box at the top of the Code window select MouseDown to insert a template for the MouseDown event handler, as shown in Figure 1.16. Add code to the event handler so that it looks like this:

```
Private Sub StepByStep1_9_MouseDown( _
 ByVal sender As Object, _
 ByVal e As System.Windows.Forms.MouseEventArgs) _
  Handles MyBase.MouseDown
    MessageBox.Show(String.Format( _
     "X ={0}, Y={1}", e.X, e.Y), _
     String.Format("The {0} mouse button hit me at:", _
     e.Button.ToString()))
End Sub
```

6. Set this form as the startup object. Run the project. Try clicking on the form with left and right mouse buttons, and you will see that the form changes its background color in addition to responding with a message box on every click.

In the previous Step By Step you added two event handlers to the newly created instance of the form's class. The form now has two event handlers registered with the MouseDown Event. You will see that the order in which the event handlers are executed is the order in which they were attached to the event.

I discussed two schemes for event handling. Can these schemes exist together? To answer this question, try Step By Step 1.12.

STEP BY STEP

1.12 Mixing the Two Event Handling Schemes

1. Open the project 306C01. In the Solution Explorer right-click on the project name and select Add, Add Windows Form from the context menu. Name the new form StepByStep1-12 and click the Open button.

2. Open the Properties window. Change the Text property of the form to Mixing Event Handling Techniques.

3. Right-click on the form and select View Code from the context menu. Enter this code after the Windows Form Designer Generated Code section:

```
' Delegate to handle the MouseDown event
Sub StepByStep_1_12_MouseDown2(ByVal sender As Object, _
 ByVal e As MouseEventArgs)
    Dim frm1_12 As Form = CType(sender, Form)
    If frm1_12.BackColor.ToArgb = _
     Color.AntiqueWhite.ToArgb Then
        frm1_12.BackColor = Color.LightCoral
    Else
        frm1_12.BackColor = Color.AntiqueWhite
    End If
End Sub
```

continues

continued

4. Expand the Windows Form Designer Generated Code
   section and modify the form's constructor to look like
   this:

```
Public Sub New()
    MyBase.New()

    'This call is required by the Windows Form Designer.
    InitializeComponent()

    'Add any initialization after the
    ➥InitializeComponent() call

    ' Add an event handler for the form's MouseDown event
    AddHandler Me.MouseDown, _
     AddressOf Me.StepByStep_1_12_MouseDown

End Sub
```

5. Set this form as the startup project and execute it. You will
   see that when you click on the form area both event handlers are executed.

REVIEW BREAK

▶ Events allow your program to respond to the changes in the
  code's environment.

▶ Custom code can be executed when an event fires by registering the code with the event. The pieces of code that respond
  to an event are called event handlers.

▶ Event handlers are registered with events through delegate
  objects.

▶ It is also possible to respond to an event by using the `Handles`
  keyword as a shortcut to creating a delegate.

BUILDING GRAPHICAL INTERFACE ELEMENTS BY USING THE SYSTEM.DRAWING NAMESPACE

The Framework Class Library provides an advanced implementation of the *Windows Graphics Design Interface (GDI+)*. These classes can be used to perform a variety of graphics-related tasks such as working with text, fonts, lines, shapes, and images. One of the main benefits of GDI+ is that it allows you to work with graphic objects without worrying about specific details of the underlying platform. The GDI+ classes are distributed among four different namespaces:

◆ System.Drawing

◆ System.Drawing.Drawing2D

◆ System.Drawing.Imaging

◆ System.Drawing.Text

All these classes reside in an assembly named `System.Drawing.dll`.

Understanding the Graphics Object

The Graphics class in the System.Drawing namespace is one of the most important classes there. It provides methods for doing various kinds of graphic manipulations. The Graphics class is a sealed class and cannot be further inherited (unlike the Form class, for example). The only way to work with the Graphics class is through its instances (Graphics objects). A Graphics object represents a GDI+ drawing surface that can be manipulated using the methods of Graphics class.

When you look in the documentation of the Graphics class you will note that no constructor is available for this class, and hence a Graphics object cannot be directly created. Despite this, you can get a Graphics object already created for you in at least four ways:

1. Through PaintEventArgs argument passed to the Paint event handler of a control or a form. The Graphics object thus received will represent the drawing surface of the object that was the source of event.

2. By calling the CreateGraphics method of a control or a form.

3. By calling the Graphics.FromHwnd method and passing to it the handle of current form.

4. By calling the static Graphics.FromImage method. This method will take an image object and return a Graphics object corresponding to that image. Once you have this Graphics object you can use it to manipulate the image.

Once you have a Graphics object available, you have access to a drawing surface. You can use this surface to draw lines, text, curves, shapes, and so on. But before you can draw you must understand the Windows Forms coordinate system.

Understanding the Windows Forms Coordinate System

The Windows Forms library treats a Windows Form as an object with a two-dimensional coordinate system (see Figure 1.19). That means that when you write text on the form, or put controls on the form, their positions will be identified by a set of points. A *point* is a pair of numbers generally represented as (x, y) where *x* and *y* respectively denote horizontal and vertical distances from the origin of the form. The *origin* of the form is the top-left corner of the Client area of the form. The *Client area* is the inner area of the form, remaining after excluding the space occupied by title bar, sizing borders, and menu (if any). The point of the origin is treated as (0, 0). The value of *x* increases to the right, and the value of *y* increases as you go down.

Two structures are available to represent points in your program—Point and PointF. These structures each represent an ordered pair of values (*x* and *y*). Point stores a pair of integer values, whereas PointF stores a pair of floating-point values. In addition to these values, these structures also provide a set of static methods and operators to perform basic operation on points.

Table 1.8 summarizes all the structures defined in the System.Drawing namespace.

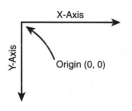

FIGURE 1.19
The Windows Forms Coordinate system.

TABLE 1.8

SYSTEM.DRAWING NAMESPACE STRUCTURES

Structure	Description
CharacterRange	A range of character positions within a string.
Color	The Color structure has 140 static properties, each representing the name of a color. It also has four properties—A, R, G, and B—to specify the values of the Alpha, Red, Green, and Blue portions of the color. A Color value can be created using any of the three static constructors FromArgb, FromKnownColor, or FromName.
Point	Stores an ordered pair of integers x and y that defines a point in a two-dimensional plane. A Point value can be created using its constructor. This structure also provides you with a set of methods and operators to work with Points.
PointF	A float version of the Point structure.
Rectangle	Stores the location and size of a rectangular region. It can be created using a point and a size. *Point* represents the top-left corner and the *Size* specifies its width and length from the given point.
RectangleF	A float version of the Rectangle structure.
Size	Represents the size of a rectangular region with an ordered pair of width and height.
SizeF	A float version of the Size structure.

Drawing Text on a Form

The Graphics class provides a DrawString method that can be invoked on a Graphics object to render a text string on the drawing surface. There are six forms in which the DrawString method can be used. Step By Step 1.13 will show you three ways.

STEP BY STEP

1.13 Drawing Text on the Form

1. Open the project 306C01. In the Solution Explorer right-click on the project name and select Add Windows Form from the context menu. Name the new form StepByStep1-13 and click the Open button.

2. Open the Code view. Use the combo boxes to create an event handler for the form's Paint event. Modify this event handler to look like this:

```
Private Sub StepByStep1_13_Paint(ByVal sender As Object, _
 ByVal e As System.Windows.Forms.PaintEventArgs) _
 Handles MyBase.Paint
    Dim grfx As Graphics = e.Graphics
    Dim strText As String = String.Format( _
     "Form Size is: Width={0}, Height={1}", Width,
     Height)
    grfx.DrawString(strText, Font, Brushes.Black, 0, 0)
End Sub
```

3. Set this form as the startup object. Run the project. The form will display a string of text in black, showing the width and height of the form. Figure 1.20 shows the result.

FIGURE 1.20
Drawing text on a Windows Form using the DrawString method of the Graphics class.

Why did I choose to write the code within an event handler in the preceding exercise? The foremost reason is that Paint event handler provides access to the Graphics object. Secondly, the Paint event is fired whenever the form is redrawn, including when the form is first shown and when the form is restored from minimized state, as well as when the form is shown after a window overlapping it is removed. So a Paint event handler is an appropriate place to put the code that you want to be executed whenever a form is redrawn.

The code gets the Graphics object through the Graphics property of the PaintEventArgs argument of the Paint event handler. The next step is to call its DrawString method to draw text on the form. The DrawString method used here takes five arguments and has the following signature:

```
Public Sub DrawString(string, Font, Brush, float, float);
```

1. The first argument is the string to be displayed. I used the String.Format method to format the string.

2. The second argument is the font of the string. In this exercise I chose the default font of the current form through its Font property.

3. The third parameter is the type of brush. The Brushes enumeration provides a variety of Brush objects, each with a distinct color. I chose the Brushes.Black value to draw text in black.

4. The fourth and fifth properties are used to specify the (x, y) location for the point that marks the start of string on the form. Both of these values are required to be of float type. The 0 value that the code contains will be implicitly converted to a float value.

You might have noticed that when you resized the form in the last exercise it did not trigger the Paint event. An obvious idea for improving this form is to have it dynamically reflect the size of the form as we resize it. Can you guess what event you should handle to do that? You are right if you guessed the Resize event. See Step By Step 1.14 for a walk-through.

STEP BY STEP

1.14 Using the Invalidate Method

1. Open the project 306C01. In the Solution Explorer, right-click the project name and select Add Windows Form from the context menu. Name the new form StepByStep1-14 and click the Open button.

2. Open the Code view. Use the combo boxes to create an event handler for the form's Paint event. Modify this event handler to look like this:

```
Private Sub StepByStep1_14_Paint(ByVal sender As Object, _
 ByVal e As System.Windows.Forms.PaintEventArgs) _
 Handles MyBase.Paint
    Dim grfx As Graphics = e.Graphics
    Dim strText As String = String.Format( _
```

continues

EXAM TIP

Unicode Support and DrawString
GDI+ (and hence the Windows Forms library) has full support for Unicode, making it possible to draw text in any language supported by the operating system.

continued

```
   "Form Size is: Width={0}, Height={1}", Width, Height)
   grfx.DrawString(strText, Font, Brushes.Black, 0, 0)
End Sub
```

3. Add an event handler for the form's `Resize` event:

```
Private Sub StepByStep1_14_Resize(ByVal sender As Object, _
 ByVal e As System.EventArgs) Handles MyBase.Resize
   Invalidate()
End Sub
```

4. Set the form as the startup object. Run the project, and you will notice that the form constantly modifies the text as it is resized.

INVALIDATE Method Call When you call the Invalidate method without any parameters, the Paint event is called for the entire area. If only a particular portion of the control needs refreshed, calling Invalidate for the entire area is overly taxing on application performance. In this case, call Invalidate with a Rectangle parameter that specifies the portion of the control that you are interested in refreshing.

Now the program works as desired. They key is the `Invalidate` method. Calling the `Invalidate` method causes a `Paint` message to be sent to the form. As a result, the `Paint` event handler is called. So this handy method can be called any time to execute the code in the `Paint` event handler. In this exercise, the code makes a call to the `Invalidate` method whenever the form is resized. The `Invalidate` method is available in various forms. It is also possible to refresh a specific portion of the form using one of these forms.

It's not unusual to want to repaint a form whenever it's resized. The Windows Forms library designers provided a shortcut for this with the ResizeRedraw property, a protected property that the Form class inherits from the Control class. When set to True, this property will instruct a control (or a form in this case) to redraw itself when resized. The default value of this property is False. Step By Step 1.15 shows the usage of ResizeRedraw.

STEP BY STEP

1.15 Using the `ResizeRedraw` Property

1. Open the project 306C01. In the Solution Explorer right-click the project name and select Add Windows Form from the context menu. Name the new form StepByStep1-15 and click the Open button.

2. Open the Code view. Use the combo boxes to create an event handler for the form's `Paint` event. Modify this event handler to look like this:

```
Private Sub StepByStep1_15_Paint(ByVal sender As Object, _
 ByVal e As System.Windows.Forms.PaintEventArgs) _
 Handles MyBase.Paint
    Dim grfx As Graphics = e.Graphics
    Dim strText As String = String.Format( _
      "Form Size is: Width={0}, Height={1}", Width, Height)
    grfx.DrawString(strText, Font, Brushes.Black, 0, 0)
End Sub
```

3. Expand the Windows Form Designer Generated Code section. Modify the constructor of the form so the modified version looks like this:

```
Public Sub New()
    MyBase.New()

    'This call is required by the Windows Form Designer.
    InitializeComponent()

    'Add any initialization after the
  ➥InitializeComponent() call

    ' Paint when resized
    Me.ResizeRedraw = True

End Sub
```

4. Set the form as the startup object. Run the project, and you will notice that the form paints its drawing surface whenever you resize the form (just as it did in the previous Step By Step, although the implementation is different).

The form's constructor is a good place to set this property.

As one more enhancement to Step By Step 1.15, you can center this text programmatically within the form. What's involved in that? First, you need to find the coordinates of the center of the form. The horizontal distance can be found by dividing the width of the Client area (`ClientSize.Width`) by two, and the vertical distance can be found by dividing the height of the Client area (`ClientSize.Height`) by two.

The `ClientSize` properties give you access to a `Size` structure representing the size of the Client area of the form. However, this won't center the text onscreen because now the text will start from center; depending on how long it is it will be more on the right side. You need to adjust the coordinates of the center point according to the size of our string. Beware here that size of string can vary depending on what font you have chosen for the text. A safe way to determine string size is to use `MeasureString` method of the Graphics object. It can be used as shown in the following code segment:

```
Dim stringSize As SizeF = grfx.MeasureString(str, Font)
```

Then the modified coordinates for placing the string can be calculated as x=(`ClientSize.Width`–`stringSize.Width`)/2 and y=(`ClientSize.Height`–`stringSize.Height`)/2.

An alternative approach is to make use of the `StringFormat` object in the following signature of the `DrawString` method:

```
Public Sub DrawString(string, Font, Brush, _
  PointF, StringFormat);
```

The `StringFormat` argument lets you specify the text alignment and spacing options for the text. Step By Step 1.16 uses this form of `DrawString` to center text onscreen:

STEP BY STEP

1.16 Drawing Text on a Form

1. Open the project `306C01`. In the Solution Explorer right-click on the project name and select Add Windows Form from the context menu. Name the new form `StepByStep1-16` and click the Open button.

2. Open the Code view of the form. Add an event handler for the `Paint` event. Modify the event handler to look like this:

```
Private Sub StepByStep1_16_Paint(ByVal sender As Object, _
  ByVal e As System.Windows.Forms.PaintEventArgs) _
  Handles MyBase.Paint
    Dim grfx As Graphics = e.Graphics
    Dim strText As String = String.Format( _
    "Form Size is: Width={0}, Height={1}", Width, Height)
```

```
    Dim pt As PointF = New PointF(ClientSize.Width / 2, _
      ClientSize.Height / 2)

    ' Set the horizontal and vertical alignment
    ' using StringFormat object
    Dim strFormat As StringFormat = New StringFormat()
    strFormat.Alignment = StringAlignment.Center
    strFormat.LineAlignment = StringAlignment.Center

    ' Create Font and Brush objects
    Dim fntArial As Font = New Font("Arial", 12)
    Dim brushColor As Brush = New SolidBrush(Me.ForeColor)

    ' Call the DrawString method
    grfx.DrawString(strText, fntArial, _
      brushColor, pt, strFormat)

End Sub
```

3. Expand the Windows Form Designer Generated Code section. Modify the constructor of the form so that the modified version looks like this:

```
Public Sub New()
    MyBase.New()

    'This call is required by the Windows Form Designer.
    InitializeComponent()

    'Add any initialization after the
    ➥InitializeComponent() call

    ' Paint when resized
    Me.ResizeRedraw = True

End Sub
```

4. Set the form as the startup object. Run the project and Resize the form. Notice that the text is displayed in the center of the form.

The code begins by calculating the center coordinates of the form. Once you have the coordinates of center, call `StringAlignment.Center` to horizontally center the string at that point. `StringAlignment` is an enumeration available in the System.Drawing namespace to specify the location of the alignment of the text.

By default, when the DrawString method draws a string, it aligns the top of string with its x coordinate value. This won't make much difference if the height of the text itself is not big, but as you increase the size of font, you will notice the text is hanging down starting from x-axis. To center the text vertically within its own line, set the LineAlignment property of the StringFormat object to StringAlignment.Center.

The code creates a new Font object and specifies a font name and size. Rather than using the brush specified by Brushes.Black value, this code creates a brush object that takes the value of its color from the current form's ForeColor property. If you change the ForeColor of the form using the Properties window, the change will automatically reflect here. Using a brush based on the ForeColor of the form is a good idea as compared to using an absolute value like Brushes.Black for a brush. For example, if the form designer chooses the BackColor of the form to be black and ForeColor to be white, text drawn using Brushes.Black won't be visible but the brush made from ForeColor would be visible.

Drawing Shapes

The Graphics class allows you to draw various graphical shapes such as Arc, Curve, Pie, Ellipse, Rectangle, Image, Path, and Polygon. Table 1.9 lists some important drawing methods of Graphics class.

TABLE 1.9

IMPORTANT DRAWING METHODS OF THE GRAPHICS CLASS

Method Name	Description
DrawArc	Draws an arc that represents a portion of an ellipse
DrawBezier	Draws a Bézier curve defined by four Points
DrawBeziers	Draws a series of Béziers
DrawClosedCurve	Draws a closed curve defined by an array of Points
DrawCurve	Draws a curve defined by an array of Points
DrawEllipse	Draws an ellipse defined by a bounding rectangle specified by a pair of coordinates, a height, and a width

Method Name	Description
DrawIcon	Draws the image represented by the specified Icon object at the given coordinates
DrawImage	Draws an Image object at the specified location preserving its original size
DrawLine	Draws a line connecting the two points
DrawLines Points	Draws a series of line segments that connect an array of
DrawPath	Draws a GraphicsPath object
DrawPie	Draws a pie shape defined by an ellipse and two radial lines
DrawPolygon	Draws a polygon defined by an array of Points
DrawRectangle height	Draws a rectangle specified by a Point, a width, and a
DrawRectangles	Draws a series of rectangles
DrawString	Draws the given text string at the specified location with the specified Brush and Font objects

You will be using some of these methods in Step By Step 1.17 to draw shapes on a form's surface.

STEP BY STEP

1.17 Using the Draw Methods of the Graphics Class

1. Open the project 306C01. In the Solution Explorer right-click the project name and select Add Windows Form from the context menu. Name the new form StepByStep1-17 and click the Open button.

2. Open the Code view of the form. At the top of the Code view add the following line of code:

```
Imports System.Drawing.Drawing2D
```

3. Add a handler for the Paint event of the form. Modify the code in the Paint event handler to look like this:

```
Private Sub StepByStep1_17_Paint(ByVal sender As Object, _
 ByVal e As System.Windows.Forms.PaintEventArgs) _
```

continues

FIGURE 1.21
Calling Draw methods of the Graphics class.

continued

```
Handles MyBase.Paint
    Dim grfx As Graphics = e.Graphics
    ' Set the Smoothing mode to SmoothingMode.AntiAlias
    grfx.SmoothingMode = SmoothingMode.AntiAlias
    ' Create Pen objects
    Dim penYellow As Pen = New Pen(Color.Blue, 20)
    Dim penRed As Pen = New Pen(Color.Red, 10)
    ' Call Draw methods
    grfx.DrawLine(Pens.Black, 20, 130, 250, 130)
    grfx.DrawEllipse(penYellow, 20, 10, 100, 100)
    grfx.DrawRectangle(penRed, 150, 10, 100, 100)
End Sub
```

4. Set this form as the startup object. Run the project and you will see the form as displayed in Figure 1.21.

The Draw methods used in the previous exercise take five arguments:

◆ The first argument to each method is the Pen object it uses to draw the shape. You can create a Pen object in several ways. The simplest way is to use a ready-made Pen from the Pens class. You can also create a Pen object using the Pen class constructor. Table 1.10 lists the different Pen-related classes available in the System.Drawing namespace.

◆ The second and third arguments are the x and y coordinates of the upper-left corner where the desired shape is drawn.

◆ The fourth and fifth parameters indicate the width and height of the desired shape. In case of DrawLine, these indicates the x and y coordinates of the ending point of the line drawn.

TABLE 1.10

CLASSES RELATED TO PEN IN SYSTEM.DRAWING NAMESPACE

Class	Description
Pen	Defines an object used to draw lines and curves.
Pens	Provides 140 static properties, each representing a Pen of a standard color.
SystemPens	Provides a set of static properties each named after a Windows display element. Each of these properties returns a Pen object representing the color of a Windows display element with a width of 1.

The reason you must include a reference to the System.Drawing.Drawing2D namespace in Step By Step 1.17 is that in the above program you are using an enumeration named SmoothingMode. This enumeration class is defined in the namespace System.Drawing.Drawing2D, so a reference to the namespace must be present in the program if the for the VB .NET compiler to find the class.

The Graphics object has a property named SmoothingMode; it can take any of the values of the SmoothingMode enumeration type. Table 1.11 summarizes these values. This property specifies the quality of rendering. The Windows Forms library supports antialiasing, which if chosen will produce text and graphics that appear smoother.

NOTE

Antialiasing Antialiasing is a technique for rendering images in which partially transparent pixels are drawn close to the opaque pixels present at the edges of the drawing. This will actually make the edges kind of fuzzy, but this effect makes the edges appear smoother to human eyes as compared to its original form. Because extra calculations are involved, antialiasing makes rendering graphics slower.

TABLE 1.11

SmoothingMode ENUMERATION MEMBERS

Member Name	Description
AntiAlias	Antialiased rendering
Default	Same as None
HighQuality	High quality, low performance rendering (same as AntiAlias)
HighSpeed	High performance, low quality rendering (same as None)
Invalid	Invalid mode (raises exception)
None	No antialiasing

In addition to the Draw methods, the Graphics class also provides a variety of Fill methods (see Table 1.12). These methods can be used to draw a solid shape on the form (see Step By Step 1.18).

TABLE 1.12

FILL METHODS OF THE GRAPHICS CLASS

Method Name	Description
FillClosedCurve	Fills the interior of a closed curve defined by an array of Points
FillEllipse	Fills the interior of an ellipse defined by a bounding rectangle
FillPath	Fills the interior of a GraphicsPath object

continues

TABLE 1.12 | *continued*

FILL METHODS OF THE GRAPHICS CLASS

Method Name	Description
FillPie	Fills the interior of a pie section defined by an ellipse and two radial lines
FillPolygon	Fills the interior of a polygon defined by an array of points
FillRectangle	Fills the interior of a rectangle specified by a Point, a width, and a height
FillRectangles	Fills the interiors of a series of rectangles
FillRegion	Fills the interior of a Region object

STEP BY STEP

1.18 Using the Fill Methods of the Graphics Object

1. Open the project 306C01. In the Solution Explorer right-click on the project name and select Add Windows Form from the context menu. Name the new form StepByStep1-18 and click the Open button.

2. Open the Code view of the form. Add a handler for the Paint event of the form. Modify the code in the Paint event handler to look like this:

```
Private Sub StepByStep1_18_Paint(ByVal sender As Object, _
 ByVal e As System.Windows.Forms.PaintEventArgs) _
 Handles MyBase.Paint
    Dim grfx As Graphics = e.Graphics
    ' Create Brush objects
    Dim brushRed As Brush = New SolidBrush(Color.Red)
    Dim brushYellow As Brush = _
     New SolidBrush(Color.FromArgb(200, Color.Yellow))
    ' Call Fill methods
    grfx.FillEllipse(brushRed, 20, 10, 80, 100)
    grfx.FillRectangle(brushYellow, 60, 50, 100, 100)
End Sub
```

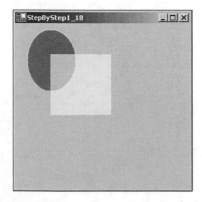

FIGURE 1.22
Using Fill methods of the Graphics class.

3. Set this form as the startup object. Run the project and a red ellipse and yellow rectangle overlaying will appear on the form as in Figure 1.22.

The `Fill` methods use `Brush` objects to fill the drawing object. Other than that, their syntax looks very similar to the syntax of corresponding `Draw` methods.

Note the call used to create the yellow brush in the previous exercise. This form of the constructor uses alpha blending of the yellow color to get the transparent yellow color used to produce an overlay effect.

You used a `SolidBrush` object in this exercise to fill shapes. Other types of brushes can be used to create fancy filling effects. Table 1.13 lists the different types of brushes and Step By Step 1.19 provides a walk-through on using them.

TABLE 1.13

TYPES OF BRUSHES IN SYSTEM.DRAWING AND SYSTEM.DRAWING.DRAWING2D NAMESPACE

Class	Description
Brush	This class is an abstract base class that is used to created brushes such as `SolidBrush`, `TextureBrush`, and `LinearGradientBrush`. These brushes are used to fill the interiors of graphical shapes such as rectangles, ellipses, pies, polygons, and paths. This class is a member of the `System.Drawing` namespace.
Brushes	Provides 140 static properties, one for name of each standard color. This class is a member of the `System.Drawing` namespace.
HatchBrush	Allows you to fill the region using one of pattern from a large number of patterns available in `HatchStyle` enumeration. This class is a member of the `System.Drawing.Drawing2D` namespace.
LinearGradientBrush	Creates both two-color gradients and multicolor gradients. By default the gradient is a linear gradient changing from one color to another color along the specified line. This class is a member of the `System.Drawing.Drawing2D` namespace.
SolidBrush	Defines a brush of a single color. Brushes are used to fill graphics shapes, such as rectangles, ellipses, pies, polygons, and paths. This class is a member of the `System.Drawing` namespace.

continues

TABLE 1.13   *continued*

TYPES OF BRUSHES IN SYSTEM.DRAWING AND
SYSTEM.DRAWING.DRAWING2D NAMESPACE

Class	Description
SystemBrushes	Provides a set of static properties each named after a Windows display element. Each of these properties returns a SolidBrush object representing the color respective Windows display element. This class is a member of the System.Drawing namespace.
TextureBrush	Each property of the TextureBrush class is a Brush object that uses an image to fill the interior of a shape. This class is a member of the System.Drawing namespace.

STEP BY STEP

1.19 Using Different Brush types

1. Open the project 306C01. In the Solution Explorer right-click the project name and select Add Windows Form from the context menu. Name the new form StepByStep1-19 and click the Open button.

2. Open the Code view of the form. At the top of the Code view add the following line of code:

```
Imports System.Drawing.Drawing2D
```

3. Add a handler for the Paint event of the form. Modify the code in the Paint event handler to look like this:

```
Private Sub StepByStep1_19_Paint(ByVal sender As Object, _
 ByVal e As System.Windows.Forms.PaintEventArgs) _
 Handles MyBase.Paint
    Dim grfx As Graphics = e.Graphics

    ' Create a HatchBrush object
    ' Call FillEllipse method by passing
    ' the created HatchBrush object
```

```
Dim hb As HatchBrush = _
 New HatchBrush(HatchStyle.HorizontalBrick, _
Color.Blue, Color.FromArgb(100, Color.Yellow))
grfx.FillEllipse(hb, 20, 10, 100, 100)

' Create a TextureBrush object
' Call FillEllipse method by passing
' the created TextureBrush object
Dim img As Image = New Bitmap("sunset.jpg")
Dim tb As Brush = New TextureBrush(img)
grfx.FillEllipse(tb, 150, 10, 100, 100)

' Create a LinearGradientBrush object
' Call FillEllipse method by passing
' the created LinearGradientBrush object
Dim lb As LinearGradientBrush = _
 New LinearGradientBrush( _
 New Rectangle(80, 150, 100, 100), _
 Color.Red, Color.Yellow, _
 LinearGradientMode.BackwardDiagonal)
   grfx.FillEllipse(lb, 80, 150, 100, 100)
End Sub
```

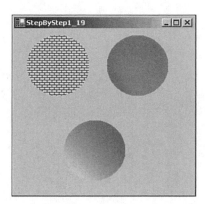

FIGURE 1.23
Creating fancy objects using different Brush types.

4. Set this form as the startup object. Run the project. You will notice that ellipses filled in various styles are displayed on the form as in Figure 1.23.

You used three different brush objects in the previous exercise. The TextureBrush class is part of the System.Drawing namespace, while the other two classes (HatchBrush and LinearGradientBrush) are members of the System.Drawing.Drawing2D namespace.

Using HatchBrush you filled the ellipse with HorizontalBrick HatchStyle. The TextureBrush uses an image to fill the interior of a shape. In this code, I'm assuming the image is in the same directory as the .EXE file. If you have the image in some other directory, you must change the path in the Bitmap constructor. The Bitmap name is a bit misleading, as it is actually capable of creating images from a variety of image formats, including .BMP, .GIF, .JPG, and .PNG.

In the previous exercise the code sets the gradient direction from upper-right corner to the lower-left corner of the rectangle encapsulating the ellipse. Table 1.14 lists the enumeration values for LinearGradientMode:

TABLE 1.14	

LINEARGRADIENTMODE ENUMERATION

Member Name	*Description*
BackwardDiagonal	Specifies a gradient from upper-right to lower-left
ForwardDiagonal	Specifies a gradient from upper-left to lower-right
Horizontal	Specifies a gradient from left to right
Vertical	Specifies a gradient from top to bottom

Working with Images

In addition to working with simple shapes and colors, the Graphics class also supports working with more complex image files. You can either work with existing image files, or, as in Step By Step 1.20, you can compose your own images directly in code.

STEP BY STEP

1.20 Creating and Rendering Images

1. Open the project 306C01. In the Solution Explorer right-click on the project name and select Add Windows Form from the context menu. Name the new form StepByStep1-20 and click the Open button.

2. Open the Code view of the form. At the top of the Code view add the following lines of code:

```
Imports System.Drawing.Drawing2D
Imports System.Drawing.Imaging
```

3. Add a handler for the Paint event of the form. Modify the code in the Paint event handler to look like this:

```
Private Sub StepByStep1_20_Paint(ByVal sender As Object, _
 ByVal e As System.Windows.Forms.PaintEventArgs) _
 Handles MyBase.Paint
    Dim grfx As Graphics = e.Graphics
    grfx.DrawImage(New Bitmap("SampleImage.png"), _
    ClientRectangle)
End Sub
```

4. Expand the Windows Form Designer Generated Code section. Modify the form's constructor to look like this:

```
Public Sub New()
    MyBase.New()

    'This call is required by the Windows Form Designer.
    InitializeComponent()

    'Add any initialization after the
    ➥InitializeComponent() call
    ' Create a Bitmap object
    Dim bmp As Bitmap = New Bitmap(800, 600, _
     PixelFormat.Format32bppArgb)
    ' Create a Graphics object using FromImage method
    Dim grfx As Graphics = Graphics.FromImage(bmp)
    ' Call the Fill Rectangle method
    ' to create an outer rectangle
    grfx.FillRectangle(New SolidBrush(Color.White), _
     New Rectangle(0, 0, 800, 600))
    ' Create Font and RectangleF object
    Dim fntText As Font = New Font("Verdana", 20)
    Dim rect As RectangleF = _
     New RectangleF(100, 100, 250, 300)
    ' Fill the InnerRectangle
    ' Add the text to the Inner Rectangle
    grfx.FillRectangle(New SolidBrush( _
     Color.AliceBlue), rect)
    grfx.DrawString("Sample Text", fntText, _
     New SolidBrush(Color.Blue), rect)
    ' Draw a closed curve
    Dim penBlack As Pen = New Pen(Color.Black, 20)
    penBlack.DashStyle = DashStyle.Dash
    penBlack.StartCap = LineCap.Round
    penBlack.EndCap = LineCap.Round
    grfx.DrawClosedCurve(penBlack, New Point() { _
     New Point(50, 50), _
     New Point(400, 50), _
     New Point(400, 400), _
     New Point(50, 400)})
    ' Save the newly created image file
    bmp.Save("SampleImage.png", ImageFormat.Png)

End Sub
```

5. Set this form as the startup object. Run the project. The code will create an image and render it in the form as in Figure 1.24.

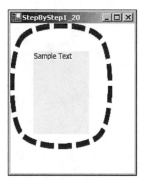

FIGURE 1.24
A bitmap image created entirely in code and then rendered to a form.

You can see the result in Figure 1.24. Step By Step 1.20 first creates an image and then renders it on the form's surface. The image creation code is written in the form's constructor, meaning it is executed before the application creates the form object. Three keys steps relate to image manipulation:

1. The first step is to create a `Bitmap` object to use to work on images. This code creates the object by specifying its size in pixels and specifying a format value from the `PixelFormat` enumeration. The `PixelFormat` enumeration belongs to the System.Drawing.Imaging namespace. The value `Format32bppArgb` specifies that 32 bits of data are associated with each pixel in the image. Of these 32 bits, 8 bits are used for each component (alpha, red, green, and blue) of the pixel.

2. Once you have a `Bitmap` object, you can get a Graphics object from it. This `Graphics` object can be used to draw on the surface of the drawing.

3. Once the image is ready, the `Save` method can be called on the `Bitmap` object. It supports a variety of formats for saving the graphics; these formats are available as static public properties of the `ImageFormat` class. The `ImageFormat` class is a member of `System.Drawing.Imaging` namespace. Some of the possible formats include BMP, GIF, Icon, JPEG, PNG, TIFF, WMF, and so forth.

The rest of the code draws a piece of text and a curved line on the image before saving it. Note the various properties of the `Pen` object that you used in Step By Step 1.20. The code uses this customized `Pen` object to create a boundary around the image. Table 1.15 summarizes some important properties of the `Pen` class. (Guided Practice Exercise 1.3 offers another opportunity to develop your skills.)

TABLE 1.15

Pen CLASS PROPERTIES

Property	Description
Alignment	Alignment for this Pen object
Brush	Brush object that determines attributes of this Pen object
Color	Color of this Pen object

Property	*Description*
DashCap	Cap style used at the end of the dashes that make up dashed lines
DashPattern	Array of custom dashes and spaces
DashStyle	Style used for dashed lines
EndCap	Cap style used at the end of lines
LineJoin	Join style for the ends of two consecutive lines
PenType	Style of lines
StartCap	Cap style used at the beginning of lines
Width	Width of this Pen object

GUIDED PRACTICE
EXERCISE 1.3

You are a Windows developer for SpiderWare Inc. The Windows application you are working on should have a form that allows users to create new designs for Spider-Webs. The requirement itself is simple: the form must have a white background on which a user can design using a thin black pen. Users often make mistakes while designing, so a mechanism to erase should be part of the design. Users say that they will be comfortable using the left mouse button for drawing and right mouse button for erasing. You also noted that users of your application all have high-end machines, and they want sharper looking designs.

How would you design such a form?

Try this on your own first. If you get stuck or would like to see one possible solution, read the following steps:

1. Open the project 306C01. Add a Windows Form by the name GuidedPracticeExercise1-3 to this project.

2. Open the Properties window for this form. Change the form's BackColor property to White.

3. Open the Code view of the form and insert this line at the top of the form's module:

```
Imports System.Drawing.Drawing2D
```

continues

continued

4. Add a line of code after the Windows Form Designer Generated Code:

```
Dim ptPrevPosition As Point = New Point(-1, -1)
```

5. Add an event handler for the form's MouseMove event. Modify the MouseMove event handler to look like this:

```
Private Sub GuidedPracticeExercise1_3_MouseMove( _
 ByVal sender As Object, _
 ByVal e As System.Windows.Forms.MouseEventArgs) _
 Handles MyBase.MouseMove
    If (ptPrevPosition.X = -1) Then
        ' Set the previous position x-y coordinates to
        ' the current x-y coordinates
        ptPrevPosition = New Point(e.X, e.Y)
    End If
    Dim ptCurrPosition As Point = New Point(e.X, e.Y)
    ' Get the Graphics object by
    ' calling Graphics.FromHwnd method
    Dim g As Graphics = Graphics.FromHwnd(Me.Handle)
    g.SmoothingMode = SmoothingMode.AntiAlias
    ' Check if the left mouse button is pressed
    If (e.Button = MouseButtons.Left) Then
        ' Draw a line from the previous
        ' position to current position
        g.DrawLine(New Pen(Color.Black), _
         ptPrevPosition, ptCurrPosition)
        ' Check whether right mouse button is pressed
    ElseIf (e.Button = MouseButtons.Right) Then
        ' Draw a line from the previous
        ' position to current position
        ' usingthe form's BackColor
        g.DrawLine(New Pen(Me.BackColor, 4), _
         ptPrevPosition, ptCurrPosition)
    End If
    ' Set the Previous position to current position
    ptPrevPosition = ptCurrPosition
End Sub
```

6. Set the form as startup object and execute the program.

If you had difficulty following this exercise, review the sections titled "Event Handling" and "Drawing Shapes." The text and examples presented in these sections should help in relearning this material. After review, try this exercise again.

▶ Windows Forms follow a two-dimensional coordinate system. A point is an addressable location in this coordinate system.

▶ The Graphics object gives access to a drawing surface. It can be used to draw lines, text, curves, and a variety of shapes.

▶ The ResizeRedraw property, when set to True, instructs the form to redraw itself when it is resized. It's a good programming practice to design forms that resizes their contents based on their size. The Resize event of the form can also be used to program the resizing logic.

▶ The Graphics class provides a set of Draw methods that can be used to draw shapes like rectangles, ellipses, curves, and so forth on a drawing surface. The Graphics class also provides a set of Fill methods to create solid shapes.

▶ An object of the Bitmap class gives access to image manipulation. The System.Drawing namespace classes can understand a variety of image formats.

CHAPTER SUMMARY

The .NET Framework is a standards-based, multilanguage platform for developing next generation applications. Visual Studio .NET provides a productive integrated development environment (IDE) for developing .NET Framework applications.

The .NET Framework class libraries include classes for developing Windows-based desktop and distributed applications. Visual Studio .NET provides a Windows Forms Designer that allows you to visually drag and drop components and create applications. Various exercises in this chapter helped you familiarize yourself with the development environment and its key concepts.

A Windows Form is where you assemble the user interface of your application. Form is a class that provides you various properties through which you can get or set its characteristics.

KEY TERMS

- Application
- Attributes
- Class
- Constructor
- Delegate
- Enumeration
- Event
- Event handling

continues

CHAPTER SUMMARY   *continued*

- Field
- Framework Class Library
- Garbage collection
- GDI+
- Inheritance
- Intermediate language
- JIT compilation
- Managed code
- Namespace
- .NET Framework
- Override
- Property
- Structure
- Visual Inheritance
- Windows Forms Designer

In this chapter you learned how to manipulate a form's properties and how to add a custom property to a form. You also learned how to derive from an existing form and extend the functionality of an existing form by adding your own properties and methods.

Event handling plays a key role in user-interface–based programming; through event handling you respond to various events fired as a result of user actions and make the programs interactive. I discussed various ways to handle events in this chapter. In the next chapter you will see how to define your own events.

You also learned how to use the classes from the .NET Framework that implement graphic functionality. You saw how to draw text, lines, and shapes and work with other key graphic elements like Brush, Color and Pen.

In the next chapter I'll talk more about various user interface elements that allow rapid development of a powerful and interactive Windows application.

APPLY YOUR KNOWLEDGE

Exercises

1.1   Responding to Keyboard Input

The Windows Forms libraries provide controls like TextBox and RichTextBox to process keyboard input from the user. But sometimes you want to program the keyboard yourself. In this exercise you will learn how to capture keyboard events and respond to them by designing a very basic text editor named *NEN (Not Even Notepad)* that lets you type on a form surface and edit the text using the Backspace key.

Estimated Time: 20 minutes.

1. Create a new Visual Basic .NET Windows application in the Visual Studio .NET IDE.

2. Add a new form to your Visual Basic .NET project. Change the Text property of the form to Not Even Notepad and change its BackColor property to White.

3. In the Code view add the following namespace reference at the top:

   ```
   Imports System.Text
   ```

4. Declare a private variable just before the form's constructor code:

   ```
   Private sbText As StringBuilder
   ```

5. In the constructor, initialize this private variable by including following line of code

   ```
   sbText = New StringBuilder()
   ```

6. Add the following code to the KeyPress event handler of the form

   ```
   Private Sub Exercise1_1_KeyPress(ByVal sender
   As Object, _
    ByVal e As System.Windows.Forms.KeyPressEv-
   entArgs) _
    Handles MyBase.KeyPress
       ' Check which key is pressed
       Select Case e.KeyChar
           Case Chr(8)
               ' Backspace key is pressed
               If (sbText.Length > 0) Then
                   sbText.Remove(sbText.Length -
                   1, 1)
               End If
           Case Chr(10), Chr(13)
               ' Enter key is pressed
               sbText.Append(vbCrLf)
           Case Else
               ' Other keys are pressed
               sbText.Append(e.KeyChar)
       End Select
       ' Paint the form
       Invalidate()
   End Sub
   ```

7. In the form's Paint event handler add the following code

   ```
   Private Sub Exercise1_1_Paint(ByVal sender As
   Object, _
    ByVal e As System.Windows.Forms.PaintEven-
   tArgs) _
    Handles MyBase.Paint
       Dim grfx As Graphics = _
         CType(sender, Form).CreateGraphics()
       grfx.DrawString(sbText.ToString(), _
         Font, Brushes.Black, _
         RectangleF.op_Implicit(ClientRectangle))
   End Sub
   ```

APPLY YOUR KNOWLEDGE

8. Set the form as the startup object of the project. Execute the application. You will see a form onscreen. The form doesn't show a blinking cursor, but if you click on it and start typing, it will show what you type. You can press Enter to start a new line or the Backspace key to make changes, as shown in Figure 1.25.

FIGURE 1.25
The Not Even Notepad text editor.

The KeyPress event is fired when you press a key on the keyboard. In its event handler the code uses these keys to modify a StringBuilder object that stores the text for this small editor. Then it calls the Invalidate method, which in turn generates a call to the Paint method that actually draws the text on the screen. So in fact every key-press forces a total repaint of the form. In the next chapter I'll talk about better ways of doing this task.

1.2   Getting a List of Installed Fonts

Several Windows applications allow you to change the font of displayed text. They will normally give you a list of fonts installed on your system to choose from. How do they get this list? The following exercise shows you how to work with font-related classes in the System.Drawing namespace to display a list of installed fonts.

Estimated Time: 15 minutes.

1. Add a new form to your Visual Basic .NET project.

2. Change the Text property of the form to List of Installed Fonts and change its BackColor property to White.

3. Add a Paint event handler to this form and add the following code to it:

```
Private Sub Exercise1_2_Paint(ByVal sender As
Object, _
 ByVal e As System.Windows.Forms.PaintEven-
tArgs) _
   Handles MyBase.Paint
     ' Set the y coordinate to 0
     Dim intYCoord As Integer = 0

     ' Create a Black color SolidBrush
     Dim br As SolidBrush = New
SolidBrush(Color.Black)

     ' Iterate through the FontFamily.Families
     Dim i As Integer
     For i = 0 To FontFamily.Families.Length - 1

       Dim fs As FontStyle = FontStyle.Regular
```

APPLY YOUR KNOWLEDGE

```
            ' Check whether Regular style is
available
        If Not (FontFamily.Families(i). _
        IsStyleAvailable(FontStyle.Regular))
Then
            fs = FontStyle.Italic
            ' Check whether Italic style is
available
        If Not (FontFamily.Families(i). _

IsStyleAvailable(FontStyle.Italic)) Then
            fs = FontStyle.Bold
            ' If bold isn't available,
give up
            If Not
(FontFamily.Families(i). _

IsStyleAvailable(FontStyle.Bold)) Then
                GoTo NextFont
            End If
        End If
    End If

        ' Create a Font object and Draw the
Font Name
        Dim fnt As Font = _
        New
Font(FontFamily.Families(i).Name, 12, fs)
        Dim strFontName As String = _
        FontFamily.Families(i).Name
        e.Graphics.DrawString(strFontName, _
        fnt, br, 0, intYCoord)
        ' Increase the y Cooridnate by the
Font Height
        intYCoord += Font.Height
    NextFont:
    Next

    End Sub
```

4. Insert the Main method and set the form as the startup object of the project. Execute the application; you will see a form displaying a list of fonts, with each font name displayed in its own font. When you increase the height of the form, you can see more lines listing the fonts, as shown in Figure 1.26.

FIGURE 1.26
A form that enumerates all the fonts on the system.

The FontFamily.Families method returns an array of FontFamily objects. The code iterates over this array to display each font name in its own font style. If you remove the FontStyle checks used in this program you'll get a runtime error because not all fonts support all font styles.

You probably can't see all the fonts because the list of fonts usually contains more fonts than the number of lines you can display, even on a maximized form. You'll see how to make the contents of a form scroll in the next chapter.

1.3 Creating Nonrectangular Forms

All the forms you created in this chapter were rectangular. The Windows Forms library also allows you to create nonrectangular forms. Nonrectangular forms can be used in various applications such as games, device simulation, and multimedia applications. In this exercise you will see how to create a nonrectangular form.

APPLY YOUR KNOWLEDGE

Estimated Time: 10 minutes.

1. Add a new form to your Visual Basic .NET project.

2. In the Properties window for the form, change the `FormBorderStyle` to `None` and change the `BackColor` to `FireBrick`.

3. Switch to the Code view and include the following using directive at top of the code:

```
Imports System.Drawing.Drawing2D
```

4. Modify the constructor for the form as follows:

```
Public Sub New()
    MyBase.New()

    'This call is required by the Windows
Form Designer.
    InitializeComponent()

    'Add any initialization after the
➥InitializeComponent() call
    ' Create a GraphicsPath object
    ' Add an ellipse to the GraphicsPath
object
    ' Set the Form's Region property
    ' to the GraphicsPath region
    Dim gp As GraphicsPath = New Graphic-
sPath()
    gp.AddEllipse(25, 25, 250, 250)
    Me.Region = New Region(gp)

End Sub
```

5. Set the form as the startup object of the project. Run the application; you will see a circular red form.

This code first defines an elliptical region using the `GraphicsPath` object. This object is then used to set the `Region` property of the form. The `Region` property will instruct the operating system to hide any portion of the form that lies outside this elliptical region. As a result, the form is displayed as an ellipse.

Review Questions

1. Describe the difference between a public field and a public property.

2. What is the purpose of organizing classes in namespaces?

3. What property would you use to control the shape of the mouse pointer when it enters the Client area of a Windows Form?

4. How can you add a custom property to a form?

5. What is Visual Inheritance?

6. What are different approaches for event handling? What is the difference between them?

7. What is the ResizeRedraw property? When should you set it to True for a Windows Form?

8. Name at least two ways by which you can create a Graphics object for a Windows Form

9. What is the difference between a Pen object and a Brush object?

Exam Questions

1. You are designing a Windows Form that will work like a splash screen, giving the welcome message and product information when the application starts. What properties would you set on the form to make it look like a splash screen?

   A. Set the FormBorderStlye property to FormBorderStyle.SizableToolWindow, StartPosition property to FormStartPosition.CenterScreen.

APPLY YOUR KNOWLEDGE

B. Set the FormBorderStyleProperty to Fixed3D, MinimizeBox to False, MaximizeBox to False, ControlBox to False and StartPosition to CenterScreen.

C. Set the FormBorderStyle property to None, set StartPosition to CenterScreen and TopMost property to True.

D. Set the TopMost property to True, ShowInTaskbar to False, BackColor to Desktop and StartPosition to CenterScreen.

2. You are designing a graphical Windows application to allow your users to design their homes' interiors. Users are very particular about getting good quality printing of their designs and want a fast performing application. What should you do while using a Graphics object to create lines and curves?

A. Set the SmoothingMode property of the Graphics object to AntiAlias.

B. Set the SmoothingMode property of the Graphics object to HighSpeed.

C. Set the SmoothingMode property of the Graphics object to HighQuality.

D. Set the SmoothingMode property of the Graphics object to Laser.

3. You are a Windows developer for a major component vendor. Your company is planning to launch a product that will provide a set of sophisticated Windows Forms. Your customers can inherit their forms from these forms to speed up their development work. In one of the forms you have certain properties that are for advanced use only.

You don't want these properties to be displayed in the Properties window, but you would like programmers to see these properties via the IntelliSense help. Which of the following attributes would you use for these properties?

A. `<Browsable(true), _`
`EditorBrowsable(EditorBrowsableState.Never)>`

B. `<Browsable(false), _`
`EditorBrowsable(EditorBrowsableState.Always)>`

C. `<Browsable(true), _`
`EditorBrowsable(EditorBrowsableState.Always)>`

D. `<Browsable(false), _`
`EditorBrowsable(EditorBrowsableState.Never)>`

4. You are a Windows developer for a company developing shareware software. Your task is to develop Personal Information Management software that will run on a Windows platform. The main form of the application has various controls placed on it. You want to resize all the controls when the form is resized. Which of the following options would you choose?

A. Write the resizing logic for each control in its own Resize event handler and set the ResizeRedraw property to True for each one of them.

B. Write the resizing logic in the form's Paint event handler.

C. Write the resizing logic in the form's Paint event handler and set the form's ResizeRedraw property to True.

D. Write the resizing logic for each control in its own Paint event handler and set the ResizeRedraw property to True for each one of them.

APPLY YOUR KNOWLEDGE

5. You are developing a Windows application containing a single Windows Form. You need to do some initializations that will change the appearance of the form and assign values to some fields when the application starts. Where should you put your code?

   A. In the InitializeComponent method

   B. In the form's constructor

   C. In a custom procedure

   D. In the form's Dispose method

6. You are drawing a big line of text on your form displaying the company name. You would like to fill the text with the image a of company logo. Which Brush should you use?

   A. SolidBrush

   B. TextureBrush

   C. HatchBrush

   D. ImageBrush

7. You want to make a Windows Form completely transparent when it is displayed. What should you do?

   A. Set TransparencyKey property to 0%.

   B. Set TransparencyKey property to 100%.

   C. Set Opacity property to 0%.

   D. Set Opacity property to 100%.

8. You can see a property in the Properties window for a Windows Form but cannot modify it. What could be the cause?

   A. The Browsable attribute for the property must be False.

   B. The property is a private property.

   C. The Set accessor of the property is private.

   D. The Set accessor of the property is not implemented.

9. Which of the following methods can be used for getting a Graphics object for a Windows Form?

   A. Graphics.FromForm

   B. Graphics.FromImage

   C. Graphics.FromHwnd

   D. Graphics.CreateObject

10. Which one of the following points has coordinate x=0 and y=0 for a Windows Form:

    A. Top-left corner of Client area of form

    B. Center of the Client area of form

    C. Top-right corner of Client area of form

    D. Center of the user's screen

11. You want to change the property of a form so that all text placed on it will appear in bold. Which of the following statements would you use in form's constructor?

    A. `this.Font.Bold = true;`

    B. `this.Font = new Font(this.Font, FontStyle.Bold);`

    C. `this.Font.FontStyle = FontStyle.Bold;`

    D. `this.Font = new Font(this.Font, this.Font.Bold);`

12. You are designing an interactive Windows application to respond to several user actions.

You would like to change the form's appearance when the user moves a mouse over the form. You have written an event handler that implements this change and want it to attach to MouseMove event. What statement should you use in your form's constructor?

A. `AddHandler Me.MouseMove, Me.MouseMoveHandler`

B. `RemoveHandler Me.MouseMove, Me.MouseMoveHandler`

C. `RemoveHandler Me.MouseMove, AddressOf Me.MouseMoveHandler`

D. `AddHandler Me.MouseMove, AddressOf Me.MouseMoveHandler`

13. You want to create a Windows application capable of manipulating image files in GIF, JPG, and PNG formats. Which class you should use in your program?

    A. Bitmap

    B. Image

    C. Icon

    D. Metafile

14. You are using objects of HatchBrush class in your program but have forgotten to include the reference of its namespace System.Drawing.Drawing2D through a using directive at the top of program. Which of the following statement holds true for this scenario?

    A. You will get a compile-time error while compiling the Import statements.

    B. You will get an error at runtime while executing the Import statements.

    C. The compilation should be okay if you refer to the HatchBrush class as System.Drawing.Drawing2D.HatchBrush in your program.

    D. The compilation should be okay if you refer to all HatchBrush objects by prefixing them with System.Drawing.Drawing2D namespace.

15. You are creating an object of the GraphicsPath class in your program. When you compile the program, you get an error saying that the type or namespace name cannot be found. What should you do?

    A. Add reference to System.Drawing.dll in your program.

    B. Include an Imports System.Drawing statement at top of your program.

    C. Include an Imports System.Drawing.Drawing2D statement at the top of your program.

    D. Include an Imports System.Drawing.Imaging statement at the top of your program.

Answers to Review Questions

1. A property, unlike a field, does not have any storage location associated with it. Generally (but not necessarily), a property uses a private field to store its data and exposes its value through a pair of accessors named Get and Set that are used for read and write operations, respectively. These accessors can encapsulate program logic that will run when the property is read or written. A property is the preferred way to expose class characteristics.

APPLY YOUR KNOWLEDGE

2. Namespaces solves two problems: first, they help organize the classes by logically grouping them. Secondly, proper use of namespaces allows you to uniquely identify a class, thereby avoiding naming conflicts that you might have otherwise encountered.

3. The Cursor property of a form can be used to specify the default mouse pointer shape for a form.

4. You can add a custom property by defining a public property in a form class using the VB .NET syntax for property declaration. The Get and Set accessors of the property define what happens when you attempt to read or write the property value.

5. Visual Inheritance is the process that lets you inherit a visual element like a form or a control based on an already existing element. Visual Inheritance reuses existing code and maintains consistency between visual elements.

6. I discussed two approaches to event handling in this chapter. The first one, which is preferred by Visual Basic .NET, is to override the base class event procedure. The second is to register an event handler with an event using a delegate object. The second approach has the benefit of allowing you to attach multiple handlers to the same event, whereas the first approach requires less coding on your part.

7. The ResizeRedraw property indicates whether a form will redraw itself if resized. The Form class inherits this property from the Control class. This property when set to True for a form will cause form's Paint event to be fired whenever the form size is changed. This property is especially useful when you want to create a form whose elements resize proportionally with the form.

8. You can create a Graphics object for a control by calling CreateGraphics method on its instance. Alternatively, you can also get a Graphics object by calling the static method FromHwnd of the Graphics class. You need to pass the handle of a specific form to this method. You can get handle of a form through its Handle property.

9. Brush is an abstract class used to create classes that would fill interiors of shapes such as rectangle, ellipse, and so forth. SolidBrush, TextureBrush, and LinearGradientBrush are implementations of the Brush class that can be used to create Brush objects. A Pen object is used to draw lines and curves. A Pen object can use a Brush object to apply various fill styles to the lines it draws.

Answers to Exam Questions

1. **C.** When you set the FormBorderStyle property to None through the Properties window, the form will have neither the title bar nor borders displayed. In addition, splash screens are generally displayed on the center of the screen and are not resizable. Given these facts, **C** is the correct answer.

2. **B.** SmoothingMode has no effect whatsoever on printing quality. Antialiasing involves extra work and makes applications slower. So to increase speed in this case, select the HighSpeed option. The HighSpeed value is same as the AntiAlias value so is not required in this case.

3. **B.** Setting the Browsable attribute of a property to False hides the property from the Properties window. The EditorBrowsable attribute specifies whether the property will be available through IntelliSense help. So the correct answer is **B**.

4. **C.** Setting the ResizeRedraw property to True for a form fires its Paint event whenever the form is resized. Programming the Resize event for each control won't work, as when the form is resized, the control is not resized, anyway.

5. **B.** A form's constructor is the ideal place to put all initialization, as it ensures that all initialization is done at the time the form is created. Although InitializeComponent procedure is also called from form's constructor it is not recommended to put code there, as it can interfere with Windows Forms Designer working.

6. **B.** Only TextureBrush can fill using an image. There is no such brush as an ImageBrush.

7. **C.** Opacity sets the transparency level for a form, whereas TransparencyKey will only make those form areas transparent which match a specified color. The use of TransparencyKey is also wrong here.

8. **D.** You can make a property read only by not implementing the property's Set accessor. The Browsable attribute just hides or shows the property in the Properties window; the question mentions that you can already see the property in Properties window. Finally, you cannot set the access modifiers, such as public or private on accessor functions; you can only apply them to a property as a whole.

9. **C.** Graphics.Hwnd is the function that gets a Graphics object for a Windows Form. Graphics.FromImage can only get the Graphics object for an image file. The other two methods are nonexistent.

10. **A.** The top-left corner of the Client area has coordinates of (0, 0) for a Windows Form.

11. **B.** You cannot directly set the Bold property of a Font object, as its set accessor is not available. So the only way to set the Font's Bold property is by calling its constructor to create a new Font object and then use this newly created object.

12. **D.** To add an event handler, use the AddHandler keyword and pass the address of the delegate function that will handle the events.

13. **A.** Image is an abstract class, it so won't help you much in image-related operations. Bitmap is the implementation of Image class that can work with several types of image formats including GIF, JPG, and PNG formats.

14. **C.** When you are not including an Import directive for a namespace, you need to fully qualify any class belonging to that namespace in your program. The compiler only needs to qualify the class names, not the object names; therefore answer **D** is not correct. Problems with namespace qualifications can only lead to a compile-time error, not to a runtime error, so answer **B** is also not correct. Missing a using directive will not give compile error at the using statements, but it might give error later in the program if it is unable to uniquely identify a class, so answer **A** is incorrect.

15. **C.** GraphicsPath class belongs to System.Drawing.Drawing2D namespace. This namespace must be included with a using directive to uniquely identify GraphicsPath class in your program.

APPLY YOUR KNOWLEDGE

Suggested Readings and Resources

1. Chappell, David. *Understanding .NET.* Addison Wesley, 2001.

2. Cisco, Steve. *Migrating to Visual Basic .NET.* M&T Books, 2002.

3. Siler, Brian and Jeff Spotts. *Special Edition Using Microsoft Visual Basic .NET.* Que, 2002.

4. Windows Forms Community Site. http://www.windowsforms.net/.

5. Windows Forms FAQ. http://www.syncfusion.com/FAQ/winforms/.

6. Visual Studio .NET Combined Help Collection:

   • Drawing and Editing Images

   • Handling and Raising Events

   • Introduction to Windows Forms

   • .NET Framework SDK

   • Visual Basic .NET Programmer's Reference

This chapter covers the following Microsoft-specified objectives for the Creating User Services section of the Visual Basic .NET Windows-Based Applications exam:

Add controls to a Windows Form.

- **Set properties on controls.**

- **Load controls dynamically.**

- **Write code to handle control events and add the code to a control.**

- **Create menus and menu items.**

▶ Controls are the most visible part of a Windows application. The purpose of this objective is to test your knowledge of working with the most common Windows Forms controls. That includes working with their properties, methods and events.

Implement navigation for the user Interface (UI).

- **Configure the order of tabs.**

▶ When placing controls on a form, you need to provide a logical order of keyboard-based navigation for the controls. This exam objective covers how to achieve this using Visual Studio .NET.

CHAPTER 2

Controls

► Experiment with the controls in the Visual Studio .NET toolbox and examine their properties. Tables throughout this chapter will help you understand the key members in the interfaces of these controls. The Windows Forms QuickStarts (which are installed as part of the .NET Framework SDK) also contain excellent reference material and control samples.

► Know how to handle events for Windows Forms controls. Make sure you read the discussion on event handling in Chapter 1.

► You should know how to create controls dynamically. See Step By Step 2.2 and 2.4 to get hands-on experience in loading controls dynamically.

► Know how to create menus and menu items. This includes creating both a main menu for your application as well as context menus.

INTRODUCTION

This chapter extends the concepts presented in Chapter 1 and discusses various aspects of user interface programming in more detail.

I'll start by teaching you how to add various controls to a Windows Form, how to set their properties, and how to program the events associated with these controls.

You'll also learn how to use common dialog boxes in your application and how to create a custom dialog box for your specific requirements when common dialog boxes won't do.

This chapter also covers most of the commonly used controls available in the Visual Studio .NET Toolbox. Controls are explained with examples to help you understand and appreciate how they function.

Finally, I'll show you how to create main menus and context menus for Windows applications and how to associate menu items with specific actions.

ADDING CONTROLS TO A WINDOWS FORM

You can place controls on the surface of any container object. Container objects include Windows Forms, Panel controls, and GroupBox controls.

You can add controls to a form either programmatically or by using the Windows Forms Designer. While the Windows Forms Designer provides you with an easy-to-use interface for adding controls on a form, you might find times when your application's functionality requires you to create controls in code.

Adding Controls Using Windows Forms Designer

Add controls to Windows Form.

The Windows Forms Designer provides a toolbox with a variety of commonly used controls. You can drag and drop controls from the toolbox to a form and arrange them as required (see Step By Step 2.1). The Toolbox window can be activated by selecting Toolbox from the View menu or by pressing Ctrl+Alt+X. You will find a rich set of controls listed on the Windows Forms tab of the toolbox, as shown in Figure 2.1. From the toolbox you can use any of three ways to add controls to a form or other container object:

FIGURE 2.1
Windows Forms Designer Toolbox.

◆ **Adding controls to Forms: Method 1**—Select a control from the toolbox and draw it on the container surface by following these steps:

1. Select a control by clicking on the control's icon in the Toolbox window (see Figure 2.1).

2. Release the mouse button and move the mouse pointer to the position on the container where you want to draw the control.

3. Hold down the mouse button and draw a rectangle on the container surface to indicate the size and position for the control instance.

◆ **Adding controls to Forms: Method 2**—Drag the control directly from the toolbox to the desired location on the form.

1. Select a form or other container control where you want to add a control.

2. Drag the control's icon from the toolbox and drop it at the desired location on the container control. The control will be added with its default size.

◆ **Adding controls to Forms: Method 3**—Add the control to the form by double-clicking in the toolbox.

1. Select a form or other container control where you want to add a control.

2. Double-click the control's icon in the toolbox to add the control to the top-left corner of the form or other container control in its default size. You can later use the mouse or properties of the control to modify its position and size.

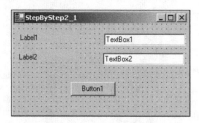

FIGURE 2.2
Using Windows Forms Designer to add controls to a form.

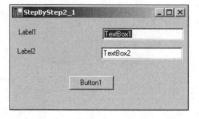

FIGURE 2.3
What you see at design time is what you get at runtime.

STEP BY STEP

2.1 Adding Controls to a Windows Form Using Windows Forms Designer

1. Create a new Visual Basic .NET Windows Application project in the Visual Studio .NET IDE.

2. Add a new Windows Form to the project.

3. Select the Toolbox window. From the Windows Forms tab of the Toolbox, place two controls each of type Label and TextBox and a control of type Button on the form's surface. Arrange the controls as shown in Figure 2.2.

4. Set the form as the startup object for the project.

5. Run the project. You will see a Windows Form as shown in Figure 2.3. You can navigate between controls using the Tab key or by clicking on them with the mouse.

Adding Controls Dynamically

It is also possible to add controls to a form programmatically. While doing so, you must remember to add code to do the following three things:

1. Create a private variable to represent each of the controls you want to place on the form.

2. In the form's constructor place code to instantiate each control and to customize each control using its properties, methods, or events.

3. Add each control to the form's control collection.

Step By Step 2.2 demonstrates this process.

STEP BY STEP

2.2 Adding Controls to a Windows Form Programmatically

1. Add a new Windows Form to your Visual Basic .NET project.

2. Switch to the Code view and add the following variables just below the Windows Forms Designer generated code:

```
' Create variables to hold controls
Dim lblName, lblPassword As Label
Dim txtName, txtPassword As TextBox
Dim btnLogin As Button
```

3. Expand the Windows Forms Designer Generated region. Modify the New() procedure as follows:

```
Public Sub New()
    MyBase.New()

    'This call is required by the Windows Form Designer.
    InitializeComponent()

    'Add any initialization after the
    ' InitializeComponent() call
    ' apecify the form's size
    Me.ClientSize = New System.Drawing.Size(272, 182)

    'Set up the label the Name textbox
    Dim lblName As Label = New Label()
    lblName.Text = "Name: "
    ' Specify the location for the control
    ' the default location will be (0, 0) otherwise
    lblName.Location = New Point(16, 16)

    ' Set up the label for the Password textbox
    Dim lblPassword As Label = New Label()
    lblPassword.Text = "Password: "
    lblPassword.Location = New Point(16, 80)

    ' Set up a Name textbox
    Dim txtName As TextBox = New TextBox()
    txtName.Location = New Point(152, 16)

    ' Set up a Password textbox
    Dim txtPassword As TextBox = New TextBox()
    txtPassword.Location = New Point(152, 80)
    txtPassword.PasswordChar = "*"
```

continues

continued

```
' Set up a command button
Dim btnLogin As Button = New Button()
btnLogin.Text = "Login"
btnLogin.Location = New Point(96, 128)

' Add controls to the form
' Method 1: Specify the current form as
' parent container for a control
lblName.Parent = Me

' Method 2: Add a control to form's control
  collection
Me.Controls.Add(txtName)

' Method 3: Add an array of controls to form's
' control collection
Me.Controls.AddRange(New Control() { _

    lblPassword, txtPassword, btnLogin})
```

4. Set the form as the startup object for the project.

5. Run the project. The form will be displayed as shown in Figure 2.4.

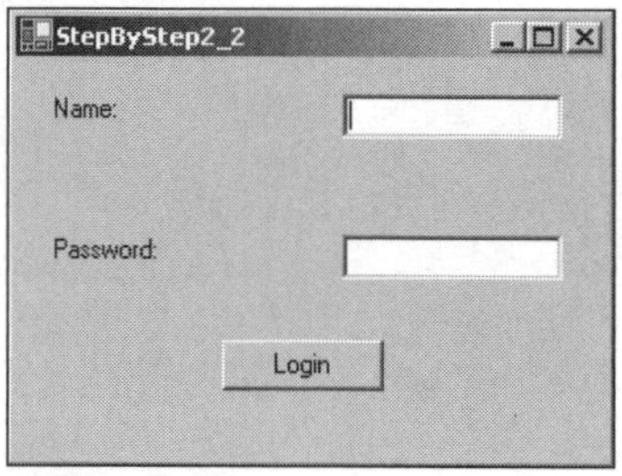

FIGURE 2.4
A form with controls loaded programmatically.

When creating controls programmatically, you must specify the location and size of the controls numerically, as compared to placing the controls via the Windows Forms designer. In lieu of this small inconvenience, the Code view allows you to add more functionality and power to a Windows Form. Many projects will benefit from a mix of these two methods.

The examples in this section add controls to a Windows Form, because the form is the container control that you are most familiar with after Chapter 1. You can easily apply these concepts to any of the container controls. A container control has a property named Controls, which is a collection of Control objects that the container control contains. When you add or remove a control to a container, it is added to or removed from the container's Controls collection.

EXAM TIP

Adding Control to a Container Control While creating controls programmatically, you must remember to associate them to a parent container control. If you don't, controls will be created but will not be displayed.

SETTING PROPERTIES OF CONTROLS

Add controls to a Windows Form

- **Set properties on controls.**

In Chapter 1, I discussed how to work with properties of a Form object. You learned how to manipulate these properties both through the Properties window at design time and through code at runtime. The same principle carries over to Windows Forms controls. You will recall from the inheritance hierarchy of a form that a form is also a control, because it derives from the Control class. That accounts for many of the similarities between forms and controls.

Some of the properties and methods of controls are similar to those of a form. Controls can also have additional properties depending on their specific functionality.

To set a property for a control using the Properties window, follow these steps:

1. Select the control and make it the active object by clicking it.

2. If necessary, show the Properties window by pressing F4 or selecting View, Properties Window.

3. Activate the Properties window, select a property from the given list, and modify it by selecting or entering a new value.

To set a property for a control within code, follow these steps:

1. Switch to the Code view. Select the event in which you want to write the code.

2. Use the ControlObject.PropertyName syntax to access the property for a control's object. Here ControlObject is the name of the object for the control. This can be name of the control itself, or of any object that references the control. PropertyName is any valid property name for a given control. In the Code view you can select valid property names from the IntelliSense help.

Important Common Properties of Controls

In this section, I will talk about several important properties shared by many of the standard controls:

- ◆ Anchor
- ◆ Dock
- ◆ Enabled
- ◆ Font
- ◆ Location

- ◆ Name
- ◆ Size
- ◆ TabIndex and TabStop
- ◆ Visible

Anchor

When a form is resized, you might want to resize and move the controls it contains to make good use of the form's real estate. You can achieve this by anchoring your control to the edges of its container control with the Anchor property. Figure 2.5 shows the Anchor property in the Properties window, and Figure 2.6 shows the graphical interface that Visual Studio .NET provides for setting this property. The default value of Anchor is Top, Left. That specifies that the control is anchored to the top and left edges of its container. See Step By Step 2.4 later in this chapter for an example of this property in use.

FIGURE 2.5▶
Click the down arrow in the Anchor property to display an anchoring window.

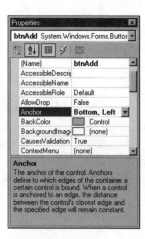

FIGURE 2.6▲
The dark bars in the Anchoring window indicate the sides to which the control is anchored.

Dock

Sometimes you need a control to span an entire side (left, right, top, or bottom) of its parent control. The Dock property of the control achieves this behavior. Figure 2.7 shows the Dock property in the Properties window, and Figure 2.8 shows the graphical interface that Visual Studio .NET provides for setting this property. The default value of the Dock property is None. This property is mainly used with controls like StatusBar or ToolBar but is not limited to them. You'll see an example of docking a label control in Step By Step 2.4 later in this chapter.

FIGURE 2.7◀
Click the down arrow in the Dock property to display a Docking window.

FIGURE 2.8▲
Click the edge where you want the control docked.

Enabled

The Enabled property of a control is a Boolean value (True/False) that can be used to determine whether a control can respond to user interactions. A disabled control (that is, one with the Enabled property set to False) will not receive focus, will not generate any events, and will appear dimmed or "grayed out." The default value of the Enabled property is True for nearly all controls. One exception is the Timer control, whose Enabled property is False by default.

Font

The Font property sets the font of any text displayed by the control. The value of this property is an instance of the Font class. When you select the Font property in the Properties window for a control, you see a browse button (marked with an ellipsis). Clicking on this button invokes a Font dialog box, as shown in Figure 2.9, which can be used to conveniently manipulate the Font property.

NOTE

Only Minor Changes   Many of the common control properties are the same in VB .NET as they were in VB6 (and earlier versions). You should at least skim this section of the chapter, because there are some changes in the way these properties work, and there are new properties as well. But if you understand control properties in VB6 you're well prepared for controls in VB .NET.

FIGURE 2.9
The Font dialog box allows you to set the Font property of a control.

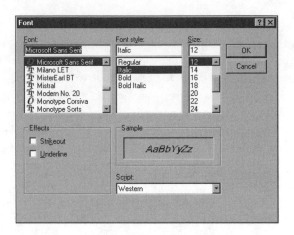

> **NOTE**
>
> **Programmatically Setting a Font Object's Property** The Font object is immutable. If you try to programmatically set one of its properties you will get a compilation error: `Property or indexer cannot be assigned to`—it `is read only`. To work around this, you can create a new Font object with the required properties and assign this newly created object to the Font property.

Location

The Location property specifies the location of the top-left corner of the control with respect to top-left corner of its container control. The value of this property is an instance of the Point class. The unit of measure of the Location property is pixels.

Name

A control's Name property can be used to manipulate the control programmatically. When you place a control on a container object using the visual designer, it names the control automatically. These automatic names are based on the control type. For instance, Label controls will be named Label1, Label2, and so on. If you create a control programmatically, its name is an empty string by default. It's good programming practice to give a meaningful name to a control. Most programmers use Hungarian notation in which the name of each control begins with a lowercase prefix that is an abbreviation for the name of the control. For example, an instance of a TextBox storing a customer name can be named txtCustomerName.

Size

The Size property sets or gets height and width of a control. The value of this property is of data type Size. (Size is a Structure that has properties named Height and Width that respectively store the height and width of the control.) Like the Location property, the Size property is measured in pixels.

You can also manipulate the height and width of a control individually using the control's Height and Width properties.

The Control class has a protected property named DefaultSize that specifies the default size of the control. The default size is used to draw a control if the size of the control is not explicitly specified. You can override this property in your program to specify a different default size for the control.

NOTE

Derived Properties Four other properties depend on the Location, Height, and Width properties: Left, Right, Top, and Bottom. Left is the same as Location.X; Right is the same as Location.X,+Width; Top is same as Location.Y; and Bottom is same as Location.Y+Height.

TabIndex and TabStop

The Tab key is used for keyboard navigation from one control to another on a Windows Form. The TabIndex property of a control is an integer value that specifies the order in which controls will receive focus when the user presses the Tab key. You should organize controls so that the TabIndex values increase as the user moves through the controls in a logical order.

If you do not want a control to receive the focus when a user presses the Tab key, you can set the control's TabStop property to False. The default value of this property is True, which allows the control to participate in keyboard navigation through the Tab key.

The TabIndex property has no effect if the TabStop property for the control is set to False.

Text

The Text property is a string that indicates the text associated with a control. Different controls can use the Text property differently. For example, a Form control will display the value of its Text property in the form's title bar, and a Label control displays the value of its Text property on the face of the control. In some cases, the user can manipulate the Text property of the control at runtime. For example, the TextBox and RichTextBox controls display the value of their Text properties in an input box that can be changed by the user.

The Text property can also provide a keyboard shortcut to some controls. An ampersand (&) in front of a character marks it as the access key for that control. If you assign &Save to the Text property of a Button control, the s in the name will be underlined. Because this is a standard Windows convention, you can assume that when a user sees this, he will know that he can press the button by pressing the Alt+S key combination.

N O T E **Visually Displaying an Ampersand in the Text Property**   What if you would like to display an ampersand (&) in a control's text property rather than to have it function as an access key? If the control is a Label control, you can set its UseMnemonic property to False. When UseMnemonic is False, the control will not interpret the ampersand as an access key modifier. But only the Label and LinkLabel controls have a UseMnemonic property. What about other controls, such as a Button? You can use a double ampersand (&&) in the Text property to represent a single ampersand. This trick will work with any standard control.

N O T E **Control Transparency**   No property directly allows you to set the transparency value for a control. But you can use the BackColor property of a control and set a color using the Color.FromArgb method. The Color.FromArgb method lets you specify an alpha component that controls transparency.

Some controls, such as a Label control, cannot receive the focus. If you assign a keyboard access key for such a control, the focus will instead go to a control with the next higher TabIndex value. You can use this behavior to your advantage: To identify controls like a TextBox, a RichTextBox, a TreeView, or a ListView, you can place a Label beside them. You can then associate an access key with the Label control and keep the TabIndex property of the Label and the corresponding control in immediate succession. This way when the user presses the access key for the Label, it will transfer focus to the control with the next higher TabIndex value, and the corresponding control will receive the focus.

Visible

The Visible property determines whether a control will actually be displayed. The Visible property is a Boolean value, set to True by default. When you set it to False, you still see the control in the Form designer, but users of the application won't see the control at runtime. Setting the Visible property to False does not remove the control from its container's Controls collection. (You'll learn more about the Controls collection later in this chapter.)

Configuring the Order of Tabs

Implement navigation for the user interface (UI)

- **Configure the order of tabs.**

Many people use the keyboard for navigating between the various controls on a form. A Windows user expects to move from one control to another in a logical order by using the Tab key. The Visual Studio .NET Forms designer provides a Tab Order Wizard to allow you to conveniently set the order in which the controls will receive focus when the Tab key is pressed. See Step By Step 2.3 for an exercise in configuring tab order.

STEP BY STEP

2.3 Configuring the Order of Tabs

1. Add a Windows Form to your Visual Basic .NET application.

2. Place two Label controls on the form and set their Text properties to &Name and &Department.

3. Place two TextBox controls, a GroupBox control, and two CheckBox controls on the form. Clear the Text property for both the TextBox controls. Set the Text properties for the CheckBox controls to &Bachelor's degree and &Master's degree. Set the Text property for the GroupBox control to Qualifications.

4. Add two Button controls to the form and set their Text properties to &Save and Save && &Close. Resize and arrange all controls as shown in Figure 2.10.

5. Select Tab Order from the View menu and number the controls as shown in Figure 2.11. You can change a tab order number by clicking on it. Select View, Tab Order again when you're done.

6. Set the form as the startup object for the project.

7. Run the project. Use the Tab key to navigate from one control to another. Use the keyboard access keys to directly jump to a control.

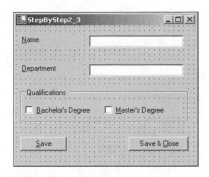

FIGURE 2.10
Controls that implement keyboard access keys.

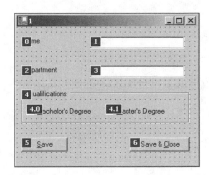

FIGURE 2.11
Configuring the order of tabs.

HANDLING CONTROL EVENTS

Add controls to a Windows Form

- **Write code to handle control events and add the code to a control.**

- **Load controls dynamically.**

Event handling for a control is similar to event handling for a Windows Form, which you learned about in Chapter 1. Each control inherits a basic set of events from the System.Windows.Forms.Control class. Each control type also has a set of events specific to its own functionality. Every control has a default event associated with it. For instance, the Click event is the default event for a Button control; the Load event is the default event for a form; and the CheckedChanged event is the default event for a CheckBox control.

When you double-click a control in the visual designer, it automatically attaches an event handler to the default event for the control and displays the empty event handler in the code view of the form. You can handle an event other than the default event by selecting the control and the event from the combo boxes at the top of the Code view.

In the next example you'll see both dynamic control generation and event handling. Step By Step 2.4 creates a Windows Form that presents two Buttons labeled Add and Remove. When you click on the Add button, the code in its Click event handler will dynamically add a new Button object to this. When you click on the Remove button, the code in its Click event handler removes the most recently created Button. Figure 2.12 shows this form.

The example will illustrate the following points related to handling events:

◆ Attaching an event handler to a control's event

◆ Adding custom code to an event handler

◆ Attaching a single event handler to several controls

◆ Attaching an event programmatically

You'll get additional practice in setting control properties and handling events in Guided Practice Exercise 2.1.

STEP BY STEP

2.4 Programming Control Events

1. Add a Windows Form to your Visual Basic .NET project.

2. Place a Label control on the form and name it lblStatus. Change the Dock property of the control to Top; set its Font property to size 12 and italic; clear the Text property; and change the TextAlign property to MiddleCenter.

3. Place another Label control on the form and name it lblStack. Change the Dock property of the control to Bottom; set its Font property to size 16 and bold; change the Text property to A Button Stack; and finally change the TextAlign property to MiddleCenter.

4. Place a Button control on the form. Name it `btnAdd`, set its `Text` property to `&Add` and its `Anchor` property to `Bottom, Left`.

5. Place another `Button` control on the form. Name it `btnRemove`. Set its `Text` property to `&Remove` and its `Anchor` property to `Bottom, Right`.

6. Switch to the Code view and add the following code directly after the Windows Forms Designer generated code:

```
' Stores the top of stack value
Dim intTos As Integer
' Stores initial control count
Dim intInitCtrlCount As Integer
```

7. Expand the Windows Forms Designer Generated Code region and add the following code in the Form's New method code after the call to the InitializeComponent method:

```
'Add any initialization after the InitializeComponent() call
' Initially the stack is empty
intTos = 0
' Get the initial control count. Be sure to put this
' statement after the call to the InitializeComponent method
intInitCtrlCount = Me.Controls.Count
' Redraw form if it is resized
Me.ResizeRedraw = True
```

8. Using the combo boxes in the Code window, add an event handler for the form's `Paint` event. Add the following code to the event handler:

```
Private Sub StepByStep2_4_Paint(ByVal sender As Object, _
 ByVal e As System.Windows.Forms.PaintEventArgs) _
 Handles MyBase.Paint
    ' Gets the Graphics object for the form
    Dim grfx As Graphics = e.Graphics
    ' Draw a line, end-to-end on the form
    grfx.DrawLine(Pens.Black, 0, _
     Me.lblStack.Location.Y - 5, _
     Me.Width, Me.lblStack.Location.Y - 5)
    ' Set the location for Add and remove buttons so
      that
    ' they get repositioned after the form is
      resized.
    Me.btnAdd.Location = _
     New Point(0, Me.lblStack.Location.Y - 40)
```

continues

NOTE

Setting a Property for Multiple Controls To set a property for multiple controls to the same value simultaneously, click each control while pressing the Ctrl key. This will select all the clicked controls. Then invoke the Properties window and set the property. The property you set will be applied to all the controls. Logically enough, when you invoke the Properties window while multiple controls are selected, it will only show those properties that all the selected controls have in common.

continued

```
    Me.btnRemove.Location = _
      New Point(Me.Width - Me.btnRemove.Width - 7, _
      Me.lblStack.Location.Y - 40)
End Sub
```

9. Insert the following event handler in the code; you will later attach it programmatically to the dynamically created Button objects:

```
' This event handler will handle the Click event of all of
' the buttons in the stack
Private Sub Button_Click(ByVal sender As System.Object, _
 ByVal e As System.EventArgs)
    ' Cast the object to a Button
    Dim btnSender As Button = CType(sender, Button)
    ' Change the lblStatus to show that
    ' this button was clicked.
    lblStatus.Text = "Status: " & _
     btnSender.Text & " is clicked."
End Sub
```

10. In the Design view, double-click the Add button. This will attach an event handler for the Click event (the default event for a button). Modify this event handler as follows:

```
Private Sub btnAdd_Click(ByVal sender As System.Object, _
 ByVal e As System.EventArgs) Handles btnAdd.Click
'If stack is not yet full
    If (intTos < 8) Then
        Dim btnSender As Button = CType(sender, Button)
        ' Create a new Button to add to the Stack
        Dim btnNew As Button = New Button()
        btnNew.Name = "Element" & intTos
        btnNew.Text = "Element " & intTos
        btnNew.Location = New Point( _
        (Me.Width - btnNew.Width) / 2, _
        btnSender.Location.Y - btnSender.Height * intTos)
        ' Attach a event handler to the
        ' Click event of newly created button
        AddHandler btnNew.Click, AddressOf Me.Button_Click

        ' Add the Button to the Container's
        ' Control collection
        Me.Controls.Add(btnNew)
        lblStatus.Text = "Status: Element " & _
         intTos & " added."
        intTos += 1
    Else
```

```
        ' Stack is full, can't add a button
        lblStatus.Text = "Status: Stack is full!"
    End If
End Sub
```

11. In the Design view, double-click the Remove button. In
its `Click` event handler code, insert the following lines:

```
Private Sub btnRemove_Click(ByVal sender As System.Object, _
 ByVal e As System.EventArgs) Handles btnRemove.Click
    Dim btnSender As Button = CType(sender, Button)
    ' Current control count in the Form's Control collection
    Dim intCtrlCount As Integer = Me.Controls.Count
    ' If any new buttons were created in the stack
    If (intCtrlCount > intInitCtrlCount) Then
        ' Remove the most recetly added control
        ' in the collection
        Me.Controls.Remove(Me.Controls( _
        Me.Controls.Count - 1))
        ' Adjust the top of stack
        intTos -= 1
        lblStatus.Text = "Status: Element " & _
        intTos & " removed."
    Else
        ' Stack is empty, Can't remove a button
        lblStatus.Text = "Status: Stack is empty!"
    End If
End Sub
```

12. Set this form as the startup object for the project.

13. Run the project. Click the Add and Remove buttons. You
will see that the Button controls are dynamically created
and removed. When you click on one of the dynamically
created button controls, its `Click` event is fired, and it will
display a message on the top Label control, as shown in
Figure 2.12.

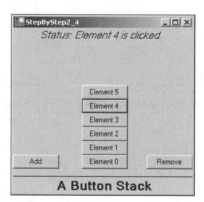

FIGURE 2.12
Adding and removing controls dynamically.

Step By Step 2.4 also illustrated these important aspects of dynamic
control creation:

◆ You can dynamically add or remove controls to a container by
using the `Add` and `Remove` methods of the container object's
`Controls` collection.

◆ You can access the dynamically added control objects by index in the `Controls` collection.

◆ By attaching a single event handler to a group of controls, you can provide them with a common behavior.

You'll see several more examples of event handling later in this chapter. Event-driven programming is one of the key patterns of Windows application development, and you should understand it thoroughly.

REVIEW BREAK

▶ Controls can be added to a form in two ways: You can use the Windows Forms Designer or create them in code.

▶ The Windows Forms Designer in the Microsoft Visual Studio .NET IDE allows you to add controls to a form and manipulate them in an easy manner.

▶ The Visual Studio .Net toolbox provides a varierty of controls and components to create common Windows GUI elements.

▶ While creating controls programmatically, be sure to add them to their parent container's Controls collection.

▶ The properties of controls can be set at design time using the Properties window or at runtime by accessing them as ControlName.PropertyName in the code.

▶ Some of the important properties of the controls, such as Anchor, Dock, Enabled, Font, Location, Name, Size, TabIndex, TabStop, and Visible, are shared by most common Windows Forms controls.

▶ The Tab Order Wizard provides a convenient way to set the TabIndex property of controls to implement logical keyboard-based navigation in the form using the Tab key.

▶ Control programming is event driven. Events are fired when the user interacts with a control. To take specific action when an event occurs, write an event handler method and attach it to the event of a control via its delegate.

▶ You can attach an event handler to an event by using the AddHandler statement.

GUIDED PRACTICE EXERCISE 2.1

In this exercise you will create the Windows form shown in Figure 2.13. The controls on this form are grouped in two GroupBox container controls. The Console GroupBox allows you to manipulate controls in the Playground GroupBox. In the Console area, you can choose a type of control from the combo box and click on the Hide button to hide all controls of that type in the Playground container. Similarly, when you click on the Show button, it restores the visibility of all controls of the selected type.

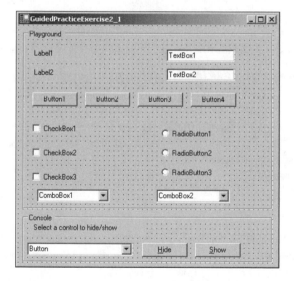

FIGURE 2.13

A form that hides and shows controls at run-time.

Try this on your own first. If you get stuck or would like to see one possible solution, follow these steps:

1. Add a new form to your Visual Basic .NET Project.

2. Place two GroupBox controls on the form. Change their NAME property to GRPCONSOLE and GRPPLAYGROUND.

continues

continued

Add and arrange controls on these group boxes as shown in Figure 2.13. You might find the options from the Format menu, shown in Figure 2.14, useful in designing this form.

FIGURE 2.14
Format menu options allow you to arrange controls.

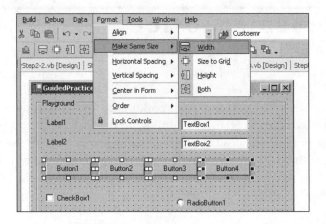

3. Name the combo box inside the Console GroupBox cboControls and name the Buttons btnHide and btnShow.

4. Invoke the Properties window for cboControls control and select its Items property. Click the Builder button to invoke the String Collection Editor, as shown in Figure 2.15. Add the following values to the editor and then close it.

```
Button
CheckBox
ComboBox
Label
TextBox
RadioButton
```

FIGURE 2.15
String Collection Editor.

5. Double-click the btnShow button to open the form's code module. Enter this code to handle the Click events of the btnShow and btnHide buttons:

```
Private Sub btnShow_Click(ByVal sender As System.Object, _
  ByVal e As System.EventArgs) Handles btnShow.Click
      ' Check each control in the
      ' grpPlayground container control
      Dim ctrl As Control
      For Each ctrl In Me.grpPlayground.Controls
```

```
        ' Check the type of the control
        If (ctrl.GetType().ToString() = _
        "System.Windows.Forms." & _
        Me.cboControls.SelectedItem) Then
            ' Show the control
            Me.grpPlayground.Controls( _
            Me.grpPlayground.Controls. _
            IndexOf(ctrl)).Visible = True
        End If
    Next
End Sub

Private Sub btnHide_Click(ByVal sender As System.Object, _
ByVal e As System.EventArgs) Handles btnHide.Click
    ' Check each control in the
    ' grpPlayground container control
    Dim ctrl As Control
    For Each ctrl In Me.grpPlayground.Controls
        ' Check the type of the control
        If (ctrl.GetType().ToString() = _
        "System.Windows.Forms." & _
        Me.cboControls.SelectedItem) Then
            ' Show the control
            Me.grpPlayground.Controls( _
            Me.grpPlayground.Controls. _
            IndexOf(ctrl)).Visible = False
        End If
    Next
End Sub
```

6. Set the form as the startup object for the project.

7. Run the project and experiment with the user interface. When you click on the Hide button after selecting a control type from the ComboBox, it will hide all controls of that type from the Playground GroupBox. Similarly, clicking the Show button will display the selected controls.

DIALOG BOXES

A dialog box is used to prompt the user for input. This input can be used by the application for its own processing. You can either use one of the existing dialog box components provided by the Windows Forms library or create a dialog box to meet your custom application requirements. I'll cover both of these scenarios in this section.

Common Dialog Boxes

The Windows Forms library provides the following "canned" dialog boxes ready to use in your Windows applications:

◆ **ColorDialog**—Displays a list of colors and returns a property containing the color selected by the user

◆ **FontDialog**—Displays a dialog box that allows the user to select a font and to set its properties such as size, style and special effects

◆ **OpenFileDialog**—Allows the user to browse files and folders on her computer and select one or more files

◆ **PageSetupDialog**—Allows the user to select various page-layout–related settings

◆ **PrintDialog**—Allows the user to select various print-related options and sends the specified document to the selected printer

◆ **PrintPreviewDialog**—Allows the user to preview a file before printing

◆ **SaveFileDialog**—Allows the user to browse the files and folders on his computer and select a name for a file to be saved

These classes are also referred to as Windows Forms *dialog components*. These dialog boxes provide the same functionality used by the Windows operating system. Each dialog class is derived from the CommonDialog class, which provides the basic functionality for displaying a dialog box.

The dialog classes each provide a method named ShowDialog that presents the dialog box to the user. Each of the dialog classes has a set of properties that stores the data relevant to the particular dialog box. Step By Step 2.5 offers an opportunity to practice working with the dialog boxes provided in the Windows Forms library.

STEP BY STEP

2.5 Common Dialog Boxes

1. Add a Windows Form to your Visual Basic .NET project.

2. Place five Button controls to the form. Name them `btnOpen`, `btnSave`, `btnClose`, `btnColor`, and `btnFont`; and change their `Text` properties to `&Open...`, `&Save...`, `Clos&e`, `&Color...`, and `&Font...`, respectively.

3. Place a RichTextBox control on the form and name it `rtbText`. Figure 2.16 shows a design for this form.

4. Drag and drop the following components from the toolbox to the form: OpenFileDialog, SaveFileDialog, ColorDialog, and FontDialog. Because these are components, they won't be added to the form, but will rather appear on the component tray beneath the form (see Figure 2.16).

5. Switch to the Code view and add the following statement at the top of the form's module:

```
Imports System.IO
```

6. Double-click on the Open button to attach an event handler to this control's `Click` event. Add the following code to the event handler:

```
Private Sub btnOpen_Click(ByVal sender As System.Object, _
 ByVal e As System.EventArgs) Handles btnOpen.Click
    ' Allow the user to select only *.rtf files
    OpenFileDialog1.Filter = "Rich Text Files (*.rtf)|*.rtf"
    If OpenFileDialog1.ShowDialog() = DialogResult.OK Then
        ' Load the file contents to the RichTextBox
        rtbText.LoadFile(OpenFileDialog1.FileName, _
        RichTextBoxStreamType.RichText)
    End If
End Sub
```

continues

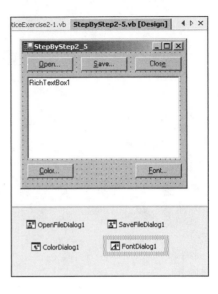

FIGURE 2.16
Windows Form with component tray.

> **NOTE**
>
> **Nonvisual Controls** Controls such as common dialog box controls do not provide a runtime user interface. Instead of being displayed on the form's surface, they are displayed on the component tray at the bottom of the form. Once a control has been added to the component tray, you can select the component and set its properties just as with any other control on the form. These nonvisual controls implement the IComponent interface and therefore are also sometimes referred to as components.

continued

7. Add the following code to handle the `Click` event of the Save button:

```
Private Sub btnSave_Click(ByVal sender As System.Object, _
 ByVal e As System.EventArgs) Handles btnSave.Click
    ' Default choice to save file is
    ' *.rtf but user can select
    ' All Files to save with another extension
    SaveFileDialog1.Filter = _
    "Rich Text Files (*.rtf)|*.rtf|All Files (*.*)|*.*"
    If SaveFileDialog1.ShowDialog() = DialogResult.OK Then
        ' Save the RichText content to a file
        rtbText.SaveFile(SaveFileDialog1.FileName, _
        RichTextBoxStreamType.RichText)
    End If
End Sub
```

8. Add the following code to handle the `Click` event of the Close button:

```
Private Sub btnClose_Click(ByVal sender As System.Object, _
 ByVal e As System.EventArgs) Handles btnClose.Click
    ' Close the form
    Me.Close()
End Sub
```

9. Add the following code to handle the `Click` event of the Color button:

```
Private Sub btnColor_Click(ByVal sender As System.Object, _
 ByVal e As System.EventArgs) Handles btnColor.Click
    If ColorDialog1.ShowDialog() = DialogResult.OK Then
        ' Change the color of the selected text
        ' If no text is selected, change the active color
        rtbText.SelectionColor = ColorDialog1.Color
    End If
End Sub
```

10. Add the following code to handle the `Click` event of the Font button:

```
Private Sub btnFont_Click(ByVal sender As System.Object, _
 ByVal e As System.EventArgs) Handles btnFont.Click
    If FontDialog1.ShowDialog() = DialogResult.OK Then
        ' Change the font of selected text
        ' If no text is selected, change the active font
        rtbText.SelectionFont = FontDialog1.Font
    End If
End Sub
```

EXAM TIP

FilterIndex Property The FilterIndex property of OpenFileDialog and SaveFileDialog components determines the index of the currently selected filter in the list of filters specified by the dialog box's Filter property. Be aware that this index is one-based; in other words, the first filter in the list of filters has an index of one instead of zero.

11. Set this form as the startup object for the project.

12. Run the project. Click on the Open button and select an RTF file to open. You can experiment with changing the color and font and save the file. Figure 2.17 shows this form in action.

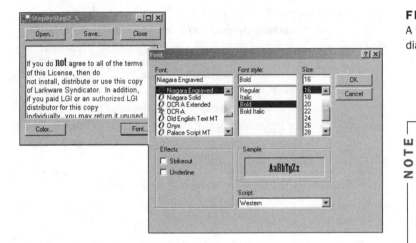

FIGURE 2.17
A file being edited with the help of a common dialog box.

The `Filter` property of the OpenFileDialog and SaveFileDialog components specifies the choices that will appear in the Files of Type drop-down list of these dialog boxes. This property can be used to filter the type of files the user can select from the dialog box.

You will learn about the printing-related dialog components in Chapter 11 "Printing."

Creating a Custom Dialog Box

If you need to create dialog boxes other than those already provided by the Windows Forms library, you can create a custom form and set it to behave as a dialog box. You can make your dialog box as rich as your requirements dictate by adding controls and code to it, as in Step By Step 2.6.

NOTE

Retrieving File Extensions The OpenFileDialog and SaveFileDialog components each has a FileName property that returns the name of selected file. How can you get just the extension for this file? You can do this using the Extension property of the FileInfo class:

```
Dim fiFileInfo As FileInfo
= _
  new FileInfo(openFileDia-
  log1.FileName)
MessageBox.Show(fiFile-
Info.Extension)
```

Similarly, if you want just the name of file without any extensions, you can use the Name property of the FileInfo class:

```
Dim fiFileInfo As FileInfo
= _
  new FileInfo(openFileDia-
  log1.FileName)
MessageBox.Show(fiFile-
Info.Name)
```

STEP BY STEP

2.6 Creating a Custom Dialog Box

1. Add a new form to your Visual Basic .NET project. Name this form frmDialog.

2. Set the ControlBox property of the form to False, the FormBorderStyle property to FixedDialog, the ShowIntaskBar property to False, the StartPosition property to CenterParent, and the Text property to A Custom Dialog Box.

3. Place two Button controls (btnOK and btnCancel) and a TextBox control named txtDialogText on the form. Set the Text properties of the Button controls to &OK and &Cancel. Set the Text property of the TextBox to Dialog Text.

4. Modify the form's New method as follows:

```
Public Sub New()
    MyBase.New()

    'This call is required by the Windows Form Designer.
    InitializeComponent()

    'Add any initialization after the
    ' InitializeComponent() call
    ' Configure OK button
    btnOK.DialogResult = _
     System.Windows.Forms.DialogResult.OK
    ' Configure Cancel button
    btnCancel.DialogResult = _
     System.Windows.Forms.DialogResult.Cancel

End Sub
```

5. Add the following code to create a property that holds the text entered in the TextBox control:

```
Private mstrMessage As String
Public Property Message() As String
    Get
        Message = mstrMessage
    End Get
    Set(ByVal Value As String)
        mstrMessage = Value
    End Set
End Property
```

6. Add an event handler for the Click event of the OK button and add the following code to it:

```
Private Sub btnOK_Click(ByVal sender As System.Object, _
 ByVal e As System.EventArgs) Handles btnOK.Click
    mstrMessage = txtDialogText.Text
End Sub
```

7. Add another Windows Form to the project.

8. Place a Button and a Label control on the new form. Name the Button control btnInvokeDialog and change its Text property to Invoke Dialog. Name the Label control lblDialogResult and change its Text property to Click the button to invoke a custom dialog box.

9. Attach an event handler to the Click event of btnInvokeDialog and add the following code to it:

```
Private Sub btnInvokeDialog_Click( _
 ByVal sender As System.Object, _
 ByVal e As System.EventArgs) Handles btnInvokeDialog.Click
    ' Create the custom dialog box
    Dim dlgCustom As frmDialog = New frmDialog()
    ' Present dialog box to the user
    dlgCustom.ShowDialog()

    If dlgCustom.DialogResult = DialogResult.OK Then
        ' Display the message in the
        ' label if the user pressed OK
        Me.lblDialogResult.Text = dlgCustom.Message
    Else
        ' Indicate that user cancelled the dialog box
        Me.lblDialogResult.Text = "Dialog box was cancelled"
    End If
End Sub
```

10. Set this form as the startup object for the project.

11. Run the project. Click the Invoke Dialog button. The custom dialog box will be displayed. Enter some text in the TextBox and click on the OK button. The text you enter will be displayed on the parent form's label control, as shown in Figure 2.18.

FIGURE 2.18
A custom dialog box and its results.

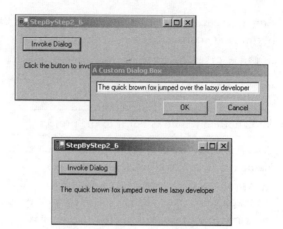

The `ShowDialog` method displays a form as a modal dialog box. Each button on the form should have its `DialogResult` property set to one of the members of the `DialogResult` enumeration. When the user clicks the button, the form's `DialogResult` property is set to the `DialogResult` of the button. The form will close automatically after the button's `Click` event handler (if any) executes, and the result will be available to the calling code.

REVIEW BREAK

▶ A dialog box prompts the user for input. A few built-in dialog boxes are available, such as the ColorDialog, FontDialog, OpenFileDialog, and SaveFileDialog classes. These function just like the Windows operating system's dialog boxes.

▶ You can also build custom dialog boxes to meet custom requirements by creating a form and setting a few properties of the form to enable it to behave like a dialog box.

▶ Dialog boxes can be of two types: modal and modeless. You can call the ShowDialog and Show methods of the Form class to create modal and modeless dialog boxes, respectively.

COMMON WINDOWS FORMS CONTROLS

Add controls to a Windows Form: Set properties on controls.

Add controls to a Windows Form: Write code to handle control events and add the code to a control.

The Windows Forms library comes with a whole array of commonly used GUI elements that you can assemble on a Windows Form to create Windows applications. These GUI elements (known as Windows Forms controls) are mostly derived from the System.Windows.Forms.Control class. As a virtue of this inheritance, these controls share many common properties, methods, and events; in addition, the controls can also have their own specific sets of properties, methods, and events that provide a distinct behavior. Figure 2.19 shows a hierarchy of important classes that derive from the Control class.

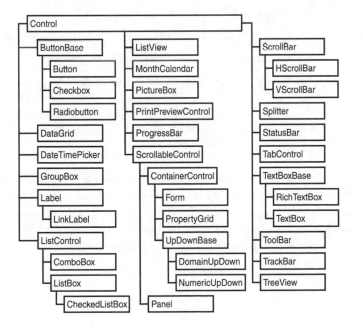

FIGURE 2.19
The Windows Forms controls hierarchy.

In this section I'll talk about some important controls available in the Windows Forms Designer toolbox. Each control has its own purpose and strengths in enabling a robust and functional user interface.

Label and LinkLabel

A Label control displays read-only information to the user. It is generally used to label other controls or to provide runtime information such as messages or statistics. You can display both text and an image on a Label using its Text and Image properties, respectively. Table 2.1 shows some properties of the Label class that you should be familiar with.

TABLE 2.1

IMPORTANT MEMBERS OF THE LABEL CLASS

Member	Type	Description
Image	Property	Image displayed on the Label.
Font	Property	Font in which the text is displayed on the Label.
Text	Property	The text displayed on the Label.
TextAlign	Property	Alignment of the text displayed on the Label. You can choose one of three horizontal positions (Center, Left, or Right) and one of three vertical positions (Bottom, Middle, or Top).

The LinkLabel control is derived from the Label control. In addition to the behavior of a Label, a LinkLabel can also show one or more hyperlinks (links to resources). Table 2.2 summarizes the important properties and events for a LinkLabel control, and Step By Step 2.7 provides the opportunity to use a LinkLabel control.

TABLE 2.2

IMPORTANT MEMBERS OF THE LINKLABEL CLASS

Member	Type	Description
ActiveLinkColor	Property	Color used to display an active link.
DisabledLinkColor	Property	Color used to display a disabled link.
Links	Property	Returns the collection of Link objects in the LinkLabel. The Link class contains information about the hyperlink. Its LinkData property allows you to associate a URL with the hyperlink.
LinkArea	Property	Specifies which portion of text in the LinkLabel is treated as part of the link.
LinkBehavior	Property	Specifies how the link will appear when mouse pointer is placed over it.
LinkClicked	Event	The default event, generated when the link is clicked. Inside its event handler, the LinkLabelLinkClickedEventArgs parameter will provide data for the event.
LinkColor	Property	Color used to display a link.
VisitedLinkColor	Property	Color used to display a visited link.

STEP BY STEP

2.7 Using a LinkLabel Control

1. Add a new form to your Visual Basic .NET project.

2. Place two LinkLabel controls to the form. Change their Name properties to lnkWinForms and lnkPrograms and their Text properties to Windows Forms Community Website and Launch Calculator | Open C: Drive.

3. Switch to the Code view. Modify the form's New method as follows:

```
Public Sub New()
    MyBase.New()
```

continues

continued

```
'This call is required by the Windows Form Designer.
InitializeComponent()

'Add any initialization after
' the InitializeComponent() call
' Add a link for Calculator in
' the first half of LinkLabel
lnkPrograms.Links.Add(0, _
 "Launch Calculator".Length, "calc.exe ")
' Add a link for C: Drive in
' the second half of LinkLabel
lnkPrograms.Links.Add(lnkPrograms. _
 Text.IndexOf("Open C: Drive"), _
 "Open C: Drive".Length, "c:\\")

' Autosize the control based on its contents
lnkPrograms.AutoSize = True

End Sub
```

4. Double-click on the lnkWinForms LinkLabel to attach a `LinkClicked` event handler. Add the following code to the event handler:

```
Private Sub lnkWinForms_LinkClicked( _
 ByVal sender As System.Object, _
 ByVal e As System.Windows.Forms. _
 LinkLabelLinkClickedEventArgs) _
 Handles lnkWinForms.LinkClicked
    lnkWinForms.LinkVisited = True
    ' Go to Windows Forms Community Website
    System.Diagnostics.Process.Start("IExplore", _
    "http://www.windowsforms.net")
End Sub
```

5. Double-click on the lnkPrograms LinkLabel to attach a `LinkClicked` event handler to it. Add the following code to the event handler:

```
Private Sub lnkPrograms_LinkClicked( _
 ByVal sender As System.Object, _
 ByVal e As System.Windows.Forms. _
 LinkLabelLinkClickedEventArgs) _
 Handles lnkPrograms.LinkClicked
    ' Launch the program stored in the hyperlink

System.Diagnostics.Process.Start(e.Link.LinkData.ToString())
End Sub
```

6. Set this form as the startup object for the project.

7. Run the project and click the links. The form will take the appropriate action by either navigating to the Web site, launching the Calculator, or opening the folder (see Figure 2.20).

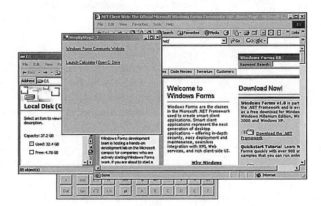

FIGURE 2.20
A LinkLabel control can be used to link to a Web page, an application, or a folder.

The System.Diagnostic.Process class provides the ability to start and stop processes running on your computer. Its Start method actually starts a given process. The Start method is static, so it lets you create the process without creating an instance of the System.Diagnostic.Process class. The LinkLabelLinkClickedEventArgs object passed to the LinkClicked event handler contains a Link object that corresponds to the Link being clicked. The LinkData property of this Link object represents the data associated with the Link.

TextBox and RichTextBox

The TextBox and RichTextBox classes both derive from the TextBoxBase class. The TextBoxBase class implements the basic functionality used by both the TextBox and RichTextBox classes.

A TextBox control provides an area into which the user can input text. Depending on how you set the properties of this control, you can use it for multiline text input or in a mode that masks the characters entered by user with a specific character such as an asterisk (*). Table 2.3 summarizes the important members of the TextBox class.

TABLE 2.3

IMPORTANT MEMBERS OF THE TEXTBOX CLASS

Member	Type	Description
AcceptReturn	Property	Works only if the text box accepts multiline input. Represents a Boolean value in which True indicates that pressing an Enter key in a multiline textbox will insert a new line.
CharacterCasing	Property	Determines whether and how the TextBox control needs to modify the case of the characters as they are entered. The value of this property can be Lower, Normal, or Upper. Default value is Normal, which does not modify the entered characters.
MultiLine	Property	Indicates whether the text box can accept multiple lines of input. The default value of this property is False.
PasswordChar	Property	The PasswordChar character masks each character in the text box by the specified character. It is usually set when the text box is used for sensitive information, such as a password, in which the characters should appear masked. If no character is specified, the normal text is displayed.
ReadOnly	Property	When set to True, this property makes the text box appear with a gray background, and its text cannot be edited.
ScrollBars	Property	Specifies which scroll bars (none, horizontal, vertical, or both) should appear in a multiline text box.
Text	Property	Text contained in the text box.
TextChanged	Event	The default event. Occurs when the value of the control's Text property changes.
WordWrap	Property	Determines whether the control can automatically wrap words to next line. The default value is True. Works only if the MultiLine property is set to True.

The RichTextBox control, as the name suggests, is a text box with rich formatting capabilities. It can read and write Rich Text Format (RTF) files. It can display its contents with rich character and paragraph formatting. Any portion of the control can be displayed in various formats with the help of its properties. Table 2.4 summarizes the important members of the RichTextBox class.

TABLE 2.4

IMPORTANT MEMBERS OF THE RICHTEXTBOX CLASS

Member	Type	Description
DetectUrls	Property	Controls whether the control will automatically detect and format URLs.
Rtf	Property	A version of the text from the control that contains all the RTF formatting codes.
SelectionColor	Property	Color of the currently selected text.
SelectionFont	Property	Font of the currently selected text.
SelectedRtf	Property	Currently selected RTF text.
TextChanged	Event	The default event. Occurs when the value of the control's Text property changes.
WordWrap	Property	Determines whether the control can automatically wrap words to next line if required.
ZoomFactor	Property	Current zoom level.

Step By Steps 2.5 and 2.18 demonstrate the use of the RichTextBox control.

PictureBox

A PictureBox can display graphics from a metafile, icon, bitmap, JPEG, PNG, or GIF file. Table 2.5 summarizes the important members of the PictureBox class.

TABLE 2.5

IMPORTANT MEMBERS OF THE PICTUREBOX CLASS

Member	Type	Description
Click	Event	The default event. Occurs when the control is clicked.
Image	Property	Represents the image that the picture box is displaying.
SizeMode	Property	Indicates how the image is displayed. Holds one of the `PictureBoxSizeMode` enumeration values: AutoSize (picture box is auto-sized to the image size), CenterImage (image is displayed in the center of the picture box), Normal (image is placed in the upper-left corner of the picture box), or StretchImage (image is stretched or shrunken to fit picture box size).

Step By Steps 2.8 and 2.16 demonstrate the use of the PictureBox control.

GroupBox and Panel

A GroupBox is a container control that can contain other controls. It is mostly used to arrange controls and group like controls together and does not include scrollbars. Table 2.6 summarizes the important members of the GroupBox class.

TABLE 2.6
IMPORTANT MEMBERS OF THE GROUPBOX CLASS

Member	Type	Description
Controls	Property	Collection of controls contained in the group box.
Text	Property	Caption of the group box.

The Panel is another container control that can contain other controls. It is mostly used to arrange controls and group like controls together. It has built-in scrollbar support. You cannot provide a caption for the Panel control. Table 2.7 summarizes the important members of the Panel class.

TABLE 2.7
IMPORTANT MEMBERS OF THE PANEL CLASS

Member	Type	Description
AutoScroll	Property	Indicates whether the scrollbars should be displayed when the display of all the controls exceeds the area of the Panel.
Controls	Property	Collection of controls contained in the Panel.

Practice using the GroupBox and Panel controls in Step By Step 2.8.

STEP BY STEP

2.8 Using GroupBox and Panel Controls

1. Add a Windows Form to your Visual Basic .NET project.

2. Place a Label control and a Button control on the form. Set the `Text` property of the Label control to `Click button to open a picture file:`. Set the `Name` of the Button control to `btnBrowse` and its `Text` to `Browse....` Also add an OpenFileDialog control to the form with the Name `ofdPicture`.

3. Place a GroupBox control on the form, and place three Label controls in the GroupBox control. Set the `Name` property to grpFile and the `Text` property to `File Statistics`. Name the three label controls `lblSize`, `lblDateModified`, and `lblDateAccessed`.

4. Place a Panel control on the Form and add a PictureBox control to it. Set the `Name` property of the Panel control to `pnlImage` and its `AutoScroll` property to True. Set the `Name` property of the PictureBox to `pbImage` and its `SizeMode` property to AutoSize.

5. Switch to the Code view and add the following statement at the top of the form's module.

```
Imports System.IO
```

6. Double-click the btnBrowse Button to attach a `Click` event handler to it. Add the following code to the event handler:

```
Private Sub btnBrowse_Click( _
 ByVal sender As System.Object, _
 ByVal e As System.EventArgs) Handles btnBrowse.Click
    ' Set filters for graphics files
    ofdPicture.Filter = _
    "Image Files (BMP, GIF, JPEG, etc.)|" & _
    "*.bmp;*.gif;*.jpg;*.jpeg;*.png;*.tif;*.tiff|" & _
    "BMP Files (*.bmp)|*.bmp|" & _
    "GIF Files (*.gif)|*.gif|" & _
    "JPEG Files (*.jpg;*.jpeg)|*.jpg;*.jpeg|" & _
    "PNG Files (*.png)|*.png|" & _
    "TIF Files (*.tif;*.tiff)|*.tif;*.tiff|" & _
    "All Files (*.*)|*.*"
    If ofdPicture.ShowDialog() = DialogResult.OK Then
```

continues

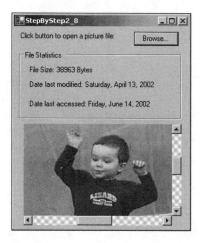

FIGURE 2.21
Panel and GroupBox control showing an image
and a file's statistics.

continued

```
        ' Get file information
        Dim file As FileInfo = New FileInfo( _
         ofdPicture.FileName)
        lblSize.Text = String.Format( _
         "File Size: {0} Bytes", _
         file.Length.ToString())
        lblDateModified.Text = String.Format( _
         "Date last modified: {0}", _
         file.LastWriteTime.ToLongDateString())
        lblDateAccessed.Text = String.Format( _
         "Date last accessed: {0}", _
         file.LastAccessTime.ToLongDateString())
        ' Load the file contents in the PictureBox
        Me.pbImage.Image = New Bitmap(ofdPicture.FileName)
    End If
End Sub
```

7. Set this form as the startup object for the project.

8. Run the project and click on the Browse button. It will prompt you to open an image file. Select an appropriate image file and click OK. The panel shows the image, and the GroupBox shows the file statistics, as shown in Figure 2.21. You will also notice that the panel includes scrollbars if the image size exceeds the panel area.

Button, CheckBox, and RadioButton

A Button object initiates a specific action when the user clicks it. The Button class derives from the ButtonBase class. The ButtonBase class provides common functionality to the Button, CheckBox, and RadioButton classes.

The CheckBox and RadioButton controls maintain state. They can be on or off (selected or unselected, checked or unchecked). These controls are generally used in groups. Check boxes allow the user to select one or more options from a group of options, while a group of radio buttons is used to select one of many mutually exclusive options. If you want to place two groups of radio buttons on your form with each group allowing an independent selection, you must place each group in a different container control. The GroupBox control is a popular choice to group RadioButton controls.

Tables 2.8, 2.9, and 2.10 summarize the important members of the Button, CheckBox, and RadioButton classes, respectively. Step By Step 2.9 provides an opportunity to practice with RadioButton and CheckBox controls.

TABLE 2.8

IMPORTANT MEMBERS OF THE BUTTON CLASS

Member	Type	Description
Image	Property	Image displayed on the Button.
Text	Property	Text displayed on the Button.
Click	Event	The default event. Fires when the Button control is clicked.

TABLE 2.9

IMPORTANT MEMBERS OF THE CHECKBOX CLASS

Member	Member	Description
Checked	Property	Returns True if the CheckBox has been checked, otherwise False.
CheckedChanged	Event	Default event for the CheckBox control. This event is raised every time a check box is either checked or unchecked.
CheckState	Property	State of the check box. Its value is one of the three CheckState enumeration values: Checked, Unchecked, or Indeterminate.
ThreeState	Property	Indicates whether the check box allows the three states Checked, Unchecked, and Indeterminate. If set to False, the CheckState can be set to Indeterminate only in code and not through the user interface.
Text	Property	Text displayed along with the check box.

NOTE

Checked Property Doesn't Always Indicate Checked State If the ThreeState property of the check box is True, the Checked property returns True for the Checked as well as the Indeterminate CheckState. The CheckState property should be used to determine the current state of the check box in this case.

TABLE 2.10

IMPORTANT MEMBERS OF THE RADIOBUTTON CLASS

Member	Type	Description
Checked	Property	Indicates whether the radio button is checked. Returns True if checked, False otherwise.
CheckedChanged	Event	Default event of RadioButton. This event is raised every time that this control is checked or unchecked.
Text	Property	Text displayed along with the RadioButton.

STEP BY STEP

2.9 Using CheckBox and RadioButton Controls

1. Add a new form to your Visual Basic .NET project.

2. Add three GroupBox controls to the form. Change their Name properties to grpSampleText, grpEffects and grpFontSize. Add a Label control to the grpSampleText GroupBox. Add two CheckBox controls to the grpEffects GroupBox. Add three RadioButton controls to the grpFontSize GroupBox. Arrange the controls and change their Text properties as shown in Figure 2.22.

3. Change the Name property of the Label control to lblSampleText. Change the Name property of two CheckBox controls to cbStrikeout and cbUnderline. Change the Name property of RadioButton controls to rb12Points, rb14Points, and rb16Points.

4. Add the following code to the form to handle events:

```
Private Sub cbStrikeout_CheckedChanged( _
 ByVal sender As System.Object, _
 ByVal e As System.EventArgs) _
Handles cbStrikeout.CheckedChanged
    ' Toggle the Strikeout FontStyle of lblSampleText
    lblSampleText.Font = New Font(lblSampleText.Font.Name, _
     lblSampleText.Font.Size, lblSampleText.Font.Style Xor _
     FontStyle.Strikeout)
End Sub
```

NOTE

AutoCheck Property When the AutoCheck property of a check box or a radio button is True, the Checked (and the CheckState in case of CheckBox) property and the appearance of the control are automatically changed when the user clicks the control. You can set this property to False and write code in the Click event handler to have these controls behave in a different manner.

```
Private Sub cbUnderline_CheckedChanged( _
 ByVal sender As System.Object, _
 ByVal e As System.EventArgs) _
 Handles cbUnderline.CheckedChanged
    ' Toggle the Underline FontStyle of lblSampleText
    lblSampleText.Font = New Font(lblSampleText.Font.Name, _
      lblSampleText.Font.Size, lblSampleText.Font.Style Xor _
      FontStyle.Underline)
End Sub

Private Sub rb12Points_CheckedChanged( _
 ByVal sender As System.Object, _
 ByVal e As System.EventArgs) _
 Handles rb12Points.CheckedChanged
    ' Change the font size of lblSampleText to 12
    lblSampleText.Font = _
      New Font(lblSampleText.Font.Name, 12, _
      lblSampleText.Font.Style)
End Sub

Private Sub rb14Points_CheckedChanged( _
 ByVal sender As System.Object, _
 ByVal e As System.EventArgs) _
 Handles rb14Points.CheckedChanged
    ' Change the font size of lblSampleText to 14
    lblSampleText.Font = _
      New Font(lblSampleText.Font.Name, 14, _
      lblSampleText.Font.Style)
End Sub

Private Sub rb16Points_CheckedChanged( _
 ByVal sender As System.Object, _
 ByVal e As System.EventArgs) _
 Handles rb16Points.CheckedChanged
    ' Change the font size of lblSampleText to 16
    lblSampleText.Font = _
      New Font(lblSampleText.Font.Name, 16, _
      lblSampleText.Font.Style)
End Sub
```

5. Set the form as the startup object for the project.

6. Run the project. Click the CheckBox controls to change the style of the sample text. You can select both of the CheckBox controls at the same time. Click on the RadioButton controls to change the size of the text. You can only select one of the RadioButton controls at a time. Figure 2.22 shows this form in action.

EXAM TIP

FontStyle Enumeration and Bitwise Operations The FontStyle enumeration has a FlagAttribute attribute to allow bitwise operations on FontStyle values. When you use an expression such as

```
lblSampleText.Font.Style
Or FontStyle.Underline
```

the operator will turn on all the bits representing the Underline style, returning a FontStyle value that adds Underline to the existing FontStyle of lblSampleText.

The following expression involves a bitwise exclusive OR (XOR) operation:

```
lblSampleText.Font.Style
Xor FontStyle.Underline
```

This expression returns a FontStyle value that toggles the Underline FontStyle of the label. If the label was already underlined, the new value will have it removed; if it was not underlined already, the Underline bits will be set in the new value.

FIGURE 2.22
Using CheckBox and RadioButton controls.

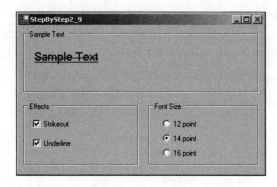

ListBox, CheckedListBox, and ComboBox

A ListBox control allows you to select one or more values from a given list of values. It derives from the ListControl class, which provides common functionality for the ListBox and ComboBox controls. Table 2.11 summarizes the important members of the ListBox class.

TABLE 2.11

IMPORTANT MEMBERS OF THE LISTBOX CLASS

Member	Type	Description
ColumnWidth	Property	Width of column in a multicolumn list box.
ItemHeight	Property	Height of an item in list box.
Items	Property	A collection of objects representing the list of items in a list box.
FindString	Method	Finds the first item in the list box that starts with the specified string.
FindStringExact	Method	Finds the first item in the list box that exactly matches the specified string.
MultiColumn	Property	Specifies whether the list box supports multiple columns.
SelectedIndex	Property	Index of the currently selected item.
SelectedIndexChanged	Event	The default event. Occurs when the SelectedIndex property changes.

Member	Type	Description
SelectedIndices	Property	Collection of indexes of the currently selected items.
SelectedItem	Property	Currently selected item.
SelectedItems	Property	Collection of currently selected items.
SelectionMode	Property	Indicates the number of items that can be selected. The values are specified by the SelectionMode enumeration. They can be MultiSimple (allows multiple selections), MultiExtended (allows multiple selections with the help of Ctrl, Shift and arrow keys), None (no selection) and One (allows single selection).
Sorted	Property	Indicates whether the items are sorted alphabetically.

The CheckedListBox control derives from the ListBox control and inherits most of the features of the ListBox class. You can practice using both these controls in Step By Step 2.10. A CheckedListBox displays a list of items to be selected along with a check box for each item. The user selects the items by clicking the check box associated with the item. As a CheckedListBox contains a check box for each item, it implies that one or more items can be selected from the list box. The CheckedListBox cannot be controlled by properties to allow only single item selections. Table 2.12 summarizes the important members of the CheckedListBox class.

TABLE 2.12

IMPORTANT MEMBERS OF THE CHECKEDLISTBOX CLASS

Member	Type	Description
CheckedIndices	Property	Collection of indexes of the currently checked items.
CheckedItems	Property	Collection of currently checked items.
ItemCheck	Event	Occurs when an item is checked or unchecked.
SelectionMode	Property	Indicates the number of items that can be checked. The value is specified by the SelectionMode enumeration and can be only None (no selection) or One (allow multiple selections).

STEP BY STEP

2.10 Using ListBox and CheckedListBox Controls

1. Add a new form to your Visual Basic .NET project.

2. Add two Label controls, a CheckedListBox control, a ListBox control, and a Button control to the form. Arrange them as shown in Figure 2.23. Change the Label control's Text properties to Select Scripts and Selected Scripts. Change the Button control's Name property to btnDone and its Text property to Done.

3. Change the ListBox control's Text property to lbSelectedScripts and its SelectionMode to MultiExtended. Name the CheckedListBox control clbScripts. Select its Items property and click the Build button (marked with an ellipsis). Add the following strings in the String Collection Editor:

```
Latin
Greek
Cyrillic
Armenian
Hebrew
Arabic
Devanagari
Bengali
Gurmukhi
Gujarati
Oriya
Tamil
Telugu
Kannada
Malayalam
Thai
Lao
Georgian
Tibetan
Japanese Kana
```

4. Switch to the Code view and add this line of code at the top of the Form's module:

```
Imports System.Text
```

5. Add an event handler for the CheckedListBox control's `ItemCheck` event:

```
Private Sub clbScripts_ItemCheck(ByVal sender As Object, _
 ByVal e As System.Windows.Forms.ItemCheckEventArgs) _
 Handles clbScripts.ItemCheck
    ' Get the item that was just checked or unchecked
    Dim item As String = clbScripts.SelectedItem.ToString()
    If e.NewValue = CheckState.Checked Then
        ' Checked: Add to the ListBox
        lbSelectedScripts.Items.Add(item)
    Else
        ' Unchecked: Remove from the ListBox
        lbSelectedScripts.Items.Remove(item)
    End If
End Sub
```

6. Double-click the btnDone control and add the following code to handle the `Click` event of the Button control:

```
Private Sub btnDone_Click(ByVal sender As System.Object, _
 ByVal e As System.EventArgs) Handles btnDone.Click
    Dim sbLanguages As StringBuilder = New StringBuilder()
    If lbSelectedScripts.SelectedItems.Count > 0 Then
        sbLanguages.Append( _
        "You Selected:" & vbCrLf & vbCrLf)
        ' If there were items selected in ListBox
        ' create a string of their names
        Dim item As String
        For Each item In lbSelectedScripts.SelectedItems
            sbLanguages.Append(item & vbCrLf)
        Next
    Else
        ' No items selected
        sbLanguages.Append("No items selected from List
        Box")
    End If
    MessageBox.Show(sbLanguages.ToString(), _
      "Selection Status", _
      MessageBoxButtons.OK, MessageBoxIcon.Information)
End Sub
```

7. Set the form as the startup object for the project.

8. Run the project. Double-click the check box to select items from the CheckedListBox control. The selected scripts are then added to the ListBox control. Select some items from the ListBox control and click the button. A message box will show the selected scripts from the ListBox control (see Figure 2.23).

FIGURE 2.23
Using ListBox and CheckedListBox controls.

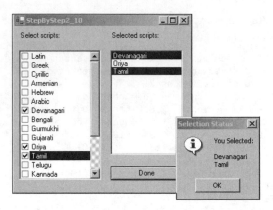

A ComboBox control is similar to a ListBox control with an editing field. The combo box appears as an editing text box with a down arrow at the right end of the box. When you click the arrow, the ComboBox control displays a drop-down list containing predefined items. The user can only select a single item from the combo box. A combo box allows you to enter new text or select from the list of existing items in the combo box. Table 2.13 summarizes the members of the ComboBox class that you should be familiar with. Step By Step 2.12 and Guided Practice Exercise 2.2 provide opportunities to practice using the ComboBox control.

TABLE 2.13

IMPORTANT MEMBERS OF THE COMBOBOX CLASS

Member	Type	Description
DrawMode	Property	Specifies how the combo box items are drawn. It has one of the values from the DrawMode enumeration. The value Normal specifies that the list of items is drawn by the system itself. The other two values (OwnerDrawFixed and OwnerDrawVariable), specify that the elements are drawn by your own program (preferably in the DrawItem event handler). The former specifies that elements will all be the same size, whereas the later specifies a variable size.
DropDownStyle	Property	Represents the style of the combo box. Its values are specified by the DropDownStyle enumeration: DropDown (default style, click the arrow button to display the items and the text portion is editable), DropDownList (click the arrow button to display the items but the text portion is not editable) and Simple (no arrow button, the list portion is always visible and the text portion is also editable).
DropDownWidth	Property	Width of the drop-down list portion of the combo box.
Items	Property	Collection of items in the ComboBox control.
MaxDropDownItems	Property	Represents the maximum number of items the drop-down list portion can display. If the number of items is more than this property, a scrollbar appears.

Member	Type	Description
MaxLength	Property	Indicates the maximum length of text allowed to be entered in the editable portion.
SelectedIndex	Property	Index of the currently selected item.
SelectedIndexChanged	Event	The default event. Occurs when the selected index property changes.
SelectedItem	Property	Currently selected item.
SelectedText	Property	Currently selected text in the editable portion.
Sorted	Property	Indicates whether the items are sorted alphabetically.

STEP BY STEP

2.11 Using the ComboBox Control

1. Add a new Windows Form to your Visual Basic .NET project.

2. Place a Label control with its Text property set to Select or Enter a Color, a ComboBox control with the Name cboColor, and Button control with the Name btnSet on the form. Set the text of the Button control to Set Form's Back Color.

3. Change the ComboBox control's Sorted property to True and add the following strings to the Items collection with the String Collection Editor:

```
Violet
Indigo
Blue
Green
Yellow
Orange
Red
White
```

4. Double-click the btnSet control and add the following code to handle the Click event of the Button control:

```
Private Sub btnSet_Click(ByVal sender As System.Object, _
 ByVal e As System.EventArgs) Handles btnSet.Click
    Me.BackColor = Color.FromName(cboColor.Text)
End Sub
```

5. Set the form as the startup object for the project.

continues

EXAM TIP

SelectedIndex Property with No Selection The SelectedIndex property in the ListBox, CheckedListBox, and ComboBox will return −1 (negative one) if no item is selected.

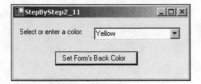

FIGURE 2.24
Setting a background color with a ComboBox control.

continued

6. Run the project. Select a color from the list of colors in the combo box or enter a new color in the combo box. Click the button. The Form's background color will change to the color selected or entered in the combo box. Figure 2.24 shows the result.

GUIDED PRACTICE EXERCISE 2.2

In this exercise you will create the Windows Form shown in Figure 2.25. The idea is to create a font sampler such as those normally used by word processing applications. The form contains a combo box that displays a list of fonts installed in your system, but the items in the combo box are displayed in their respective fonts. The form also contains a label control that displays the sample of the font chosen by the user from the combo box.

To achieve the object of this exercise, you must change the `DrawMode` property of the combo box to handle the rendering by programming a `DrawItem` event handler. This exercise gives practice on how to work with owner-drawn controls that display custom rendering.

Try this on your own first. If you get stuck or would like to see one possible solution, follow these steps:

1. Add a new form to your Visual Basic .NET Project.

2. Place two Label controls on the form. Set the `Text` property of the first Label control to `Select a Font`. Set the `Name` property of the second Label control `lblSampleText`; set its `Text` property to `Sample Text`, and set its font to Microsoft Sans Serif, Regular, size 14.

3. Place a ComboBox control on the form. Set the `Name` property to `cboFont`, the `DrawMode` property to `OwnerDrawVariable`, and `DropDownStyle` property to `DropDownList`. Set the font size of the ComboBox control to 14 point.

4. Double-click the form and add the following code to handle the Load event of the form:

```
Private Sub GuidedPracticeExercise2_2_Load( _
 ByVal sender As System.Object, _
 ByVal e As System.EventArgs) Handles MyBase.Load
    ' Add a list of System Fonts to th eComboBox
    cboFont.Items.AddRange(FontFamily.Families)
End Sub
```

5. Add the following procedure to the form's code:

```
Private Function GetFontStyle( _
 ByVal ff As FontFamily) As FontStyle
    Dim fs As FontStyle = FontStyle.Regular
    ' Check whether Regular style is available
    If Not (ff.IsStyleAvailable(FontStyle.Regular)) Then
        fs = FontStyle.Italic
        ' Check whether Italic style is available
        If Not (ff.IsStyleAvailable(FontStyle.Italic))
Then
            fs = FontStyle.Bold
        End If
    End If
    Return fs
End Function
```

6. Create an event handler for the DrawItem event of the ComboBox control:

```
Private Sub cboFont_DrawItem(ByVal sender As Object, _
 ByVal e As System.Windows.Forms.DrawItemEventArgs) _
 Handles cboFont.DrawItem
    ' This DrawItem event handler is invoked
    ' to draw an item in a ComboBox
    ' If that  ComboBox is in an OwnerDraw DrawMode.

    Dim cboFont As ComboBox = CType(sender, ComboBox)
    ' do nothing if there is no data
    If e.Index = -1 Then
        Return
    End If
    If sender Is Nothing Then
        Return
    End If

    ' Make a FontFamily object from the name
    ' of the font currently being drawn
    Dim ff As FontFamily = _
     CType(cboFont.Items(e.Index), FontFamily)

    ' Create a Font object that will
    ' be used to draw the text in ComboBox
    Dim fnt As Font = _
     New Font(ff.Name, 12, GetFontStyle(ff))
```

continues

continued

```
' If the item is selected,
' draw the correct background color
e.DrawBackground()
e.DrawFocusRectangle()

' DrawItemEventArgs gives access
' to ComboBox Graphics object
Dim g As Graphics = e.Graphics

' Draw the name of the font in the same font
g.DrawString(ff.Name, fnt, _
  New SolidBrush(e.ForeColor), _
  e.Bounds.X, e.Bounds.Y + 4)
End Sub
```

7. Double-click the combo box and add the following code to handle the SelectedIndexChanged event of the combo box control:

```
Private Sub cboFont_SelectedIndexChanged( _
 ByVal sender As System.Object, _
 ByVal e As System.EventArgs) _
 Handles cboFont.SelectedIndexChanged
    ' Get the FontFamily object
    ' for current ComboBox selection
    Dim ff As FontFamily = _
      CType(CType(sender, ComboBox).SelectedItem, _
      FontFamily)
    ' Create a Font object and Draw the Font Name
    lblSampleText.Font = New Font(ff.Name, _
      lblSampleText.Font.Size, GetFontStyle(ff))
End Sub
```

8. Set the form as the startup object for the project.

9. Run the project. The combo box displays all the available fonts drawn in their own fonts. The Label's text is also updated to display the text in the selected font, as shown in Figure 2.25

FIGURE 2.25
ComboBox displaying font data.

REVIEW BREAK

▶ The LinkLabel control is derived from the Label control. The LinkLabel control allows you to add links to the control. The Links property of the LinkLabel contains a collection of all the links referred to by the control.

▶ The TextBox control can be displayed as an ordinary text box, a password text box (in which each character is masked by the character provided in the PasswordChar property), or as a multiline text box (by setting its MultiLine property to True). The RichTextBox control provides enriched formatting capabilities compared to a TextBox control. It can also be drawn as a single- or multiline text box. By default, the RichTextBox control has its MultiLine property set to True.

▶ GroupBox and Panel controls are container controls used to group other controls. The Controls property of these controls contains a collection of their child controls.

▶ In a group of CheckBox controls, you can check multiple check boxes. In a group of RadioButton controls, you can select only a single radio button at a time.

▶ The CheckBox control allows you to set three check states (Checked, Unchecked, and Indeterminate), if the ThreeState property is set to True.

▶ The ComboBox control allows you to select a value from a predefined list of values. You can also enter a value in the ComboBox control. The ListBox control will only allow you to select a value from the list of values displayed.

▶ The CheckedListBox control derives from the ListBox control and inherits its functionality. However, a CheckedListBox control displays a check box along with each item in the list of items to be checked. The CheckedListBox control allows only two values for the SelectionMode property: None (no selection) or One (allows multiple selections).

DomainUpDown and NumericUpDown

The DomainUpDown and NumericUpDown controls both inherit from the System.Windows.Forms.UpDownBase class. Use these controls to select a value from the (generally) ordered collection of values by pressing up and down buttons of the control. You can also enter a value directly in these controls, unless the ReadOnly property is set to True. See Step By Step 2.12 for practice.

The DomainUpDown allows you to select from a collection of objects. When an item is selected, its value is converted to string and returned by the control. Table 2.14 summarizes the important members of the DomainUpDown class.

TABLE 2.14

IMPORTANT MEMBERS OF THE DOMAINUPDOWN CLASS

Member	Type	Description
Items	Property	Represents the collection of objects assigned to the control.
ReadOnly	Property	Indicates whether you can enter the value directly, as opposed to by pressing the up and down buttons.
SelectedIndex	Property	Index value of the selected item in the Items collection.
SelectedItem	Property	The selected item value based on the SelectedIndex.
SelectedItemChanged	Event	The default event. Occurs when the SelectedIndex property is changed.
Sorted	Property	Determines whether the Items collection is sorted.
Wrap	Property	Determines whether the SelectedIndex property resets to the first or to the last item if the user continues past the end of the list.

The NumericUpDown control contains a single numeric value that can be increased or decreased by clicking on the up or down buttons of the control. You can specify the Minimum, Maximum, and Increment values to control the range of values in this control. Table 2.15 summarizes the important members of the NumericUpDown class.

TABLE 2.15

IMPORTANT MEMBERS OF THE NUMERICUPDOWN CLASS

Member	Type	Description
Increment	Property	Increases or decreases the Value property by this increment when the up or down button is clicked.
Maximum	Property	Maximum allowed value.
Minimum	Property	Minimum allowed value.
ReadOnly	Property	Indicates whether you can change the values directly rather than by selecting them by pressing the up and down buttons.
ThousandsSeparator	Property	Determines whether a thousands separator should be used when appropriate.
Value	Property	Value assigned to the control.
ValueChanged	Event	The default event. Occurs when the Value property is changed.

STEP BY STEP

2.12 Using DomainUpDown and NumericUpDown Controls

1. Add a new Windows Form to your Visual Basic .NET project.

2. Add three Label controls, one DomainUpDown control, and one NumericUpDown control to the form and arrange them as shown in Figure 2.26.

3. Name the DomainUpDown control dudColor. Set its Text property to Black, its UpDownAlign property to Left, and its Wrap property to True. Select its Items property; click on the builder button and in the String Collection Editor add the following values:

Violet
Indigo
Blue

continues

continued

```
Green
Yellow
Orange
Red
Black
White
```

4. Name the NumericUpDown control `nudSize`. Set its `Maximum` property to `30`, its `Minimum` property to `2`, its `Increment` property to `2` and its `Value` property to `12`. Set its `ReadOnly` property to `True`.

5. Name the Label placed at bottom `lblSampleText`. Change its `Text` property to `Sample Text` and its `TextAlign` property to `MiddleCenter`.

6. Add event handlers for the default events of the DomainUpDown and NumericUpDown controls:

```
Private Sub dudColor_SelectedItemChanged( _
 ByVal sender As System.Object, _
 ByVal e As System.EventArgs) _
 Handles dudColor.SelectedItemChanged
    ' Typecast the object to DomainUpDown
    Dim dudColor As DomainUpDown = _
    CType(sender, DomainUpDown)
    ' Change color of lblsampleText to selected color
    lblSampleText.ForeColor = Color.FromName(dudColor.Text)
End Sub

Private Sub nudSize_ValueChanged( _
 ByVal sender As System.Object, _
 ByVal e As System.EventArgs) Handles nudSize.ValueChanged
    ' Typecast the object to NumericUpDown
    Dim nudSize As NumericUpDown = _
    CType(sender, NumericUpDown)
    ' Change the font of lblSampleText to selected font
    lblSampleText.Font = _
    New Font(lblSampleText.Font.FontFamily, _
    CType(nudSize.Value, Double))
End Sub
```

7. Set this form as the startup object for the project.

8. Run the project. Click on the up and down buttons of the UpDown controls. Note that their respective event handlers fire and change the appearance of the Text property of lblSampleText control, as shown in Figure 2.26. You will notice that you can enter a desired color in the DomainUpDown control by typing, because its ReadOnly property is False.

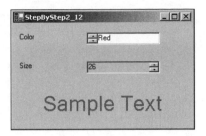

FIGURE 2.26
Using the DomainUpDown and NumericUpDown controls.

MonthCalendar and DateTimePicker

The MonthCalendar control provides a user-friendly interface to select a date or a range of dates. Table 2.16 summarizes the members of the MonthCalendar class that you should be familiar with.

TABLE 2.16

IMPORTANT MEMBERS OF THE MONTHCALENDAR CLASS

Member	Type	Description
CalendarDimensions	Property	Number of columns and rows of months displayed.
DateChanged	Event	The default event. Occurs when the date selected in the control changes.
DateSelected	Event	Occurs when a date is selected in the control.
FirstDayOfWeek	Property	Represents the first day of the week displayed by the calendar.
MaxDate	Property	Maximum allowable date to be selected.
MaxSelectionCount	Property	Maximum number of days that can be selected.
MinDate	Property	Minimum allowable date to be selected.
SelectionEnd	Property	End date of the selected range of dates.
SelectionRange	Property	Selected range of dates.
SelectionStart	Property	Start date of the selected range of dates.
ShowToday	Property	Indicates whether today's date should be displayed in the bottom of the control.
ShowTodayCircle	Property	Indicates whether today's date should be circled.

continues

TABLE 2.16		*continued*

IMPORTANT MEMBERS OF THE MONTHCALENDAR CLASS

Member	*Type*	*Description*
ShowWeekNumbers	Property	Indicates whether the week numbers (1–52) should be displayed at the beginning of each row of days.
TodayDate	Property	Represents the today's date.

The DateTimePicker control allows the user to select a date and time in different formats. The Format property determines the format in which the control displays the date and time. You can also display a custom date and time format with the DateTimePicker control by setting the Format property to DateTimePickerFormat.Custom and the CustomFormat property to the custom format desired. Table 2.17 summarizes the important members of the DateTimePicker class.

TABLE 2.17

IMPORTANT MEMBERS OF THE DATETIMEPICKER CLASS

Member	*Type*	*Description*
CustomFormat string.	Property	Represents the custom date and time format
Format	Property	Specifies the format of date and time displayed in the control. The values are specified by the DateTimePickerFormat enumeration: Custom, Long (default), Short, and Time. The Long, Short, and Time display the date in the value formats set by the operating system. The Custom value lets you specify your own custom format.
FormatChanged	Event	Occurs when the Format property changes.
MaxDate	Property	Maximum allowable date and time to be selected.
MinDate	Property	Minimum allowable date and time to be selected.
ShowCheckBox	Property	Indicates whether a check box should be displayed at the left of the selected date.
ShowUpDown	Property	Indicates whether an up-down control should be displayed to allow the user to make selections other than the default calendar control.

Member	Type	Description
Value	Property	Represents the value of the date and time selected.
ValueChanged	Event	The default event. Occurs when the Value property changes.

Step By Step 2.13 provides an opportunity to further familiarize yourself with the MonthCalendar and DateTimePicker controls.

STEP BY STEP

2.13 Using MonthCalendar and DateTimePicker Controls

1. Add a Windows Form to your Visual Basic .NET project.

2. Place three Label controls, one MonthCalendar control (named mcTravelDates), one DateTimePicker control (named dtpLaunchDate), and two RadioButton controls (named rbLongDate and rbShortDate) on the form and arrange them as shown in Figure 2.27. Name the Label placed adjacent to the MonthCalendar control lblTravelDates.

3. Switch to the Code view and add this line of code at the top of the module:

```
Imports System.Text
```

4. Add an event handler for the DateSelected event of the MonthCalendar control. Add the following code to the event handler:

```
Private Sub mcTravelDates_DateSelected( _
 ByVal sender As Object, _
 ByVal e As System.Windows.Forms.DateRangeEventArgs) _
 Handles mcTravelDates.DateSelected
    Dim sbMessage As StringBuilder = New StringBuilder()
    With sbMessage
        .Append("StartDate: " & vbCrLf)
        .Append(e.Start.ToShortDateString() & vbCrLf)
        .Append("End Date: " & vbCrLf)
        .Append(e.End.ToShortDateString)
    End With
    Me.lblTravelDates.Text = sbMessage.ToString()
End Sub
```

continues

continued

5. Attach event handlers to the default events of the RadioButton controls. Add the following code to the event handlers:

```
Private Sub rbLongDate_CheckedChanged( _
 ByVal sender As System.Object, _
 ByVal e As System.EventArgs) _
 Handles rbLongDate.CheckedChanged
    If rbLongDate.Checked Then
        dtpLaunchDate.Format = DateTimePickerFormat.Long
    End If
End Sub

Private Sub rbShortDate_CheckedChanged( _
 ByVal sender As System.Object, _
 ByVal e As System.EventArgs) _
 Handles rbShortDate.CheckedChanged
    If rbShortDate.Checked Then
        dtpLaunchDate.Format = DateTimePickerFormat.Short
    End If
End Sub
```

6. Set this form as the startup object for the project.

7. Run the project. Select a range of dates from the MonthCalendar control and a date from the DateTimePicker control. The label adjacent to the MonthCalendar control will display the start date and end date from the range of the dates selected (see Figure 2.27). You can also change the format of the date shown by the DateTimePicker control by clicking the radio buttons.

FIGURE 2.27
Using MonthCalendar and DateTimePicker controls.

TreeView and ListView

The TreeView control displays a hierarchical collection of nodes. Each node is represented by a TreeNode object. TreeNode objects can have their own collection of nodes, thus forming a hierarchical structure. Table 2.18 summarizes the important members of the TreeView class.

TABLE 2.18

IMPORTANT MEMBERS OF THE TREEVIEW CLASS

Member	Type	Description
AfterCheck	Event	Occurs after a tree node is checked.
AfterCollapse	Event	Occurs after a tree node is collapsed.
AfterExpand	Event	Occurs after a tree node is expanded.
AfterSelect	Event	The default event. Occurs after a tree node is selected.
CheckBoxes	Property	Indicates whether a check box should appear along with each item in the control.
ImageList	Property	Represents the ImageList control that contains node icons.
Nodes	Property	Collection of Tree nodes in the control.
Scrollable	Property	Indicates whether the scroll bars should be displayed when needed. The default value is True.
SelectedNode	Property	Represents the currently selected node.
Sorted	Property	Indicates whether the tree nodes are sorted.

The ListView control displays a list of items. Each item in the list can have a name, an icon, and additional columns of text associated with it.

Table 2.19 summarizes the important members of the ListView class.

TABLE 2.19

IMPORTANT MEMBERS OF THE LISTVIEW CLASS

Member	Type	Description
Activation	Property	Indicates how an item can be activated: OneClick (single click), Standard (double-click), or TwoClick (double-click, item color changes when mouse hovers over it). These values are defined in the ItemActivation enumeration.
CheckBoxes	Property	Indicates whether a check box should appear along with each item in the control.
CheckedIndices	Property	Collection of indexes of the currently checked items.
CheckedItems	Property	Collection of currently checked items.
ItemActivate	Event	Occurs when an item is activated.

continues

TABLE 2.19   *continued*

IMPORTANT MEMBERS OF THE LISTVIEW CLASS

Member	Type	Description
ItemCheck	Event	Occurs when an item's check state changes.
Items	Property	Collection of items displayed by the ListView control.
LargeImageList	Property	Represents the ImageList control to display large icons.
MultiSelect	Property	Indicates whether multiple items can be selected.
Scrollable	Property	Indicates whether the scroll bar will be added when the list of items exceeds the size of the client area. The default value is True.
SelectedIndexChanged	Event	Default event. Occurs when the selected index changes.
SelectedIndices	Property	Collection of indexes of the currently selected items.
SelectedItems	Property	Collection of currently selected items.
SmallImageList	Property	Represents the ImageList control to display small icons.
Sorting	Property	Represents the sort order of items in the control from the SortOrder enumeration: Ascending, Descending, or None (default).
View	Property	Represents how items are displayed. The values are specified by the View enumeration, as seen here: **Details**—Items are displayed with multicolumn information about the item. **LargeIcon**—Default value, item appears with a large icon along with a label below it in multi-columns. **List**—Single column list in which a small icon is displayed with a label on its right. **SmallIcon**—Small icon with a label on its right displayed in multicolumns.

The familiar interface of Windows Explorer uses both a TreeView and a ListView to present the folders and folder contents in its left and right pane, respectively. In Step By Step 2.14, I also attempt to provide a similar functionality, but on a smaller scale.

STEP BY STEP

2.14 Using TreeView and ListView Controls

1. Add a new Windows Form to your Visual Basic .NET project.

2. Place a TreeView control (tvwDirectories), a ListView control (lvwFiles) and an ImageList (ilSmallIcons) control on the form. The ImageList control will be added to the component tray.

3. Set the ColorDepth property of the ImageList control to Depth8Bit. Select the Images property and click the build button to invoke the Image Collection Editor. Click the Add button, and an Open File dialog will appear. Select a small icon image to represent items in a List View and click Open. The file will be added to the Members list box in the Image Collection Editor along with its index as shown in Figure 2.28. Click OK to close the Image Collection Editor.

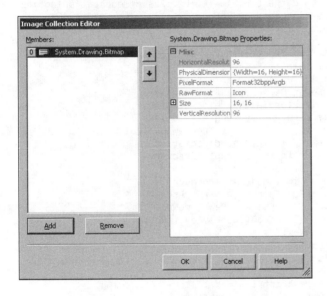

FIGURE 2.28
Adding images to an image list using the Image Collection Editor.

4. Change the View property of the ListView control to List and the SmallImageList property to ilSmallIcons.

5. Switch to Code view and add these lines to the top of the form's module:

```
Imports System.Text
Imports System.IO
```

continues

continued

6. Add code to handle events:

```vb
Private Sub StepByStep2_14_Load( _
 ByVal sender As System.Object, _
 ByVal e As System.EventArgs) Handles MyBase.Load
    tvwDirectories.Nodes.Add("C:\")
    ' Load the TreeView with C: drive contents
    RefreshTreeView("C:\", tvwDirectories.Nodes(0))
End Sub

Private Sub tvwDirectories_AfterSelect( _
 ByVal sender As Object, _
 ByVal e As System.Windows.Forms.TreeViewEventArgs) _
 Handles tvwDirectories.AfterSelect
    ' Load the TreeView with
    ' subdirectories of current selection
    RefreshTreeView(e.Node.Text, e.Node)
    ' Load the ListView with files of current selection
    RefreshListView(e.Node.Text)
End Sub

Sub RefreshTreeView(ByVal strDir As String, _
 ByVal tnRoot As TreeNode)
    ' Get directory information
    Dim strDirArray() As String = _
     Directory.GetDirectories(strDir)
    If strDirArray.Length <> 0 Then
        ' Populate the TreeVew control
        ' with all subdirectories
        ' in the current directory
        Dim d As String
        Dim tnNode As TreeNode
        For Each d In strDirArray
            tnNode = New TreeNode
            tnRoot.Nodes.Add(tnNode)
        Next
    End If
End Sub

Sub RefreshListView(ByVal strDir As String)
    lvwFiles.Items.Clear()
    ' Get file information
    Dim files() As FileInfo = _
     New DirectoryInfo(strDir).GetFiles()
    ' Populate the ListView with all files
    ' in the current directory
    Dim f As FileInfo
    Dim newFile As ListViewItem
    For Each f In files
        newFile = lvwFiles.Items.Add(f.Name)
        newFile.ImageIndex = 0
    Next
End Sub
```

7. Set the form as the startup object for the project.

8. Run the project. The TreeView control will display the C: node and the ListView will display the files in that directory. As you expand the directory structure, the ListView will be updated, as shown in Figure 2.29.

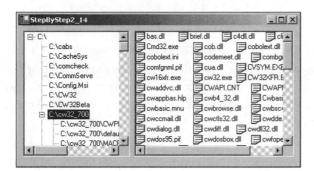

FIGURE 2.29
TreeView and ListView controls showing a directory listing.

Step By Step 2.14 also uses an ImageList component. This component stores a list of images that can be used by other Windows Forms controls such as the ListView. The Images property of an ImageList component is a collection that stores the list of images, and the ImageIndex property provides an index to those images.

Timer, TrackBar, and ProgressBar

The Timer control is used when an event must be generated at user-defined intervals. Table 2.20 summarizes the important members of the Timer class.

TABLE 2.20

IMPORTANT MEMBERS OF THE TIMER CLASS

Member	Type	Description
Enabled	Property	Indicates whether the timer is currently running.
Interval	Property	Represents the time in milliseconds between Tick events of the timer. The default value is 100 milliseconds.
Start	Method	Starts the Timer control.

continues

> **EXAM TIP**
>
> **System.Windows.Forms.Timer Versus System.Timers.Timer** You should always use the Timer class from the System.Windows.Forms namespace in your Windows Forms. This class is optimized to work with forms. The System.Timers.Timer class fires its Tick event from another thread and can cause indeterminate results in a forms-based application.

TABLE 2.20   *continued*

IMPORTANT MEMBERS OF THE TIMER CLASS

Member	Type	Description
Stop	Method	Stops the Timer control.
Tick	Event	Occurs when the timer interval elapses and the timer is enabled.

The TrackBar control provides an intuitive way to select a value from a given range by providing a scroll box and a scale of value. The user can slide the scrollbar on the scale to point to the desired value. Table 2.21 summarizes the important members of the TrackBar class.

TABLE 2.21

IMPORTANT MEMBERS OF TRACKBAR CLASS

Member	Type	Description
LargeChange	Property	Indicates the number of units by which the Value property changes when the scroll box is moved a large distance.
Maximum	Property	Upper bound of the track bar's range.
Minimum	Property	Lower bound of the track bar's range.
Orientation	Property	Specifies Horizontal or Vertical orientation of the control.
Scroll	Event	The default event. Occurs when the scroll box is moved by a keyboard or mouse action.
SmallChange	Property	Indicates the number of units by which the Value property changes when the scroll box is moved a small distance.
TickFrequency	Property	Represents the frequency within which ticks are drawn in the control.
TickStyle	Property	Represents how the control appears. The values are specified by the TickStyle enumeration: Both, BottomRight, None, or TopLeft.
Value	Property	Represents the scroll box's current position in the control.
ValueChanged	Property	Occurs when the Value property changes.

A ProgressBar control is usually displayed to indicate the status of a lengthy operation, such as installing an application, copying a file, or printing a document. Table 2.22 shows some important members of the ProgressBar class.

TABLE 2.22

IMPORTANT MEMBERS OF THE PROGRESSBAR CLASS

Member	Type	Description
Maximum	Property	Upper bound of the progress bar's range.
Minimum	Property	Lower bound of the progress bar's range.
Value	Property	Represents the current position of the control.

Step By Step 2.15 gives an example of using the TrackBar and ProgressBar controls. The example simulates a lengthy operation with the help of a Timer control. You can control the speed with which the simulated process executes with the help of a TrackBar control that changes the Interval property of Timer control to set the time in which it will generate Tick events.

STEP BY STEP

2.15 Using Timer, TrackBar, and ProgressBar Controls

1. Add a new Windows Form to your Visual Basic .NET project.

2. Place a Timer control in the form to add to the component tray. Name the Timer control tmrTimer and set its Enabled property to True.

3. Place four Label controls, one ProgressBar control, and one TrackBar control on the form and arrange them as shown in Figure 2.30.

4. Name the ProgressBar control prgIndicator and the TrackBar control trkSpeed. On the TrackBar control, set the Maximum property to 1000, TickFrequency to 100, TickStyle to Top,Left, and Value to 100.

continues

continued

NOTE

No Line and Shape Controls Unlike earlier versions of Visual Studio, you won't find Line or Shape controls in the toolbox of Visual Studio .NET because all controls in the Visual Studio .Net toolbox must be windowed. The Line and Shape controls are windowless and hence were removed. What can you do about this? To draw a simple line, you can set the BorderStyle property of a label control with its Height property set to 1 (or more if you want a thicker line). For advanced lines and shapes, you can use the powerful GDI+ classes available in the Windows Forms library (refer to Chapter 1 for a discussion of the System.Drawing namespace).

5. Name a Label control to lblMessage. Change one of the Label's Size, Height property to 1 and BorderStyle property to Fixed3D to display it as a Line.

6. Add code to handle events:

```
Private Sub tmrTimer_Tick(ByVal sender As System.Object, _
 ByVal e As System.EventArgs) Handles tmrTimer.Tick
    If prgIndicator.Value < prgIndicator.Maximum Then
        ' Increase the progress indicator
        prgIndicator.Value += 5
    Else
        ' Reset the progress bar indicator
        prgIndicator.Value = prgIndicator.Minimum
    End If
    lblMessage.Text = "Percentage Complete: " _
     & prgIndicator.Value & "%"
End Sub

Private Sub trkSpeed_Scroll(ByVal sender As System.Object, _
 ByVal e As System.EventArgs) Handles trkSpeed.Scroll
    Dim trkSpeed As TrackBar = CType(sender, TrackBar)
    If trkSpeed.Value >= 1 Then
        ' Set timer value based on user's selection
        tmrTimer.Interval = trkSpeed.Value
    End If
End Sub
```

7. Set this form as the startup object for the project.

8. Run the project. Slide the TrackBar control: The Progress bar progresses at different speeds depending on the time interval set by the Track bar. Figure 2.30 shows this form in action.

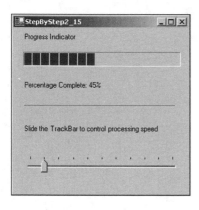

FIGURE 2.30
Using Timer, TrackBar, and ProgressBar controls.

HScrollBar and VScrollBar

The HScrollBar and VScrollBar controls display horizontal and vertical scroll bars, respectively. These classes inherit their properties and other members from the ScrollBar class, which provides the basic scrolling functionality.

Usually controls like the Panel, TextBox, ComboBox, and so on include their own scrollbars. But some controls, such as the PictureBox, do not have built-in scrollbars. You can use the HScrollBar and VScrollBar controls to associate scrollbars with such controls (see Step By Step 2.16). Table 2.23 summarizes the important members of the ScrollBar class inherited by both of the scrollbar classes.

TABLE 2.23

IMPORTANT MEMBERS OF SCROLLBAR CLASS

Member	Type	Description
LargeChange	Property	Indicates the amount by which the Value property changes when the scroll box is moved a large distance.
Maximum	Property	Upper bound of the scrollbar's range.
Minimum	Property	Lower bound of the scrollbar's range.
Scroll	Event	The default event. Occurs when the scroll box is moved by a keyboard or mouse action.
SmallChange	Property	Indicates the amount by which the Value property changes when the scroll box is moved a small distance.
Value	Property	Represents the current position of the control.
ValueChanged	Event	Occurs when the Value property changes either by the Scroll event or programmatically.

STEP BY STEP

2.16 Using HScrollBar and VScrollBar Controls

1. Add a new Windows Form to your Visual Basic .NET project.

2. Place a PictureBox control, an HScrollBar control, and a VScrollBar control on the form. Name the PictureBox control pbImage and set its SizeMode to AutoSize. Select the Image property and click on the Ellipsis button. This will prompt with an Open File dialog box. Select the Image you want to display in the form.

3. Name the HScrollBar control hscr and set its Dock prop-

continues

continued

erty to Bottom. Change the `Name` property of the
VScrollBar control to `vscr` and set its `Dock` property to
`Right`.

4. Add the following code to handle events on the form:

```
Private Sub vScroll_Scroll(ByVal sender As System.Object, _
 ByVal e As System.Windows.Forms.ScrollEventArgs) _
 Handles vscr.Scroll
    ' Scroll the image vertically
    pbImage.Top = vscr.Bottom - pbImage.Height - _
    CInt(getVScrollAdjustment())
End Sub


Private Function getVScrollAdjustment() As Double
    ' Calculate vertical scroll bar changes
    Dim vPos As Double = CDbl(vscr.Value - vscr.Minimum)
    Dim vDiff As Double = CDbl(vscr.Height - pbImage.Height)
    Dim vTicks As Double = CDbl(vscr.Maximum - vscr.Minimum)
    getVScrollAdjustment = (vDiff / vTicks) * vPos
End Function

Private Sub hScroll_Scroll(ByVal sender As System.Object, _
 ByVal e As System.Windows.Forms.ScrollEventArgs) _
 Handles hscr.Scroll
    ' Scroll the image horizontally
    pbImage.Left = hscr.Right - pbImage.Width - _
    CInt(getHScrollAdjustment())
End Sub

Private Function getHScrollAdjustment() As Double
    ' Calculate horizontal scroll bar changes
    Dim hPos As Double = CDbl(hscr.Value - hscr.Minimum)
    Dim hDiff As Double = CDbl(hscr.Width - pbImage.Width)
    Dim hTicks As Double = CDbl(hscr.Maximum - hscr.Minimum)
    Return (hDiff / hTicks) * hPos
End Function
```

5. Set this form as the startup object for the project.

6. Run the project. The form will display the image, and the
scrollbars docked on the right and bottom can be used to
scroll through the image if the image size exceeds the form
size. Figure 2.31 shows this form.

FIGURE 2.31
Using scrollbars to scroll through a
Picture box.

TabControl

The TabControl displays a collection of tabbed pages. Each tabbed
page can contain its own controls; therefore, this control can be useful in organizing a number of controls. You'll come across tabbed
pages mostly in wizards and other forms that need to display many
controls in a limited space. For example, Visual Studio .NET itself
displays all the opened files in tabbed pages. Table 2.24 summarizes
the important members of the TabControl class.

TABLE 2.24

IMPORTANT MEMBERS OF THE TABCONTROL CLASS

Member	Type	Description
Alignment	Property	Represents the area where the tabs will be aligned, whether Bottom, Left, Right, or Top (default).
ImageList	Property	Represents the image list from which images are displayed on tabs.
MultiLine	Property	Indicates whether tabs can be displayed in multiple rows.
SelectedIndex	Property	Represents the index of the selected tab page.
SelectedIndexChanged	Property	Default event. Occurs when the selected index changes.

continues

TABLE 2.24	*continued*	
IMPORTANT MEMBERS OF THE TABCONTROL CLASS		
Member	*Type*	*Description*
SelectedTab	Property	The selected tab page.
TabCount	Property	Count of the tabs in the control.
TabPages	Property	Collection of tab pages in the control.

Step By Step 2.17 uses a Tab Control to build a message box by prompting for the caption and the message in one tab page, the message box buttons in a second tab page, and the icon to be displayed in a third tab page.

FIGURE 2.32
The TabPage Collection Editor.

STEP BY STEP

2.17 Using the TabControl Control

1. Add a new Windows Form to your Visual Basic .NET project.

2. Place a TabControl (tabDemo) on the form. Select the TabPages property and click the build button to invoke the TabPage Collection Editor. Click the Add button to add a TabPage to the control. Name the TabPage tbpMessage and change its Text property to Message. Add two more TabPages: tbpButtons with Text property Buttons and tbpIcons with Text property Icons. Figure 2.32 shows the TabPage Collection Editor after adding the tab pages. Click OK to close the TabPage Collection Editor.

3. Place two Label controls and two TextBox controls (txtMessage and txtCaption) on the Message tab page. Add five RadioButton controls (rbOK, rbOKCCancel, rbRetryCancel, rbYesNo, and rbYesNoCancel) to the Buttons tab page. Place five RadioButton controls (rbError, rbInformation, rbNone, rbQuestion, and rbWarning) on the Icons tab page. Place a GroupBox on the form and four RadioButton controls (rbLeft, rbRight, rbTop, and rbBottom) inside it. Place a Button Control (btnShow) on the form. Arrange all the controls and set their Text properties as shown in Figure 2.33.

4. Switch to Code view and add two declarations after the Windows Forms Designer generated region:

```
Dim mbbButtons As MessageBoxButtons
Dim mbiIcon As MessageBoxIcon
```

5. Modify the form's New method as follows:

```
Public Sub New()
    MyBase.New()

    'This call is required by the Windows Form Designer.
    InitializeComponent()

    ' Add any initialization after the
    ' InitializeComponent() call
    ' Initial setting for MessageBox button
    mbbButtons = MessageBoxButtons.OK
    ' Initial setting for MessageBox icon
    mbiIcon = MessageBoxIcon.Information

    ' Hook up the events
    AddHandler rbBottom.CheckedChanged, _
     AddressOf rbAlign_CheckedChanged
    AddHandler rbTop.CheckedChanged, _
     AddressOf rbAlign_CheckedChanged
    AddHandler rbLeft.CheckedChanged, _
     AddressOf rbAlign_CheckedChanged
    AddHandler rbRight.CheckedChanged, _
     AddressOf rbAlign_CheckedChanged

    AddHandler rbOKCancel.CheckedChanged, _
     AddressOf rbButtons_CheckedChanged
    AddHandler rbRetryCancel.CheckedChanged, _
     AddressOf rbButtons_CheckedChanged
    AddHandler rbYesNo.CheckedChanged, _
     AddressOf rbButtons_CheckedChanged
    AddHandler rbYesNoCancel.CheckedChanged, _
     AddressOf rbButtons_CheckedChanged
    AddHandler rbOK.CheckedChanged, _
     AddressOf rbButtons_CheckedChanged

    AddHandler rbNone.CheckedChanged, _
     AddressOf rbIcon_CheckedChanged
    AddHandler rbError.CheckedChanged, _
     AddressOf rbIcon_CheckedChanged
    AddHandler rbInformation.CheckedChanged, _
     AddressOf rbIcon_CheckedChanged
    AddHandler rbQuestion.CheckedChanged, _
     AddressOf rbIcon_CheckedChanged
    AddHandler rbWarning.CheckedChanged, _
     AddressOf rbIcon_CheckedChanged

End Sub
```

continues

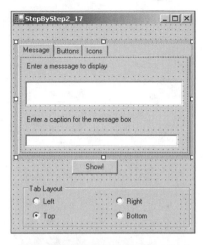
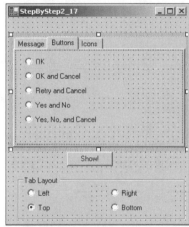
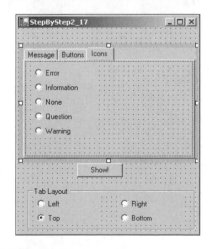

FIGURE 2.33
Three tab pages on a single form.

continued

6. Add the following code in the Code view:

```
' This event handler is used by the RadioButtons
' that set the TabControl's alignment
Private Sub rbAlign_CheckedChanged(ByVal sender As Object, _
ByVal e As System.EventArgs)
    ' Cast sender object to a RadioButton
    Dim rbAlign As RadioButton = CType(sender, RadioButton)
    If rbAlign.Checked Then
        ' Set the alignment of TabControl based
        ' on which RadioButton was checked.
        If rbAlign Is rbLeft Then
            tabDemo.Alignment = TabAlignment.Left
        ElseIf rbAlign Is rbRight Then
            tabDemo.Alignment = TabAlignment.Right
        ElseIf rbAlign Is rbBottom Then
            tabDemo.Alignment = TabAlignment.Bottom
        Else
            tabDemo.Alignment = TabAlignment.Top
        End If
    End If
End Sub

' This event handler is used by the RadioButtons
' on the Buttons tab
Private Sub rbButtons_CheckedChanged( _
ByVal sender As Object, _
ByVal e As System.EventArgs)
    ' find the RadioButton that was checked
    ' from the Buttons tab and create a
    ' MessageBoxButtons objects corresponding to it.
    If sender Is rbOKCancel Then
        mbbButtons = MessageBoxButtons.OKCancel
    ElseIf sender Is rbRetryCancel Then
        mbbButtons = MessageBoxButtons.RetryCancel
    ElseIf sender Is rbYesNo Then
        mbbButtons = MessageBoxButtons.YesNo
    ElseIf sender Is rbYesNoCancel Then
        mbbButtons = MessageBoxButtons.YesNoCancel
    Else
        mbbButtons = MessageBoxButtons.OK
    End If
End Sub

' This event handler is used by the RadioButtons
' on the Icon tab
Private Sub rbIcon_CheckedChanged(ByVal sender As Object, _
ByVal e As System.EventArgs)
    ' find the RadioButton that was checked
    ' from the Icon tab and create a
    ' MessageBoxIcon objects corresponding to it.
```

```
    If sender Is rbError Then
        mbiIcon = MessageBoxIcon.Error
    ElseIf sender Is rbWarning Then
        mbiIcon = MessageBoxIcon.Warning
    ElseIf sender Is rbNone Then
        mbiIcon = MessageBoxIcon.None
    ElseIf sender Is rbQuestion Then
        mbiIcon = MessageBoxIcon.Question
    Else
        mbiIcon = MessageBoxIcon.Information
    End If
End Sub
```

7. Double-click the Button control and add the following
code to handle the `Click` event of the Button control:

```
Private Sub btnShow_Click(ByVal sender As System.Object, _
 ByVal e As System.EventArgs) Handles btnShow.Click
    MessageBox.Show(txtMessage.Text, txtCaption.Text, _
    mbbButtons, mbiIcon)
End Sub
```

8. Set this form as the startup object for the project.

9. Run the project. Enter the message and caption of the
message in the Message tab page; select the desired button
from the Buttons tab page; and select the desired icon
from the Icons tab page. Click the Show Button to see a
message box appear with the desired message, caption,
button, and icon. You are also able to align tabs to different directions depending on the radio button selected
from the Tab Layout group box.

REVIEW BREAK

▶ The DomainUpDown and NumericUpDown controls allow
you to select from a list of defined values by pressing Up and
Down buttons. You can also enter a value in the controls,
unless their ReadOnly property is set to True.

▶ The DateTimePicker control allows you to select a date and
time, and the MonthCalendar control allows you to select a
date or range of dates. The SelectionStart, SelectionEnd, and
SelectionRange properties return the start date, end date, and
range of dates selected.

continues

continued

▶ The TreeView displays data in a hierarchical collection of nodes. Each node is represented by a TreeNode object. The AfterSelect event of the TreeView control occurs when a node is selected and the SelectedNode property is set with the new selection.

▶ The ListView control displays items in different views, such as List, Details, SmallIcon, and LargeIcon, similar to the view options of the Windows Explorer.

▶ Scrollbars can be associated with controls to provide scrolling functionality.

▶ The TabControl control provides a user interface that can save space as well as organize a number of controls. You usually see TabControls in wizards.

CREATING MENUS AND MENU ITEMS

Add controls to Windows Form: Create menus and menu items.

Windows applications use menus to provide organized collections of commands that can be performed by the user. Menus can inform the user of the application's capabilities as well as its limitations. If a program has properly organized menus, users can easily find common commands as well as less familiar features. Users can also learn shortcut keys from a well-designed menu structure.

Because menus have so many benefits to the user, you should be well versed in their creation and the functions they provide. In this section, I'll present a discussion of the menu-related classes: MainMenu, MenuItem, and ContextMenu. I'll also discuss two controls (StatusBar and ToolBar controls) often used in conjunction with menus.

All three menu-related classes (MainMenu, MenuItem and ContextMenu) derive from the Menu class. The MainMenu class is used to create an application's top level menu. The ContextMenu class is used to create a shortcut menu that appears when the user right-clicks on a control. Both MainMenu and ContextMenu classes have a MenuItems property. MenuItems is a collection of MenuItem objects, each representing an individual menu item.

The menu item itself also has a MenuItems collection that can store submenus, thereby creating a hierarchical menu structure. Table 2.25 summarizes the members of the MenuItem class that you should be familiar with.

TABLE 2.25

IMPORTANT MEMBERS OF THE MENUITEM CLASS

Member	Type	Description
Checked	Property	Indicates whether a check mark or a radio button should appear near the menu item.
Click	Event	This event is fired when the user clicks on the menu item.
DrawItem	Event	Occurs when a request is made to draw an owner-drawn menu item. DrawItem only occurs when the OwnerDraw property is set to true.
Enabled	Property	Indicates whether the menu item is enabled.
MenuItems	Property	The collection of MenuItem objects associated with this menu. This property can be used to create hierarchical submenus.
OwnerDraw	Property	Indicates whether you can provide your own custom code to draw a menu item instead of allowing Windows to handle it in a standard way.
Parent	Property	The Parent with which this menu item is associated. You must specify a Parent for a MenuItem object; otherwise it will not be displayed.
PerformClick	Method	Generates the Click event for this menu item as if the user has clicked it.
Popup	Event	This event occurs just before displaying a submenu corresponding to the menu item. This event handler is generally used to add, remove, enable, disable, check, or uncheck menu items based on the state of an application just before they are displayed.
RadioCheck	Property	Indicates whether the menu item should display a radio button instead of a check mark when its Checked property is true.
Select	Event	Fires when the user selects a menu item by navigating to it.
Shortcut	Property	Specifies the shortcut key combination associated with the menu item.
Text	Property	Specifies the caption of menu item.

MainMenu

The MainMenu object is the container control for a form's main menu. The main menu is displayed just below the form's title bar. Visual Studio .NET provides an easy-to-use menu designer to help in quickly designing a main menu for your form.

A Windows Form can have just one MainMenu object associated with it. The Menu property of the form points to this object. After creating a menu, be sure to set the Menu property of the form to the name you want to displayed on it.

The most important member of the MainMenu class is MenuItems, a collection of MenuItem objects. I will now create a simple word processing program to give a good overview of how menus are used in a Windows application. Later in the chapter I'll extend this example with additional controls.

You'll learn the following skills from Step By Step 2.18:

◆ How to add a menu and submenus to a form.

◆ How to use Checked and RadioButton menu items and how to select and deselect them based on user actions.

◆ How to associate keyboard access keys and shortcuts with menu items.

◆ How to write event handlers for performing actions when the user clicks on a menu item.

STEP BY STEP

2.18 Creating a Main Menu for a Form

1. Add a new Windows Form to your Visual Basic .NET project.

2. Place a Panel on the form and set its Dock property to Fill and its AutoScroll property to True.

3. Add a RichTextBox control to the Panel. Name it rtbText and change its Dock property to Fill.

4. From the Toolbox, drop a MainMenu control on the form. Change its Name property to mnuMainMenu. Change the form's Menu property to mnuMainMenu.

5. Using the WYSIWYG menu designer, add a top level menu item. Set its Text to &File and name it mnuFile. Add the menu items listed in Table 2.26 to it. Figure 2.34 shows the menu designer.

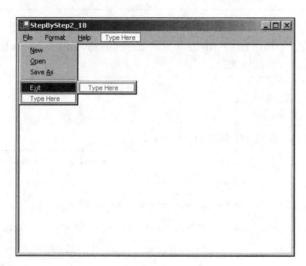

EXAM TIP

Separators   To add a separator (horizontal line) to a menu, right-click on the menu and select Insert Separator.

FIGURE 2.34
Menu designer.

TABLE 2.26

FILE MENU ITEMS

Text	*Name*	*Shortcut*
&New	MnuFileNew	Ctrl+N
&Open...	mnuFileOpen	Ctrl+O
Save &As...	mnuFileSaveAs	Ctrl+S
E&xit	mnuFileExit	None

6. Create a second top-level menu item with the Text property F&ormat and the Name property mnuFormat. Add the menu items listed in Table 2.27 to it.

continues

continued

TABLE 2.27

FORMAT MENU ITEMS

Text	Name	Shortcut
&Color	MnuFormatColor	None
&Font	MnuFormatFont	None

7. Set up the Format, Color submenu with the items listed in Table 2.28.

TABLE 2.28

FORMAT, COLOR MENU ITEMS

Text	Name	Shortcut	RadioCheck
&All Colors...	mnuFormatAllColors	None	False
&Black	mnuFormatColorBlack	Ctrl+Shift+B	True
Bl&ue	mnuFormatColorBlue	Ctrl+Shift+U	True
&Green	mnuFormatColorGreen	Ctrl+Shift+G	True
&Red	mnuFormatColorRed	Ctrl+Shift+R	True

8. Set up the Format, Font menu with the items listed in Table 2.29.

TABLE 2.29

FORMAT, FONT MENU ITEMS

Text	Name	Shortcut
&All Fonts...	mnuFormatFontAllFonts	None
&Bold	mnuFormatFontBold	Ctrl+B
&Italic	mnuFormatFontItalic	Ctrl+I
&Underline	mnuFormatFontUnderline	Ctrl+U

9. Name the third top-level menu `mnuHelp`, and set its Text property to &Help. Add a single menu item to it named `mnuHelpAbout`, and set its Text property to &About.

10. Insert separators after the `All Colors...` and `All Fonts...` menu items.

11. From the toolbox, drop four dialog components on the form: an OpenFileDialog, a SaveFileDialog, a FontDialog, and a ColorDialog. Change their `Name` properties to `dlgOpenFile`, `dlgSaveFile`, `dlgFont`, and `dlgColor`, respectively.

12. Double-click on the File, New menu item. Add the following code to the event handler:

```
Private Sub mnuFileNew_Click( _
 ByVal sender As System.Object, _
 ByVal e As System.EventArgs) Handles mnuFileNew.Click
    rtbText.Clear()
End Sub
```

13. Add the following code to the `Click` event handler of File, Open menu item:

```
Private Sub mnuFileOpen_Click( _
 ByVal sender As System.Object, _
 ByVal e As System.EventArgs) Handles mnuFileOpen.Click
    ' Allow the user to select only *.rtf files
    dlgOpenFile.Filter = "Rich Text Files (*.rtf)|*.rtf"
    If dlgOpenFile.ShowDialog() = DialogResult.OK Then
        ' Load the file contents in the RichTextBox
        rtbText.LoadFile(dlgOpenFile.FileName, _
        RichTextBoxStreamType.RichText)
    End If
End Sub
```

14. Double-click the File, Save As menu item to attach a `Click` event handler to it. Add the following code to the event handler:

```
Private Sub mnuFileSaveAs_Click( _
 ByVal sender As System.Object, _
 ByVal e As System.EventArgs) Handles mnuFileSaveAs.Click
    ' Default choice to save file
    ' is *.rtf but user can select
    ' All Files to save with other extension
    dlgSaveFile.Filter = _
    "Rich Text Files (*.rtf)|*.rtf|All Files (*.*)|*.*"
```

continues

continued

```
        If dlgSaveFile.ShowDialog() = DialogResult.OK Then
            ' Save the RichText content to a file
            rtbText.SaveFile(dlgSaveFile.FileName, _
            RichTextBoxStreamType.RichText)
        End If
End Sub
```

15. Double-click the File, Exit menu item to attach a `Click` event handler to it. Add the following code to the event handler:

```
Private Sub mnuFileExit_Click( _
 ByVal sender As System.Object, _
 ByVal e As System.EventArgs) Handles mnuFileExit.Click
    Me.Close()
End Sub
```

16. Double-click the Format - Color - All Colors... menu item to attach a `Click` event handler to it. Add the following code to the event handler:

```
Private Sub mnuFormatAllColors_Click( _
 ByVal sender As System.Object, _
 ByVal e As System.EventArgs) _
 Handles mnuFormatAllColors.Click
    If dlgColor.ShowDialog() = DialogResult.OK Then
        ' Change the color of selected text
        ' If no text selected, change the active color
        rtbText.SelectionColor = dlgColor.Color
    End If
End Sub
```

17. Insert the following event handler in the code and associate it with the `Click` event of Format, Color, Black; Format, Color, Blue; Format, Color, Green; and Format, Color, Red menu items:

```
Private Sub mnuFormatColorItem_Click( _
 ByVal sender As Object, ByVal e As System.EventArgs)
    Dim mnuItem As MenuItem = CType(sender, MenuItem)
    ' Get color name
    ' Remember to get rid of the ampersand
    rtbText.SelectionColor = Color.FromName( _
    mnuItem.Text.Replace("&", ""))
    ' uncheck all menu items inside color menu
    Dim m As MenuItem
    For Each m In mnuItem.Parent.MenuItems
        m.Checked = False
    Next
    ' just check the clicked menu
    mnuItem.Checked = True
End Sub
```

18. Insert the following event handler in the code and associate it with the Popup event of the Format, Color menu items:

```
Private Sub mnuFormatColor_Popup( _
 ByVal sender As Object, ByVal e As System.EventArgs)
    Dim mnuItem As MenuItem = CType(sender, MenuItem)
    ' for all menu items inside color menu
    Dim m As MenuItem
    For Each m In mnuItem.MenuItems
    if m.Text.Replace("&", "") = _
     rtbText.SelectionColor.Name Then
            ' If it is the selected color, check it
            m.Checked = True
        Else
            ' otherwise uncheck it
            m.Checked = False
        End If
    Next
End Sub
```

19. Double-click on the Format, Font, All Fonts... menu item to attach a Click event handler to it. Add the following code to the event handler:

```
Private Sub mnuFormatFontAllFonts_Click( _
 ByVal sender As System.Object, _
 ByVal e As System.EventArgs) _
 Handles mnuFormatFontAllFonts.Click
    If dlgFont.ShowDialog() = DialogResult.OK Then
        ' Change the font of selected text
        ' If no text selected, change the active font
        rtbText.SelectionFont = dlgFont.Font
    End If
End Sub
```

20. Insert the following event handler in the code and associate it with the Click event of the Format, Font, Bold; Format, Font, Italic; and Format, Font, Underline menu items:

```
Private Sub mnuFormatFontItem_Click( _
 ByVal sender As Object, _
 ByVal e As System.EventArgs)
    Dim mnuItem As MenuItem = CType(sender, MenuItem)
    mnuItem.Checked = Not mnuItem.Checked
    Dim fsStyle As FontStyle
    ' Set the FontStyle selected by user in fsStyle
    Select Case mnuItem.Text.Replace("&", "")
        Case "Bold"
            fsStyle = FontStyle.Bold
        Case "Italic"
            fsStyle = FontStyle.Italic
```

continues

continued

```
        Case "Underline"
            fsStyle = FontStyle.Underline
        Case Else
            fsStyle = FontStyle.Regular
    End Select
    ' Create a font object, toggle the FontStyle
    ' and set the new font on selection
    rtbText.SelectionFont = New Font( _
     rtbText.SelectionFont.FontFamily, _
     rtbText.SelectionFont.Size, _
     rtbText.SelectionFont.Style Xor fsStyle)
End Sub
```

21. Insert the following event handler in the code and associate it with the `Popup` event of the Format, Font menu items:

```
Private Sub mnuFormatFont_Popup( _
 ByVal sender As Object, _
 ByVal e As System.EventArgs)
    ' Set the check boxes on format menu to reflect
    ' users selection of Font
    mnuFormatFontBold.Checked = rtbText.SelectionFont.Bold
    mnuFormatFontItalic.Checked = _
     rtbText.SelectionFont.Italic
    mnuFormatFontUnderline.Checked = _
     rtbText.SelectionFont.Underline
End Sub
```

22. Double-click on the Help, About menu item to attach a `Click` event handler to it. Add the following code to the event handler:

```
Private Sub mnuHelpAbout_Click( _
 ByVal sender As System.Object, _
 ByVal e As System.EventArgs) Handles mnuHelpAbout.Click
    Dim frm As frmAbout = New frmAbout()
    ' Display an About dialog box.
    frm.ShowDialog(Me)
End Sub
```

23. Add a new Windows Form to the project. Name this form `frmAbout`. Change its `ControlBox` property to `False`, its `FormBorderStyle` property to `FixedDialog`, its `ShowInTaskbar` property to `False`, and its `Text` property to `About`.

24. Place a rich text box and a button on the form. Name them `rtbText` and `btnClose`, respectively. Arrange the controls as shown in Figure 2.35

25. Add a following code to the About form's `Load` event handler:

```
Private Sub frmAbout_Load(ByVal sender As System.Object, _
 ByVal e As System.EventArgs) Handles MyBase.Load
    If (File.Exists("About.rtf")) Then
        ' Load content from a file
        rtbText.LoadFile("About.rtf")
    Else
        ' When file not available, just link to a Website
        rtbText.Text = _
        "Please visit http://www.microsoft.com/net " & _
        "to learn how this product was developed"
    End If
End Sub
```

26. Add the following code to the `LinkClicked` event handler of `rtbText`:

```
Private Sub rtbText_LinkClicked(ByVal sender As Object, _
 ByVal e As System.Windows.Forms.LinkClickedEventArgs) _
 Handles rtbText.LinkClicked
    ' Start internet explorer to open the link
    System.Diagnostics.Process.Start("IExplore", e.LinkText)
End Sub
```

27. Add the following code to the `Click` event handler of `btnClose`:

```
Private Sub btnClose_Click(ByVal sender As System.Object, _
 ByVal e As System.EventArgs) Handles btnClose.Click
    ' Get rid of this form
    Me.Close()
End Sub
```

28. Set the word processing form as the startup object for the project.

29. Run the project. Open or create a rich text file. Use the Format menu to format your text. Also use keyboard access keys and shortcut keys to select menu items. Figure 2.36 shows this form in action.

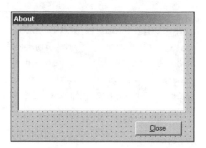

FIGURE 2.35
Help, About dialog box.

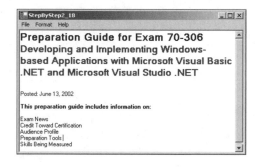

FIGURE 2.36
Using menus in a Windows application.

EXAM TIP

WordWrap Property and Scrollbars
When the WordWrap property of a rich text box is True (the default value), the horizontal scrollbars are not displayed, regardless of the setting of its Scrollbars property.

EXAM TIP

RadioCheck Property Setting the RadioCheck property to True does not implicitly set mutual exclusion for menu items; you are still able to check several of them together. You must set the mutual exclusion programmatically. The Popup event is an appropriate place to check a menu item and uncheck all other menu items in that group.

You might be wondering why I placed a panel on the form and placed the rich text box on the panel. Actually, this example will work without using the panel. But having a Panel control as the container is helpful when you want to use other controls, such as a status bar or a toolbar, in your application. The panel makes it easy to divide the form's real estate and avoid any overlap problems.

ContextMenu

A ContextManu control is typically used to provide users with a small context-sensitive menu based on the application's current state and user's current selection. A context menu is invoked when the user right clicks on a control.

The ContextMenu class provides the functionality for creating a context menu. A context menu is simpler than a main menu because a context menu has only one top-level menu that displays all the menu items. Of course, you can have submenus and other functions such as hide, show, enable, disable, check, and uncheck available in a context menu.

A context menu is associated with a particular control (or a form). You can have several ContextMenu objects in your application, each working in a different context. You must associate a ContextMenu object with a control by assigning it to a control's ContextMenu property.

The process of creating a context menu is very similar to that of creating a main menu. In the next example, I will extend the application created in Step By Step 2.18 by adding a context menu for basic editing operations such as cut, copy, and paste. You will learn the following skills from Step By Step 2.19:

- ◆ How to create a context menu and its items
- ◆ How to associate a context menu with a control
- ◆ How to enable and disable menu items based on application state
- ◆ How to work with the Clipboard class

STEP BY STEP

2.19 Creating a Context Menu for a Form

1. Make a copy of the form from Step By Step 2.18 in your Visual Basic .NET project.

2. From the toolbox, drag and drop a ContextMenu control to the form to add to the component tray. Select its properties and change its name to `mnuContextMenu`.

3. Change the `ContextMenu` property of `rtbText` object to `mnuContextMenu`.

4. Select the ContextMenu control and notice that the context menu appears on the form in place of the main menu. Create menu items in the context menu as shown in Figure 2.37, defining their properties as shown in Table 2.30.

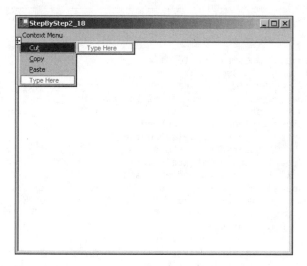

FIGURE 2.37
Menu designer showing context menu.

TABLE 2.30

CONTEXT MENU ITEMS

Text	Name	Shortcut
Cu&t	MnuContextCut	Ctrl+X
&Copy	MnuContextCopy	Ctrl+C
&Paste	MnuContextpaste	Ctrl+V

continues

continued

5. Double-click on the Cut menu item to add an event handler. Add the following code:

```
Private Sub mnuContextCut_Click( _
 ByVal sender As System.Object, _
 ByVal e As System.EventArgs) Handles mnuContextCut.Click
    ' Set the clipboard with current selection
    Clipboard.SetDataObject(rtbText.SelectedRtf, True)
    ' Delete the current selection
    rtbText.SelectedRtf = ""
End Sub
```

6. Add the following event handler for the `Click` event handler of the Copy menu item:

```
Private Sub mnuContextCopy_Click( _
 ByVal sender As System.Object, _
 ByVal e As System.EventArgs) Handles mnuContextCopy.Click
    ' Set the clipboard with current selection
    Clipboard.SetDataObject(rtbText.SelectedRtf, True)
End Sub
```

7. Add the following code to the `Click` event handler of Paste menu item:

```
Private Sub mnuContextPaste_Click( _
 ByVal sender As System.Object, _
 ByVal e As System.EventArgs) Handles mnuContextPaste.Click
    ' DataObject provides format-independent
    ' data transfer mechanism
    ' Get data from clipboard and
    ' store it in a DataObject object
    Dim doClipboard As DataObject = _
     CType(Clipboard.GetDataObject(), DataObject)
    ' only if clipboard had any data
    If doClipboard.GetDataPresent(DataFormats.Text) Then
        ' get the string data from DataObject object
        Dim text As String = CStr( _
         doClipboard.GetData(DataFormats.Text))
        If text <> " then" Then
            ' If there was some text to paste
            ' paste it in RTF format
            rtbText.SelectedRtf = text
        End If
    End If
    End Sub
```

8. Double-click on the `mnuContextMenu` object in the component tray, to add an event handler for its `Popup` event. Add
code to handle this event:

```
Private Sub mnuContextMenu_Popup( _
 ByVal sender As System.Object, _
 ByVal e As System.EventArgs) Handles mnuContextMenu.Popup
    ' Initially disable all menu items
    mnuContextCut.Enabled = False
    mnuContextCopy.Enabled = False
    mnuContextPaste.Enabled = False
    ' If there was any selected text
    If Not rtbText.SelectedText.Equals("") Then
        ' enable the cut and copy menu items
        mnuContextCut.Enabled = True
        mnuContextCopy.Enabled = True
    End If
    Dim doClipboard As DataObject = _
     CType(Clipboard.GetDataObject(), DataObject)
    ' if there is text data on clipboard,
    ' enable the Paste menu item
    If doClipboard.GetDataPresent(DataFormats.Text) Then
        mnuContextPaste.Enabled = True
    End If
End Sub
```

9. Set the form as the startup object for the project.

10. Run the project. Open or create a rich text file. Select
some text, right-click, and copy it to the clipboard. Paste
it at a different location. You will also see that the Cut,
Copy, and Paste menu items are enabled and disabled
depending on the context. For instance, if no text is
selected, the Cut and Copy menu items will be disabled.
Figure 2.38 shows a context menu at runtime.

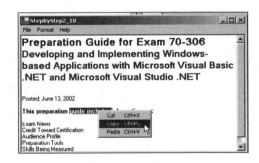

FIGURE 2.38
Using a context menu in a Windows application.

Although the Clipboard operations implemented here will work
within this application, they can fail when pasting data from another
application because I have not implemented error handling. This is
one of the topics I will cover in Chapter 3, "Error Handling for the
User Interface." For now, you can modify the application you just
created in Guided Practice Exercise 2.3.

GUIDED PRACTICE EXERCISE 2.3

In this exercise you need to extend the application created in Step By Step 2.19 by adding an Edit menu as a top-level menu in the form's main menu. In addition to cut, copy, and paste, you need to implement an undo and a redo menu item.

Try this on your own first. If you get stuck or would like to see one possible solution, follow the steps below.

1. Make a copy of the form from Step By Step 2.19 in your Visual Basic .NET project.

2. Select `mnuContextMenu` in the component tray. In the context menu select all the menu items by pressing the Ctrl key while selecting them. Right-click and select Copy to copy them to the clipboard. Now select `mnuMainMenu`, right-click on the top-level Format menu, and select Insert New from its shortcut menu to create a new menu item just before Format menu. Change its text to `&Edit` and name the new menu `mnuEdit`. Right-click in the menu list of this newly created menu, and select paste from the shortcut menu. All the context menu items will be copied here.

3. Change the `Name` properties of the menu items Cut, Copy, and Paste to `mnuEditCut`, `mnuEditCopy`, and `mnuEditPaste`. Also change their `Shortcut` properties to Ctrl+X, Ctrl+C and Ctrl+V, respectively.

4. Add code to the form to reuse the existing event handlers for the new menu items. You can put this code in the form's `New` method:

```
AddHandler mnuEditCopy.Click, AddressOf
mnuContextCopy_Click
AddHandler mnuEditCut.Click, AddressOf
mnuContextCut_Click
AddHandler mnuEditPaste.Click, _
 AddressOf mnuContextPaste_Click
```

5. Insert another menu item just before the Edit, Cut menu item. Change its `Text` property to `&Undo`, its `Name` property to `mnuEditUndo`, and its `Shortcut` property to Ctrl-Z. Similarly, add another menu item for Redo and set the `Text` to `&Redo`, the `Name` to `mnuEditRedo`, and the `Shortcut` as Ctrl+Y.

Insert a separator bar set Undo and Redo apart from other menu items in the edit menu.

6. Add event handlers for the `Click` events of `mnuEditUndo` and `mnuEditRedo` menu items and modify the code as given here:

```
Private Sub mnuEditUndo_Click( _
 ByVal sender As System.Object, _
 ByVal e As System.EventArgs) Handles mnuEditUndo.Click
    rtbText.Undo()
End Sub

Private Sub mnuEditRedo_Click( _
 ByVal sender As System.Object, _
 ByVal e As System.EventArgs) Handles mnuEditRedo.Click
    rtbText.Redo()
End Sub
```

7. Add the following code to handle the `Popup` event of `mnuEdit`:

```
Private Sub mnuEdit_Popup(ByVal sender As Object, _
 ByVal e As System.EventArgs) Handles mnuEdit.Popup
    ' Initially disable all menu items
    mnuEditUndo.Enabled = False
    mnuEditRedo.Enabled = False
    mnuEditCut.Enabled = False
    mnuEditCopy.Enabled = False
    mnuEditPaste.Enabled = False

    ' If there was any selected text
    If Not rtbText.SelectedText.Equals("") Then
        ' enable the cut and copy menu items
        mnuEditCut.Enabled = True
        mnuEditCopy.Enabled = True
    End If
    Dim doClipboard As DataObject = _
     Clipboard.GetDataObject()
    ' if there is text data on clipboard,
    ' enable the Paste menu item
    If doClipboard.GetDataPresent(DataFormats.Text) Then
        mnuEditPaste.Enabled = True
    End If
    ' Check whether Undo is possible
    If rtbText.CanUndo Then
        mnuEditUndo.Enabled = True
    End If
    ' Check whether Redo is possible
    If rtbText.CanRedo Then
        mnuEditRedo.Enabled = True
    End If
End Sub
```

8. Set the form as the startup object for the project.

continues

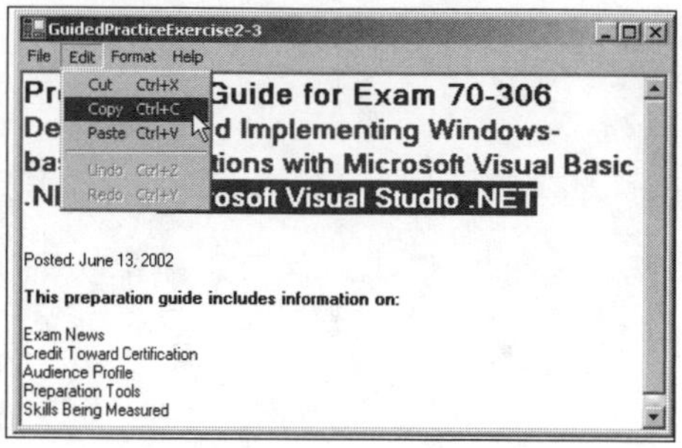

FIGURE 2.39
Using menus in a Windows application.

NOTE

Layering of Controls   Z-order specifies the visual layering of controls
along a form's z-axis. A control at the
top (lowest value) of the z-order overlaps other controls, whereas other
controls overlap a control that is at
the bottom of the z-order. You can set
the z-order of a control with respect to
its container control by right-clicking
on the control and selecting either
Send to back or Bring to front from
the shortcut menu.

---

continued

9. Run the project. Open or create a rich text file. Select some
   text, select Edit, Copy to copy text to the Clipboard. Perform
   some cut, copy, and paste operations. Selecting Edit, Undo
   will undo the changes in the document. Figure 2.39 shows the
   application.

StatusBar

A StatusBar control displays information such as help messages or
status messages. A status bar is normally docked at the bottom of the
form. When you add a StatusBar control from the toolbox to a
form, be sure to set the z-order of the control by right-clicking the
status bar and selecting Send to Back from its shortcut menu. When
you do this you won't see the StatusBar overlapping other controls at
the bottom of the form.

One of the most important properties for a status bar is the Panels
property, a collection of StatusBarPanel objects. Panels divide a status bar into multiple areas that can display information such as the
status of Caps Lock, Num Lock, or Insert keys; the current date and
time; or other information. Table 2.31 summarizes the important
members of the StatusBarPanel class, and in Step By Step 2.20, you
can create your own status bar.

TABLE 2.31

IMPORTANT MEMBERS OF THE STATUSBARPANEL CLASS

Member	Type	Description
Alignment	Property	Specifies the alignment of text and icon within the panel (can be one of the Center, Left, or Right values of the HorizontalAlignment enumeration).
AutoSize	Property	Specifies how the panel sizes itself. This property can take a value None, Contents, or Spring of the StatusBarPanelAutosize enumeration.

Member	Type	Description
BorderStyle	Property	Specifies the border style. BorderStyle can have one of the values None, Raised, or Sunken from the StatusBarPanelBorderStyle enumeration.
Icon	Property	Specifies the icon to be displayed in the status bar.
Style	Property	Specifies whether the StatusBarPanel object is OwnerDraw or Text (System-drawn). The OwnerDraw style can give custom rendering to a StatusBarPanel object.
ToolTipText	Property	Specifies the ToolTip.

STEP BY STEP

2.20 Creating a Status Bar for a Form

1. Make a copy of the form from Guided Practice Exercise 2.3 in your Visual Basic .NET project.

2. Select the form by clicking its title bar. Double-click the StatusBar control in the toolbox to add it to the form. Name the StatusBar object sbStatus and clear its Text property. Change its ShowPanels property to True.

3. Select the status bar. Right-click it and select Send to Back from the shortcut menu.

4. Select the Panels property of the status bar. Click the Build button and create three StatusBarPanel objects using the StatusBarPanel Collection Editor as shown in Figure 2.40. Name the first object sbpHelp, change its AutoSize property to Spring, and empty its Text property. Name the second object sbpDate and change its Alignment property to Right, its AutoSize property to Contents, its ToolTipText to Current System Date. Empty the Text property. Name the third and final object sbpTime; change its Alignment property to Right, its AutoSize property to Contents, and its ToolTipText to Current System Time. Empty its Text property.

continues

NOTE

AutoSize Property StatusBarPanel objects with their AutoSize property set to StatusBarPanelAutoSize.Contents have priority placement over StatusBarPanel objects with their AutoSize property set to StatusBarPanelAutoSize.Spring. A StatusBarPanel with AutoSize set to Spring will be shortened if the StatusBarPanel with AutoSize set to Contents resizes itself to take more space on the StatusBar.

NOTE

Icon Positioning on a Status Bar Panel The icon is always positioned on the left side of panel's text, irrespective of the text's alignment.

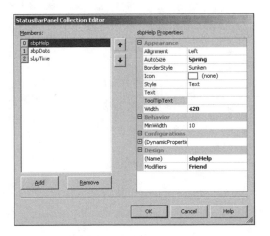

FIGURE 2.40
StatusBarPanel Collection Editor.

continued

5. Add a Timer control to the form, name it `tmrTimer`,
change its `Enabled` property to `True`, and set the `Interval`
property to `1000`. Add code to handle the `Tick` events:

```
Private Sub tmrTimer_Tick(ByVal sender As System.Object, _
 ByVal e As System.EventArgs) Handles tmrTimer.Tick
    Dim dtNow As DateTime = DateTime.Now
    ' display current date in the status bar panel
    sbpDate.Text = dtNow.ToLongDateString()
    ' display current time in the status bar panel
    sbpTime.Text = dtNow.ToShortTimeString()
End Sub
```

6. Insert the following procedure:

```
Private Sub mnuItem_Select( _
 ByVal sender As Object, ByVal e As System.EventArgs)
    ' Get the menu item sending the event
    Dim mnuItem As MenuItem = CType(sender, MenuItem)
    Dim strHelp As String
    ' Check which menu it is and set the appriate help text.
    Select Case mnuItem.Text.Replace("&", "")
        Case "New"
            strHelp = "Create a new document"
        Case "Open..."
            strHelp = "Open an existing document"
        Case "Save As..."
            strHelp = _
              "Save the active document with a new name"
        Case "Exit"
            strHelp = "Quit the application"
        Case "Undo"
            strHelp = "Undo the last action"
        Case "Redo"
            strHelp = "Redo the last undone action"
        Case "Cut"
            strHelp = "Cut the selection to the clipboard"
        Case "Copy"
            strHelp = "Copy the selection to the clipboard"
        Case "Paste"
            strHelp = "Insert clipboard contents"
        Case "Color"
            strHelp = "Select a color"
        Case "Font"
            strHelp = "Select a font"
        Case Else
            strHelp = ""
    End Select
    sbpHelp.Text = strHelp
End Sub
```

7. Add code to use `mnuItem_Select` as the event handler for the `Select` event of all the menu items, including the top-level menus. You can add this code to the form's `New` method:

```
AddHandler mnuEdit.Select, AddressOf mnuItem_Select
AddHandler mnuEditCopy.Select, AddressOf mnuItem_Select
AddHandler mnuEditCut.Select, AddressOf mnuItem_Select
AddHandler mnuEditPaste.Select, AddressOf mnuItem_Select
AddHandler mnuEditRedo.Select, AddressOf mnuItem_Select
AddHandler mnuEditUndo.Select, AddressOf mnuItem_Select
AddHandler mnuFile.Select, AddressOf mnuItem_Select
AddHandler mnuFileExit.Select, AddressOf mnuItem_Select
AddHandler mnuFileNew.Select, AddressOf mnuItem_Select
AddHandler mnuFileOpen.Select, AddressOf mnuItem_Select
AddHandler mnuFileSaveAs.Select, AddressOf mnuItem_Select
AddHandler mnuFormat.Select, AddressOf mnuItem_Select
AddHandler mnuFormatAllColors.Select, _
 AddressOf mnuItem_Select
AddHandler mnuFormatColor.Select, AddressOf mnuItem_Select
AddHandler mnuFormatColorBlack.Select, _
 AddressOf mnuItem_Select
AddHandler mnuFormatColorBlue.Select, _
 AddressOf mnuItem_Select
AddHandler mnuFormatColorGreen.Select, _
 AddressOf mnuItem_Select
AddHandler mnuFormatColorRed.Select, _
 AddressOf mnuItem_Select
AddHandler mnuFormatFont.Select, AddressOf mnuItem_Select
AddHandler mnuFormatFontAllFonts.Select, _
 AddressOf mnuItem_Select
AddHandler mnuFormatFontBold.Select, _
 AddressOf mnuItem_Select
AddHandler mnuFormatFontItalic.Select, _
 AddressOf mnuItem_Select
AddHandler mnuFormatFontUnderline.Select, _
 AddressOf mnuItem_Select
AddHandler mnuHelp.Select, AddressOf mnuItem_Select
AddHandler mnuHelpAbout.Select, AddressOf mnuItem_Select
```

8. Add the following event handler in the code:

```
Protected Overrides Sub OnMenuComplete( _
 ByVal e As System.EventArgs)
    ' Reset the help text on status bar after the
    ' Menu is closed
    sbpHelp.Text = ""
End Sub
```

9. Set this form as the startup object for the project.

continues

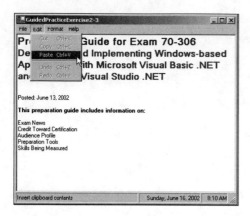

FIGURE 2.41
Using Status Bar.

continued

10. Run the project. The system date and time are on the on the status bar. As you navigate through various menu items, you'll see their helps in the status bar, as shown in Figure 2.41.

ToolBar

The ToolBar class can be used to create a Windows toolbar. This control is normally docked on the top of the form, just below its menu bar. When you add a ToolBar control from the toolbox to a form, make sure to set the z-order of the control by right-clicking the toolbar and selecting Send to Back from its shortcut menu. When you do this, you won't see the toolbar overlapping other controls at the top of the form. Table 2.32 summarizes the important members of the ToolBar class.

TABLE 2.32

IMPORTANT MEMBERS OF THE TOOLBAR CLASS

Member	Type	Description
Buttons	Property	A collection of ToolBarButton objects. Each ToolbarButton represents a button on the ToolBar object.
ButtonClick	Event	Occurs when a Toolbar button is clicked.
ImageList	Property	Specifies the ImageList object storing the icons that will be displayed on the ToolBarButton objects.
SendToBack	Method	Sends the toolbar to the back of the z-order.
ShowToolTips	Property	Specifies whether the toolbar should show ToolTips.

Normally the toolbar buttons represent a shortcut to a task that could also be performed by selecting a menu item. In that case, when you respond to the ButtonClick event of a ToolBar object, you can simply invoke the code for the corresponding menu item.

A menu item can be programmatically invoked by calling the PerformClick method of the MenuItem object. So all you must know is which menu to invoke for a particular Toolbar button. The Toolbar button provides a useful property for this, the Tag property. You can use this property to store any object that must be associated with a Toolbar button. Step By Step 2.21 shows how to do this.

STEP BY STEP

2.21 Creating a Toolbar for a Form

1. Add a copy of the form from Step By Step 2.20 to your Visual Basic .NET application.

2. Select the form by clicking its title bar. Double-click the ToolBar control in the toolbox to add it to the form. Name the ToolBar object tbarToolBar, and change the Height and Width of its ButtonSize property to 16 each. Change its ShowToolTips property to True.

3. Drop an ImageList (imgToolBarIcons) object on your form. In its Images property add images for New, Open, Save, Cut, Copy, Paste, Undo, and Redo operations. The appropriate icons are in the c:\Program Files\Microsoft Visual Studio .NET\Common7\Graphics\Bitmaps\ Tbr_W95 directory if you've done a full install of Visual Studio.NET. Set the ImageList property of the ToolBar control to imgToolBarIcons.

4. Select the ToolBar control's Buttons property. Click the build button to open the ToolBarButton Collection Editor window. Using this window, add buttons for New, Open, Save, Cut, Copy, Paste, Undo, and Redo operations as in Figure 2.42. Name them tbarFileNew, tbarFileOpen, tbarFileSaveAs, tbarEditCut, tbarEditCopy, tbarEditPaste, tbarEditUndo, and tbarEditRedo. Select an image for them from the ImageIndex property and give them an appropriate ToolTipText. You can also add a separator between the Toolbar buttons by adding a Toolbar button and setting its Style property to Separator. The toolbar should look as shown in Figure 2.42.

continues

FIGURE 2.42
A toolbar with buttons.

continued

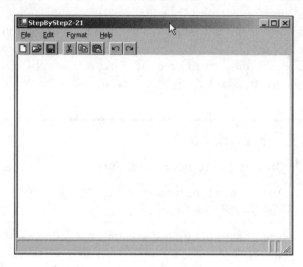

5. Add the following code to the form's New method:

```
' Store the references to menu items in the toolbar buttons
tbarFileNew.Tag = mnuFileNew
tbarFileOpen.Tag = mnuFileOpen
tbarFileSaveAs.Tag = mnuFileSaveAs
tbarEditCut.Tag = mnuEditCut
tbarEditCopy.Tag = mnuEditCopy
tbarEditPaste.Tag = mnuEditPaste
tbarEditUndo.Tag = mnuEditUndo
tbarEditRedo.Tag = mnuEditRedo
```

6. Double-click on the toolbar and add an event handler for its ButtonClick event:

```
Private Sub tbarToolbar_ButtonClick( _
 ByVal sender As System.Object, _
 ByVal e As System.Windows.Forms. _
 ToolBarButtonClickEventArgs) _
 Handles tbarToolbar.ButtonClick
    Dim tbarButton As ToolBarButton = e.Button
    ' Get the related menu item from the
    ' toolbar buton's tag property
    Dim mnuItem As MenuItem = tbarButton.Tag
    ' Generate the click event for related menu item
    mnuItem.PerformClick()
End Sub
```

7. Set this form as the startup object for the project.

8. Run the project. You'll see the toolbar, as shown in Figure 2.43. Click on various toolbar buttons to perform the indicated tasks.

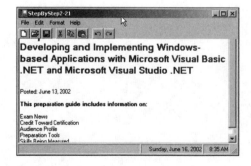

FIGURE 2.43
Toolbar on a Windows Form.

In this case, the toolbar buttons map directly to menu items. Clicking a menu toolbar button is the same as clicking on the corresponding menu item (or pressing the accelerator key for that item).

Disabling a menu item will disable its toolbar button as well, but will not change the appearance of the button. If you want the button to "look" disabled, you must do this programmatically.

CREATING MULTIPLE-DOCUMENT INTERFACE (MDI) APPLICATIONS

So far in this chapter I have created single-document interface (SDI) applications only. These applications allow the user to work with only one window at a time. Several large Windows applications such as Microsoft Excel and Visual Studio.Net allow users to work with several open windows at the same time. These applications are called multiple-document interface (MDI) applications. The main application window of an MDI application acts as the Parent window that can open several child windows. You need to know the following main points about an MDI application:

◆ The child windows are limited to their parent window. In other words, you cannot move child windows outside of the main application window.

◆ The parent window can open several types of child windows. As an example, Visual Studio .NET allows you to work with several types of document windows at the same time.

◆ The child windows can be opened, closed, maximized, or minimized independent of each other. When the Parent window is closed, the child windows are automatically closed.

◆ The MDI frame should always have a menu. One of the menus that a user always expects to see in an MDI application is the Window menu that allows users to manipulate various windows opened in an MDI container form (see Figure 2.44).

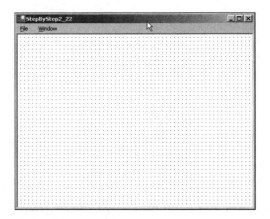

FIGURE 2.44
MDI container form.

The Windows Forms in an MDI application are also created using the standard System.Windows.Forms.Form class. To create an MDI parent form, create a regular Windows Form and change its IsMdiContainer property to True. To create an MDI child form, create a regular windows form and assign the name of the parent MDI object to its MdiParent property. Table 2.33 summarizes the important members of the Form class related to the MDI forms.

TABLE 2.33

IMPORTANT MEMBERS OF THE FORM CLASS RELATED TO MDI APPLICATIONS

Member	Type	Description
ActiveMDiChild	Property	Currently active MDI child window
IsMdiContainer	Property	Indicates whether the form is a container for MDI child forms
MdiChildActivate	Event	Occurs when an MDI child form is activated or closed within an MDI application
MdiChildren	Property	Array of forms representing the MDI child form of this form
MdiParent	Property	Specifies the MDI parent form for the current form
LayoutMdi	Method	Arranges the MDI child forms with an MDI parent form

Step By Step 2.22 shows how to create an MDI application. I will create a form similar to the one created in Step by Step 2.18 and use that as an MDI child window.

You'll learn the following from this exercise:

- ◆ How to create an MDI parent form
- ◆ How to create an MDI child form
- ◆ How to convert an existing SDI application to an MDI application
- ◆ How to merge menus between MDI parent and child windows
- ◆ How to create Windows menus that allow you to load and rearrange MDI child forms

STEP BY STEP

2.22 Creating an MDI Application

1. Add a copy of the form from Step By Step 2.18 to your Visual Basic .NET project. Name this new form `frmMdiChild`.

2. Select the main menu of the new form. Change the `MergeType` property of its File menu to `MergeItems`. Select the File, New and File, Open menu items and change their `MergeType` property to `Remove`.

3. Rename the File, E&xit menu item to `&Close`. Change the `MergeOrder` property for the File, Save As; File, Close; Format; and Help menu items to `5`, `3`, `10`, and `30`, respectively. Change the `MergeOrder` property for the separator in the File menu to `4`.

4. Switch to the Code view, and after the default `New` method, add another constructor with the following code:

```
Public Sub New(ByVal fileName As String)
    MyBase.New()

    'This call is required by the Windows Form Designer.
    InitializeComponent()

    'Add any initialization after the
    ' InitializeComponent() call
    AddHandler mnuFormatColorBlack.Click, _
     AddressOf mnuFormatColorItem_Click
    AddHandler mnuFormatColorBlue.Click, _
     AddressOf mnuFormatColorItem_Click
    AddHandler mnuFormatColorRed.Click, _
     AddressOf mnuFormatColorItem_Click
    AddHandler mnuFormatColorGreen.Click, _
     AddressOf mnuFormatColorItem_Click

    AddHandler mnuFormatColorBlack.Popup, _
     AddressOf mnuFormatColor_Popup
    AddHandler mnuFormatColorBlue.Popup, _
     AddressOf mnuFormatColor_Popup
    AddHandler mnuFormatColorRed.Popup, _
     AddressOf mnuFormatColor_Popup
    AddHandler mnuFormatColorGreen.Popup, _
     AddressOf mnuFormatColor_Popup
```

continues

continued

```
    AddHandler mnuFormatFontBold.Click, _
     AddressOf mnuFormatFontItem_Click
    AddHandler mnuFormatFontUnderline.Click, _
     AddressOf mnuFormatFontItem_Click
    AddHandler mnuFormatFontItalic.Click, _
     AddressOf mnuFormatFontItem_Click

    AddHandler mnuFormatFontBold.Popup, _
     AddressOf mnuFormatFont_Popup
    AddHandler mnuFormatFontUnderline.Popup, _
     AddressOf mnuFormatFont_Popup
    AddHandler mnuFormatFontItalic.Popup, _
     AddressOf mnuFormatFont_Popup

    rtbText.LoadFile(fileName, _
     RichTextBoxStreamType.RichText)
End Sub
```

5. Add another Windows Form to your Visual Basic .NET project. Change its `IsMdiContainer` property to `True`.

6. Add a MainMenu component to this form. Create a top-level menu item, change its `Text` property to `&File`, and name it `mnuFile`. Add the following menu items to it: `&New` (`mnuFileNew`), `&Open...` (`mnuFileOpen`), separator, and `E&xit` (`mnuFileExit`). Change their `MergeOrder` property to `1`, `2`, `6`, and `7`, respectively.

7. Add another top-level menu. Change its `Text` property to `&Window` and its name to `mnuWindow`. Change its `MdiList` property to true. Add the following menu items to it: `Tile &Horizontally` (`mnuWindowTileHorizintally`), `Tile &Vertically` (`mnuWindowTileVertically`), and `&Cascade` (`mnuWindowCascade`).

8. Double-click the File, New menu item and add the following event handler to its `Click` event:

```
Private Sub mnuFileNew_Click( _
 ByVal sender As System.Object, _
 ByVal e As System.EventArgs) Handles mnuFileNew.Click
    ' create a new instance of the child form
    Dim f As frmMdiChild = New frmMdiChild()
    ' set its MdiParent
    f.MdiParent = Me
    f.Text = "New Document"
    ' Display the child window
    f.Show()
End Sub
```

9. Double-click the File, Open menu item and add the following event handler to it:

```
Private Sub mnuFileOpen_Click( _
 ByVal sender As System.Object, _
 ByVal e As System.EventArgs) Handles mnuFileOpen.Click
    ' Allow to select only *.rtf files
    dlgOpenFile.Filter = "Rich Text Files (*.rtf)|*.rtf"
    If dlgOpenFile.ShowDialog() = DialogResult.OK Then
        ' create the child form by
        ' loading the given file in it
        Dim f As frmMdiChild = _
         New frmMdiChild(dlgOpenFile.FileName)
        ' Set the current form as its parent
        f.MdiParent = Me
        ' Set the file's title bar text
        f.Text = dlgOpenFile.FileName
        ' display the form
        f.Show()
    End If
End Sub
```

10. Add event handlers for the other menu items:

```
Private Sub mnuFileExit_Click( _
 ByVal sender As System.Object, _
 ByVal e As System.EventArgs) Handles mnuFileExit.Click
    Me.Close()
End Sub

Private Sub mnuWindowTileHorizontally_Click( _
 ByVal sender As System.Object, _
 ByVal e As System.EventArgs) _
 Handles mnuWindowTileHorizontally.Click
    ' Tile child windows horizontally
    Me.LayoutMdi(MdiLayout.TileHorizontal)
End Sub

Private Sub mnuWindowTileVertically_Click( _
 ByVal sender As System.Object, _
 ByVal e As System.EventArgs) _
 Handles mnuWindowTileVertically.Click
    ' Tile child windows horizontally
    Me.LayoutMdi(MdiLayout.TileVertical)
End Sub

Private Sub mnuWindowCascade_Click( _
 ByVal sender As System.Object, _
 ByVal e As System.EventArgs) Handles mnuWindowCascade.Click
    ' Tile child windows horizontally
    Me.LayoutMdi(MdiLayout.Cascade)
End Sub
```

continues

continued

11. Add the following event handler for the Popup event of the mnuWindow menu item:

```
Private Sub mnuWindow_Popup(ByVal sender As Object, _
ByVal e As System.EventArgs) Handles mnuWindow.Popup
    ' code to enable and disable Window menu items
    ' depending on whether any child windows are open
    If (Me.MdiChildren.Length > 0) Then
        mnuWindowTileHorizontally.Enabled = True
        mnuWindowTileVertically.Enabled = True
        mnuWindowCascade.Enabled = True
    Else
        mnuWindowTileHorizontally.Enabled = False
        mnuWindowTileVertically.Enabled = False
        mnuWindowCascade.Enabled = False
    End If
End Sub
```

12. Set this form as the startup object for the project.

13. Run the project. From the File menu you can open an existing document or create a new document. Click on the Window menu and select various options to arrange the child windows, as shown in Figure 2.45.

FIGURE 2.45
Working with an MDI application.

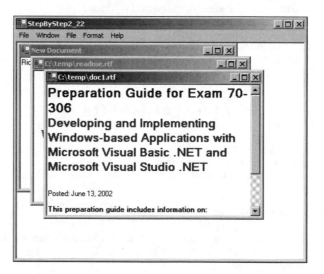

The default MergeType property for MenuItem objects is Add, which means that the MenuItem objects will all be added together to the MDI Parent window. If you don't want to include some of the menu items, you can set their MergeType property to Remove. The MergeOrder properties for the MenuItem objects specify the order in which they will appear on the parent MDI form.

Another interesting property of MenuItem objects used with MDI applications is the MdiList property. When this property is set to True, the MenuItem will be populated with a list of MDI child windows displayed within the associated form.

▶ Two types of menus exist in Windows applications. The main menu groups all the available commands and options in a Windows application. A context menu specifies a relatively small list of options that applies to a control depending on the application's current context.

▶ You can make keyboard navigation possible between menu items by including keyboard access keys in the Text property of menu items. You can also associate shortcut keys with a menu. Pressing a shortcut key directly invokes a command.

▶ The Clipboard object consists of two public static methods: GetDataObject and SetDataObject. These get and set the data from the Clipboard.

▶ The StatusBar control creates a standard windows status bar in your applications. You can use a status bar to display various messages and help text to the user.

▶ ToolBars allows you to create a set of small buttons that are identified by icons. Toolbars generally provide a shortcut to an operation available in the application's main menu. Toolbars are commonplace in Windows applications and make your application simple to use.

▶ An MDI Application allows multiple documents or windows to be open simultaneously.

CHAPTER SUMMARY

KEY TERMS

- Clipboard
- Context menu
- Main menu
- MDI form
- Tab order
- ToolTip
- SDI form
- Z-Order

Visual Studio .NET allows controls to be added to forms in two ways. The easier way is to use Visual Studio .NET's Windows Forms Designer. The other way is to write code to create controls and load them dynamically in the applications.

Visual Studio .NET comes with whole array of Windows Forms controls. You can set their properties at design time and runtime. This makes event handling easy by automatically wiring up event handlers with the controls.

Visual Studio .NET comes with full-fledged menu controls needed by almost every application. It allows you to create main menus as well as context menus. MDI Forms support is extensive, allowing you to merge the menu items of the parent MDI window with the menus of the child windows.

By now you should be familiar with the rich library of Windows Forms controls. I discussed most of the common windows controls used by the applications. The .NET Framework SDK also allows you to create your own controls. A number of such custom controls are already available from several control vendors. In Chapter 3, "Error Handling for the User Interface," I'll show you how to create your own User controls and use them in your applications.

APPLY YOUR KNOWLEDGE

Exercises

2.1 Adding ToolTips to Controls

Some Windows Forms controls, such as the TabControl, ToolBarButton, and StatusBarPanel controls, have a ToolTipText property to show ToolTips. But other commonly used controls do not have any built-in property to contain ToolTip text. That's the job of the ToolTip component.

In this exercise you will learn how to set ToolTips for a form.

Estimated Time: 25 minutes.

1. Create a new Visual Basic .NET Windows Application in the Visual Studio .NET IDE.

2. Add a new form to your Visual Basic .NET application. Change the Text property of the form to Find, the FormBorderStyle property to Fixed3D, and the TopMost property to True. Set the MaximizeBox, MinimizeBox, and ShowInTaskBar properties to False.

3. Place a ToolTip component on the form to add to the component tray. Name the component tTip.

4. Place a Label control, one TextBox control (txtTextToFind), two button controls (btnFind and btnCancel), one CheckBox control (chkMatchCase), and a group box with two RadioButton controls (rbUp and rbDown) on the form. Arrange the controls as shown in Figure 2.46.

5. You will find a property named ToolTip on tTip in the Properties window for each control. Enter an appropriate ToolTip message for each control in the ToolTip on tTip property.

6. Set the form as the startup object of the project.

7. Run the project. The ToolTip message will be displayed when you hover over the control, as shown in Figure 2.46.

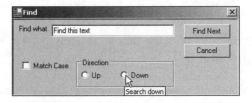

FIGURE 2.46
ToolTips on a form.

2.2 Dynamically Creating Menu Items

While creating menus in Windows applications, you might be required to add menu items dynamically. The following exercise shows how to create menu items dynamically. The exercise shows a list of the recent files opened by application.

Estimated Time: 40 minutes.

1. Add a new form to your Visual Basic .NET project.

2. Place a MainMenu control (mnuMainMenu) and an OpenFileDialog (dlgOpenFile) control on the form.

3. Using the menu designer, add a top-level menu item. Set its Text to &File and name it mnuFile. Add three menu items: &Open (mnuFileOpen), Recent &Files (mnuFileRecentFiles), and E&xit (mnuExit)

4. Set the Menu property of the form to mnuMainMenu.

APPLY YOUR KNOWLEDGE

5. Add the following code to the form:

```
Imports System.Collections

' Store recently used file list
' in an ArrayList
Private alRecentFiles As ArrayList
' Maximum number to files to store
Private Const intListSize = 4
```

6. Add the following code to the New method of the form:

```
' Create an ArrayList of given size
alRecentFiles = New ArrayList(intListSize)
```

7. Add the following code to handle the Click events of the menu items:

```
Private Sub mnuFileExit_Click( _
 ByVal sender As System.Object, _
 ByVal e As System.EventArgs) _
 Handles mnuFileExit.Click
    Me.Close()
End Sub

Private Sub mnuFileOpen_Click( _
 ByVal sender As System.Object, _
 ByVal e As System.EventArgs) _
 Handles mnuFileOpen.Click
    If dlgOpenFile.ShowDialog() = _
    DialogResult.OK Then
        ' Find if the file already exists
        ' in the ArrayList
        Dim pos As Integer = _
        alRecentFiles.IndexOf( _
        dlgOpenFile.FileName)
        ' If it exists then remove it
        If pos >= ) Then
            alRecentFiles.RemoveAt(pos)
        End If

        ' If you have exceeded the size
        ' of ArrayList
        ' delete the oldest item from it
        If alRecentFiles.Count >= _
        intListSize Then
            alRecentFiles.RemoveAt( _
            intListSize - 1)
        End If
```

```
        ' Add the recently opened file
        ' to the queue of recent files
        alRecentFiles.Insert(0, _
        dlgOpenFile.FileName)

        ' do some processing here...
        MessageBox.Show("You selected   " & _
        dlgOpenFile.FileName, _
        "File Opened", _
        MessageBoxButtons.OK, _
        MessageBoxIcon.Information)
    End If
End Sub

' Handle click events in recent files
Private Sub mnuFileRecentFilesItem_Click( _
 ByVal sender As Object, _
 ByVal e As System.EventArgs)
    Dim mnuItem As MenuItem = _
    CType(sender, MenuItem)
    MessageBox.Show("You selected " & _
    mnuItem.Text.Substring(2), _
    "File Opened", _
    MessageBoxButtons.OK, _
    MessageBoxIcon.Information)
End Sub
```

8. Add a PopUp event handler for the mnuFile menu item:

```
Private Sub mnuFile_Popup( _
 ByVal sender As Object, _
 ByVal e As System.EventArgs) _
 Handles mnuFile.Popup
    ' Check if there are any
    ' file names in the list
    If alRecentFiles.Count > 0 Then
        ' Clear old recent file list
        mnuFileRecentFiles.MenuItems.Clear()
        ' Use this number to add keyboard
        ' shortcut to menu items
        ' Most recent file has
        ' shortcut of 1,
        ' next file has shortcut of 2...
        Dim intFileCount As Integer = 1
        Dim strFileName As String
        For Each strFileName _
        In alRecentFiles
            ' Create a menu item to in the
            ' File - Recent Files menu
            Dim mnuItem As MenuItem = _
            New MenuItem()
```

APPLY YOUR KNOWLEDGE

```
          ' Set the MenuItem text
          ' with a shortcut key
          mnuItem.Text = String.Format( _
            "&{0} {1}", _
            intFileCount, strFileName)
          intFileCount += 1
          ' attach an event handler
          ' to this menu item
          AddHandler mnuItem.Click, _
            AddressOf _
            mnuFileRecentFilesItem_Click
          ' Add the recently used file in
          ' the File - Recent files menu
          mnuFileRecentFiles. _
            MenuItems.Add(mnuItem)
      Next
      ' Now that there are some files in
      ' the File - Recent Files menu,
      ' Enable it.
      mnuFileRecentFiles.Enabled = True
    Else
      ' If there are no recent files,
      ' disable the menu item
      mnuFileRecentFiles.Enabled = False
    End If
End Sub
```

9. Set the form as the startup object of the project.

10. Run the project. Open a few files using the File, Open menu, and click on the Recent Files menu item. The recently opened files are added as submenu items to the Recent Files menu item, as shown in Figure 2.47.

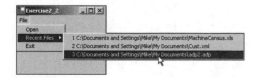

FIGURE 2.47
The files I opened have been added as a submenu to the Recent Files menu item.

Review Questions

1. Where can controls be placed in a form? What are the two ways to add controls?

2. What is the shortcut way to create an event handler for the default event of a control?

3. When should you choose a combo box instead of a list box in your application?

4. What different modes of selection are possible in a list box control?

5. What are the roles of the TabIndex and TabStop properties?

6. How can you create modal and modeless dialog boxes?

7. What different styles can be used to draw a combo box?

8. What is the use of the Tag property of a control?

9. When does the PopUp event of the menu fire? What is the major use of this event?

10. What is the difference between the DateTimePicker control and the MonthCalendar control? What must you do to display a custom format in DateTimePicker control?

11. What is an MDI application?

12. How do you merge the menu items of child window with those of the parent MDI window?

Exam Questions

1. You are designing a data entry form that contains several Label and TextBox controls. You have placed a label and a text box beside each other.

The text box is used for entering the ZIP code, and the label just identifies it. When the user presses the Alt+Z key combination, the focus should shift to the text box for entering ZIP code. What should you do? (Select all that apply.)

A. Set the TabIndex property of the text box to one higher than the TabIndex property of the label.

B. Set the TabIndex property of the label to one higher than the TabIndex property of the text box.

C. Change the label's Text property to ^Zip Code.

D. Change the label's Text property to &Zip Code.

E. Set the UseMnemonic property of the label to True.

F. Set the UseMnemonic property of the label to False.

2. You are designing a Windows application with a variety of controls on its user interface. You want to prevent the user from being able to give focus to some of the controls under any circumstance. Which of the following options should you use?

A. Set the controls' TabIndex property to 0.

B. Set the controls' TabStop property to 0.

C. Set the controls' TabStop property to False.

D. Set the controls' Enabled property to False.

3. You are using a CheckedListBox control on one of the Windows Forms of your application. You want to allow the user to select multiple items from this CheckedListBox. Which value of SelectionMode property should you choose?

A. SelectionMode.None

B. SelectionMode.One

C. SelectionMode.MultiSimple

D. SelectionMode.MultiExtended

4. You are using a TreeView control on one of your Windows Forms. When the user clicks a Tree node to select it, you need to get the newly selected node in your program. Which of the following will give you the correct result?

A. Use the SelectedNode property in the Click event handler of the TreeView control.

B. Use the SelectedNode property in the DoubleClick event handler of the TreeView control.

C. Use the SelectedNode property in the BeforeSelect event handler of the TreeView control.

D. Use the SelectedNode property in the AfterSelect event handler of the TreeView control.

5. You are using a CheckBox control on a Windows Form. The application requires that users either check or uncheck the check box, but your program should be also capable of setting the check box to Indeterminate state depending on the application's current state. Which of the following will satisfy these requirements?

A. Set the ThreeState property of the check box to False.

B. Set the ThreeState property of the check box to True.

APPLY YOUR KNOWLEDGE

C. Set the CheckState property to CheckState.Checked.

D. Set the CheckState property to CheckState.Unchecked.

6. You are designing a menu that has some mutually exclusive options. You have set the RadioCheck property of all the menu items to True and their OwnerDraw property to false. Still, you are able to check multiple items from the menu when you run the program. Which of the following events should you program to set the mutual exclusion between menu items?

   A. Click

   B. Select

   C. Popup

   D. DrawItem

7. You have placed a rich text box on a Windows Form. You want both a horizontal scrollbar and a vertical scrollbar to appear with the control in all cases. Which of the following choices should you make? (Select two.)

   A. Set the ScrollBars property to RichTextScrollBars.Both.

   B. Set the ScrollBars property to RichTextScrollBars.ForcedBoth.

   C. Set the WordWrap property to False.

   D. Set the WordWrap property to True.

8. You are modifying an existing Windows Form application. You have placed a TextBox control on an existing panel. When you run the program, the text box appears to be disabled. Which of following could be the reasons? (Select all that apply.)

A. The Enabled property of text box is False.

B. The ReadOnly property of text box is True.

C. The Enabled property of panel is False.

D. The Enabled property of form is False.

9. Your application represents an XML document in a TreeView control. You are working on a module that gathers all data from the tree and stores it back in an XML document. Which of the following properties gives you access to the entire collection of items in the TreeView?

   A. Controls

   B. Container

   C. Nodes

   D. TopNode

10. You want to apply a Bold FontStyle to a Label control's Text displayed on your form. This should not affect any other FontStyle (such as italic or underline) that the control might already have. Which of the following expression will return the correct FontStyle value?

A. `lblSampleText.Font.Style Or _`
   `   FontStyle.Bold`

B. `lblSampleText.Font.Style Xor _`
   `   FontStyle.Bold`

C. `lblSampleText.Font.Style And _`
   `   FontStyle.Bold`

D. `lblSampleText.Font.Style Or _`
   `   (FontStyle.Underline And _`
   `   FontStyle.Italic)`

APPLY YOUR KNOWLEDGE

11. You are creating a graphic application in which you will manipulate a variety of image formats. You have created an OpenFileDialog object in your program and have set its Filter property as:

```
ofdPicture.Filter="Image Files (BMP, " & _
 "GIF, JPEG, etc.)|*.bmp;*.gif;*.jpg;" & _
 "*.jpeg;*.png;*.tif;*.tiff|BMP Files " & _
 "(*.bmp)|*.bmp|GIF Files (*.gif)|" & _
 "*.gif|JPEG Files (*.jpg;*.jpeg)|" & _
 "*.jpg;*.jpeg|PNG Files (*.png)|" & _
 "*.png|TIF Files (*.tif;*.tiff)|" & _
 "*.tif;*.tiff|All Files (*.*)|*.*"
```

You have created a button with its Text property set to Open Image.... When you click this button, the Open File dialog box should display the GIF Files as its first choice in the list of File Types. Which value for FilterIndex property must you select to achieve this in the event handler of button's Click event?

   A. 0

   B. 1

   C. 2

   D. 3

12. You are developing a purchase order form. The form has a View menu with several menu items. One of the menu items has its Name property set to mnuViewComments, the Text property set as C&omments, and the Shortcut property set as CtrlO. You don't want to allow users to view comments unless they have first created some comments. Which of the following solutions should you select for this?

   A. In the Popup event of the View menu, set the Visible property of mnuViewComments to True if number of comments > 0; otherwise set the Visible property to False.

   B. In the Click event of the View menu, set the Visible property of mnuViewComments to True if number of comments > 0; otherwise set the Visible property to False.

   C. In the Popup event of the View menu, set the Enabled property of mnuViewComments to True if number of comments > 0; otherwise set the Enabled property to False.

   D. In the Popup event of the mnuViewComments menu item, set its Enabled property to True if number of comments > 0; otherwise set the Enabled property to False.

13. You are designing a form that needs to display a date in a long date format. This might not be the operating system's native format. Which format property of the DateTimePickerFormat enumeration should you select?

   A. DateTimePickerFormat.Short

   B. DateTimePickerFormat.Long

   C. DateTimePickerFormat.Time

   D. DateTimePickerFormat.Custom

14. Assume that the menu designer has been already used to create a menu structure for a form. For menus to provide functionality required, how are the menu items assigned program code?

   A. By attaching an event handler to the Click event of each menu item

B. By attaching an event handler to the Select event of each menu item

C. By attaching an event handler to the Popup event of each menu item

D. By attaching an event handler to the DrawItem event of each menu item

15. You are designing an MDI application in which the parent container and the child window each has its own menu structure. You need to suppress some of the menu items in the child window that collide with parent menu items. Which of the following options should you select?

A. Set the MergeType property to MergeType.Remove for the items that need to be suppressed.

B. Set the Visible property to False for the items that need to be suppressed.

C. Set the MergeOrder property to 0 for the items that need to be suppressed.

D. Set the MdiList property to False for the items that need to be suppressed.

Answers to Review Questions

1. Controls are placed on any container control or directly in a form. You can add controls to a container control either by using the Windows Forms Designer or by hand coding them.

2. Double-clicking the control in the Design view will wire an event handler to the default event of the control.

3. A combo box can save space on a form because the full list is not displayed until the user clicks the down arrow (unless its DropDownStyle property is set to ComboBoxStyle.Simple). Another reason for choosing a combo box might be that it contains a text box field, so choices not in its list can be typed in (unless the DropDownStyle property is set to ComboBoxStyle.DropDownList).

4. The different modes of selection possible in a list box are multiple selections (SelectionMode.MultiSimple); multiple selections with the help of Ctrl, Shift, and arrow keys (SelectionMode.MultiExtended); single selection (SelectionMode.One); and no selection (SelectionMode.None).

5. The TabIndex property of a control specifies the order in which controls receive focus when the user presses the Tab key. The TabStop property indicates whether the control can receive focus by pressing the Tab key.

6. Modal and modeless dialog boxes are created in the same way but are displayed by calling different methods. Modal dialog boxes are displayed by calling Form.ShowDialog method, and calling Form.Show method shows modeless dialog boxes.

7. The combo box can be represented in different styles by setting its DropDownStyle property to different values of the DropDownStyle enumeration. It can appear as DropDown, which is the default style (in which you click the arrow button to display the items, and the text portion is editable), as DropDownList (in which it displays the list of items when the arrow button is clicked, but you cannot edit the text portion), or as Simple (in which the list portion is always visible without any arrow buttons, and the text portion is also editable).

APPLY YOUR KNOWLEDGE

8. The Tag property is commonly used to store data associated with a control. For example, you can store a reference to a MenuItem object in a ToolBarButton object's Tag property. By doing this you have a reference available to the corresponding menu item that can be used to perform an action on the MenuItem object when the ToolBarButton object is clicked. If using the Properties window, you can only assign a string to the Tag property, but in your program, you are free to assign any type derived from Object class to the Tag property.

9. The Popup event of a menu is fired just before displaying its menu items. If a menu has no items in its submenu, the Popup event is not fired.

10. The MonthCalendar allows you to select a range of dates, while the DateTimePicker control allows you to select a date and time. To display a date in a custom format, the Format property should be set to DateTimePicker.Custom, and the custom format should be assigned to the CustomFormat property of the DateTimePicker control.

11. MDI applications consist of an MDI form that acts as a master form and that can open any number of child forms. A form must have its IsMdiContainer property set to True before it can work as an MDI container.

12. Menu items of child windows are automatically merged with menu items of the MDI window depending upon the settings of the MergeType property and the MergeOrder property. As a side note, if you want to merge two menus that are not part of an MDI application, you can use the MergeMenu method of the MainMenu or ContextMenu classes.

Answers to Exam Questions

1. **A, D, E.** A Label control cannot receive focus. Instead it transfers it to the control having next higher TabIndex (Answer **A**). The mnemonic character & (not the ^ character) specifies the keyboard shortcut key (Answer **D**). The UseMnemonic property should be true if the mnemonic character identifies the adjacent character as shortcut key. If UseMnemonic is set to False, & will not have any special meaning and will be displayed as it is (Answer **E**).

2. **D.** To prevent the user from giving focus to a control under any circumstance, you must set the control's Enabled property to False. All other options will only affect the user's navigation with the Tab key. The user could still use the mouse as long as the Enabled property was True.

3. **B.** The CheckedListBox only supports two values for the SelectionMode property: SelectionMode.None, which does not allow any selection, and SelectionMode.One, in which multiple selections are allowed. If the other two selection modes are set through the properties Window, the IDE generates an error message. If set programmatically, they will raise an ArgumentException.

4. **D.** The Click and DoubleClick events are inherited from the Control class, and they occur before the new selection is set to the SelectedNode property. The BeforeSelect event is also fired just before a Tree node is selected. Therefore, accessing a SelectedNode property in these events will return the old selection. The correct event to program is the AfterSelect event because this event is fired after the newly selected node is set in the SelectedNode property.

APPLY YOUR KNOWLEDGE

5. **A.** When the ThreeState property is set to False, the check box can be set to an Indeterminate state only through the program and not by any user interaction.

6. **C.** The Popup event is fired just before a menu's list of items is displayed. You can use this event to check or uncheck menu items. Remember that setting the RadioCheck property to True does not implicitly set mutual exclusion for menu items; you can still check several of them together. So the Popup event is the right place to check the appropriate item and uncheck all others.

7. **B, C.** If the WordWrap property of a rich text box is True (which is the default setting), the horizontal scrollbar is not displayed, regardless of the setting in the ScrollBars property. So, if you need to display the horizontal scrollbar, you need to set WordWrap as False. If you also want to display scrollbars all the time, setting the ScrollBars property to RichTextScrollBars.ForcedBoth will do that provided that the WordWrap property is False.

8. **A, C, D.** A Control's Enabled property will depend on its parent container controls. If the text box is disabled, it might be because its own Enabled property is False, or because any of its parent controls' (Panel as well as the Form) Enabled properties are False.

9. **C.** The Nodes property of a TreeView control gets the collection of TreeNode objects in the TreeView. As opposed to this, the TopNode gets just the first fully visible node in the TreeView.

10. **A.** The FontStyle enumeration has a FlagAttribute attribute that allows bitwise operations on FontStyle values. When you use an expression such as

`lblSampleText.Font.Style Or FontStyle.Bold`

the FontStyle.Bold represents all Bold bits set as 1. The result of bit-wise OR operation with a value 1 is always 1, and hence the above expression will return a FontStyle value that adds Bold to the existing FontStyle of lblSampleText.

11. **D.** The FilterIndex property specifies the filter currently selected in the file dialog box. It is a one-based index, so the GIF Files have an index of 3 in this example.

12. **C.** You should set the Enabled property of mnuViewComments to True if number of comments > 0; otherwise, set it to False. When the menu item is disabled, the user will be unable to select it from the menu or by pressing the shortcut key associated with it. The Visible property hides the menu item from display, but the shortcut key will still work because the menu item itself is enabled.

13. **D.** You must select DateTimePickerFormat.Custom, as the other three will always display date/time according to the settings in the operating system.

14. **A.** The action associated with a menu item is performed when the user clicks the menu, so you must program the event handler of its Click event to do the associated task.

15. **A.** Set the MergeType property to MergeType.Remove to suppress the menu from appearing in the Mdi container's main menu. If you set it to visible, although the menu item will be hidden, it can still be invoked by pressing its associated shortcut key.

APPLY YOUR KNOWLEDGE

Suggested Readings and Resources

1. Grimes, Richard. *Developing Applications with Visual Studio .NET*. Addison Wesley, 2002.

2. Siler, Brian and Jeff Spotts. *Special Edition Using Microsoft Visual Basic .NET*. Que, 2002.

3. Visual Studio .NET Combined Help Collection

   - Menus in Windows Forms

   - Multiple-Document Interface (MDI) Applications

- What's New in Windows Forms and Controls

- Windows Forms Controls

- Windows Forms Walkthroughs

4. Windows Forms FAQ http://www.syncfusion.com/FAQ/winforms/

5. Windows Forms QuickStart Tutorial

   - Building Applications

   - Control Reference

   - Getting Started

This chapter covers the following Microsoft-specified objectives for the Creating User Services section of the Visual Basic .NET Windows-Based Applications exam:

Implement error handling in the UI.

- **Create and implement custom error messages.**

- **Create and implement custom error handlers.**

- **Raise and handle errors.**

▶ When you run a Windows application, it might encounter problems that should not crop up in the normal course of operations. For example, a file might be missing, or a user might enter nonsensical values. A good Windows application must recover gracefully from these problems instead of abruptly shutting down. This exam objective covers the use of exception handling to create robust and fault tolerant applications. The Microsoft .NET Framework provides some predefined exception classes to help you catch these unusual situations in your programs. You can also create your own exception handling classes and error messages that are specific to your own applications.

Validate user input.

▶ It's a truism of computer programming that garbage-in is garbage-out. The best place to avoid incorrect data in an application is at the source, right where the data enters. The Windows Forms library includes an ErrorProvider control, which can be used to display messages, icons, and other information in response to data entry errors. This exam objective covers the ErrorProvider control and various other input validation techniques.

CHAPTER 3

Error Handling for the User Interface

STUDY STRATEGIES

▶ Review the "Exception Handling Statements" and "Best Practices for Exception Handling" sections of the Visual Studio .NET Combined Help Collection.

▶ Experiment with code that uses Try, Catch, and Finally blocks. Use these blocks with various combinations and inspect the differences in your code's output.

▶ Know how to create custom Exception classes and custom error messages in your program.

▶ Experiment with the ErrorProvider component, the Validating event, and other validation techniques. Use these tools in various combinations to validate data entered in the controls.

INTRODUCTION

The .NET Framework adopts the Windows structured exception handling model. Exception handling is an integral part of the .NET Framework. The Common Language Runtime and your code can throw exceptions within an application, across languages, and across machines. Visual Basic .NET provides a structured method for handling exceptions with the use of the Try, Catch, Finally, and Throw statements. The .NET Framework Class Library provides a huge set of exception classes to deal with various unforeseen or unusual conditions in the normal execution environment. If you feel the need to create custom Exception classes to meet specific requirements of your application, you can derive from the ApplicationException class.

Every program must validate the data it receives before it proceeds with further data processing or storage. In this chapter I'll discuss the various techniques you can use to validate data and maintain the integrity of your application. This isn't just a matter of ensuring that your application delivers the proper results. If you don't validate input, your application can represent a serious security hole on the system.

UNDERSTANDING EXCEPTIONS

An exception occurs when a program encounters any serious problem such as running out of memory or attempting to read from a file that no longer exists. These problems are not necessarily caused by a coding error, but can result from the violation of assumptions that you might have made about the execution environment.

When a program encounters an exception, its default behavior is to throw the exception, which generally translates to abruptly terminating the program after displaying an error message. This is not a characteristic of a robust application and won't make your program popular with users. Your program should be able to handle these exceptional situations and if possible gracefully recover from them. This process is called *exception handling*. The proper use of exception handling can make your programs robust and easy to develop and maintain. If you don't use exception handling properly, you might end up having a program that performs poorly, is harder to maintain, and can potentially mislead its users.

Whenever possible, an application should fail to a safe state when an exception occurs. You should attempt to prevent your program from doing any damage in case of failure. For example, if you can't be sure that a particular file is no longer needed, don't delete that file if an exception occurs.

Step By Step 3.1 shows the effect of an unhandled exception in an application. Later in this chapter you'll learn how to handle exceptions.

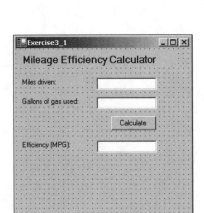

FIGURE 3.1
Mileage Efficiency Calculator.

STEP BY STEP

3.1 Exception in a Windows Application

1. Create a new Visual Basic .NET Windows Application.

2. Add a new Windows Form to the project.

3. Place three TextBox controls (txtMiles, txtGallons, and txtEfficiency), four Label controls, and a Button control (btnCalculate) on the form's surface. Figure 3.1 shows a design for this form.

4. Add the following code to the Click event handler of btnCalculate:

```
Private Sub btnCalculate_Click( _
 ByVal sender As System.Object, _
 ByVal e As System.EventArgs) Handles btnCalculate.Click
    ' This code has no error checking. If something
    ' Goes wrong at run time, it will throw an exception
    Dim decMiles As Decimal = _
     Convert.ToDecimal(txtMiles.Text)
    Dim decGallons As Decimal = _
     Convert.ToDecimal(txtGallons.Text)
    Dim decEfficiency As Decimal = decMiles / decGallons
    txtEfficiency.Text = _
     String.Format("{0:n}", decEfficiency)
End Sub
```

5. Set the form as the startup object for the project.

6. Run the project. Enter values for miles and gallons and click the Calculate button to calculate the mileage efficiency as expected. Now enter the value zero in the gallons text box and click the button. You will see the program abruptly terminate after displaying the error message shown in Figure 3.2.

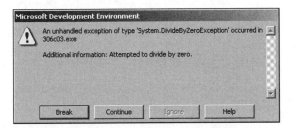

FIGURE 3.2
DivideByZeroException thrown by the development environment.

When you run an application from the development environment and the program throws an exception, the development environment gives you the opportunity to analyze the problem by debugging the program. If you compile the application and launch it from Windows Explorer, the program will terminate after displaying a message box with error message and some debugging information as shown in Figure 3.3.

The CLR views an *exception* as an object that encapsulates information about any problems that occurred during program execution. The .NET Framework Class Library provides two categories of exceptions:

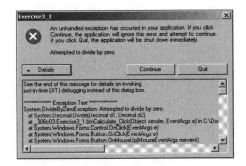

FIGURE 3.3
DivideByZeroException thrown outside the development environment.

◆ ApplicationException: Represents the exceptions thrown by the user programs.

◆ SystemException: Represents the exceptions thrown by the CLR.

Both of these exception classes derive from the base Exception class. The Exception class implements common functionality for exception handling. Neither the ApplicationException class nor the SystemException class adds any new functionality to the Exception class. These classes exist just to differentiate exceptions in user programs from exceptions in the CLR. Table 3.1 lists the important properties of all three classes.

TABLE 3.1

IMPORTANT MEMBERS OF THE EXCEPTION CLASS

Property	Description
HelpLink	A URL to the help file associated with this exception.
InnerException	Specifies an exception associated with this exception. This property is helpful when a series of exceptions is involved. Each new exception can preserve the information about the previous exception by storing it in the InnerException property.
Message	A message that explains the error and possibly offers ways to resolve it.
Source	The name of the application that caused the error.
StackTrace	Specifies where an error occurred. If debugging information is available, the stack trace includes the source file name and program line number.
TargetSite	The method that threw the exception.

HANDLING EXCEPTIONS

Implement error handling in the UI: Raise and handle errors.

Implement error handling in the UI: Create and implement custom error messages.

Abruptly terminating the program when an exception occurs is not a good idea. Your application should be able to handle the exception and (if possible) recover from it. If recovery is not possible you can take other steps, such as notifying the user and then gracefully terminating the application.

The .NET Framework allows exception handling to interoperate among languages and across machines. You can throw an exception in code written in VB .NET and catch it in code written in C#, for example. In fact, the .NET framework also allows you to handle common exceptions thrown by legacy COM applications and legacy nonCOM Win32 applications.

Exception handling is such an integral part of .NET framework that when you look up a method in the product documentation, a section will always specify what exceptions a call to that method might throw.

You can handle exceptions in Visual Basic .NET programs by using a combination of the exception handling statements: Try, Catch, Finally, and Throw. In this section of the chapter I'll show how to use these statements.

The Try Block

You should place the code that can cause exception in a Try block. A typical Try block will look like this:

```
Try
    ' Code that may cause an exception
End Try
```

You can place any valid Visual Basic .NET statements inside a Try block. That can include another Try block or a call to a method that places some of its statement inside a Try block. Thus at runtime you can have a hierarchy of Try blocks placed inside each other. When an exception occurs at any point, the CLR will search for the nearest Try block that encloses this code. The CLR will then pass control of the application to a matching Catch block (if any) and then to the Finally block associated with this Try block.

A Try block cannot exist on its own; it must be immediately followed by one or more Catch blocks or by a Finally block.

The Catch Block

You can have several Catch blocks immediately following a Try block. Each Catch block handles an exception of a particular type. When an exception occurs in a statement placed inside a Try block, the CLR looks for a matching Catch block capable of handling that type of exception. The formula that CLR uses to match the exception is simple. It will look for the first Catch block with either an exact match for the exception or for any of the exception's base classes.

NOTE

Unhandled Exceptions   If No Catch block matches a particular exception, that exception becomes an unhandled exception. The unhandled exception is propagated back to the code that called the current method. If the exception is not handled there, it will propagate further up the hierarchy of method calls. If the exception is not handled anywhere, it goes to the CLR for processing. The Common Language Runtime's default behavior is to terminate the program immediately.

For example, a DivideByZeroException will match with any of these exceptions: DivideByZeroException, ArithmeticException, SystemException, and Exception (progressively more general classes from which DivideByZeroException is derived). In the case of multiple Catch blocks, only the first matching Catch block will be executed. All other Catch blocks will be ignored.

When you write multiple Catch blocks, you must arrange them from specific exception types to more general exception types. For example, the Catch block for catching DivideByZeroException should always precede the Catch block for catching ArithmeticException because the DivideByZeroException derives from ArithmeticException and is therefore more specific. You'll get a compiler error if you do not follow this rule.

A Try block need not necessarily have a Catch block associated with it, but in that case it must have a Finally block associated with it. Step by Step 3.2 demonstrates the use of multiple Catch blocks to keep a program running gracefully despite errors.

STEP BY STEP

3.2 Handling Exceptions

1. Add a new Windows Form to your Visual Basic .NET project.

2. Create a form similar to the one in Step By Step 3.1 with the same names for controls (see Figure 3.1).

3. Add the following code to the Click event handler of btnCalculate:

```
Private Sub btnCalculate_Click( _
 ByVal sender As System.Object, _
 ByVal e As System.EventArgs) Handles btnCalculate.Click
    ' put all the code that may require graceful
    ' error recovery in a try block
    Try
        Dim decMiles As Decimal = _
         Convert.ToDecimal(txtMiles.Text)
        Dim decGallons As Decimal = _
         Convert.ToDecimal(txtGallons.Text)
        Dim decEfficiency As Decimal = decMiles /
        decGallons
```

```
            txtEfficiency.Text = _
             String.Format("{0:n}", decEfficiency)
            ' each  try block should at least
            ' have one catch or finally block
            ' catch blocks should be in order
            ' of specific to the generalized
            ' exceptions otherwise compilation
            ' generates an error
        Catch fe As FormatException
            Dim msg As String = String.Format( _
             "Message: {0}\n Stack Trace:\n {1}", _
             fe.Message, fe.StackTrace)
            MessageBox.Show(msg, fe.GetType().ToString())
        Catch dbze As DivideByZeroException
            Dim msg As String = String.Format( _
             "Message: {0}\n Stack Trace:\n {1}", _
             dbze.Message, dbze.StackTrace)
            MessageBox.Show(msg, dbze.GetType().ToString())
            ' catches all CLS-compliant exceptions
        Catch ex As Exception
            Dim msg As String = String.Format( _
             "Message: {0}\n Stack Trace:\n {1}", _
             ex.Message, ex.StackTrace)
            MessageBox.Show(msg, ex.GetType().ToString())
            ' catches all other exception including
            ' non-CLS-compliant exceptions
        Catch
            ' just rethrow the exception to the caller
            Throw
        End Try
    End Sub
End Sub
```

4. Set the form as the startup object for the project.

5. Run the project. Enter values for miles and gallons and click the Calculate button to calculate the mileage efficiency as expected. Now enter the value zero in the gallons control and run the program. You will see that instead of abruptly terminating the program (as in the earlier example), the program shows a message about a DivideByZeroException (see Figure 3.4). After you dismiss the message, the program will continue running. Now enter some alphabetic characters in the fields instead of numbers and hit the calculate button again. This time you'll get a FormatException message and the program will continue to run. Now try entering a very large value for both the fields. If the values are large enough, the program will encounter an OverflowException, but since the program is catching all types of exceptions it will continue running.

FIGURE 3.4
DivideByZeroException.

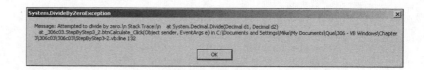

```
System.DivideByZeroException                                                    ×
  Message: Attempted to divide by zero.\n Stack Trace:\n   at System.Decimal.Divide(Decimal d1, Decimal d2)
        at _306c03.StepByStep3_2.btnCalculate_Click(Object sender, EventArgs e) in C:\Documents and Settings\Mike\My Documents\Que\306 - VB Windows\Chapter
  3\306c03\306c03\StepByStep3-2.vb:line 132
                                        OK
```

The program in Step By Step 3.2 displays a message box when an exception occurs. The StackTrace property lists the methods that led up to the exception in the reverse order of their calling sequence to help you understand the flow of logic of the program. In a real application, you might choose to try to automatically fix the exceptions as well.

When you write a Catch block to catch exceptions of the general Exception type, it will catch all CLS-compliant exceptions. That includes all exceptions unless you're interacting with legacy COM or Win32 API code. If you want to catch all exceptions, CLS-compliant or not, you can use a Catch block with no specific type. This Catch block must be last in the list of Catch blocks because it is the most generic.

If you are thinking that it's a good idea to catch all sorts of exceptions in your code and suppress them as soon as possible, think again. A good programmer will only catch an exception in code if the answer is yes to one or more of these questions:

◆ Will I attempt to recover from this error in the Catch block?

◆ Will I log the exception information in system event log or any other log file?

◆ Will I add relevant information to the exception and rethrow it?

◆ Will I execute cleanup code that must run even if an exception occurs?

If you answered no to all those questions, you should not catch the exception but rather just let it go. In that case, the exception will propagate up to the code that is calling your code. Possibly that code will have a better idea of what to do with the exception.

The Throw Statement

A Throw statement explicitly generates an exception in your code. You can use Throw to handle execution paths that lead to undesired results.

You should not throw an exception for anticipated cases, such as the user entering an invalid username or password. This occurrence can be handled in a method that returns a value indicating whether the logon was successful. If you don't have enough permissions to read records from the user table, that's a better candidate to raise an exception because a method to validate users should normally have read access to the user table.

Using exceptions to control the normal flow of execution is bad for two reasons:

1. It can make your code difficult to read and maintain because using Try and Catch blocks to deal with exceptions forces you to separate the regular program logic between separate locations.

2. It can make your programs slower because exception handling consumes more resources than just returning values from a method.

You can use the Throw statement in two ways. In its simplest form, you can just rethrow an exception that you've caught in a Catch block:

```
Catch ex As Exception
    ' TODO: Add code to write to the event log
    Throw
```

This usage of the Throw statement rethrows the exception that was just caught. It can be useful when you don't want to handle the exception yourself but want to take other actions (such as recording the error in an event log or sending an email notification about the error) when the exception occurs. Then you can pass the exception unchanged to the next method in the calling chain.

The second way to use a Throw statement is to throw explicitly created exceptions. For example, this code creates and throws an exception:

```
Dim strMessage As String = _
  "EndDate should be greater than the StartDate"
Dim exNew As ArgumentOutOfRangeException = _
  New ArgumentOutOfRangeException(strMessage)
Throw exNew
```

In this example I first created a new instance of the Exception object and associated a custom error message with it Then I threw the newly created exception.

> **EXAM TIP**
>
> **Custom Error Messages**   When creating an exception class, you should use the constructor that allows you to associate a custom error message with the exception instead of using the default constructor. The custom error message can pass specific information about the cause of the error and a possible way to resolve it.

You are not required to put this usage of the Throw statement inside a Catch block because you're just creating and throwing a new exception rather than rethrowing an existing one. You will typically use this technique in raising your own custom exceptions. I'll show how to do that later in this chapter.

An alternate way to throw an exception is to throw it after wrapping it with additional useful information, for example:

```
Catch ane As ArgumentNullException
    ' TODO: Add code to create an entry in the log file
    Dim strMessage As String = "CustomerID cannot be null"
    Dim aneNew As ArgumentNullException = _
     New ArgumentNullException(strMessage)
    Throw aneNew
```

You might need to catch an exception that you cannot handle completely. You would then perform any required processing and throw a more relevant and informative exception to the calling code, so that it can perform the rest of the processing. In this case, you can create a new exception whose constructor wraps the previously caught exception in the new exception's InnerException property. The calling code will now have more information available to handle the exception appropriately.

Because InnerException is also an exception, it might also store an exception object in its InnerException property, so what you are propagating is a chain of exceptions. This information can be very valuable at debugging time because it allows you to trace the problem to its origin.

The Finally Block

The Finally block contains the code that always executes whether any exception occurred. You can use the Finally block to write cleanup code to maintain your application in a consistent state and preserve the external environment. As an example you can write code to close files, database connections, or related I/O resources in a Finally block.

It is not necessary for a Try block to have an associated Finally block. However, if you do write a Finally block, you cannot have more than one, and the Finally block must appear after all the Catch blocks.

Step By Step 3.3 illustrates the use of the Finally block.

EXAM TIP

No Code in Between Try, Catch, and Finally Blocks When you write Try, Catch, and Finally blocks, they must be in immediate succession. You cannot write any code between the blocks, although you can place comments between them.

STEP BY STEP

3.3 Using a Finally Block

1. Add a new Windows Form to your Visual Basic .NET project.

2. Place two TextBox controls (txtFileName and txtText), two Label controls, and a Button control (btnSave) on the form's surface and arrange them as shown in Figure 3.5.

3. Double-click the Button control to open the form's module. Enter a reference at the top of the module:

```
Imports System.IO
```

4. Enter this code to handle the Button's Click event:

```
Private Sub btnSave_Click(ByVal sender As System.Object, _
 ByVal e As System.EventArgs) Handles btnSave.Click
    ' A StreamWriter writes characters to a stream
    Dim sw As StreamWriter
    Try
        sw = New StreamWriter(txtFilename.Text)
        ' Attempt to write the textbox contents in a file
        Dim strLine As String
        For Each strLine In txtText.Lines
            sw.WriteLine(strLine)
        Next
        ' This line only executes if
        ' there were no exceptions so far
        MessageBox.Show( _
          "Contents written, without any exceptions")
        ' Catches all CLS-complaint exceptions
    Catch ex As Exception
        Dim msg As String = String.Format( _
      "Message: {0}\n Stack Trace:\n {1}", _
      ex.Message, ex.StackTrace)
        MessageBox.Show(msg, ex.GetType().ToString())
        GoTo endit
        ' The finally block is always
        ' executed to make sure that the
        ' resources get closed whether or
        ' not an exception occurs.
        ' Even if there is a goto statement
        ' in catch or try block the
        ' final block is first executed before
        ' the control goes to the label
```

FIGURE 3.5
An application to test a Finally block.

continues

continued

```
        Finally
            If Not sw Is Nothing Then
                sw.Close()
            End If
            MessageBox.Show( _
             "Finally block always executes " & _
             "whether or not exception occurs")
        End Try
EndIt:
        MessageBox.Show("Control is at label: end")
End Sub
```

5. Set the form as the startup object for the project.

6. Run the project. Enter a file name and some text. Watch the order of the messages and note that the message box from the `Finally` block will always be displayed prior to the message box from the end label.

Step By Step 3.3 illustrates that the `Finally` block always executes, even if a transfer of control statement, such as `GoTo`, is within a `Try` or `Catch` block. The compiler will not allow a transfer of control statement within a `Finally` block.

The `Finally` statement can be used in a `Try` block with no `Catch` block. For example:

```
Try
    ' Write code to allocate some resources
Finally
    ' Write code to Dispose all allocated resources
End Try
```

This usage ensures that allocated resources are properly disposed of no matter what happens in the `Try` block.

EXAM TIP

Finally Block Always Executes If you have a Finally block associated with a Try block, the code in the Finally block will always execute, regardless of whether an exception occurs.

NOTE

Throwing Exceptions from a Finally Block Although throwing exceptions from a Finally block is perfectly legitimate, you should avoid doing so. A Finally block there might already have an unhandled exception waiting to be handled.

REVIEW BREAK

▶ An exception occurs when a program encounters any unexpected problem during normal execution.

▶ The Framework Class Library (FCL) provides two main types of exceptions: SystemException and ApplicationException. A SystemException represents an exception thrown by the Common Language Runtime while an ApplicationException represents an exception thrown by the your own code.

▶ The System.Exception class is the base class for all CLS-compliant exceptions and provides the common functionality for exception handling.

▶ A Try block consists of code that might raise an exception. A Try block cannot exist on its own but should be immediately followed by one or more Catch blocks or a Finally block.

▶ The Catch block handles any exception raised by the code in the Try block. The runtime looks for a matching Catch block to handle the exception and uses the first Catch block with either the exact same exception or any of the exception's base classes.

▶ If multiple Catch blocks are associated with a Try block, then the Catch blocks should be arranged in order from specific to general exception types.

▶ The Throw statement is used to raise an exception.

▶ The Finally block is used to enclose any code that needs to be run irrespective of whether an exception is raised.

CUSTOM EXCEPTIONS

Implement error handling in the UI: Create and implement custom error messages.

Implement error handling in the UI: Create and implement custom error handlers.

In most cases, .NET's built-in exception classes, combined with custom messages that you create when instantiating a new exception, will suffice your exception handling requirements. However, in some cases you need exception types specific to the problem you are solving.

The .NET Framework allows you to define custom exception classes. To make your custom Exception class work well with the .NET exception handling framework, Microsoft recommends that you consider the following when you're designing a custom exception class:

◆ Create an exception class only if no existing exception class satisfies your requirement.

> **EXAM TIP**
>
> **Use ApplicationException As Base Class for Custom Exceptions** Although you can derive directly from the Exception class, Microsoft recommends that you derive any custom exception class you create for your Windows application from the ApplicationException class.

◆ Derive all programmer-defined exception classes from the System.ApplicationException class.

◆ End the name of custom exception class with the word Exception (for example, `MyOwnCustomException`).

◆ Implement three constructors with the signatures shown in the following code:

```
Public Class MyOwnCustomException
    Inherits ApplicationException

    ' Default constructor
    Public Sub New()

    End Sub

    ' Constructor accepting a single string message
    Public Sub New(ByVal message As String)
        MyBase.New(message)
    End Sub

    ' Constructor accepting a string message
    ' and an inner exception
    ' that will be wrapped by this custom exception class
    Public Sub New(ByVal message As String, _
     ByVal inner As Exception)
        MyBase.new(message, inner)
    End Sub

End Class
```

Step By Step 3.4 shows how to create a custom exception.

STEP BY STEP

3.4 Creating a Custom Exception

1. Add a new Windows Form to your Visual Basic .NET project.

2. Place two Label controls, a TextBox control named `txtDate`, and a Button control named `btnIsLeap` on the form. Figure 3.6 shows a design for this form. Name the empty Label control `lblResults`.

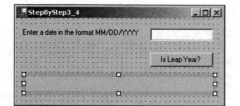

FIGURE 3.6
Leap Year Finder.

3. Add a new class to your project. Add code to create a custom exception class:

```
Public Class MyOwnInvalidDateFormatException
    Inherits ApplicationException

    ' Default constructor
    Public Sub New()

    End Sub

    ' Constructor accepting a single string message
    Public Sub New(ByVal message As String)
        MyBase.New(message)
        Me.HelpLink = _
            "file://MyOwnInvalidDateFormatExceptionHelp.htm"
    End Sub

    ' Constructor accepting a string
    ' message and an inner exception
    ' that will be wrapped by this custom exception class
    Public Sub New(ByVal message As String, _
     ByVal inner As Exception)
        MyBase.new(message, inner)
        Me.HelpLink = _
            "file://MyOwnInvalidDateFormatExceptionHelp.htm"
    End Sub

End Class
```

4. Add a second new class to your project. Add code to create a class named LeapDate:

```
Public Class LeapDate
    ' This class does elementary date handling for the
    ' leap year form
    Private day, month, year As Integer

    Public Sub New(ByVal strDate As String)
        If strDate.Trim().Length = 10 Then
            ' Input data might be in invalid
            ' format; in that case
            ' the Convert.ToDateTime method will fail
            Try
                Dim dt As DateTime = _
                 Convert.ToDateTime(strDate)
                day = dt.Day
                month = dt.Month
                year = dt.Year
                ' Catch any exception, attach
                ' it to the custom exception and
                ' throw the custom exception
```

continues

continued

```
                    Catch e As Exception
                        Throw New MyOwnInvalidDateFormatException( _
                        "Custom Exception: Invalid Date Format", e)
                    End Try
                Else
                    ' bad input, throw a custom exception
                    Throw New MyOwnInvalidDateFormatException( _
                    "The input does not match  the required " & _
                    "format: MM/DD/YYYY")
                End If
            End Sub


            ' Find if the given date belongs to a leap year
            Public Function IsLeapYear() As Boolean
                IsLeapYear = (year Mod 4 = 0) And _
                ((year Mod 100 <> 0) Or (year Mod 400 = 0))
            End Function
        End Class
```

---

5. Add the following event handler for the `Click` event of `btnIsLeap`:

```
Private Sub btnIsLeap_Click(ByVal sender As System.Object, _
 ByVal e As System.EventArgs) Handles btnIsLeap.Click
    Try
        Dim dt As LeapDate = New LeapDate(txtDate.Text)
        If dt.IsLeapYear() Then
            lblResult.Text = "This date is in a leap year"
        Else
            lblResult.Text = _
                "This date is NOT in a leap year"
        End If
        ' Catch the custom exception and
        ' display an appropriate message
    Catch dte As MyOwnInvalidDateFormatException
        Dim msg As String
        ' If some other exception was also
        ' attached with this exception
        If Not dte.InnerException Is Nothing Then
            msg = String.Format( _
            "Message:" & vbCrLf & "{0}" & _
            vbCrLf & vbCrLf & "Inner Exception:" & _
            vbCrLf & "{1}", _
            dte.Message, dte.InnerException.Message)
```

```
      Else
          msg = String.Format("Message:" & _
          vbCrLf & "{0}" & _
          vbCrLf & vbCrLf & _
          "Help Link:" & vbCrLf & "{1}", _
          dte.Message, dte.HelpLink)
      End If
      MessageBox.Show(msg, dte.GetType().ToString())
  End Try
End Sub
```

FIGURE 3.7
Custom error message thrown by the custom exception.

6. Set the form as the startup object for the project.

7. Run the project. Enter a date and click the button. If the date was in the correct format, you'll see a result displayed in the Results label. Otherwise, you'll get a message box showing the custom error message thrown by the custom exception, as shown in Figure 3.7.

In Guided Practice Exercise 3.1 you'll create a custom defined Exception class that helps implement custom error messages and custom error handling in your programs.

GUIDED PRACTICE EXERCISE 3.1

Your goal is to create a keyword-searching application. The application should ask for a filename and a keyword and search for the keyword in the file. The application should then display the number of lines that contain the keyword. The application assumes that the entered keyword will be a single word. If not, you must create and throw a custom exception for that case.

Try this on your own first. If you get stuck or would like to see one possible solution, follow these steps:

1. Add a new form to your Visual Basic .NET Project.

2. Place three Label controls, two TextBox controls, and two Button controls on the form, arranged as shown in Figure 3.8. Name the TextBox for accepting filenames `txtFileName` and the Browse button `btnBrowse`. Name the TextBox for accepting keywords `txtKeyword` and the search button `btnSearch`. Name the results label `lblResult`.

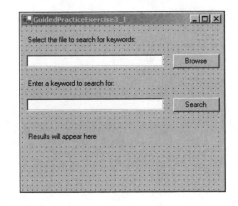

FIGURE 3.8
Form allowing a keyword search in a file.

continues

continued

3. Add an OpenFileDialog control to the form and change its name to `dlgOpenFile`.

4. Create a new class named `BadKeywordFormatException` that derives from `ApplicationException` and place the following code in it:

```
Public Class BadKeywordFormatException
    Inherits ApplicationException

    ' Default constructor
    Public Sub New()

    End Sub

    ' Constructor accepting a single string message
    Public Sub New(ByVal message As String)
        MyBase.New(message)
    End Sub

    ' Constructor accepting a string
    ' message and an inner exception
    ' that will be wrapped by this custom exception class
    Public Sub New(ByVal message As String, _
     ByVal inner As Exception)
        MyBase.new(message, inner)
    End Sub

End Class
```

5. Create a method named `GetKeywordFrequency` in the form's module. This class accepts a filename and returns the number of lines containing the keyword. Add the following code to the method:

```
Private Function GetKeywordFrequency( _
 ByVal strPath As String) As Integer
    If Me.txtKeyword.Text.Trim().IndexOf(" ") >= 0 Then
        Throw New BadKeywordFormatException( _
         "The keyword must only have a single word")
    End If

    Dim count As Integer = 0
    If File.Exists(strPath) Then
        Dim sr As StreamReader = _
         New StreamReader(txtFileName.Text)
        Do While (sr.Peek() > -1)
            If sr.ReadLine().IndexOf(txtKeyword. _
             Text) >= 0 Then
                count += 1
            End If
```

```
        Loop
    End If
    GetKeywordFrequency = count
End Function
```

6. Add the following code to the Click event handler of the
   btnBrowse button:

```
Private Sub btnBrowse_Click(ByVal sender As
System.Object, _
 ByVal e As System.EventArgs) Handles btnBrowse.Click
    If dlgOpenFile.ShowDialog() = DialogResult.OK Then
        txtFileName.Text = dlgOpenFile.FileName
    End If
End Sub
```

7. Add the following code to the Click event handler of the
   btnSearch Button:

```
Private Sub btnSearch_Click(ByVal sender As
System.Object, _
 ByVal e As System.EventArgs) Handles btnSearch.Click
    If txtKeyword.Text.Trim().Length = 0 Then
        MessageBox.Show( _
          "Please enter a keyword to search", _
          "Missing Keyword")
        Exit Sub
    End If
    Try
    lblResult.Text = String.Format("The keyword: '{0}'" & _
      "was found in {1} lines", _
        txtKeyword.Text, _
         GetKeywordFrequency(txtFileName.Text))
    Catch bkfe As BadKeywordFormatException
        Dim msg As String = _
          String.Format("Message:" & vbCrLf & _
          "{0}" & vbCrLf & vbCrLf & "StackTrace:" & _
          vbCrLf & "{1}", _
          bkfe.Message, bkfe.StackTrace)
        MessageBox.Show(msg, bkfe.GetType().ToString())
    End Try
End Sub
```

8. Set the form as the startup object for the project.

9. Run the project. Click the Browse button and select an existing file. Enter a keyword to search for in the file and press the
   Search button. If the keyword entered is in wrong format
   (contains a space) then the custom exception will be raised.

MANAGING UNHANDLED EXCEPTIONS

Managed applications (that is, applications that use the services of the CLR) execute in an isolated environment called an AppDomain. The AppDomain class provides a set of events that allows you to respond when an assembly is loaded, when an application domain is about to be unloaded, or when an application throws an unhandled exception. I'll discuss the AppDomain class in more detail in Chapter 4, "Creating and Managing Components and Assemblies," but for now I'll use its UnhandledException event. This event fires when no other exception handler catches an exception. The CLR passes this event an instance of the UnhandledExceptionArgs class. The properties of the UnhandledExceptionEventArgs class are listed in Table 3.2.

TABLE 3.2

IMPORTANT PROPERTIES OF THE UNHANDLEDEXCEPTIONEVENTARGS CLASS

Property	Description
ExceptionObject	It gets the unhandled exception object corresponding to the current domain.
IsTerminating	It has a Boolean value that indicates whether the Common Language Runtime is terminating.

You can attach an event handler to this event to take custom actions such as logging the exception-related information. A log maintained over a period can help analyze and find patterns that can give you useful debugging information. You can log the information related to an event in several ways:

- ◆ Windows event log
- ◆ Custom log files
- ◆ Databases such as SQL Server 2000
- ◆ Email notifications

Among these ways, the Windows event log offers a very robust way of event logging. It requires the minimum infrastructure for logging the event. The other cases are not as fail-safe because your application can lose connectivity with a database or with the SMTP server, because or you might have problems writing an entry in a custom log file.

The .NET Framework provides access to the Windows event log through the EventLog class. Windows 2000 (and later versions) has three default logs: Application, System, and Security. You can use the EventLog class to create custom event logs. These event logs can be easily viewed using the Windows Event Viewer utility.

You should know about the important members of the EventLog class listed in Table 3.3. See Step By Step 3.5 to use the event log to log unhandled exceptions.

TABLE 3.3

IMPORTANT MEMBERS OF THE EVENTLOG CLASS

Member	Type	Description
Clear	Method	Removes all entries from the event log to make it empty
CreateEventSource	Method	Creates an event source that you can use to write to a standard or custom event log
Entries	Property	Gets the contents of the event log
Log	Property	The name of the log to read from or write to
MachineName	Property	The name of the computer on which to read or write events
Source	Property	The event source name to register and use when writing to the event log
SourceExists	Method	Specifies whether the event source exists on a computer
WriteEntry	Method	Writes an entry in the event log

NOTE

When Not to Use the Event Log   The Windows event log is not available on older version of Windows, such as Windows 98. If your application needs to support those computers, you might want to create a custom error log in a file. Also, in case of a distributed application, you might want to log all events centrally in a SQL Server database. To make the scheme more robust, you could choose to log locally if a database is not available and transfer the log to the central database when it is available again.

STEP BY STEP

3.5 Logging Unhandled Exceptions in the Windows Event Log

1. Add a new Windows Form to your Visual Basic .NET project.

2. Place three TextBox controls (txtMiles, txtGallons, and txtEfficiency) and a Button (btnCalculate) on the form's surface and arrange them as was shown in Figure 3.1. Add the label controls as necessary.

3. Double-click the Button control and add the following code to handle its Click event:

```
Private Sub btnCalculate_Click( _
 ByVal sender As System.Object, _
 ByVal e As System.EventArgs) _
 Handles btnCalculate.Click
   ' This code has no error checking. If something
   ' goes wrong at runtime, it will throw an exception
   Dim decMiles As Decimal = Convert.ToDecimal( _
    txtMiles.Text)
   Dim decGallons As Decimal = Convert.ToDecimal( _
    txtGallons.Text)
   Dim decEfficiency As Decimal = _
    decMiles / decGallons
   txtEfficiency.Text = String.Format( _
    "{0:n}", decEfficiency)
End Sub
```

4. Add the following event handler to the end of the form's module:

```
Private Sub UnhandledExceptionHandler( _
 ByVal sender As Object, _
 ByVal ue As UnhandledExceptionEventArgs)
   Dim unhandledException As Exception = +
    CType(ue.ExceptionObject, Exception)

   ' If no event source exist, create an event source
   If Not EventLog.SourceExists( _
    "Mileage Efficiency Calculator") Then
      EventLog.CreateEventSource( _
       "Mileage Efficiency Calculator", _
       "Mileage Efficiency Calculator Log")
   End If
```

```
' Create an EventLog instance and assign its source.
Dim el As EventLog = New EventLog()
el.Source = "Mileage Efficiency Calculator"

' Write an informational entry to the event log.
el.WriteEntry(unhandledException.Message)
MessageBox.Show( _
    "An exception occurred: Created an entry in the log
file")
End Sub
```

5. Modify the form's New method as follows:

```
Public Sub New()
    MyBase.New()

    'This call is required by the Windows Form Designer.
    InitializeComponent()

    ' Add any initialization after the
    ' InitializeComponent() call
    ' Create an AppDomain object
    Dim adCurrent As AppDomain = AppDomain.CurrentDomain
    ' Attach the UnhandledExceptionEventHanlder
    ' to the UnhandledException of the AppDomain object
    AddHandler adCurrent.UnhandledException, _
        AddressOf UnhandledExceptionHandler

End Sub
```

6. Set the form as the startup object for the project.

7. Run the project. Enter a zero for the number of gallons and click the button. An unhandled exception will occur, and a message box will be displayed notifying you that the exception has been logged. You can view the logged message by selecting Start, Control Panel, Administrative Tools, Event Viewer. The Event Viewer will display the Mileage Efficiency Calculator Log in the left pane of the window as shown in Figure 3.9. The right pane of the window shows the events that have been logged. You can double-click an event to view its description and other properties as shown in Figure 3.10.

NOTE

Refreshing the List of Event Logs   If you have the Event Viewer open already when you run this code, you'll need to close and reopen it to see the new event log category.

FIGURE 3.9▶
EventViewer showing the
MileageEfficiencyCalculatorLog.

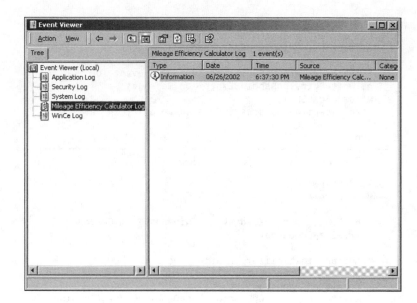

FIGURE 3.10▲
Event Properties of a particular event.

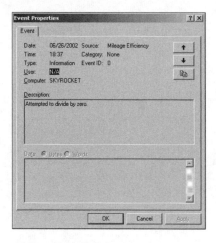

R E V I E W   B R E A K

▶ If the existing exception classes do not satisfy your exception handling requirements, you can create new exception classes specific to your application. Custom exceptions should be derived from the ApplicationException class.

▶ You can use the UnhandledException event of the AppDomain class to manage unhandled exceptions.

▶ You can use the EventLog class to log events to the Windows event log.

USER INPUT VALIDATION

Validate user input.

It's a truism of the computer world that garbage-in is garbage-out. When designing an application that interacts with the user to accept data, you must ensure that the entered data is acceptable to the application.

The most obvious time to ensure the validity of data is at the time of data entry itself. You can use various techniques for validating data, including these:

◆ Restrict the values that a field can accept by using standard controls like combo boxes, list boxes, radio buttons and check boxes. These allow users to select from a set of given values rather than permitting free keyboard entry.

◆ Capture the user's keystrokes and analyze them for validity. Some fields might require the user to enter only alphabetic values but no numeric values or special characters; in that case, you can accept the keystrokes for alphabetic characters while rejecting others.

◆ Restrict entry in some data fields by enabling or disabling them depending on the state of other fields.

◆ Analyze the contents of the data field as a whole and warn the user of any incorrect values when the user attempts to leave the field or close the window.

You saw how to use the various controls to limit input in Chapter 2, "Controls." I'll cover the rest of the techniques in this section.

Keystroke-Level Validation

When you press a key on a control, three events take place in the following order:

1. KeyDown

2. KeyPress

3. KeyUp

You can add code to the event handlers for these events to perform keystroke-level validation. You will choose which event to handle based on the order in which the events are fired and the information passed in the event argument of the event handler.

The KeyPress event happens after the KeyDown event but before the KeyUp event. Its event handler receives an argument of type KeyPressEventArgs. Table 3.4 lists the properties of the KeyPressEventArgs class.

TABLE 3.4

IMPORTANT PROPERTIES OF THE KEYPRESSEVENTARGS CLASS

Property	Description
Handled	Setting this property to True indicates that the event has been handled.
KeyChar	Gets the character value corresponding to the key.

The KeyPress event only fires if the key pressed generates a character value. This means you won't get a KeyPress event from keys such as function keys, control keys, and the cursor movement keys; you must use the KeyDown and KeyUp events to trap those keys.

The KeyDown and KeyUp events occur when a user presses and releases a key on the keyboard. The event handlers of these events receive an argument of the KeyEventArgs type; this argument provides the properties listed in Table 3.5.

TABLE 3.5

IMPORTANT PROPERTIES OF THE KEYEVENTARGS CLASS

Property	Description
Alt	Returns True if Alt key is pressed, otherwise False.
Control	Returns True if Ctrl key is pressed, otherwise False.
Handled	Indicates whether the event has been handled.
KeyCode	Gets the keyboard code for the event. Its value is one of the values specified in the Keys enumeration.
KeyData	Gets the key code for the pressed key, along with modifier flags that indicate the combination of Ctrl, Shift, and Alt keys that were pressed at the same time.
KeyValue	Gets an integer representation of the KeyData property.
Modifiers	Gets the modifier flags that indicate which combination of modifier keys (Ctrl, Shift, and Alt) were pressed.
Shift	Returns True if Shift key is pressed, otherwise False.

The KeyPreview Property

By default, only the active control will receive keystroke events. The Form object also has KeyPress, KeyUp, and KeyDown events, but they are fired only when all the controls on the form are either hidden or disabled. However, you can modify this behavior.

When you set the KeyPreview property of a form to True, the form will receive all three events (KeyDown, KeyPress, and KeyUp) just before the active control receives them. This allows you to set up a two-tier validation on controls. If you want to discard a certain type of characters at the form level itself, you can set the Handled property for the event argument to True (This will not allow the event to propagate to the active control.); otherwise, the events will propagate to the active control. You can then use keystroke events at the control level to perform field-specific validation such as restricting the field to only numeric digits.

Field-Level Validation

Field-level validation ensures that the value entered in the field as a whole is in accordance with the application's requirement. If it isn't, you can alert the user to the problem. Appropriate times to perform field-level validations are

◆ When the user attempts to leave the field.

◆ When the content of the field changes for any reason. This isn't always a feasible strategy. For example, if you're validating a date to be formatted as "mm/dd/yy", it won't be in that format until all the keystrokes are entered.

When a user enters and leaves a field, events occur in the following order:

1. Enter

2. GotFocus

3. Leave

4. Validating

5. Validated

6. LostFocus

The Validating Event

The Validating event is the ideal place for performing field-level validation logic on a control. The event handler for the Validating event receives an argument of type CancelEventArgs. Its only property is the Cancel property. When set to True, this property cancels the event.

Inside the Validating event, you can write code to

◆ Programmatically correct any errors or omissions made by the user.

◆ Show error messages and alerts to the user so that he can fix the problem.

Inside the Validating event, you might also want to retain the focus in the current control, thus forcing user to fix the problem before proceeding further. You can use either of the following techniques to do this:

◆ Use the Focus method of the control to transfer the focus back to the field.

◆ Set the Cancel property of the CancelEventArgs object to True. This will cancel the Validating event, leaving the focus in the control.

A related event is the Validated event. The Validated event is fired just after the Validating event and enables you to take actions after the control's contents have been validated.

The CausesValidation Property

When you use the Validating event to retain the focus in a control by canceling the event, you must also consider that you are making your control *sticky*.

Consider what can happen if you force the user to remain in a control until the contents of that control are successfully validated. Now when the user clicks on the Help button in the toolbar to see what is wrong, nothing will happen unless the user makes a correct entry. This can be an annoying situation for users and one that you want to avoid in your application.

The CausesValidation property comes to your rescue here. The default value of the CausesValidation property for any control is True, meaning that the Validating event will fire for any control requiring validation before the control in question receives focus.

When you want a control to respond irrespective of the validation status of other controls, set the CausesValidation property of that control to False. So in the previous example, the Help button in the toolbar should have its CausesValidation property set to False.

ErrorProvider

The ErrorProvider component in the Visual Studio .Net toolbox is useful when showing validation-related error messages to the user. The ErrorProvider component can display a small icon next to a field when the field contains an error. When the user hovers the mouse pointer over the icon, it also displays an error message as a ToolTip. This is a better way of displaying error messages as compared to the old way of using message boxes because it eliminates at least two serious problems with message boxes:

◆ If you have errors in multiple controls, several message boxes popping up simultaneously can annoy or scare users.

◆ After the user dismisses a message box, the error message is no longer available for reference.

Table 3.6 lists some important members of the ErrorProvider class that you should be familiar with.

> **NOTE**
>
> **Validating Event and Sticky Forms** The Validating event also fires when you close a form. If you set the Cancel property of the CancelEventArgs object to True inside this event, it will cancel the close operation as well.
>
> This problem has a work-around: Inside the Validating event you should set the Cancel property of CancelEventArgs argument to True only if the mouse pointer is in the form's Client area. The close box is in the title bar outside the client Area of form. Therefore, when the user clicks the close box, the Cancel property will not be set to True.

TABLE 3.6

IMPORTANT MEMBERS OF THE ERRORPROVIDER CLASS

Member	Type	Description
BlinkRate	Property	Specifies the rate at which the error icon flashes.
BlinkStyle	Property	Specifies a value indicating when the error icon flashes.
ContainerControl	Property	Specifies the parent control of the ErrorProvider control.
GetError	Method	Returns the error description string for the specified control.

continues

TABLE 3.6		*continued*

IMPORTANT MEMBERS OF THE ERRORPROVIDER CLASS

Member	Type	Description
Icon	Property	Specifies an icon to display next to a control. The icon is displayed only when an error description string has been set for the control.
SetError	Method	Sets the error description string for the specified control.
SetIconAlignment	Method	Sets the location to place an error icon with respect to the control. It has one of the ErrorIconAlignment values.
SetIconPadding	Method	Sets the amount of extra space to leave between the specified control and the error icon.

The ErrorProvider object displays an error icon next to a field when you set the error message string. The error message string is set by the SetError method. If the error message is empty, no error icon is displayed and the field is considered to be correct. You'll see how to use the ErrorProvider component in Step By Step 3.6.

STEP BY STEP

3.6 Using the ErrorProvider Control and Other Validation Techniques

1. Add a new Windows Form to your Visual Basic .NET project.

2. Place three TextBox controls (txtMiles, txtGallons, and txtEfficiency) and a Button (btnCalculate) on the form's surface and arrange them as was shown in Figure 3.1. Add the label controls as necessary.

3. Add an ErrorProvider (ErrorProvider1) control to the form. The ErrorProvider control will be displayed in the component tray.

4. Double-click the form and add the following code to handle the form's Load event:

```
Private Sub StepByStep3_6_Load( _
 ByVal sender As System.Object, _
 ByVal e As System.EventArgs) Handles MyBase.Load
    ' Set the ErrorProvider's Icon
    ' alignment for the textbox controls
    ErrorProvider1.SetIconAlignment( _
     txtMiles, ErrorIconAlignment.MiddleLeft)
    ErrorProvider1.SetIconAlignment( _
     txtGallons, ErrorIconAlignment.MiddleLeft)
End Sub
```

5. Add code to handle the `Validating` events of the `txtMiles`
and `txtGallons` controls:

```
Private Sub txtMiles_Validating(ByVal sender As Object, _
 ByVal e As System.ComponentModel.CancelEventArgs) _
 Handles txtMiles.Validating
    Try
        Dim decMiles As Decimal = _
         Convert.ToDecimal(txtMiles.Text)
        ErrorProvider1.SetError(txtMiles, "")
    Catch ex As Exception
        ErrorProvider1.SetError(txtMiles, ex.Message)
    End Try
End Sub

Private Sub txtGallons_Validating(ByVal sender As Object, _
 ByVal e As System.ComponentModel.CancelEventArgs) _
 Handles txtGallons.Validating
    Try
        Dim decGallons As Decimal = _
         Convert.ToDecimal(txtGallons.Text)
        If (decGallons > 0) Then
            ErrorProvider1.SetError(txtGallons, "")
        Else
            ErrorProvider1.SetError(txtGallons, _
             "Please enter a positive non-zero value")
        End If
    Catch ex As Exception
        ErrorProvider1.SetError(txtGallons, ex.Message)
    End Try
End Sub
```

6. Add the following code to the `Click` event handler of
`btnCalculate`:

```
Private Sub btnCalculate_Click( _
 ByVal sender As System.Object, _
 ByVal e As System.EventArgs) Handles btnCalculate.Click
    ' Check whether the error description is not empty
    'for either of the textbox controls
```

continues

continued

```
If (ErrorProvider1.GetError(txtMiles) <> "") Or _
 (ErrorProvider1.GetError(txtGallons) <> "") Then
    Exit Sub
End If
Try
    Dim decMiles As Decimal = _
     Convert.ToDecimal(txtMiles.Text)
    Dim decGallons As Decimal = _
     Convert.ToDecimal(txtGallons.Text)
    Dim decEfficiency As Decimal = decMiles / decGallons
    txtEfficiency.Text = _
     String.Format("{0:n}", decEfficiency)
Catch ex As Exception
    Dim msg As String = _
     String.Format("Message: {0}" & vbCrLf & _
     "Stack Trace:" & vbCrLf & "{1}", _
     ex.Message, ex.StackTrace)
    MessageBox.Show(msg, ex.GetType().ToString())
End Try
End Sub
```

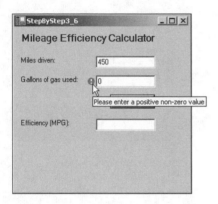

FIGURE 3.11
ErrorProvider control showing the error icon and the error message.

7. Set the form as the startup object for the project.

8. Run the project. Enter values for miles and gallons and run the program. It will calculate the mileage efficiency as expected. You will notice that when you enter an invalid value into any of the TextBox controls, the error icon starts blinking. It will display an error message when the mouse is hovered over the error icon, as shown in Figure 3.11.

Enabling Controls Based On Input

One of the useful techniques for restricting user input is the selective enabling and disabling of controls. Some common cases in which this is useful are

◆ Your application might have a Check Here If You Want to Ship to a Different Location check box. When the user checks the check box, you should allow her to enter values in the fields for a shipping address. Otherwise, the shipping address is same as the billing address.

◆ In a Find dialog box, you have two buttons labeled Find and Cancel. You want to keep the Find button disabled initially and enable it only when the user enters some search text in the text box.

The Enabled property for a control is True by default. When you set it to False, the control cannot receive the focus and will appear grayed out.

For some controls, such as the TextBox, you can also use the ReadOnly property to restrict user input. One advantage of using the ReadOnly property is that the control will still be able to receive focus so that users will be able to scroll through the text in the control if it is not completely visible. In addition, users can also select and copy the text to the clipboard if the ReadOnly property is true.

Other Properties for Validation

In addition to already mentioned techniques, the CharacterCasing and MaxLength properties allow you to enforce some restrictions on the user input.

The CharacterCasing Property

The CharacterCasing property of a TextBox control changes the case of characters in the text box as required by your application. For example, you might want to convert all characters entered in a text box used for entering a password to lowercase to avoid case confusion.

This property can be set to CharacterCasing.Lower, CharacterCasing.Normal (the default value) or CharacterCasing.Upper.

The MaxLength Property

The MaxLength property of a TextBox or a ComboBox specifies the maximum number of characters the user can enter into the control. This property comes in handy when you want to restrict the size of some fields such as a telephone number or a ZIP code.

MaxLength   The MaxLength property only affects the text entered into the control interactively by the user. Programmatically, you can set the value of the Text property to a value that is larger than the value specified by the MaxLength property. So you can use the MaxLength property to limit user input without limiting the text that you can programmatically display in the control.

When the MaxLength property is zero (the default), the number of characters that can be entered is limited only by the available memory. In practical terms, this means that the number of characters is generally unlimited.

In Guided Practice Exercise 3.2 you will learn to use some of the validation tools such as the Enabled property, the Focus method of the TextBox control, and the ErrorProvider control.

GUIDED PRACTICE EXERCISE 3.2

In this exercise, your job is to add some features to the keyword searching application you created in Guided Practice Exercise 3.1. The Keyword text box and the Search button should be disabled when the application is launched. These controls should be enabled as the user progresses through the application. The application assumes that the entered keyword must be a single word. If it is not, you must display an error icon and set the error message. The keyword control should not lose focus unless the user enters valid data in the text box.

Try this on your own first. If you get stuck, or would like to see one possible solution, follow these steps:

1. Add a new form to your Visual Basic .NET Project.

2. Place three Label controls, two TextBox controls, and two Button controls on the form, arranged as was shown in Figure 3.8. Name the text box for accepting file names txtFileName and the Browse button btnBrowse. Name the text box for accepting keywords txtKeyword and the search button btnSearch. Name the results label lblResult.

3. Add an OpenFileDialog control to the form and change its name to dlgOpenFile. Add an ErrorProvider (ErrorProvider1) control to the form. The ErrorProvider control will be placed in the component tray.

4. Double-click the form and add the following code to handle the Form's Load event:

```
Private Sub GuidedPracticeExercise3_2_Load( _
 ByVal sender As System.Object, _
 ByVal e As System.EventArgs) Handles MyBase.Load
```

```
    ' Disable the Keyword textbox and Search button
    txtKeyword.Enabled = False
    btnSearch.Enabled = False
    ErrorProvider1.SetIconAlignment( _
     txtKeyword, ErrorIconAlignment.MiddleLeft)
End Sub
```

5. Attach TextChanged and Validating event handlers to the
   txtKeyword control by adding the following code:

```
Private Sub txtKeyword_TextChanged(ByVal sender As Object, _
 ByVal e As System.EventArgs) Handles
txtKeyword.TextChanged
    If txtKeyword.Text.Length = 0 Then
        btnSearch.Enabled = False
    Else
        btnSearch.Enabled = True
    End If
End Sub


Private Sub txtKeyword_Validating(ByVal sender As Object, _
 ByVal e As System.ComponentModel.CancelEventArgs) _
 Handles txtKeyword.Validating
    If txtKeyword.Text.Trim().IndexOf(" ") >= 0 Then
        ErrorProvider1.SetError(txtKeyword, _
         "You may only search with a single word")
        txtKeyword.Focus()
        txtKeyword.Select(0, txtKeyword.Text.Length)
    Else
        ErrorProvider1.SetError(txtKeyword, "")
    End If
End Sub
```

6. Create a method named GetKeywordFrequency that accepts a
   string and returns the number of lines containing it. Add the
   following code to the method:

```
Private Function GetKeywordFrequency( _
 ByVal strPath As String) As Integer
    Dim count As Integer = 0
    If File.Exists(strPath) Then
        Dim sr As StreamReader = _
         New StreamReader(txtFileName.Text)
        Do While (sr.Peek() > -1)
            If sr.ReadLine().IndexOf( _
             txtKeyword.Text) >= 0 Then
                count += 1
            End If
        Loop
    End If
    GetKeywordFrequency = count
End Function
```

continues

continued

7. Add the following code to the `Click` event handler of the `btnBrowse` button:

```
Private Sub btnBrowse_Click(ByVal sender As System.Object, _
 ByVal e As System.EventArgs) Handles btnBrowse.Click
    If dlgOpenFile.ShowDialog() = DialogResult.OK Then
        txtFileName.Text = dlgOpenFile.FileName
        txtKeyword.Enabled = True
        txtKeyword.Focus()
    End If
End Sub
```

8. Add the following code to the `Click` event handler of the `btnSearch` button:

```
Private Sub btnSearch_Click(ByVal sender As System.Object, _
 ByVal e As System.EventArgs) Handles btnSearch.Click
    If ErrorProvider1.GetError(txtKeyword) <> "" Then
        Exit Sub
    End If
    Try
    lblResult.Text = String.Format( _
     "The keyword: '{0}', found in {1} lines", _
     txtKeyword.Text, _
     GetKeywordFrequency(txtFileName.Text))
    Catch ex As Exception
        Dim msg As string = _
         String.Format("Message:" & vbCrLf & "{0}" & _
         vbCrLf & vbCrLf & "StackTrace:" & vbCrLf & "{1}", _
         ex.Message, ex.StackTrace)
        MessageBox.Show(msg, ex.GetType().ToString())
    End Try
End Sub
```

9. Set the form as the startup object for the project.

10. Run the project. Note that the Keyword text box and the Search button are disabled. Click the Browse button and select an existing file to enable the Keyword text box. Enter the keyword to search in the file to enable the Search button. Click the Search button. If the keyword entered is in wrong format (if it contains a space), the ErrorProvider control will show the error message and the icon.

▶ It is generally a good practice to validate user input at the time of data entry. Thoroughly validated data will result in consistent and correct data stored by the application.

▶ When a user presses a key three events are generated: KeyDown, KeyPress, and KeyUp in that order.

▶ The Validating event is the ideal place for storing the field-level validation logic for a control.

▶ The CausesValidation property specifies whether validation should be performed. If False, the Validating and Validated events are suppressed.

▶ The ErrorProvider component in the Visual Studio .Net toolbox shows validation-related error messages to the user.

▶ A control cannot receive the focus and appears grayed out if its Enabled property is set to False.

CHAPTER SUMMARY

The .NET Framework includes thorough support for exception handling. In fact, it allows you to raise exceptions in one language and catch them in a program written in another language. A Try block should enclose any code that can cause exceptions. A Catch block is used to handle the exceptions raised by the code in the Try block, and the Finally block contains code that will be executed irrespective of the occurrence of an exception.

The Framework Class Library (FCL) provides a large number of Exception classes that represent most of the exceptions that your program can encounter. If you prefer to create your own custom exception class, you can do so by deriving your exception class from the ApplicationException class.

You also learned variety of ways in which to validate user input. The Windows Forms library includes an ErrorProvider component to inform the user of errors. You can also associate custom icons and error messages with the ErrorProvider object.

KEY TERMS

- Exception
- Exception handling
- Input validation

APPLY YOUR KNOWLEDGE

Exercises

3.1   Handling Exceptions

Recall Step By Step 2.5 ("Common Dialog Boxes") from Chapter 2. This Step By Step demonstrated the use of common dialog boxes by creating a simple rich text editor. This editor allows you to open and save a rich text file. You can edit the text or change its fonts and colors. The program worked fine in all cases unless you tried to open or save a file that was already open; in this case the program throws a `System.IO.IOException`.

The objective of this exercise is to make a more robust version of this program that generates a warning about the open file rather than abruptly terminating the program.

Estimated Time: 15 minutes.

1. Create a new Visual Basic .NET Windows application.

2. Add a Windows Form to the project. Name this form `Exercise3_1`.

3. Place five Button controls to the form. Name them `btnOpen`, `btnSave`, `btnClose`, `btnColor`, and `btnFont` and change their Text property to `&Open...`, `&Save...`, `Clos&e...`, `&Color...`, and `&Font...`, respectively. Place a RichTextBox control and name it `rtbText`. Arrange all controls as shown in Figure 3.12.

FIGURE 3.12
A simple rich text editor.

4. Drag and drop the following components from the Toolbox to the form: OpenFileDialog, SaveFileDialog, ColorDialog, and FontDialog.

5. Switch to the Code view and add the following line of code at the top of the form's module:

```
Imports System.IO
```

6. Double-click on the Open button to attach an event handler to its `Click` event. Add the following code to the event handler:

```
Private Sub btnOpen_Click( _
 ByVal sender As System.Object, _
 ByVal e As System.EventArgs) _
 Handles btnOpen.Click
    ' Allow the user to select
    ' only *.rtf files
    OpenFileDialog1.Filter = _
     "Rich Text Files (*.rtf)|*.rtf"
    If OpenFileDialog1.ShowDialog() = _
     DialogResult.OK Then
        Try
            ' Load the file contents
            ' in the RichTextBox
            rtbText.LoadFile( _
             OpenFileDialog1.FileName, _
             RichTextBoxStreamType.RichText)
        Catch ioe As System.IO.IOException
            MessageBox.Show(ioe.Message, _
             "Error opening file")
        End Try
    End If
End Sub
```

7. Add the following code to handle the `Click` event of the Save button:

```
Private Sub btnSave_Click( _
 ByVal sender As System.Object, _
 ByVal e As System.EventArgs) _
 Handles btnSave.Click
    ' Default choice to save file
    ' is *.rtf but user can select
    ' All Files to save with other extension
    SaveFileDialog1.Filter = _
     "Rich Text Files (*.rtf)|*.rtf|" & _
      "All Files (*.*)|*.*"
    If SaveFileDialog1.ShowDialog() = _
     DialogResult.OK Then
        Try
            ' Save the RichText
            ' content to a file
            rtbText.SaveFile( _
             SaveFileDialog1.FileName, _
             RichTextBoxStreamType.RichText)
        Catch ioe As System.IO.IOException
            MessageBox.Show(ioe.Message,_
             "Error saving file")
        End Try
    End If
End Sub
```

8. Add the following code to handle the `Click` event of the Close button:

```
Private Sub btnClose_Click( _
 ByVal sender As System.Object, _
 ByVal e As System.EventArgs) _
 Handles btnClose.Click
    ' Close the form
    Me.Close()
End Sub
```

9. Add the following code to handle the `Click` event of the Color button:

```
Private Sub btnColor_Click( _
 ByVal sender As System.Object, _
 ByVal e As System.EventArgs) _
 Handles btnColor.Click
    If ColorDialog1.ShowDialog() = _
     DialogResult.OK Then
        ' Change the color of selected text
        ' If no text selected,
        ' change the active color
```

```
        rtbText.SelectionColor = _
         ColorDialog1.Color
    End If
End Sub
```

10. Add the following code to handle the `Click` event of the Font button:

```
Private Sub btnFont_Click( _
 ByVal sender As System.Object, _
 ByVal e As System.EventArgs) _
 Handles btnFont.Click
    If FontDialog1.ShowDialog() = _
     DialogResult.OK Then
        ' Change the font of selected text
        ' If no text selected,
        ' change the active font
        rtbText.SelectionFont = _
         FontDialog1.Font
    End If
End Sub
```

11. Set this form as the startup object for the project.

12. Run the project. Click on the Open button and try to open an already opened file. You'll see an error message warning about the file being already open, as shown in Figure 3.13.

FIGURE 3.13
Error message warning user about an already open file.

3.2 Validating User Input

One of the techniques for input validation is to force the user to fix an erroneous field before allowing her to move to another field. To achieve this, you can set the Cancel property of the CancelEventArgs argument of the Validating event of a field to True.

APPLY YOUR KNOWLEDGE

In this exercise, you'll create a login form (see Figure 3.14) that accepts a username and a password. It forces the user to enter the username. The user should be also able to close the application by clicking the Cancel button irrespective of the validation status of the fields.

Estimated Time: 15 minutes.

1. Add a new form to your Visual Basic .NET application.

2. Place three Label controls, two TextBox controls named txtUserName and txtPassword, two Button controls named btnLogin and btnCancel and an ErrorProvider component named ErrorProvider1 on the form. The ErrorProvider component will be placed in the component tray. Arrange the controls in the form as shown in Figure 3.14.

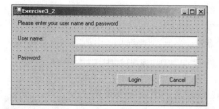

FIGURE 3.14
The login form.

3. Change the ControlBox property of the form to False, the CharacterCasing property of the txtPassword control to Lower and the CausesValidation property of btnCancel to False.

4. Double-click the form to add an event handler for the Load event:

```
Private Sub Exercise3_2_Load( _
 ByVal sender As System.Object, _
 ByVal e As System.EventArgs) _
 Handles MyBase.Load
   ErrorProvider1.SetIconAlignment( _
    txtUserName, _
    ErrorIconAlignment.MiddleLeft)
```

```
   ErrorProvider1.SetIconAlignment( _
    txtPassword, _
    ErrorIconAlignment.MiddleLeft)
End Sub
```

5. Declare the following variable outside a method block in the class:

```
' closingFlag is used to check
' if user has clicked on the Close button
Private closingFlag As Boolean = False
```

6. Add the following code to the Click event handler of the Cancel button:

```
Private Sub btnCancel_Click( _
 ByVal sender As System.Object, _
 ByVal e As System.EventArgs) _
 Handles btnCancel.Click
    closingFlag = True
    Me.Close()
End Sub
```

7. Add the following code to the Click event handler of the Login button:

```
Private Sub btnLogin_Click( _
 ByVal sender As System.Object, _
 ByVal e As System.EventArgs) _
 Handles btnLogin.Click
    Dim strMessage As String = _
     String.Format( _
      "The following information:" & _
      vbCrLf & vbCrLf & "UserName: {0}" & _
      vbCrLf & vbCrLf & _
      "Password: {1}" & vbCrLf & vbCrLf & _
      " can be now passed to " & _
      "  the middle-tier for validation", _
     txtUserName.Text, txtPassword.Text)
    MessageBox.Show(strMessage, _
     "User Input Validation Succeeded")
End Sub
```

8. Add code to handle the Validating events of the txtUserName and txtPassword controls:

```
Private Sub txtUserName_Validating( _
 ByVal sender As Object, _
 ByVal e As System.ComponentModel. _
 CancelEventArgs) _
 Handles txtUserName.Validating
    If Not closingFlag Then
        If txtUserName.Text.Trim(). _
        Length = 0 Then
```

APPLY YOUR KNOWLEDGE

```
        ErrorProvider1.SetError( _
         txtUserName, _
         "Please enter a value " & _
         "for this field")
        e.Cancel = True
    ElseIf txtUserName.Text.Trim(). _
      IndexOf(" ") >= 0 Then
        ErrorProvider1.SetError( _
         txtUserName, _
         "You can NOT have spaces " & _
         "in this field")
        txtUserName.Select(0, _
         txtUserName.Text.Length)
        e.Cancel = True
    End If
  End If
End Sub

Private Sub txtPassword_Validating( _
 ByVal sender As Object, _
 ByVal e As System.ComponentModel. _
 CancelEventArgs) _
 Handles txtPassword.Validating
    If Not closingFlag Then
        If txtPassword.Text.Trim(). _
          Length = 0 Then
            ErrorProvider1.SetError( _
             txtPassword, _
             "Please enter a value " & _
             "for this field")
            e.Cancel = True
        ElseIf txtPassword.Text.Trim(). _
          IndexOf(" ") >= 0 Then
            ErrorProvider1.SetError( _
             txtPassword, _
             "You can NOT have spaces " & _
             "in this field")
            txtPassword.Select(0, _
             txtPassword.Text.Length)
            e.Cancel = True
        End If
    End If
End Sub
```

9. Add code to handle the `Validated` event of the `txtUserName` and `txtPassword` controls:

```
Private Sub txtUserName_Validated( _
 ByVal sender As Object, _
 ByVal e As System.EventArgs) _
 Handles txtUserName.Validated
    ErrorProvider1.SetError(txtUserName, "")
End Sub
```

```
Private Sub txtPassword_Validated( _
 ByVal sender As Object, _
 ByVal e As System.EventArgs) _
 Handles txtPassword.Validated
    ErrorProvider1.SetError(txtPassword, "")
End Sub
```

10. Set this form as the startup object for the project.

11. Run the project. If you click directly on the Login button, you will be forced to enter a username. However, you can click the Cancel button to close the application even without entering a valid username.

Review Questions

1. What is the default behavior of the .NET framework when an exception is raised?

2. Which is the base class of all the exceptions that provides the basic functionality for exception handling? What are the two main types of exception classes and their purposes?

3. Explain the Message and InnerException properties of the Exception class.

4. What is the purpose of Try and Catch blocks?

5. How many Catch blocks can be associated with a single Try block? How should they be arranged?

6. What is the importance of the Finally block?

7. Can you associate custom error messages with the exception types defined by the CLR? If yes, how can you do this?

8. What are some of the points you should consider before creating custom exceptions?

9. What is the importance of the Validating event?

10. Explain the purpose of the ErrorProvider component.

APPLY YOUR KNOWLEDGE

Exam Questions

1. You are creating a data import utility for a personal information system that you designed recently. When the record in the source data file is not in the required format, your application needs to throw a custom exception. You will create an exception class with the name InvalidRecordStructureException. Which of the following classes would you choose as the base class for your custom exception class?

   A. ApplicationException

   B. Exception

   C. SystemException

   D. InvalidFilterCriteriaException

2. You are assisting your colleague in solving the compiler error that his code is throwing. The problematic portion of his code is

```
Try
    Dim success As Boolean = GenerateNewton-
Series(500, 0)
    ' more code here
Catch dbze As DivideByZeroException
    ' exception handling code
Catch nfne As NotFiniteNumberException
    ' exception handling code
Catch ae As ArithmeticException
    ' exception handling code
Catch e As OverflowException
    ' exception handling code
End Try
```

To remove the compilation error, which of the following ways would you modify the code?

A.

```
Try
    Dim success As Boolean = GenerateNewton-
Series(500, 0)
    ' more code here
```

```
Catch dbze As DivideByZeroException
    ' exception handling code
Catch ae As ArithmeticException
    ' exception handling code
Catch e As OverflowException
    ' exception handling code
End Try
```

B.

```
Try
    Dim success As Boolean = GenerateNewton-
Series(500, 0)
    ' more code here
Catch dbze As DivideByZeroException
    ' exception handling code
Catch ae As Exception
    ' exception handling code
Catch e As OverflowException
    ' exception handling code
End Try
```

C.

```
Try
    Dim success As Boolean = GenerateNewton-
Series(500, 0)
    ' more code here
Catch dbze As DivideByZeroException
    ' exception handling code
Catch nfne As NotFiniteNumberException
    ' exception handling code
Catch e As OverflowException
    ' exception handling code
Catch ae As ArithmeticException
    ' exception handling code
End Try
```

D.

```
Try
    Dim success As Boolean = GenerateNewton-
Series(500, 0)
    ' more code here
Catch dbze As DivideByZeroException
    ' exception handling code
Catch nfne As NotFiniteNumberException
    ' exception handling code
Catch ae As Exception
    ' exception handling code
Catch e As OverflowException
    ' exception handling code
End Try
```

APPLY YOUR KNOWLEDGE

3. You need to debug a program containing some exception handling code. To understand the program better, you created a stripped down version of it and included some MessageBox statements that give clues about the flow of its execution. The program has the following code:

```
Try
    Dim num As Integer = 100
    dim den as Integer  = 0)
    MessageBox.Show("Message1")
    Try
        Dim res As Integer = num / den
        MessageBox.Show("Message2")
    Catch ae As ArithmeticException
        MessageBox.Show("Message3")
    End Try
Catch dbze As DivideByZeroException
    MessageBox.Show("Message4")
Finally
    MessageBox.Show("Message5")
End Try
```

Which of these is the order of messages that you receive?

A.

```
Message1
Message2
Message3
Message4
Message5
```

B.

```
Message1
Message3
Message5
```

C.

```
Message1
Message4
Message5
```

D.

```
Message1
Message2
Message4
Message5
```

4. What is the output displayed by the MessageBox in the following code segment?

```
Try
    Try
        Throw _
            New ArgumentOutOfRangeException()
    Catch ae As ArgumentException
        Throw New ArgumentException( _
        "Out of Range", ae)
    End Try
Catch ex As Exception
    MessageBox.Show( _
      ex.InnerException.GetType().ToString())
End Try
```

A. System.Exception

B. System.ApplicationException

C. System.ArgumentException

D. System.ArgumentOutOfRangeException

5. The Validating event of a text box in your Windows application contains the following code. The MyValidatingCode method validates the contents of the text box. If the contents are invalid, this method throws an exception and retains the focus in the text box. The line numbers in the code sample are for reference purpose only.

```
01  Private Sub TextBox1_Validating( _
02    ByVal sender As System.Object, _
03    ByVal e As System.EventArgs) _
04    Handles TextBox1.Validating
05      Try
06          MyValidatingCode()
07      Catch ex As Exception
08
09          TextBox1.Select(0,
            ➥textBox1.Text.Length)
10          ErrorProvider1.SetError(textBox1,
            ➥ex.Message)
11      End Try
12  End Sub
```

Which of the following line of code should be in line 8?

APPLY YOUR KNOWLEDGE

A. `e.Cancel = True`

B. `e.Cancel = False`

C. `TextBox1.CausesValidation = True`

D. `TextBox1.CausesValidation = False`

6. You have designed a Windows Form that works as a login screen. The form has two TextBox controls named `txtUserName` and `txtpassword`. You want to ensure that the user can only enter lowercase characters in the controls. Which of the following methods should you use?

   A. Set the form's KeyPreview property to True and program the KeyPress event of the form to convert uppercase letters to lowercase letters.

   B. Create a single event handler attached to the KeyPress event of both txtUserName and txtpassword. Program this event handler to convert the uppercase letters to lowercase.

   C. Use the CharacterCasing property of the controls.

   D. Use the Char.ToLower method in the TextChanged event handlers of the controls.

7. You must create a custom exception class in your Windows application. You have written the following code for the exception class:

```
Public Class KeywordNotFound
    Inherits ApplicationException

    Public Sub New()
        ' Code here
    End Sub

    Public Sub New( _
     ByVal message As String, _
     ByVal inner As Exception)
        MyBase.New(message, inner)
        ' Code here
    End Sub

End Class
```

A code review suggests that that you did not followed some of the best practices for creating a custom exception class. Which of these changes should you make? (Select two.)

   A. Name the exception class KeywordNotFoundException.

   B. Derive the exception class from the base class Exception instead of ApplicationException.

   C. Add one more constructor to the class with the following signature:

```
Public Sub New(ByVal message As String)
    MyBase.New(message)
    ' Code here
End Sub
```

   D. Add one more constructor to the class with the following signature:

```
Public Sub New(ByVal inner As Exception)
    MyBase.New(inner)
    ' Code here
End Sub
```

   E. Derive the exception class from the base class SystemException instead of ApplicationException.

8. In your Windows application, you have created a dialog box that allows the user to set options for the application. You have also created a Help button that the user can press to get help on various options in the dialog box. You validate the data entered by the user in a TextBox control labeled Complex Script; if the user enters an invalid value in this text box, you set the focus back in the control by setting the cancel property of the CancelEventArgs object to True. While testing the application, you discovered that once you enter invalid data in the text box, you could not click on the Help button without correcting the data first. What should you do to correct the problem?

A. Set the CausesValidation property of the text box to False.

B. Set the CausesValidation property of the text box to True.

C. Set the CausesValidation property of the Help button to False.

D. Set the CausesValidation property of the Help button to True.

9. You are writing exception handling code for an order entry form. When the exception occurs, you want to get information about the sequence of method calls and the line number in the method where the exception occurs. Which property of your exception class can help you?

A. HelpLink

B. InnerException

C. Message

D. StackTrace

10. Your code uses the Throw statement in this fashion:

```
Catch e As Exception
    Throw
```

Which of these statements is true about this code?

A. The Throw statement catches and rethrows the current exception.

B. The Throw statement catches, wraps, and then rethrows the current exception.

C. The Throw statement must be followed by an exception object to be thrown.

D. The Throw statement transfers control to the Finally block following the Catch block.

11. You are creating a Windows Form that works as a login screen for an Order Entry system designed for the sales department of your company. Which of the following strategies should you follow?

A. Design a ValidateUser method. Throw a new custom exception named EmployeeNotFound when the entered username is not in the database.

B. Design a ValidateUser method. Throw an ArgumentException exception when the user types special characters in the User name or Password text boxes.

C. Design a ValidateUser method. It returns True if the username and password are correct; otherwise it returns False.

D. Design a ValidateUser method. Throw an ApplicationException when the entered username is not in the database.

12. You want to capture all the exceptions that escape from the exception handling code in your application and log them to Windows event log. Which of the following techniques would you use?

A. Write all the code of the application inside a Try block, attach a generic Catch block to that Try block, and handle the exception there.

B. Write all the code of the application inside a Try block, attach a Catch block that catches the super type of all exceptions (the Exception objects), and write code to make entries in the event log there.

C. Program the ProcessExit event handler of the AppDomain class.

D. Program the UnhandledException event handler of the AppDomain class.

APPLY YOUR KNOWLEDGE

13. Which of the following is generally the most robust way to record the unhandled exceptions in your application?

    A. Create an entry in Windows event log.

    B. Create an entry in the application's custom event log.

    C. Create an entry in a table in Microsoft SQL Server 2000 database.

    D. Send an email using SMTP.

14. The structured exception handling mechanism of the .NET Framework allows you to handle which of the following types of exceptions? (Select all that apply.)

    A. Exceptions from all CLS-compliant languages

    B. Exceptions from non-CLS–compliant languages

    C. Exceptions from unmanaged COM code

    D. Exceptions from unmanaged nonCOM code

15. What is the result of executing this code snippet?

    ```
    Const someVal1 As Int32 = Int32.MaxValue
    Const someVal2 As Int32 = Int32.MaxValue
    Dim result As Int32

    result = someVal1 * someVal2
    ```

    A. The code will generate an OverflowException.

    B. The code will execute successfully without any exceptions.

    C. The code will cause a compile-time error

    D. The code executes successfully but the value of the variable result is truncated.

Answers to Review Questions

1. The .NET framework terminates the application after displaying an error message when an exception is raised.

2. The Exception class is the base class that provides common functionality for exception handling. The two main types of exceptions derived from Exception class are SystemException and ApplicationException. SystemException represents the exceptions thrown by the common language runtime, whereas ApplicationException represents the exceptions thrown by user code.

3. The Message property describes the current exception. The InnerException property represents an exception object associated with the exception object; this property is helpful when a series of exceptions are involved. Each new exception can preserve information about a previous exception by storing it in InnerException property.

4. The Try block encloses code that might raise an exception. The Catch block handles any exception raised by the code in the Try block.

5. Zero or more Catch blocks can be associated with a single Try block. If no Catch block is associated with a Try block, a Finally block should follow the Try block; otherwise a compile-time error occurs. The Catch blocks should be arranged from specific to general exception types to avoid a compile-time error.

6. The code contained by the Finally block always executes regardless of any exception in the application. Therefore, you can use the Finally block to write cleanup code to complete tasks, such as closing data connections, closing files, and so on, that need to be performed regardless of whether an exception occurred.

7. Yes, you can associate custom error messages with the exception classes defined by the Common Language Runtime to provide more meaningful information to the caller code. The constructor of these classes that accepts the exception message as its parameter can be used to pass the custom error message.

8. Custom exceptions should be derived from ApplicationException and should be created only if existing classes do not meet the requirements of your application. They should have a name ending with the word Exception and should implement the three constructors (default, Message, and Message and Exception) of their base class.

9. The Validating event is the ideal place to store the field-level validation logic for a control. The Validating event handler can be used to cancel the event if validation fails, thus forcing the focus to the control. This forces the user to enter correct data.

10. The ErrorProvider component in the Visual Studio .Net toolbox can be used to show validation-related error icons and error messages to the user.

Answers to Exam Questions

1. **A.** When creating a class for handling custom exceptions in your programs, the best practice is to derive it from the ApplicationException class. The SystemException class is for system-defined exceptions. The Exception class is the base class for both ApplicationException and SystemException classes and should not generally be derived from directly.

2. **C.** When you have multiple Catch blocks associated with a Try block, you must write them in order from the most specific to the most general one. The Catch block corresponding to the ArithmeticException should come at the end because it is a more general class than the three (DivideByZeroException, NotFiniteNumberException and the OverFlowException) classes derived from it.

3. **B.** When an exception occurs in a Try block, it will search for a matching Catch block associated with that Try block. In this case, the ArithmeticException generates a match for DivideByZeroException because DivideByZeroException is derived from ArithmeticException, and the exception is handled right there. In all cases the Finally block is executed.

4. **D.** The message box displays System.ArgumentOutOfRangeException because you caught and wrapped that exception in the InnerException property of the exception caught later by the outer Catch block.

5. **A.** When you want to retain the focus inside a control after the Validating event is processed, you must set the Cancel property of the CancelEventArgs argument in the Validating event, so the correct answer is e.Cancel = True. The CausesValidation property has a different purpose: It decides whether a Validating event will be fired for a control.

6. **C.** The CharacterCasing property when set to CharacterCasing.Lower for a text box will convert all uppercase letters to lowercase as you type them. It is the preferred way to enforce either lowercase or uppercase input in a text box.

APPLY YOUR KNOWLEDGE

7. **A, C.** The best practices for exception handling recommend that you end the name of your exception class with the word Exception. In addition, an exception class must implement three standard contructors. The missing constructor is the one given in option **C.**

8. **C.** When you want a control to respond regardless of the validation statuses of other controls, set the CausesValidation property of that control to True. Then the Help button should have its CausesValidation property set to False.

9. **D.** The StackTrace property of the Exception class and the classes that derive from it contains information about the sequence of method calls and the line numbers in which the exception occurred. Therefore, it is the right property to use.

10. **A.** The Throw statement just catches and throws the current exception.

11. **C.** It is obvious that user can make typing mistakes while typing her username or password. You should not throw exceptions for these situations; you should rather design a ValidateUser method that returns a result indicating whether the login was successful.

12. **D.** To capture all unhandled exceptions for an application, you must program the UnhandledEvent event handler of its AppDomian class.

13. **A.** Logging to the Windows event handler is the most robust solution because the other solutions have more assumptions that can fail. Sometimes your application can loose connectivity with the database or with the SMTP server, or you might have problems writing an entry in a custom log file.

14. **A, B, C, D.** The .NET Framework allows you to handle all types of exceptions including cross-language exceptions for both CLS- and nonCLS-complaint languages. It also allows you to handle exceptions from unmanaged code, both COM and nonCOM.

15. **C.** Since you are multiplying two maximum possible values for integers, the result cannot be stored inside an integer. The compiler will detect it and will flag a compile-time error.

Suggested Readings and Resources

1. Ritcher, Jeffery. *Applied Microsoft .NET Framework Programming.* Microsoft Press, 2001.

2. Siler, Brian and Jeff Spotts. *Special Edition Using Visual Basic .NET.* Que, 2002.

3. Visual Studio .NET Combined Help Collection

   - Best Practices for Exception Handling
   - Exception Handling Statements
   - Exception Management in .NET

This chapter covers the following Microsoft-specified objectives for the Creating and Managing Components and .NET Assemblies section of the Visual Basic .NET Windows-Based Applications exam:

Create a Windows control.

- **Create a Windows control by using visual inheritance.**

- **Host a Windows control inside Microsoft Internet Explorer.**

▶ The Microsoft .NET Framework allows programmers to create many types of reusable components. This objective requires you to know how to create components that derive from the three important base classes for controls: Component, Control, and UserControl. The Microsoft .NET Framework also supports extensibility by allowing you to create new controls that extend the functionality of existing controls through a technique known as Visual Inheritance. In addition to hosting controls in a Windows Form, you should also know how to host them in Microsoft Internet Explorer.

Create and modify a .NET assembly.

- **Create and implement satellite assemblies.**

- **Create resource-only assemblies.**

▶ Assemblies are the basic .NET unit for reuse, versioning, security, and deployment of components and applications. This objective requires you to know about creating and modifying assemblies. This chapter will help you learn various important concepts related to assemblies, such as private and shared assemblies, single-file and multifile assemblies, and resource-only and satellite assemblies.

CHAPTER 4

Creating and Managing Components and .NET Assemblies

This chapter also covers the following Microsoft-specified objective for the Creating User Services section of the Visual Basic .NET Windows-Based Applications exam:

Create, implement, and handle events.

▶ User interface programming in a Windows-based application is mostly event driven. Events allow you to respond to changes in the environment of your application. In this exam objective you are required to know how to create and implement your own events.

▶ Review the "Component Authoring Walkthroughs" and the "Component Authoring— Decision Chart" sections of the Visual Studio .NET Combined Help Collection. The Visual Studio .NET Combined Help Collection is installed as part of the Visual Studio .NET installation.

▶ Create reusable components in the different ways described in the chapter and inspect the differences between them. Host these components in a form and test the components.

▶ Experiment with creating controls by inheriting from existing user-created controls through Visual Inheritance.

▶ Practice hosting Windows controls in Microsoft Internet Explorer.

▶ Experiment with creating your own events and implementing them.

▶ Review the "Programming with Assemblies" and the "Creating Satellite Assemblies" sections of the Visual Studio .NET Combined Help Collection.

▶ Know how to create and manage different types of assemblies in the .NET Framework.

▶ Experiment with creating satellite assemblies. You'll find information about satellite assemblies in Chapter 8, "Globalization," as well as in this chapter.

INTRODUCTION

Visual Basic .NET provides a rich collection of components. You can use these components to quickly create user interfaces and functionality for your Windows applications. For more advanced or customized functionality, you can also create your own custom components or purchase them from a component vendor. These custom-created components can encapsulate user interface and business logic and can be directly plugged in to your application.

The .NET Framework allows you to create components in several different ways:

◆ You can create a nonvisual component by deriving from the Component class.

◆ You can create a control that draws its own User Interface by deriving from the Control class or any of its derived classes.

◆ You can create a composite control based on other existing controls by deriving from the UserControl class or any of its derived classes.

Using Visual Basic .NET helps you extend the user interface functionality by allowing you to create new controls that inherit from existing Windows controls. This technique is called *Visual Inheritance*.

Such components cannot run by themselves. They need to be hosted in a container. The preferred place to host Windows controls is on a Windows Form, though you can also host controls inside Microsoft Internet Explorer.

Assemblies are the basic unit for reuse, versioning, security, and deployment for components created using the .NET Framework. An *assembly* is a collection of types and resources that together form a logical unit of functionality. Different types of assemblies that you should be aware of include single-file and multifile assemblies, private and shared assemblies, static and dynamic assemblies, and satellite and resource-only assemblies.

In this chapter I'll show how to create and manage components, events, and assemblies in your .NET applications.

CREATING AND MANAGING .NET COMPONENTS

Create a Windows control.

You can create components in the .NET Framework from three main classes:

- ◆ The Component class
- ◆ The Control class
- ◆ The UserControl class

The most general of these three classes is the Component class. It is the base class for all components in the .NET Framework. The Component class belongs to the System.ComponentModel namespace. You can derive directly from the Component class to create nonvisual components such as the Timer component or the EventLog component.

The Control class extends the Component class and enables you to create components with visual representations. The Control class belongs to the System.Windows.Forms namespace. Most of the Windows controls, including Form, Label, and Button, inherit from this class. The Control class by itself gives very basic functionality, including getting user input through keyboard and mouse, participating in the message loop that allows event handling, and security.

You might also want to design a control by assembling existing controls. In this case, you won't need a custom Paint method. Instead, the goal is to assemble custom functionality by having a group of controls work together. The .NET Framework provides the UserControl class for this purpose. The UserControl class belongs to the System.Windows.Forms namespace.

The UserControl class provides an empty control. You can create a new control by assembling existing controls on the surface of a UserControl. The UserControl class derives from the ContainerControl class that in turn indirectly derives from the Control class. Because the UserControl class is derived from the ContainerControl class, it is capable of acting as a container control.

> **EXAM TIP**
>
> **Control Class and Painting**   The Control class does not implement any method to paint controls, so when you derive from this class, you need to implement your own rendering logic by overriding the Paint method of the Control class. This is a desirable thing if you want to design a control with a different user interface from common Windows controls.

When you create a class deriving directly or indirectly from the Component class, you create a .NET component. I'll use the term control for components deriving from the Control class or any of its child classes (that includes the UserControl class). I will refer the components that do not render any user interface simply as components.

In this section, I'll start by discussing how to create a control based on the UserControl class. Later I'll discuss how can you design controls that derive from the Control class and render their own UI. Finally, I'll show how to create a nonvisual component by deriving directly from the Component class.

Creating Components by Extending the UserControl Class

To create a control using Visual Studio .NET, you will create a Windows Control Library project. This type of project allows you to package one or more controls in a .dll file. This .dll file can be then used by other applications to instantiate the controls contained within it.

By default Visual Studio .NET helps create controls based on the UserControl class. When you create the Control Library Project, it will automatically add a class derived from UserControl to the project. The Design view for this class shows a borderless, captionless gray area where you can assemble your control by selecting controls from the toolbox.

I'll start in Step By Step 4.1 by creating a ColorMixer control. This control allows you to select the Red, Green, and Blue values to create a desired color.

NOTE

Working with Multiple Projects I'll organize project files in this chapter in a way different from the earlier chapters because I'm going to create various types of projects in this chapter. I'll create a solution for this chapter and create a project in the solution for each Step By Step.

STEP BY STEP

4.1 Creating Components by Extending the UserControl Class

1. Launch Visual Studio .NET, Select File, New, Blank Solution and name the new solution 306C04.

---

2. In the Solution Explorer window, right-click the name of the solution and select Add, New Project. Select Visual Basic projects from the Project Types tree and then select Windows Control Library from the list of templates on the right. Name the project StepByStep4-1. You will see that the designer shows the control as a captionless, borderless form.

3. In the Solution Explorer window, change the name of the UserControl1.vb file to ColorMixer.vb. Right-click the control surface and select View Code from its context menu. Change the name of the class in the code from UserControl1 to ColorMixer.

4. Drag and drop a GroupBox control, three Label controls and three TrackBar controls from the toolbox to the UserControl design surface. Arrange them as shown in Figure 4.1. Name the TrackBar controls tbRed, tbGreen and tbBlue. Change their Maximum property to 255, their Orientation to Vertical, their TickFrequency to 15, and their TickStyle to Both.

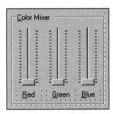

FIGURE 4.1
Creating a ColorMixer User Control.

5. Switch to the Code view. Add a namespace reference at the top of the class:

```
Imports System.ComponentModel
```

6. Add code to create three properties for the control and link them to properties of the constituent controls:

```
<Category("Color"), Description("Value of Red Color")> _
Public Property Red() As Integer
    Get
        Red = tbRed.Value
    End Get
    Set(ByVal Value As Integer)
        tbRed.Value = Value
    End Set
End Property

<Category("Color"), Description("Value of Green Color")> _
Public Property Green() As Integer
    Get
        Green = tbGreen.Value
    End Get
```

continues

FIGURE 4.2
UserControl in Solution Explorer.

> **Z O T E**
>
> **Project Name and DLL Name**
> Although the DLL file is not required to
> have the same name as the project,
> Visual Studio .NET will keep them syn-
> chronized. If you want a different
> name, you can use the command-line
> compilation tools to generate the DLL
> file with any name you wish.

> **Z O T E**
>
> **Visual Studio .NET Editions**   The
> templates for creating Windows
> Control Library and the Class Library
> projects are not part of the Visual
> Studio .NET Standard Edition feature
> set. You must have Visual Studio .NET
> Professional edition or higher to use
> these templates. You can still create
> such projects using the Framework
> SDK tools if you like, but you won't
> get the support of the Visual Studio
> .NET IDE.

---

continued

```
        Set(ByVal Value As Integer)
            tbGreen.Value = Value
        End Set
End Property

<Category("Color"), Description("Value of Blue Color")> _
Public Property Blue() As Integer
    Get
            Blue = tbBlue.Value
    End Get
    Set(ByVal Value As Integer)
            tbBlue.Value = Value
    End Set
End Property
```

7. Select Build, Build StepByStep4-1 from the main menu.
   This step generates the code for your control and packages
   it into a StepByStep4-1.dll. The DLL file is located in the
   bin directory of your project. You can navigate to it
   through the Solution Explorer window. Select the project
   and click the Show All Files button in the Solution
   Explorer toolbar, as shown in Figure 4.2.

When you build the project, it creates a DLL file named
StepByStep4-1.dll. This DLL file contains the code for the
ColorMixer control.

Although in the previous example StepByStep4-1.dll contains the
definition of only one control, you're not limited to one control per
library. You can always add more control definitions by adding more
user controls to the project.

Although Step By Step 4.1 creates the control, you can't see it in
action yet for two reasons. First, a control can't exist by itself. It
needs to be placed inside a parent container control such as a
Windows Form. Second, the code in DLL files can't instantiate itself
as no Sub Main or other entry point is in the DLL.

In Step By Step 4.2, I'll create a Windows Application project that
hosts the ColorMixer control on a form.

STEP BY STEP

4.2 Hosting the ColorMixer Control in a Windows Application

1. Right-click the solution name in Solution Explorer and select Add, Add New Project from its menu. Select Windows Application as the template for the new project and name it `StepByStep4-2`.

2. In the Solution Explorer window, right-click Form1.vb and rename it `TestColorMixer.vb`. Open the Properties window for this form and change its name and `Text` properties to `TestColorMixer`.

3. In the Solution Explorer window, right-click project StepByStep4-2 and select Add Reference from its context menu. In the Add Reference dialog box, select the Projects tab, select the Project Name StepByStep4-1 from the list view, and click the Select button (see Figure 4.3). The selected Project will be copied to the Selected Components list. Click OK. You will now see a reference to StepByStep4-1 in the Reference node of your project in Solution Explorer, as shown in Figure 4.4.

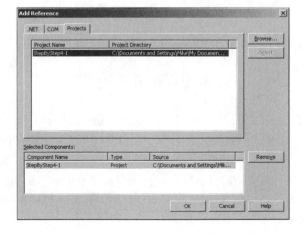

FIGURE 4.3
Add Reference dialog box.

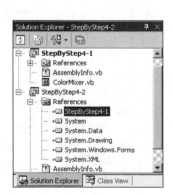

FIGURE 4.4
Solution Explorer showing the reference added to the project.

continues

continued

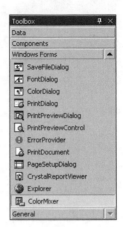

FIGURE 4.5
Toolbox showing the ColorMixer user control.

4. Scroll down the list of controls in the Windows Forms section of the toolbox until you find a control named ColorMixer, as shown in Figure 4.5. Double-click the control to add it to the form. Accept the default name ColorMixer1 for the control and activate the Properties window. Arrange the properties by category by clicking the Categorized toolbar button on the Properties window. Look for the Color Category and set the Red, Green, and Blue properties to 100 each as shown in Figure 4.6.

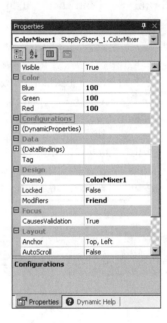

FIGURE 4.6
Properties window showing the properties of the Color Category.

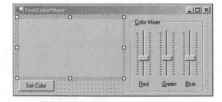

FIGURE 4.7
Form to test ColorMixer control.

5. Add a Label control named lblColorSample and a Button control named btnSetColor to the form and arrange the controls as shown in Figure 4.7.

6. Double-click the Button control to attach an event handler to the Click event and add the following code to the handler:

```
Private Sub btnSetColor_Click( _
 ByVal sender As System.Object, _
 ByVal e As System.EventArgs) Handles btnSetColor.Click
    lblColorSample.BackColor = _
     Color.FromArgb(ColorMixer1.Red, _
       ColorMixer1.Green, ColorMixer1.Blue)
End Sub
```

7. In the Solution Explorer window, right-click the name of the solution and select Properties. In the Solution Property pages, select StepByStep4-2 as the Single Startup Project. Click OK. Set TestColorMixer as the start object for the StepByStep4-2 project.

8. Run the project. You will see the form hosting a ColorMixer control. You can work with the Red, Green, and Blue track bars to select the color values and then click the Set Color button. The label will show the color made from the Red, Green, and Blue values you selected.

The previous Step By Step demonstrated that a custom-created control can be used just like any standard Windows Form control. You can drag and drop it from the toolbox to the form's surface and set its properties just like those of any standard Windows control.

But think about the functionality of this example for a moment. Wouldn't it be nice if the form could automatically reflect changes in the control as they happen? You'd like the label to somehow subscribe to changes in the ColorMixer control and have its BackColor changed as soon as there is any change in the ColorMixer. That would eliminate the need to press the button every time after making changes.

You can't do this by simply handling the events of the TrackBar controls, because the TrackBars are private controls within the ColorMixer control and not accessible outside the ColorMixer control. The solution is to have the class ColorMixer publish a Changed event, so that all interested classes could subscribe to it. I'll tell you how to do that in the next section.

REVIEW BREAK

▶ The Microsoft .NET Framework allows programmers to create reusable code components. You can create a Windows component for use on forms by deriving from Component, Control, or UserControl classes or any of their derived classes.

▶ If you want to create a control by assembling existing controls and wish to add custom-defined functionality to them, you should inherit from the UserControl class. You should create a Windows Control Library template to create a user control.

continues

continued

> ► You can drag and drop a custom component from the toolbox to a form's surface and set its properties just as you can with any standard Windows component.

Creating and Implementing Events

Create, implement, and handle events.

Events in Visual Basic .NET are based on a publisher-subscriber model. The class that implements an event is called the publisher of the event. The publisher announces that other classes can subscribe to the event by attaching appropriate event handlers to the event. The class publishing the event will register all event handlers with itself and takes the responsibility of invoking them all when the event occurs.

An *event handler* is a method with a specific signature that the publisher class is capable of registering. By convention, most event handlers take two arguments. The first argument specifies the object on which the event occurred (in other words, the publisher of event), and the second argument contains information related to the event; the second argument is an object of a type EventArgs or of a class derived from EventArgs. For example, here's how you might define a ColorMixerEventArgs class that contains information about the event occuring on ColorMixer control:

```
Public Class ColorMixerEventArgs
    Inherits EventArgs
    Public ReadOnly Red, Green, Blue As Integer
    Public Sub New(ByVal Red As Integer, _
     ByVal Green As Integer, _
     ByVal Blue As Integer)
        Me.Red = Red
        Me.Green = Green
        Me.Blue = Blue
    End Sub
End Class
```

By convention, a class derived from EventArgs is assigned a name ending with EventArgs. When a Changed event occurs in the ColorMixer control, it would like to pass the Red, Green, and Blue color values to its subscribers. So the above class does exactly that: It derives from EventArgs, and its constructor provides a mechanism to store event-related data in its object.

Events in Visual Basic .NET are implemented using delegates. A
delegate is a special class whose object is capable of storing references
to methods of a particular signature. If you have a background of
C/C++ programming, you'll recognize delegates as similar to function pointers. In Visual Basic .NET, a delegate is defined like this:

```
' Define the prototype of the callback method
Public Delegate Sub ChangedEventHandler( _
 ByVal sender As Object, _
 ByVal args As ColorMixerEventArgs)
```

The signature of the delegate essentially specifies the signature of the
event handler methods that it can generate a call-back on.

The event itself is declared using the type of the appropriate
delegate:

```
' Define the event
Public Event Changed As ChangedEventHandler
```

The event member internally manages a linked list of delegates.
When an event occurs, it will scan this linked list and invoke the
event handler identified by the delegate object for each item in the
list.

When the actual event occurs, the class that publishes the event
takes the responsibility of notifying all its subscribers that the event
occurred by executing the event handlers attached to it. The following code example shows how the publisher class does this:

```
' Notify the registered objects of event
Protected Sub OnChanged(ByVal e As ColorMixerEventArgs)
    RaiseEvent Changed(Me, e)
End Sub
```

When the actual event occurs, the publisher class just needs to call
this OnChanged method. The RaiseEvent keyword handles the job
of checking to see whether any event handlers are registered for the
event and passes the supplied objects to each of them.

When a subscriber wishes to subscribe an event, it needs to take the
following steps:

1. Implement an event handler with the signature specified by
   the delegate object of the event.

2. Attach the event handler to the event. You can do this with
   the Handles keyword or with the AddHandler method, as you
   saw in Chapter 2, "Controls."

In Step By Step 4.3, I'll create a new version of the ColorMixer control that I'll call ColorMixerWithEvents. This version will implement a Changed event in the control using the techniques I just discussed.

STEP BY STEP

4.3 Creating a User Control That Publishes Events

1. Create a new project in this chapter's solution using the Windows Control Library template. Name the project StepByStep4-3. Delete the default UserControl1.vb class from the new project.

---

2. Using the Solution Explorer window, drag the ColorMixer.vb control from StepByStep4-1 to this project. While dragging, hold the Ctrl key so that the control is copied to the current project instead of being moved. Change the name of the control to ColorMixerWithEvents.vb. Switch to the Code view and change all instances of ColorMixer to ColorMixerWithEvents.

---

3. Add the following code at the end of class ColorMixerWithEvents:

```
Public Class ColorMixerEventArgs
    Inherits EventArgs
    Public ReadOnly Red, Green, Blue As Integer
    Public Sub New(ByVal Red As Integer, _
     ByVal Green As Integer, _
     ByVal Blue As Integer)
        Me.Red = Red
        Me.Green = Green
        Me.Blue = Blue
    End Sub
End Class

' Define the prototype of the callback method
Public Delegate Sub ChangedEventHandler( _
 ByVal sender As Object, _
 ByVal args As ColorMixerEventArgs)
```

```
' Define the event
Public Event Changed As ChangedEventHandler

' Notify the registered objects of event
Protected Sub OnChanged(ByVal e As ColorMixerEventArgs)
    RaiseEvent Changed(Me, e)
End Sub

Private Sub tbRed_ValueChanged(ByVal sender As Object, _
 ByVal e As System.EventArgs) Handles tbRed.ValueChanged
    Dim args As ColorMixerEventArgs = _
     New ColorMixerEventArgs(tbRed.Value, _
     tbGreen.Value, tbBlue.Value)
    OnChanged(args)
End Sub

Private Sub tbGreen_ValueChanged(ByVal sender As Object, _
 ByVal e As System.EventArgs) Handles tbGreen.ValueChanged
    Dim args As ColorMixerEventArgs = _
     New ColorMixerEventArgs(tbRed.Value, _
     tbGreen.Value, tbBlue.Value)
    OnChanged(args)
End Sub

Private Sub tbblue_ValueChanged(ByVal sender As Object, _
 ByVal e As System.EventArgs) Handles tbBlue.ValueChanged
    Dim args As ColorMixerEventArgs = _
     New ColorMixerEventArgs(tbRed.Value, _
     tbGreen.Value, tbBlue.Value)
    OnChanged(args)
End Sub
```

4. Select the project StepByStep4-3 in the Solution Explorer and select Build, Build Step By Step 4-3 from the main menu to generate a StepByStep4-3.dll file that contains the code for ColorMixerWithEvents.

Step By Step 4.3 created a class that publishes a Changed event. Step By Step 4.4 creates a Windows Application that will host this class and subscribe to its Changed event. You'll get additional practice in publishing and subscribing to events in Guided Practice Exercise 4.1.

STEP BY STEP

4.4 Creating a Windows Application That Subscribes to Events

1. Create a new Windows Application project in your solution and name it StepByStep4-4.

2. In the Solution Explorer window, right-click Form1.vb and rename it TestColorMixerWithEvents. Open the Properties window for this form and change its Name and Text properties to TestColorMixerWithEvents.

3. In the toolbox, click the Windows Form section and scroll down the list of Windows Form controls until you find a control named ColorMixerWithEvents. Double-click the control to add it to the form and automatically add a reference to the appropriate project as well. Accept the default name of the control, ColorMixerWithEvents1. Add a GroupBox control and a Label control named lblColorSample to the form. Set the Label control's Dock property to Fill and arrange the controls as shown in Figure 4.8.

4. Add code to handle the Changed event for the ColorMixerWithEvents1 control:

```
Private Sub ColorMixerWithEvents1_Changed( _
 ByVal sender As Object, _
 ByVal args As StepByStep4_3.ColorMixerWithEvents. _
 ColorMixerEventArgs) _
 Handles ColorMixerWithEvents1.Changed
    lblColorSample.BackColor = _
     Color.FromArgb(args.Red, args.Green, args.Blue)
End Sub
```

5. Set the form as the startup object for the project. Right-click the project in Solution Explorer and select Set As Startup Project from its context menu.

6. Run the Project to see the form hosting the ColorMixerWithEvents control. Work with the Red, Green, and Blue track bars to select the color values. You will see that the label control changes its color as you change the value of any track bar.

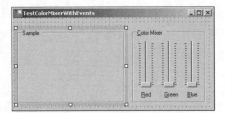

FIGURE 4.8
A form to test events from a custom UserControl.

▶ A Delegate is a special type that can store a reference to a method having a specific signature. Events are objects whose type is Delegate.

▶ To create and implement an event, you must take the following steps:

1. Define the EventArgs class that will contain the event-related data. This is required only if you want to pass specific event-related information to the event handlers.

2. Create a Delegate object that can store a reference to the event handler.

3. Define the event itself as an object of delegate type.

4. Define a method that notifies the registered objects of the event. Usually this method has name such as OnChanged, where *Changed* is the event name.

5. Call the method defined in the above step whenever the event occurs.

GUIDED PRACTICE
EXERCISE 4.1

In this exercise you will create a composite control by assembling two command buttons as shown in Figure 4.9. You should be able to drag the buttons at runtime and generate two events, CrashEnter and CrashLeave. The CrashEnter event will be fired when the two buttons overlap each other. The CrashLeave event will be fired when the overlap is removed. You will host this control on a Windows Form, where you will display a red message saying Crash! whenever the control overlaps and will clear the message when the overlapping is removed.

continues

continued

Try this on your own first. If you get stuck or would like to see one possible solution, follow these steps:

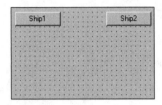

FIGURE 4.9
Creating the ButtonShips control.

1. Create a new project using the Windows Control Library template in the solution for this chapter. Name the project `GuidedPracticeExercise4-1`.

2. In the Solution Explorer window, change the name of theUserControl1.vb file to ButtonShips.vb. Right-click the control surface and select View Code from its context menu. Change the name of the class from UserControl1 to ButtonShips.

3. Place two Button controls (`btnShip1` and `btnShip2`) on the form as shown in Figure 4.9.

4. Switch to Code view and define the following variables:

   ```
   ' Specifies whether mousebutton is pressed or not
   Private isMouseDown As Boolean
   ' Stores the position of last mouse movement
   Private ptLast As Point
   ' Are the buttons overlapping?
   Private inCrash As Boolean
   ```

5. Double-click the control and add the following code to the `Load` event handler of the control:

   ```
   Private Sub ButtonShips_Load( _
    ByVal sender As System.Object, _
    ByVal e As System.EventArgs) Handles MyBase.Load
        ' Put the buttons in default locations
        btnShip1.Location = New Point(0, 0)
        btnShip2.Location = New Point( _
         Me.Width - btnShip2.Width, 0)
   End Sub
   ```

6. Add the following code to the class definition to create the events `CrashEnter` and `CrashLeave` and the methods `OnCrashEnter` and `OnCrashLeave` that will help notify subscribers when the events occur. Note that the events use the default `EventHandler` delegate type provided by the .NET Framework:

   ```
   ' Define the CrashEnter event
   Public Event CrashEnter As EventHandler

   ' Notify any registered objects of the CrashEnter event
   Protected Sub OnCrashEnter(ByVal e As EventArgs)
       RaiseEvent CrashEnter(Me, e)
   End Sub
   ```

```
' Define the CrashLeave event
Public Event CrashLeave As EventHandler

' Notify any registered objects of the CrashLeave event
Protected Sub OnCrashLeave(ByVal e As EventArgs)
    RaiseEvent CrashLeave(Me, e)
End Sub
```

7. Add the following `AnyButton_MouseDown`, `AnyButton_MouseUp` and `AnyButton_MouseMove` event handlers to the class:

```
Private Sub AnyButton_MouseDown(ByVal sender As Object, _
 ByVal e As System.Windows.Forms.MouseEventArgs)
    isMouseDown = True
    ' Save the position of mouse down
    ptLast = New Point(e.X, e.Y)
End Sub

Private Sub AnyButton_MouseUp(ByVal sender As Object, _
 ByVal e As System.Windows.Forms.MouseEventArgs)
    isMouseDown = False
End Sub

Private Sub AnyButton_MouseMove(ByVal sender As Object, _
 ByVal e As System.Windows.Forms.MouseEventArgs)
    If Not isMouseDown Then
        Exit Sub
    End If

    ' Find the button causing the move operation
    Dim btn As Button = CType(sender, Button)

    ' Set the button's new positions
    btn.Top = btn.Top + (e.Y - ptLast.Y)
    btn.Left = btn.Left + (e.X - ptLast.X)

    Dim btn1Rect As Rectangle = _
     New Rectangle(btnShip1.Location, btnShip1.Size)
    Dim btn2Rect As Rectangle = _
     New Rectangle(btnShip2.Location, btnShip2.Size)

    ' Check for intersection or lack thereof
    If btn1Rect.IntersectsWith(btn2Rect) Then
        If Not inCrash Then
            Me.OnCrashEnter(New EventArgs())
            inCrash = True
        End If
    Else
        If (inCrash) Then
            Me.OnCrashLeave(New EventArgs())
            inCrash = False
        End If
    End If
End Sub
```

continues

continued

8. Add code to the control's `New` procedure to attach the event handlers to the MouseDown, MouseUp, and MouseMove events of the two buttons:

```
Public Sub New()
    MyBase.New()

    'This call is required by the Windows Form Designer.
    InitializeComponent()

    ' Add any initialization after
    ' the InitializeComponent() call
    AddHandler btnShip1.MouseDown, _
     AddressOf AnyButton_MouseDown
    AddHandler btnShip1.MouseUp, _
     AddressOf AnyButton_MouseUp
    AddHandler btnShip1.MouseMove, _
     AddressOf AnyButton_MouseMove
    AddHandler btnShip2.MouseDown, _
     AddressOf AnyButton_MouseDown
    AddHandler btnShip2.MouseUp, _
     AddressOf AnyButton_MouseUp
    AddHandler btnShip2.MouseMove, _
     AddressOf AnyButton_MouseMove

End Sub
```

9. Select Build, Build GuidedPracticeExercise4-1 from the main menu. This step generates the code for your control and packages it into a GuidedPracticeExercise4-1.dll. The DLL file is located in the bin directory of your project.

10. Add a new project to the solution. Select the Windows Application template and name the project `GuidedPracticeExercise4-1Test`.

11. In the Solution Explorer window, right-click Form1.vb and rename it as TestButtonShips. Open the Properties window for this form and change its Name and Text properties to TestButtonShips. Switch to the Code view of the form and change the class name to `TestButtonShips` instead of Form1.

12. Using the Solution Explorer window, add a reference to GuidedPracticeExercuse4-1.dll.

13. Add a GroupBox control and a Label control named `lblResults` control to the form. Place a ButtonShips control in the group box and set its Dock property to Fill. Arrange the controls as shown in Figure 4.10.

14. Attach event handlers for the `CrashEnter` and `CrashLeave` events of the ButtonShips control and add the following code to the event handlers:

```
Private Sub ButtonShips1_CrashEnter( _
 ByVal sender As Object, _
 ByVal e As System.EventArgs) _
 Handles ButtonShips1.CrashEnter
     lblResults.Text = "Crash!"
End Sub

Private Sub ButtonShips1_CrashLeave( _
 ByVal sender As Object, _
 ByVal e As System.EventArgs) _
 Handles ButtonShips1.CrashLeave
     lblResults.Text = ""
End Sub
```

15. Set the form as the startup object for the project, and the GuidedPracticeExercise4-1Test project as the startup project for the solution.

16. Run the project to see the form hosting the ButtonShips control. Drag the Ship1 and Ship2 buttons around the form. Whenever they overlap the label displays `Crash!` as shown in Figure 4.10. The label erases when they are moved away from each other.

FIGURE 4.10
ButtonShips control in action.

Extending a Control Through Visual Inheritance

Create a Windows control: Create a Windows control by using visual inheritance

Recall from Chapter 1, "Introducing Windows Forms," that it is possible to inherit a form from another form. When you inherit, you get all the functionality of the base form, allowing you to reuse its design and code. The same concept of inheritance also applies to controls. The technique of inheriting one visual object from another visual object is also known as *Visual Inheritance*.

To demonstrate how Visual Inheritance can help in extending the functionality of existing controls, I'll create a new control that derives from ColorMixerWithEvents and add a color sampler to it (see Step By Step 4.5).

FIGURE 4.11
Inheritance Picker dialog box.

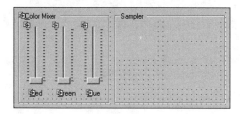

FIGURE 4.12
Inherited user control with new controls added.

STEP BY STEP

4.5 Extending a Control Through Visual Inheritance

1. Create a new project based on the Windows Control Library template and name it StepByStep4-5.

2. Right-click the UserControl1.vb file and select Delete from the context menu.

3. Right-click the project name and select Add, Add Inherited Control. Name the control ColorMixerX.vb and click the Open button. From the Inheritance Picker dialog box select the component named ColorMixerWithEvents as shown in Figure 4.11. Click the OK button to see a control surface that includes the contents of the ColorMixerWithEvents control.

4. Add a GroupBox and four Label controls (lblSampler, lblRed, lblGreen, and lblBlue) as shown in Figure 4.12. Change the Text property of the GroupBox control to Sampler and change the Text property of the Label controls to an empty string.

5. Switch to the Code view and add the following lines of code in the control's constructor after the call to the IntializeComponent method:

```
' Set the initial display for the control
    lblSampler.BackColor = _
    Color.FromArgb(Me.Red, Me.Green, Me.Blue)
    lblRed.Text = String.Format("R: {0}", Me.Red)
    lblGreen.Text = String.Format("G: {0}", Me.Green)
    lblBlue.Text = String.Format("B: {0}", Me.Blue)
```

6. Add this code to handle the Changed event of the control:

```
Private Sub ColorMixerX_Changed(ByVal sender As Object, _
 ByVal args As StepByStep4_3. _
 ColorMixerWithEvents.ColorMixerEventArgs) _
```

```
Handles MyBase.Changed
    lblSampler.BackColor = _
     Color.FromArgb(args.Red, args.Green, args.Blue)
    lblRed.Text = String.Format("R: {0}", args.Red)
    lblGreen.Text = String.Format("G: {0}", args.Green)
    lblBlue.Text = String.Format("B: {0}", args.Blue)
End Sub
```

7. Select Build, Build Step By Step 4-5 from the main menu to generate a StepByStep4-5.dll file that contains the code for ColorMixtureX control.

Now I'll test the inherited control ColorMixerX in Step By Step 4.6.

STEP BY STEP

4.6 Creating a Windows Application That Hosts the Inherited Control

1. Add a new Windows Application project and name it `StepByStep4-6`.

2. In the Solution Explorer window, right-click Form1.vb and rename it as `TestColorMixerX`. Open the Properties window for this form and change its `Name` and `Text` properties to `TestColorMixerX`. Switch to the Code view of the form and change the class name to `TestColorMixerX` instead of `Form1`.

3. Using the Solution Explorer window, add a reference to StepByStep4_5.dll.

4. Drag the ColorMixerX control from the toolbox and drop it on the form. Add a GroupBox control and a Label control (`lblDrawingBoard`) to the group box. Change the label's `BackColor` property to System, Window and its `Dock` property to Fill. Arrange the controls as shown in Figure 4.13.

5. Switch to the Code view and add the following statement at the top of the code:

```
Imports System.Drawing.Drawing2D
```

continues

continued

6. Add the following code that declares some new variables and modify the form's constructor as shown:

```
' Specifies whether mouse button is pressed
Dim isMouseDown As Boolean
' Stores the position of the last mouse movement
Dim ptLast As Point
' Stores the current color
Dim clrSelected As Color

Public Sub New()
    MyBase.New()

    'This call is required by the Windows Form Designer.
    InitializeComponent()

    ' Set the value of color when form is initialized
    clrSelected = Color.FromArgb( _
     ColorMixerX1.Red, ColorMixerX1.Green, _
     ColorMixerX1.Blue)
End Sub
```

7. Add the following code to the event handler for the Changed event of the ColorMixerX1 control:

```
Private Sub ColorMixerX1_Changed(ByVal sender As Object, _
 ByVal args As StepByStep4_3. _
 ColorMixerWithEvents.ColorMixerEventArgs) _
 Handles ColorMixerX1.Changed
    clrSelected = Color.FromArgb(ColorMixerX1.Red, _
     ColorMixerX1.Green, ColorMixerX1.Blue)
End Sub
```

8. Add code to handle mouse events on the lblDrawingBoard control:

```
Private Sub lblDrawingBoard_MouseDown( _
 ByVal sender As Object, _
 ByVal e As System.Windows.Forms.MouseEventArgs) _
 Handles lblDrawingBoard.MouseDown
    isMouseDown = True
    ptLast = New Point(e.X, e.Y)
End Sub

Private Sub lblDrawingBoard_MouseMove( _
 ByVal sender As Object, _
 ByVal e As System.Windows.Forms.MouseEventArgs) _
 Handles lblDrawingBoard.MouseMove
    If Not isMouseDown Then
        Exit Sub
    End If
```

```
    Dim ptCurr As Point = New Point(e.X, e.Y)
    Dim g As Graphics = Me.lblDrawingBoard.CreateGraphics()
    g.SmoothingMode = SmoothingMode.AntiAlias
    g.DrawLine(New Pen(clrSelected, 2), ptLast, ptCurr)
    ptLast = ptCurr
    g.Dispose()

End Sub

Private Sub lblDrawingBoard_MouseUp( _
 ByVal sender As Object, _
 ByVal e As System.Windows.Forms.MouseEventArgs) _
 Handles lblDrawingBoard.MouseUp
    isMouseDown = False
End Sub
```

9. Set the form as the startup object for the project and set the project as the startup project for the solution.

10. Run the project to see the form hosting a ColorMixerX control. Select your preferred color from the ColorMixerX control to see that you can draw on the drawing board with the selected color, as shown in Figure 4.13

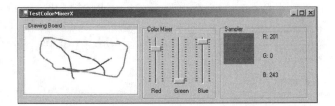

FIGURE 4.13
Picking a color from the ColorMixerX control to draw on the drawing board with the selected color.

Note that when you add a reference to StepByStep4_5.dll in this project, in addition to this file, Visual Studio .NET also copies the DLL containing its base class (StepByStep4_3.dll) to the bin folder. This is to ensure that all the classes in the inheritance chain are available at runtime.

Hosting a Windows Control Inside Internet Explorer

Create a Windows control: Host a Windows control inside Microsoft Internet Explorer.

In addition to hosting the controls in a Windows Form, you can host a Windows Forms control inside Internet Explorer (see Step By Step 4.7). Inside Internet Explorer the control is rendered as an object, but (unlike an ActiveX object) it requires no registration. The assembly containing the Windows control should reside either in Global Assembly Cache (which you'll learn more about later in this chapter) or in the same virtual directory where the Web page that renders the control is saved.

You need to take the following steps to host a Windows control in Internet Explorer:

◆ Create a virtual directory on the Web server that will deliver the control to the browser. Ensure that the directory has its permissions set to Scripts Only. If the permission is set as Scripts & Executables, your control might not work properly.

◆ Copy the assemblies (DLL file) that contains the control to the virtual directory if this assembly is not in the Global Assembly Cache.

◆ Create an HTML (or ASPX) document in the virtual directory and add an object tag referencing the control to the document. Assign the ClassID property, the assembly (DLL) path, and the name of the control to be hosted with a # (pound sign) between them as follows:

```
classid="http://localhost/306C04VD/
➥ StepByStep4_5.dll#StepByStep4_5.ColorMixerX"
```

STEP BY STEP

4.7 Hosting a Windows Control Inside Internet Explorer

1. Create a new directory 306C04VD under the c:\Inetpub\wwwroot path on your computer.

2. Open Internet Services Manager by selecting Start, Settings, Control Panel, Administrative Tools, Internet Services Manager. Double-click the Web server under which you want to create the virtual directory. Right-click the Web site and select New, Virtual Directory to open the Virtual Directory Creation Wizard. Read the Welcome message and click Next. The wizard will prompt for an alias for Virtual Directory. Type 306C04VD and click Next.

NOTE

IIS Versions   These directions assume that you're using IIS 5.0, as shipped with Windows 2000. The steps might differ slightly on IIS 6.0 in Windows .NET Server.

Type the path to the directory, `c:\Inetpub\wwwroot\306C04VD` in the Directory text box. You can also click the Browse button and browse through the directory. Click Next; you will be prompted to select access permissions for the directory. Select the default permissions as shown in Figure 4.14. Click Next and then Finish to complete the creation of the virtual directory.

3. Copy the StepByStep4-5.dll and StepByStep4-3.dll from the StepByStep4-5 project's bin directory into the 306C04VD directory.

4. Create a new HTML file `StepByStep4-7.htm` in the 306C04VD directory.

5. Insert the following code in the HTML file:

```
<html>
    <body>
        <object id="colorMixerX1"
            classid="http://localhost/306C04VD/
➥ StepByStep4-5.dll#StepByStep4_5.ColorMixerX"
            height="300" width="300">
        </object>
    </body>
</html>
```

6. Launch Internet Explorer, and type `http://localhost/306C04VD/StepByStep4-7.htm` into the Address bar. Note the ColorMixerX Windows Forms control hosted in the Internet Explorer as shown in Figure 4.15.

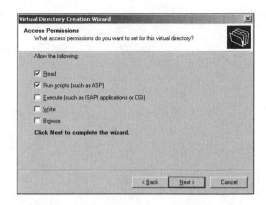

FIGURE 4.14
Access Permissions in the Virtual Directory Creation Wizard.

> **NOTE**
>
> **Web Server Required**   You'll need to have a Web server available to you to host Windows controls inside Microsoft Internet Explorer.

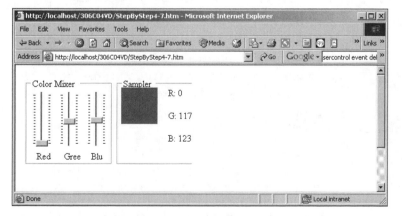

FIGURE 4.15
Internet Explorer hosting ColorMixerX Windows control.

Creating Components by Extending the Control Class

Another way to create a control is by extending it directly from the Control class instead of the UserControl class. You will most likely to do this when you want to design a control with a unique User Interface that you cannot just create by assembling existing controls.

When you create a control by extending it from the Control class, the control does not have any default UI. You must handle the control's Paint event to render its UI.

Visual Studio .NET does not provide any template to create a control directory from the Control class. To deal with this, I will use the template for the UserControl and modify it to extend from the Control class rather than the UserControl class.

In Step By Step 4.8, I'll demostrate the process of creating a custom control by designing a digital clock that renders its own user interface.

STEP BY STEP

4.8 Creating a Control That Renders Its Own User Interface

1. Create a new project based on the Windows Control Library template. Name the project `StepByStep4-8`.

2. Rename the UserControl1.vb file to `DigitalClock.vb`.

3. Switch to the Code view. Change the name of the class from UserControl1 to `DigitalClock`. Change the class declaration so that its base class is now `Control` instead of `System.Windows.Forms.UserControl`. After making changes the class header should look like this:

```
Public Class DigitalClock
    Inherits Control
```

4. Switch back to the Design view, and note that the gray, borderless box for creating controls is gone. Instead, a message will tell you to add components from the Server Explorer or the Toolbox window.

5. Open the toolbox and double-click a Timer control. Note that the message on the Design window vanishes and the Timer control is placed there. Set the `Enabled` property of the Timer control to True and the `Interval` property to `1000`. Add an event handler for the Timer control's `Tick` event:

```
Private Sub Timer1_Tick(ByVal sender As System.Object, _
 ByVal e As System.EventArgs) Handles Timer1.Tick
    Invalidate()
End Sub
```

6. Add an event handler for the DigitalClock control's `SizeChanged` event:

```
Private Sub DigitalClock_SizeChanged( _
 ByVal sender As Object, _
 ByVal e As System.EventArgs) Handles MyBase.SizeChanged
    Invalidate()
End Sub
```

7. Add an event handler for the `Paint` event of DigitalControl:

```
Private Sub DigitalClock_Paint(ByVal sender As Object, _
 ByVal e As System.Windows.Forms.PaintEventArgs) _
 Handles MyBase.Paint
    Dim g As Graphics = e.Graphics
    Dim strTime As String = DateTime.Now.ToString("T")

    ' Get the current string size
    Dim sf As SizeF = g.MeasureString(strTime, Font)

    ' Get the scaling factor
    Dim scale As Double = Math.Min( _
     ClientSize.Width / sf.Width, _
     ClientSize.Height / sf.Height)

    ' Scale the font as per new control size
    Dim f As Font = New Font(Font.FontFamily, _
     scale * Font.SizeInPoints)

    ' Get the string size for the scaled font size
    sf = g.MeasureString(strTime, Font)

    ' Find the position to draw the string
    Dim pos As PointF = New PointF(( _
     ClientSize.Width - sf.Width) / 2, _
     (ClientSize.Height - sf.Height) / 2)

    ' Draw the time string
    g.DrawString(strTime, Font, _
     New SolidBrush(ForeColor), pos)
End Sub
```

continues

continued

8. Select Build, Build StepByStep4-8 from the main menu to generate a StepByStep4-8.dll file that contains the code for DigitalClock control.

Note that, when you modify the UserControl template to extend the class from Control instead of UserControl, Visual Studio .NET will remove the borderless gray Control area. Also, when you place controls from the toolbox on the form, they will be placed on that big empty area with no particular placement and no visual representation of the underlying control.

Another important point from this exercise is the use of the event handler for the SizeChanged event of the control. The SizeChanged event is fired when you change the size of the control either at design-time or at runtime. If you don't include this event handler, when you resize the control after placing it in its container, it won't paint itself back corectly. I have included a call to the Invalidate method that will ensure that the Paint method is called every time the size of control is changed.

In Step By Step 4.9, I'll host the DigitalClock control in a Windows form.

STEP BY STEP

4.9 Creating a Windows Application That Hosts the DigitalClock

1. Add a new Windows Application project named `StepByStep4-9`.

2. In the Solution Explorer window, right-click Form1.vb and rename it as TestDigitalClock. Open the Properties window for this form and change its `Name` and `Text` properties to TestDigitalClock.

3. Using the Solutions Explorer window, add a reference for StepByStep4_8.dll.

4. Right-click the Toolbox window and select Add Tab. Name the new tab My Custom Controls. Right-click the My Custom Controls tab and select Customize Toolbox. Click the .NET Framework Components tab, and click the Browse button to add a reference to StepByStep4_8.dll. Click OK to add the DigitalClock control to the My Custom Controls tab in the toolbox.

5. Drag the DigitalClock control from the toolbox and drop it on the form. Resize the control and note that the control will repaint itself with text of appropriate size.

6. Set the project StepByStep4_9 as the Startup Project.

7. Run the Project to see the form hosting DigitalClock control showing the current time as in Figure 4.16.

FIGURE 4.16
Form showing the Digital Clock custom control.

You'll get additional practice in creating custom controls in Guided Practice Exercise 4.2, later in the chapter.

Creating Components by Extending the Component Class

When you don't need a visual representation for your components, you can extend them from the most basic component class, the Component class itself. A familiar example of a nonvisual component is the Timer component. It does not have any user interface to show on a form, but it does provide useful properties and events that can be used by its container to customize and control its behavior.

> **EXAM TIP**
>
> **Component Projects** Visual Studio .NET does not include a template to create a project for a Component. You can work around this by using a Class Library project template to create a project and then add a Component class to it. Step By Step 4.10 demonstrates this technique.

STEP BY STEP

4.10 Creating a RandomNumberGenerator Component

1. Create a new project based on the Class Library template and name it StepByStep4-10.

continues

continued

2. Select and right-click Class1.vb in the solution Explorer, and select Delete from the context menu to delete this file from the project.

3. In the Solution Explorer, right-click the project name (StepByStep4-10) and select Add, Add New Item. In the Add New Item dialog, select Component Class as the template for the item. Name it `RandomNumberGenerator.vb` as shown in Figure 4.17.

FIGURE 4.17
Adding a Component class.

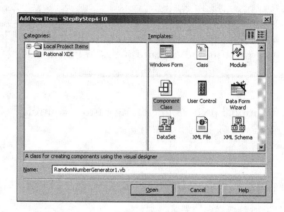

4. Add the following code just after the Component Designer generated code:

```
' Stores minValue and maxValue
Private mminValue As Integer = 1
Private mmaxValue As Integer = 100
```

5. Add the code for a pair of properties:

```
' Get or set the minimum value for the random number
Public Property MinValue() As Integer
    Get
        MinValue = mminValue
    End Get
    Set(ByVal Value As Integer)
        mminValue = Value
    End Set
End Property

' Get or set the maximum value for the random number
Public Property MaxValue() As Integer
    Get
        MaxValue = mmaxValue
    End Get
```

```
    Set(ByVal Value As Integer)
        mmaxValue = Value
    End Set
End Property
```

6. Add a method named `GetRandomNumber`:

```
Public Function GetRandomNumber() As Integer
    Dim r As Random = New Random()
    GetRandomNumber = r.Next(MinValue, MaxValue)
End Function
```

7. In the Solution Explorer window, navigate to the project StepByStep4-10 and right-click on Reference node. Select Add Reference from the context menu. In the Add Reference dialog double-click the component named System.Drawing.dll in the .NET tab and click OK, as shown in Figure 4.18. This will add a reference to System.Drawing.dll to this project.

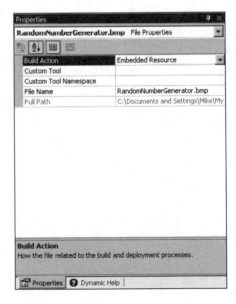

FIGURE 4.18
Adding a reference to a .NET DLL.

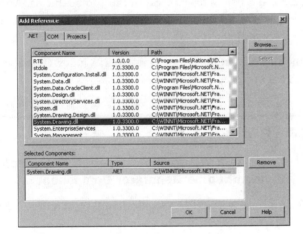

8. Insert a reference at the top of the code:

```
Imports System.Drawing
```

9. Select any 16×16 pixel BMP file (if you have a 16×16 ICO file just rename it to BMP). Change its name to `RandomNumberGenerator.bmp` and add it to the project. After the BMP file appears in the Solution Explorer window right-click it and select Properties from the menu. In the Properties sheet, set the Build Action to Embedded Resources as shown in Figure 4.19.

FIGURE 4.19
Setting the Build Action for a resource.

continues

continued

NOTE

Sample Graphics   Visual Studio .NET installs a small library of sample graphics files including icon, bitmap, and video files, available in the Common7\Graphics subfolder of your Visual Studio .NET installation folder. The selection isn't great, but it will get you started.

10. Add the following attribute just before the class declaration.

```
<ToolboxBitmap(GetType(RandomNumberGenerator))> _
```

11. Select Build, Build StepByStep4-10 from the main menu. This will generate a StepByStep4_10.dll file that contains the code for the RandomNumberGenerator component.

It is possible to change the Toolbox icon for a control or a component using the ToolboxBitMapAttribute class. This class belongs to the System.Drawing namespace. Because the component does not have a UI, Visual Studio .NET does not automatically include a reference to the System.Drawing.dll, as it would do with a UserControl class or a Form class. To have access to the ToolboxBitmapAttribute class, I decided to add the reference to System.Drawing.dll library manually in Step By Step 4.10.

To see the component in action, I created a Windows application project in Step By Step 4.11.

STEP BY STEP

4.11 Creating a Windows Application That Uses the RandomNumberGenerator Component

1. Add a new Windows Application project and name it StepByStep4-11.

2. In the Solution Explorer window, right-click Form1.vb and rename it TestRandomNumberGenerator. Open the Properties window for the form and change its Name and Text properties to TestRandomNumberGenerator.

3. Using the Solutions Explorer window, add a reference for StepByStep4-10.dll.

4. Activate the Toolbox window and click the My Custom Controls tab. Right-click the Toolbox window and select Customize Toolbox, the .NET Framework Components tab, Browse. Add a reference to StepByStep4-10.dll. Click OK to add the RandomNumberGenerator component to the My Custom Controls tab in the toolbox as shown in Figure 4.20.

5. Drag the Random Number Generator control from the toolbox and drop it on the form to see that the component is added to the Component tray, rather than placed on the form. Use the Properties window to change its MinValue to 500 and MaxValue to 1000 (see Figure 4.21).

6. Add a label (lblResults) and a button (btnGenerate) to the form. Set the label's Text property to an empty string and the button's Text property to Generate a Random Number!. Double-click the button to add an event handler for its Click event. Add the following code to the event handler:

```
Private Sub btnGenerate_Click( _
 ByVal sender As System.Object, _
 ByVal e As System.EventArgs) Handles btnGenerate.Click
    lblResults.Text = _
      String.Format("The next random number is: {0}", _
      RandomNumberGenerator1.GetRandomNumber())
End Sub
```

7. Set the form as the startup object for the project and the project as the startup project for the solution.

8. Run the Project. Each time you click the button you'll get a random number between 500 and 1000, as shown in Figure 4.22.

FIGURE 4.20
A component showing custom icon in the toolbox.

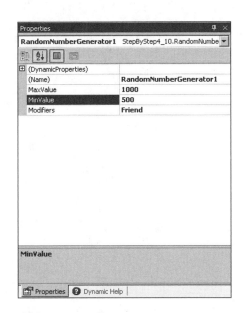

FIGURE 4.21▲
Properties for the custom-created component.

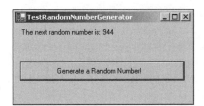

FIGURE 4.22◀
A form generating random number using a component.

▶ The technique of inheriting one visual object from another visual object is *Visual Inheritance*. When you inherit from a control using visual inheritance, you get all the functionality and user interface of the base control, which allows you to reuse code.

▶ When controls are hosted inside Internet Explorer, they are rendered as object elements that do not require any registration, unlike ActiveX objects. The classID should be assigned the assembly (DLL) path and the control name to be hosted, separated with a # (pound sign).

▶ Controls can be hosted inside Internet Explorer if the assemblies exist in the same virtual directories where the Web page resides or in the Global Assembly Cache.

▶ When you create a control by extending it from the Control class, the control does not have a default user interface. You must handle the control's Paint event to render its user interface.

▶ When you don't need a visual representation for your components, you can extend them from the Component class. It does not have a user interface to show on a form but does provide useful properties and events that can be used by its container to customize and control its behavior.

GUIDED PRACTICE EXERCISE 4.2

In this exercise you will create a custom control that derives from the TextBox control. The derived control will be called a NumericTextBox because it only allows digital input. If you type any characters other than digits, they will be simply ignored.

Try this on your own first. If you get stuck or would like to see one possible solution, follow these steps:

1. Create a new project with the Windows Control Library template. Name the project GuidedPracticeExercise4-2.

2. In the Solution Explorer window, change the name of UserControl1.vb file to `NumericTextBox.vb`. Switch to the Code view, and change the name of the class from UserControl1 to `NumericTextBox`. Change the class declaration so that its base class is `System.Winmdows.Forms.TextBox` instead of `System.Windows.Forms.UserControl`, After making changes, the class header should look like this:

```
Public Class NumericTextBox
    Inherits System.Windows.Forms.TextBox
```

3. Switch back to the Design view and note that the gray, borderless box for creating controls is gone. Instead a message will tell you to add components from the Server Explorer or the Toolbox window.

4. Switch back to Code view and add a `KeyPress` event handler for the control:

```
Private Sub NumericTextBox_KeyPress( _
 ByVal sender As Object, _
 ByVal e As System.Windows.Forms.KeyPressEventArgs) _
 Handles MyBase.KeyPress
    If Not (Char.IsDigit(e.KeyChar)) Then
        e.Handled = True
    Else
        e.Handled = False
    End If
End Sub
```

5. Select Build, Build GuidedPracticeExercise4-2 from the main menu to generate a GuidedPracticeExercise4-2.dll file that contains the code for NumericTextBox control.

6. Add new Windows Application project named `GuidedPracticeExercise4-2Test.`

7. In the Solution Explorer window, right-click Form1.vb and rename it TestNumericTextBox. Open the Properties window for this form and change its `Name` and `Text` properties to TestNumericTextBox.

8. Using the Solutions Explorer window, add a reference to GuidedPracticeExercise4-2.dll.

9. Right-click the Toolbox window and select the My Custom Controls tab created in the previous exercises. Right-click in the My Custom Controls tab and select Customize Toolbox.

continues

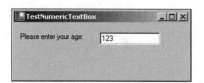

FIGURE 4.23
Form showing the NumericTextBox that accepts only numeric data.

continued

Select the .NET Framework Components tab, Browse, and add a reference to GuidedPracticeExercise4_2.dll. Click OK to add the NumericTextBox control to the My Custom Controls tab in the toolbox.

10. Drag the NumericTextBox control from the toolbox and drop it on the form. Add a label to the form as shown in Figure 4.23.

11. Set the form as the startup object for the project and the project as the startup project for the solution.

12. Run the Project to see the form hosting a NumericTextBox which allows the user to enter only numeric text as shown in Figure 4.23.

CREATING AND MANAGING .NET ASSEMBLIES

Create and modify a .NET assembly.

A Windows application often consists of several different files; it typically includes the DLL and EXE files that contain the application code, the GIF, BMP, or ICO file that contains graphics, and other data files such as those storing strings in several languages for multilingual support. A Windows application created using the .NET Framework groups together a logical collection of such files into what is called an *assembly*. The reason I use the term *logical* here is that these files are not physically combined into a single large file. Even when these files are part of an assembly, they maintain their own physical existence. In fact, you can't tell by looking at a file that it belongs to a particular assembly.

One of the files in the assembly contains a special piece of information called the *assembly manifest*. The manifest contains the metadata for the assembly. When the Common Language Runtime loads an assembly it first reads the manifest to get the following information:

◆ The Name and version of the assembly.

◆ The files that make up the assembly, including their names and hash values.

◆ The compile-time dependency of this assembly on other assemblies.

◆ The culture or language that an assembly supports.

◆ The set of permissions required for the assembly to run properly.

An assembly is the basic unit of deployment, scoping, versioning and security in the .NET Framework. Microsoft uses assemblies to deliver these benefits to .NET:

◆ Each assembly has a version number. All the types and resources in an assembly share the same version number to make it easy for applications to refer to the correct version of files and avoid problems like the infamous "DLL Hell," where installing a new version of a shared library breaks older applications.

◆ The self-describing nature of assemblies makes it possible to deploy applications using the zero-impact XCOPY installation. There's nothing to register and no system files to change.

◆ Assemblies define a security boundary, allowing the Common Language Runtime to restrict a set of operations to be executed depending on the identity and origin of the assembly.

Assemblies exist in different forms depending on how they are used. One way to classify assemblies is with these categories:

◆ Single-file and multifile assemblies

◆ Static and dynamic assemblies

◆ Private and shared assemblies

◆ Satellite and resource-only assemblies

The following sections discusses each of these categories.

Single-file and Multifile Assemblies

A single-file assembly has just a single EXE or DLL file. This file consists of code, any embedded resources, and the assembly manifest of the assembly. A single-file assembly is something you are already familiar with because when you were building your projects in the Step By Step exercises, the output DLL or EXE file was nothing but a single-file assembly. Step By Step 4.12 shows how to view the contents of an assembly file.

NOTE

Microsoft Intermediate Language Disassembler The *MSIL Disassembler* can be used to view the metadata and disassembled code for .NET libraries, modules, and executables in a hierarchical Tree view. Looking at MSIL can reveal lots of information about the inner workings of a program or a component, and it can be a useful learning and debugging tool.

STEP BY STEP

4.12 Viewing Assembly Contents

1. Activate the Solution Explorer window. Click the Show All Files tool button from its toolbar. Navigate to the bin folder of project StepByStep4-11.

2. Right-click StepByStep4-10.dll it and select Open With from its context menu. In the Open With dialog box (see Figure 4.24), select Ildasm.exe, Open. If Ildasm is not on the list, click the Add button and browse for it, as shown in Figure 4.25; you'll find it in the FrameworkSDK\bin folder inside the Visual Studio .NET installation. This step will launch Microsoft Intermediate Language Disassembler, showing the contents of StepByStep4_10.dll (see Figure 4.26).

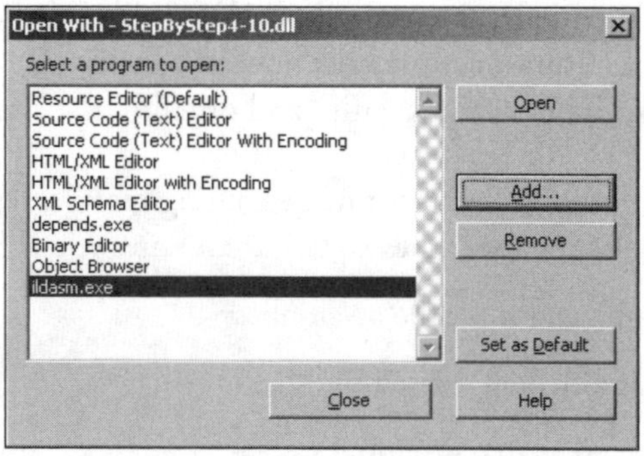

FIGURE 4.24 ▶
Selecting the application for opening a DLL file.

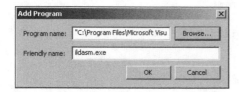

FIGURE 4.25 ▲
Adding ildasm.exe to the Open With list.

FIGURE 4.26
Microsoft Intermediate Language Disassembler.

3. Expand the nodes to see the methods and constructors defined inside the class. Double-clicking a Method node will open a window showing disassembled code for the method.

4. On the top of the hierarchy you will find a node titled MANIFEST. Double-click it to open the metadata information for this assembly (see Figure 4.27). You will see that manifest contains references to other assemblies, version information, and values among other information.

```
MANIFEST                                                          _|□|x|
.assembly extern mscorlib
{
  .publickeytoken = (B7 7A 5C 56 19 34 E0 89 )           // .z`
  .ver 1:0:3300:0
}
.assembly extern Microsoft.VisualBasic
{
  .publickeytoken = (B0 3F 5F 7F 11 D5 0A 3A )           // .?_
  .ver 7:0:3300:0
}
.assembly extern System
{
  .publickeytoken = (B7 7A 5C 56 19 34 E0 89 )           // .z`
  .ver 1:0:3300:0
}
.assembly extern System.Data
{
  .publickeytoken = (B7 7A 5C 56 19 34 E0 89 )           // .z`
  .ver 1:0:3300:0
}
.assembly extern System.Xml
{
  .publickeytoken = (B7 7A 5C 56 19 34 E0 89 )           // .z`
```

FIGURE 4.27
Assembly manifest.

You might also find it useful to add an Ildasm entry for EXE files as well as DLL files. Alternatively, you can launch ILDASM from the .NET Framework command prompt and use its menus to open any assembly that you wish to inspect.

A multifile assembly can include multiple files in one assembly. You should have at least one DLL or EXE file among these files. You can choose to attach the assembly manifest with any of these files, or you can keep it in a separate file of its own. Unfortunately Visual Studio .NET does not support the creation of multifile assemblies, so you must use the command-line tools from the .NET Framework SDK to do so. Step By Step 4.13 provides a walk-through of this process.

STEP BY STEP

4.13 Creating a Multifile Assembly

1. Create a new project based on the Empty Project template and name it StepByStep4-13. Right-click the project, select Properties, and use the project's Property page to change its Output Type to Class Library.

2. Right-click the project and select Add, Add Class from the context menu. Add a new class named MathLib.vb, as shown in Figure 4.28. Wrap this class in a Namespace declaration. Add a shared method named Add to the class. The code should look like this:

```
Namespace StepByStep4_13

    Public Class MathLib

        Public Shared Function Add(ByVal first As_
        Integer, _
         ByVal second As Integer) As Integer
            Add = first + second
        End Function

    End Class

End Namespace
```

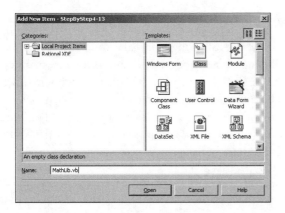

FIGURE 4.28
Adding a class to a project.

3. Add another class to the project. Name this class `StringLib` and place it in the same Namespace as MathLib. Add a shared method named `Concat`:

```
Namespace StepByStep4_13

    Public Class StringLib
        Public Shared Function Concat( _
        ByVal firstHalf As String, _
        ByVal secondHalf As String) As String
            Concat = firstHalf + secondHalf
        End Function

    End Class

End Namespace
```

4. From the Windows Start menu select Programs, Microsoft Visual Studio .NET, Visual Studio .NET Tools, Visual Studio .NET Command Prompt to open a command window ready to execute .NET Framework command-line tools.

5. Navigate to the folder containing StepByStep4-13. Give the following command to compile the StringLib.vb file as a module that is not part of any assembly yet. This command will generate a file named StringLib.netModule:

```
vbc /t:module StringLib.vb
```

continues

continued

6. Type the following command to open StringLib.netModule in Ildasm. Open its manifest, and note that this manifest is not an assembly manifest because no `.assembly` directive is in it. An `.assembly extern` directive points to another assembly named mscorlib (the core .NET Framework file), but that's different and doesn't make this file an assembly.

```
ildasm StringLib.netModule
```

7. Use a command similar to Step 5 to compile MathLib.vb file into a module. If you inspect the MathLib.netModule file through Ildasm, you will again note that this file is just a module and not an assembly.

8. Type the following command to invoke the Assembly Linker, al.exe. This command will read both the module files and create an assembly:

```
al StringLib.netmodule MathLib.netmodule
➥  /out:Utils.dll /t:library
```

9. Open the Utils.dll file in Ildasm and note that Utils.dll is a file that contains just the manifest and no code. Inspect the manifest to see that it has an `.assembly Utils` directive that identifies this manifest as an assembly manifest for an assembly named Utils. The `.assembly` directive is followed by two `.file` directives that identify other files of this assembly.

So, is Utils.dll *the* assembly? No, it is not. It just specifies the assembly manifest. The assembly actually consists of three files: the Utils.dll, which stores the assembly manifest, the MathLib.netModule file, and the StringLib.netModule file. Thus, this is a logical assembly and not a physical one (captured in a single file). Although the three files, Utils.dll, MathLib.netModule, and StringLib.netModule, are three distinct files physically, logically they belong to the same assembly named Utils.

Although you can't create multifile assemblies using Visual Studio .NET, you can use them within a Visual Stuio .NET project. I'll demonstrate how to do this in Step By Step 4.14.

STEP BY STEP

4.14 Creating a Windows Application That Uses a Multifile Assembly.

1. Add a new Windows Application project to your solution and name it StepByStep4-14.

2. In the Solution Explorer window, right-click Form1.vb and rename it TestMultiFileAssembly. Open the Properties window for this form and change its Name and Text properties to TestMultiFileAssembly.

3. In the Solutions Explorer window, right-click the project name and select Add Reference. In the Add Reference dialog, browse for the file Utils.dll (in the folder of project StepByStep4-13) and add a reference to it. Adding this reference will copy the all the files of the assembly as identified by the assembly manifest in Utils.dll in the bin\Utils folder of the current project. You can verify this by clicking on the Show All Files tool button of Solution Explorer and navigating to the bin\Utils folder of the current project.

4. Arrange controls on the form as shown in Figure 4.29. In the first group box, name the TextBox controls txtFirst and txtSecond; name the Button btnAdd, and name the Label at the bottom of the group box lblAddResult. For the second group box, name the TextBox controls txtFirstHalf and txtSecondHalf; name the Button btnConcat and the Label at the bottom lblConcatResult.

5. Add the following event handling code to the Click event of btnAdd:

```
Private Sub btnAdd_Click(ByVal sender As System.Object, _
  ByVal e As System.EventArgs) Handles btnAdd.Click
    Dim intAddResult As Integer = _
    StepByStep4_13.MathLib.Add( _
    Convert.ToInt32(txtFirst.Text), _
    Convert.ToInt32(txtSecond.Text))
    lblAddResult.Text = String.Format(" _
    The Result of Addition is: {0}", _
    intAddResult)
End Sub
```

continues

continued

6. Add the following event handling code to the `Click` event of btnConcat:

```
Private Sub btnConcat_Click(ByVal sender As System.Object, _
 ByVal e As System.EventArgs) Handles btnConcat.Click
    lblConcatResult.Text = _
    "The Result of concatenation is: " & _
    StepByStep4_13.StringLib.Concat( _
    txtFirstHalf.Text, txtSecondHalf.Text)
End Sub
```

7. Set the form as the startup object for the project and the project as the startup project for the solution.

8. Run the Project. Enter two integer values in the top group box and click the Add button to invoke the MathLib.Add method from the MathLib.netModule file. Now enter two string values in the bottom group box and click the Concat button to invoke the StringLib.Concat method from the StringLib.netModule file. You will see output similar to Figure 4.29.

FIGURE 4.29
A Windows application using multifile assembly.

Static and Dynamic Assemblies

When you compile programs using Visual Studio .NET or through the command-line compiler, they emit the files that make up an assembly. These files are physically stored on disk. Such an assembly is called a *static assembly*.

However, it is also possible to create and execute assemblies on-the-fly (while a program is still under execution). Such assemblies are called *dynamic assemblies*. A common usage of dynamic assemblies can be seen in ASP .NET. While executing ASPX files, the ASP .NET process creates corresponding assemblies at runtime. If needed, dynamic assemblies can be saved to disk to be later loaded again. The classes used to create dynamic assemblies are available in the System.Reflection.Emit namespace. I won't cover that namespace in this text because it isn't required by the exam objectives, but if you are interested, you might want to look at the documentation for the System.Reflection.Emit namespace.

Private and Shared Assemblies

Assemblies can be deployed using two different approaches:

◆ You can deploy an assembly for use with a single application. When an assembly is deployed this way, it is called a *private assembly.*

◆ You can deploy an assembly for use with several applications. When an assembly is deployed in the shared mode, it is called a *shared assembly.*

Here are some fast facts about private assemblies:

◆ Private assemblies are intended to be only used by the application they are deployed with.

◆ Private assemblies are deployed in the directory (or a subdirectory) where the main application is installed.

◆ Typically, a private assembly is written by the same company that writes the main application that uses the private assembly.

Because of the localized nature of a private assembly, the runtime does not impose a strict versioning policy with them. How the application developers version and name their assembly is more or less left to them.

On the other hand, a shared assembly can be used by more than one application. All the shared assemblies on a computer are stored in a special place called the Global Assembly Cache (GAC) to be accessible by all applications. Because of the shared nature of the GAC, the Common Language Runtime imposes special security and versioning requirements on any assembly installed in the GAC.

Here are some fast facts about shared assemblies and the Global Assembly Cache:

◆ All assemblies are installed in GAC must have a strong name. A *strong name* consists of an assembly's name, a version number, a culture, a public key, and a digital signature. Having a strong name ensures an assembly's identity.

◆ The Common Language Runtime checks for the assembly's integrity before installing it in the GAC and ensures that an assembly has not been tampered with by checking the strong name of the assembly.

NOTE

XCOPY Deployment and Global Assembly Cache When your application needs to refer to assemblies in the Global Assembly Cache, you can no longer deploy the applications using just the XCOPY command. Now you also need to install the assembly in the Global Assembly Cache of the target machine. In this case, you should use an installer program (such as Windows Installer 2.0) that understands how to work with the GAC.

NOTE

Private Assemblies Versus Shared Assemblies As a general rule of thumb, you should always deploy your assemblies as private assemblies. Install the assemblies in the Global Assembly Cache only if you are explicitly required to share them with other applications.

◆ The GAC is capable of maintaining multiple copies of an assembly with the same name but different versions.

◆ The runtime can determine what version of an assembly to load based on the information in an application's configuration file or the machinewide configuration file (machine.config). You'll learn more about this in Chapter 15, "Configuring a Windows Application."

To view the contents of the GAC, follow Steps By Step 4.15.

STEP BY STEP

4.15 Viewing Contents of Global Assembly Cache

1. Launch Windows Explorer and navigate to the system folder of your computer (such as C:\Windows or C:\WINNT). Open the subfolder named Assembly.

2. You are now seeing the contents of Global Assembly Cache (see Figure 4.30). The .NET Framework installs a Windows shell extension called the Assembly Cache Viewer (Shfusion.dll) that allows you to easily view the contents of GAC. Select the System.Security assembly. Right-click it and select Properties from the context menu to see information related to this assembly as shown in Figure 4.31.

FIGURE 4.30
Viewing the Global Assembly Cache.

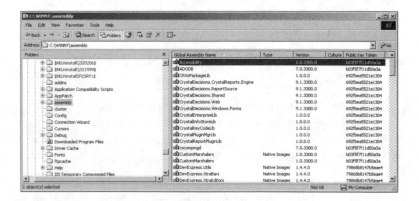

FIGURE 4.31
Properties for an assembly installed in Global Assembly Cache.

I'll talk more about the Global Assembly Cache in Chapter 13, "Deploying a Windows Application," in which you will learn how to deploy your own assemblies in the Global Assembly Cache. You'll also learn in Chapter 15, "Configuring a Windows Application," how to use configuration files to control which version of an assembly is loaded by your application.

Satellite and Resource-Only Assemblies

Create and modify a .NET assembly: Create and implement satellite assemblies.

Create and modify a .NET assembly: Create resource-only assemblies.

A Windows application typically contains resources such as images and strings in addition to code. These resources can be translated into various cultures and languages. When you add these files to a Visual Studio .NET Project, their default Build type is Content. When you compile the project, the assemblies contain just code, metadata, and links to files that exist externally. This means that the resource files will be distributed with the application as separate files, and all these files must be available at runtime for your application to function correctly.

NOTE

Native Assembly Versus JIT-Compiled Assembly   Assemblies store code in the MSIL (Microsoft intermediate language) format. When a method is invoked for the first time, the Common Language Runtime will Just In Time–compile that method into native machine code. The native code is stored in memory and directly used for any subsequent calls to this method. In the JIT compilation mode, a method is slow when it is called for the first time because an additional step of compilation is involved, but any subsequent calls to that method will run as fast as native code itself.

When you view the GAC, note that some assemblies have their type marked as *native images*, meaning these assemblies were precompiled in native code before they were installed in the GAC. The advantage of using a native image is that even the first call of any method in an assembly will be as fast as its subsequent calls. You too can create a native image for your assembly by using the Native Image Generator tool (NGEN.EXE) installed as part of .NET Framework SDK.

Another way to package the resource files with your application is to embed them into the assembly itself. To achieve this, when you add the resource files to your project, set their Build type as Embedded Resources instead of Content. You can do this through the Properties window by accessing the properties of these files. When the Build type is set to Embedded Resources, the contents of the resource file will be included in the assembly itself at the compile-time. Visual Studio .NET does this in the following three steps:

1. It creates an XML resource file with an extension resx. This file stores the resources as key-value pairs, for example the name of a resource file and its location.

2. At the time of compilation, all resources referenced by the resx file are embedded into a binary file with the extension resources.

3. The binary resource file is embedded into the the code assembly.

Of course, all these steps can be done manually. The resx file is an XML file, so you can manually create it using any text editor. It can be compiled into a resources file using the Resource Generator tool (resgen.exe). A resources file can be embedded to an assembly using the VBC compiler's /resource option.

These steps create an assembly that contains both code as well as resource. Assemblies created in such a way are not dependent on external resource files but have all necessary information stuffed into themselves. Recall that in Step By Step 4.10 you embedded a resource file named RandomNumberGenerator.bmp. When Visual Studio compiled that project to create StepByStep4_10.dll it actually followed the three previously mentioned steps. You can go to this project's folder and search for resx file and resources files. The resx file and the resources files will have file names the same as the name of the class; only the extension differs. Also view the DLL file in Ildasm to see how it differs from the other files.

Another way to attach resources in an application is by creating resource-only assemblies. These assemblies just contain resources without any code.

With the exception of satellite assemblies, Visual Studio .NET does not give direct support to create a resource-only assembly. However, you can use the command-line tools provided by the .NET Framework to create such assemblies.

The .NET Framework provides various classes in the
System.Resources namespace that can be used to work with resource
files. Some important classes of this namespace are listed in Table 4.1.

TABLE 4.1

**SOME IMPORTANT CLASSES THAT DEAL WITH
RESOURCES**

Class	Explanation
ResourceManager	Provides access to resources at runtime. You can use this class to read information from resource-only assemblies.
ResourceReader	Enables you to read resources from a binary resource file.
ResourceWriter	Enables you to write resources to a binary resource file.
ResXResourceReader	Enables you to read resource information from an XML-based resx file.
ResXResourceWriter	Enables you to write resource information to an XML-based resx file.

Step By Step 4.16 will use some of these classes to write an application
that will show how to programatically generate resx and resource files
from given resources. The objective is to create resource files for storing the flags of different countries. You can get these graphics from the
common7\graphics\icons\flag folder from your Visual Studio .NET
installation. For the purposes of this example, I renamed those files
with their corresponding two letter ISO country codes.

STEP BY STEP

4.16 Creating Resource Files

1. Add a new Windows Application project to your solution
   and name it StepByStep4-16.

2. In the Solution Explorer window, right-click Form1.vb
   and rename it GenerateResourceFiles. Open the
   Properties window for this form and change its Name and
   Text properties to GenerateResourceFiles.

continues

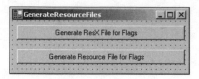

FIGURE 4.32
A form that generates Flags.resx and
Flags.resources files.

continued

3. In the Solution Explorer, right-click the project and select Add, New Folder. Name the folder Flags. Right-click the Flags folder and select Add, Add Existing Item and add all the icon files of country flags to this folder.

4. Place two Button controls on the form as shown in Figure 4.32 and name them btnGenerateResX and btnGenerateResources.

5. Place the following directives at the top of the code:

```
Imports System.Resources
Imports System.IO
```

6. Add an event handler for the Click event of btnGenerateResX and add the following code to it:

```
Private Sub btnGenerateResx_Click( _
 ByVal sender As System.Object, _
 ByVal e As System.EventArgs) Handles btnGenerateResx.Click
    ' Create a ResXResourceWriter object
    Dim rsxw As ResXResourceWriter = _
     New ResXResourceWriter("Flags.resx")
    ' the EXE will be placed in bin folder so refer to
    ' Flags folder from there
    Dim strFile As String
    Dim strCountryCode As String
    Dim img As Image
    For Each strFile In Directory.GetFiles( _
      "..\Flags", "*.ico")
        strCountryCode = _
         strFile.Substring(strFile.Length - 6, 2)
        img = Image.FromFile(strFile)
        ' Store the Key-Value pair.
        rsxw.AddResource(strCountryCode, img)
    Next
    rsxw.Close()
    MessageBox.Show("Flags.resx file generated")
End Sub
```

7. Add an event handler for the Click event of btnGenerateResources and add the following code to it:

```
Private Sub btnGenerateResources_Click( _
 ByVal sender As System.Object, _
 ByVal e As System.EventArgs) _
 Handles btnGenerateResources.Click
    ' Create a ResourceWriter object
    Dim rw As ResourceWriter = _
     New ResourceWriter("Flags.resources")
    ' The EXE will be placed in bin folder so refer to
    ' the Flags folder from there
```

```
    Dim strFile As String
    Dim strCountryCode As String
    Dim img As Image
    For Each strFile In Directory.GetFiles( _
     "..\Flags", "*.ico")
        strCountryCode = _
         strFile.Substring(strFile.Length - 6, 2)
        img = Image.FromFile(strFile)
        ' Store the Key-Value pair.
        rw.AddResource(strCountryCode, img)
    Next
    rw.Close()
    MessageBox.Show("Flags.resources file generated")
End Sub
```

8. Set the form as the startup object for the project and set the project as the startup project for the solution.

9. Run the Project. Click each of the buttons to create both a Flags.resx file and a Flags.resources file. The location of these files will be the same as the location of the project's EXE file.

This exercise creates both a RESX file and a resources file to demonstrate the capability of the ResXResourceWrite and ResourceWriter classes. Note that the Flags.resources file was not generated by compiling the Flags.resx file, but directly using the ResourceWriter class. You could also create a RESX file into a resources file from the command line by using the following command:

```
    resgen Flags.resx
```

Although the Flags.resources file has resources embedded in binary format, it is not an assembly. To create an assembly from this file, you can use the Assembly Linker tool (al.exe) as shown in Step By Step 4.17.

STEP BY STEP

4.17 Creating a Resource-Only Assembly

1. Select State, Programs, Microsoft Visual Studio .NET, Visual Studio .NET Tools, Visual Studio .NET Command Prompt to open a command window ready to execute .NET Framework command-line tools.

continues

continued

2. Change directory to where your project's EXE file is stored. Give the following command to compile the Flags.resources file as a resource-only assembly:

```
al /embed:Flags.resources /out:Flags.Resources.dll
```

Now that you know how to create a resource-only assembly, let me show you how to use it from a Windows application. I'll demonstrate this in the Step By Step 4.18. In this exercise you should especially focus on the use of the ResourceManager class to load the resources from resource-only assemblies.

STEP BY STEP

4.18 Using Resource-Only Assemblies.

1. Crete a new Windows Application project and name it StepByStep4-18.

2. In the Solution Explorer window, right-click Form1.vb and rename it GetCountryFlag.vb. Open the Properties window for this form and change its Name and Text properties to GetCountryFlag.

3. Add a TextBox control named txtCountryCode, a PictureBox control named pbFlag, a Button control named btnGetFlag, and a Label control to the form. Arrange the controls on form as shown in Figure 4.33.

4. Place the following statements at the top of the code:

```
Imports System.Reflection
Imports System.Resources
```

5. Add an event handler for the Click event of btnGetFlag and add the following code to it:

```
Private Sub btnGetFlag_Click( _
ByVal sender As System.Object, _
ByVal e As System.EventArgs) Handles btnGetFlag.Click
    Dim rm As ResourceManager = _
    New ResourceManager("Flags", _
    System.Reflection.Assembly.LoadFrom( _
    "Flags.resources.dll"))
```

```
pbFlag.Image = CType(rm.GetObject( _
   txtCountryCode.Text.ToUpper()), Bitmap)
End Sub
```

6. Set the form as the startup object for the project and set the project as the startup project for the solution.

7. Copy the Flags.resources.dll file to the `bin` folder for this project.

8. Run the Project. Enter `US` in the text box and click the Get Flag button. The appropriate flag will be loaded into the picture box from the resource assembly.

FIGURE 4.33
Reading resources from a resource-only assembly.

A common use of resource-only assemblies is to store language and culture-specific information. A Windows application designed for international usage might package resource information for each locale in a separate assembly file. When a user downloads the application, she can ignore the assemblies for other cultures. Skipping the unncessary files can significantly reduce the user's download time for the application.

Resource-only assemblies that store culture-specific information are also known as *satellite assemblies*.

Step By Step 4.19 demostrates how Visual Studio .NET can be used to generate satellite assemblies for different cultures.

STEP BY STEP

4.19 Generating Culture-Specific Satellite Assemblies

1. Add a new Windows Application to your solution and name it `StepByStep4-19`.

2. Drag and drop a Label and a PictureBox control to the form. Write some text in the Label and assign an image to Images property of PictureBox. The actual contents of the Label and the PictureBox does not matter because I'm just demonstrating the creation of satellite assemblies.

continues

continued

3. Set the `Localizable` property of form to True. Set the `Language` property to Hindi (India).

4. In the Solution Explorer window click the Show All Files button to see all files for this project. Click the + sign next to Form1.vb to see the set of files attached to it with extension RESX. These files are the XML-based resource files for storing the culture information for each language you select.

5. Go back to the form properties, and set the language property to Japanese. Note that this adds a resx file for Japanese culture in the Solution Explorer.

6. Set the project as the startup project.

7. Run the project. Navigate to the bin folder to see that new folders specific to the selected language are created there. Expand the hi-IN folder to see its contents, and you will see a file named StepByStep4_19.resources.dll, as shown in Figure 4.34. This is the satellite assembly created by compiling the resources listed in its corresponding resx file. Open the file in Ildasm to view its contents. Figure 4.35 shows the assembly manifest.

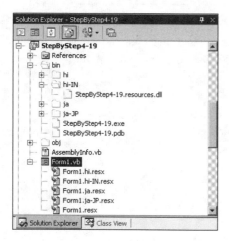

FIGURE 4.34
Generating satellite assemblies through Visual Studio .NET.

FIGURE 4.35
Assembly manifest for a satellite assembly.

```
MANIFEST                                                                    _ □ X
.assembly 'StepByStep4-19.resources'
{
  .hash algorithm 0x00008004
  .ver 1:0:916:22519
  .locale = (68 00 69 00 2D 00 49 00 4E 00 00 00 )              // h.i.-.I.N.
}
.mresource public 'StepByStep4_19.Form1.hi-IN.resources'
{
}
.module 'StepByStep4-19.resources.dll'
// MVID: {8E39B372-C00E-4339-AC22-A68CBC8BE4EA}
.imagebase 0x00400000
.subsystem 0x00000003
.file alignment 512
.corflags 0x00000001
// Image base: 0x03210000
```

I'll cover the topic of satellite assemblies and globalization of applications in great detail in Chapter 8, "Globalization."

For now, note that Visual Studio .NET automatically creates a satellite assembly for the localized resx file in the correct directory location, which is identified by its culture name. The resx is an XML-based configuration file that contains the resource information. Its format allows you to edit and modify this file using any Text editor. Visual Studio .NET also comes with a built-in Resource Editor that allows you to edit resx files.

REVIEW BREAK

▶ Assemblies are the basic unit for reuse, versioning, security, and deployment of components created using the .NET Framework. Each assembly includes an assembly manifest to store the assembly's metadata.

▶ Depending on the number of files that make up an assembly, it is a single-file or a multifile assembly.

▶ A private assembly is an assembly available only to clients in the same directory structure as the assembly, while a shared assembly can be referenced by more than one application and is stored in the machinewide Global Assembly Cache. A shared assembly must be assigned a cryptographically strong name.

▶ Resource-only assemblies are those assemblies that contain just resources and no code. Resource-only assemblies that store culture-specific information are known as satellite assemblies.

CHAPTER SUMMARY

KEY TERMS

- Assembly
- Assembly manifest
- Assembly metadata
- Component
- Custom Control
- Delegate
- Global Assembly Cache (GAC)
- Metadata
- Private assembly
- Resource-only assembly
- Satellite assembly
- Shared assembly
- Strong Name
- User Control

Building an efficient Visual Basic .NET application requires you to create and manage .NET components and assemblies. As applications grow ever more complex, it's necessary to build them effectively by creating reusable components. The Microsoft .NET Framework allows programmers to create reusable components. You can create a Windows component by deriving from Component, Control, and UserControl, or any of their derived classes. The choice of base class mostly depends on what functionality you want to borrow and the type of component you want to create.

The Microsoft .NET Framework also supports extensibility of components by allowing you to create new controls through a technique known as Visual Inheritance. In addition to hosting controls in a Windows Form, you can also host them in Microsoft Internet Explorer without much effort.

Assemblies are the basic unit for reuse, versioning, security, and deployment of components created using the .NET Framework. Assemblies are self-describing: They store their metadata within them in the assembly manifest.

Assemblies can be classified various ways: single-file and multifile assemblies, static and dynamic assemblies, private and shared assemblies, and satellite and resource-only assemblies.

Shared assemblies can be shared across applications and are stored in the machinewide Global Assembly Cache. Resource-only assemblies are those assemblies that contain just resources and no code. Resource-only assemblies that store culture-specific information are known as satellite assemblies.

APPLY YOUR KNOWLEDGE	

Exercises

4.1   Creating the Odometer User Control

In this exercise you'll practice creating a new control from existing controls.

Estimated Time: 20 minutes.

1. Launch Visual Studio .NET. Select File, New, Blank Solution and name the new solution `306C04Exercises`.

2. Add a new Windows Control Library project to the solution. Name the project `Exercise4-1`.

3. Drag and drop three Label controls (`lblHundred`, `lblTen` and `lblUnit`) and a Timer component (`Timer1`) to the form. Set the Enabled property of the Timer control to `True`.

4. Switch to Code view and define a property in the class definition:

```
Public Property ScrollInterval() As Integer
    Get
        ScrollInterval = Timer1.Interval
    End Get
    Set(ByVal Value As Integer)
        Timer1.Interval = Value
    End Set
End Property
```

5. Double-click the Timer component in the component tray to attach the default `Tick` event and add the following code to the event handler:

```
Private Sub Timer1_Tick( _
 ByVal sender As System.Object, _
 ByVal e As System.EventArgs) _
 Handles Timer1.Tick
    Dim intUnit As Integer = _
     Convert.ToInt32(lblUnit.Text)
    intUnit += 1
    If intUnit >= 9 Then
        intUnit = 0
        Dim intTen As Integer = _
         Convert.ToInt32(lblTen.Text)
        intTen += 1
```

```
        If intTen >= 9 Then
            intTen = 0
            Dim intHundred As Integer = _
             Convert.ToInt32( _
             lblHundred.Text)
            intHundred += 1
            If intHundred >= 9 Then
                intHundred = 0
            End If
            lblHundred.Text = _
             intHundred.ToString()
        End If
        lblTen.Text = intTen.ToString()
    End If
    lblUnit.Text = intUnit.ToString()
End Sub
```

6. Select Build, Build Exercise4-1 from the main menu. This step generates the code for your control and packages it into Exercise4-1.dll. The DLL file is located in the bin directory of your project.

7. Add a new Windows Application project and name it Exercise4-1Test.

8. In the Solution Explorer window, right-click Form1.vb and rename it `TestOdometer`. Open the Properties window for this form and change its `Name` and `Text` properties to `TestOdometer`.

9. Using the Solutions Explorer window, add a reference for Exercuse4-1.dll.

10. Place an Odometer control on the form from the toolbox.

11. Set the form as the startup object for the project, and set Exercise4-1Test as the startup project.

12. Run the project to see the form hosting an Odometer control as shown in Figure 4.36.

FIGURE 4.36
Odometer user control in action.

APPLY YOUR KNOWLEDGE

4.2 Getting Types in an Assembly

The classes in the System.Reflection namespace along with the System.Type class allow you to obtain information about loaded assemblies at runtime. This information includes the types defined within the assembly such as classes, interfaces, and value types. In this exercise you will use these classes to enumerate types in an assembly selected by the user.

Estimated Time: 20 minutes.

1. Add a new Windows Application project named `Exercise4-2` to your solution.

2. In the Solution Explorer window, right-click Form1.vb and rename it GetTypes. Open the Properties window for this form and change its Name and Text properties to GetTypes.

3. Place a Label control, a TextBox control (`txtAssemblyName`), a Button control (`btnLoadAssembly`), and a ListBox control (`lbTypes`) on the form as shown in Figure 4.37. Also add an OpenFileDialog component and name it `dlgOpen`.

4. Switch to Code view and add the following line of code to the top of the form's module:

```
Imports System.Reflection
```

5. Add code to handle the `Click` event of the Button control:

```
Private Sub btnLoadAssembly_Click( _
  ByVal sender As System.Object, _
  ByVal e As System.EventArgs) _
  Handles btnLoadAssembly.Click
    If dlgOpen.ShowDialog() = _
    DialogResult.OK Then
        txtAssemblyName.Text = _
        dlgOpen.FileName
        ' Load the Assembly
        Dim assem As [Assembly] = _
        System.Reflection.Assembly. _
        LoadFrom(txtAssemblyName.Text)
```

```
        ' Get all the types in the assembly
        Dim types() As Type = _
        assem.GetTypes()
        lbTypes.Items.Clear()

        Dim typ As Type

        For Each typ In types
            ' Dump the FullName of the
            ' Type to the ListBox
            lbTypes.Items.Add(typ.FullName)
        Next
    End If
End Sub
```

6. Set the form as the startup form for the project and set the project as the startup project for the solution.

7. Run the project. Click the Load Assembly button and select an assembly to load. All the Types in the assembly with their full names will appear in the ListBox, as shown in Figure 4.37.

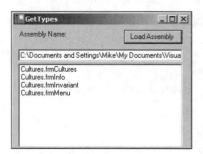

FIGURE 4.37
Getting the Types from an assembly.

Review Questions

1. What are the three different ways in which Windows components can be created?

2. What is the usual signature of an event handler?

APPLY YOUR KNOWLEDGE

3. What steps must be performed to create and implement an event?

4. How do you set the classID value when creating object elements to render a Windows control in a Web page?

5. When you create a control by inheriting from Control class, what is the extra step you need to do?

6. How can you assign a custom Toolbox icon to a component?

7. What is the purpose of the assembly manifest?

8. What type of assemblies should be stored in the Global Assembly Cache?

9. What are resource-only and satellite assemblies?

Exam Questions

1. You want to decrease the time it takes for a component to load for the first time. Which of the following tools can help you?

   A. gacutil.exe

   B. resgen.exe

   C. sn.exe

   D. ngen.exe

2. You have converted your application's assembly files to native images using the Native Image Generation tool (ngen.exe). Which of the following statements hold true for your assemblies? (Select two.)

   A. Applications that use a native assembly will run faster for the initial run.

   B. Applications using a native assembly will have consistently faster performance as compared to a JIT-compiled assembly.

   C. The native assemblies are portable. You should be able to use them on any machine that has the Common Language Runtime installed on it.

   D. The native assemblies can be used in debugging scenarios.

3. You have developed a graphics application. Before you create a setup program you want to package some of the image files in a satellite assembly. You have created an XML-based resource file for these files and named it App.resx. Which of the following steps would you take to convert this file in a satellite assembly?

   A. Use the vbc.exe tool followed by the al.exe tool.

   B. Use the resgen.exe tool followed by the al.exe tool.

   C. Use the resgen.exe tool followed by the vbc.exe tool.

   D. Use the vbc.exe tool followed by the resgen.exe tool.

4. You have developed a utility network library that will be used by several applications in your company. How should you deploy this library?

   A. Sign the library using the Strong Name tool (sn.exe) and place it in Global Assembly Cache.

   B. Sign the library using the File Signing tool (signcode.exe) and place it in Global Assembly cache.

APPLY YOUR KNOWLEDGE

C. Sign the library using both the Strong Name tool and the File Signing tool and place it in the bin directory of each application using it.

D. Keep the library at a central place such as C:\CommonComponents and use each application's configuration files to point to it.

5. You are a programmer for a popular gaming software publishing company. The company has recently designed a series of games using the .NET Framework. All these new game applications share some components. Some of these components are shipped in the box with the application and others are deployed over the Internet. Which of the following commands will you use for these components before packaging them for deployment.

A. Use sn.exe to sign the components.

B. Use signcode.exe to sign the components.

C. Use sn.exe followed by signcode.exe to sign your components.

D. Use signcode.exe followed by sn.exe to sign your components.

6. You want to implement a versioning policy on all the components of your windows application. Which of the following options will you use?

A. Use the File Signing Tool (signcode.exe) to assign the version information.

B. Use the resgen.exe tool to create a resource file containing version information.

C. Create an XML-based configuration file that maintains version information for each component.

D. Use the Strong Name tool (sn.exe) to assign a Strong Name to all the assemblies.

7. You are designing a Contact Management system for the salespersons of your company. You note that you will be often required to create forms capable of accepting and validating addresses including information like Name, Street Name, State, Country, and ZIP code by displaying controls such as a TextBox or a ComboBox. You think it is a good idea to package your address input and validation code in a component so you can reuse your efforts in several forms throughout the application. Which of the following classes would you prefer to be the base class of your component?

A. System.Windows.Forms.Control

B. System.Windows.Forms.UserControl

C. System.Windows.Forms.Form

D. System.ComponentModel.Component

8. You are creating a time-tracking application to be used companywide. Several forms in this application show the user a clock. The clock has the look and action of an analog clock with a circular face and hands of different size for the hour, minute, and second. You decided to code the analog clock as a reusable component. Which of the following classes would you choose as the base class for creating this control?

A. System.Windows.Forms.Control

B. System.Windows.Forms.UserControl

C. System.Windows.Forms.Form

D. System.ComponentModel.Component

APPLY YOUR KNOWLEDGE

9. You are using the C# language compiler from the command line. You want to compile a C# program but do not want the compiler to write an assembly manifest in it. Which of the compiler option would you choose?

   A. /target:exe

   B. /target:library

   C. /target:module

   D. /target:winexe

10. You have defined a custom component for your application that manages user authentication. This component raises an Authenticated event whenever a user is successfully authenticated. At that point, you must make the user's name and SID (security identifier) available to the control container. How should you do this?

   A. Place the user's name and SID in properties of the component for the container to retrieve.

   B. Pass the user's name and SID as parameters of the Authenticated event.

   C. Define global variables in a separate module and place the values in those variables.

   D. Define a custom AuthenticatedEventArgs class that inherits from the EventArgs class, and pass it as a parameter of the Authenticated event.

11. One of your colleagues is trying to host a control in Internet Explorer. He has created the control and tested it successfully on a Windows Form, but he can't make it show up in Internet Explorer.

The name of the control is SolidControls.ColorMixer, and it is stored in a DLL named SolidControlsLib.dll. Your colleague has also placed both the HTML page and the DLL in the same virtual directory.

He shows you the HTML file that he has designed to host this control. Part of his HTML code is as listed here (line numbers are for reference purpose only).

```
01: <html>
02:     <body>
03:         <object id="colorMixerX1"
04: classid="http://localhost/WebDir/
    ➥SolidControlsLib.dll"
05:             height="300" width="300">
06:         </object>
07:     </body>
08: </html>
```

What changes would you suggest to make this control work in Internet Explorer?

   A. Change the code in line 4 to:

```
classid="http://localhost/WebDir/
➥ SolidControlsLib.dll#SolidControls.
➥ColorMixer"
```

   B. Change the code in line 4 to:

```
classid="http://localhost/WebDir/
➥SolidControlsLib.dll
➥ ?SolidControls.ColorMixer"
```

   C. Change the code in line 4 to:

```
classid="SolidControls.ColorMixer"
```

   D. Change the code in line 4 to:

```
classid="http://localhost/WebDir/
➥SolidControlsLib.dll?
➥ classid=SolidControls.ColorMixer"
```

APPLY YOUR KNOWLEDGE

12. You have designed a UserControl by assembling five TextBox controls and two Button controls. You do not want the client application to be able to access the contained objects within your control. Which modifiers should you use with your contained objects to achieve this goal? (Select two.)

    A. Private

    B. Friend

    C. Protected

    D. Public

13. You are designing a component to enable your applications to interact with the computers in a network. The component does not have any visual representation but should provide you a design-time interface that will help a client application designer to set its properties and behavior. Which of the following types is your best choice as the base class for creating this control?

    A. System.Windows.Forms.Control

    B. System.Windows.Forms.UserControl

    C. System.Windows.Forms.Form

    D. System.ComponentModel.Component

14. Your Windows application is using some graphics files. You want to embed the graphics files in the application's EXE itself so that you don't have to distribute additional files with your application. What should you do?

    A. Create a satellite assembly for storing graphics.

    B. Set the BuildAction property of the graphics files to Content.

    C. Set the BuildAction property of the graphics files to Compile.

    D. Set the BuildAction property of the graphics files to Embedded Resources.

15. Which of the following statements is true for a multifile assembly?

    A. Each file in a multifile assembly must contain an assembly manifest.

    B. Only one of the files in the multifile assembly can contain the assembly manifest.

    C. You can find the assembly to which a file belongs by opening that file with the MSIL Dissambler (ildasm.exe).

    D. You can have two files with the same name but different versions in a multifile assembly without any versioning conflicts.

Answers to Review Questions

1. The three different ways in which Windows components can be created are

    • Creating a nonvisual component by deriving from the Component class.

    • Creating a control that paints its own UI by deriving from the Control class or any of its derived classes.

    • Creating a composite control based on existing controls by deriving from the UserControl class or any of its derived classes.

APPLY YOUR KNOWLEDGE

2. The event handler method usually contains two parameters The first is the object on which the event occurred, and the second is the object of type System.EventArgs (or one of its derived classes) that contains event-related data.

3. To create and implement an event, you must take the following steps:

   • Define the EventArgs class that will contain the event-related data. This is required only if you want to pass specific event-related information to the event handlers.

   • Create a Delegate object to store a reference to the event handler. This is required only if you want to pass specific event-related information to the event handlers.

   • Define the event itself as an object of the Delegate type.

   • Define a method that notifies the registered objects of the event. Usually this method has a name such as OnChanged, where Changed is an event name.

   • Call the method defined in the above step whenever the event occurs.

4. The classID should be assigned the assembly (DLL) path and the control name to be hosted, separated with a # (pound sign).

5. When you create a control by inheriting from the Control class, the control does not have a UI. Therefore, the Paint event should be handled to paint the desired user interface for the control.

6. You can assign a custom Toolbox icon with a component by associating the ToolBoxBitmap attribute with the class definition.

The bitmap file (16×16) should have the same base name as that of the component, should reside in the same folder as the class file, and should have a BMP file extension.

7. An assembly manifest stores the assembly's metadata. The metadata provides self-describing information like the name and version of the assembly, the files that are part of the assembly and their hash values, the files' dependencies on other assemblies, and so on. This subset of information in the manifest makes assemblies self-sufficient.

8. Shared assemblies (those used by more than one application) should be stored in the machinewide Global Assembly Cache. Shared assemblies are digitally signed and have a strong name.

9. Resource-only assemblies are those that contain just resources and no code. Resource-only assemblies that store culture-specific information are known as satellite assemblies.

Answers to Exam Questions

1. **D.** The Native Image Generator tool (ngen.exe) converts Microsoft intermediate language to processor-specific native code. These native assemblies will load faster the first time the code is called because the work JIT compiler would do normally has been already done by the ngen tool. The other three choices are not relevant because gacutil.exe allows you to view and manipulate the contents of Global Assembly Cache. The resgen.exe is the Resource Generator tool that is used to compile XML-based resource files (resx files) into binary .resources files. The sn.exe is used to assign assemblies with a strong name so they can be placed in the Global Assembly Cache.

APPLY YOUR KNOWLEDGE

2. **A and D.** The native assemblies will load faster the first time because the work JIT compiler would do normally has been already done by the ngen tool, but for subsequent usage the native assemblies would show the same performance as their JIT-compiled equivalents. The natively generated assemblies are processor-specific: They can't be ported across a different processor architecture. The ngen.exe tool provides a /debug switch to generate native assemblies for debugging scenarios.

3. **B.** To create a satellite assembly, you first compile the XML-based resource file into a binary resource file using the Resource Generator tool (resgen.exe). Then you use the Assembly Generation tool (al.exe) to create a satellite assembly.

4. **A.** If an assembly is used by several applications, it is a good idea to place the assembly in the Global Assembly Cache because GAC provides benefits including versioning and security checks. To place an assembly in GAC you must assign a strong name to it. You can use the sn.exe tool to assign a strong name. The File Signing tool (signcode.exe) can digitally sign an assembly with a third-party software publisher's certification. It is not a requirement for an assembly to be placed in GAC.

5. **C.** Since your components are being shared between several games published by your company, they are good candidates to be placed in the Global Assembly Cache of the target machine. Before a component can be placed in GAC, it must be signed using the Strong Name tool (sn.exe). Your company is also deploying software over the Internet; in this case, it is a good idea to digitally sign your code with a software publisher's certificate obtained by a respected certification authority.

Once you obtain the certificate you can use sign-code.exe to sign your component. When you are using both sn.exe and signcode.exe with your assembly, you should always use sn.exe before using signcode.exe.

6. **D.** Versioning is done only for the assemblies having a Strong Name, so you must sign your components using the Strong Name tool (sn.exe) before they can participate in versioning.

7. **B.** The System.Windows.Forms.UserControl class provides the functionality to quickly create a reusable component by assembling existing Windows Controls.

8. **A.** You should inherit from the Control class if you want to provide a custom graphical representation of your control or functionality not available through standard controls.

9. **C.** You will use /target:module. This is the only option that instructs the VB .NET compiler not to include an assembly manifest in the compiled code.

10. **D.** Using a class derived from EventArgs to pass event parameters is preferable to using individual arguments because it's more readily extended in case you need to pass additional parameters in the future.

11. **A.** The correct usage is to give·the classID a string with the virtual path to the control and the namespace-qualified name of the control class, separated by a pound sign (#).

12. **A and B.** When you declare the contained objects within a control as Friend or Private, they are not accessible to the client application for direct manipulation. See "Creating and Managing .NET Components."

APPLY YOUR KNOWLEDGE

13. **D.** Components that provide no visual interface should derive directly from the System.ComponentModel.Component class.

14. **D.** When you set the Build Action property of a graphics file to Embedded Resources, the file is embedded with the main project output, whether that output is a DLL or an EXE.

15. **B.** Only one of the files in a multifile assembly can contain the assembly manifest. You cannot find the name of the assembly to which a file belongs by viewing it in ILDASM because only the assembly manifest contains this information. It is not possible to have two files with the same name in an assembly, and the most elementary unit of versioning is the assembly itself, so the files contained in it cannot have additional versions.

Suggested Readings and Resources

1. Box, Don. *Essential .NET Vol.1: The Common Language Runtime.* Addison Wesley, 2002.

2. Grimes, Richard. *Developing Applications With Visual Studio .NET.* Addison Wesley, 2002.

3. Richter, Jeffery. *Applied Microsoft .NET Framework Programming.* Microsoft Press, 2001.

4. Visual Studio .NET Combined Help Collection

   - Component Authoring Decision Chart
   - Component Authoring Walkthroughs
   - Creating Satellite Assemblies
   - Programming with Assemblies

This chapter covers the following Microsoft-specified objectives for the Creating User Services section of the Visual Basic .NET Windows-Based Applications exam:

Display and Update Data.

- **Transform and filter data.**

- **Bind data to the UI.**

▶ Nearly every Windows application deals with data in one way or another. The purpose of this objective is to teach you some of the skills involved in making this data available on the user interface (UI) of a Windows-based application. That includes both getting the data that the user wants to see (transforming and filtering) and tying the data to the user interface (data binding). In Chapter 6, "Consuming and Manipulating Data," you'll learn more about programming with data; this objective deals with the parts of the process that you can actually see onscreen.

CHAPTER 5

Data Binding

STUDY STRATEGIES

▶ Read the sections on data binding carefully, even if you think you already know all about data binding. In the .NET world, the concept of data binding has been generalized and improved from what existed in earlier Microsoft development environments.

▶ In previous Microsoft development environments, many writers and trainers recommended avoiding data binding due to performance issues and a lack of flexibility. Microsoft has removed the bulk of these limitations in Visual Studio .NET. Even if you ignored data binding in the past, you should expect to be tested on it this time.

▶ Ensure that you understand the difference between *simple* and *complex data binding*, and the syntax used for each.

▶ Practice working with Server Explorer. You should know how to connect your application to any data source and how to select and display the data that you want to show to the end user.

INTRODUCTION

Now that you know how to put together a user interface in Visual Basic .NET, it's time to turn to the functionality behind the user interface. One of the most important parts of developing almost any application is to connect the *data model* of the application to the user interface. *Data model* is a general term: it might refer to data stored in a database, or to an array of values, or to items contained in an object from the System.Collections namespace. The data model is internal to the application and contains information that is known to the application.

To be useful to the end users of your application, the data model must somehow be connected to the user interface. One of the easiest ways to make a connection between the data model and the user interface is to bind the data to the user interface. *Binding* refers to the process of making a link between controls on the user interface and data stored in the data model. As the user views and manipulates controls, the application takes care of translating his actions into reading and writing data from the data model.

Sometimes the data model contains more information than you want to show to the user. For example, you might have a list of 10,000 customers in the data model. Most likely the user wants to see the orders from a single customer or a small group of customers. So, your application will need to filter (limit) the amount of information that it shows from the data model to avoid overwhelming the user. You might also need to transform the data from an internal representation (for example, a customer code) to something more user friendly (such as a customer name) in the process of moving it from the data model to the user interface.

In this chapter I'll cover all these topics using a broad concept of data. In the next chapter, I'll drill into the use of ADO.NET, focusing on data stored in databases.

BIND DATA TO THE UI

Display and Update Data: Bind data to the UI.

Binding data (sometimes called *data binding*) is the process of creating a link between a data model and the user interface of an application.

The data model can be any source of data within the application: It might be an array of values, an XML file, or data stored in a database. The user interface consists of the controls contained on the forms in your application.

The .NET Framework includes extremely flexible data binding capabilities. In this section you'll learn about many of those capabilities:

◆ Simple data binding

◆ Complex data binding

◆ One-way and two-way data binding

◆ The BindingContext object

◆ The DataForm Wizard

Simple Data Binding

Simple data binding means connecting a single value from the data model to a single property of a control. For example, you might bind the Vendor name from a list of vendors to the Text property of a TextBox control (see Step By Step 5.1).

STEP BY STEP

5.1 Using Simple Data Binding to Display a Vendor Name

1. Place a TextBox control on a new VB .NET form. Name the control txtVendorName.

---

2. Double-click the form and enter code in the form's Load event:

```
Private Sub StepByStep5_1_Load(ByVal sender As System.Object, _
 ByVal e As System.EventArgs) Handles MyBase.Load

    ' Create an array of vendor names
    Dim astrVendorNames() As String = _
     {"Microsoft", "Rational", "Premia"}
    ' Bind the array to the textbox
    txtVendorName.DataBindings.Add("Text", astrVendorNames, "")

End Sub
```

---

3. Set the form as the startup object for the project.

4. Run the project. The text box is now bound to the array and will display the first value from the array.

Looking at the code in the previous Step By Step, you can see that the .NET Framework supplies an object model for binding on the next to last line of code. The control has a ControlDataBindings collection (accessed through its DataBindings property), which contains instances of the `Binding` class. By default no Binding objects are in the collection, so when you create a control, it's not bound. To bind the control, you can add a new Binding object to the collection by using its `Add` method.

Because the `Add` method is creating a new instance of the `Binding` class, it takes the same parameters as the constructor for that class:

◆ The name of the property to bind to

◆ The data source to bind

◆ The navigation path to the particular data

In this particular example, the navigation path is empty because only one thing to bind to is in this array.

Now that you've seen simple data binding in action, it's time to explore the topic in a bit more depth. I'll start by looking at which entities can be bound to the user interface. Then you'll see which properties you can bind to those entities. Finally, I'll explain the architecture that the .NET Framework uses to manage simple data binding. You can work directly with the objects that handle data binding connections if you need to interact with the data binding process from your code.

Bindable Entities

In the previous example, the Text property of the TextBox control was bound to an element from an array. The Binding class can accept many other data sources, including

◆ An instance of any class that implements the IBindingList or ITypedList interface. These include the DataSet, DataTable, DataView, and DataViewManager classes.

◆ Any class that implements the IList interface on an indexed collection of objects. In particular, this applies to classes that inherit from System.Array, including VB .NET arrays.

◆ A strongly typed IList of strongly typed objects. For example, you can bind to an array of Vendor objects.

Binding to a strongly typed IList of strongly typed objects is a convenient way to handle data from an object-oriented data model (see Step By Step 5.2).

STEP BY STEP

5.2 Using Simple Data Binding with a Strongly Typed IList

1. Add a new class named Vendor.vb to your VB .NET project. Enter this code in the class:

```
Public Class Vendor

    Private mstrVendorName As String

    Public Property VendorName() As String
        Get
            VendorName = mstrVendorName
        End Get
        Set(ByVal Value As String)
            mstrVendorName = Value
        End Set
    End Property

    Sub New(ByVal VendorName As String)
        mstrVendorName = VendorName
    End Sub

End Class
```

2. Place a TextBox control on a new VB .NET Form. Name the control txtVendorName.

3. Double-click the form and enter code in the form's Load event:

```
Private Sub StepByStep5_2_Load( _
 ByVal sender As System.Object, _
 ByVal e As System.EventArgs) Handles MyBase.Load
```

```
' Create an array of vendor objects
Dim aVendors(3) As Vendor
aVendors(0) = New Vendor("Microsoft")
aVendors(1) = New Vendor("Rational")
aVendors(2) = New Vendor("Premia")

' Bind the array to the textbox
txtVendorName.DataBindings.Add( _
  "Text", aVendors, "VendorName")

End Sub
```

> **NOTE**
>
> **Navigation Path for Objects** This list of steps demonstrates how to use the navigation path (the third parameter to the DataBindings.Add call) to specify a particular property of an object to bind to a control.

4. Set the form as the startup object for the project.

5. Run the project. The text box is now bound to the array and will display the first value from the array.

At this point, you might think that binding makes only the first element of a data source available on the user interface. In fact, bound controls are designed to let the user move through an entire collection of data. Later in this chapter you'll learn the details of the BindingContext object, which enables you to manipulate the data behind a bound control. But as a preview, Figure 5.1 shows a form that lets you scroll through the data in a strongly typed Ilist, and Step By Step 5.3 gives more information on using the BindingContext object.

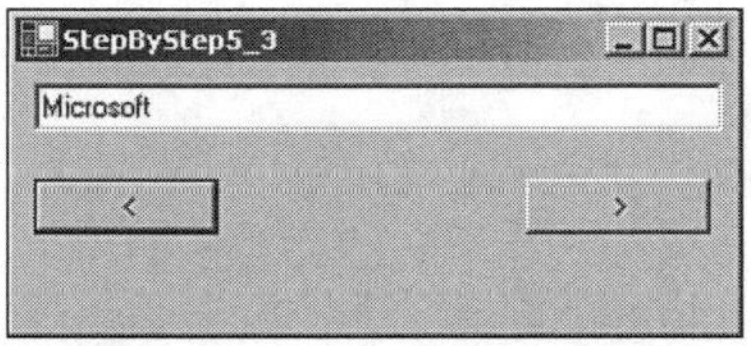

FIGURE 5.1
This form includes a bound TextBox control and two Button controls that let the user scroll through the data.

STEP BY STEP

5.3 Scrolling Through Data with the BindingContext Object

1. Place a TextBox control on a new VB .NET Form. Name the control txtVendorName.

2. Place a Button control on the form. Name the control btnPrevious and set its Text property to <.

3. Place a second Button control on the form. Name the control btnNext and set its Text property to >.

continues

continued

4. Double-click the form and enter code in the form's `Load` event:

```
' Create an array of vendor objects
Dim maVendors(3) As Vendor

Private Sub StepByStep5_3_Load( _
 ByVal sender As System.Object, _
 ByVal e As System.EventArgs) Handles MyBase.Load

    ' Initialize the vendors array
    maVendors(0) = New Vendor("Microsoft")
    maVendors(1) = New Vendor("Rational")
    maVendors(2) = New Vendor("Premia")

    ' Bind the array to the textbox
    txtVendorName.DataBindings.Add( _
     "Text", maVendors, "VendorName")

End Sub
```

5. Add this code to handle the `Click` events from the two buttons:

```
Private Sub btnPrevious_Click(ByVal sender As Object, _
 ByVal e As System.EventArgs) Handles btnPrevious.Click
    ' Move to the previous item in the data source
    Me.BindingContext(maVendors).Position -= 1
End Sub

Private Sub btnNext_Click(ByVal sender As Object, _
 ByVal e As System.EventArgs) Handles btnNext.Click
    ' Move to the next item in the data source
    Me.BindingContext(maVendors).Position += 1
End Sub
```

6. Set the form as the startup object for the project.

7. Run the project. The text box is now bound to the array and will display the first value from the array. You can use the two buttons to move to different values within the array.

Properties That Can Be Bound

Just as the .NET Framework allows flexibility in the source of bound data, it allows flexibility on the user interface. You can use simple data binding with any control that has a DataBindings property, which includes any control derived from System.Windows.Forms.Control.

In practice, that's almost any control you can drop on a Windows form.

You can bind just about any property of these controls to an item of data. This gives enormous flexibility in building a user interface that depends on data. For example, you can bind an array of DateTime values to the Value property of a DateTimePicker control (see Step By Step 5.4).

STEP BY STEP

5.4 Binding Data to a DateTimePicker Control

1. Place a DateTimePicker control on a new VB .NET form. Name the control dtBound.

2. Place a Button control on the form. Name the control btnPrevious and set its Text property to <.

3. Place a second Button control on the form. Name the control btnNext and set its Text property to >.

4. Double-click the form and enter code in the form's Load event:

```
' Create an array of dates
Dim madtBound() As Date = _
 {DateTime.Today, DateTime.Today.AddDays(1), _
  DateTime.Today.AddDays(2), DateTime.Today.AddDays(3), _
  DateTime.Today.AddDays(4), DateTime.Today.AddDays(5)}

Private Sub StepByStep5_4_Load( _
 ByVal sender As System.Object, _
 ByVal e As System.EventArgs) Handles MyBase.Load

    ' Bind the array to the date/time picker
    dtBound.DataBindings.Add("Value", madtBound, "")

End Sub
```

5. Add this code to handle the Click events from the two buttons:

```
Private Sub btnPrevious_Click(ByVal sender As Object, _
 ByVal e As System.EventArgs) Handles btnPrevious.Click
    ' Move to the previous item in the data source
    Me.BindingContext(mdtBound).Position -= 1
End Sub
```

continues

continued

```
Private Sub btnNext_Click(ByVal sender As Object, _
 ByVal e As System.EventArgs) Handles btnNext.Click
    ' Move to the next item in the data source
    Me.BindingContext(mdtBound).Position += 1
End Sub
```

6. Set the form as the startup object for the project.

7. Run the project. The `DateTimePicker` control is now bound to the array and will display the first value from the array. You can use the two buttons to move to different values within the array.

If you think creatively, you can find many ways to use simple data binding beyond simply displaying text in a text box. Some possibilities:

◆ Display a set of photos by binding to the Image property of a PictureBox control.

◆ Show the relative magnitude of quantities with the Value property of a ProgressBar control.

◆ Color-code an area of a form by binding the BackColor property of a Panel control.

The Architecture of Data Binding

When you use data binding to connect a control to a data source, the .NET Framework creates a pair of objects to manage the binding: a *CurrencyManager object* and a *BindingContext object*. Depending on the number of controls on the form and the data to which they are bound, a single form might involve several of each of these objects.

The CurrencyManager object is responsible for keeping track of which piece of data from a data source is currently bound to the user interface. Although so far you've only seen one bound control on each form, a single form can contain multiple bound controls. If all the controls are bound to the same data source, they can share a CurrencyManager. But a single form can involve multiple CurrencyManager objects as well. Suppose, for example, that you built a form with an array of Vendor objects bound to one control and an array of dates bound to another control. In that case, the form would have two CurrencyManager objects.

Any bound form will also have at least one BindingContext object. The job of the BindingContext object is to keep track of the various CurrencyManager objects on the form. The Item property of the BindingContext object returns a CurrencyManager object. Consider this line of code:

```
Me.BindingContext(mdtBound).Position += 1
```

That tells the BindingContext for the form to return a CurrencyManager object for the mdtBound data source and then to increment the Position property of the CurrencyManager object. The CurrencyManager encapsulates the knowledge of how to move the pointer within the data array when the Position property is changed.

In addition to forms, container controls (such as the GroupBox, Panel, or TabControl controls) can have their own BindingContext objects. Using these separate BindingContext objects, you can create forms that have independently scolling views of the same data.

You'll see the CurrencyManager object in more depth later in this chapter. But first, let's look at another variety of data binding: complex data binding.

R E V I E W   B R E A K

▶ Simple data binding refers to connecting a single entity in the data model to a single property of a control on the user interface.

▶ Any class that implements the IBindingList, ITypedList, or IList interface can deliver data via simple data binding.

▶ You can bind to almost any property of any control.

▶ The form uses CurrencyManager and BindingContext objects to keep track of data binding.

Complex Data Binding

In *complex data binding*, you bind a user interface control to an entire collection of data, rather than to a single data item. A good example of complex data binding is the DataGrid control.

Figure 5.2 shows a bound DataGrid control displaying data from the Suppliers table in the SQL Server 2000 Northwind database.

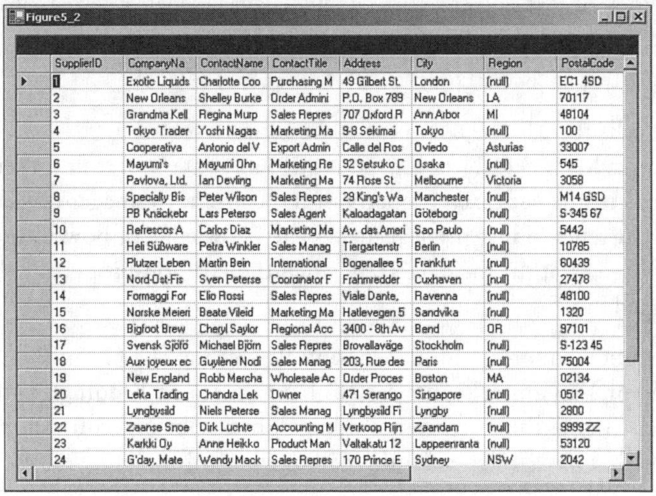

FIGURE 5.2

By using complex data binding, you can see an entire collection of data on the user interface at one time. Here a DataGrid control displays the Northwind Suppliers table.

EXAM TIP

Database Terminology Some literature refers to the rows of a database table as *records* or *tuples* and the columns as *fields* or *attributes*.

NOTE

The Northwind Sample Database Whenever I've used data from a database in this book, I've used the Northwind sample database that comes as part of SQL Server 2000. Visual Studio .NET includes MSDE, a stripped-down version of SQL Server that you can use if you don't have the full version installed. See your Visual Studio CD's readme file for information on installing MSDE. You can also find the Northwind sample database in any version of Microsoft Access, but the Access version does not ship with Visual Studio .NET. The code in this book assumes you're using the SQL Server version.

You'll learn how to build this form later in the chapter, but for now, concentrate on its features. The DataGrid is a single control that displays many pieces of data. In this case, the data is taken from the rows and columns of the Suppliers table in a SQL Server 2000 database. You can click on any cell in the DataGrid and edit the data the cell contains. If you've properly programmed your form, these edits will be reflected in the underlying data.

Obviously, complex data binding is a powerful tool for transferring large amounts of data from a data model to a user interface. In this section we'll dig into the mechanics of complex data binding with two examples:

◆ Binding to a ComboBox or ListBox

◆ Binding to a DataGrid

Binding to a ComboBox or ListBox

The ComboBox and ListBox controls both provide ways for the user to select one item from a list of data. The difference between the two is that in the ListBox the list is visible at all times, whereas in the ComboBox the list is hidden until the user clicks the drop-down arrow at the end of the box. Either of these controls can be loaded with an entire list of data via complex data binding.

Step By Step 5.5 explores the process of binding data to the list in a ListBox Control.

STEP BY STEP

5.5 Binding Data to the List in a ListBox Control

1. Place a ListBox control on a new VB .NET form. Name the control `lbExams`.

2. Add a new class named `Exam.vb` to your VB .NET project. Enter this code in the class:

```
Public Class Exam

    Private mstrExamNumber As String
    Private mstrExamName As String

    Public ReadOnly Property ExamNumber() As String
        Get
            ExamNumber = mstrExamNumber
        End Get
    End Property

    Public ReadOnly Property ExamName() As String
        Get
            ExamName = mstrExamName
        End Get
    End Property

    Sub New(ByVal ExamNumber As String, _
     ByVal ExamName As String)
        mstrExamNumber = ExamNumber
        mstrExamName = ExamName
    End Sub

End Class
```

3. Double-click the form and enter code in the form's `Load` event:

```
Private Sub StepByStep5_5_Load(ByVal sender As System.Object, _
ByVal e As System.EventArgs) Handles MyBase.Load

    ' Create an array of exams
    Dim aExams() As Exam = _
     {New Exam("305", "Web Applications With VB.NET"), _
      New Exam("306", "Windows Applications With _
      VB.NET"), _
      New Exam("310", "XML With VB.NET"), _
      New Exam("315", _
```

continues

continued

```
        "Web Applications With Visual C# .NET"), _
        New Exam("316", _
        "Windows Applications With Visual C# .NET"), _
        New Exam("320", "XML With Visual C# .NET")}

    ' Bind the array to the listbox
    With lbExams
        .DataSource = aExams
        .DisplayMember = "ExamName"
    End With

End Sub
```

4. Set the form as the startup object for the project.

5. Run the project. The ListBox control will display the `ExamName` property of every object in the array.

This Step By Step works by first creating an array of Exam objects that contains all the information you'd like to display in the list portion of a ListBox. It then sets the `DataSource` property of the ListBox to the name of the array and the `DisplayMember` property to the name of the object property that supplies the text for the list. The result is a ListBox that allows the user to choose from a list of exam names.

As it stands, this example doesn't do anything with the data after the user chooses an item from the list. But frequently you'll use a complex data bound ListBox or ComboBox in conjunction with a simple data bound control such as a TextBox. By selecting a row in the ListBox, the user can choose a value for the TextBox.

You can think of the ListBox in this case as a little pump that moves data from one part of the data model to another. Step By Step 5.6 shows how to set this up.

STEP BY STEP

5.6 Using a ListBox with Two Data Bindings

1. Start with the form from Step By Step 5.5. Add two Label controls, two Button controls, and two TextBox controls. Name the TextBox controls `txtCandidateName` and `txtExamNumber`. Name the buttons `btnPrevious` and `btnNext`. Arrange the controls as shown in Figure 5.3.

2. Add a new class named `Candidate.vb` to your VB .NET project. Enter this code in the class:

```
Public Class Candidate

    Private mstrExamNumber As String
    Private mstrCandidateName As String

    Public Property ExamNumber() As String
        Get
            ExamNumber = mstrExamNumber
        End Get
        Set(ByVal Value As String)
            mstrExamNumber = Value
        End Set
    End Property

    Public Property CandidateName() As String
        Get
            CandidateName = mstrCandidateName
        End Get
        Set(ByVal Value As String)
            mstrCandidateName = Value
        End Set
    End Property

    Sub New(ByVal CandidateName As String, _
     Optional ByVal ExamNumber As String = "")
        mstrCandidateName = CandidateName
        mstrExamNumber = ExamNumber
    End Sub

End Class
```

FIGURE 5.3
Design a form with a bound ListBox control and other controls to see the effect of the data binding.

3. Modify the form's module to include this code:

```
' Create an array of candidates
Private maCandidates() As Candidate = _
 {New Candidate("Bill Gates", "305"), _
  New Candidate("Steve Ballmer", "320")}


Private Sub StepByStep5_6_Load( _
 ByVal sender As System.Object, _
 ByVal e As System.EventArgs) Handles MyBase.Load

    ' Create an array of exams
    Dim aExams() As Exam = _
     {New Exam("305", "Web Applications With VB.NET"), _
      New Exam("306", "Windows Applications With _
      VB.NET"), _
      New Exam("310", "XML With VB.NET"), _
      New Exam("315", _
      "Web Applications With Visual C# .NET"), _
      New Exam("316", _
      "Windows Applications With Visual C# .NET"), _
      New Exam("320", "XML With Visual C# .NET")}
```

continues

continued

```
' Bind the array to the listbox
With lbExams
    .DataSource = aExams
    .DisplayMember = "ExamName"
    .ValueMember = "ExamNumber"
End With

'Bind the candidates to the textboxes
txtCandidateName.DataBindings.Add( _
 "Text", maCandidates, "CandidateName")
txtExamNumber.DataBindings.Add( _
 "Text", maCandidates, "ExamNumber")

' And bind the exam number to the listbox value
lbExams.DataBindings.Add( _
 "SelectedValue", maCandidates, "ExamNumber")

End Sub

Private Sub btnPrevious_Click( _
 ByVal sender As System.Object, _
 ByVal e As System.EventArgs) Handles btnPrevious.Click
    Me.BindingContext(maCandidates).Position -= 1
End Sub

Private Sub btnNext_Click(ByVal sender As System.Object, _
 ByVal e As System.EventArgs) Handles btnNext.Click
    Me.BindingContext(maCandidates).Position += 1
End Sub
```

4. Set the form as the startup object for the project.

5. Run the project. As you move through the Candidate records, the ListBox will show the exam name that matches the exam number for the candidate. If you change the value in the Listbox or in the txtExamNumber control, the change will be reflected in the other control as soon as the change is committed (by tabbing to another control).

Understanding this example is crucial for the effective use of ComboBox and ListBox controls in your applications. That can be a little tricky, because the ListBox control is bound to two different things. Let's review how it all fits together:

◆ The ListBox in this example draws the list of items to display from the array of Exam objects. The list portion of the listbox is complex bound to this array. The complex binding is managed by setting the DataSource, DisplayMember, and ValueMember properties of the ListBox.

◆ The two TextBox controls are simple bound to different elements in the array of Candidate objects. As you move through that array (with the btnNext and btnPrevious controls), the data displayed in those TextBox controls changes. This is, by the way, a two-way link. If you change the data in one of the TextBox controls, it's also changed in the array, as you can see by changing an entry, scrolling to another candidate, and scrolling back.

◆ The SelectedValue property of the ListBox is also simple bound to an element in the array of Candidate objects. This sets up the link between the two arrays. As you choose an item from the list in the ListBox, your choice is automatically pushed to the bound value from the Candidate array.

◆ Because the SelectedValue property of the ListBox and the Text property of the txtExamNumber text box are bound to the same value, they automatically stay synchronized when either one is updated.

◆ You can use the DisplayMember and ValueMember properties of the ListBox control to show one value while binding another, as in the previous example.

Binding to a DataGrid

The DataGrid also provides a way to display many rows from a data model simultaneously. The DataGrid is designed to let you see an entire collection of data (often called a *result set*) at one time (see Step By Step 5.7).

STEP BY STEP

5.7 Binding an Array of Objects to a DataGrid

1. Place a DataGrid control on a new VB .NET form. Name the control dgExams.

continues

continued

2. Double-click the form and enter code in the form's `Load` event:

```
Private Sub StepByStep5_7_Load( _
 ByVal sender As System.Object, _
 ByVal e As System.EventArgs) Handles MyBase.Load

    ' Create an array of exams
    Dim aExams() As Exam = _
     {New Exam("305", "Web Applications With VB.NET"), _
      New Exam("306", "Windows Applications With _
      VB.NET"), _
      New Exam("310", "XML With VB.NET"), _
      New Exam("315", "Web Applications With Visual C# _
      .NET"), _
      New Exam("316", "Windows Applications With Visual _
      C# .NET"), _
      New Exam("320", "XML With Visual C# .NET")}

    ' Bind the array to the datagrid
    dgExams.DataSource = aExams

End Sub
```

3. Set the form as the startup object for the project.

4. Run the project. The DataGrid will display all the information from the `aExams` array.

The DataGrid control is a mainstay of data display for Visual Basic .NET forms. As such, it is extremely configurable. Visual Studio .NET includes several interfaces for setting the display propeties of a DataGrid. First, you can set individual properties to control the look of the DataGrid in the Properties window. Second, you can use AutoFormats to apply a whole new look to a DataGrid quickly (see Step by Step 5.8).

STEP BY STEP

5.8 Applying an AutoFormat to a DataGrid

1. Select a DataGrid control on a Visual Basic .NET form with the form open in the Visual Studio .NET Designer.

2. Click the AutoFormat hyperlink, located directly under the Properties list in the Properties window. This will open the Auto Format dialog box.

3. Select a format from the list and click OK to apply the new format to the DataGrid control. Figure 5.4 shows some contrasting AutoFormats.

When you need more precise formatting for a DataGrid control than the Auto Format dialog box allows, or when you just don't care for the look of any of the AutoFormats, you can set individual display properties for the DataGrid control. Table 5.1 lists the properties you can use to control the look of the DataGrid control.

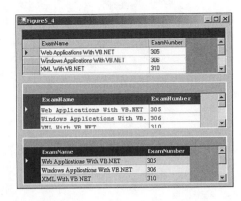

FIGURE 5.4
The three DataGrid controls on this form have had three different AutoFormats applied. Though each is bound to the same array of objects, they look different.

TABLE 5.1

DataGrid Control Display Properties

Property	Explanation
AlternatingBackColor	Background color to use for even-numbered rows in the grid.
BackColor	Background color to use for odd-numbered rows in the grid.
BackgroundColor	Color to use for any portion of the control that's not filled with data.
BorderStyle	Select from None, FixedSingle, or Fixed3D for the borders of the control.
CaptionBackColor	Background color for the caption portion of the control.
CaptionFont	Font for the caption portion of the control.
CaptionText	Text to display in the caption portion of the control.
CaptionVisible	Boolean property that controls whether a caption will be displayed.
ColumnHeadersVisible	Boolean property that controls whether each column will have a header.
FlatMode	Boolean property that controls whether the grid will have a 3D or a flat appearance.
Font	Font for text in the control.

continues

TABLE 5.1	*continued*

DATAGRID CONTROL DISPLAY PROPERTIES

Property	Explanation
ForeColor	Foreground color for text in the control.
GridlineColor	Color for the lines of the grid.
GridlineStyle	Select from None or Solid.
HeaderBackColor	Background color for column and row headers.
HeaderFont	Font for column and row headers.
HeaderForeColor	Foreground color for column and row headers.
LinkColor	Color to use for hyperlinks between sections of the control.
ParentRowBackColor	Background color to use for the Parent Rows area.
ParentRowsForeColor	Text color to use for the Parent Rows area.
ParentRowsLabelStyle	Select from None, TableName, ColumnName, or Both.
ParentRowsVisible	Boolean property that controls whether the Parent Rows area will be visible.
PreferredColumnWidth	Default width for columns, in pixels.
PreferredRowHeight	Default height for rows, in pixels.
RowHeadersVisible	Boolean property that controls whether each row will have a header.
RowHeaderWidth	Default width of row headers, in pixels.
SelectionBackColor	Background color for any selected cells.
SelectionForeColor	Text color for any selected cells.

Figure 5.5 shows a complex data bound DataGrid control displaying data from several database tables simultaneously to help you understand where each of the areas mentioned in Table 5.1 is located. You'll learn how to bind database tables to the DataGrid later in this chapter. In the meantime, you can integrate your knowledge of the DataGrid control with data binding in Guided Practice Exercise 5.1

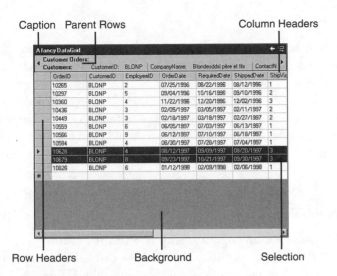

Caption   Parent Rows

Column Headers

Row Headers

Background

Selection

FIGURE 5.5
Location of formatting areas on the DataGrid control.

GUIDED PRACTICE
EXERCISE 5.1

In this exercise, you'll work with employee data from Skylark Spaceways. This exercise will help you review the basic syntax of both simple and complex data binding, and in addition uses the DataGrid control. Table 5.2 shows the data you need to manage.

TABLE 5.2

SKYLARK SPACEWAYS EMPLOYEE ROSTER

Employee Number	Employee Name	Position	Home Planet
1	E.E. Smith	CEO	Earth
2	Melanie "Jets" Riggs	Chief Pilot	Mars
3	William Danforth	Pilot	Mars
4	Blaise Canton	Engineer	Luna
5	Amanda Timmel	CFO	Earth

continues

continued

Your task is to display this data in two ways. First, create a form that displays information about one employee at a time with buttons to scroll through the list. To save space, the form will show the employee name and position in TextBox controls. However, it should also make the home planet information available as a ToolTip on the Employee Name text box. A button on this form should open a second form. The second form should display the entire employee roster in grid form.

Try this on your own first. If you get stuck, or would like to see one possible solution, follow these steps:

1. Create a form populated with two TextBox controls (txtEmployeeName and txtPosition), two Label controls, and three Button controls, arranged as shown in Figure 5.6. Also add a ToolTip control to this form.

2. Create a new class in the project using this code:

```
Public Class Employee

    Private mintEmployeeNumber As Integer
    Private mstrEmployeeName As String
    Private mstrPosition As String
    Private mstrHomePlanet As String

    Public Property EmployeeNumber() As Integer
        Get
            EmployeeNumber = mintEmployeeNumber
        End Get
        Set(ByVal Value As Integer)
            mintEmployeeNumber = Value
        End Set
    End Property

    Public Property EmployeeName() As String
        Get
            EmployeeName = mstrEmployeeName
        End Get
        Set(ByVal Value As String)
            mstrEmployeeName = Value
        End Set
    End Property
```

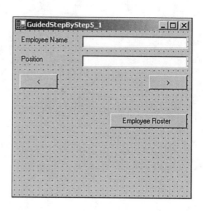

FIGURE 5.6
Design a form to display employee data.

```
    Public Property Position() As String
        Get
            Position = mstrPosition
        End Get
        Set(ByVal Value As String)
            mstrPosition = Value
        End Set
    End Property

    Public Property HomePlanet() As String
        Get
            HomePlanet = mstrHomePlanet
        End Get
        Set(ByVal Value As String)
            mstrHomePlanet = Value
        End Set
    End Property

    Sub New(ByVal EmployeeNumber As Integer, _
     ByVal EmployeeName As String, _
     ByVal Position As String, ByVal HomePlanet As _
     String)
        mintEmployeeNumber = EmployeeNumber
        mstrEmployeeName = EmployeeName
        mstrPosition = Position
        mstrHomePlanet = HomePlanet
    End Sub
End Class
```

3. Add code behind this form to handle data creation, data binding, and navigation:

```
' Create and stock an array of data
Dim maEmployees() As Employee = _
 {New Employee(1, "E.E. Smith", "CEO", "Earth"), _
  New Employee(2, "Melanie ""Jets"" Riggs", _
  "Chief Pilot", "Mars"), _
  New Employee(3, "William Danforth", "Pilot", "Mars"), _
  New Employee(4, "Blaise Canton", "Engineer", "Luna"), _
  New Employee(5, "Amanda Timmel", "CFO", "Earth")}

Private Sub GuidedStepByStep5_1_Load( _
 ByVal sender As System.Object, _
 ByVal e As System.EventArgs) Handles MyBase.Load

    ' Bind data to the ui
    txtEmployeeName.DataBindings.Add( _
      "Text", maEmployees, "EmployeeName")
    txtEmployeeName.DataBindings.Add( _
      "Tag", maEmployees, "HomePlanet")
    txtPosition.DataBindings.Add("Text", _
      maEmployees, "Position")
```

continues

continued

```
' Transfer the home planet info to the tooltip
ToolTip1.SetToolTip(txtEmployeeName, _
 txtEmployeeName.Tag)

End Sub

Private Sub btnPrevious_Click(ByVal sender As Object, _
 ByVal e As System.EventArgs) Handles btnPrevious.Click
    Me.BindingContext(maEmployees).Position -= 1
    ToolTip1.SetToolTip(txtEmployeeName, _
     txtEmployeeName.Tag)
End Sub

Private Sub btnNext_Click(ByVal sender As Object, _
 ByVal e As System.EventArgs) Handles btnNext.Click
    Me.BindingContext(maEmployees).Position += 1
    ToolTip1.SetToolTip(txtEmployeeName, _
     txtEmployeeName.Tag)
End Sub

Private Sub btnRoster_Click(ByVal sender As
System.Object, _
 ByVal e As System.EventArgs) Handles btnRoster.Click
    Dim f As New GuidedStepByStep5_1a()
    f.dgEmployees.DataSource = maEmployees
    f.Show()
End Sub
End Class
```

4. Create a second form and name it GuidedStepByStep5_1a (or give it any name you like, and revise the code in the btnRoster_Click event in step 3 to match). Place a single DataGrid control on this form. Name the DataGrid Control dgEmployees.

5. Set the first form as the project's startup form and test your work. You should be able to scroll through employees, view the home planet information in a ToolTip, and open a grid containing all the employee information.

If you had difficulty following this exercise, review the sections titled "Simple Data Binding" and "Complex Data Binding." The text and examples should help you relearn the material and understand what happened in this exercise. After review, try this exercise again.

▶ Complex data binding binds a user interface control to an entire collection of data.

▶ To use complex data binding with a ListBox or ComboBox control, set the control's `DataSource` and `DisplayMember` properties.

▶ A ListBox or ComboBox control can act to pull values from one data source and place them in another.

▶ You can cause a ListBox or ComboBox control to display one value while binding another by using the `DisplayMember` and `ValueMember` properties of the control.

▶ The DataGrid control displays an entire array of data in rows and columns. You specify the data to display by setting the `DataSource` property of the DataGrid control.

▶ The properties of the DataGrid control include many flexible formatting options.

One-Way and Two-Way Data Binding

Data binding in Windows forms can be *one-way* or *two-way*. In one-way data binding, the bound property of the control reflects changes to the data model, but changes to the control are not written back to the data model. For example, if you display a list of customers in a ComboBox control, the act of selecting a customer from the ComboBox does not modify the list.

In two-way data binding, changes to the control are written back to the data model. For example, if a TextBox control is bound to the `CustomerName` property of a Customer object, changing the text in the text box changes the corresponding property of the object.

Simple data binding on Windows forms is automatically two-way. Any changes you make to the data on the form are automatically transmitted back to the data model. However, note that the data model might not be the ultimate data source. The most common exception to this comes when using the ADO.NET classes to access data from a database and place it in a data model. Changes to bound data on a form are written back to the data model, but they are not automatically returned to the database (though you can write code to do this).

NOTE Using the DataAdapter to Update the Data Source To transmit changes from a data model back to the original data source, you'll usually use the `Update` method of the DataAdapter object. For more detailed information on the DataAdapter object, refer to Chapter 6, "Consuming and Manipulating Data," and to the section "Object Design from Server Explorer" later in this chapter.

The BindingContext and CurrencyManager Classes

You saw the BindingContext and CurrencyManager classes earlier in the chapter, when I discussed the overall architecture of data binding. Now that you've seen both simple and complex data binding in action, it's time to look at the BindingContext and CurrencyManager classes in somewhat more detail. In many applications, you can let Visual Basic .NET manage these objects for you, but sometimes it's useful to work directly with these objects. For instance, the CurrencyManager class provides event hooks to let you react to modifications that the user makes to bound data.

The BindingContext class exists primarily as a means to retrieve the CurrencyManager objects on a form. Table 5.3 shows the important interface members of the BindingContext class.

TABLE 5.3

MEMBERS OF THE BINDINGCONTEXT CLASS

Member	Type	Description
Contains	Method	Indicates whether the BindingContext contains a specific BindingManagerBase object
Item	Property	Returns a BindingManagerBase object

The BindingManagerBase class is an abstract class that is implemented in both the CurrencyManager class and the PropertyManager class. You've already seen the CurrencyManager class. The PropertyManager class manipulates the current value of an individual property, rather than the property of the current object in a list; you'll seldom have any reason to use the PropertyManager class. Table 5.4 shows the important interface members of the BindingManagerBase class.

TABLE 5.4

MEMBERS OF THE BINDINGMANAGERBASE CLASS

Member	Type	Description
AddNew	Method	Adds a new object to the underlying list
Bindings	Property	Gets the collection of Bindings being managed by this class
CancelCurrentEdit	Method	Cancels any edit in progress
Count	Property	Gets the number of rows managed by the class
Current	Property	Gets the current object
CurrentChanged	Event	Occurs when the bound value changes
EndCurrentEdit	Method	Commits any edit in progress
GetItemProperties	Method	Gets a list of item properties for the current object in the list
Position	Property	Gets or sets the position in the underlying list that is bound with this class
PositionChanged	Event	Occurs when the Position property changes
RemoveAt	Method	Removes the object at the specified position from the underlying list
ResumeBinding	Method	Resumes data binding
SuspendBinding	Method	Suspends data binding

The CurrencyManager class implements most of the interfaces of the BindingManagerBase class and adds a few more of its own. Table 5.5 lists the important interface members of the CurrencyManager class.

TABLE 5.5

MEMBERS OF THE CURRENCYMANAGER CLASS

Member	Type	Description
AddNew	Method	Adds a new object to the underlying list
Bindings	Property	Gets the collection of Bindings being managed by this class

TABLE 5.5   *continued*

MEMBERS OF THE CURRENCYMANAGER CLASS

Member	Type	Description
CancelCurrentEdit	Method	Cancels any edit in progress
Count	Property	Gets the number of rows managed by the class
Current	Property	Gets the current object
CurrentChanged	Event	Occurs when the bound value changes
EndCurrentEdit	Method	Commits any edit in process
GetItemProperties	Method	Gets a list of item properties for the current object in the list
ItemChanged	Event	Occurs when the current item has been altered
List	Property	Gets the Ilist interface from the data source
Position	Property	Gets or sets the position in the underlying list that is bound with this class
PositionChanged	Event	Occurs when the Position property changes
Refresh	Method	Repopulates the bound controls
RemoveAt	Method	Removes the object at the specified position from the underlying list
ResumeBinding	Method	Resumes data binding
SuspendBinding	Method	Suspends data binding

EXAM TIP

Understanding the Binding Objects
There's no need to memorize every detail of the BindingContext, BindingManagerBase, and CurrencyManager objects. Instead, concentrate on knowing the overall uses of these objects. The BindingContext is your hook to retrieve the CurrencyManager object. The BindingManagerBase class supplies the Position property that lets you see where you are in a set of bound data. The CurrencyManager class supplies the event hooks that let you interact with user-initiated data changes.

In addition to manipulating the Position property, you'll likely find the CurrencyManager class most useful for managing events on data bound forms. Of course, because this class doesn't have a visual, control-based representation, you'll need to set up these events in code. Listing 5.1 shows how to create delegates and respond to the events of the CurrencyManager class.

LISTING 5.1

TRAPPING EVENTS FOR THE CURRENCYMANAGER CLASS

```
' Create an array of vendor objects
Dim maVendors(3) As Vendor
```

```vb
Private Sub Listing5_1_Load(ByVal sender As System.Object, _
 ByVal e As System.EventArgs) Handles MyBase.Load

    ' Initialize the vendors array
    maVendors(0) = New Vendor("Microsoft")
    maVendors(1) = New Vendor("Rational")
    maVendors(2) = New Vendor("Premia")

    ' Bind the array to the textbox
    txtVendorName.DataBindings.Add("Text", _
     maVendors, "VendorName")

    Dim cm As CurrencyManager = _
    Me.BindingContext(maVendors)

    AddHandler cm.CurrentChanged, _
     AddressOf CurrencyManager_CurrentChanged
    AddHandler cm.ItemChanged, _
     AddressOf CurrencyManager_ItemChanged
    AddHandler cm.PositionChanged, _
     AddressOf CurrencyManager_PositionChanged

End Sub

Private Sub CurrencyManager_CurrentChanged( _
 ByVal sender As Object, _
 ByVal e As EventArgs)
    ' Handle event
End Sub

Private Sub CurrencyManager_ItemChanged( _
 ByVal sender As Object, _
 ByVal e As System.Windows._
 Forms.ItemChangedEventArgs)
    ' Handle event
End Sub

Private Sub CurrencyManager_PositionChanged( _
 ByVal sender As Object, _
  ByVal e As System.EventArgs)
    ' Handle Event
End Sub
```

The names of the `CurrencyManager` events can be a bit confusing. The `ItemChanged` event is fired when the data itself is changed by an external factor. For example, if you modify the data in an array, and that array is bound to the user interface, the ItemChanged event will fire.

The CurrentChanged event fires when the data is changed on the user interface. That's true whether the user changes the data by typing in a control or the CurrencyManager changes the data by responding to a change of the Position property. Finally, the PositionChanged event fires when the Position property is changed. In practice, you'll see a CurrentChanged event whenever you see a PositionChanged event, but you can also get CurrentChanged events without a change of Position. Get more experience with CurrencyManager events in Step By Step 5.9.

STEP BY STEP

5.9 Using CurrencyManager Events

1. Create a form populated with two TextBox controls (txtEmployeeName and txtPosition), two Label controls, and two Button controls (btnPrevious and btnNext). Also add a ToolTip control to this form. Figure 5.7 shows the form in Design mode.

2. Double-click the form and enter code behind the form:

FIGURE 5.7
Design a form to demonstrate
CurrencyManager events.

```
' Create and stock an array of data
Dim maEmployees() As Employee = _
 {New Employee(1, "E.E. Smith", "CEO", "Earth"), _
  New Employee(2, "Melanie ""Jets"" Riggs", _
  "Chief Pilot", "Mars"), _
  New Employee(3, "William Danforth", "Pilot", "Mars"), _
  New Employee(4, "Blaise Canton", "Engineer", "Luna"), _
  New Employee(5, "Amanda Timmel", "CFO", "Earth")}

Private Sub StepByStep5_9_Load(ByVal sender As System.Object, _
 ByVal e As System.EventArgs) Handles MyBase.Load

    ' Bind data to the ui
    txtEmployeeName.DataBindings.Add( _
     "Text", maEmployees, "EmployeeName")
    txtEmployeeName.DataBindings.Add( _
     "Tag", maEmployees, "HomePlanet")
    txtPosition.DataBindings.Add( _
     "Text", maEmployees, "Position")

    ' Set the initial tooltip
    ToolTip1.SetToolTip(txtEmployeeName, _
     txtEmployeeName.Tag)
```

```
     ' Set up an event to update the tooltip
     Dim cm As CurrencyManager = _
      Me.BindingContext(maEmployees)
     AddHandler cm.PositionChanged, _
      AddressOf CurrencyManager_PositionChanged

End Sub

Private Sub btnPrevious_Click(ByVal sender As Object, _
 ByVal e As System.EventArgs) Handles btnPrevious.Click
     Me.BindingContext(maEmployees).Position -= 1
End Sub

Private Sub btnNext_Click(ByVal sender As Object, _
 ByVal e As System.EventArgs) Handles btnNext.Click
     Me.BindingContext(maEmployees).Position += 1
End Sub

Private Sub CurrencyManager_PositionChanged( _
 ByVal sender As Object, ByVal e As System.EventArgs)
     ToolTip1.SetToolTip(txtEmployeeName, _
      txtEmployeeName.Tag)
End Sub
```

---

3. Set the form as the startup object for the project.

---

4. Run the project. As you scroll through the records, you'll see that the ToolTip for the Employee Name TextBox control is synchronized by the PositionChanged event code.

If you compare the code in this Step By Step with the code from the Guided Practice Exercise earlier in the chapter, you'll see that using the event can save you from writing duplicate code in every procedure in which you might change the Position property of the CurrencyManager.

Using the Data Form Wizard

Now that you've seen the mechanics of data binding, it's time to explore one of the tools that Visual Basic .NET offers for automatic data binding: the *Data Form Wizard*. In this section, you'll see how to use the Wizard to build both a single-table form and a multiple-table form. These will help ease into the broad topic of using data from databases, which will occupy the rest of this chapter and all the next one.

A CRASH COURSE IN DATABASES

Although this exam doesn't have any objectives that explicitly demand database knowledge, you can't pass it without knowing something about databases. These days, databases are part of the pervasive understructure of computing. You're expected to understand the basics, just as you understand the basics of files and folders.

Data stored in relational databases warrants particular attention. A *relational database* (such as Microsoft SQL Server, which is used in the examples in this book) stores data in tables, each of which represents instances of a particular entity. An *entity* is anything you're tracking in the database: a customer, an order, an employee, or a supplier, for example. A single database can contain many tables; in this case, you might have tables named Customers, Orders, Employees, and Suppliers.

Each table contains one row (or record) for each instance of an entity: if you have fifty customers, then the Customers table will have fifty rows. Each row consists of a number of columns (or fields) that describe the entity. For example, the fields in a Customers table might be:

- Customer Number

- Customer Name

- City

- State

In a well-designed database, each entity can be identified by a column or combination of columns called the *primary key*. For example, the primary key for the Customers table could be the Customer Number column. Each customer then has a unique and unchanging Customer Number. If you know the Customer Number, you can use it to look up all the other information the database stores about that customer.

The reason SQL Server is called a relational database is that it understands that entities stored in different tables are related.

Think about customers and orders, for example: Each order is placed by a single customer. You can indicate this by storing the Customer Number (the primary key of the Customers table) in the Orders table. The columns of the Orders table might be:

- Order Number

- Customer Number

- Order Date

- Delivery Date

In this case, the Order Number is the primary key (the unique identifying column) of the Orders table. The Customer Number in the Orders table serves to relate each order to a corresponding row in the Customers table. The Customer Number is called a *foreign key* in the Orders table. To specify a relation between tables, name the two tables and the columns that match between them. Relations can be one-to-many (one customer can place many orders) or one-to-one (one employee has at most one pension).

In addition to tables, databases can contain other objects, including views and stored procedures (which can provide a subset of information from one or more tables), and users and groups (which control the security of database objects).

If you've never worked with a database, it can be a bit confusing at first. But if you work through the examples carefully, it should become clear to you.

NOTE For more information on relational database design and terminology, refer to Que Publishing's *SQL Server 2000 Programming* by Carlos Rojas and Fernando Guerrero (ISBN: 0-7897-2449-9).

Building a Single-Table Data Form

Start by building a data form that displays data from a single table—the Customers table in the Northwind sample database—in Step By Step 5.10.

STEP BY STEP

5.10 Building a Single-Table Data Form

1. Select Project, Add New Item. In the Add New Item dialog box, select the Data Form Wizard (see Figure 5.8). Name the new form StepByStep5-10.vb and click Open.

continues

continued

FIGURE 5.8
Launch the Data Form Wizard.

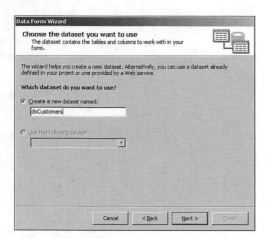

FIGURE 5.9
Create a new dataset.

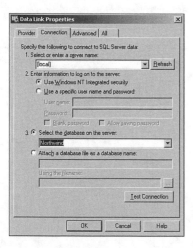

FIGURE 5.10
Connecting to the Northwind sample database.

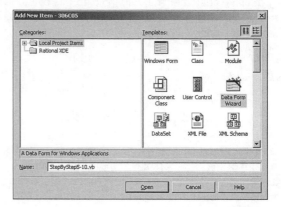

2. Read the Welcome panel of the wizard and click Next.

3. The next panel helps you choose a dataset to use with the data form. A *dataset* is a .NET Framework object that you can think of as representing one or more tables from a database (it's actually more flexible than that, but that's enough for this example). On this panel, shown in Figure 5.9, choose to create a new dataset named dsCustomers. Click Next.

4. The next panel helps you choose or build a data connection. A *data connection* tells Visual Basic .NET which database contains the data that you want to retrieve. You haven't set up any data connections yet, so click the New Connection button to open the Data Link Properties dialog box.

5. Click on the Provider tab of the Data Link Properties dialog box and select the Microsoft OLE DB Provider for SQL Server.

6. Click on the Connection tab of the Data Link Properties dialog box and enter the information you need to use the Northwind database, as shown in Figure 5.10.

7. Click OK on the Data Link Properties dialog box to create the connection and return to the Data Form Wizard. Select the new connection in the combo box (it will have a name such as MACHINENAME.dbo.Northwind) and click Next.

8. On the Choose Tables or Views panel, select the Customers table in the Available Items list and click the > button to move it to the Selected Items list, as shown in Figure 5.11. Click Next.

9. On the Choose Tables and Columns to Display on the Form panel, leave all the columns in the table selected, and click Next.

10. On the Choose the Display Style panel shown in Figure 5.12, select the Single Record style and check all the optional checkboxes. Click Finish.

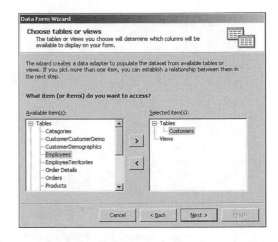

FIGURE 5.11
Choose a table as a data source.

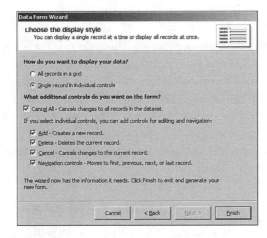

11. Set the new form as the default form for the project and run the project to experiment with the data form.

FIGURE 5.12
Choose a display style for the data form.

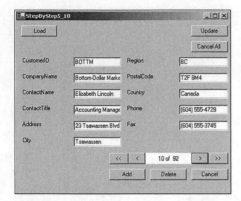

FIGURE 5.13
The finished data form displays all the data from the Customers table. It also provides ways to delete rows, add rows, and save changes back to the original database.

Figure 5.13 shows the finished data form created by this Step By Step. It contains 10 buttons, with these functions:

- ◆ **Load**—Load all the data from the database and bind it to the form.

- ◆ **Update**—Save all changes to the database.

- ◆ **Cancel All**—Discard all changes without changing the database.

- ◆ <<—Move to the first row.

- ◆ <—Move to the previous row.

- ◆ >—Move to the next row.

- ◆ >>—Move to the last row.

- ◆ **Add**—Add a new row.

- ◆ **Delete**—Delete the current row.

- ◆ **Cancel**—Cancel changes to the current row.

You might want to browse through the code that the wizard created behind this form. Be warned, though, that over 600 lines of code are involved in implementing this functionality! Obviously, the Data Form Wizard can save a lot of time building data bound forms. As you continue through the book, you'll learn more about database objects and the code you can use to manipulate them. For now, I'll stick to the relatively easy user interface tools to explore what you can do with data binding.

Building a Multiple-Table Data Form

The Data Form Wizard can also build a form that displays data from more than one table (see Step By Step 5.11).

STEP BY STEP

5.11 Building a Multiple-Table Data Form

   1. Select Project, Add New Item. In the Add New Item dialog box, select the Data Form Wizard. Name the new form StepByStep5-11.vb and click Open.

2. Read the Welcome panel of the wizard and click Next.

3. On the Choose a Dataset panel, choose to create a new dataset named dsCustOrders. Click Next.

4. On the Choose a Data Connection panel, select the data connection that you created in the previous Step By Step and click Next.

5. On the Choose Tables or Views panel, select the Customers table in the Available Items list and click the > button to move it to the Selected Items list. Also select the Orders table and click the > button to move it to the Selected Items list. Click Next.

6. The next panel will help specify the relationship between the two tables, Customers and Orders. Name the new relationship relCustomerOrders. Select Customers as the parent table and Orders as the child table. Select CustomerID as the key field in each table. Figure 5.14 shows the wizard at this point. Click the > button to create the new relationship, and then click Next.

7. On the Choose Tables and Columns to Display on the Form panel, leave all columns in both tables selected, and click Next.

8. On the Choose the Display Style panel, select the All Records in a Grid style, and check the Cancel All checkbox. Click Finish.

9. Set the new form as the default form for the project and run the project to experiment with the data form.

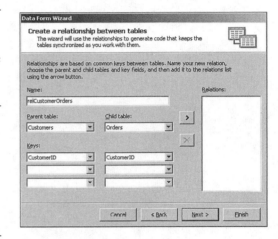

FIGURE 5.14
Create a relationship between tables.

NOTE

Relationships Creating a relationship between tables tells the wizard which fields to treat as primary and foreign keys. Refer to "A Crash Course in Databases" earlier in the chapter to review this concept.

As you select different Customer rows in the upper DataGrid control on this form, the lower DataGrid control will change to show only the Order rows for that Customer. Figure 5.15 shows an example.

FIGURE 5.15
This two-table data form uses one DataGrid
control for each table and uses code to keep
the two DataGrid controls synchronized.

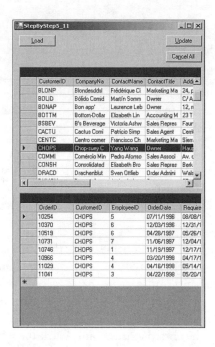

Once again, you'll find a tremendous amount of code (about 500
lines) behind this form. And once again I'll leave it for future
inspection.

REVIEW BREAK

▶ In one-way data binding, data from the data model is displayed on the form, but changes to the form do not affect the
data model.

▶ In two-way data binding, data from the data model is displayed on the form, and changes to the form are also written
back to the database.

▶ The .NET Framework uses BindingContext and
CurrencyManager objects to manage data binding.

▶ You can use events of the CurrencyManager object to help you
react to changes in bound data.

▶ The Data Form Wizard helps create data bound forms, both
simple and complex, quickly. These forms draw their data
from a relational database such as SQL Server.

TRANSFORM AND FILTER DATA

Display and Update Data: Transform and filter data.

The second test objective for this chapter covers transforming and filtering data. Especially when dealing with data from a database, you might find that it's not in the exact form that you'd like to display to the user. Perhaps the Customer table has 5,000 rows, and you'd like to pull out the single row that interests your users. Perhaps you'd like to show customer names with orders, but the Orders table only stores the CustomerID. This section looks at a few of the tools that the .NET Framework offers for manipulating database data.

First, I'll dig into the Server Explorer, which allows direct interaction with SQL Server or other databases. Then I'll look at some of the ways you can filter and transform data.

Using Server Explorer

By default, the Server Explorer window in Visual Studio .NET is displayed as a small vertical tab to the left of the toolbox. When you hover over this tab, the Server Explorer will slide out to cover the toolbox. Figure 5.16 shows the two states of the Server Explorer window.

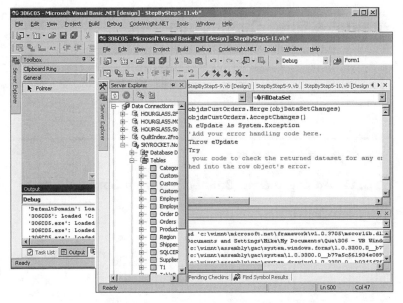

FIGURE 5.16
The Server Explorer is normally displayed as a small vertical tab. When you hover over this tab, the window slides out to cover the toolbox.

Although you'll use the Server Explorer to work with databases, it's really a general-purpose tool for managing server resources of many types. Table 5.6 lists the resources you can manage with Server Explorer.

TABLE 5.6

RESOURCES THAT YOU CAN MANAGE WITH SERVER EXPLORER

Resource Type	Represents
Data connection	A connection to a particular database
Crystal Services	Options for Crystal Reports
Event logs	Windows event logs
Message queues	Windows message queues
Performance counters	Windows performance counters
Services	Windows services
SQL Servers	Microsoft SQL Servers

To work with bound data, use the Data Connection node in Server Explorer and its children.

Adding a Data Connection

You've already seen that you can add a data connection to your project from within the Data Form Wizard. Those data connections are automatically available in Server Explorer as well. You can also add a data connection directly from Server Explorer (see Step By Step 5.12).

STEP BY STEP

5.12 Adding a Data Connection from Server Explorer

1. Open Server Explorer.

2. Right-click the Data Connections node and select Add Connection to open the Data Link Properties dialog box.

3. Fill in the connection information for your data source. The dialog box defaults to the Microsoft OLE DB Provider for SQL Server, but you can change that on the Provider tab if you like.

4. Click OK to create the data connection.

Visual Studio .NET remembers your data connections across sessions and projects. Any data connection you've created appears in Server Explorer in all your projects unless you right-click the Data Connection and choose Delete.

Object Design from Server Explorer

Even without bringing SQL Server objects into your Visual Basic .NET projects, you can manipulate them from Server Explorer. For example, Step By Step 5.13 shows you how you can edit a SQL Server table from Server Explorer. Visual Studio .NET provides wide-ranging design options for SQL Server objects. Table 5.7 summarizes your options in this area.

EXAM TIP

Supported Connection Types You probably noticed that the Data Link Properties dialog box gives many choices on the Provider tab. In addition to SQL Server, connections using the Oracle or Jet providers are also fully supported by .NET. Other providers might work, but there's no guarantee, and you should test your application carefully if you decide to use another provider.

EXAM TIP

Visual Studio Focuses on Data, Not Management The objects you can edit from Visual Studio are those that can bring back data to your application. SQL Server contains many objects (such as users, groups, and alerts) that are used for server management. To work with these objects, use SQL Server's own design tools.

TABLE 5.7

MANIPULATING SQL SERVER OBJECTS FROM SERVER EXPLORER

Object	Edit Data?	Design?	Create New?
Database Diagram	N/A	Yes	Yes
Table	Yes	Yes	Yes
View	Yes	Yes	Yes
Stored Procedure	Yes	Yes	Yes
Function	Yes	Yes	Yes

STEP BY STEP

5.13 Editing a SQL Server Table from Server Explorer

1. Open Server Explorer.

2. Expand the tree under Data Connections to show a SQL Server data connection that points to the Northwind sample database, then the Tables node of the SQL Server, then individual tables.

3. Right-click on the Products table and select Retrieve Data. The data stored in the table will appear within your Visual Studio .NET workspace, as shown in Figure 5.17.

FIGURE 5.17

Edit SQL Server data directly within Visual Studio .NET.

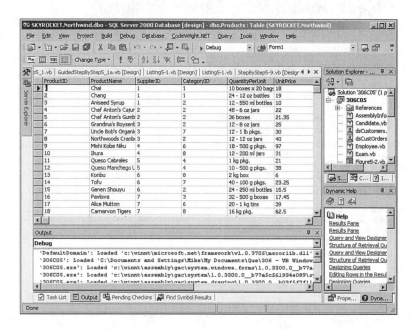

4. As you work with the data, you can edit, add, and delete values from the table.

5. Close the window that displays the Products data.

6. Reopen Server Explorer and find the Products table again. Right-click on the table and select Design Table. Visual Studio .NET will display information relating to the design of the table, as shown in Figure 5.18.

This information includes such things as the name and data type of each column in the table.

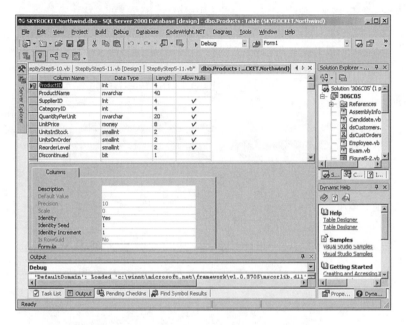

7. Close the editing window when you're done examining the design information for the table.

Drag-and-Drop Operations from Server Explorer

The Server Explorer can also act as a source for drag-and-drop operations. Different visual data objects are created, depending on what sort of object you drag from Server explorer:

◆ Dragging and dropping a database creates a SqlConnection object.

◆ Dragging and dropping a Table, View, Table Column, or View Column creates a SqlDataAdapter object.

◆ Dragging and dropping a stored procedure or table-valued function creates a SqlCommand object.

These three objects are members of the System.Data.SqlClient namespace. You'll learn more about this namespace in Chapter 6, "Consuming and Manipulating Data." In this chapter, I'll concentrate more on what you can do with the objects than with the code that creates and supports them.

Figure 5.19 shows the appearance of the created objects on a Visual Basic .NET form. This figure also includes a DataSet object; you'll see how to generate a DataSet object in the Form designer shortly.

FIGURE 5.19
Visual data objects created in the Form designer.

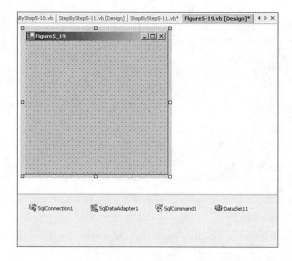

As you might guess from their placement below the form's design surface, these visual data objects are not visible at runtime. At design time, they provide access to instances of their underlying class. For example, the SqlConnection1 object in the designer is a visual representation of an instance of the SqlConnection class. If you view the code behind the form, and expand the Windows Form Designer Generated Code region, you'll find the declaration that Visual Basic .NET created when you dropped the object on the form:

```
Friend WithEvents SqlConnection1 _
    As System.Data.SqlClient.SqlConnection
```

What can you use these visual data objects for? Well, they can provide a fast way to design a form that has a DataGrid control complex bound to data in a SQL Server table. Explore this in Step By Step 5.14.

EXAM TIP

Friend and WithEvents The Friend keyword makes this object accessible from anywhere in the assembly that contains this code. The WithEvents keyword makes it possible to connect event handlers to this object.

STEP BY STEP

5.14 Binding a DataGrid Control to a SQL Server Table

1. Place a DataGrid control on a new VB .NET form. Name the control dgCustomers. Set the CaptionText property of this control to Customers.

2. Open Server Explorer.

3. Expand the tree under Data Connections to show a SQL Server data connection that points to the Northwind sample database, then the Tables node of the SQL Server, then individual tables.

4. Drag the Customers table from Server Explorer and drop it on the form. This will create two visual data objects, SqlConnecton1 and SqlDataAdapter1.

5. Select the SqlDataAdapter1 object. Click the Generate Dataset link below the Properties window.

6. In the Generate Dataset window, choose to use the existing dsCustomers dataset. Click OK. Figure 5.20 shows this dialog box.

7. Set the DataSource property of the DataGrid control to DsCustomers1. Set the DataMember property of the DataGrid control to Customers.

8. Double-click the form and enter code in the form's Load event:

```
Private Sub StepByStep5_14_Load( _
 ByVal sender As System.Object, _
 ByVal e As System.EventArgs) Handles MyBase.Load
    ' Move the data from the database to the DataGrid
    SqlDataAdapter1.Fill(DsCustomers1, "Customers")
End Sub
```

9. Set the form as the startup object for the project.

10. Run the project. The DataGrid will display all the data from the Customers table.

FIGURE 5.20
Generate a dataset.

Although you only had to write one line of code for the previous Step By Step, you actually created a number of ADO.NET objects along the way. Here's a rundown of how all the pieces fit together.

◆ The `SqlConnection1` object is an instance of the `SqlConnection` class. This object represents a connection to the SQL Server database.

◆ The `SqlDataAdapter1` object is an instance of the `SqlDataAdapter` class. This class encapsulates all the tools necessary to extract data via a SqlConnection and to write changes back to the data source.

◆ The Generate Dataset dialog box created an XSD file, dsCustomers.xsd. This is an XML Schema Design file that represents the structure of the Customers table to the .NET Framework.

◆ The `DsCustomers1` object is an instance of the dataset represented by the dsCustomers.xsd file.

◆ The call to the `Fill` method of the `SqlDataAdapter1` object tells it to extract all the rows from the Customers table and to place them in the `DsCustomers1` object. You can think of the `SqlDataAdapter` class as a two-way pump that can move data from the underlying database to the data model within your application and back.

◆ Setting the `DataSource` and `DataMember` properties of the DataGrid control uses complex data binding to show the contents of the `DsCustomers1` object on the user interface.

Filtering Data

Filtering data refers to selecting only some data from a larger body of data to appear on the user interface of a form. This can be a critical part of avoiding information overload for end users of an application. In most cases, users are not going to need to see every row of data in a database or even every row from a specific table. More often, they need only a small subset of the larger data body. In this section, I'll look at two different ways to filter data in your applications. You can filter data by building a DataView on the client or by using a server-based view to deliver only the desired data to the client.

Filtering with a DataView

The first filtering method you'll learn is using the `DataView` object (see Step By Step 5.15). A `DataView` starts with the data in a `DataSet` and lets you choose which data from the `DataSet` to work with.

To understand the `DataView`, you need to know a little about the internal structure of the `DataSet` object. A `DataSet` contains two collections. The Tables collection is made up of `DataTable` objects, each one representing data from a single table in the datasource. The Relations collection is made up of DataRelation objects, each one representing the relation between two `DataTable` objects.

The DataView object supplies one more piece of this puzzle: It represents a bindable, customized view of a DataTable. You can sort or filter the records from a DataTable to build a DataView.

STEP BY STEP

5.15 Using a DataView to Filter Data

1. Place a DataGrid control on a new VB .NET Form. Name the control `dgCustomers`. Set the `CaptionText` property of this control to `Customers`.

2. Open Server Explorer.

3. Expand the tree under Data Connections to show a SQL Server data connection that points to the Northwind sample database, then the Tables node of the SQL Server, then individual tables.

4. Drag the Customers table from Server Explorer and drop it on the form. This will create two visual data objects, `SqlConnection1` and `SqlDataAdapter1`.

5. Select the `SqlDataAdapter1` object. Click the Generate Dataset link below the Properties window.

6. In the Generate Dataset window, choose to use the existing dsCustomers dataset. Click OK.

continues

continued

7. Double-click the form and enter code in the form's Load event:

```
Private Sub StepByStep5_15_Load(ByVal sender As System.Object, _
 ByVal e As System.EventArgs) Handles MyBase.Load
    ' Move the data from the database to the DataSet
    SqlDataAdapter1.Fill(DsCustomers1, "Customers")

    ' Create a dataview to filter the Customers table
    Dim dvCustomers As DataView = _
     New DataView(DsCustomers1.Tables("Customers"))
    ' Apply a sort to the dataview
    dvCustomers.Sort = "ContactName"
    ' Apply a filter to the dataview
    dvCustomers.RowFilter = "Country = 'France'"
    ' and bind the results to the grid
    dgCustomers.DataSource = dvCustomers

End Sub
```

8. Set the form as the startup object for the project.

9. Run the project. The DataGrid will display only the data from customers in France, because the code sets the RowFilter property to return only those customers. Note that they're also sorted by the ContactName column, as shown in Figure 5.21, because the Sort property of the DataView is set to the ContactName column name.

FIGURE 5.21
This DataGrid was populated by binding it to a DataView that filters and sorts the records from the Customers table.

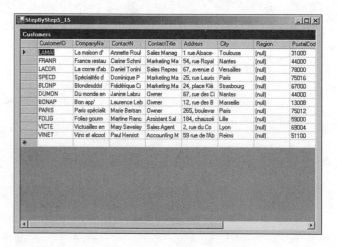

Filtering at the Server

The DataView class provides a useful way to filter data, but it's inefficient if you're working with large amounts of data because all the data is first retrieved from the database server and stored on the client. So if 10 million rows of data are on the server, a DataView will retrieve all 10 million rows. After that, the DataView can be used to quickly select a subset of the data. But what if you'll never need all the data? In that case, you're better off filtering on the server rather than retrieving all the data you'll never need. One way to do this is by basing a SqlDataAdapter object on a view instead of a table (see Step By Step 5.16).

STEP BY STEP

5.16 Using a Server-Side View to Filter Data

1. Place a DataGrid control on a new VB .NET Form. Name the control dgCustomers. Set the CaptionText property of this control to Customers.

2. Open Server Explorer.

3. Expand the tree under Data Connections to show a SQL Server data connection that points to the Northwind sample database, then the Views node of the SQL Server.

4. Right-click on the Views node and select New View.

5. In the Add Table dialog box, select the Customers table. Click Add, then Close. This will put you in the view designer within Visual Studio .NET.

6. Click the checkboxes for All Columns, ContactName, and Country in the column listing.

7. Fill in the details of the view as shown in Figure 5.22.

continues

continued

FIGURE 5.22
Create a new SQL Server view using the Design tools within Visual Studio .NET.

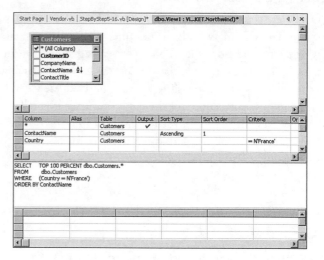

8. Click the Save button and save the view as vwFranceCustomers. Close the Design window for the view.

9. Drag the vwFranceCustomers view from Server Explorer and drop it on the form. You'll get a configuration error because the view is read-only. That's not a problem because we're not writing any data back to the database; click OK to create two visual data objects, SqlConnection1 and SqlDataAdapter1.

10. Select the SqlDataAdapter1 object. Click the Generate Dataset link below the Properties window.

11. In the Generate Dataset window, choose to use the existing dsCustomers dataset. Click OK.

12. Set the DataSource property of the DataGrid control to DsCustomers1. Set the DataMember property of the DataGrid control to vwFranceCustomers.

13. Double-click the form and enter code in the form's Load event:

```
Private Sub StepByStep5_16_Load(ByVal sender As Object, _
    ByVal e As System.EventArgs) Handles MyBase.Load
```

```
' Move the data from the database to the DataGrid
   SqlDataAdapter1.Fill(DsCustomers1, "vwFranceCustomers")
End Sub
```

14. Set the form as the startup object for the project.

15. Run the project. The DataGrid will display only the data from customers in France. Note that they're also sorted by the ContactName column, as shown in Figure 5.21.

The previous Step By Step will display the same results as the version before. However, behind the scenes, things are different. Instead of retrieving all the rows of the Customers table from the server, this version retrieves only the rows that belong on the display. If you're operating over a slow network or Internet connection, this sort of server-side filtering can save a good deal of time.

Transforming Data with Lookups

Finally, we'll take a brief look at another server-side technique: transforming data by applying lookups. A *lookup* is a technique for replacing one column of data with another column from the same table. For example, given a customer ID value, you could look up the corresponding customer name.

Figure 5.23 shows a DataGrid control bound to the Orders table.

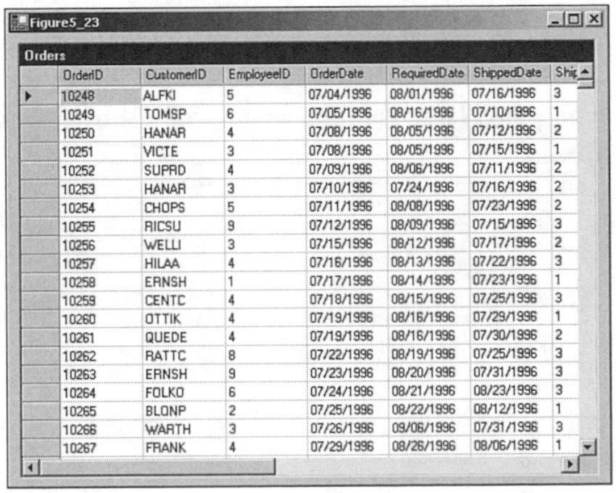

FIGURE 5.23
This DataGrid control is bound to the Orders table. Note that only the Customer ID is displayed to identify the customers.

One problem with this particular form is that it only displays Customer ID values, and no other information about the customers. What if you wanted to view customer names instead? The answer is to use a new view to retrieve data from the server as in Step By Step 5.17. Then review what you've learned in the past few sections with Guided Practice Exercise 5.2.

STEP BY STEP

5.17 Using a Server-Side View to Transform Data

1. Place a DataGrid control on a new VB .NET form. Name the control dgOrders. Set the CaptionText property of this control to Orders.

2. Open Server Explorer.

3. Expand the tree under Data Connections to show a SQL Server data connection that points to the Northwind sample database, then the Views node of the SQL Server.

4. Right-click on the Views node and select New View.

5. In the Add Table dialog box, select the Customers table and click Add. Select the Orders table, click Add, and click Close to access the view designer within Visual Studio .NET.

6. Click the checkboxes for CompanyName in the Customers table and all columns except for CustomerID in the Orders table.

7. In the grid, drag the OrderID column above the CompanyName column. Figure 5.24 shows the completed view.

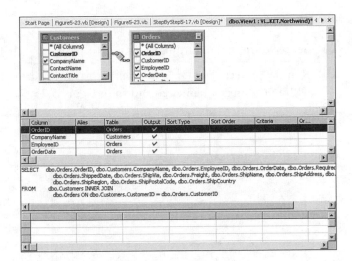

8. Click the Save button and save the view as vwCustOrders. Close the Design window for the view.

9. Drag the vwCustOrders view from Server Explorer and drop it on the form. You'll get a configuration error because the view is read-only. That's not a problem because we're not writing any data back to the database; click OK to create objects. This will create two visual data objects, SqlConnection1 and SqlDataAdapter1.

10. Select the SqlDataAdapter1 object. Click the Generate Dataset link below the Properties window.

11. In the Generate Dataset window, create a new dataset named dsOrders. Click OK.

12. Set the DataSource property of the DataGrid control to DsOrders1. Set the DataMember property of the DataGrid control to vwCustOrders.

13. Double-click the form and enter code in the form's Load event:

```
Private Sub StepByStep5_17_Load(ByVal sender As System.Object, _
ByVal e As System.EventArgs) Handles MyBase.Load
    ' Load the data
    SqlDataAdapter1.Fill(DsOrders1, "vwCustOrders")
End Sub
```

continues

continued

14. Set the form as the startup object for the project.

15. Run the project. The DataGrid will display order data with full company names, as shown in Figure 5.25.

FIGURE 5.25
Customer IDs transformed into customer names.

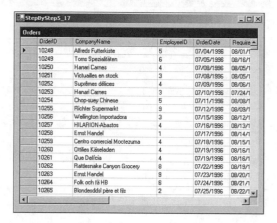

GUIDED PRACTICE EXERCISE 5.2

In this exercise, you'll be working with Order and Order Detail data from the Northwind sample database. Design a form that lets the user select from a list of orders and then displays all the order detail data for the selected order. The list of orders should be presented in a ComboBox control, and the corresponding order detail data should be shown on a DataGrid control.

Try this on your own first. If you get stuck or would like to see one possible solution, follow these steps:

1. Create a form populated with a ListBox control named lbOrders and a DataGrid control named dgOrderDetails.

2. Open Server Explorer.

3. Expand the tree under Data Connections to show a SQL Server data connection that points to the Northwind sample database, then the Tables node of the SQL Server, then individual tables.

4. Drag the Orders table from Server Explorer and drop it on the form. This will create two visual data objects: `SqlConnection1` and `SqlDataAdapter1`. Drag the Order Details table from Server Explorer and drop it on the form to create one more object, `SqlDataAdapter2`.

5. Select the `SqlDataAdapter1` object. Click the Generate Dataset link below the Properties window.

6. In the Generate Dataset window, select to use the existing dsOrders dataset. Click OK.

7. Select the `SqlDataAdapter1` object. Click the Generate Dataset link below the Properties window.

8. In the Generate Dataset window, select to create a new dsOrderDetails Dataset. Click OK.

9. Double-click the form and enter code for the form:

```
Dim dvOrderDetails As DataView

Private Sub GuidedStepByStep5_2_Load( _
 ByVal sender As System.Object, _
 ByVal e As System.EventArgs) Handles MyBase.Load

    ' Load the dataset for the DataGrid
    SqlDataAdapter2.Fill(DsOrderDetails1, "Order Details")
    ' and set up a dataview
    dvOrderDetails = New DataView( _
     DsOrderDetails1.Tables("Order Details"))

    ' Load the dataset for the listbox
    SqlDataAdapter1.Fill(DsOrders1, "Orders")
    ' And bind it
    With lbOrders
        .DataSource = DsOrders1
        .DisplayMember = "Orders.OrderID"
        .ValueMember = "Orders.OrderID"
    End With

End Sub

Private Sub lbOrders_SelectedIndexChanged( _
 ByVal sender As Object, _
 ByVal e As System.EventArgs) _
 Handles lbOrders.SelectedIndexChanged

    ' When a new item is selected in the listbox,
    ' filter the dataview
```

continues

continued

```
' Note that the SelectedItem returns
' a DataRow object; the OrderID
' is at the first indexed column position in the object.
dvOrderDetails.RowFilter = "OrderID = " & _
    lbOrders.SelectedItem(0)
dgOrderDetails.DataSource = dvOrderDetails

End Sub
```

10. Set the form as the startup object for the project.

11. Run the project. The ListBox control will display all order numbers from the database. The DataGrid will display the order details for the selected order. Figure 5.26 shows the final form.

FIGURE 5.26
Order and Order Detail information on a single form.

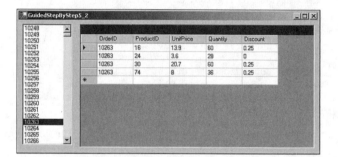

If you had difficulty following this exercise, review the sections titled "Using Server Explorer" and "Filtering with a DataView", as well as the material earlier in the chapter on complex data binding. The text and examples should help you relearn this material and understand what happened in this exercise. After review, try the exercise again.

REVIEW BREAK

▶ The Server Explorer provides a powerful tool for working with SQL Server data.

▶ You can edit and design SQL Server objects directly within Visual Studio .NET.

▶ The DataView object offers client-side sorting and filtering capabilities for data bound objects.

▶ Views on the server can be an efficient way to filter or transform data.

CHAPTER SUMMARY

Nearly every Windows application deals with data in one form or another. Often this data is contained in a database, but it can be in a simple array, in an array of objects, or in many other forms. The form the data is in is known as the data model of the application.

Data binding gives a means to connect data stored in the database with the user interface of your application. In this chapter, you saw many of the tools Visual Basic .NET provides for data binding, including simple and complex data binding, the Data Form Wizard, and the Server Explorer.

Data binding in the .NET Framework is much more flexible than in any previous development environment. You can bind any class that implements IList, IBindingList, or ITypedList to the user interface. And any property of a user interface control can potentially be bound to data.

You also saw some programmatic approaches to data, including the use of the `BindingContext` and `CurrencyManager` classes and the creation of SQL Server views to filter or transform data. Trapping events from the `CurrencyManager` class provides you with additional flexibility to handle complex binding scenarios.

KEY TERMS

- Column
- Complex data binding
- Data binding
- Foreign key
- One-way data binding
- Primary key
- Relation
- Relational database
- Result set
- Row
- Simple data binding
- Table
- Two-way data binding

Exercises

5.1   Use Simple Data Binding to Display Information from an Array

This exercise shows how to populate an array in code and then use simple data binding to display the information on the user interface.

Estimated Time: 20 minutes.

1. Create a new Visual Basic .NET project to use for the exercises in the remainder of this chapter.

2. Add a new class file to the project. Name the class `Computer.vb`. Enter this code in the class file to create a class with three properties and a constructor:

```
Public Class Computer

    Private mstrComputerName As String
    Private mstrCPU As String
    Private mintRAM As Integer

    Public Property ComputerName() As String
        Get
            ComputerName = mstrComputerName
        End Get
        Set(ByVal Value As String)
            mstrComputerName = Value
        End Set
    End Property

    Public Property CPU() As String
        Get
            CPU = mstrCPU
        End Get
        Set(ByVal Value As String)
            mstrCPU = Value
        End Set
    End Property

    Public Property RAM() As Integer
        Get
            RAM = mintRAM
        End Get
        Set(ByVal Value As Integer)
            mintRAM = Value
        End Set
    End Property
```

```
    Sub New(ByVal ComputerName As String, _
      ByVal CPU As String, _
      ByVal RAM As Integer)
        mstrComputerName = ComputerName
        mstrCPU = CPU
        mintRAM = RAM
    End Sub

End Class
```

3. Add a new form to the project. Place Label, TextBox, and Button controls on the form as shown in Figure 5.27. Name the TextBox controls `txtComputerName`, `txtCPU`, and `txtRAM`. Name the Button controls `txtPrevious` and `txtNext`.

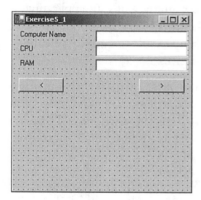

FIGURE 5.27
Design of the form for Exercise 5.1.

4. Add code to the form to create and initialize an array of Computer objects and then to bind the array to the user interface:

```
' Create and fill an array of
' computer objects
Private maComputers() As Computer = _
 {New Computer("Frodo", "PIII-866", 512), _
  New Computer( _
    "Samwise", "PIII-500", 256), _
  New Computer( _
    "Meriadoc", "K6-350", 128), _
  New Computer("Peregrine", "K6-350", 128)}
```

APPLY YOUR KNOWLEDGE

```
Private Sub Exercise5_1_Load( _
 ByVal sender As System.Object, _
 ByVal e As System.EventArgs) _
 Handles MyBase.Load
    ' Bind data to the user interface
    txtComputerName.DataBindings.Add( _
    "Text", _maComputers, "ComputerName")
    txtCPU.DataBindings.Add("Text", _
      maComputers, "CPU")
    txtRAM.DataBindings.Add("Text", _
      maComputers, "RAM")
End Sub
```

5. Add code to the form to handle navigation:

```
Private Sub btnPrevious_Click( _
 ByVal sender As System.Object, _
 ByVal e As System.EventArgs) _
 Handles btnPrevious.Click
    Me.BindingContext(maComputers). _
      Position -= 1
End Sub

Private Sub btnNext_Click( _
 ByVal sender As System.Object, _
 ByVal e As System.EventArgs) _
 Handles btnNext.Click
    Me.BindingContext(maComputers). _
      Position += 1
End Sub
```

6. Set the form as the startup form for the project and run the project. The information from the data model will appear on the user interface, and you'll be able to use the buttons to scroll through the different records.

5.2 Use Simple Data Binding to Display Information from a Database

This exercise shows how to connect to a database using Server Explorer and then bind some of the information from the database to the user interface using simple data binding.

Estimated Time: 30 minutes.

> **NOTE**
>
> **Creating the Database Connection** This exercise assumes you've already used Server Explorer to connect to a copy of the SQL Server 2000 Northwind sample database. If you haven't, refer to Step By Step 5.10, particularly steps 4–6 and the accompanying Exam Tip, to build a connection. Then you can proceed with this exercise.

1. Add a new form to the Visual Basic .NET project.

2. Hover over the Server Explorer tab until the Server Explorer appears.

3. Expand the tree in the Server Explorer to locate the Orders table in the Northwind sample database. Drag the Orders table from Server Explorer and drop it on the form.

4. Click on the SqlDataAdapter1 object. Click the Generate Dataset link in the Properties window. Create a new dataset named dsOrders and click OK.

5. Place Label, TextBox, DateTimePicker, and Button controls on the form as shown in Figure 5.28. Name the TextBox controls txtOrderID and txtCustomerID. Name the DateTimePicker control dtOrderDate. Name the Button controls txtPrevious and txtNext.

APPLY YOUR KNOWLEDGE

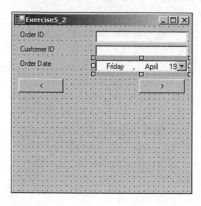

FIGURE 5.28
Design of the form for Exercise 5.2.

6. Add code to the form to fill the dataset and then bind selected items from the dataset to the user interface:

```
Private Sub Exercise5_2_Load( _
 ByVal sender As System.Object, _
 ByVal e As System.EventArgs) _
 Handles MyBase.Load
    ' Fill the dataset
    SqlDataAdapter1.Fill(DsOrders1, _
     "Orders")
    ' Bind it to the user interface
    txtOrderID.DataBindings.Add("Text", _
     DsOrders1, "Orders.OrderID")
    txtCustomerID.DataBindings.Add( _
     "Text", DsOrders1, "Orders.CustomerID")
    dtOrderDate.DataBindings.Add( _
     "Value", DsOrders1, "Orders.OrderDate")
End Sub
```

7. Add code to the form to handle navigation:

```
Private Sub btnPrevious_Click( _
 ByVal sender As System.Object, _
 ByVal e As System.EventArgs) _
 Handles btnPrevious.Click
    Me.BindingContext(DsOrders1, _
     "Orders").Position -= 1
End Sub

Private Sub btnNext_Click( _
 ByVal sender As System.Object, _
```

```
 ByVal e As System.EventArgs) _
 Handles btnNext.Click
    Me.BindingContext(DsOrders1, _
     "Orders").Position += 1
End Sub
```

8. Set the form as the startup form for the project and run the project. The information from the data model will appear on the user interface, and you'll be able to use the buttons to scroll through the rows of the database table.

As this Exercise shows, you're not forced to use complex data binding when you use data from a database. Simple data binding works just as well. However, some syntactical complexities are introduced because the DataSet object can contain more than one bindable object (remember, a DataSet contains a collection of one or more DataTable objects). The code in this Exercise shows how to specify the database column to bind when adding a Binding, and how to specify the proper CurrencyManager in your navigation code.

5.3   Use Complex and Simple Data Binding with a Combo Box

In this exercise, you'll use complex data binding to fill the list in a ComboBox control, and simple data binding to retrieve the value that the user selects from the list.

Estimated Time: 10 minutes.

1. Add a new form to the Visual Basic .NET project. Place a ComboBox control named cboComputers and a TextBox control named txtRAM on the form.

2. Add code to the form to create an array and set up data bindings:

```
Private Sub Exercise5_3_Load( _
 ByVal sender As System.Object, _
 ByVal e As System.EventArgs) _
 Handles MyBase.Load
```

```
' Create and initialize an array
Dim maComputers() As Computer = _
  {New Computer( _
    "Frodo", "PIII-866", 512), _
   New Computer( _
    "Samwise", "PIII-500", 256), _
   New Computer( _
    "Meriadoc", "K6-350", 128), _
   New Computer( _
    "Peregrine", "K6-350", 128)}
  ' Bind the array to the ComboBox list
With cboComputers
    .DataSource = maComputers
    .DisplayMember = "ComputerName"
    .ValueMember = "RAM"
End With
  ' Bind the TextBox to
  ' the value in the ComboBox
txtRAM.DataBindings.Add( _
  "Text", cboComputers, "SelectedValue")
End Sub
```

3. Set the form as the startup form for the project and run the project. The information from the data model will appear on the user interface. When you select a computer name in the ComboBox control, you'll see the RAM value for that computer displayed in the TextBox control.

This exercise shows you yet another twist on simple data binding: binding a property from one control (the TextBox, in this case) to a value delivered by another control (the ComboBox). This is just one more demonstration of the flexibility of data binding in the .NET Framework.

5.4 Create a Master-Detail Data Form

This exercise lets you practice with the Visual Basic .NET Data Form Wizard. You'll build a data form that shows all the employees in the Northwind sample database. When the user selects a particular employee, the form will display the orders that employee has taken.

Estimated Time: 15 minutes.

1. Select Project, Add New Item. In the Add New Item dialog box select the Data Form Wizard. Name the new form Exercise5-4.vb and click Open.

2. Read the Welcome panel of the wizard and click Next.

3. On the Choose a Dataset panel, select to create a new dataset named dsEmpOrders. Click Next.

4. On the Choose a Data Connection panel, select the data connection to the Northwind sample database and click Next.

5. On the Choose Tables or Views panel, select the Employees table in the Available Items list and click the > button to move it to the Selected Items list. Also select the Orders table and click the > button to move it to the Selected Items list. Click Next.

6. On the Create a Relationship Between Tables panel, name the new relationship relEmpOrders. Select Employees as the parent table and Orders as the child table. Select EmployeeID as the key field in each table. Click the > button to create the new relationship and click Next.

7. On the Choose Tables and Columns to Display on the Form panel, leave all the columns in both tables selected and click Next.

8. On the Choose the Display Style panel, select the All Records in a Grid style and check the Cancel All check box. Click Finish.

9. Set the new form as the default form for the project and run the project to experiment with the data form. Figure 5.29 shows the completed form.

APPLY YOUR KNOWLEDGE

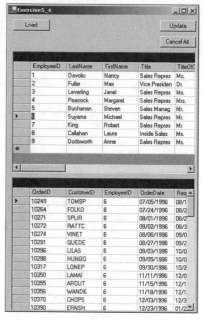

FIGURE 5.29
Browsing data with the form created in Exercise 5.4.

5.5   Use a DataView to Filter Data at Run Time

This exercise will guide you through building a form with a DataGrid whose display can be filtered at runtime. The DataGrid will display customers from a country selected by the user.

Estimated Time: 40 minutes.

1. Add a new form to the Visual Basic .NET project.

2. Hover your cursor over the Server Explorer tab until the Server Explorer appears.

3. Expand the tree in the Server Explorer to locate the Customers table in the Northwind sample database. Drag the Customers table from Server Explorer and drop it on the form.

4. Click on the `SqlDataAdapter1` object. Click the Generate Dataset link in the Properties window. Create a new dataset named `dsCustomers` and click OK.

5. Reopen Server Explorer.

6. Right-click on the Views node and select New View.

7. In the Add Table dialog box, select the Customers table, click Add, then click Close. This will put you in the view designer within Visual Studio .NET.

8. Click the checkbox for Country in the column listing.

9. Fill in the details of the view as shown in Figure 5.30.

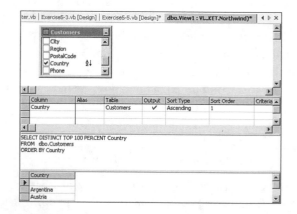

FIGURE 5.30
Create a new SQL Server view to select the country names from the Customers table.

APPLY YOUR KNOWLEDGE

EXAM TIP

SELECT DISTINCT The use of the DISTINCT keyword in the SQL statement tells SQL Server to not return any duplicates when running this view. You'll need to add the DISTINCT keyword by typing it in to the SQL string.

10. Click the Save button and save the view as vwCustomerCountries. Close the Design window for the view.

11. Drag the vwCustomerCountries view from Server Explorer and drop it on the form. You'll get a configuration error because the view is read-only. That's not a problem because we're not writing any data back to the database; click OK to create objects. This will create one more visual data object, SqlDataAdapter2.

12. Select the SqlDataAdapter1 object. Click the Generate Dataset link below the Properties window.

13. In the Generate Dataset window, choose to create a new dsCountries dataset. Click OK.

14. Place a ComboBox control named cboCountries on the form. Place a DataGrid control named dgCustomers on the form.

15. Add code to the form to fill both DataSet objects and to set up a DataView:

```
Dim mdvCustomers As DataView

Private Sub Exercise5_5_Load( _
  ByVal sender As System.Object, _
  ByVal e As System.EventArgs) _
  Handles MyBase.Load
```

```
    ' Fill the dataset of countries
    ' and bind it to the combo box
    SqlDataAdapter2.Fill(DsCountries1, _
      "Countries")
    With cboCountries
        .DataSource = _
          DsCountries1.Tables("Countries")
        .DisplayMember = "Country"
        .ValueMember = "Country"
    End With
    ' Fill the dataset of customers
    ' and set up a dataview
    SqlDataAdapter1.Fill(DsCustomers1, _
      "Customers")
    mdvCustomers = _
      New DataView(DsCustomers1. _
      Tables("Customers"))
End Sub
```

16. Add code to the form to apply a filter to the DataView whenever the selection in the ComboBox changes:

```
Private Sub _
cboCountries_SelectedIndexChanged( _
  ByVal sender As Object, _
  ByVal e As System.EventArgs) _
  Handles cboCountries.SelectedIndexChanged
    ' Apply a filter to the dataview
    If Not mdvCustomers Is Nothing Then
        mdvCustomers.RowFilter = _
          "Country = '" & _
          cboCountries.SelectedItem(0) & "'"
        ' And bind the result to the datagrid
        dgCustomers.DataSource = _
          mdvCustomers
    End If
End Sub
```

17. Set the form as the startup form for the project and run the project. As you select countries in the ComboBox, customers from the selected country will be displayed on the DataGrid.

Review Questions

1. Describe the difference between a database and a data model.

APPLY YOUR KNOWLEDGE

2. Describe the difference between simple and complex data binding.

3. What is the purpose of the BindingContext object?

4. What is the purpose of the CurrencyManager object?

5. Name and briefly explain two ways to filter data.

6. Name three interfaces that support simple data binding.

7. How do the DataSource, DisplayMember, and ValueMember properties of the ComboBox work together?

8. Name at least two SQL Server objects that you can design from within Visual Studio .NET.

9. Which is more efficient for filtering data, a server-side view or a DataView object?

Exam Questions

1. The data model for your application includes an array of Product objects named Products. Each Product object exposes public properties named ProductNumber and ProductName. You'd like to provide an interface that allows users to select the ProductNumber and see the corresponding ProductName. What should you do?

   A. Create two TextBox controls. Bind the `ProductNumber` property to one TextBox control and the ProductNumber to the other TextBox control. Provide navigation buttons to allow the user to scroll through the data.

   B. Create a DataGrid control. Bind the Products array to the DataGrid control.

   C. Create a ComboBox control. Set the Products array as the DataSource of the control. Bind the DisplayMember property to the ProductNumber property, and bind the ValueMember property to the ProductName property. Bind a text box on the form to the SelectedValue property of the ComboBox control.

   D. Create a TextBox control and a Label control. Bind the ProductNumber property to the TextBox control and the ProductName property to the Label control.

2. Your application's data model represents orders in a strongly typed IList of Order objects. You've used simple data binding to display the pertinent fields from the Order objects on a form. The form includes buttons to allow the user to navigate through the Order objects. What must you do in the handler for the buttons' click events?

   A. Increment or decrement the Item property of the BindingContext object for your form.

   B. Call the DataBindings.Add and the DataBindings.Remove methods to move through the objects.

   C. Call the ResumeBinding and SuspendBinding methods of the CurrencyManager object that manages the data source.

   D. Increment or decrement the Position property of the CurrencyManager object that manages the data source.

3. Your application includes a form that displays employee names in a simple-bound TextBox control. You'd like to add a ToolTip to the TextBox control, with the ToolTip displaying the title of the employee. The employee names and employee titles are both supplied by the same IList. How can you do this?

APPLY YOUR KNOWLEDGE

A. Bind the employee title to the Tag property of the TextBox control. In the event handler for the PositionChanged event of the CurrencyManager object, call the ToolTip's SetToolTip method to copy the value from the Tag property to the ToolTip.

B. Bind the employee title to the Name property of the ToolTip control.

C. Bind the employee title to the Tag property of the TextBox control. In the event handler for the CurrentChanged event of the CurrencyManager object, call the ToolTip's SetToolTip method to copy the value from the Tag property to the ToolTip.

D. Bind the employee title to the Tag property of the TextBox control. In the event handler for the ItemChanged event of the CurrencyManager object, call the ToolTip's SetToolTip method to copy the value from the Tag property to the ToolTip.

4. Your application includes a database table that contains a list of course numbers and course names. You've used Server Explorer to create a SqlConnection object and a SqlDataAdapter object to access this data. You've created a dataset named dsCourses1 to hold this data. Your form includes code to fill the dataset when it's loaded.

   Now you'd like to display the list of courses in a ListBox control named lbCourses on your form. The ListBox should show the course names and return the course numbers. Which of these code snippets should you use?

A.
```
With lbCourses
    .DataSource = DsCourses1
    .DisplayMember = "CourseName"
    .ValueMember = "CourseNumber"
End With
```

B.
```
With lbCourses
    .DataSource = _
    DsCourses1.Tables("Courses")
    .DisplayMember = "CourseName"
    .ValueMember = "CourseNumber"
End With
```

C.
```
With lbCourses
    .DataSource = _
    DsCourses1.Tables("Courses")
    .DisplayMember = "CourseName"
    .SelectedItem = "CourseNumber"
End With
```

D.
```
With lbCourses
    .DataBindings.Add("DisplayMember", _
    DsCourses1, "CourseName")
    .DataBindings.Add("ValueMember", _
    DsCourses1, "CourseNumber")
End With
```

5. Your application includes a ListBox control named lbEmployees that displays a list of employees. The DisplayMember property of the ListBox is bound to the EmployeeName column of the Employees database table. The ValueMember property of the ListBox is bound to the EmployeeNumber column of the Employees database table.

   Your form also contains a TextBox control named txtEmployeeNumber. This control uses simple data binding to display the EmployeeNumber column from the Orders table in your database.

APPLY YOUR KNOWLEDGE

When the user selects a new employee name in the ListBox, you want to display the corresponding EmployeeNumber value in the txtEmployeeNumber control. What should you do?

A. Use the SelectedIndexChanged event of the ListBox to copy the data from the ListBox to the text box.

B. Use simple data binding to bind the ValueMember property of the ListBox to the Text property of the text box.

C. Use simple data binding to bind the SelectedValue property of the ListBox to the EmployeeNumber column of the Orders table.

D. Use simple data binding to bind the SelectedValue property of the ListBox to the EmployeeNumber column of the Employees table.

6. Your application requires data from a database named College. The database includes two tables. The Departments table includes columns DepartmentID and DepartmentName. The Courses table includes columns DepartmentID, CourseName and CourseNumber. The DepartmentID column is a primary key for the Departments table and a foreign key for the Courses table.

A form in your application needs to display a list of CourseName values, together with the DepartmentName value for each course. This form does not need any other data. How should you retrieve only this data from the database?

A. Use Server Explorer to create a new SQL Server view that joins the two tables and returns only the required fields. Drag this view and drop it on a form to create a DataAdapter that returns the required data. Build a dataset from the DataAdapter and bind the dataset to your form.

B. Drag both the Departments table and the Courses table from Server Explorer and drop them on your form to create two separate DataAdapters. Use the DataAdapters to fill a single DataSet. Build a DataView from the DataSet and use the DataView to filter the data.

C. Drag both the Departments table and the Courses table from Server Explorer and drop them on your form to create two separate DataAdapters. Use the two DataAdapters to create two separate DataSets. Bind the DataSet of Course information to a DataGrid. Bind the DataSet of Department information to a ComboBox. Use the value in the ComboBox to filter the information displayed on the DataGrid.

D. Use Server Explorer to create a new SQL Server table that includes only the necessary information. Copy the data from the two separate tables to this table. Drag and drop this table from Server Explorer to your form to create a DataAdapter. Build a DataSet from the DataAdapter and bind the DataSet to your form.

APPLY YOUR KNOWLEDGE

7. Your application includes a SqlDataAdapter object named SqlDataAdapter1 that was created by dragging and dropping the Physicians table from a database to your form. Your application also includes a DataSet named dsPhysicians1, based on this SqlDataAdapter. What line of code should you use to load the data from the database into the DataSet?

   A. `dsPhysicians =`
`sqlDataAdapter1.Fill("Physicians")`

   B. `SqlDataAdapter1.Fill("DsPhysicians1",`
`"Physicians")`

   C. `SqlDataAdapter1.Fill(DsPhysicians1)`

   D. `SqlDataAdapter1.Fill(DsPhysicians1,`
`"Physicians")`

8. The application that you're designing will display employee information on a DataGrid control using complex data binding. Your database contains a table of departments and a table of employees. The Employees table has a foreign key that points back to the Departments table. The application will communicate with the database via a slow WAN link. The list of departments changes approximately once every two months.

The form will display all the employees from a single department. Although users will only view one department at a time, they will frequently need to view several departments during the course of a session with the application.

How should you design the filtering for this form?

  A. Build one view on the server for each department. At runtime, have the program use the appropriate view to retrieve the requested department.

B. Each time the user requests a department, retrieve all the data into a DataSet. Then delete all rows from the DataSet that do not apply to this department.

C. Retrieve all the data into a DataSet. Use a DataView with its RowFilter property set at runtime to retrieve individual departments as needed.

D. Build one form for each department. Each form should be based on a view that returns only the employees for that department. At runtime, open the appropriate form. Hide the form when the user is done so that it can be opened more quickly if it's needed a second time.

9. Your application is connected to a SQL Server database that contains customer and order information. You have a form in your application that fills a DataSet with information from the Orders table that includes the CustomerID. The DataSet is displayed on the form by using complex data binding to a DataGrid.

Now you've been asked to display the CustomerName column from the Customers table in the DataGrid, instead of the CustomerID column. How should you proceed?

A. Create a view in the SQL Server database that combines the Customers and Orders tables. Replace the dataset on the form with a new DataSet based on this new view. Bind the new DataSet to the DataGrid.

B. Add a second DataSet to the form. Base the second DataSet on the Customers table from the database. Use each DataSet to fill the appropriate columns of the DataGrid.

APPLY YOUR KNOWLEDGE

C. Create a DataView in code from the existing DataSet. Filter the DataView to remove the CustomerID column.

D. Add an array of Customer objects to your application and initialize it in code with customer names and IDs. Use a view to join this array to the existing DataSet.

10. You're using simple data binding to display a DateTime value (that includes a time part) in a TextBox control. Your application uses two-way data binding, so that the user can edit the value in the control and have changes saved back to the data model. Unfortunately, users are not always careful, and you have a problem when invalid dates (such as February 30, 2004) are entered in the text box. How should you fix this problem?

A. Write an event handler for the TextChanged event of the TextBox control. Check the Text of the control in this event handler to see if it's a valid date. If not, revert to the original date.

B. Replace the TextBox control on the form with a DateTimePicker control. Use simple data binding to bind the data to the control's Value property.

C. Replace the TextBox control on the form with a DateTimePicker control. Use simple data binding to bind the data to the control's Tag property.

D. Replace the TextBox control on the form with a MonthCalendar control. Use simple data binding to bind the data to the control's Value property.

11. You are working with a complex form that uses Panel controls to organize a large amount of data.

The form displays information from six different data sources. Some of the panels contain data from more than one data source.

You have added navigation buttons to scroll through the data in one particular data source. The navigation buttons increment and decrement the Position property of a CurrencyManager object. You test the form, and the buttons do not appear to scroll the data in that data source. What could be the problem? (Choose two.)

A. Too many controls are on the form for your code to be executed.

B. You retrieved the CurrencyManager through the Form's BindingContext object, but the Panel control has its own BindingContext object.

C. This particular CurrencyManager object does not support a Position property.

D. The BindingContext object you're using has more than one CurrencyManager object, and you're working with the wrong one.

12. The data model of your application includes a task list that can have anywhere from one to eight items in it. Each item is characterized by five pieces of information. You need to display the entire task list on a single form. Your users want to be able to see all tasks at one time. What should you do?

A. Use simple data binding to display a single task in individual TextBox controls. Provide navigation buttons to scroll through the task list.

B. Use the System.Reflection.Emit namespace to create the appropriate number of TextBox controls at runtime. Use simple data binding to bind each task to a different set of controls.

APPLY YOUR KNOWLEDGE

C. Use complex data binding to display the task list in a ComboBox control.

D. Use complex data binding to display the task list in a DataGrid control.

13. You have created an array of Car objects named aCars. Each Car object has a Model property and a Year property. You want to display all the Model values in a ListBox control named lbCars. Which code snippet should you use for this purpose?

A.

```
With lbCars
    .DataSource = aCars
    .ValueMember = Model
End With
```

B.

```
With lbCars
    .DataSource = aCars
    .DisplayMember = Model
End With
```

C.

```
With lbCars
    .DataSource = aCars
    .DisplayMember = "Model"
End With
```

D.

```
With lbCars
    .DataSource = aCars
    .ValueMember = "Model"
End With
```

14. You have an XML file containing information on customers. You plan to make this information available to your users by using simple data binding to controls on the user interface. What must you do?

A. Transfer the data from the XML file to a data structure that implements the IList, IBindingList, or ITypedList interfaces.

B. Create an XML Web Service to retrieve information from the file.

C. Store the XML file in a SQL Server database.

D. Set the Tag property of each control that you will use for data binding to XML.

15. Your data model includes an array of Date values named gadtMain. You've created a form that includes a DateTimePicker control named dtMain. Which line of code can you use to bind the control to the array?

A. `dtMain.DataBindings.Add("Value", gadtMain, "")`

B. `dtMain.DataBindings.Add("Format", gadtMain, "")`

C. `dtMain.DataBindings.Add("Value", gadtMain, "Date")`

D. `dtMain.DataBindings.Add("Format", gadtMain, "Date")`

Answers to Review Questions

1. A database is a location, such as a SQL Server database, where you can store data outside of your application. A data model is the representation of data within your application.

2. Simple data binding means connecting a single value from the data model to a single property of a control. Complex data binding means connecting a user interface control to an entire collection of data, rather than to a single data item.

3. The BindingContext object provides access to the CurrencyManager objects on a form.

APPLY YOUR KNOWLEDGE

4. The CurrencyManager object is responsible for keeping track of which piece of data from a data source is currently bound to the user interface.

5. You can filter data by creating a DataView object and setting its RowFilter property, or by creating a view on the database server. In the first case, all the data is returned from the server to your application, and then filtered in your application. In the second case, the data is filtered on the server, and only the filtered data is returned to your application.

6. Any object that implements the IList, IBindingList, or ITypedList interfaces can be used as a data-binding source.

7. The DataSource property of a ComboBox control specifies the data that will be displayed in the list portion of the ComboBox. The DisplayMember property specifies the exact column of data that will be shown in the list. The ValueMember property specifies the exact column of data that will be returned by the SelectedValue property of the ComboBox.

8. You can design SQL Server database diagrams, tables, views, stored procedures, and functions from within Visual Studio .NET.

9. Which alternative is more efficient depends on what your application is doing with the data. If you only need a small portion of the data, it's more efficient to filter the data on the server with a server-side view. But if your communications link with the server is slow or if you will need a variety of different subsets of the data, it can be more efficient to perform filtering on the client with a DataView.

Answers to Exam Questions

1. **C.** Binding the ComboBox control to both the data source and a TextBox control lets the ComboBox transfer data from the source to the TextBox. Answer **A** requires searching for the data rather than choosing it. Answer **B** displays all the data at once. Answer **D** does not have any provision for choosing a ProductNumber.

2. **D.** To move through the list of items, you must change the Position property of the appropriate CurrencyManager object. The Item property of the BindingContext is used to return a CurrencyManager. The Add and Remove methods make and break bindings. The ResumeBinding and SuspendBinding methods control whether data binding is active.

3. **A.** The value displayed by the ToolTip can only be set with the SetToolTip method. It can't be bound directly. The appropriate event for renewing the ToolTip is the PositionChanged event, which fires whenever a record becomes current.

4. **B.** The code in **B** performs the required task. Answer **A** does not properly specify which data from the dataset to use. Answer **C** neglects to bind the ValueMember property, which controls the value of the ListBox. Answer **D** uses simple data binding syntax, which will not display an entire list of data.

5. **C.** This is the only choice that will satisfy the conditions. For review, see the section "Binding to a ComboBox or ListBox" and Step By Step 5.6.

6. **A.** Answers **B** and **C** return too much data to the client. Answer **D** results in storing duplicate data on the server, which is inefficient and prone to error.

APPLY YOUR KNOWLEDGE

7. **D.** In a call to the Fill method of a SqlDataAdapter object, you must specify the DataSet to fill as an object and the table to fill as a string.

8. **C.** Answers **A** and **D** require maintenance programming every time the list of departments changes. Answer **B** will retrieve more data than necessary over the slow WAN line.

9. **A.** Answers **B** and **C** are unworkable. Answer **D** requires you to maintain the code to synchronize the array with the actual data in the database. Only answer **A** lets you set up the DataGrid so that it's automatically kept up-to-date.

10. **B.** You must use a DateTimePicker rather than a MonthCalendar because the latter doesn't let you specify a time. Validating the data in the text box won't work, because the text box will still attempt to save the bad value to the database before validating. When you're binding a DateTimePicker, the Value property is the one that controls the displayed date.

11. **B, D.** All CurrencyManager objects support a Position property, and it would take a truly astronomical number of controls to cause problems with .NET's code execution.

12. **D.** Answers **A** and **C** result in only one task being visible at a time. Answer **B** uses complicated programming where a single data binding call will suffice.

13. **C.** You must set the DataSource and DisplayMember properties of the ListBox to cause it to display anything. The DisplayMember property is a string, not an object.

14. **A.** Only this answer will produce data that can be bound.

15. **A.** The Value property of the DateTimePicker control is what you bind when you want to display a particular value. You don't need a navigation path (the third parameter to DataBindings.Add) when you're binding to an array of simple types.

Suggested Readings and Resources

1. .NET Framework SDK Documentation
   - System.Data Namespace
   - System.Windows.Forms Namespace

2. Windows Forms QuickStart Tutorial
   - Databinding in Windows Forms
   - Control topics including ComboBox, DateTimePicker, and DataGrid.

3. Visual Studio .NET Combined Help Collection
   - Windows Forms Data Architecture

This chapter covers the following Microsoft-specified objectives for the Consuming and Manipulating Data section of the Visual Basic .NET Windows-Based Applications exam:

Consuming and Manipulating Data.

- **Access and manipulate data from a Microsoft SQL Server database by creating and using ad hoc queries and stored procedures.**

- **Access and manipulate data from a data store. Data stores include relational databases, XML documents, and flat files. Methods include XML techniques and ADO .NET.**

- **Handle data errors.**

▶ Visual Basic .NET includes a variety of ways to manipulate data and to move it from place to place. The Visual Studio .NET IDE offers tight integration with Microsoft SQL Server, making it easy to work with SQL Server data, either interactively or programmatically. The .NET Framework also offers several entire namespaces to deal with data in its various forms. These include

- System.IO for dealing with file-based storage.

- System.Data, System.Data.SqlClient, and System.Data.OleDb (which collectively make up ADO.NET) for using data from relational databases.

- System.Xml for working with XML files.

In this chapter you'll learn about these many ways to manipulate data within your application.

C H A P T E R 6

Consuming and Manipulating Data

▶ You should understand how to construct and interpret simple Transact SQL statements including SELECT, INSERT, UPDATE, and DELETE, as well as SQL Server stored procedures. Spend some time practicing with the Visual Data Tools inside .NET or with another query front end such as SQL Server Query Analyzer. Be sure to work with the raw T-SQL, not just the graphical tools.

▶ For file-based access, understand the difference between a stream and a backing store. Practice reading and writing data with FileStream, StreamReader, and StreamWriter objects.

▶ Sometimes you'll come across the claim that ADO.NET is just an evolutionary improvement on classic ADO, and that your knowledge of classic ADO will help you learn ADO.NET. This is not true! ADO.NET is an entirely new model for working with data. Pay attention to the uses and functions of the ADO.NET objects, and don't get confused by the similarity of names between these objects and classic ADO objects.

▶ Know which objects are part of the System.Data namespace (and so shared by all data providers) and which are part of specific data provider namespaces such as System.Data.SqlClient and System.Data.OleDb.

▶ You'll need to know the classes contained within a DataSet and the methods available to manipulate them. Be sure you understand when to use a strongly typed DataSet and how this affects the syntax of DataSet operations.

▶ You should also know how to read and write XML data using the classes from the System.Xml namespace. Understand how to synchronize an XML document with a DataSet and some of the reasons that you might want to do this.

INTRODUCTION

Now that you've seen some of the techniques available for dealing with data directly from the user interface of a Visual Basic .NET Windows application, it's time to take a more detailed look at the facilities that the .NET Framework offers for working with data. Data is at the core of many .NET applications, and the Microsoft developers spent many hours building a flexible set of tools for working with data in your code.

I'll look at three main types of data in this chapter:

◆ Data stored in databases such as Microsoft SQL Server

◆ Data stored in disk files

◆ Data stored in XML

The .NET Framework offers specialized ways to deal with each of these types of data.

Many parts of ADO.NET are specially optimized to work with Microsoft SQL Server as a database, so you must understand the language, Transact-SQL (T-SQL), that's used to communicate with SQL Server. I'll start the chapter by reviewing the basic parts of the T-SQL language that you must know to communicate effectively with SQL Server. You'll also see how to use a small part of ADO.NET to send T-SQL statements to SQL Server and receive the results of the statements.

Once you know T-SQL, you can look at ways to manipulate a variety of data. Data stored in files is handled by the classes in the System.IO namespace. The .NET Framework handles file data as part of a more general concept of streams and backing stores. A *backing store* is any place you can store data (including a disk file), and a *stream* represents that data's movements from place to place.

Data stored in databases is the target of ADO.NET, a subset of the .NET Framework that uses objects from the System.Data namespace and related namespaces. The DataSet object is the central object here, representing an entire relational database in a single object (with many constituent objects). You'll see how to create DataSet objects and fill them with data, and then see some of the many ways to work with that data.

Data stored in XML is handled by the System.Xml namespace. XML is a key part of the .NET Framework, and the classes in this namespace give you flexibility to read and write such data.

I'll close the chapter with a look at handling data errors. In particular, you'll see how the .NET error-trapping mechanisms let you deal with common database and multi-user data errors.

ACCESS AND MANIPULATE SQL SERVER DATA

Consuming and Manipulating Data: Access and manipulate data from a Microsoft SQL Server(TM) database by creating and using ad hoc queries and stored procedures.

You might be a bit surprised to find a Microsoft SQL Server objective on a Visual Basic .NET certification exam, but this really makes perfect sense. Many Visual Basic .NET applications require a database to enable them to store data on a permanent basis, and SQL Server is one of the best databases to use with .NET. As you'll see later in this chapter, an entire namespace (System.Data.SqlClient) is devoted to efficient communication between .NET applications and SQL Server.

The objects in System.Data.SqlClient, though, won't do you any good unless you understand the language used to communicate with SQL Server, *Transact-SQL (T-SQL)*. T-SQL is Microsoft's implementation of SQL (Structured Query Language), which is defined by a standard from the American National Standards Institute (ANSI). The core of T-SQL is based on the ANSI SQL-92 standard. SQL-92 defines a query-oriented language in which you submit queries to the database and get back a result set consisting of rows and columns of data. Other queries cause changes to the database (for example, adding, deleting, or updating a row of data) without returning any result set.

You can submit T-SQL to a SQL Server database for processing in two ways. First, you can write *ad-hoc queries*, SQL statements that are executed directly. Second, you can write *stored procedures*, SQL statements that are stored on the server as a named object. The .NET Framework includes facilities for running both ad hoc queries and stored procedures.

SQL Statement Formatting You'll usually see SQL keywords (such as SELECT, INSERT, UPDATE, and DELETE) formatted entirely in uppercase. I'll follow that convention in this book, but uppercase formatting isn't required by SQL Server. You might see these same keywords in mixed case or lowercase on an exam. As far as SQL Server is concerned, there's no difference between SELECT, Select, and select.

SQL Dialects Microsoft SQL Server isn't the only product that implements the SQL-92 standard. Other products, including Microsoft Access and Oracle, also use SQL-92–based query languages. However, databases differ in their treatment of SQL in many subtle ways. Most databases contain extensions to SQL-92 (keywords that are only understood by that particular database), and most don't implement the entire SQL-92 standard. The SQL statements in this chapter are from the shared core of SQL-92 that's identical in nearly all database products, so they should work whether you're using SQL Server, Access, or Oracle (among others). But as you study the more advanced features of SQL Server, you should keep in mind that T-SQL statements will not necessarily run without changes on other database servers.

Using Ad Hoc Queries

Ad hoc T-SQL queries provide an extremely flexible way to retrieve data from a SQL Server database or to make changes to that database. In this section of the chapter, I'll show several ways to send an ad hoc query to SQL Server. Then you'll learn the basics of the four main T-SQL statements that help manipulate SQL Server data:

◆ SELECT statements allow you to retrieve data stored in the database.

◆ INSERT statements allow you to add new data to the database.

◆ UPDATE statements allow you to modify data already in the database.

◆ DELETE statements allow you to delete data from the database.

Running Queries

When learning T-SQL, it's useful to be able to send queries to a SQL Server database and to see the results (if any) that the server returns. You should be aware of the many ways to communicate with SQL Server. I'll show you four of them in this section:

◆ Using the Visual Studio .NET IDE

◆ Using Osql

◆ Using SQL Query Analyzer

◆ Using a Visual Basic .NET Application

Using the Visual Studio .NET IDE

When you just need to run a query in the course of working with a project, you can run it directly from the Visual Studio .NET IDE. Step by Step 6.1 shows you how.

STEP BY STEP

6.1 Running a Query from the Visual Studio .NET IDE

1. Open a Visual Basic .NET Windows Application in the Visual Studio .NET IDE.

2. Open Server Explorer.

3. Expand the tree under Data Connections to show a SQL Server data connection that points to the Northwind sample database, then the Views node of the SQL Server.

4. Right-click the Views node and select New View.

5. Click Close on the Add Table dialog box.

6. In the SQL pane of the View Designer (the area that displays the text SELECT FROM) type this SQL statement (replacing the existing text):

```
SELECT * FROM Employees
```

7. Select Query, Run from the Visual Studio menu, or click the Run Query button on the View toolbar to send the SQL statement to SQL Server and display the results, as shown in Figure 6.1.

> **NOTE**
>
> **The Northwind Sample Database** Whenever I've used data from a database in this book, I've used the Northwind sample database that comes as part of SQL Server 2000. Visual Studio .NET includes MSDE, a stripped-down version of SQL Server that you can use if you don't have the full version installed. See your Visual Studio CD's readme file for information on installing MSDE.

> **NOTE**
>
> **Creating Data Connections** If you need a refresher on creating SQL Server data connections, refer to Chapter 5, "Data Binding," especially Step By Step 5.10, "Building a Single-Table Data Form," and Step By Step 5.12, "Adding a Data Connection from Server Explorer."

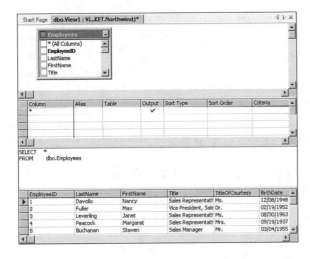

FIGURE 6.1
Running an ad hoc query directly from the Visual Studio .NET IDE.

When you run the query, Visual Studio .NET sends the SQL statement to the SQL Server that was specified by the database connection you chose in step 3. The server then processes the query (this particular query tells it to return all columns in all rows of the Employees table) and sends the results back to the client (in this case, Visual Studio .NET). The IDE then displays the results formatted as a grid.

SQL Statement Formatting If you refer to Figure 6.1, you'll see that Visual Studio .NET made some changes to the SQL statement that you typed. The original statement was

```
SELECT * FROM Employees
```

The statement that Visual Studio .NET turns this into is

```
SELECT      *
FROM        dbo.Employees
```

I'd like to elaborate on two points here: First, SQL Server doesn't care about whitespace. You can insert spaces, tabs, or new lines between any SQL keywords without changing the statement. Second, every SQL Server object (such as the Employees table) has an owner. The default owner is a user named *dbo* (for database owner). You can add the name of the owner of an object to the object when referring to it. In the case of SQL statements on the exam, it's likely that every object will be owned by dbo, so don't get thrown if you see the dbo prefix on a table name.

The View Designer in Visual Studio .NET displays up to four panes. From top to bottom, these are

1. The Diagram pane, which displays the tables involved in the query and the relations between these tables, as well as all the columns that the tables contain

2. The Grid pane, which shows the columns that have been selected as part of the query, as well as additional sorting and filtering information.

3. The SQL pane, which shows the actual SQL statement that will be executed.

4. The Results pane, which shows the results (if any) after the query has been executed.

The View toolbar includes buttons used to hide or show any of these four panes. For this chapter, you'll only need the SQL Results panes.

Using Osql

A second option for executing ad hoc queries is to use one of the utilities that ships as a part of SQL Server. The MSDE version of SQL Server that's shipped with Visual Studio .NET includes one of these utilities, osql. Osql is a command-line utility that can execute SQL Server queries (see Step By Step 6.2).

STEP BY STEP

6.2 Running a Query from Osql

1. Open a Windows command prompt.

2. To launch Osql and log in using Windows integrated authentication, type `osql -E`.

3. To execute a query in osql, you must first tell it which database to use. Type `use Northwind`.

4. Next you must enter the query to execute. Type `SELECT FirstName, LastName FROM Employees`.

5. Finally, you must tell osql to execute the SQL statements that you just entered. Type GO.

6. When you're done with osql, type exit.

Here's the entire osql session, including the prompts from osql:

```
C:\>osql -E
1> use Northwind
2> SELECT FirstName, LastName FROM Employees
3> GO
 FirstName  LastName
 ---------  --------------------
 Nancy      Davolio
 Max        Fuller
 Janet      Leverling
 Margaret   Peacock
 Steven     Buchanan
 Michael    Suyama
 Robert     King
 Laura      Callahan
 Anne       Dodsworth

(9 rows affected)
1> exit

C:\>
```

I chose a slightly different query for the osql session than I used in Step By Step 6.1. The SELECT query in Step By Step 6.2 specifies two columns from the table (FirstName and LastName), telling SQL Server to return only the contents of those two columns. If you execute SELECT * FROM Employees in osql, you might get a bit of a shock because the Employees table includes a bitmap image column, and the contents of that column will fill a command session with junk characters.

Using SQL Query Analyzer

Although osql can be convenient for quick queries, it doesn't offer much in the way of tools. SQL Server also offers a full-featured query environment called SQL Query Analyzer (see Step By Step 6.3).

EXAM TIP

Obtaining SQL Query Analyzer SQL Query Analyzer is not included in the MSDE version of SQL Server. It's a part of all the other editions of SQL Server, so if you have another edition installed, you'll have SQL Query Analyzer available. Otherwise, you can download the 120-day trial version of SQL Server 2000 from http://www.microsoft.com/sql/evaluation/trial/2000/default.asp. This version also contains SQL Query Analyzer.

STEP BY STEP

6.3 Running a Query from SQL Query Analyzer

1. Select Start, Programs, Microsoft SQL Server, Query Analyzer.

2. SQL Query Analyzer will launch and display the Connect to SQL Server dialog box. To choose a SQL Server to work with, you can type the name of a SQL Server, or type the special name (local) to use a SQL Server on the same computer as SQL Query Analyzer. You can also use the browse button to list all servers on the network. After selecting a server and filling in your authentication information, click OK.

3. Select the Northwind database from the databases combo box on the SQL Query Analyzer toolbar.

4. Type a query in the Query window:

```
SELECT * FROM Employees
```

5. Select Query, Execute, click the Execute button on the toolbar, or press F5 to run the query. This will send the SQL statement to SQL Server and display the results, as shown in Figure 6.2.

FIGURE 6.2

Running an ad hoc query in SQL Query Analyzer.

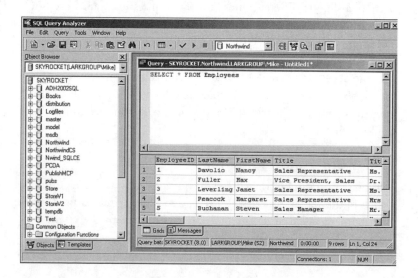

SQL Query Analyzer offers an extremely flexible environment for running ad hoc queries. The features of SQL Query Analyzer include

◆ Multiple open query windows

◆ An Object Browser to see the structure of SQL Server objects

◆ Performance analysis

◆ Templates for common queries

For more information on using SQL Query Analyzer, refer to SQL Server Books Online, the help file installed as part of SQL Server.

Using a Visual Basic .NET Application

As a final alternative for executing ad hoc queries, Step By Step 6.4 shows how to build your own Visual Basic .NET form to execute any query.

STEP BY STEP

6.4 Running a Query from a Custom Form

1. Add a new form to your Visual Basic .NET project.

2. Open Server Explorer.

3. Expand the tree under Data Connections to show a SQL Server data connection that points to the Northwind sample database. Drag and drop the data connection to the form to create a SqlConnection1 object on the form. This object represents a connection to SQL Server.

4. Add a TextBox control named txtQuery, a Button control named btnExecute, and a DataGrid control named dgResults to the form. Set the Multiline property of the TextBox to True. Set the CaptionVisible property of the DataGrid to False.

5. Double-click the Button control to open the form's module. Enter two statements at the top of the module to make the ADO.NET objects available:

```
Imports System.Data
Imports System.Data.SqlClient
```

continues

continued

6. Enter this code to execute the query when you click the Button control:

```
Private Sub btnExecute_Click( _
 ByVal sender As System.Object, _
 ByVal e As System.EventArgs) Handles btnExecute.Click
    ' Create a SqlCommand to represent the query
    Dim cmd As SqlCommand = SqlConnection1.CreateCommand
    cmd.CommandType = CommandType.Text
    cmd.CommandText = txtQuery.Text
    ' Create a SqlDataAdapter to talk to the database
    Dim da As SqlDataAdapter = New SqlDataAdapter()
    da.SelectCommand = cmd
    ' Create a DataSet to hold the results
    Dim ds As DataSet = New DataSet()
    ' Fill the DataSet
    da.Fill(ds, "Results")
    ' And bind it to the DataGrid
    dgResults.DataSource = ds
    dgResults.DataMember = "Results"
End Sub
```

7. Set the form as the startup object for the project.

8. Run the project. Enter a query in the text box: SELECT * FROM Employees.

9. Click the button to run the code, retrieving the results to the DataGrid, as shown in Figure 6.3.

FIGURE 6.3
Running an ad hoc query from a custom form.

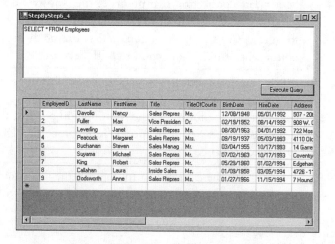

You'll learn about the ADO.NET objects that this example uses later in this chapter, starting in the section "The ADO.NET Object Model." For now I'll give a quick preview of the objects I just used:

◆ The SqlConnection object represents a connection to a database.

◆ The SqlCommand object represents a single query that you can send to the server.

◆ The DataSet object represents the results of one or more queries.

◆ The SqlDataAdapter object acts as a pipeline between the SqlConnection and DataSet objects.

The code uses these objects to retrieve data from the SQL Server to the DataSet and uses the SQL statement that you typed to know which data to retrieve. It then uses complex data binding (which you learned about in Chapter 5) to display the results on the user interface in the DataGrid control.

The SELECT Statement

Now that you know a variety of ways to execute ad hoc queries, it's time to dig into the T-SQL language to see some of the possible queries, starting with the SELECT statement.

The basic SQL statement is the SELECT statement. This statement is used to create a result set. In skeleton form, a SELECT looks like this:

```
SELECT field_list
FROM table_list
WHERE where_clause
GROUP BY group_by_clause
HAVING having_clause
ORDER BY sort_clause
```

Each of those lines of code is called a *clause*. The SELECT and FROM clauses are required, and the rest are optional. Here's an example of a SQL statement containing only the required clauses:

```
SELECT OrderID, CustomerID
FROM Orders
```

The result set for this statement contains the values of the OrderID and CustomerID fields from every record in the Orders table.

EXAM TIP

Practice Using SQL You can use any of the methods you saw in the preceding section to execute the statements you're about to learn. You *should* execute enough of these statements to get a good idea of how the T-SQL language works. Just reading the descriptions here is no substitute for actually practicing with T-SQL. You're sure to see some SQL statements on the exam.

Other results are attainable by the SELECT clause besides just lists of fields. You've already seen the shortcut for all fields:

```
SELECT *
FROM Orders
```

You can also perform calculations in the SELECT clause:

```
SELECT OrderID,
CAST(ShippedDate - OrderDate AS integer) AS Delay
FROM Orders
```

The expression ShippedDate - OrderDate calculates the number of days between the two dates. The CAST function tells SQL Server to return the result as an integer. If you try that example, you'll see the AS clause supplies a name for the calculated column. If you omit AS Delay, the query will still work, but SQL Server will return the calculation without assigning a name to the column.

You're also not limited to fields from a single table. For instance, you might try retrieving information from both the Customers and Orders tables with this query:

```
SELECT OrderID, Customers.CustomerID
FROM Orders, Customers
```

Customers.CustomerID is what's known as a *fully qualified name*, specifying both the table name and the field name. This is necessary because both the Customers and the Orders tables contain fields named CustomerID, and you need to tell SQL Server which one you want to display.

If you try the previous query, though, you'll get more than 75,000 records back—many more than the number of orders in the database! That's because the query as written, while it includes all the proper tables, doesn't tell SQL Server how to relate those tables.

The name for this sort of query is a *cross-product* query. SQL Server constructs the result set by including one row in the output for each row in each combination of input table rows. That is, there's an output row for the first order and the first customer, for the first order and the second customer, and so on. A more useful query, of course, matches each order with the corresponding customer.

That's the job of the INNER JOIN keyword. INNER JOIN tells SQL Server how to match two tables. Here's how the syntax looks for a fixed version of the original query:

```
SELECT OrderID, Customers.CustomerID
FROM Orders INNER JOIN Customers
ON Orders.CustomerID = Customers.CustomerID
```

This rewrite tells SQL Server to look at each row in the Orders table and match it with all rows in the Customers table where the CustomerID of the order equals the CustomerID of the customer. Because CustomerIDs are unique in the Customers table, this is tantamount to including only a single row for each order in the result set.

The INNER JOIN keyword can appear more than once in a query for more than two tables to join. For example, here's a query to show EmployeeIDs along with Order and CustomerIDs:

```
SELECT Orders.OrderID, Customers.CustomerID,
Employees.EmployeeID
FROM Employees INNER JOIN
(Customers INNER JOIN Orders
ON Customers.CustomerID = Orders.CustomerID)
ON Employees.EmployeeID = Orders.EmployeeID
```

Note the use of parentheses to specify the order in which the joins should be performed.

The basic SELECT query allows you to see all of the data in a table. For example:

```
SELECT * FROM Orders
```

That query returns every bit of data in the Orders table: every column, every row. You've already seen that you can use a field list to limit the number of columns returned:

```
SELECT OrderID, CustomerID, EmployeeID FROM Orders
```

But what if you only want to see some of the rows in the table? That's where the WHERE clause comes into the picture. You can think of a WHERE clause as making a simple, yes-or-no decision for each row of data in the original table, deciding whether to include that row in the result set.

NOTE

One Keyword or Two? Even though it's two words, INNER JOIN is referred to as a single SQL keyword because you can't have INNER in T-SQL unless you immediately follow it with JOIN.

The simplest form of the WHERE clause checks for the exact contents of a field. For example:

```
SELECT * FROM Orders
WHERE ShipCountry = 'Brazil'
```

This query looks at every row in the Orders table and determines whether the ShipCountry field contains the exact value Brazil. If so, the row is included in the results. If not, it's discarded. However, WHERE clauses need not be exact. This is also a valid SQL statement:

```
SELECT * FROM Orders
WHERE Freight > 50
```

In this case, you'll get all the rows where the amount in the Freight field is greater than 50.

Note, by the way, that Brazil goes in quotation marks while 50 doesn't. That's simply a syntax matter: Text and date data need quotation marks, numeric columns don't.

You're free to combine multiple tests in a single WHERE clause. For example:

```
SELECT * FROM Orders
WHERE ShipCountry = 'Brazil'
 AND Freight > 50
 AND OrderDate <= '12/31/97'
```

This retrieves all orders that went to Brazil, had more than $50 of freight charges, and were shipped before the end of 1997. The key is that the entire WHERE clause must be a single logical predicate. That is, by evaluating all the pieces, the result must be a True or False value. Rows for which the WHERE clause evaluates to True are included in the results; rows for which it evaluates to False are excluded.

You can also use wild cards in a WHERE clause. Consider this simple SELECT statement:

```
SELECT * FROM Customers
WHERE CustomerID = 'BLONP'
```

If you run that query, you'll find that it returns the record for Blondel pere et fils, the customer that is assigned the CustomerID BLONP. So far, that's easy. But what if you remember that the CustomerID starts with B, but not what it is exactly? That's when you'd use a wildcard:

```
SELECT * FROM Customers
WHERE CustomerID LIKE 'B%'
```

The % wildcard matches zero or more characters, so the result of this query is to retrieve all of the customers whose CustomerIDs begin with *B*. Note the switch from = to LIKE when using a wildcard (if you searched for `CustomerID = 'B%'`, you'd only find a customer with that exact ID). Now suppose you almost remember the CustomerID, but not quite: Is it BLOND or BLONP? Try this query:

```
SELECT * FROM Customers
WHERE CustomerID LIKE 'BLON_'
```

The _ wildcard matches precisely one character—so that would match BLONA, BLONB, and so on. If you're sure that it's either *D* or *P*, you can try the following:

```
SELECT * FROM Customers
WHERE CustomerID LIKE 'BLON'''
```

The '' is a character set wildcard. The square brackets tell SQL Server to match any one of the characters listed in the set. You can also use a dash in a character set to indicate a range:

```
SELECT * FROM Customers
WHERE CustomerID LIKE 'BLON[D-P]'
```

That matches BLOND, BLONE, and so on, through BLONP. You can also invert a character set with the ^ character. For example:

```
SELECT * FROM Customers
WHERE CustomerID LIKE 'BLON[^A-O]'
```

That matches BLONP, BLONQ, and so on but not BLONA, BLONB, or anything else that would match the character set without the ^ character.

SQL is a set-oriented language; by default, the database engine is free to return the set of results in any order it likes. To guarantee a sort order, include an ORDER BY clause in your SQL statement. For example, to see the customers from Venezuela in Postal Code order, you could use this statement:

```
SELECT * FROM Customers
WHERE Country = 'Venezuela'
ORDER BY PostalCode
```

That's the basic ORDER BY clause: a field name to sort by. You can use two keywords to modify this: ASC, for ascending sort (the default), and DESC, for descending sort. So, you could write the previous SQL statement as:

```
SELECT * FROM Customers
WHERE Country = 'Venezuela'
ORDER BY PostalCode ASC
```

Or you could get the customers sorted in reverse postal code order with this statement:

```
SELECT * FROM Customers
WHERE Country = 'Venezuela'
ORDER BY PostalCode DESC
```

You're not limited to sorting by a single field. For example, you might want to see the entire Customer list, sorted first by country and then by postal code within country:

```
SELECT * FROM Customers
ORDER BY Country, PostalCode
```

You can specify on a field-by-field basis the order of the sort:

```
SELECT * FROM Customers
ORDER BY Country ASC, PostalCode DESC
```

That would sort by country in ascending order, and then by postal code in descending order within each country.

You can also calculate a sort. For example, you can sort the customers by the length of their company name:

```
SELECT * FROM Customers
ORDER BY Len([CompanyName])
```

Here the square brackets tell the Len() function that it's being passed a column name, and to retrieve that column value for each row as the input to the function. In fact, the calculation need not have anything to do with the fields returned by the SELECT statement:

```
SELECT * FROM Customers
ORDER BY 2+2
```

That's a perfectly valid SQL statement, though the effect is to put the records in whatever order the database engine decides it wants to use.

So far, all the SELECT statements you've seen in this chapter have returned results where each row corresponds to one row in the underlying tables. However, it's possible (and indeed common) to use SQL to return aggregate, summarized information.

For example, suppose you want to know how many customers you have in each country. Here's a query that will give you the answer:

```
SELECT Count(CustomerID) AS CustCount, Country
FROM Customers
GROUP BY Country
```

You can think of the GROUP BY clause as creating "buckets" in this case, one for each country. As the database engine examines each record, it tosses it in the appropriate bucket. After this process is done, it counts the number of records that ended up in each bucket and outputs a row for each one. Figure 6.4 shows the start of the result set from this query.

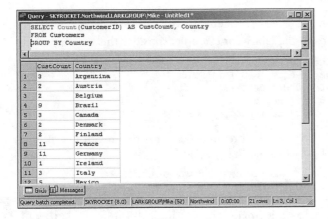

FIGURE 6.4
Result set from a query that includes a
GROUP BY clause.

You can use ORDER BY in conjunction with GROUP BY. In this case, you could sort by the number of customers in each country:

```
SELECT Count(CustomerID) AS CustCount, Country
FROM Customers
GROUP BY Country
ORDER BY Count(CustomerID) DESC
```

Or by the country name:

```
SELECT Count(CustomerID) AS CustCount, Country
FROM Customers
GROUP BY Country
ORDER BY Country
```

Count() in these SQL statements is an *aggregate function*, one that returns a result based on a number of rows. T-SQL supports a number of aggregate functions. Here are some of the most common:

◆ Count()—Number of records

◆ Sum()—Total value of records

◆ Avg()—Average value of records

◆ Min()—Smallest record

◆ Max()—Largest record

You can also group on more than one field. For example:

```
SELECT Count(CustomerID) AS CustCount, Region, Country
FROM Customers
GROUP BY Region, Country
```

That statement sets up one bucket for each combination of region and country and categorizes the customers by both fields simultaneously.

So far, the GROUP BY statements you've seen have included all the records in the table. For example, consider this query:

```
SELECT ProductID,
Sum(Quantity) AS TotalSales
FROM [Order Details]
GROUP BY ProductID
ORDER BY Sum(Quantity) DESC
```

That query returns a result set that has one row for each product found in the Order Details table, with the ProductID and the total quantity of that product that was ordered.

As stated, that query uses all the rows in the Order Details table to come up with its totals. You can limit this to use only part of the table in two ways.

First, you can use a WHERE clause to limit the rows from the original query that will be included in the totals:

```
SELECT ProductID,
Sum(Quantity) AS TotalSales
FROM [Order Details]
WHERE Quantity > 10
GROUP BY ProductID
ORDER BY Sum(Quantity) DESC
```

That will have the same effect as the first query, except that it will just ignore any row in the Order Details table that has a quantity of 10 or under.

The other way to limit the results is by filtering the totals with a HAVING clause:

```
SELECT ProductID, Sum(Quantity) AS TotalSales
FROM [Order Details]
GROUP BY ProductID
HAVING Sum(Quantity) > 1000
ORDER BY Sum(Quantity) DESC
```

A HAVING clause filters the results, rather than the input. That is, the last query will sum everything from the Order Details table and then show you rows where the total is greater than 1,000.

> **NOTE**
>
> **Quoting Names**   This query uses square brackets to quote the name of the Order Details table because the table name has a space in it, and without the quoting, SQL Server would try to interpret it as two names.

You can also combine the two types of filtering:

```
SELECT ProductID, Sum(Quantity) AS TotalSales
FROM [Order Details]
WHERE Quantity > 10
GROUP BY ProductID
HAVING  Sum(Quantity) > 1000
ORDER BY Sum(Quantity) DESC
```

That searches the source table for rows where the quantity is greater than 10 and then only keeps those rows where the total is over 1,000.

Note that WHERE and HAVING go in two different places in the SQL statement. The order of clauses is fixed, not optional.

The INSERT Statement

The purpose of the INSERT statement is to add a row or multiple rows to a table through executing a SQL statement.In its simplest form, the insert query lists a target table and a set of values to insert. For example, this query adds a new row to the Order Details table:

```
INSERT INTO [Order Details]
VALUES (10248, 1, 12.00, 5, 0)
```

This simple form of the statement has two drawbacks. First, knowing which field is getting which piece of data is difficult: The values are inserted into the table fields in the order that the fields show up in Design view, but you must remember (in this example) that the quantity is the fourth field. Second, if you use this format, you must supply a value for every field. This is a problem when you want the default value for a field or when a field can't have data inserted into it (for example, an identity field, whose values are automatically generated by SQL Server). To get around these problems, a second format explicitly lists the fields for the target table:

```
INSERT INTO [Order Details]
   (OrderID, ProductID, UnitPrice, Quantity, Discount)
VALUES (10248, 2, 12.00, 5, 0)
```

Here, the first set of parentheses holds a column list, and the second set holds the values to insert. If a field has a default value, can be null, or is an identity field, you can leave it out of the field list:

```
INSERT INTO Products
   (ProductName, SupplierID, CategoryID)
VALUES ('Turnips', 25, 7)
```

This works even though no value is specified for most of the fields in the Products table. Also, you can rearrange the field list as long as you rearrange the value list to match:

```
INSERT INTO Products
   (SupplierID, ProductName, CategoryID)
VALUES (20, 'Lettuce',  7)
```

The insert query isn't limited to inserting a single record. A second format inserts the results of a SELECT statement into the target table. For example, this query will insert a product from every supplier into the Products table:

```
INSERT INTO Products (SupplierID, ProductName,
CategoryID )
SELECT SupplierID, 'Trout', 8
FROM Suppliers
```

This works by building the results of the SELECT statement and then putting each row returned by the SELECT into the target table. Of course, the columns still need to match up properly.

The UPDATE Statement

Another useful SQL statement is the UPDATE statement. As you can probably guess, the purpose of an UPDATE query is to update data. For example, you could update a field in a record in Northwind with this query:

```
UPDATE Customers
  SET ContactName = 'Maria Anderson'
  WHERE CustomerID = 'ALFKI'
```

In this query, the UPDATE keyword introduces an update query. The SET keyword tells SQL Server what to update. Here it's setting a field equal to a literal value. The WHERE clause tells SQL Server which row in the table to update.

You're not limited to updating a single record. If the WHERE clause selects multiple records, they'll all be updated:

```
UPDATE Customers
  SET Country = 'United States'
  WHERE Country = 'USA'
```

You can even update every row in a table, by leaving out the WHERE clause:

```
UPDATE Products
  SET Discontinued = False
```

This will update every row in the Products table, even those where the Discontinued field already has the value False.

You can also update more than one field at a time with an UPDATE query:

```
UPDATE Customers
  SET ContactName = 'Maria Anders', City = 'Berlin'
  WHERE CustomerID = 'ALFKI'
```

And you can update with the result of an expression:

```
UPDATE Products
  SET UnitPrice = UnitPrice * 1.1
```

If only it were so simple to raise prices in real life! Finally, you can update based on joined tables:

```
UPDATE Suppliers INNER JOIN Products
  ON Suppliers.SupplierID = Products.SupplierID
  SET Discontinued = 1
  WHERE Suppliers.Country = 'Italy'
```

That has the effect of discontinuing all the products that are imported from Italy.

The DELETE Statement

The DELETE statement removes data from a table. The rule for constructing a delete query is simple: Construct a select query to select the records you want to delete, and change the SELECT keyword to DELETE. Remove any * identifier from the SELECT clause as well. That's it!

To avoid destroying existing data, I'll use another query to set the stage. The SELECT INTO statement is used to create a new table. For example, this statement creates a table named BadCustomers with all the data from the existing Customers table:

```
SELECT * INTO BadCustomers
FROM Customers
```

Here's a select query to select a single row from the new table:

```
SELECT * FROM BadCustomers WHERE CustomerID = 'GODOS'
```

Now change the SELECT * clause to DELETE:

```
DELETE FROM BadCustomers WHERE CustomerID = 'GODOS'
```

If you run this query, it will delete the specified row.

There's no need for a WHERE clause if you want to get really extreme:

```
DELETE FROM BadCustomers
```

That statement deletes all the rows from the BadCustomers table.

R E V I E W   B R E A K

▶ Transact-SQL is the Microsoft SQL Server dialect of the ANSI SQL-92 standard query language.

▶ You can execute T-SQL statements from a variety of interfaces, including the Visual Studio .NET IDE, osql, SQL Query Analyzer, or custom applications.

▶ SELECT statements retrieve data from tables in a database.

▶ INSERT statements add new data to tables in a database.

▶ UPDATE statements modify existing data in tables in a database.

▶ DELETE statements remove data from tables in a database.

Using Stored Procedures

> **EXAM TIP**
>
> **When to Use Stored Procedures**
> In almost every case, stored procedures are preferable to ad hoc queries in production applications. The only time you should consider using ad hoc queries is when you're writing an application that must allow completely free-form querying by the end user. Otherwise, the additional development time required to implement stored procedures will be worth it in the end.

When you use an ad hoc query to interact with SQL Server, the SQL statements in the query are completely transient. They vanish as soon as you close whatever tool you've used to execute the query. By contrast, stored procedures are queries stored permanently on the SQL Server itself. Stored procedures have two main benefits. First, you can save complex SQL statements for future execution so that you don't have to re-create them from scratch. Second, SQL Server compiles stored procedures so that they run faster than ad hoc queries.

In this section, you'll see how to create and run stored procedures. I'll also discuss parameters, which make stored procedures more flexible, and the @@IDENTITY variable, which can supply useful information any time you use a stored procedure to insert data into a table with an identity column.

Creating a Stored Procedure

T-SQL includes a CREATE PROCEDURE keyword to create stored procedures. You can run CREATE PROCEDURE statements from any interface that allows you to enter and execute T-SQL (see Step By Step 6.5).

STEP BY STEP

6.5 Creating a Stored Procedure from the Visual Studio .NET IDE

1. Open a Visual Basic .NET Windows application in the Visual Studio .NET IDE.

2. Open Server Explorer.

3. Expand the tree under Data Connections to show a SQL Server data connection that points to the Northwind sample database, then the Stored Procedures node of the SQL Server.

4. Right-click the Stored Procedures node and select New Stored Procedure.

5. Replace the boilerplate code in the Stored Procedure designer with this code:

```
CREATE PROCEDURE procFranceCustomers
AS
    SELECT * FROM Customers
    WHERE Country = 'France'
```

6. Click the Save button to save the stored procedure to the database.

7. Select Database, Run Stored Procedure to run the CREATE PROCEDURE statement. This creates the stored procedure in the database.

8. Now you can execute the new procFranceCustomers stored procedure from any tool that allows you to execute SQL Statements. For example, Figure 6.5 shows the results of executing this stored procedure in the custom form you built in Step By Step 6.4.

FIGURE 6.5
The results of running a stored procedure are
the same as the results of running the T-SQL
statements contained in the stored procedure.

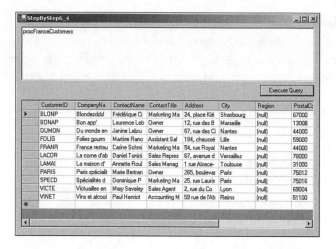

You can see two separate executing steps in this process. Executing
the CREATE PROCEDURE statement (which is itself an ad hoc query) is
necessary to create the stored procedure. After that has been done,
you can execute the stored procedure itself to return results.

Running Stored Procedures from .NET

Executing a stored procedure from .NET is very similar to executing
an ad hoc query. The difference is that you supply the name of the
stored procedure instead of the actual SQL as the CommandText
property of a SqlCommand object (see Step By Step 6.6).

STEP BY STEP

6.6 Running a Stored Procedure from Visual Basic .NET

1. Add a new form to your Visual Basic .NET project.

2. Open Server Explorer.

3. Expand the tree under Data Connections to show a SQL
Server data connection that points to the Northwind
sample database. Drag and drop the data connection to
the form. This will create a SqlConnection1 object on the
form.

4. Add a DataGrid control named `dgResults` to the form.

5. Double-click the form to open the form's module. Enter two statements at the top of the module to make the ADO.NET objects available:

```
Imports System.Data
Imports System.Data.SqlClient
```

6. Enter this code to execute the stored procedure when you load the form:

```
Private Sub StepByStep6_6_Load( _
 ByVal sender As System.Object, _
 ByVal e As System.EventArgs) Handles MyBase.Load
    ' Create a SqlCommand to represent the stored
      procedure
    Dim cmd As SqlCommand = SqlConnection1.CreateCommand
    cmd.CommandType = CommandType.StoredProcedure
    cmd.CommandText = "procFranceCustomers"
    ' Create a SqlDataAdapter to talk to the database
    Dim da As SqlDataAdapter = New SqlDataAdapter()
    da.SelectCommand = cmd
    ' Create a DataSet to hold the results
    Dim ds As DataSet = New DataSet()
    ' Fill the DataSet
    da.Fill(ds, "Customers")
    ' And bind it to the DataGrid
    dgResults.DataSource = ds
    dgResults.DataMember = "Customers"
End Sub
```

7. Set the form as the startup object for the project.

8. Run the project. This will run the code, retrieving the results to the DataGrid, as shown in Figure 6.6.

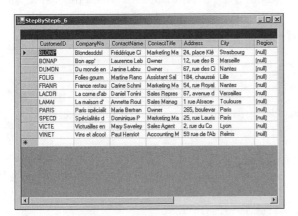

FIGURE 6.6
Displaying results from a stored procedure.

Stored procedures are not limited to containing SELECT statements. You can place any SQL statement inside a stored procedure. For example, you might use this SQL statement to create a stored procedure to update the Customers table:

```
CREATE PROCEDURE procExpandCountry
AS
UPDATE Customers
 SET Country = 'United States'
 WHERE Country = 'USA'
```

When your stored procedure doesn't return a result set, you need to use a slightly different code structure to execute it (see Step By Step 6.7). Guided Practice Exercise 6.1 offers additional practice in this technique.

STEP BY STEP

6.7 Running a Stored Procedure That Does Not Return Results

1. Add a new form to your Visual Basic .NET project.

2. Open Server Explorer.

3. Expand the tree under Data Connections to show a SQL Server data connection that points to the Northwind sample database. Drag and drop the data connection to the form. This will create a SqlConnection1 object on the form.

4. Use a tool such as SQL Query Analyzer or the Visual Studio .NET IDE to create a stored procedure with this code:

```
CREATE PROCEDURE procExpandCountry
AS
UPDATE Customers
 SET Country = 'United States'
 WHERE Country = 'USA'
```

5. Place a Button control on the form and name it btnExecute.

6. Double-click the Button control to open the form's module. Enter this statement at the top of the module to make the ADO.NET objects available:

```
Imports System.Data.SqlClient
```

7. Enter this code to execute the stored procedure when you click the button:

```
Private Sub btnExecute_Click( _
 ByVal sender As System.Object, _
 ByVal e As System.EventArgs) Handles btnExecute.Click
    ' Create a SqlCommand to represent the stored
      procedure
    Dim cmd As SqlCommand = SqlConnection1.CreateCommand
    cmd.CommandType = CommandType.StoredProcedure
    cmd.CommandText = "procExpandCountry"
    ' Open the connection and execute the stored
      procedure
    SqlConnection1.Open()
    cmd.ExecuteNonQuery()
    ' Close the connection
    SqlConnection1.Close()
    MessageBox.Show("SQL statement was executed.")
End Sub
```

8. Set the form as the startup object for the project.

9. Run the project and click the button to execute the stored procedure and display a message box when the stored procedure has completed its work.

The ExecuteNonQuery method of the SqlCommand object can be used to execute any ad hoc query or stored procedure that doesn't return any results.

Using Parameters in Stored Procedures

The examples that you've seen so far don't begin to tap the real power of stored procedures. SQL Server supports *parameterized stored procedures*, which allow you to pass information to the stored procedure at runtime (you can think of these as the T-SQL analog of Visual Basic .NET functions). For example, this SQL statement defines a stored procedure that returns the total sales for a particular customer, with the CustomerID specified at runtime:

```
CREATE PROC procCustomerSales
   @CustomerID char(5),
   @TotalSales money OUTPUT
AS
   SELECT @TotalSales = SUM(Quantity * UnitPrice)
   FROM ((Customers INNER JOIN Orders
   ON Customers.CustomerID = Orders.CustomerID)
   INNER JOIN [Order Details]
   ON Orders.OrderID = [Order Details].OrderID)
   WHERE Customers.CustomerID = @CustomerID
```

EXAM TIP

Opening and Closing Connections
When you call the methods of the SqlDataAdapter object, the .NET Framework will automatically open and close the associated SqlConnection object as necessary. For any other operation (such as using the SqlCommand.ExecuteNonQuery method) you must explicitly call the SqlConnection.Open and SqlConnection.Close methods in your code.

In this SQL statement, both `@CustomerID` and `@TotalSales` are variables (called parameters in T-SQL). To use the stored procedure, you must supply a value for the `@CustomerID` parameter. The `@TotalSales` parameter is marked as an `OUTPUT` parameter; it returns a value from the stored procedure to the calling code.

In the .NET Framework, the SqlCommand object has a collection of Parameters to let you manage parameterized stored procedures (see Step By Step 6.8).

STEP BY STEP

6.8 Running a Parameterized Stored Procedure

1. Add a new form to your Visual Basic .NET project.

2. Open Server Explorer.

3. Expand the tree under Data Connections to show a SQL Server data connection that points to the Northwind sample database. Drag and drop the data connection to the form to create a SqlConnection1 object on the form.

4. Use a tool such as SQL Query Analyzer or the Visual Studio .NET IDE to create a stored procedure with this code:

```
CREATE PROC procCustomerSales
  @CustomerID char(5),
  @TotalSales money OUTPUT
AS
  SELECT @TotalSales = SUM(Quantity * UnitPrice)
  FROM ((Customers INNER JOIN Orders
  ON Customers.CustomerID = Orders.CustomerID)
  INNER JOIN [Order Details]
  ON Orders.OrderID = [Order Details].OrderID)
  WHERE Customers.CustomerID = @CustomerID
```

5. Place two label controls, two TextBox controls (`txtCustomerID` and `txtTotalSales`) and a Button control (`btnGetTotalSales`) on the form, as shown in Figure 6.7.

6. Double-click the Button control to open the form's module. Enter these two statements at the top of the module to make the ADO.NET objects available:

```
Imports System.Data.SqlClient
Imports System.Data.SqlTypes
```

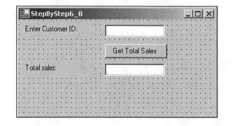

FIGURE 6.7
Designing a form to execute a parameterized stored procedure.

7. Enter this code to execute the stored procedure when you click the button:

```
Private Sub btnGetTotalSales_Click( _
 ByVal sender As System.Object, _
 ByVal e As System.EventArgs) Handles btnGetTotalSales.Click
    ' Create a SqlCommand to represent the stored
      procedure
    Dim cmd As SqlCommand = SqlConnection1.CreateCommand
    cmd.CommandType = CommandType.StoredProcedure
    cmd.CommandText = "procCustomerSales"
    ' Add the input parameter and set its value
    cmd.Parameters.Add(New SqlParameter( _
      "@CustomerID", SqlDbType.Text, 5))
    cmd.Parameters("@CustomerID").Value =
    txtCustomerID.Text
    ' Add the output parameter and set its direction
    cmd.Parameters.Add(New SqlParameter( _
      "@TotalSales", SqlDbType.Money))
    cmd.Parameters("@TotalSales").Direction =_
      ParameterDirection.Output
    ' Execute the stored procedure and
    ' display the formatted results
    SqlConnection1.Open()
    cmd.ExecuteNonQuery()
    txtTotalSales.Text = String.Format("{0:c}", _
      cmd.Parameters("@TotalSales").Value)
    SqlConnection1.Close()
End Sub
```

8. Set the form as the startup object for the project.

9. Run the project and enter a CustomerID from the Customers table in the first text box. Click the button to execute the stored procedure and return the total sales for this customer in the second text box.

In ADO.NET, parameters are represented by SqlParameter objects. This code uses two different forms of the constructor for SqlParameters. The first takes the parameter name, the parameter data type, and the size of the parameter; the second omits the parameter size (because the money type has a fixed size). The code works by setting the Value property of the @CustomerID parameter, executing the SqlCommand object, and then retrieving the Value property of the @TotalSales parameter.

The @@IDENTITY Variable

A SQL Server table can have a single *identity* column. An identity column is a column whose value is assigned by SQL Server itself whenever you add a new row to the table. The purpose of the identity column is to guarantee that each row in the table has a unique primary key.

If you're working with a table that contains an identity column, you'll often want to add a new row to the table and then immediately retrieve the value of the identity column for the new row. SQL Server provides a variable named @@IDENTITY for just this purpose. The @@IDENTITY variable returns the most recently assigned identity column value.

Step By Step 6.9 shows how to use a stored procedure to insert a new row in a table and return the value of the identity column so that your code can continue to work with the new row.

STEP BY STEP

6.9 Retrieving a New Identity Value

1. Add a new form to your Visual Basic .NET project.

2. Open Server Explorer.

3. Expand the tree under Data Connections to show a SQL Server data connection that points to the Northwind sample database. Drag and drop the data connection to the form to create a SqlConnection1 object on the form.

4. Use a tool such as SQL Query Analyzer or the Visual Studio .NET IDE to create a stored procedure with this code:

```
CREATE PROC procInsertShipper
  @CompanyName nvarchar(40),
  @ShipperID int OUTPUT
AS
  INSERT INTO Shippers (CompanyName)
    VALUES (@CompanyName)
  SELECT @ShipperID = @@IDENTITY
```

This stored procedure contains two SQL statements. The first inserts a row into the Shippers table, and the second retrieves the value of the identity column for the new row.

5. Place two label controls, two TextBox controls (txtCompanyName and txtShipperID) and a Button control (btnAddShipper) on the form.

6. Double-click the Button control to open the form's module. Enter these two statements at the top of the module to make the ADO.NET objects available:

```
Imports System.Data.SqlClient
Imports System.Data.SqlTypes
```

7. Enter this code to execute the stored procedure when you click the button:

```
Private Sub btnAddShipper_Click( _
 ByVal sender As System.Object, _
 ByVal e As System.EventArgs) Handles btnAddShipper.Click
    ' Create a SqlCommand to represent the stored
    ' procedure
    Dim cmd As SqlCommand = SqlConnection1.CreateCommand
    cmd.CommandType = CommandType.StoredProcedure
    cmd.CommandText = "procInsertShipper"
    ' Add the input parameter and set its value
    ' cmd.Parameters.Add(New SqlParameter( _
    "@CompanyName", SqlDbType.VarChar, 40))
    cmd.Parameters("@CompanyName").Value = _
    txtCompanyName.Text
    ' Add the output parameter and set its direction
    ' cmd.Parameters.Add(New SqlParameter( _
    "@ShipperID", SqlDbType.Int))
    cmd.Parameters("@ShipperID").Direction = _
    ParameterDirection.Output
    ' Execute the stored procedure and display the
    ' result
    SqlConnection1.Open()
    cmd.ExecuteNonQuery()
    txtShipperID.Text = cmd.Parameters("@ShipperID").Value
    SqlConnection1.Close()
End Sub
```

8. Set the form as the startup object for the project.

9. Run the project and enter a company name for the new shipper in the first text box. Click the button to execute the stored procedure and return the identity value assigned to the new shipper in the second text box.

Step By Step 6.9 uses the same code pattern as Step By Step 6.8.

The variable names and control names are different, but the two Step By Steps show a common pattern for using stored procedures in your code:

1. Create a SqlCommand object to represent the stored procedure.

2. Create SqlParameter objects to represent the parameters of the stored procedure.

3. Supply values for any input parameters.

4. Open the SqlConnection for this stored procedure.

5. Execute the stored procedure using the ExecuteNonQuery method of the SqlCommand object.

6. Retrieve values of any output parameters.

7. Close the SqlConnection.

GUIDED PRACTICE EXERCISE 6.1

In this exercise, you'll be designing a form to enter new products into the Northwind database. Table 6.1 shows the columns that the Products table contains.

TABLE 6.1

NORTHWIND PRODUCTS TABLE

Column Name	Data Type	Nullable?	Identity?
ProductID	int	No	Yes
ProductName	nvarchar(40)	No	No
SupplierID	int	Yes	No
CategoryID	int	Yes	No
QuantityPerUnit	nvarchar(20)	Yes	No
UnitPrice	money	Yes	No
UnitsInStock	smallint	Yes	No
UnitsOnOrder	smallint	Yes	No
ReorderLevel	smallint	Yes	No
Discontinued	bit	No	No

Allow the user to enter at least the product name and CategoryID, to add the product to the table, and to see the ProductID that's assigned to the new row in the table. You might optionally allow the user to input any other data that you like.

Valid values for the CategoryID column can be determined by retrieving the CategoryID values from the Categories table, which also contains a CategoryName column. You should use a ComboBox control to display valid CategoryID values.

Try this on your own first. If you get stuck or would like to see one possible solution, follow these steps:

1. Add a new form to your Visual Basic .NET project.

2. Open Server Explorer.

3. Expand the tree under Data Connections to show a SQL Server data connection that points to the Northwind sample database. Drag and drop the data connection to the form to create a SqlConnection1 object on the form.

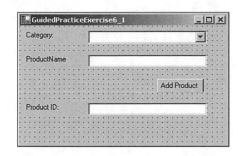

FIGURE 6.8
Designing a form to enter product information.

4. Add Label controls, a ComboBox control (cboCategoryID), a Button control (btnAddProduct), and two TextBox controls (txtProductName and txtProductID) to the form. Figure 6.8 shows a design for the form.

5. Use a tool such as SQL Query Analyzer or the Visual Studio .NET IDE to create a stored procedure with this code:

```
CREATE PROC procInsertProduct
  @ProductName nvarchar(40),
  @CategoryID int,
  @ProductID int OUTPUT
AS
  INSERT INTO Products (ProductName, CategoryID)
    VALUES (@ProductName, @CategoryID)
  SELECT @ProductID = @@IDENTITY
```

6. Double-click the form to open the form's module. Enter these three statements at the top of the module to make the ADO.NET objects available:

```
Imports System.Data
Imports System.Data.SqlClient
Imports System.Data.SqlTypes
```

continues

continued

7. Enter code to fill the list in the ComboBox control when the form is opened:

```
Private Sub GuidedPracticeExercise6_1_Load( _
 ByVal sender As System.Object, _
 ByVal e As System.EventArgs) Handles MyBase.Load
    ' Retrieve data for the combo box
    Dim cmdCategories As SqlCommand = _
     SqlConnection1.CreateCommand()
    cmdCategories.CommandType = CommandType.Text
    cmdCategories.CommandText = _
     "SELECT CategoryID, CategoryName " & _
     "FROM Categories ORDER BY CategoryName"
    Dim ds As DataSet = New DataSet()
    Dim da As SqlDataAdapter = New SqlDataAdapter()
    da.SelectCommand = cmdCategories
    da.Fill(ds, "Categories")
    With cboCategoryID
        .DataSource = ds.Tables("Categories")
        .DisplayMember = "CategoryName"
        .ValueMember = "CategoryID"
    End With
End Sub
```

8. Enter this code to execute the stored procedure when you click the button:

```
Private Sub btnAddProduct_Click( _
 ByVal sender As System.Object, _
 ByVal e As System.EventArgs) Handles btnAddProduct.Click
    ' Create a SqlCommand to represent the stored
       procedure
    Dim cmd As SqlCommand = SqlConnection1.CreateCommand
    cmd.CommandType = CommandType.StoredProcedure
    cmd.CommandText = "procInsertProduct"
    ' Add the input parameters and set their values
    cmd.Parameters.Add(New SqlParameter( _
     "@ProductName", SqlDbType.VarChar, 40))
    cmd.Parameters("@ProductName").Value = _
     txtProductName.Text
    cmd.Parameters.Add(New SqlParameter( _
     "@CategoryID", SqlDbType.Int))
    cmd.Parameters("@CategoryID").Value = _
     cboCategoryID.SelectedValue
    ' Add the output parameter and set its direction
    cmd.Parameters.Add(New SqlParameter( _
     "@ProductID", SqlDbType.Int))
    cmd.Parameters("@ProductID").Direction = _
     ParameterDirection.Output
    ' Execute the stored procedure and display the result
    SqlConnection1.Open()
    cmd.ExecuteNonQuery()
```

```
    txtProductID.Text =
cmd.Parameters("@ProductID").Value
    SqlConnection1.Close()
End Sub
```

9. Set the form as the startup object for the project.

10. Run the project. Select a category for the new product from the combo box. Enter a name for the new product in the first text box. Click the button. The form will execute the stored procedure and return the identity value assigned to the new shipper in the second text box.

If you had difficulty following this exercise, review the sections titled "Running Queries," "The SELECT Statement," "The INSERT statement," and "Using Stored Procedures," as well as the material on "Complex Data Binding" in Chapter 5. The text and examples should help you relearn this material and understand what just happened in this exercise. After review, try the exercise again.

ACCESS AND MANIPULATE DATA

Consuming and Manipulating Data: Access and manipulate data from a data store. Data stores include relational databases, XML documents, and flat files. Methods include XML techniques and ADO .NET.

Although it's only a single test objective, this particular objective covers an immense amount of functionality within the .NET Framework. You'll need to know how to work with three types of data:

◆ File-based data

◆ Relational database data

◆ XML data

The .NET Framework includes namespaces and classes optimized for each of these types of data.

Data stored in files is handled by the classes in the System.IO namespace. The .NET Framework handles file data as part of a more general concept of streams and backing stores. A *backing store* is any place you can store data (including a disk file), and a *stream* represents that data's movements from place to place.

Data stored in databases is the target of ADO.NET, a subset of the .NET Framework that uses objects from the System.Data namespace and related namespaces. The DataSet object is the central object here, representing an entire relational database in a single object (with many constituent objects). You'll see how to create DataSet objects and fill them with data, and then some of the many ways to work with that data.

Data stored in XML is handled by the System.Xml namespace. XML is a key part of the .NET Framework, and the classes in this namespace give the flexibility to read and write such data.

The major topics that I'll cover for this objective include:

◆ Reading and writing disk files

◆ The ADO.NET object model

◆ Manipulating data with ADO.NET

◆ XML Basics

◆ Working with XML Documents and Data

Working with Disk Files

The oldest form of data you're likely to work with in the .NET Framework is the simple disk file. This is sometimes called a *flat file*, to distinguish it from more structured forms of storage such as relational databases and XML files.

The .NET Framework includes complete support for working with flat files. In this section, I'll show how to invoke the standard Windows Open File dialog, introduce the concepts of streams and backing stores, and demonstrate the classes from the System.IO namespace that you can use to manipulate data stored in disk files.

Browsing for Files

When writing code to work with disk files, it's convenient to be able to locate the files of interest by browsing. Fortunately, the .NET Framework provides a class, System.Windows.Forms.OpenFileDialog, specifically for this purpose (see Step By Step 6.10).

STEP BY STEP

6.10 Browsing for a File

1. Add a new form to your Visual Basic .NET project.

2. Place a Button control named btnBrowse and a TextBox control named txtFilename on the form.

3. Double-click the Button control to open the form's module. Enter this statement at the top of the module:

```
Imports System.Windows.Forms
```

4. Enter this code to handle the Click event of the Button control:

```
Private Sub btnBrowse_Click(ByVal sender As System.Object, _
 ByVal e As System.EventArgs) Handles btnBrowse.Click
    Dim dlgOpen As New OpenFileDialog()
    dlgOpen.Title = "Select a File"
    dlgOpen.Filter = _
     "Text files (*.txt)|*.txt|All Files(*.*)|*.*"
    If dlgOpen.ShowDialog = DialogResult.OK Then
        txtFilename.Text = dlgOpen.FileName
    End If
End Sub
```

5. Set the form as the startup object for the project.

6. Run the project and click the button. The File Open dialog box provided by Windows will open. Select a file in the dialog box and click OK. The name of the file will appear in the TextBox control.

When you click the Browse button, the form creates a new OpenFileDialog object and sets some of its properties. The Title property sets the caption of the dialog box. The Filter property controls the entries in the Files of Type combo box on the dialog box.

This property is a set of strings separated by vertical bar characters. The strings alternate between the text that the user should see and the filter that should be in effect when the corresponding text is selected.

Streams and Backing Stores

File-based input and output in the .NET Framework revolves around the twin concepts of *streams* and *backing stores*. A stream represents a flow of raw data. A backing store represents some place you can put data. A backing store might be a file—but it might also be a network connection, an Internet address, or even a section of memory. The .NET Framework contains classes to let you work with data from any of these backing stores.

You'll find classes for working with streams and backing stores in the System.IO namespace. In this section, I'll show how to use five of these classes that apply directly to working with disk files. The FileStream class gives you a stream-oriented view of a disk file. The FileStream class treats files as a raw, typeless stream of bytes. For cases in which you know more about the structure of the file, you might find the BinaryReader and BinaryWriter or StreamReader and StreamWriter classes to be more convenient to use. After working with these classes individually, you can use Guided Practice Exercise 6.2 to compare their performance.

Using the FileStream Class

The FileStream class treats a file as a stream of bytes. For example, you can use this class as a way to make a backup copy of a file (see Step By Step 6.11).

STEP BY STEP

6.11 Using FileStream Objects to Back Up a File

1. Add a new form to your Visual Basic .NET project.

2. Place two Label controls, a Button control named btnBrowse and two TextBox controls (txtFilename and txtBackupname) on the form. Figure 6.9 shows the design of the form.

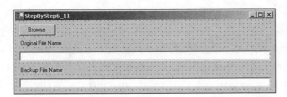

FIGURE 6.9
A form to make backup copies of files.

3. Double-click the Button control to open the form's module. Enter this statement at the top of the module:

```
Imports System.IO
```

4. Enter this code to handle the Click event of the Button control:

```
Private Sub btnBrowse_Click(ByVal sender As System.Object, _
ByVal e As System.EventArgs) Handles btnBrowse.Click
    ' Browse for a file to back up
    Dim dlgOpen As New OpenFileDialog()
    dlgOpen.Title = "Select a File to back up"
    dlgOpen.Filter = "All Files(*.*)|*.*"
    If dlgOpen.ShowDialog = DialogResult.OK Then
        ' Display the original and backup file names
        txtFilename.Text = dlgOpen.FileName
        txtBackupName.Text = dlgOpen.FileName & ".bak"
        ' Open the file for reading as a stream
        Dim fsIn As FileStream = _
         File.OpenRead(dlgOpen.FileName)
        ' Open the file for writing as a stream
        Dim fsOut As FileStream = _
         File.OpenWrite(dlgOpen.FileName & ".bak")
        ' Copy all data from in to out, byte-by-byte
        Dim b As Int16
        Do While ((b = fsIn.ReadByte()) > -1)
            fsOut.WriteByte(CType(b, Byte))
        Loop
        ' Clean up
        fsOut.Flush()
        fsOut.Close()
        fsIn.Close()
    End If
End Sub
```

5. Set the form as the startup object for the project.

6. Run the project and click the button. The File Open dialog box provided by Windows will open. Select a file in the dialog box and click OK. The name of the file will appear in the first TextBox control, and the name of the file will appear in the second TextBox control. If you check your hard drive, you'll find a copy of the selected file with the extension bak.

WARNING

Data Loss Danger! Be careful when testing this program. It doesn't check for the existence of the backup file, so it will overwrite any existing file without warning.

The code creates two FileStream objects, one each for the input and output files, by using static methods of the File object (which represents a disk file). It then reads bytes from the input file and writes those bytes to the output file. Note the difference between the ReadByte method, which returns an int, and the WriteByte method, which writes a byte. That's because the ReadByte method uses the special value -1 (which can't be stored in a byte) to indicate that it's reached the end of the data.

When the code is done writing, it calls the Flush method of the output stream to ensure that all the data has actually been written to the disk. Then it closes both the input and output streams.

Table 6.2 shows some of the methods and properties of the FileStream object that you should be familiar with.

TABLE 6.2

FileStream Object Members

Member	Type	Description
CanRead	Property	Indicates whether you can read from this FileStream
CanSeek	Property	Indicates whether you can seek to a particular location in this FileStream
CanWrite	Property	Indicates whether you can write to this FileStream
Close	Method	Closes the FileStream and releases associated resources
Flush	Method	Writes any buffered data to the backing store
Length	Property	Length of the FileStream in bytes
Position	Property	Gets the position within the FileStream
Read	Method	Reads a sequence of bytes
ReadByte	Method	Reads a single byte
Seek	Method	Sets the FileStream to a specified position
Write	Method	Writes a sequence of bytes
WriteByte	Method	Writes a single byte

Although the code in Step By Step 6.11 performs the desired task, it's not very efficient. Using a buffer to hold data allows the operating system to optimize file activity for increased speed (see Step By Step 6.12).

STEP BY STEP

6.12 Using FileStream Objects with a Buffer

1. Add a new form to your Visual Basic .NET project.

2. Place two Label controls, a Button control named btnBrowse and two TextBox controls (txtFilename and txtBackupname) on the form.

3. Double-click the Button control to open the form's module. Enter this statement at the top of the module:

```
Imports System.IO
```

4. Enter this code to handle the Click event of the Button control:

```
Private Sub btnBrowse_Click(ByVal sender As System.Object, _
ByVal e As System.EventArgs) Handles btnBrowse.Click
    ' Browse for a file to back up
    Dim dlgOpen As New OpenFileDialog()
    dlgOpen.Title = "Select a File to back up"
    dlgOpen.Filter = "All Files(*.*)|*.*"
    If dlgOpen.ShowDialog = DialogResult.OK Then
        ' Display the original and backup file names
        txtFilename.Text = dlgOpen.FileName
        txtBackupName.Text = dlgOpen.FileName & ".bak"
        ' Open the file for reading as a stream
        Dim fsIn As FileStream = _
         File.OpenRead(dlgOpen.FileName)
        ' Open the file for writing as a stream
        Dim fsOut As FileStream = _
         File.OpenWrite(dlgOpen.FileName & ".bak")
        ' Copy all data from in to out, using a 4K
          buffer
        Dim buf(4096) As Byte
        Dim intBytesRead As Integer
        Do While ((intBytesRead = _
         fsIn.Read(buf, 0, 4096)) > 0)
            fsOut.Write(buf, 0, intBytesRead)
        Loop
        ' Clean up
        fsOut.Flush()
        fsOut.Close()
        fsIn.Close()
    End If
End Sub
```

5. Set the form as the startup object for the project.

continues

continued

6. Run the project and click the button. The File Open dialog box provided by Windows will open. Select a file in the dialog box and click OK. The name of the file will appear in the first TextBox control, and the name of the file will appear in the second TextBox control. If you check your hard drive, you'll find a copy of the selected file with the extension bak. If you experiment with large files, you should be able to see a speed difference between this version of the code and the one from Step By Step 6.11.

The FileStream.Read method takes three parameters:

◆ A buffer to hold the data being read

◆ An offset in the buffer where newly read bytes should be placed

◆ The maximum number of bytes to read

The Read method returns the number of bytes that were actually read. Similarly, the Write method takes three parameters:

◆ A buffer to hold the data being written

◆ An offset in the buffer where bytes to write begin

◆ The number of bytes to write

Using the StreamReader and StreamWriter Classes

The FileStream class is your best option when you don't care (or don't know) about the internal structure of the files with which you're working. But in many cases, you have additional knowledge that lets you use other objects. Text files, for example, are often organized as lines of text separated by end of line characters. The StreamReader and StreamWriter classes provide tools for manipulating such files (see Step By Step 6.13).

STEP BY STEP

6.13 Using StreamWriter and StreamReader Objects

1. Add a new form to your Visual Basic .NET project.

2. Place a Button control named btnCreateFile and a ListBox control named lbLines on the form.

3. Double-click the Button control to open the form's module. Enter this statement at the top of the module:

```
Imports System.IO
```

4. Enter this code to handle the Click event of the Button control:

```
Private Sub btnCreateFile_Click( _
 ByVal sender As System.Object, _
 ByVal e As System.EventArgs) Handles btnCreateFile.Click
    ' Create a new file to work with
    Dim fsOut As FileStream = _
     File.Create("c:\temp\test.txt")
    ' Create a StreamWriter to handle writing
    Dim sw As StreamWriter = New StreamWriter(fsOut)
    ' And write some data
    sw.WriteLine("There was a young lady named Bright")
    sw.WriteLine("Whose speed was much faster than
    light")
    sw.WriteLine("She set out one day")
    sw.WriteLine("In a relative way")
    sw.WriteLine("And returned on the previous night")
    sw.Flush()
    sw.Close()

    ' Now open the file for reading
    Dim fsIn As FileStream = _
     File.OpenRead("c:\temp\test.txt")
    ' Create a StreamReader to handle reading
    Dim sr As StreamReader = New StreamReader(fsIn)
    ' And read the data
    Do While sr.Peek > -1
        lbLines.Items.Add(sr.ReadLine())
    Loop
    sr.Close()
End Sub
```

5. Set the form as the startup object for the project.

6. Run the project and click the button. The c:\temp\test.txt file will be created on your hard drive, and the ListBox control will show the contents of the file, as shown in Figure 6.10.

FIGURE 6.10
Contents of a file written by a StreamWriter and then read by a StreamReader.

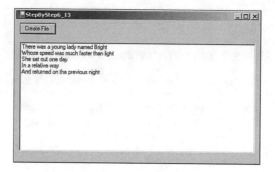

You can think of the StreamWriter and StreamReader classes as providing additional functionality that is not available with the FileStream class alone. The FileStream object handles opening a particular disk file and then serves as a parameter to the constructor of the StreamWriter or StreamReader. This code first opens a StreamWriter and calls its WriteLine method multiple times to write lines of text to the file. It then creates a StreamWriter that uses the same text file. The code makes use of the Peek method of the StreamReader to watch for the end of the file. This method returns the next byte in the file without actually reading it or returns –1 if no more data is to be read. As long as there's data to read, the ReadLine method of the StreamReader can read it to place in the list box.

In addition to the methods that you see in this example, the StreamWriter has a Write method that writes output without adding a new line character. The StreamReader class implements Read and ReadToEnd methods to offer additional functionality for reading data. The Read method reads a specified number of characters. The ReadToEnd method reads all the remaining characters to the end of the stream.

Using the BinaryReader and BinaryWriter Classes

For files with a known internal structure, the BinaryReader and BinaryWriter classes offer streaming functionality oriented toward particular data types (see Step By Step 6.14).

STEP BY STEP

6.14 Using BinaryWriter and BinaryReader Objects

1. Add a new form to your Visual Basic .NET project.

2. Place a Button control named btnCreateFile and a ListBox control named lbData on the form.

3. Double-click the Button control to open the form's module. Enter this statement at the top of the module:

```
Imports System.IO
```

4. Enter this code to handle the Click event of the Button control:

```
Private Sub btnCreateFile_Click( _
 ByVal sender As System.Object, _
 ByVal e As System.EventArgs) Handles btnCreateFile.Click
    ' Create a new file to work with
    Dim fsOut As FileStream = _
     File.Create("c:\temp\test.dat")
    ' Create a BinaryWriter to handle writing
    Dim bw As BinaryWriter = New BinaryWriter(fsOut)
    ' And write some data
    Dim intData1 As Integer = 7
    Dim dblData2 As Decimal = 3.14159
    Dim strData3 As String = "Pi in the Sky"
    bw.Write(intData1)
    bw.Write(dblData2)
    bw.Write(strData3)
    bw.Flush()
    bw.Close()

    ' Now open the file for reading
    Dim fsIn As FileStream = _
     File.OpenRead("c:\temp\test.dat")
    ' Create a BinaryReader to handle reading
    Dim br As BinaryReader = New BinaryReader(fsIn)
    ' And read the data
    lbData.Items.Add("Integer: " & br.ReadInt32())
    lbData.Items.Add("Decimal: " & br.ReadDecimal())
    lbData.Items.Add("String: " & br.ReadString())
    br.Close()
End Sub
```

5. Set the form as the startup object for the project.

6. Run the project and click the button. The c:\temp\test.dat file will be created on your hard drive, and the ListBox control will show the contents of the file, as shown in Figure 6.11.

FIGURE 6.11
Contents of a file written by a BinaryWriter and then read by a BinaryReader.

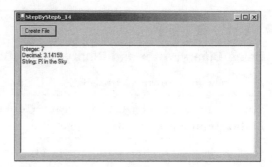

Like the StreamWriter and the StreamReader, the BinaryWriter and BinaryReader add additional functionality to the basic FileStream object. BinaryWriter and BinaryReader are oriented toward writing and reading particular types of data. The BinaryWriter.Write method has overloads for many data types, so it can handle writing almost anything to a file. The BinaryReader class has methods for reading all those different data types; this code shows the ReadInt32, ReadDecimal, and ReadStringmethods in action.

GUIDED PRACTICE EXERCISE 6.2

In this exercise, you'll write a set of decimal numbers to two different file formats: a text file with each number on a separate line and a binary file. After writing the files, you can see which file format is more efficient for this particular data. The following shows the data to be written to text and binary files.

Value
4.981273
45.92847
1.099
0.47162
2.44801
17.2323
490.00901
12.1234
23.022
1.034782

Try this on your own first. If you get stuck or would like to see one possible solution, follow these steps:

1. Add a new form to your Visual Basic .NET project.

2. Place a Button control named btnCreateFiles and a ListBox control named lbResults on the form.

3. Double-click the Button control to open the form's module. Enter this statement at the top of the module:

```
Imports System.IO
```

4. Enter this code to handle the Click event of the Button control:

```
Private Sub btnCreateFiles_Click( _
 ByVal sender As System.Object, _
 ByVal e As System.EventArgs) Handles
btnCreateFiles.Click
    ' Create a new text file to work with
    Dim fsOut As FileStream = _
     File.Create("c:\temp\TextTest.txt")
    ' Create a StreamWriter to handle writing
    Dim sw As StreamWriter = New StreamWriter(fsOut)
    ' And write some data
    sw.WriteLine("4.981273")
    sw.WriteLine("45.92847")
    sw.WriteLine("1.099")
    sw.WriteLine("0.47162")
    sw.WriteLine("2.44801")
    sw.WriteLine("17.2323")
    sw.WriteLine("490.00901")
    sw.WriteLine("12.1234")
    sw.WriteLine("23.022")
    sw.WriteLine("1.034782")
    sw.Flush()
    lbResults.Items.Add( _
     "Text file length = " & fsOut.Length)
    sw.Close()

    ' Create a new binary file to work with
    fsOut = File.Create("c:\temp\BinaryTest.dat")
    ' Create a BinaryWriter to handle writing
    Dim bw As BinaryWriter = New BinaryWriter(fsOut)
    ' And write some data
    bw.Write(4.981273)
    bw.Write(45.92847)
    bw.Write(1.099)
    bw.Write(0.47162)
    bw.Write(2.44801)
    bw.Write(17.2323)
    bw.Write(490.00901)
```

continues

continued

```
bw.Write(12.1234)
bw.Write(23.022)
bw.Write(1.034782)
bw.Flush()
lbResults.Items.Add( _
  "Binary file length = " & fsOut.Length)
bw.Close()

End Sub
```

FIGURE 6.12
Relative lengths of the same data in a text file and in a binary file.

5. Set the form as the startup object for the project.

6. Run the project and click the button. The two files will be created on your hard drive, and the ListBox control will show the lengths of the files, as shown in Figure 6.12.

If you had difficulty following this exercise, review the sections titled "Using the StreamReader and StreamWriter Classes" and "Using the BinaryReader and BinaryWriter Classes." The text and examples should help you relearning the material and understand what happened in this exercise. After review, try this exercise again.

The ADO.NET Object Model

ADO.NET is the overall name for the set of classes (spread across a number of namespaces including System.Data, System.Data.Common, System.Data.SqlTypes, System.Data.SqlClient, and System.Data.OleDb) that the .NET Framework provides for working with data in relational databases.

The ADO.NET object model is broken up into two distinct sets of objects—data provider objects and DataSet objects— because the .NET Framework separates the task of using data from the task of storing data. The DataSet objects provide a memory-resident, disconnected set of objects that you can load with data. The data provider objects handle the task of working directly with data sources. One of the provider objects, the DataAdapter object, serves as a conduit between the two sets of objects. By using a DataAdapter, you can load data from a database into a DataSet and later save changes back to the original data source.

In generic terms, the data provider objects manage the database for your application, and the DataSet objects manage the data model for the application.

Data Providers and Their Objects

You should know about five main data provider objects:

- Connection
- Command
- Parameter
- DataReader
- DataAdapter

You've actually seen most of these objects already, but not with those names because those are the generic names for the classes defined in System.Data.Common. Each data provider has implementations of these objects with specific names.

A data provider is a namespace that implements these five classes (and some other classes and enumerations) for use with a particular database. For example, I've been using the SQL Server data provider, which is implemented in the System.Data.SqlClient namespace. In this namespace, the object names are as follows:

- SqlConnection
- SqlCommand
- SqlParameter
- SqlDataReader
- SqlDataAdapter

But the SQL Server data provider is not the only alternative for retrieving data in ADO.NET. The .NET Framework also ships with the OLE DB data provider, implemented in the System.Data.OleDb namespace. In this namespace, the corresponding object names are as follows:

- OleDbConnection
- OleDbCommand

E X A M T I P

Not All OLE DB Is Equal Though from the name it seems that the OLE DB data provider should work with any existing OLE DB provider, that's not the case. It's only designed to work with the SQL Server, Jet 4.0, and Oracle OLE DB providers. Other providers might work but are not supported.

◆ OleDbParameter

◆ OleDbDataReader

◆ OleDbDataAdapter

Although the .NET Framework includes only two data providers, other alternatives exist. For example, Microsoft has made an ODBC data provider available for download and has announced plans to release an Oracle provider. Third parties are also planning to release other providers.

I'll continue to use the SQL Server data provider objects in all my examples, but you should keep in mind that the techniques you learn to work with objects from this namespace will also work with objects from other data provider namespaces.

The SqlConnection Object

The SqlConnection object represents a single persistent connection to a SQL Server data source. ADO.NET automatically handles connection pooling, which contributes to better application performance. When you call the Close method of a SqlConnection object, it is returned to a connection pool. Connections in a pool are not immediately destroyed by ADO.NET. Instead, they're available for reuse if another part of your application requests a SqlConnection that matches in details a previously closed SqlConnection.

Table 6.3 shows the most important members of the SqlConnection object.

TABLE 6.3

SQLCONNECTION OBJECT MEMBERS

Member	Type	Description
BeginTransaction	Method	Starts a new transaction on this SqlConnection
Close	Method	Returns the SqlConnection to the connection pool
ConnectionString	Property	Specifies the server to be used by this SqlConnection
CreateCommand	Method	Returns a new SqlCommand object that executes via this SqlConnection
Open	Method	Opens the SqlConnection

So far, all the SqlConnection objects you've seen in this book have been created by dragging and dropping from Server Explorer. But it's easy to create them in code yourself (see Step By Step 6.15).

STEP BY STEP

6.15 Creating a SqlConnection in Code

1. Add a new form to your Visual Basic .NET project.

2. Place a Button control named btnConnect and a TextBox control named txtConnectionString on the form.

3. Double-click the Button control to open the form's module. Enter this statement at the top of the module:

```
Imports System.Data.SqlClient
```

4. Enter this code to handle the Click event of the Button control:

```
Private Sub btnConnect_Click( _
 ByVal sender As System.Object, _
 ByVal e As System.EventArgs) Handles btnConnect.Click
    Dim cnn As SqlConnection = New SqlConnection()
    cnn.ConnectionString = "Data Source=(local);" & _
     "Initial Catalog=Northwind;Integrated
     Security=SSPI"
    cnn.Open()
    txtConnectionString.Text = cnn.ConnectionString
    cnn.Close()
End Sub
```

5. Set the form as the startup object for the project.

6. Run the project and click the button. The code will connect to the SQL Server database on the local computer and echo the connection string to the TextBox control.

The SqlCommand and SqlParameter Objects

You've already seen the SqlCommand and SqlParameter objects used in quite a few examples. The SqlCommand represents something that can be executed. This could be an ad hoc query string or a stored procedure name. The SqlParameter object represents a single parameter to a stored procedure.

> **EXAM TIP**
>
> **The Parts of a Connection String** You should know how to construct a SQL Server connection string for use with the SqlConnection object. The string has three parts. First is the Data Source, which is the name of the server to which you'd like to connect. You can use "(local)" as a shortcut name for the SQL Server instance running on the same computer as this code. Second is the Initial Catalog, which is the name of the database on the server to use. Third is authentication information. This can either be "Integrated Security=SSPI" to use Windows authentication, or "User ID=*username*;Password=*password*" to use SQL Server authentication. Other optional parameters exist, but these three are the most important.

Table 6.4 shows the most important members of the SqlCommand object.

TABLE 6.4

SqlCommand Object Members

Member	Type	Description
CommandText	Property	Statement to be executed by the SqlCommand
CommandType	Property	Enumeration indicating what type of command this SqlCommand represents
Connection	Property	SqlConnection through which this SqlCommand executes
CreateParameter	Method	Creates a new SqlParameter for this SqlCommand
ExecuteNonQuery	Method	Executes a SqlCommand that does not return a result set
ExecuteReader	Method	Executes a SqlCommand and places the results in a SqlDataReader
ExecuteScalar	Method	Executes a SqlCommand and returns the first column of the first row of the result set
ExecuteXmlReader	Method	Executes a SqlCommand and places the results in an XmlReader object
Parameters	Property	Collection of SqlParameter objects for this SqlCommand

Step By Step 6.16 gives an example of using the ExecuteScalar, which provides you with an easy way to retrieve a single value (such as an aggregation) from a database.

STEP BY STEP

6.16 Using the ExecuteScalar Method

1. Add a new form to your Visual Basic .NET project.

2. Place a Button control named btnCount, a TextBox control named txtCountry, and a Label control named lblResults on the form. Figure 6.13 shows the design of this form.

3. Double-click the Button control to open the form's module. Enter this statement at the top of the module:

```
Imports System.Data.SqlClient
```

4. Enter this code to handle the `Click` event of the Button control:

```
Private Sub btnCount_Click(ByVal sender As System.Object, _
 ByVal e As System.EventArgs) Handles btnCount.Click
    ' Connect to the database
    Dim cnn As SqlConnection = New SqlConnection()
    cnn.ConnectionString = "Data Source=(local);" & _
     "Initial Catalog=Northwind;Integrated Security=SSPI"
    ' Create a new ad hoc query to count
    ' customers in the selected country
    Dim cmd As SqlCommand = cnn.CreateCommand
    cmd.CommandType = CommandType.Text
    cmd.CommandText = _
     "SELECT COUNT(*) FROM Customers WHERE _
      Country = '" & _
      txtCountry.Text & "'"
    ' Use ExecuteScalar to return results
    cnn.Open()
    lblResults.Text = "There are " & _
    cmd.ExecuteScalar() & _
     " customers in " & txtCountry.Text
    cnn.Close()
End Sub
```

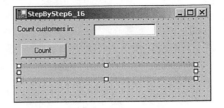

FIGURE 6.13
Designing a form to demonstrate the ExecuteScalar method.

5. Set the form as the startup object for the project.

6. Run the project. Enter a country name such as France and click the button. The code will connect to the SQL Server database on the local computer and fill in the Label control's text with a string that includes the results of the ad hoc query.

The SqlDataReader Object

The SqlDataReader object is designed to be the fastest possible way to retrieve a result set from a database. SqlDataReader objects can only be constructed by calling the ExecuteReader method of a Command object (see Step By Step 6.17). The result set contained in a SqlDataReader is forward-only, read-only. That is, you can only read the rows in the result set sequentially from start to finish, and you can't modify any of the data.

STEP BY STEP

6.17 Using a SqlDataReader

1. Add a new form to your Visual Basic .NET project.

2. Place a Button control named `btnGetCustomers` and a ListBox control named `lbCustomers` on the form.

3. Double-click the Button control to open the form's module. Enter this statement at the top of the module:

```
Imports System.Data.SqlClient
```

4. Enter this code to handle the `Click` event of the Button control:

```
Private Sub btnGetCustomers_Click( _
 ByVal sender As System.Object, _
 ByVal e As System.EventArgs) Handles btnGetCustomers.Click
    ' Connect to the database
    Dim cnn As SqlConnection = New SqlConnection()
    cnn.ConnectionString = "Data Source=(local);" & _
      "Initial Catalog=Northwind;Integrated Security=SSPI"
    ' Create a new ad hoc query to retrieve customer names
    Dim cmd As SqlCommand = cnn.CreateCommand
    cmd.CommandType = CommandType.Text
    cmd.CommandText = _
      "SELECT CompanyName FROM Customers ORDER BY
      CompanyName"
    ' Dump the data to the user interface
    cnn.Open()
    Dim dr As SqlDataReader = cmd.ExecuteReader
    Do While dr.Read()
        lbCustomers.Items.Add(dr.GetString(0))
    Loop
    ' Clean up
    dr.Close()
    cnn.Close()
End Sub
```

5. Set the form as the startup object for the project.

6. Run the project and click the button. The code will connect to the SQL Server database on the local computer and fill the ListBox control with a list of customers from the database.

EXAM TIP

Stored Procedures for Speed You could improve the performance of this code even more by using a stored procedure instead of an ad hoc query to deliver the customer names.

You can think of the SqlDataReader as a data structure that can contain one row of data at a time. Each call to the SqlDataReader.Read method loads the next row of data into this structure. When there are no more rows to load, the Read method returns False, which tells you that you've reached the end of the data. To retrieve individual columns of data from the current row, the SqlDataReader provides a series of methods (such as the GetString method used in the code above) that take a column number and return the data from that column. There's also a GetValue method for use with any column, but the typed methods are faster.

Table 6.5 shows the most important members of the SqlDataReader object. You don't need to memorize all the data methods (others aren't even shown in this table), but you should understand the pattern that they represent.

TABLE 6.5

SqlDataReader Object Members

Member	Type	Description
Close	Method	Closes the SqlDataReader
GetBoolean	Method	Gets a Boolean value from the specified column
GetByte	Method	Gets a byte value from the specified column
GetChar	Method	Gets a character value from the specified column
GetDateTime	Method	Gets a date/time value from the specified column
GetDecimal	Method	Gets a decimal value from the specified column
GetDouble	Method	Gets a double value from the specified column
GetFloat	Method	Gets a float value from the specified column
GetGuid	Method	Gets a GUID value from the specified column
GetInt16	Method	Gets a 16-bit integer value from the specified column
GetInt32	Method	Gets a 32-bit integer value from the specified column
GetInt64	Method	Gets a 64-bit integer value from the specified column
GetString	Method	Gets a string value from the specified column
GetValue	Method	Gets a value from the specified column
GetValues	Method	Gets an entire row of data and places it in an array of objects
IsDbNull	Method	Indicates whether a specified column contains a Null value
Read	Method	Loads the next row of data into the SqlDataReader

EXAM TIP

Close Your SqlDataReaders! The SqlDataReader makes exclusive use of its SqlConnection object as long as it is open. You won't be able to execute any other SqlCommand objects on that connection as long as the SqlDataReader is open. Always call SqlDataReader.Close as soon as you're done retrieving data.

The SqlDataAdapter Object

The final data provider object I'll consider, the SqlDataAdapter, provides a bridge between the data provider objects and the DataSet objects you'll learn about in the next section. You can think of the SqlDataAdapter as a two-way pipeline between the data in its native storage format and the data in a more abstract representation (the DataSet) designed for manipulation in your application.

Table 6.6 shows the most important members of the SqlDataAdapter object.

TABLE 6.6

SQLDATAADAPTER OBJECT MEMBERS

Member	Type	Description
DeleteCommand	Property	SqlCommand used to delete rows from the data source
Fill	Method	Transfers data from the data source to a DataSet
InsertCommand	Property	SqlCommand used to insert rows into the data source
SelectCommand	Property	SqlCommand used to retrieve rows from the data source
Update	Method	Transfers data from a DataSet to the data source
UpdateCommand	Property	SqlCommand used to update rows in the data source

---

You've seen the SqlDataAdapter used in many samples in Chapter 5 and earlier in this chapter. Later in this chapter (in the "Using Datasets" section) you'll learn more about using the SqlDataAdapter in conjunction with the DataSet to manipulate data.

The DataSet Objects

The second set of ADO.NET objects are the DataSet objects, which are all contained in the System.Data namespace. Unlike the data provider objects, there's only one set of DataSet objects. The DataSet objects represent data in an abstract form that's not tied to any particular database implementation. In this section, I'll introduce you to the DataSet and the other objects that it contains:

- ◆ DataSet
- ◆ DataTable
- ◆ DataRelation
- ◆ DataRow
- ◆ DataColumn
- ◆ DataView

The DataSet Object

The DataSet itself is a self-contained memory-resident representation of relational data. A DataSet contains other objects, such as DataTables and DataRelations, that hold the actual data and information about the design of the data. The DataSet is designed to be easy to move between components. In particular, specific methods convert a DataSet to an XML file and vice versa.

Table 6.7 shows the most important members of the DataSet object.

TABLE 6.7

DATASET OBJECT MEMBERS

Member	Type	Description
AcceptChanges	Method	Marks all changes in the DataSet as having been accepted
Clear	Method	Removes all data from the DataSet
GetChanges	Method	Gets a DataSet that contains only the changed data in this DataSet
GetXml	Method	Gets an XML representation of the DataSet
GetXmlSchema	Method	Gets an XSD representation of the DataSet
Merge	Method	Merges two DataSets
ReadXml	Method	Loads the DataSet from an XML file
ReadXmlSchema	Method	Loads the DataSet's schema from an XSD file
Relations	Property	A collection of DataRelation objects
Tables	Property	A collection of DataTable objects
WriteXml	Method	Writes the DataSet to an XML file
WriteXmlSchema	Method	Writes the DataSet's schema to an XSD file

As you can see, several of the DataSet methods deal with XML and XSD files. You'll learn more about these files in the "XML Basics" section later in this chapter.

The DataTable Object

The DataTable object represents a single table within the DataSet. A single DataSet can contain many DataTable objects. Table 6.8 shows the most important members of the DataTable object.

TABLE 6.8

DATATABLE OBJECT MEMBERS

Member	Type	Description
ChildRelations	Property	A collection of DataRelation objects that refer to children of the DataTable
Clear	Method	Removes all data from the DataTable
ColumnChanged	Event	Fires when the data in any row of a specified column has been changed
ColumnChanging	Event	Fires when the data in any row of a specified column is about to be changed
Columns	Property	A collection of DataColumn objects
Constraints	Property	A collection of Constraint objects
NewRow	Method	Creates a new, blank row in the DataTable
ParentRelations	Property	A collection of DataRelation objects that refer to parents of the DataTable
PrimaryKey	Property	An array of DataColumn objects that provide the primary key for the DataTable
RowChanged	Event	Fires when any data in a DataRow has been changed
RowChanging	Event	Fires when any data in a DataRow is about to be changed
RowDeleted	Event	Fires when a row has been deleted
RowDeleting	Event	Fires when a row is about to be deleted
Rows	Property	A collection of DataRow objects
Select	Method	Selects an array of DataRow objects that meet specified criteria
TableName	Property	The name of the DataTable

As you can see, you can manipulate a DataTable as either a collection of DataColumn objects or a collection of DataRow objects. The DataTable also provides events that you can use to monitor data changes. For example, you might bind a DataTable to a DataGrid and use these events to track the user's operations on the data within the DataGrid.

The DataRelation Object

As I mentioned earlier, the DataSet can represent an entire relational database. The DataRelation object stores information on the relations between DataTables within a DataSet. Table 6.9 shows the most important members of the DataRelation object.

TABLE 6.9

DATARELATION OBJECT MEMBERS

Member	Type	Description
ChildColumns	Property	Collection of DataColumn objects that define the foreign key side of the relation
ChildKeyConstraint	Property	Returns a ForeignKeyConstraint object for the relation
ChildTable	Property	DataTable from the foreign key side of the relation
ParentColumns	Property	Collection of DataColumn objects that define the primary key side of the relation
ParentKeyConstraint	Property	Returns a PrimaryKeyConstraint object for the relation
ParentTable	Property	DataTable from the primary key side of the relation
RelationName	Property	Name of the DataRelation

The DataRow Object

Continuing down the object hierarchy from the DataSet past the DataTable, you come to the DataRow. As you can guess by now, the DataRow represents a single row of data. When you're selecting, inserting, updating, or deleting data in a DataSet, you'll normally work with DataRow objects.

Table 6.10 shows the most important members of the DataRow object.

DATAROW OBJECT MEMBERS

Member	Type	Description
BeginEdit	Method	Starts editing the DataRow
CancelEdit	Method	Discards an edit in progress
Delete	Method	Deletes the DataRow from its parent DataTable
EndEdit	Method	Ends an edit in progress, saving the changes
Item	Property	Returns the data from a particular column in the DataRow
IsNull	Method	Returns True if a specified column contains a Null value
RowState	Property	Returns information on the current state of a DataRow (for example, whether it has been changed since it was last saved to the database)

The DataColumn Object

The DataTable also contains a collection of DataColumn objects. A DataColumn represents a single column in the DataTable. By manipulating the DataColumn objects, you can determine and even change the structure of the DataTable.

Table 6.11 shows the most important members of the DataColumn object.

DATACOLUMN OBJECT MEMBERS

Member	Type	Description
AllowDbNull	Property	Indicates whether the DataColumn can contain Null values
AutoIncrement	Property	Indicates whether the DataColumn is an identity column
ColumnName	Property	Name of the DataColumn

Member	Type	Description
DataType	Property	Data type of the DataColumn
DefaultValue	Property	Default value of this DataColumn for new rows of data
MaxLength	Property	Maximum length of a text DataColumn
Unique	Property	Indicates whether values in the DataColumn must be unique across all rows in the DataTable

The DataView Object

Finally, the DataView object represents a view of the data contained in a DataTable. A DataView might contain every DataRow from the DataTable, or it might be filtered to contain only specific rows. Filtering can be done by SQL expressions (returning, for example, only rows for customers in France) or by row state (returning, for example, only rows that have been modified). You'll see one example of this filtering in Guided Practice Exercise 6.3.

Table 6.12 shows the most important members of the DataView object.

TABLE 6.12

DataView Object Members

Member	Type	Description
AddNew	Method	Adds a new row to the DataView
AllowDelete	Property	Indicates whether deletions can be performed through this DataView
AllowEdit	Property	Indicates whether updates can be performed through this DataView
AllowNew	Property	Indicates whether insertions can be performed through this DataView
Count	Property	Number of rows in this DataView
Delete	Method	Deletes a row from this DataView
Find	Method	Searches for a row in the DataView
FindRows	Method	Returns an array of rows matching a filter expression
Item	Property	Returns a DataRowView object representing a particular row in the DataView
Sort	Method	Sorts the data in a DataView

REVIEW BREAK

▶ The ADO.NET object model includes both database-specific data provider classes and database-independent DataSet classes.

▶ Data providers contain implementations of the Connection, Command, Parameter, DataReader, and DataAdapter objects optimized for a particular database product.

▶ The SqlConnection object represents a connection to a SQL Server database.

▶ The SqlCommand object represents a command that can be executed.

▶ The SqlParameter object represents a parameter of a stored procedure.

▶ The SqlDataReader object provides a fast way to retrieve a result set from a command.

▶ The SqlDataAdapter object implements a two-way pipeline between the database and the data model.

▶ The DataSet represents an entire relational database in memory. It's composed of DataTable, DataRelation, DataRow, and DataColumn objects.

▶ The DataView object provides a filtered row of the data from a DataTable.

Using DataSets

Now that you've seen the ADO.NET objects, it's time to see what you can do with them. Of course, in a single chapter I can't possibly cover everything you can do with ADO.NET. So I'm going to concentrate on some of the basic operations, including

◆ Populating a DataSet from a database

◆ Moving around in DataSets and retrieving data

◆ Using strongly typed DataSets

◆ Using DataSets with multiple tables

◆ Finding and sorting data in DataSets

◆ Editing data with ADO.NET

◆ Updating data

◆ Adding data

◆ Deleting data

If you're interested in exploring ADO.NET in more depth, you'll find a list of references at the end of the chapter.

Populating a DataSet from a Database

Before you can do anything with data in a DataSet, you must get the data into the DataSet (see Step By Step 6.18). In general, you can follow a four-step pattern to move data from the database to a DataSet object:

1. Create a SqlConnection object to connect to the database.

2. Create a SqlCommand object to retrieve the desired data.

3. Assign the SqlCommand to the SelectCommand property of a SqlDataAdapter object.

4. Call the Fill method of the SqlDataAdapter object.

STEP BY STEP

6.18 Filling a DataSet

1. Add a new form to your Visual Basic .NET project.

2. Place a Button control named btnLoad and a DataGrid control named dgProducts on the form. Set the Caption property of the DataGrid control to Products.

3. Double-click the Button control to open the form's module. Enter these statements at the top of the module:

```
Imports System.Data
Imports System.Data.SqlClient
```

continues

continued

4. Enter this code to handle the `Click` event of the Button control:

```
Private Sub btnLoad_Click(ByVal sender As System.Object, _
 ByVal e As System.EventArgs) Handles btnLoad.Click
     ' Create a SqlConnection
     Dim cnn As SqlConnection = _
      New SqlConnection("Data Source=(local);" & _
      "Initial Catalog=Northwind;Integrated
       Security=SSPI")
     ' Create a SqlCommand
     Dim cmd As SqlCommand = cnn.CreateCommand()
     cmd.CommandType = CommandType.Text
     cmd.CommandText = _
      "SELECT * FROM Products ORDER BY ProductName"
     ' Set up the DataAdapter and fill the DataSet
     Dim da As SqlDataAdapter = New SqlDataAdapter()
     da.SelectCommand = cmd
     Dim ds As DataSet = New DataSet()
     ' Display the data on the user interface
     da.Fill(ds, "Products")
     dgProducts.DataSource = ds
     dgProducts.DataMember = "Products"
End Sub
```

5. Set the form as the startup object for the project.

6. Run the project and click the button. The code will connect to the SQL Server database on the local computer and fill the DataGrid control with the result of executing the SQL statement, as shown in Figure 6.14.

FIGURE 6.14

A DataGrid control bound to data stored in a DataSet.

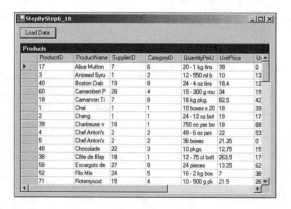

This sample demonstrates a couple of shortcuts that you can use in your ADO.NET code. First, the constructor for the SqlConnection object has an overloaded form that lets you supply the connection string when you create the object. Second, this code doesn't call the Open and Close methods of the SqlConnection explicitly. Instead, it lets the SqlDataAdapter make those calls when it needs the data. Doing this not only cuts down the amount of code that you need to write, it also improves the scalability of your application by keeping the SqlConnection open for the shortest possible period of time.

Moving Around in DataSets and Retrieving Data

If you're familiar with classic ADO, you're used to *Recordsets*: collections of records that have a pointer to a current record. In classic ADO, you move through a Recordset with code such as this:

```
Do Until rst.EOF
    rst.MoveNext
Loop
```

DataSets have no equivalent to this code because DataSets have no concept of a current record pointer. Instead, you move through a DataSet by working with the collections that the DataSet contains (see Step By Step 6.19).

> **EXAM TIP**
>
> **Choose a Table Name** The second parameter to the DataAdapter.Fill method is the name of the DataTable. The DataTable will be created from the data supplied by the SelectCommand. The DataTable name does not have to match the table name in the underlying database. This example would work just as well if you placed data from the Products table into a DataTable named Starship (although that would be a pretty poor idea from the standpoint of code maintainability).

STEP BY STEP

6.19 Moving Through a DataSet

1. Add a new form to your Visual Basic .NET project.

2. Place a Button control named `btnLoadData` and a ListBox control named `lbData` on the form.

3. Double-click the Button control to open the form's module. Enter these statements at the top of the module:

```
Imports System.Data
Imports System.Data.SqlClient
```

continues

continued

4. Enter this code to handle the `Click` event of the Button control:

```
Private Sub btnLoadData_Click( _
 ByVal sender As System.Object, _
 ByVal e As System.EventArgs) Handles btnLoadData.Click
    ' Create a SqlConnection
    Dim cnn As SqlConnection = _
     New SqlConnection("Data Source=(local);" & _
     "Initial Catalog=Northwind;Integrated Security=SSPI")
    ' Create a SqlCommand
    Dim cmd As SqlCommand = cnn.CreateCommand()
    cmd.CommandType = CommandType.Text
    cmd.CommandText = _
     "SELECT * FROM Customers WHERE Country = 'France'"
    ' Set up the DataAdapter and fill the DataSet
    Dim da As SqlDataAdapter = New SqlDataAdapter()
    da.SelectCommand = cmd
    Dim ds As DataSet = New DataSet()
    da.Fill(ds, "Customers")
    ' Dump the contents of the DataSet
    Dim dt As DataTable
    Dim dr As DataRow
    Dim dc As DataColumn
    lbData.Items.Add("DataSet: " & ds.DataSetName)
    For Each dt In ds.Tables
        lbData.Items.Add("  DataTable: " & dt.TableName)
        For Each dr In dt.Rows
            lbData.Items.Add("    DataRow")
            For Each dc In dt.Columns
                lbData.Items.Add("      " & dr(dc))
            Next
        Next
    Next
End Sub
```

5. Set the form as the startup object for the project.

6. Run the project and click the button. The code will dump the contents of the DataSet to the ListBox control, as shown in Figure 6.15.

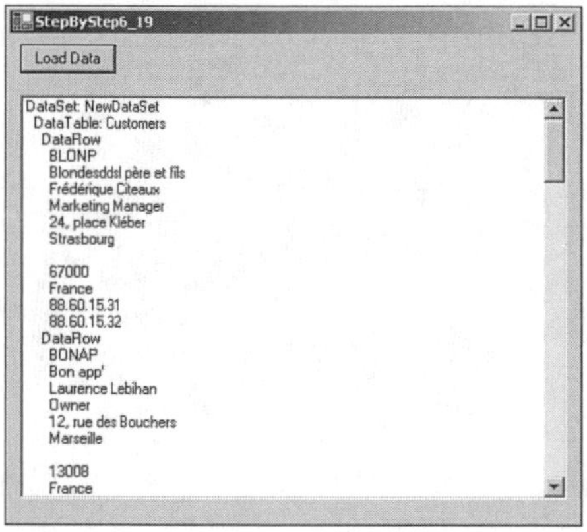

FIGURE 6.15
Dumping the contents of a DataSet to a ListBox control.

This sample shows how to visit every piece of data in a DataSet by a proper selection of nested `For Each` loops. It also shows a general syntax for retrieving data: Locate the data row and column whose intersection contains the data that you're interested in, and use the dr(dc) syntax to retrieve the actual data value.

You can use a variety of other syntaxes to retrieve data. Given a DataTable variable named dt that refers to the data from the Customer table, for example, any of these statements will retrieve the value in the first column of the first row of data in the DataTable:

```
dt.Rows(0).Item(0)
dt.Rows(0)(0)
dt.Rows(0).Item("CustomerID")
dt.Rows(0)("CustomerID")
dt.Rows(0)!CustomerID
```

Using Strongly Typed DataSets

All the syntaxes you saw in the previous section for retrieving data have one thing in common: They're all *late-bound*. That is, the .NET Framework doesn't know until runtime that "CustomerID" is a valid column name. One of the innovations of ADO.NET is a provision to create strongly typed DataSets. In a strongly typed DataSet, columns actually become properties of the row. This allows you to write an early-bound version of the data-retrieval expression:

```
dt.Rows(0).CustomerID
```

In addition to being faster than the late-bound syntaxes, the early-bound syntax has the advantage of making column names show up in IntelliSense tips as you type code.

You've already seen quite a few strongly typed DataSets, although I didn't emphasize this while I was using them. Any time you use the Generate DataSet link in the Properties window for a SqlDataAdapter object on a form, Visual Studio .NET builds a strongly typed DataSet. You can also build strongly typed DataSets by using the XSD designer, as in Step By Step 6.20.

STEP BY STEP

6.20 Designing a Strongly Typed DataSet

1. Select Project, Add New Item in your Visual Basic .NET project.

2. In the Add New Item dialog box, select the DataSet template. Name the new DataSet Suppliers.xsd. Click Open to create the XSD file, and open it in the Designer.

continues

FIGURE 6.16
A strongly typed DataSet open in the XSD Designer.

continued

3. Open Server Explorer.

4. Expand the tree under Data Connections to show a SQL Server data connection that points to the Northwind sample database, then the Tables node of the SQL Server. Drag the Suppliers table from Server Explorer and drop it on the design surface for the DataSet. Figure 6.16 shows the resulting XSD Design view. The *E* icons for each column of the table indicate that those columns have been rendered as XML elements.

5. Save the DataSet. At this point, your project will contain a new class named Suppliers, which is a strongly typed DataSet that you can use in code.

6. Add a new form to your Visual Basic .NET project.

7. Place a Button control named `btnLoadData` and a ListBox control named `lbData` on the form.

8. Double-click the Button control to open the form's module. Enter these statements at the top of the module:

```
Imports System.Data
Imports System.Data.SqlClient
```

9. Enter this code to handle the `Click` event of the Button control:

```
Private Sub btnLoadData_Click(ByVal sender As System.Object, _
 ByVal e As System.EventArgs) Handles btnLoadData.Click
    ' Create a SqlConnection
    Dim cnn As SqlConnection = New SqlConnection("Data
    Source=(local);" & _
    "Initial Catalog=Northwind;Integrated Security=SSPI")
    ' Create a SqlCommand
    Dim cmd As SqlCommand = cnn.CreateCommand()
    cmd.CommandType = CommandType.Text
    cmd.CommandText = "SELECT * FROM Suppliers"
    ' Set up the DataAdapter and fill the DataSet
    Dim da As SqlDataAdapter = New SqlDataAdapter()
    da.SelectCommand = cmd
    Dim ds As Suppliers = New Suppliers()
    da.Fill(ds, "Suppliers")
```

```
' Dump the contents of the DataSet
Dim suppRow As Suppliers.SuppliersRow
For Each suppRow In ds.Suppliers
    lbData.Items.Add(suppRow.SupplierID & " " &
    suppRow.CompanyName)
Next
End Sub
```

10. Set the form as the startup object for the project.

11. Run the project and click the button. The code will display two columns from the DataSet in the ListBox control, as shown in Figure 6.17.

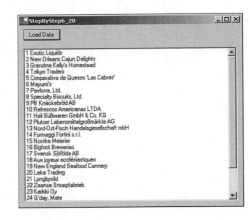

FIGURE 6.17
Data dumped from a strongly typed DataSet.

Using the Suppliers class to define the DataSet in this case gives several syntactical benefits. You can refer to the Suppliers DataTable as a property of the DataSet. You can also refer to the columns in the DataRows in this DataTable as properties of the DataRow. The strongly typed DataSet automatically defines a class named SuppliersRow to represent one DataRow with strong typing.

DataSets with Multiple Tables

Every DataSet you've seen so far in this chapter has contained a single DataTable. But DataSets are not limited to a single DataTable; in fact, no practical limit exists on the number of DataTables that a DataSet can contain. By using multiple DataAdapter objects, you can connect a single DataSet to more than one table in the SQL Server database (see Step By Step 6.21). You can also define DataRelation objects to represent the relationship between the DataTables in the DataSet.

STEP BY STEP

6.21 Building a DataSet Containing Multiple DataTables

1. Add a new form to your Visual Basic .NET project.

2. Place a Button control named btnLoadData and a DataGrid control named dgMain on the form.

continues

continued

> **3.** Double-click the Button control to open the form's module. Enter these statements at the top of the module:

```
Imports System.Data
Imports System.Data.SqlClient
```

> **4.** Enter this code to handle the `Click` event of the Button control:

```
Private Sub btnLoadData_Click( _
 ByVal sender As System.Object, _
 ByVal e As System.EventArgs) Handles btnLoadData.Click
    ' Create a SqlConnection and a DataSet
    Dim cnn As SqlConnection = _
     New SqlConnection("Data Source=(local);" & _
     "Initial Catalog=Northwind;Integrated Security=SSPI")
    Dim ds As DataSet = New DataSet()

    ' Add the customers data to the DataSet
    Dim cmdCustomers As SqlCommand = cnn.CreateCommand()
    cmdCustomers.CommandType = CommandType.Text
    cmdCustomers.CommandText = "SELECT * FROM Customers"
    Dim daCustomers As SqlDataAdapter = New SqlDataAdapter()
    daCustomers.SelectCommand = cmdCustomers
    daCustomers.Fill(ds, "Customers")

    ' Add the Orders data to the DataSet
    Dim cmdOrders As SqlCommand = cnn.CreateCommand()
    cmdOrders.CommandType = CommandType.Text
    cmdOrders.CommandText = "SELECT * FROM Orders"
    Dim daOrders As SqlDataAdapter = New SqlDataAdapter()
    daOrders.SelectCommand = cmdOrders
    daOrders.Fill(ds, "Orders")

    ' Add the Order Details data to the DataSet
    Dim cmdOrderDetails As SqlCommand = cnn.CreateCommand()
    cmdOrderDetails.CommandType = CommandType.Text
    cmdOrderDetails.CommandText = _
     "SELECT * FROM [Order Details]"
    Dim daOrderDetails As SqlDataAdapter = _
     New SqlDataAdapter()
    daOrderDetails.SelectCommand = cmdOrderDetails
    daOrderDetails.Fill(ds, "OrderDetails")

    ' Add Relations
    Dim relCustOrder As DataRelation = _
     ds.Relations.Add("CustOrder", _
     ds.Tables("Customers").Columns("CustomerID"), _
     ds.Tables("Orders").Columns("CustomerID"))
```

```
Dim relOrderOrderDetails As DataRelation = _
 ds.Relations.Add("OrderOrderDetails", _
 ds.Tables("Orders").Columns("OrderID"), _
 ds.Tables("OrderDetails").Columns("OrderID"))

' And show the data on the user interface
dgMain.DataSource = ds
dgMain.DataMember = "Customers"

End Sub
```

5. Set the form as the startup object for the project.

6. Run the project and click the button. The code will load all three database tables into the DataSet and then display the customers' information on the DataGrid, as shown in Figure 6.18.

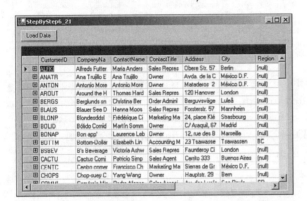

FIGURE 6.18
Customers' data from a multitable DataSet.

This code uses three different SqlDataAdapter objects to move data from three different database tables into a single DataSet. The data from each SqlDataAdapter is stored in a separate DataTable. You could also use a single SqlDataadapter object for the same purpose, by changing its SelectCommand property each time you want to load a separate table. The code then adds DataRelation objects to specify the relationships between these DataTables. The Add method of the DataSet.Relations collection takes three parameters:

1. A name for the DataRelation object to be created

2. The DataColumn object representing the primary key side of the relationship

3. The DataColumn object representing the foreign key side of the relationship

Although the DataGrid in this example initially displays only the Customer data, all the data is available. The DataGrid control contains built-in logic to help navigate between related DataTables in a DataSet. If you click the + sign to the left of a row of Customer data, the DataGrid will show a list of the relationships that involve that row, as shown in Figure 6.19.

FIGURE 6.19

Viewing the relationships for a row of customer data.

The name of the relationship is a hot link. Clicking the link loads all the related rows on the other side of that relationship into the DataGrid, as shown in Figure 6.20. Note that the Parent Rows area of the DataGrid contains information on the Customers row where the navigation started.

FIGURE 6.20

Orders data from a multitable DataSet.

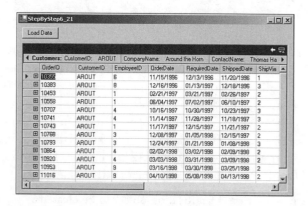

Because this DataSet has another level of detail, you can repeat the process. Click the + sign next to an order to see the relations in which that order is involved, as shown in Figure 6.21.

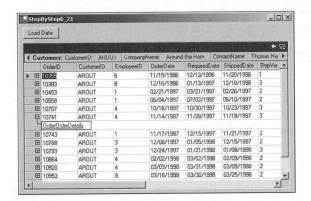

FIGURE 6.21
Drilling into an order.

Finally, clicking the hotlink beneath an order will reveal all the Order Detail rows for that order, as shown in Figure 6.22. The Parent Rows area now contains the details on both the customer and the order that were used to get to this point.

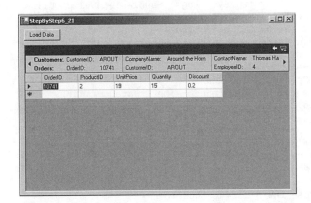

FIGURE 6.22
Orders data from a multitable DataSet.

Finding and Sorting Data in DataSets

The .NET Framework offers several object-oriented ways to find and sort data. In this section, I'll show how to use two of these ways: the DataTable.Select method and the filtering and sorting capabilities of the DataView object.

The Select method of the DataTable object is a convenient way to find particular DataRow objects within the DataTable (see Step By Step 6.22). This method extracts an array of DataRow objects that you can work with.

STEP BY STEP

6.22 Using the DataTable.Select Method

1. Add a new form to your Visual Basic .NET project.

2. Place a Button control named btnSelect, a TextBox control named txtCountry, and a ListBox control named lbSelected on the form.

3. Double-click the Button control to open the form's module. Enter these statements at the top of the module:

```
Imports System.Data
Imports System.Data.SqlClient
```

4. Enter this code to handle the Click event of the Button control:

```
Private Sub btnSelect_Click(ByVal sender As System.Object, _
 ByVal e As System.EventArgs) Handles btnSelect.Click
    ' Create a SqlConnection
    Dim cnn As SqlConnection = _
     New SqlConnection("Data Source=(local);" & _
     "Initial Catalog=Northwind;Integrated
     Security=SSPI")
    ' Create a SqlCommand
    Dim cmd As SqlCommand = cnn.CreateCommand()
    cmd.CommandType = CommandType.Text
    cmd.CommandText = "SELECT * FROM Customers"
    ' Set up the DataAdapter and fill the DataSet
    Dim da As SqlDataAdapter = New SqlDataAdapter()
    da.SelectCommand = cmd
    Dim ds As DataSet = New DataSet()
    da.Fill(ds, "Customers")
    ' Use the Select method to
    ' get a sorted array of DataRows
    Dim adr() As DataRow = ds.Tables("Customers").Select( _
     "Country = '" & txtCountry.Text & _
      "'", "ContactName ASC")
    ' Dump the result to the user interface
    lbSelected.Items.Clear()
    Dim dr As DataRow
    For Each dr In adr
        lbSelected.Items.Add(dr(0) & _
        " " & dr(1) & " " & dr(2))
    Next
End Sub
```

5. Set the form as the startup object for the project.

6. Run the project. Enter a country name and click the button. You'll see the first three columns from DataRows for customers in that country, as shown in Figure 6.23.

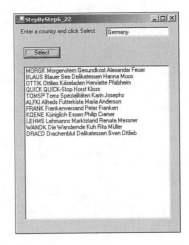

FIGURE 6.23
Results of using the DataTable.Select method.

The Select method of the DataTable constructs an array of DataRows based on up to three factors: a filter expression, a sort expression, and a state constant.

Filter expressions are essentially SQL WHERE clauses constructed according to these rules:

◆ Column names containing special characters should be enclosed in square brackets.

◆ String constants should be enclosed in single quotes.

◆ Date constants should be enclosed in pound signs.

◆ Numeric expressions can be specified in decimal or scientific notation.

◆ Expressions can be created using AND, OR, NOT, parentheses, IN, LIKE, comparison operators, and arithmetic operators.

◆ The + operator is used to concatenate strings.

◆ Either * or % can be used as a wildcard to match any number of characters. Wildcards can be used only at the start or end of strings.

◆ Columns in a child table can be referenced with the expression `Child.Column`. If the table has more than one child table, use the expression `Child(RelationName).Column` to choose a particular child table.

◆ The Sum, Avg, Min, Max, Count, StDev, and Var aggregates can be used with child tables.

◆ Supported functions include CONVERT, LEN, ISNULL, IIF, and SUBSTRING.

In the sample code, the filter expression is built by concatenating the text from the txtCountry control with a column comparison.

If you don't specify a sort order in the Select method, the rows are returned in primary key order or in the order of addition if the table doesn't have a primary key. You can also specify a sort expression consisting of one or more column names and the keywords ASC or DESC to specify ascending or descending sorts. For example, this is a valid sort expression:

```
Country ASC, CompanyName DESC
```

That expression will sort first by country in ascending order, and then by company name within each country in descending order.

Finally, you can also select DataRows according to their current state by supplying one of the DataViewRowState constants. Table 6.13 shows these constants.

TABLE 6.13

DataViewRowState Constants

Constant	Meaning
Added	New rows that have not yet been committed
CurrentRows	All current rows, whether unchanged, modified, or new
Deleted	Deleted rows
ModifiedCurrent	Modified rows
ModifiedOriginal	Original data from modified rows
None	No rows
OriginalRows	Original data, including rows that have been modified or deleted
Unchanged	Rows that have not been changed

EXAM TIP

DataTable to Array   You can quickly create an array that holds all the content of a DataTable by calling the Select method with no parameters:

```
Dim adr() As DataRow =
dt.Select()
```

You can also sort and filter data by using a DataView (See Step By Step 6.23). The DataView has the same structure of rows and columns as a DataTable, but it also lets you specify sorting and filtering options as properties of the DataView object. Typically you'll create a DataView by starting with a DataTable and specifying options to include a subset of the rows in the DataTable.

STEP BY STEP

6.23 Using a DataView to Sort and Filter Data

1. Add a new form to your Visual Basic .NET project.

2. Place a Button control named `btnLoad` and a DataGrid control named `dgCustomers` on the form.

3. Double-click the Button control to open the form's module. Enter these statements at the top of the module:

```
Imports System.Data
Imports System.Data.SqlClient
```

4. Enter this code to handle the `Click` event of the Button control:

```
Private Sub btnLoad_Click(ByVal sender As System.Object, _
 ByVal e As System.EventArgs) Handles btnLoad.Click
    ' Create a SqlConnection
    Dim cnn As SqlConnection = _
     New SqlConnection("Data Source=(local);" & _
     "Initial Catalog=Northwind;Integrated
      Security=SSPI")
    ' Create a SqlCommand
    Dim cmd As SqlCommand = cnn.CreateCommand()
    cmd.CommandType = CommandType.Text
    cmd.CommandText = "SELECT * FROM Customers"
    ' Set up the DataAdapter and fill the DataSet
    Dim da As SqlDataAdapter = New SqlDataAdapter()
    da.SelectCommand = cmd
    Dim ds As DataSet = New DataSet()
    da.Fill(ds, "Customers")
    ' Create a DataView based on the Customers DataTable
    Dim dv As DataView = _
     New DataView(ds.Tables("Customers"))
    dv.RowFilter = "Country = 'France'"
    dv.Sort = "CompanyName ASC"
    dgCustomers.DataSource = dv
End Sub
```

5. Set the form as the startup object for the project.

6. Run the project and click the button. The DataGrid will display only the customers from France, sorted in ascending order by company name.

The constructor for the DataView specifies the DataTable that includes the data from which the DataView can draw. By setting the RowFilter, Sort, and RowStateFilter properties of the DataView, you can control which rows are available in the DataView, as well as the order in which they are presented. I didn't use the RowStateFilter property in Step By Step 6.23. RowStateFilter allows you to select, for example, only rows that have been changed since the DataTable was loaded.

GUIDED PRACTICE EXERCISE 6.3

In this exercise, you'll fill a DataSet with customer and order data. Then you'll allow the user to select a customer and display a DataView containing only that customer's orders on the user interface.

Your form should include a bound ComboBox control to allow the user to select a CustomerID value. When the user selects a new value in the combo box, you should initialize the DataView and bind it to a DataGrid for display.

Try this on your own first. If you get stuck or would like to see one possible solution, follow these steps:

1. Add a new form to your Visual Basic .NET project.

2. Add a Label control, a ComboBox control (cboCustomers), and a DataGrid control (dgOrders) to the form. Figure 6.24 shows a design for the form.

3. Double-click the form to open the form's module. Enter these two statements at the top of the module to make the ADO.NET objects available:

```
Imports System.Data
Imports System.Data.SqlClient
```

4. Enter code to fill the list in the ComboBox control and initialize a DataSet of orders when the form is opened:

```
' Create a SqlConnection
Dim mcnn As SqlConnection = _
 New SqlConnection("Data Source=(local);" & _
 "Initial Catalog=Northwind;Integrated Security=SSPI")
' DataSet to hold order information
 Dim mdsOrders As DataSet = New DataSet()
```

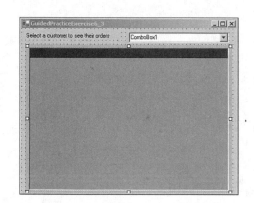

FIGURE 6.24
Designing a form to retrieve order information by customers.

```
Private Sub GuidedPracticeExercise6_3_Load( _
 ByVal sender As System.Object, _
 ByVal e As System.EventArgs) Handles MyBase.Load
     ' Get all of the orders
     Dim cmdOrders As SqlCommand = mcnn.CreateCommand
     cmdOrders.CommandType = CommandType.Text
     cmdOrders.CommandText = "SELECT * FROM Orders"
     Dim daOrders As SqlDataAdapter = New SqlDataAdapter()
     daOrders.SelectCommand = cmdOrders
     daOrders.Fill(mdsOrders, "Orders")
     ' Retrieve data for the combo box
     Dim cmdCustomers As SqlCommand = mcnn.CreateCommand()
     cmdCustomers.CommandType = CommandType.Text
     cmdCustomers.CommandText = _
       "SELECT CustomerID, CompanyName " & _
       "FROM Customers ORDER BY CompanyName"
     Dim ds As DataSet = New DataSet()
     Dim da As SqlDataAdapter = New SqlDataAdapter()
     da.SelectCommand = cmdCustomers
     da.Fill(ds, "Customers")
     With cboCustomers
         .DisplayMember = "CompanyName"
         .ValueMember = "CustomerID"
         .DataSource = ds.Tables("Customers")
     End With
 End Sub
```

5. Enter this code to load the correct orders when you select a
   value in the combo box:

```
Private Sub cboCustomers_SelectedIndexChanged( _
 ByVal sender As System.Object, _
 ByVal e As System.EventArgs) _
 Handles cboCustomers.SelectedIndexChanged
     ' Create a DataView containing
     ' the orders for the selected customer
     Dim dv As DataView = New DataView( _
       mdsOrders.Tables("Orders"))
     dv.RowFilter = "CustomerID = '" & _
       cboCustomers.SelectedValue & "'"
     dgOrders.DataSource = dv
 End Sub
```

6. Set the form as the startup object for the project.

7. Run the project. Select a customer from the combo box to
   display that customer's orders in the DataGrid.

continues

continued

If you had difficulty following this exercise, review the sections titled "Running Queries," "The SELECT Statement," and "Finding and Sorting Data in DataSets," as well as the material on "Complex Data Binding" in Chapter 5. The text and examples should help you relearning this material and help understand what just happened in this exercise. After review, try this exercise again.

You could meet the requirements of this particular exercise in many other ways. For example, you could create stored procedures to retrieve the customer or order information (or both), or you could create a new DataSet whenever you need a set of orders rather than building a DataView on an existing DataSet. As you practice with ADO.NET, it's so flexible that you can almost always find alternative ways to do things.

Editing Data with ADO.NET

Now that you know how to retrieve data with ADO.NET, there's one other important database-related topic to cover: editing data. ADO.NET supports all the normal database operations of updating existing data, adding new data, and deleting existing data.

As you read this section, keep in mind the distinction between the data model and the database. As you work with data in the DataSet and its subsidiary objects, you're altering the data in the data model. These changes will not be reflected in the underlying database until and unless you call the Update method of the DataAdapter method. So far, I've only been using the SqlDataAdapter to move data fro the database to the data model; in this section, you'll see how to move data back from the data model to the database.

Updating Data

Updating data is easy: Just assign a new value to the item in the data row that you want to change—but there's more to finishing the job.

For the Update method of the SqlDataAdapter to write changes back to the database, you must set its UpdateCommand property to an appropriate SqlCommand object. Step By Step 6.24 will show you how.

STEP BY STEP

6.24 Updating Data with a SqlDataAdapter

1. Add a new form to your Visual Basic .NET project.

2. Place a Button control named btnUpdate on the form.

3. Double-click the Button control to open the form's module. Enter these statements at the top of the module:

```
Imports System.Data
Imports System.Data.SqlClient
```

4. Enter this code to load data when the form is opened:

```
' Create some ADO.NET objects
Dim mcnn As SqlConnection = New SqlConnection( _
 "Data Source=(local);" & _
 "Initial Catalog=Northwind;Integrated Security=SSPI")
Dim mds As DataSet = New DataSet()
Dim mda As SqlDataAdapter = New SqlDataAdapter()

Private Sub StepByStep6_24_Load( _
 ByVal sender As System.Object, _
 ByVal e As System.EventArgs) Handles MyBase.Load
    ' Create a SqlCommand to select data
    Dim cmdSelect As SqlCommand = mcnn.CreateCommand()
    cmdSelect.CommandType = CommandType.Text
    cmdSelect.CommandText = _
     "SELECT CustomerID, ContactName FROM Customers"
    ' Create a SqlCommand to update data
    Dim cmdUpdate As SqlCommand = mcnn.CreateCommand()
    cmdUpdate.CommandType = CommandType.Text
    cmdUpdate.CommandText = "UPDATE Customers SET " & _
     "ContactName = @ContactName WHERE " & _
    "CustomerID = @CustomerID"
    cmdUpdate.Parameters.Add("@ContactName", _
     SqlDbType.NVarChar, _
     30, "ContactName")
    cmdUpdate.Parameters.Add( _
     "@CustomerID", SqlDbType.NChar, _
     5, "CustomerID")
    cmdUpdate.Parameters("@CustomerID").SourceVersion = _
     DataRowVersion.Original
```

continues

continued

```
' Set up the DataAdapter and fill the DataSet
    mda.SelectCommand = cmdSelect
    mda.UpdateCommand = cmdUpdate
    mda.Fill(mds, "Customers")
End Sub
```

5. Enter this code to handle the `Click` event of the Button control:

```
Private Sub btnUpdate_Click(ByVal sender As System.Object, _
 ByVal e As System.EventArgs) Handles btnUpdate.Click
    ' Prompt the user for a customer ID
    Dim strCustomerID As String = _
     InputBox("Enter Customer ID to modify:")
    ' Get just that customer's DataRow
    Dim adrEdit() As DataRow = _
     mds.Tables("Customers").Select( _
       "CustomerID = '" & strCustomerID & "'")
    ' Make sure there's some data
    If UBound(adrEdit) > -1 Then
        ' Prompt for new data and put it in the DataRow
        adrEdit(0)("ContactName") = _
         InputBox("Enter new contact name", , _
         adrEdit(0)("ContactName"))
        ' And save the changes
        mda.Update(mds, "Customers")
    End If
End Sub
```

6. Set the form as the startup object for the project.

7. Run the project and click the button. The code will prompt you for a CustomerID value. Enter a CustomerID (such as ALFKI) and click OK. The code will prompt you for a contact name. Enter a new contact name and click OK to write the change back to the database. You can verify the change by running the program a second time and changing the same customer's data.

The Update method of the SqlDataAdapter is syntactically similar to the Fill method. It takes as its parameters the DataSet to be reconciled with the database and the name of the DataTable to be saved. You don't have to worry about which rows or columns of data were changed. The SqlDataAdapter automatically locates the changed rows. It executes the SqlCommand specified in its UpdateCommand property for each of those rows.

In this particular case, the UpdateCommand property has two para-meters. The SqlParameter objects are created using a version of the constructor that takes four parameters rather than the three you saw earlier in the chapter. The fourth parameter is the name of a DataColumn which contains the data to be used in this particular parameter. Note also that you can specify whether a parameter should be filled in from the current data in the DataSet (the default) or from the original version of the data before any edits were made. In this case, the @CustomerID parameter is being used to locate the row to edit in the database, so the code uses the original value of the column as the value for the parameter.

Adding Data

To add data to the database, you must supply a SqlCommand for the InsertCommand property of the SqlDataAdapter, as in Step By Step 6.25.

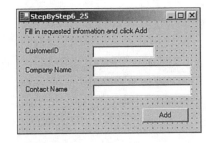

FIGURE 6.25
Designing a form to add new customers to the database.

STEP BY STEP

6.25 Adding Data with a SqlDataAdapter

1. Add a new form to your Visual Basic .NET project.

2. Place four Label controls, three TextBox controls (txtCustomerID, txtCompanyName, and txtContactName) and a Button control (btnAdd) on the form. Figure 6.25 shows a design for the form.

3. Double-click the Button control to open the form's mod-ule. Enter these statements at the top of the module:

```
Imports System.Data
Imports System.Data.SqlClient
```

4. Enter this code to load data when the form is opened:

```
' Create some ADO.NET objects
Dim mcnn As SqlConnection = _
 New SqlConnection("Data Source=(local);" & _
 "Initial Catalog=Northwind;Integrated Security=SSPI")
Dim mds As DataSet = New DataSet()
Dim mda As SqlDataAdapter = New SqlDataAdapter()
```

continues

continued

```
Private Sub StepByStep6_25_Load( _
 ByVal sender As System.Object, _
 ByVal e As System.EventArgs) Handles MyBase.Load
    ' Create a SqlCommand to select data
    Dim cmdSelect As SqlCommand = mcnn.CreateCommand()
    cmdSelect.CommandType = CommandType.Text
    cmdSelect.CommandText = _
     "SELECT CustomerID, CompanyName, " & _
     "ContactName FROM Customers"
    ' Create a SqlCommand to insert data
    Dim cmdInsert As SqlCommand = mcnn.CreateCommand()
    cmdInsert.CommandType = CommandType.Text
    cmdInsert.CommandText = "INSERT INTO Customers " & _
     "(CustomerID, CompanyName, ContactName) " & _
     "VALUES(@CustomerID, @CompanyName, @ContactName)"
    cmdInsert.Parameters.Add( _
     "@CustomerID", SqlDbType.NChar, _
     5, "CustomerID")
    cmdInsert.Parameters.Add( _
     "@CompanyName", SqlDbType.NVarChar, _
     40, "CompanyName")
    cmdInsert.Parameters.Add( _
     "@ContactName", SqlDbType.NVarChar, _
     30, "ContactName")
    cmdInsert.Parameters("@CustomerID").SourceVersion = _
     DataRowVersion.Original
    ' Set up the DataAdapter and fill the DataSet
    mda.SelectCommand = cmdSelect
    mda.InsertCommand = cmdInsert
    mda.Fill(mds, "Customers")
End Sub
```

5. Enter this code to handle the Click event of the Button control:

```
Private Sub btnAdd_Click(ByVal sender As System.Object, _
 ByVal e As System.EventArgs) Handles btnAdd.Click
    ' Create a new DataRow
    Dim dr As DataRow = mds.Tables("Customers").NewRow()
    ' Set values
    dr(0) = txtCustomerID.Text
    dr(1) = txtCompanyName.Text
    dr(2) = txtContactName.Text
    ' And append the new row to the DataTable
    mds.Tables("Customers").Rows.Add(dr)
    ' Now save back to the database
    mda.Update(mds, "Customers")
    MessageBox.Show("Row added!")
End Sub
```

6. Set the form as the startup object for the project.

7. Run the project. Enter data in the text boxes and click the button. The code will add the new row to the database.

As you can see, adding a new DataRow to a DataTable has several steps. First, call the NewRow method of the DataTable to return a DataRow object that has the proper schema for that particular DataTable. Then you can set the values of the individual items in the DataRow. Finally, call the Add method of the DataTable to actually append this DataRow to the DataTable.

Of course, appending the DataRow to the DataTable doesn't make any changes to the database. For that you must call the Update method of the SqlDataAdapter once again. If the SqlDataAdapter finds any new rows in its scan of the database, it will call the SqlCommand specified by its InsertCommand property once for each new row. It's this SqlCommand actually permanently saves the data.

Deleting Data

The Rows collection of the DataTable object supports a Remove method that deletes an entire DataRow from the DataTable. To persist the changes to the database, you'll need to call the Update method of the SqlDataAdapter as in Step By Step 6.26.

STEP BY STEP

6.26 Deleting Data with a SqlDataAdapter

1. Add a new form to your Visual Basic .NET project.

2. Place a Button control named btnDelete on the form.

3. Double-click the Button control to open the form's module. Enter these statements at the top of the module:

```
Imports System.Data
Imports System.Data.SqlClient
```

4. Enter this code to load data when the form is opened:

```
' Create some ADO.NET objects
Dim mcnn As SqlConnection = _
 New SqlConnection("Data Source=(local);" & _
 "Initial Catalog=Northwind;Integrated Security=SSPI")
Dim mds As DataSet = New DataSet()
Dim mda As SqlDataAdapter = New SqlDataAdapter()

Private Sub StepByStep6_26_Load( _
 ByVal sender As System.Object, _
 ByVal e As System.EventArgs) Handles MyBase.Load
```

continues

continued

```
' Create a SqlCommand to select data
Dim cmdSelect As SqlCommand = mcnn.CreateCommand()
cmdSelect.CommandType = CommandType.Text
cmdSelect.CommandText = _
 "SELECT CustomerID, ContactName FROM Customers"
' Create a SqlCommand to delete data
Dim cmdDelete As SqlCommand = mcnn.CreateCommand()
cmdDelete.CommandType = CommandType.Text
cmdDelete.CommandText = "DELETE FROM Customers " & _
 "WHERE CustomerID = @CustomerID"
cmdDelete.Parameters.Add( _
 "@CustomerID", SqlDbType.NChar, _
 5, "CustomerID")
cmdDelete.Parameters("@CustomerID").SourceVersion = _
 DataRowVersion.Original
' Set up the DataAdapter and fill the DataSet
mda.SelectCommand = cmdSelect
mda.DeleteCommand = cmdDelete
mda.Fill(mds, "Customers")
End Sub
```

5. Enter this code to handle the `Click` event of the Button control:

```
Private Sub btnDelete_Click(ByVal sender As System.Object, _
 ByVal e As System.EventArgs) Handles btnDelete.Click
    ' Prompt the user for a customer ID
    Dim strCustomerID As String = _
     InputBox("Enter Customer ID to delete:")
    ' Find the specified row and delete it
    Dim dr As DataRow
    For Each dr In mds.Tables("Customers").Rows
        If dr(0) = strCustomerID Then
            mds.Tables("Customers").Rows.Remove(dr)
            Exit For
        End If
    Next
    ' Save the changes
    mda.Update(mds, "Customers")
    MessageBox.Show("Row deleted!")
End Sub
```

6. Set the form as the startup object for the project.

7. Run the project and click the button. The code will prompt you for a CustomerID value. Enter a CustomerID (such as ALFKI) and click OK. That customer will be deleted from the DataSet and from the database.

Note that the deletion command uses the original value of the CustomerID column to locate the correct row to delete from the database.

Editing with a DataGrid

The examples you just saw of editing, adding, and deleting rows are functional but somewhat tedious. Fortunately, easier methods can set these operations up in the user interface. If you bind a DataSet to a DataGrid control, as in Step By Step 6.27, you'll find that the DataGrid enables you to perform all three of the fundamental editing operations:

◆ To update the data in a row, click in the column to be updated and type a new value.

◆ To add a new row, scroll to the end of the list and type the values for the row into the last row of the DataGrid.

◆ To delete a row, click on the record selector to the left of the row and press the Delete key on the keyboard.

If you do use a DataGrid for editing, you should supply SqlCommand objects to handle all the editing operations.

STEP BY STEP

6.27 Editing Data Through a DataGrid Control

1. Add a new form to your Visual Basic .NET project.

2. Place a DataGrid control named dgCustomers and a Button control named btnSaveChanges on the form.

3. Double-click the Button control to open the form's module. Enter these statements at the top of the module:

```
Imports System.Data
Imports System.Data.SqlClient
```

4. Enter this code to load data when the form is opened:

```
' Create some ADO.NET objects
Dim mcnn As SqlConnection = _
 New SqlConnection("Data Source=(local);" & _
 "Initial Catalog=Northwind;Integrated Security=SSPI")
```

continues

continued

```
Dim mds As DataSet = New DataSet()
Dim mda As SqlDataAdapter = New SqlDataAdapter()

Private Sub StepByStep6_27_Load( _
 ByVal sender As System.Object, _
 ByVal e As System.EventArgs) Handles MyBase.Load
    ' Create a SqlCommand to select data
    Dim cmdSelect As SqlCommand = mcnn.CreateCommand()
    cmdSelect.CommandType = CommandType.Text
    cmdSelect.CommandText = _
      "SELECT CustomerID, CompanyName, " & _
      "ContactName FROM Customers"
    ' Create a SqlCommand to update data
    Dim cmdUpdate As SqlCommand = mcnn.CreateCommand()
    cmdUpdate.CommandType = CommandType.Text
    cmdUpdate.CommandText = "UPDATE Customers SET " & _
      "CompanyName = @CompanyName, " & _
      "ContactName = @ContactName " & _
      "WHERE CustomerID = @CustomerID"
    cmdUpdate.Parameters.Add("@ContactName", _
      SqlDbType.NVarChar, _
      30, "ContactName")
    cmdUpdate.Parameters.Add("@CompanyName", _
      SqlDbType.NVarChar, _
      40, "CompanyName")
    cmdUpdate.Parameters.Add("@CustomerID", _
      SqlDbType.NChar, _
      5, "CustomerID")
    cmdUpdate.Parameters("@CustomerID").SourceVersion = _
      DataRowVersion.Original
    ' Create a SqlCommand to insert data
    Dim cmdInsert As SqlCommand = mcnn.CreateCommand()
    cmdInsert.CommandType = CommandType.Text
    cmdInsert.CommandText = "INSERT INTO Customers " & _
      "(CustomerID, CompanyName, ContactName) " & _
      "VALUES(@CustomerID, @CompanyName, @ContactName)"
    cmdInsert.Parameters.Add("@CustomerID", _
      SqlDbType.NChar, _
      5, "CustomerID")
    cmdInsert.Parameters.Add("@CompanyName", _
      SqlDbType.NVarChar, _
      40, "CompanyName")
    cmdInsert.Parameters.Add("@ContactName", _
      SqlDbType.NVarChar, _
      30, "ContactName")
    cmdInsert.Parameters("@CustomerID").SourceVersion = _
      DataRowVersion.Original
    ' Create a SqlCommand to delete data
    Dim cmdDelete As SqlCommand = mcnn.CreateCommand()
    cmdDelete.CommandType = CommandType.Text
    cmdDelete.CommandText = "DELETE FROM Customers " & _
      "WHERE CustomerID = @CustomerID"
```

```
cmdDelete.Parameters.Add("@CustomerID", _
 SqlDbType.NChar, _
 5, "CustomerID")
cmdDelete.Parameters("@CustomerID").SourceVersion = _
 DataRowVersion.Original
' Set up the DataAdapter and fill the DataSet
mda.SelectCommand = cmdSelect
mda.UpdateCommand = cmdUpdate
mda.InsertCommand = cmdInsert
mda.DeleteCommand = cmdDelete
mda.Fill(mds, "Customers")
' And bind the data to the DataGrid
dgCustomers.DataSource = mds
dgCustomers.DataMember = "Customers"
End Sub
```

5. Enter this code to handle the Click event of the Button control:

```
Private Sub btnSaveChanges_Click(_
 ByVal sender As System.Object, _
 ByVal e As System.EventArgs) _
 Handles btnSaveChanges.Click
    ' Persist all changes from the data model to the
    database
    mda.Update(mds, "Customers")
End Sub
```

6. Set the form as the startup object for the project.

7. Run the project. Make some changes in the DataGrid and click the Save Changes button. If you run the project a second time, you should find that all the changes were saved to the database.

Although Step By Step 6.27 has a lot of code, it's just a combination of the code you saw in the previous three examples. To set up a SqlDataAdapter to handle all possible changes, you must supply all the necessary SqlCommand objects. The Update method of the SqlDataAdapter calls the appropriate SqlCommand object for each change.

REVIEW BREAK

▶ Changing data in a DataSet can be done by treating the items in the DataSet like any other variable.

continues

continued

▶ To persist changes from the data model to the underlying database you must call the Update method of the SqlDataAdapter object.

▶ The UpdateCommand property of the SqlDataAdapter object specifies a SqlCommand object to be executed for all changed rows.

▶ The InsertCommand property of the SqlDataAdapter object specifies a SqlCommand object to be executed for all new rows.

▶ The DeleteCommand property of the SqlDataAdapter object specifies a SqlCommand object to be executed for all deleted rows.

▶ The DataGrid control can provide a convenient way to handle data changes on the user interface.

Using XML Data

The final type of data you'll learn about in this chapter is XML data. XML (Extensible Markup Language) is an entire family of closely related standards. For example, an XSD (XML Schema Definition) file is a special type of XML file optimized for storing schema information. You saw XSD files in action in the section on strongly typed DataSets earlier in the chapter.

In this section of the chapter, I'll introduce you to the basic terminology and format of XML files. Then you'll see the XmlDocument and XmlNode classes, which are part of the System.Xml namespace. These classes provide an internal representation of XML that your .NET applications can make use of. Finally, to tie things together, you'll see how to synchronize data in a DataSet with data in an XmlDocument.

XML Basics

If you're already familiar with XML, you might want to skip this section, but if you're still confused about the whole XML thing, follow along. You'll find that the basics are not that difficult, though some people seem determined to make XML harder than it has to be.

NOTE

XML Training   This chapter contains enough information on XML for you to pass the 70-306 exam, but it barely scratches the surface of XML's complexity. For much more information on XML and related topics, see *MCSD Training Guide: Exam 70-310*, which will be published in early 2003.

First, a definition: *XML* is just human-readable data combined with human-readable metadata. That is, XML files are in regular text, so you can read them. And they contain both data (such as information about customers) and descriptions of that data.

Here's a concrete example to start with. This XML file represents data for two customers:

```
<?xml version="1.0" encoding="UTF-8"?>
<!-- Customer list for Bob's Tractor Parts -->
<Customers>
    <Customer CustomerNumber="1">
        <CustomerName>Lambert Tractor Works</CustomerName>
        <CustomerCity>Millbank</CustomerCity>
        <CustomerState>WA</CustomerState>
    </Customer>
    <Customer CustomerNumber="2">
        <CustomerName><![CDATA[Joe's Garage]]>
        </CustomerName>
        <CustomerCity>Doppel</CustomerCity>
        <CustomerState>OR</CustomerState>
    </Customer>
</Customers>
```

Even without knowing anything about XML, you can make some observations just by looking at the file. In particular, XML consists of tags (which are contained within angle brackets) and data. Tags come in pairs, with each opening tag matched by a closing tag. The closing tag has the same text as the opening tag, prefixed with a forward slash.

The first statement you'll find in an XML file is the *XML declaration*:

```
<?xml version="1.0" encoding="UTF-8"?>
```

The declaration gives three facts about this document:

◆ It's an XML document.

◆ It conforms to the XML 1.0 specification.

◆ It uses the UTF-8 character set (a standard set of characters for the western alphabet).

Tags in an XML document contain the names of elements. If you're familiar with HTML, you'll know that some elements have names dictated by the HTML specification. For example, the <H1> tag specifies a first-level heading. XML takes a different approach.

You can make up any name you like for an element, subject to some simple naming rules:

◆ Names can contain any alphanumeric character.

◆ Names can contain underscores, hyphens, and periods.

◆ Names must not contain any whitespace.

◆ Names must start with a letter or underscore.

A start tag together with an end tag and the content between them defines an *element*. For example, here's a single element from the sample document:

```
<CustomerState>OR</CustomerState>
```

That defines an element whose name is CustomerState and whose value is OR.

Elements can be nested, but they cannot overlap. So this is legal XML, defining an element named Customer with three child elements:

```
<Customer CustomerNumber="1">
    <CustomerName>Lambert Tractor Works</CustomerName>
    <CustomerCity>Millbank</CustomerCity>
    <CustomerState>WA</CustomerState>
</Customer>
```

But this is not legal XML because the CustomerCity and CustomerState elements overlap:

```
<Customer CustomerNumber="1">
    <CustomerName>Lambert Tractor Works</CustomerName>
    <CustomerCity>Millbank</CustomerState>
    <CustomerState>WA</CustomerCity>
</Customer>
```

Every XML document contains a single root element. The root element in the sample document is named Customers. The effect of these rules (nesting is okay, overlapping is not, and the document contains a single root element) is that any XML document can be represented as a tree of nodes.

Elements can contain attributes. An *attribute* is a piece of data that further describes an element. For example, the sample document includes this opening tag for an element:

```
<Customer CustomerNumber="1">
```

That declares an element named Customer. The Customer element includes an attribute whose name is CustomerNumber and whose value is 1.

XML documents can contain one or more *namespace* declarations. The sample document does not declare a namespace. Here's the syntax for a namespace declaration:

```
<Customers xmlns:tr="urn:schemas-tractor-repair">
```

The namespace is declared as part of the root tag for the document. In this particular case, the namespace (introduced with the special xmlns characters) defines a prefix of tr for tags within the namespace. The urn (Uniform Resource Name) value is an arbitrary string whose purpose is to distinguish this namespace from other namespaces.

XML namespaces serve the same purpose as .NET namespaces: They help cut down on naming collisions. After declaring the tr namespace, an XML document could use a tag such as

```
<tr:CustomerState>OR</tr:CustomerState>
```

That indicates that this CustomerState tag is from the tr namespace and should not be confused with any other CustomerState tag.

XML offers two ways to deal with special characters in data. First, for individual characters you can use entity references. Five entity references are defined in the XML standard:

◆ &lt translates to < (opening angle bracket).

◆ &gt translates to > (closing angle bracket).

◆ &amp translates to & (ampersand).

◆ &apos translates to ' (apostrophe).

◆ &quot translates to " (quotation mark).

You can also use a CDATA section to hold any arbitrary data, whether the data contains special characters or not. The sample document uses this approach to store a customer name containing an apostrophe:

```
<CustomerName><![CDATA[Joe's Garage]]>
</CustomerName>
```

Finally, an XML document can contain comments. Comments are set off by the opening string <! — and the closing string —>. Here's an example:

```
<!-- Customer list for Bob's Tractor Parts -->
```

A great deal more complexity is available in XML than I've covered in this section. But these basics are more than enough to understand most of the XML you're likely to run across until you start working with XML in depth.

Using the XmlDocument Class

XML documents on disk are just disk files, so you could read them with the System.IO classes that you learned about earlier in the chapter. But XML is so central to the .NET Framework that the Framework provides classes especially for working with XML.

To understand the .NET Framework representation of an XML document, you can start with the concept of a node. A node is one item in an XML document: It might be an attribute, a comment, an element, or something else. In the System.Xml namespace, nodes are represented by XmlNode objects. Table 6.14 shows the most important members of the XmlNode object.

TABLE 6.14

XMLNODE OBJECT MEMBERS

Member	Type	Description
AppendChild	Method	Adds a new child node to the end of the node's list of children.
Attributes	Property	A collection of the attributes of the node.
ChildNodes	Property	A collection of child nodes of the node.
FirstChild	Property	The first child node of the node.
InnerText	Property	The value of the node and all its children.
InnerXml	Property	XML representing just the children of the node.
InsertAfter	Method	Inserts a new node after the node.
InsertBefore	Method	Inserts a new node before the node.
LastChild	Property	The last child node of the node.
Name	Property	The name of the node.

Member	Type	Description
NextSibling	Property	The next child node of the node's parent node.
NodeType	Property	The type of node. The XmlNodeType enumeration includes values for all possible node types.
OuterXml	Property	XML representing the node and all its children.
ParentNode	Property	The parent of the node.
PrependChild	Method	Adds a new child node to the start of the node's list of children.
PreviousSibling	Method	The previous child node of the node's parent node.
RemoveAll	Method	Removes all children of the node.
RemoveChild	Method	Removes a specified child of the node.
ReplaceChild	Method	Replaces a child node with a new node.
Value	Property	Value of the node.

> **EXAM TIP**
>
> **Get the Big Picture** Don't worry about memorizing the complete list of XmlNode members. Instead, concentrate on understanding the big picture: There are rich methods for navigating the tree of nodes and for altering existing nodes.

XmlNode objects are collected into an XmlDocument object. As you can probably guess, XmlDocument is the object in the System.Xml namespace that represents an entire XML document. Table 6.15 shows the most important members of the XmlDocument object.

TABLE 6.15

XmlDocument Object Members

Member	Type	Description
CreateAttribute	Method	Creates a new attribute node
CreateElement	Method	Creates a new element node
CreateNode	Method	Creates a new XmlNode object
DocumentElement	Property	Returns the XmlNode object that represents the root node of the document
GetElementsByTagName	Method	Returns a list of all elements with the specified tag name
Load	Method	Loads an XML document
LoadXml	Method	Loads a string of XML
Save	Method	Saves the XmlDocument as a file or stream
WriteTo	Method	Saves the XmlDocument to an XmlWriter

You can use the XmlDocument and XmlNode objects to display the contents of any XML document, as Step By Step 6.28 demontrates.

STEP BY STEP

6.28 Displaying the Contents of an XML Document

1. Add a new form to your Visual Basic .NET project.

2. Place a ListBox control named lbNodes and a Button control named btnLoadXml on the form.

3. Double-click the Button control to open the form's module. Enter these statements at the top of the module:

```
Imports System.Xml
```

4. Enter this code to load data when the button is clicked:

```
Private Sub btnLoadXml_Click( _
 ByVal sender As System.Object, _
 ByVal e As System.EventArgs) Handles btnLoadXml.Click
    ' Browse for an XML file
    Dim dlgOpen As New OpenFileDialog()
    dlgOpen.Title = "Select a File"
    dlgOpen.Filter = _
     "XML files (*.xml)|*.xml|All Files(*.*)|*.*"
    If dlgOpen.ShowDialog = DialogResult.OK Then
        ' Hook up to the disk file
        Dim xtr As New XmlTextReader(dlgOpen.FileName)
        xtr.WhitespaceHandling = WhitespaceHandling.None
        Dim xd As XmlDocument = New XmlDocument()
        ' Load the file into the XmlDocument
        xd.Load(xtr)
        ' Add an item representing
        ' the document to the ListBox
        lbNodes.Items.Add("XML Document")
        ' Find the root node, and add
        ' it together with its children
        Dim xnod As XmlNode = xd.DocumentElement
        AddWithChildren(xnod, 1)
    End If
End Sub

Private Sub AddWithChildren( _
 ByVal xnod As XmlNode, ByVal intLevel As Integer)
    ' Adds a node to the ListBox,
    ' together with its children.
    ' intLevel controls the depth of indenting
    Dim xnodWorking As XmlNode
    Dim tnodWorking As TreeNode
    Dim tnodAttribute As TreeNode
```

```
    Dim strIndent As String = New String(" ", 2 * intLevel)
    ' Get the value of the node (if any)
    Dim strValue As String = CType(xnod.Value, String)
    If Len(strValue) > 0 Then
        strValue = " : " & strValue
    End If
    ' Add the node details to the ListBox
    lbNodes.Items.Add(strIndent & xnod.Name & strValue)
    ' For an element node, retrieve the attributes
    If xnod.NodeType = XmlNodeType.Element Then
        Dim mapAttributes As XmlNamedNodeMap = _
         xnod.Attributes
        Dim xnodAttribute As XmlNode
        ' Add the attrbutes to the ListBox
        For Each xnodAttribute In mapAttributes
            lbNodes.Items.Add(strIndent & "  " & _
             xnodAttribute.Name & " : " & _
             xnodAttribute.Value)
        Next
    End If
    ' If there are any child nodes,
    ' call this procedure recursively
    If xnod.HasChildNodes Then
        xnodWorking = xnod.FirstChild
        Do Until IsNothing(xnodWorking)
            AddWithChildren(xnodWorking, intLevel + 1)
            xnodWorking = xnodWorking.NextSibling
        Loop
    End If
End Sub
```

5. Set the form as the startup object for the project.

6. Run the project. Click the button and browse to an XML file. The contents of the XML will be dumped to the ListBox control, as shown in Figure 6.26.

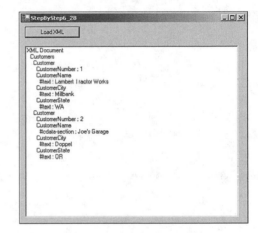

FIGURE 6.26

Viewing a list of nodes from an XML file.

As you can see in Figure 6.26, the object model implemented in the XmlDocument and XmlNode objects has access to the entire contents of the XML file. This code uses an XmlTextReader object to read the disk file into the XmlDocument object. The XmlTextReader has very similar functionality to the StreamReader and BinaryReader objects that you saw earlier in the chapter, except that it's designed to pipe data from a disk file to an XmlDocument object. The XmlTextReader also has other XML-specific features. For example, the WhitespaceHandling property setting in this code tells it not to create nodes for extra whitespace in the XML file.

The code uses the DocumentElement property of the XmlDocument object to find the node at the root of the tree representation of the XML. After that, it's just a matter of recursively calling a procedure that adds information about the node to the ListBox control.

One bit of added complexity in the code is necessary to deal with attributes. Attribute nodes are not included in the ChildNodes collection of a node in the XmlDocument. Instead, you can use the Attributes property of the XmlNode object to get a collection of attribute nodes only. The code uses an XmlNamedNodeMap object to hold this collection; this object can hold an arbitrary collection of XmlNode objects of any type.

You can also modify an XML document through the XmlDocument object, as in Step By Step 6.29. To do so, you must modify the individual XmlNode objects and then write the file back out to disk.

STEP BY STEP

6.29 Modifying an XML File in Code

1. Add a new form to your Visual Basic .NET project.

2. Place a Button control named btnModify on the form.

3. Double-click the Button control to open the form's module. Enter this statement at the top of the module:

```
Imports System.Xml
```

4. Enter this code to load and modify data when the button is clicked:

```
Private Sub btnModify_Click(ByVal sender As System.Object, _
 ByVal e As System.EventArgs) Handles btnModify.Click
    ' Browse for an XML file
    Dim dlgOpen As New OpenFileDialog()
    dlgOpen.Title = "Select a File"
    dlgOpen.Filter = _
    "XML files (*.xml)|*.xml|All Files(*.*)|*.*"
    If dlgOpen.ShowDialog = DialogResult.OK Then
        ' Hook up to the disk file
        Dim xtr As New XmlTextReader(dlgOpen.FileName)
        xtr.WhitespaceHandling = WhitespaceHandling.None
        Dim xd As XmlDocument = New XmlDocument()
```

```
        ' Load the file into the XmlDocument
        xd.Load(xtr)
        xtr.Close()
        ' Find the root node, and modify
        ' it together with its children
        Dim xnod As XmlNode = xd.DocumentElement
        ModifyWithChildren(xnod)
        ' Write the modified file to disk
        Dim xtw As XmlTextWriter = _
         New XmlTextWriter(dlgOpen.FileName & _
         ".new", System.Text.Encoding.UTF8)
        xd.WriteTo(xtw)
        xtw.Flush()
        xtw.Close()
        MessageBox.Show("Done!")
    End If
End Sub

Private Sub ModifyWithChildren(ByVal xnod As XmlNode)
    ' Sets all CustomerCity nodes to uppercase
    Dim xnodWorking As XmlNode
    Dim tnodWorking As TreeNode

    If xnod.Name = "CustomerCity" Then
        xnod.FirstChild.Value = _
          xnod.FirstChild.Value.ToUpper
    End If
    ' If there are any child nodes,
    ' call this procedure recursively
    If xnod.HasChildNodes Then
        xnodWorking = xnod.FirstChild
        Do Until IsNothing(xnodWorking)
            ModifyWithChildren(xnodWorking)
            xnodWorking = xnodWorking.NextSibling
        Loop
    End If
End Sub
```

5. Set the form as the startup object for the project.

6. Run the project. Click the button and browse to an XML file. The code will make a copy of the XML file with the added extension .new. The copy will have all the CustomerState values converted to uppercase.

Writing the XML file out uses one new class, the XmlTextWriter. This class connects an XmlDocument to a backing store for output, similar to the StreamWriter you saw earlier in the chapter.

Treating XML As Relational Data

You can also treat an XML document as relational data. To do this, you can use an XmlDataDocument class, which inherits from the XmlDocument. The key feature of the XmlDataDocument class is that it can be synchronized with a DataSet, as in Step By Step 6.30. Guided Practice Exercise 6.4 will give you additional practice in using XML documents and databases together.

STEP BY STEP

6.30 Reading an XML Document into a DataSet

1. Add a new form to your Visual Basic .NET project.

2. Place a Button control named btnLoadXml and a DataGrid named dgXml on the form.

3. Double-click the Button control to open the form's module. Enter this statement at the top of the module:

```
Imports System.Xml
```

4. Enter this code to load data when the button is clicked:

```
Private Sub btnLoadXml_Click( _
 ByVal sender As System.Object, _
 ByVal e As System.EventArgs) Handles btnLoadXml.Click
    ' Browse for an XML file
    Dim dlgOpen As New OpenFileDialog()
    dlgOpen.Title = "Select a File"
    dlgOpen.Filter = _
     "XML files (*.xml)|*.xml|All Files(*.*)|*.*"
    If dlgOpen.ShowDialog = DialogResult.OK Then
        ' Hook up to the disk file
        Dim xtr As New XmlTextReader(dlgOpen.FileName)
        Dim xdd As XmlDataDocument = New XmlDataDocument()
        ' Get the DataSet
        Dim ds As DataSet = xdd.DataSet
        ' Read the schema of the file
        ' to initialize the DataSet
        ds.ReadXmlSchema(xtr)
        xtr.Close()
        xtr = New XmlTextReader(dlgOpen.FileName)
        xtr.WhitespaceHandling = WhitespaceHandling.None
        ' Load the file into the XmlDataDocument
        xdd.Load(xtr)
        xtr.Close()
        ' And display it on the DataGrid
        dgXml.DataSource = ds
    End If
End Sub
```

5. Set the form as the startup object for the project.

6. Run the project. Click the button and browse to an XML file. The code will load the XML file into the DataSet and display it on the user interface, as shown in Figure 6.27.

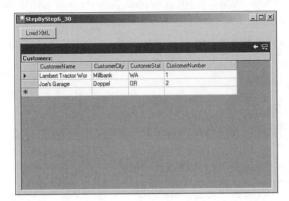

FIGURE 6.27
An XML File displayed as a DataSet.

For the DataSet to properly represent the XML, it must have the same schema (structure) as the XML file. In this example, I've ensured that by using the ReadXmlSchema method of the DataSet to load the schema from the same XML file that the XmlDataDocument holds. The XmlTextReader must be closed and reopened after reading the schema because it's a forward-only object.

The synchronization between the XmlDataDocument and the DataSet is two-way. If you derive a DataSet from an XmlDataDocument, modify the DataSet, and then write the XmlDataDocument back to disk, the changes you made in the DataSet will be reflected in the XML file.

> **NOTE**
>
> **DataSet to XML** You can also go in the other direction: If you've already got a DataSet in your code, you can create the equivalent XML document by calling an overloaded constructor of the XmlDataDocument class:
>
> ```
> Dim xdd As XmlDataDocument
>     = New XmlDataDocument(ds)
> ```

GUIDED PRACTICE EXERCISE 6.4

Northwind Traders has a new European partner who doesn't use Microsoft SQL Server for data storage. However, it can import an XML file to its system. In this exercise, retrieve all the Customers from France, allow the user to edit the customer information on a form, and then save the edited version as an XML file. The edits should *not* be saved to your own database.

continues

continued

Try this on your own first. If you get stuck or would like to see one possible solution, follow these steps:

1. Add a new form to your Visual Basic .NET project.

2. Place a DataGrid control named `dgCustomers` and a Button control named `btnSave` on the form.

3. Double-click the Button control to open the form's module. Enter these statements at the top of the module:

```
Imports System.Data
Imports System.Data.SqlClient
Imports System.Xml
```

4. Enter this code to load the data when the form is opened:

```
Private Sub GuidedPracticeExercise6_4_Load( _
 ByVal sender As System.Object, _
 ByVal e As System.EventArgs) Handles MyBase.Load
    ' Create a SqlConnection
    Dim cnn As SqlConnection = _
     New SqlConnection("Data Source=(local);" & _
     "Initial Catalog=Northwind;Integrated
      Security=SSPI")
    ' Create a SqlCommand
    Dim cmd As SqlCommand = cnn.CreateCommand()
    cmd.CommandType = CommandType.Text
    cmd.CommandText = _
     "SELECT * FROM Customers WHERE Country = 'France'"
    ' Set up the DataAdapter and fill the DataSet
    Dim da As SqlDataAdapter = New SqlDataAdapter()
    da.SelectCommand = cmd
    Dim ds As DataSet = New DataSet()
    da.Fill(ds, "Customers")
    ' Show the data on the user
    ' interface so the user can edit it
    dgCustomers.DataSource = ds
    dgCustomers.DataMember = "Customers"
End Sub
```

5. Enter this code to save the file when the user clicks the button:

```
Private Sub btnSave_Click(ByVal sender As System.Object, _
 ByVal e As System.EventArgs) Handles btnSave.Click
    ' Create an XmlDataDocument from the DataSet
    Dim xdd As XmlDataDocument = _
     New XmlDataDocument(dgCustomers.DataSource)
    ' And save it to a disk file
    Dim xtw As XmlTextWriter = _
     New XmlTextWriter("c:\temp\FranceCust.xml", _
     System.Text.Encoding.UTF8)
```

```
      xdd.WriteTo(xtw)
      xtw.Flush()
      xtw.Close()
      MessageBox.Show("Wrote file c:\temp\FranceCust.xml")
   End Sub
```

6. Run the project. The French customers will appear on the user interface. Edit some of the data and click the Save button. Open the c:\temp\FranceCust.xml file and verify that it contains the edited data.

If you had difficulty following this exercise, review the sections titled "Using the XmlDocument Class" and "Treating XML As Relational Data." The text and examples should help you relearn this material and help understand what just happened in this exercise. After review, try this exercise again.

You could employ several alternatives for meeting the requirements of this Guided Practice Exercise. You could choose to save the DataSet directly instead of working with an XmlDataDocument by working with the DataSet.WriteXml method. If you'd like to let the user browse for a file name instead of hard-coding the file name, refer to the .NET Framework documentation for information on the System.Windows.Forms.SaveFileDialog class.

HANDLE DATA ERRORS

Consuming and Manipulating Data: Handle data errors.

Although I've been leaving error trapping out of the code so far in this chapter for simplicity, in real life you can't afford to do that. You should always check for errors in any production code, so that you can take corrective action if something goes wrong. In this section I'll show how to deal with two groups of data errors. First, you might attempt an operation that causes an error from the underlying database. Second, in a multiuser situation you can have errors caused by two or more users editing the same row of data.

Handling Database Errors

Many things can go wrong when working with a database. You might try to add a duplicate value to a column that only allows unique values, or you might try to write to a table that you don't have permission to modify. In serious cases, the database server itself might run out of disk space. These are just a few of the thousands of specific conditions that can trigger SQL Server errors.

The System.Data.SqlClient namespace includes two objects to help handle SQL Server-specific errors. These are the SqlException class, which inherits from System.Exception, and the SqlError class, which represents a single SQL Server error. Step by Step 6.31 shows how you can use these objects to handle SQL Server errors.

STEP BY STEP

6.31 Trapping SQL Server Errors

1. Add a new form to your Visual Basic .NET project.

2. Place a Button control named btnNew.

3. Double-click the Button control to open the form's module. Enter this statement at the top of the module:

```
Imports System.Data.SqlClient
```

4. Enter this code to handle the button's Click event:

```
Private Sub btnNew_Click( _
 ByVal sender As System.Object, _
 ByVal e As System.EventArgs) Handles btnNew.Click
    Try
        ' Create a SqlConnection
        Dim cnn As SqlConnection = _
         New SqlConnection("Data Source=(local);" & _
         "Initial Catalog=Northwind; " & _
         "Integrated Security=SSPI")
        ' Create a SqlCommand
        Dim cmd As SqlCommand = cnn.CreateCommand()
        cmd.CommandType = CommandType.Text
        cmd.CommandText = "INSERT INTO Customers " & _
         "(CompanyName) VALUES ('New Company')"
        ' And execute it
        cnn.Open()
        cmd.ExecuteNonQuery()
        cnn.Close()
    Catch SqlEx As SqlException
```

```
            ' Handle SQL Server specific errors
            Dim err As SqlError
            For Each err In SqlEx.Errors
                MessageBox.Show("SQL Error " & _
                    err.Number & ": " & err.Message)
            Next
        Catch Ex As Exception
            ' Handle general errors
            MessageBox.Show("Non-SQL Exception " & Ex.Message)
        End Try
End Sub
```

5. Set the form as the startup object for the project.

6. Run the project. Click the button. You'll get a message box that informs you of error 515, Cannot insert the value NULL into column 'CustomerID', table 'Northwind.dbo.Customers'; column does not allow nulls. INSERT fails. When you dismiss this message box, you'll get a second message box that informs you of error 3621, `The statement has been terminated.`

> **EXAM TIP**
>
> **Trap All the Errors** This code actually has two different Catch statements. The first one will catch exceptions packaged as SqlException objects. But even if you're writing data access code, it's possible for nondata-related errors to occur. That's why a second Catch statement uses the generic Exception object. Any time you write code to catch exceptions of a specific type, you should remember to include a general-purpose Catch statement as well, just in case.

As you can see in the code, the SqlException object exposes an Errors property. This property is a collection of SqlError objects, each of which contains a SQL Server error. A single SQL Server operation can raise multiple errors, as it did in this case. You should place a similar error trap in any procedure that uses the classes from System.Data.SqlClient.

Handling Multiuser Errors

You must be aware of a second class of errors when writing database code—though actually, these are better thought of as "potentially unexpected outcomes" than as errors. Whenever you have more than one user updating the same data, concurrency issues can arise. The basic question is who wins in case of multiple updates.

Here's how the problem arises: suppose both Alice and Bob are working with data from the Customers table in a SQL Server database. They've both downloaded a DataSet containing the table to their local computers, and both are making edits in a DataGrid control. Alice changes the address of the first customer in the table, because she's working on a stack of change of address requests.

Meanwhile, Bob changes the contact name for the first customer, because he's updating the sales records. So now there are three versions of the row: the original one that's still on the SQL Server, the one with a new address that's on Alice's computer, and the one with the new contact name that's on Bob's computer. Now Bob saves his changes by calling the Update method of the SqlDataAdapter, so the SQL Server database contains the new contact name.

What happens when Alice saves her changes?

The answer is it depends. When you're creating the SqlCommand object that will be used for the UpdateCommand property of a SqlDataAdapter, it's up to you to choose between two different strategies for dealing with such conflicts:

◆ With optimistic concurrency control, an update to a row will succeed only if no one else has changed that row after it was loaded into the DataSet.

◆ With "last one wins" concurrency control, an update to a row always succeeds, whether another user has edited the row or not (as long as the row still exists).

You've already seen how to implement "last one wins" concurrency control in Step By Step 6.24. Consider the SQL statement that the code in that example uses to update the database:

```
UPDATE Customers
SET ContactName = @ContactName
WHERE CustomerID = @CustomerID
```

The key observation to make is the WHERE clause: The only column it looks at is the CustomerID column. CustomerID is the primary key of this table, a value that should never change. As long as that one column has not been changed, the UPDATE statement will succeed, no matter what might have changed about other columns in the same table. Step by Step 6.32 shows you how to use this technique for optimistic concurrency control.

STEP BY STEP

6.32 Implementing Optimistic Concurrency Control

1. Add a new form to your Visual Basic .NET project.

2. Place a Button control named btnUpdate on the form.

3. Double-click the Button control to open the form's module. Enter these statements at the top of the module:

```
Imports System.Data
Imports System.Data.SqlClient
```

4. Enter this code to load data when the form is opened:

```
' Create some ADO.NET objects
Dim mcnn As SqlConnection = _
 New SqlConnection("Data Source=(local);" & _
 "Initial Catalog=Northwind;Integrated Security=SSPI")
Dim mds As DataSet = New DataSet()
Dim mda As SqlDataAdapter = New SqlDataAdapter()

Private Sub StepByStep6_32_Load( _
 ByVal sender As System.Object, _
 ByVal e As System.EventArgs) Handles MyBase.Load
    ' Create a SqlCommand to select data
    Dim cmdSelect As SqlCommand = mcnn.CreateCommand()
    cmdSelect.CommandType = CommandType.Text
    cmdSelect.CommandText = _
     "SELECT CustomerID, ContactName FROM Customers"
    ' Create a SqlCommand to update data
    Dim cmdUpdate As SqlCommand = mcnn.CreateCommand()
    cmdUpdate.CommandType = CommandType.Text
    cmdUpdate.CommandText = "UPDATE Customers SET " & _
     "ContactName = @ContactName " & _
     "WHERE CustomerID = @CustomerID AND " & _
     "ContactName = @ContactNameOrig"
    cmdUpdate.Parameters.Add("@ContactName", _
     SqlDbType.NVarChar, _
     30, "ContactName")
    cmdUpdate.Parameters.Add("@CustomerID", _
     SqlDbType.NChar, _
     5, "CustomerID")
    cmdUpdate.Parameters("@CustomerID").SourceVersion = _
     DataRowVersion.Original
    cmdUpdate.Parameters.Add("@ContactNameOrig", _
     SqlDbType.NVarChar, _
     30, "ContactName")
    cmdUpdate.Parameters( _
     "@ContactNameOrig").SourceVersion = _
     DataRowVersion.Original
    ' Set up the DataAdapter and fill the DataSet
    mda.SelectCommand = cmdSelect
    mda.UpdateCommand = cmdUpdate
    mda.Fill(mds, "Customers")
End Sub
```

5. Enter this code to handle the Click event of the Button control:

```
Private Sub btnUpdate_Click(ByVal sender As System.Object, _
 ByVal e As System.EventArgs) Handles btnUpdate.Click
```

continues

continued

```
      ' Prompt the user for a customer ID
      Dim strCustomerID As String = _
       InputBox("Enter Customer ID to modify:")
      ' Get just that customer's DataRow
      Dim adrEdit() As DataRow = _
       mds.Tables("Customers").Select( _
       "CustomerID = '" & strCustomerID & "'")
      ' Make sure there's some data
      If UBound(adrEdit) > -1 Then
          ' Prompt for new data and put it in the DataRow
          adrEdit(0)("ContactName") = _
           InputBox("Enter new contact name", , _
           adrEdit(0)("ContactName"))
          ' And save the changes
          mda.Update(mds, "Customers")
      End If
End Sub
```

6. Set the form as the startup object for the project.

7. Run the project and click the button. The code will prompt you for a CustomerID value. Enter a CustomerID (such as ALFKI) and click OK. The code will prompt you for a contact name. Enter a new contact name and click OK. This will write the change back to the database, as you can verify by running the program a second time and changing the same customer's data.

The only difference between this version of the update code and the earlier version is in the UPDATE SQL statement, which now has a different WHERE clause:

```
UPDATE Customers
SET ContactName = @ContactName
WHERE CustomerID = @CustomerID AND
ContactName = @ContactNameOrig
```

The new WHERE clause will only find a row to update if both the CustomerID and ContactName are unchanged from what they were when the row was originally loaded. If you'd like to experiment with this, you can run two copies of the code at the same time. Load the data in both copies, then change the contact name with one copy. You'll find that you cannot then change the contact name with the second copy.

EXAM TIP

Retrieve Whole Tables Strictly speaking, you can only enforce optimistic concurrency control if you check every column of the table in the WHERE clause. If you only retrieve a few columns, it's possible to miss a change in a column that you didn't retrieve.

- Every real-world application should include error trapping. Data manipulation adds some special requirements to error trapping code.

- The SqlException and SqlError objects provide the means to retrieve SQL Server-specific error information.

- You can choose when you're designing update commands between optimistic concurrency and "last one wins" concurrency.

CHAPTER SUMMARY

The .NET Framework offers an incredible amount of flexibility for consuming and manipulating data. In this chapter, you've seen a broad survey of various techniques for dealing with data. As you continue to work with Visual Basic .NET, you'll discover more advanced techniques in all these areas.

SQL Server is an important data source for .NET applications. To deal effectively with SQL Server data, you must have an understanding of the T-SQL language. In this chapter, you learned the basics of T-SQL, including the SELECT, INSERT, UPDATE, and DELETE statements. You also saw how to execute SQL in ad hoc queries and in stored procedures.

The .NET Framework also includes classes for manipulating disk files. These classes are part of the System.IO namespace, which treats data as streams that are supplied by backing stores. You learned how to browse for files as well as how to read and write files.

The major part of the chapter dealt with the ADO.NET objects, which span multiple namespaces. ADO.NET includes both data provider objects, which are tied to specific data sources, and DataSet objects, which provide a purely abstract view of relational data. After seeing the object model, you learned how to apply it to a number of problems, including loading and saving data, finding and sorting data, and editing data.

KEY TERMS

- Ad hoc query
- Attribute
- Backing store
- CDATA Section
- Data provider
- DataSet
- Element
- Identity
- "Last one wins" concurrency control
- Optimistic concurrency control
- OSQL
- Parameter
- Schema
- SQL-92

continues

CHAPTER SUMMARY   *continued*

- SQL Query Analyzer

- Stored procedure

- Stream

- Transact-SQL

- XML

- XML Declaration

- XML Namespace

You also saw the key classes used for dealing with XML. These classes, XmlNode and XmlDocument, are contained in the System.Xml namespace. XML data can also be loaded into DataSet objects, allowing you to treat XML files as relational databases.

Finally, you learned about some of the key issues involved in error handling for data-oriented applications. These include which classes are available for catching SQL Server errors and the issues surrounding multiuser concurrency control.

APPLY YOUR KNOWLEDGE

Exercises

6.1 Preselecting Data with Parameterized Stored Procedures

One of the biggest issues in working with server-side data such as SQL Server data is to minimize the amount of data you load into your application. This is because communications with such servers are typically comparatively slow, while the servers themselves have enough processing power to quickly locate the exact data you want. In this exercise, you'll see how to minimize the amount of data retrieved by using a series of stored procedures with parameters

Estimated Time: 30 minutes.

1. Create a new Visual Basic .NET project for the exercises in this chapter.

2. Add a new form to the project.

3. Place a ComboBox control named cboCustomers, a Button control named btnLoad, and a DataGrid control named dgMain on the form.

4. Double-click the button to open the form's module. Enter these statements at the top of the module:

```
Imports System.Data
Imports System.Data.SqlClient
```

5. Use a tool such as SQL Query Analyzer to create this stored procedure:

```
CREATE PROC procCustomerList
AS
SELECT CustomerID, CompanyName
FROM Customers
ORDER BY CompanyName
```

6. Use a tool such as SQL Query Analyzer to create this stored procedure:

```
CREATE PROC procCustomerDetails
  @CustomerID char(5)
AS
SELECT * FROM Customers
WHERE CustomerID = @CustomerID
```

7. Use a tool such as SQL Query Analyzer to create this stored procedure:

```
CREATE PROC procOrdersForCustomer
  @CustomerID char(5)
AS
SELECT * FROM Orders
WHERE CustomerID = @CustomerID
```

8. To minimize load time, the form will start by loading only the customer list into the ComboBox control. Enter this code to load the customer list:

```
Dim mcnn As SqlConnection = _
 New SqlConnection( _
 "Data Source=(local);" & _
 "Initial Catalog=Northwind;" & _
 "Integrated Security=SSPI")

Private Sub Exercise6_1_Load( _
 ByVal sender As System.Object, _
 ByVal e As System.EventArgs) _
 Handles MyBase.Load
    ' Load the customer list
    Dim cmdCustomers As SqlCommand = _
     mcnn.CreateCommand
    cmdCustomers.CommandType = _
     CommandType.StoredProcedure
    cmdCustomers.CommandText = _
     "procCustomerList"
    mcnn.Open()
    Dim ds As DataSet = New DataSet()
    Dim da As SqlDataAdapter = _
     New SqlDataAdapter()
    da.SelectCommand = cmdCustomers
    da.Fill(ds, "Customers")
    With cboCustomers
        .DataSource = ds.Tables("Customers")
        .DisplayMember = "CompanyName"
        .ValueMember = "CustomerID"
    End With
    mcnn.Close()
End Sub
```

APPLY YOUR KNOWLEDGE

9. When the user clicks the Load button, you'll use the other stored procedures to load only the data of interest. Enter this code to build the DataSet and bind it to the DataGrid:

```
Private Sub btnLoad_Click( _
 ByVal sender As System.Object, _
 ByVal e As System.EventArgs) _
 Handles btnLoad.Click
    ' Create a new DataSet
    Dim ds As DataSet = New DataSet()
    ' Load only the customer of interest
    Dim cmdCustomer As SqlCommand = _
     mcnn.CreateCommand()
    cmdCustomer.CommandType = _
     CommandType.StoredProcedure
    cmdCustomer.CommandText = _
     "procCustomerDetails"
    cmdCustomer.Parameters.Add(New _
     SqlParameter("@CustomerID", _
      SqlDbType.Text, 5))
    cmdCustomer.Parameters( _
     "@CustomerID").Value = _
     cboCustomers.SelectedValue
    Dim daCustomer As SqlDataAdapter = _
     New SqlDataAdapter()
    daCustomer.SelectCommand = cmdCustomer
    daCustomer.Fill(ds, "Customers")
    ' Load the orders for this customer
    Dim cmdOrders As SqlCommand = _
     mcnn.CreateCommand()
    cmdOrders.CommandType = _
     CommandType.StoredProcedure
    cmdOrders.CommandText = _
     "procOrdersForCustomer"
    cmdOrders.Parameters.Add(New _
     SqlParameter("@CustomerID", _
      SqlDbType.Text, 5))
    cmdOrders.Parameters( _
     "@CustomerID").Value = _
     cboCustomers.SelectedValue
    Dim daOrders As SqlDataAdapter = _
     New SqlDataAdapter()
    daOrders.SelectCommand = cmdOrders
    daOrders.Fill(ds, "Orders")
    ' Relate the two DataTables
    Dim relCustOrder As DataRelation = _
     ds.Relations.Add("CustOrder", _
     ds.Tables("Customers"). _
     Columns("CustomerID"), _
     ds.Tables("Orders"). _
     Columns("CustomerID"))
    ' Bind the data to the user interface
    dgMain.DataSource = ds
    dgMain.DataMember = "Customers"
End Sub
```

10. Set the form as the startup form for the project.

11. Run the project. Select a customer from the list in the combo box and then press the Load button. The form will display only the information for that customer, as shown in Figure 6.28.

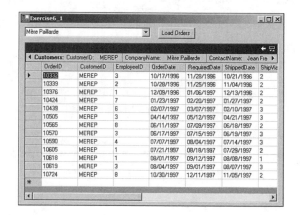

FIGURE 6.28
Retrieving data on a particular customer and their orders.

6.2 Transferring Database Data to a Disk File

The DataSet object has facilities for saving data as XML, but sometimes file size is more important than the readability that XML brings to the table. In this exercise, you'll retrieve data from a database and then use the BinaryWriter class to write it out as a compact disk file.

APPLY YOUR KNOWLEDGE

Estimated Time: 20 minutes.

1. Add a new form to your Visual Basic .NET project.

2. Place a ComboBox control named `cboProducts` and a button control named `btnWrite` on the form.

3. Double-click the button to open the form's module. Enter these statements at the top of the module:

```
Imports System.Data
Imports System.Data.SqlClient
Imports System.IO
```

4. The form will initialize the list of products at load time. Enter this code to load the list of products:

```
Dim mcnn As SqlConnection = _
 New SqlConnection( _
 "Data Source=(local);" & _
 "Initial Catalog=Northwind;" & _
 "Integrated Security=SSPI")

Private Sub Exercise6_2_Load( _
 ByVal sender As System.Object, _
 ByVal e As System.EventArgs) _
 Handles MyBase.Load
    ' Load the customer list
    Dim cmd As SqlCommand = _
     mcnn.CreateCommand()
    cmd.CommandType = CommandType.Text
    cmd.CommandText = _
     "SELECT ProductName, ProductID " & _
     "FROM Products ORDER BY ProductName"
    mcnn.Open()
    Dim ds As DataSet = New DataSet()
    Dim da As SqlDataAdapter = _
     New SqlDataAdapter()
    da.SelectCommand = cmd
    da.Fill(ds, "Products")
    With cboProducts
        .DataSource = ds.Tables("Products")
        .DisplayMember = "ProductName"
        .ValueMember = "ProductID"
    End With
    mcnn.Close()
End Sub
```

5. Enter this code to handle the button's `Click` event. This code retrieves the `DataRow` of interest and then uses a `BinaryWriter` to move it, field by field, to a disk file. The code uses the `SaveFileDialog` class to prompt for a file name.

```
Private Sub btnWrite_Click( _
 ByVal sender As System.Object, _
 ByVal e As System.EventArgs) _
 Handles btnWrite.Click
    ' Get a file name to use
    ' when saving the file
    Dim sfd As SaveFileDialog = _
     New SaveFileDialog()
    sfd.Title = "Choose save file"
    If sfd.ShowDialog() = _
     DialogResult.OK Then
        ' Get the full data on
        ' the selected product
        Dim cmdProduct As SqlCommand = _
         mcnn.CreateCommand()
        cmdProduct.CommandType = _
         CommandType.Text
        cmdProduct.CommandText = _
         "SELECT * FROM Products " & _
         "WHERE ProductID = @ProductID"
        cmdProduct.Parameters.Add(New _
         SqlParameter("@ProductID", _
         SqlDbType.Int))
        cmdProduct.Parameters( _
         "@ProductID").Value = _
         cboProducts.SelectedValue
        ' Open a BinaryWriter
        Dim fsOut As FileStream = _
         New FileStream(sfd.FileName, _
         FileMode.Create)
        Dim bw As BinaryWriter = _
         New BinaryWriter(fsOut)
        ' Get the data into a DataRow
        Dim da As SqlDataAdapter = _
         New SqlDataAdapter()
        da.SelectCommand = cmdProduct
        Dim ds As DataSet = New DataSet()
        da.Fill(ds, "Products")
        Dim dr As DataRow = ds.Tables( _
         "Products").Rows(0)
```

APPLY YOUR KNOWLEDGE

```
        ' And write the data
        Dim intI As Integer
        For intI = 0 To 9
            bw.Write(dr(intI))
        Next
        bw.Flush()
        bw.Close()
        MessageBox.Show("Data written")
    End If
End Sub
```

6. Set the form as the startup form for the project.

7. Run the project. Select a customer from the list in the combo box and click the Write button to save the corresponding `DataRow` through a `BinaryWriter` class.

6.3   Updating Multiple Tables

You've seen how to load data from more than one table into the same DataSet, and how to update a database with changes that were made to a DataSet. In this exercise you'll combine the two and write code to update multiple tables that are contained in a single DataSet.

Estimated Time: 25 minutes.

1. Add a new form to your Visual Basic .NET project.

2. Place a DataGrid control named `dgMain` and a button control named `btnUpdate` on the form.

3. Double-click the button to open the form's module. Enter these statements at the top of the module:

```
Imports System.Data
Imports System.Data.SqlClient
```

4. Enter this code to load data when the form is opened:

```
Dim mcnn As SqlConnection = _
  New SqlConnection( _
  "Data Source=(local);" & _
  "Initial Catalog=Northwind;" & _
  "Integrated Security=SSPI")
Dim mds As DataSet = New DataSet()
Dim mdaCust As SqlDataAdapter = _
  New SqlDataAdapter()
Dim mdaOrders As SqlDataAdapter = _
  New SqlDataAdapter()


Private Sub Exercise6_3_Load( _
 ByVal sender As System.Object, _
 ByVal e As System.EventArgs) _
 Handles MyBase.Load
    ' Create a SqlCommand
    ' to select Customer data
    Dim cmdSelect As SqlCommand = _
     mcnn.CreateCommand()
    cmdSelect.CommandType = CommandType.Text
    cmdSelect.CommandText = _
     "SELECT CustomerID, CompanyName, " & _
     "ContactName FROM Customers"
    ' Create a SqlCommand to
    ' update Customer data
    Dim cmdUpdate As SqlCommand = _
     mcnn.CreateCommand()
    cmdUpdate.CommandType = CommandType.Text
    cmdUpdate.CommandText = _
     "UPDATE Customers SET " & _
     "CompanyName = @CompanyName, " & _
     "ContactName = @ContactName " & _
     "WHERE CustomerID = @CustomerID"
    cmdUpdate.Parameters.Add( _
     "@ContactName", _
     SqlDbType.NVarChar, _
     30, "ContactName")
    cmdUpdate.Parameters.Add( _
     "@CompanyName", _
     SqlDbType.NVarChar, _
     40, "CompanyName")
    cmdUpdate.Parameters.Add( _
     "@CustomerID", _
     SqlDbType.NChar, _
     5, "CustomerID")
    cmdUpdate.Parameters("@CustomerID"). _
     SourceVersion = _
     DataRowVersion.Original
```

APPLY YOUR KNOWLEDGE

```
' Create a SqlCommand to
' insert Customer data
Dim cmdInsert As SqlCommand = _
 mcnn.CreateCommand()
cmdInsert.CommandType = CommandType.Text
cmdInsert.CommandText = _
 "INSERT INTO Customers " & _
 "(CustomerID, CompanyName, " & _
 "ContactName) " & _
 "VALUES(@CustomerID, " & _
 "@CompanyName, @ContactName)"
cmdInsert.Parameters.Add( _
 "@CustomerID", _
 SqlDbType.NChar, _
 5, "CustomerID")
cmdInsert.Parameters.Add( _
 "@CompanyName", _
 SqlDbType.NVarChar, _
 40, "CompanyName")
cmdInsert.Parameters.Add( _
 "@ContactName", _
 SqlDbType.NVarChar, _
 30, "ContactName")
cmdInsert.Parameters( _
 "@CustomerID").SourceVersion = _
 DataRowVersion.Original
' Create a SqlCommand to
' delete Customer data
Dim cmdDelete As SqlCommand = _
 mcnn.CreateCommand()
cmdDelete.CommandType = CommandType.Text
cmdDelete.CommandText = _
 "DELETE FROM Customers " & _
 "WHERE CustomerID = @CustomerID"
cmdDelete.Parameters.Add( _
 "@CustomerID", SqlDbType.NChar, _
 5, "CustomerID")
cmdDelete.Parameters("@CustomerID"). _
 SourceVersion = _
 DataRowVersion.Original
' Set up the DataAdapter
' and fill the DataSet
mdaCust.SelectCommand = cmdSelect
mdaCust.UpdateCommand = cmdUpdate
mdaCust.InsertCommand = cmdInsert
mdaCust.DeleteCommand = cmdDelete
mdaCust.Fill(mds, "Customers")

' Now set up the commands for Orders
Dim cmdSelectOrders As SqlCommand = _
 mcnn.CreateCommand()
cmdSelectOrders.CommandType = _
 CommandType.Text
cmdSelectOrders.CommandText = _
 "SELECT OrderID, CustomerID, " & _
 "OrderDate FROM Orders"
' Create a SqlCommand to
' update Order data
Dim cmdUpdateOrders As SqlCommand = _
 mcnn.CreateCommand()
cmdUpdateOrders.CommandType = _
 CommandType.Text
cmdUpdateOrders.CommandText = _
 "UPDATE Orders SET " & _
 "CustomerID = @CustomerID, " & _
 "OrderDate = @OrderDate " & _
 "WHERE OrderID = @OrderID"
cmdUpdateOrders.Parameters.Add( _
 "@CustomerID", SqlDbType.NChar, _
 5, "CustomerID")
cmdUpdateOrders.Parameters.Add( _
 "@OrderDate", SqlDbType.DateTime)
cmdUpdateOrders.Parameters( _
 "@OrderDate").SourceColumn = _
 "OrderDate"
cmdUpdateOrders.Parameters.Add( _
 "@OrderID", SqlDbType.Int)
cmdUpdateOrders.Parameters( _
 "@OrderID").SourceColumn = "OrderID"
cmdUpdateOrders.Parameters( _
 "@CustomerID").SourceVersion = _
 DataRowVersion.Original
' Create a SqlCommand to
' insert Order data
Dim cmdInsertOrders As SqlCommand = _
 mcnn.CreateCommand()
cmdInsertOrders.CommandType = _
 CommandType.Text
cmdInsertOrders.CommandText = _
 "INSERT INTO Orders " & _
 "(CustomerID, OrderDate) " & _
 "VALUES(@CustomerID, @OrderDate)"
cmdInsertOrders.Parameters.Add( _
 "@CustomerID", SqlDbType.NChar, _
 5, "CustomerID")
cmdInsertOrders.Parameters.Add( _
 "@OrderDate", SqlDbType.DateTime)
cmdInsertOrders.Parameters( _
 "@OrderDate").SourceColumn = _
 "OrderDate"
```

APPLY YOUR KNOWLEDGE

```
' Create a SqlCommand to
' delete Order data
Dim cmdDeleteOrders As SqlCommand = _
  mcnn.CreateCommand()
cmdDeleteOrders.CommandType = _
  CommandType.Text
cmdDeleteOrders.CommandText = _
  "DELETE FROM Orders " & _
  "WHERE OrderOD = @OrderID"
cmdDeleteOrders.Parameters.Add( _
  "@OrderID", SqlDbType.Int)
cmdDeleteOrders.Parameters( _
  "@OrderID").SourceColumn = "OrderID"
cmdDeleteOrders.Parameters( _
  "@OrderID").SourceVersion = _
  DataRowVersion.Original
' Add orders to the DataSet
mdaOrders.SelectCommand = _
  cmdSelectOrders
mdaOrders.UpdateCommand = _
  cmdUpdateOrders
mdaOrders.InsertCommand = _
  cmdInsertOrders
mdaOrders.DeleteCommand = _
  cmdDeleteOrders
mdaOrders.Fill(mds, "Orders")
' Relate the two tables
Dim relCustOrder As DataRelation = _
  mds.Relations.Add("CustOrder", _
  mds.Tables("Customers").Columns( _
  "CustomerID"), _
  mds.Tables("Orders").Columns( _
  "CustomerID"))
' And bind the data to the DataGrid
dgMain.DataSource = mds
dgMain.DataMember = "Customers"
End Sub
```

5. Enter this code to handle the button's `Click` event. This code calls the Update property of each of the DataTables in the DataSet.

```
Private Sub btnUpdate_Click( _
 ByVal sender As System.Object, _
 ByVal e As System.EventArgs) _
 Handles btnUpdate.Click
   ' Update both datatables
   mdaCust.Update(mds, "Customers")
   mdaOrders.Update(mds, "Orders")
End Sub
```

6. Set the form as the startup form for the project.

7. Run the project. Make as many updates as you like and click OK to make the updates a permanent part of the database.

Review Questions

1. Describe the difference between an ad hoc query and a stored procedure.

2. List and describe the four basic T-SQL statements.

3. Name four ways to execute SQL statements.

4. In a T-SQL SELECT statement, what is the difference between the WHERE clause and the HAVING clause?

5. What is the purpose of the @@IDENTITY variable?

6. What is a stream? What is a backing store?

7. How should you decide between using a StreamReader object and using a BinaryReader object?

8. Describe the difference between the data provider objects and the DataSet objects.

9. Which ADO.NET object do you use to execute a stored procedure?

10. Which ADO.NET object transfers data between the database and the data model?

11. What are the advantages of strongly typed DataSets?

12. Which XML object can you synchronize with a DataSet object?

13. Name and describe the two main types of concurrency control that you can implement in .NET.

Exam Questions

1. Your SQL Server database contains a table, Sales, with these columns:

   SalesID (int, identity)

   StoreNumber (int)

   DailySales (int)

   You want to see a list of each store with its total daily sales. The list should be filtered to only include stores whose total daily sales are more than 10. Which SQL statement should you use?

   A. `SELECT StoreNumber, DailySales FROM Sales WHERE DailySales > 10`

   B. `SELECT StoreNumber, SUM(DailySales) FROM Sales WHERE DailySales > 10 GROUP BY StoreNumber`

   C. `SELECT StoreNumber, SUM(DailySales) FROM Sales GROUP BY StoreNumber HAVING SUM(DailySales) > 10`

   D. `SELECT StoreNumber, SUM(DailySales) FROM Sales WHERE DailySales > 10 GROUP BY StoreNumber HAVING SUM(DailySales) > 10`

2. Your SQL Server database contains a table, Sales, with these columns:

   SalesID (int, identity)

   StoreNumber (int)

   DailySales (int)

   You want to see a list of each store with its total daily sales. The list should be filtered to only include rows from the table where the daily sales are more than 10. Which SQL statement should you use?

   A. `SELECT StoreNumber, DailySales FROM Sales WHERE DailySales > 10`

   B. `SELECT StoreNumber, SUM(DailySales) FROM Sales WHERE DailySales > 10 GROUP BY StoreNumber`

   C. `SELECT StoreNumber, SUM(DailySales) FROM Sales GROUP BY StoreNumber HAVING SUM(DailySales) > 10`

   D. `SELECT StoreNumber, SUM(DailySales) FROM Sales WHERE DailySales > 10 GROUP BY StoreNumber HAVING SUM(DailySales) > 10`

3. Your SQL Server database contains a table, Experiments, with the following columns:

   ExperimentID (int, identity)

   ExperimentType (char(1))

   ExperimentDate (datetime)

   You wish to delete all rows from the table where the ExperimentType value is either "A" or "C". You do not wish to delete any other rows. Which SQL statement should you use?

   A. `DELETE FROM Experiments WHERE ExperimentType LIKE '[AC]'`

   B. `DELETE FROM Experiments WHERE ExperimentType LIKE '[A-C]'`

   C. `DELETE FROM Experiments WHERE ExperimentType LIKE 'A' OR 'C'`

   D. `DELETE * FROM Experiments WHERE ExperimentType IN ('A', 'C')`

APPLY YOUR KNOWLEDGE

4. Your SQL Server database contains a table, Sales, with these columns:

SalesID (int, identity)

StoreNumber (int)

DailySales (int)

You wish to create a stored procedure that accepts as inputs the store number and daily sales, inserts a new row in the table with this information, and returns the new identity value. Which SQL statement should you use?

A.

```
CREATE PROCEDURE procInsertSales
  @StoreNumber int,
  @DailySales int,
  @SalesID int
AS
  INSERT INTO Sales (StoreNumber, DailySales)
  VALUES (@StoreNumber, @DailySales)
  SELECT @SalesID = @@IDENTITY
```

B.

```
CREATE PROCEDURE procInsertSales
  @StoreNumber int,
  @DailySales int,
  @SalesID int OUTPUT
AS
  INSERT INTO Sales (SalesID, StoreNumber,
DailySales)
  VALUES (@SalesID, @StoreNumber, @Dai-
lySales)
```

C.

```
CREATE PROCEDURE procInsertSales
  @StoreNumber int,
  @DailySales int,
  @SalesID int OUTPUT
AS
  INSERT INTO Sales (SalesID, StoreNumber,
DailySales)
  VALUES (0, @StoreNumber, @DailySales)
  SELECT @SalesID = @@IDENTITY
```

D.

```
CREATE PROCEDURE procInsertSales
  @StoreNumber int,
  @DailySales int,
  @SalesID int OUTPUT
AS
  INSERT INTO Sales (StoreNumber, DailySales)
  VALUES (@StoreNumber, @DailySales)
  SELECT @SalesID = @@IDENTITY
```

5. Your application has two FileStream objects. The fsIn object is open for reading, and the fsOut object is open for writing. Which code snippet will copy the contents of fsIn to fsOut using a 2K buffer?

A.

```
Dim buf(2048) As Integer
Dim intBytesRead As Integer
Do While ((intBytesRead = _
fsIn.Read(buf, 0, 2048)) > 0)
    fsOut.Write(buf, 0, intBytesRead)
Loop
' Clean up
fsOut.Flush()
fsOut.Close()
fsIn.Close()
```

B.

```
Dim buf(2048) As Integer
Dim intBytesRead As Integer
Do While ((intBytesRead = _
fsIn.Read(buf, 0, 2048)) > 1)
    fsOut.Write(buf, 0, intBytesRead)
Loop
' Clean up
fsOut.Flush()
fsOut.Close()
fsIn.Close()
```

C.

```
Dim buf(2048) As Byte
Dim intBytesRead As Integer
Do While ((intBytesRead = _
fsIn.Read(buf, 0, 2048)) > 0)
    fsOut.Write(buf, 0, intBytesRead)
Loop
```

APPLY YOUR KNOWLEDGE

```
' Clean up
fsOut.Flush()
fsOut.Close()
fsIn.Close()
```

D.

```
Dim buf(2048) As Byte
Dim intBytesRead As Integer
Do While ((intBytesRead = _
fsIn.Read(buf, 0, 2048)) > 1)
    fsOut.Write(buf, 0, intBytesRead)
Loop
' Clean up
fsOut.Flush()
fsOut.Close()
fsIn.Close()
```

6. Your application includes 15 double-precision floating point numbers that you wish to write out to a disk file. You'd like to minimize the size of the disk file. Which object should you use to write the file?

   A. FileStream

   B. StreamWriter

   C. BinaryWriter

   D. XmlTextWriter

7. Your application needs to return the total number of customers in the database. What is the fastest way to do this?

   A. Write ad hoc SQL to return the total number of customers. Use the SqlCommand.ExecuteScalar method to execute the SQL statement.

   B. Write ad hoc SQL to return the total number of customers. Use the SqlDataAdapter.Fill method to execute the SQL statement.

   C. Create a stored procedure to return the total number of customers. Use the SqlCommand.ExecuteScalar method to execute the stored procedure.

   D. Create a stored procedure to return the total number of customers. Use the SqlDataAdapter.Fill method to execute the stored procedure.

8. Your application needs to retrieve a list of customer balances from a SQL Server database. The application will move through the list once, processing each balance in turn. The application does not need to write to the database. Which object should you use to hold the list in the data model?

   A. DataSet

   B. SqlDataReader

   C. DataTable

   D. DataView

9. Your SQL Server database contains customer and order information. The Order table includes a foreign key that refers to the Customer table. You have loaded the Customer and Order tables into a single DataSet through two separate SqlDataAdapter objects. The DataSet is bound to a DataGrid on your application's user interface. When you run the application, only customer information appears in the DataGrid. You have verified that orders are in the database. What is the most likely cause of this problem?

   A. You must use a single SqlDataAdapter object to load both tables.

   B. You have neglected to create a DataRelation object in the DataSet.

   C. No orders for the first customer are displayed on the DataGrid.

   D. The DataGrid can only display information from a single table.

APPLY YOUR KNOWLEDGE

10. Your application uses a SqlDataReader object to retrieve information on customer balances. When you find a past-due balance, you want to write a new entry to a billing table by executing a stored procedure in the same database. You have used a SqlCommand object to represent the stored procedure. Calling the ExecuteNonQuery method of the SqlCommand object is causing an error. What is the most likely cause of this error?

    A. You must use a SqlDataAdapter object to execute the stored procedure.

    B. You must use an ad hoc SQL statement rather than a stored procedure to insert new rows in a database.

    C. You are using the ExecuteNonQuery method of the SqlCommand object and should be using the ExecuteScalar method instead.

    D. You are using the same SqlConnection object for both the SqlDataReader object and the SqlCommand object, and the SqlDataReader is still open when you try to execute the SqlCommand.

11. Your application allows the user to edit product data on a DataGrid control. The DataGrid is bound to a DataSet. The DataSet is filled through a SqlDataAdapter object. The InsertCommand, UpdateCommand, and DeleteCommand properties of the SqlDataAdapter are set to SqlCommand objects, and you have tested the SQL in those SqlCommand objects.

    When users exit the application, none of their changes are saved to the database, and they do not receive any errors. What could be the problem?

    A. You have neglected to call the SqlDataAdapter.Update method in your code.

    B. The users do not have permission to write to the database.

    C. You have neglected to fill the DataSet from the DataGrid after the users finish editing the data.

    D. The DataSet is a read-only object.

12. Your application includes a DataSet that contains a DataTable named Suppliers. This DataTable contains all rows from the Suppliers table in your database. You want to bind an object to a DataGrid on a form such that the DataGrid displays only the Suppliers from Pennsylvania. What should you do?

    A. Create a filtered array by calling the DataTable.Select method on the Suppliers DataTable and bind the array to the DataGrid.

    B. Create a new SqlCommand object to retrieve only suppliers from Pennsylvania. Use a new SqlDataAdapter to fill a new DataSet with these suppliers. Bind the new DataSet to the DataGrid.

    C. Use a For Each loop to move through the entire Suppliers DataTable. Each time you find a DataRow representing a supplier from Pennsylvania, bind that DataRow to the DataGrid.

    D. Create a filtered DataView from the Suppliers DataTable and bind the DataView to the DataGrid.

APPLY YOUR KNOWLEDGE

13. You allow users to edit Product information on a DataGrid bound to a DataSet. When the user clicks the Update button on the form, you call the SqlDataAdapter.Update method to persist the changes from the DataSet to the underlying database.

    Users reports that new records and updated rows are saved properly, but that deleted rows are reappearing the next time they run the application. What could be the problem?

    A. The users do not have permission to update the underlying table.

    B. The Update method does not delete rows.

    C. Someone is restoring an old version of the database between the two executions of the program.

    D. The DeleteCommand property of the SqlDataAdapter points to a SqlCommand object that does not properly delete rows.

14. Your application recursively calls the FirstChild and NextChild methods of XmlNode objects to visit every node in an XML file. When you find a node that includes customer name information, you store the information. The application is not returning all the customer names from the file. What could be the problem?

    A. The XML file is not well formed.

    B. The XML file has more than one root node.

    C. The customer name information is stored in XML attributes.

    D. The HasChildNodes property is not properly set on all nodes.

15. Your application reads an XML file from disk into an XmlDocument object and then modifies some of the nodes in the document. Which object should you use to write the modified XmlDocument object back to disk?

    A. XmlTextWriter

    B. FileStream

    C. StreamWriter

    D. BinaryWriter

16. You have designed your application to use optimistic concurrency control. Alice and Bob each retrieve the Products table to the application at 8:00 AM. The initial price of a Widget is $3. At 8:05 AM, Alice changes the price of a Widget to $4 and saves her changes to the database. At 8:10 AM, Bob changes the price of a Widget to $5 and saves his changes to the database. What will be the price of a Widget in the database at 8:11 AM if no one makes any other changes?

    A. $3

    B. $4

    C. $5

    D. $9

Answers to Review Questions

1. An ad hoc query consists of SQL statements that are sent to the server. A stored procedure consists of SQL statements permanently stored on the server.

APPLY YOUR KNOWLEDGE

2. The SELECT statement retrieves data; the UPDATE statement updates existing data; the INSERT statement adds new data; and the DELETE statement deletes data.

3. Using the Visual Studio IDE, through osql, through SQL Query Analyzer, or with your own home-grown solutions.

4. The WHERE clause restricts the output of the statement. The HAVING clause restricts the rows used as input to an aggregate.

5. The @@IDENTITY variable returns the last identity value to have been assigned to a table.

6. A stream is a file viewed as a list of bytes. A backing store is a place where data can be stored.

7. The StreamReader is most useful when dealing with a line-oriented text file. The BinaryWriter is most useful when you're working with a file in a particular format.

8. There are multiple sets of platform- and product-specific data provider objects. A single set of DataSet objects holds abstract data not directly associated with any database.

9. The SqlCommand object can be used to execute a stored procedure.

10. The SqlDataAdapter object is the pipeline between the data model and the DataSet.

11. Strongly typed DataSets give the benefit of IntelliSense at design time. They also provide faster data binding than automatic DataSets.

12. The XmlDataDocument object can be synchronized with a DataSet.

13. With optimistic concurrency control, an update to a row will succeed only if no one else has changed that row after it was loaded into the DataSet. With "last one wins" concurrency control, an update to a row always succeeds, whether another user has edited the row or not (as long as the row still exists).

Answers to Exam Questions

1. **C.** The GROUP BY clause is required to obtain aggregate numbers. The HAVING clause filters the results after the aggregation has been performed. The answers containing the WHERE clause are incorrect because WHERE filters the input to the aggregations.

2. **B.** The GROUP BY clause is required to obtain aggregate numbers. The WHERE clause filters rows before aggregating them. The answers containing the HAVING clause are incorrect because HAVING filters the results after aggregation.

3. **A.** Answer **B** would also delete rows with an ExperimentType of B. Answer **C** would take the OR of "A" and "C" before evaluating the LIKE clause. DELETE * is not valid T-SQL syntax.

4. **D.** Answer **A** does not indicate that @SalesID is an output parameter. Answers **B** and **C** attempt to insert values into the identity column, rather than letting SQL Server assign the new value.

5. **C.** The Read method will return the number of bytes read, so answers **B** and **D** will fail when there is 1 byte in the file. The Read method reads to a byte array, so answers **A** and **B** will fail because the buffer has the wrong data type.

APPLY YOUR KNOWLEDGE

6. **B.** The BinaryWriter provides a compact format for data storage on disk, as long as you don't need the data to be human-readable. All the other objects will store the data as ASCII text, which will take more space.

7. **C.** Stored procedures execute faster than the corresponding ad hoc SQL statements because stored procedures are stored in the database in compiled form. The ExecuteScalar method is faster than filling a DataSet for returning a single value.

8. **B.** The SqlDataReader gives a fast, forward-only, read-only view of the data. It's ideal for processing all rows once without extra overhead.

9. **B.** Even though the two tables are related in the database, you must still tell the DataSet what the relation is by creating a DataRelation object.

10. **D.** While a SqlDataReader object is open, you cannot execute other commands on the SqlConnection that the SqlDataReader is using.

11. **A.** If you do not call the SqlDataAdapter.Update method, all changes to the data model will be lost. Answer **B** would return an error to the users.

Answer **C** is incorrect because a bound DataSet automatically reflects changes to the DataGrid. Answer **D** is incorrect because DataSets are designed to be edited.

12. **D.** Answers **A** and **C** do not give objects that can be bound to the DataGrid. Answer **B** will work, but retrieving the data from the database a second time will be slower than filtering it from the existing DataTable.

13. **D.** If answers **A** or **C** were the case, none of the changes would be saved. Answer **B** is simply incorrect.

14. **C.** By default, XML attributes do not appear as part of the XmlNodes collections that are traversed by the FirstChild and NextChild methods. If answers **A** or **B** were the case, you would be unable to load the file into an XmlDocument. Answer **D** is incorrect because HasChildNodes is automatically set by the .NET Framework.

15. **A.** The XmlTextWriter is designed to write XML files, preserving the proper XML structure.

16. **B.** With optimistic concurrency control, Bob's change will not be written to the database.

Suggested Readings and Resources

1. Delaney, Kalen. *Inside SQL Server 2000.* Microsoft Press, 2000.

2. Gunderloy, Mike. *ADO and ADO.NET Programming.* Sybex, 2002.

3. .NET Framework SDK Documentation:
   - Accessing Data with ADO.NET

4. SQL Server Books Online
   - Transact-SQL Reference

5. Vaughn, Bill. *ADO.NET and ADO Examples and Best Practices for VB Programmers.* Apress, 2002.

6. Visual Studio .NET Combined Help Collection, "Accessing Data" section.

This chapter covers the following Microsoft-specified objective for the Consuming and Manipulating Data section of the Visual Basic .NET Windows-Based Applications exam:

Instantiate and Invoke a Web service or component.

- **Instantiate and Invoke a Web service.**

▶ Although the exam has only a single objective relating to Web services, this is a major area of .NET. Since the release of .NET, it's easier than ever to build, deploy, and use Web services. In this chapter you'll first learn what Web services are and how they fit into the overall .NET architecture. Then you'll see how to perform basic Web service tasks:

- Create a Web service.

- Discover a Web service.

- Instantiate and invoke a Web service.

CHAPTER 7

Web Services

STUDY STRATEGIES

▶ Use ASP.NET to create a simple Web service. Then use the wsdl.exe tool to create a proxy class for that Web service and instantiate the Web service within your application. Ensure that you understand how to make all the pieces of the process work together.

▶ Use the registry at `http://www.uddi.org/` to explore some available Web services.

▶ If you're reviewing references on Web services to study for the exam, ensure that they're specifically about Microsoft's approach to Web services. Although Web services are broadly interoperable between manufacturers, implementation differences exist.

▶ Use a tool such as the .NET WebService Studio to inspect SOAP message and WSDL files to see what's happening as you interact with a Web service.

INTRODUCTION

You've probably already heard quite a bit of hype about *Web services* in conjunction with .NET. In fact, Microsoft has gone so far as to sometimes describe the .NET Framework as "an XML Web services platform that will enable developers to create programs that transcend device boundaries and fully harness the connectivity of the Internet." You might also run across a lot of complex and confusing explanations of the architecture of these Web services. But at their most basic level, Web services are simple: They are a means for interacting with objects over the Internet.

Seen in that light, Web services are part of a natural progression:

1. Object-oriented languages such as C++ and C# let two objects within the same application interact.

2. Protocols such as COM let two objects on the same computer, but in different applications, interact.

3. Protocols such as DCOM let two objects on different computers, but the same local network, interact.

4. Web services let two objects on different computers, even if they're only connected by the Internet, interact.

In this chapter I'll introduce Web services as they exist in the .NET Framework. You'll see how to build and use Web services in your .NET applications, and learn about the major protocols to use when you communicate with a Web service.

UNDERSTANDING WEB SERVICES

Instantiate and Invoke a Web service.

Before I get into the nuts and bolts of actually working with Web services, I'll give an overview of how they work. The key to understanding Web services is to know something about the protocols that make them possible:

- ◆ SOAP
- ◆ UDDI
- ◆ WSDL

One important thing to realize is that, by default, all communication between Web services servers and their clients is through XML messages transmitted over the HTTP protocol. This has several benefits. First, because Web services messages are formatted as XML, they're reasonably easy for human beings to read and understand. Second, because those messages are transmitted over the pervasive HTTP protocol, they can normally reach any machine on the Internet without worrying about firewalls.

SOAP

For Web services to manipulate objects through XML messages, there must be a way to translate objects (as well as their methods and properties) into XML. This is called SOAP (Simple Object Access Protocol). SOAP encapsulates object calls as XML sent via HTTP.

Using SOAP to communicate with Web services has two major advantages. First, because HTTP is so pervasive, it can travel to any point on the Internet, regardless of intervening hardware or firewalls. Second, because SOAP is XML-based, it can be interpreted by a wide variety of software on many operating systems. Although you'll only work with the Microsoft implementation of Web services in this chapter, numerous Web services tools from other vendors can interoperate with Microsoft-based Web services.

Here's a typical SOAP message sent from a Web services client to a Web services server:

> **EXAM TIP**
>
> **SOAP Over Other Protocols** You'll often read that SOAP messages travel over HTTP. While this is the default for SOAP as implemented by Visual Studio .NET, it's not a part of the SOAP specification. SOAP messages could be sent by email or FTP without losing their content. As a practical matter, SOAP today uses HTTP in almost all cases.

```
<?xml version="1.0" encoding="utf-8"?>
<soap:Envelope
  xmlns:soap="http://schemas.xmlsoap.org/soap/envelope/"
  xmlns:soapenc="http://schemas.xmlsoap.org/soap/encoding/"
  xmlns:tns="http://www.capeclear.com/AirportWeather.wsdl"
  xmlns:types="http://www.capeclear.com/
    AirportWeather.wsdl/encodedTypes"
  xmlns:xsi="http://www.w3.org/2001/XMLSchema-instance"
  xmlns:xsd="http://www.w3.org/2001/XMLSchema">
  <soap:Body soap:encodingStyle=
    "http://schemas.xmlsoap.org/soap/encoding/">
    <q1:getLocation
      xmlns:q1="capeconnect:AirportWeather:Station">
      <arg0 xsi:type="xsd:string">KSEA</arg0>
    </q1:getLocation>
  </soap:Body>
</soap:Envelope>
```

Even without digging into this file in detail, you can see some obvious points:

◆ The SOAP message consists of an envelope and a body.

◆ This particular message invokes a method named `getLocation` from a specified URL.

◆ The method takes a single parameter, `arg0`, which is transmitted as an XML element.

Here's the SOAP message back from the server:

```
<?xml version="1.0" encoding="utf-8"?>
<SOAP-ENV:Envelope
  xmlns:SOAP-ENV="http://schemas.xmlsoap.org/soap/envelope/"
  xmlns:xsd="http://www.w3.org/2001/XMLSchema"
  xmlns:cc1="http://www.capeclear.com/AirportWeather.xsd"
  xmlns:xsi="http://www.w3.org/2001/XMLSchema-instance"
  xmlns:SOAP-ENC=
      "http://schemas.xmlsoap.org/soap/encoding/">
  <SOAP-ENV:Body SOAP-ENV:encodingStyle=
    "http://schemas.xmlsoap.org/soap/encoding/">
    <cc2:getLocationResponse
      xmlns:cc2="capeconnect:AirportWeather:Station"
      SOAP-ENC:root="1">
      <return xsi:type="xsd:string">
        Seattle, Seattle-Tacoma International Airport,
        WA, United States</return>
    </cc2:getLocationResponse>
  </SOAP-ENV:Body>
</SOAP-ENV:Envelope>
```

In the response message, the `getLocationResponse` element is the result of the call to the object on the server. It includes a string wrapped up as an XML element.

Disco and UDDI

Before you can use a Web service, you need to know where to find the service. Handling such requests is the job of several protocols, including Disco and UDDI. These protocols allow you to communicate with a Web server to discover the details of the Web services available at that server.

> **NOTE**
> **XML Files** If you need a refresher on the parts of an XML file, refer to Chapter 6, "Consuming and Manipulating Data."

WSDL

The other prerequisite for using a Web service is knowing the SOAP messages that it can receive and send. You can obtain this knowledge by parsing WSDL files. WSDL (Web Services Description Language) is a standard by which a Web service can tell clients what messages it accepts and which results it will return.

Here's a portion of a WSDL file:

```
<?xml version="1.0" encoding="utf-16"?>
<definitions
  xmlns:http="http://schemas.xmlsoap.org/wsdl/http/"
  xmlns:soap="http://schemas.xmlsoap.org/wsdl/soap/"
  xmlns:s="http://www.w3.org/2001/XMLSchema"
  xmlns:s0="http://www.capeclear.com/AirportWeather.xsd"
  xmlns:soapenc="http://schemas.xmlsoap.org/soap/encoding/"
  xmlns:tns="http://www.capeclear.com/AirportWeather.wsdl"
  xmlns:tm="http://microsoft.com/wsdl/mime/textMatching/"
  xmlns:mime="http://schemas.xmlsoap.org/wsdl/mime/"
  targetNamespace=
    "http://www.capeclear.com/AirportWeather.wsdl"
  name="AirportWeather"
  xmlns="http://schemas.xmlsoap.org/wsdl/">
  <types>
    <s:schema targetNamespace=
        "http://www.capeclear.com/AirportWeather.xsd">
      <s:complexType name="WeatherSummary">
        <s:sequence>
          <s:element minOccurs="1" maxOccurs="1"
            name="location" nillable="true"
            type="s:string" />
          <s:element minOccurs="1" maxOccurs="1"
            name="wind" nillable="true" type="s:string" />
          <s:element minOccurs="1" maxOccurs="1"
            name="sky" nillable="true" type="s:string" />
          <s:element minOccurs="1" maxOccurs="1"
            name="temp" nillable="true" type="s:string" />
          <s:element minOccurs="1" maxOccurs="1"
            name="humidity" nillable="true"
            type="s:string" />
          <s:element minOccurs="1" maxOccurs="1"
            name="pressure" nillable="true"
            type="s:string" />
          <s:element minOccurs="1" maxOccurs="1"
            name="visibility" nillable="true"
            type="s:string" />
        </s:sequence>
      </s:complexType>
    </s:schema>
  </types>
<message name="getHumidity">
  <part name="arg0" type="s:string" />
</message>
```

EXAM TIP

Exposure Is Optional While UDDI and WSDL files make it possible to interact with Web services without prior knowledge, these files are not required for a Web service to function. You can make a Web service available on the Internet without a UDDI or WSDL file. In that case, only clients who already know the expected message formats and location of the Web service can use it.

```
<message name="getHumidityResponse">
  <part name="return" type="s:string" />
</message>
<message name="getLocation">
  <part name="arg0" type="s:string" />
</message>
<message name="getLocationResponse">
  <part name="return" type="s:string" />
</message>
<message name="getOb">
  <part name="arg0" type="s:string" />
</message>
...
```

WSDL files define everything about a Web service:

◆ The data types it can process

◆ The methods it exposes

◆ The URLs through which those methods can be accessed

Invoking Your First Web Service

At this point, I'd like to show a Web service in action. Step By Step 7.1 shows how to use a Web service, in this case one supplied by Microsoft's TerraService geographical information server.

STEP BY STEP

7.1 Invoking a Web Service

1. Open a Visual Basic .NET Windows application in the Visual Studio .NET IDE.

2. Right-click the References folder in Solution Explorer and select Add Web Reference to open the Add Web Reference dialog box.

3. `http://live.capescience.com/wsdl/AirportWeather.wsdl` into the Address bar of the Add Web Reference dialog box and press Enter to connect to the Airport Weather Web service and download the information shown in Figure 7.1.

continues

WARNING

Working with the Internet Most of the examples in this chapter assume you're working on a computer connected to the Internet. It's okay if a proxy server is between you and the Internet, as long as you can connect to Web sites.

NOTE

Airport Codes You can find a list of four-letter ICAO airport codes to use with this Web service at `http://www.house747.freeserve.co.uk/aptcodes.htm`. Codes for airports in the United States all start with K; codes for Canadian airports all start with C.

WARNING

Web Service Stability Web services come and go, and there's no guarantee that the one I'm using in this chapter will still be available when you go to test it. If the Airport Weather Web service doesn't seem to be available, one good way to find others is to use your favorite search engine to look for the term "Web service examples."

continued

FIGURE 7.1
Connect to a Web service over the Internet.

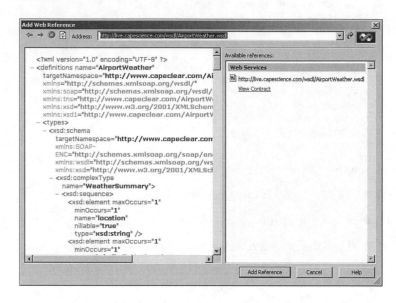

FIGURE 7.2
Create a form to invoke a Web service.

4. Click the Add Reference button.

5. Add a new form to your Visual Basic .NET project.

6. Place a Label control, a TextBox control named `txtCode`, a Button control named `btnGetSummary`, and a ListBox control named `lbResults` on the Form. Figure 7.2 shows this form in Design view.

7. Double-click the Button control to open the form's module. Enter this code to invoke the Web service when the user clicks the button:

```
Private Sub btnGetSummary_Click( _
 ByVal sender As System.Object, _
 ByVal e As System.EventArgs) Handles btnGetSummary.Click
    ' Connect to the Web service by declaring
    ' a variable of the appropriate type
    Dim aw As com.capescience.live.AirportWeather = _
    New com.capescience.live.AirportWeather()

    ' Call the Web service to get the summary
    ' for the entered airport
    Dim ws As com.capescience.live.WeatherSummary = _
    aw.getSummary(txtCode.Text)
```

```
' Display some of the properties
' filled in by the Web service
With lbResults.Items
    .Clear()
    .Add(ws.location)
    .Add("Temperature: " & ws.temp)
    .Add("Visibility: " & ws.visibility)
    .Add("Wind: " & ws.wind)
End With
End Sub
```

8. Set the form as the startup object for the project.

9. Run the project and fill in values for the four TextBox controls. Click the button. After a brief pause while the Web service is invoked, you'll see some information in the ListBox control, as shown in Figure 7.3. This information is delivered from the server where the Web service resides, as properties of the WeatherSummary object.

FIGURE 7.3
Invoke a Web service from a Windows form.

You'll learn more about the techniques in the previous Step By Step in the rest of the chapter, but you should be able to see the broad outlines of Web services already. In one sense, not much is new here, compared to invoking any other object. After setting a reference to the server, you can create objects from that server, invoke their methods, and examine the results. You could do the same with objects from a .NET library on your own computer.

But in another sense, revolutionary work is going on here, even though you don't see most of it happening. When you create the Web reference, for example, Visual Studio .NET reads the appropriate WSDL file to determine which classes and methods are available from the remote server. When you call a method on an object from that server, the .NET infrastructure translates your call and the results into SOAP messages and transmits them without any intervention on your part.

REVIEW BREAK

▶ Web services provide the means to create objects and invoke their methods even though your only connection to the server is via the Internet.

continues

continued

- ▶ Communication with Web services is via XML messages transported by the HTTP protocol.

- ▶ Because they communicate over HTTP, Web services are typically not blocked by firewalls.

- ▶ The Simple Object Access Protocol (SOAP) encapsulates object-oriented messages between Web service clients and servers.

- ▶ The Universal Description, Discovery, and Integration protocol (UDDI) allows you to find Web services by connecting to a directory.

- ▶ The Web Services Description Language (WSDL) lets you retrieve information on the classes and methods supported by a particular Web service.

CREATING WEB SERVICES

To better understand Web services, you should be familiar with both sides of the conversation. In this section, you'll learn how to create a Web service using the tools built into ASP.NET. Although this material won't appear directly on the exam, it will help enhance your understanding of the skills that the exam does measure.

Creating a Web Service Project

To create a Web service, you can build an ASP.NET project in Visual Studio .NET (see Step By Step 7.2). Guided Practice Exercise 7.1 will give you additional practice in this technique.

NOTE

Web Server Required You'll need a Web server available to you to complete these exercises.

STEP BY STEP

7.2 Creating a Web Service

1. Create a new project in Visual Studio .NET. Select the ASP.NET Web Service template and name the new project StringProc, as shown in Figure 7.4. Replace HOURGLASS with the name of your own Web server.

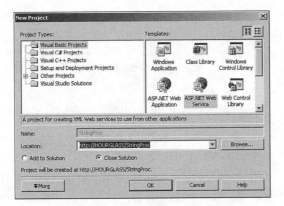

FIGURE 7.4
Create a new Web service project.

2. Right-click the Service1.asmx file in Solution Explorer and rename it `Strings.asmx`.

3. Click the hyperlink on the Strings.asmx design surface to switch to Code view. Enter this code for the class (Don't alter the Web services designer generated code.):

```
Imports System.Web.Services

<WebService(Namespace:="http://NetExam.org/StringProc")> _
Public Class Strings
    Inherits System.Web.Services.WebService

    <WebMethod()> Public Function ToUpper( _
     ByVal inputString As String) _
     As String
        ToUpper = inputString.ToUpper()
    End Function

    <WebMethod()> Public Function ToLower( _
     ByVal inputString As String) _
     As String
        ToLower = inputString.ToLower()
    End Function

End Class
```

4. Save the project.

5. Select Build, Build Solution to create the Web service on the server.

You now have a functioning Web service on your Web server. Congratulations! Although lots of plumbing is involved in properly hooking up a Web service, Visual Studio .NET protects you from having to set up any of this plumbing. Instead, you only have to do three things:

1. Build your project from the ASP.NET Web Service template.

2. Mark the classes that should be available via the Web service with the WebService attribute.

3. Mark the methods that should be available via the Web service with the WebMethod attribute.

Testing the Web Service Project

Visual Studio .NET includes built-in tools for testing a Web service project without building any client applications for the Web service. Step By Step 7.3 shows how to use these tools, which can save time when you're debugging a Web service.

STEP BY STEP

7.3 Testing a Web Service

  1. Start with the Web service project from Step by Step 7.2. Run the project to launch a browser and open the test page shown in Figure 7.5.

FIGURE 7.5
Web service test page.

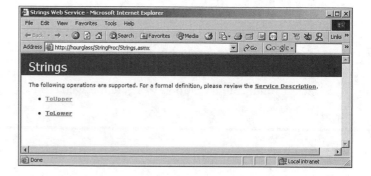

2. Click the Service Description link on the test page to view the WSDL for this Web service. Click the Back button in the browser to return to the test page.

3. Click the ToUpper link on the test page to open a page for testing the ToUpper method, as shown in Figure 7.6.

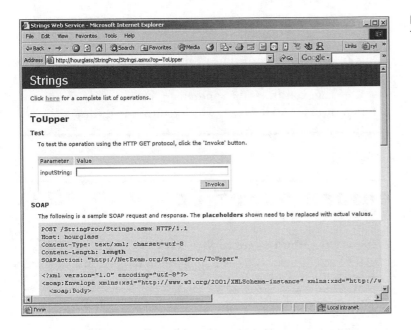

FIGURE 7.6
Test page for a Web method.

4. The Web Method test page shows the SOAP and other messages that the Web service understands. It also contains a form to allow you to test the Web method.

5. Enter a string with mixed upper- and lowercase characters in the inputString prompt.

6. Click the Invoke button. A second browser window will open, as shown in Figure 7.7, with the XML message that the Web service sends back when you call the ToUpper method on your test string.

continues

continued

FIGURE 7.7
Testing a Web Method.

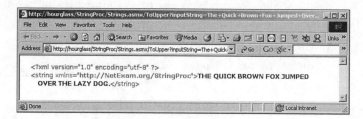

7. You can also experiment with the ToLower method in the same way. When you click the Invoke button, the test page constructs the appropriate XML message and passes it to the Web service, which returns the results.

GUIDED PRACTICE EXERCISE 7.1

In this exercise, you'll connect a Web service to a SQL Server database. The goal is to allow a client application to perform a database lookup via the Web service.

Specifically, the tasks you need to perform are the following:

1. Build a Web service that exposes a single class named Customer. The Customer class should expose a Web method named GetCustomers. The GetCustomers Web method should accept a country name and return a dataset that contains all the customers from that country. Use the data from the Customers table of the Northwind sample database.

2. Build a client application that uses the Web service from step 1. The user should be able to enter a country name and see all the customers from that country.

Try this on your own first. If you get stuck or would like to see one possible solution, follow these steps:

1. Create a new project in Visual Studio .NET. Select the ASP.NET Web Service template and name the new project Northwind.

2. Right-click the Service1.asmx file in Solution Explorer and rename it to `Customer.asmx`.

3. Click the hyperlink on the Strings.asmx design surface to switch to Code view. Change the name of the class to Customer and enter this code at the top of the file:

```
Imports System.Web.Services
Imports System.Data
Imports System.Data.SqlClient
```

4. Enter this code to create the GetCustomers Web method:

```
<WebMethod()> Public Function GetCustomers( _
 ByVal Country As String) As DataSet
    ' Create a SqlConnection
    Dim cnn As SqlConnection = _
     New SqlConnection("Data Source=(local);" & _
     "Initial Catalog=Northwind;Integrated Security=SSPI")
    ' Create a SqlCommand
    Dim cmd As SqlCommand = cnn.CreateCommand()
    cmd.CommandType = CommandType.Text
    cmd.CommandText = _
     "SELECT * FROM Customers WHERE Country = '" & _
     Country & "'"
    ' Set up the DataAdapter and fill the DataSet
    Dim da As SqlDataAdapter = New SqlDataAdapter()
    da.SelectCommand = cmd
    Dim ds As DataSet = New DataSet()
    da.Fill(ds, "Customers")
    ' And return it to the client
    GetCustomers = ds
End Function
```

5. Select Build, Build Solution to create the Web service on the server.

6. Now you can build the client application. Open your Windows application for this chapter and add a new form to the project.

7. Place a Label control, a TextBox control named txtCustomers, a Button control named btnGetCustomers, and a DataGrid control named dgCustomers on the form. Figure 7.8 shows the design of this form.

8. Right-click the References folder in Solution Explorer and select Add Web Reference to open the Add Web Reference dialog box.

FIGURE 7.8
Design a form to test the GetCustomers Web method.

continues

9. Type `http://`*YourServerName*`/Northwind/Customer.asmx` (substituting your own Web server name) into the Address bar of the Add Web Reference dialog box and press Enter to connect to the server and download the information about the Northwind Web service.

10. Click the Add Reference button.

11. Double-click the Button control on the form to open the form's module. Enter this code at the top of the module:

```
Imports System.Data
Imports System.Data.SqlClient
```

12. Enter this code to handle the Button's click event. You'll need to replace the name `hourglass` with the name of your own Web server:

```
Private Sub btnGetCustomers_Click( _
 ByVal sender As System.Object, _
 ByVal e As System.EventArgs) Handles
 btnGetCustomers.Click
    ' Create a DataSet to hold the customers of interest
    Dim dsCustomers As DataSet
    ' Connect to the Web service and retrieve customers
    Dim cust As hourglass.Customer = _
     New hourglass.Customer()
    dsCustomers = cust.GetCustomers(txtCountry.Text)
    ' Bind the results to the user interface
    dgCustomers.DataSource = dsCustomers
    dgCustomers.DataMember = "Customers"
End Sub
```

13. Set the form as the startup object for the project.

14. Run the project and enter a country name (such as France). Click the button. After a brief delay while the project contacts the Web service, the DataGrid will fill with data as shown in Figure 7.9.

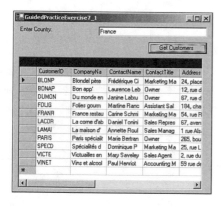

FIGURE 7.9
Data supplied by the GetCustomers Web method.

As this exercise shows, you can return complex objects from a Web service as easily as you can return simple types. The Web service takes care of all the details of converting the `DataSet` to an XML representation, wrapping it in a SOAP message, sending it to the client, and reconstituting the `DataSet` there.

DISCOVERING WEB SERVICES

One of the problems with Web services is simply finding them. Because Web services aren't installed on your computer, you need some way to determine the messages they accept and the services they provide. The usual term for this process is *discovery*, which encompasses both finding Web services and determining their interfaces. You should know about three protocols in this area:

◆ Disco

◆ UDDI

◆ WSDL

Disco and UDDI

Disco is a Microsoft standard for the creation of discovery documents. A Disco document is kept at a standard location on a Web services server and contains paths and other helps for retrieving useful information, such as the WSDL file that describes a service.

UDDI (Universal Description, Discovery, and Integration) is a method for finding services by referring to a central directory. These can be Web services, URIs for information, or any other online resource. UDDI registries are sites that contain information available via UDDI; you can search such a registry to find information about Web services.

UDDI registries come in two forms, public and private. A public UDDI registry is available to all via the Internet and serves as a central repository of information about Web and other services for businesses. A private UDDI registry follows the same specifications as a public UDDI registry but is located on an intranet for the use of workers at one particular enterprise.

> **NOTE**
>
> **The UDDI Project** The UDDI specification is being developed jointly by several industry partners including Microsoft and IBM. For more information and a public directory, visit `http://www.uddi.org`.

Using the Web Services Discovery Tool (disco.exe)

When you set a Web reference inside of Visual Studio .NET, the software handles the details of discovery automatically, but you can also get into the details of the process yourself.

One of the tools included in the .NET Framework SDK (and also in Visual Studio .NET) is the Web Services Discovery tool, disco.exe (see Step By Step 7.4). This is a command-line tool that will assist you in the discovery process.

STEP BY STEP

7.4 Using the Web Services Discovery Tool

1. Select Start, Programs, Microsoft Visual Studio .NET, Visual Studio .NET Tools, Visual Studio .NET Command Prompt. This will open a command prompt window and set up the environment so that you can use any of the command-line tools from the .NET Framework SDK.

2. Enter the following command to discover the details of the Airport Weather Web service:

`disco http://live.capescience.com/wsdl/AirportWeather.wsdl`

As you can see, you need to know the base address of the Web service to use this tool.

3. The tool will contact the Web service and (in this case) create two files of results: AirportWeather.wsdl and results.discomap.

4. Open the files in Visual Studio .NET to see the results of the discovery process.

5. The results.discomap file is an XML file that shows you the name of the other file and the URL from which its content was retrieved.

6. The AirportWeather.wsdl file is an XML file that contains information on the interface of the Web service.

This includes details of the messages, parameters, and objects with which you can interact. This file gives Visual Studio .NET the details it needs to let you use a Web service from your code.

▶ Disco is Microsoft's standard format for discovery documents, which contain information on Web services.

▶ UDDI, the Universal Description, Discovery, and Integration protocol, is a multi-vendor standard for discovering online resources, including Web services.

▶ The Web Services Discovery tool, disco.exe, can retrieve discovery information from a server that exposes a Web service.

INSTANTIATING AND INVOKING WEB SERVICES

After discovering a Web service and retrieving information about its interface, you can instantiate an object representing that Web service and then invoke its methods. In this section you'll see two methods to integrate Web services into your applications and learn about testing a Web service as a consumer.

Creating Proxy Classes with the Web Services Description Language Tool (wsdl.exe)

The .NET Framework SDK includes the Web Services Description Language tool, wsdl.exe. This tool can take a WSDL file and generate a corresponding proxy class that you can use to invoke the Web service (see Step By Step 7.5).

STEP BY STEP

7.5 Using the Web Services Description Language Tool

1. Select Start, Programs, Microsoft Visual Studio .NET, Visual Studio .NET Tools, Visual Studio .NET Command Prompt. This will open a command prompt window and set the environment so that you can use any of the command-line tools from the .NET Framework SDK.

2. Navigate to the folder that contains the WSDL file that you created in Step By Step 7.4.

3. Enter the following command to create a proxy class to call the Airport Weather Web service:

```
wsdl /language:VB /out:aw.vb AirportWeather.wsdl
```

4. The tool will read the WSDL file and create a new file named aw.vb.

5. Add the aw.vb file to your Visual Studio .NET Windows application project by selecting File, Add Existing Item.

6. Add a new form to your Visual Basic .NET project.

7. Place a Label control, a TextBox control named `txtCode`, a Button control named `btnGetSummary`, and a ListBox control named `lbResults` on the Form. Use the same form design that you saw in Figure 7.2.

8. Double-click the Button control to open the form's module. Enter this code to invoke the Web service when the user clicks the button:

```
Private Sub btnGetSummary_Click( _
 ByVal sender As System.Object, _
 ByVal e As System.EventArgs) Handles btnGetSummary.Click
     ' Connect to the Web service by declaring
     ' a variable of the appropriate type
     Dim aw As AirportWeather = _
      New AirportWeather()

     ' Call the Web service to get the summary
     ' for the entered airport
     Dim ws As WeatherSummary = _
      aw.getSummary(txtCode.Text)
```

```
' Display some of the properties
' filled in by the Web service
With lbResults.Items
    .Clear()
    .Add(ws.location)
    .Add("Temperature: " & ws.temp)
    .Add("Visibility: " & ws.visibility)
    .Add("Wind: " & ws.wind)
End With
End Sub
```

9. Set the form as the startup object for the project.

10. Run the project and fill in a value for the airport code. Click the button. After a brief pause while the Web service is invoked, you'll see some information in the ListBox control, as shown in Figure 4.3. This information is delivered from the server where the Web service resides, as properties of the WeatherSummary object. The difference between this and the version that you saw at the start of the chapter is that this code defines the objects that it uses explicitly rather than discovering them at runtime. The AirportWeather and WeatherSummary objects are proxy objects that pass calls through to the Web service and return results from the Web service.

Table 7.1 shows some of the command-line options you can use with wsdl.exe. You don't need to memorize this material, but you should be familiar with the overall capabilities of the tool. You can use either the path to a local WSDL or Disco file or the URL of a remote WSDL or Disco file with this tool.

TABLE 7.1

COMMAND-LINE OPTIONS FOR WSDL.EXE

Option	Meaning
/domain:*DomainName*	Domain name to use when connecting to a server that requires authentication.
/language:*LanguageCode*	Specifies the language for the generated class. The LanguageCode parameter can be CS (for C#), VB (for VB .NET) or JS (for Jscript).
/namespace:*Namespace*	Specifies a namespace for the generated class.

continues

TABLE 7.1	*continued*

COMMAND-LINE OPTIONS FOR WSDL.EXE

Option	*Meaning*
/out:*Filename*	File name for the generated output. If not specified, the file name will be derived from the Web service name.
/password:*Password*	Password to use when connecting to a server that requires authentication.
/protocol	Specifies the default protocol to use in the class. Choose from SOAP (the default), HttpGet, or HttpPost.
/proxy: *url*	Proxy server to use for HTTP Get requests.
/proxydomain:*DomainName*	Domain name to use when connecting to a proxy server that requires authentication.
/password:*Password*	Password to use when connecting to a proxy server that requires authentication.
/username:*Username*	User name to use when connecting to a proxy server that requires authentication.
/server	Generates a class to create a server based on the input file. By default, the tool generates a client proxy object.
/username:*Username*	User name to use when connecting to a server that requires authentication.
/?	Displays full help on the tool.

Using Web References

As an alternative to using the Web Service Discovery tool and the Web Service Description Language tool to create explicit proxy classes, you can simply add a Web reference to your project to enable the project to use the Web service. You've seen Web references several times in this chapter, starting with Step By Step 7.1.

In fact, there's no difference in the end result between using the tools to create a proxy class and adding a Web reference. That's because behind the scenes the Web reference creates its own proxy class. To see this, click the Show All Files toolbar button within Solution Explorer, and then expand the Solution Explorer node for a Web reference. You'll see a set of files similar to that shown in Figure 7.10.

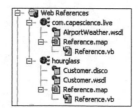

FIGURE 7.10
Files generated by adding a Web reference.

The .disco, .wsdl, and .map files are the same files that would be generated by running the Web Service Discovery tool on the URL of the Web reference. The .vb file defines the proxy objects to be used with the Web service represented by this Web reference, as you can see by opening this file. The major difference between this file and the proxy that you generated with the Web Services Description Language tool is that the auto-generated file uses a namespace based on the name of the Web reference.

Testing a Web Service

If you'd like to test a Web service without building an entire client application, you can use a testing tool. Several of these tools are readily available:

◆ NetTool is a free Web services proxy tool from CapeClear. You can get a copy from `http://capescience.capeclear.com/articles/using_nettool/`.

◆ The .NET WebService Studio tool comes from Microsoft. You can download a free copy from `http://www.gotdotnet.com/team/tools/web_svc/default.aspx`.

◆ XML Spy includes a SOAP debugger that can be used to test Web services. You can download a trial copy of this XML editor and toolkit from `http://www.xmlspy.com/default.asp`.

All three of these tools work in the same basic way: They intercept SOAP messages between Web services clients and servers so that you can inspect and, if you like, alter the results. In Step By Step 7.6 you'll use one of these tools to see a Web service in action.

E X A M   T I P

Why Use a Web Reference? The major benefit of using a Web reference (as opposed to constructing proxy classes with the command-line tools) is that it's easier to update the proxy classes if the Web service changes. All you need to do in that case is right-click the Web reference node in Solution Explorer and select Update Web Reference.

S T E P   B Y   S T E P

7.6 Testing a Web Service Without a Client Project

1. Download the .NET WebService Studio tool from `http://www.gotdotnet.com/team/tools/web_svc/default.aspx` and install it on your computer.

2. Launch the WebServiceStudio.exe application.

continues

continued

3. Enter `http://live.capescience.com/wsdl/`
`AirportWeather.wsdl` as the WSDL endpoint and click the
Get button.

4. The tool will read the WSDL file from the Web service
and construct the necessary proxy classes to invoke it.
Click the GetSummary entry on the Invoke tab to use the
GetSummary Web method.

5. In the Input section, select the arg0 item. You can now
enter a value for this item in the Value section. Enter an
airport code such as "KSEA" for the value.

6. Click the Invoke button. The tool will send a SOAP message to the Web service using your chosen parameters and
then display the results, as shown in Figure 7.11.

FIGURE 7.11
Invoking a Web service with the .NET
WebService Studio tool.

7. Click the Request/Response tab to view the outgoing and
incoming SOAP messages.

8. Click the WSDLs & Proxy tab to see the WSDL file and the generated proxy class for this Web service.

▶ You can generate proxy classes for a Web service manually using the Web Services Description Language tool.

▶ You can generate proxy classes for a Web service automatically by setting a Web reference to point to the Web service.

▶ You can test and debug a Web service without a client application using one of several SOAP proxy tools.

CHAPTER SUMMARY

Web service support is one of the most significant advances in the .NET architecture. The .NET Framework supports both creating and consuming Web services through command-line tools as well as through the Visual Studio .NET IDE.

Web services provide a way to invoke objects over the Internet. A Web service can expose one or more Web methods, each of which can accept parameters and return objects.

Web services use protocols and standards including SOAP, Disco, UDDI, and WSDL to communicate. These protocols are designed to use HTTP as their transmission mechanism, so they are generally not blocked by firewalls.

The .NET Framework includes command-line tools to aid in the discovery and use of Web services. Visual Studio .NET wraps these tools in the simple act of setting a Web reference. Either method produces local proxy classes that you can use to send messages to a Web service and that will return the results from the Web service to the rest of your application.

KEY TERMS

- Disco
- SOAP
- UDDI
- Web method
- Web reference
- Web service
- WSDL

APPLY YOUR KNOWLEDGE

Exercises

7.1 Calling a Web Service Asynchronously

Depending on the speed of your Internet connection, you might have noticed that the Web service client applications you constructed earlier in this chapter "freeze" when you invoke the Web service. That's because by default these applications use synchronous methods to communicate with the Web service, waiting for the SOAP response before allowing any other code to execute. But the proxy classes constructed by .NET include asynchronous methods as well. In this exercise, you'll learn how to call a Web service asynchronously.

Estimated Time: 30 minutes.

1. Open a Visual Basic .NET Windows application in the Visual Studio .NET IDE.

2. Right-click on the References folder in Solution Explorer and select Add Web Reference to open the Add Web Reference dialog box.

3. Type http://hourglass/StringProc/Strings.asmx?wsdl into the Address bar of the Add Web Reference dialog box and press Enter. This connects to the StringProc Web service and creates the appropriate proxy classes, as you learned in this chapter.

4. Click the Add Reference button.

5. Add a new form to your Visual Basic .NET project.

6. Place a TextBox control named txtInput, a Button control named btnUpperCase, and a TextBox control named txtOutput on the form.

7. Double-click the Button control to open the form's module. Enter this code to invoke the Web service when the user clicks the button:

```
Private strUpperCase As String

Private Sub btnUpperCase_Click( _
 ByVal sender As System.Object, _
 ByVal e As System.EventArgs) _
 Handles btnUpperCase.Click
   ' Connect to the Web service
   Dim objStrings As hourglass.Strings = _
   New hourglass.Strings()

   ' Invoke the Web service. This may
   ' take some time
   ' so call it asynchronously.
   ' First, create a callback function
   Dim wcb As New AsyncCallback( _
   AddressOf WebServiceCallback)
   ' And then initiate the asynchronous call
   objStrings.BeginToUpper( _
   txtInput.Text, wcb, objStrings)
End Sub

Public Sub WebServiceCallback( _
 ByVal ar As IAsyncResult)
   ' This function will get called
   ' when the Web service call is done

   ' Retrieve the state of the proxy object
   dim objStrings as hourglass.Strings = _
   ar.AsyncState
   ' Call the End method to finish
   ' processing
   txtOutput.Text = _
   objStrings.EndToUpper(ar)
End Sub
```

8. Set the form as the startup object for the project.

9. Run the project and fill in a value for the input string. Click the button. Wait a few moments, and the output box will show the uppercase version of the input string. Note that while you're waiting (after the initial delay while the form contacts the Web service with the Begin call), you can still drag the form around the screen, which shows that it is not blocked by the Web service call.

APPLY YOUR KNOWLEDGE

If you compare the code for this exercise with the code you saw in Step By Step 7.1, you'll find some significant changes. In the .NET Framework, callback functions manage asynchronous Web service calls. When you add a Web reference, the proxy class includes Begin and End methods for each Web method. In this case, those are the `BeginToUpper` and `EndToUpper` methods.

The Begin method takes all the same parameters as the underlying Web method, plus two others. The first is the address of a callback function, and the second is an object whose properties should be available in the callback function. When you call the Begin method, the .NET Framework launches the call to the Web service in the background. When the Web method call completes, the Callback function will be invoked. The code in this exercise shows how to retrieve the original object and use its End method to finish the work of using the Web service.

Review Questions

1. What is the purpose of a Web service proxy class?

2. Describe the general purpose of SOAP.

3. Describe the general purpose of Disco and UDDI.

4. Describe the general purpose of WSDL.

5. Can a Web service exist without a WSDL file?

6. Explain two ways in which you can create proxy classes for a Web service.

7. List three steps involved in building a Web service using Visual Studio .NET.

8. What tools can you use to make local copies of the configuration files for a Web service?

9. How can you test a Web service without building a client application?

10. What is the advantage of sending SOAP messages over the HTTP protocol?

Exam Questions

1. You want to use a Web service that supplies inventory level information in your application. You know the URL of the asmx file published by the Web service. What step should you take first?

   A. Open the asmx file in a Web browser.

   B. Run the XML Schema Definition tool.

   C. Run the Web Service Discovery tool.

   D. Copy the asmx file to your client project.

2. Your application includes a Web reference to a Web service that delivers customer information as an object with multiple properties. The developer of the Web service has added a new property named CreditRating to the object. What should you do to be able to use the CreditRating property in your code?

   A. Create an entirely new client application and add a Web reference for the Web service to the new application.

   B. Delete and re-create the Web reference in the existing application.

   C. Update the Web reference in the existing application.

   D. Use a generic Object variable to hold customer information, so you can call any property you like.

APPLY YOUR KNOWLEDGE

3. You have created a Web service to return financial information using ASP.NET. One of the methods in your Web service is defined with this code:

```
Public Function Cash() As Double
    ' Calculations omitted
End Function
```

Potential consumers of your Web service report that although they can set a reference to the Web service, the Cash method is not available. What could be the problem?

A. The asmx file for the Web service is not available on your Web server.

B. The Web service class is not marked with the <WebService> attribute.

C. The Cash method is not marked with the <WebMethod> attribute.

D. Web services can only return string values.

4. You have created a new Web service to perform financial calculations. You're working in an ASP.NET project within the Visual Studio .NET environment. What's the easiest way to test your new Web service to ensure that it's returning the proper results?

A. Cut and paste the code into a Windows application project and test it in the new project.

B. Run the Web service project and use the test page that it opens in the browser.

C. Use a tool such as WebService Studio to send SOAP requests directly to the server.

D. Have a large number of beta testers use the application, and monitor the server for odd behavior.

5. Your application uses a Web service named Northwind. The Northwind Web service includes a Web method named Suppliers that returns a DataSet containing all the company's suppliers. What data type should you use to declare an object to hold the result of the Suppliers method?

A. Suppliers.DataSet

B. Dataset

C. Northwind.DataSet

D. DataRow()

6. You're using the Web Services Discovery tool to determine information about a Web service on a particular server. You receive the error message, `The HTML document does not contain Web service discovery information`. What could be the problem?

A. The server address that you typed does not exist.

B. The server requires authentication, and you have entered improper credentials.

C. The Web Services Discovery tool works only on your local computer.

D. No WSDL or Disco file is available at the address that you typed.

7. You are using the Web Services Description Language tool to create a proxy class for a Web service. The Web service exposes a class named Customer. You already have a Customer class in your application. What should you do to allow both classes to coexist in the same application?

A. Use the /namespace option of the Web Services Description Language tool to specify a unique namespace for the new class.

APPLY YOUR KNOWLEDGE

B. Rename the existing class.

C. Use the /out option of the Web Services Description Language tool to specify a unique output file name for the new class.

D. Manually edit the generated proxy class to change the class name it contains.

8. You have used a UDDI registry to locate a Web service that might be able to supply information for your business. You want to test the interface of the Web service to ensure that it meets your requirements before you invest the effort to build a client application. How should you proceed?

A. Use the Web Service Discovery tool to download the WSDL file for the Web service and inspect it in an XML editor.

B. Use the Web Service Description Language tool to create a proxy class for the Web service and inspect the class using a text editor.

C. Craft SOAP messages in an XML editor and use them to test the Web service.

D. Use a tool such as the .NET WebService Studio to exercise the interface of the Web service.

9. Your application calls a Web service that performs complex, time-consuming calculations. Users complain that the user interface of the application freezes while it's recalculating. What can you do to fix this problem?

A. Move the application to a faster computer.

B. Install a faster link to the Internet.

C. Install more memory in the computer.

D. Use asynchronous calls to invoke the Web service.

10. One of your business partners has informed you that she's making her inventory information available via a Web service. You do not know the URL of the Web service. How can you discover the URL?

A. Use the Web Service Discovery tool to download the information.

B. Use the Web Service Description Language tool to create a proxy class.

C. Use a UDDI Registry to locate the Web service.

D. Use a search engine to explore your partner's Web site.

11. What must a developer of a client application that uses a Web service do to make a Web service available asynchronously?

A. Nothing. The client can always call a Web service asynchronously.

B. Use a separate Thread object for each invocation of the Web service.

C. Provide callback functions to invoke the Web service.

D. Host the Web service on an IIS 6.0 server.

12. You are invoking a Web service that returns a dataset object. Which project requires a reference to the System.Data namespace?

A. The client project

B. The Web service project

C. Both the client project and the Web service project

D. Neither project

APPLY YOUR KNOWLEDGE

13. Your application invokes a Web service named Northwind that includes a Web method named GetOrders. GetOrders returns a DataSet containing order information. What must you do to use this dataset in your client application?

    A. Create a new DataSet object and use the ReadXml method of the DataSet to initialize it from the returning SOAP message.

    B. Obtain an XSD file that specifies the schema of the DataSet. Use this XSD file to instantiate a DataSet from the returned data from the GetOrders method.

    C. Assign the return value from the GetOrders method to an array of DataRow variables. Loop through the array to build the DataSet.

    D. Assign the return value from the GetOrders method to a DataSet variable.

14. You have used the Web Services Discovery tool to retrieve information about a Web service named ZipcodeService. Which file will contain the URL for any documentation of the ZipcodeService Web service?

    A. disco.exe

    B. results.discomap

    C. ZipcodeService.wsdl

    D. ZipcodeService.disco

15. You have used the Web Services Description Language tool to create a proxy class for a Web service. When you add the proxy class to your project, you discover that it is coded in the C# language. What must you do to get the proxy class in VB .NET instead of C#?

    A. Manually convert the C# code to VB .NET code.

    B. Rerun the tool, specifying the /language:VB option.

    C. Rerun the tool, specifying the /namespace:VB option.

    D. Select File, Save As and save the file with the .vb extension.

Answers to Review Questions

1. A Web service proxy class is an object you can create on the client to communicate with a Web service. The proxy accepts messages, forwards them to the Web service, and returns the results of those messages.

2. SOAP is designed to encapsulate objects as XML messages. These objects can then be sent via HTTP or other standard communications channels.

3. Disco and UDDI are designed to help you discover the interface details of a Web service.

4. WSDL exists to supply information on the interface of a Web service.

5. A Web service can exist without a WSDL file, but you must know the exact incoming SOAP message that the Web service expects before you can use it.

6. You can create proxy classes for a Web service by using the disco.exe and wsdl.exe tools, or by creating a Web reference within Visual Studio .NET.

7. To build a Web service you must create a new Web service application, mark the classes to be exposed with the <WebService> attribute, and mark the methods to be exposed with the <WebMethod> attribute.

8. The disco.exe tool will make local copies of the configuration files for a Web service. Creating a new Web reference will also create these files.

9. You can use a tool such as .NET WebService Studio to test a Web service without building a client application.

10. Using HTTP as the transport protocol for SOAP messages means that these messages can take advantage of pervasive Internet connectivity to reach their destination.

Answers to Exam Questions

1. **C.** The Web Service Discovery tool will retrieve copies of the files you need to proceed with this project.

2. **C.** The Update Web Reference menu item for a Web reference will refresh local configuration information from the server that hosts the Web service.

3. **C.** All exposed methods of a Web service must be marked with the <WebMethod> attribute.

4. **B.** When you're creating a Web service in ASP.NET, running the project will open a testing form in a browser window.

5. **B.** The client needs to declare the same data type that the server is returning, in this case the DataSet object.

6. **D.** The Web Services Discovery tool requires the URL to a Disco or WSDL file to function.

7. **A.** Specifying a unique namespace for the new object removes the chance that it can clash with a preexisting object name.

8. **D.** By using an automated tool you can avoid tedious and error-prone inspection of the XML files.

9. **D.** Speeding up the client computer will do nothing to speed up the Web service, which runs on the server computer.

10. **C.** UDDI Registries exist so you can find business services by browsing or searching.

11. **A.** Building the proxy class, either with wsdl.exe or by setting a Web reference, automatically creates methods to invoke the Web service asynchronously.

12. **C.** Web services client and server applications must agree on the definition of the data to be exchanged.

13. **D.** The only thing you must do to use a complex variable returned by the Web service is to declare an instance of the same data type in the client application.

14. **D.** The Disco file is the only one that contains pointers to nonXML resources.

15. **B.** The /language option controls the output language of the wsdl.exe tool.

APPLY YOUR KNOWLEDGE

Suggested Readings and Resources

1. Basiura, Russ, et al. *Professional ASP.NET Web Services*. Wrox, 2001.

2. Cerami, Ethan. *Web Services Essentials*. O'Reilly, 2002.

3. .NET Framework SDK Documentation

   • XML Web Services Created Using ASP.NET and XML Web Service Clients

4. Scribner, Kenn and Mark C. Stiver. *Applied SOAP: Implementing .NET XML Web Services*. Sams, 2001.

5. Short, Scott. *Building XML Web Services for the Microsoft .NET Platform*. Microsoft Press, 2000.

6. Visual Studio .NET Combined Help Collection

This chapter covers the following Microsoft-specified objectives for the Creating User Services section of the Visual Basic .NET Windows-Based Applications exam:

Implement Globalization.

- **Implement localizability for the UI.**

- **Convert existing encodings.**

- **Implement right-to-left and left-to-right mirroring.**

- **Prepare culture-specific formatting.**

Validate User Input.

- **Validate non-Latin user input.**

▶ The goal of this particular exam objective is to test your ability to produce what Microsoft calls *world-ready* applications. A world-ready application is one that can be translated for a new culture with minimum recoding (ideally, with no recoding at all). This means you need some way to deal with issues such as

- Different currency symbols for different countries

- Changes of language on the user interface

- Different rules for presenting numbers (for instance, what punctuation is used when formatting a number)

- Cultures that read right-to-left instead of left-to-right

The .NET Framework offers good support for the process of producing world-ready applications.

CHAPTER 8

Globalization

▶ Review the "Globalization" section of the Common Tasks QuickStart tutorial. The QuickStart tutorials are installed as part of the .NET Framework installation.

▶ Experiment with code that uses the CurrentCulture and CurrentUICulture properties.

Set these cultures to several different values and inspect the differences in your code's output.

▶ Change the mirroring of a complex form from one of your own applications and watch how its properties change at runtime.

INTRODUCTION

In the pre-Internet days, it wasn't unusual to design an application to be used in only a single country. Large companies such as Microsoft might produce Windows or Office in a dozen or more languages, but that was unusual. The majority of applications were written in a single human language, and all the users and developers spoke the same language.

These days, though, that approach can seriously limit the market for your software. Most developers need to think from the beginning of a project about translating a user interface into multiple languages, a process known as *localization*. With the Internet as a marketing tool, there's no telling where your next customer will come from.

In support of this new way of working, the .NET Framework provides excellent capabilities for localizing applications. Localization goes far beyond simply translating the text on a user interface. Some of the topics you need to consider include:

- ◆ Translating user interface text, message boxes, and so on.

- ◆ Using encodings to translate characters from one representation to another.

- ◆ Using mirroring to change the direction of text in controls on the user interface.

- ◆ Formatting items such as currency and dates that are presented differently in different locales.

- ◆ Managing data sorts to take different alphabets into account.

In this chapter, you'll learn about the concepts and techniques the .NET Framework makes available for localization. You'll need a basic understanding of the entire process to pass the globalization section of the certification exam.

Understanding Localization and Globalization

If you consider the process of developing an application for multiple locations around the world (say, the United States, Singapore, and Peru), you can see two basic ways to undertake the job:

◆ Write three completely different sets of source code, one for each location where the application will be used.

◆ Write one set of source code and build in the ability to customize the application for different locations.

The first of these alternatives is likely to be prohibitively expensive. Using three different sets of source code will require three times as many developers, testers, and managers as building a single version of the application. Perhaps worse, a bug that's found and fixed in one version might slip through the cracks and ship in another version. If you later needed to ship a version for a fourth location, you'd have to repeat the entire process again.

Not surprisingly, Visual Basic .NET encourages the second approach. An application built from a single code base can be easily customized for multiple locations by using techniques such as locale-aware formatting functions and resource files. You don't have to worry about different versions getting out of sync (because they're built from the same source code), and building a new version requires no work beyond translating strings into a new language.

The Localization Process

The technical term for the entire process of preparing an application for shipment in a new location-specific version is *localization*. Microsoft divides this process of preparing a world-ready application into three phases:

1. Globalization

2. Localizability

3. Localization

Flexible Terms   Although in theory the terms *globalization*, *localizability*, and *localization* are precise and distinct, in practice they tend to be used interchangeably. Indeed, even the objectives for the certification exam are not careful in how they use these terms.

Globalization is the first step in the process. In the globalization stage, you identify all the localizable resources in the application and separate them from the executable code so that they can be modified easily. Ideally, you'll perform the globalization step during the design phase, so the resources will always remain separate from the code.

Localizability is the second step in the process. In the localizability stage, you ensure that translating the application for a new location won't require design changes. If you've planned for localization from the beginning, localizability will typically be part of your quality assurance (QA) process.

Localization is the final step in the process. In the localization phase, you customize your application for new locales. This consists primarily of translating resources you identified during the globalization phase.

What Should Be Localized?

Obviously, you must modify text that shows on the user interface when you're localizing an application. This includes text on forms, text in error messages, text in message boxes, and any other text shown to the user. But many other items might need to be localized in any given application. Here's a list of resources that are commonly localized, depending on the target locale:

◆ Menu item text.

◆ Form layouts. Text in German, for example, averages nearly twice as long as the same text in English. You might need to move and resize controls to accommodate this.

◆ The display format for dates and times.

◆ The display format for currency.

◆ The display format for numbers (for example, some countries use commas as the thousands separator in long numbers).

◆ Data input fields (What if you're asking for a ZIP Code in a country other than the United States?).

◆ Maps, road signs, photos, or other graphics with local content.

◆ Shortcut keys. Not every character you know appears on every keyboard.

◆ Calendars. Countries such as Korea and Saudi Arabia use completely different calendars from each other.

◆ Alphabetical order.

You'll need to use some judgment in deciding which of these really need to be localized in your application. You might decide, for example, that a set of general-purpose data entry fields can serve your needs for collecting addresses, rather than trying to research address formats worldwide.

IMPLEMENTING LOCALIZATION FOR THE USER INTERFACE

Implement Globalization: Implement localizability for the UI.

Implement Globalization: Prepare culture-specific formatting.

The System.Globalization namespace in the .NET Framework provides most of the support in .NET for localization in Visual Basic .NET applications. I'll start looking at localization code by exploring some of the concepts and classes you'll need to understand to build your own world-ready applications.

The two key pieces to keep in mind are cultures and resource files. A *culture* is an identifier for a particular locale. A *resource file* is a place you can store some culture-dependent resources such as strings and bitmaps (.NET handles translating other resources, such as date formats, automatically).

Understanding Cultures

Before you can start localizing applications, you must understand the concept of a *culture*. A culture, in .NET terms, is a more precise identifier than a location or a language. A culture identifies everything that might need to be localized in an application, which requires you to know more than just the language. For example, just knowing that an application uses English as its user interface language doesn't give you enough information to completely localize it:

Should you format dates and currency amounts in that application in a way appropriate to the United States, to the United Kingdom, to Canada, to Australia, or to New Zealand (among other possibilities)? Similarly, just knowing the location isn't enough: If an application will be used in Switzerland, four possibilities exist for the user interface language. Each combination of location and language identifies a culture.

About Culture Codes

Cultures are identified by abbreviations called *culture codes*. A full culture code consists of a neutral culture code (written in lower case), followed by one or more subculture codes (written in mixed case or upper case). Here are a few culture codes as examples:

- ◆ `de`—Identifies the German culture. This is a *neutral* culture, a culture that does not specify a subculture code. Neutral cultures generally do not provide sufficient information to localize an application.

- ◆ `en-GB`—Identifies the English (United Kingdom) culture. This is a *specific* culture, a culture that provides enough information to localize an application (in this case, for English speakers in Great Britain).

- ◆ `az-AZ-Cyrl`—An example of a specific culture with two subculture codes. This particular culture refers to the Azeri language in Azerbaijan, written with Cyrillic characters.

The CultureInfo Class

The .NET Framework represents cultures with the `System.Globalization.CultureInfo` class. This class lets you retrieve a wide variety of information about any particular culture (see Step By Step 8.1).

STEP BY STEP

8.1 Retrieving Culture Information

1. Open a Visual Basic .NET Windows Application in the Visual Studio .NET IDE.

2. Add a new form to your Visual Basic .NET project.

3. Place a Button control named `btnGetInfo`, a TextBox control named `txtCulture`, and a ListBox control named `lbInfo` on the form.

4. Double-click the Button control to open the form's module. Enter a reference to the `System.Globalization` namespace at the top of the code module:

```
Imports System.Globalization
```

5. Enter code to handle the button's `Click` event:

```
Private Sub btnGetInfo_Click( _
 ByVal sender As System.Object, _
 ByVal e As System.EventArgs) Handles btnGetInfo.Click
    ' Create a CultureInfo object for the specified
    culture
    Dim ci As CultureInfo = New CultureInfo(txtCulture.Text)
    ' Dump information about the culture
    With lbInfo.Items
        .Clear()
        .Add("Display Name: " & ci.DisplayName)
        .Add("English Name: " & ci.EnglishName)
        .Add("Native Name: " & ci.NativeName)
        ' Get day names
        .Add("Day Names:")
        Dim strDayNames() As String = _
         ci.DateTimeFormat.DayNames
        Dim strDay As String
        For Each strDay In strDayNames
            .Add("  " & strDay)
        Next
        ' Get the current year
        .Add("Current year: " & _
         ci.Calendar.GetYear(DateTime.Today))
        ' And the currency symbol
        .Add("Currency symbol: " & _
         ci.NumberFormat.CurrencySymbol)
    End With
End Sub
```

6. Set the form as the startup object for the project.

7. Run the project and enter the name of a culture in the text box. Click the button. The form will retrieve and display some of the information that the `CultureInfo` object can return, as shown in Figure 8.1.

FIGURE 8.1
Retrieving information about a culture.

Enumerating Cultures   You might want a list of all supported cultures. The static `CultureInfo.GetCultures` method returns an array of `CultureInfo` objects that you can enumerate to get that list.

The `THREAD` Object   The `Thread` object is a member of the `System.Threading` namespace, which allows you to write multithreaded applications. Multithreading is an advanced topic that I won't cover in this book. A normal Windows application has a single thread of execution, represented by the `Thread.CurrentThread` object.

This example works by creating a `CultureInfo` object to represent the specified culture. It then uses properties of the `CultureInfo` object (and of the objects that it contains, such as the `DateTimeFormat`, `NumberFormat`, and `Calendar` objects) to retrieve information about that culture. This information is useful in localizing applications, and it's all built right into the .NET Framework.

The `CultureInfo` class is the key to localizing your applications. After you've retrieved the proper `CultureInfo` object, you can derive a wide variety of information from it.

The CurrentCulture and CurrentUICulture Properties

The .NET Framework handles localization on a thread-by-thread basis. Each thread has two properties used for determining the culture to use: `CurrentCulture` and `CurrentUICulture`. You can set or view these properties on the `Thread.CurrentThread` object.

The `CurrentUICulture` property tells the CLR which culture to use when choosing resources for the user interface. You'll see later in this chapter how to provide multiple sets of resources for the CLR to use.

The `CurrentCulture` property is also used by the CLR to manage localization, but in a different way. The `CurrentCulture` property dictates the formats for dates, times, currency, and numbers, as well as other culture-specific functionalities, such as string comparison rules and casing rules.

The Invariant Culture

One more culture that you should know about is the *invariant culture*. This is a special culture that doesn't have an abbreviation. The invariant culture has two purposes:

◆ Interacting with other software, such as system services, in which no user is directly involved.

◆ Storing data in a culture-independent format that won't be displayed directly to end users.

You can use two ways to create a `CultureInfo` object that represents the invariant culture:

```
Dim ciInv As CultureInfo = New CultureInfo("")
Dim ciInv As CultureInfo = CultureInfo.InvariantCulture
```

R E V I E W   B R E A K

▶ Localization is a three-step process that consists of globalization (identifying resources), localizability (verifying separation
of resources from code), and localization (translating
resources).

▶ Many resources need to be localized, including user interface
text, dates, times, currency amounts, and calendars.

▶ Cultures are identified by culture codes. Neutral culture codes
specify only a location, and cannot be used for localization.
Specific culture codes specify both a location and a language
and provide enough information for localization.

▶ The CultureInfo object represents a culture in the .NET
Framework.

Displaying Localized Information

Now that you know how culture information is stored in the .NET
Framework, you're ready to see its use in code in Step By Step 8.2.

STEP BY STEP

8.2 Displaying Localized Information

1. Add a new form to your Visual Basic .NET project.

2. Place a Label control, a ComboBox control
(`cboSelectCulture`), and four TextBox controls
(`txtCulture`, `txtDate`, `txtCurrency`, and `txtNumber`) on
the form.

continues

continued

3. Double-click the Button control to open the form's module. Enter references at the top of the code module:

```
Imports System.Globalization
Imports System.Threading
```

4. Enter code to handle events in the form's module:

```
Private Sub StepByStep8_2_Load( _
 ByVal sender As System.Object, _
 ByVal e As System.EventArgs) Handles MyBase.Load
    ' Stock the combo box
    Dim ci As CultureInfo
    For Each ci In CultureInfo.GetCultures( _
     CultureTypes.SpecificCultures)
        cboSelectCulture.Items.Add(ci.Name)
    Next
    ' Display the name of the default culture
    txtCulture.Text = Thread.CurrentThread. _
     CurrentCulture.EnglishName
    ' Display some data
    DisplayData()
End Sub

Private Sub cboSelectCulture_SelectedIndexChanged( _
 ByVal sender As System.Object, _
 ByVal e As System.EventArgs) _
 Handles cboSelectCulture.SelectedIndexChanged
    ' Create an appropriate CultureInfo
    ' object for the thread
    Thread.CurrentThread.CurrentCulture = _
     New CultureInfo(cboSelectCulture.Text)
    ' Display the name of the culture
    txtCulture.Text = Thread.CurrentThread. _
     CurrentCulture.EnglishName
    ' Refresh the display of the data
    DisplayData()
End Sub

Private Sub DisplayData()
    Dim dtNow As Date = DateTime.Now
    Dim dblcurrency As Double = 13472.85
    Dim dblnumber As Double = 1409872.3502

    txtDate.Text = dtNow.ToLongDateString()
    txtCurrency.Text = dblcurrency.ToString("c")
    txtNumber.Text = dblnumber.ToString("n")

End Sub
```

5. Set the form as the startup object for the project.

6. Run the project. Select a culture from the combo box. The form will refresh to display localized information, as shown in Figure 8.2.

When you select a culture from the combo box, the code uses that information to create a `CultureInfo` object assigned to the `CurrentCulture` property of the `CurrentThread`. It then calls a method to display some data on the form. Note that the display method simply uses the `ToLongDateString` and `ToString` methods to format the data that it displays. You don't have to do anything special to tell these methods which culture to use. They automatically use the culture specified by the `CurrentCulture` property.

Setting Culture Properties

When setting the CurrentCulture and CurrentUICulture properties, you have two choices: You can set them based on information stored in the user's operating system, or you can provide a user interface to let the user choose a culture for formatting.

To use the culture of the operating system, you don't have to do anything. If the application is being executed on the Multiple User Interface (MUI) version of Windows 2000 or Windows XP, the .NET Framework will automatically default to the culture currently selected by the user. If the application is executed on another version of Windows, the .NET Framework will automatically default the culture to the language used by the operating system.

Although letting the .NET Framework choose the appropriate culture is the easy way to handle things, it's not always workable because the user might be using a version of Windows that doesn't match the user's own preferred language. For example, in a public kiosk, setting your application might execute on the English version of Windows XP but need to cater to users with a wide variety of language preferences.

If you want to let the user choose the culture to use, you can follow a strategy similar to the one you just saw: Provide a control to select a culture, and update the CurrentCulture property when the user makes a selection from this control. You'll see an example of this technique when you work through Guided Practice Exercise 8.1.

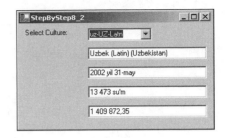

FIGURE 8.2
Displaying localized information.

EXAM TIP

No Localized Business Rules
Although this sample code changes the currency symbol when you select a new culture, it makes no attempt to convert the currency value into local units. The built-in localization support in the .NET Framework deals strictly with the user interface, not with business rules.

Working with Resource Files

So far you've seen how to use the CurrentCulture property to handle localized formatting of things such as currency, dates, and numbers. But localizing the text displayed on the user interface is perhaps even more important. The .NET Framework offers support for user interface localization through its ability to select a set of user interface resources at runtime. You can select three different places to store localized user interface resources:

◆ **External resource files**—These are created from plain text files containing key-value pairs by the resgen.exe tool. External resource files are useful when you're depending on an outside contractor to provide localized text, because their source files are simple text files.

◆ **Satellite assemblies**—These are created by compiling external resource files into dynamic link libraries (DLLs). Satellite assemblies are most useful when you want to supply additional languages after shipping a product. Satellite assemblies must be created with the command-line tools from the .NET Framework SDK. You can't create satellite assemblies by using Visual Studio .NET.

◆ **Assembly resource files**—These are specially formatted XML files that contain localized text. Visual Studio .NET allows you to work directly with assembly resource files.

For most applications, assembly resource files will be the easiest of these alternatives to work with. In this section, I'll demonstrate how to use Visual Studio .NET to localize the user interface of a simple application.

Localizing Forms in the Designer

The easiest way to localize user interface resources is to use the Windows Forms Designer. Step By Step 8.3 will show you how.

STEP BY STEP

8.3 Localizing a Form in the IDE

1. Add a new form to your Visual Basic .NET project. Name it `StepByStep8-3.vb`.

2. Place a Label control, three RadioButton controls, and a Button control on the form. It doesn't matter what you name these controls, because they're only going to be used to demonstrate localization. Set the text of the controls as shown in Figure 8.3.

3. Set the Localizable property of the form to True. Set the Language property of the form to French (France).

4. Change the text of the controls to the French translations, as shown in Figure 8.4. Note that I've also resized the Button control so that the French text will fit.

5. Add another new form to your Visual Basic .NET project. Name this form `StepByStep8-3a.vb`.

6. Place a ComboBox control named `cboCulture` and a Button control named `btnOpenForm` on the form.

7. Double-click the Button control to open the form's module. Enter references at the top of the code module:

```
Imports System.Globalization
Imports System.Threading
```

8. Enter code to handle events in the form's module:

```
Private Sub StepByStep8_3a_Load( _
 ByVal sender As System.Object, _
 ByVal e As System.EventArgs) Handles MyBase.Load
    ' Put language choices in the combo box
    cboCulture.Items.Add("English")
    cboCulture.Items.Add("French")
End Sub

Private Sub btnOpenForm_Click( _
 ByVal sender As System.Object, _
 ByVal e As System.EventArgs) Handles btnOpenForm.Click
    Dim f As New StepByStep8_3()
    f.Show()
End Sub
```

continues

FIGURE 8.3
Designing the form in English.

FIGURE 8.4
Designing the form in French.

continued

```
Private Sub cboCulture_SelectedIndexChanged( _
 ByVal sender As System.Object, _
 ByVal e As System.EventArgs) _
 Handles cboCulture.SelectedIndexChanged
    ' When the user selects a language,
    ' change the UI culture
    Select Case cboCulture.Text
        Case "English"
            Thread.CurrentThread.CurrentUICulture = _
             New CultureInfo("en-US")
        Case "French"
            Thread.CurrentThread.CurrentUICulture = _
             New CultureInfo("fr-FR")
    End Select
End Sub
```

9. Set the StepByStep8-3a.vb form as the startup object for the project.

10. Run the project. Click the Open Form button. Select French in the combo box and click the button again. Figure 8.5 shows the results of this procedure.

FIGURE 8.5
Two versions of the same form.

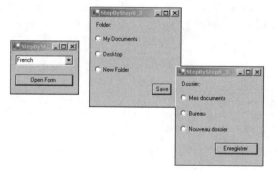

When you select a value from the combo box on the first form, the code behind that form sets the CurrentUICulture to a new CultureInfo object representing the selected culture. Once you've done this, the .NET Framework automatically uses that culture when creating new forms and the controls on those forms. It does this by using resources that were automatically compiled into satellite assemblies when you localized the form in the designer.

If you click the Show All Files button in Solution Explorer and expand the tree, you'll find the files shown in Figure 8.6. As you can see, the designer created a .resx file (containing the localized resources) and a .dll file (the satellite assembly) for each culture that you selected in the designer.

Creating Resource Files

As an alternative to creating satellite assemblies with the Windows Forms Designer, you can create your own assembly resource files to hold localizable strings. Step By Step 8.4 demonstrates this approach.

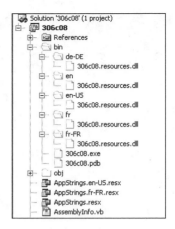

FIGURE 8.6
Localized files in Solution Explorer.

STEP BY STEP

8.4 Localizing a Form with Resource Files

1. Add a new form to your Visual Basic .NET project.

2. Place a Label control named lblFolder, three RadioButton controls (rbMyDocuments, rbDesktop, and rbNewFolder), a ComboBox control named cboCulture, and a Button control named btnSave on the form. Figure 8.7 shows this form in Design view.

3. Select Project, Add New Item. Select the Assembly Resource File template. Name the new item AppStrings.resx and click Open to create the file.

4. The new file will open in the Visual Studio IDE with a grid-based editing interface. Enter names and values to identify all the text strings on the user interface, as shown in Figure 8.8. You can optionally enter a comment for each string. The Type and Mimetype columns are not used for localizing strings.

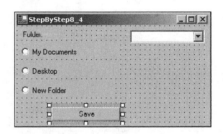

FIGURE 8.7
A form to be localized at runtime.

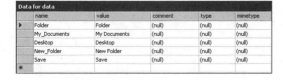

FIGURE 8.8
Entering invariant resources.

Data for data					
name	value	comment	type	mimetype	
Folder	Dossier	(null)	(null)	(null)	
My_Documents	Mes documents	(null)	(null)	(null)	
Desktop	Bureau	(null)	(null)	(null)	
New_Folder	Nouveau dossier	(null)	(null)	(null)	
Save	Enregistrer	(null)	(null)	(null)	

FIGURE 8.9
Entering French resources.

5. Add two more assembly resource files to your project. The first, named `AppStrings.en-US.resx`, should contain another copy of the strings in English. The second, named `AppStrings.fr-FR.resx`, should contain the strings in French, as shown in Figure 8.9. The Name column is the same in the English and French versions; only the value column changes.

6. Double-click the ComboBox control to open the form's module. Enter references at the top of the code module:

```
Imports System.Globalization
Imports System.Resources
Imports System.Threading
```

7. Enter code to handle events in the form's module:

```
Private Sub StepByStep8_4_Load( _
 ByVal sender As System.Object, _
 ByVal e As System.EventArgs) Handles MyBase.Load
    ' Put language choices in the combo box
    cboCulture.Items.Add("English")
    cboCulture.Items.Add("French")
    ' Initialize the UI text
    SetUIText()
End Sub

Private Sub cboCulture_SelectedIndexChanged( _
 ByVal sender As System.Object, _
 ByVal e As System.EventArgs) _
 Handles cboCulture.SelectedIndexChanged
    ' When the user selects a language,
    ' change the UI culture
    Select Case cboCulture.Text
        Case "English"
            Thread.CurrentThread.CurrentUICulture = _
             New CultureInfo("en-US")
        Case "French"
            Thread.CurrentThread.CurrentUICulture = _
             New CultureInfo("fr-FR")
    End Select
    ' Initialize the UI text
    SetUIText()
End Sub

Private Sub SetUIText()
    Dim rm As ResourceManager = _
     New ResourceManager("_306c08.AppStrings", _
     GetType(StepByStep8_4).Assembly)
    lblFolder.Text = rm.GetString("Folder")
    rbMyDocuments.Text = rm.GetString("My_Documents")
    rbDesktop.Text = rm.GetString("Desktop")
    rbNewFolder.Text = rm.GetString("New_Folder")
    btnSave.Text = rm.GetString("Save")
End Sub
```

NOTE

Finding the Project Namespace This code assumes that your VB .NET project is named 306c08. If it has some other name, you must alter the first parameter to the constructor for the ResourceManager object. This parameter is the root namespace of your project. You can find the name of the root namespace by right-clicking the Project node in Solution Explorer. Select Properties, and you'll find the root namespace in the General section.

8. Set the form as the startup object for the project.

9. Run the project. As you select languages in the combo box, the user interface will be refreshed with the appropriate resources.

The naming of the resource files in this example follows a required pattern. The .NET Framework looks for several specific files when loading resources, depending on the base name of the resources and the selected culture. The base name is the second part of the first parameter to the `ResourceManager` constructor, in this case `AppStrings`. When the `CurrentUICulture` is set to a `CultureInfo` object representing the fr-FR (French in France) culture, the .NET Framework will check for resources in three possible files, in this order:

1. **A specific culture file**—In this case, AppStrings.fr-FR.resx

2. **A neutral culture file**—In this case, AppStrings.fr.resx

3. **An invariant culture file**—In this case, AppStrings.resx

In other words, the .NET Framework will fall back on increasingly more general resources in trying to load resources for a form.

Localizing Resources at Runtime

Runtime user interface resources are actually loaded by an instance of the `System.Resources.ResourceManager` class. After you've initialized a `ResourceManager` object by calling one of the class's constructors, you can use two methods to retrieve localized resources:

◆ `GetObject`—returns an object from the appropriate resource file.

◆ `GetString`—returns a string from the appropriate resource file.

If you're just dealing with text displayed directly on a form, the satellite assembly approach (which you saw in Step By Step 8.3) and the assembly resource file approach (which you saw in Step By Step 8.4) are equivalent, but sometimes one approach is preferred to the other.

If you need to move and resize controls, the satellite assembly approach is more convenient because you can move and resize the controls directly in the Windows Forms Designer. If you need to move and resize controls when using assembly resource files, you must store position and size information somewhere and apply them to the controls' properties in code yourself.

On the other hand, assembly resource files offer a substantial benefit in that they allow you to easily localize text that doesn't appear directly on the user interface. Message box and other informative text, for example, is most easily localized using an assembly resource file.

Assembly resource files also let you change text on-the-fly, whereas satellite assemblies are only used when a form is first created.

You can also consider hybrid solutions for complex applications: using satellite assemblies to localize controls and embedding assembly resource files to localize other resources in the same project.

GUIDED PRACTICE EXERCISE 8.1

In this exercise, you'll combine the two types of localization that you've seen in this chapter by using both the CurrentCulture and the CurrentUICulture properties in a single project.

The goal of this exercise is to build a form that displays the current date. The form should offer two choices:

1. A choice between long date and short date display formats

2. A choice between two different cultures on the user interface

Try this on your own first. If you get stuck or would like to see one possible solution, follow these steps:

1. Add a new form to your Visual Basic .NET Project. Name the form `GuidedPracticeExercise8-1.vb`.

2. Place a ComboBox control named `cboCulture`, two RadioButton controls named `rbLongDate` and `rbShortDate`, and a TextBox control named `txtDate` on your form. Set the Checked property of `rbLongDate` to True. Figure 8.10 shows a design for this form.

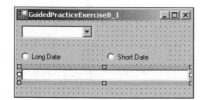

FIGURE 8.10
A form to display localized dates.

3. Add a new assembly resource file to your project. Name the file `GPE1.resx`. Enter two strings in the file. The first one should be named `strLongDate` and have the value Long Date. The second should be named `strShortDate` and have the value Short Date.

4. Add a second assembly resource file to your project. Name the file `GPE1.en-US.resx`. This file should have the same contents as the `GPE1.resx` file.

5. Add a third assembly resource file to your project. Name the file `GPE1.de-DE.resx`. In this file, use the value Langes Datum for the `strLongDate` resource and the value Kurzes Datum for the `strShortDate` resource.

6. Double-click the ComboBox control to open the form's code module. Enter these references at the top of the file:

```
Imports System.Globalization
Imports System.Resources
Imports System.Threading
```

7. Enter this code to manage events on the form:

```
Private Sub cboCulture_SelectedIndexChanged( _
 ByVal sender As System.Object, _
 ByVal e As System.EventArgs) _
 Handles cboCulture.SelectedIndexChanged
    ' Set the current cultures to the selected culture
    Thread.CurrentThread.CurrentCulture =
     New CultureInfo(cboCulture.Text)
    Thread.CurrentThread.CurrentUICulture = _
     New CultureInfo(cboCulture.Text)
    ' Refresh the display
    DisplayData()
End Sub

Private Sub GuidedPracticeExercise8_1_Load( _
 ByVal sender As System.Object, _
 ByVal e As System.EventArgs) Handles MyBase.Load
    ' Put some choices in the combo box
    cboCulture.Items.Add("en-US")
    cboCulture.Items.Add("de-DE")
    ' Refresh the display
    DisplayData()
End Sub

Private Sub rbLongDate_CheckedChanged( _
 ByVal sender As System.Object, _
 ByVal e As System.EventArgs) _
 Handles rbLongDate.CheckedChanged
```

continues

continued

```
        ' Refresh the display
        DisplayData()
    End Sub

    Private Sub rbShortDate_CheckedChanged( _
     ByVal sender As System.Object, _
     ByVal e As System.EventArgs) _
     Handles rbShortDate.CheckedChanged
        ' Refresh the display
        DisplayData()
    End Sub

    Private Sub DisplayData()
        ' Reformat the date according to the user's choices
        If rbLongDate.Checked Then
            txtDate.Text = DateTime.Today.ToLongDateString()
        Else
            txtDate.Text = DateTime.Today.ToShortDateString()
        End If
        ' Update the user interface text
        Dim rm As ResourceManager = _
         New ResourceManager("_306c08.GPE1", _
         GetType(GuidedPracticeExercise8_1).Assembly)
        rbLongDate.Text = rm.GetString("strLongDate")
        rbShortDate.Text = rm.GetString("strShortDate")
    End Sub
```

8. Set the form as the startup object for the project.

9. Run the project and experiment with the user interface. You can select either English or German, and both the user interface text and the date formats change accordingly.

CONVERTING EXISTING ENCODINGS

Implement Globalization: Convert existing encodings.

Many schemes have been developed for representing the characters in a language as numeric codes within a computer. These schemes are referred to as encodings. For example, the venerable ASCII encoding represents common Latin characters as numeric codes ranging from 0 to 127. The .NET Framework provides support for encodings through the System.Text.Encoding class.

Understanding Unicode and Encodings

Internally, the .NET Framework's preferred encoding for characters is 16-bit Unicode, otherwise known as UTF-16. This encoding represents characters as 16-bit numbers, giving it the capability to represent approximately 65,000 distinct characters—enough to represent every character commonly in use. Additional features of the full Unicode specification allow for the representation of another million characters.

Over time, Windows has been moving toward Unicode as the basis for encoding characters, but this wasn't always the case. Earlier versions of Windows used *code pages* to represent character sets. A code page could hold 256 characters, and the system supplied different code pages for different character sets, such as Greek characters or Latin characters.

Although Unicode is the native character encoding for .NET, the .NET Framework supports conversion to and from older encodings, such as ASCII and code pages, for compatability with older applications.

> **WARNING**
>
> **Unicode Isn't Everywhere** Even though Unicode is the default character encoding for .NET, you won't find Unicode in every file that you work with. In particular, XML documents default to the UTF-8 character set.

> **NOTE**
>
> **Unicode Details** You can find everything you'll ever need to know about Unicode at the Unicode home page, `http://www.unicode.org`.

Converting Encodings

The System.Text namespace contains classes designed to let you convert characters from the UTF-16 Unicode encoding to other encodings, and vice versa (see Step By Step 8.5).

STEP BY STEP

8.5 Converting Character Encodings

1. Add a new form to your Visual Basic .NET project.

2. Place two Label controls, a TextBox control named txtUnicode, a Button control named btnConvert, and a ListBox control named lbAscii on the form.

3. Double-click the ComboBox control to open the form's module. Enter a reference at the top of the code module:

```
Imports System.Text
```

---

continues

4. Enter code to handle the button's `Click` event:

```
Private Sub btnConvert_Click( _
 ByVal sender As System.Object, _
 ByVal e As System.EventArgs) Handles btnConvert.Click
    ' Get an encoding object for ascii
    Dim encASCII As ASCIIEncoding = New ASCIIEncoding()
    ' Convert the string to an array of ASCII bytes
    Dim bytEncodedCharacters() As Byte
    bytEncodedCharacters = _
     encASCII.GetBytes(txtUnicode.Text)
    Dim i As Integer
    For i = 0 To bytEncodedCharacters.Length - 1
        lbASCII.Items.Add(bytEncodedCharacters(i))
    Next
End Sub
```

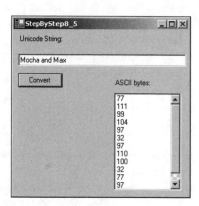

FIGURE 8.11
Converting Unicode characters to ASCII bytes.

5. Set the form as the startup object for the project.

6. Run the project. Enter some text in the TextBox control and click the button to convert the Unicode text from the TextBox into a series of ASCII byte codes and to display those codes in the ListBox, as shown in Figure 8.11

This code sample uses the `GetBytes` method of the `ASCIIEncoding` object to convert a Unicode string into an array of ASCII bytes. Although I didn't use it in this example, a matching `GetChars` method will convert ASCII bytes into Unicode text.

The `ASCIIEncoding` class is a subclass of `System.Text.Encoding`. Table 8.1 lists the other available subclasses that help convert to and from other encodings.

TABLE 8.1

ENCODING CLASSES IN THE SYSTEM.TEXT NAMESPACE

Class	Use
ASCIIEncoding	Converts characters between Unicode and ASCII.
Encoding	General-purpose class. The Encoding.GetEncoding static method returns encodings that can be used for legacy code page compatibility.
UnicodeEncoding	Converts characters to and from Unicode encoded as consecutive bytes in either big-endian or little-endian order.
UTF7Encoding	Converts characters to and from seven-bit Unicode encoding.
UTF8Encoding	Converts characters to and from eight-bit Unicode encoding.

IMPLEMENTING MIRRORING

Implement Globalization: Implement right-to-left and left-to-right mirroring.

Many differences exist between human languages, beyond the use of different character sets. One of the most important differences is whether the language reads from left to right (like English) or from right to left (like Arabic). The .NET Framework supports both reading directions.

Understanding Mirroring

The process of switching a user interface between a left-to-right language such as German or English and a right-to-left language such as Hebrew or Arabic is called *mirroring*. Mirroring in the Windows environment involves changes beyond simply reversing the order of text strings. Figure 8.12, for example, shows part of the user interface from Arabic Windows.

As you can see, the entire format of the Windows user interface is reversed when you use mirroring. The close, minimize, and other buttons appear at the upper left of the window. Menus appear to the right of the menu bar. Combo box arrows are located to the left of the combo box, and check box text to the left of the check box.

FIGURE 8.12
Mirroring in the Windows user interface.

Mirroring in .NET

The .NET Framework offers partial support for mirroring through the RightToLeft property of forms (see Step By Step 8.6).

STEP BY STEP

8.6 Mirroring a Form

1. Add a new form to your Visual Basic .NET project.

2. Place a TextBox control, a ComboBox control, a CheckBox control, a RadioButton control, and a MainMenu control on the form. Add some items to the MainMenu control. Figure 8.13 shows what the form might look like in Design mode.

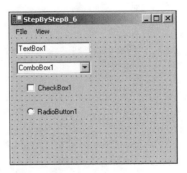

FIGURE 8.13
Preparing a form to test mirroring.

continues

FIGURE 8.14
Right-to-left form.

continued

3. Set the `RightToLeft` property of the form to Yes.

4. Set the form as the startup object for the project.

5. Run the project. You'll see that the form is partially mirrored, as shown in Figure 8.14.

Mirroring in .NET manages most of the essentials. The form's text moves to the right end of the title bar. Controls fill from right to left as you enter text. ComboBox, RadioButton, and CheckBox controls reverse their appearance as well. Menus show up at the right end of the menu bar.

But the mirroring support is imperfect. The system menu and the other window buttons (such as the close and minimize buttons) don't switch positions. Controls are not mirrored to the opposite position on the form from their initial design (although, of course, you can manage that by using satellite assemblies to hold alternate form resources, as you saw earlier in the chapter).

> **EXAM TIP**
>
> **Mirroring Part of a Form**   If you only want to mirror part of a form, you can set the `RightToLeft` property to Yes on individual controls instead of on the entire form.

> **NOTE**
>
> **True Mirroring**   To completely mirror a form, you can call the `SetProcessDefaultLayout` Windows API call.

VALIDATING NON-LATIN USER INPUT

Validate User Input: Validate non-Latin user input.

Another area in which world-ready applications can require code changes is in handling character strings, specifically in string indexing and data sorting. These areas require the most coding attention for non-Latin characters (such as Arabic, Hebrew, or Cyrillic characters) but can be important when dealing with Latin characters as well.

String Indexing

String indexing refers to the process of extracting single characters from a text string. You might think you could simply iterate through the data that makes up the string 16 bits at a time, treating each 16 bits as a separate character. But it turns out that things aren't that simple in the Unicode world.

Unicode supports surrogate pairs and combining character sequences. A *surrogate pair* is a set of two 16-bit codes that represents a single character from the extended 32-bit Unicode character space. A *combining character* sequence is a set of more than one 16-bit codes that represents a single character. Combining character sequences are often used to combine diacritical marks such as accents with base characters.

This presents a problem: If characters in a string aren't all the same length, how can you move smoothly from one to the next? The answer, of course, is to use a class from the .NET Framework that knows how to perform this task. The System.Globalization.StringInfo class is designed to iterate through the elements in a string (see Step By Step 8.7).

STEP BY STEP

8.7 Iterating with the StringInfo Class

1. Add a new form to your Visual Basic .NET project.

2. Place a TextBox control named txtText, a Button control named btnIterate, and a ListBox control named lbIterate on the form.

3. Double-click the button to open the form's module. Enter a reference at the top of the module:

```
Imports System.Globalization
```

4. Add code to handle the Click event of the button:

```
Private Sub btnIterate_Click( _
 ByVal sender As System.Object, _
 ByVal e As System.EventArgs) Handles btnIterate.Click
    lbIterate.Items.Clear()
    ' Get an iterator for the entered text
    Dim iter As TextElementEnumerator = _
     StringInfo.GetTextElementEnumerator(txtTest.Text)
    ' The iterator starts before the string, have to move
    ' it forward once to reach the first element
    iter.MoveNext()
    Do
        lbIterate.Items.Add( _
          "Element " & iter.ElementIndex & _
          ": " & iter.Current)
    Loop While (iter.MoveNext)
End Sub
```

continues

FIGURE 8.15
String decomposed by the StringInfo class.

continued

5. Set the form as the starting object for the project.

6. Run the project. Paste or enter any text you like in the TextBox and click the Button control. The code will split the string into its constituent characters, as shown in Figure 8.15.

This code uses the static GetTextElementEnumerator method of the StringInfo class. Given any Unicode string, this method returns an iterator that you can use to move through the string one character at a time, properly handling surrogate pairs and combining characters. The iterator has a MoveNext method that returns zero when it has exhausted the characters in the string. The Current property of the iterator returns a single character from the current position of the iterator.

Comparing and Sorting Data

Another area in which you might need to alter code to produce a world-ready application is in working with string. Different cultures use different alphabetical orders to sort strings, and different cultures compare strings differently. For example, the single-character ligature *æ* is considered to match the two characters *ae* in some cultures but not in others.

For the most part, you needn't do any special programming to account for these factors in the .NET Framework. To make your application world-ready, you're more likely to need to remove old code—for example, code that assumes that characters are properly sorted if you sort their ASCII character numbers. Specifically, the .NET Framework provides these culture-aware features:

◆ The String.Compare method compares strings according to the rules of the CultureInfo referenced by the CurrentCulture property.

◆ The `CultureInfo.CompareInfo` object can search for substrings according to the comparison rules of the current culture.

◆ The `Array.Sort` method sorts the members of an array by the alphabetical order rules of the current culture.

◆ The `SortKey.Compare` method also compares strings according to the rules of the current culture.

▶ Internally, .NET applications use 16-bit Unicode (UTF-16) as their preferred character encoding.

▶ The `System.Text.Encoding` class and its subclasses allow you to convert text from one encoding to another.

▶ In some languages, the user interface is read from right to left instead of from left to right. Converting a form for one of these languages is *mirroring*.

▶ The .NET Framework provides partial support for mirroring through the `RightToLeft` property on forms and controls.

▶ To iterate through the elements of a string in a world-ready application, you should use the `GetTextElementEnumerator` method of the `StringInfo` class.

▶ Searching, sorting, and comparing strings in a world-ready application requires using standard objects and methods rather than clever programming tricks.

CHAPTER SUMMARY

KEY TERMS

- Culture
- Culture code
- Encoding
- Globalization
- Localizability
- Localization
- Resource file
- Unicode

The .NET Framework was designed to help develop world-ready applications quickly and consistently. The localization process includes globalization (planning for localized versions), localizability (testing to make sure resources can be localized), and localization (actually translating the resources).

The .NET Framework contains a number of useful localization classes in the `System.Globalization` namespace. Key among these classes is the `CultureInfo` class, which provides the capability for .NET applications to properly display dates, times, currencies, and other culture-specific data.

Visual Studio .NET provides several ways to localize the user interface of an application, including satellite assemblies and assembly resource files. You can create satellite assemblies by manipulating user interface elements directly in the Visual Studio IDE. Assembly resource files require you to list resources in special files, which can be loaded at runtime.

Other important globalization topics include encoding (translating from one representation of text characters to another), mirroring (handling right-to-left language input and output), and working with character sorts, comparisons, and iteration.

APPLY YOUR KNOWLEDGE

Exercises

8.1 Using Localized Calendars

In addition to the features you saw earlier in the chapter, the CultureInfo class can supply localized calendars for different cultures. In this exercise, you'll see how to retrieve culture-specific calendar information.

Estimated Time: 20 minutes.

1. Open a Visual Basic .NET Windows Application in the Visual Studio .NET IDE.

2. Add a new form to the application.

3. Place a Label control, a ComboBox control named cboCultures, and a ListBox control named lbInfo on the form.

4. Double-click the ComboBox control to open the form's module. Add a line of code to the top of the module:

```
Imports System.Globalization
```

5. Add code to handle the Load event of the form and the SelectedIndexChanged event of the ComboBox control:

```
Private Sub Exercise8_1_Load( _
 ByVal sender As System.Object, _
 ByVal e As System.EventArgs) _
 Handles MyBase.Load
    ' Fill the combo box with cultures
    Dim ci As CultureInfo
    For Each ci In CultureInfo. _
     GetCultures( _
     CultureTypes.SpecificCultures)
        cboCultures.Items.Add(ci.Name)
    Next
End Sub
```

```
Private Sub _
 cboCultures_SelectedIndexChanged( _
 ByVal sender As System.Object, _
 ByVal e As System.EventArgs) _
 Handles cboCultures.SelectedIndexChanged
    ' Get the selected CultureInfo
    ' and some other objects
    Dim ci As CultureInfo = _
 New CultureInfo(cboCultures.Text)
    Dim cal As Calendar = ci.Calendar
    Dim dtfi As DateTimeFormatInfo = _
     ci.DateTimeFormat
    lbInfo.Items.Clear()
    Dim dt As DateTime = DateTime.Today
    ' List the culture and the calendar
    With lbInfo.Items
        .Add("The culture is " & _
         ci.EnglishName)
        .Add("The calendar is " & _
         cal.GetType.ToString)
        ' Get the current day,
        ' month, and year
        .Add("Today is day " & _
         cal.GetDayOfMonth(dt))
        .Add(" of month " & _
         cal.GetMonth(dt))
        .Add(" of year " & cal.GetYear(dt))
        .Add("This is day " & _
         cal.GetDayOfWeek(dt) & _
         " of the week")
        .Add("The day name is " & _
         dtfi.DayNames( _
         cal.GetDayOfWeek(dt)))
        .Add("The month name is " & _
         dtfi.MonthNames( _
         cal.GetMonth(dt) - 1))
        .Add("There are " & + 
         cal.GetMonthsInYear( _
         cal.GetYear(dt)) & _
         " months in this year")
    End With
End Sub
```

6. Set the form as the startup object for the project.

7. Run the project. Select cultures from the combo box to see some of their calendar information in the ListBox control, as shown in Figure 8.16. You might try ar-SA, he-IL, and th-TH to get some sense of the calendars that the .NET Framework supports.

APPLY YOUR KNOWLEDGE

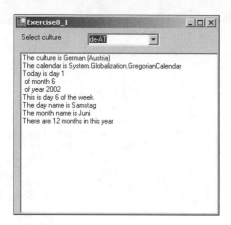

FIGURE 8.16
Calendar information from the CultureInfo class.

This exercise shows some of the methods available from the `Calendar` class(and its subclasses, such as `GregorianCalendar`). Following is a more extensive list of the available methods of the `Calendar` class. Their use should be self-evident from their names.

- AddDays
- AddHours
- AddMilliseconds
- AddMinutes
- AddMonths
- AddSeconds
- AddWeeks
- AddYears
- GetDayOfMonth
- GetDayOfWeek
- GetDayOfYear
- GetDaysInMonth

- GetDaysInYear
- GetEra
- GetHour
- GetMilliseconds
- GetMinute
- GetMonth
- GetMonthsInYear
- GetSecond
- GetWeekOfYear
- GetYear
- IsLeapDay
- IsLeapMonth
- IsLeapYear
- ToDateTime
- ToFourDigitYear

8.2   Retrieving Region Information

Another part of the `System.Globalization` namespace is the `RegionInfo` object. This object provides some additional information on a particular geographic region. In this exercise, you'll see how to retrieve the information available from the `RegionInfo` object.

Estimated Time: 15 minutes.

1. Open a Visual Basic .NET Windows Application in the Visual Studio .NET IDE.

2. Add a new form to the application.

3. Place a Label control, a ComboBox control named `cboCultures`, and a ListBox control named `lbInfo` on the form.

APPLY YOUR KNOWLEDGE

4. Double-click the ComboBox control to open the form's module. Add a line of code to the top of the module:

```
Imports System.Globalization
```

5. Add code to handle the Load event of the Form and the SelectedIndexChanged event of the ComboBox control:

```
Private Sub Exercise8_2_Load( _
 ByVal sender As System.Object, _
 ByVal e As System.EventArgs) _
  Handles MyBase.Load
    ' Fill the combo box with cultures
    Dim ci As CultureInfo
    For Each ci In CultureInfo.GetCultures( _
CultureTypes.SpecificCultures)
        cboCultures.Items.Add(ci.Name)
    Next
End Sub

Private Sub _
 cboCultures_SelectedIndexChanged( _
 ByVal sender As System.Object, _
 ByVal e As System.EventArgs) _
 Handles cboCultures.SelectedIndexChanged
    ' Attempt to get the correct RegionInfo
    Dim rgi As RegionInfo = _
     New RegionInfo( _
     cboCultures.Text.Substring( _
     cboCultures.Text.Length - 2))
    lbInfo.Items.Clear()
    ' List the regioninfo
    With lbInfo.Items
        .Add("The region is " & rgi.Name)
        .Add("Display Name: " & _
        rgi.DisplayName)
        .Add("English Name: " & _
        rgi.EnglishName)
        .Add("Currency symbol: " & _
        rgi.CurrencySymbol)
        If rgi.IsMetric Then
            .Add("Region uses " & _
            "metric measurements.")
        Else
            .Add("Region does not " & _
            "use metric measurements.")
        End If
        .Add("ISO Currency symbol: " & _
        rgi.ISOCurrencySymbol)
        .Add("ISO three-letter code: " & _
        rgi.ThreeLetterISORegionName)
    End With
End Sub
```

6. Set the form as the startup object for the project.

7. Run the project. Select cultures from the combo box to see some of their region information in the ListBox control, as shown in Figure 8.17.

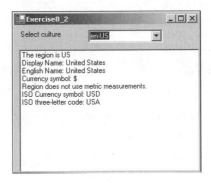

FIGURE 8.17
Region information from the RegionInfo class.

Regions are identified by two-letter codes assigned by the International Standards Organization (ISO). These codes usually match the subculture codes, so this example cheats and uses the rightmost two characters of culture codes to locate regions.

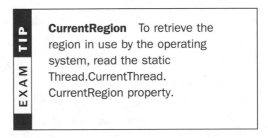

EXAM TIP

CurrentRegion To retrieve the region in use by the operating system, read the static Thread.CurrentThread.CurrentRegion property.

Review Questions

1. What might need to be localized in a world-ready application?

2. Name and briefly describe the three steps of the localization process.

3. Describe the differences between neutral, specific, and invariant cultures.

4. What is the difference between the CurrentCulture property and the CurrentUICulture property of the currently executing thread?

5. Explain the naming standard for resx files.

6. What properties must you set to directly localize a form within the Visual Studio .NET IDE?

7. What advantages do assembly resource files have over satellite assemblies?

8. How many bits does a single UTF-16 character consist of?

9. What should change when a form is mirrored?

10. What class can you use to iterate through a string character by character in all cases?

Exam Questions

1. Your application displays order information, including the total cost of each order. You are beginning to sell this application in multiple countries. How should you ensure that the correct currency symbol is used in all cases?

   A. Allow the user to select a culture from a list. Create a CultureInfo object based on the user's selection and assign it to the Thread.CurrentThread.CurrentCulture property. Use the ToString method to format currency amounts.

   B. Accept the Thread.CurrentThread.CurrentCulture property as it is set when you run your application. Use the ToString method to format currency amounts.

   C. Prompt the user for a currency symbol and store it in the registry.

   D. Allow the user to select a currency symbol from a list of supported symbols.

2. Your application allows users to select a culture such as English, French, or Spanish from an options dialog box. Users complain that some information is not displayed correctly, even after selecting the proper culture. What could be the problem?

   A. They are running your application on an English-only version of Windows.

   B. You're using a neutral CultureInfo to retrieve information instead of a specific CultureInfo.

   C. The users have not yet installed .NET Framework SP1.

   D. Your application is constructed as an executable file rather than a satellite library.

3. Users want to include the day of the week when your application displays dates. They want this to be in the language of their Windows installation. What can you do to address this need? (Select two.)

   A. Use the DateTime.ToLongDateString() method to format dates.

   B. Use the CultureInfo.DateTimeFormat property to retrieve the names of the weekdays, and select the proper name from that array.

APPLY YOUR KNOWLEDGE

C. Force the user to enter the day of the week whenever he enters a date into the system.

D. Use the RegionInfo object to retrieve the names of the weekdays, and select the proper name from that array.

4. Your user wants to see French dates and currencies displayed in an application but wants the user interface to remain in English. How can you accomplish this?

A. Set the CurrentCulture property to a CultureInfo representing the fr-FR culture, and set the CurrentUICulture property to a CultureInfo representing the en-US culture.

B. Set the CurrentCulture property to a CultureInfo representing the en-US culture, and set the CurrentUICulture property to a CultureInfo representing the fr-FR culture.

C. Set the CurrentCulture property to a CultureInfo representing the fr-FR culture, and set the CurrentUICulture property to a CultureInfo representing the fr-FR culture.

D. Set the CurrentCulture property to a CultureInfo representing the en-US culture, and set the CurrentUICulture property to a CultureInfo representing the en-US culture.

5. Your application is named 1st_Class_Tracer. You are using embedded assembly resource files to localize the application. When you try to compile the localized application, you receive an error message. What could be the problem?

A. This application must use satellite assemblies rather than assembly resource files.

B. You did not include resources for every possible culture in your application.

C. You did not include a means for the user to switch cultures in your application.

D. You used 1st_Class_Tracer rather than _1st_Class_Tracer as the namespace for your resources.

6. You are using satellite assemblies to hold localization resources for the user interface of your application. The application's main form includes a menu that lets users select English, French, Spanish, or German as the user interface language. When the user makes a selection, your code creates an appropriate CultureInfo object and assigns it to the Thread.CurrentThread.CurrentUICulture property.

Users report that the user interface does not change languages when they make a selection from the menu. What can you do to fix this bug?

A. Instruct the users to close and reopen the application after making a selection.

B. Switch to assembly resource files to hold the resources. Use a ResourceManager object to extract the resources whenever they're needed.

C. Verify that your code contains the correct Namespace name for your application in the module that selects the resources to use.

D. Spawn a second copy of the main form, this one with the correct user interface language.

7. Your application includes three assembly resource files: Strings.resx contains the default (English) resources; Strings.en-US.resx contains the English resources; Strings.France.resx contains the French resources. Users report that they are getting the default English user interface when they've selected the option for a French user interface.

APPLY YOUR KNOWLEDGE

What should you do?

A. Instruct users to close and reopen the application after selecting a new user interface language.

B. Add French resources to the Strings.resx file.

C. Rename the French resource file to Strings.fr-FR.resx.

D. Delete the Strings.en-US.resx file from the project.

8. Your application contains Unicode strings encoded in the UTF-16 format. You want to save a copy of those strings to disk in the UTF-8 format. What should you do?

A. Use the Unicode.GetBytes method to perform the conversion.

B. Use the Unicode.GetChars method to perform the conversion.

C. Use the UTF8Encoding.GetBytes method to perform the conversion.

D. Use the UTF8Encoding.GetChars method to perform the conversion.

9. You are localizing a Windows Form for use in Saudi Arabia (the ar-SA culture). Which of these steps should you perform as part of the process? (Select two.)

A. Set the Tag property to ar-SA.

B. Set the Language property to Arabic (Saudi Arabia)

C. Set the Localizable property to False

D. Set the RightToLeft property to Yes

10. A dialog box in your application reports the number of characters in a particular data entry form. You're dividing the number of bits taken up by the data by 16 to arrive at this figure. Users of the localized version in Saudi Arabia complain that the number of characters is consistently overestimated, What should you do?

A. Divide the number of bits by 32 to arrive at a more accurate figure.

B. Use the String.Length method to retrieve the actual length of the string.

C. Divide the number of bits by 8 to arrive at a more accurate figure.

D. Use a GetTextElementEnumerator object to enumerate the characters.

11. Arabic-speaking users of your application want to see dates displayed with the Arabic calendar. How can you accomplish this?

A. Retrieve a Calendar object from Thread.CurrentThread.CurrentCulture, and use its methods to format the dates.

B. Retrieve a Calendar object from Thread.CurrentThread.CurrentUICulture, and use its methods to format the dates.

C. Retrieve a DateTime object from Thread.CurrentThread.CurrentCulture, and use its methods to format the dates.

D. Retrieve a DateTime object from Thread.CurrentThread.CurrentUICulture, and use its methods to format the dates.

APPLY YOUR KNOWLEDGE

12. You are shipping an application to France and Russia and using satellite assemblies to hold form localization resources. Now you need to start shipping to Spain. If the application is run on the Spanish version of Windows, you want to show the user interface in Spanish. What should you do?

    A. Create an assembly resource file to hold the user interface text translated into Spanish.

    B. Build a new project containing only the Spanish version of the form, and build this new project to sell in Spain.

    C. Set the form's language to Spanish (Spain) in the IDE and translate the controls.

    D. Create a new CultureInfo object for the Spanish (Spain) culture. Assign this object to the Thread.CurrentThread.CurrentUICulture property.

13. Your application contains an options dialog box that allows the user to select a culture for localizing dates, times, and currency. What should you do to ensure that all possible valid choices are available in this dialog box?

    A. Retrieve the list of supported cultures by using the static CultureInfo.GetCultures method.

    B. Look up the list of available cultures in the .NET Framework help, and hard-code that list into your application.

    C. Retrieve the list of supported cultures from the Windows Registry.

    D. Allow users to enter cultures as they need them, and store a list of entered cultures for future use.

14. You are writing an application on a system that uses US English Windows (culture code en-US). The application will run on a system that uses Japanese Windows (culture code jp-JP). The application will send information to the services of Windows on the target computer. Which culture should you use to format your application's output?

    A. en-US

    B. jp-JP

    C. jp

    D. The Invariant Culture

15. Your application needs to search for substrings in longer strings. This searching should be culture-aware. What should you use to perform these searches?

    A. CultureInfo.CompareInfo

    B. Array.Sort

    C. InStr

    D. IndexOf

Answers to Review Questions

1. Items that might need to be localized include text on the user interface; form layouts; date, time, and currency formats; data input fields; graphics with local content; shortcut keys; calendars; and alphabetical order.

2. The three steps are globalization (identification of resources to be localized), localizability (verification that localizable resources have been separated from code), and localization (translation of localized resources).

APPLY YOUR KNOWLEDGE

3. A neutral culture specifies a culture but not a subculture. A specific culture specifies a culture and one or more subcultures. The invariant culture does not specify either a culture or a subculture.

4. The CurrentCulture property is used by culture-aware functions such as ToString(). The CurrentUICulture is used to locate appropriate resources to display on the user interface.

5. A default resource file has a name such as MyResources.resx. A neutral resource file has a name such as MyResources.fr.resx. A specific resource file has a name such as MyResources.fr-FR.resx. When searching for resources to load, the .NET runtime will first try to find a specific resource file, then a neutral resource file, then a default resource file.

6. You must set the Localizable property and the Language property to directly localize a form.

7. You can extract resources from an assembly resource file via a ResourceManager object at any time. Satellite assemblies are only used when a form is loaded.

8. Usually, a single UTF-16 character consists of 16 bits. However, due to surrogate characters and composed characters, a single UTF-16 character can consist of 32 bits or more.

9. When a form is mirrored, the location of controls should be flipped from one side of the form to the other; menus and the caption bar text should move to the right; and controls should fill with data starting at the right.

10. The StringInfo class supports iterating through any string, regardless of culture.

Answers to Exam Questions

1. **A.** Allowing the user to choose a culture is better than accepting the existing culture of the application, because the user might be running on a version of Windows that's not appropriate for her culture. There's no need to prompt or store a currency symbol when all necessary currency symbols are stored in the .NET Framework.

2. **B.** Neutral cultures do not contain enough information to properly localize an application. You should be using the appropriate specific culture instead.

3. **A, B.** The RegionInfo object does not expose weekday names, and forcing the user to enter days when you've already got them available is pointless. Both the DateTime class and the CultureInfo class can supply the information you need.

4. **A.** The CurrentCulture property controls formatting, and the CurrentUICulture property controls user interface resource loading.

5. **D.** The namespace for resources must exactly match the namespace that .NET assigns to the project. For a project whose name begins with a digit, .NET prepends an underscore to come up with the project name.

6. **B.** Satellite assemblies are only used when a form is first opened. For more responsive resource switching you should switch to using assembly resource files.

7. **C.** Naming for assembly resource files must follow the scheme the .NET Framework expects. Otherwise, it cannot find the resource file.

APPLY YOUR KNOWLEDGE

8. **C.** The GetBytes method translates from Unicode characters to bytes appropriate for the Encoding object in use.

9. **B, D.** The Tag property has no effect on the localization process (or on anything else), and the Localizable property must remain set to True for you to localize a form.

10. **D.** The simple division-by-sixteen algorithm does not take into account composed characters.

11. **A.** The Calendar object contains localized date and time formatting resources. The CurrentCulture property, not the CurrentUICulture property, controls which CultureInfo object supplies formatting information.

12. **C.** If you set the language property and translate the controls, .NET will automatically build the necessary resources for you.

13. **A.** To get a list of cultures that .NET can work with, you should retrieve .NET's own list by iterating over the CultureInfo.GetCultures property.

14. **D.** Always use the Invariant Culture for communication with services of Windows, no matter what language of Windows is involved.

15. **A.** Array.Sort does not locate substrings. The Instr() method is obsolete and only works in VB6 or earlier versions. IndexOf can find substrings but is not culture-aware.

Suggested Readings and Resources

1. Barwell, Fred, et al., *Professional VB.NET*, 2nd ed. Wrox, 2002.

2. Symmonds, Nick, *Internationalization and Localization Using Microsoft .NET*. Apress, 2001.

3. Resources and Localization Using the .NET Framework SDK tutorial (`http://msdn.microsoft.com/library/default.asp?url=/library/en-us/cptutorials/html/resources_and_localization_using_the__net_framework_sdk.asp`)

4. Visual Studio .NET Combined Help Collection
   - Developing World Ready Applications topic

This chapter covers the following Microsoft-specified objectives for the Creating User Services section of the Visual Basic .NET Windows-Based Applications exam:

Add controls to a Windows Form.

- **Instantiate and invoke an ActiveX control.**

Instantiate and invoke a Web service or component.

- **Instantiate and invoke a COM or COM+ component.**

- **Call native functions by using platform invoke.**

▶ Although the .NET Framework can handle nearly all your application development needs, most organizations will already have accumulated a large amount of useful code. It doesn't make sense to simply throw away this legacy code and rewrite everything from scratch. Fortunately, if you've followed recommendations to encapsulate your code into components over the years, you don't need to abandon old code to start getting the benefits of .NET. Instead, you can make use of .NET's interoperability features to use several types of legacy code:

- ActiveX controls can be placed on Windows Forms.

- COM and COM+ components can be instantiated and invoked by .NET code.

- The .NET platform invoke capability (usually referred to as PInvoke) can be used to call the Windows Application Programming Interface (API).

Using these interoperability features, you can ease your migration to .NET development. Using legacy components from .NET code means you can migrate an application piecemeal rather than trying to do it all at once.

CHAPTER 9

Working with Legacy Code

STUDY STRATEGIES

▶ Convert several ActiveX controls for use in .NET. Try both the ActiveX Control Importer and the Visual Studio .NET tools for converting the ActiveX controls.

▶ If you have an existing COM or COM+ object to work with, create a runtime callable wrapper for the object to investigate the conversion process. If you don't have any existing objects, you can build one with Visual Basic 6.0.

▶ Experiment with PInvoke to invoke some common Windows API calls.

INTRODUCTION

Migrating to a new development platform can be a painful process. In extreme cases, you might have to throw away the results of years of work when you decide it's time for a new set of tools. This can make switching to a new platform a difficult decision.

Fortunately, Microsoft recognized the need to provide easy migration paths from previous versions of its tools to the .NET world. In particular, if you heeded the advice to use COM for intercomponent communications and to design your applications as a set of COM servers and clients, you'll find the upgrade path to .NET much smoother. That's because the .NET Framework includes good support for interoperating with existing COM-based code.

From .NET components, you can easily instantiate and call COM components such as ActiveX controls or COM libraries. (In fact, interoperability works in the other direction too, with COM components able to call .NET code, though I won't cover those techniques here). Combine this with an existing modular architecture, and you get an easy migration path: Move one module at a time from COM to .NET, and use the .NET interoperability features so that the components can continue to talk to one another.

In this chapter, you'll learn about the facilities that the .NET Framework provides for using COM components and other legacy code. In particular, you'll learn about the tools and techniques necessary to call ActiveX controls, COM components, or Windows API code from the .NET Framework.

USING ACTIVEX CONTROLS

Add controls to a Windows Form: Instantiate and invoke an ActiveX control.

With their roots in the Visual Basic custom control standard, ActiveX controls have become a major means of delivering encapsulated functionality to Windows applications. The key advance underlying ActiveX controls is that they have a standard set of interfaces through which they communicate with the hosting form. By supporting these interfaces, any application can make use of any ActiveX control, without any knowledge of the internal workings of that control.

This concept has become so popular that thousands of ActiveX controls are available commercially. You can find controls to display unusual graphs, controls that implement common Internet protocols, controls that emulate spreadsheets, and many more.

But in the .NET world, an ActiveX control is useless. Windows Forms can only contain instances of classes derived from the `System.Windows.Forms.Control` class. ActiveX controls, having been built using previous technologies, do not derive from this class. So how can you possibly use an ActiveX control on a Windows Form?

The answer lies in the creation of a wrapper. In programming terms, a *wrapper* is a layer of software whose job it is to translate one set of interfaces into another. The `System.Windows.Forms` namespace contains a wrapper class, `AxHost`, whose job it is to make ActiveX controls available to Windows Forms. To a Windows Form, this class appears to be a regular Windows Forms control. To an ActiveX control, this class appears to be an ActiveX control container. When the form sends a message to the control, or vice versa, the wrapper class translates the message so that the recipient component can understand it.

The AxHost class needs to be customized to work with a particular ActiveX control. That customization is the job of the Windows Forms ActiveX Control Importer, a utility that ships with the .NET Framework.

The Windows Forms ActiveX Control Importer

To illustrate the Windows Forms ActiveX Control Importer, I'll show you in Step By Step 9.1 how to use the SysInfo control, which ships as a part of Visual Basic 6.0 on a Windows Form.

STEP BY STEP

9.1 Using the Windows Forms ActiveX Control Importer

1. Create a new folder on your hard drive to house the imported control.

2. Launch a .NET command prompt by selecting Start, Programs, Microsoft Visual Studio .NET, Visual Studio .NET Tools, Visual Studio .NET Command Prompt.

3. Inside the Command Prompt window, navigate to the folder that you created in step 1.

4. Enter this command line to run the Importer:

```
aximp c:\winnt\system32\sysinfo.ocbx
```

5. The Importer will list the names of the files it creates as part of the import process:

```
SysInfoLib.dll
AxSysInfoLib.dll
```

6. Open a Visual Basic .NET Windows application and add a new form to the project. Name the new form `StepByStep9-1.vb`.

7. Right-click the References node in Solution Explorer and select Add Reference. Select the COM tab in the Add Reference dialog box. Browse to the folder you created in step 1. Add references to both `SysInfoLib.dll` and `AxSysInfoLib.dll`.

8. Right-click the form and select View Code. Expand the Windows Form Designer Generated Code region. Modify the code for the form as follows:

```
Public Class StepByStep9_1
    Inherits System.Windows.Forms.Form

#Region " Windows Form Designer generated code "

    Public Sub New()
        MyBase.New()

        'This call is required by the Windows Form
        Designer.
        InitializeComponent()

        ' Add any initialization after the
        ' InitializeComponent() call

    End Sub
```

continues

> **WARNING**
>
> **Check the Path** You might need to modify the command line for the Importer if you're running on an operating system other than Windows NT 4.0 or Windows 2000.

continued

```vb
'Form overrides dispose to clean up the component list.
Protected Overloads Overrides _
 Sub Dispose(ByVal disposing As Boolean)
    If disposing Then
        If Not (components Is Nothing) Then
            components.Dispose()
        End If
    End If
    MyBase.Dispose(disposing)
End Sub

'Required by the Windows Form Designer
Private components As System.ComponentModel.IContainer

'NOTE: The following procedure is
' required by the Windows Form Designer
'It can be modified using the Windows Form Designer.
'Do not modify it using the code editor.
Friend WithEvents SysInfo1 As AxSysInfoLib.AxSysInfo

<System.Diagnostics.DebuggerStepThrough()>
Private Sub InitializeComponent()
    Dim resources As _
     System.Resources.ResourceManager = _
     New System.Resources.ResourceManager( _
     GetType(StepByStep9_1))
    Me.SysInfo1 = New AxSysInfoLib.AxSysInfo()
    CType(Me.SysInfo1, _
     System.ComponentModel. _
     ISupportInitialize).BeginInit()
    Me.SuspendLayout()
    '
    'SysInfo1
    '
    Me.SysInfo1.Enabled = True
    Me.SysInfo1.Name = "SysInfo1"
    Me.SysInfo1.OcxState = CType(resources.GetObject( _
     "SysInfo1.OcxState"), _
     System.Windows.Forms.AxHost.State)
    Me.SysInfo1.Size = New System.Drawing.Size(38, 38)
    Me.SysInfo1.TabIndex = 0
    '
    'StepByStep9_1
    '
    Me.AutoScaleBaseSize = _
     New System.Drawing.Size(5, 13)
    Me.ClientSize = New System.Drawing.Size(292, 273)
    Me.Controls.AddRange( _
     New System.Windows.Forms.Control() {Me.SysInfo1})
```

```
            Me.Name = "StepByStep9_1"
            Me.Text = "StepByStep9_1"
            CType(Me.SysInfo1, System.ComponentModel. _
              ISupportInitialize).EndInit()
            Me.ResumeLayout(False)

        End Sub

    #End Region

        Private Sub StepByStep9_1_Load( _
          ByVal sender As System.Object, _
          ByVal e As System.EventArgs) Handles MyBase.Load
            MessageBox.Show(SysInfo1.OSVersion)
        End Sub
    End Class
```

FIGURE 9.1
ActiveX Control on a Windows Form.

9. Switch back to the Design view of the form. You should see an instance of the SysInfo control, as shown in Figure 9.1

10. Set the form as the startup object for the project.

11. Run the project. The MessageBox statement will display the major version number of the operating system.

Although the Windows Forms ActiveX Control Importer does the work of building the necessary wrapper classes for you, you still must do a lot of work to use those classes. Because the Importer does not add the control to the toolbox in Visual Studio .NET, you must write all the code to initialize the code yourself. Getting this code right can be tricky. Fortunately, you'll see an easier way to bring an ActiveX control into your .NET Windows application project in the next section.

Importing Controls with the Toolbox

If using Visual Studio .NET to build your Visual Basic .NET applications (and I assume you are), you needn't bother with the Windows Forms ActiveX Control Importer. Instead, you can use the toolbox to add any ActiveX control from your system to the .NET environment (see Step By Step 9.2). This method takes care of most of the work for you.

ActiveX Control Properties ActiveX control properties are directly integrated into the Properties window. You can also click the ActiveX-Properties hyperlink at the bottom of the Properties window to open a property sheet for the control.

FIGURE 9.2
Adding an ActiveX control to the Visual Studio .NET toolbox.

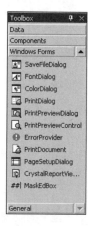

FIGURE 9.3
An ActiveX control in the Visual Studio .NET toolbox.

STEP BY STEP

9.2 Using the Toolbox to Add an ActiveX Control

1. Create a new form in your Visual Basic .NET application.

2. Right-click the toolbox and select Customize Toolbox.

3. Select the COM Components tab in the Customize Toolbox dialog box.

4. Scroll down the list of components, which will include all the ActiveX controls registered on your computer, until you find the control you want to add to your project. Click the check box for the control. Figure 9.2 shows the process of adding the Microsoft Masked Edit control.

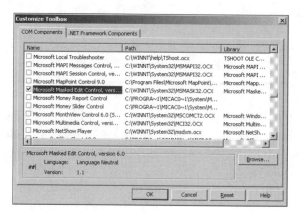

5. Click OK to add the control to the toolbox.

6. The new control will appear at the bottom of the toolbox, as shown in Figure 9.3. You can drag and drop the control to a form as with any native .NET control. Place an instance of the Masked Edit control on your form. Set the Mask property of the Masked Edit control to ##/##/##.

7. Run the project. The form will only accept the numeric characters allowed by the Masked Edit control.

Using ActiveX Controls on Windows Forms

As you've probably guessed by now, using ActiveX controls on Windows Forms is easy. Just import the ActiveX control to .NET (either by running the Windows Forms ActiveX Control Importer or by adding the control to the toolbox) and you can treat it as if it were a native .NET control. But you should consider a few things before you use ActiveX controls in your .NET applications.

First and foremost, recognize that an inevitable performance decrease occurs when you use ActiveX controls on a .NET form. The wrapper architecture, while it does allow you to seamlessly use an ActiveX control, imposes this performance penalty because every call to the control is actually a call to the wrapper class, which then must call the control itself after suitably transforming the parameters of the call. Thus your code must do twice as much work to interact with an ActiveX control as with a native .NET control. If you're only using a few ActiveX controls in a limited number of forms, this performance decrease might be unnoticeable, but if you overuse ActiveX controls, it will add up.

Some ActiveX control properties can change names when you import the control to .NET to avoid conflicts with existing objects. You're most likely to see this happen if your control has a property named `State`; such a property will be named `CtlState` after the import.

Because ActiveX controls are not managed code, they don't get any of the protection that the Common Language Runtime brings to your .NET applications. An ActiveX control is free to access memory that doesn't belong to it or to indulge in other buggy behavior that can crash your entire application.

Finally, using ActiveX controls makes deploying your .NET applications more difficult. In addition to installing the .NET Framework and your own application, you must ensure that the target machine has a copy of the ActiveX control properly installed and registered.

Because of these drawbacks, you should use ActiveX controls sparingly (if at all). Before importing an ActiveX control into your project, consider whether a native .NET control can fill your requirements.

REVIEW BREAK

▶ You can use the Windows Forms ActiveX Control Importer to create wrapper classes. These wrapper classes let you host the ActiveX control on a .NET Windows Form.

▶ You can also import an ActiveX control to a Visual Studio .NET project by adding it to the toolbox.

▶ After they're imported, ActiveX controls can be used just like native .NET controls.

▶ ActiveX controls impose a performance penalty and have other drawbacks.

Using COM Components

Instantiate and invoke a Web service or component

• **Instantiate and invoke a COM or COM+ component.**

Using ActiveX controls on a Windows Form is a special case of a more general problem: using legacy COM code from a .NET application. To see why you might want to do this, consider the task of migrating an entire application from Visual Basic 6.0 to Visual Basic .NET. Although Microsoft does offer a migration utility, it does not do a perfect job. You're likely to spend a considerable amount of time cleaning up and fixing migrated code. For a large application, this can represent a formidable barrier to migration. Still, sometimes migration is the best path. Guided Practice Exercise 9.1 examines the tradeoffs involved here.

Fortunately, if you implemented your VB6 project using a component architecture, you don't have to do a "big bang" migration all at once. .NET components can call COM components, and COM components can call .NET components. This means that you can migrate one component (a control, a class library, and so on) at a time and still keep all your code working together.

Why might you want to undertake such a gradual migration? There are four basic reasons for maintaining part of a system in COM components while moving other parts to .NET components:

◆ It takes time to learn enough about Visual Basic .NET and the .NET Framework to be productive. While making your way up the learning curve, you might have to continue developing existing COM components.

◆ You might have components that can't be easily moved to .NET because they use language features no longer supported, or because of other implementation quirks.

◆ It takes time to move code from one system to the other. Unless you can afford extended downtime, a gradual move lets you write the converted code at a slower pace.

◆ Your application might depend on third-party controls or libraries for which you do not have the source code.

In this section of the chapter, you'll learn how to encapsulate COM components for use from .NET applications. As with ActiveX controls, both command-line and GUI tools can work with COM components. Before seeing those tools, though, you should know a bit more about wrapper classes.

Understanding Runtime Callable Wrappers

As you probably already know, Visual Basic .NET creates code that operates within the .NET Common Language Runtime (CLR). Code that operates within the CLR is called *managed code*. Managed code benefits from the services that the CLR offers, including garbage collection, memory management, and support for versioning and security.

Code that does not operate within the CLR is called *unmanaged code*. Code created by tools before .NET is by definition unmanaged code. COM components are unmanaged code, because COM was designed before the CLR existed, and COM components don't make use of any of its services.

Managed code expects that all the code with which it interacts will use the CLR. This is an obvious problem for COM components.

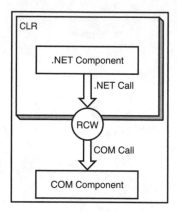

FIGURE 9.4
The architecture of a runtime callable wrapper.

How can you take a component that was developed before the advent of .NET and make it look like a .NET component to other .NET components? The answer is to use a *proxy*. In general terms, a proxy accepts commands and messages from one component, modifies them, and passes them to another component. The particular type of proxy that allows you to use COM components within a .NET application is called a *runtime callable wrapper (RCW)*, a proxy that can be called by the CLR.

Figure 9.4 shows schematically how the pieces fit together.

To see how COM works, you'll need a COM library. Step By Step 9.3 shows you how to build a simple one.

STEP BY STEP

9.3 Building a COM DLL

1. Launch Visual Basic 6.0. Create a new ActiveX DLL project.

2. Select the Project1 node in the Project Explorer window and rename it MyCustomer.

3. Select the Class1 node in the Project Explorer window and rename it Balances.

4. Add this code to the Balances class:

```
Option Explicit

Private mintCustomerCount As Integer
Private macurBalances(1 To 10) As Currency

' Create a read-only CustomerCount property
Public Property Get CustomerCount() As Integer
    CustomerCount = mintCustomerCount
End Property

' Create a GetBalance method
Public Function GetBalance( _
 CustomerNumber As Integer) As Currency
    GetBalance = macurBalances(CustomerNumber)
End Function

' Initialize the data
Private Sub Class_Initialize()
    Dim intI As Integer
```

```
      mintCustomerCount = 10

      For intI = 1 To 10
          macurBalances(intI) = Int(Rnd(1) * 100000) / 100
      Next intI

End Sub
```

5. Save the Visual Basic project.

6. Select File, Build MyCustomer.dll to create the COM
component.

> **NOTE**
>
> **If You Don't Have VB 6.0** You can
> still test COM interoperability by work-
> ing with a COM library already
> installed on your computer. A variety
> of Microsoft components, including
> Office, SQL Server, and ADO, install
> COM libraries.

Using TLBIMP

The task of using COM components from .NET is made substan-
tially easier by the fact that COM components, like .NET components, have metadata to describe their interfaces. For .NET
components, this metadata is embedded in the assembly manifest.
For COM components, the metadata is stored in a type library. A
type library can be a separate file, or (as with Visual Basic 6 class
libraries) it can be embedded within another file.

The .NET Framework includes a tool, the *Type Library Importer*,
that can create an RCW from COM metadata contained in a type
library (see Step By Step 9.4).

STEP BY STEP

9.4 Using the Type Library Importer

1. Launch a .NET command prompt by selecting Start,
Programs, Microsoft Visual Studio .NET, Visual Studio
.NET Tools, Visual Studio .NET Command Prompt.

2. Inside the Command Prompt window, navigate to the
folder that contains the MyCustomers.dll COM library.

3. Enter this command line to run the Type Library
Importer:

```
tlbimp MyCustomer.dll /out:NETMyCustomer.dll
```

continues

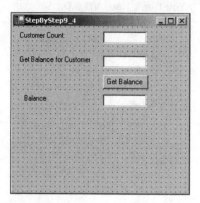

FIGURE 9.5
A form to test the use of a COM component.

continued

4. Add a new form to your Visual Basic .NET application.

5. Place three labels, a TextBox control named `txtCustomerCount`, a TextBox control named `txtCustomerNumber`, a Button control named `btnGetBalance`, and a TextBox control named `txtBalance` on the form. Figure 9.5 shows the design of this form.

6. Right-click the References node in Solution Explorer and select Add Reference.

7. Click the Browse button in the Add Reference dialog box. Browse to the NETMyCustomer.dll file that you created in step 3. Click OK to add the reference to the project.

8. Double-click the Button control to open the form's module. Enter this line of code at the top of the module:

```
Imports NETMyCustomer
```

9. Enter this code within the module:

```
Dim B As Balances

Private Sub StepByStep9_4_Load( _
 ByVal sender As System.Object, _
 ByVal e As System.EventArgs) Handles MyBase.Load
    B = New Balances()
    txtCustomerCount.Text = B.CustomerCount
End Sub

Private Sub btnGetBalance_Click( _
 ByVal sender As System.Object, _
 ByVal e As System.EventArgs) Handles btnGetBalance.Click
    txtBalance.Text =
 B.GetBalance(txtCustomerNumber.Text)
End Sub
```

10. Set the form as the startup object for the project.

11. Run the project. The form will display the customer count in the first TextBox control. Enter a number between 1 and 10 in the customer number TextBox control and click the Button control to see that customer's balance.

In the previous Step By Step, you used the Type Library Importer to create a runtime callable wrapper for the COM type library.

This RCW is a library that you can add to your .NET project as a reference. After you've done that, the classes in the COM component can be used just like native .NET classes. When you use a class from the COM component, .NET makes the call to the RCW, which in turn forwards the call to the original COM component and returns the results to your .NET managed code.

The Type Library Importer supports a set of command-line options. Table 9.1 shows the available options.

TABLE 9.1

OPTIONS FOR THE TYPE LIBRARY IMPORTER

Option	Meaning
/asmversion:*versionNumber*	Specifies the version number for the created assembly
/delaysign	Prepares the assembly for delay signing
/help	Displays help on command-line options
/keycontainer:*containerName*	Signs the assembly with the strong name from the specified key container
/keyfile:*filename*	Signs the assembly with the strong name from the specified key file
/namespace:*namespace*	Specifies the namespace for the created assembly
/out:filename	Specifies the name of the created assembly
/primary	Produces a primary interop assembly
/publickey:*filename*	Specifies the file containing a public key used to sign the resulting file
/reference:*filename*	Specifies a file to be used to resolve references from the file being imported
/silent	Suppresses information that would otherwise be displayed on the command line during conversion
/strictref	Refuses to create the assembly if one or more references cannot be resolved
/sysarray	Imports COM SafeArrays as instances of the System.Array.Class type
/unsafe	Creates interfaces without Net security checks
/verbose	Displays additional information on the command line during conversion
/?	Displays help on command-line options

EXAM TIP

Options Overview You don't need to memorize all the options to the Type Library Importer. You should know that most of the options deal with the security of the resulting RCW and the code that it contains.

Using COM Components Directly

As with ActiveX controls, the Visual Studio .NET interface provides a streamlined way to use a COM component from your .NET code. Step by Step 9.5 demonstrates this easy direct reference method.

STEP BY STEP

9.5 Using Direct Reference with a COM Library

1. Add a new form to your Visual Basic .NET application.

2. Place three labels, a TextBox control named txtCustomerCount, a TextBox control named txtCustomerNumber, a Button control named btnGetBalance, and a TextBox control named txtBalance on the form. Refer to Figure 9.5 for the design of this form.

3. Right-click the References node in Solution Explorer and select Add Reference.

4. Select the COM tab in the Add Reference dialog box. Scroll down the list of COM components until you come to the MyCustomer library. Select the MyCustomer library, click Select, and then click OK.

5. Double-click the Button control to open the form's module. Enter this line of code at the top of the module:

```
Imports MyCustomer
```

6. Enter this code within the module:

```
Dim B As MyCustomer.Balances

Private Sub StepByStep9_5_Load( _
 ByVal sender As System.Object, _
 ByVal e As System.EventArgs) Handles MyBase.Load
    B = New MyCustomer.Balances()
    txtCustomerCount.Text = B.CustomerCount
End Sub

Private Sub btnGetBalance_Click( _
 ByVal sender As System.Object, _
 ByVal e As System.EventArgs) Handles btnGetBalance.Click
    txtBalance.Text = B.GetBalance(txtCustomerNumber.Text)
End Sub
```

7. Set the form as the startup object for the project.

8. Run the project. The form will display the customer count in the first TextBox control. Enter a number between 1 and 10 in the customer number TextBox control and click the Button control to see that customer's balance.

When you directly reference a COM library from the Visual Studio .NET IDE, the effect is almost the same as if you had used the Type Library Importer to import the same library. Visual Studio .NET creates a new namespace with the name of the original library and then exposes the classes from the library within that namespace.

Although you can use either of the two methods you've seen to call a COM component from a .NET component, circumstances can call for one method over the other:

◆ For a COM component that you wrote yourself, and that will only be used in a single Visual Basic .NET project, use the easiest method: direct reference from your .NET project. This method is only suitable for a truly private component that does not need to be shared.

◆ If a COM component is shared among multiple projects, use the Type Library Importer, so you can sign the resulting assembly and place it in the Global Assembly Cache (GAC). Shared code must be signed.

◆ If you need to control details of the created assembly, such as its name, namespace, or version number, you must use the Type Library Importer. The direct reference method gives no control over these details.

> **WARNING**
>
> **Only Import Your Own Code** You should not use either one of these methods on code written by another developer, because you are not allowed to sign code written by someone else. If you need to use a COM component from another developer, you should obtain a primary interop assembly (PIA) from the original developer of the component. Microsoft supplies PIAs for all their own common libraries. For example, there's an ADODB PIA for when you want to use the legacy ADO library.

USING COM+ COMPONENTS

COM+ is the Component Services layer of Windows 2000 and later operating systems. COM+ supplies a number of services to components running under Windows. These include:

◆ Role-based security

◆ Object pooling and reusability

◆ Queued components for asynchronous calls

◆ Transactional processing

◆ A publish-and-subscribe events model

Despite the significant differences between COM+ and straight COM, you needn't do anything differently using a COM+ component from when using a COM component. To the consumer, a COM+ component looks much like a COM component. The Type Library Importer and Visual Studio .NET can both create wrappers for COM+ components using the same procedures that they use for COM components.

GUIDED PRACTICE EXERCISE 9.1

In this exercise, you'll compare the performance of two implementations of the same code, using a COM library for one implementation and a native .NET class for the other implementation. You should pick some code that takes a reasonably long time to run, so you can detect any differences between the two.

Try this on your own first. If you get stuck or would like to see one possible solution, follow these steps:

1. Launch Visual Basic 6.0. Create a new ActiveX DLL project.

2. Select the Project1 node in the Project Explorer window and rename it Numeric.

3. Select the Class1 node in the Project Explorer window and rename it to Primes.

4. Add this code to the Primes class:

```
Option Explicit

Public Function HighPrime(Max As Long) As Long
        Dim a() As Byte
        Dim lngI As Long
        Dim lngJ As Long

        ReDim a(Max)

        ' In the array, 1 indicates a prime,
        ' 0 indicates nonprime. Start by marking
        multiples
```

EXAM TIP

Timing Code   To tell how long a piece of code takes to run, you can use arithmetic with two instances of the DateTime class to produce a TimeSpan object.

```
        ' of 2 as nonprime
        For lngI = 0 To Max
            If lngI Mod 2 = 0 And lngI <> 2 Then
                a(lngI) = 0
            Else
                a(lngI) = 1
            End If
        Next lngI
        ' Now execute the usual
        ' sieve of erasthones algorithm
        For lngI = 3 To Sqr(Max) Step 2
            If a(lngI) = 1 Then
                ' This is a prime, so
                ' eliminate its multiples
                For lngJ = lngI + lngI To Max Step lngI
                    a(lngJ) = 0
                Next lngJ
            End If
        Next lngI
        ' Find the largest prime by working backwards
        For lngI = Max To 1 Step -1
            If a(lngI) = 1 Then
                HighPrime = lngI
                Exit For
            End If
        Next lngI

    End Function
```

5. Save the Visual Basic project.

6. Select File, Build Numeric.dll to create the COM component.

7. In your Visual Basic .NET project, right-click the References node of Solution Explorer and select Add Reference.

8. Select the COM tab in the Add Reference dialog box. Scroll down the list of COM components until you come to the Numeric library. Select the Numeric library, click Select, and then click OK.

9. Add a new class to your Visual Basic .NET project. Name the class `Primes.vb`.

10. Add this code to the `Primes.vb` class:

```
Public Class Primes
    Public Function HighPrime(ByVal Max As Long) As Long
        Dim a() As Byte
        Dim intI As Integer
        Dim intJ As Integer

        ReDim a(Max)
```

continues

continued

```
' In the array, 1 indicates a prime,
' 0 indicates nonprime. Start by marking
  multiples
' of 2 as nonprime
For intI = 0 To Max
    If intI Mod 2 = 0 And intI <> 2 Then
        a(intI) = 0
    Else
        a(intI) = 1
    End If
Next intI
' Now execute the usual
' sieve of erasthones algorithm
For intI = 3 To System.Math.Sqrt(Max) Step 2
    If a(intI) = 1 Then
        ' This is a prime, so
        ' eliminate its multiples
        For intJ = intI + intI To Max Step intI
            a(intJ) = 0
        Next intJ
    End If
Next intI
' Find the largest prime by working backwards
For intI = Max To 1 Step -1
    If a(intI) = 1 Then
        HighPrime = intI
        Exit For
    End If
Next intI

    End Function

End Class
```

11. Add a new form to your Visual Basic .NET Project. Name the form `GuidedPracticeExercise9-1.vb`.

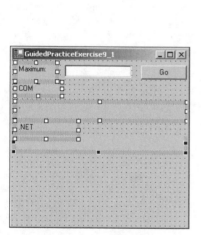

FIGURE 9.6
A form to compare execution speed.

12. Place five Label controls, a Button control, and a TextBox control on the form. Name the two blank Label controls `lblCOMresults` and `lblNETresults`. Name the Button control `btnGo`, and name the TextBox control `txtMaximum`. Figure 9.6 shows a design for this form.

13. Double-click the Button control to open the form's module. Add this statement to the top of the module:

```
Imports Numeric
```

14. Add this code to run when the Button control is clicked:

```
Private Sub btnGo_Click(ByVal sender As System.Object, _
 ByVal e As System.EventArgs) Handles btnGo.Click
    Dim lngHighPrime As Long
```

```
        Dim COM_Primes As Numeric.Primes = New
        Numeric.Primes()
        Dim dt1 As DateTime = DateTime.Now
        lngHighPrime = COM_Primes.HighPrime(txtMaximum.Text)
        Dim ts1 As TimeSpan = DateTime.Now.Subtract(dt1)
        lblCOMresults.Text = "High prime = " & _
         lngHighPrime.ToString() & _
          " took " & ts1.Ticks.ToString & " ticks"

        Dim NET_Primes As Primes = New Primes()
        Dim dt2 As DateTime = DateTime.Now
        lngHighPrime = NET_Primes.HighPrime(txtMaximum.Text)
        Dim ts2 As TimeSpan = DateTime.Now.Subtract(dt2)
        lblNETresults.Text = "High prime = " & _
         lngHighPrime.ToString() & _
          " took " & ts2.Ticks.ToString & " ticks"

    End Sub
```

15. Set the form as the startup object for the project.

16. Run the project. Enter a fairly large number in the TextBox control and click the Button control. The code will find the largest prime number smaller than the number you entered, first with the COM library and then with the native .NET class. It will display the relative execution times for the two versions, as shown in Figure 9.7.

FIGURE 9.7
Comparing the execution speed of two classes.

USING PLATFORM INVOKE

Instantiate and invoke a Web service or component.

Call native functions by using platform invoke.

So far, you've seen interoperability between managed code and unmanaged code by way of method calls to classes in COM libraries. A second way .NET can interoperate with unmanaged code is through functional calls to unmanaged libraries. The *platform invoke* (often abbreviated PInvoke) feature of .NET allows .NET code to call functions from unmanaged libraries such as the Windows API (see Step By Step 9.6).

WARNING

The Pitfalls of Performance In this particular example, the .NET class was about 20% faster than the COM class, but timing performance on Windows is notoriously difficult for several reasons. First, although you can measure things down to the timer tick, the hardware does not provide precise, to-the-tick numbers. Second, because of caching and other programs in memory, timings tend not to be repeatable. Finally, it's hard to write exactly equivalent COM and .NET code. Nevertheless, repeated runs of a program such as this example can give general information on which of two alternatives is faster.

STEP BY STEP

9.6 Using Platform Invoke with the Windows API

1. Add a new module to your Visual Basic .NET application. Name the new module `API.vb`.

2. Add this code to the `API.vb` module:

```
Public Module API

    Declare Auto Function GetComputerName Lib _
    "kernel32" ( _
    ByVal lpBuffer As String, _
    ByRef nSize As Integer) As Integer

End Module
```

3. Add a new form to your Visual Basic .NET application.

4. Place a Label control named `lblComputerName` on the form.

5. Double-click the form to open its module. Enter this line of code at the top of the module:

```
Imports System.Text
```

6. Enter this code within the module:

```
Private Sub StepByStep9_6_Load( _
 ByVal sender As System.Object, _
 ByVal e As System.EventArgs) Handles MyBase.Load

    Dim buf As String = New String(CChar(" "), 128)
    Dim len As Integer = buf.Length
    Dim ret As Integer


    ret = GetComputerName(buf, len)

    lblComputerName.Text = "This computer is named " & _
      buf.ToString.SubString(1, len)

End Sub
```

7. Set the form as the startup object for the project.

8. Run the project. The form will display the name of the computer where the code is run, as shown in Figure 9.8.

FIGURE 9.8
Calling the Windows API.

If you've used the Windows API from Visual Basic 6.0, PInvoke will look very familiar. The Declare statement (which must be contained in a module or a class module) tells the CLR where to find an API function by specifying the name of the library (in this case kernel32.dll) and the name of the function (in this case GetComputerName). Once the function is declared, you can use it within Visual Basic .NET just like any other function.

Note the use of the Auto modifier in the function declaration. You might know that many Windows API calls come in two versions, depending on the character set you're using. For example, GetComputerName really exists as GetComputerNameA (for ANSI characters) and GetComputerNameW (for Unicode characters). The Auto modifier instructs the .NET Framework to use the appropriate version of the API call for the platform where the code is running.

PInvoke can also handle API calls that require structures as parameters (see Step By Step 9.7). For example, the GetWindowRect API call fills in a structure consisting of four members that indicate the position of a window onscreen.

STEP BY STEP

9.7 Using Platform Invoke with a Struct Parameter

1. Add this statement to the top of the API.vb module:

```
Imports System.Runtime.InteropServices
```

2. Add this code to the API.vb module:

```
<StructLayout(LayoutKind.Explicit)> _
Public Structure Rect
    <FieldOffset(0)> Public left As Integer
    <FieldOffset(4)> Public top As Integer
    <FieldOffset(8)> Public right As Integer
    <FieldOffset(12)> Public bottom As Integer
End Structure

Declare Function GetWindowRect Lib "user32" ( _
 ByVal hwnd As IntPtr, ByRef lpRect As Rect) As Integer
```

3. Add a new form to your Visual Basic .NET application.

4. Place a Button control named btnGetCoordinates, four Label controls, and four TextBox controls (txtTop, txtBottom, txtLeft, and txtRight) on the form.

continues

continued

5. Double-click the Button control to open the form's module. Enter this code within the module:

```
Private Sub btnGetCoordinates_Click( +
 ByVal sender As System.Object, _
 ByVal e As System.EventArgs) _
 Handles btnGetCoordinates.Click
    Dim r As Rect
    Dim ret As Integer
    Dim hwnd As IntPtr
    hwnd = Me.Handle

    ret = GetWindowRect(hwnd, r)
    If ret Then
        txtTop.Text = r.top.ToString
        txtBottom.Text = r.bottom.ToString
        txtLeft.Text = r.left.ToString
        txtRight.Text = r.right.ToString
    End If

End Sub
```

6. Set the form as the startup object for the project.

7. Run the project. Move and resize the form, then click the button. The form will report its own coordinates, as shown in Figure 9.9.

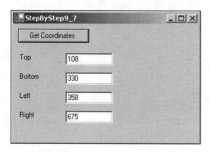

FIGURE 9.9
Information returned by the Windows API in a structure.

The tricky part of this code lies in the declaration of the structure. The StructLayout attribute tells the VB .NET compiler that you'll explicitly specify the location of the individual fields within the structure. The FieldOffset attribute specifies the starting byte of each field within the structure. Using these attributes, you can ensure that .NET constructs the same structure that the API function is expecting to receive.

R E V I E W   B R E A K

▶ Using COM or COM+ components from .NET managed code requires the creation of a runtime callable wrapper (RCW).

▶ You can create an RCW for a COM component by using the Type Library Importer, or by directly referencing the COM component from your .NET code.

▶ To use COM components you did not create, you should obtain a primary interop assembly (PIA) from the creator of the component.

▶ RCWs impose a performance penalty on COM code.

▶ You can use the .NET Platform Invoke (PInvoke) facility to call functions from Windows libraries, including the Windows API.

CHAPTER SUMMARY

Although the .NET Framework is extensive, it is not all-encompassing. Many projects need a mix of old (COM or Windows) components and new (.NET) components. Even if all the necessary facilities are available within the .NET Framework, it might not be feasible to migrate an entire existing application to .NET at once.

The .NET Framework and Visual Studio .NET include a variety of features designed to make using legacy components easier. In this chapter, you saw three of those features:

KEY TERMS
- Platform invoke
- Managed code
- Runtime callable wrapper (RCW)
- Unmanaged code

◆ The capability to use ActiveX controls on a Windows Form

◆ The capability to instantiate and invoke objects from a COM component

◆ The capability to call functions from a Windows API or other DLL

You can create a wrapper for an ActiveX control by using the Windows Forms ActiveX Control Importer or by adding the control directly to the Visual Studio .NET toolbox. Either method will create wrapper classes to help host the control. The wrapper classes present the interfaces of the Control class to the Windows Form, while presenting the interfaces of an ActiveX control container to the control.

continues

COM components also depend on wrappers, called runtime callable wrappers (RCWs) to work with .NET. An RCW is a proxy that sends data back and forth between the COM component and .NET components. You can create RCWs with the Type Library Importer command-line tool or by adding the COM component to the references collection of your .NET project.

You might also need to call functions from the Windows API or other DLLs. The .NET Platform Invoke functionality lets you do this. By using the `Declare` keyword, you can tell the .NET Framework where to find a function call and what parameters to send to the call.

APPLY YOUR KNOWLEDGE

Exercises

9.1   Embedding a Web Browser Control

One ActiveX control you might find useful on Windows Forms is the WebBrowser control, which uses the Internet Explorer rendering engine to display Web pages. In this exercise, you'll see how to embed this control in a Windows Form.

Estimated Time: 15 minutes.

1. Open a Visual Basic .NET Windows Application in the Visual Studio .NET IDE.

2. Right-click the toolbox and select Customize Toolbox.

3. Select the COM Components tab in the Customize Toolbox dialog box.

4. Scroll down the list of components, which will include all the ActiveX controls registered on your computer, until you find the Microsoft Web Browser. Click the check box for the control and click OK to add the control to the toolbox.

5. Add a new form to the application.

6. Place a TextBox control named txtURL, a Button control named btnGo, and a Web Browser control named Browser1 on the form.

7. Double-click the Button control to open the form's module. Add this code to the module:

```
Private Sub Exercise9_1_Load( _
 ByVal sender As System.Object, _
 ByVal e As System.EventArgs) _
  Handles MyBase.Load
    ' Initialize the browser
    ' to a default URL
    Browser1.Navigate2( _
      "http://www.quepublishing.com/")
End Sub
```

```
Private Sub btnGo_Click( _
 ByVal sender As System.Object, _
 ByVal e As System.EventArgs) _
 Handles btnGo.Click
    ' Navigate to the specified URL
    Browser1.Navigate2(txtURL.Text)
End Sub
```

8. Set the form as the startup object for the project.

9. Run the project. Wait for the default Web page to load, or enter a URL and click the button to navigate to that URL, as shown in Figure 9.10.

FIGURE 9.10
Using the WebBrowser ActiveX control.

9.2   Using StringBuilder with API Calls

You might already know that instances of the String class in .NET are immutable. The .NET Framework allows you to pass a String as a buffer to an API call, but for the return value to be properly displayed in the string, it must destroy the variable and create a new one. In this Exercise, you'll rewrite the code from Step By Step 9.6 to use a StringBuilder instead of a String. The advantage of the StringBuilder class is that it allows modifying an existing string.

Estimated Time: 15 minutes.

APPLY YOUR KNOWLEDGE

1. Add a new module to your Visual Basic .NET application. Name the new module `API.vb`.

2. Add this code to the `API.vb` module:

```
Imports System.Text

Module API

    Declare Auto Function _
    GetComputerName Lib "kernel32" ( _
    ByVal lpBuffer As StringBuilder, _
    ByRef nSize As Integer) As Integer

End Module
```

3. Add a new form to your Visual Basic .NET application.

4. Place a Label control named `lblComputerName` on the form.

5. Double-click the Form to open its module. Enter this line of code at the top of the module:

```
Imports System.Text
```

6. Enter this code within the module:

```
Private Sub Exercise9_2_Load( _
 ByVal sender As System.Object, _
 ByVal e As System.EventArgs) _
 Handles MyBase.Load

    Dim buf As StringBuilder = _
    New StringBuilder(128)
    Dim len As Integer = buf.Capacity
    Dim ret As Integer

    ret = GetComputerName(buf, len)

    lblComputerName.Text = _
      "This computer is named " & _
      buf.ToString

End Sub
```

7. Set the form as the startup object for the project.

8. Run the project. The form will display the name of the computer where the code is run, as was shown in Figure 9.8.

EXAM TIP

StringBuilder Convenience When you use a StringBuilder object as a buffer for a Windows API call, you needn't worry about the length of the returned string. The .NET Framework automatically truncates the returned string at the first null character.

Review Questions

1. What must you do to use an ActiveX control on a form in a Visual Basic .NET Windows application?

2. What are the advantages and disadvantages of using ActiveX controls on a .NET form?

3. Name some reasons to use COM components in a .NET project.

4. What is the purpose of a runtime callable wrapper?

5. How can you create a runtime callable wrapper?

6. What should you consider when choosing how to create a runtime callable wrapper?

7. What extra steps must you take to use a COM+ component in a .NET application, as compared to using a COM component?

8. What's the difference between COM interoperability and PInvoke?

9. What is the purpose of the Auto modifier in a Declare statement?

APPLY YOUR KNOWLEDGE

Exam Questions

1. Your application uses an instance of the Microsoft Masked Edit ActiveX control to collect data from users. You deploy your application via xcopy to the users' computers. Some of the users report that the main form of the application won't load. You've checked, and those users do have the .NET Framework installed. What could be the problem?

    A. The Microsoft Masked Edit control is not installed on the problem computers.

    B. The RCW for the ActiveX control must be registered on the problem computers.

    C. The problem computers are not connected to the Internet.

    D. Service Pack 1 for the .NET Framework is not installed on the problem computers.

2. You've imported a TriState ActiveX control to the .NET toolbox and inserted an instance of it, named Control1, on your form. This control exposes a property named State that can be set to 0, 1, or 2. Which line of code can you use to set the State property of Control1 to 2?

    A. `Control1.CtlState = 2`

    B. `Control1.ActiveXState = 2`

    C. `Control1.AxState = 2`

    D. `Control1.State = 2`

3. You are responsible for migrating an existing Visual Basic 6 application to Visual Basic .NET. The existing application consists of 8 COM server components and a single client user interface component that instantiates and invokes objects from the server components.

You'd like to give the user interface of the application an overhaul and migrate to VB .NET with low risk and minimal downtime. How should you proceed?

    A. Use the Visual Basic Migration Wizard to bring all the existing code into Visual Basic .NET.

    B. Bring only the user interface code into Visual Basic .NET. Use COM interop to call the existing COM servers form the .NET user interface code. Migrate the servers one by one.

    C. Bring all the servers into Visual Basic .NET. Use COM interop to call the migrated servers from the existing user interface code.

    D. Cut and paste all the existing code into Visual Basic .NET.

4. Your company supplies a COM component to provide advanced data analysis for your clients. Some of your clients are moving to .NET and require a runtime callable wrapper for your component. How should you proceed?

    A. Use the Visual Basic Migration Wizard to bring the code into .NET, and recompile it.

    B. Use the Type Library Importer to create and sign a primary interop assembly for your component.

    C. Set a reference to your component from any Visual Basic .NET project to create the runtime callable wrapper for your component.

    D. Create a class that uses PInvoke to call functions from your component.

5. You wrote a COM component to supply random numbers in a specific distribution to a simple statistical client program. Now you're moving that client program to .NET. The COM component is used nowhere else, and you have not shipped copies to anyone else. You want to call the objects in the COM server from your new .NET client. How should you proceed?

   A. Set a direct reference from your .NET client to the COM server.

   B. Use the Type Library Importer to create an unsigned RCW for the COM component.

   C. Use the Type Library Importer to create a signed RCW for the COM component.

   D. Use PInvoke to instantiate classes from the COM component.

6. You have written several applications for your own use, all of which share classes from a COM component that you also wrote. You are moving the applications to .NET but intend to leave the COM component untouched. How should you proceed?

   A. Set a direct reference from each application to the existing COM component.

   B. Use the Type Library Importer to create an unsigned RCW for the COM component. Place a copy of this RCW in each application's directory.

   C. Use PInvoke to call functions from the existing COM component in each application.

   D. Use the Type Library Importer to create a signed RCW for the COM component. Place this RCW in the Global Assembly Cache.

7. Your application uses a communications library from a third-party developer. This library is implemented as a COM component. You are migrating your application to .NET. What should you do to continue to use the classes and methods within the communications library?

   A. Obtain a primary interop assembly from the developer of the library. Install the PIA in the Global Assembly Cache.

   B. Use the Type Library Importer to create a signed runtime callable wrapper for the library. Install the RCW in the Global Assembly Cache.

   C. Use the Type Library Importer to create an unsigned runtime callable wrapper for the library. Install the RCW in the Global Assembly Cache.

   D. Create wrapper code that uses PInvoke to call functions from the library. Import this wrapper code into your application.

8. Your Visual Basic .NET application uses functions from a Visual Basic 6.0 COM library implemented as a DLL via a runtime callable wrapper. You built the RCW by directly referencing the COM DLL. Users are complaining of poor performance. Which of these changes is most likely to improve the performance of your application?

   A. Recompile the Visual Basic 6.0 library as an EXE file.

   B. Switch your .NET application from Visual Basic .NET to C#.

   C. Use the Type Library Importer to create a new runtime callable wrapper.

APPLY YOUR KNOWLEDGE

D. Rewrite the Visual Basic 6.0 library as a native .NET library.

9. Your project contains the following API declaration:

```
Declare Auto Function GetComputerName _
Lib "kernel32" ( _
 ByVal lpBuffer As String, _
 ByRef nSize As Integer) As Integer
```

The project also contains code to use this API to display the computer name:

```
Private Sub ShowName()
    Dim buf As String = New String("")
    Dim len As Integer
    Dim ret As Integer
    ret = GetComputerName(buf, len)
    MessageBox.Show(buf.ToString)
End Sub
```

Users report that no computer name is displayed. What could be the problem?

A. You used an immutable String rather than a StringBuilder to hold the computer name.

B. The users' computers have no name set in their network properties.

C. You neglected to initialize the String to hold any characters.

D. You are not truncating the returned string at the returned length.

10. Your application uses the GetComputerName API function. This function exists in kernel32.dll in both ANSI and Unicode versions. Your declaration is as follows:

```
Declare Function GetComputerName _
Lib "kernel32" ( _
 ByVal lpBuffer As String, _
 ByRef nSize As Integer) As Integer
```

Your code is failing with a System.EntryPointNotFoundException exception whenever you call this function. What should you do to fix this failure?

A. Supply the full path for kernel32.dll.

B. Add the Auto modifier to the declaration.

C. Declare the function as GetComputerNameA instead of GetComputerName.

D. Declare the function as GetComputerNameW instead of GetComputerName.

11. You want to use the SysInfo ActiveX control in your Visual Basic .NET application. How can you make this control available for your Windows Forms? (Select two.)

A. Use the Type Library Importer.

B. Use the Windows Forms ActiveX Control Importer.

C. Add the control directly to the Visual Basic .NET toolbox.

D. Add a reference to the control's library.

12. You are using three classes from a COM component in your Visual Basic .NET application. You want to give the runtime callable wrapper for the COM component the same version number as the rest of your components when you ship your application. What should you do?

A. Use PInvoke to call functions from the COM component, thus eliminating the RCW.

B. Directly import the COM component into the References list. Right-click the reference and select Properties to set the version number.

APPLY YOUR KNOWLEDGE

C. Recompile the existing COM library with the desired version number before creating the RCW.

D. Use the Type Library Importer with the /asmversion option to explicitly set the version of the RCW.

13. You are planning to use two classes from a COM component in your .NET application. You'd like to place these two classes into a namespace named ComComponents. What must you do?

A. Set a direct reference to the COM component. Create an empty class file in your .NET project. Specify the ComComponents namespace in that file and import the wrapper class.

B. Use the Type Library Importer with the /namespace option to set the namespace within the RCW.

C. Use the Type Library Importer with the /out option to create a file with the desired name.

D. Use PInvoke within a Namespace declaration to import the classes.

14. Your application will use functions from a COM+ component that makes use of COM+ for publish-and-subscribe events and object pooling. Which of these methods can you use to access the classes in the COM+ component? (Select two.)

A. Use PInvoke to declare the functions within the COM+ component.

B. Add the COM+ component directly to the Visual Basic .NET toolbox.

C. Set a direct reference to the COM+ component.

D. Use the Type Library Importer to create a runtime callable wrapper for the COM+ component.

15. You have an existing COM component that contains shared classes. These classes encapsulate functionality that you want to use in your .NET application. How can you use these classes while maintaining the benefits of managed code such as type safety and automatic garbage collection?

A. Use the Type Library Importer with the /strictref option to create a runtime callable wrapper for the COM component.

B. Call the methods from the COM component directly via platform invoke.

C. Add a direct reference to the COM component.

D. Rewrite the COM component as a .NET component.

Answers to Review Questions

1. Use the Windows Forms ActiveX Control Importer to create a set of wrapper classes for the control, or add the control directly to the Visual Studio .NET toolbox.

2. The advantage of using an ActiveX control is that it can provide functionality not otherwise available to .NET applications. The disadvantages are that ActiveX controls impose a performance penalty, that they are unmanaged code, and that they make the distribution of your application more complex.

APPLY YOUR KNOWLEDGE

3. You might use COM components in a .NET project because you need to migrate an existing application in small pieces, or because the COM components contain unique functionality for which you do not have source code.

4. Runtime callable wrappers provide a proxy between .NET applications and COM components. The RCW translates .NET calls into COM calls and returns the COM results as .NET results.

5. You can create a runtime callable wrapper by using the Type Library Importer or by adding a direct reference to the COM component.

6. When deciding how to create an RCW, consider whether you own the source code for the COM component, whether the RCW needs to go into the Global Assembly Cache, and how many .NET applications will make use of the COM component.

7. You needn't take any extra steps. For purposes of calling from a .NET application, COM components and COM+ components are identical.

8. COM interoperability allows you to instantiate COM classes within a .NET application and to invoke their members. PInvoke allows you to call functions from a DLL.

9. The Auto modifier tells the CLR to select the correct version, ANSI or Unicode, of an API for the particular platform where you are running the code.

Answers to Exam Questions

1. **A.** RCWs install by xcopy, just like any other .NET assembly. .NET does not require the Internet to run, nor do RCWs depend on Service Pack 1. When you add an ActiveX control to your application, you must ensure that that ActiveX control is installed on the target computers using its own setup.

2. **A.** Any property named State will be renamed to CtlState to avoid conflicts with the AxHost.State class.

3. **B.** Moving all the code will take longer than moving part of the code and introduces additional risk. Because you'd like to rewrite the user interface, you should move that component to .NET before the server components.

4. **B.** As the vendor of the component, it's your responsibility to supply the PIA.

5. **A.** For components that you wrote, and that are used in a single project, the simplest method of creating the RCW is best.

6. **D.** Shared libraries should be places in the Global Assembly Cache. Code must be signed before it can be placed in the GAC, and only the Type Library Importer can sign an RCW.

7. **A.** Because you did not write the code for the communications library, the proper way to proceed is to obtain a PIA from the original author.

8. **D.** Changing from a DLL to an EXE or from VB .NET to C# will have no significant effect on performance. RCWs are the same no matter how they're created. But rewriting the library into .NET will probably speed it up because it eliminates the extra calls in the proxy layer.

APPLY YOUR KNOWLEDGE

9. **C.** Although strings are generally immutable, the .NET Framework lets them change in PInvoke calls. All computers must have a name set. Not truncating the string might display bad data, but it would display some data. The code as it exists supplies a zero-character buffer to the API call.

10. **B.** The Auto modifier is necessary to tell the CLR to use the ANSI or Unicode versions of the function as appropriate to the operating system.

11. **B, C.** These are the two methods for using an ActiveX control within a .NET project.

12. **D.** Only the Type Library Importer can explicitly set the version number for an RCW.

13. **B.** Only the Type Library Importer can set the namespace for an RCW.

14. **C, D.** You can use COM+ components through the same techniques that you use with COM components.

15. **D.** Only managed code benefits from the features of the CLR. The only way to turn the component into managed code is to rewrite it in .NET.

Suggested Readings and Resources

1. Nathan, Adam. *.NET and COM: The Complete Interoperability Guide.* Sams Publishing, 2002.

2. Troelsen, Andrew. *Visual Basic .NET and the .NET Platform.* Apress, 2001.

3. Visual Studio .NET Combined Help Collection:

   • "Interoperating with Unmanaged Code"

This chapter covers the following Microsoft-specified objectives for the Creating User Services section of the Visual Basic .NET Windows-Based Applications exam:

Implement online user assistance.

Implement accessibility features.

▶ Perhaps at one time an application was finished when the code functioned properly, but that is certainly no longer the case. Users and managers alike expect more than properly functioning code in a useful and usable application. From the process of defining requirements right through the necessity to supply post-installation support, applications exist as part of a wide range of features and activities. In this chapter, I'll look at two of the necessary parts of shipping any complex Windows application:

- *User assistance* refers to the process of providing help within an application through a variety of means.

- *Accessibility* refers to the coding you must do to make your application usable by those with disabilities.

Developers sometimes think of user assistance and accessibility features as the icing on the cake that can be left out if they're in a hurry. That's a fundamental misunderstanding of the importance of these features. User assistance and accessibility should be designed into your applications right from the start and implemented as a matter of course with each new feature that you add.

CHAPTER 10

User Assistance and Accessibility

▶ Use the standalone HTML Help Workshop or the integrated Help Workshop to create an HTML Help file for one of your own applications. Ensure that you understand how to create help topics and how to hook them up to the user interface.

▶ Use the ToolTip component to add ToolTips to one of your own applications.

▶ Review the documentation from the HTML Help SDK to get an idea of the advanced capabilities of HTML Help.

▶ Refer to the topic "Walkthrough: Creating an Accessible Windows Application" in the Visual Studio .NET Combined Help Collection for another example of setting accessibility properties.

▶ Use the testing strategies described in this chapter to evaluate some existing Windows applications for accessibility.

INTRODUCTION

Building the best program in the world is useless if no one but the original developer can use it. As applications grow ever more complex, it's incumbent upon their developers to provide help for end users of the applications. Visual Studio .NET provides strong support for two specific types of help: *user assistance* and *accessibility*.

User assistance refers to the type of help you get from the traditional help file: a set of short topics designed to teach you what you need to know to effectively use the capabilities of an application. Windows forms are designed to integrate with *HTML Help*, Microsoft's current standard for building application help. They also support more immediate help through the use of *ToolTips*, short messages that pop up when the user hovers his cursor over a control.

Accessibility refers to ensuring that users with disabilities can work with your application. In the United States alone over thirty million people have some disability that can affect their ability to use software, according to government figures. Windows and the .NET Framework include a variety of tools and techniques to help you make your application accessible to these users.

In this chapter, you'll learn how to create HTML Help files and how to integrate those files with your applications. You'll also learn how to design an application for accessibility, as well as methods for implementing and testing accessibility.

SELECTING A HELP COMPILER

You have two choices when creating an HTML Help file using Microsoft tools. As I write this, in mid 2002, the latest released version of HTML Help is HTML Help 1.3. This version is installed with Visual Studio .NET and has been in use for some time now.

An alternative if you'd like more modern-looking help is HTML Help 2, which is in beta as I write this chapter and should ship some time in 2003. This new version is readily available, and you might choose to work with it.

If company policy or personal preference dictates that you use only released software, HTML Help 1.3 is probably your best bet. If you don't mind being on the cutting edge, you can download HTML Help 2. Of course, after HTML Help 2 is released it will be the current version, suitable for everyone. Fortunately, HTML Help 2 includes tools to convert HTML Help 1.3 projects, so if you decide to wait you won't lose any of the effort that you put into writing HTML Help 1.3 files.

I'll discuss both versions of HTML Help in this chapter, starting with the older HTML Help 1.3.

> **WARNING**
>
> **Context-Sensitive Help**   As of this writing, Microsoft has documented how to create HTML Help 2 files but has not yet released the API necessary to call them from a Visual Basic .NET form. If you require context-sensitive help in your applications, you should stick with HTML Help 1.3 until HTML Help 2 is released.

CREATING HTML HELP 1.3

Implement online user assistance.

Several standards for help files have been in various versions of Windows. The standard help for .NET applications is HTML Help, Microsoft's familiar multiple-pane help, whose contents are created in HTML. If you install Visual Studio .NET, it will install the HTML Help Software Development Kit (SDK) version 1.3 by default. This SDK contains the tools and documentation you need to create your own help files. Figure 10.1 shows a typical HTML Help file (in this case, the help for the HTML Help SDK itself).

> **EXAM TIP**
>
> **Latest Version**   If you didn't install the HTML Help SDK, or if you want to check for a later version, visit the HTML Help download page on the MSDN Web site at http://msdn.microsoft.com/library/default.asp?url=/library/en-us/htmlhelp/html/hwMicrosoftHTMLHelpDownloads.asp.

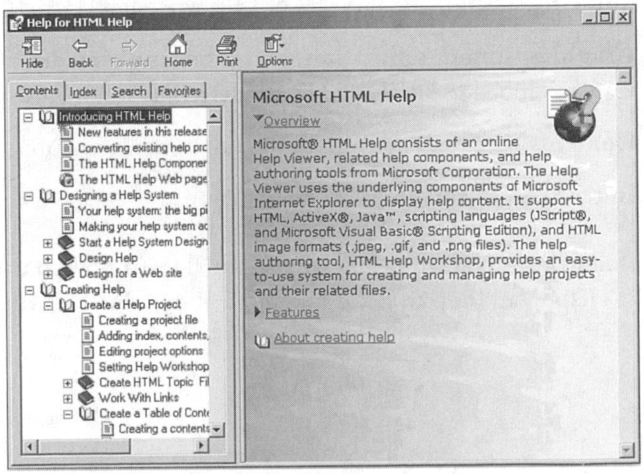

FIGURE 10.1
An HTML Help file.

The HTML Help SDK includes a number of components:

◆ **HTML Help Workshop**—An IDE for developing HTML Help files

◆ **HTML Help ActiveX Control and HTML Help Java Applet**—Components that can be used for advanced navigation in HTML Help files

◆ **HTML Help Viewer**—A host application that can display HTML Help files

◆ **HTML Help Image Editor**—Captures screenshots and performs graphics-editing tasks

◆ **HTML Help program**—Executes HTML Help files outside of the browser

◆ **HTML Help Compiler**—Converts files from the HTML Help Workshop into actual HTML Help files

◆ **HTML Help Authoring Guide**—Contains help for developers of HTML Help files

A number of files go into a full HTML Help system. These files can all be created and manipulated within HTML Help Workshop. The parts of an HTML Help system include the following:

◆ **A help project file**—Determines the overall structure of the HTML help file

◆ **Topic files**—Individual pieces of help written as HTML files

◆ **Graphics, sound, animation, and other multimedia files**—Can be embedded within HTML Help files

◆ **Contents files**—Contain table of contents information

◆ **Index files**—Contain index information

In the following sections of this chapter, you'll learn how to use HTML Help Workshop to build and test a simple HTML Help file.

Creating a Help Project

The first step in creating an HTML Help file is to create a new help project. Step By Step 10.1 will guide you through this process.

STEP BY STEP

10.1 Creating a Help Project File

1. Launch HTML Help Workshop by selecting Start, Programs, HTML Help Workshop, HTML Help Workshop.

2. Select File, New. In the New dialog box, select Project as the type of file to create and click OK.

3. This will launch the New Project Wizard. Read the introductory panel and click Next.

4. On the Destination panel of the New Project Wizard, name the new project file Random.hhp. Browse to choose an appropriate location for this file. Click Next.

5. Leave the check boxes on the Existing Files panel of the New Project Wizard unchecked and click Next.

6. Click Finish to create the new help project file.

7. Click the Change Project Options button on the Project tab in the HTML Help Workshop IDE.

8. Set the Title property for the help file to Help for Random and click OK.

9. Click the Save button to save the help project file. Figure 10.2 shows the new file open in HTML Help Workshop.

FIGURE 10.2
New help project in HTML Help Workshop.

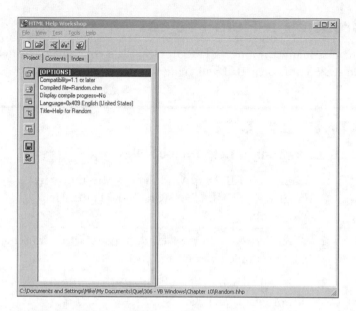

Creating Topic Files

After you've created a help project, the next step is to populate the project with topic files. Topic files are HTML pages, each of which is designed to give help to the user in a specific situation. Writing help topics requires you to know what the application will do, of course. So I'll take a detour in Step By Step 10.2 and build a simple application to deliver random numbers to the user interface. This application will serve as a test bed for help and accessibility features over the course of this chapter.

STEP BY STEP

10.2 Building an Application That Requires User Assistance

1. Launch Visual Studio .NET and create a new Visual Basic .NET Windows application.

2. Add a new form to the application. Name the form `RandomForm.vb` and set its `Text` property to `Random Number Server`.

3. Add a MainMenu control, a Label control, a TextBox control, and a Button control to the form. Name the Label control lblRange. Name the TextBox control txtRandom and clear its Text property. Name the Button control btnGetRandom and set its Text property to Get Random.

4. Add a top-level menu named mnuTools with the text &Tools. Add a menu item to this menu named mnuToolsOptions with the text &Options. Add a top-level menu named mnuHelp with the text &Help. Add a menu item to this menu named mnuHelpContents with the text &Contents.

5. Add a second from to the project. Name this form frmOptions. Set its Text property to Options, its MaximizeButton and MinimizeButton properties to False, its HelpButton property to True, and its FormBorderStyle property to FixedDialog.

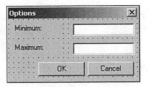

6. Place two Label controls, two TextBox controls (txtMin and txtMax), and two Button controls (btnOK and btnCancel) on frmOptions. Set the DialogResult property of btnOK to OK, and set the DialogResult property of btnCancel to Cancel. Figure 10.3 shows a design for this form.

FIGURE 10.3
An Options form for the sample project.

7. Double-click the form RandomForm to open its module. Enter this code behind the form:

```
Private mintMin = 1
Private mintMax = 1000

Private Sub mnuToolsOptions_Click( _
 ByVal sender As System.Object, _
 ByVal e As System.EventArgs) Handles mnuToolsOptions.Click
    Dim f As frmOptions = New frmOptions()
    f.txtMin.Text = CStr(mintMin)
    f.txtMax.Text = CStr(mintMax)
    f.ShowDialog()
    If f.DialogResult = DialogResult.OK Then
        mintMin = CInt(f.txtMin.Text)
        mintMax = CInt(f.txtMax.Text)
        lblRange.Text = _
         "Generate a random number between " & _
         CStr(mintMin) & " and " & CStr(mintMax)
    End If
End Sub
```

continues

continued

```
Private Sub RandomForm_Load(ByVal sender As System.Object, _
 ByVal e As System.EventArgs) Handles MyBase.Load
    mintMin = 1
    mintMax = 1000
End Sub

Private Sub btnGetRandom_Click( _
 ByVal sender As System.Object, _
 ByVal e As System.EventArgs) Handles btnGetRandom.Click
    Dim r As Random = New Random()
    txtRandom.Text = CStr(r.Next(mintMin, mintMax))
End Sub
```

8. Set RandomForm as the start object for the project.

9. Run the project. Click the Button control to get a random number. Select Tools, Options to open the Options form. Adjust the minimum and maximum and click OK. Verify that random numbers are now in the new range.

For this simple application, create three help topics:

1. An introductory topic that explains the purpose and use of the application

2. A topic that can be invoked from the main RandomForm, explaining how to generate random numbers

3. A topic that can be invoked from the frmOptions form, explaining how to set the program options

In Step By Step 10.3, you'll see how to use HTML Help Workshop to create these topics.

STEP BY STEP

10.3 Creating Help Topics.

1. In HTML Help Workshop, select File, New or click the New button on the toolbar. Select HTML File in the New dialog box and click OK.

2. Set the title of the new file to `Welcome to Random` and click OK to open the new file in the HTML Help Workshop workspace, as shown in Figure 10.4.

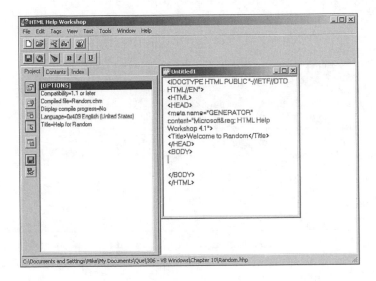

FIGURE 10.4
Creating a new HTML Help topic.

3. Modify the HTML file as follows:

```
<!DOCTYPE HTML PUBLIC "-//IETF//DTD HTML//EN">
<HTML>
<HEAD>
<meta name="GENERATOR" content="Microsoft&reg;
HTML Help Workshop 4.1">
<Title>Welcome to Random</Title>
</HEAD>
<BODY>
<h1>Welcome to the Random Server</h1>
<p>The Random Server application is designed
to serve all of your integer random
number needs. Just run the program and
click to get as many random numbers as
you would like. The numbers can be in
any range you like. Randomness guaranteed
or your money back (this application
is 100% free)!</p></BODY>
</HTML>
```

4. Select File, Save File and save this file as `Welcome.html`.

continues

> **EXAM TIP**
>
> **Creating HTML Help Topics** HTML Help topics are just standard HTML files. If you don't feel comfortable writing raw HTML, you can create these files with any HTML authoring tool you like, such as Microsoft FrontPage. Then just cut and paste the HTML into HTML Help Workshop.

continued

5. Add a second new HTML file. Give this file the title `Generating Random Numbers`. Modify its text as follows:

```
<!DOCTYPE HTML PUBLIC "-//IETF//DTD HTML//EN">
<HTML>
<HEAD>
<meta name="GENERATOR" content="Microsoft&reg;
HTML Help Workshop 4.1">
<Title>Generating Random Numbers</Title>
</HEAD>
<BODY>
<h1>Generating Random Numbers</h1>
<p><img src="Main.jpg"></p>
<p>This is the main form of the Random
Number Server. Click the button to
generate a random number in the specified
range. If you'd like to change the
range, select Tools, Options to open the
Options dialog box.</p>
</BODY>
</HTML>
```

6. Run the RandomServer project to capture an image of the main form, and click the button to display a random number.

7. Select Start, Programs, HTML Help Workshop, HTML Image Editor to launch the HTML Image Editor.

8. Select Capture, Using the Mouse in the HTML Image Editor window. HTML Image Editor will minimize. Move the mouse pointer over the main random server form and click the primary mouse button.

9. Select File, Save As. Save the captured image as `Main.jpg`. Accept the defaults in the JPG Image Options dialog box.

10. Save the HTML file as Main.htm.

11. Add a third new HTML file. Give this file the title `Setting Options`. Modify its text as follows:

```
<!DOCTYPE HTML PUBLIC "-//IETF//DTD HTML//EN">
<HTML>
<HEAD>
<meta name="GENERATOR" content="Microsoft&reg;
HTML Help Workshop 4.1">
<Title>Setting Options</Title>
</HEAD>
```

```
<BODY>
<h1>Setting Options</h1>
<p><img src="Options.jpg"></p>
<p>This is the options form of the
Random Number server. Enter the
minimum and maximum values you
would like to set for random numbers
and click OK. You can also click
Cancel to keep the settings
unchanged.</p></BODY>
</HTML>
```

12. Display the Options dialog box on the screen and capture it as `Options.jpg`.

13. Save the third HTML page as `Options.htm`.

At this point, you've created all the content you'll need for the help file for this application, but you still have tasks to perform before the help file is ready for use. The next step is to add links between topics.

Working with Links

One of the most important features of HTML is its support for hyperlinks. This is as true in an HTML Help file as it is on the World Wide Web. When the user presses F1 to display help, your job is to display the help topic that is most likely to apply to their current situation, but you need to also provide ways to quickly navigate to other topics, just in case your best guess is wrong. In Step By Step 10.4, you'll learn how to create links between topics in your HTML Help file, as well as how to insert a link to an external Web site.

STEP BY STEP

10.4 Inserting Links

1. In HTML Help Workshop, select the Welcome.htm file. Add two links to the bottom of this file by inserting this text just ahead of the `</BODY>` tag:

```
<p><a href="main.htm">Generating Random Numbers</a></p>
<p><a href="options.htm">Setting Options</a></p>
```

continues

continued

> **NOTE**
>
> **Special Link Types**   HTML Help also supports several special types of links, including a keyword link to find topics on a particular keyword and an associative link to group related topics. Refer to the HTML Help SDK documentation for more information on these links.

2. Add two links to the bottom of the Main.htm file by inserting this text just ahead of the `</BODY>` tag:

```
<p><a href="http://random.mat.sbg.ac.at/">
About random numbers</a></p>
<p><a href="options.htm">Setting Options</a></p>
```

As you can see, there isn't a lot to know about inserting links. Links in an HTML Help file use the same tags as links in any other HTML file. You can link to a local file using its name as the link target or to an external Web site by including its complete URL.

Creating a Table of Contents and an Index

Two more features that most professional help files should have are a table of contents and an index (see Step By Step 10.5).

STEP BY STEP

10.5 Creating a Table of Contents and an Index

1. In HTML Help Workshop, click File, New. In the New dialog box, select Table of Contents and click OK to open the Table of Contents editor window in the HTML Help Workshop workspace.

2. Save the table of contents file as `Table of Contents.hhc.`

3. Click the Options button on the Project tab of HTML Help Workshop. On the General tab, set the default file to Welcome.htm. On the Files tab, set the contents file to the Table of Contents.hhc file that you just created. Click OK.

4. Select Edit, Insert Topic. On the Entry tab of the Table of Contents Entry dialog box, set the Entry Title to `Welcome`.

Click the Add button. In the Path or URL dialog box, select the Random.hhp project file. Click the Browse button and browse to the Welcome.htm file. Click OK to add this file to the Welcome table of contents entry. Figure 10.5 shows the Table of Contents Entry dialog box at this point. Click OK to create the entry.

5. With the Welcome.htm file selected in the Table of Contents editor window, select Edit, Insert Heading. Click No to the prompt asking if you want to insert the new topic at the beginning of the table of contents. Set the entry title to Help Topics and click OK.

6. With the Help Topics folder selected in the Table of Contents editor window, select Edit, Insert Topic. On the Entry tab of the Table of Contents Entry dialog box, set the Entry Title to "Generating Random Numbers." Click the Add button. In the Path or URL dialog box, select the Random.hhp project file. Click the Browse button and browse to the Main.htm file. Click OK to add this file to the Welcome table of contents entry. Click OK to create the entry.

7. With the Generating Random Numbers entry selected in the Table of Contents editor window, select Edit, Insert Topic. On the Entry tab of the Table of Contents Entry dialog box, set the Entry Title to `Setting Options`. Click the Add button. In the Path or URL dialog box, select the Random.hhp project file. Click the Browse button and browse to the Options.htm file. Click OK to add this file to the Welcome table of contents entry. Click OK to create the entry. Figure 10.6 shows the completed table of contents in the Table of Contents editor. Click the Save button to save the table of contents.

8. In HTML Help Workshop, click File, New. In the New dialog box, select Index and click OK to open the Index editor window in the HTML Help Workshop workspace.

9. Save the index file as `Index.hhk`.

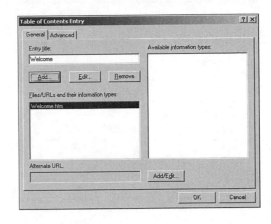

FIGURE 10.5
Creating a new table of contents entry.

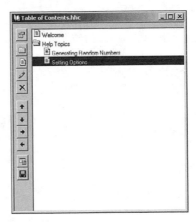

FIGURE 10.6
The Table of Contents editor.

continues

continued

10. Select Edit, Insert Keyword. Enter the keyword Random and click the Add button. In the Path or URL dialog box, select the Random.hhp project file. Click the Browse button and browse to the Main.htm file. Set the Title to Generating Random Numbers. Click OK to add this file to the Random index entry. Click the Add button again and add the Options.htm file to this keyword as well. Click OK to create the entry.

11. Select Edit, Insert Keyword. Enter the keyword Options and click the Add button. In the Path or URL dialog box, select the Random.hhp project file. Click the Browse button and browse to the Options.htm file. Set the Title to Generating Random Numbers. Click OK to add this file to the Options index entry. Click OK to create the entry.

12. Click the Options button on the Project tab of HTML Help Workshop. On the Files tab, set the index file to the index.hhk file that you just created. Click OK.

A help file for a serious application might contain hundreds of table of contents and index entries, but they're created using the same process that you just saw. The table of contents provides a structured way for the user to view the contents of the help file. The index provides a quick way for the user to search for specific information of interest.

Compiling and Testing a Help File

Now you're finally ready to build the help file and try it, which is the subject of Step By Step 10.6.

STEP BY STEP

10.6 Compiling and Testing a Help File

1. In HTML Help Workshop, save and close all the source files for the HTML Help file.

2. Click File, Compile. In the Create a Compiled File dialog box, you can select check boxes to save files or to display the finished help file when the compilation step is completed. Assign a name to the completed file and click Compile.

3. HTML Help Workshop will display a log of compile actions, as shown in Figure 10.7. If there are no errors, the end result will be a compiled help file with the extension .CHM.

4. Click the View Compiled File button on the toolbar. Browse to the HTML Help file that you just created and click View.

5. The newly created help file will open in the HTML Help viewer, as shown in Figure 10.8. You should be able to manipulate it just like any other help file.

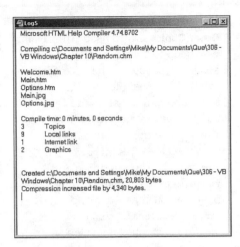

FIGURE 10.7
Compiling an HTML Help file.

FIGURE 10.8
Finished HTML Help file.

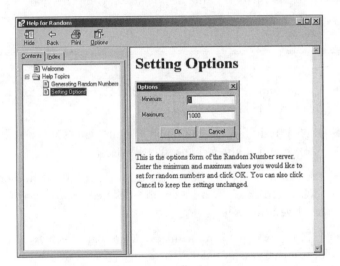

In a typical organization, three different groups will work with help files while an application is being built:

◆ User assistance specialists will create the help file.

◆ Developers will hook up the help file with the user interface (see the section "Implementing User Assistance" later in this chapter).

◆ Testers will check the work of the other two groups.

Other Choices I've used HTML Help Workshop to build a help file in this section because that help file solution ships with Visual Studio .NET, but you should be aware that a wide variety of other programs can create help files. These range from shareware programs such as FAR (`http://www.mvps.org/htmlhelpcenter/far.htm`) to full-featured commercial programs such as RoboHelp (`http://www.ehelp.com/`). If you're involved in creating help files as an ongoing activity, you should evaluate these and other alternatives.

The goal of testing a help file is to ensure that it will effectively deliver assistance to users. Here are some questions testers should ask:

◆ Does the HTML Help file compile with no error messages?

◆ Does the Help menu item in the application open the correct help file to the correct topic?

◆ Does F1 within the application bring up the correct context-sensitive help?

◆ Do all links go to the proper locations?

◆ Do all entries in the table of contents load the proper topics?

◆ Do all index entries open the proper topics?

◆ Is the formatting consistent throughout the help file?

◆ Are the spelling and grammar correct?

◆ Is the information in the help file clear, complete, and accurate?

REVIEW BREAK

▶ Visual Studio .NET includes the HTML Help SDK for the creation of HTML Help files.

▶ HTML Help files are composed of multiple HTML source files, compiled into a single .CHM file.

▶ You can create HTML Help topics with any HTML authoring tool. HTML Help Workshop provides a convenient way to organize help projects.

▶ HTML Help files can include navigation aids such as a table of contents and an index.

CREATING HTML HELP 2

The latest standard for HTML Help is HTML Help 2. Currently, you can obtain HTML Help 2 tools as part of the Visual Studio Help Integration Kit (VSHIK). The VSHIK is designed to build help files that integrate into the Visual Studio .NET shell, but you can also use it to build standalone HTML Help 2 files for your own components.

Figure 10.9 shows a typical HTML Help 2 file (in this case, a part of the help for the VSHIK itself).

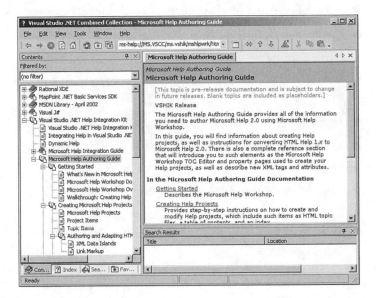

EXAM TIP

Obtaining VSHIK   You can download the VSHIK from the MSDN Web site. The VSHIK home page is located at `http:// msdn.microsoft.com/library/ default.asp?url=/library/ en-us/htmlhelp/html/ hwmscExtendingNETHelp.asp`.

FIGURE 10.9
An HTML Help 2 file.

The VSHIK includes a number of components:

◆ **Microsoft Help Workshop**—A set of tools for developing HTML Help 2 files. As you'll see in the next few sections of this chapter, these tools integrate directly into the Visual Studio .NET IDE.

◆ **The Microsoft Help Authoring Guide**—Contains help for developers of HTML Help 2 files.

◆ **The Visual Studio Help Integration Guide**—Contains help on integrating help files with Visual Studio .NET's own help. This guide will mainly be of interest to those writing tools and add-ins for Visual Studio .NET.

◆ **White papers**—Detail the process of integrating your own help into the Visual Studio .NET shell.

A number of files go into a full HTML Help 2 system. These files can all be created and manipulated within Microsoft Help Workshop. The parts of an HTML Help system include:

◆ **Topic files**—Individual pieces of help written as HTML files. You can also use text files and XML files as topic files.

◆ **Graphics, sound, animation, and other multimedia files**—Can be embedded within HTML Help files.

◆ **Table of contents files**—Contain table of contents information.

◆ **Collection Definition files**—Define the basic structure of your help file.

◆ **Include files**—Identify the topics to be included in your help file.

◆ **Index files**—Contain index information.

◆ **Virtual Topic Definition files**—Allow you to associate help keywords with Internet URLs.

◆ **Sample Definition files**—Allow you to include samples in your help files.

◆ **Attribute Definition files**—Help classify topics into categories.

Most of these files are specialized XML files. If you work with the Microsoft Help Workshop, though, you don't have to worry about the XML structure of these files. In the following sections of this chapter, you'll learn how to use Microsoft Help Workshop to build and test a simple HTML Help 2 file.

Creating a Help Project

The first step in creating an HTML Help 2 file is to create a new help project. Step By Step 10.7 will guide you through this process.

STEP BY STEP

10.7 Creating a Help 2 Project File

1. Install the Visual Studio Help Integration Kit on a computer that already has Visual Studio .NET installed.

2. Launch Visual Studio .NET. On the Start page, click the New Project button.

3. Expand the Other Projects section of the Project Types tree view and select Help Projects, as shown in Figure 10.10. Select the New Help Project template. Name the new help project `Random` and select a suitable location. Click OK.

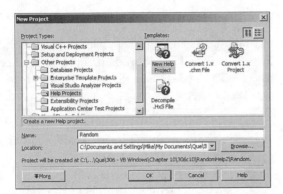

FIGURE 10.10
Creating a new HTML Help 2 file.

4. Microsoft Help Workshop will create a new project that includes a collection file with the extension HxC and an index file with the extension HxF. Right-click the project file in Solution Explorer and select Properties.

5. On the General tab of the Random Property Pages dialog box, set the Title to `Random Help` and the version to `1.0.0.0`. Click OK to save the properties.

> **NOTE**
>
> **Other Project Choices**   You can also choose to start a new HTML Help 2 project by converting an HTML Help 1.x project, decompiling a HTML Help 1.x help file, or decompiling an existing HTML Help 2 file.

Creating Topic Files

After you've created a help project, the next step is to populate the project with topic files. Topic files are HTML pages, each of which is designed to give help to the user in a specific situation. Alternatively, Microsoft Help Workshop allows you to use plain text files as topic files when you don't need the rich formatting that HTML makes possible. Topic files can also include XML data islands to define index entries and other special formatting. You'll see an example of an XML data island later when you create an index for this help file.

In Step By Step 10.8, you'll use Microsoft Help Workshop to create an HTML Help 2 version of the help topics for the Random application.

STEP BY STEP

10.8 Creating Help Topics

1. In Microsoft Help Workshop, select Project, Add New Item. Select the Help Workshop Topic Items category. Select HTML File. Name the new HTML file `Welcome.htm` and click Open.

---

2. The new HTML file will open in the Visual Studio .NET workspace. You can use all Visual Studio's editing tools to compose your HTML file visually, if you like. Alternatively, you can use the HTML tab at the bottom of the Design window to switch to HTML mode and edit the source for the page directly.

---

3. Switch to HTML view and modify the HTML file as follows:

```
<HTML xmlns:MSHelp="http://msdn.microsoft.com/mshelp">
    <HEAD>
        <meta name="vs_targetSchema" content="HTML 4.0">
        <TITLE>Welcome to Random Server</TITLE>
    </HEAD>
    <BODY>
    <h1>Welcome to the Random Server</h1>
        <p>The Random Server application is
            designed to serve all of
            your integer random number needs.
            Just run the program and
            click to get as many random
            numbers as you would like. The
            numbers can be in any range you
            like. Randomness guaranteed
            or your money back (this
            application is 100% free)!</p>
    </BODY>
</HTML></HTML>
```

> **EXAM TIP**
>
> **Existing Files** If you have existing HTML files that you'd like to add as topics to your help file, you can drag and drop them from Windows Explorer to the Solution Explorer within Visual Studio .NET.

4. Copy the Main.jpg and Options.jpg files that you created in Step By Step 10.3 to the folder that contains your HTML Help 2 project. Select Project, Add Existing Item and add these two graphics files to your project.

5. Add a second new HTML file. Name this file `Main.htm`. Use the Properties window to change the title of this document to `Generating Random Numbers`.

6. Click in the Design window and type `Generating Random Numbers`. Select this text and use the font size drop-down list on the toolbar to change it to font size 6.

7. Drag and drop an image control from the HTML toolbox to the page. Use the Properties window to change the source of the image to Main.jpg.

8. Type this help text to fill out the topic:

```
This is the main form of the Random
Number Server. Click the button to
generate a random number in the
 specified range. If you'd like to change the
range, select Tools, Options to open the Options dialog box.
```

9. Add a third new HTML file. Name this file `Options.htm`. Modify its text as follows:

```
<HTML xmlns:MSHelp="http://msdn.microsoft.com/mshelp">
    <HEAD>
        <meta name="vs_targetSchema" content="HTML 4.0">
        <TITLE>Setting Options</TITLE>
    </HEAD>
    <BODY>
        <h1>Setting Options</h1>
        <p><img src="Options.jpg"></p>
        <p>This is the options form of the Random
            Number server. Enter the minimum and
            maximum values you would like to set
            for random numbers and click OK. You can
            also click Cancel to keep the settings
            unchanged.</p>
    </BODY>
</HTML>
```

> **NOTE**
>
> **Image Capture** Unlike HTML Help Workshop, Microsoft Help Workshop does not include an integrated image capture application. A number of excellent programs are available for this purpose.

At this point, you've created all the content that you'll need for the help file for this application. As you can see, Microsoft Help Workshop offers you great flexibility in creating help content. But there are still tasks to perform before the help file is ready to be used. The next step is to add links between topics.

Working with Links

Just as in HTML Help 1.x, you can have links between topics in HTML Help 2. In fact, links help users make the most of your help file. In Step By Step 10.9, you'll learn how to create links between topics in your HTML Help file, as well as how to insert a link to an external Web site.

STEP BY STEP

10.9 Inserting Links

1. In HTML Help Workshop, select the Welcome.htm file. Switch to HTML view in the designer. Add two links to the bottom of this file by inserting this text just ahead of the `</BODY>` tag:

```
<p><a href="main.htm">Generating Random Numbers</a></p>
<p><a href="options.htm">Setting Options</a></p>
```

2. Open the Main.htm file in the designer. Type the text `About Random Numbers` at the bottom of this file. Highlight this text and select Insert, Hyperlink. In the Hyperlink dialog box, shown in Figure 10.11, type in the URL `http://random.mat.sbg.ac.at/`. Click OK to create the hyperlink.

3. Type the text `Setting Options` after the About Random Numbers hyperlink. Use the Hyperlink dialog box to link it to the options.htm file using the URL `/options.htm`. The leading slash specifies the root directory of the project.

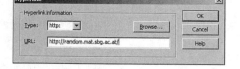

FIGURE 10.11
Inserting a hyperlink in an HTML Help 2 file.

NOTE

Special Link Types HTML Help also supports several special types of links, including a keyword link to find topics on a particular keyword and a keyword link that displays an entire list of related topics. Refer to the VSHIK documentation for more information on these links.

As you can see, there isn't a lot to know about inserting links. Links in an HTML Help file use the same tags as links in any other HTML file. You can link to a local file by using its name as the link target or to an external Web site by including its complete URL.

Creating a Table of Contents and an Index

Two more features that most professional help files should have are a table of contents and an index. Step by Step 10.10 helps you create these items.

STEP BY STEP

10.10 Creating a Table of Contents and an Index

1. In Microsoft Help Workshop, select Project, Add New Item. Select the Help Workshop Project Items category. Select the Table of Contents template. Name the file Random.HxT and click Open. The new table of contents will open in the Visual Studio Design window.

2. Drag the Welcome.htm file from Solution Explorer and drop it on top of the Global TOC node in the table of contents.

3. Right-click the default New Topic node and select Delete Node.

4. Use the Properties window to change the title of the new node to Welcome.

5. Right-click the Welcome node and select Add Blank Node. Name the new node Help Topics.

6. Right-click the Help Topics node and select Add Node From File. In the Select File for TOC dialog box, select the Main.htm file and click Open. Accept the default node title "Generating Random Numbers," which is derived from the page's <TITLE> tag.

7. Right-click the Generating Random Numbers node and select Move Node Right. Note that the Help Topics node changes from a document icon to an open book icon.

> **EXAM TIP**
>
> **Table of Contents Nodes** An HTML Help 2 table of contents must always have a Global TOC node and at least one topic node. You can't delete the default New Topic node until you've added at least one other node.

continues

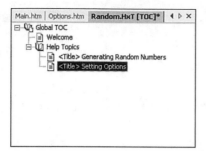

FIGURE 10.12
A table of contents in Microsoft Help Workshop.

8. Drag the Options.htm file from Solution Explorer and drop it on the Generating Random Numbers node. Accept the default title. Figure 10.12 shows the completed table of contents in the designer.

9. Select Project, Add New Item. Select the Help Workshop Project Items category. Select the Keyword Index template. Name the file `Random.HxK` and click Open. The new index will open in the Visual Studio Design window. Index files are edited as raw XML.

10. Modify the Random.HxK file as follows:

```xml
<?xml version="1.0"?>
<!DOCTYPE HelpIndex SYSTEM
"ms-help://hx/resources/HelpIndex.DTD">

<HelpIndex DTDVersion="1.0" Name="K">
  <Keyword Term="Random">
    <Jump Url="/Main.htm" />
  </Keyword>
</HelpIndex>
```

11. Open the Options.htm file in the HTML view of the designer. Add the following XML data island to the page, just before of the `</HEAD>` tag:

```xml
<xml>
  <MSHelp:Keyword Index="K" Term="Random" />
  <MSHelp:Keyword Index="K" Term="Options" />
</xml>
```

12. To set a default home page for your help file, you must add a second index, called a *Named URL index*. Select Project, Add New Item. Select the Help Workshop Project Items category and the Keyword Index template. Name the file `NamedUrlIndex.HxK` and click Open.

13. Edit the NamedUrlIndex.HxK file as follows (the only change is in the index name):

```xml
<?xml version="1.0"?>
<!DOCTYPE HelpIndex SYSTEM
"ms-help://hx/resources/HelpIndex.DTD">

<HelpIndex DTDVersion="1.0" Name="NamedUrlIndex">
  <!-- Insert keywords here -->
</HelpIndex>
```

14. Open the Welcome.htm file in HTML view and add this XML data island directly before the `</HEAD>` tag to specify this as the home page for the help file:

```
<xml>
 <MSHelp:Keyword Index="NamedURLIndex" Term="HomePage"/>
</xml>
```

> **NOTE**
>
> **Index Types**   The Name *K* within the Random.HxK file indicates that this particular index is a keyword index. You can also create an associative index that provides links between help topics (even across help files), or a context-sensitive help index. For details on these other index types, refer to the VSHIK documentation.

Note that you can define the entries that appear in a keyword index in two different ways. If you prefer to have all this information in one place, you can define all the keywords and the topics to which they jump directly within the XML index file. Alternatively, you can insert XML data islands within the help topics themselves. The latter method is often more convenient if you have multiple authors working on a single help file. All this information will be combined into a single index by the help compiler.

A help file for a serious application might contain hundreds of table of contents and index entries, but they're created using the same process that you just saw. The table of contents provides a structured way for the user to view the contents of the help file. The index provides a quick way for the user to search for specific information of interest.

Compiling and Testing a Help File

Now you're finally ready to build the help file and try it out, which is the subject of Step By Step 10.11.

STEP BY STEP

10.11 Compiling and Testing a Help File

1. In Microsoft Help Workshop, save all the source files for the HTML Help 2 file.

2. Select Build, Build Solution. The Visual Studio .NET Output window will display the results of the build.

continues

continued

3. If no build errors occurred, select Debug, Start to view the completed help file. Figure 10.13 shows the sample help file open in the HTML Help 2 viewer.

FIGURE 10.13
Finished HTML Help 2 file.

Although the process of building the help file with the new Microsoft Help Workshop differs from that of the older HTML Help Workshop, the end result is the same: a file designed to provide help to the end user. As such, you can apply the same testing rules to HTML Help 2 files that you saw earlier in the chapter for HTML Help 1.x files.

REVIEW BREAK

▶ HTML Help 2 is Microsoft's latest standard for help files.

▶ The Visual Studio Help Integration Kit includes the tools necessary to build HTML Help 2 files, including Microsoft Help Workshop.

Implementing User Assistance

Building a help file is only the first part of the job of providing user assistance. You still must make the information in the help file available to users, as well as implement the other ways in which users expect to be able to get help with your application. In this section, I'll demonstrate the three main ways in which .NET enables you to provide user assistance:

◆ By using the HelpProvider component to show a traditional help file

◆ By using the HelpProvider component to provide pop-up help for a dialog box

◆ By using the ToolTip component to provide quick help for individual controls

Although I'm focusing on the mechanics of providing user assistance in code, you should consider this just one facet of an overall user assistance strategy. Depending on your organization and the applications involved, user assistance can include any or all of the following:

◆ A readme file or other introductory material for the user to refer to even before installing the application

◆ Printed, online, or electronic documentation

◆ Email, telephone, or onsite support from a product specialist

◆ Wizards, builders, and other user interface components designed to guide the user through a process.

> **NOTE**
>
> **User Assistance with HTML Help 1.3** Because Microsoft has not yet provided a documented way to tie HTML Help 2.0 to Windows Forms, I'll use the HTML Help 1.3 format help file for the remainder of this chapter.

Using the HelpProvider Component

The HelpProvider component is designed to provide the link between your application and a help file. Like other components that do not have a runtime user interface, it is displayed in the component tray at design time. Step By Step 10.12 shows how to use this component.

STEP BY STEP

10.12 Using the HelpProvider Component

1. Open the RandomServer Visual Basic .NET application.

2. Copy the Random.chm HTML Help file that you created in Step By Step 10.6 to the bin folder of the RandomServer project.

3. Open the RandomForm.vb form in the designer. Drag and drop a HelpProvider control to the form. Accept the default name of `HelpProvider1`.

4. Set the `HelpNamespace` property of the HelpProvider component to `Random.chm`.

5. Open the Properties window for the RandomForm.vb form. Set its `HelpKeyword` on `HelpProvider1` property to `Main.htm`, its `HelpNavigator` on `HelpProvider1` property to `Topic`, and its `ShowHelp` on `HelpProvider1` property to `True`.

6. Double-click the Help, Contents menu item. Enter this code to handle the menu item's `Click` event:

```
Private Sub mnuHelpContents_Click(ByVal sender As
System.Object, _
   ByVal e As System.EventArgs) Handles mnuHelpContents.Click
      Help.ShowHelp(Me, "Random.chm")
End Sub
```

7. Open the frmOptions.vb form in the designer. Drag and drop a HelpProvider control to the form. Accept the default name of `HelpProvider1`.

8. Set the `HelpNamespace` property of the `HelpProvider` component to `Random.chm`.

9. Open the Properties window for the frmOptions.vb form. Set its `HelpKeyword` on `HelpProvider1` property to `Options.htm`, its `HelpNavigator` on `HelpProvider1` property to `Topic`, and its `ShowHelp` on `HelpProvider1` property to `True`.

10. Run the project. Press F1 with the focus on the main form of the project, and with the focus on the options form. Also try the Help, Contents menu item from the main form.

I used two different objects to provide user assistance in this example. The first, the HelpProvider component, works by extending other objects on a form to include help-related properties. The HelpNamespace property of the HelpProvider itself specifies the name of the help file to use. The HelpNavigator and HelpKeyword properties then specify the exact information to show from the help file. Table 10.1 shows the possible values for the HelpNavigator property.

TABLE 10.1

VALUES OF THE HELPPROVIDER.HELPNAVIGATOR PROPERTY

Value	Meaning
AssociateIndex	Displays the first topic listed in the index for the specified HelpKeyword.
Find	Displays the search page of the specified help file.
Index	Displays the index for the specified help file.
KeywordIndex	Displays the index for the specified HelpKeyword.
TableOfContents	Displays the table of contents for the specified help file.
Topic	Displays the topic identified by the specified HelpKeyword.

> **EXAM TIP**
>
> **Help from a Web Page**   You can also supply the URL for a Web page as the HelpNamespace property of the HelpProvider component. In this case, requests for help load the specified Web page into the browser, and the HelpKeyword property provides an anchor name to jump to on the page.

The other object I used in this example is the static Help object. This object has a ShowHelp method, which displays the contents of a specified help file and a ShowHelpIndex method, which displays the index of a specified help file. This object and its methods are useful when you want to open a help file to its default topic rather than to a specific topic.

Creating Pop-Up Help for Dialog Boxes

For dialog boxes, pop-up help (sometimes called *what's-this help*) offers an alternative to using an external help file. Dialog boxes are meant to keep the user focused on a particular task until that task is complete. Thus, a dialog box does not allow you to move to a different form within the application. Using pop-up help allows you to show help for a dialog box without making the user switch focus to another window. Step By Step 10.13 shows how to employ pop-up help.

STEP BY STEP

10.13 Displaying Pop-Up Help

1. Open the RandomServer Visual Basic .NET application.

2. If you have not already done so, open the frmOptions.vb form in the designer. Drag and drop a HelpProvider control to the form. Accept the default name `HelpProvider1`.

3. Set the `HelpNamespace` property of the HelpProvider component to `Random.chm`.

4. Set the `HelpString` property of txtMin to `Enter the minimum random value to be generated.`

5. Set the `HelpString` property of txtMax to `Enter the maximum random value to be generated.`

6. Set the `HelpString` property of btnOK to `Set the specified values, close this form, and return to the main form.`

7. Set the `HelpString` property of btnCancel to `Return to the main form without making any changes.`

8. Run the project. Open the Tools, Options dialog box. Click the Help button in the form's caption bar and click on any control. It will display the specified string, as shown in Figure 10.14.

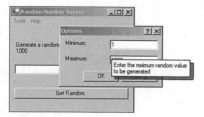

FIGURE 10.14
Displaying Pop-up Help.

Using the ToolTip Component

The third method to display user assistance on forms is to use ToolTips. ToolTips are short help strings that are displayed in a pop-up window when the user hovers the mouse over a particular control. You saw an example of using ToolTips in Chapter 2, "Controls." In Step By Step 10.14, I'll use the ToolTip component to add ToolTips to the RandomServer main form.

STEP BY STEP

10.14 Displaying ToolTips

1. Open the RandomServer Visual Basic .NET application.

2. Drag a ToolTip component from the toolbox and drop it on the RandomForm.vb form. Accept the default name of ToolTip1.

3. Set the `ToolTip on ToolTip1` property of btnGetRandom to `Click here for a random number`.

4. Set the `ToolTip on ToolTip1` property of txtRandom to `Your a random number`.

5. Run the project. Hover your mouse over the btnGetRandom and txtRandom controls to see the ToolTips. Note that the delay is longer to display the first ToolTip than to switch to a second ToolTip.

> **NOTE**
>
> **Avoid Conflicts**   Generally, you should not use ToolTips and pop-up help on the same control. Having two different pieces of assistance in the same interface tends to confuse users.

You can set four properties on the ToolTip component to control the timing of ToolTip displays:

◆ **InitialDisplay**—The time (in milliseconds) before the initial ToolTip is displayed.

◆ **AutoPopDelay**—The time (in milliseconds) that the ToolTip remains visible.

◆ **ReshowDelay**—The time (in milliseconds) before subsequent ToolTips are displayed as the mouse pointer moves between controls.

◆ **AutomaticDelay**—A single value used to set all three of the above properties. If you set AutomaticDelay, InitialDelay is set equal to AutomaticDelay; AutoPopDelay is set to ten times AutomaticDelay; and ReshowDelay is set to one-fifth of AutoDelay.

R E V I E W   B R E A K

▶ The HelpProvider component is the bridge between your .NET Windows application and an HTML Help file. With the HelpProvider component, you can associate help topics with user interface controls.

▶ You can use the HelpProvider to display topics from a help file, Web pages, or pop-up help strings. You can use more than one source of help in a single application.

▶ Pop-up help is appropriate for dialog boxes, when you don't want the users to switch focus to another task.

▶ ToolTips let you provide quick help for individual controls by popping up an unbostrusive text window.

IMPLEMENTING ACCESSIBILITY FEATURES

Implement accessibility features.

According to Microsoft, over thirty million people in the United States alone have disabilities that can be affected by the design of computer hardware and software. Although software developers have long ignored this issue, modern software design takes accessibility strongly into account. From both ethical and economic standpoints, as well as to comply with the law, designing software for accessibility simply makes sense. In fact, Microsoft has made accessibility a key feature of the Windows Logo certification program, which allows applications to display the "designed for Windows" logo.

Accessible design has five basic principles:

◆ **Flexibility**—The user interface should be flexibile and customizable, so users can adjust it to their own individual needs and preferences.

◆ **Choice of Input Methods**—Different users have different abilities and preferences when it comes to choosing a mouse or a keyboard to perform tasks. All operations in your application should be accessible to the keyboard, and basic operations should be available via the mouse as well. In the future, voice and other types of input might also be considered here.

◆ **Choice of Output Methods**—You should not depend on a single method of output (such as sound, color, or text) for important information.

◆ **Consistency**—Your application should be consistent with the Windows operating system and other applications to minimize difficulties in learning and using new interfaces.

◆ **Compatibility with Accessibility Aids**—Windows includes a number of accessibility aids such as the Magnifier (which can blow up text or graphics to a larger size) and the Onscreen Keyboard (which enables keyboard input via the mouse). Your application should not circumvent these accessibility aids.

As an example of implementing these principles, the Windows logo certification requirements includes these items:

◆ Support the standard system size, color, font, and input settings.

◆ Ensure compatibility with the High Contrast display setting. With this setting, the application can only use colors from the Control Panel or colors explicitly chosen by the user.

◆ Provide documented keyboard access to all features.

◆ It must always be obvious to the user and programmatically where the keyboard focus is located. This is necessary for the Magnifier and Narrator accessibility aids to function properly.

◆ Do not convey information by sound alone.

In this section, you'll learn more about accessible design guidelines, and see how to implement those guidelines for a Visual Basic .NET Windows application.

Understanding Accessible Design Guidelines

Table 10.2 lays out some of the important accessibility guidelines to consider for any application.

TABLE 10.2

ACCESSIBILITY GUIDELINES FOR APPLICATION DESIGN

Area	Guidelines
Color	Use color to enhance or highlight information, but do not use color as the sole means to convey important information. Remember that not all users can distinguish all colors.
Disks	Do not make the user insert or swap removable media such as disks or CD-ROMs during the normal operation of your application.
General UI	The fundamental rule of accessibility is to provide a user interface flexible enough to accommodate the varying needs and preferences of different users.
Keyboard Focus	Many accessibility aids need to identify the location of the keyboard focus to function properly. The .NET Framework will normally take care of this guideline for you.
Keyboard Input	All applications should be accessible via keyboard input. Alternative input devices often emulate the keyboard, so if your application is available via the keyboard, it will be available to these devices as well.
Layout	A label of other text should identify every item onscreen to help users who cannot see the entire screen at one time.
Mouse Input	Some people can use a mouse (or a device whose interface emulates a mouse) more easily than a keyboard. Your application should be available via the mouse.
Multitasking	Applications should not hog the CPU—Excessive consumption of processor power can interfere with accessibility aids.
Size	Follow the system metrics and allow users to resize items onscreen to accommodate their own preferences.

Area	*Guidelines*
Sound	Use sound to enhance or highlight information, but do not use sound as the sole means to convey important information. Hearing-impaired users or those in noisy environments might be unable to distinguish sound cues.
Timing	Timed events should be adjustable by the user, so that those with difficulty reading or reacting to information quickly can still use your application.

Setting Control Properties for Accessibility

Some control properties critical to implementing accessibility in your application include

◆ **AccessibleDescripton**—A description of the control that will be reported to accessibility aids.

◆ **AccessibleName**—The name of the control that will be reported to accessibility aids.

◆ **AccessibleRole**—The role of the control that will be reported to accessibility aids.

◆ **BackColor and ForeColor**—Leave these properties at their default values to use the user's selected screen colors.

◆ **BackgroundImage**—Leave this property empty to help users read text on your forms.

◆ **Font Size**—If the font size on your form is fixed, it should be set to at least ten point.

◆ **TabIndex**—You must set the TabIndex to ensure a sensible navigation path and to ensure that shortcut keys work to access controls such as TextBox controls.

◆ **Text**—Use the ampersand character to create shortcut keys and ensure keyboard access to controls.

In Step by Step 10.15, you'll begin modifying the RandomServer application for accessibility.

STEP BY STEP

10.15 Setting Control Properties for Accessibility

1. Open the RandomServer Visual Basic .NET application.

2. Open the RandomForm.vb form in the designer.

3. Open the Properties window for the form itself. Set the form's `AccessibleDescription` property to `Random number generation form` and its `AccessibleName` property to `Random Form`.

4. Select the lblRange Label control. Set its `AccessibleDescription` property to `Range of random numbers` and its `AccessibleName` property to `Range Label`.

5. Select the txtRandom TextBox control. Set its `AccessibleDescription` property to `Returned random number` and its `AccessibleName` property to `Random Number`.

6. Select the btnGetRandom Button control. Set its `Text` property to `&Get Random`, its `AccessibleDescription` property to `Get random number`, and its `AccessibleName` property to `Get Random Button`.

7. Open the frmOptions form in the designer.

8. Select the lblMinimum Label control. Set its `Text` property to `&Minimum`, its `AccessibleDescription` property to `Minimum label`, and its `AccessibleName` property to `Minimum label`.

9. Select the txtMinimum TextBox control. Set its `AccessibleDescription` property to `Minimum value for random numbers` and its `AccessibleName` property to `Minimum value`.

10. Select the lblMaximum Label control. Set its `Text` property to `Ma&ximum:`, its `AccessibleDescription` property to `Maximum label`, and its `AccessibleName` property to `Maximum label`.

11. Select the txtMaximum TextBox control. Set its `AccessibleDescription` property to `Maximum value for random numbers` and its `AccessibleName` property to `Maximum value`.

12. Select the btnOK Button control. Set its Text property to &OK, its AccessibleDescription property to OK button, and its AccessibleName property to OK button.

13. Select the btnCancel Button control. Set its Text property to &Cancel, its AccessibleDescription property to Cancel button, and its AccessibleName property to Cancel button.

14. Select View, Tab Order and verify that the Label controls directly precede the associated TextBox controls in the tab order.

Supporting High Contrast Mode

The RandomServer application uses Windows defaults for color and font everywhere, so it's already compatible with High Contrast mode. However, you might need to make changes to properties at runtime if the user has her computer set up in High Contrast mode, or if she switches to that mode at runtime. In High Contrast mode, you should:

◆ Use only system colors to display controls.

◆ Add visual cues (such as boldface or special icons) to any information ordinarily conveyed by color.

◆ Remove any background images or patterns.

You can determine programatically whether the user is in High Contrast mode by checking the value of the Boolean SystemInformation.HighContrast property. Typically, you should check this property in your form's New method and adjust control properties as necessary if the property returns True. You should also add an event handler for the SystemEvents.UserPreferenceChanged event, which is raised whenever the HighContrast property changes. Guided Practice Exercise 10.1 demonstrates the code needed to implement this technique.

Testing Application Accessibility

Before shipping an application, you should test the accessibility features. Here are some tests you should perform:

◆ Navigate your user interface using only the keyboard. Ensure that all functionality is accessible by using the keyboard alone.

◆ Select the Accessibility icon in the Control Panel. On the Display tab, check the box for High Contrast. Ensure that all your application's user interface is displayed properly in this mode and that any background images are removed.

◆ Launch Magnifier by selecting Start, Programs, Accessories, Accessibility, Magnifier. Verify that the Magnifier window follows the keyboard focus as you use the keyboard and mouse to navigate through your application.

EXAM TIP

Accessibility Tools   You can download other tools for testing Accessibility as part of the Active Accessibility SDK, which is available at `http://www.msdn.microsoft.com/library/default.asp?url=/nhp/Default.asp?contentid=28000544`.

GUIDED PRACTICE
EXERCISE 10.1

In this exercise, you'll add code to the RandomServer application to properly implement High Contrast mode.

Try this on your own first. If you get stuck or want to see one possible solution, follow these steps:

1. Open the RandomServer Visual Basic .NET application.

2. Select the RandomForm.vb form and set its `BackColor` property to `Red`.

3. Switch to the form's module and add this procedure:

```
Private Sub AdjustBackground()
    If SystemInformation.HighContrast Then
        Me.BackColor = SystemColors.Window
    Else
        Me.BackColor = Color.Red
    End If
End Sub
```

4. Add an event handler for the `UserPreferenceChanged` event:

```
Protected Sub UserPreferenceChanged_Handler( _
 ByVal sender As Object, _
 ByVal e As Microsoft.Win32.UserPreferenceChangedEvent
Args)
    AdjustBackground()
End Sub
```

5. Modify the form's `New` method to call the `AdjustBackground` procedure and the hook up the event procedure:

```
Public Sub New()
    MyBase.New()

    'This call is required by the Windows Form Designer.
    InitializeComponent()

    ' Add any initialization after the
    ' InitializeComponent() call
    AdjustBackground()
    AddHandler Microsoft.Win32.SystemEvents. _
     UserPreferenceChanged, _
     AddressOf Me.UserPreferenceChanged_Handler

End Sub
```

6. Modify the form's `Dispose` method to unhook the event procedure:

```
'Form overrides dispose to clean up the component list.
Protected Overloads Overrides Sub Dispose( _
 ByVal disposing As Boolean)
    If disposing Then
        If Not (components Is Nothing) Then
            components.Dispose()
        End If
    End If
    RemoveHandler Microsoft.Win32.SystemEvents. _
     UserPreferenceChanged, _
     AddressOf Me.UserPreferenceChanged_Handler
    MyBase.Dispose(disposing)
End Sub
```

7. Run the project. The form should show up with a red background. Select the Accessibility icon in Control Panel. On the Display tab, check the High Contrast check box. The form should change to using the system background color.

CHAPTER SUMMARY

KEY TERMS

- Accessibility
- Pop-up help
- User Assistance

User Assistance and Accessibility are important parts of building an application. Just having code that performs properly isn't enough. You must also help the user understand how to use your application effectively and accommodate users who have disabilities that affect their use of software and hardware.

Visual Studio .NET includes the HTML Help SDK as one of its components. This SDK, which includes HTML Help Workshop and other tools, will help you build HTML Help files for your applications. HTML Help is Microsoft's current standard for constructing help files and should be familiar to any Windows user.

HTML Help files are created from individual HTML files that represent help topics, as well as from other files that represent such items as the table of contents or the index of the HTML Help file. HTML Help Workshop includes editors for these items as well as a compiler to build the HTML Help file from its component parts.

Windows forms offer several ways to display text for user assistance. You can use the HelpProvider component to display a particular topic from an HTML Help file or the Help object to display the default page from a help file. The HelpProvider component also supports the creation of pop-up help for dialog box controls. Finally, the ToolTip component can display a short piece of help text related to a particular control.

Accessibility guidelines dictate the design of your application in certain areas. You must be prepared to handle either keyboard or mouse input, accessibility aids, different color schemes, and users who might not be able to process information provided in various ways. Visual Studio .NET offers excellent support for accessibility programming.

Exercises

10.1 Using a Web Page for User Assistance

Sometimes your application is so small or simple that it doesn't make sense to build an entire HTML Help file to provide user assistance. In those cases, you can use a simple Web page instead.

Estimated Time: 15 minutes.

1. Open a Visual Basic .NET Windows Application in the Visual Studio .NET IDE. Add a new form to the application.

2. Add a GroupBox control, two RadioButton controls (rbLongDate and rbShortDate), a Label control (lblDate), and a Button control (btnUpdate) to the form. Figure 10.15 shows a design for this form.

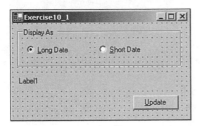

FIGURE 10.15
A simple form.

3. Double-click the form to open the form's module. Add this code to handle events on the form:

```
Private Sub Exercise10_1_Load( _
 ByVal sender As System.Object, _
 ByVal e As System.EventArgs) _
 Handles MyBase.Load
    UpdateDate()
End Sub
```

```
Private Sub UpdateDate()
    If rbLongDate.Checked Then
        lblDate.Text = _
         DateTime.Now.ToLongDateString()
    Else
        lblDate.Text = _
         DateTime.Now.ToShortDateString
    End If
End Sub

Private Sub rbLongDate_CheckedChanged( _
 ByVal sender As Object, _
 ByVal e As System.EventArgs) _
 Handles rbLongDate.CheckedChanged
    UpdateDate()
End Sub

Private Sub rbShortDate_CheckedChanged( _
 ByVal sender As Object, _
 ByVal e As System.EventArgs) _
 Handles rbShortDate.CheckedChanged
    UpdateDate()
End Sub

Private Sub btnUpdate_Click( _
 ByVal sender As System.Object, _
 ByVal e As System.EventArgs) _
 Handles btnUpdate.Click
    UpdateDate()
End Sub
```

4. Add a new HTML file to your project. Name the new file Exercise10-1.htm.

5. Switch to HTML view and enter the following HTML for this page:

```
<!DOCTYPE HTML PUBLIC
"-//W3C//DTD HTML 4.0 Transitional//EN">
<html>
    <head>
        <title>Exercise10_1</title>
        <meta name="vs_defaultClientScript"
content="JavaScript">
        <meta name="vs_targetSchema"
content="http://schemas.microsoft.com/intel-
lisense/ie5">
        <meta name="GENERATOR"
 content="Microsoft Visual Studio.NET 7.0">
        <meta name="ProgId"
content="VisualStudio.HTML">
```

APPLY YOUR KNOWLEDGE

```
        <meta name="Originator"
content="Microsoft Visual Studio.NET 7.0">
    </head>
    <body>
        <h1>Welcome to the date display
application</h1>
        <p>To use this application, just open
the form.
        It will display the date in long
        date format by default.</p>
        <p>You can switch between long date
        and short date format by selecting
        the appropriate radio button.</p>
        <h2>Updating</h2>
        <p>If you leave the application run
        ning past midnight, you can click
        the Update button to update the
        display to the current date.</p>
    </body>
</html>
```

6. Place a `HelpProvider` component on the form. Set the `HelpNamespace` property of the `HelpProvider` component to `..\Exercise10-1.htm`.

7. Set the `ShowHelp` property of the form to `True`.

8. Set the form as the startup object for the project.

9. Run the project and press F1. The HTML file will appear in a new browser window.

In addition to very short help files, this technique is also useful when the user assistance content changes rapidly. For example, you might have an application that periodically downloads updates from the Internet. Rather than download a new help file every time, you might choose to keep the user assistance on the Internet as a Web site and have a HelpProvider component to open pages from that Web site.

10.2 Augmenting Sound with the FlashWindowEx API

One of the accessibility guidelines states that you should not depend solely on sound to convey information. This exercise will show how to use the FlashWindowEx API call to notify the user visually.

Estimated Time: 15 minutes.

1. Add a new form to your Visual Basic .NET application.

2. Add two Label controls, a TextBox control named txtNumber, and a Button control named btnTest to the form. Name the blank Label control lblResults. Figure 10.16 shows a design for this form.

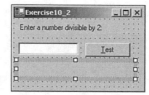

FIGURE 10.16
A form to use with FlashWindowEx.

3. Double-click the form to open the form's module. Add this code to the form:

```
Private Sub btnTest_Click( _
ByVal sender As System.Object, _
 ByVal e As System.EventArgs) _
 Handles btnTest.Click
    If CInt(txtNumber.Text) Mod 2 = 0 Then
        lblResults.Text = "OK!"
    Else
        lblResults.Text = ""
        Beep()
    End If
End Sub
```

APPLY YOUR KNOWLEDGE

4. Set the form as the startup object for the project.

5. Run the project. Enter some numbers and click the Test button. Note that for even numbers you get a message on the form, but for odd numbers the only feedback is the computer's beep.

6. Stop the project. Add a new module to the project. Enter this code in the module:

```
Module API

    ' Structure used by FlashWindowEx
    Public Structure FLASHWINFO
        ' Size of the structure
        Public cbSize As Int32
        ' Handle of the window to flash
        Public hwnd As IntPtr
        ' One of the FLASHW flags
        Public dwFlags As Int32
        ' Number of times to flash
        Public uCount As Int32
        ' Time of each flash, zero for default
        Public dwTimeout As Int32
    End Structure

    ' FlashWindowEx constants
    ' Stop flashing
    Public Const FLASHW_STOP = 0
    ' Flash the window caption
    Public Const FLASHW_CAPTION = 1
    ' Flash the taskbar button
    Public Const FLASHW_TRAY = 2
    ' Flash the caption
    ' and the taskbar button
    Public Const FLASHW_ALL = 3
    ' Flash continuously until
    ' called again with FLASHW_STOP
    Public Const FLASHW_TIMER = 4
    ' Flash continuously until window
    ' is called to the foreground
    Public Const FLASHW_TIMERNOFG = 12

    Declare Auto Function FlashWindowEx _
      Lib "user32.dll" _
      (ByRef pwfi As FLASHWINFO) As Int32

End Module
```

7. Modify the code behind the form to call the FlashWindowEx API:

```
Private Sub btnTest_Click( _
 ByVal sender As System.Object, _
 ByVal e As System.EventArgs) _
 Handles btnTest.Click
    If CInt(txtNumber.Text) Mod 2 = 0 Then
        lblResults.Text = "OK!"
    Else
        lblResults.Text = ""
        Beep()
        Dim pwfi As FLASHWINFO
        pwfi.cbSize = Marshal.SizeOf(pwfi)
        pwfi.hwnd = Me.Handle
        pwfi.dwFlags = FLASHW_ALL
        pwfi.uCount = 3
        pwfi.dwTimeout = 0
        Dim intret As Integer = _
          FlashWindowEx(pwfi)
    End If
End Sub
```

8. Run the project. Enter some numbers and click the Test button. Note that for even numbers you get a message on the form, and that for odd numbers you get a beep and a flashing caption and Taskbar button.

Review Questions

1. What methods can you use to provide user assistance within a .NET Windows application?

2. What help file formats can the HelpProvider component use?

3. What is the standard help file format for .NET applications?

4. Name some of the parts of an HTML Help system.

5. Name some areas you should test in a help file.

APPLY YOUR KNOWLEDGE

6. What tools can you use to create HTML Help topics?

7. Name two uses for the HelpProvider component.

8. What is the purpose of pop-up help?

9. Name the five basic principles of accessible design.

10. Name some of the Windows Logo certification program accessibility requirements.

Exam Questions

1. You created an HTML Help file for your application and placed it in the same folder as the application's executable file. You placed a HelpProvider component on your application's main form and set the HelpNamespace property of the HelpProvider component to refer to the HTML Help file. When you run the application and press F1, the HTML Help file displays its default topic. What must you do to display a specific topic related to the main form?

   A. Set the Name property of the main form to the name of the help topic (.htm) file.

   B. Set the Text property of the main form to the name of the help topic (.htm) file.

   C. Set the HelpKeyword property of the main form to the name of the help topic (.htm) file.

   D. Set the HelpString property of the main form to the name of the help topic (.htm) file.

2. You want to display pop-up help for controls on a dialog box form. How should you set the properties of the form?

   A. Set FormBorderStyle to FixedDialog, and HelpButton to True.

   B. Set MaximizeBox to False, MinimizeBox to False, and HelpButton to True.

   C. Set MaximizeBox to True, MinimizeBox to True, and HelpButton to True.

   D. Set ControlBox to True and HelpButton to True.

3. Your form contains a menu item named mnuHelpContents. You want to use this menu item to display the contents page of a help file named MyApp.chm. Which code snippet should you use for this purpose?

   A.

```
Private Sub mnuHelpContents_Click( _
 ByVal sender As System.Object, _
 ByVal e As System.EventArgs) _
 Handles mnuHelpContents.Click
     HelpProvider1.HelpNamespace = _
     "MyApp.chm"
End Sub
```

   B.

```
Private Sub mnuHelpContents_Click( _
 ByVal sender As System.Object, _
 ByVal e As System.EventArgs) _
 Handles mnuHelpContents.Click
     HelpProvider1.SetHelpNavigator( _
     "MyApp.chm")
End Sub
```

   C.

```
Private Sub mnuHelpContents_Click( _
 ByVal sender As System.Object, _
 ByVal e As System.EventArgs) _
 Handles mnuHelpContents.Click
     Help.ShowHelp(Me, "MyApp.chm")
End Sub
```

   D.

```
Private Sub mnuHelpContents_Click( _
 ByVal sender As System.Object, _
 ByVal e As System.EventArgs) _
 Handles mnuHelpContents.Click
     Help.ShowHelpIndex(Me, "MyApp.chm")
End Sub
```

4. You created a dialog box for which you want to display pop-up help. You set the form properties so that the Help button appears and placed a HelpProvider component on the form. For the OK button on the form, you set the HelpKeyword property to "Click here to save settings and return to the main form."

   When you click the Help button and then the OK button, no help is displayed. What must you do to display the pop-up help?

   A. Add pop-up help to every control on the form.

   B. Set the HelpNamespace property of the HelpProvider control to the name of a help file.

   C. Set the ControlBox property of the form to False.

   D. Place the help string in the HelpString property instead of the HelpKeyword property.

5. Your application provides users with quick help via ToolTips. Users complain that the ToolTips take too long to display. How can you fix this problem?

   A. Decrease the value of the AutoPopDelay property.

   B. Move the application to a faster computer.

   C. Decrease the value of the InitialDisplay property.

   D. Increase the value of the AutomaticDelay property.

6. Your application displays sales information on a form. Users complain that the application does not properly respond to the HighContrast setting on their computers. What must you do to accommodate this setting? (Select two.)

   A. Use only system colors on the form and its controls.

   B. Remove any background images or patterns from the form.

   C. Use only black and white on the form and its controls.

   D. Increase the font size on the form.

7. Your application allows data entry through a form. The form uses the system default colors and fonts throughout. When the user makes a data entry mistake, the computer beeps and the cursor remains in place. When the user saves a record, the entry colors are cleared and the cursor is returned to the first control on the form.

   What should you do to make this form more accessible?

   A. Prompt the user before clearing the form.

   B. Set the form's BackColor to white instead of depending on the system properties.

   C. Provide audio notification of saves.

   D. Provide an additional, nonaudio means of notification for data entry errors.

8. Your application will be used by people who depend on accessibility aids such as screen readers. Which properties should you explicitly set for every control? (Select two.)

   A. ForeColor

   B. AccessibleName

   C. AccessibleDescription

   D. AccessibleRole

APPLY YOUR KNOWLEDGE

9. You want your application to monitor for changes to the HighContrast setting at runtime, so it can remove a background image from a form if necessary. Which event must you trap?

   A. Me.Paint

   B. SystemEvents.PaletteChanged

   C. Me.StyleChanged

   D. SystemEvents.UserPreferenceChanged

10. You have created an application that displays financial information. The information displayed is retrieved from a Web service and changes frequently. How should you provide user assistance in interpreting this information?

    A. Place an explanation of the information on a Web page on an Internet server and use a HelpProvider component to display the information.

    B. Place an explanation of the information on a Web page on an Internet server and use a ToolTip component to display the information.

    C. Place an explanation of the information in an HTML Help file and use a HelpProvider component to display the information.

    D. Place an explanation of the information in an HTML Help file and use a ToolTip component to display the information.

11. You are developing a checkbook application. Currently, the application plays a music file when the checkbook is in balance. Which of these modifications would make the application more accessible? (Select two.)

    A. Add a message box that is also displayed when the checkbook is in balance.

    B. Allow the user to select a custom music file to play when the checkbook is in balance.

    C. Allow the user to set the volume of the music played when the checkbook is in balance.

    D. Use the FlashWindowEx API to flash the caption of the application when the checkbook is in balance.

12. You developed a complex form that performs mathematical calculations. The instructions for using the form are quite complex, and users must refer to the instructions while entering information. Which type of user assistance should you supply?

    A. Pop-up help

    B. HTML Help file

    C. ToolTips

    D. AccessibleDescription property

13. You created an HTML Help file for your application and compiled it with help topics. You are now ready to set the properties of controls on your form so that the proper help topics are displayed, but you can't find the HelpKeyword and HelpNavigator properties for the controls. What must you do?

    A. Place a HelpProvider component on the form.

    B. Place the help file in the same folder as the executable file.

    C. Place a ToolTip component on the form.

    D. Declare an instance of the Help object in the form's New method.

APPLY YOUR KNOWLEDGE

14. You created an HTML Help file for your application and connected it with a form with a HelpProvider component. The HelpString property of the txtFirstName TextBox is set to FirstName.htm. When you place the cursor in that text box and press F1, the default help for the form is displayed. What is the most likely cause of the problem?

    A. The HelpKeyword property of the control is not set to FirstName.htm.

    B. The HTML Help file does not contain a topic named FirstName.htm.

    C. The HTML Help file is not located in the proper folder.

    D. The HelpProvider component has an empty HelpNamespace property.

15. You have developed a complex dialog box with its own F1 help already implemented. Now you want to add pop-up help as a way for users to get quick reminders of the form's functionality. What should you do?

    A. Set the form's properties to show the Help button, and add HelpString properties to the controls on the form.

    B. Add a second HelpProvider component to the form, set the form's properties to show the Help button, and add HelpString properties to the controls on the form.

    C. Add a ToolTip component to the form, set the form's properties to show the Help button, and add HelpString properties to the controls on the form.

    D. Add a message box to prompt the user when they click F1. Let the user choose whether to display pop-up help or F1 help.

Answers to Review Questions

1. You can use a help file, pop-up help, or ToolTips to provide user assistance within a .NET Windows application.

2. The HelpProvider component can use HTML Help (.chm) and HTML (.htm) files.

3. .NET applications use HTML Help as their standard help file format.

4. The parts of an HTML Help system include a help project file, topic files, multimedia files, contents files, and index files.

5. The areas to test in a help file include proper compilation, context sensitivity, the validity of links in topics, the table of contents, the index, consistent formatting, spelling and grammar, and accuracy and completeness of information.

6. You can use any tool capable of saving HTML to create HTML Help topics.

7. The HelpProvider component can display F1 help or pop-up help.

8. Pop-up help is designed to provide help for modal dialog boxes without requiring the user to refocus his attention.

9. The basic principles of accessible design are flexibility, choice of input methods, choice of output methods, consistency, and compatibility with accessibility aids.

10. The Windows Logo certification program accessibility requirements include support for system size, color, font, and input settings; compatibility with the High Contrast display setting; keyboard access to all features; obvious keyboard focus; and alternatives to sound for conveying information.

APPLY YOUR KNOWLEDGE

Answers to Exam Questions

1. **C.** The correct property to connect a form or control to a particular help topic is the HelpKeyword property. The HelpString property is only used for text to be displayed as pop-up help.

2. **B.** Although the ControlBox property is normally set to True and the FormBorderStyle property to FixedDialog for dialog box forms, these properties can be set either way without affecting the Help button.

3. **C.** The static Help.ShowHelp method displays the contents of a help file.

4. **D.** The HelpKeyword property holds the topic name for regular help topics. The HelpString property holds the string to display as pop-up help.

5. **C.** The time to display a ToolTip is controlled by the InitialDelay property, and it is independent of the speed of the computer. The AutoPopDelay property controls how long the ToolTip remains onscreen. Increasing the AutomaticDelay property will make ToolTips display more slowly rather than more quickly.

6. **A, B.** The HighContrast setting is designed to aid those who need additional contrast for visibility.

7. **D.** Accessible applications should not depend on sound as the sole means of feedback.

8. **B, C.** The AccessibleDescription and AccessibleName properties provide important information for screen readers. The AccessibleRole property only needs to be set in special situations. The ForeColor property need not be set; if it's left at its default value, the user can adjust colors through the Control Panel.

9. **D.** The SystemEvents.UserPreferenceChanged event is triggered by changing the High Contrast setting.

10. **A.** Using a Web page to hold the user assistance for this application allows you to update the information frequently without sending new files to the client. A HelpProvider is more suited for extensive help information than a ToolTip.

11. **A, D.** To make an application dependent on sounds for notification more accessible, you must add nonaudio means of notification.

12. **B.** For extensive help, an HTML Help file is most appropriate. The other types of user assistance do not remain onscreen while the user works with the application.

13. **A.** The HelpKeyword and HelpNavigator properties are provided to controls by the HelpProvider component.

14. **A.** The help file is in the right place and correctly connected to the HelpProvider; otherwise the help file would not be displayed at all. For regular help, you must set the HelpKeyword property. The HelpString property is reserved for pop-up help.

15. **A.** The same HelpProvider control can provide both F1 help and pop-up help. All you must do in this case is make the changes necessary to implement the pop-up help.

APPLY YOUR KNOWLEDGE

Suggested Readings and Resources

1. Microsoft HTML Help SDK.

2. Nathan, Adam. *.NET and COM: The Complete Interoperability Guide.* Sams Publishing, 2002.

3. Visual Studio .NET Combined Help Collection

   - Application Assistance

   - Designing Accessible Applications

   - HelpProvider Component

This chapter covers the following Microsoft-specified objective for the Creating User Services section of the Visual Basic .NET Windows-Based Applications exam:

Implement print capability.

▶ Many applications require some sort of portable, permanent record of their activities. In some cases, storing a file on disk or CD-ROM can satisfy this requirement, but other applications require a printer to produce a paper record. The .NET Framework handles printing support by defining the printer as another location a Graphics object can be located and by allowing you to use the methods of the Graphics object to construct the image to be printed. Printing itself is managed by an instance of the PrintDocument class.

The Visual Studio .NET IDE adds to this basic object-oriented printing scheme by defining a number of controls for use on a Windows Form. With these controls and a minimal amount of code, you can print anything you can draw.

CHAPTER 11

Printing

STUDY STRATEGIES

▶ Use the Object Browser to drill into the System.Drawing.Printing namespace. This is the best way to learn which printer settings are under direct programmatic control via the class hierarchy.

▶ Add printing capability to one of your own applications using the PrintDocument component.

▶ Implement PrintPreviewDialog and PageSetupDialog controls in an application. Experiment with the page setup settings to understand their effects on print preview and printing.

INTRODUCTION

Printing is one area in which Visual Basic .NET differs greatly from Visual Basic 6.0. Old code that uses the Printers collection or the PrintForm method is no longer compatible with the .NET Framework. Instead, you must learn a new object-oriented way of printing.

The new method of printing is anchored by the PrintDocument class. This class represents a connection between your application and a printer, and it abstracts all the specific printer functions into a single set of methods and properties. All the complexities and details of printing are hidden within this class. After you learn how to manage the PrintDocument class, you needn't worry about the details of programming any particular printer.

The PrintDocument class raises an event for each page to be printed. Your job is to write code to handle this event by supplying the actual text or graphics to be printed. If you recall the details of drawing graphics from Chapter 1, "Introducing Windows Forms," you'll see that printing is very similar to drawing. Indeed, the classes that handle printing are contained within the System.Drawing.Printing namespace.

In this chapter, you'll learn about printing directly from Visual Basic .NET. You'll see how to use the PrintDocument component to print both text and graphics, and you'll learn about the additional controls that give access to the printing-related common dialogs that are a part of Windows.

> **NOTE**
>
> **Crystal Reports** One skill that the exam doesn't cover is using *Crystal Reports*, the high-end reporting component that ships as a part of the Enterprise Edition of Visual Studio .NET. Crystal is designed to allow you to put together flexible, data-based reports. However, it can't handle the sort of general, low-level printing chores that I'll cover in this chapter.

USING THE PRINTDOCUMENT COMPONENT

Implement print capability.

Printing in the .NET Framework is managed by the PrintDocument class. Typically, you create a new instance of the PrintDocument class, set its properties, and call its Print method. Calling the method will fire the PrintDocument.PrintPage event. You determine what will be printed by adding a handler for this event. In the PrintPage event, you can retrieve and manipulate a Graphics object that lets you treat the next page to be printed as a canvas to draw on.

By using the methods of the Graphics class, as well as associated objects (such as Font or Brush objects) you can determine what to print.

In this section, you'll see how to take advantage of this printing scheme to print both text and graphics. I'll also discuss the other events fired by the PrintDocument object that allow you to perform initialization and cleanup tasks.

Printing Text

To the .NET printing mechanism, text is just a special case of graphics. You can handle text printing by calling the DrawString method of the Graphics class (see Step By Step 11.1).

STEP BY STEP

11.1 Printing Text

1. Create a new Visual Basic .NET Windows application. Add a form to the application.

2. Place a TextBox control and a Button control on the form. Name the TextBox control txtText and set its MultiLine property to True. Name the Button control btnPrint and set its Text property to &Print.

3. Drag a PrintDocument component from the toolbox to the form. This component has no runtime image, so it will be displayed in the component tray. Set its DocumentName property to NetDocument11-1.

4. Double-click the Button control to open the form's module. Add a line of code at the top of the module:

```
Imports System.Drawing.Printing
```

5. Add code to the button's Click event handler to print the document:

```
Private Sub btnPrint_Click(ByVal sender As System.Object, _
 ByVal e As System.EventArgs) Handles btnPrint.Click
    PrintDocument1.Print()
End Sub
```

6. Add an event handler for the PrintDocument object's
PrintPage event:

```
Private Sub PrintDocument1_PrintPage( _
 ByVal sender As Object, _
 ByVal e As System.Drawing.Printing.PrintPageEventArgs) _
 Handles PrintDocument1.PrintPage
    ' Create a font to print with
    Dim fnt As Font = New Font( _
     "Arial", 10, FontStyle.Regular, _
     GraphicsUnit.Point)
    ' Print the text
    e.Graphics.DrawString(txtText.Text, _
     fnt, Brushes.Black, 0, 0)
    ' And indicate that there are no more pages
    e.HasMorePages = False
End Sub
```

7. Set the form as the startup object for the project.

8. Run the project. Enter some text in the text box and click
the Print button.

> **NOTE**
>
> **Printer Required** For this example
> (and most of the others in this chap-
> ter) to function, you need a default
> printer installed.

Step By Step 11.1 demonstrated the basic mechanics of printing in
the .NET Framework:

1. Declare an instance of the PrintDocument class. (This is what
   the PrintDocument component does when you drop it on a
   form, as you can confirm by expanding the Windows Form
   Designer generated code region.)

2. When you're ready to print, call the Print method of the
   PrintDocument object.

3. Write code in the PrintDocument object's PrintPage event handler
   to perform the actual printing. Within this event, you can retrieve
   a Graphics object that represents the page about to be printed.
   Manipulating this object lets you dictate what will be printed.

4. At the end of the PrintPage event handler, set the
   HasMorePages property of the event arguments to indicate
   whether there is at least one more page to print.

This particular example takes the text from the TextBox, including
any newline characters, and draws it on the Graphics object using
the DrawString method. It draws the string at the coordinate
(0,0)—the upper-left corner of the drawing space.

If you have more than one string of text to print, you must consider the location of each string. If you just use the code from Step By Step 11.1, the DrawString method will place each line at (0,0)—which means that they'll all overlap. You must keep track of the printing position and change the coordinate in code. Step By Step 11.2 shows how to do this.

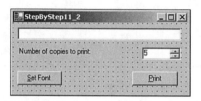

FIGURE 11.1
A form to print multiple lines of text.

STEP BY STEP

11.2 Printing Multiple Lines of Text

1. Add a new form to your Visual Basic .NET application.

2. Place a TextBox control (txtText), a Label control, a NumericUpDown control (nudCopies), a FontDialog control, and two Button controls (btnSetFont and btnPrint) on the form. Figure 11.1 shows a design for this form.

3. Drag a PrintDocument component from the toolbox to the form. Set its DocumentName property to NetDocument11-2.

4. Double-click the Button control to open the form's module. Add a line of code at the top of the module:

```
Imports System.Drawing.Printing
```

5. Add code to handle events:

```
' Create a default font to print with
Dim mfnt As Font = New Font("Arial", 10, _
 FontStyle.Regular, _
 GraphicsUnit.Point)

Private Sub btnPrint_Click(ByVal sender As System.Object, _
 ByVal e As System.EventArgs) Handles btnPrint.Click
    PrintDocument1.Print()
End Sub

Private Sub PrintDocument1_PrintPage( _
 ByVal sender As Object, _
 ByVal e As System.Drawing.Printing.PrintPageEventArgs) _
 Handles PrintDocument1.PrintPage
    ' Determine the height of the font
    Dim intFontHeight As Integer = _
     mfnt.GetHeight(e.Graphics)
    ' Vertical position for the next line of text
    Dim intCurrentY As Integer = 0
```

```
    Dim intI As Integer
    For intI = 1 To nudCopies.Value
        ' Print the text, using the selected font
        e.Graphics.DrawString(txtText.Text, mfnt, _
         Brushes.Black, 0, intCurrentY)
        intCurrentY += intFontHeight
    Next
    ' And indicate that there are no more pages
    e.HasMorePages = False
End Sub

Private Sub btnSetFont_Click( _
 ByVal sender As System.Object, _
 ByVal e As System.EventArgs) Handles btnSetFont.Click
    ' Start with the current font
    FontDialog1.Font = mfnt
    ' If the user clicks OK, set a new font
    If FontDialog1.ShowDialog = DialogResult.OK Then
        mfnt = FontDialog1.Font
    End If
End Sub
```

6. Set the form as the startup object for the project.

7. Run the project. Enter some text in the text box and use the NumericUpDown control to set the number of times to print the text. You can click the Set Font button to set the font of the text. Click the Print button to print the results.

This example showed how to calculate the printed height of a font by using the GetHeight method of the font. Note that this method takes a Graphics object as a parameter because it calculates the height for the font on that particular Graphics object, which of course represents a particular device you can print to.

Step By Step 11.2 will work as long as all the copies fit on a single page. But what if you have more copies than will fit? In that case, you must determine the page height and maintain the HasMorePages property correctly. Step by Step 11.3 shows how you can use the PrintPage method to print multiple pages of text.

STEP BY STEP

11.3 Printing Multiple Pages of Text

1. Add a new form to your Visual Basic .NET application.

2. Place a TextBox control (txtText), a Label control, a NumericUpDown control (nudCopies), a FontDialog control, and two Button controls (btnSetFont and btnPrint) on the form. You can reuse the form design you saw in Figure 11.1.

3. Drag a PrintDocument component from the toolbox to the form. Set its DocumentName property to NetDocument11-3.

4. Double-click the Button control to open the form's module. Add a line of code at the top of the module:

```
Imports System.Drawing.Printing
```

5. Add code to handle events:

```
' Create a default font to print with
Dim mfnt As Font = New Font("Arial", 10, _
 FontStyle.Regular, _
 GraphicsUnit.Point)
' Number of lines printed so far
Dim mintLines As Integer = 0

Private Sub btnPrint_Click(ByVal sender As System.Object, _
 ByVal e As System.EventArgs) Handles btnPrint.Click
    PrintDocument1.Print()
End Sub

Private Sub PrintDocument1_PrintPage( _
 ByVal sender As Object, _
 ByVal e As System.Drawing.Printing.PrintPageEventArgs) _
 Handles PrintDocument1.PrintPage
    ' Determine the height of the font
    Dim intFontHeight As Integer = _
     mfnt.GetHeight(e.Graphics)
    ' Vertical position for the next line of text
    Dim intCurrentY As Integer = 0

    Dim fPageDone As Boolean = False
    Do Until fPageDone
        ' Check to see whether there's
        ' more space on the page
        If intCurrentY <= e.MarginBounds.Height Then
```

```
            ' Increment the line number
            mintLines += 1
            If mintLines < nudCopies.Value Then
                ' Print the text, using the selected
                  font
                e.Graphics.DrawString(txtText.Text,
                mfnt, _
                  Brushes.Black, 0, intCurrentY)
                ' And increment the vertical
                ' location on the page
                intCurrentY += intFontHeight
            Else
                ' We've printed all the copies
                ' we need to print. In
                ' this case, set the flags
                ' to indicate that this page
                ' is done, but there are no more pages
                fPageDone = True
                e.HasMorePages = False
            End If
        Else
            ' We want to print another line,
            ' but there's no space
            fPageDone = True
            e.HasMorePages = True
        End If
    Loop

End Sub

Private Sub btnSetFont_Click( _
 ByVal sender As System.Object, _
 ByVal e As System.EventArgs) Handles btnSetFont.Click
    ' Start with the current font
    FontDialog1.Font = mfnt
    ' If the user clicks OK, set a new font
    If FontDialog1.ShowDialog = DialogResult.OK Then
        mfnt = FontDialog1.Font
    End If
End Sub
```

6. Set the form as the startup object for the project.

7. Run the project. Enter some text in the text box and use the NumericUpDown control to set the number of times to print the text. You can click the Set Font button to set the font of the text. Click the Print button to print the results. If necessary, the code will print multiple pages.

None of the additional complexity in this code comes from the act of printing itself; it's just the math required to manage what gets printed on each page. Table 11.1 shows all the properties of the PrintPageEventArgs object that is passed to the PrintPage event.

One of these, MarginBounds, provides a rectangular structure that represents the printable area of the page, taking the current margins into account. The code checks to see whether each line of text would extend past the bottom of the rectangle. If it would, it stops the current PrintPage event but sets the HasMorePages property to True to tell the .NET Framework there is more to print and to trigger the PrintPage event another time.

TABLE 11.1

PROPERTIES OF THE PRINTPAGEEVENTARGS CLASS

Property	Meaning
Cancel	Gets or sets a value indicating whether the print job should be cancelled
Graphics	The Graphics object representing the page to be printed
HasMorePages	Boolean value indicating whether there are more pages to print
MarginBounds	A rectangle representing the printable area of the page
PageBounds	A rectangle representing the entire page
PageSettings	An object that gets or sets page settings (such as portrait or landscape orientation)

Printing Graphics

Printing graphics is similar to printing text. The only major difference is that you use different methods of the Graphics object to print graphics (see Step By Step 11.4).

STEP BY STEP

11.4 Printing Graphics

1. Add a new form to your Visual Basic .NET application.

2. Place a Button control named `btnPrintGraphics` and a PrintDocument component on the form. Set the `DocumentName` property of the PrintDocument object to `NetDocument11-4`.

3. Double-click the Button control to open the form's module. Add code to import the necessary namespaces to the top of the module:

```
Imports System.Drawing
Imports System.Drawing.Printing
Imports System.Drawing.Drawing2D
```

4. Add code to handle events:

```
Private Sub btnPrintGraphics_Click( _
 ByVal sender As System.Object, _
 ByVal e As System.EventArgs) Handles btnPrintGraphics.Click
    PrintDocument1.Print()
End Sub


Private Sub PrintDocument1_PrintPage( _
 ByVal sender As Object, _
 ByVal e As System.Drawing.Printing.PrintPageEventArgs) _
 Handles PrintDocument1.PrintPage
    Dim grfx As Graphics = e.Graphics
    ' Set the Smoothing mode to SmoothingMode.AntiAlias
    grfx.SmoothingMode = SmoothingMode.AntiAlias
    ' Create Pen objects
    Dim penYellow As Pen = New Pen(Color.Blue, 20)
    Dim penRed As Pen = New Pen(Color.Red, 10)
    ' Call Draw methods
    grfx.DrawLine(Pens.Black, 20, 130, 250, 130)
    grfx.DrawEllipse(penYellow, 20, 10, 100, 100)
    grfx.DrawRectangle(penRed, 150, 10, 100, 100)
    ' No more pages to print
    e.HasMorePages = False
End Sub
```

5. Set the form as the startup object for the project.

6. Run the project. Click the button. The form will print a rectangle, an ellipse, and a line on the page.

NOTE

Device Independence This code is a good demonstration of how GDI+ enables you to create output without worrying about the differences between various devices. If you refer back to Chapter 1, you'll find that the code in Step By Step 1.17 is nearly identical to this code. The only difference is the addition of the setting for the HasMorePages property. Of course, if you don't have a color printer, the output will be in black and white—but you needn't handle that problem explicitly in your code.

All the methods of the Graphics object, plus associated objects such as brushes and pens, work just as well on the printed page as they do onscreen. For example, Step By Step 11.5 shows how to use a Brush object in conjunction with printing.

STEP BY STEP

11.5 Using Different Brush Types

1. Add a new form to your Visual Basic .NET application.

2. Place a Button control named btnPrintGraphics and a PrintDocument component on the form. Set the DocumentName property of the PrintDocument object to NetDocument11-5.

3. Double-click the Button control to open the form's module. Add code to import the necessary namespaces to the top of the module:

```
Imports System.Drawing
Imports System.Drawing.Printing
Imports System.Drawing.Drawing2D
```

4. Add code to handle events:

```
Private Sub PrintDocument1_PrintPage( _
 ByVal sender As Object, _
 ByVal e As System.Drawing.Printing.PrintPageEventArgs) _
 Handles PrintDocument1.PrintPage
    Dim grfx As Graphics = e.Graphics

    ' Create a HatchBrush object
    ' Call FillEllipse method by passing
    ' the created HatchBrush object
    Dim hb As HatchBrush = _
     New HatchBrush(HatchStyle.HorizontalBrick, _
    Color.Blue, Color.FromArgb(100, Color.Yellow))
    grfx.FillEllipse(hb, 40, 20, 200, 200)

    ' Create a TextureBrush object
    ' Call FillEllipse method by passing
    ' the created TextureBrush object
    Dim img As Image = New Bitmap("sunset.jpg")
    Dim tb As Brush = New TextureBrush(img)
    grfx.FillEllipse(tb, 300, 20, 200, 200)

    ' Create a LinearGradientBrush object
    ' Call FillEllipse method by passing the
    ' created LinearGradientBrush object
    Dim lb As LinearGradientBrush = _
     New LinearGradientBrush( _
     New Rectangle(160, 300, 200, 200), _
     Color.Red, Color.Yellow, _
     LinearGradientMode.BackwardDiagonal)
    grfx.FillEllipse(lb, 160, 300, 200, 200)

    e.HasMorePages = False
End Sub
```

5. Set the form as the startup object for the project.

6. Run the project. Click the button. The form will print three ellipses on the page, using three different brushes.

The Graphics Object   For more details on the Graphics object and the other drawing classes in the .NET Framework, review Chapter 1.

NOTE

Initialization and Cleanup

In addition to the PrintPage event, the PrintDocument class supplies three other events that you can learn how to use in Step By Step 11.6:

◆ The BeginPrint event fires once, before the first page of the job prints.

◆ The EndPrint event fires once, after the last page of the job has printed.

◆ The QueryPageSettings event fires immediately before each PrintPage event. During this event you can modify the QueryPageSettingsEventArgs.PageSettings property to control the page settings (for example, Portrait or Landscape mode) of the next page to be printed.

Guided Practice Exercise 11.1 will give you additional practice with these events.

STEP BY STEP

11.6 Using PrintDocument Events

1. Add a new form to your Visual Basic .NET application.

2. Place a TextBox control (txtText), a Label control, a NumericUpDown control (nudCopies), a FontDialog control, and two Button controls (btnSetFont and btnPrint) on the form. You can reuse the form design that you saw in Figure 11.1.

continues

continued

3. Drag a PrintDocument component from the toolbox to the form. Set its DocumentName property to `NetDocument11-6`. Drag a second PrintDocument component from the toolbox to the form. Set its DocumentName property to `Cover Sheet`.

4. Double-click the Button control to open the form's module. Add a line of code at the top of the module:

```
Imports System.Drawing.Printing
```

5. Add code to handle events:

```
' Create a default font to print with
Dim mfnt As Font = New Font("Arial", _
10, FontStyle.Regular, _
GraphicsUnit.Point)
' Number of lines printed so far
Dim mintLines As Integer = 0
' Number of pages printed
Dim mintPages As Integer = 0

Private Sub btnPrint_Click(ByVal sender As System.Object, _
 ByVal e As System.EventArgs) Handles btnPrint.Click
    PrintDocument1.Print()
End Sub

Private Sub PrintDocument1_PrintPage( _
 ByVal sender As Object, _
 ByVal e As System.Drawing.Printing.PrintPageEventArgs) _
 Handles PrintDocument1.PrintPage
    ' Determine the height of the font
    Dim intFontHeight As Integer = _
     mfnt.GetHeight(e.Graphics)
    ' Vertical position for the next line of text
    Dim intCurrentY As Integer = 0

    Dim fPageDone As Boolean = False
    Do Until fPageDone
        ' Check to see whether there's
        ' more space on the page
        If intCurrentY <= e.MarginBounds.Height Then
            ' Increment the line number
            mintLines += 1
            If mintLines < nudCopies.Value Then
                ' Print the text, using the selected font
                e.Graphics.DrawString(txtText.Text, mfnt, _
                 Brushes.Black, 0, intCurrentY)
```

```
                        ' And increment the vertical
                        ' location on the page
                        intCurrentY += intFontHeight
                    Else
                        ' We've printed all the copies
                        ' we need to print. In
                        ' this case, set the flags to
                        ' indicate that this page
                        ' is done, but there are no more pages
                        fPageDone = True
                        mintPages += 1
                        e.HasMorePages = False
                    End If
                Else
                    ' We want to print another line,
                    ' but there's no space
                    fPageDone = True
                    mintPages += 1
                    e.HasMorePages = True
                End If
        Loop

End Sub

Private Sub btnSetFont_Click( _
 ByVal sender As System.Object, _
 ByVal e As System.EventArgs) Handles btnSetFont.Click
    ' Start with the current font
    FontDialog1.Font = mfnt
    ' If the user clicks OK, set a new font
    If FontDialog1.ShowDialog = DialogResult.OK Then
        mfnt = FontDialog1.Font
    End If
End Sub

Private Sub PrintDocument1_BeginPrint( _
 ByVal sender As Object, _
 ByVal e As System.Drawing.Printing.PrintEventArgs) _
 Handles PrintDocument1.BeginPrint
    ' Prompt for cover sheet
    If InputBox("Print cover sheet?", , "Yes") = "Yes" Then
        PrintDocument2.Print()
    End If
End Sub

Private Sub PrintDocument1_EndPrint( _
 ByVal sender As Object, _
 ByVal e As System.Drawing.Printing.PrintEventArgs) _
 Handles PrintDocument1.EndPrint
    ' Tell the user we're done
    MessageBox.Show("Print job finished. Printed " & _
     mintPages & " page(s)")
End Sub
```

continues

```
Private Sub PrintDocument2_PrintPage( _
 ByVal sender As Object, _
 ByVal e As System.Drawing.Printing.PrintPageEventArgs) _
 Handles PrintDocument2.PrintPage
   ' Print a cover sheet for the job
   ' Create a font to print with
   Dim fnt As Font = New Font("Arial", 10, _
    FontStyle.Regular, _
    GraphicsUnit.Point)
   ' Height of a line of text
   Dim intHeight As Integer = fnt.GetHeight(e.Graphics)
   ' Print the text
   e.Graphics.DrawString("Printed at " & _
    DateTime.Now.ToShortTimeString, _
    fnt, Brushes.Black, 0, 0)
   ' Print some printer information
   e.Graphics.DrawString("Color: " & _
    e.PageSettings.Color.ToString, _
    fnt, Brushes.Black, 0, intHeight)
   e.Graphics.DrawString("Printer Name: " & _
    e.PageSettings.PrinterSettings.PrinterName, _
    fnt, Brushes.Black, 0, intHeight * 2)
   ' And indicate that there are no more pages
   e.HasMorePages = False
End Sub
```

6. Set the form as the startup object for the project.

7. Run the project. Enter some text in the TextBox control and use the NumericUpDown control to set the number of times to print the text. You can click the Set Font button to set the font of the text. Click the Print button to print the results. The code will prompt you for input as to whether it should print a cover page; answer Yes to get a cover page. If necessary, the code will print multiple pages. When printing is done, a message box will display the total number of pages printed.

> **EXAM TIP**
>
> **Altering Printer Settings**
> Remember, you can't change the printer settings in the PrintPage event. You'll need to use the QueryPageSettings event for this purpose.

> **NOTE**
>
> **Printer Capabilities**   You needn't memorize all the properties in Tables 11.2 and 11.3 for the exam, but you should have a sense of which printer settings are under the control of the .NET Framework objects.

Step By Step 11.6 builds on the code you saw in Step By Step 11.3. The additional code serves two purposes. First, if you want to print a cover page, it calls the Print method of the second PrintDocument object to do so. This code uses some of the properties of the PageSettings and PrinterSettings objects; you can find a full list of those properties in Tables 11.2 and 11.3, respectively. Second, the code tracks in a module-level variable the number of pages that have been printed and displays this number after the print job is finished.

TABLE 11.2

PROPERTIES OF THE PAGESETTINGS CLASS

Property	Meaning
Bounds	Size of the page, taking the page orientation into account
Color	Gets or sets a value indicating whether to print in color
Landscape	True if the page is in landscape orientation
Margins	Gets or sets the margins for the page
PaperSize	Gets or sets the paper size for the page
PaperSource	Gets or sets the paper source for the page
PrinterResolution	Gets or sets the resolution for this page
PrinterSettings	Returns the current PrinterSettings object

TABLE 11.3

PROPERTIES OF THE PRINTERSETTINGS CLASS

Property	Meaning
CanDuplex	True if the printer supports duplex printing.
Collate	True if the printer output is collated.
Copies	Gets or sets the number of copies to print.
DefaultPageSettings	Returns a PageSettings object for this printer.
Duplex	Gets or sets the duplex setting.
FromPage	Gets or sets the first page number to print.
InstalledPrinters	Gets the names of all printers on the system.
IsDefaultPrinter	Indicates whether this is the default printer.
IsPlotter	Indicates whether this is a plotter.
IsValid	Indicates whether the PrinterName property designates a valid printer.
LandscapeAngle	Number of degrees rotation from portrait to landscape output.
MaximumCopies	Most copies that you can print at once.
MaximumPage	Largest page number that can be selected in a print dialog.

continues

TABLE 11.3   *continued*

PROPERTIES OF THE PRINTERSETTINGS CLASS

Property	Meaning
MinimumPage	Smallest page number that can be selected in a print dialog.
PaperSizes	Paper sizes supported by the printer.
PaperSources	Paper sources supported by the printer.
PrinterName	Gets or sets the name of the printer to use. Change this property to change printers.
PrinterResolutions	Resolutions supported by the printer.
PrintRange	Page numbers specified for printing.
PrintToFile	True if output is redirected to a file.
SupportsColor	True if this printer supports color.
ToPage	Gets or sets the last page number to print.

GUIDED PRACTICE EXERCISE 11.1

In this exercise, you'll integrate your knowledge of databases with your knowledge of printing. The goal is to print the results of an arbitrary database query (expressed as a SQL statement).

Try this on your own first. If you get stuck or would like to see one possible solution, follow these steps.

1. Add a new form to your Visual Basic .NET application.

2. Place a Label control, a TextBox control named txtSQL with its MultiLine property set to True, a Button control named txtPrint, and a PrintDocument component on the form. Set the DocumentName of the PrintDocument component to SQL Query Results. Figure 11.2 shows a possible design for this form.

3. Switch to the form's module and add this code at the top of the module:

```
Imports System.Data
Imports System.Data.SqlClient
Imports System.Drawing.Printing
```

FIGURE 11.2
A form to print the results of a SQL query.

4. Add code to handle events on the form:

```vb
Dim mcnn As SqlConnection = New SqlConnection( _
 "data source=(local);initial catalog=Northwind;" & _
 "integrated security=SSPI")
Dim mds As DataSet = New DataSet()
' Number of rows of data to print
Dim mintRows As Integer = 0
' Number of rows printed
Dim mintRowsPrinted As Integer = 0

Private Sub btnPrint_Click(ByVal sender As
System.Object, _
 ByVal e As System.EventArgs) Handles btnPrint.Click
    PrintDocument1.Print()
End Sub

Private Sub PrintDocument1_PrintPage( _
 ByVal sender As Object, _
 ByVal e As System.Drawing.Printing.PrintPageEventArgs) _
 Handles PrintDocument1.PrintPage

    ' Create a font to print with
    Dim fnt As Font = New Font("Arial", _
     10, FontStyle.Regular, _
     GraphicsUnit.Point)
    ' Determine the height of the font
    Dim intFontHeight As Integer =
fnt.GetHeight(e.Graphics)
    ' Vertical position for the next line of text
    Dim intCurrentY As Integer = 0

    Dim dr As DataRow
    Dim dc As DataColumn
    Dim strPrint As String
    Dim intI As Integer

    Dim fPageDone As Boolean = False
    Do Until fPageDone
        ' Check to see whether there's
        ' more space on the page
        If intCurrentY <= e.MarginBounds.Height Then
            ' Increment the line number
            mintRowsPrinted += 1
            If mintRowsPrinted < mintRows Then
                ' Retrieve the DataRow
                dr = mds.Tables("Results"). _
                 Rows(mintRowsPrinted - 1)
                ' Print a row header
                e.Graphics.DrawString("Row Number " & _
                 CInt(mintRowsPrinted), fnt, _
                 Brushes.Black, 0, intCurrentY)
```

continues

continued

```
                         ' Build and print a string of data
                         strPrint = "   "
                         For intI = 0 To mds.Tables("Results"). _
                          Columns.Count - 1
                            dc = mds.Tables("Results").Columns(intI)
                            strPrint = strPrint & dc.ColumnName & _
                              ": " & dr(intI).ToString & " "
                              e.Graphics.DrawString(strPrint, fnt, _
                              Brushes.Black, 0, intCurrentY + _
                              intFontHeight)
                         Next
                         ' And increment the vertical
                         ' location on the page
                         intCurrentY += (2 * intFontHeight)
                     Else
                         ' We've printed all the rows
                         ' we need to print. In
                         ' this case, set the flags to
                         ' indicate that this page
                         ' is done, but there are no more pages
                         fPageDone = True
                         e.HasMorePages = False
                     End If
                 Else
                     ' We want to print another row,
                     ' but there's no space
                     fPageDone = True
                     e.HasMorePages = True
                 End If
         Loop
     End Sub

     Private Sub PrintDocument1_BeginPrint( _
      ByVal sender As Object, _
      ByVal e As System.Drawing.Printing.PrintEventArgs) _
      Handles PrintDocument1.BeginPrint
         ' Get the data to print
         Dim cmd As SqlCommand = mcnn.CreateCommand()
         cmd.CommandType = CommandType.Text
         cmd.CommandText = txtSQL.Text
         Dim da As SqlDataAdapter = New SqlDataAdapter()
         da.SelectCommand = cmd
         mcnn.Open()
         da.Fill(mds, "Results")
         mintRows = mds.Tables("Results").Rows.Count
     End Sub

     Private Sub PrintDocument1_EndPrint( _
      ByVal sender As Object, _
      ByVal e As System.Drawing.Printing.PrintEventArgs) _
      Handles PrintDocument1.EndPrint
```

```
        ' Close database connection
        mcnn.Close()
    End Sub
```

5. Set the form as the startup object for the project.

6. Run the project. Enter a query against the Northwind database such as

```
SELECT CustomerID, CompanyName
FROM Customers
WHERE Country = 'France'
```

7. Click the Print button to print the results of the query.

This exercise demonstrates another good use for the BeginPrint and EndPrint events: They can set up and destroy database objects that retrieve the data to be printed.

▶ To print in .NET, you use methods of the Graphics class. You can retrieve the appropriate instance of this class in the PrintPage event of a PrintDocument object.

▶ The PrintPage event is called once for each page to be printed. You can control whether there are more pages by setting the HasMorePages property during the event.

▶ The PrintDocument class also supports three other events: BeginPrint (which fires before the first page printed), EndPrint (which fires after the last page printed), and QueryPageSettings (which fires before each PrintPage event).

USING THE PRINTING CONTROLS

You could use the PageSettings and PrinterSettings classes directly to allow the user to set such options as the orientation of the printer or the paper tray to use, but this would require you to develop a user interface for changing such settings. Windows already has a standard Page Setup dialog box, as well as other standard printer-related dialog boxes.

Fortunately, these dialog boxes are available directly to Windows Forms. In fact, four components can come in handy when you're dealing with printing issues:

◆ The PageSetupDialog Component

◆ The PrintPreviewDialog Component

◆ The PrintPreviewControl Control

◆ The PrintDialog Component

In the remainder of this chapter, you'll see how to use these controls to add standard Windows printing features to your own applications.

The PageSetupDialog Component

The PageSetupDialog control displays the Windows Page Setup common dialog box (see Step By Step 11.7). This dialog box allows the user to set margins, paper orientation, and other characteristics of the printer that control the output.

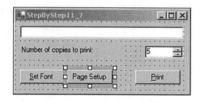

FIGURE 11.3
A form that uses the PageSetupDialog component.

STEP BY STEP

11.7 Using the PageSetupDialog Component

1. Add a new form to your Visual Basic .NET application.

2. Place a TextBox control (txtText), a Label control, a NumericUpDown control (nudCopies), a FontDialog control, a PageSetupDialog control, and three Button controls (btnPageSetup, btnSetFont, and btnPrint) on the form. Figure 11.3 shows a design for this form.

3. Drag a PrintDocument component from the toolbox to the form. Set its DocumentName property to NetDocument11-7.

4. Double-click one of the Button controls to open the form's module. Add a line of code at the top of the module:

```
Imports System.Drawing.Printing
```

5. Add code to handle events:

```
' Create a default font to print with
Dim mfnt As Font = New Font( _
 "Arial", 10, FontStyle.Regular, _
 GraphicsUnit.Point)
' Number of lines printed so far
Dim mintLines As Integer = 0

Private Sub btnPrint_Click(ByVal sender As System.Object, _
 ByVal e As System.EventArgs) Handles btnPrint.Click
    PrintDocument1.Print()
End Sub

Private Sub PrintDocument1_PrintPage( _
 ByVal sender As Object, _
 ByVal e As System.Drawing.Printing.PrintPageEventArgs) _
 Handles PrintDocument1.PrintPage
    ' Determine the height of the font
    Dim intFontHeight As Integer = _
     mfnt.GetHeight(e.Graphics)
    ' Vertical position for the next line of text
    Dim intCurrentY As Integer = 0

    Dim fPageDone As Boolean = False
    Do Until fPageDone
        ' Check to see whether there's
        ' more space on the page
        If intCurrentY <= e.MarginBounds.Height Then
            ' Increment the line number
            mintLines += 1
            If mintLines < nudCopies.Value Then
                ' Print the text, using the selected
                 font
                e.Graphics.DrawString(txtText.Text,
                mfnt, _
                 Brushes.Black, 0, intCurrentY)
                ' And increment the vertical
                ' location on the page
                intCurrentY += intFontHeight
            Else
                ' We've printed all the copies
                ' we need to print. In
                ' this case, set the flags to
                ' indicate that this page
                ' is done, but there are no more pages
                fPageDone = True
                e.HasMorePages = False
            End If
        Else
```

continues

continued

```
                    ' We want to print another line,
                    ' but there's no space
                    fPageDone = True
                    e.HasMorePages = True
            End If
        Loop

End Sub

Private Sub btnSetFont_Click( _
 ByVal sender As System.Object, _
 ByVal e As System.EventArgs) Handles btnSetFont.Click
        ' Start with the current font
        FontDialog1.Font = mfnt
        ' If the user clicks OK, set a new font
        If FontDialog1.ShowDialog = DialogResult.OK Then
            mfnt = FontDialog1.Font
        End If
End Sub

Private Sub btnPageSetup_Click( _
 ByVal sender As System.Object, _
    ByVal e As System.EventArgs) Handles btnPageSetup.Click
        ' Create a PageSettings object and send it to the dialog
        Dim pgsCustom As PageSettings = New PageSettings()
        PageSetupDialog1.PageSettings = pgsCustom
        If PageSetupDialog1.ShowDialog = DialogResult.OK Then
            PrintDocument1.DefaultPageSettings = _
            PageSetupDialog1.PageSettings
        End If
End Sub
```

6. Set the form as the startup object for the project.

7. Run the project. Enter some text in the TextBox control and use the NumericUpDown control to set the number of times to print the text. You can click the Set Font button to set the font of the text. You can also click the Page Setup button to see the Page Setup dialog box, as shown in Figure 11.4. Click the Print button to print the results.

> **NOTE**
>
> **Reused Code**   With the exception of the btnPageSetup_Click event handler, this is exactly the code that you saw in Step By Step 11.3.

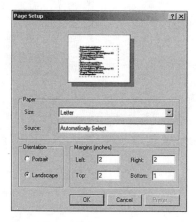

FIGURE 11.4
The Page Setup dialog box.

The PageSetupDialog component has four properties that you can use to enable or disable different sections of the dialog box:

◆ **AllowMargins**—Set this to False to disable the margin settings.

◆ **AllowOrientation**—Set this to False to disable the orientation section of the dialog box.

◆ **AllowPaper**—Set this to False to disable the paper size and source section of the dialog box.

◆ **AllowPrinter**—Set this to False to disable the printer button in the dialog box.

The PrintPreviewDialog Component

In the examples you've seen so far in this chapter, output has gone directly to the printer, but in a real application, you'll often want to provide print preview capabilities. Print preview allows users to see the results of a print job onscreen, before using time and paper to actually print it. This makes it much easier to adjust the job until it's perfect and is a convenience that Windows users have grown to expect.

The .NET Framework offers both a component and a control for print preview. I'll demonstrate the component approach first in Step By Step 11.8.

STEP BY STEP

11.8 Using the PrintPreviewDialog Component

1. Add a new form to your Visual Basic .NET application.

2. Place a TextBox control (txtText), a Label control, a NumericUpDown control (nudCopies), a FontDialog control, a PageSetupDialog control, a PrintPreviewDialog control, and four Button controls (btnPageSetup, btnSetFont, btnPreview, and btnPrint) on the form.

3. Drag a PrintDocument component from the toolbox to the form. Set its DocumentName property to NetDocument11-8. Set the Document property of the PrintPreviewDialog component to PrintDocument1.

continues

continued

4. Double-click one of the Button controls to open the form's module. Add a line of code at the top of the module:

```
Imports System.Drawing.Printing
```

5. Add code to handle events:

```
' Create a default font to print with
Dim mfnt As Font = New Font( _
"Arial", 10, FontStyle.Regular, _
GraphicsUnit.Point)
' Number of lines printed so far
Dim mintLines As Integer = 0

Private Sub btnPrint_Click(ByVal sender As System.Object, _
 ByVal e As System.EventArgs) Handles btnPrint.Click
    PrintDocument1.Print()
End Sub

Private Sub PrintDocument1_PrintPage( _
 ByVal sender As Object, _
 ByVal e As System.Drawing.Printing.PrintPageEventArgs) _
 Handles PrintDocument1.PrintPage
    ' Determine the height of the font
    Dim intFontHeight As Integer = _
     mfnt.GetHeight(e.Graphics)
    ' Vertical position for the next line of text
    Dim intCurrentY As Integer = 0

    Dim fPageDone As Boolean = False
    Do Until fPageDone
        ' Check to see whether there's
        ' more space on the page
        If intCurrentY <= e.MarginBounds.Height Then
            ' Increment the line number
            mintLines += 1
            If mintLines < nudCopies.Value Then
                ' Print the text, using the selected font
                e.Graphics.DrawString(txtText.Text, mfnt, _
                 Brushes.Black, 0, intCurrentY)
                ' And increment the vertical
                ' location on the page
                intCurrentY += intFontHeight
        Else
            ' We've printed all the copies
            ' we need to print. In
            ' this case, set the flags to
            ' indicate that this page
            ' is done, but there are no more pages
            fPageDone = True
            e.HasMorePages = False
        End If
```

```
        Else
            ' We want to print another line,
            ' but there's no space
            fPageDone = True
            e.HasMorePages = True
        End If
    Loop

End Sub

Private Sub btnSetFont_Click( _
 ByVal sender As System.Object, _
 ByVal e As System.EventArgs) Handles btnSetFont.Click
    ' Start with the current font
    FontDialog1.Font = mfnt
    ' If the user clicks OK, set a new font
    If FontDialog1.ShowDialog = DialogResult.OK Then
        mfnt = FontDialog1.Font
    End If
End Sub

Private Sub btnPageSetup_Click( _
 ByVal sender As System.Object, _
     ByVal e As System.EventArgs) Handles btnPageSetup.Click
    ' Create a PageSettings object and send it to the
    dialog
    Dim pgsCustom As PageSettings = New PageSettings()
    PageSetupDialog1.PageSettings = pgsCustom
    If PageSetupDialog1.ShowDialog = DialogResult.OK Then
        PrintDocument1.DefaultPageSettings = _
            PageSetupDialog1.PageSettings
    End If
End Sub

Private Sub btnPreview_Click( _
 ByVal sender As System.Object, _
 ByVal e As System.EventArgs) Handles btnPreview.Click
    PrintPreviewDialog1.ShowDialog()
End Sub
```

6. Set the form as the startup object for the project.

7. Run the project. Enter some text in the text box and use the NumericUpDown control to set the number of times to print the text. You can click the Set Font button to set the font of the text. You can also click the Page Setup button to see the Page Setup dialog box. Click the Preview button to see the document in Print Preview mode, as shown in Figure 11.5, or click the Print button to print the results.

FIGURE 11.5
The Print Preview dialog box.

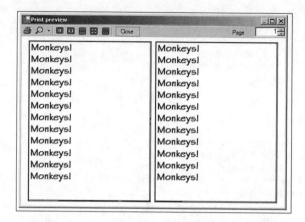

Adding print preview to this example takes only two lines of code: one to set the Document property of the PrintPreviewDialog object (so that it knows what it should display), and one to call the ShowDialog method of the component. Everything else is built into the .NET Framework and Windows itself. The Print Preview dialog offers these features:

◆ Printing from preview

◆ Adjustable zoom

◆ One-, two-, three-, four-, and six-page display modes

◆ The capability to scroll through all pages of the document being printed

If you set a breakpoint in the form's code, you'll discover that the code in the PrintDocument's events is executed in Preview mode as well as in Print mode.

The PrintPreviewControl Control

If you want more control over the presentation of print previews than you get with the PrintPreviewDialog component, you can use the PrintPreviewControl control (see Step By Step 11.9). This control can be embedded on a form to provide the core graphical functionality of the PrintPreviewDialog. (In fact, the area of the PrintPreviewDialog that presents the preview is itself a PrintPreviewControl.)

STEP BY STEP

11.9 Using the PrintPreviewControl Control

1. Add a new form to your Visual Basic .NET application.

2. Place a TextBox control (txtText), a Label control, a NumericUpDown control (nudCopies), a FontDialog control, a PageSetupDialog control, a PrintPreviewDialog control, and four Button controls (btnPageSetup, btnSetFont, btnPreview, and btnPrint) on the form.

3. Drag a PrintDocument component from the toolbox to the form. Set its DocumentName property to NetDocument11-9.

4. Double-click one of the Button controls to open the form's module. Add a line of code at the top of the module:

```
Imports System.Drawing.Printing
```

5. Add code to handle events:

```
' Create a default font to print with
Dim mfnt As Font = New Font("Arial", 10, _
 FontStyle.Regular, _
 GraphicsUnit.Point)
' Number of lines printed so far
Dim mintLines As Integer = 0

Private Sub btnPrint_Click(ByVal sender As System.Object, _
 ByVal e As System.EventArgs) Handles btnPrint.Click
    PrintDocument1.Print()
End Sub

Private Sub PrintDocument1_PrintPage( _
 ByVal sender As Object, _
 ByVal e As System.Drawing.Printing.PrintPageEventArgs) _
 Handles PrintDocument1.PrintPage
    ' Determine the height of the font
    Dim intFontHeight As Integer = _
     mfnt.GetHeight(e.Graphics)
    ' Vertical position for the next line of text
    Dim intCurrentY As Integer = 0

    Dim fPageDone As Boolean = False
    Do Until fPageDone
```

continues

continued

```
            ' Check to see whether there's _
            ' more space on the page
            If intCurrentY <= e.MarginBounds.Height Then
                ' Increment the line number
                mintLines += 1
                If mintLines < nudCopies.Value Then
                    ' Print the text, using the selected font
                    e.Graphics.DrawString(txtText.Text, mfnt, _
                    Brushes.Black, 0, intCurrentY)
                    ' And increment the vertical
                    ' location on the page
                    intCurrentY += intFontHeight
                Else
                    ' We've printed all the copies
                    ' we need to print. In
                    ' this case, set the flags
                    ' to indicate that this page
                    ' is done, but there are no more pages
                    fPageDone = True
                    e.HasMorePages = False
                End If
            Else
                ' We want to print another line,
                ' but there's no space
                fPageDone = True
                e.HasMorePages = True
            End If
        Loop

End Sub

Private Sub btnSetFont_Click( _
 ByVal sender As System.Object, _
 ByVal e As System.EventArgs) Handles btnSetFont.Click
    ' Start with the current font
    FontDialog1.Font = mfnt
    ' If the user clicks OK, set a new font
    If FontDialog1.ShowDialog = DialogResult.OK Then
        mfnt = FontDialog1.Font
    End If
End Sub

Private Sub btnPageSetup_Click( _
 ByVal sender As System.Object, _
    ByVal e As System.EventArgs) Handles btnPageSetup.Click
    ' Create a PageSettings object and send it to the dialog
    Dim pgsCustom As PageSettings = New PageSettings()
    PageSetupDialog1.PageSettings = pgsCustom
    If PageSetupDialog1.ShowDialog = DialogResult.OK Then
        PrintDocument1.DefaultPageSettings = _
        PageSetupDialog1.PageSettings
```

```
      End If
End Sub

Private Sub btnPreview_Click( _
 ByVal sender As System.Object, _
 ByVal e As System.EventArgs) Handles btnPreview.Click
    ' Expand the form to accommodate the control
    Me.Height = 425
    ' Create the control
    Dim PrintPreviewControl1 As PrintPreviewControl = _
     New System.Windows.Forms.PrintPreviewControl()
    ' Set its properties
    PrintPreviewControl1.Location = _
     New System.Drawing.Point(8, 144)
    PrintPreviewControl1.Name = "PrintPreviewControl1"
    PrintPreviewControl1.Size = _
     New System.Drawing.Size(272, 248)
    PrintPreviewControl1.Zoom = 0.3
    PrintPreviewControl1.Document = PrintDocument1
    ' And add it to the form
    Me.Controls.Add(PrintPreviewControl1)
End Sub
```

6. Set the form as the startup object for the project.

7. Run the project. Enter some text in the text box and use the NumericUpDown control to set the number of times to print the text. You can click the Set Font button to set the font of the text. You can also click the Page Setup button to see the Page Setup dialog box. Click the Preview button to see the document in Print Preview mode, as shown in Figure 11.6, or click the Print button to print the results.

FIGURE 11.6
Print preview embedded in a form.

The PrintPreviewControl control doesn't have any of the user interface of the PrintPreviewDialog beyond the print area itself, but you can manipulate the properties listed in Table 11.4 to get the same effects with whatever user interface you like.

> **WARNING**
>
> **Runtime Only** You'll notice that I created the PrintPreviewControl control dynamically at runtime. Although this control does appear in the toolbox, it won't work right if you simply drop an instance on the form and set its properties.

TABLE 11.4

SELECTED PROPERTIES OF THE PRINTPREVIEWCONTROL CONTROL

Property	Meaning
AutoZoom	Set to True to automatically change the zoom factor when the control is resized.

continues

TABLE 11.4   *continued*

SELECTED PROPERTIES OF THE PRINTPREVIEWCONTROL CONTROL

Property	Meaning
Columns	Number of columns of pages to display in preview.
Rows	Number of rows of pages to display in preview.
StartPage	The page number of the first page to display.
UseAntiAlias	Set to True to use antialiasing when displaying the print preview. Antialiasing shows higher quality text but takes longer to render.
Zoom	Zoom factor to use when displaying the preview.

> **EXAM TIP**
>
> **A Hidden PrintPreviewControl**   To programatically make changes to a PrintPreviewDialog at runtime, you can retrieve its PrintPreviewControl property and use the properties listed in Table 11.4.

The PrintDialog Component

Finally, you can use the PrintDialog component to give the user control over the printer and its properties, as demonstrated in Step By Step 11.10.

STEP BY STEP

11.10 Using the PrintDialog Component

1. Add a new form to your Visual Basic .NET application.

2. Place a TextBox control (`txtText`), a Label control, a NumericUpDown control (`nudCopies`), a FontDialog control, a PageSetupDialog control, a PrintPreviewDialog control, a PrintDialog control, and five Button controls (`btnPageSetup`, `btnSetFont`, `btnPreview`, `btnPrinter`, and `btnPrint`) on the form.

3. Drag a PrintDocument component from the toolbox to the form. Set its `DocumentName` property to `NetDocument11-10`. Set the Document property of the PrintPreviewDialog control to `PrintDocument1`.

4. Double-click one of the Button controls to open the form's module. Add a line of code at the top of the module:

```
Imports System.Drawing.Printing
```

5. Add code to handle events:

```
' Create a default font to print with
Dim mfnt As Font = New Font("Arial", 10, _
 FontStyle.Regular, _
 GraphicsUnit.Point)
' Number of lines printed so far
Dim mintLines As Integer = 0

Private Sub btnPrint_Click(ByVal sender As System.Object, _
 ByVal e As System.EventArgs) Handles btnPrint.Click
    PrintDocument1.Print()
End Sub

Private Sub PrintDocument1_PrintPage( _
 ByVal sender As Object, _
 ByVal e As System.Drawing.Printing.PrintPageEventArgs) _
 Handles PrintDocument1.PrintPage
    ' Determine the height of the font
    Dim intFontHeight As Integer = _
     mfnt.GetHeight(e.Graphics)
    ' Vertical position for the next line of text
    Dim intCurrentY As Integer = 0

    Dim fPageDone As Boolean = False
    Do Until fPageDone
        ' Check to see whether there's
        ' more space on the page
        If intCurrentY <= e.MarginBounds.Height Then
            ' Increment the line number
            mintLines += 1
            If mintLines < nudCopies.Value Then
                ' Print the text, using the selected
                ' font
                e.Graphics.DrawString(txtText.Text,
                mfnt, _
                 Brushes.Black, 0, intCurrentY)
                ' And increment the vertical
                ' location on the page
                intCurrentY += intFontHeight
            Else
                ' We've printed all the
                ' copies we need to print. In
                ' this case, set the flags to
                ' indicate that this page
                ' is done, but there are no more pages
                fPageDone = True
                e.HasMorePages = False
            End If
        Else
```

continues

continued

```
                ' We want to print another line,
                ' but there's no space
                fPageDone = True
                e.HasMorePages = True
            End If
        Loop

End Sub

Private Sub btnSetFont_Click( _
 ByVal sender As System.Object, _
 ByVal e As System.EventArgs) Handles btnSetFont.Click
        ' Start with the current font
        FontDialog1.Font = mfnt
        ' If the user clicks OK, set a new font
        If FontDialog1.ShowDialog = DialogResult.OK Then
            mfnt = FontDialog1.Font
        End If
End Sub

Private Sub btnPageSetup_Click( _
 ByVal sender As System.Object, _
     ByVal e As System.EventArgs) Handles btnPageSetup.Click
        ' Create a PageSettings object and send it to the
          dialog
        Dim pgsCustom As PageSettings = New PageSettings()
        PageSetupDialog1.PageSettings = pgsCustom
        If PageSetupDialog1.ShowDialog = DialogResult.OK Then
            PrintDocument1.DefaultPageSettings = _
              PageSetupDialog1.PageSettings
        End If
End Sub

Private Sub btnPreview_Click( _
 ByVal sender As System.Object, _
 ByVal e As System.EventArgs) Handles btnPreview.Click
        PrintPreviewDialog1.ShowDialog()
        'PrintPreviewControl1.Refresh()
End Sub


Private Sub btnPrinter_Click( _
 ByVal sender As System.Object, _
 ByVal e As System.EventArgs) Handles btnPrinter.Click
        Dim psCustom As PrinterSettings
        PrintDialog1.PrinterSettings = psCustom
        If PrintDialog1.ShowDialog = DialogResult.OK Then
            PrintDocument1.PrinterSettings = psCustom
        End If
End Sub
```

6. Set the form as the startup object for the project.

7. Run the project. Enter some text in the text box and use the NumericUpDown control to set the number of times to print the text. You can click the Set Font button to set the font of the text. You can also click the Page Setup button to see the Page Setup dialog box. Click the Preview button to see the document in Print Preview mode; click the Printer button to set properties for the printer, as shown in Figure 11.7, or click the Print button to print the results.

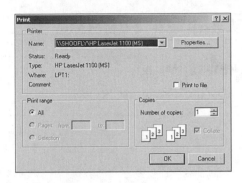

FIGURE 11.7
Using the PrintDialog class.

If you inspect the code, you'll see that the PrintDialog class is used in a similar fashion to the PageSetupDialog class. You supply a PrinterSettings variable to the PrintDialog, call its ShowDialog method, and set the returned PrinterSettings variable into the PrinterSettings property of the PrintDocument object.

REVIEW BREAK

▶ The PageSetupDialog component displays a dialog box that allows the user to set page-related printing properties.

▶ The PrintPreviewDialog component displays a preview of the document before it is printed.

▶ The PrintPreviewControl control lets you embed a print preview in a Windows Form.

▶ The PrintDialog component allows the user to set printer-related printing properties.

Chapter Summary

KEY TERM

- PrintDocument

The .NET Framework gives your applications complete printer control through a set of custom classes. The key object involved is an instance of the PrintDocument class, which represents a document to be printed. When you call the PrintDocument.Print method, it triggers the PagePrint event of the class. In this event, you can retrieve a Graphics object that represents the page to be printed, and draw on it using the familiar methods of the Graphics object.

Other events of the PrintDocument object let you manage initialization and cleanup for printing and manipulate page settings on a page-by-page basis.

The .NET Framework also provides components to allow access to the built-in common dialogs for printing. You can manipulate page settings and printer settings through these dialogs. You can also preview a document before it is printed, either in a separate dialog box or directly on a form.

APPLY YOUR KNOWLEDGE

Exercises

11.1 Printing Multiple Columns

The methods of the Graphics object give complete flexibility to place text or objects at any point in the drawing area. In this exercise, you'll use these positioning capabilities to print a database table in multiple columns. You'll also see how to use the QueryPageSettings event to force the printed output to be in Landscape mode.

Estimated Time: 25 minutes.

1. Open a Visual Basic .NET Windows Application in the Visual Studio .NET IDE. Add a new form to the application.

2. Add a Label control, a TextBox control (txtSQL), and two Button controls (btnPreview and btnPrint) to the form. Set the MultiLine property of the TextBox control to True. Figure 11.8 shows a design for this form.

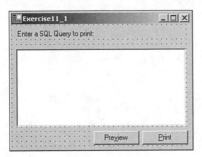

FIGURE 11.8
A form to test multiple-column printing.

3. Add a PrintDocument component and a PrintPreviewDialog component to the form. Set the DocumentName property of the PrintDocument component to SQL Query Results.

Set the Document property of the PrintPreviewDialog component to PrintDocument1.

4. Double-click one of the buttons to open the form's module. Enter this code at the top of the module:

```
Imports System.Data
Imports System.Data.SqlClient
Imports System.Drawing.Printing
```

5. Add code to handle the Button and Printing events:

```
Dim mcnn As SqlConnection = _
 New SqlConnection( _
 "data source=(local);" & _
 "initial catalog=Northwind; " & _
 "integrated security=SSPI")
Dim mds As DataSet = New DataSet()
' Number of rows of data to print
Dim mintRows As Integer = 0
' Number of rows printed
Dim mintRowsPrinted As Integer = 0

Private Sub btnPrint_Click( _
 ByVal sender As System.Object, _
 ByVal e As System.EventArgs) _
 Handles btnPrint.Click
    PrintDocument1.Print()
End Sub

Private Sub PrintDocument1_PrintPage( _
 ByVal sender As Object, _
 ByVal e As System.Drawing.Printing. _
 PrintPageEventArgs) _
 Handles PrintDocument1.PrintPage

    ' Create some fonts to print with
    Dim fnt As Font = New Font("Arial", _
     10, FontStyle.Regular, _
     GraphicsUnit.Point)
    Dim fntHeader As Font = _
     New Font("Arial", _
     10, FontStyle.Bold, _
     GraphicsUnit.Point)
    ' Determine the height of the font
    Dim intFontHeight As Integer = _
     fnt.GetHeight(e.Graphics)
```

APPLY YOUR KNOWLEDGE

```
' Vertical position for
' the next line of text
Dim intCurrentY As Integer = 0

Dim dr As DataRow
Dim dc As DataColumn
Dim strPrint As String
Dim intI As Integer

Dim fPageDone As Boolean = False

' Print a header row first
For intI = 0 To mds.Tables( _
  "Results").Columns.Count - 1
    dc = mds.Tables("Results"). _
      Columns(intI)
    e.Graphics.DrawString( _
      dc.ColumnName, fntHeader, _
      Brushes.Black, intI * 200, 0)
Next
' And increment the vertical
' location on the page
intCurrentY += intFontHeight

Do Until fPageDone
    ' Check to see whether there's
    ' more space on the page
    If intCurrentY <= _
    e.MarginBounds.Height Then
        ' Increment the line number
        mintRowsPrinted += 1
        If mintRowsPrinted < _
        mintRows Then
            ' Retrieve the DataRow
          dr = mds.Tables("Results"). _
            Rows(mintRowsPrinted - 1)
            ' And print its data
          strPrint = "  "
          For intI = 0 To _
          mds.Tables("Results"). _
          Columns.Count - 1
              e.Graphics. _
                DrawString(dr(intI). _
                ToString, fnt, _
                Brushes.Black, _
                intI * 200, _
                intCurrentY)
          Next
          ' And increment the vertical
          ' location on the page
          intCurrentY += intFontHeight
        Else
```

```
            ' We've printed all the rows
            ' we need to print. In
            ' this case, set the flags
            ' to indicate that this page
            ' is done, but there
            ' are no more pages
            fPageDone = True
            e.HasMorePages = False
        End If
    Else
        ' We want to print another row,
        ' but there's no space
        fPageDone = True
        e.HasMorePages = True
    End If
Loop
End Sub

Private Sub PrintDocument1_BeginPrint( _
 ByVal sender As Object, _
 ByVal e As System.Drawing.Printing. _
 PrintEventArgs) _
 Handles PrintDocument1.BeginPrint
    ' Get the data to print
    Dim cmd As SqlCommand = _
      mcnn.CreateCommand()
    cmd.CommandType = CommandType.Text
    cmd.CommandText = txtSQL.Text
    Dim da As SqlDataAdapter = _
      New SqlDataAdapter()
    da.SelectCommand = cmd
    mcnn.Open()
    da.Fill(mds, "Results")
    mintRows = mds.Tables( _
      "Results").Rows.Count
End Sub

Private Sub PrintDocument1_EndPrint( _
 ByVal sender As Object, _
 ByVal e As System.Drawing.Printing. _
 PrintEventArgs) _
 Handles PrintDocument1.EndPrint
    ' Close database connection
    mcnn.Close()
End Sub

Private Sub btnPreview_Click( _
 ByVal sender As System.Object, _
 ByVal e As System.EventArgs) _
 Handles btnPreview.Click
    PrintPreviewDialog1.ShowDialog()
End Sub
```

APPLY YOUR KNOWLEDGE

```
Private Sub _
 PrintDocument1_QueryPageSettings( _
 ByVal sender As Object, _
 ByVal e As System.Drawing.Printing. _
 QueryPageSettingsEventArgs) _
 Handles PrintDocument1.QueryPageSettings
    ' Put the page into landscape mode
    e.PageSettings.Landscape = True
End Sub
```

6. Set the form as the startup object for the project.

7. Run the project. Enter a SQL query such as

```
SELECT CustomerID, CompanyName, ContactName
FROM Customers
WHERE Country = 'Germany'
```

8. Click the Preview button or the Print button to see how the results are formatted.

This code works by placing columns every two inches (200 graphics units) across the page. The page is forced to Landscape mode by setting the PageSettings.Landscape property to True to make room for the maximum possible number of columns. From there, it's simple math to calculate the x,y coordinate for printing each string to the Graphics object.

Of course, this sample has limitations. The most notable is that it doesn't have any way to check whether all the columns will fit on the page or whether the text will fit into the columns. If you need to print arbitrary data on the page, you should investigate the Graphics.MeasureString method, which can return the size of the rectangle needed to print a given string of text to a particular Graphics object with a given font and brush.

11.2 Setting Preview Properties

This exercise will show how to use the properties of the PrintPreviewControl class to customize the initial view of a document in Print Preview mode.

Estimated Time: 15 minutes.

1. Add a new form to your Visual Basic .NET application.

2. Add a TextBox control named txtText, three Label controls, three NumericUpDown controls (nudCopies, nudRows, and nudColumns), and three Button controls (btnSetFont, btnPreview, and btnPrint) to the form. Figure 11.9 shows a design for this form.

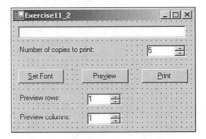

FIGURE 11.9
A form to experiment with preview properties.

3. Double-click the form to open the form's module. Add this code to the top of the module:

```
Imports System.Drawing.Printing
```

4. Add code to handle events to the form:

```
' Create a default font to print with
Dim mfnt As Font = New Font("Arial", 10, _
 FontStyle.Regular, _
 GraphicsUnit.Point)
' Number of lines printed so far
Dim mintLines As Integer = 0

Private Sub btnPrint_Click( _
 ByVal sender As System.Object, _
 ByVal e As System.EventArgs) _
 Handles btnPrint.Click
    PrintDocument1.Print()
End Sub
```

APPLY YOUR KNOWLEDGE

```
Private Sub PrintDocument1_PrintPage( _
 ByVal sender As Object, _
 ByVal e As System.Drawing.Printing. _
 PrintPageEventArgs) _
 Handles PrintDocument1.PrintPage
    ' Determine the height of the font
    Dim intFontHeight As Integer = _
     mfnt.GetHeight(e.Graphics)
    ' Vertical position for
    ' the next line of text
    Dim intCurrentY As Integer = 0

    Dim fPageDone As Boolean = False
    Do Until fPageDone
        ' Check to see whether there's
        ' more space on the page
        If intCurrentY <= _
         e.MarginBounds.Height Then
            ' Increment the line number
            mintLines += 1
            If mintLines < _
             nudCopies.Value Then
                ' Print the text,
                ' using the selected font
                e.Graphics.DrawString( _
                 txtText.Text, mfnt, _
                 Brushes.Black, 0, _
                 intCurrentY)
                ' And increment the vertical
                ' location on the page
                intCurrentY += intFontHeight
            Else
                ' We've printed
                ' all the copies
                ' we need to print. In
                ' this case, set the flags
                ' to indicate that this page
                ' is done, but there
                ' are no more pages
                fPageDone = True
                e.HasMorePages = False
            End If
        Else
```

```
            ' We want to print another line,
            ' but there's no space
            fPageDone = True
            e.HasMorePages = True
        End If
    Loop

End Sub

Private Sub btnSetFont_Click( _
 ByVal sender As System.Object, _
 ByVal e As System.EventArgs) _
 Handles btnSetFont.Click
    ' Start with the current font
    FontDialog1.Font = mfnt
    ' If the user clicks OK, set a new font
    If FontDialog1.ShowDialog = _
     DialogResult.OK Then
        mfnt = FontDialog1.Font
    End If
End Sub

Private Sub btnPreview_Click( _
 ByVal sender As System.Object, _
 ByVal e As System.EventArgs) _
 Handles btnPreview.Click
    ' Set up the specified rows and columns
    PrintPreviewDialog1. _
     PrintPreviewControl.Rows _
     = nudRows.Value
    PrintPreviewDialog1. _
     PrintPreviewControl.Columns = _
     nudColumns.Value
    ' And show the preview
    PrintPreviewDialog1.ShowDialog()
End Sub
```

5. Set the form as the startup object for the project.

6. Run the project. Enter text and a repeat count for the document. Enter a number of rows and columns and click Preview to see the preview. Figure 11.10 shows a sample preview at three rows by three columns.

APPLY YOUR KNOWLEDGE

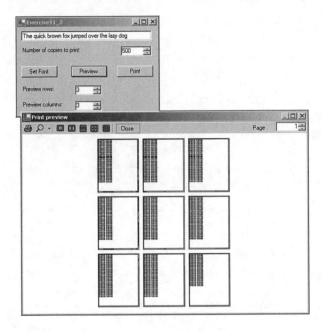

FIGURE 11.10
Custom print preview.

Review Questions

1. What method should you call to print a document from a .NET Windows Form?

2. What events does the PrintDocument object support?

3. How can you print multiple pages from a PrintDocument object?

4. How can you determine the height of a string of text on the printed page?

5. What is the difference between drawing on a Windows Form and printing graphics via the PrintDocument class?

6. What happens when you try to print colored graphics to a black and white printer?

7. What common dialog boxes does the .NET Framework supply to aid in printing?

8. How can you enable the user to set paper orientation without allowing them to change printers?

Exam Questions

1. Your application is printing a number of copies of a text string, using this code:

```
Private Sub PrintDocument1_PrintPage( _
 ByVal sender As Object, _
 ByVal e As System.Drawing. _
 Printing.PrintPageEventArgs) _
 Handles PrintDocument1.PrintPage
    ' Determine the height of the font
    Dim intFontHeight As Integer = _
    mfnt.GetHeight(e.Graphics)
    ' Vertical position for
    ' the next line of text
    Dim intCurrentY As Integer = 0

    Dim fPageDone As Boolean = False
    Do Until fPageDone
        ' Check to see whether there's
        ' more space on the page
        If intCurrentY <= _
        e.MarginBounds.Height Then
            ' Increment the line number
            mintLines += 1
            If mintLines < _
            nudCopies.Value Then
                ' Print the text,
                ' using the selected font
                e.Graphics.DrawString( _
                txtText.Text, mfnt, _
                Brushes.Black, 0, _
                intCurrentY)
                ' And increment the vertical
                ' location on the page
                intCurrentY += intFontHeight
        Else
```

APPLY YOUR KNOWLEDGE

```
                   ' Nothing left to print
                   fPageDone = True
               End If
           Else
               ' We want to print another line,
               ' but there's no space
               fPageDone = True
           End If
       Loop
End Sub
```

The application prints one page and then stops, regardless o the number of lines you've told it to print. What should you do to fix this code?

A. Set e.HasMorePages to True when there is more to print but no space.

B. Set e.HasMorePages to False when there is more to print but no space.

C. Set e.MarginBounds.Height to a value greater than the length of the page to force another page.

D. Set e.PageBounds.Height to a value greater than the length of the page to force another page.

2. Your application contains the following code:

```
Private Sub PrintDocument1_PrintPage( _
 ByVal sender As Object, _
 ByVal e As System.Drawing.Printing. _
 PrintPageEventArgs) _
 Handles PrintDocument1.PrintPage
     ' Create a font to print with
     Dim fnt As Font = New Font("Arial", _
       10, FontStyle.Regular, _
       GraphicsUnit.Point)
     ' Print the text 5 times
     Dim intI As Integer
     For intI = 1 To 5
         e.Graphics.DrawString( _
           txtText.Text, _
           fnt, Brushes.Black, 0, 0)
     Next
     ' And indicate that
     ' there are no more pages
     e.HasMorePages = False
End Sub
```

When you call the Print method of the PrintDocument1 object, only a single line of text is printed on the form. What could be the reason you don't see five lines of output?

A. The printer is incompatible with Windows.

B. The code prints the line of text five times in the same place.

C. You must create a new Font object for each line of text.

D. You must set the HasMorePages property to True.

3. You have designed a form that includes this code to print 10 copies of a line of text:

```
Private Sub PrintDocument1_PrintPage( _
 ByVal sender As Object, _
 ByVal e As System.Drawing.Printing. _
 PrintPageEventArgs) _
 Handles PrintDocument1.PrintPage
     ' Create a font to use
     Dim mfnt As Font = New Font( _
       "Arial", 10, _
       FontStyle.Regular, _
       GraphicsUnit.Point)
     ' Determine the height of the font
     Dim intFontHeight As Integer = _
       mfnt.GetHeight(Me.CreateGraphics())
     ' Vertical position for
     ' the next line of text
     Dim intCurrentY As Integer = 0

     Dim intI As Integer
     For intI = 1 To 10
         ' Print the text,
         ' using the selected font
         e.Graphics.DrawString( _
           txtText.Text, _
           mfnt, Brushes.Black, 0, _
           intCurrentY)
         intCurrentY += intFontHeight
     Next
     ' And indicate that
     ' there are no more pages
     e.HasMorePages = False
End Sub
```

APPLY YOUR KNOWLEDGE

When you execute the code, it prints 10 copies of the text string, but the line spacing is wrong. What could be the problem?

A. The printer is incompatible with the .NET Framework.

B. A font height retrieved using the form's Graphics object will not necessarily match a font height for the printer's Graphics object.

C. You must append a vbCrLf character to the end of each text string to reset the print position.

D. You must set e.HasMorePages to True before printing.

4. You want to ensure that all pages of your document are printed in Portrait mode, no matter what settings the user has chosen. How should you do this?

A. Set the DefaultPageSettings.Landscape property to False in the PrintPage event.

B. Display the Page Setup dialog box to the user, with instructions to select Portrait mode.

C. Set the PageBounds property to reflect a portrait page in the BeginPrint event.

D. Set the PageSettings.Landscape property to False in each QueryPageSettings event.

5. Your code is printing numbers on a page using a font defined at the module level:

```
Private Sub PrintDocument1_PrintPage( _
 ByVal sender As Object, _
 ByVal e As System.Drawing.Printing. _
 PrintPageEventArgs) _
 Handles PrintDocument1.PrintPage
    Dim intFontHeight As Integer = _
     mfnt.GetHeight(Me.CreateGraphics())
```

```
    ' Vertical position for
    ' the next line of text
    Dim intCurrentY As Integer = 0

    Dim intI As Integer = 0
    Do Until intCurrentY > _
     e.PageBounds.Height
        intI += 1
        ' Print the text,
        ' using the selected font
        e.Graphics.DrawString(CStr(intI), _
         mfnt, _
         Brushes.Black, 0, intCurrentY)
        intCurrentY += intFontHeight
    Loop
    MessageBox.Show("Printed " & _
     CStr(intI) & " lines")
    ' And indicate that
    ' there are no more pages
    e.HasMorePages = False
End Sub
```

When you run this code, it claims to print 26 lines, but on inspecting the printed page you find that only 24 lines are on the page. How should you fix this problem?

A. Fix the off-by-one error in the loop.

B. Declare the Font object within the event procedure.

C. Check the MarginBounds.Height property instead of the PageBounds.Height property.

D. Initialize intCurrentY to intFontHeight instead of to zero.

6. Your application needs to print information retrieved from a Web service across the Internet. The information is delivered in a single method call from the Web service, but you must break it up into multiple pages during printing. In which event of the PrintDocument object should you retrieve the information?

A. PagePrint

B. QueryPrintSettings

C. EndPrint

D. BeginPrint

7. You developed complex logic within the PrintPage event of a PrintDocument object to print your company logo using graphics primitives. You'd like to reuse this logic on multiple forms. What should you do?

  A. Cut and paste your custom logic to individual PrintDocument instances on each form.

  B. Move your logic to a Public procedure in a module and call that procedure from each PrintDocument instance.

  C. Keep one form open with a PrintDocument object and use that PrintDocument object for every print job.

  D. Derive a class from the PrintDocument object, override the PagePrint event, and put your logic in that event. Use an instance of the derived class whenever you need to print.

8. Users of your application want to select the margins and paper orientation of their print jobs. Which component should you add to your form to enable this easily?

  A. PrintDocument

  B. PrintDialog

  C. PrintPreviewDialog

  D. PageSetupDialog

9. You are using a PrintPreviewDialog component in your application to display print jobs before they are printed. Users want to view eight pages at a time in the print preview, but that isn't one of the choices on the toolbar of the Print Preview dialog box. How can you display eight pages in print preview? (Select two.)

  A. Set the PrintPreviewDialog.PrintPreviewControl.Rows and PrintPreviewDialog.PrintPreviewControl.Columns settings to 2 and 4 respectively before showing the dialog.

  B. Use the PageSetupDialog class to reduce the size of the pages so that more will fit in the display.

  C. Use a PrintPreviewControl control to create your own custom Print Preview dialog box.

  D. Use two PrintPreviewDialog components and display four pages in each one.

10. Your application uses an instance of the PageSetupDialog component to allow users to set the margins of their print jobs. All print jobs are sent to a departmental printer with multiple paper trays. The accounting department complains that your users are using the check stock from one of the reserved paper trays. What can you do to prevent users from printing from that tray?

  A. Set the AllowPaper property of the PageSetupDialog to False before showing it.

  B. Set the AllowPrinter property of the PageSetupDialog to False before showing it.

  C. Set the AllowMargins property of the PageSetupDialog to False before showing it.

  D. Set the AllowPaper property of the PageSetupDialog to True before showing it.

11. Your application creates and displays a PrintPreviewControl control at runtime.

APPLY YOUR KNOWLEDGE

Users want the display in this control automatically sized to fit when the control is resized. What should you do?

A. Set the UseAntiAlias property to True.

B. Set the UseAntiAlias property to False.

C. Set the AutoZoom property to True.

D. Set the AutoZoom property to False.

12. Your application needs to print the contents of a database table. The print job might span multiple pages, depending on the number of rows in the table. In which event of the PrintDocument control should you connect to the database?

A. PagePrint

B. QueryPrintSettings

C. EndPrint

D. BeginPrint

13. You must print the contents of a TextBox control from your form. You have added a PrintDocument component to the form and created a Button control that calls the Print method of the PrintDocument component. When you click the button, nothing prints. What must you do?

A. Add code to the PagePrint event of the PrintDocument to tell it what to print.

B. Add a PrintDialog component to your form.

C. Add code to the BeginPrint event of the PrintDocument to tell it what to print.

D. Add a PrintPreviewDialog component to your form.

14. Your application allows the user to print documents and then places an entry in the Windows event log with the total number of pages for each document. In which event of the PrintDocument object should you place the event log code?

A. BeginPrint

B. EndPrint

C. QueryPageSettings

D. PagePrint

15. Your application lets the user select a font for printing. Users complain that when they select a large font the lines on the printed page overlap. What should you do to fix this problem?

A. Call the Graphics.MeasureString method to get the width of the text before it is printed.

B. Set the AutoZoom property of the associated PrintPreviewDialog component to True.

C. Check the size of the font that the user selects and reduce it if it is too large.

D. Call the Font.GetHeight method to determine the vertical size of the font.

Answers to Review Questions

1. The Print method of the PrintDocument class is used to print from a .NET Windows Form.

2. The PrintDocument class supports the BeginPrint (fired once before printing starts), QueryPageSettings (fired before each page is printed), PagePrint (fired when each page is printed) and EndPrint (fired once when printing is finished) events.

APPLY YOUR KNOWLEDGE

3. Set the HasMorePages property to True within the PagePrint event to have the event fired again to print another page.

4. Use the GetHeight method of the Font object to determine the height of a font.

5. The only difference between drawing on a form and drawing on the printed page is the Graphics object you use. After you have the appropriate Graphics object, the code is exactly the same.

6. Windows will take care of the details of reducing the color to something the printer can handle.

7. The .NET Framework gives you common dialog boxes to handle page setup, printer setup, and print preview.

8. Call the PageSetupDialog with the AllowPrinters property set to False to allow the user to set paper orientation without allowing them to switch printers.

Answers to Exam Questions

1. **A.** To indicate to the PrintDocument class that it should print another page, set the HasMorePages property to True in the PagePrint event.

2. **B.** The DrawString method takes an x and a y argument as its last two parameters. If you don't vary these parameters, the method will continue printing in the same place.

3. **B.** All print operations must be carried out with the printer's Graphics object, which can be retrieved from the arguments to the PrintPage event.

4. **D.** The QueryPageSettings event is the appropriate place to change page settings. When the PrintPage event fires, it's too late to change any settings for that page.

5. **C.** The PageBounds property returns a rectangle that represents the entire page. The MarginBounds property returns a rectangle that represents the printable area of the page.

6. **D.** The BeginPrint event is appropriate for one-time actions that must be performed before a print job starts delivering output.

7. **D.** Using a derived class allows you to encapsulate and reuse the custom logic without duplicating code or losing any of the object-oriented benefits of the PrintDocument class.

8. **D.** The PageSetupDialog includes sections for setting margins and orientation.

9. **A, C.** The Rows and Columns properties of the PrintPreviewControl control let you customize the display of thumbnails. You can either create your own instance of this control or retrieve the control from the built-in PrintPreviewDialog component.

10. **A.** To disable a section of the Page Setup dialog box, set the corresponding variable to False before showing the dialog box.

11. **C.** Setting the AutoZoom property to True tells the control to display the document as large as it can, based on the current size of the control.

12. **D.** By connecting to the database in the BeginPrint event, you can ensure that the data is available for the duration of the print job.

13. **A.** The Print method triggers the PagePrint event, which is how the actual work of printing occurs.

APPLY YOUR KNOWLEDGE

14. **B.** The EndPrint event is appropriate for actions that must be performed once when a print job is finished.

15. **D.** If you use the Font.GetHeight method to get the height of the font, you can calculate the proper spacing of printed lines for that font.

Suggested Readings and Resources

1. Cornell, Gary and Jonathan Morrison. *Programming VB. NET: A Guide for Experienced Programmers.* Apress, 2002.

2. Grundgeiger, Dave. *Programming Visual Basic .NET.* O'Reilly, 2002.

3. Siler, Brian and Jeff Spotts. *Special Edition Using Microsoft Visual Basic .NET.* Que, 2002.

4. Visual Studio .NET Combined Help Collection

   • Windows Forms Print Support

5. Windows Forms Quickstarts

   • Working With Printing

This chapter covers the following Microsoft-specified objective for the "Testing and Debugging" section of the Visual Basic .NET Windows-Based Applications exam:

Create a unit test plan.

▶ Before you release a product or a component, the software needs to pass through several different types of tests. This objective requires you to know the different types of testing that a product should undergo to verify its robustness, reliability, and correctness. These tests should be executed with a designed test plan, which ensures that the product thoroughly meets its goals and requirements.

Implement tracing.

- **Add trace listeners and trace switches to an application.**

- **Display trace output.**

▶ Tracing helps in displaying informative messages while an application is running, so you can get a fair idea of how the application is progressing. This objective requires you to know how to use the properties and methods of the Trace class, attach trace listeners, and apply trace switches. Using trace switches, you can change the detail level of messages that are displayed by the Trace class without recompiling programs. You can do this by just editing the Extensible Markup Language (XML) configuration file for a program.

CHAPTER 12

Testing and Debugging a Windows Application

Debug, rework, and resolve defects in code.

- **Configure the debugging environment.**

- **Create and apply debugging code to components and applications.**

- **Provide multicultural test data to components and applications.**

- **Execute tests.**

- **Resolve errors and rework code.**

▶ The process of debugging helps you locate logical or runtime errors in an application. This objective requires you to know the various tools and windows available in Visual Basic .NET to enable easy and effective debugging. These debugging tools and windows help a great deal in locating errors, executing test code, and fixing defects.

▶ Review the "Introduction to Instrumentation and Tracing" and the "Using the Debugger" sections of the Visual Studio .NET Combined Help Collection.

▶ Try calling the different methods of the Trace and Debug classes. Note the difference in the output when you run a program using the Debug and Release configurations.

▶ Experiment with attaching predefined and custom-made listeners to the Trace object. Refer to Step By Step 12.2 and Guided Practice Exercise 12.1 for examples.

▶ Know how to implement trace switches and conditional compilation in a Windows application. Refer to Step By Step 12.3 and Step By Step 12.4 for examples.

▶ Experiment with the different types of debugging windows available in Visual Basic .NET. Understand their advantages and learn to use them effectively. They can be a great help in resolving errors.

INTRODUCTION

Building a quality Windows application requires thorough testing to ensure that the application has the minimum possible defects. Therefore, you need to create an effective test plan. Complex applications require multiple levels of testing, including unit testing, integration testing, and regression testing.

Tracing is the process of monitoring an executing program. You trace a program by placing tracing code in the program with the help of the Trace and Debug classes. The tracing messages can be sent to a variety of destinations, including the Output window, a text file, an event log, or any other custom-defined trace listener, where they can be recorded to analyze the behavior of the program. Trace switches can be used to change the types of messages being generated without recompiling the application.

The process of testing may reveal various logical errors, or bugs, in a program. The process of finding the exact location of these errors may be time-consuming. Visual Basic .NET provides a rich set of debugging tools that makes this process very convenient.

In this chapter I'll first discuss the creation of test plans and various common testing techniques. I'll then discuss how to put tracing code in a program to monitor its execution. Finally, I'll talk about the debugging capabilities of Visual Studio .NET.

TESTING

Testing is the process of executing a program with the intention of finding errors (bugs). By *error* I mean any case in which the program's actual results fail to match the expected results. Expected results may include not just the correctness of the program but also other attributes, such as usability, reliability, and robustness. The process of testing may be manual, automated, or a mix of both techniques.

In today's increasingly competitive world, testing is more important than ever. A software company cannot afford to ignore the importance of testing. If a company releases buggy code, not only will it end up spending more time and money in fixing and redistributing the corrected code, but it will also lose the goodwill and business of potential customers. In the Internet world, the competition is not even next door: It is just a click away!

> **NOTE**
>
> **Correctness, Robustness, and Reliability**   *Correctness* refers to the ability of a program to produce expected results when the program is given a set of valid input data. *Robustness* is the ability of a program to cope with invalid data or operation. *Reliability* is the ability of a program to produce consistent results on every use.

Creating a Test Plan

Create a unit test plan.

A *test plan* is a document that guides the whole process of testing. A good test plan typically includes the following information:

◆ Which software component needs to be tested

◆ What parts of a component's specification are to be tested

◆ What parts of a component's specification are not to be tested

◆ What approach needs to be followed for testing

◆ Who will be responsible for each task in the testing process

◆ What the schedule is for testing

◆ What the criteria are for a test to fail or pass

◆ How the test results will be documented and disseminated

Executing Tests

Debug, rework, and resolve defects in code

- **Execute tests.**

Incremental testing (sometime also called *evolutionary testing*) is a modern approach to testing that has proven very useful for rapid application development (RAD). The idea of incremental testing is to test the system as you build it. There are three levels of testing involved:

◆ **Unit testing**—Involves testing an elementary unit of an application (usually a class).

◆ **Integration testing**—Tests the integration of two or more units or the integration between subsystems of those units.

◆ **Regression testing**—Usually involves the process of repeating the unit and integration tests whenever a bug is fixed, to ensure that no old bugs have recurred and that no new bugs have been introduced.

Unit Testing

Units are the smallest building blocks of an application. In Visual Basic .NET these building blocks are often components or class definitions. *Unit testing* involves performing basic tests at the component level, to ensure that each unique execution path in the component behaves exactly as documented in its specifications.

NOTE

NUnit   NUnit is a simple framework that enables you to write repeatable tests in any .NET language. For more information visit `http://nunit.sourceforge.net`.

Often the same person who writes the component also does unit testing for it. Unit testing typically requires writing special programs that use the component or class being tested. These programs are called *test drivers*, and they are used throughout the testing process but are not part of the final product.

Some of the major benefits of unit testing are as follows:

◆ It allows you to test parts of an application without waiting for the other parts to be available.

◆ It allows you to test exceptional conditions that are not easily reached by external inputs in a large integrated system.

◆ It simplifies the debugging process by limiting the search for bugs to a smaller unit than the complete application.

◆ It avoids lengthy compile-build-debug cycles when debugging difficult problems.

◆ It enables you to detect and remove defects at a much lower cost than with other, later, stages of testing.

Integration Testing

Integration testing verifies that the major subsystems of an application work well with each other. The objective of integration testing is to uncover the errors that might result because of the way units integrate or interface with each other.

Visualize a whole application as a hierarchy of components; integration testing can be performed in any of the following ways:

◆ **Bottom-up approach**—With this approach, testing progresses from the smallest subsystem and then gradually progresses up in the hierarchy to cover the whole system. This approach may require you to write a number of test-driver programs that test the integration between subsystems.

◆ **Top-down approach**—This approach starts with the top-level system to test the top-level interfaces and gradually comes down and tests smaller subsystems. You might be required to write *stubs* (that is, dummy modules that just mimic the interface of a module but have no functionality) for the modules that are not yet ready for testing.

◆ **Umbrella approach**—This approach focuses on testing the modules that have a high degree of user interaction. Normally in the umbrella approach, stubs are used in place of process-intensive modules. This approach enables you to release GUI-based applications early, allowing you to gradually increase functionality. The reason it is called *umbrella* is that when you look at the application hierarchy (as shown in Figure 12.1), the input/output modules are generally present on the edges, forming an umbrella shape.

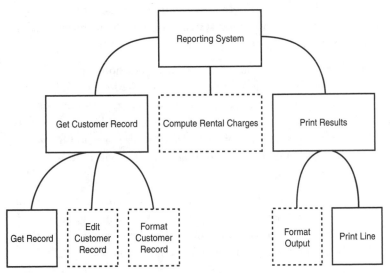

FIGURE 12.1
A hierarchy of subsystems to be tested.

> **NOTE**
>
> **Limitations of Testing** Testing can show the presence of errors, but it can never confirm their absence. Various factors—for example, the complexity of the software, requirements such as interoperability with various software and hardware, and globalization issues such as support for various languages and culture—can create excessive input data and too many execution paths to be tested. Many companies do their best to capture most of the test cases by using automation (that is, using computer programs to find errors) and beta testing (that is, involving product enthusiasts to find errors). Despite the efforts invested, errors still exist in shipping products, as any user of software well knows.

Regression Testing

Regression testing should be performed any time a program is modified, either to fix a bug or to add a feature. The process of regression testing involves running all the previous tests plus any newly added test cases, to test the added functionality. Regression testing has three main goals:

◆ Verify that all known bugs are corrected.

◆ Verify that no old bugs have been reintroduced.

◆ Verify that the program has no new bugs.

Testing International Applications

Debug, rework, and resolve defects in code

- **Provide multicultural test data to components and applications.**

Testing an application designed for international usage involves checking the country and language dependencies of each locale for which the application has been designed. While testing international application, you need to consider the following:

- ◆ You should test the application's data and user interface to make sure that they conform to the locale's standards for date and time, numeric values, currency, list separators, and measurements.

- ◆ If you are developing for Windows 2000 or Windows XP, you should test your application on as many language and culture variants as necessary to cover your entire market for the application. These operating systems support the languages used in more than 120 cultures/locales.

- ◆ You should use Unicode for your application. Applications that use Unicode run fine on Windows 2000 and XP without any changes being made. If instead your application uses Windows code pages, you need to set the culture/locale of the operating system according to the localized version of the application that you are testing, and then you need to reboot after each change.

- ◆ While testing a localized version of an application, you should make sure that you use input data in the language supported by the localized version. This makes the testing scenario similar to the scenario in which the application will actually be used.

For more discussion on support for globalization in a Windows application, refer to Chapter 8, "Globalization."

▶ Testing is the process of executing a program with the intention of finding errors. You should design an effective test plan to ensure that your application is free from all detectable defects and errors.

▶ Unit testing ensures that each unit of an application functions as desired. It is the lowest level of testing.

▶ Integration testing ensures that different units of an application function as expected by the test plan after they are integrated.

▶ Whenever code is modified or a new feature is added in an application, you should run all the existing test cases, along with a new set of test cases, to check the new feature. This is called regression testing, and it helps in developing robust applications.

TRACING

Debug, rework, and resolve defects in code

- **Create and apply debugging code to components and applications.**

The process of testing can reveal the presence of errors in a program, but to find the actual causes of these problems, sometimes you need the program to generate information about its own execution. Analysis of this information may help you understand why the program is behaving in a particular way and may lead to resolution of the error.

This process of collecting information about a program's execution is called *tracing*. Tracing is done in Visual Basic .NET by generating messages about the program's execution with the use of Debug and Trace classes.

The Trace and Debug classes have several things in common:

◆ They both belong to the System.Diagnostics namespace.

◆ They both have members with the same names.

◆ All their members are static.

◆ They are conditionally compiled (that is, their statements are included in the object code only if a certain symbol is defined).

The only difference between the Debug and Trace class is that the Debug class depends on the DEBUG symbol and the Trace class depends on the TRACE symbol.

Visual Basic .NET provides two basic configurations for a project: *Debug* and *Release*. Debug is the default configuration. When you compile a program using the Debug configuration, both the TRACE and DEBUG symbols are defined, as shown in Figure 12.2. When you compile a program in the Release configuration, only the TRACE symbol is defined. You can switch between the Debug and Release configurations by using the Solution Configurations combo box on the standard toolbar (as shown in Figure 12.3) or by using the Configuration Manager dialog box (as shown in Figure 12.4) from the project's Property Pages window.

FIGURE 12.2
A project's Property Pages window.

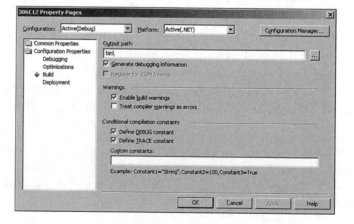

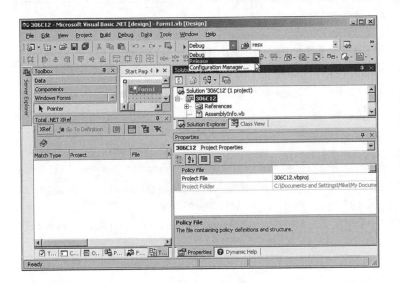

FIGURE 12.3◄
The Solutions Configuration combo box on the standard toolbar.

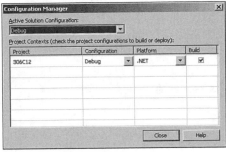

FIGURE 12.4▲
The Configuration Manager dialog box.

You can, of course, change the symbols that are available for a configuration by making changes to the project's Property Pages window. Later in this section, I will show you how to make those changes from within the program and through the command-line compilation options.

When you compile a program using the Debug configuration, both code using the Debug class and code using the Trace class is included in the compiled code. When you run such a program, you get messages that are generated using both Debug and Trace classes. When a program is compiled using the Trace configuration, it does not include any calls to the Debug class. Thus when such a program is executed, you get only the messages that are generated using the Trace class.

Table 12.1 summarizes the members of both the Trace and Debug classes.

NOTE

Tracing Helps in Resolving Hard-to-Reproduce Errors When programs run in the production environment, they sometimes report errors (mostly related to performance or threading problems) that are difficult to reproduce from a simulated testing environment. Tracing the production application can help you get runtime statistics of the program. This may help you trap these hard-to-reproduce errors.

TABLE 12.1

MEMBERS OF Debug AND Trace CLASSES

Member	*Type*	*Description*
Assert	Method	Checks for a condition and displays a message if the condition is false.

continues

TABLE 12.1	*continued*	

MEMBERS OF Debug AND Trace CLASSES

Member	*Type*	*Description*
AutoFlush	Property	Specifies whether Flush should be called on the Listeners collection after every write.
Close	Method	Flushes the output buffer and then closes the Listeners collection.
Fail	Method	Displays an error message.
Flush	Method	Flushes the output buffer and causes buffered data to be written to the Listeners collection.
Indent	Method	Increases the current IndentLevel property by one.
IndentLevel	Property	Specifies the indent level.
IndentSize	Property	Specifies the number of spaces in an indent.
Listeners	Property	Specifies a collection of Listeners that is monitoring the trace output.
Unindent	Method	Decreases the current IndentLevel property by one.
Write	Method	Writes the given information to the trace listeners in the Listeners collection.
WriteIf	Method	Writes the given information to the trace listeners in the Listeners collection only if a condition is true.
WriteLine	Method	Same as Write, but appends a newline character after the information.
WriteLineIf	Method	Same as WriteIf, but appends a newline character after the information.

Using Trace and Debug to Display Information

Implement tracing

- **Display trace output.**

Step By Step 12.1 demonstrates how to use some of the methods of the Trace and Debug classes.

STEP BY STEP

12.1 Using the `Trace` and `Debug` Classes to Display Debugging Information

1. Launch Visual Studio .NET, and Select File, New, Blank Solution. Name the solution `306C12`.

2. In the Solution Explorer window, right-click the name of the solution and select Add, New Project. Select Visual Basic projects from the Project Types tree, and then select Windows Application from the list of templates on the right. Name the project `StepByStep12-1`.

3. In the Solution Explorer window, right-click `Form1.vb` and rename it `FactorialCalculator.vb`. Open the Properties window for this form and change its `Name` property to `FactorialCalculator` and its `Text` property to `Factorial Calculator 12-1`.

4. Add three `Label` controls, two `TextBox` controls (`txtNumber` and `txtFactorial`), and a `Button` control (`btnCalculate`) to the form. Arrange the controls as shown in Figure 12.5.

5. Add the following code to the `Click` event handler of `btnCalculate`:

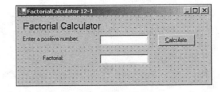

FIGURE 12.5
The Factorial Calculator.

```
Private Sub btnCalculate_Click( _
 ByVal sender As System.Object, _
 ByVal e As System.EventArgs) Handles btnCalculate.Click

    ' Write a debug message
    Debug.WriteLine("Inside Button Click event handler")
    ' Start indenting messages now
    Debug.Indent()
    Dim intNumber As Integer = _
     Convert.ToInt32(txtNumber.Text)
    ' Make a debug assertion
    Debug.Assert(intNumber >= 0, "Invalid value", _
     "negative value in debug mode")
    ' Write a trace assertion
    Trace.Assert(intNumber >= 0, "Invalid value", _
     "negative value in trace mode")

    Dim intFac As Integer = 1
    Try
        Dim i As Integer
        For i = 2 To intNumber
            intFac = intFac * i
```

continues

continued

```
            ' Write a debug message
            Debug.WriteLine(i, _
              "Factorial Program Debug, Value of i")
        Next
        txtFactorial.Text = intFac.ToString()
    Catch ex As System.OverflowException
        ' Write a trace message
        Trace.WriteLine("There was an overflow", _
          "Factorial Program Trace")
        ' Write a debug message
        Debug.WriteLine("There was an overflow", _
          "Factorial Program Debug")
        intFac = 0
    Catch ex As Exception
        ' Write a trace message
        Trace.WriteLine( _
          "An unknown exception was thrown", _
          "Factorial Program Trace")
        ' Write a debug message
        Debug.WriteLine( _
          "An unknown exception was thrown", _
          "Factorial Program Debug")
        intFac = 0
    End Try

    ' Write a conditional message
    Trace.WriteLineIf(intFac = 0, "Unable to calculate", _
      "Factorial Program Trace")
    Debug.WriteLineIf(intFac = 0, "Unable to calculate", _
      "Factorial Program Trace")
    ' Decrease the indent level
    Debug.Unindent()

    ' Write a debug message
    Debug.WriteLine("Done with computations,
    ➥returning...")
End Sub
```

---

6. Set the form as the startup object for the project. Run the project. Keep the program running and switch to the Visual Studio .NET integrated development environment (IDE). Select View, Other Windows, Output. Switch to the running program, enter 5 in the text box, and click the Calculate button. You will see the debug messages generated by the program, as shown in Figure 12.6.

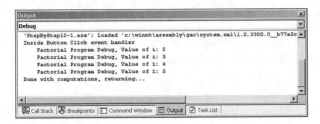

FIGURE 12.6
The Output window.

7. Enter the value 100 and click the Calculate button. Messages by both the Debug class and the Trace class are displayed in the Output window. Note that the default configuration is the Debug configuration where both TRACE and DEBUG symbols are defined.

8. Enter a negative value such as -1 and click the Calculate button. This causes the assertion to fail, and you see a dialog box showing the assertion failed message, as shown in Figure 12.7. This message box is generated by the Debug.Assert method in your code. The dialog box gives you three choices: Abort, to terminate the program; Retry, to break the program execution so that you can debug the program; and Ignore, to continue the execution as if nothing has happened. Click Ignore, and you will see another Assertion Failed dialog box, this one generated by the Trace.Assert method in your code. Click the Abort button to terminate the program execution.

FIGURE 12.7
The Assertion Failed dialog box.

9. From the Solution Configurations combo box, select the Release configuration. The result is configured so that only the TRACE symbol is defined. Run the program again.

continues

continued

Enter value 5 and click the Calculate button. You will find that the factorial has been calculated but there are no messages in the Output window. Enter the value 100 and click the Calculate button. You will now see the trace message about overflow in the Output window. Finally, try calculating the factorial of -1; you will see just one dialog box, showing the assertion failed message. Click the Abort button to terminate the program.

Note from Step By Step 12.1 that you can use the Debug and Trace methods to display messages based on a Boolean condition (by using their WriteIf and WriteLineIf methods). This can be a very useful technique if you are trying to understand the flow of logic of a program. Step By Step 12.1 also demonstrated the use of the Assert method; the Assert method tests your assumption about a condition at a specific place in the program. When an assertion fails, the Assert method pinpoints the code that is violating your assumptions. A related method is Fail; like the Assert method, the Fail method displays a dialog box, but it does not work conditionally. The Fail method signals unconditional failure in a branch of code execution. You can use the Fail method to catch the program when it does something that you think should be impossible.

Trace Listeners

Implement tracing

- **Add trace listeners and trace switches to an application.**

Listeners are the classes that are responsible for forwarding, recording, or displaying the messages generated by the Trace and Debug classes. You can have multiple listeners associated with the Trace and Debug classes by adding multiple Listener objects to their Listeners property. The Listeners property is a collection that is capable of holding objects of any type derived from the TraceListener class.

The TraceListener class is an abstract class that belongs to the System.Diagnostics namespace, and it has three implementations:

◆ **DefaultTraceListener**—An object of this class is automatically added to the Listeners collection of the Trace and Debug classes. Its behavior is to write messages to the Output window.

◆ **TextWriterTraceListener**—An object of this class writes messages to any class that derives from the Stream class. You can use a TextWriterTraceListener object to write messages to the console or to a file.

◆ **EventLogTraceListener**—An object of this class writes messages to the Windows event log.

If you want a listener object to perform differently from these three listener classes, you can create your own class that inherits from the TraceListener class. When doing so, you must at least implement the Write and WriteLine methods.

In Step By Step 12.2 you create a custom listener class that inherits from the `TraceListener` class to send debug and trace messages through email.

> **EXAM TIP**
>
> **The Same Listeners for Debug and Trace** Messages sent through the Debug and Trace objects are directed through each listener in the Listeners collection. Debug and Trace share the same Listeners collection, so any listener defined in the Trace.Listeners collection will also be defined in the Debug.Listeners collection.

STEP BY STEP

12.2 Creating a Custom TraceListener Object

1. Create a new Windows application project in your solution. Name the project `StepByStep12-2`.

2. In the Solution Explorer window, right-click `Form1.vb` and select Delete from the context menu.

3. Using the Solution Explorer window, drag the `FactorialCalculator.vb` form from the `StepByStep12_1` project to the new project. While dragging, hold down the Ctrl key so that the form is copied to the current project instead of being moved. Change the `Text` property of the form to `Factorial Calculator 12-2`.

4. Add to the project a reference to `System.Web.dll`.

continues

continued

5. Add a new class to the project. Name the class
EmailTraceListener.vb and add the following code to it:

```
Imports System
Imports System.Diagnostics
Imports System.Text
Imports System.Web.Mail

Public Class EmailTraceListener
    Inherits TraceListener

    ' Mmessage log will be sent to this address
    Private mstrMailTo As String
    ' Storage for the message log
    Private mmessage As StringBuilder

    Public Sub New(ByVal MailTo As String)
        mstrMailTo = MailTo
    End Sub

    ' A custom listener must override Write method
    Public Overloads Overrides Sub Write( _
     ByVal message As String)
        If mmessage Is Nothing Then
            mmessage = New StringBuilder()
        End If
        mmessage.Append(message)
    End Sub

    ' A custom listener must override WriteLine method
    Public Overloads Overrides Sub WriteLine( _
     ByVal message As String)
        If mmessage Is Nothing Then
            mmessage = New StringBuilder()
        End If
        mmessage.Append(message)
        mmessage.Append(vbCrLf)
    End Sub

    ' Use the close method to send the mail.
    Public Overrides Sub Close()
        Flush()
        Dim msg As MailMessage = New MailMessage()
        msg.To = mstrMailTo
        msg.Subject = _
         "Factorial Program Debug/Trace output"
        If Not mmessage Is Nothing Then
            msg.Body = mmessage.ToString()
        Else
            msg.Body = ""
        End If
```

```
        ' Send the mail
        SmtpMail.Send(msg)
    End Sub

    Public Overrides Sub Flush()
        ' Nothing much to do here
        ' Just call the base class's implementation
        MyBase.Flush()
    End Sub

End Class
```

6. Add the following code to the Load event of the FactorialCalculator form, replacing *Insert@youraddress.here* with a real address that can receive email messages:

```
Private Sub FactorialCalculator_Load( _
 ByVal sender As System.Object, _
 ByVal e As System.EventArgs) Handles MyBase.Load
    Trace.Listeners.Add(New EmailTraceListener( _
    "Insert@youraddress.here"))
End Sub
```

7. Add the following code to handle the Closing event of the FactorialCalculator form:

```
Private Sub FactorialCalculator_Closing( _
 ByVal sender As Object, _
 ByVal e As System.ComponentModel.CancelEventArgs) _
 Handles MyBase.Closing
    ' Call the Close method for all listeners
    Trace.Close()
End Sub
```

8. Set the form as the startup object for the project and set the project as the startup project for the solution.

9. Run the project, using the default Debug configuration. Enter a value and click the Calculate button. Close the form. Both Debug and Trace messages appear on the Output window, and they are also emailed to the specified address, using the local SMTP server. Run the project again in the Release mode. Enter a large value, say 100, and click the Calculate button. You will see the overflow message in the Output window. Close the form. While you are closing it, an email message is sent to the specified email address that contains the trace overflow message.

> **NOTE**
> **Sending Email Messages** The types in the System.Web.Mail namespace can be used from any managed application, including both Web and Windows applications. This functionality is supported only in the Windows 2000, Windows XP Professional, and Windows .NET Server operating systems. For other operating systems, you can send email messages by manually establishing an SMTP connection through the System.NET.TcpClient class. In addition, several component vendors sell custom SMTP client classes.

Trace Switches

Implement tracing

- **Add trace listeners and trace switches to an application.**

So far, you have learned that the Trace and Debug classes can be used to display valuable information related to program execution. You have also learned that it is possible to capture the messages in a variety of formats by using TraceListener objects. In this section, you'll learn how to control the nature of messages that you get from a program.

Trace switches allow you to set the parameters that can control the level of tracing that needs to be done in a program. These switches are set in an XML-based external configuration file. This is especially useful when the application is in production mode. You may not normally want your application to generate any trace messages. However, if the application has problems or you just want to check on the health of the application, you can instruct the application to emit a particular type of trace information by just changing the configuration file. There's no need to recompile the application. The application will automatically pick up the changes from the configuration file the next time you run the application.

There are two predefined classes for creating trace switches: the BooleanSwitch class and the TraceSwitch class. Both of these classes derive from the abstract Switch class. You can also define your own trace switch class by deriving a class from the Switch class.

The BooleanSwitch class is used to differentiate between two modes of tracing: trace-on and trace-off. Its default value is zero, which corresponds to the trace-off state. A class value set to any nonzero value corresponds to a trace-on state.

Unlike the BooleanSwitch class, the TraceSwitch class provides five different levels of tracing switches. These levels are defined by the TraceLevel enumeration, listed in Table 12.2. The default value of TraceLevel for a trace switch is 0 (Off).

TABLE 12.2

THE TraceLevel ENUMERATION

Enumerated Value	Integer Value	Type of Tracing
Off	0	None
Error	1	Only error messages
Warning	2	Warning messages and error messages
Info	3	Informational messages, warning messages, and error messages
Verbose	4	Verbose messages, informational messages, warning messages, and error messages

EXAM TIP

Out-of-Range Values for BooleanSwitch and TraceSwitch For a BooleanSwitch object, if any nonzero (negative or positive) value is specified in the configuration file, the Enabled property of the object is set to True. For a TraceSwitch object, if a value greater than 4 is specified, the Level property of the object is set to TraceLevel.Verbose (4). But if a negative value is specified for a TraceSwitch object, a StackOverflow exception will occur at runtime.

Table 12.3 displays the important properties of the TraceSwitch class.

TABLE 12.3

IMPORTANT PROPERTIES OF THE TraceSwitch CLASS

Property	Description
Description	Describes the switch (inherited from Switch).
DisplayName	Identifies the switch (inherited from Switch).
Level	Specifies the trace level that helps in selecting which trace and debug messages will be processed. Its value is one of the TraceLevel enumeration values (refer Table 12.2)
TraceError	Returns True if Level is set to Error, Warning, Info, or Verbose; otherwise, returns False.
TraceInfo	Returns True if Level is set to Info or Verbose; otherwise, returns False.
TraceVerbose	Returns True if Level is set to Verbose; otherwise, returns False.
TraceWarning	Returns True if Level is set to Warning, Info, or Verbose; otherwise, returns False.

Step By Step 12.3 demonstrates how to use trace switches in a Windows application.

STEP BY STEP

12.3 Using the `TraceSwitch` Class

1. Create a new Windows application project in your solution. Name the project `StepByStep12-3`.

2. In the Solution Explorer window, right-click `Form1.vb` and select Delete from the context menu.

3. Using the Solution Explorer window, drag the `FactorialCalculator.vb` form from the `StepByStep12-1` project to the new project. While dragging, hold down the Ctrl key so that the form is copied to the current project instead of being moved. Change the `Text` property of the form to `Factorial Calculator 12-3`.

4. Modify the `Click` event handler for the `btnCalculate` button so that it looks like this:

```
Private Sub btnCalculate_Click( _
 ByVal sender As System.Object, _
 ByVal e As System.EventArgs) Handles btnCalculate.Click

    Dim ts As TraceSwitch = _
       New TraceSwitch("FactorialTrace", _
       "Trace the factorial application")

    If ts.TraceVerbose Then
        ' Write a debug message
        Debug.WriteLine( _
        "Inside Button Click event handler")
    End If

    ' Start indenting messages now
    Debug.Indent()
    Dim intNumber As Integer = _
     Convert.ToInt32(txtNumber.Text)

    If ts.TraceError Then
        ' Make a debug assertion
        Debug.Assert(intNumber >= 0, "Invalid value", _
         "negative value in debug mode")
        ' Write a trace assertion
        Trace.Assert(intNumber >= 0, "Invalid value", _
         "negative value in trace mode")
    End If
```

```
    Dim intFac As Integer = 1
    Try
        Dim i As Integer
        For i = 2 To intNumber
            intFac = intFac * i
            If ts.TraceInfo Then
                ' Write a debug message
                Debug.WriteLine(i, _
                  "Factorial Program Debug, Value of i")
            End If
        Next
        txtFactorial.Text = intFac.ToString()
    Catch ex As System.OverflowException
        If ts.TraceWarning Then
            ' Write a trace message
            Trace.WriteLine("There was an overflow", _
             "Factorial Program Trace")
            ' Write a debug message
            Debug.WriteLine("There was an overflow", _
             "Factorial Program Debug")
        End If
        intFac = 0
    Catch ex As Exception
        If ts.TraceWarning Then
            ' Write a trace message
            Trace.WriteLine( _
             "An unknown exception was thrown", _
             "Factorial Program Trace")
            ' Write a debug message
            Debug.WriteLine( _
             "An unknown exception was thrown", _
             "Factorial Program Debug")
        End If
        intFac = 0
    End Try

    If ts.TraceWarning Then
        ' Write a conditional message
        Trace.WriteLineIf(intFac = 0, _
         "Unable to calculate", _
         "Factorial Program Trace")
        Debug.WriteLineIf(intFac = 0, _
         "Unable to calculate", _
         "Factorial Program Trace")
    End If
    ' Decrease the indent level
    Debug.Unindent()

    If ts.TraceVerbose Then
        ' Write a debug message
        Debug.WriteLine( _
         "Done with computations, returning...")
    End If
End Sub
```

continues

continued

5. In the Solution Explorer, select View All Files from the toolbar. Right-click the `bin` folder for this project and select Add, Add New Item. Choose to create an XML file. Name the XML file `StepByStep12-3.exe.config`.

6. Use the XML editor to modify this new file so that it looks like this:

```
<?xml version="1.0" encoding="utf-8" ?>
<configuration>
    <system.diagnostics>
        <switches>
            <add name="FactorialTrace" value="4" />
        </switches>
    </system.diagnostics>
</configuration>
```

7. Set the form as the startup object for the project and set the project as the startup project for the solution.

8. Run the project, using the default `Debug` configuration. Enter a value `5`; all messages appear on the Output window. Try entering a negative value and then a large value. You'll see all the error and warning messages. Close the form. Modify the XML file to change the value of `FactorialTrace` to 3. You will now see all messages except the ones with `TraceLevel` set to `Verbose`. Repeat the process with values of `FactorialTrace` in the configuration file changed to 2, 1, and 0.

Having the ability to change the number of messages in a trace file can be very handy with a production application. You can leave many Trace statements in the code and use the configuration file to control which Trace statements are active. A value of zero in the file suppresses all the tracing output.

Conditional Compilation

The Visual Basic .NET programming language provides a set of pre-processing directives. You can use these directives to skip sections of source files for compilation, to report errors and warnings, or to mark distinct regions of the source code.

Table 12.4 summarizes the preprocessing directives available in Visual Basic .NET.

TABLE 12.4

VISUAL BASIC .NET PREPROCESSING DIRECTIVES

Directives	Description
#If, #Else, #ElseIf, and #End If	These directives conditionally skip sections of code. The skipped sections are not the part of compiled code.
#Const	This directive defines a preprocessor constant. This constant can be used only within a conditional compilation directive, not in regular code.
#ExternalSource and #End ExternalSource	These directives are used by the compiler to track line numbers for compiler error messages. You won't use them in your own code.
#Region and #End Region	These directives mark sections of code. A common example of these directives is the code generated by the Windows Forms Designer. This marking can be used by visual designers such as Visual Studio .NET to show, hide, and format code.

In addition to the preprocessing directives, Visual Basic .NET also provides a ConditionalAttribute class.

You can mark a method as conditional by applying the Conditional attribute to it. The Conditional attribute takes one argument that specifies a symbol. The conditional method is either included or omitted from the compiled code, depending on the definition of the specified symbol at that point. If the symbol definition is available, then the call to that method is included; otherwise, the method call is excluded from the compiled code.

Careful use of conditional compilation directives as well as methods with Conditional attributes allows you to keep debugging-related code in the source code while you're developing an application but exclude it from the compiled version. That way, no extraneous messages are generated in shipping code, and production programs do not encounter a performance hit due to processing of additional code. If you want to resolve some errors, you can easily activate the debugging code by defining a symbol and recompiling the program.

NOTE

The VB Preprocessor There is no separate preprocessor in the Visual Basic .NET compiler. The lexical analysis phase of the compiler processes all the preprocessing directives. This contrasts with languages such as C and C++, which use a separate preprocessor to take care of conditional compilation.

EXAM TIP

The Conditional Method A method must be a Sub rather than a Function to have the Conditional attribute applied to it.

Step By Step 12.4 demonstrates the use of the `ConditionalAttribute` attribute, along with the usage of conditional compilation directives.

STEP BY STEP

12.4 Using Conditional Compilation

1. Create a new Windows application project in your solution. Name the project `StepByStep12-4`.

2. In the Solution Explorer window, right-click `Form1.vb` and select Delete from the context menu.

3. Using the Solution Explorer window, drag the `FactorialCalculator.vb` form from the `StepByStep12-1` project to the new project. While dragging, hold down the Ctrl key so that the form is copied to the current project instead of being moved. Change the `Text` property of the form to `Factorial Calculator 12-4`.

4. Add the following two conditional methods to the class definition:

```
<Conditional("DEBUG")> _
Public Sub InitializeDebugMode()
    Label1.Text = "Factorial Calculator: Debug Mode"
End Sub

<Conditional("TRACE")> _
Public Sub InitializeReleaseMode()
    Label1.Text = "Factorial Calculator Version 1.0"
End Sub
```

5. Add an event handler to the form's `Load` event and add the following code:

```
    Private Sub FactorialCalculator_Load( _
    ByVal sender As System.Object, _
    ByVal e As System.EventArgs) Handles MyBase.Load
#If Debug Then
        Debug.WriteLine("Program started in debug mode")
        InitializeDebugMode()
#Else
        Trace.WriteLine("Program started in release mode")
        InitializeReleaseMode()
#End If
    End Sub
```

6. Set the form as the startup object for the project and set the project as the startup project for the solution.

7. Run the project, using the default Debug configuration. The heading of the form displays "Factorial Calculator: Debug Mode" (see Figure 12.8). The Output window displays the string "Program started in debug mode." Close the program, and then start it again in the Release mode. A different heading appears for the form and a different message appears in the Output window (see Figure 12.9) .

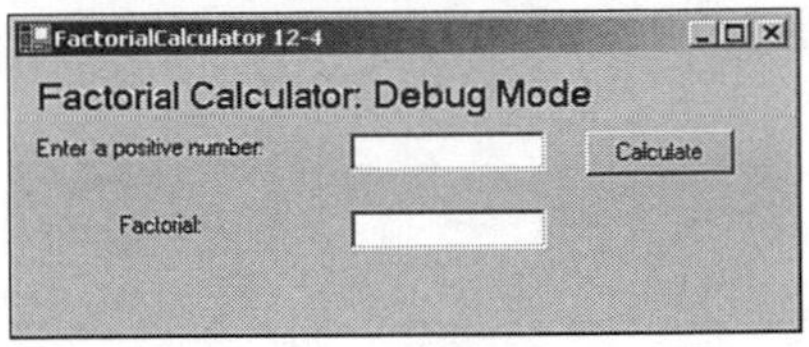

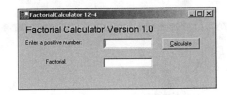

FIGURE 12.8
A program conditionally compiled for Debug configuration.

FIGURE 12.9
A program conditionally compiled for Release configuration.

The DEBUG and TRACE symbols can be defined for the compiler in the following ways:

◆ Modifying the project's Property Pages window.

◆ Using the #Const directive in the beginning of the code file.

◆ Using the /define (/d for short) option with the command-line Visual Basic .NET compiler (vbc.exe).

Step By Step 12.4 demonstrates conditional compilation with the DEBUG and TRACE symbols. You can also use any other custom defined symbols you like to perform conditional compilation.

GUIDED PRACTICE EXERCISE 12.1

In this exercise, you will add an EventLogTraceListener object to the Factorial Calculator program so that it writes all Trace and Debug messages to the Windows event log.

You should try doing this on your own first. If you get stuck, or if you'd like to see one possible solution, follow these steps:

1. Create a new project, using the Windows Application template in your solution. Name the project GuidedPracticeExercise12-1.

2. In the Solution Explorer window, right-click Form1.vb and select Delete from the context menu.

continues

3. Using the Solution Explorer window, drag the
   `FactorialCalculator.vb` form from the `StepByStep12-1` project to the new project. While dragging, hold down the Ctrl
   key so that the form is copied to the current project instead of
   being moved. Change the `Text` property of the form to
   `Factorial Calculator Guided 12-1`.

4. Double-click the form to add an event handler for the `Load`
   event. Add the following code to the event handler:

```
Private Sub FactorialCalculator_Load( _
 ByVal sender As System.Object, _
 ByVal e As System.EventArgs) Handles MyBase.Load
    ' Add a event log listener to the Listeners collection
    Trace.Listeners.Add(New EventLogTraceListener( _
    "FactorialCalculator"))
End Sub
```

5. Set the form as the startup object for the project and set the
   project as the startup project for the solution.

6. Run the project. Enter a value for finding a factorial, and then
   click the Calculate button. Close the program. Select View,
   Server Explorer. In the Server Explorer window, navigate to
   your computer, and expand the Event Logs, Application,
   FactorialCalculator node. You will see that the messages generated by the `Trace` and `Debug` classes have been added to the
   Application event log, as shown in Figure 12.10.

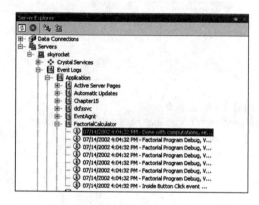

FIGURE 12.10
Viewing the Windows event log from the Server
Explorer window.

REVIEW BREAK

▶ The `Trace` and `Debug` classes can be used to display informative
  messages in an application when the `DEBUG` and `TRACE` symbols
  are defined, respectively, at the time of compilation.

▶ By default, both the `TRACE` and `DEBUG` symbols are defined in the
  `Debug` configuration for compilation and only the `TRACE` symbol
  is defined for the `Release` configuration of compilation.

▶ Listeners are objects that receive trace and debug output. By
  default, there is one listener, `DefaultTraceListener`, attached
  to the `Trace` and `Debug` classes. This listener displays the messages in the Output window.

▶ Debug and Trace objects share the same Listeners collection. Therefore, any Listener object added to the Trace.Listeners collection is also added to the Debug.Listeners collection.

▶ Trace switches allows you to change the type of messages traced by a program, depending on a value stored in the XML configuration file. You need not recompile the application for this change to take effect; you just restart it. You need to implement code to display the messages, depending on the value of the switch.

▶ Visual Basic .NET preprocessor directives allow you to define symbols in an application, mark regions of code, and conditionally skip code for compilation.

▶ The Conditional attribute allows you to conditionally add or skip a method for compilation, depending on the value of the symbol passed as a parameter to the attribute.

DEBUGGING

Debug, rework, and resolve defects in code

- **Configure the debugging environment.**

Debugging is the process of finding the causes of errors in a program, locating the lines of code causing the errors, and then fixing those errors.

Without good tools, the process of debugging can be very time-consuming and tedious. Thankfully, Visual Studio .NET is loaded with a large set of tools to help you with various debugging tasks.

NOTE

Runtime Errors and Compile-Time Errors   *Compile-time errors* are produced when a program does not comply with the syntax of the programming language. These errors are easy to find and are generally pointed out by compilers themselves. *Runtime errors* occur in programs that are compiled successfully but do not behave as expected. The process of testing and debugging applies to runtime errors only. Testing reveals these errors, and debugging repairs them.

Stepping Through Program Execution

A common technique for debugging is the step-by-step execution of a program, sometimes called *stepping*. This systematic execution allows you to track the flow of logic to ensure that the program is following the path of execution that you expect it to follow. If it does not, you can immediately identify the location of problem.

Stepping also gives you an opportunity to monitor a program's state before and after a statement is executed. This includes checking the values in variables, records in a database, and other changes in the environment. Visual Studio .NET provides tools to make these tasks convenient.

The Debug menu provides three options for step execution of a program, as listed in Table 12.5. The keyboard shortcuts listed in Table 12.5 correspond to the Visual Basic settings of the Visual Studio IDE. If you have personalized the keyboard scheme either through the Tools, Options, Environment, Keyboard menu or through the Visual Studio .NET Start Page, you might have a different keyboard mapping. You can check out the keyboard mappings available for your customization through Visual Studio .NET's context sensitive help.

TABLE 12.5

DEBUG OPTIONS FOR STEP EXECUTION

Debug Menu Item	Keyboard Shortcut	Description
Step Into	F8	You use this option to execute the code in single-step mode. If a method call is encountered, the program execution steps into the code of the function and executes the method in single-step mode.
Step Over	Shift+F8	You use this option when a method call is encountered and you do not want to step into the method code. When this option is selected, the debugger executes the entire method without any step-by-step execution (interruption), and then it steps to the next statement after the method call.
Step Out	Ctrl+Shift+F8	You use this option inside a method call to execute the rest of the method without stepping, and you resume step execution mode when control returns to the calling method.

STEP BY STEP

12.5 Trying Step-By-Step Execution of a Windows Application

1. Set the project StepByStep12_4 as the startup project for the solution.

2. Select Debug, Step Into. The program pauses its execution at the first executable statement and shows it highlighted, as shown in Figure 12.11. An arrow also appears on the left margin of the code, pointing to the next statement to be executed.

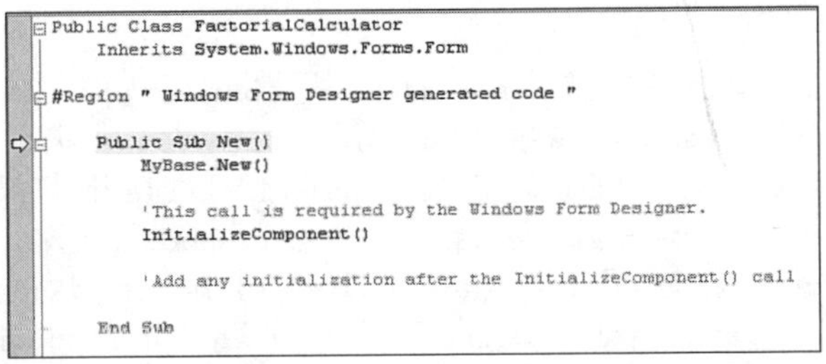

```
Public Class FactorialCalculator
    Inherits System.Windows.Forms.Form

#Region " Windows Form Designer generated code "

    Public Sub New()
        MyBase.New()

        'This call is required by the Windows Form Designer.
        InitializeComponent()

        'Add any initialization after the InitializeComponent() call

    End Sub
```

FIGURE 12.11
Stepping through a program's execution.

3. Press F8 to proceed to the next step. The debugger proceeds through the constructor for the form. Press F8 a couple more times.

4. Drag the yellow arrow in the margin one line up. This way you can instruct the debugger to change the statement that will be executed next. Press F11 two times to see the effect of dragging the arrow back. Now press Ctrl+Shift+F8. The New method finishes executing, and you see the form onscreen.

5. Enter a positive number in the form and click the Calculate button. The form calculates the factorial and displays it almost instantly. Note that the application is no longer running in step mode. When you press F8 either on the form or in the Code view, it has no effect.

The lesson from Step By Step 12.5 is that when you start an application in step mode, after the form is launched, you cannot really go back to the step-by-step execution of the code. To step into the code of various event handlers of a form, you need to mark breakpoints in the code, as described in the following section.

Setting Breakpoints

Breakpoints are markers in code that signal the debugger to pause execution. When the debugger pauses at a breakpoint, you can take as much time as you like to analyze variables, data records, and other settings in the environment to determine the state of the program. You can also choose to execute the program in single-step mode from this point on.

If you place a breakpoint in the Click event handler of a button, the program pauses when you click the button and the execution reaches the point where you have set the breakpoint. You can then step through the execution of the rest of the event handler. After the handler code is over, control is transferred back to the form being executed. This time, if you click another button and a breakpoint is not set in its event handler, the program is no longer under single-step execution. Therefore, you must set breakpoints at all the places where you would like execution to pause.

STEP BY STEP

12.6 Working with Breakpoints

1. Create a new Windows application project in your solution. Name the project StepByStep12-6.

2. In the Solution Explorer window, right-click Form1.vb and select Delete from the context menu.

3. Using the Solution Explorer window, drag the FactorialCalculator.vb form from the StepByStep12-1 project to the new project. While dragging, hold down the Ctrl key so that the form is copied to the current project instead of being moved. Change the Text property of the form to Factorial Calculator 12-6.

4. Set the form as the startup form for the project and set the project as the startup project for the solution.

5. Add the following method to the class:

```
Private Function Factorial( _
 ByVal intNumber As Integer) As Integer
     Dim intFac As Integer = 1
     Dim i As Integer

     For i = 2 To intNumber
         intFac = intFac * i
     Next
     Factorial = intFac
End Function
```

6. Modify the Click event handler of btnCalculate so that it looks like this:

```
Private Sub btnCalculate_Click( _
 ByVal sender As System.Object, _
 ByVal e As System.EventArgs) Handles btnCalculate.Click
     Dim intNumber, intFactorial As Integer
     Try
         intNumber = Convert.ToInt32(txtNumber.Text)
         intFactorial = Factorial(intNumber)
         txtFactorial.Text = intFactorial.ToString()
     Catch ex As Exception
         Debug.WriteLine(ex.Message)
     End Try
End Sub
```

7. In the Click event handler, right-click the beginning of the line that makes the call to the Factorial method and select Insert Breakpoint from the context menu. The line of code is highlighted with red, and a red dot appears in the left margin, as shown in Figure 12.12. You can also create a breakpoint by clicking in the left margin, next to the line where you'd like the breakpoint to be set.

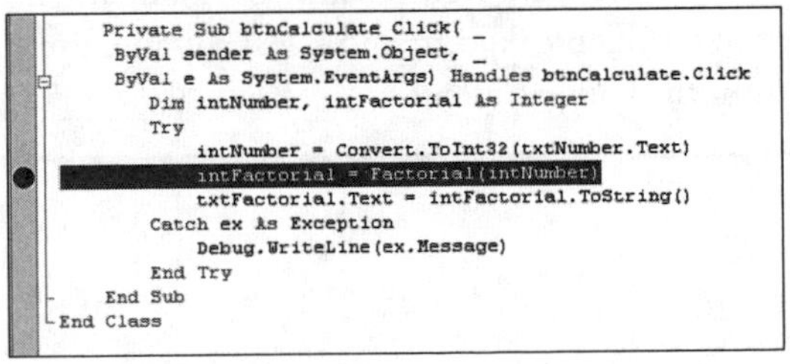

FIGURE 12.12
Setting a breakpoint.

continues

NOTE

The Disassembly Window Shows Assembly Code Instead of MSIL Although Visual Basic .NET programs are compiled to Microsoft Intermediate Language (MSIL), they are just-in-time compiled to native assembly code only at the time of their first execution. This means the executing code is never in IL; it is always in native code. Thus you will always see native code instead of IL in the Disassembly window.

FIGURE 12.13
The Breakpoints window gives you convenient access to all breakpoint-related tasks.

NOTE

The Debug Configuration Breakpoints and other debugging features are available only when you compile your program using the Debug configuration.

NOTE

Disabling Versus Removing a Breakpoint When you remove a breakpoint, you lose all information related to it. Alternatively, you can choose to disable a breakpoint. Disabling a breakpoint does not pause the program at that point, but still, Visual Basic .NET will remember the breakpoint settings. At any time, you can select Enable Breakpoint to reactivate the breakpoint.

8. Execute the project. The Factorial form appears. Enter a value and click the Calculate button. The execution pauses at the location where you have marked the breakpoint.

9. Press F8 to step into the code of `Factorial` function. Hover the mouse pointer over various variables in the `Factorial` function. You will see the current values of the variables.

10. Select Debug, Windows, Breakpoints. The Breakpoints window opens, as shown in Figure 12.13. Right-click the breakpoint listed in the window and select Go to Disassembly. The Diassembler opens, showing you the object code of the program, along with the disassembled source code.

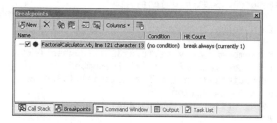

11. Close the Disassembly window. From the Debug menu, select Step Out to automatically execute the rest of the factorial function and start the step mode again in the event handler at the next statement. Step through the execution until you see the form again.

12. Select Stop Debugging from the Debug menu. This ends the debugging session and terminates the application.

13. In the Code view, right-click the statement where you have set the breakpoint and select Disable Breakpoint from the context menu.

In addition to using the method described in Step By Step 12.6, you can set a breakpoint by choosing New Breakpoint from the Debug menu or from the context menu in a module. The New Breakpoint dialog box (see Figure 12.14) has four tabs that allow you to set a breakpoint in a function, in a file, at an address in the object code, or when the data value (that is, the value of a variable) changes.

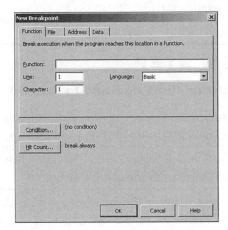

FIGURE 12.14
The New Breakpoint dialog box.

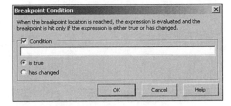

FIGURE 12.15
The Breakpoint Condition dialog box.

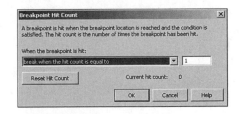

FIGURE 12.16
The Breakpoint Hit Count dialog box.

Clicking the Condition button opens the Breakpoint Condition dialog box, as shown in Figure 12.15. The Condition dialog box allows you to set, at runtime, a breakpoint that is based on a value of an expression.

Clicking the Hit Count button in the New Breakpoint dialog box opens a Breakpoint Hit Count dialog box, as shown in Figure 12.16. This dialog box enables you to break the program execution only if the specified breakpoint has been hit a given number of times. This can be especially helpful if you have a breakpoint inside a lengthy loop and you want to step-execute the program only toward the end of the loop.

Analyzing Program State to Resolve Errors

Debug, rework, and resolve defects in code

- **Resolve errors and rework code.**

When you break the execution of a program, the program is stuck at a particular state in its execution cycle. You can use various debugging tools to analyze the values of variables, the results of expressions, or the path of execution to help identify the cause of the error that you are debugging.

Step By Step 12.7 demonstrates various Visual Basic .NET debugging tools, including the Watch1, Autos, Locals, Me, Immediate, and Call Stack windows.

STEP BY STEP

12.7 Analyzing Program State to Resolve Errors

1. Create a new Windows application project in your solution. Name the project StepByStep12-7.

2. In the Solution Explorer window, right-click Form1.vb and select Delete from the context menu.

3. Using the Solution Explorer window, drag the FactorialCalculator.vb form from the StepByStep12-6 project to the new project. While dragging, hold down the Ctrl key so that the form is copied to the current project instead of being moved. Change the Text property of the form to Factorial Calculator 12-7.

4. Set the form as the startup form for the project and set the project as the startup project for the solution.

5. Change the code in the Factorial method to the following (note that I have introduced a logical error that I will later "discover" through debugging):

```
Private Function Factorial( _
 ByVal intNumber As Integer) As Integer
    Dim intFac As Integer = 1
    Dim i As Integer

    For i = 2 To intNumber + 1
        intFac = intFac * i
    Next
    Factorial = intFac
End Function
```

6. Run the program, enter the value 5 in the text box, and click the Calculate button. The result is not correct. This program needs to be debugged.

7. Set a breakpoint in the `Click` event handler of `btnCalculate` at the line where a call to the `Factorial` function is being made. Execute the program, enter the value 5 again, and click the Calculate button.

8. Press the F8 key to step into the `Factorial` function. Select Debug, Windows, Watch, Watch1 to add a watch window. Similarly, select Debug, Windows and add the Locals, Autos, Me, Immediate, and Call Stack windows. Pin down the windows so that they always remain in view and are easy to watch as you step through the program.

9. Look at the Call Stack window (see Figure 12.17). It shows the method call stack, giving you information about the path the code has taken to reach its current point of execution. The currently executing method is at the top of the stack, with an arrow pointing to it. When this method quits, the next entry in the stack will be the method receiving the control of execution.

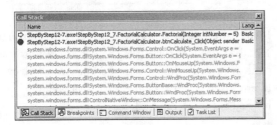

continues

NOTE

Two Modes of the Command Window
The Command window has two modes: the Command mode and the Immediate mode (see Figure 12.21). When you invoke the Command window by selecting View, Other Windows, Command Window, it is invoked in Command mode. In Command mode, the window can be used to issue commands such as Edit to edit the text in the file. You can use regular expressions with the Edit command to make editing operations extremely quick and effective. The Command window shows a > prompt.

On the other hand, when you invoke the Command window by selecting Debug, Window, Immediate, you can use it to evaluate expressions in the currently debugged program. The Immediate mode does not show any prompt. You can switch from Immediate mode to Command mode by typing >cmd, and you can switch from Command mode to Immediate mode by typing the immed command.

FIGURE 12.17
The Call Stack window.

10. Look at the Me window, which is shown in Figure 12.18. This window allows you to examine the members associated with the current object (the Factorial form). You can scroll down to find the `txtNumber` object. If you need to, you can change the values of these objects here.

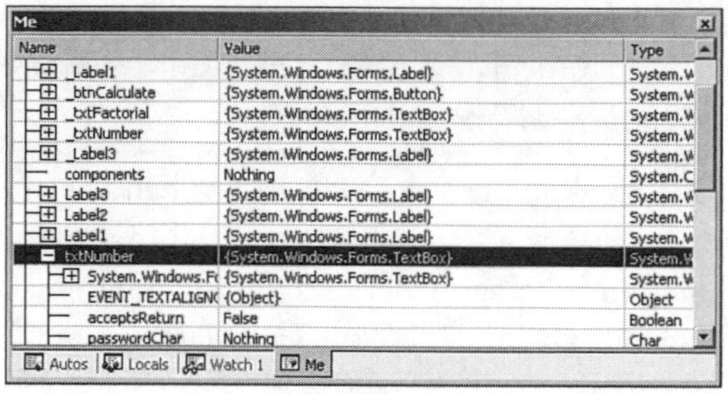

FIGURE 12.18
The Me window.

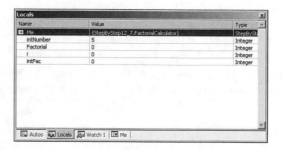

11. Activate the Autos window, which is shown in Figure 12.19. It displays the variables in the current statement and in the previous statement. The debugger determines this for you automatically, hence the name of the window.

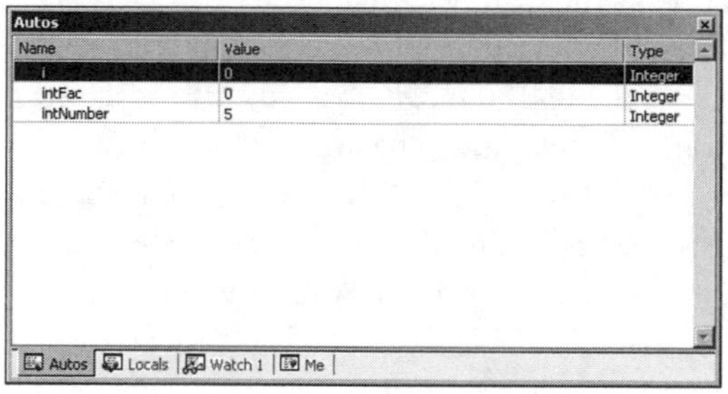

FIGURE 12.19
The Autos window.

12. Invoke the Locals window, which is shown in Figure 12.20. It displays the variables that are local to the current context (that is, the current method under execution) with their current values. Figure 12.20 shows the local variables in the Factorial method.

FIGURE 12.20
The Locals window.

13. Activate the Immediate window. Type `?intNumber` and click Enter. Visual Studio .NET immediately evaluates and displays the current value of this variable in the next line. Now type the expression `?Factorial(intNumber)`. The Immediate window calls the `Factorial` function for the given value and prints the result. The Immediate window can therefore be used to print values of variables and expressions while you are debugging a program.

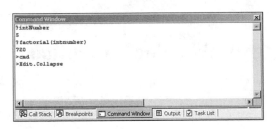

No Break-Edit-Continue Capability
In Visual Basic 6.0, you could edit the code of a running program, and the new code would be used immediately, without a restart. This Break-Edit-Continue capability is not present in Visual Basic .NET.

FIGURE 12.21
Two modes of the Command window.

14. Invoke the Watch1 window (see Figure 12.22). Select the variable `intFac` in the code and drag and drop it to the Watch1 window. You can also double-click the next available row and add a variable to it. Add the variables `i` and `intNumber` to the Watch1 window.

15. Step through the execution of the program by pressing the F8 key. Continue observing the way the values change in the Watch1 (or Autos or Locals) window. After a few steps, the method terminates, but note that it executes until the value of `i` is `6`, rather than stopping at `5`. This is the cause of the wrong output in your program.

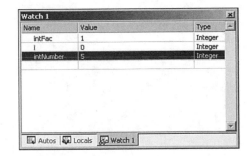

FIGURE 12.22
The Watch1 window.

16. Change the `For` statement to run from 2 to `intNumber`. Press F8 to step through the program. The Unable to Apply Code Changes dialog box appears, as shown in Figure 12.23. The dialog box appears because after you have identified the problem and corrected the code, the source code is different from the compiled version of the program. If you choose to continue at this stage, your source code and the program in execution are different, and this may mislead you. I recommend that you always restart the program rather than continuing. Click the Restart button. The code is recompiled, and the program starts again.

FIGURE 12.23
The Unable to Apply Code Changes dialog box.

continues

continued

17. Enter the value 5 and click the Continue button. The program breaks into the debugger again because the breakpoint is still active. Step through the program and watch the values of variables. The loop is executed for the correct number of times, and you get the correct factorial value.

NOTE

Support for Cross-Language Debugging   Visual Studio .NET support debugging projects that contain code written in several managed languages. The debugger can transparently step in and step out from one language to another, making the debugging process smooth for you as a developer. Visual Studio .NET also extends this support to nonmanaged languages, but with minor limitations.

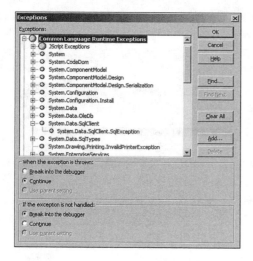

FIGURE 12.24
The Exceptions dialog box.

Debugging When an Exception Occurs

You can control the way the debugger behaves when it encounters a line of code that throws an exception. You can control this behavior through the Exceptions dialog box, shown in Figure 12.24, which is invoked via the Debug, Exceptions menu option. The Exceptions dialog box allows you to control the debugger's behavior for each type of exception defined in the system. In fact, if you have defined your own exceptions, you can add them to this dialog box.

There are two levels at which you can control the behavior of the debugger when it encounters an exception:

◆ **If the exception is thrown**—You can instruct the debugger to either continue or break the execution of the program when an exception is thrown. The default setting for Common Language Runtime exceptions is to continue the execution, possibly in the anticipation that there will be an exception handler.

◆ **If the exception is not handled**—If the program that you are debugging fails to handle an exception, you can instruct the debugger to either ignore it and continue or to break the execution of the program. The default setting for CLR exceptions is to break the execution, warning the programmer of a possible problematic situation.

GUIDED PRACTICE
EXERCISE 12.2

The later versions of the Factorial Calculator program (refer to Step By Steps 12.6 and 12.7) catch any exceptions so that the users don't complain about annoying exception messages. In this exercise you have to configure the debugger from Step By Step 12.7 so that when a reported exception occurs, you get an opportunity to analyze the program.

You should try doing this on your own first. If you get stuck, or if you'd like to see one possible solution, follow these steps:

1. Open the Windows application project StepByStep12-7. Set this project as the active project in the solution.

2. Activate the Exceptions dialog box by selecting Debug, Exceptions.

3. In the Exception dialog box, click the Find button. Enter System.FormatException and click the OK button. This quickly takes you to the desired exception in the Exception Tree view.

4. In the When the Exception Is Thrown group box, select Break Into the Debugger.

5. Repeat steps 3 and 4 for System.OverFlowException. Click OK to close the Exceptions dialog box.

6. Run the project and enter a nonnumeric value in the textbox. This causes a System.FormatException error, and the debugger prompts you to either break or continue the execution, rather than automatically throwing execution into the Catch block. Select Break. You can now note the values of various variables at this stage, either by hovering the mouse pointer over them or by adding the variables to the Watch window. On the next run of the program, enter a very large value. This causes a System.OverFlowException error to be thrown. Select Break when prompted by the debugger, and then analyze the values of various variables.

Debugging a Running Process

Up to this point, you have only seen examples of debugging programs by starting them from the Visual Studio .NET environment. The Visual Studio .NET debugging environment also allows you to debug processes that are started outside the debugging environment.

To access external processes from Visual Studio .NET, you need to invoke the Processes dialog box, shown in Figure 12.25, which you can do in two ways:

◆ When you have a solution open in Visual Studio .NET, you can invoke the Processes dialog box by selecting Debug, Processes.

◆ When there is no solution open in Visual Studio .NET, the Debug menu is not displayed. However, you can invoke the Processes dialog box by selecting Tools, Debug Processes.

FIGURE 12.25
The Processes dialog box.

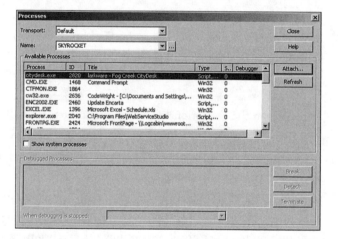

Step By Step 12.8 demonstrates how to attach the debugger to a process that is being executed.

STEP BY STEP

12.8 Attaching the Debugger to a Process That Is Being Executed

1. Using Windows Explorer, navigate to the bin folder inside the project folder for StepByStep12-7. Double-click the executable (EXE) file to launch the program.

2. Start a new instance of Visual Studio .NET. Select Tools, Debug Processes. The Processes dialog box appears, as shown in Figure 12.25. You might have a different process list from what is shown in the figure.

3. Select the process named `StepByStep12-7.exe` and click the Attach button. This invokes an Attach to Process dialog box, as shown in Figure 12.26. Select Common Language Runtime as the program type and uncheck all the other choices. Click the OK button. You now see the selected process in the Debugged Processes section of the Processes dialog box.

4. Click the Break button to break into the running process. Click the Close button to close the Processes dialog box for now.

5. You see both the Diassembly window and the source code window open in the debugging environment. Switch to the source code window. Set a breakpoint on the line of code that makes a call to the `Factorial` method. Press F8 to step into the program.

6. Enter the value 5 in the form and click the Calculate button. The debugger breaks the execution when the breakpoint is reached.

7. Use the Watch, Locals, and Autos windows to analyze variables and step through the program execution.

8. When the factorial result is displayed, invoke the Processes window again by selecting Debug, Processes. From the list of debugged processes, select `StepByStep12-7` and click the Detach button.

9. Click the Close button to close the Processes dialog box. Note that `StepByStep12-7.exe` is still executing as it was when you intiated the debugging process.

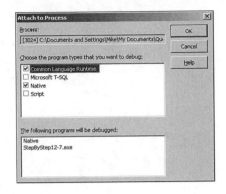

FIGURE 12.26
The Attach to Process dialog box.

Debugging a Remote Process

The process of debugging a remote process is almost the same as debugging an already running process. The only difference is that, prior to selecting a running process from the Processes dialog box, you must select the remote machine name from the Name drop-down list box in the Processes dialog box.

Before you can debug a process remotely, you need to perform a one-time configuration on the remote machine (where the processes are running). You can do this in two ways:

◆ Install Visual Studio .NET on the remote machine.

◆ Install the Remote Components Setup on the remote machine (you can start this from the Visual Studio .NET Setup Disc 1).

Using either of these methods, you can set up Machine Debug Manager (mdm.exe) on the remote computer. mdm.exe runs as a background service on the computer, providing remote debugging support. In addition, when you use either of these methods, you must add the logged-on user to the Debugger Users group. A user needs to be a member of this group in order to remotely access this computer. You can later add other usernames to this group by using the Computer Management MMC Snap-in on the remote computer.

If SQL Server is installed on the remote machine, the setup process just described will also configure the machine for SQL Server Stored Procedures debugging. I'll demonstrate SQL Server Stored Procedure debugging in Exercise 12.2, at the end of this chapter.

For information on more complex remote debugging configurations and requirements, refer to the "Setting Up Remote Debugging" topic in the Visual Studio .NET Combined Help Collection.

Debugging Code in DLL Files

The process of debugging a dynamic link library (DLL) file is similar to the process of debugging an EXE file. There is one difference, though: The code in a DLL file cannot be directly invoked, so you need to have a calling program that calls various methods/components from the DLL files.

You typically need to take the following steps to debug code in a DLL file:

1. Launch the EXE file that uses the components or methods in the DLL file.

2. Launch Visual Studio .NET and attach the debugger to the EXE file. Set a breakpoint where the method in the DLL file is called. Continue with the execution.

3. The execution breaks when the breakpoint is reached. At this point, select Debug, Step Into to step into the code of the DLL file. Execute the code in the DLL file in step mode while you watch the value of its variables.

In addition, if the code files are executing on a remote machine, you should make sure that the remote machine is set up with remote debugging support, as explained in the section "Debugging a Remote Process," earlier in this chapter.

REVIEW BREAK

▶ Debugging is the process of finding the causes of errors in a program, locating the lines of code causing the errors, and then fixing those errors.

▶ The three options available while performing step-by-step execution are Step Into, Step Over, and Step Out.

▶ Breakpoints allow you to mark code that signals the debugger to pause execution when it encounters them. You can choose to continue step-by-step execution or resume normal execution by clicking F5 or the Resume button.

▶ The various tool windows, such as Me, Locals, Autos, Watch, and Call Stack, can be of great help in tracking the execution path and the status of variables when debugging an application in Visual Studio .NET.

▶ When an exception is thrown by an application, you can either choose to continue execution or break into the code with the debugger (that is, you can start debugging operations such as step-by-step execution). You can customize this behavior for each exception object by using the Exceptions dialog box.

continues

continued

▶ You can attach a debugger to a running process (local or remote) with the help of the Processes dialog box.

CHAPTER SUMMARY

KEY TERMS

- Debugging
- Testing
- Tracing

This chapter begins by discussing the various types of tests and how important testing is for an application. You have learned that designing and executing a comprehensive test plan is desirable, to ensure that an application is robust, correct, and reliable.

The .NET Framework provides various classes and techniques to implement tracing in applications. Tracing helps in displaying informative messages during execution of a program. The Trace and Debug classes provide different methods to generate messages at specific locations in code. Classes derived from the TraceListener class process these messages. You have seen how trace switches can be applied to an application to give you control over the type of tracing information generated by an application, without even recompiling the application.

Later in the chapter, I discuss the various preprocessor directives available in Visual Basic .NET. You have learned how methods can be conditionally compiled by using the `Conditional` attribute.

The compiler can generally identify compile-time errors without assistance. The tough job is to find logical and runtime errors in an application. Visual Basic .NET offers some powerful tools for debugging. In this chapter, you have seen a broad survey of the various tools available for debugging. You have also seen how to debug an already running process, debug from a remote machine, debug DLL files, and debug SQL Server stored procedures. As you continue to work with Visual Basic .NET, you'll discover more benefits from debugging in all these areas.

Exercises

12.1 Creating a Custom Trace Switch

The TraceSwitch and BooleanSwitch classes are two built-in classes that provide trace switch functionality. If you need different trace levels or different implementations of the Switch class, you can inherit from the Switch class and implement your own custom trace switch.

This exercise shows you how to create a custom trace switch. You will create a FactorialSwitch class that can be set with four values (Negative (-1), Off (0), Overflow (1), and Both (2)) for the Factorial Calculator form. The class will have two properties: Negative and Overflow.

Estimated Time: 25 minutes.

1. Launch Visual Studio .NET. Select File, New, Blank Solution and name the new solution 306C12Exercises.

2. Add a new Windows application project to the solution. Name the project Exercise12-1.

3. Delete Form1.vb from the new project.

4. Using the Solution Explorer window, drag the FactorialCalculator.vb form from the StepByStep12-1 project to this project. While dragging, hold down the Ctrl key so that the form is copied to the current project instead of being moved. Change the Text property of the form to Factorial Calculator Exercise 12_1.

5. Add a new class to the project. Name the class FactorialSwitch and modify the class definition with the following code:

```
Imports System
Imports System.Diagnostics

Public Enum FactorialSwitchLevel
    Negative = -1
    Off = 0
    Overflow = 1
    Both = 2
End Enum

Public Class FactorialSwitch
    Inherits Switch

    Public Sub New( _
     ByVal DisplayName As String, _
     ByVal Description As String)
        MyBase.New(DisplayName, Description)
    End Sub

    Public Property Negative() As Boolean
        Get
            ' Return true if
            ' the SwitchSetting
            ' is Negative or Both
            If ((SwitchSetting = -1) Or _
             (SwitchSetting = 2)) Then
                Return True
            Else
                Negative = False
            End If
        End Get
        Set(ByVal Value As Boolean)

        End Set
    End Property

    Public Property Overflow() As Boolean
        Get
            ' Return true if
            ' the SwitchSetting
            ' is Overflow or Both
            If ((SwitchSetting = 1) Or _
             (SwitchSetting = 2)) Then
                Return True
            Else
                Negative = False
            End If
        End Get
        Set(ByVal Value As Boolean)

        End Set
    End Property
End Class
```

APPLY YOUR KNOWLEDGE

6. Open `FactorialCalculator.vb` in the Code view. Change the `Click` event handler of the `btnCalculate` control so that it looks like this:

```
Private Sub btnCalculate_Click( _
 ByVal sender As System.Object, _
 ByVal e As System.EventArgs) Handles _
 btnCalculate.Click

    Dim facSwitch As FactorialSwitch = _
    New FactorialSwitch("FactorialTrace", _
    "Trace the factorial application")

    Dim intNumber As Integer = _
    Convert.ToInt32(txtNumber.Text)

    If facSwitch.Negative Then
        ' Make a debug assertion
        Debug.Assert(intNumber >= 0, _
        "Invalid value", _
         "negative value in debug mode")
    End If

    Dim intFac As Integer = 1
    Dim i As Integer
    Try
        For i = 2 To intNumber
            intFac = intFac * i
        Next
    Catch ex As Exception
        If facSwitch.Overflow Then
            ' Write a debug message if
            ' the condition is true
            Debug.WriteLineIf(intFac < 1, _
            "There was an overflow", _
            "Factorial Program Debug")
        End If
    End Try

    txtFactorial.Text = intFac.ToString()
End Sub
```

7. In the Solution Explorer window, select View All Files from the toolbar. Navigate to the `bin` folder. Right-click the `debug` folder and select Add, Add New Item. Choose to create an XML file, and name the XML file `Exercise12-1.exe.config`.

8. In the XML editor, type the following configuration data in the XML file:

```
<?xml version="1.0" encoding="utf-8" ?>
<configuration>
    <system.diagnostics>
        <switches>
            <add name="FactorialTrace"
value="2" />
        </switches>
    </system.diagnostics>
</configuration>
```

9. Set the form as the startup form for the project and set the project as the startup project for the solution.

10. Run the project, using the default `Debug` configuration. The Negative Assertion dialog box is displayed only if the switch is set with the value `-1` or 2. Similarly, the overflow message is displayed in the Output window only if the switch value is set to 1 or 2.

The value set in the configuration file can be accessed through `SwitchSetting` property of the `Switch` class. This property's `Negative` and `Overflow` properties return `True` or `False`, depending on the value of the `SwitchSetting` property.

12.2 Debugging SQL Server Stored Procedures Using Visual Basic .NET

You can perform step-by-step execution of SQL Server stored procedures in Visual Basic .NET. This exercise shows you how.

Estimated Time: 30 minutes.

1. Add a new Windows application project to your solution. Name the project `Exercise12-2`.

2. Change the name of the `Form1.vb` form to `MostExpensiveProducts.vb`.

APPLY YOUR KNOWLEDGE

3. Select Project, Properties. Select Debugging under the Configuration Properties node in the left pane of the Property Pages window. In the right pane, under the Debugging node, check the box to enable SQL Server debugging, as shown in Figure 12.27. Click OK.

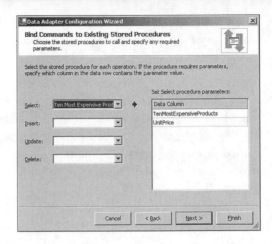

FIGURE 12.28
Binding commands to existing stored procedures.

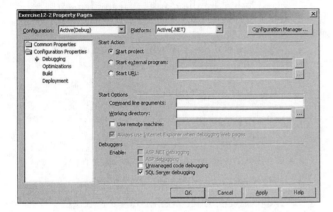

FIGURE 12.27
A Property Pages window showing debugging properties.

4. Drag a `SqlDataAdapter` component from the Data tab of the toolbox to the form. This launches the Data Adapter Configuration Wizard. Click Next. Select the Northwind database connection that was created in Chapters 5, "Data Binding," and 6, "Consuming and Manipulating Data," or use the New Connection button to create a Northwind database connection. Click Next.

5. Choose the Use Existing Stored Procedures option in the Choose a Query type page. Click Next. Select Ten Most Expensive Products from the Select combo box, as shown in Figure 12.28. Click Next and then click Finish. This creates a `SqlConnection` component in the component tray.

6. Select the `SqlDataAdapter1` component. Right-click and select Generate DataSet from the context menu. Create a new `DataSet1` component and choose the Ten Most Expensive Products stored procedure from the checked list box. Click OK. This creates a `DataSet11` component in the component tray.

7. Place a `Button` control(`btnGetProducts`) and a `DataGrid` control (`DataGrid1`) on the form. Change the `DataSource` property of `DataGrid1` to `DataSet1`, and change the `DataMember` property to `Ten Most Expensive Products`.

8. Add the following code to the `Click` event of the `Button` control:

```
Private Sub btnGetProducts_Click( _
 ByVal sender As System.Object, _
 ByVal e As System.EventArgs) Handles _
 btnGetProducts.Click
    SqlDataAdapter1.Fill(Me.DataSet11)
End Sub
```

APPLY YOUR KNOWLEDGE

9. Insert a breakpoint in the Click event handler, at the point of the call to the Fill method of the sqlDataAdapter1 object.

10. Open the Server Explorer window. Open the Data Connections node, and drill down to the stored procedure Ten Most Expensive Products. Right-click the stored procedure and select Edit Stored Procedure. Insert a breakpoint in the first code line of the stored procedure, as shown in Figure 12.29.

FIGURE 12.29
A Property Pages window showing debugging properties.

11. Run the project. Click the Get Products button. Notice that the program starts step-by-step execution as soon as it encounters the breakpoint in the Fill method call line. Press F8. You are taken to the stored procedure code, where you can perform step-by-step execution.

This exercise teaches you how to debug SQL Server stored procedures by using step-by-step execution. In Figure 12.29, notice that the Select statement is enclosed in a blue outline; this indicates a single executable SQL statement. You can use various tools, such as the Watch and Locals windows, to keep track of the values of the variables defined in the stored procedures during step-by-step execution. These tools are of great help when you debug complex stored procedures.

Review Questions

1. For what do you use a test plan?

2. What is the purpose of the Assert method in the Debug and Trace classes?

3. What is the main purpose of the TraceListener class? What are the classes that implement TraceListener in the Framework Class Library?

4. What are the two built-in trace switches in the .NET Framework Class Library?

5. What is the main advantage of trace switches?

6. What types of methods can be marked with the Conditional attribute?

7. What is the purpose of the #const preprocessor directive?

8. What are the three commands for stepping through code while debugging?

9. What happens when you put a breakpoint in code?

10. Name some of the different tool windows that are available for debugging.

11. How can you attach the debugger to a running process in Visual Basic .NET?

12. To verify that remote debugging is enabled on a system, what should you check?

Exam Questions

1. Your task in your current project is to perform unit testing. Which activities should you perform as part of this task?

APPLY YOUR KNOWLEDGE

A. Locate and fix errors.

B. Run the application with carefully planned test data and check whether it works according to its specification.

C. Run a module with carefully planned test data and check whether it works according to its specification.

D. Verify that a program module integrates well with other modules in an application.

2. Which of the following actions enables tracing for a Visual Basic .NET application? (Select all that apply.)

A. Compile the Windows application with the /define:TRACE option.

B. Add the #Const TRACE=1 statement at the top of the source code.

C. Start the application with the /define:TRACE option.

D. Add the following code to the application's configuration file and then execute the Windows application:

```
<system.diagnostics>
    <switches>
        <add name="TraceLevelSwitch"
        value="1" />
    </switches>
</system.diagnostics>
```

3. You are developing a Windows application using Microsoft Visual Studio .NET. You have included the following line at the top of the source code:

```
#Const DEBUG=0
```

Which of the following statements are true with respect to program execution? (Select two.)

A. You will see the trace messages while running the program in the Debug configuration.

B. You will see the trace messages while running the program in the Release configuration.

C. You will see only the trace messages generated by the methods of the Debug class.

D. You will not see any trace messages.

4. You have added the following statement to the Load event handler of a single-form Windows application:

```
Trace.Listeners.Add( _
    New TextWriterTraceListener("TraceLog.txt"))
```

Which of the following statements are true with respect to program execution? (Select three.)

A. TextWriterTraceListener listens to all messages generated by the methods of the Debug and Trace classes.

B. TextWriterTraceListener listens only to the messages generated by the methods of the Trace classes.

C. All the trace messages are stored in a file named TraceLog.txt.

D. The trace messages are displayed in the Output window while the program is run in either the Debug or Release configurations.

5. You have the following lines of code in a Visual Basic .NET program:

```
TraceSwitch myTraceSwitch = _
    new TraceSwitch("SwitchOne", _
    "The first switch")
myTraceSwitch.Level = TraceLevel.Info
```

APPLY YOUR KNOWLEDGE

Which of the following expressions in your program will evaluate to False?

A. myTraceSwitch.TraceInfo

B. myTraceSwitch.TraceWarning

C. myTraceSwitch.TraceError

D. myTraceSwitch.TraceVerbose

6. You want to control the tracing and debug output of a Windows application without recompiling your code. Which of the following classes enables you to do this?

A. TraceListener

B. TraceSwitch

C. Trace

D. Debug

7. You are asked to implement tracing in a Windows application such that the application displays both warning and error messages when the application is run by using the Debug configuration, but that only displays error messages when run by using the Release configuration of Visual Basic .NET. Which of the following code segments best solves this requirement?

A.

```
Dim traceSwitch As TraceSwitch  = _
 New TraceSwitch("MySwitch",_
  "Error and Warning Switch")

#If DEBUG
   traceSwitch.Level = TraceLevel.Warning
#Else
   traceSwitch.Level = TraceLevel.Error
#End If

Trace.WriteLineIf( _
 traceSwitch.TraceWarning, _
  "Warning Message")
Trace.WriteLineIf( _
 traceSwitch.TraceError, "Error Message")
```

B.

```
Dim traceSwitch As TraceSwitch  = _
 New TraceSwitch("MySwitch",_
  "Error and Warning Switch")

#If DEBUG
   traceSwitch.Level = TraceLevel.Warning
#else
   traceSwitch.Level = TraceLevel.Error
#End If

Debug.WriteLineIf( _
 traceSwitch.TraceWarning, _
  "Warning Message")
Debug.WriteLineIf(traceSwitch.TraceError, _
  "Error Message")
```

C.

```
Dim traceSwitch As TraceSwitch  = _
 New TraceSwitch("MySwitch",_
  "Error and Warning Switch")

#If TRACE
   traceSwitch.Level = TraceLevel.Warning
#else
   traceSwitch.Level = TraceLevel.Error
#End If

Trace.WriteLineIf( _
 traceSwitch.TraceWarning, _
  "Warning Message")
Trace.WriteLineIf(traceSwitch.TraceError, _
  "Error Message")
```

D.

```
Dim traceSwitch As TraceSwitch  = _
 New TraceSwitch("MySwitch",_
  "Error and Warning Switch")

#If TRACE
   traceSwitch.Level = TraceLevel.Error
#Else
   traceSwitch.Level = TraceLevel.Warning
#End If

Trace.WriteLineIf( _
 traceSwitch.TraceWarning, _
  "Warning Message")
Trace.WriteLineIf( _
 traceSwitch.TraceError, "Error Message")
```

APPLY YOUR KNOWLEDGE

8. The configuration file of a Windows application has the following contents:

```
<system.diagnostics>
    <switches>
        <add name="BooleanSwitch" value="-1" />
        <add name="TraceLevelSwitch"
            value="33" />
    </switches>
</system.diagnostics>
```

You are using the following statements to create switch objects in your code:

```
BooleanSwitch booleanSwitch = _
 new BooleanSwitch("BooleanSwitch", "Boolean
Switch")
TraceSwitch traceSwitch = _

 new TraceSwitch("TraceLevelSwitch", "Trace
Switch")
```

Which of the following option is correct regarding the values of these switch objects?

A. The booleanSwitch.Enabled property is set to False and traceSwitch.Level is set to TraceLevel.Verbose.

B. The booleanSwitch.Enabled property is set to True and traceSwitch.Level is set to TraceLevel.Verbose.

C. The booleanSwitch.Enabled property is set to False and traceSwitch.Level is set to TraceLevel.Error.

D. The booleanSwitch.Enabled property is set to False and traceSwitch.Level is set to TraceLevel.Info.

9. You are developing a Windows application. Your application's configuration files have the following code:

```
Dim ts As TraceSwitch = New TraceSwitch( _
 "TraceLevelSwitch", _
 "Trace the application")

<Conditional("DEBUG")> _
Private Sub Method1()
    Trace.WriteLineIf(ts.TraceError, _
     "Message 1", "Message 2")
End Sub

<Conditional("TRACE")> _
Private Sub Method2()
    Trace.WriteLine("Message 3")
End Sub

Private Sub btnCalculate_Click( _
 ByVal sender As System.Object, _
 ByVal e As System.EventArgs) _
 Handles btnCalculate.Click
    If ts.TraceWarning Then
        Trace.WriteLine("Message 10")
        Method1()
    Else
        Trace.WriteLineIf(ts.TraceInfo, _
         "Message 20")
        Method2()
    End If

    If (ts.TraceError) Then
        Trace.WriteLineIf(ts.TraceInfo, _
         "Message 30")
        Trace.WriteLineIf(ts.TraceVerbose, _
         "Message 40")
    End If
End Sub
```

What tracing output will be generated when you run your program in debug mode and click the btnCalculate button?

APPLY YOUR KNOWLEDGE

A.

```
Message 10
Message 1
Message 2
Message 30
```

B.

```
Message 10
Message 2: Message 1
Message 30
```

C.

```
Message 10
Message 2
Message 30
Message 40
```

D.

```
Message 20
Message 3
Message 30
Message 40
```

10. You have the following segment of code in your program:

```
Dim traceListener As EventLogTraceListener = _
  new EventLogTraceListener("TraceLog")

Trace.Listeners.Add(traceListener)
Debug.Listeners.Add(traceListener)

Trace.WriteLine("Sample Message")
Debug.WriteLine("Sample Message")
```

When you debug the program through Visual Studio .NET, how many times will the message "Sample Message" be written to the trace log?

A. 1

B. 2

C. 3

D. 4

11. Which of the following statements are true for remote debugging of processes? (Select two.)

A. Both the local and remote machines must have Visual Studio.NET installed.

B. Only the local machine needs Visual Studio.NET.

C. Remote components setup is required on the local machine.

D. Remote components setup is required on the remote machine.

12. While you are debugging in Visual Studio .NET, you want to watch only the values of variables that you are using in the current statement and in the previous statement. Which of the following debugger windows provides the easiest way to watch these variables?

A. Autos

B. Locals

C. Me

D. Watch

13. You want to debug a remote process. The remote machine does not have Visual Studio .NET installed on it. Which of the following options should you choose?

A. Start the process on the remote machine first, and then launch Visual Studio .NET on the local machine. Attach a debugger to the running process. Break into the execution of the remote process.

B. Open the project of the remote process in Visual Studio .NET, set a breakpoint, and then execute the process.

APPLY YOUR KNOWLEDGE

C. Copy the remote application project to the local machine and debug it by using the Visual Studio .NET debugger.

D. Open the project of the remote process in Visual Studio .NET on the remote machine and then set a breakpoint. Run Visual Studio .NET on the local machine and attach the debugger to the project.

14. You have created a DLL file project in Visual Studio .NET. How do you debug the code for this file?

   A. Open the DLL file project, set the breakpoint at the desired location, and start the debugger.

   B. Create an EXE project that uses the DLL file, and then start the debugger.

   C. Create an EXE project that uses the DLL file, set the breakpoint in the EXE project, and start the debugger

   D. Select the DLL file through the Processes dialog box and attach the debugger to it. Click the Break button to break the execution into the DLL code.

15. You want to debug a remote process running on a Windows 2000 Server computer that is not in the domain of your local computer. The remote server has a full installation of Visual Studio .NET. The two domains do not have two-way trust established, but you do have a username and password on the remote Windows 2000 server. Which of the following options allows you to debug a process on that machine?

A. Ask the administrator of the remote machine to start the Machine Debug Manager service, and then launch Visual Studio .NET on your local machine and attach the debugger to the remote process.

B. Ask the administrator of the remote machine to include your username and password in the Debugger Users group, and then launch Visual Studio .NET on your local machine and attach the debugger to the remote process.

C. Use Terminal Server to log in to the remote machine. Launch Visual Studio on the remote machine and debug the process by attaching the debugger to it.

D. Use Terminal Server to log in to the remote machine. Launch Visual Studio on the local machine and debug the process by attaching the debugger to it.

Answers to Review Questions

1. The test plan is a document that guides the process of testing. The document clearly specifies the different testing approaches, the test cases, the validation criteria of the tests, and so on.

2. The Assert method takes a condition as its first parameter, and then it displays an Assertion Failed dialog box if the condition evaluates to False.

3. TraceListener is an abstract class that provides the functionality to receive trace and debug messages. DefaultTraceListener, TextWriterTraceListener, and EventLogTraceListener are the three built-in classes that implement TraceListener.

APPLY YOUR KNOWLEDGE

4. The FCL supplies the BooleanSwitch and TraceSwitch classes. You can also create additional trace switch classes of your own.

5. You can easily change the value of trace switches by editing the application configuration (XML) file, using any text editor. To make these changes take effect, you need not recompile the application; you just need to restart it.

6. To apply the Conditional attribute to a method, the method should have no return value.

7. The #Const preprocessing directives lets you define a constant in code. This constant can be used only by other preprocessor directives—not by regular Boolean statements.

8. The three commands that allow you to step through code are Step Into (steps into each statement of the method called), Step Over (performs the entire method call in one step), and Step Out (steps out of the method call).

9. When the debugger encounters a breakpoint in code, it pauses the execution of the application. You can resume execution by using stepping commands.

10. Visual Studio .NET provides a variety of tools to ease debugging processes, such as Me, Locals, Autos, Watch, Call Stack, and Breakpoints.

11. To attach a debugger to a running process, open Visual Basic .NET, Invoke the Processes dialog box, select the process from the list of processes, and click the Attach button.

12. You should verify that the remote machine has the Machine Debug Manager (mdm.exe) running as a background process to enable debugging support. You should also verify that you are a member of the Debugger Users group in order to remotely access the machine for debugging.

Answers to Exam Questions

1. **C.** A unit test involves running a module against carefully planned test data and checking whether it works according to its specification. Debugging is the process of locating and fixing errors. When you run a complete application against test data, you are performing system testing. Checking whether modules integrate well is a task involved in integration testing.

2. **A, B.** To enable tracing in a Windows application, you must have either TRACE or DEBUG symbols defined in the application. There are two ways to do this. One way is to compile the program with a /define:TRACE switch and another is by define the symbol at the top of the source code by using the #define compilation directive. Refer to the section "Conditional Compilation" for more information.

3. **A, B.** When you develop a Windows application using Visual Studio .NET, two project configurations are set for you: the default Debug configuration, which has both TRACE and DEBUG symbols defined, and the Release configuration, which has just one symbol, TRACE, defined. So even if you remove the definition of the DEBUG symbol by using a compiler directive, you still have a TRACE symbol defined for both the Debug and Release configurations. After you remove the definition of the DEBUG symbol, you don't see any tracing messages generated by the Debug class, but because the TRACE symbol is still defined, you can see messages generated by the methods of the Trace class.

4. **A, C, D.** When you add a listener in the Trace.Listeners collection, it listens to the messages generated by both the Trace and Debug classes.

APPLY YOUR KNOWLEDGE

When the new listener is added, it is added to the Listeners collection; it already has a DefaultTraceListener object that sends messages to the Output window, and it is still active and listening to the Trace messages. Therefore, you get messages in TraceLog.txt as well as in the Output window.

5. **D**. Setting the Level property of a trace switch to TraceLevel.Info allows it to capture all informational, warning, and error messages, but not the verbose messages. Thus the TraceInfo, TraceWarning, and TraceError properties of the switch return True but the TraceVerbose property returns False.

6. **B**. The TraceSwitch class provides a multilevel switch that allows you to control tracing and debugging output of a Windows application without recompiling the code. You can cause the changes in behavior by just changing the application's configuration file.

7. **A**. In answer **A**, for the Debug configuration where the DEBUG symbol is defined, the Level property of TraceSwitch is set to TraceLevel.Warning. This causes both the TraceWarning and TraceError properties of this object to be True. Using the Debug configuration causes both messages to be displayed. In the Release configuration, where only the TRACE symbol is defined, the Level property of TraceSwitch is set to TraceLevel.Error. This causes the TraceWarning property to return False and the TraceError property to return True, causing only the error messages to be displayed.

8. **B**. For BooleanSwitch, a value of 0 corresponds to Off, and any nonzero value corresponds to On.

For TraceSwitch, any number greater than 4 is treated as Verbose. From the values given in the configuration file, you know that the booleanSwitch object will have its Enabled property set as True and the traceSwitch object will have its Level property set to TraceLevel.Verbose.

9. **B**. The XML file has the value for the TraceLevelSwitch set to 3; this sets the Level property as TraceLevel.Info, which causes the TraceError, TraceWarning, and TraceInfo properties of TraceSwitch to be True. Only the TraceVerbose property will evaluate to False. Also, the third parameter to the WriteLineIf method is used to categorize the output by stating its value followed by a colon (:) and then the trace message.

10. **D**. The message SampleMessage will be written four times. This is because two instances of EventLogTraceListeners are added to the Listeners collection. So any message generated by the Trace and Debug classes will be listened to twice. When the program is running in Debug mode, both the Trace and Debug statements are executed. The net effect is that the Trace.WriteLine and Debug.WriteLine messages will both be written twice, making four entries in the trace log.

11. **B, D**. For remote debugging, Visual Studio .NET is not required on the remote machine. In that case, you need to run Remote Components setup on the remote machine. For the local machine you need to have Visual Studio .NET to be able to debug the remote processes.

12. **A**. The Autos window gives you the most convenient access because it automatically at every step displays names and values of all variables in the current statement and the previous statement.

APPLY YOUR KNOWLEDGE

13. **A.** To debug a remote process, first the process needs to be started on the remote machine. You can then open Visual Studio on the local machine and attach the debugger to the running process. After the debugger is attached, you can break into the code of remote process and do step-by-step execution or set a breakpoint.

14. **C.** A DLL project cannot be instantiated by itself, so you need to first create an EXE project that calls the classes and methods from the DLL file. You then need to set the breakpoint on the EXE project and start the debugger. When the code steps on to a method inside the DLL file, you can use the step into function to debug the code in a DLL file.

15. **C.** If your local machine's domain does not have a two-way trust relationship with the remote computer's domain, you are not able to debug a remote process from your local computer. The only option you have is to log on to the remote machine by using terminal services, start Visual Studio on the remote machine, and use Visual Studio to attach a debugger on the process that is running on the same machine. Then, you debug as if you were debugging a process running on your local machine.

Suggested Readings and Resources

1. Windows Forms QuickStart Tutorial: "Tracing Topics Under Diagnostics" in "How Do I" section

2. Visual Studio .NET Combined Help Collection"

   • Introduction to Instrumentation and Tracing

   • Using the Debugger

3. Burton, Kevin. *.NET Common Language Runtime Unleashed.* Sams Publishing, 2002.

4. Grimes, Richard. *Developing Applications with Visual Studio .NET.* Addison-Wesley, 2002.

This chapter covers the following Microsoft-specified objectives for the "Deploying a Windows-Based Application" section of the Visual Basic .NET Windows-Based Applications exam:

Deploy a Windows-based application.

- **Use setup and deployment projects**

▶ Microsoft Visual Basic .NET ships with a new project category, setup and deployment projects. These projects contain templates that help in building user-friendly installation packages for different types of applications. This objective requires you to know how to create various setup projects that help in deploying Windows applications.

Create a setup program that installs an application and allows for the application to be uninstalled.

- **Register components and assemblies.**

- **Perform an install-time compilation of a Windows-based application.**

▶ Visual Studio .NET creates installation packages based on the Microsoft Windows Installer technology. Microsoft Windows Installer 2.0 takes handles the execution of the tasks involved in installing, uninstalling, and repairing Windows applications. You have to just focus on what files need to be installed, where they should be located, what Registry entries need to be made, what type of user interface should be displayed to the end user during the installation, and whether any custom code should be executed during the installation. This objective requires you to know how to deploy components and assemblies and also how to perform native compilation (that is, compiling .NET assemblies to processor-specific native code) of assemblies at the time of installation.

CHAPTER 13

Deploying a Windows Application

Add assemblies to the Global Assembly Cache.

▶ The .NET Framework allows you to place *shared assemblies* (that is, assemblies intended to be used by more than one application) in a central location called the Global Assembly Cache (GAC). Assemblies that are placed in GAC must have strong names. This objective requires you to know how to assign a strong name to an assembly and how to install files in the GAC on the target machine during deployment.

Plan the deployment of a Windows-based application.

- **Plan a deployment that uses removable media.**

- **Plan a Web-based deployment.**

- **Plan a network-based deployment.**

- **Ensure that the application conforms to Windows Installer requirements and Windows Logo Program requirements.**

▶ This objective requires you to know the various techniques that you can use to deploy applications. You can choose to deploy an application through removable media such as floppy disks, CDs, or DVDs; you can use a network-based deployment; or you can have your installation package available over the Web, so that the end user can download the package over the Internet. This objective requires you to know what is involved in creating applications that conform to the Windows Installer and Windows Logo Program requirements.

Verify security policies for a deployed application.

- **Launch a remote application (URL remoting)**

▶ You can deploy a Windows application on a network server or a Web server. This deployment method does not require you to install the application on each desktop that will use it. At runtime users can launch the application by typing the uniform resource locator (URL) in the Internet Explorer address bar. All necessary files are then downloaded to the user's computer and can be executed from there. This type of deployment is called *zero-impact deployment* because there is no installation required on the client machines. However, security is a concern with code downloaded from the Internet. This objective requires you to know how to configure a security policy for the target machine in order to allow good code while restricting bad code from executing on the user's computer.

STUDY STRATEGIES

▶ Review the "Deployment Concepts" and the "Deploying Applications" sections of the Visual Studio .NET Combined Help Collection.

▶ Experiment with using setup projects and merge module projects to deploy Windows applications. Understand when you should choose to create a setup project versus a merge module project.

▶ Work with the different editors that are available in the setup and merge module projects and thoroughly understand the purpose of each of these editors.

▶ Experiment with the Strong Name tool (sn.exe) to create a public/private key pair and then use the key pair to assign a strong name to an assembly. Work with the delay-signing feature to understand the scenarios in which it can be helpful.

▶ Experiment with placing assemblies in the GAC. Understand the steps performed by the Common Language Runtime to locate assemblies.

▶ Experiment with the creation of a custom action to compile assemblies into machine-specific code at install time.

▶ Understand the runtime security policy and how you can use it to your advantage to allow useful applications to run while you're blocking malicious code.

▶ Understand the various ways to deploy a Windows application, and understand the benefits and shortcomings of these methods. Understand when you would use XCOPY deployment or a Windows Installer–based installation package.

▶ Understand the requirements of the Windows Logo Program and other logo programs run by Microsoft.

INTRODUCTION

After you have developed and tested a Windows application, the next step is to deploy the application so that the end user can run it. You need to keep in mind the complexity and requirements of the application in order to choose the right deployment tool. The .NET Framework simplifies the deployment model by making it possible to deploy simple applications by using nothing more than an XCOPY command. However, for applications that are packaged and shipped to the user, Microsoft recommends the use of Microsoft Windows Installer technology.

This chapter discusses how to use Visual Studio .NET to create Windows Installer–based setup and deployment projects. You'll learn about both setup projects (which are used to package Windows applications) and merge module projects (which are used to package shared components).

Chapter 4, "Creating and Managing Components and .NET Assemblies," introduces the concept of shared assemblies. *Shared assemblies* are components that are shared between several applications. This chapter delves into the details of creating and installing shared assemblies.

The .NET Framework provides a new model for deploying Windows applications, the *no-touch* (or *zero-impact*) deployment model. This chapter explores how to use this installation model to execute a Windows application by just pointing to a URL. I'll also discuss how to configure security on a client machine to deal with the hazards of malicious mobile code while executing the code that you really want to execute.

I'll also talk about various ways in which an application can be deployed. Finally, I'll discuss the Windows Logo Program and the requirements that must be met in order for a Windows-based application to be qualified for using the Certified for Windows and Designed for Microsoft Windows XP logos.

DEPLOYMENT TOOLS

A *deployment tool* helps you set up an application on the user's computer. Choosing the right deployment tool is important because the correct tool not only makes the process of deployment simpler but also minimizes the total cost of ownership for the application's users. The choice of tool also depends on the nature of the application. For installing simple applications, sometimes a tool as simple as the XCOPY command can be used. For sophisticated requirements, you might use a tool that creates a Windows Installer–based setup package for the application.

XCOPY Deployment

The .NET Framework simplifies deployment by making zero-impact installation and XCOPY deployment feasible. For a .NET application that uses only managed code and private assemblies, the application can be installed by just copying all files to the desired destination. No Registry entries need to be created, and no files need to be copied to the Windows system directory (thereby causing zero impact on the configuration of user's computer).

However, there are scenarios in which XCOPY is not sufficient as a deployment tool. The following are some common installation tasks that are difficult or impossible to perform by using the XCOPY command:

- Creating shortcuts
- Allowing users to select features during installation
- Copying files to relative paths on the target machine that differ from the paths on the source machine
- Adding assemblies to the GAC
- Creating or configuring databases during an installation
- Adding custom event logs or performance counters to the target machine
- Checking whether the .NET Framework redistributable file is installed on the target machine

◆ Presenting a user-friendly and branded user interface

◆ Allowing license key management and user registration

For the scenarios listed above, the preferred alternative is to use Microsoft Windows Installer–based installation programs instead of using XCOPY for deploying an application.

Microsoft Windows Installer

Microsoft Windows Installer is an installation and configuration service that is built in to the Windows operating system. It gives you complete control over installation of an application, a component, or an update.

The Windows Installer includes many built-in actions for performing installations. In addition to the standard actions such as installing files, creating shortcuts to files, making Start menu entries, and writing Registry entries, the Installer also offers several advanced features, some of which are listed here:

◆ It provides the ability to take custom actions during application installation. For example, you might want to run a SQL script to install a database during application installation.

◆ It provides "on-demand" installation of features. This capability allows the user to install, at a later stage, a feature that was not installed during the application's original installation. On-demand installation does not force the user to run the entire installation package—just to add a single feature.

◆ It provides the ability to roll back an installation. The Windows Installer allows an undo operation for every operation that is performed during an application installation. If it encounters any error while installing an application, it can uninstall everything that was installed during the installation.

◆ It allows you to uninstall an application without breaking any other application that depends on it.

◆ It allows you to fix an application or one of its components if it becomes corrupted. This way, users spend less time uninstalling and reinstalling applications.

NOTE

Microsoft Windows Installer Although the Windows Installer service is included in all current versions of Windows, you might need to install a redistributable installation in order to get the latest version. Later in this chapter you will see how to create a Windows Installer bootstrapper to ensure that the Windows Installer service is updated (if necessary) on target machines.

NOTE

Windows Installer Requirements Windows Installer version 2.0 (the version used to install .NET applications) requires Windows NT 4.0 with Service Pack 6 or later, Windows XP, Windows .NET Server, Windows 2000, or Windows Me. Earlier Windows Installer versions require Windows NT 4.0 with Service Pack 3 or later, Windows XP, Windows 2000, or Windows Me. Windows Installer is also available as a redistributable file for Windows NT 4.0, Windows 95, and Windows 98. It can be downloaded from www.microsoft.com/msdownload/platformsdk/sdkupdate/psdkredist.htm.

NOTE

> **Using Windows Installer**   Microsoft recommends the use of the Windows Installer service to install and configure .NET applications on an end user's system.

The Windows Installer service manages all installed components on a system by keeping a database of information about every application that it installs, including files, Registry keys, and components.

When you create an installation program for the Windows Installer service, you create a Windows Installer (.msi) package. This package includes a number of database tables that describe the application to the Windows Installer service. When this package is executed on the target machine, the Windows Installer service installs the program by reading the installation information stored in the Windows Installer package.

There are several ways to create a Windows Installer package. The most basic option is to manually create it, using the Windows Installer Software Development Kit (SDK), but for most practical requirements you should instead use a visual tool that can help you with the process. In this chapter, I will use Visual Studio .NET setup and deployment projects to create setup packages, using the Windows Installer technology. A lot of people also use installation tools from independent vendors, such as InstallShield or Wise Solutions. Specialized tools from these and other vendors provide you with a much higher level of customization and ease for creating Windows Installer–based setup programs.

DEPLOYING A WINDOWS APPLICATION

Deploy a Windows-based application

- **Use setup and deployment projects.**

Microsoft Visual Studio .NET allows you to create Windows Installer–based installation packages. It offers four types of deployment project templates:

◆ **Setup Project**—Used to create installation packages for deploying Windows-based applications.

◆ **Web Setup Project**—Used to create installation packages for deploying Web-based applications.

◆ **Merge Module Project**—Used to create installation packages for components that may be shared by multiple applications.

◆ **Cab Project**—Used to package ActiveX components so that they can be downloaded over the Internet.

Visual Studio .NET also has a Setup Wizard that helps you interactively create deployment projects. This chapter mainly discusses setup projects and merge module projects. For more details on the other two types of projects, refer to *MCAD/MCSD Training Guide: Visual Basic .NET Web-Based Applications.*

Before you delve into the details of creating deployment projects with the help of Visual Studio .NET, you will need to create an application that can be deployed. In Step By Step 13.1 you create a simple Windows application named NetSql that returns the result of any SELECT query from the SQL Server Northwind database. This application will then serve as a testbed for exploring various deployment features over the course of this chapter.

> **NOTE**
>
> **Setup Projects Versus Web Setup Projects**   The main distinction between a setup project and a Web setup project is where the files are deployed. A setup project (usually) installs files to the Program Files directory on the target computer, whereas the Web setup project installs files into a virtual directory of a Web server.

STEP BY STEP

13.1 Building an Application That Needs to Be Deployed

1. Launch Visual Studio .NET. Select File, New, Blank Solution and name the new solution 306C13.

2. In the Solution Explorer window, add a Visual Basic .NET Windows application project to the solution. Name the project NetSql.

3. Delete the default Form1.vb. Add a new form named NetSql.vb.

4. Open the Server Explorer. Expand the tree under Data Connections to show a SQL Server data connection that points to the Northwind sample database. Drag and drop the data connection to the form to create a SqlConnection1 object on the form. This object represents a connection to SQL Server.

continues

continued

5. Place a TextBox control named `txtQuery`, a Button control named `btnExecute`, and a DataGrid control named `dgResults` on the form. Set the `Multiline` property of the TextBox control to `True`. Set the `CaptionVisible` property of the DataGrid control to `False`.

6. Switch to the Code view. Add these statements at the top of the form's module:

```
Imports System.Data.SqlClient
Imports System.IO
```

7. Add the following member declaration in the class definition:

```
Private Shared query As String = ""
```

8. Add the following code to the Load event handler of the form:

```
Private Sub NetSql_Load(ByVal sender As System.Object, _
 ByVal e As System.EventArgs) Handles MyBase.Load
    ' Check for command-line arguments
    Dim args() As String = Environment.GetCommandLineArgs
    If UBound(args, 1) > 0 Then
        ' Assume the first argument to be a file
        ' Load the file contents
        Dim sr As StreamReader = New _
        StreamReader(args(1))
        query = sr.ReadToEnd()
        sr.Close()
    End If
    txtQuery.Text = query
End Sub
```

9. Enter this code to execute the query when the Button control is clicked:

```
Private Sub btnExecute_Click( _
 ByVal sender As System.Object, _
 ByVal e As System.EventArgs) Handles btnExecute.Click
    ' Create a SqlCommand to represent the query
    Dim cmd As SqlCommand = _
    SqlConnection1.CreateCommand()
    cmd.CommandType = CommandType.Text
    cmd.CommandText = txtQuery.Text
    ' Create a SqlDataAdapter to talk to the database
    Dim da As SqlDataAdapter = New SqlDataAdapter()
    da.SelectCommand = cmd
    ' Create a DataSet to hold the results
    Dim ds As DataSet = New DataSet()
    Try
```

```
      ' Fill the DataSet
      da.Fill(ds, "Results")
      ' And bind it to the DataGrid
      dgResults.DataSource = ds
      dgResults.DataMember = "Results"
    Catch ex As Exception
      MessageBox.Show(ex.Message, _
 "Error executing query", _
        MessageBoxButtons.OK, MessageBoxIcon.Error)
    End Try
End Sub
```

10. Change the solution configuration to `Release` mode. Run the application. Enter a `SELECT` query for the Northwind database in the text box.

11. Click the button. The code runs, returning the results to the DataGrid control, as shown in Figure 13.1.

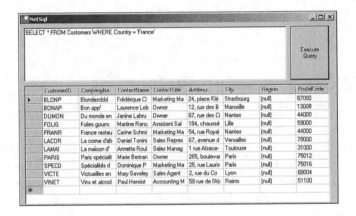

FIGURE 13.1
The `NetSql` application returning `SELECT` query results from the Northwind database.

12. Next you need to add a few files that will be required when you deploy the application. Launch WordPad, and create a `Readme.rtf` file with the following text:

```
NetSql Version 1.0
This application allows you to SELECT data from the
Northwind database. Just type any valid SELECT
statement and you will see the results of the
query instantly!
```

13. Create another file with the name `License.rtf` that contains the following text:

```
NetSql End User License Agreement
You should carefully read the following terms
and conditions before using this software.
```

continues

continued

```
If you do not agree to any of the terms of this
License, then do not install, distribute or
 use this copy of NetSql.
This software, and all accompanying files,
data and materials, are distributed "AS IS"
and with no warranties of any kind, whether
express or implied. Good data processing
procedure dictates that any program be
thoroughly tested with non-critical data
before relying on it.  The user must
assume the entire risk of using the program.
© All rights reserved.
```

Now that you have created an application, the following section demonstrates how to create a setup project for installing this application.

Creating a Setup Project

Visual Studio .NET provides the Setup Project template to create an installer for a Windows application. It also provides the Setup Wizard, which gives you an interactive interface that helps you create different types of setup and deployment projects. Step By Step 13.2 guides you through the process of creating a simple installer, using the Setup Wizard for the NetSql application that you created in Step By Step 13.1.

STEP BY STEP

13.2 Creating a Setup Project for the NetSql Project by Using the Setup Wizard

1. In the Solution Explorer, right-click Solution and select Add, New Project. Select Setup and Deployment projects from the Project Types tree and then select Setup Wizard from the list of templates on the right, as shown in Figure 13.2.

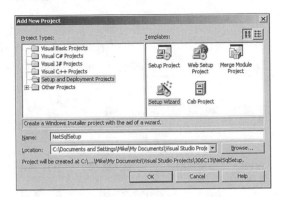

FIGURE 13.2
Adding new setup project via the Setup Wizard.

2. Name the project `NetSqlSetup`. Click OK. The Setup Wizard appears. The first screen that appears is the Welcome screen. Click Next.

3. The second screen is the Choose a Project Type screen. Choose Create a Setup for Windows Application in the first group of options, as shown in Figure 13.3. Click Next.

4. The third page is the Choose Project Outputs to Include screen. Select Primary Output from `NetSql`, as shown in Figure 13.4. Click Next.

5. The fourth page is the Choose Files to Include screen. Click the Add button and include the `Readme.rtf` and `License.rtf` files from the `NetSql` project folder. After you include the files, the screen looks as shown in Figure 13.5. Click Next.

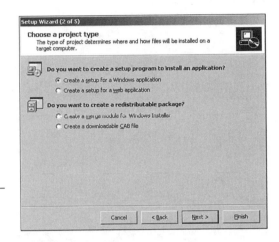

FIGURE 13.3
The Choose a Project Type Setup Wizard screen.

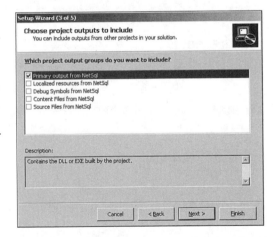

FIGURE 13.4
The Choose Project Outputs to Include Setup Wizard screen.

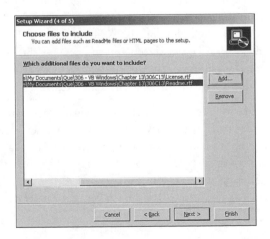

FIGURE 13.5
The Choose Files to Include Setup Wizard screen.

continues

continued

6. The fifth and last page is the Create Project screen, as shown in Figure 13.6. Click Finish to create the project.

FIGURE 13.6
The Create Project Setup Wizard screen.

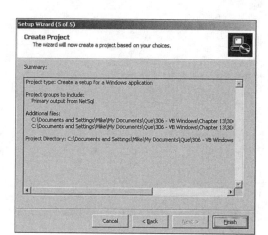

7. Select the new project `NetSqlSetup` in the Solution Explorer. Activate the Properties window. Set `Manufacturer` to `NetSql Software`, `ProductName` to `NetSql`, and `Title` to `NetSql Installer`, as shown in the Figure 13.7.

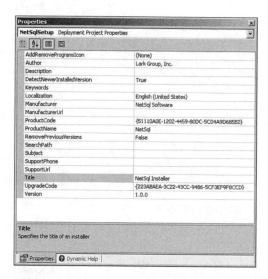

FIGURE 13.6
The Create Project Setup Wizard screen.

8. Build the `NetSqlSetup` project. Open Windows Explorer and navigate to the `Release` folder inside the project folder. Run `setup.exe`. Alternatively, on the development machine, you can install by right-clicking the project in the Solution Explorer and choosing the Install option from the context menu. This opens the `NetSql` Setup Wizard. Click Next on the Welcome screen. The Select Installation Folder screen appears next, as shown in Figure 13.8. Select the default settings and click Next. Click Next again to start the installation. Click Close.

FIGURE 13.7
Project properties of the `NetSqlSetup` deployment project.

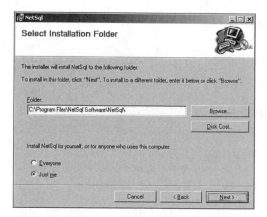

9. Open Windows Explorer and navigate to the installation folder path. If you have not changed the default settings during installation, the path is `C:\Program Files\NetSql Software\NetSql`. Run the `NetSql.exe` file from the folder. The `NetSql` application is launched. Enter a query and click the button to get the results of the query.

FIGURE 13.8
The Select Installation Folder screen during the installation process.

10. Select Start, Settings, Control Panel, Add/Remove Programs to open Add/Remove Programs dialog box. Select the Change or Remove Programs icon from the left pane and select NetSql from the right pane. Click the Remove button to uninstall the NetSql application and click Yes. The NetSql application is uninstalled from your application. Alternatively, on the development machine, you can uninstall by right-clicking the project in the Solution Explorer and choosing the Uninstall option from the context menu.

Step By Step 13.2 illustrates the process of creating a setup project. When the project is compiled, the output files are placed in the bin\Release folder (that is, the active configuration folder). The contents of the folder are an installer package (.msi), executables (.exe), and initialization (.ini) files. The .msi file is the installation package, in the Microsoft Windows Installer format. If the Windows Installer service is installed on your computer, you can directly start the installation by double-clicking this file. The executable files are setup.exe, InstMsiA.exe, and InstMsiW.exe. setup.exe (also called the Windows Installer bootstrapper) bootstraps the installation process by first testing for the presence of the Windows Installer service on the target machine. If the Windows Installer service is not installed, setup.exe first installs it, using either InstMsiA.exe (for Windows 9x and Me) or InstMsiW.exe (for Windows NT/2000/XP/.NET) and then instructs the Windows Installer service to execute the installation, based on the information stored in the installation package (that is, the .msi file). The setup.ini file stores the initialization settings, such as the name of the installation database, for the bootstrap file setup.exe.

There is one catch here. This setup project will only work on computers on which the .NET Framework Common Language Runtime has been already installed. In fact, when you build the setup project, you will see the following message in the Output window of Visual Studio .NET:

> WARNING: This setup does not contain the .NET Framework which must be installed on the target machine by running dotnetfx.exe before this setup will install. You can find dotnetfx.exe on the Visual Studio .NET 'Windows Components Update' media. Dotnetfx.exe can be redistributed with your setup.

On the other hand when you look at the setup project folder in the Solution Explorer, you will see that the Setup Wizard has created a Detected Dependencies folder and included a file named dotnetfxredist_x86_enu.msm in it. But the Exclude property of this file is set to True; this is basically just a placeholder module that stops Visual Studio .NET from automatically including in the project the .NET Framework files from your installation of the .NET Framework. If you try changing the Exclude property of the dotnetfxredist_x86_enu.msm file to False, Visual Studio .NET won't allow you to, and you will get an error when you build the project:

ERROR: dotNETFXRedist_x86_enu.msm must not be used to redistribute the .NET Framework. Please exclude this merge module.

Ideally, you should leave the Exclude property at its default value of True for the dotNETFXRedist_x86_enu.msm dependency.

The .NET Framework cannot be included in a Windows Installer setup package that is created using the Visual Studio .NET deployment tools. It must be installed separately. There are several ways you can do this, including the following:

◆ Ask the user to run setup for the .NET Framework from the Windows Component Upgrade CD-ROM that comes with Visual Studio .NET

◆ Ask user to download the .NET Framework from the Microsoft MSDN Download Center or from the Microsoft Windows Update Web site, http://windowsupdate.microsoft.com.

◆ Use the .NET Framework bootstrapper (setup.exe), which checks for the availability of the .NET Framework, and install it if it is not already installed.

Of course, for a professional installation you would not want to leave it to the users to perform a manual installation of the .NET Framework. Using a bootstrapper setup.exe file is a good idea. Microsoft provides a sample bootstrapper setup.exe file that you can readily use in your projects. I will tell you where to get and how to use this bootstrapper setup.exe file later in this chapter, in Exercise 13.1. For now let's assume that the .NET Framework is available on the machine where you will deploy your applications.

You can modify the configuration settings for a setup project by selecting the project in Solution Explorer and choosing Project, Properties from the main menu. This opens up the project's Property Pages dialog box, as shown in Figure 13.9.

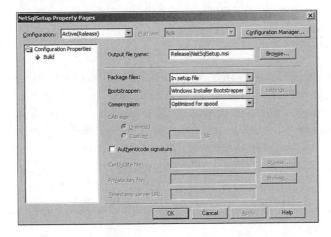

FIGURE 13.9
The project's Property Pages dialog box, showing configuration properties of the NetSqlSetup project.

As shown in Figure 13.9, there are five main configuration properties:

◆ **Output file name**—Specifies the name of the output file for the installation package (.msi file).

◆ **Package files**—Specifies how to package the files. The options are As Loose Uncompressed Files, In Setup File, and In Cabinet File(s). If the In Cabinet File(s) option is selected, then you can also specify the maximum size of the .cab files.

◆ **Bootstrapper**—Specifies whether any bootstrap file needs to be created for launching the installation program. A bootstrap is required when the target machine does not have the Windows Installer service already installed. The None option generates only the installation package (.msi file). The Windows Installer Bootstrapper option creates a setup.exe file that is capable of installing the Windows Installer service if it is not already installed.

◆ **Compression**—Specifies whether to optimize the installation files for size or speed or whether no optimization is required. The value Optimized for Speed uses a faster compression algorithm that unpacks the files quickly at install time. A faster compression algorithm usually results in a larger installation files.

The value Optimized for Size uses a compression algorithm that runs slowly but uses tightly pack the files. If the value None is selected, no optimization is performed.

◆ **Authenticode signature**—Allows you to specify the file that contains the Authenticode certificate, the private key file, and the timestamp server URL (which is provided by the certification authority).

The output files generated can be deployed (that is, copied) to any target machine and then be installed and later uninstalled. When an application is uninstalled, all the actions performed by the installer application during the installation on the target machine are undone, leaving the target machine in its original state. You can also choose to repair or reinstall the application that was installed by clicking the Change button in the Add/Remove Programs dialog box.

REVIEW BREAK

▶ Although the .NET Framework supports XCOPY deployment, XCOPY is not sufficient for advanced deployment requirements. For advanced requirements, you should instead choose a Microsoft Windows Installer–based installation package to deploy applications.

▶ Microsoft Windows Installer 2.0 is the built-in installation and configuration service of the Windows operating system. It addition to having several advanced installation features, it also provides features such as the ability to roll back the installation process, uninstall an application, and repair a component or an application.

▶ Visual Studio .NET provides four types of deployment templates: Setup Project (for Windows-based applications), Web Setup Project (for Web-based applications), Merge Module Project (for shared components and assemblies), and CAB Project (for ActiveX components to be downloaded over the Internet). It also provides the Setup Wizard, which helps in creating installation packages for any of these deployment projects.

Customizing Setup Projects

Deploy a Windows-based application:

• Use setup and deployment projects.

When you are creating a professional application, you don't want the user to have to navigate to the installation folder to run the application. You instead want to create menu options and shortcuts in the target machine so that the end user can easily run the application. You might also like the installation program to provide different custom features and actions while performing installation.

Visual Studio .NET provides several different editors to customize various aspects of the installation process:

◆ File System Editor

◆ Registry Editor

◆ File Types Editor

◆ User Interface Editor

◆ Custom Actions Editor

◆ Launch Conditions Editor

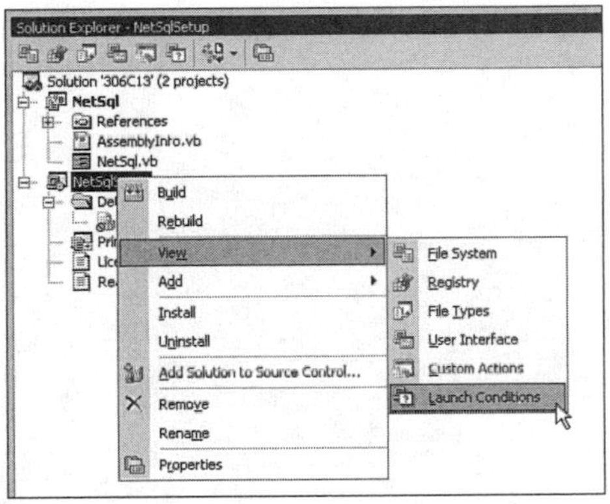

FIGURE 13.10
You can launch various editors for a setup project via the Solution Explorer.

You can view an editor by either choosing its icon from the Solution Explorer or by right-clicking a project in the Solution Explorer and then selecting View and the respective editor option from the shortcut menu, as shown in Figure 13.10.

Using the File System Editor

The File System Editor provides a mapping of the file system on the target machine. Each folder is referred to with special names that are converted to represent the folder on the target machine during the installation process. For example, the special folder User's Desktop will be converted to the actual desktop path on the target machine at the time of installation.

You can add special folders by selecting the File System on Target Machine node in the left pane of the File System Editor and choosing the Add Special Folder option from the context menu.

There are many options for special folders, such as Application Folder, Common Files Folder, Program Files Folder, User's Desktop, System Folder, User's Startup Folder, and many others, each of which represents a particular folder on the target machine.

In Step By Step 13.3, you will add menu items to the Windows program menu to launch the application and display the contents of the Readme.rtf file. You will also create a shortcut to the application on the user's desktop and associate icons with the menu items and shortcuts.

STEP BY STEP

13.3 Using the File System Editor

1. Select the NetSqlSetup project in the Solution Explorer. Right-click the project node and select Add, File from the context menu. the Add Files dialog box appears. Add two icon files to represent the NetSql application and the Readme file.

2. Right-click the NetSqlSetup project in the Solution Explorer and select View, File System. Select Application Folder under the File System on Target Machine node in the left pane of the editor.

3. Right-click Primary Output from NetSql (Active) and select Create Shortcut to Primary Output from NetSql (Active), as shown in Figure 13.11. Alternatively, you can select Primary Output from NetSql (Active) and then select Action, Create Shortcut to Primary Output from NetSql (Active) from the Visual Studio .NET menu. Rename the Shortcut Run NetSql.

FIGURE 13.11
Creating shortcuts via the File System Editor.

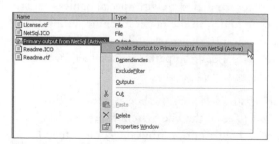

4. Move the shortcut you just created to the `User's Desktop` folder, either by dragging and dropping or by choosing Cut and then Paste from the context menu.

5. Open the Properties window for the shortcut and select the `Icon` property. Click the ellipsis (...) button. The Icon dialog box appears.

6. Click the Browse button in the Icon dialog box. The Select Item in Project dialog box appears. Select `NetSql.ico` from the Application Folder list, as shown in Figure 13.12. Click OK. Select the icon from the Current Icon box, as shown in Figure 13.13, and click OK.

7. Right-click the `User's Programs Menu` folder in the left pane of the editor and select Add, Folder. Rename the new folder `NetSql`.

8. Create shortcuts for the `Readme.rtf` file and Primary Output from NetSql (Active). Move the shortcuts to the newly created folder `NetSql` under the `User's Programs Menu` folder. Name the newly created shortcuts `Read Me` and `Run NetSql`, respectively.

9. Set the `Icon` properties of the new shortcuts to `ReadMe.ico` and `NetSql.ico`, following steps 5 and 6.

10. Build the `NetSqlSetup` project. Right-click the project in the Solution Explorer and select the Install option. Install the project.

11. The desktop should now contain a shortcut to run the `NetSql` application, with an icon attached to the shortcut. Double-click the shortcut to verify that it works as expected.

12. Select Start, Programs, NetSql. The shortcuts named `Read Me` and `NetSql` appear as options in the menu. Click them to verify that they work as desired.

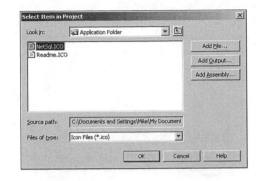

FIGURE 13.12
The Select an Item in Project dialog box.

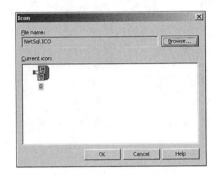

FIGURE 13.13
The Icon dialog box.

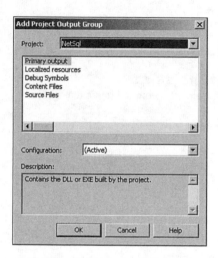

FIGURE 13.14
The Add Project Output Group dialog box.

GUIDED PRACTICE
EXERCISE 13.1

In this exercise, you will create a setup project by using the Setup Project template rather than the Setup Wizard. The project will install the NetSql application and create shortcuts for the NetSql executable file and the Readme.rtf file on the user's desktop.

This exercise will give you practice in creating setup projects using the Setup Project template. You should first attempt this exercise on your own. If you would later like to see one of the possible solutions, follow these steps:

1. In the Solution Explorer window, right-click the solution and select Add, New Project. Select Setup and Deployment Projects from the Project Types tree and then select Setup Project from the list of templates on the right. Name the project GuidedPracticeExercise13-1.

2. In the Solution Explorer window, right-click the project and select Add, Project Output from the context menu. The Add Project Output Group dialog box appears, as shown in Figure 13.14. Select NetSql as the project and select Primary Output from the list box. Click OK.

3. Right-click the project and select Add, File from the context menu. The Add Files dialog box appears. Navigate to the NetSql project folder and add the Readme.rtf file.

4. Open the File System Editor by clicking the File System Editor icon in the Solution Explorer. Select Application Folder under the File System on Target Machine node in the left pane of the editor.

5. Right-click the Readme.rtf file and select Create Shortcut to Readme.rtf. Rename the shortcut Read Me. Move the shortcut you just created to the User's Desktop folder.

6. Add another shortcut to Primary Output from NetSql (Active) and move it to the User's Desktop folder.

7. Select the new project in the Solution Explorer. Activate the Properties window. Set Manufacturer to NetSql SoftwareGPE and set ProductName to NetSqlGPE.

8. Build the `GuidedPracticeExercise13_1` project. Right-click the project in the Solution Explorer and select the Install option. Install the project.

9. The desktop now contains two shortcuts to the `NetSql` application and the `Readme` file. Double-click the shortcuts to verify that they work as expected.

Using the Registry Editor

The Registry Editor allows you to specify Registry keys, subkeys, and values that are added to the Registry in the target machine during installation. You can also use the Registry Editor to import Registry files. Importing a Registry file can merge an entire set of Registry keys in a single operation, rather than require you to create them one by one.

STEP BY STEP

13.4 Using the Registry Editor

1. Select the `NetSqlSetup` project in the Solution Explorer. Open the Registry Editor by clicking the Registry Editor icon in the Solution Explorer.

2. In the left pane, select the `HKEY_LOCAL_MACHINE` node, then select `Software`, and then select `[Manufacturer]`. Right-click the selected node and select New, DWORD Value, as shown in Figure 13.15. Name the key value `FreeWare`. Change the `Value` property of the `FreeWare` key to 1 in the Properties window.

3. Build the `NetSqlSetup` project. Right-click the project in the Solution Explorer and select the Install option. Install the project.

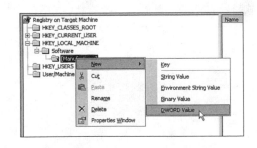

FIGURE 13.15
Adding Registry keys via the Registry Editor.

continues

continued

4. Select Start, Run and type regedit in the Open text box. Click OK. The Registry Editor launches. In the left pane of the editor, select MyComputer, HKEY_LOCAL_MACHINE, Software, NetSql Software to view the FreeWare value that you added, as shown in Figure 13.16.

FIGURE 13.16
Viewing the Registry key value added in the Registry Editor.

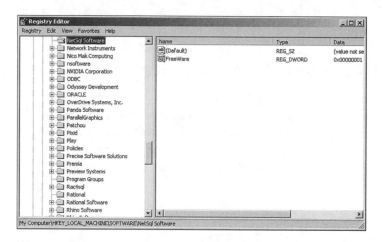

> **WARNING**
>
> **Working with the Registry**   Be extra careful when working with the Windows Registry. Take special care with the DeleteAtUninstall property of the Registry. Setting DeleteAtUninstall to True for the wrong key (such as HKEY_LOCAL_MACHINE\ SOFTWARE), for example, might have very bad consequences for your computer.

Using the File Types Editor

The File Types Editor provides the facility to associate file extensions and actions with an application. For example, files with the extension qry and the open action of the file can be associated with the NetSql application, so that the application is launched whenever the user opens a .qry file. Step By Step 13.5 shows you how.

STEP BY STEP

13.5 Using the File Types Editor

1. Select the NetSqlSetup project in the Solution Explorer. Open the File Types Editor by clicking the File Types Editor icon in the Solution Explorer.

2. Select the `File Types on Target Machine` node and choose Action, Add File Type. Open the Properties window, select the `Command` property, and click the ellipsis (…) button. The Select Item in Project dialog box appears. Select `Primary Output from NetSql (Active)` from the `Application Folder` node and click OK.

3. Change the `Name` property to `QueryFiles`, the `Description` property to `Query Files`, and the `Extensions` property to `qry;sql` in the Properties window for the newly added file type, as shown in Figure 13.17.

4. Build the `NetSqlSetup` project. Right-click the project in the Solution Explorer and select the Install option. Install the project.

5. Create a new file with the following SQL SELECT statement:

```
SELECT * FROM EMPLOYEES
```

6. Save the file to the desktop, with a `qry` or `sql` extension. Open the file from the desktop. The file launches the `NetSql` application. Interestingly, the text box in the application contains the query stored in the file. This happens because of the query member declaration and the code you added in the `Load` event handler of the `NetSql.vb` class in Step By Step 13.1.

FIGURE 13.17
Associating file types via the File Types Editor.

The `Command` property specifies the executable file to be invoked when an action occurs on the file with one of the specified extensions. By default the Open action, with the verb `open`, is added to the file type. You can also add custom actions by using different verbs, such as `print` and `edit`.

Using the User Interface Editor

The User Interface Editor allows you to customize the user interface that is provided to the user during the installation process. The *user interface* is the various dialog boxes that appear during the installation process. The user interface provided to the user is divided into three stages: start, progress, and end. You can add different types of dialog boxes for each stage. Each stage allows only certain types of dialog boxes to be added.

> **NOTE**
>
> **The LicenseFile and ReadmeFile Properties** The LicenseFile and ReadmeFile properties of the User Interface dialog box only work with Rich Text Format (RTF) files. If you specify a file of any other format, you won't get any error message, but the contents of the file will not be displayed.

The User Interface Editor displays the user interface that is applicable to both end-user installation and administrative installation. You can customize the user interface for both types of installations. The administrative installation occurs when you run the MSIEXEC command-line tool with the /a option. You will find more details about administrative installation later in the chapter.

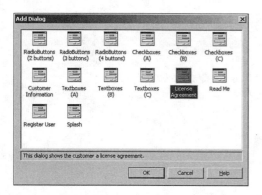

FIGURE 13.18
The Add Dialog dialog box, for adding dialog boxes in the User Interface Editor.

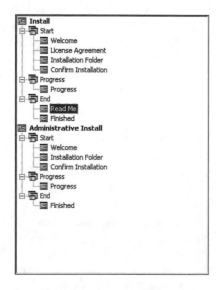

FIGURE 13.19
Customizing the user interface of the installation program via the User Interface Editor.

STEP BY STEP

13.6 Using the User Interface Editor

1. Select the NetSqlSetup project in the Solution Explorer. Open the User Interface Editor by clicking the User Interface Editor icon in the Solution Explorer.

2. Right-click the Start node under the Install tree and select Add Dialog from the context menu. The Add Dialog dialog box appears. Select License Agreement, as shown in Figure 13.18. Click OK. Right-click License Agreement and choose Move Up twice to move the License Agreement dialog box to appear directly after the Welcome dialog box. Select the LicenseFile property in the Properties window, Select (Browse...) from the drop-down list. The Select Item in Project dialog box appears. Navigate to the Application folder and select License.rtf.

3. Add a Read Me dialog box to the End node under the Install tree. Move the Read Me dialog box before the Finished dialog box. The dialog boxes should appear in the User Interface Editor as shown in Figure 13.19. Set the ReadmeFile property to Readme.rtf.

4. Build the NetSqlSetup project. Right-click the project in the Solution Explorer and select the Install option. Install the project. A License Agreement screen appears. When you select I Agree, the Next button is enabled, as shown in Figure 13.20. The Read Me screen then appears, before the Close screen is shown.

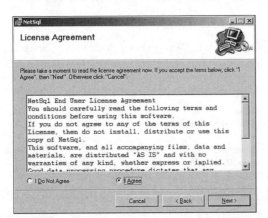

FIGURE 13.20
The License Agreement screen, which appears during the installation process.

Using the Custom Actions Editor

The Custom Actions Editor allows you to run compiled DLL or EXE files or assemblies at the end of the installation. These files can be used to perform custom actions that are vital but were not carried out during the installation. If a custom action fails, the entire installation process is rolled back. For example, you might have to install the database required by your application during the installation process.

There are four phases in which custom action can be performed: install, commit, rollback, and uninstall. In Step By Step 13.7 you will create a simple custom action to launch the NetSql application when the installation ends.

STEP BY STEP

13.7 Using the Custom Actions Editor

1. In the Solution Explorer window, right-click Solution and select Add, New Project. Select the Visual Basic Projects node from the Project Types tree and then select Empty Project from the list of templates on the right. Name the project LaunchNetSql.

2. Right-click the new project in the Solution Explorer and select Add, Add Module from the context menu. Name the module LaunchNetSql.vb.

continues

continued

3. Right-click the References node in the Solution Explorer and select Add Reference. Add a reference to System.dll.

4. Modify the class definition so that it looks like this:

```
Imports System
Imports System.Diagnostics

Module LaunchNetSql
    Public Sub Main()
        ' Create a ProcessStartInfo object
        Dim psi As System.Diagnostics.ProcessStartInfo = _
        New ProcessStartInfo()
        Dim args() As String = _
        Environment.GetCommandLineArgs
        Dim intI As Integer
        Dim strTemp As String = ""
        ' May need to concatenate args together if there
        ' are spaces in the path to the file
        If UBound(args, 1) > 0 Then
            For intI = 1 To UBound(args)
                strTemp = strTemp & " " & args(intI)
            Next
            psi.FileName = strTemp.Trim() & "NetSql.exe "
            Process.Start(psi)
        End If
    End Sub
End Module
```

NOTE

The Process and ProcessInfo Classes
I'll discuss the Process and ProcessInfo classes in detail in Chapter 14, "Maintaining and Supporting a Windows Application."

5. Right-click the LaunchNetSql project in the Solution Explorer and select Properties. The Property Pages dialog box appears. In the left pane select the General node under the Common Properties tree. Set the Output Type property to Windows Application. Click OK. Build the LaunchNetSql project.

6. In the Solution Explorer window, right-click the NetSqlSetup project and select Add, Project Output from the context menu. The Add Project Output Group dialog box appears. Select LaunchNetSql as project and select Primary Output from the list box. Click OK.

7. Select the NetSqlSetup project in the Solution Explorer. Open the Custom Actions Editor by clicking the Custom Actions Editor icon in the Solution Explorer.

8. Select the `Install` node under the `Custom Actions` tree. Select Action, Add Custom Action. The Select Item in Project dialog box appears. Navigate to the `Application` folder and select Primary Output from LaunchNetSql (Active). Rename the action `LaunchNetSql`.

9. Select the custom action `LaunchNetSql` and open the Properties window. Set the `Arguments` property to `[TARGETDIR]` and the `InstallerClass` property to `False`, as shown in Figure 13.21.

10. Build the `NetSqlSetup` project. Right-click the project in the Solution Explorer and select the Install option. Install the project. The `NetSql` application is launched after the installation process is completed.

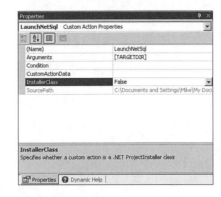

FIGURE 13.21
Adding custom actions via the Custom Actions Editor.

In Step By Step 13.7, the `Arguments` property is used to pass any command-line arguments to the custom action that is launched. This property is set to the Windows Installer property `[TARGETDIR]`, which maps to the directory where the application is installed on the target machine. This argument is passed to the `LaunchNetSql` application so that it knows the path of the `NetSql` application. Note that the `InstallerClass` property is set to `False`. This is because the `LaunchNetSql` class does not inherit from the `Installer` class. The .NET Framework provides the `Installer` class to provide a base for custom installations. I'll talk more about the `Installer` class later in the chapter.

Using the Launch Conditions Editor

The Launch Conditions Editor allows you to set conditions to be evaluated when the installation begins on the target machine. If the conditions are not met, the installation stops. For example, say you would like to install your Visual Basic .NET application only if the .NET Framework Common Language Runtime exists on the target machine. This condition is by default added by Visual Studio .NET. You might also need to perform other checks, such as whether a particular file exists on the target machine or whether a particular Registry key value exists on the target machine.

The Launch Conditions Editor allows you to perform searches on a target machine for a file, in a Registry key, or on Windows Installer components. For example, you can determine whether the Microsoft Data Access Components (MDAC) is installed on the target machine by searching in the Registry for a particular Registry key value.

You can add conditions to be evaluated for the search performed on the target machine. If the conditions fail, the installation ends. For example, you can add a condition that the MDAC installed should be 2.7 or higher in order for the installation to continue, by checking against the Registry key value retrieved by the Registry search. You'll learn how to do this in Step By Step 13.8.

STEP BY STEP

13.8 Using the Launch Conditions Editor

1. Select the `NetSqlSetup` project in the Solution Explorer. Open the Launch Conditions Editor by clicking the Launch Conditions Editor icon in the Solution Explorer.

2. Select the `Requirements on Target Machine` node and select Action, Add Registry Launch Condition. Two nodes are added, one under the `Search Target Machine` node and another under the `Launch Conditions` node.

3. Select the newly created node under the `Search Target Machine` node and open the Properties window. Set the `Name` property to `Search for MDAC Support`, the `Property` property to `MDACSUPPORT`, the `Root` property to `vsdrrHKLM`, the `RegKey` property to `Software\Microsoft\DataAccess`, and the `Value` property to `FullInstallVer`, as shown in Figure 13.22.

4. Select the newly created node under the `Launch Conditions` node and open the Properties window. Set the `Name` property to `MDACSupport`, the `Condition` property to `MDACSUPPORT >= "2.7"`, and the `Message` property to `You must have MDAC version 2.7 or higher installed on this computer. Please contact the administrator for installation information.`, as shown in Figure 13.23.

FIGURE 13.22
Adding a Registry search via the Launch Conditions Editor.

FIGURE 13.23
Adding a launch condition via the Launch Conditions Editor.

5. Build the NetSqlSetup project. Right-click the project in the Solution Explorer and select the Install option. Install the project. If the target computer does not have MDAC 2.7 or higher installed, the installation process of the NetSql project fails. Instead, you get the error message set in the Message property of the launch condition.

> **NOTE**
>
> **The Condition Property** Setup and deployment project editor elements—such as folders, files, Registry keys, custom actions, and launch conditions—have a Condition property. The Condition property consists of a valid conditional statement in the form of a string that evaluates to either True or False.
>
> The conditional statement is executed during installation, and if it returns True, the action associated with that particular element is performed on the target machine. For example, a condition is applied to the Registry key value, and if it evaluates to False during installation, that particular key value will not be entered in the Registry on the target machine.

GUIDED PRACTICE
EXERCISE 13.2

In this exercise, you will add a few sample files to the NetSqlSetup project and then provide an option to include or omit installation of sample files on the target machine. You will use the User Interface Editor to provide the user interface to select or deselect this option. You will use the Condition properties of the files to check whether the sample option is selected by the end user.

This exercise will give you practice in how to perform conditional deployment. You should first attempt this exercise on your own. If you would later like to see one of the possible solutions, follow these steps:

1. Open the NetSql project in the Solution Explorer.

2. Add a sample query file, CustomersFromBrazil.sql, with the following text, to the NetSql project:

```
SELECT *
FROM Customers
WHERE Country = 'Brazil'
ORDER BY CompanyName
```

continues

continued

3. Add another sample query file,
   `TenMostExpensiveProducts.qry`, with the following text, to the
   `NetSql` project:

   ```
   SELECT TOP 10
   Products.ProductName AS
   TenMostExpensiveProducts,
   Products.UnitPrice
   FROM Products
   ORDER BY Products.UnitPrice DESC
   ```

4. Open the File System Editor of the `NetSqlSetup` project. Select
   `Application Folder` and then select Add, Folder from the context menu. Rename the newly added folder `Samples`.

5. Select the `Samples` folder and choose Add, File option from the
   context menu. The Add Files dialog box appears. Navigate to
   the sample query files created in the previous steps and add
   them to the `Samples` folder.

6. Open the User Interface Editor of the `NetSqlSetup` project.
   Right-click the `Start` node under the `Install` tree and select
   Add Dialog from the context menu. The Add Dialog dialog
   box appears. Select Radio Buttons (2 Buttons). Click OK.
   Place the newly added dialog box in between the License
   Agreement and Installation Folder dialog boxes.

7. Set the properties `BannerText` to `NetSql Samples`, `BodyText` to
   `Do you want to install samples?`, `Button1Label` to `Yes`,
   `Button1Value` to `1`, `Button2Label` to `No`, `Button2Value` to `2`,
   `ButtonProperty` to `NETSQLSAMPLES`, and `DefaultValue` to `1`, as
   shown in Figure 13.24.

8. Open the File System Editor and select the `Samples` folder.
   Change the `Condition` properties of both the sample files to
   `NETSQLSAMPLES=1`.

9. Build the `NetSqlSetup` project. Right-click the project in the
   Solution Explorer and select the Install option. Install the project. The NetSql Samples dialog box is displayed during the
   installation process, with the Yes option selected, as shown in
   the Figure 13.25.

FIGURE 13.24
Properties of the Radio Buttons dialog box.

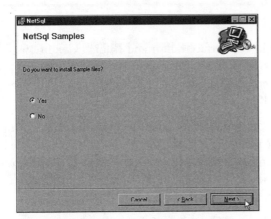

FIGURE 13.25
The NetSql Samples dialog box appears during the installation process.

10. If you choose the option Yes in the NetSql Samples dialog box, sample files appear in the `Samples` folder, under the installation folder (that is, `C:\Program Files\NetSql Software\NetSql\Samples`, if you did not change the folder during installation). On the other hand, if you choose the No option in the NetSql Samples dialog box, the `Samples` folder and the sample files are not installed.

R E V I E W   B R E A K

▶ The File System Editor provides a mapping of the file system on the target machine. The folders are referred to by special names that during the installation process are converted to represent the folders as per the file system on the target machine.

▶ The Registry Editor allows you to specify Registry keys, sub keys, and values that are added to the Registry on the target machine during installation.

▶ The File Types Editor allows you to register one or more file extensions with a Windows application.

▶ The User Interface Editor allows you to customize the user interface that is provided to the user during the installation process. Different types of user interfaces are available for end user installation and administrative installation.

continues

continued

▶ The User Interface Editor and Launch Conditions Editor elements provide special properties (such as `Property` and `ButtonProperty`), whose value can be evaluated to perform the installation according to the end user's choice.

▶ The Custom Actions Editor allows you to add custom actions to be performed during the installation process. It allows you to run `.dll`, `.exe`, `assembly`, and `scripts` files. Custom actions can be performed during four phases: install, commit, rollback, and uninstall.

▶ The Launch Conditions Editor allows you to set conditions to be evaluated when the installation begins on the target machine. If these conditions are not met, the installation stops.

SHARED ASSEMBLIES

Add assemblies to the Global Assembly Cache.

In Chapter 4 I briefly discuss shared assemblies. In this section I will explore more about shared assemblies and how to deploy them.

A shared assembly is shared among multiple applications on a machine. It is therefore stored at a central location, called the GAC, and enjoys special services, such as file security, shared location, and side-by-side versioning.

Because shared assemblies are all installed at a central location, distingushing them with just a filename is not enough. You would not like your application to break when some other vendor installs an assembly with the same name in the GAC. To avoid this possibility, Microsoft requires you to assign a strong name to each assembly before placing it in the GAC.

Assigning a Strong Name to an Assembly

An assembly is identified by its text name (usually the name of the file, without the file extension), version number, and culture information.

However, these pieces of information do not guarantee that an assembly will be unique. There might be a case in which two software publishers use the same identity for an assembly, thereby causing applications that use those assemblies to behave abnormally. You can greatly reduce the possibility of this problem occurring by assigning a strong name to an assembly. A strong name strengthens an assembly's identity by qualifying it with the software publisher's identity. The .NET Framework uses a standard cryptography technique known as *digital signing* to ensure uniqueness of an assembly.

The process of digital signing involves two related pieces of binary data: the public key and the private key. The *public key* represents the software publisher's identity and is freely distributed. While you are creating a strongly named assembly, the public key is stored in the assembly manifest, along with other identification information, such as the name, version number, and culture of the assembly. This scheme is not foolproof because, after all, the public key is available freely, and nobody can stop a software publisher from using some other company's public key. To verify that only the legitimate owner of the public key has created the assembly, an assembly is signed with the publisher's private key. The *private key* is assumed to be only known to the publisher of the assembly. The processes of signing an assembly and verifying its signature work like this:

◆ **Signing an assembly**—You create a signature computing a cryptographic hash from the contents of the assembly. The hash is encoded with the private key. This signature is then stored within the assembly.

◆ **Verifying the signature**—When the Common Language Runtime verifies an assembly's identity, it reads the public key from the assembly manifest and uses it to decrypt the cryptographic hash that is stored in the assembly. It then recalculates the hash for the current contents of the assembly. If the two hashes match, this it ensures two things: the contents of the assembly were not tampered with after the assembly was signed and only the party that has a private key associated with the public key stored in the assembly has signed the assembly.

You can easily generate public/private key pairs by using the Strong Name tool (sn.exe), which is available in the .NET Framework SDK.

NOTE

Signing a Multifile Assembly If an assembly consist of multiple files, just the file containing the assembly manifest needs to be signed. This is because the assembly manifest already contains file hashes for all the files that constitute the assembly implementation. You can easily determine whether a file is tampered with by matching its actual hash with what is stored in the assembly manifest.

STEP BY STEP

13.9 Creating a Public/Private Key Pair, Using the Strong Name Tool (`sn.exe`)

1. From the Visual Studio .NET program group in the Windows Start menu, launch the Visual Studio .NET command prompt.

2. Issue the following command to create a pair of public/private keys:

```
sn -k RandNumCorpKeys.snk
```

3. Both the public and private keys are created and stored in a file named `RandNumCorpKeys.snk`, as shown in Figure 13.26. Note the directory where this file is created, because you will be using it in Step By Step 13.10.

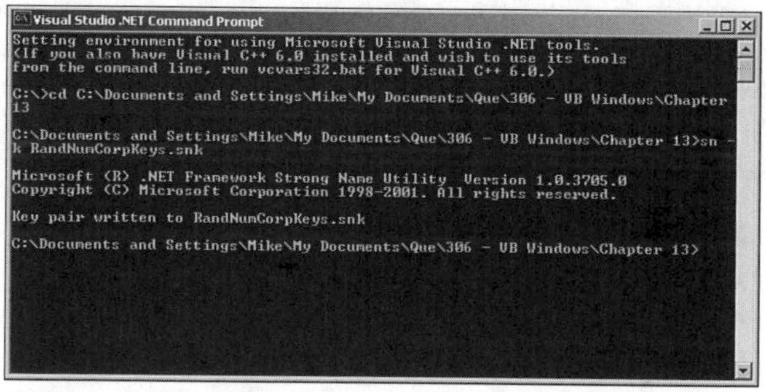

FIGURE 13.26

Creating a public/private key pair by using the Strong Name tool.

In Step By Step 13.10 you will create a strongly named assembly, and you will use the key file generated in Step By Step 13.9 to digitally sign the assembly.

STEP BY STEP

13.10 Creating a Component with a Strong Name

1. Create a new Visual Basic .NET Class Library project in solution `306C13`. Name the project `RandomNumberGenerator`.

2. Add a component class to the project and name it RandomNumberGenerator.vb. Delete Class1.vb.

3. Switch to the Code view. Add a reference to System.Drawing.dll and insert the following code at the top of the module:

```
Imports System.Drawing
```

4. Add an icon for the component and name it RandomNumberGenerator.bmp. Set its Build Action property to Embedded Resources.

5. Add the following attribute just before the class declaration to set the Toolbox icon:

```
<ToolboxBitmap(GetType(RandomNumberGenerator))> _
```

6. Add the following code after the Component Designer Generated Code section:

```
Private mminValue As Integer = 1
Private mmaxValue As Integer = 100

Public Property MinValue() As Integer
    Get
        MinValue = mminValue
    End Get
    Set(ByVal Value As Integer)
        mminValue = Value
    End Set
End Property

Public Property MaxValue() As Integer
    Get
        MaxValue = mmaxValue
    End Get
    Set(ByVal Value As Integer)
        mmaxValue = Value
    End Set
End Property

Public Function GetRandomNumber() As Integer
    Dim r As Random = New Random()
    GetRandomNumber = r.Next(MinValue, MaxValue)
End Function
```

7. Add to this project the RandNumCorpKeys.snk file that was generated in Step By Step 13.9.

continues

continued

8. Open the `AssemblyInfo.vb` file. Scroll down the file and change the `AssemblyVersion` and `AssemblyKeyFile` attributes as shown here:

```
<Assembly: AssemblyVersion("1.0")>
<Assembly: AssemblyKeyFile("..\..\RandNumCorpKeys.snk")>
```

9. Build the project. The file `RandomNumberGenerator.dll` is generated, and a strong name is assigned to it based on the specified key file.

Note that in Step By Step 13.10 you changed the `AssemblyVersion` attribute of the assembly from `1.0.*` to `1.0`. The assembly's version consists of up to four parts:

```
<major>.<minor>.<build>.<revision>
```

If you want to use a fixed value, you can hard-code it. The default value of the version uses an asterisk in place of the build and revision numbers. This changes the build and revision each time you compile the project. The build will be calculated as the number of days since January 1, 2000, and the revision will be calculated as the number of seconds since midnight modulo 2.

At runtime the CLR will use this information to load the assembly. In next few examples, you will frequently compile the projects, thereby changing the version of the assembly if you use the default version property. The GAC allows you to install multiple versions of the same assembly. For this chapter, you will hard-code the version of the application's assembly to keep matters simple.

In Step By Step 13.10 you used Visual Studio .NET to attach a strong name to an assembly. If you want to do this manually, you can use the Assembly Linker tool (`al.exe`) with the `-keyfile` option.

Adding an Assembly to the GAC

After you have associated a strong name with an assembly, you can place the assembly in the GAC. There are several ways you can add an assembly to the GAC. Using the Windows Installer is the recommended approach, but there are some quick alternatives, too.

However, you should use these quick approaches only for development purpose; they are not recommended for installing assemblies on the end user's computer.

Using Windows Installer

Using Microsoft Windows Installer is the preferred way of adding assemblies to the GAC. Windows Installer maintains reference counts for assemblies in the GAC and provides uninstallation support. I will tell you how to add assemblies using Windows Installer technology through the setup and deployment projects of Visual Stuido .NET a little later in this chapter.

Using Windows Explorer

When the .NET Framework is installed, the Assembly Cache Viewer Shell extension (shfusion.dll) is also installed. This extension allows you to view the complex structure of the GAC folder in a navigable and understandable manner. Because it is integrated with Windows Shell, you can view and manage the GAC's contents with the help of Windows Explorer.

STEP BY STEP

13.11 Adding an Assembly to the GAC by Using Windows Explorer

1. Open Windows Explorer. Navigate to the assembly cache folder, which is usually `c:\WINNT\assembly` or `C:\Windows\assembly` (see Figure 13.27).

2. Using Windows Explorer, drag the `RandomNumberGenerator.dll` file created in Step By Step 13.10 and drop it in the assembly cache folder.

3. In the assembly cache folder, select Properties from the shortcut menu of `RandomNumberGenerator.dll`. The Properties dialog box appears, as shown in Figure 13.28.

> **NOTE**
>
> **Working with the GAC** You need to have administrative privileges on a computer in order to manage its GAC.

> **NOTE**
>
> **The Assembly Cache Folder** The assembly cache folder actually contains two caches, the GAC and the Native Image Cache. When you view the assembly cache folder using Windows Explorer, the Assembly Cache Viewer Shell extension shows you a combined list of both caches. You can identify whether the assembly is from the GAC or from the Native Image Cache by looking at the Type field in the list. When you add an assembly to this folder by using Windows Explorer, the assembly is added to the GAC. You will learn about the Native Image Cache and how to add assemblies to it later in this chapter.

FIGURE 13.27
The Assembly Cache Viewer Shell extension enables you to view and manage the contents of the assembly cache by using Windows Explorer.

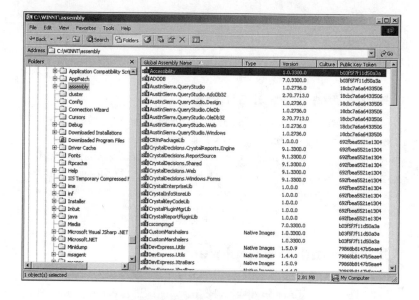

FIGURE 13.28
Viewing properties of the RandomNumberGenerator assembly installed in the GAC.

If you want to remove a file from the GAC, you just delete it from Windows Explorer by selecting File, Delete or by selecting Delete from the shortcut menu.

Using the .NET Framework Configuration Tool

You can use the .NET Framework Configuration tool (`mscorcfg.msc`) to manage assemblies in the GAC. Step By Step 13.12 guides you through the process of adding an assembly by using .NET Framework Configuration tool.

STEP BY STEP

13.12 Adding an Assembly to the GAC by Using the .NET Framework Configuration Tool

1. Open the Administrative Tools section of the Windows Control Panel. Open the tool named Microsoft .NET Framework Configuration. Select the `Assembly Cache` folder in the left pane under the `My Computer` node (see Figure 13.29).

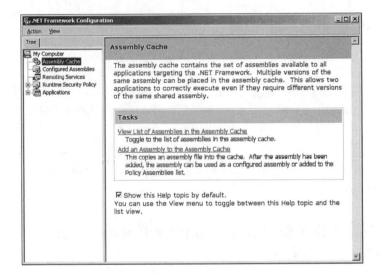

FIGURE 13.29
The .NET Framework Configuration tool allows you to manage the GAC.

2. In the right pane, click the hyperlink title Add an Assembly to the Assembly Cache. The Add an Assembly dialog box appears. Navigate to the file `RandomNumberGenerator.dll` in the `RandomNumberGenerator` project and click the OK button.

3. Click the other hyperlink titled, View List of Assemblies in the Assembly Cache. A list of installed assemblies appears. Ensure that `RandonNumberGenerator` is in this list, as shown in Figure 13.30.

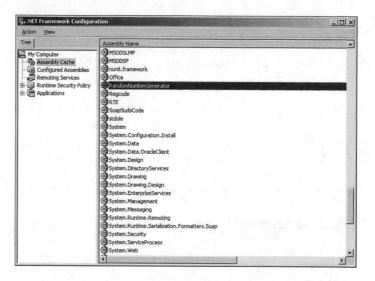

To uninstall an assembly by using the .NET Framework
Configuration tool, you just select Action, Delete or select Delete
from the assembly's shortcut menu.

In addition to helping you add or remove assemblies, this tool also
helps you configure an assembly and manage its runtime security
policy.

Using the Global Assembly Cache Tool (gacutil.exe)

gacutil.exe is a command-line tool that is specially useful for adding
and removing assemblies from the GAC via a program script or a
batch file.

STEP BY STEP

13.13 Adding an Assembly to the GAC by Using the Global Assembly Cache Tool

1. From the Visual Studio .NET program group in the
Windows Start menu, launch the Visual Studio .NET
command prompt.

2. Change the directory to the folder where the
   `RandomNumberGenerator.dll` file resides in the
   `RandomNumberGenerator` project—in this case, the project's
   `bin` directory.

3. Issue the following command to install the assembly to
   the GAC, as shown in Figure 13.31:

```
gacutil /i RandomNumberGenerator.dll
```

FIGURE 13.31
Adding an assembly to the GAC by using the
Global Assembly Cache tool.

You can list all the assemblies in the GAC by using the `gacutil.exe`
tool with the `/l` option. You can use the `/u` option with the name of
the assembly (without the file extension) to uninstall the assembly
from the GAC:

```
gacutil /u RandomNumberGenerator
```

You can also choose to uninstall from the GAC an assembly of a specific version and specific culture by specifying its version, culture,
and public key, along with the name of the assembly:

```
gacutil /u RandomNumberGenerator,Version=1.0.0.0,
➥Culture=neutral,PublicKeyToken=f26af4dbb33881b1
```

Referencing an Assembly from the GAC

Normally when you reference an assembly in a Windows application
project, you can invoke the Add Reference dialog box and browse to
the desired assembly. But after you have added an assembly to the
GAC, this approach does not work. This is because the GAC has a
complex structure that cannot be directly enumerated by the Add
Reference dialog box.

When you view the GAC by using the tools mentioned in the previous section, you see an abstraction of its structure. If you instead switch to the command prompt and change the directory to the GAC folder, you see that the GAC is actually made up of various subdirectories, one for each assembly. Each of these directories has subdirectories, whose names depend on the assembly's version and public key. Finally, each subdirectory stores the actual assembly file with some additional assembly information. Figure 13.32 shows how the GAC entry is made for the RandomNumberGenerator component on my computer.

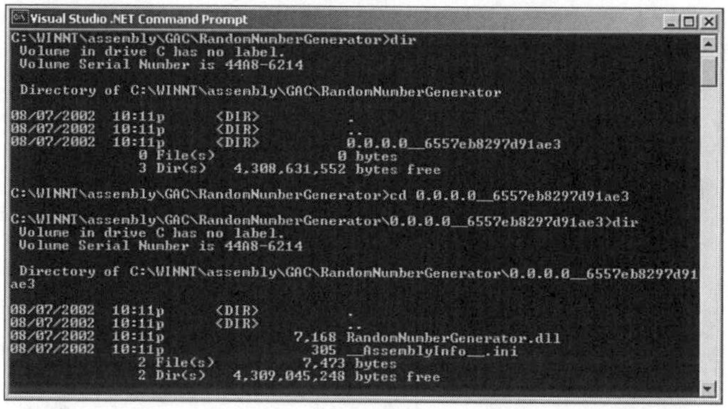

FIGURE 13.32
Exploring the GAC by using the Command window.

A good practice is to keep a copy of the assemblies installed in the GAC somewhere outside the GAC, where it is easily accessible via a pathname. You can then easily reference these assemblies through the Add Reference dialog box by browsing to that path. In fact, the .NET Framework uses the same techniques for all the assemblies stored in the GAC. It also stores a copy of those files in the folder where the .NET Framework is installed.

Step By Step 13.4 shows how to instruct Visual Studio .NET to add assemblies stored in a custom folder to its Add Reference dialog box.

STEP BY STEP

13.14 Displaying an Assembly in the Add Reference Dialog Box

1. Open the Registry Editor by launching `Regedit.exe` from the Run dialog box (which you access by selecting Start, Run).

2. In the Registry Editor, browse to the key named
`HKEY_LOCAL_MACHINE\SOFTWARE\Microsoft\.NETFramework\`
`AssemblyFolders`.

3. Create a new key and name it `MyAssemblies`.

4. Double-click the default value in this key and change its
value data to the location of `RandomNumberGenerator.dll`
in the `bin\Release` folder of the `RandomNumberGenerator`
project, as shown in Figure 13.33.

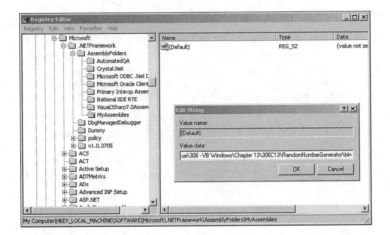

FIGURE 13.33
Setting the default value via the Edit String
dialog box.

5. Close the Registry Editor and close all instances of Visual
Studio .NET.

Step By Step 13.15 shows how to create a small Windows application that loads the components that you just installed in the GAC.
Before starting with these steps, make sure that you have already
installed the file `RandomNumberGenerator.dll` in the GAC.

STEP BY STEP

13.15 Creating a Windows Application That Uses the RandomNumberGenerator Component

1. Add a new Visual Basic .NET Windows application project to the solution 306C13 and name it RandomNumberApplication.

2. In the Solution Explorer window, add a new form named RandomNumberApplication.vb. Delete the default form Form1.vb.

3. Using the Add Reference dialog box, add a reference to RandomNumberGenerator.dll. Set the Copy Local property of the RandomNumberGenerator.dll file to False.

4. Activate the toolbox. Click the My Custom Controls tab. Right-click the toolbox and select Customize Toolbox. Click on .NET Framework Components tab and select RandomNumberGenerator.dll.

5. Drag the RandomNumberGenerator control from the toolbox and drop it on the form. Change its MinValue property to 500 and MaxValue to 1000.

6. Add a Label control (lblResults) and a Button control (btnGenerate) to the form. Set the label's text property to empty and the button's Text property to Generate a Random Number!. Double-click the Button control to add an event handler for its Click event. Add the following code to the event handler:

```
Private Sub btnGenerate_Click( _
 ByVal sender As System.Object, _
 ByVal e As System.EventArgs) Handles btnGenerate.Click
    lblResults.Text = String.Format( _
    "The next random number is: {0}", _
    RandomNumberGenerator1.GetRandomNumber())
End Sub
```

7. Set the project RandomNumberApplication as the startup project and set the form as the startup object for the project.

8. Run the solution. A random number in the range of 500 and 1000 is generated every time you press the button, as shown in Figure 13.34.

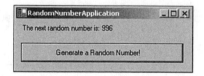

FIGURE 13.34

A form that generates random numbers by using the RandomNumberGenerator component installed in the GAC.

No matter which copy of the assembly you use to add a reference, the application will load the assembly from the GAC rather than load the copy in the application folder. To understand what I mean by this, you need to understand how the CLR locates assemblies.

How the Common Language Runtime Locates Assemblies

The CLR uses the following steps to locate an assembly:

1. It tries to determine the version of the assembly to be located. (This information may be available in the application's configuration files.)

2. It checks whether the assembly is already loaded. If the requested assembly has been loaded in one of the previous calls, it uses the already loaded assembly.

3. It checks the GAC. If the assembly is in the GAC, it loads the assembly from there.

4. If there is a <codebase> element specified in the application's configuration file, the CLR locates the assembly by using the path specified by the <codebase> element.

5. If there is no <codebase> element specified in the configuration files and if there is no culture information available for the assembly, the Common Language Runtime checks the following locations (in the order listed here) for the assembly:

```
[ApplicationBase]\[AssemblyName].dll
[ApplicationBase]\[AssemblyName]\[AssemblyName].dll
[ApplicationBase]\[PrivatePath1]\[AssemblyName].dll
[ApplicationBase]\[PrivatePath1]\[AssemblyName]\[Assem-
blyName].dll
[ApplicationBase]\[PrivatePath2]\[AssemblyName].dll
[ApplicationBase]\[PrivatePath2]\[AssemblyName]\[Assem-
blyName].dll
   .
   .
   .
```

In this case, ApplicationBase is the root directory where the application is installed. AssemblyName is the text name of the assembly. PrivatePath1, PrivatePath2, and so on are the user-defined subdirectories specified either in the application's configuration file, using the <probing> element, or via the AppendPrivatePath property for an application domain.

6. If there is no <codebase> element specified in the configuration files and if the culture information is available, the Common Language Runtime checks the following locations (in the order listed here) for the assembly:

```
[ApplicationBase]\[culture]\[AssemblyName].dll
[ApplicationBase]\[culture]\[AssemblyName]\
[AssemblyName].dll
[ApplicationBase]\[culture]\[PrivatePath1]\
[AssemblyName].dll
[ApplicationBase]\[culture]\[PrivatePath1]\
[AssemblyName]\[AssemblyName].dll
[ApplicationBase]\[culture]\[PrivatePath2]\
[AssemblyName].dll
[ApplicationBase]\[culture]\[PrivatePath2]\
[AssemblyName]\[AssemblyName].dll
.
.
.
```

In this case ApplicationBase is the root directory where the application is installed. AssemblyName is the text name of the assembly. PrivatePath1, PrivatePath2, and so on are the user-defined subdirectories specified either in the application's configuration file, using the <probing> element, or via the AppendPrivatePath property for an application domain.

In the case of an assembly that is stored in the GAC, these rules ensure that the GAC copy is always the one used.

Delay Signing an Assembly

In Step By Step 13.10, when you signed an assembly you used a key file that contained both the public key and the private key for a company. But the private key ensures that the assembly is signed only by its advertised publisher. Thus in most companies the private key is stored securely, and only a few people have access to it.

If the keys are highly protected, it might be difficult to frequently access the assembly when multiple developers of a company are building assemblies several times a day. To solve this problem, the .NET Framework uses the delay signing technique for assemblies.

When you use delay signing, you use only the public key to build an assembly. Associating public keys with an assembly allows you to place the assembly in the GAC and complete most of the development and testing tasks with the assembly.

Later, when you are ready to package the assembly, someone who is authorized can sign the assembly with the private key. Signing with the private key ensures that the CLR will provide tamper protection for the assembly. The following list summarizes the various steps involved in delay signing:

1. *Extracting a public key from the public/private key pair*—To extract the public key from a file that stores the public/private key pair, you can use the strong name tool:

   ```
   sn.exe -p RandNumCorpKeys.snk RandNumCorpPublicKey.snk
   ```

   At this stage, the `RandNumCorpPublicKey.snk` file can be freely distributed to the development team, and the `RandNumCorpKeys.snk` file that contains both the private and public keys can be stored securely (possibly on a hardware device such as a smart card).

2. *Delay signing an assembly using Visual Studio .NET*—To use delay signing in a Visual Studio .NET project, you modify the following two attributes of the project's `AssemblyInfo.vb` file and build the assembly:

   ```
   <Assembly: AssemblyDelaySign(True)>
   <Assembly: AssemblyKeyFile("RandNumCorpPublicKey.snk")>
   ```

3. *Turning off verification for an assembly in the GAC*—By default, of the GAC verifies each assembly for its strong name. If an assembly is not signed using a private key, this verification fails. For development and testing purposes, you can relax this verification for an assembly by issuing the following command:

   ```
   sn.exe -Vr RandomNumberGenerator.dll
   ```

   After you execute this command, the GAC always skips the verification for this assembly in future.

4. *Signing a delay-signed assembly with the private key*—When you are ready with the deployment of a delay-signed assembly, you need to sign it with the company's private key:

   ```
   sn.exe -R RandomNumberGenerator.dll RandNumCorpKeys.snk
   ```

5. *Turning on verification for an assembly in the GAC*—Finally, you can instruct the GAC to turn on verification for an assembly by using the following command:

   ```
   sn.exe -Vu RandomNumberGenerator.dll
   ```

Delay Signing, Using the Assembly Linker Tool

The Assembly Linker tool (al.exe) generates an assembly with an assembly manifest from the given modules or resource files. Remember that a module is a Microsoft Intermediate Language (MSIL) file without an assembly manifest.

While generating an assembly, you can also instruct the Assembly Linker tool to sign or delay sign an assembly with the given public/private key file. When you al.exe for delay signing, you use the arguments listed in Table 13.1.

TABLE 13.1

ARGUMENTS PASSED TO al.exe FOR DELAY SIGNING

Argument	Description
`<sourcefiles>`	You replace `<sourcefiles>` with the names of one or more complied modules that will be the parts of the resulting assembly.
`/delay[sign][+|-]`	You can use either the `delay` argument or the `delay[sign]` argument for delay signing. The option + is used to delay sign the assembly by storing just the public key manifest in the assembly manifest. The - option is used to fully sign an assembly by using both public and private keys. If you do not use either + or -, the default value of - is assumed.
`/keyf[ile]:<filename>`	You can use either `keyf` or `keyfile` to specify the key file. You replace `<filename>` with the name of the file that stores the key(s).
`/out:<filename>`	You replace `<filename>` with the desired name of the output assembly file.

EXAM TIP

The Strong Name and the Authenticode Signature An assembly signed with a strong name does not automatically assert a company's identity, such as its name. For that purpose you can use an Authenticode signature, in which case the company's identity is asserted by a third-party certification authority (such as Verisign or Thawte). You can use the File Signing tool (signcode.exe) to attach an authenticode signature to the assembly.

An important thing to know is the order of commands when signing an assembly using both sn.exe and signcode.exe. You must sign your assembly with the Strong Name tool (sn.exe) before you sign it with the File Signing tool (signcode.exe).

Assume that you want to create an assembly by linking two modules, Sample1.netmodule and Sample2.netmodule. The public key file is SamplePublicKey.snk and the name of the desired output assembly is SignedSample.exe. You use the al.exe command, in the following form:

```
al.exe Sample1.netmodule,Sample2.netmodule /delaysign+
➡/keyfile:SamplePublicKey.snk /out:SignedSample.exe
```

Creating a Setup Project for Distributing Components

Create a setup program that installs an application and allows for the application to be uninstalled: Register components and assemblies.

You will now see how to create a setup project for distributing a component such as the RandomNumberGenerator component. The process of packaging a component is different from the process of packaging Windows applications. When you have a component that will be shared among multiple applications, you should package it as a merge module (that is, an .msm file). A merge module includes the actual component, such as a .dll file, along with any related setup logic, such as adding resources, Registry entries, custom actions, and launch conditions.

When you modify a component to release new versions, you create a new merge module for each new version. You should create a new merge module for each successive version of a component in order to avoid version conflicts.

A merge module cannot be directly installed. Instead, when an application uses a component for which a merge module exists, the merge module is merged into the installer for the application.

STEP BY STEP

13.16 Creating a Merge Module Project by Using the Setup Wizard to Package a Shared Component for Deployment

1. In the Solution Explorer window, right-click Solution and select Add, New Project. Select the Setup and Deployment Projects node from the Project Types tree, and then select Setup Wizard from the list of templates on the right. Name the project RandomNumberMergeModule.

2. The first screen that appears is the Welcome screen. Click Next. The second page is the Choose a Project Type screen. Choose the Create a Merge Module for Windows Installer option in the second group (Do You Want to Create a Redistributable Package?). Click Next.

continues

continued

3. The third page is the Choose Project Outputs to Include screen. Select Primary Output from `RandomNumberGenerator`. Click Next. Click Next on the fourth screen, and then click Finish.

4. Open the File System Editor for the merge module project. Add the new folder `RandNumCorp` to the `Common Files` folder. Move the `Primary Output from RandomNumberGenerator (Active)` file in the `Common Files` folder to the `RandNumCorp` folder.

5. Select the `File System on Target Machine` node and choose Add Special Folder, Global Assembly Cache Folder from the context menu. Select the `Global Assembly Cache` folder and select Add, Project Output from the context menu.

6. The Add Project Output Group dialog box appears. Select the `RandomNumberGenerator` project and select Primary Output from the list of items to be added and click OK.

7. Open the Registry Editor. Select the `HKEY_LOCAL_MACHINE` node and add new keys to the node, hierarchically, in the order `HKEY_LOCAL_MACHINE`, `Software`, `Microsoft`, `.NETFramework`, `AssemblyFolders`, `RandNumCorp`, as shown in Figure 13.35.

FIGURE 13.35
Setting the keys and value in the Registry Editor to add an assembly in the Add Reference dialog box.

8. Add a new string value to the newly added `RandNumCorp` key. Select the value and invoke the Properties window.

Empty the `Name` property. When you empty the `Name` property, the default name of the value is set as shown in Figure 13.35. Set the `Value` property to `[CommonFilesFolder]RandNumCorp\`, where `CommonFilesFolder` is where the assembly file copy is stored.

9. Build the `RandomNumberMergeModule` project. Open Windows Explorer and navigate to the `Release` folder inside the project folder. Notice that the merge module `RandomNumberMergeModule.msm` has been created.

If you later want to distribute the component from Step By Step 13.16 with a Windows application, you can just add the merge module to your application's setup project.

GUIDED PRACTICE EXERCISE 13.3

In this exercise, you will create a setup project that will install the Windows application `RandomNumberApplication` and include the merge module `RandomNumberMergeModule` to install the component `RandomNumberGenerator.dll`.

This exercise will give you practice in creating installers for applications that have components that are packaged as merge modules. You should first attempt this exercise on your own. If you would later like to see one of the possible solutions, follow these steps:

1. In the Solution Explorer window, right-click Solution and select Add, New Project. Select `Setup and Deployment Projects` from the `Project Types` tree and then select Setup Wizard from the list of templates on the right. Name the project `RandomNumberAppSetup`. Click OK. The Setup Wizard launches. The first page that appears is the Welcome screen. Click Next.

2. The second page is the Choose a project type screen. Choose Create a Setup for Windows Application in the first group of options. Click Next.

continues

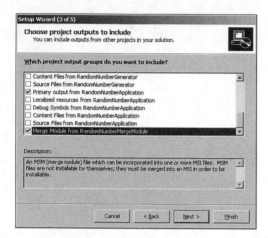

FIGURE 13.36
The Choose Project Outputs to Include Setup
Wizard screen.

continued

3. The third page is the Choose Project Outputs to Include screen. Select Primary output from RandomNumberApplication and Merge Module from RandomNumberMergeModule, as shown in Figure 13.36. Click Next, Next, and then Finish to create the project.

4. You'll see that the Application folder in the File System Editor has two files: Primary Output from RandomNumberApplication (Active) and RandomNumberGenerator.dll. RandomNumberGenerator.dll is included because by default the dependencies of the RandomNumberApplication project are included as well. Set the Exclude property of RandomNumberGenerator.dll to True because RandomNumberMergeModule already places the assembly copy into the GAC.

5. Select the setup project RandomNumberAppSetup in the Solution Explorer. Activate the Properties window. Set Manufacturer to Random Number Corporation, ProductName to Random Number Application, and Title to Random Number Application.

6. Build the RandomNumberAppSetup project. Open Windows Explorer and navigate to the Release folder inside the project folder. Run setup.exe and install the project.

7. Open Windows Explorer and navigate to the assembly cache folder (which is typically C:\Winnt\assembly or C:\Windows\assembly). Scroll down the assemblies, and you will notice that the RandomNumberGenerator assembly has been added to the GAC. Now navigate to C:\Program Files\Common Files\RandNumCorp ([CommonFilesFolder]RandNumCorp), and you will find a copy of RandomNumberGenerator.dll in this folder.

8. Open the Registry Editor by launching Regedit.exe from the Run dialog box (which you access by selecting Start, Run). In the Registry Editor, browse to the key named HKEY_LOCAL_MACHINE\SOFTWARE\Microsoft\.NETFramework\ AssemblyFolders. You will notice that a key with RandNumCorp is created, with the default value being the C:\Program Files\ Common Files\RandNumCorp ([CommonFilesFolder]RandNumCorp). This all happens due to the actions performed in Step By Step 13.16.

9. Close all instances of Visual Studio .NET (if any are opened). Launch Visual Studio .NET. Open the Add Reference dialog box by loading any Windows application. Select the .NET tab, and browse through it. You will notice that a reference to `C:\Program Files\Common Files\RandNumCorp\` `RandomNumberGenerator.dll` is added, as shown in Figure 13.37.

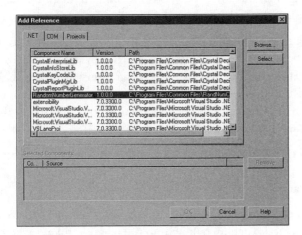

FIGURE 13.37
The Add Reference dialog box showing a reference to the RandomNumberGenerator component.

10. Navigate to the installation folder. If you did not change the default settings during installation, the path is `C:\Program` `Files\Random Number Corporation\Random Number` `Application`. You will notice that only the `RandomNumberApplication.exe` file exists in the folder. Run the file from the folder. The Random Number application is launched. Click the button, and a random number is displayed in the label. Enter a query and click the button to get the results of the query. The application loads the `RandomNumberGenerator` assembly from the GAC.

REVIEW BREAK

▶ Shared assemblies are used by multiple applications on a machine. They are placed in the GAC and enjoy special priviliges such as file security (because they are placed in the `System` folder), shared location, and side-by-side versioning.

continues

continued

▶ You generate public/private key pairs by using the Strong Name tool (`sn.exe`). These pairs can be used to digitally sign assemblies.

▶ You can add a shared assembly to the GAC by using Windows Explorer, the .NET Framework Configuration tool, the Global Assembly Cache tool, or the Installer tool.

▶ The best way to add an assembly during deployment is to use Microsoft Windows Installer, which provides an assembly reference-counting feature. When you uninstall an application, assemblies used by that application are removed only if they are not used by any other applications that are still on the computer.

▶ When viewed in Windows Explorer, the assembly cache folder in the `System` folder displays assemblies from the GAC and Native Image Cache.

▶ The Common Language Runtime searches the GAC to locate assemblies before looking into the files and folders where the assembly is installed. Thus shared assemblies placed in the GAC are efficient because the CLR does not engage itself in looking into the `<codebase>` and `<probing>` elements of the applicable configuration files.

▶ Delay signing allows you to place a shared assembly in the GAC by just signing the assembly with the public key. This allows the assembly to be signed with the private key at a later stage, when the development process is complete and the component or assembly is ready to be deployed. This process allows developers to work with shared assemblies as if they were strongly named, and it also secures the private key of the signature from being accessed at different stages of development.

▶ Merge modules allow you to create reusable components that help in deploying shared components. Merge modules cannot be directly installed. When an application uses a component for which a merge module exists, the merge module is merged into the installer for the application.

CREATING INSTALLATION COMPONENTS

Create a setup program that installs an application and allows for the application to be uninstalled: Perform an install-time compilation of a Windows-based application.

When you develop an application by using Visual Studio .NET, you use several resources, such as databases, event logs, performance counters, and message queues. However, when you install the program on a user's machine, these resources might not be present on the target machine. A good installation program ensures that all the resources that are required by an application exist on the target machine.

The .NET Framework provides an Installer class that is defined in the System.Configuration.Install namespace. This class is specifically designed to help you perform customized installation actions such as those just mentioned. In this section I will explore various ways in which you can use the Installer class to create powerful installation programs.

I will show you how to use the predefined installation classes that are available with several components of Visual Studio .NET. I will also show you how to create your own classes that extend the Installer class to perform specialized tasks at the time of installation.

Understanding the Installer Class

The System.Configuration.Install.Installer class works as a base class for all the custom installers in the .NET Framework. Some of the important members of the Installer class that I will discuss in this chapter are listed in Table 13.2.

TABLE 13.2

IMPORTANT MEMBERS OF THE Installer CLASS

Member Name	Type	Description
Commit	Method	Executes the code in the Commit method if the Install method executes successfully.
Install	Method	Performs the specified actions during an application's installation.

continues

TABLE 13.2	*continued*

IMPORTANT MEMBERS OF THE Installer CLASS

Member Name	Type	Description
Installers	Property	Specifies a collection of Installer objects that are needed for this Installer instance to successfully install a component.
Rollback	Method	Calls the code in Rollback method if the Install() method fails for some reason, to undo any custom actions performed during the Install method.
Uninstall	Method	Performs the specified actions when a previously installed application is uninstalled.

You can derive a class from the Installer class and override the methods listed in Table 13.2 to perform any custom actions.

If you want the derived Installer class to execute when an assembly is installed via a setup project or the Installer tool (installutil.exe), you need to decorate the class with RunInstallerAttribute set to True:

```
<RunInstaller(True)]>
```

The Installer classes provide the infrastructure for making installation a trasactional process. If an error is encountered during the Install method, the Rollback method will undo all the changes, to leave the machine in a clean state, as it was before the process of installation started. The Rollback method must know the order in which the installation steps were performed and exactly what changes were made so that it can undo those changes in the right order.

Similarly, when an application is uninstalled, the Uninstall method of the Installer class is called. Again, the responsibility of the Uninstall method is to undo the changes done by the installation process so that the machine is left clean, as if the program had never been installed on it.

How does the Install method communicate its installation information with the Rollback and Uninstall methods? This question becomes especially interesting when you see that the Install and Uninstall methods are not called in the same process. Install is called when the application is installed, and Uninstall is called when the application is uninstalled. These two events might occur over the course of several days, with computer restarts occuring in between.

The Install method communicates the installation state by persisting it in a file with the extension .InstallState. This file is placed in the installation directory of the application. The Installer class makes this file available to each of the Install, Commit, Rollback, and Uninstall methods by passing an IDictionary object to the contents of this file. Content in the .InstallState file is used by the Rollback and Uninstall method to perform the required cleanup operation.

Working with Predefined Installation Components

Most of the components that are available through the Server Explorer have predefined installation components associated with them. For example, when you create an instance of the EventLog component in project, you can add to the project an installer that corresponds to it. When you set the properties of an EventLog object in a program, those properties are remembered by the Installer component and will be reproduced on the target machine when the application is deployed.

In Step By Step 13.17, I'll show you how to create the required event log resources on the target machine at the time of installation, with the help of predefined installation components.

STEP BY STEP

13.17 Using a Predefined Component to Install an Event Source on a Target Computer

1. Add a new Visual Basic .NET Windows application project to the solution 306C13. Name the project `EventLogApplication`.

2. Rename the `Form1.vb` file `EventLogApplication.vb` in the project. Switch to the Code view of the form and modify all references to `Form1` so that they refer to `EventLogApplication` instead.

continues

FIGURE 13.38
Adding an Installer class for the EventLog component through the Add Installer hyperlink in the Properties window.

continued

3. Open the Server Explorer. Expand the tree under the Event Logs node. Drag and drop the Application event log to the form. This creates an EventLog1 object that you can see in the component tray.

4. Access the properties of the EventLog1 object. Change the Source property to EventLogApplication. Click the Add Installer link just above the description area in the Properties window, as shown in Figure 13.38, to add a new class named ProjectInstaller.vb to the project. In the Design view, you can see that ProjectInstaller.vb contains an object named EventLogInstaller1. This is the installation component for the event log created in the EventLogApplication.vb form.

5. Switch to the Code view of ProjectInstaller.vb. Note the use of the following attribute with the ProjectInstaller class:

```
<RunInstaller(True)>
```

This attribute specifies whether the ProjectInstaller class should be invoked during the execution of an assembly. View the Component Designer Generated Code section for this class. You will find all the necessary coding for installing an event log or event source on the target machine.

6. Switch to the Design view of EventLogApplication.vb. Add a TextBox control (txtMessage) and a Button control (btnWrite) to the form. Double-click the Button control to attach an event handler to its Click event. Add the following code to the event handler:

```
Private Sub btnWrite_Click( _
 ByVal sender As System.Object, _
 ByVal e As System.EventArgs) _
 Handles btnWrite.Click
    EventLog1.WriteEntry(txtMessage.Text)
End Sub
```

7. Build your project using the Debug mode. Run the project. Enter a value in the text box and click the button. Open the Server Explorer. Expand the Event Logs and the Application node. You will see a new source added to the Application event log with a message that you give when you run the program.

8. Build your project using the `Release` mode. The project is now ready for deployment.

As described in Step By Step 13.17, when you click the Add Installer link for an `EventLog` component, a `ProjectInstaller` class is created in your project; the installation component for the `EventLog` component is then added to this class. If you add additional installation components (for example, a `PerformanceCounter` installation component) to this project, they will be all added to this `ProjectInstaller` class. These additional installation components are actually added to the `Installers` collection of the `ProjectInstaller` class. When you compile the project to build an EXE or a DLL file, the `ProjectInstaller` class becomes part of the output assembly.

Deploying an Assembly That Contains Installation Components

There are two ways you can deploy an assembly that contains installation components:

◆ By using a setup and deployment project

◆ By using the Installer tool (installutil.exe)

I will show you how to deploy an application that contains installation components by using both the techniques in the following sections.

Deploying an Installation Component by Using the Setup Project

To deploy an application that contains installation components, you need to create a setup project as you would normally do. However, you need to use the Custom Actions Editor to deploy the additional resources needed for the application. At the time of deployment, the deployment project will execute the ProjectInstaller class as part of its custom installation action, to create component resources. Step By Step 13.18 shows you how.

STEP BY STEP

13.18 Using a Setup Project to Install Component Resources

1. Add a new setup project to the solution. Name the project `EventLogApplicationSetup`.

2. Right-click the `EventLogApplicationSetup` project in the Solution Explorer. Select Add, Project Output from the shortcut menu. In the Add Project Output Group dialog box, select Primary Output of EventLogApplication project.

3. Open the Custom Actions Editor for the `EventLogApplicationSetup` project. Right-click the `Custom Actions` node, and select Add Custom Action from the shortcut menu. This opens the Select Item in Project dialog box. From the `Application` folder select `Primary Output from EventLogApplication(Active)`. Click OK. The primary output is added to all four nodes under custom actions: `Install`, `Commit`, `Rollback`, and `Uninstall`.

4. Select the new project in the Solution Explorer. Activate the Properties window. Set `Manufacturer` to `EventLog Application` and set `ProductName` to `EventLogApplication`.

5. Build the `EventLogApplicationSetup` project. Take the project's output to a computer that does not already have an event source for `EventLogApplication`. Run the installation. The setup program installs `EventLogApplication` along with the required event source.

6. Run the application's executable file from the installation folder. Enter some text and click the button. Launch the Event Viewer from the Administrative Tools section of the Windows Control Panel. Select the Application log under the `Event Viewer` node. Your event log entries appear in the right pane of the Event Viewer.

Deploying an Installation Component by Using the Installer Tool (installutil.exe)

You can use the command-line Installer tool (installutil.exe) to install the assemblies that contain additional component resources.

To install the resources contained in an assembly named Assembly1.dll, you can use the following form of the installutil.exe command:

```
installutil.exe Assembly1.dll
```

You can also install resources contained in multiple assemblies together, like this:

```
installutil.exe Assembly1.dll Assembly2.dll Assembly3.dll
```

If you instead want to launch the uninstaller for installation classes stored in an assembly, you use the /u or /uninstall option with the command, like this:

```
installutil.exe /u Assembly1.dll
```

> **EXAM TIP**
>
> **installutil.exe Performs Installation in a Transactional Manner** If you are installing components from multiple assemblies by using the installutil.exe command, if any of the assemblies fails to install, installutil.exe will roll back the installations of all other assemblies.

Working with Installer Classes

You can add your own Installer classes to a project to perform custom actions during installation, such as compiling the code to native image format or creating a database on a target computer. These compiled Installer classes from your project are then added to the deployment project as custom actions that are run at the end of the installation. The following are typical actions that you would perform while creating a custom Installer class:

- ◆ Inherit a class from the Installer class.

- ◆ Makes sure that RunInstallerAttribute is set to true in the derived class.

- ◆ Override the Install, Commit, Rollback, and Uninstall methods to perform any custom actions.

- ◆ In a setup project, use the Custom Actions Editor to invoke this derived class to do the required processing.

- ◆ If needed, pass arguments from the Custom Actions Editor to the custom Installer class by using the CustomActionData property.

In the following section, I'll show you how to use these actions to create a custom installation program that translates the MSIL assemblies to native images by using the Native Code Generation tool (ngen.exe) tool.

Performing Install-Time Compilation

Create a setup program that installs an application and allows for the application to be uninstalled: Perform an install-time compilation of a Windows-based application.

When assemblies are loaded at runtime, the CLR compiles the requested MSIL code into native code by using a technique known as just-in-time (JIT) compilation. The advantage of JIT compilation is that the next time a piece of code is called, it need not be converted again to the native code, and it in turn executes faster.

Because of JIT compilation, an application that executes a lot of startup code is rather slow when it starts. You can solve this problem by precompiling the MSIL code to native code. The best time to do this conversion is at installation time because at that time the compilation can be done according to the exact architecture of the machine that will execute the code.

You can compile from MSIL to native code by using the Native Code Generation tool (ngen.exe) on the target machine. If you are using this tool at the install time, you typically have to take the following steps:

1. Find the location where the .NET Framework Common Language Runtime is installed on the target computer. This is the path where ngen.exe is located.

2. Execute ngen.exe for each assembly that you want to compile into native code. Your assemblies may be present either in a common location, such as the Common Files folder, or in a location specified by the user at the time of compilation. You need to determine this path so that you can create the correct command line for calling ngen.exe.

Step By Step 13.19 shows how to create a custom Installer class that runs ngen.exe and how to call the class from a setup project.

STEP BY STEP

13.19 Adding a Custom Action to Perform Install-Time Compilation

1. In the Solution Explorer, add a Visual Basic .NET Class Library project to the solution. Name the project `GenerateNativeImage`.

2. Right-click the project `GenerateNativeImage` and choose Add, Add New Item from the context menu. The Add New Item dialog box appears. Select Installer Class from the right pane, as shown in Figure 13.39. Name it `GenerateNativeImage.vb`.

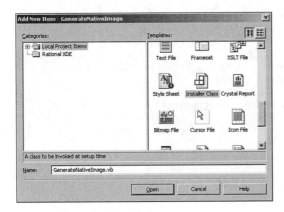

FIGURE 13.39
Adding an Installer class via the Add New Item dialog box.

3. Open `GenerateNativeImage.vb` in the Code view. Add the following code at the top of the file:

```
Imports System.Diagnostics
Imports System.Runtime.InteropServices
```

4. Add the following code after the Component Designer Generated Code section in the class definition:

```
' Gets the install directory for the version of the
' runtime that is loaded in the current process
Private Declare Function GetCORSystemDirectory Lib _
  "mscoree.dll" (<MarshalAs(UnmanagedType.LPWStr)> _
  ByVal Buffer As System.Text.StringBuilder, _
  ByVal BufferLength As Integer, _
  ByRef Length As Integer) As Integer
```

continues

continued

```
Public Overrides Sub Install( _
 ByVal savedState As System.Collections.IDictionary)
    ' Call the Install method of the base class
    MyBase.Install(savedState)
    ' Get the arguments to pass to the class
    Dim strArgs As String = _
    Me.Context.Parameters.Item("Args")
    If strArgs = "" Then
        Throw New InstallException( _
        "No arguments specified")
    End If

    ' Declare a StringBuilder to hold the path
    'of the ngen.exe on the target machine
    Dim strPath As StringBuilder = New _
    StringBuilder(1024)
    Dim intSize As Integer

    ' Call the mscoree.dll's GetCORSystemDirectory method
    GetCORSystemDirectory(strPath, _
    strPath.Capacity, intSize)

    ' Run the ngen process with the arguments
    ' passed to the class
    Dim si As ProcessStartInfo = _
    New ProcessStartInfo(strPath.ToString() & _
        "ngen.exe ", "\"" + strArgs + " \ "")
    si.WindowStyle = ProcessWindowStyle.Hidden
    Try
        Dim p As Process = Process.Start(si)
        p.WaitForExit()
    Catch ex As Exception
        Throw New InstallException(ex.Message)
    End Try
End Sub

Public Overrides Sub Commit( _
 ByVal savedState As System.Collections.IDictionary)
    ' Call the Commit method of the base class
    MyBase.Commit(savedState)
End Sub

Public Overrides Sub Rollback( _
 ByVal savedState As System.Collections.IDictionary)
    ' Call the Rollback method of the base class
    MyBase.Rollback(savedState)
End Sub

Public Overrides Sub Uninstall( _
 ByVal savedState As System.Collections.IDictionary)
    ' Call the Uninstall method of the base class
    MyBase.Uninstall(savedState)
End Sub
```

5. Build the `GenerateNativeImage` project.

6. Select the `RandomNumberMergeModule` project in the Solution Explorer. Open the File System Editor for the merge module project. Move to the `RandNumCorp` folder in the `Common Files Folder` node. Add `Primary Output from GenerateNativeImage (Active)` to the folder by selecting Action, Add, Project Output.

7. Open the Custom Actions Editor for the merge module project. Select the `Custom Actions` node and select Add Custom Action from the context menu. The Select Item in Project dialog box appears. Select `Primary Output from GenerateNativeImage (Active)` by navigating to the `Common Files Folder - RandNumCorp` folder. Click OK. `Primary Output from GenerateNativeImage (Active)` is added to all four nodes under `Custom Actions`.

8. Select the newly added custom action under the `Install` node. Open the Properties window and set the `CustomActionData` property to `/Args="[CommonFilesFolder]RandNumCorp\RandomNumberGenerator.dll"`.

9. Build the `RandomNumberAppSetup` project and install it.

10. A precompiled native image of the `RandomNumberGenerator` assembly is added to the Native Image Cache, as shown in Figure 13.40.

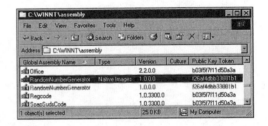

FIGURE 13.40
The Native Image Cache, which is centrally stored in the assembly cache along with the GAC.

In Step By Step 13.19, note the usage of the `CustomActionData` property of the Custom Actions Editor. This property is used to pass installation data from a setup program to the custom `Installer` class.

Another important thing to note from Step By Step 13.19 is the use of term *Native Image Cache*. The Common Language Runtime stores all natively compiled assemblies in a central area called the Native Image Cache, which is stored in a separate folder inside the assembly cache folder (usually `c:\WINNT\assembly` or `c:\Windows\assembly`) along with the GAC, as shown in Figure 13.40. You can identify whether the assembly is from the GAC or from the Native Image Cache by examining the Type field in the list. You can also list the contents of the Native Image Cache by using the `/show` option with `ngen.exe`, as shown in Figure 13.41.

FIGURE 13.41
Using ngen.exe to view the contents of the
Native Image Cache.

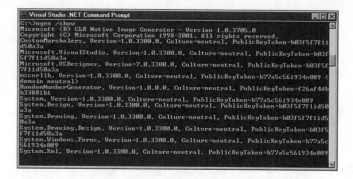

R E V I E W   B R E A K

▶ The System.Configuration.Install.Installer class is a base
class for all the custom installers in the .NET Framework.

▶ The Installer class method Install() is called when an
application is installed, and Uninstall() is called when an
application is uninstalled. The Commit() method is executed if
the Install() method executes successfully, and the
Rollback() method is executed if the Install() method is not
executed successfully.

▶ If you add predefined installation components (for example, a
PerformanceCounter installation component) to a setup project, they will be all added to the ProjectInstaller class. They
are actually added to the Installers collection of the
ProjectInstaller class.

▶ You can add your own custom Installer classes to a project to
perform custom actions—such as compiling code to native
image format or creating a database on a target computer—
through the Custom Actions Editor during installation.

▶ You can compile from MSIL to native by using the Native
Image Generation tool (ngen.exe). The assemblies that are
compiled into machine-specific native code are placed in the
Native Image Cache.

URL REMOTING

Verify security policies for a deployed application: Launch a remote application (URL remoting).

The .NET Framework provides a zero-impact (or no-touch) deployment model for deploying Windows applications. The idea of zero-impact deployment is to keep all the necessary code and configuration files on a Web server and execute the application by just pointing to the URL of the EXE file from Internet Explorer on each user's computer—rather than installing the application on each user's computer. Launching a remote application with a URL is also known as *URL remoting*.

This Web-based deployment model does not require the .NET Framework to be installed on the server machine (the server is not even required to be running Windows). All the required code and configuration files are downloaded from the Web server and are executed on the local machine. Of course, the local machine must have the .NET Framework installed on it.

This deployment model is very exciting because it gives you the ease of maintenance that is available from a Web application in addition to the rich user interface of Windows Forms. This is certainly a big shift from how Windows applications were traditionally deployed.

Launching a Remote Application

Step By step 13.20 shows you how to deploy a simple Windows Forms application on a Web server and launch it by refering to its URL (that is, URL remoting).

STEP BY STEP

13.20 Launching a Remote Application

1. In the Solution Explorer, add a Visual Basic .NET Windows application project to the solution. Name the project SimpleUI.

---

continues

continued

2. Rename the `Form1.vb` file `SimpleUI.vb` in the project.

3. Place a `TextBox` control named `txtMessage`, a `Button` control named `btnDisplay`, and a `Label` control named `lblMessage` on the form. Set the `TextAlign` property of the `Label` control to `MiddleCenter` and the `Font` property to a bigger size.

4. Add the following code to the `Click` event handler of the `Button` control:

```
Private Sub btnDisplay_Click( _
 ByVal sender As System.Object, _
 ByVal e As System.EventArgs) Handles btnDisplay.Click
    lblMessage.Text = txtMessage.Text
End Sub
```

5. Set the `SimpleUI` project as the startup project. Run the project. Enter some text in the text box and click the button. Text is displayed in the `Label` control.

6. Copy the `SimpleUI.exe` file to a Web server directory (such as `c:\inetpub\wwwroot`)

7. Launch Internet Explorer. Navigate to `http://localhost/SimpleUI.exe`. (This path may be different if you have a different server or path.)

8. If your Web server is local or within an intranet zone, the `SimpleUI` application is launched as shown in Figure 13.42. If instead you browse to a Web server over the Internet (using an address such as `http://myserver.com/SimpleUI.exe`), you will get a security exception error message. I will discuss how to deal with this security exception later in this chapter.

NOTE

IEExec.exe   When you launch a remote application using a URL, no process is started by the name of the application. This is because a process with the name IEExec.exe launches the application. If you look at the current processes through Windows Task Manager, you will find one copy of IEExec.exe running for each application that was launched through a URL.

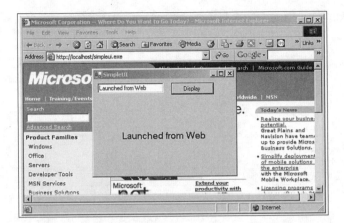

FIGURE 13.42
Launching a remote application from Internet Explorer.

The Download Cache

The code downloaded from a URL is cached in a central location called the download cache. Unlike the GAC, download cache always remembers the original locations from which the stored contents were downloaded. Therefore, the next time a request is made for the remote content, the download cache will check the time stamp of the requested assemblies on the server. If it finds requested assemblies with newer dates, it will download them; otherwise, the already downloaded assemblies in the download cache are used. This behavior makes the download cache useful for the files coming from the Internet; with Internet files, the download time may be slow, and caching the files may eliminate the additional time required to download an already downloaded file.

The download cache also isolates assemblies from other assemblies that are downloaded by other users or applications. The download cache is physically stored in a directory that is private to a user. For example, on my computer, the download cache is stored in the C:\Documents and Settings\Mike\Local Settings\Application Data\assembly\dl folder. The folder and subfolders in the download cache have cryptic names and do not easily convey the information about the cache contents. To easily read the contents of the download cache, open Windows Explorer and navigate to the assembly cache folder. You will find the download cache as a subfolder attached to the assembly cache folder (see Figure 13.43). This folder is not physically in that location, but shfusion.dll shows it there for easy access. If you want to see the contents of the Download Cache by using the command line, you can use gacutil.exe with the /ldl switch (see Figure 13.44) .

FIGURE 13.43

Using Windows Explorer to view the contents of the Download Cache.

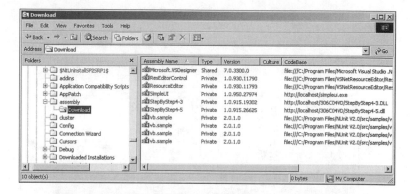

FIGURE 13.44

Using the Command window to view the contents of the Download Cache.

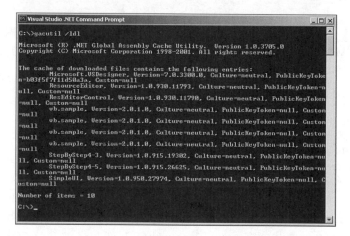

The Code Access Security Policy

Downloading code from remote sources may be a security risk. To help protect computers from malicious mobile code, the .NET Framework provides a security mechanism called code access security. It allows code to be trusted to varying degrees, depending on where the code originates, the publisher, the strong name, and the security zone.

To view the current code access security policy on your machine, follow the steps in Step By Step 13.21.

STEP BY STEP

13.21 Exploring the Code Access Security Policy for a Computer

1. Open the Administrative Tools section of the Windows Control Panel. Open the .NET Framework Configuration tool.

2. Expand the `Runtime Security Policy` node, the `Machine` node, the `Code Groups` node, and the `All_Code` node. Select the `My_Computer_Zone` node. In the right pane, click the hyperlink Edit Code Group Properties. You'll see the Properties window (see Figure 13.45). Select the Permission Set tab. Note that the default permission set for this code group is `FullTrust`.

3. In the left pane of the .NET Framework Configuration tool, select `LocalIntranet_Zone` and on the right pane, click the hyperlink Edit Code Group Properties. Select the Permission Set tab in the Properties window. Note that this code group is not fully trusted. It has only a partial set of permissions, as defined by the `LocalIntranet` permission set (see Figure 13.46).

4. Access the properties for `Internet_Zone`. Note that its permission set is set to `Nothing`.

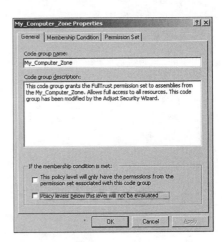

FIGURE 13.45
The My_Computer_Zone code group granting full trust to code originating from the local computer.

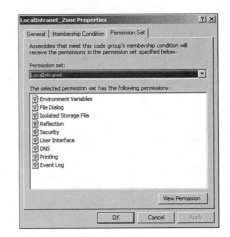

FIGURE 13.46
The LocalIntranet_Zone code group grants partial trusted to only selected permissions.

When the Common Language Runtime executes code, it can determine the code's origin by looking at the URL or path used to invoke the code. This information is used to classify the code in one of the predefined zones, which are listed in Table 13.3.

TABLE 13.3

CODE ACCESS SECURITY ZONES

Code Origin	Code Group
From a file path on local computer, such as `c:\inetpub\wwwroot\simpleUI.exe` or `c:\MyDir\SimpleUI.exe`	My_Computer_Zone

continues

TABLE 13.3	*continued*

CODE ACCESS SECURITY ZONES

Code Origin	Code Group
From a network share, such as `\\server1\share1\SimpleUI.exe`, or from a Web server that is local within the network, such as `http://server1/SimpleUI.exe` or `http://192.168.1.1/SimpleUI.exe`	LocalIntranet_Zone
From Internet addresses, such as `www.myserver.com/SimpleUI.exe` or `http://207.46.197.100/SimpleUI.exe`	Internet_Zone

As described in Step By Step 13.21, the My_Computer_Zone code group has the FullTrust permission set associated with it. The LocalIntranet_Zone code group is only partially trusted, as defined by the LocalIntranet permission set. The Internet_Zone code group has a permission set of Nothing. In Step By Step 13.18, when you used the URL http://localhost/SimpleUI.exe, the runtime determined from the URL that the code was coming from LocalIntranet_Zone. The assembly SimpleUI.exe was therefore only partially trusted. Still, it executed successfully because all its code was within the boundary of the permission set assigned to it. But if you would have uploaded SimpleUI.exe to a Web server addressable from the Internet and accessed the program by using a URL such as www.myserver.com/SimpleUI.exe, the runtime would have determined from the address that the code was downloaded from the Internet and would have applied to it the permission set for Internet_Zone, which is Nothing. As you can guess, the execution of the program would fail and throw a security exception.

This behavior might look different from the behavior described in the product documentation installed with the final release of the .NET Framework SDK or Visual Studio .NET. Actually, following the Bill Gates initiative for Trustworthy Computing, the .NET Framework team decided to tighten the default security policy in the .NET Framework. Some of those changes were reflected in Version 1 of the .NET Franework, and other security changes were made part of Service Pack 1 of Microsoft .NET Framework. If you have not yet installed Service Pack 1 or later, I recommend that you do so before proceeding with rest of the chapter.

NOTE

.NET Framework Service Pack 1
The .NET Framework Service Pack 1 is widely distributed as part of Microsoft Windows Update service. You can also easily check for updates by using Visual Studio .NET by selecting Help, Check for Updates. Alternatively, you can download Service Pack 1 from `http://msdn.microsoft.com/netframework/downloads/sp`.

One of the significant changes in Service Pack 1 is the change of permission set for Internet_Zone from Internet permission set to Nothing, thereby totally disabling the execution of mobile code originating from the Internet. That means that the mobile code will not unintentionally execute. If you are sure that an assembly coming from the Internet is safe, you can increase the level of trust and permissions associated with it by using the .NET Framework Configuration tool (I will cover how to do that a little later in this chapter). In that case you could execute code coming from Internet, too.

Changes to Caller Trust

Another important last-minute change to Version 1 release of the .NET Framework that resulted from the Trustworthy Computing initiative was to ensure that by default, any strong-named assembly can be called only from an assembly that is granted full trust by the security policy. This change protects strong-named assemblies from any possible misuse by partially trusted code.

The program SimpleUI.exe uses several assemblies from the .NET Framework: System.dll, System.Data.dll, System.Drawing.dll, System.Windows.Forms, and System.XML.dll. All these assemblies are strong-named assemblies. When you executed SimpleUI.exe from a local Web server in Step By Step 13.20, it was partially trusted because the code originated from LocalIntranet_Zone. In Step By Step 13.20, you observed that SimpleUI.exe executed successfully. This means that a partially trusted assembly (such as SimpleUI.exe) was able to call strong-named assemblies (such as System.Windows.Forms). Doesn't this violate the statement "any strong-named assembly can be called only from an assembly that is granted full trust by the security policy"?

The answer to this question can be explained with the help of the newly introduced (in Service Pack 1) AllowPartiallyTrustedCallersAttribute attribute. The .NET Framework has marked the following assemblies with this attribute:

◆ Accessibility.dll

◆ IEExecRemote.dll

> **NOTE**
>
> **Version 1 Security Changes**   The .NET Framework team made some security-related changes just before shipping Version 1 of the .NET Framework. Some of these changes did not made it into the product document that is installed with the .NET Framework SDK. To get an overview of these changes, you can refer to the Version 1 Security Changes whitepaper at http://msdn.microsoft.com/library/en-us/dnnetsec/html/v1securitychanges.asp.

- ◆ mscorlib.dll

- ◆ Microsoft.VisualBasic.dll

- ◆ System.dll

- ◆ System.Data.dll

- ◆ System.Drawing.dll

- ◆ System.Web.Services.dll

- ◆ System.Windows.Forms.dll

- ◆ System.XML.dll

When a programmer decorates a strong-named assembly with AllowPartiallyTrustedCallersAttribute, it instructs the Common Language Runtime to allow calling of the given strong-named assembly from a partially trusted assembly. The advantage of this attribute is that now partially trusted assemblies can provide more functionality without making the user explicitly increase the trust level associated with them. But this has security considerations, too. As a programmer, before you mark an assembly with AllowPartiallyTrustedCallersAttribute, you must thoroughly test the assembly to make sure that it cannot be potentially misused by malicious callers to cause harm on users' computers. You can mark an assembly with AllowPartiallyTrustedCallersAttribute by using Visual Studio .NET by writing the following line of code in the AssemblyInfo.vb file of a project:

```
<Assembly: AllowPartiallyTrustedCallersAttribute>
```

This attribute belongs to the System.Security namespace. You would also have to include the following statement at the top of AssemblyInfo.vb

```
Imports System.Security
```

Now let's take a look at another assembly that we used earlier in this chapter: NetSql.exe. This assembly calls only those assemblies from the.NET Framework that are marked with assemblies to AllowPartiallyTrustedCallersAttribute listed previously. You can copy Netsql.exe to a local Web server in your network and execute it from Internet Explorer by using a URL such as http://localhost/NetSql.exe.

You will find that the execution fails with a security exception, as shown in Figure 13.47. What's the reason? What is NetSql.exe doing differently than SimpleUI.exe?

FIGURE 13.47

The failed execution of the partially trust assembly NetSql.exe.

The answer is that some of the types in assemblies marked with AllowPartiallyTrustedCallersAttribute may require stronger permissions. One such type being used by the NetSql.exe assembly is System.Data.SqlClient.SqlConnection. This is the reason NetSql.exe, which is a partially trusted assembly (as it is loaded from the LocalIntranet_Zone), ia not granted permission to execute. To get a complete list of the types in assemblies marked with AllowPartiallyTrustedCallersAttribute that require stronger permissions to execute, see http://msdn.microsoft.com/library/en-us/dnnetsec/html/Aptcatypes.asp.

Setting the Runtime Security Policy for an Assembly

If you want to execute NetSql.exe, you have to configure the runtime security policy to increase the trust associated with NetSql.exe. Step By Step 13.22 shows the process.

STEP BY STEP

13.22 Setting the Runtime Security Policy for an Assembly

1. Open the Administrative Tools section of the Windows Control Panel. Open the .NET Framework Configuration tool. Select the Runtime Security Policy folder in the left pane, under the My Computer node, as shown in Figure 13.48.

FIGURE 13.48

Using the .NET Framework Configuration to configure the runtime security policy for an assembly.

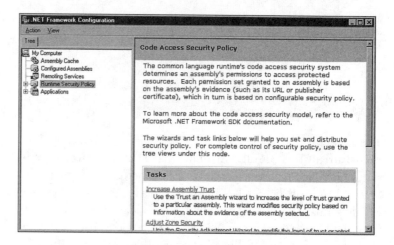

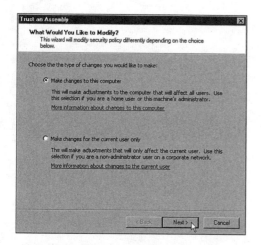

FIGURE 13.49

Using the Trust an Assembly Wizard to trust an assembly for the logged-on user or for all users.

2. From the list of tasks in the right pane, click the hyperlink Increase Assembly Trust. The Trust an Assembly Wizard appears, as shown in Figure 13.49. Choose the option Make Changes to This Computer and click the Next button.

3. In the next screen, type the URL for the NetSql.exe assembly, as shown in Figure 13.50. Click the Next button.

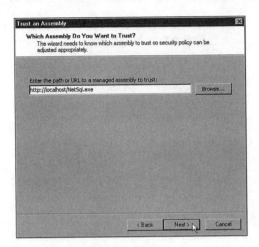

FIGURE 13.50
Specifying the path or URL of the assembly to be trusted.

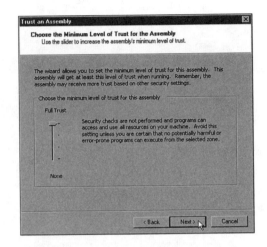

FIGURE 13.51
Selecting from one of the four values to set the minimum level of trust for an assembly.

4. The next screen asks you to select the minimum level of trust you want to associate with the assembly. You will see a slider, which can take four positions: Nothing, Internet, Local Intranet, and Full Trust. Change the default Nothing level to Full Trust, as shown in Figure 13.51.

5. Click the Next button. The final screen shows a summary of the operation. Click the Finish button to close the wizard.

6. Open Internet Explorer and navigate to the URL of NetSql.exe. NetSql.exe is invoked from the Web server.

In addition to using the method described in Step By Step 13.22, you can set the trust for an assembly by using a Microsoft .NET Framework Wizards shortcut, which you access from the Administrative Tools section of the Windows Control Panel (see Figure 13.52).

If you have a strong-named assembly, users will see an additional screen in the Trust an Assembly Wizard, as shown in Figure 13.53. In this screen, you can choose to set a level of trust for all assemblies from the same publisher or all assemblies that have the same public key.

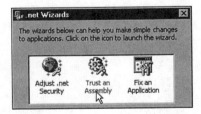

FIGURE 13.52
Using a Microsoft .NET Framework Wizards shortcut to trust an assembly.

FIGURE 13.53

Using the Trust an Assembly Wizard to trust all assemblies from the same publisher or all assemblies that have the same public key.

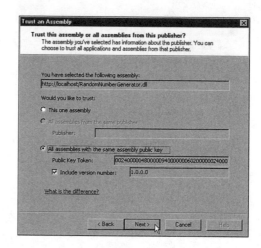

Setting the Runtime Security Policy for a Zone

There is another way to adjust security for executing code in the .NET Framework: by using the Security Adjustment Wizard to modify the level of trust granted to all assemblies that are coming from a particular zone, such as Internet, Local Intranet, or My Computer. Step By Step 13.23 uses this wizard to grant full trust to all assemblies coming from the Local Intranet zone.

STEP BY STEP

13.23 Setting the Runtime Security Policy for a Zone

1. Open the Microsoft .NET Configuration Wizards dialog box from the Administrative Tools section of the Windows Control Panel. Click the Adjust .NET Security icon. The Security Adjustment Wizard appears, as shown in Figure 13.54. (You can also invoke this wizard from the .NET Framework Configuration tool.) Choose Make Changes to This Computer and click the Next button.

2. In the next screen, select the Local Intranet zone and increase its level of trust to Full Trust, as shown in Figure 13.55. Click Next to continue.

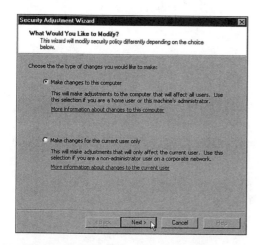

FIGURE 13.54

Using the Security Adjustment Wizard to modify the level of trust granted to all assemblies coming from a particular zone.

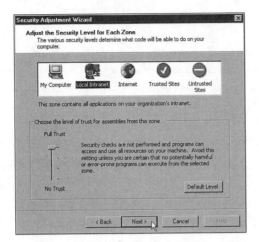

FIGURE 13.55
Increasing the level of trust for the Local Intranet zone.

3. The next screen summarizes the changes made to the security policy for various zones. Click Finish to close the wizard.

4. To confirm your changes, copy `RandomNumberGenerator.dll` and `RandomNumberApplication.exe` to the local Web server. Invoke them from a Web browser, using a URL such as `http://localhost/RandomNumberApplication.exe`. You will see that the application seccessfully executes.

When you set the runtime security policy for a zone, it has much wider implications than setting permissions for a single assembly because it will affect all the assemblies in that zone. Therefore, you need to be careful when you set the policy for a zone.

I'll talk more about code access security and application configuration in Chapter 14.

WARNING

Increasing Trust for the Internet Zone Be aware that increasing the trust level for the Internet zone increases the chance of malicious code altering your computer over the Internet. Normally it is not a recommended practice to do so. If you want to trust code from selected Internet sites that you trust, a better option is to add those sites to the Trusted Sites zone (by using Internet Explorer, Tools, Internet Options, Security) and then set the trust level for the Trusted Sites zone.

REVIEW BREAK

▶ URL remoting provides a zero-impact deployment model for deploying a Windows application. The code and configuration files reside on a Web server, and you can execute the application by just pointing to the URL of the EXE file from Internet Explorer on the end user's computer.

continues

continued

▶ Code that is downloaded from a URL is cached in a central location called the download cache. When a subsequent request to the same content is made, the download cache checks the timestamp of the requested assemblies on the server and downloads the file from the server only if the timestamp is changed. Otherwise, it displays the cached copy to the user.

▶ Code access security allows code to be trusted to varying degrees, depending on where the code originates, the publisher, the strong name, and the security zone.

▶ If `AllowPartiallyTrustedCallersAttribute` is associated with a strong name assembly, it allows even partially trusted code to call this assembly.

▶ The .NET Framework Configuration tool can be used to configure the runtime security policy for an assembly or a zone.

METHODS OF DEPLOYMENT

After you have created a setup package, you can deploy your application from any location that's accessible to all the application's potential users. You can use one of several deployment methods:

◆ Deployment via removable media

◆ Network-based deployment

◆ Web-based deployment

The following sections discuss each of these deployment options.

Deployment via Removable Media

Plan the deployment of a Windows-based application: Plan a deployment that uses removable media.

The most common examples of removable media are floppy disks, CD-ROMs, and DVDs. Deployment via removable media is suitable in three situations:

◆ When users are in many locations, without any common central connection.

◆ When not all users have access to the Internet.

◆ When application size is huge and not all users have access to high-speed Internet connections.

Deployment via removable media is becoming more outdated every day. It involves costs for media as well as replication and distribution that can easily be eliminated by using other deployment options. But deployment via removable media is still the "lowest common denominator" solution and covers the maximum number of users.

Deployment projects in Visual Studio .NET can be used to create packages divided across multiple files each with small size, as specified by the developer. These small-sized files can be copied to floppy disks or CD-ROMs and distributed to users.

To create a setup project for removable media, you create a setup project as you would normally do. Right-click the project in the Solution Explorer and select Properties from the shortcut menu. In the Properties window, change Package Files to In Cabinet File(s). This enables the CAB Size option. Set the CAB size to Custom and set the size depending on your media size, as shown in Figure 13.56.

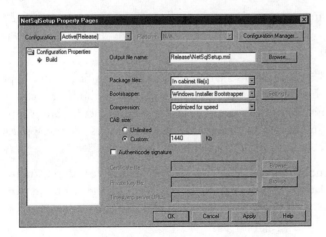

FIGURE 13.56
Setting the setup project configuration properties to create an installation package in cabinet files of size 1440Kb.

Now build the setup project, which will create a Windows Installer package (.msi file) and one or more CAB files, depending on the size of the application. If the Bootstrapper option is set to Windows Installer Bootstrapper, the setup project will also create a setup.exe file.

When you copy all these files to the removable media, copy setup.exe and the .msi file to the first disk and then copy each CAB file to a separate disk.

Network-Based Deployment

Plan the deployment of a Windows-based application: Plan a network-based deployment.

Network-based installation is useful in a scenario in which multiple users are sharing a common network. In this case, the applications can be installed via a shared network folder. This kind of deployment method is very common in corporate environments.

While creating a setup project for a network-based deployment, you would create a single setup package instead of creating multiple CAB files. After you build the setup project, you copy all the setup files to a shared folder on the network and publish the address of the folder to the users. You might also want to make the network share a read-only share so that users cannot modify the setup files.

Administrative Installation for Network-Based Deployment

By using the administrative installation of a Windows Installer package, you can deploy an application to a network for use by a workgroup.

An administrative installation installs a source image of the application onto the network. Users in a workgroup who have access to this administrative image can then install the product from this source. After installation has been done, when the users run the application, it will use most of the files directly from the network.

A Windows Installer package can be executed for administrative installation from the command line by using the /a option with the MSIEXEC command, as in this example:

```
MSIEXEC /a netsql.msi
```

Web-Based Deployment

Plan the deployment of a Windows-based application: Plan a Web-based deployment.

Web-based deployment is the most popular form of deployment, especially for small-sized applications. With the growth of high-speed Internet connections, you will see this form of deployment in much higher demand than the removable media form of deployment. It offers several advantages over other forms of application deployment:

◆ It reduces the cost of media, replication, and distribution.

◆ Management of software updates is simple. You can program an application so that it can automatically check for updates on the Web, or you can instruct users to download setup files from a Web page.

Creating a setup package for Web-based deployment is similar to doing so for a network-based deployment. After the setup files are created, rather than copy them to a network share, you copy them to a virtual directory on a Web server. You might also want to password-protect the deployment Web site so that only authorized users can download the application.

REVIEW BREAK

▶ You should select a deployment method that is convenient and accessible to all the application's users.

▶ You can create installation packages in multiple cabinet files by choosing the In Cabinet File(s) option in the Properties window.

▶ You can execute an administrative installation by using the MSIEXEC command with the /a option. This installs a source image of the application onto the network that users in that workgroup can use to install the application.

▶ Web-based deployment reduces the cost of media, replication, and distribution. It also makes the management of software updates simple.

WINDOWS LOGO PROGRAM REQUIREMENTS

Plan the deployment of a Windows-based application: Ensure that the application conforms to Windows Installer requirements and Windows Logo Program requirements.

Microsoft provides logo programs to ensure the compatibility of applications with the Microsoft operating systems. The logo programs provide guidelines to developers for writing applications that interoperate properly with Windows, providing greater stability, better maintenance, and improved management features. To earn a logo, an application must meet predefined specifications, and an independent lab must test it to confirm its compliance with the specification.

Microsoft currently offers different certification programs for applications designed for the Windows 2000 and Windows XP operating systems:

◆ The Certified for Windows logo program

◆ The Designed for Microsoft Windows XP logo program

In addition to these operating system logo programs, Microsoft administers a variety of other logo programs for specific types of applications.

> **NOTE**
>
> **Windows .NET Server** With the release of Windows .NET Server, there will be another certification program that will certify applications designed for Windows .NET Server. Very likely, though, complying with the Windows 2000 and Windows XP requirements will prepare you well for this new program.

The Certified for Windows Logo Program

The Certified for Windows logo program certifies an application for the Microsoft Windows 2000 operating system. To get this logo, applications must conform to the technical requirements defined in the application specifications for Windows 2000. After an independent testing lab successfully tests the application and the vendor signs the logo license agreement with Microsoft, the application may carry the Certified for Microsoft Windows logo.

The application specification for developing server-based applications differs from the application specification for desktop-based applications.

You can get the complete specifications for both desktop-based and server-based applications by visiting the Certified for Windows Program home page, at http://msdn.microsoft.com/certification. For your quick reference, I have summarized the main points for developing logo-compliant desktop applications in the following list:

◆ **Windows Fundamentals**—Describes the requirements for consistent and stable functionality of a Windows application:

- Perform primary functionality and maintain stability

- Provide 32-bit components and document any 16-bit code

- Support long filenames and UNC paths

- Support printers with long filenames and UNC paths

- Do not read from or write to Win.ini, System.ini, Autoexec.bat, or Config.sys on any Windows operating system that is based on NT technology

- Ensure that nonhidden files outside your application directory have associated file types, icons, descriptions, and actions

- Correctly perform Windows version checking

- Support AutoPlay of CDs

- Ensure that any kernel mode drivers that your application installs pass verification testing on Windows 2000

- Ensure that any hardware drivers included with your application pass Windows Hardware Quality Labs (WHQL) testing

◆ **Windows Installer Service**—Describes the requirements for implementing the Windows Installer service, ensuring that the application can be easily deployed in a corporate environment:

- Install using a Windows Installer–based package that passes validation testing

- Observe the rules for componentization

- Identify shared components

- Install to Program Files by default

- Properly support Add/Remove Programs

- Ensure that your application supports advertising

- Ensure correct uninstall support

◆ **Component Sharing**—Describes the requirements for handling shared components so that applications can coexist with one another:

  - Do not attempt to replace files that are protected by Windows file protection

  - (For component producers) Build side-by-side components

  - (For application developers) Consume and install side-by-side components

  - /Install any non–side-by-side shared files to the correct locations

◆ **Data and Settings Management**—Describes the requirements to ensure that applications support roaming users, multiple users per machine, and simplified machine replacement. Applications that meet these requirements can also operate properly in a secure Windows environment:

  - Default to My Documents for storage of user-created data

  - Correctly classify and store application data

  - Degrade gracefully on access denied

  - Run in a secure Windows environment

  - Adhere to system-level group policy settings

  - Ensure that applications that create .adm files properly store their ADM file settings in the Registry

◆ **User Interface Fundamentals**—Describes the requirements to provide an accessible user interface:

  - Support standard system size, color, font, and input settings

  - Ensure compatibility with the high-contrast mode

  - Provide documented keyboard access for all features

  - Expose the location of the keyboard focus

  - Do not rely exclusively on sound

- Do not place shortcuts to documents, help, or uninstallation in the Start menu

- Support multiple monitors

◆ **OnNow/ACPI Support**—Describes the requirements for ensuring that an application can participate in systemwide power management:

- For applications allowed to prevent sleep when busy, indicate busy application status properly

- In the nonconnected state, ensure that the application allows sleep and resumes normally

- In the connected state, handle sleep notifications properly

- Handle wake from normal sleep without losing data

- Properly handle wake from critical sleep

◆ **Application Migration**—Describes requirements for ensuring that an application continues to function correctly after the user upgrades to Windows 2000:

- Ensure that applications continue to function after upgrade to Windows 2000 Professional without reinstallation

The Designed for Microsoft Windows XP Logo Program

The Designed for Microsoft Windows XP logo program certifies an application for the Microsoft Windows XP operating system. To get the logo, applications must conform to the technical requirements defined in the Designed for Microsoft Windows XP application specifications. After an independent testing lab successfully tests the application and the vendor signs the logo license agreement with Microsoft, the application may carry the Designed for Microsoft Windows XP logo.

You can get the complete specifications for the Designed for Microsoft Windows XP logo program from the Windows Logo Program Web site, at `www.microsoft.com/winlogo`.

NOTE

Designed for Windows XP— Optimized Status If a product meets an extra set of requirements in addition to the core requirements mentioned in the Designed for Microsoft Windows XP application specifications, the product will achieve Designed for Windows XP—Optimized status. The product will still display the Designed for Windows XP logo, but it will enjoy additional marketing benefits such as better placement in the Windows product catalog.

For your quick reference, I have summarized the main points of this logo certification in the following list:

◆ **Windows Fundamentals**—Describes the requirements for consistent and stable functionality of a Windows application:

- Perform primary functionality and maintain stability

- Ensure that any kernel-mode drivers that the application installs pass verification testing on Windows XP

- Ensure that any device or filter drivers included with the application pass Windows Hardware Compatibility Testing (HCT)

- Correctly perform Windows version checking

- Support Fast User Switching and Remote Desktop

- Support new visual styles

- Support switching between tasks

◆ **Installation Requirements**—Describes the requirements for installing and uninstalling applications in Microsoft Windows XP to ensure that the application does not degrade the performance of the operating system or other applications:

- Do not attempt to replace files that are protected by Windows file protection

- Migrate from earlier versions of Windows

- Do not overwrite nonproprietary files with older versions

- Do not inappropriately require a reboot

- Install to Program Files by default

- Install any shared files that are not side-by-side to the correct locations

- Properly support Add/Remove Programs

- Support All Users installations

- Support Autorun for CDs and DVDs

◆ **Data and Settings Management**—Describes the requirements to ensure that applications support the infrastructure provided by Windows XP for state separation of user data, user settings, and computer settings:

- Default to the correct location for storing user-created data

- Correctly classify and store application data

- Deal gracefully with access-denied scenarios

- Support running as a limited user

The .NET Connected Logo Program

Microsoft recently launched another logo program that is based on Microsoft .NET technology. This logo program, announced in July 2002, is called the .NET Connected logo program. This logo program certifies the applications that expose and/or consume Extensible Markup Language (XML) Web services. There are two levels of compliance for participation in the .NET Connected logo program:

◆ **The Base-Level .NET Connected level**—This is the base level of the .NET Connected logo program. A certified application is identified by a silver .NET Connected logo. This program certifies applications that were built using the Microsoft .NET Framework and that expose and/or consume XML Web services that comply with industry XML standards. Certified applications must ensure that they can share information with other applications across programming languages and platforms.

◆ **The Premium-Level .NET Connected level**—This is the premium level of the.NET Connected logo program. A certified application is identified by a gold logo. This program certifies advanced-level applications that were built using the .NET Framework and that expose and/or consume XML Web services that comply with industry XML standards. Certified applications use the full capabilities of the .NET programming model for developing XML-based services that provide multi-language support and added security, as well as enhanced flexibility, reliability, and performance.

You can learn more about the .NET Connected logo program from the program's Web site, www.microsoft.com/net/logo.

> **NOTE**
>
> **The Optimized for Microsoft .NET Development Logo Program** Microsoft has started another logo program related to the .NET Connected logo program that has a blue Optimized for Microsoft .NET Development logo. This logo is used to identify products and services specifically designed for developers who are programming for the Microsoft .NET platform.

CHAPTER SUMMARY

KEY TERMS

- Delayed signing
- Deployment
- Merge module
- Native compilation
- Native Image Cache
- URL remoting

The chapter focuses on how to deploy Windows-based applications. Some simple applications are as easy to deploy as just copying the files from one location to another, whereas some applications are complex and require reliance on the Microsoft Windows Installer service. This chapter discusses how to create setup projects to deploy Windows-based applications. It also discusses how to use various types of editors provided in the setup and deployment projects to perform specific tasks. Through these editors you can perform various tasks on the target machine, such as placing files in multiple folders (including the GAC), creating Registry keys and values in the Registry Editor, associating file types with the application, checking on dependencies, performing custom actions at different phases (such as during install, commit, rollback, and uninstall), and customizing the user interface of the installation process.

This chapter also discusses shared assemblies. You have learned how to use the Strong Name tool (sn.exe) to digitally sign an assembly. You can also use the Strong Name to perform delayed signing for an assembly. This chapter also discusses how you can add assemblies to the GAC through Windows Explorer, the Microsoft .NET Framework Configuration tool, the Global Assembly Cache tool (gacutil.exe), and the Microsoft Windows Installer (via setup and deployment projects).

You have also learned how to precompile a Windows application during installation by creating an Installer class and adding the class to the custom actions.

The .NET Framework allows you to launch a remote application through the browser by just pointing to its URL. The Web server need not have the .NET Framework installed. It just needs to have a copy of the executable file placed in a virtual directory. However, the clients should have .NET Framework because the code is executed on their machines. This chapter shows how to set runtime security policies to include trust on the code that is executed over the network (an intranet or the Internet). It also summarizes the different ways in which Windows applications can be deployed.

Finally, this chapter discusses the Windows logo programs and Windows Installer requirements for Windows applications. You should make sure that your application conforms to these requirements in order to get the Certified for Windows 2000 logo or the Designed for Microsoft Windows XP logo. You might also want to pursue some of the other logo programs that are discussed.

APPLY YOUR KNOWLEDGE

Exercises

13.1 Using Microsoft's Sample .NET Framework Bootstrapper

The setup projects created in this chapter assume that the .NET Framework is already installed on the target machine. You cannot use Visual Studio .NET setup and deployment projects to package the required .NET Framework along with a setup package. The .NET Framework has to be installed on a target machine by using a .NET Framework redistributable file (dotnetfx.exe) that is available through one of the following:

◆ The Windows Component Upgrade CD-ROM that comes with Visual Studio .NET

◆ The Microsoft MSDN Download Center (http://msdn.microsoft.com/downloads/sample.asp?url=/MSDN-FILES/027/001/829/msdncomposite-doc.xml) or the Microsoft Windows Update Web site (http://windowsupdate.microsoft.com)

Ideally, you would like a Windows application's installation program to perform a test for availability of the .NET Framework on the target machine. If the .NET Framework is not already installed, then you need to install it by using the .NET Framework redistributable file (dotnetfx.exe).

In this exercise you will learn how to use Microsoft's sample .NET Framework bootstrapper setup.exe file along with a setup package generated through Visual Studio .NET to check for the availability of the .NET Framework on the user's machine and install it by using the .NET Framework redistributable file if it is not already installed.

Estimated Time: 20 minutes.

1. Open the solution 306C13. In the Solution Explorer, select the NetSqlSetup project.

2. Right-click the project and select Properties from the shortcut menu. In the NetSqlSetup project's Property Pages dialog box, change the Bootstrapper option to None. Click OK and build the project. Only the NetSqlSetup.msi file is created. It is created in the bin\Release folder of the NetSqlSetup project.

3. Download the setup.exe bootstrapper sample from http://msdn.microsoft.com/downloads/sample.asp?url=/msdn-files/027/001/830/msdncompositedoc.xml.

4. Install the downloaded sample. It will install two files on your computer: setup.exe and settings.ini. Copy both of the files to the bin\Release folder of the NetSqlSetup project.

5. Open the settings.ini file in any text editor. Change its contents so that it looks as follows:

```
[Bootstrap]
Msi=NetSqlSetup.msi
'LanguageDirectory=jpn
'ProductName=testproductname
'DialogText=
'CaptionText=
'ErrorCaptionText=
FxInstallerPath=d:\dotNetFramework
```

The value of FxInstallerPath is the path where you have stored the .NET Framework redistributable file dotnetfx.exe. You can change the value to the actual path that you have.

6. Open the setup.exe file. The installation is bootstrapped by the sample setup.exe file. It first tests for the availability of the .NET Framework. If the .NET Framework is not installed, it uses the path specified in FxInstallerPath to install the .NET Framework. Note that there are no bootstrap files for installing Microsoft Windows Installer.

APPLY YOUR KNOWLEDGE

This is because that check is a part of the .NET Framework installation and is automatically performed by `dotnetfx.exe`.

13.2 Creating a Database Script During Installation

In this chapter you have learned that the Custom Actions Editor allows you to perform custom actions during the installation process. In this exercise, you will create a custom action to run the Northwind database installation script during installation of the `NetSql` project. You will use `osql`, a command-line utility, to run the SQL script. This exercise assumes that you have Microsoft SQL Server installed on your machine.

Estimated Time: 20 minutes.

1. Open the solution `316C13`. Add a Visual Basic .NET Class Library project to the solution. Name the project `InstallNorthwind`.

2. Add the Northwind database installation script `instnwnd.sql` file (which is usually available in the Microsoft SQL Server installation directory) to the project.

3. Right-click the project `InstallNorthwind` and choose Add, Add New Item from the context menu. The Add New Item dialog box appears. Add an `Installer` class named `InstallNorthwind.vb` to the project.

4. Open the `InstallNorthwind.vb` file in the Code view. Add the following directive:

   ```
   Imports System.Diagnostics
   ```

5. Add the following code after the Component Designer Generated Code section in the class definition:

```vb
Public Overrides Sub Install( _
 ByVal savedState As _
 System.Collections.IDictionary)
    ' call the Install method of the base
    ' class
    MyBase.Install(savedState)
    Dim strSqlFilePath As String = _
     Me.Context.Parameters.Item("Args")

    ' Run the osql process to run the data
    ' base script
    Dim psi As ProcessStartInfo = _
     New ProcessStartInfo("osql.exe ", _
     "-E -i " & "\"" &  strSqlFilePath & _
     " \ "")
    psi.WindowStyle = _
    ProcessWindowStyle.Hidden
    Try
        Dim p As Process = Process.Start(psi)
        p.WaitForExit()
    Catch e As Exception
        ' throw InstallException with
        ' the original exception message
        Throw New InstallException( _
         e.Message + strSqlFilePath)
    End Try
End Sub

Public Overrides Sub Commit( _
 ByVal savedState As _
 System.Collections.IDictionary)
    ' Call the Commit method of the base
    ' class
    MyBase.Commit(savedState)
End Sub

Public Overrides Sub Rollback( _
 ByVal savedState As _
 System.Collections.IDictionary)
    ' Call the Rollback method of the base
    ' class
    MyBase.Rollback(savedState)
End Sub

Public Overrides Sub Uninstall( _
 ByVal savedState As _
 System.Collections.IDictionary)
    ' Call the Uninstall method of the base
    ' class
    MyBase.Uninstall(savedState)
End Sub
```

APPLY YOUR KNOWLEDGE

6. Build the `InstallNorthwind` project.

7. Select the `NetSqlSetup` project in the Solution Explorer. Open the File System Editor for the merge module project. Select the `Application Folder` node and add `Primary Output from InstallNorthwind (Active)` to the folder by selecting Action, Add, Project Output.

8. Open the Custom Actions Editor for the `NetSqlSetup` project. Select the `Custom Actions` node and select Add Custom Action from the context menu. The Select Item in Project dialog box appears. Select `Primary Output from InstallNorthwind (Active)` by navigating to the `Application Folder` node. Click OK. `Primary Output from InstallNorthwind (Active)` is added to all the four nodes under `Custom Actions`.

9. Select the newly added custom action under the `Install` node. Move it before the `Launch NetSql` custom action. Open the Properties window and set the `CustomActionData` property to `/Args="[TARGETDIR]instnwnd.sql"`.

10. Build the `NetSqlSetup` project. Install the project. This time during installation, the Northwind database installation script is also executed.

Review Questions

1. What are the advantages and disadvantages of XCOPY deployment?

2. What are the different parts of an assembly version?

3. What is the purpose of the File System Editor?

4. How can you customize the user interface of an installation process?

5. When can you call custom actions?

6. What are shared assemblies?

7. Where is the GAC located on a machine? How can you add items to the GAC?

8. For what is delay signing used?

9. When should you use a merge module project?

10. How can you convert MSIL code into native code? Where are the precompiled assemblies placed?

11. What is the purpose of the CustomActionData property in the Custom Actions Editor?

12. Define URL remoting.

13. Name some ways you can deploy a Windows application.

Exam Questions

1. You have created a database-driven Windows application. Using Microsoft SQL Server, you have also generated an installation script for your database. This script is stored in a file named `InstData.sql`. You want to deploy this application on your client's computer. When the application is deployed, the database should also be created on the user's computer. You are creating a setup project by using Visual Studio .NET. Which of the following action should you take to create the database while deploying your application on the client's machine?

   A. Create a component that derives from the Installer class. Override its Install method to create the database. Add the component to the Install node of the Custom Actions Editor in the setup project.

APPLY YOUR KNOWLEDGE

B. Create a component that derives from the Installer class. Override its Install method to create the database. Add the component to the Commit node of the Custom Actions Editor in the setup project.

C. Copy the InstData.sql file to the Application Folder node on the File System on Target Machine node by using the File System Editor. Add InstData.sql to the Install node of the Custom Actions Editor in the setup project.

D. Create a component that derives from the Installer class. Override its Install method to create the database. Add the component to the Launch Conditions Editor in the setup project.

2. You are creating a setup project for a Windows application. In the Property Pages dialog box for the setup project, you have set the compression property to Optimized for Speed. Which of the following options will be true as a result of this configuration option? (Select two.)

A. All assemblies in the application will be pre-compiled to native code so that they run faster.

B. Resulting assemblies will be of larger size.

C. The setup package will be of larger size.

D. The setup project will run faster.

3. You have developed a database-intensive Windows application. When the application is installed on the user's computer, the required database must also be installed. The execution of the program cannot continue without the database. Therefore, if setup of the database fails, you would like to roll back the installation process.

Which of the following editors would you use in the setup project to ensure that the database is properly installed on the target machine?

A. File System Editor

B. Custom Actions Editor

C. Launch Conditions Editor

D. Registry Editor

4. You have created a Windows application that uses some components that are not shared by other applications. Each of these components creates its own assemblies, and all these assemblies have strong names associated with them. The application that uses these components is not required to load a specific version of these components. You do not want to store the assembly directly under the application's installation folder. Which of the following options is the best approach to store the assembly files for the application's components?

A. Store the components in the GAC.

B. Store the components anywhere you like and specify the path to them by using the <codebase> element in the application's configuration file.

C. Store the assemblies in one of the subdirectories under the application's installation directory and specify this subdirectory as part of the <probing> element in the application's configuration file.

D. Store the components in the Windows System directory.

5. When you install a Windows application on a target machine, you want to store the Readme.txt file in the directory that the user selects to install the application. You also want to create a shortcut for the Readme.txt file on the desktop of the target machine.

APPLY YOUR KNOWLEDGE

While creating a setup project, which of the following actions would you take in the File System Editor to achieve this? (Select all that apply.)

A. Move the shortcut to the Readme.txt file from the Application Folder node to the User's Desktop node in the File System on Target Machine node.

B. Add the Readme.txt file to the Application Folder node of the File System on Target Machine node.

C. Create a shortcut to the Readme.txt file that is available in the Application Folder node of the File System on Target Machine node.

D. Add the Readme.txt file to the User's Desktop node in the File System on Target Machine node.

E. Move the shortcut to the Readme.txt file from the User's Desktop node to the Application Folder node in the File System on Target Machine node.

6. You have written a component that will be shared among multiple applications. You want to install the component to the GAC. Which of the following tools would you use to achieve this? (Select two.)

A. sn.exe

B. gacutil.exe

C. ngen.exe

D. installutil.exe

7. You are a developer in a large manufacturing company. You are developing a complex inventory control application with a team of 15 other developers.

You have written two program modules, inv1234.vb and inv5678.vb, that are generic and will be used from several other applications within the company. You compiled both the program modules by using the Visual Basic .NET compiler to produce the inv1234.netmodule and inv5678.netmodule files. You now want to link both of the compiled modules into an assembly that you will install in the GAC to test some Windows forms that depend on this assembly. You have decided to make the name of the assembly InvLib.dll. You do not have access to the private key of the company, although you have access to the company's public key. The public key is stored in a file named BigCoPublic.snk. When the testing is completed, your project manager will use the private key (stored in the BigCoPrivate.snk file) to fully sign all the assemblies in the accounting software application. Which of the following commands would you choose to successfully sign your assembly?

A.

```
al.exe inv1234.netmodule,inv5678.netmodule
➡ /delaysign /keyfile:BigCoPublic.snk
➡/out:InvLib.dll
```

B.

```
al.exe inv1234.netmodule,inv5678.netmodule
➡ /delaysign+ /keyfile:BigCoPublic.snk
➡/out:InvLib.dll
```

C.

```
al.exe inv1234.netmodule,inv5678.netmodule
➡ /delaysign- /keyfile:BigCoPublic.snk
➡/out:InvLib.dll
```

D.

```
csc.exe inv1234.vb,inv5678.vb /delaysign
➡ /keyfile:BigCoPublic.snk /out:InvLib.dll
```

APPLY YOUR KNOWLEDGE

8. You are using the Installer tool (installutil.exe) to install server resources by executing the installer components in three assemblies. You issued the following command:

   ```
   installutil Assembly1.exe Assembly2.exe
   Assembly3.exe
   ```

   During execution of this command, the installation of Assembly3 failed. Which of the following will happen?

   A. Only Assembly1.exe will be installed.

   B. Only Assembly2.exe will be installed.

   C. Both Assembly1.exe and Assembly2.exe will be installed.

   D. None of the assemblies will be installed.

9. You have written a Windows application for the time entry system of your company. All the employees of your company will use this application. For easy deployment, you are planning to copy the application to the Company's Web server and publish its URL on the company's intranet Web site. At a minimum, which of the following action would you take in order to ensure that users can use this application?

   A. Install the .NET Framework on all users' computers.

   B. Install the .NET Framework on the Web server.

   C. Install the .NET Framework on all users' computers as well as the Web server.

   D. Install Visual Studio .NET on the Web server and install the .NET Framework on users' computers.

10. You have designed a Windows application that will help users plan, manage, and file their income taxes. Because this market is competitive, you want to list the application in the Microsoft Windows catalog. Which of the following requirements must the application satisfy in order to get listed in the Windows catalog? (Select all that apply.)

   A. Install to program files by default.

   B. Properly support Add/Remove Programs.

   C. Support Autorun for CDs and DVDs.

   D. Fix all known bugs in the software.

11. You want to create a customized setup program for a Windows application. One of the screens shown during installation should be available only from the administrative installation of the Microsoft Windows Installer package. Other setup options are available for both regular and administrative installations. Which of the following editors would allow you to create such an installation program?

   A. File System Editor

   B. User Interface Editor

   C. Custom Actions Editor

   D. Launch Conditions Editor

12. You have used native compilation option for several assemblies in your Windows application. During the testing of the application, you found that one of several parameters on the order entry forms is displayed incorrectly. You determined that classes involved in the problem are part of the Native Image Cache. You want to analyze the contents of the Native Image Cache on the user's computer to see if the correct versions of the assemblies are installed there.

Which of the following methods can you use to view the contents of the Native Image Cache? (Select all that apply.)

A. Use the Assembly Cache Viewer shell extension (shfusion.dll).

B. Use the Global Assembly Cache tool (gacutil.exe).

C. Use the Native Image Generation tool (ngen.exe).

D. Use the Assembly Binding Log Viewer (fuslogvw.exe)

13. You work as a software developer for a big pharmacy. You are writing some components that will be shared across several applications throughout the company. You want to place an assembly named CommonComponents.dll in the GAC for testing purpose. You do not have access to the company's private key, but you have stored the company's public key in the assembly manifest of CommonComponents.dll. Which of the following commands you are required to run to place your assembly in the GAC? (Select all that apply.)

A. sn.exe -Vr CommonComponents.dll

B. sn.exe -Vu CommonComponents.dll

C. gacutil.exe /i CommonComponents.dll

D. gacutil.exe /u ComoonComponents.dll

14. You have created a Windows-based calendaring system that allows the salespersons at your company to synchronize their schedules with a central database on the company's Web site. Most of the time, salespersons are out of the office, participating in various sales events across the globe.

They would like to access your application from their laptops, wherever they are. The company has standardized that all laptops will be Windows XP Professional, with the .NET Framework installed; all laptops use Internet Explorer as the default browser.

To deploy your application, you have uploaded to the company's Web server all the necessary files, including the main application file calendar.exe and several DLL files that implement other important functionality that is required for the application to run. To inform the salespersons about the application, you are planning to send an email message to all of them, with the URL of the application, www.BigSalesCompany.com/Cal/Calendar.exe. You also want to give them instructions on configuring their computers so that the application runs properly. Which of the following instructions would ensure the minimum security risk for all salespersons? (Select all that apply.)

A. Using the .NET Framework Configuration Wizard, set the trust level for www.BigSalesCo.com/cal/Calendar.exe assembly to Full Trust.

B. Using the .NET Framework Configuration Wizard, increase the trust level for My Computer to Full Trust.

C. Using Internet Explorer, add the company Web site to the Trusted Sites list.

D. Using the .NET Framework Configuration Wizard, increase the trust level for Internet Zone to Full Trust.

E. Using the .NET Framework Configuration Wizard, increase the trust level for Trusted Sites Zone to Full Trust.

APPLY YOUR KNOWLEDGE

15. You are designing a Windows application that will be downloaded to users' computers from your company's Web server. After it is installed on a user's computer, the application may request and download more components from the Web site, as needed to meet the user's requirements. The application uses several components that need to be installed in the GAC on the user's machine. You want to sign your components with a cryptographic digital signature as well with an Authenticode signature, where the identity of your company is certified through an independent certifying authority. Which of the following options would you use for signing the components before they are packaged for deployment?

    A. Use sn.exe to sign the assemblies.

    B. Use signcode.exe to sign the assemblies.

    C. Use sn.exe followed by signcode.exe to sign the assemblies.

    D. Use signcode.exe followed by sn.exe to sign the assemblies.

Answers to Review Questions

1. XCOPY deployment is suitable for deploying small and simple applications that contain private assemblies. XCOPY deployment makes zero impact on the configuration of the target machine. However, it lacks most of the amenities provided by the Microsoft Windows Installer, such as copying files and shortcuts in different places on the target machine, associating file types with extensions, allowing custom actions to be performed during the installation process, providing the ability to roll back the installation process, uninstalling an application, repairing a component or an application, checking for dependencies and rolling back the installation process when the dependencies do not exists, and providing a user interface. Further, XCOPY deployment is not suitable when you want to place components or assemblies of an application in the GAC.

2. The different parts of an assembly version are <major>.<minor>.<build>.<revision>.

3. The File System Editor provides a mapping of the file system on the target machine. The folders are referred to by special names that during the installation process are converted to represent the folder as per the file system on the target machine.

4. The User Interface Editor allows you to create your own user interface for the installation process. There are three stages of installation: start, progress, and end. The editor allows you to add different varieties of dialog boxes to each of the different stages. It provides special properties whose values can be evaluated to perform the installation according to the end user's choice.

5. Custom actions can be performed in four phases: install, commit, rollback, and uninstall.

6. Shared assemblies are shared by multiple applications on a machine and are placed in the GAC. A shared assembly should have a strong name, consisting of its text name (usually the name of the file, without the file extension), version number, culture information, and public key token. The developer assigns a public key token by digitally signing an assembly.

APPLY YOUR KNOWLEDGE

7. The GAC is located in the assembly folder under the system folder on a machine. You can view shared assemblies in the GAC by navigating to the assembly folder in Windows Explorer. You can add shared assemblies to the GAC through Windows Explorer, the .NET Framework Configuration tool (mscorcfg.msc), the Global Assembly Cache tool (gacutil.exe), or the Windows Installer.

8. Delay signing is a process that allows you to place a shared assembly in the GAC by just signing the assembly with the public key. This allows the assembly to be signed with the private key at a later stage, when the development process is complete and the component or assembly is ready to be deployed.

9. Merge modules should be used to package components with their related resources, Registry entries, custom actions, and launch conditions. Merge modules cannot be installed directly; rather, they are merged into an installer project.

10. You can compile from MSIL to native code by using the Native Image Generation tool (ngen.exe). The assemblies that are compiled into machine-specific native code are placed in the Native Image Cache.

11. The CustomActionData property is used to pass custom data from a setup program to the custom Installer class.

12. URL remoting provides a zero-impact deployment model for deploying a Windows application. The code and configuration files reside on a Web server, and you can execute the application by just pointing to the URL of the EXE file from Internet Explorer on the end user's computer.

13. You can deploy applications in the following ways:

   • Deployment via removable media

   • Network-based deployment

   • Web-based deployment

Answers to Exam Questions

1. **A.** You can use the Custom Actions Editor to take custom actions such as actions related to database installation during application setup. If you have an Installer class or a program that creates databases, it must be added to the Install node of the Custom Actions Editor.

2. **C, D.** When you modify a setup project's property, it does not affect the size or the speed of the installed assemblies. Instead, the setup program compresses the assemblies by using a compression algorithm that is optimize for speed. As a result, you will have a lower compression ratio, resulting in large setup packages that will execute faster.

3. **B.** The Custom Actions Editor allows you to execute custom actions such as database installations while running the setup program. It also has provisions for performing installation rollbacks if installation operations fail.

4. **C.** If the components are not shared between applications, it is not a good idea to store the components in the GAC. You could use the <codebase> element in the application's configuration file, but in that case you must specify a version of assembly. The application in question is not specific about versions, so a good place to store the assemblies is in a folder inside the application's installation folder, specifying the location via the <probing> element in the application's configuration file.

APPLY YOUR KNOWLEDGE

5. **A, B, C.** To copy the Readme.txt file to the installation directory selected by the user at install time, you would add it to the Application Folder node in the File System on Target Machine node. To create a shortcut, you first create a shortcut to the Readme.txt file stored in the Application Folder node in the File System on Target Machine node. Then, you move this shortcut from the Application Folder node to the User's Desktop node in the File System on Target Machine node.

6. **A, B.** When you want to install a component to the GAC, you first assign it a strong name, which you do by using the Strong Name tool (sn.exe). You can place a strong-named assembly in the GAC by using the Global Assembly Cache tool (gacutil.exe).

7. **B.** You can use the al.exe command to link already compiled modules into an assembly. The process of including a public key in the assembly and signing it a private key at a later stage is called *delay signing*. You can perform delay signing on an assembly by using al.exe with the /delay+ switch.

8. **D.** installutil.exe performs installation in a transactional manner. If one of the assemblies fails to install, installutil.exe rolls back the installations of all other assemblies. So if installation of Assembly3.exe fails, none of the assemblies will be installed.

9. **A.** You only have to install the .NET Framework on all user computers. It is not required to have the .NET Framework or Visual Studio .NET installed on the Web server.

10. **A, B, C.** To be listed in the Windows catalog, an application must meet the requirements mentioned in the specifications of the Windows logo program. You are not required to fix all known bugs to be listed in the Windows catalog.

11. **B.** You can customize the user interface of an installation program by using the User Interface Editor for both the regular installation and the administrative installation.

12. **A, B, C.** The Native Image Cache can be viewed with all these tools except for the Assembly Binding Log Viewer (fuslogvw.exe), which is used to display failed assembly binds.

13. **A, C.** You have to first turn off the verification for partially signed assemblies. You can do this by using the sn.exe tool with the -Vr switch. Next, you can install the assembly to the GAC by using /i switch with the gacutil.exe command.

14. **C, E.** In this scenario, the content is coming from the Web, but all the content is hosted on a single site. The minimum-risk solution would be to add the company to the Trusted Sites list and then increase the trust level for trusted sites to Full Trust.

15. **C.** sn.exe is used to sign an assembly with a cryptographic digital certificate, and signcode.exe is used to sign an assembly with an Authenticode signature. When both are used together to sign an assembly, you should always use sn.exe before using signcode.exe.

APPLY YOUR KNOWLEDGE

Suggested Readings and Resources

1. The Visual Studio .NET Combined Help Collection:

   - Deploying Applications and Components

   - Deployment Walkthroughs

   - Creating Installation Components

2. Richter, Jeffrey. *Applied Microsoft .NET Framework Programming.* Microsoft Press, 2002.

3. Version 1 Security Changes for the .NET Framework, `http://msdn.microsoft.com/library/en-us/dnnetsec/html/v1securitychanges.asp`.

4. Certified for Windows Program, `http://msdn.microsoft.com/certification`.

5. Designed for Windows Logo Program, `www.microsoft.com/winlogo`.

6. The .NET Connected Logo, `www.microsoft.com/net/logo`.

This chapter covers the following Microsoft-specified objectives for the "Maintaining and Supporting a Windows-Based Application" section of the Visual Basic .NET Windows-Based Applications exam:

Optimize the performance of a Windows-based application.

▶ This exam objective requires you to know about the techniques of optimizing a Windows application for performance. Although the .NET Framework is itself optimized for many common tasks, you'll still find that the choices you make in your code are critical for performance. Code that deals with databases is often a good candidate for optimization due to the sheer number of choices for data access. User interface code is also critical because it's the part of the application that's most visible to the user.

Diagnose and resolve errors and issues.

▶ After an application has been deployed, you would ideally expect it to run smoothly. However, experience shows that even a well-tested application may misbehave for various reasons. You may be able to pinpoint problems if you log the behavior of your application. You might also want to design applications that can fine-tune themselves according to their environment. For example, you might want to create an application that can start or stop itself in response to performance measurements. The .NET Framework provides you with a variety of components and tools to publish, record, and analyze an application's performance. This exam objective requires you to know about the classes in the System.Diagnostics namespace that help you design an application that is easy to manage and maintain.

CHAPTER 14

Maintaining and Supporting a Windows Application

STUDY STRATEGIES

▶ Review the "Performance Tips and Tricks in .NET Applications" whitepaper from the Visual Studio .NET Combined Help Collection. This paper is also available online, at http://msdn.microsoft.com/library/en-us/dndotnet/html/dotnetperftips.asp.

▶ Try out the walkthrough exercises related to the Process, EventLog, and PerformanceCounter classes from the "Visual Basic and Visual C# Walkthroughs" section of the Visual Studio .NET Combined Help Collection.

▶ Review the Design Goals—Performance section of the "Designing Distributed Applications" topic from the Visual Studio .NET Combined Help Collection.

INTRODUCTION

The System.Diagnostics namespace provides various classes that help in managing and monitoring a Windows application. In this chapter, I'll focus on three of these classes:

◆ **Process**—The Process class provides information about the processes that are running on a computer. You can also use this class to access process information for computers across a network. This class also facilitates starting and stopping a process on a local computer.

◆ **EventLog**—The EventLog class allows you to read from and write to a Windows event log. Your applications can monitor an event log to take action when an entry is written to the log. An application may also publish its own events that may be of interest to other applications or to the system administrator.

◆ **PerformanceCounter**—The PerformanceCounter class can be used to get performance data for running processes. You can also use this class to publish performance data over a network.

In addition to these classes, I'll show you how to use a number of supporting classes to monitor and manage processes, event logs, and performance counters. The System.Diagnostics namespace provides other classes, such as Trace and Debug, that help you test and debug applications. For more information on the Trace and Debug classes, see Chapter 12, "Testing and Debugging a Windows Application."

In the latter part of this chapter, I'll also discuss various techniques that may help you improve the performance of applications.

MANAGING A WINDOWS PROCESS

Diagnose and resolve errors and issues.

A *process* is an application that is being executed. Each running process is uniquely identified on a computer with a process identifier (PID). When a process executes, it consumes resources such as processor time and memory. Managing a Windows process involves getting execution information about the running processes. You can also programmatically start or stop processes.

The System.Diagnostics namespace provides several classes that help with process management. The key to working with processes is the Process class. This class represents an instance of a process. You can create instances of the Process class programmatically, or you can use the Process component from the Windows Forms Designer's toolbox. Programmatic access is especially useful for dynamically representing multiple running processes.

Starting and Stopping Processes

To start a process, you can use the Start method of the Process class. This method is available in both static and nonstatic versions. To use the nonstatic version of the Start method, you must create an instance of the Process class, set its StartInfo property to specify the necessary startup information (such as the executable filename, arguments, environment variables, and working directory), and call the Start method of this instance. The static version of the Start method returns an instance of a created process. You pass the static version a ProcessStartupInfo object or other arguments, such as the application's filename and environment.

Two methods can stop a process: CloseMainWindow and Kill. The CloseMainWindow method requests a normal shutdown of a program. This is equivalent to closing an application by clicking the close icon in the application's main window. CloseMainWindow can only stop processes that participate in the Windows message loop and that have user interfaces. On the other hand, the Kill method causes an abnormal program termination by forcibly killing an application. Using Kill is the way to stop processes that do not have user interfaces or that do not participate in the Windows message loop (such as MS-DOS–based programs).

Table 14.1 lists the members of the Process class that are useful for starting and stopping processes.

NOTE

Starting and Stopping a Process The Process class allows you to start and stop processes on the local machine only. Although you can use the Process class to access process information for remote machines, you cannot start or stop processes on a remote machine by using this class.

WARNING

Be Careful with Kill Using the Kill method is the equivalent of using Task Manager to kill a process that is hung. If you use this method to kill a process, the process won't have a chance to save data or clean up resources that it's using.

TABLE 14.1

MEMBERS OF THE Process CLASS THAT ARE USEFUL FOR STARTING AND STOPPING PROCESSES

Member	Type	Description
CloseMainWindow	Method	Closes a process that has a user interface by sending a close message to the main window of the process.
EnableRaisingEvents	Property	Specifies whether the Exited event should be raised when the process terminates.
ExitCode	Property	Holds a value specified by the process when it exits.
Exited	Event	Occurs when the process exits.
ExitTime	Property	Specifies the time at which the process exited.
GetProcessById	Method	Returns a Process object that represents an already running process with a given PID.
GetProcesses	Method	Returns an array of Process objects in which each element represents an already existing process.
GetProcessesByName	Method	Returns an array of Process objects in which each element represents an already running process with a specified process name.
HasExited	Property	Indicates whether the process has been terminated.
Id	Property	Acts as the unique identifier of the process.
Kill	Method	Immediately stops the process.
StartInfo	Property	Specifies the properties to pass to the Start method of the process.
WaitForExit	Method	Sets the length of time to wait for the process to exit and blocks the current thread of execution until that time has elapsed or the process has exited.
WaitForInputIdle	Method	Causes a Process object to wait for the process to enter an idle state.

Step By Step 14.1 shows how to start and stop a process.

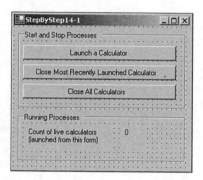

FIGURE 14.1
A form to start and stop processes.

STEP BY STEP

14.1 Starting and Stopping a Process

1. Launch Visual Studio .NET, and Select File, New, Blank Solution.

2. Add a Visual Basic .NET Windows application project to the solution. Name the project StepByStep14-1.

3. Rename the Form1.vb form StepByStep14-1.vb in the project. Switch to the Code view of the form and modify all references to Form1 so that they refer to StepByStep14-1 instead.

4. Place two GroupBox controls, three Button controls (btnLaunchCalculator, btnCloseRecentCaclulator, and btnCloseAllCalculators), and two Label controls (one named lblLiveCalculators) on the form and arrange the controls as shown in Figure 14.1.

5. Switch to the Code view. Add the following statement at the top of the form's module:

```
Imports System.Diagnostics
```

6. Add the following code directly after the Windows Form Designer Generated Code section:

```
' Declare an ArrayList to hold the
' process id of calculators
Dim arrCalculators As ArrayList = New ArrayList()
```

7. Add the following event handler to the code:

```
' Handles the Exited event of the Calculator process
Private Sub Calculator_Exited(ByVal sender As Object, _
ByVal e As System.EventArgs)
    ' Remove the process that has exited from the
    ' ArrayList
    ' Decrement the count of the live calculators
    Dim p As Process = CType(sender, Process)
    arrCalculators.RemoveAt(arrCalculators.IndexOf(p.Id))
    lblLiveCalculators.Text = _
      (Int32.Parse(lblLiveCalculators.Text) - 1).ToString()
End Sub
```

8. Add the following code to handle the events of the Button
controls:

```
Private Sub btnLaunchCalculator_Click( _
 ByVal sender As System.Object, _
 ByVal e As System.EventArgs) _
 Handles btnLaunchCalculator.Click
    ' Create a new process "calc.exe "
    ' Add an event handler to the
    ' Exited event of the process
    Dim prcCalculator As Process = New Process()
    prcCalculator.StartInfo.FileName = "calc.exe "
    prcCalculator.EnableRaisingEvents = True
    AddHandler prcCalculator.Exited, _
     AddressOf Calculator_Exited

    ' Start the process
    prcCalculator.Start()
    ' Wait for process to enter idle state
    prcCalculator.WaitForInputIdle()
    ' Add the Process Id of the calculator to the
    ' ArrayList
    arrCalculators.Add(prcCalculator.Id)
    ' Increment the count of the live calculators
    lblLiveCalculators.Text = _
     (Int32.Parse(lblLiveCalculators.Text) + 1).ToString()
End Sub

Private Sub btnCloseRecentCalculator_Click( _
 ByVal sender As System.Object, _
 ByVal e As System.EventArgs) _
 Handles btnCloseRecentCalculator.Click
    If arrCalculators.Count > 0 Then
        ' Pick up the last process id from the ArrayList
        Dim intId As Integer = _
         CInt(arrCalculators(arrCalculators.Count - 1))
        Try
            ' Get the Process object through the process
            ' id
            ' Close the process by closing the window
            Dim p As Process = _
             Process.GetProcessById(intId)
            p.CloseMainWindow()
        Catch ex As Exception
            Trace.WriteLine(ex.Message)
        End Try
    End If
End Sub

Private Sub btnCloseAllCalculators_Click( _
 ByVal sender As System.Object, _
 ByVal e As System.EventArgs) _
 Handles btnCloseAllCalculators.Click
```

continues

continued

```
' Get all the processes by name "calc"
Dim arrCalculators() As Process = _
 Process.GetProcessesByName("calc")

' Close each process by closing the window
Dim prcCalculator As Process
For Each prcCalculator In arrCalculators
    prcCalculator.CloseMainWindow()
Next
End Sub
```

9. Set the form as the startup object for the project and set the project as the startup project for the solution.

10. Run the project. Click the Launch a Calculator button several times. Multiple calculator windows are opened, and the "live calculators" label keeps updating the count of the live calculators that are opened from this application. Click the Close Most Recently Launched Calculator button to close the last calculator process started.

11. Close a calculator by clicking its close button. Note that this program receives a notification of the calculator's Exit event, and the count of live calculators is reduced by 1 by the Exited event-handling code.

12. Start a Windows calculator from the Windows Start menu; position it separately onscreen to distinctly identify it from other calculator opened by your program. Click the Close Most Recently Launched Calculator button, and note that the only last calculator started from this program closes, and the calculator that was externally started is still active. Now click the Close All Calculators button, and note that all the calculators are closed, whether or not they were opened from this program.

Getting Process Information

You can create an instance of the Process class for any of the processes running on the local or a remote machine. You can then use this object to get details about the running process. Some examples of execution details include the current processor usage, the memory usage, and whether the process is responding.

Access to this information in an application might help you decide if you need to increase or decrease processing in the application, based on the current system load. This information might also help you terminate or restart misbehaving processes. Table 14.2 lists some important properties of the Process class for getting information about processes.

TABLE 14.2

IMPORTANT PROPERTIES OF THE Process CLASS FOR GETTING INFORMATION ABOUT PROCESSES

Property	Description
MachineName	Specifies the name of the computer on which the process is running.
MainModule	Specifies the main module of the process.
MainWindowTitle	Specifies the caption of the main window of the process.
Modules	Specifies what modules have been loaded by the associated process.
PriorityClass	Specifies the priority class for the process.
ProcessName	Specifies the name of the process.
ProcessorAffinity	Specifies the processors on which the threads in this process can be scheduled to run.
Responding	Indicates whether the user interface of the process is responding.
StandardError	Provides access to a StreamReader object through which you can read error output from the process.
StandardInput	Provides access to a StreamWriter object through which you can write input to the process.
StandardOutput	Provides access to a StreamReader object through which you can read output from the process.
StartTime	Specifies the time at which the process was started.
Threads	Gets the threads that are running in the associated process.
TotalProcessorTime	Specifies the total processor time spent on this process.
UserProcessorTime	Specifies the total user processor time spent on this process.
VirtualMemorySize	Specifies the size of the process's virtual memory.
WorkingSet	Specifies the physical memory usage of the process.

I will use some of these classes in Step By Step 14.2 to display information about the processes that are running on local and remote computers.

STEP BY STEP

14.2 Getting Process Information

1. Add a Visual Basic .NET Windows application project to the solution. Name the project StepByStep14-2.

2. Delete the default form from the project. Add a new form named StepByStep14-2.

3. Place three Label controls, one TextBox control (txtMachine), one Button control (btnLoad), and two ListView controls (lvwProcesses and lvwProcessInfo) on the form. Set the View properties of the ListView controls to Details. Select the Columns property of the lvwProcesses control and click the Build button. The ColumnHeader Collection Editor dialog box appears. Add two column headers, Process Name (chProcessName) and Process ID (chProcessId), as shown in Figure 14.2. Add to the lvwProcessInfo control two column headers, Property (chProperty) and Value (chValue).

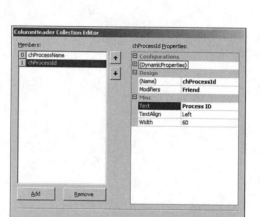

FIGURE 14.2
The ColumnHeader Collection Editor.

4. Switch to the Code view. Add the following statement at the top of the form's module:

```
Imports System.Diagnostics
```

5. Add the following code directly after the Windows Form Designer Generated Code section:

```
' Create a string member to hold the Machine Name
Private strMachineName As String
```

6. Add this code to handle events for the form:

```
Private Sub StepByStep14_2_Load( _
 ByVal sender As System.Object, _
 ByVal e As System.EventArgs) Handles MyBase.Load
    ' Set the textbox with the System ComputerName
    strMachineName = SystemInformation.ComputerName
    txtMachine.Text = strMachineName
End Sub
```

```
Private Sub btnLoad_Click(ByVal sender As System.Object, _
 ByVal e As System.EventArgs) Handles btnLoad.Click
    ' Get the Machine name
    ' Clear the list view controls
    strMachineName = txtMachine.Text
    lvwProcesses.Items.Clear()
    lvwProcessInfo.Items.Clear()
    Try
        ' Get all the processes
        Dim arrProcesses() As Process = _
         Process.GetProcesses(strMachineName)
        Dim p As Process
        For Each p In arrProcesses
            ' Add each process into the lvwProcesses
            Dim lvwItem As ListViewItem = _
                New ListViewItem(New String() _
                {p.ProcessName, p.Id.ToString()})
            lvwProcesses.Items.Add(lvwItem)
        Next
    Catch ex As Exception
        MessageBox.Show(ex.Message)
    End Try
End Sub

Private Sub lvwProcesses_SelectedIndexChanged( _
 ByVal sender As Object, ByVal e As System.EventArgs) _
 Handles lvwProcesses.SelectedIndexChanged
    lvwProcessInfo.Items.Clear()
    ' Get the PID of the selected process
    Dim intProcessId As Integer = _
     Convert.ToInt32(Me.lvwProcesses. _
     FocusedItem.SubItems(1).Text)
    Try
        Dim p As Process = _
         Process.GetProcessById(intProcessId, _
         strMachineName)

        ' Add Process information to the
        ' lvwProcessInfo(Control)
        Dim lvwItem As ListViewItem = New ListViewItem( _
            New String() {"StartTime", _
            p.StartTime.ToString()})
        lvwProcessInfo.Items.Add(lvwItem)

        lvwItem = New ListViewItem( _
            New String() {"TotalProcessorTime", _
            p.TotalProcessorTime.ToString()})
        lvwProcessInfo.Items.Add(lvwItem)

        lvwItem = New ListViewItem( _
            New String() {"VirtualMemorySize", _
            p.VirtualMemorySize.ToString()})
        lvwProcessInfo.Items.Add(lvwItem)
```

continues

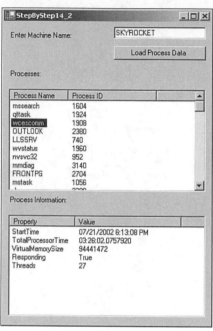

FIGURE 14.3
A form that displays process information.

continued

```
      If strMachineName = _
      SystemInformation.ComputerName Then
          lvwItem = New ListViewItem( _
              New String() {"Responding", _
              p.Responding.ToString()})
          lvwProcessInfo.Items.Add(lvwItem)

          lvwItem = New ListViewItem( _
              New String() {"Threads", _
              p.Threads.Count.ToString()})
          lvwProcessInfo.Items.Add(lvwItem)
      End If
    Catch ex As Exception
      Debug.WriteLine(ex.Message)
    End Try
End Sub
```

7. Set the form as the startup form for the project and set the project as the startup project for the solution.

8. Run the project. Your system computer name appears in the text box. Change the value if you want and then click the Load Process Data button. A list of all the running processes appears in the Processes list. Select a process from the list; its information appears in the Process Information control, as shown in Figure 14.3.

> **NOTE**
>
> **Processes on a Remote Computer**
> You must have administrative privileges on the remote computer in order to get process information for that computer.

GUIDED PRACTICE EXERCISE 14.1

In this exercise, you will work with the Process component that is available in the Windows Forms toolbox. Using this component is a convenient way to create processes in Windows Forms applications. Your objective is to create a form with two Button controls. When you click the Launch Editor button, the program should launch Windows Notepad. When you click the Close Editor button, the program should close the editor. The program should allow you to launch only one instance of the editor at a time.

You should try doing this on your own first. If you get stuck, or if you'd like to see one possible solution, follow these steps:

1. Add a Visual Basic .NET Windows application project to the solution. Name the project `GuidedPracticeExercise14-1`.

2. Rename the `Form1.vb` form `GuidedPracticeExercise14-1.vb` in the project. Switch to the Code view of the form and modify all references to `Form1` so that they refer to `GuidedPracticeExercise14_1` instead.

3. Place two `Button` controls (`btnLaunch` and `btnClose`) on the form. Select the Components tab in the toolbox and drag a `Process` component onto the form.

4. Change the `Name` property of the `Process` component to `prcEditor` and set its `EnableRaisingEvents` property to `True`. Expand the `StartInfo` property so that you can access its sub-properties. Change the `FileName` property to `Notepad.exe`.

5. Add the following code to handle the `Exited` event of `prcEditor`:

```
Private Sub prcEditor_Exited( _
 ByVal sender As System.Object, _
 ByVal e As System.EventArgs) Handles prcEditor.Exited
    btnClose.Enabled = False
    btnLaunch.Enabled = True
End Sub
```

6. Add the following code to handle the `Click` events of the Button controls:

```
Private Sub btnLaunch_Click( _
 ByVal sender As System.Object, _
 ByVal e As System.EventArgs) Handles btnLaunch.Click
    ' Start the process
    prcEditor.Start()
    btnClose.Enabled = True
    btnLaunch.Enabled = False
End Sub

Private Sub btnClose_Click( _
 ByVal sender As System.Object, _
 ByVal e As System.EventArgs) Handles btnClose.Click
    ' Kill the process
    prcEditor.Kill()
End Sub
```

7. Set the form as the startup object for the project and set the project as the startup project for the solution.

continues

continued

8. Run the project. Click the Launch Editor button to launch a copy of Notepad, as shown in Figure 14.4. Click the Close Editor button to close the editor window.

FIGURE 14.4
A form that launches Notepad.

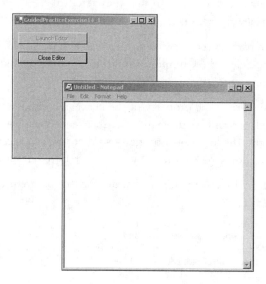

REVIEW BREAK

▶ A process is an application that is being executed. Each running process is uniquely identified on a computer with a PID.

▶ The Process class provides a large set of properties that can get information about running processes on a local or remote machine.

WORKING WITH EVENT LOGS

Event logging is the standard way in Windows for applications to leave records of their activities. You can easily monitor the behavior of an application by using the Event Viewer utility to analyze its messages in the event log. You can also view events from within the Visual Studio .NET environment. You can access event logs through the Server Explorer.

The Framework Class Library provides a set of classes that are designed to work with event logs. With the help of these classes, you can programmatically read from or write to the event logs. Programmatic access may even allow you to automate some of the administrative tasks associated with an application.

By default, three event logs are available: Application, Security, and System. Other applications or operating system components such as Active Directory may include other event logs. Table 14.3 lists the important members of the EventLog class.

TABLE 14.3

IMPORTANT MEMBERS OF THE EventLog CLASS

Member	Type	Description
CreateEventSource	Method	Opens an event source so an application can write event information.
Delete	Method	Removes a log resource.
DeleteEventSource	Method	Removes an application's event source from the event log.
EnableRaisingEvents	Property	Specifies whether the EventLog object receives notifications for the EntryWritten event.
Entries	Property	Gets the contents of an event log.
EntryWritten	Event	Occurs when an entry is written to an event log on the local computer.
Exists	Method	Determines whether the specified log exists.
GetEventLogs	Method	Creates an array of the event logs.
Log	Property	Specifies the name of the log to read from or write to.
LogDisplayName	Property	Specifies an event log's friendly name.
LogNameFromSourceName	Method	Gets the name of the log to which the specified source is registered.
MachineName	Property	Specifies the name of the computer on which to read or write events.
Source	Property	Specifies the source to register and use when writing to an event log.
SourceExists	Method	Finds whether a given event source exists.
WriteEntry	Method	Writes an entry in an event log.

Each application that is interested in interacting with an event log must register an event source with the log. When an event source is registered, its information is stored in the system registry and is available across application restarts.

The CreateEventSource method allows you to register an application with an event log. If the event log does not already exist, this method will create it for you.

Writing to Event Logs

The WriteEntry method of the EventLog object allows you to write messages to the event log specified by the event source. If you haven't called CreateEventSource, WriteEntry will create the event source for you.

You can write different types of messages (information, error, and so on) to an event log. These types are specified by the values in the EventLogEntryType enumeration.

The sample application in Step By Step 14.3 demonstrates how to create an event log, register an application with an event log, unregister an application with an event log, write to an event log, and delete an event log.

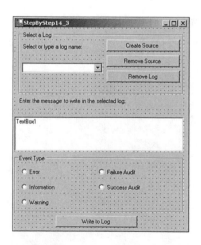

FIGURE 14.5
Form to create and write to event log.

STEP BY STEP

14.3 Creating and Writing to an Event Log

1. Add a Visual Basic .NET Windows application project to the solution. Name the project StepByStep14-3.

2. Rename the Form1.vb form StepByStep14-3.vb. Switch to the Code view of the form and modify all references to Form1 so that they refer to StepByStep14_3 instead.

3. Place two GroupBox controls, three Label controls, one TextBox control (txtMessage, with its MultiLine property set to True), four Button controls (btnCreate, btnRemoveSource, btnRemoveLog, and btnWrite), one ComboBox control (cbEventLogs), and five RadioButton controls (rbError, rbInformation, rbFailureAudit, rbSuccessAudit, and rbWarning) on the form. Arrange the controls as shown in Figure 14.5.

4. Switch to the Code view. Add this code to the top of the form's module:

```
Imports System.Diagnostics
```

5. Add the following code directly after the Windows Form Designer Generated Code section:

```
' Create a member to hold EventLogEntryType
Private eletEntryType As EventLogEntryType = _
 EventLogEntryType.Error
```

6. Add a new method named `PopulateLogNames` and an event handler for the form's `Load` event:

```
Private Sub PopulateLogNames()
    cbEventLogs.Items.Clear()
    ' Add eventlogs in to the combo box.
    Dim el As EventLog
    For Each el In EventLog.GetEventLogs()
        cbEventLogs.Items.Add(el.Log)
    Next
End Sub

Private Sub StepByStep14_3_Load( _
 ByVal sender As System.Object, _
 ByVal e As System.EventArgs) _
 Handles MyBase.Load
    PopulateLogNames()
End Sub
```

7. Add handlers for the `Click` events of the Button controls:

```
Private Sub btnCreate_Click( _
 ByVal sender As System.Object, _
 ByVal e As System.EventArgs) Handles btnCreate.Click
    If cbEventLogs.Text <> "" Then
        Dim strSourceName As String = _
         "StepByStep14-3_" & cbEventLogs.Text
        ' Check whether the Source already exists
        If Not EventLog.SourceExists(strSourceName) Then
            Try
                ' Create event source and the event log
                EventLog.CreateEventSource(_
                strSourceName, _
                 cbEventLogs.Text)
                PopulateLogNames()
                MessageBox.Show( _
                 "Created EventSource for " & _
                 "Selected EventLog")
            Catch ex As Exception
                MessageBox.Show(ex.Message)
            End Try
        Else
```

continues

continued

```
            MessageBox.Show( _
              "You already have an EventSource attached", _
              "Cannot Create EventSource")
        End If
    End If
End Sub

Private Sub btnRemoveSource_Click( _
 ByVal sender As System.Object, _
 ByVal e As System.EventArgs) Handles btnRemoveSource.Click
    If cbEventLogs.Text <> "" Then
        Dim strSourceName As String = _
          "StepByStep14-3_" & cbEventLogs.Text
        If EventLog.SourceExists(strSourceName) Then
            ' Delete the Event Source
            EventLog.DeleteEventSource(strSourceName)
            MessageBox.Show("Deleted the EventSource")
        Else
            MessageBox.Show( _
              "There is no EventSource for the EventLog")
        End If
    End If
End Sub

Private Sub btnRemoveLog_Click( _
 ByVal sender As System.Object, _
 ByVal e As System.EventArgs) Handles btnRemoveLog.Click

    Dim strLogName As String = cbEventLogs.Text.ToUpper()
    ' Do not delete system created logs
    If strLogName = "APPLICATION" Or _
     strLogName = "SECURITY" Or strLogName = "SYSTEM" Then
        Dim strMessage As String = _
          "This program does not allow deleting system" & _
          "created event logs"
        MessageBox.Show(strMessage, "Dangerous Operation")
        Exit Sub
    End If
    ' If the log exists
    If EventLog.Exists(cbEventLogs.Text) Then
        ' Confirm deletion from user
        Dim strMessage As String = "Are you sure?"
        If (MessageBox.Show(strMessage, _
          "Confirm Deletion", _
          MessageBoxButtons.YesNo) = DialogResult.Yes) Then
            Try
```

```
                    ' Delete the Event Log
                    EventLog.Delete(cbEventLogs.Text)
                    PopulateLogNames()
                Catch ex As Exception
                    MessageBox.Show(ex.Message, _
                     "Error Deleting EventLog")
                End Try
            End If
        Else
            MessageBox.Show("Event log does not exist", _
              "Cannot Delete EventLog")
        End If
End Sub

Private Sub btnWrite_Click( _
 ByVal sender As System.Object, _
 ByVal e As System.EventArgs) Handles btnWrite.Click
    If cbEventLogs.Text <> "" Then
        Dim strSourceName As String = "StepByStep14-3_" & _
          cbEventLogs.Text
        ' If Source exists
        If EventLog.SourceExists(strSourceName) Then
            Try
                ' Write an entry into event log
                EventLog.WriteEntry(strSourceName, _
                  txtMessage.Text, _
                  eletEntryType)
                MessageBox.Show( _
                  "Entry Written to the log Successfully")
            Catch ex As Exception
                MessageBox.Show(ex.Message, _
                  "Cannot Write to selected EventLog")
            End Try
        Else
            MessageBox.Show("No such event source", _
              "Event logging Failed")
        End If
    Else
        MessageBox.Show("Please Select a log to write to.")
    End If
End Sub
```

> **WARNING**
>
> **Deleting an Event Log**   You should use the Delete method to delete an event log cautiously. When an event log is deleted, all event sources that are registered with it are also deleted, so no application can continue writing to that log. Do not attempt to delete an event log created by Windows or any other important application; if you do, those applications might crash or behave in unexpected ways.

8. Add code to handle the CheckedChanged events of the RadioButton controls:

```
Private Sub rbError_CheckedChanged( _
 ByVal sender As System.Object, _
 ByVal e As System.EventArgs) _
 Handles rbError.CheckedChanged
    eletEntryType = EventLogEntryType.Error
End Sub
```

continues

continued

```
Private Sub rbInformation_CheckedChanged( _
 ByVal sender As System.Object, _
 ByVal e As System.EventArgs) _
 Handles rbInformation.CheckedChanged
    eletEntryType = EventLogEntryType.Information
End Sub

Private Sub rbWarning_CheckedChanged( _
 ByVal sender As System.Object, _
 ByVal e As System.EventArgs) _
 Handles rbWarning.CheckedChanged
    eletEntryType = EventLogEntryType.Warning
End Sub

Private Sub rbFailureAudit_CheckedChanged( _
 ByVal sender As System.Object, _
 ByVal e As System.EventArgs) _
 Handles rbFailureAudit.CheckedChanged
    eletEntryType = EventLogEntryType.FailureAudit
End Sub

Private Sub rbSuccessAudit_CheckedChanged( _
 ByVal sender As System.Object, _
 ByVal e As System.EventArgs) _
 Handles rbSuccessAudit.CheckedChanged
    eletEntryType = EventLogEntryType.SuccessAudit
End Sub
```

9. Set the project StepByStep14_3 as the startup project.

10. Run the project. Enter a name in the ComboBox control to create a source and connect to the event log. Select from the combo box the log that you want to write to, enter a message in the message text box, and select the type of the message from the radio button options. Click the Write to Log button to write to the event log.

11. To view the logged messages, navigate to the Server Explorer, expand the Servers node, and then select and expand the node corresponding to your computer. Right-click the Events node and select Launch Event Viewer from the shortcut menu. Figure 14.6 shows a custom event log created with this application.

NOTE

The Security Log   The security log is read-only. This is necessary to prevent malicious applications from filling the security log with nonsensical alerts to hide their tracks.

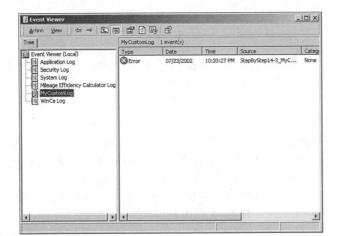

FIGURE 14.6
The Event Viewer, showing the event logs.

Reading and Monitoring Event Logs

To read the contents of an event log, you can access the Entries property of the EventLog object. This property returns an EventLogEntryCollection object, and each of the elements in this object gives you access to an individual event log entry.

You can monitor an event log by registering an event handler for its EntryWritten event. But before that, you have to set the EnableRaisingEvents property of the EventLog object to True.

> **NOTE**
> **Reading Entries from Remote Machines** Although the EventLog class allows you to access event log entries for remote machines, it does not allow you to dynamically get notification for entries written to event logs on remote machines. You can only attach an event handler to the EntryWritten event for the event logs on the local computer.

GUIDED PRACTICE EXERCISE 14.2

In this exercise, you will create a Windows form similar to the one shown in Figure 14.7. Your objective is to select an event log and get its content. The application should be able to get dynamic notifications of any messages written to the event log after you first read it. You can test this application by using it along with the program that you wrote in Step By Step 14.3, which writes to an event log.

You should try doing this on your own first. If you get stuck, or if you'd like to see one possible solution, follow these steps:

1. Add a Visual Basic .NET Windows application project to the solution. Name the project GuidedPracticeExercise14-2.

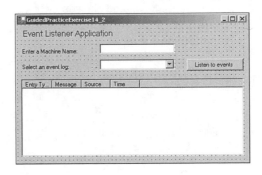

FIGURE 14.7
A form for listening to events from an event log.

continues

continued

2. Rename the `Form1.vb` form `GuidedPracticeExercise14-2.vb` in the project. Switch to the Code view of the form and modify all references to `Form1` so that they refer to `GuidedPracticeExercise14_2` instead.

3. Place three `Label` controls, one `TextBox` control (`txtMachineName`), one `Button` control (`btnListen`), one `ComboBox` control (`cbEventLogs`), and one `ListView` control (`lvwEvents`) on the form. Set the `View` property of `lvwEvents` to `Details`. Add to the `ListView` control four column headers with the `Text` properties of Entry Type (`chEntryType`), Message (`chMessage`), Source (`chSource`), and Time (`chTime`). Arrange the controls as shown in Figure 14.7.

4. Add a new method named `PopulateLogNames` and a handler for the form's `Load` event:

```
private void PopulateLogNames()
Private Sub PopulateLogNames()
    cbEventLogs.Items.Clear()
    Dim el As EventLog
    For Each el In EventLog.GetEventLogs( _
      txtMachineName.Text)
        cbEventLogs.Items.Add(el.Log)
    Next
End Sub


Private Sub GuidedPracticeExercise14_2_Load( _
 ByVal sender As System.Object, _
 ByVal e As System.EventArgs) Handles MyBase.Load
    ' Add eventlogs in to the combo box.
    PopulateLogNames()
End Sub
```

5. Attach an event handler to the `Leave` event of the `txtMachineName` control:

```
Private Sub txtMachineName_Leave( _
 ByVal sender As Object, _
 ByVal e As System.EventArgs) Handles
txtMachineName.Leave
    Try
        ' Add event logs in to the combo box.
        PopulateLogNames()
    Catch ex As Exception
      MessageBox.Show("Please try a different machine", _
          "Cannot Access Event Log")
      txtMachineName.Focus()
      txtMachineName.SelectAll()
    End Try
End Sub
```

6. Add an event handler for the Button control:

```vb
private void btnListen_Click(object sender, _
 System.EventArgs e)
Private Sub btnListen_Click( _
 ByVal sender As System.Object, _
 ByVal e As System.EventArgs) Handles btnListen.Click
    Dim el As EventLog = New EventLog( _
     cbEventLogs.Text, txtMachineName.Text)
    lvwEvents.Items.Clear()

    ' Check if the machine to listen for
    ' events from is the local machine
    If (txtMachineName.Text = _
     SystemInformation.ComputerName) Or _
     (txtMachineName.Text = ".") Then
        ' Allow the Event log to raise events
        el.EnableRaisingEvents = True
        ' Add an event handler for the EntryWritten
        ' event
        AddHandler el.EntryWritten, _
         AddressOf eventLog_EntryWritten
    Else
        MessageBox.Show("Can't receive notification " & _
         "from remote computers. Will just show the " & _
         "current event log contents.")
    End If
    Dim ele As EventLogEntry
    For Each ele In el.Entries
        ' Add the entry in to the list view
        AddEntryToListView(ele)
    Next
End Sub

Private Sub eventLog_EntryWritten( _
 ByVal source As Object, ByVal e As EntryWrittenEventArgs)
    ' Add the entry in to the list view
    AddEntryToListView(e.Entry)
End Sub

Public Sub AddEntryToListView(ByVal ele As EventLogEntry)
    Try
        Dim lviItem As ListViewItem = _
         New ListViewItem(New String() _
         {ele.EntryType.ToString(), _
         ele.Message.Trim(), _
         ele.Source, _
         ele.TimeGenerated.ToString()})
        lvwEvents.Items.Add(lviItem)
    Catch ex As Exception
        Debug.WriteLine(ex.Message)
    End Try
End Sub
```

continues

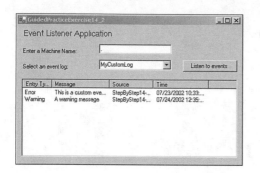

FIGURE 14.8
Listening to events from an event log.

continued

7. Set the form as the startup object for the project. In the Solution Explorer, right-click the solution and select Properties from the context menu. Select Startup Project from the left pane and choose the Multiple Startup projects option. Select Start Action for `StepByStep14-3` and `GuidedPracticeExercise14-2` to set both projects as startup projects.

8. Run the application. In the form `GuidedPracticeExercise14-2`, select the desired log from the combo box and click the Listen to Events button. A list of events that are already in the log appears. Use the `StepByStep14-3` form to add events to log. Watch the `GuidedPracticeExercise14-2` form (see Figure 14.8), and you'll see that events are added to the form as you save them to the log.

WORKING WITH PERFORMANCE COUNTERS

Performance counters are the Windows way of collecting performance data from running processes. Microsoft Windows itself provides several hundred performance counters, each of which monitors a particular system parameter. In addition, the various .NET server products, such as SQL Server and Exchange Server, and applications such as the .NET Framework, also publish their own custom performance counters.

Windows organizes performance counters in categories. Each category defines a specific set of performance counters. For example, there are categories such as Memory, Processor, and PhysicalDisk. The Memory category has various counters, such as Available Bytes, Cache Bytes, and Committed Bytes.

Some categories are further divided into instances. For example, the Process category is divided into several instances, each representing a running process on the computer. A new instance is added to the category whenever a new process is started and removed when a process is killed.

Each instance can have performance counters (such as I/O Read Bytes/sec) that specify the activity of that particular process. Usually all the instances in a category have the same list of performance counters. Of course each of the performance counters has unique performance data associated with it.

The PerformanceCounter class allows you to read performance samples for processes that are running on the local computer or on remote machines. By using this class, an application can even publish its own performance counters to inform the world about its performance level.

Table 14.4 lists the important members of the PerformanceCounter class.

TABLE 14.4

IMPORTANT MEMBERS OF THE PerformanceCounter CLASS

Member	Type	Description
CategoryName	Property	Specifies the performance counter category name.
Close	Method	Closes the performance counter and frees all the resources.
CounterHelp	Property	Describes the performance counter.
CounterName	Property	Specifies the name of the performance counter.
CounterType	Property	Specifies the type of the performance counter.
Decrement	Method	Decrements the value of the performance counter by one.
Increment	Method	Increments the value of the performance counter by one.
IncrementBy	Method	Increments or decrements the value of the performance counter by a specified amount.
InstanceName	Property	Specifies the instance name.
MachineName	Property	Specifies the computer name.
NextSample	Method	Gets a sample for the performance counter and returns the raw, or uncalculated, value for it.
NextValue	Method	Gets a sample for the performance counter and returns the calculated value for it.
RawValue	Property	Gets a sample for the performance counter and returns its raw, or uncalculated, value.

continues

NOTE

Performance Counters on Remote Machines   You can read existing performance counters on remote computers, but you can create custom performance counters only on the local machine.

| TABLE 14.4 | | *continued* |

IMPORTANT MEMBERS OF THE PerformanceCounter CLASS

Member	Type	Description
ReadOnly	Property	Indicates whether the performance counter is in read-only mode.
RemoveInstance	Method	Deletes an instance from the PerformanceCounter object.

Reading Performance Data of Running Processes

The process of reading a performance counter value is referred to as *sampling* the performance counter. When you sample a performance counter, you get a value that specifies the performance level of the process being monitored at that particular instant. The value of a performance counter may vary rapidly. A good way to analyze a performance counter is to graph the sample values over time. Windows provides the Performance Monitoring tool (perfmon.exe) for this very purpose. You can quickly launch this tool by executing perfmon.exe by selecting Windows Start, Run and typing perfmon.exe in the Run dialog box. You can also access it through the Performance option in the Administrative Tools section of the Windows Control Panel.

Although tools such as perfmon.exe make it simple for administrators to monitor the performance of an application, it is sometime also useful to read values programmatically. This can be useful, for example, when you want a program to monitor the performance of another program and take actions, depending on the performance data from that program. For example, you might want to run a processor-intensive SalesAnalysis application at a time when the critical DownloadWebOrders process is idle.

You can easily access the performance monitors installed on a computer through the Server Explorer in Visual Studio. NET. You can drag and drop the performance counter of your choice to create an instance of the PerformanceCounter component. Step By Step 14.4 demonstrate how to use an instance of the PerformanceCounter component to monitor the currently available memory on a computer.

STEP BY STEP

14.4 Reading Performance Data

1. Add a Visual Basic .NET Windows application project to the solution. Name the project `StepByStep14-4`.

2. Rename the `Form1.vb` form `StepByStep14-4.vb` in the project. Switch to the Code view of the form and modify all references to `Form1` so that they refer to `StepByStep14_4` instead.

3. Place a `Label` control and a `ListView` control (`lvwPerformance`) on the form. Change the `View` property of the `ListView` control to `Details`. Add to the `ListView` control four column headers with the `Text` properties of Counter Name (`chChounterName`), Counter Type (`chCounterType`), Time Stamp (`chTimeStamp`), and Raw Value (`chRawValue`).

4. Drag a `Timer` component onto the form. Set the `Enabled` property to `True` and the `Interval` property to `1000`.

5. Open the Server Explorer and select the server from the `Servers` node. Select the Available Bytes performance counter by navigating to Performance Counters , Memory, Available Bytes from the `Servers` node (see Figure 14.9). Drag the Available Bytes counter to the form. Name the counter `pcMemory`.

6. Switch to the Code view. Add the following code to the top of the form's module:

```
Imports System.Diagnostics
```

7. Attach an event handler to the `Tick` event of the `Timer` control and add the following code in the event handler:

```
Private Sub Timer1_Tick(ByVal sender As System.Object, _
 ByVal e As System.EventArgs) Handles Timer1.Tick
    ' Get the next performance data
    ' Add the data to the listview
   Dim csSample As CounterSample = pcMemory.NextSample()
   Dim lviItem As ListViewItem = _
    New ListViewItem(New String() _
    {pcMemory.CounterName, _
    csSample.CounterType.ToString(), _
    csSample.TimeStamp.ToString(), _
    csSample.RawValue.ToString()})
```

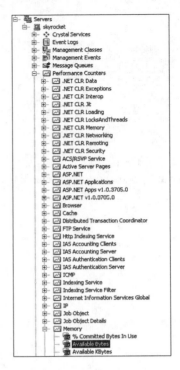

FIGURE 14.9
The Available Bytes performance counter in the Server Explorer.

continues

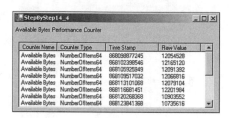

FIGURE 14.10
The Available Bytes performance counter.

continued

```
        lvwPerformance.Items.Add(lviItem)
End Sub
```

8. Set the form as the startup object for the project and set the project as the startup project for the solution.

9. Run the project. Every second a new performance value is added as a new row to the list view, as shown in Figure 14.10.

Publishing Performance Data

The .NET Framework allows applications to create their own custom performance counters and publish their performance data. This performance data can then be monitored from the Performance Monitoring tool (perfmon.exe), or it can be monitored through another application, such as the one you will create at the end of this chapter, in Exercise 14.2.

Visual Studio .NET makes it easy for you to create new performance categories and counters: It provides the Performance Counter Builder Wizard, which is available via the Server Explorer. In Step By Step 14.5, you will create a Windows application that publishes its performance and allows you to manually increase or decrease its performance.

STEP BY STEP

14.5 Publishing Performance Data

1. Add a Visual Basic .NET Windows application project to the solution. Name the project StepByStep14-5.

2. Rename the Form1.vb form StepByStep14-5.vb in the project. Switch to the Code view of the form and modify all references to Form1 so that they refer to StepByStep14_5 instead.

3. Place three `Label` controls (one named `lblCurrentLevel`), one `TextBox` control (`txtLevel`), and three `Button` controls (`btnInc`, `btnDec`, and `btnSet`) on the form. Arrange the controls as shown in Figure 14.11.

4. Open the Server Explorer. Select from the `Servers` node the server on which you want to create a performance counter. Right-click the `Performance Counters` node and select Create New Category. The Performance Counter Builder dialog box appears. Enter values in the dialog box as shown in Figure 14.12 and then click OK.

FIGURE 14.11
Publishing performance data.

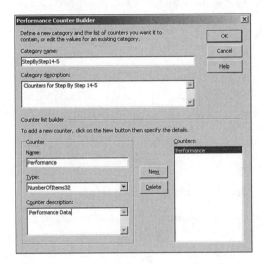

FIGURE 14.12
The Performance Counter Builder dialog box.

> **NOTE**
>
> **Creating a Custom Performance Counter** When you create a new performance counter, you must specify a completely new category for your local computer. It is not possible to add a new performance counter to an existing category; however, you can add several performance counters to a new custom category.
>
> It is also possible to create performance counter categories programmatically by using the PerformanceCounterCategory.Create method.

5. Select the new `StepByStep14-5` performance counter from the `Performance Counters` node in the Server Explorer. Drag the performance counter that appears under the `StepByStep14-5` node to the form. Set the `Name` property of the counter to `pc14_5` and set its `ReadOnly` property to `False`.

6. Switch to Code view. Add this line of code to the top of the form's module:

```
Imports System.Diagnostics
```

7. Add the following code to handle the Button controls' events:

continues

continued

```
Private Sub btnInc_Click(ByVal sender As System.Object, _
 ByVal e As System.EventArgs) Handles btnInc.Click
    pc14_5.Increment()
    lblCurrentLevel.Text = pc14_5.NextValue().ToString()
End Sub

Private Sub btnDec_Click(ByVal sender As System.Object, _
 ByVal e As System.EventArgs) Handles btnDec.Click
    pc14_5.Decrement()
    lblCurrentLevel.Text = pc14_5.NextValue().ToString()
End Sub

Private Sub btnSet_Click(ByVal sender As System.Object, _
 ByVal e As System.EventArgs) Handles btnSet.Click
    ' Set the performance counter value
    pc14_5.RawValue = Int32.Parse(txtLevel.Text)
    lblCurrentLevel.Text = pc14_5.NextValue().ToString()
End Sub
```

8. Attach Load and Closed event handlers to the form and add the following code in the event handlers:

```
Private Sub StepByStep14_5_Load( _
 ByVal sender As System.Object, _
  ByVal e As System.EventArgs) Handles MyBase.Load
    lblCurrentLevel.Text = pc14_5.NextValue().ToString()
End Sub

Private Sub StepByStep14_5_Closed( _
 ByVal sender As Object, _
 ByVal e As System.EventArgs) Handles MyBase.Closed
    pc14_5.RawValue = 0
End Sub
```

9. Set the form as the startup object for the project and set the project as the startup project for the solution.

10. Run the project. Enter a number in the text box and click the Set button. The label immediately reflects this as the current value of the performance counter. Click the increment and decrement buttons and notice the value changing in the label.

▶ The event log provides a central repository for various issues that an application may encounter while it is executing. Using an event log to record such messages not only makes the job of system administrator easier, but it also allows other applications to take appropriate action when an entry is written to a log.

▶ Multiple event sources can write into an event log. However, an event source can be used to write into only one event log.

▶ By default, events of the Process and EventLog classes are not enabled. You can set the EnableRaisingEvents property to True in order to instruct these classes to raise events.

▶ Performance counters are organized in categories. Each category defines a specific set of performance counters.

▶ The process of reading a performance counter value is called sampling the performance counter. The process of updating a performance counter value is called publishing a performance counter.

DESIGNING A WINDOWS APPLICATION FOR PERFORMANCE

Optimize the performance of a Windows-based application.

You should design and develop an application for good performance early in its development cycle. Removing any performance glitches early in the development cycle is much less expensive than removing them later on. The cost of rewriting modules, modifying code, and redistributing applications goes up as an application moves beyond design and into implementation.

A common practice for ensuring the quality of code is to do frequent code reviews. You should also plan to test alternative ways of implementing your code, to determine the performance impact of your choices.

The following are some of the commonly acknowledged best practices for writing high-performing applications by using the .NET Framework:

◆ **Use boxing and unboxing**—When a value type (such as a structure) is copied to a reference type (such as a class), the compiler needs to create an object on the heap and copy the value of the value type from the stack to this newly created object on the heap. This process is called *boxing*, and it requires more overhead than a simple copy from value type to value type. When you copy a reference type to a value type, the value of object from the heap is copied to the value type in the stack. This process is called *unboxing*. You should be aware of the overhead involved in boxing and unboxing, and while designing an application, you should choose data types that minimize this overhead.

◆ **Use StringBuilder instead of String**—The String type is immutable. That means that after a string is created, it can't be modified. When you modify a string, the Common Language Runtime in fact creates a new string, based on your modifications, and returns it. The original string still hangs around in memory, waiting to be garbage collected. If an application is extensively modifying strings, you should consider using the System.Text.StringBuilder class. This class stores the string as an array of characters. The StringBuilder object is mutable and does in-place modification of strings. Using StringBuilder may help you achieve noticeable performance gains in an application that uses many string manipulations.

◆ **Use AddRange with collections**—A large number of collection classes provide the AddRange method, which you can use to add an array of items to a collection. Using AddRange is much faster than adding elements by repeatedly calling the Add method inside a loop.

◆ **Use native compilation to reduce startup time**—When you compile a program by using the Visual Basic .NET compiler, the compiler generates Microsoft Intermediate Language (MSIL) code. When the program is loaded, this MSIL code is compiled into native code by the just-in-time (JIT) compiler as it executes. When a method is called for the first time, it is slower than usual because of the additional step of compilation.

Successive calls to the method are faster than the initial call because the code has already been converted to native code. Although this behavior will meet your requirements most of the time, you might want to optimize your application's performance even when the functions are loaded for the first time. In such a case, you should consider using the Native Code Generation tool (ngen.exe) to convert an application to native code before deploying it on the target machine. This way you will get maximum performance at all the times. For example, Microsoft precompiles several libraries of the .NET Framework, including mscorlib.dll, System.Drawing.dll, and System.Windows.Forms.dll, before deploying them on your machine because these classes are used by most applications.

◆ **Be careful about throwing exceptions**—Throwing exceptions is a costly operation. You should be very careful when you throw exceptions from programs. You should use them only to signify exceptional error cases. You should not use exceptions just to manage normal program flow.

◆ **Avoid using unmanaged code**—Calls to unmanaged components involve costly marshalling operations, and therefore the performance of these program may deteriorate. For maximum performance, you should rewrite the unmanaged components by using one of the languages supported by the Common Language Runtime. If a rewrite is not possible, you should monitor the use of unmanaged components and see if you can reduce the number of calls between the managed and unmanaged code, possibly by doing more work in each call rather than making frequent calls to do small tasks.

◆ **Make fewer calls across processes**—Working with distributed applications involves the additional overhead of negotiating network- and application-level protocols. Network speed may also be a bottleneck. The best approach is to get more done with fewer calls across the network. Reducing the number of calls is critical when you're creating high-performance distributed applications.

◆ **Compile the application in the Release configuration**—When you are ready to deploy an application, you should compile it in Release mode rather than the default Debug mode.

Deploying an application that is compiled by using the Debug mode may cause it to run slowly because of the presence of extra debugging code.

◆ **Avoid automatic scaling of images**—One of the overloads of the Graphics.DrawImage method allows you to specify an image and a point for the upper-left corner of the image. In such a case, because the height and width of the image are not specified, GDI+ attempts to auto-scale the image, and auto-scaling slows down the rendering of the image. To boost performance in this case, you should specify the height and width of the image, in addition to other parameters.

◆ **Use smart clipping and invalidation**—You can achieve better painting performance by redrawing only the areas of a form that have become invalidated. Using regions can help you exclude or paint only the specified areas of a form. Also, you should consolidate all your painting logic inside the OnPaint and OnPaintBackground methods. You should avoid painting in the event handlers for the Resize, Load, and Show events.

◆ **Avoid sophisticated painting**— When you use advanced painting features such as anti-aliasing or alpha-blending, more processing is required, and this leads to relatively slow performance of the application.

◆ **Use the optimized managed providers**—System.Data.OleDb is a generic provider that can access data exposed by any OleDb provider. Managed providers are specifically optimized for some databases. For example, when you use System.Data.OleDb to connect to a SQL Server database, it first passes your request to the OLE DB COM components, which in turn translate the requests to SQL Server's native Tabular Data Stream (TDS) format. When you use System.Data.SqlClient, it directly constructs the TDS packets and communicates with SQL Server. The removal of the extra translation step increases data access performance significantly. So if you are connecting to a SQL Server database, you should prefer System.Data.SqlClient to the generic System.Data.OleDb. Similarly, you should use System.Data.OracleClient for connecting to an Oracle database.

NOTE

The Managed Provider for Oracle
The Oracle managed provider is an add-on to the .NET Framework. You can download it from www.microsoft.com/downloads/release.asp?releaseid=40032.

◆ **Prefer stored procedures over SQL statements**—When working with SQL Server, you should prefer using stored procedures over using a set of SQL statements given as a text command. This is because stored procedures are highly optimized for server-side data access and their use usually improves data access performance significantly.

◆ **Tune the database**—Keeping up-to-date indexes also greatly helps in improving performance for a database-intensive Windows application. You can run SQL Server's Profiler and Index Tuning Wizard to avoid bottlenecks due to indexing. Also, you can use SQL Server Query Analyzer to optimize a query's performance.

◆ **Use DataReader when possible**—If you are reading a table sequentially, you should prefer using DataReader over DataSet. DataReader is a read-only, forward-only stream of data that increases application performance and reduces system overhead because only one row is in memory at a time.

◆ **Use connection pooling for the SQL Server .NET Data Provider**—The slowest database operation is establishing a connection with the database. The SQL Server .NET Data Provider provides connection pooling to improve performance when connecting to database. This means old connection information is stored in a connection pool, and it is reused during the next connection, thereby allowing significant performance gains. A connection pool is created based on the connection string in the connection. Each connection pool is associated with a distinct connection string. When a new connection is opened, if the connection string is not an exact match to an existing pool, a new pool is created.

◆ **Use auto-generated commands**—The SqlCommandBuilder and OleDbCommandBuilder classes provide a means of automatically generating commands used to reconcile changes made to a data set. Although automatic generation of INSERT, UPDATE, and DELETE statements for changes to the data set makes database updates very convenient, it makes extra trips to the server to get the schema information.

EXAM TIP

User Identity and Connection Pooling For connection pooling to work, multiple connections to a database must use exactly the same connection strings. If you are including user identity and password information in the connection string, the connection string for user Mahesh will not match with user Mary, and you will instead form two separate connection pools. To obtain maximum performance gains, you must use a single identity and password in the connection string to a database.

◆ **Use transactions**—Distributed transactions may have significant performance overhead. As a rule of thumb, you should use transactions only when required and keep transactions as short-lived as possible.

◆ **Improve perceived performance**—This last technique has more to do with human behavior than with actual performance of an application. Studies have shown that showing an active splash screen upon application startup may make your application appear as if it is loading faster. Similarly, showing a progress bar for long operation keeps users informed and in communication with the application. You should use these techniques to improve the perceived performance of your application.

CHAPTER SUMMARY

KEY TERMS

- Boxing
- Performance counter
- Process
- Unboxing

This chapter discusses the use of the Process, EventLog, PerformanceCounter, and related classes that help in managing and monitoring Windows applications.

This chapter also discusses some of the well-known techniques to optimize the performance of a Windows application. If you judiciously use these techniques while designing and developing an application, you might see a significant performance gain in your application.

APPLY YOUR KNOWLEDGE

Exercises

14.1 Getting Module Information for a Process

When a process executes, it usually loads several other modules (generally DLL files) to help it perform its functions. By using the Process class, you can also determine what modules are loaded by an application. For each module, you can also determine various details, such as the version number, entry point address, and memory size.

In this exercise, you will work with the ProcessModule class and the ProcessModuleCollection class to get information about the modules loaded by a process that is executing.

Estimated Time: 25 minutes.

1. Launch Visual Studio .NET. Select File, New, Blank Solution and name the new solution 306C14Exercises.

2. Add a new Visual Basic .NET Windows application project to the solution. Name the project Exercise14-1.

3. Rename the Form1.vb form Exercise14-1.vb in the project. Switch to the Code view of the form and modify all references to Form1 so that they refer to Exercise14_1 instead.

4. Place four Label controls, two TextBox controls (txtMachine and txtModuleInfo), one Button control (btnLoad), one ListBox control (lbModules), and a ListView control (lvwProcesses) on the form. Set the MultiLine property of txtModuleInfo to True. Set the View property of lvwProcesses to Details. Add to the ListView control two column headers with Text properties of Process Name (chProcessName) and PID (chProcessId). Arrange the controls as shown in Figure 14.13.

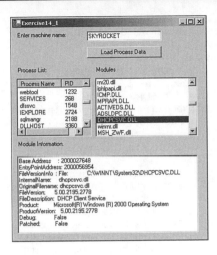

FIGURE 14.13
Process modules information.

5. Switch to the Code view. Add the following code at the top of the form's module:

```
Imports System.Diagnostics
Imports System.Text
```

6. Add the following code directly after the Windows Form Designer Generated Code section:

```
' Create a string member to hold the Machine
' Name
Private strMachineName As String
```

7. Add the following code to handle events on the form:

```
Private Sub Exercise14_1_Load( _
  ByVal sender As System.Object, _
  ByVal e As System.EventArgs) _
  Handles MyBase.Load
    ' Set the text box with
    ' the System ComputerName
    strMachineName = _
      SystemInformation.ComputerName
    txtMachine.Text = strMachineName
End Sub
```

APPLY YOUR KNOWLEDGE

```vbnet
Private Sub btnLoad_Click( _
 ByVal sender As System.Object, _
 ByVal e As System.EventArgs) _
 Handles btnLoad.Click
    ' Get the Machine name
    ' Clear the listview, listbox
    ' and textbox controls
    strMachineName = txtMachine.Text
    lvwProcesses.Items.Clear()
    lbModules.Items.Clear()
    txtModuleInfo.Clear()
    Try
        ' Get all the processes
        Dim arrProcesses() As Process = _
        Process.GetProcesses( _
          strMachineName)
        Dim p As Process
        For Each p In arrProcesses
            ' Add each process into
            ' the lvwProcesses
            Dim lvwItem As ListViewItem = _
            New ListViewItem(New String() _
            {p.ProcessName, _
            p.Id.ToString()})
            lvwProcesses.Items.Add(lvwItem)
        Next
    Catch ex As Exception
        MessageBox.Show(ex.Message)
    End Try
End Sub

Private Sub _
 lvwProcesses_SelectedIndexChanged( _
 ByVal sender As Object, _
 ByVal e As System.EventArgs) _
 Handles lvwProcesses.SelectedIndexChanged
    lbModules.Items.Clear()
    txtModuleInfo.Clear()
    Dim intProcessId As Integer = _
     Convert.ToInt32(lvwProcesses. _
     FocusedItem.SubItems(1).Text)
    Try
        Dim p As Process = _
         Process.GetProcessById( _
          intProcessId, strMachineName)
        Dim pm As ProcessModule
        For Each pm In p.Modules
            lbModules.Items.Add( _
             pm.ModuleName)
        Next
    Catch ex As Exception
        Debug.WriteLine(ex.Message)
    End Try
End Sub

Private Sub _
 lbModules_SelectedIndexChanged( _
 ByVal sender As Object, _
 ByVal e As System.EventArgs) _
 Handles lbModules.SelectedIndexChanged
    txtModuleInfo.Clear()
    Dim intProcessId As Integer = _
     Convert.ToInt32( _
     lvwProcesses.FocusedItem. _
     SubItems(1).Text)
    Try
        ' Get the Process Id
        ' of the selected process
        Dim p As Process = _
         Process.GetProcessById( _
          intProcessId, strMachineName)
        ' Get the Modules of
        ' the selected process
        ' Display module information
        Dim pm As ProcessModule
        For Each pm In p.Modules
            If pm.ModuleName = _
             lbModules.SelectedItem. _
             ToString() Then
                Dim sb As StringBuilder = _
                New StringBuilder()
                sb.Append(String.Format( _
                "Base Address    : {0}" _
                & vbCrLf, _
                pm.BaseAddress. _
                ToString()))
                sb.Append(String.Format( _
                "EntryPointAddress: {0}" _
                & vbCrLf, _
                pm.EntryPointAddress))
                sb.Append(String.Format( _
                "FileVersionInfo  : {0}" _
                & vbCrLf, _
                pm.FileVersionInfo. _
                ToString()))
                sb.Append(String.Format( _
                "ModuleMemorySize : {0}", _
                pm.ModuleMemorySize. _
                ToString()))
                txtModuleInfo.Text = _
                sb.ToString()
                Exit For
            End If
        Next
    Catch ex As Exception
        Debug.WriteLine(ex.Message)
    End Try
End Sub
```

8. Set the form as the startup object for the project and set the project as the startup project for the solution.

9. Run the project. Your computer name appears in the Enter Machine Name text box. Change the value if you want and then click the Load Process Data button. A list of all the running processes appears in the Process List list view. Select a process from the list. Its modules are listed in the list box. Select a module from the list box to obtain its information, as shown in Figure 14.13.

14.2 Getting Performance Information

Performance counters are categorized either by the operating system or by the application that created them. Each performance counter category may also have zero or more instances. When a category has instances, you must specify the instance name along with the category when you want to read the value of a performance counter.

In this exercise, you will create a performance counter explorer that is similar to perfmon.exe. Rather than displaying graphs, though, it will just list the raw value of the performance counter once every second.

Estimated Time: 35 minutes.

1. Add a new Visual Basic .NET Windows application project to the solution. Name the project Exercise142.

2. Rename the Form1.vb form Exercise14-2.vb in the project. Switch to the Code view of the form and modify all references to Form1 so that they refer to Exercise14_2 instead.

3. Place two TextBox controls (txtMachineName and txtDescription), one ComboBox control (cbCategories), two ListBox controls (lbCounters and lbInstances), and a ListView control (lvwPerformance) on the form.

Set the View property of lvwPerformance to Details. Add to the ListView control four column headers with Text properties of Counter Name (chChounterName), Counter Type (chCounterType), Time Stamp (chTimeStamp), and Raw Value (chRawValue). Arrange the controls as shown in Figure 14.14.

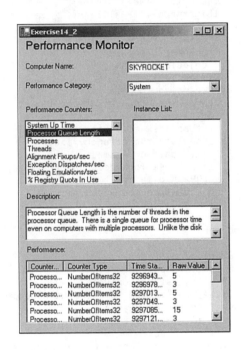

FIGURE 14.14
The Performance Monitor project.

4. Drag a Timer component to the form. Set its Enabled property to False and set its Interval property to 1000.

5. Switch to the Code view. Add this code at the top of the form's module:

```
Imports System.Diagnostics
```

APPLY YOUR KNOWLEDGE

6. Add the following code directly after the Windows Form Designer Generated Code section:

```
' Currently selected performance counter
Private pcCurrent As PerformanceCounter

Private Sub PopulateCategoryList()
    cbCategories.Items.Clear()
    lvwPerformance.Items.Clear()
    lbCounters.Items.Clear()
    lbInstances.Items.Clear()

    ' Get all the Performance
    ' Counter category
    ' objects for the given machine
    Dim pcc() As _
     PerformanceCounterCategory = _
     PerformanceCounterCategory. _
     GetCategories( _
     txtMachineName.Text)
    ' Populate the category list
    ' with category names
    Dim p As PerformanceCounterCategory
    For Each p In pcc
        cbCategories.Items.Add( _
          p.CategoryName)
    Next
End Sub


' Event handler for
' SelectedIndexChaged event
' of both listbox controls
Private Sub ListBox_SelectedIndexChanged( _
 ByVal sender As Object, _
 ByVal e As System.EventArgs)
    Timer1.Enabled = False
    Dim lb As ListBox = CType( _
     sender, ListBox)
    ' Select the appropriate item
    If lb.Name = "lbCounters" Then
        If lbInstances.Items.Count > 0 And _
        lbInstances.SelectedIndex = -1 Then
            lbInstances.SelectedIndex = 0
        End If
    Else
        If lbCounters.Items.Count > 0 And _
         lbCounters.SelectedIndex = -1 Then
            lbCounters.SelectedIndex = 0
        End If
    End If
```

```
    lvwPerformance.Items.Clear()
    Dim pcc As _
     PerformanceCounterCategory = _
     New PerformanceCounterCategory( _
     CStr(cbCategories.SelectedItem))
    Dim pc As PerformanceCounter
    ' get the PerformanceCounter object
    ' based on current selections
    pc = New PerformanceCounter( _
     pcc.CategoryName, _
     CStr(lbCounters.SelectedItem), _
     CStr(lbInstances.SelectedItem), _
     txtMachineName.Text)
    pcCurrent = pc
    ' Display Description
    ' of selected counter
    txtDescription.Text = pc.CounterHelp
    ' Enable the timer so that it can
    ' update performance
    ' data for the selected counter,
    ' every second
    Timer1.Enabled = True
End Sub
```

7. Add the following event-handling code to the form:

```
Private Sub Exercise14_2_Load( _
 ByVal sender As System.Object, _
 ByVal e As System.EventArgs) _
 Handles MyBase.Load
    ' Get the name of the local computer
    txtMachineName.Text = _
     SystemInformation.ComputerName
    ' Populate performance category list
    PopulateCategoryList()
    ' Hook up listbox events
    AddHandler _
     lbCounters.SelectedIndexChanged, _
     AddressOf ListBox_SelectedIndexChanged
    AddHandler _
     lbInstances.SelectedIndexChanged, _
     AddressOf ListBox_SelectedIndexChanged
End Sub

Private Sub txtMachineName_Leave( _
 ByVal sender As Object, _
 ByVal e As System.EventArgs) _
 Handles txtMachineName.Leave
    ' Disable the timer
    ' so that no performance
    ' data is updated
```

APPLY YOUR KNOWLEDGE

```
        Timer1.Enabled = False
        Try
            ' Re-populate the category
            ' list if a machine name
            ' is changed
            PopulateCategoryList()
        Catch ex As Exception
            ' Alert user about
            ' incorrect machine name
            MessageBox.Show( _
             "Please try a different name")
            txtMachineName.Focus()
            txtMachineName.SelectAll()
        End Try
    End Sub


    Private Sub _
     cbCategories_SelectedIndexChanged( _
     ByVal sender As Object, _
     ByVal e As System.EventArgs) _
     Handles cbCategories.SelectedIndexChanged
        ' Disable the timer
        ' so that no performance
        ' data is updated
        Timer1.Enabled = False
        lbCounters.Items.Clear()
        lbInstances.Items.Clear()
        lvwPerformance.Items.Clear()

        ' Get PerformanceCounter Categories
        ' from the selected machine
        Dim pcc As _
         PerformanceCounterCategory = _
         New PerformanceCounterCategory( _
         cbCategories.SelectedItem.ToString(), _
         txtMachineName.Text)
        Dim arrInstanceNames() As String = _
         pcc.GetInstanceNames()
        lbInstances.Items.AddRange( _
         arrInstanceNames)

        Dim pc As PerformanceCounter
        If arrInstanceNames.Length = 0 Then
            For Each pc In pcc.GetCounters()
                lbCounters.Items.Add( _
                 pc.CounterName)
            Next
        Else
            For Each pc In pcc.GetCounters( _
             arrInstanceNames(0))
                lbCounters.Items.Add( _
                 pc.CounterName)
            Next
        End If
    End Sub
```

```
    Private Sub Timer1_Tick( _
     ByVal sender As System.Object, _
     ByVal e As System.EventArgs) _
     Handles Timer1.Tick
        ' Get the current performance data
        ' for the selected counter
        Dim csSample As CounterSample = _
         pcCurrent.NextSample()
        ' Populate details in lvwPerformance
        Dim lviItem As ListViewItem = _
         New ListViewItem(New String() _
         {pcCurrent.CounterName, _
         csSample.CounterType.ToString(), _
         csSample.TimeStamp.ToString(), _
         csSample.RawValue.ToString()})
        lvwPerformance.Items.Add(lviItem)
    End Sub
```

8. Set the form as the startup object for the project and set the project as the startup project for the solution.

9. Run the project. Your system computer name appears in the computer name text box. Change the value if you want and then select a performance category from the combo box. A list of all the performance counters of the performance category selected in the Performance Counters list box appears, and a list of the instances listed in the Instances List appears. Select the desired performance counter and instance. The most recent data of the selected performance counter is added as a new row to the ListView control every second, as shown in Figure 14.14.

Review Questions

1. How do you stop a process that has a user interface? How do you stop a process that does not have a user interface?

2. What types of messages can you write into an event log?

APPLY YOUR KNOWLEDGE

3. Explain the terms *sampling a performance counter* and *publishing a performance counter*.

4. What is the purpose of the Native Code Generation tool (ngen.exe)?

5. When should you prefer using a SqlDataReader object to using a DataSet object for reading data?

Exam Questions

1. You have developed a database-intensive Windows Forms application for a large pharmaceutical company. The database for the application uses SQL Server 2000. Users of your application are complaining about the consistently slow nature of some reports. Which of the following actions would you take to increase the performance of this application? (Select two.)

   A. Compile the application to native code by using ngen.exe.

   B. Run the SQL Server Index Tuning Wizard.

   C. Convert all ad hoc SQL statements to SQL Server stored procedures.

   D. Add a PerformanceMonitor component to the code.

2. You have recently deployed an expense reporting system in your company. The application relies heavily on its SQL Server database. All employees in the company have similar access permissions to the database. You have created the application in such a way that it uses the employee's logon name and password in the connection string to connect to SQL Server. Users of the application have reported significantly slow performance.

Your task is to optimize the performance of this application. Which of the following steps should you take?

   A. Compile the application to native code by using ngen.exe.

   B. Run the SQL Server Index Tuning Wizard.

   C. Increase the maximum size of the connection pool.

   D. Use the same connection string for each user.

3. You are designing a database-intensive Windows application for a large publishing house. You want to get maximum performance from the SQL queries that run to populate a combo box from a SQL Server database. Which of the following code segments would give you the fastest performance?

   A.

```
Dim conn As SqlConnection = _
 New SqlConnection(connStr)
conn.Open()
Dim ds As DataSet = New DataSet()
Dim ad As SqlDataAdapter = _
 New SqlDataAdapter( _
 "SELECT * FROM authors", conn)
ad.Fill(ds)
End Sub
```

   B.

```
Dim conn As OleDbConnection = _
 New OleDbConnection(connStr)
conn.Open()
Dim ds As DataSet = New DataSet()
Dim ad As OleDbDataAdapter = _
New OleDbDataAdapter( _
 "SELECT * FROM authors", conn)
ad.Fill(ds)
```

APPLY YOUR KNOWLEDGE

C.

```
Dim conn As SqlConnection = _
  New SqlConnection(connStr)
Dim cmd As SqlCommand = _
  New SqlCommand( _
  "SELECT * FROM authors", connStr)
conn.Open()
Dim rdr As SqlDataReader
rdr = cmd.ExecuteReader()
```

D.

```
Dim conn As OleDbConnection = _
  New OleDbConnection(connStr)
Dim cmd As OleDbCommand = _
  New OleDbCommand( _
  "SELECT * FROM authors", connStr)
conn.Open()
Dim rdr As OleDbDataReader
rdr = cmd.ExecuteReader()
```

4. You are working on a process management application that launches a Windows form, passes some keystrokes to the form, and then closes the application. Which method of the Process object is the best method to use to close this application?

   A. Close

   B. CloseMainWindow

   C. Dispose

   D. Kill

5. You have developed a Windows application that calls a large number of methods when the application is started. The application is database intensive and uses SQL Server as its database. Users are complaining about the slow startup time of the application. You want to improve the performance of the application. What should you do?

   A. Use ngen.exe.

   B. Use gacutil.exe.

   C. Use the SQL Server Index Tuning Wizard.

   D. Increase the size of the connection pool.

6. You are designing a Windows application that monitors the application log. The application watches for any Error events from a shipping and labeling application. Your application contains this code, but you are not receiving any notifications for the error:

```
Dim el As EventLog = New _
EventLog("Application", ".")
AddHandler el.EntryWritten, AddressOf _
EventLog_EntryWritten
```

What should you do so this code will be notified of new event log entries?

   A. Set el.Enabled to True.

   B. Set el.EnableRaisingEvents to True.

   C. Set el.Enabled to False.

   D. Set el.EnableRaisingEvents to False.

7. Which of the following statements are true with respect to Windows performance counters? (Select two.)

   A. Performance counters are categorized into performance counter categories.

   B. Each performance counter category has zero or more instances associated with it.

   C. Each performance counter category has one or more instances associated with it.

   D. Each performance counter must have exactly one instance associated with it.

8. Which of the following statement is false with respect to the EventLog class?

   A. You cannot write to any event log on a remote machine.

   B. You can write to all event logs on a local machine.

APPLY YOUR KNOWLEDGE

C. You cannot get event-driven notifications when an entry is written to an event log on a remote machine.

D. You can get event-driven notifications when an entry is written to an event log on a local machine.

9. You have created an expense reporting system for a small manufacturing company. All computers in the company use Microsoft Excel as their default spreadsheet. Which of the following code examples will open the ExpenseReport.xls file by using Microsoft Excel on a user's computer?

A.
```
Process.Start(new ProcessStartInfo( _
  "ExpenseReport.xls"))
```

B.
```
Process.Start(new ProcessStartInfo( _
  "Excel ExpenseReport.xls"))
```

C.
```
Process.Start(new ProcessStartInfo( _
  "Excel ExpenseReport"))
```

D.
```
Process.Start(new ProcessStartInfo( _
  "Excel", "ExpenseReport.xls"))
```

10. You have created an expense reporting system for a small manufacturing company. The system allows users to launch expense files for editing in Microsoft Excel. Generally, the employees will keep an editing session open for a long time; meanwhile, they need to select other options from the expense reporting system to verify what they are editing. You want to know when the user has finished editing the file so that you can archive the file for later retrieval. Which of the following members of the Process class would allow you to monitor for the end of the editing session? (Select two.)

A. WaitForExit

B. HasExited

C. Exited

D. EnableRaisingEvents

11. You recently developed an expense reporting system. When you deployed the application, you found that some of the features of the application are not working as expected. You suspected that the application was using old versions of some of its components. You then created a small test application to get all the modules loaded by the application. Your program contains the following segment of code (line numbers are for reference only):

```
1  Dim p As Process = Process.Start( _
2    new ProcessStartInfo( _
     "ExpenseReport.exe "))
3
4  Dim pmc As ProcessModuleCollection = _
5    Process.GetProcessById(p.Id).Modules
```

When you analyzed the resulting collection of modules, you noted that not all the modules actually being used by the application were added to the ProcessModuleCollection object. Which of the following statements should you add as line 3?

A. p.Refresh()

B. p.WaitForInputIdle()

C. p.WaitForExit()

D. p.CreateObjRef()

12. You have written an application that publishes its own custom performance counter. You want to decrease the value of a performance counter by 5. Which of the following methods is the best method to use to do this?

APPLY YOUR KNOWLEDGE

A. Decrement

B. Increment

C. IncrementBy

D. NextValue

13. You want to determine whether a given event log exists on a remote machine. Which of the following methods is the most efficient method to use to determine this?

    A. Exists

    B. SourceExists

    C. GetEventLogs

    D. LogNameFromSourceName

14. You want to create a high-performing graphic application. You have created several variations of a method that draws an image. Which of the following methods would have the best performance?

    A.

```
Public Sub DrawSampleImage( _
 e As PaintEventArgs )
    Dim newImage As Image = _
     Image.FromFile("SampImag.jpg")
    Dim ulCorner As Point = _
     New Point(100, 100)
    e.Graphics.DrawImage(newImage, ulCorner)
End Sub
```

    B.

```
Public Sub DrawSampleImage( _
 ByVal e As PaintEventArgs)
    Dim newImage As Image = _
     Image.FromFile("SampImag.jpg")
    Dim x As Integer = 100
    Dim y As Integer = 100
    e.Graphics.DrawImage(newImage, x, y)
End Sub
```

C.

```
Public Sub DrawSampleImage( _
 ByVal e As PaintEventArgs)
    Dim newImage As Image = _
     Image.FromFile("SampImag.jpg")
    Dim destRect As Rectangle = _
     New Rectangle(100, 100, 450, 150)
    e.Graphics.DrawImage(newImage, destRect)
End Sub
```

D.

```
Public Sub DrawSampleImage( _
 ByVal e As PaintEventArgs)
    Dim newImage As Image = _
     Image.FromFile("SampImag.jpg")
    Dim x As Double = 100.0
    Dim y As Double = 100.0F
    e.Graphics.DrawImage(newImage, x, y)
End Sub
```

15. Which of the following coding constructs would have a major impact on an application's performance and should therefore be used cautiously?

    A. try

    B. catch

    C. finally

    D. throw

Answers to Review Questions

1. The CloseMainWindow method of the Process class stops the processes that participate in the Windows message loop and have user interfaces, and the Kill method of the Process class stops processes that do not have user interfaces or do not participate in the Windows message loop. You can also use the Kill method to kill applications that have interfaces.

APPLY YOUR KNOWLEDGE

2. The different types of messages that can be written into an event log are specified by the values of the EventLogEntryType enumeration. The possible types are Error, FailureAudit, Information, SuccessAudit, and Warning.

3. The process of reading a performance counter value is called sampling the performance counter. The process of updating a performance counter value is called publishing a performance counter.

4. The Native Code Generation tool (ngen.exe) is used to convert an application to native code before it is deployed on the target machine.

5. SqlDataReader provides high-performance data access for reading forward-only, read-only data. You should use a SqlDataReader object instead of a DataSet object when you are reading data sequentially and updates are not required.

Answers to Exam Questions

1. **B, C.** SQL Server's Index Tuning Wizard identifies any bottlenecks that are due to indexing. Using SQL Server stored procedure significantly improves data access performance.

2. **D.** Using different usernames and passwords when connecting to SQL Server creates a unique connection string at each database connection. This eliminates any gain that you may have from connection pooling. To get the maximum benefit from connection pooling, you must use the same connection string every time you connect to the database.

3. **C.** When you are working with a SQL Server database, using the SQL Server managed provider gives better performance than its OleDb counterpart.

Also, when doing sequential read-only operations such as populating a combo box, the SqlDataReader object gives better performance than the SqlDataAdapter object.

4. **B.** The preferred way to close an application that has a user interface is to use the CloseMainWindow method.

5. **A.** At application startup time, JIT compilation involves additional overhead. Therefore, if a large number of methods are called at startup, compiling the application to native code by using ngen.exe may improve performance.

6. **B.** The default value for EnableRaisingEvents is False. If this property is set to False, it will not raise the EntryWritten event for the event log. You should therefore set its value to True.

7. **A, B.** Performance counters are categorized into various performance counter categories. Each performance counter category has zero or more instances associated with it.

8. **B.** Although it is possible to write to the event logs on the local machine, it is not possible to write to all of them. The security log is created by the operating system itself and is read-only. You cannot write to it, even on a local machine.

9. **A.** When you specify a filename, when the process is started, the operating system takes the default action based on the file extension. Because Excel is the default spreadsheet used in the company, when the process starts, the file will be automatically opened by Excel.

10. **C, D.** You can attach an event handler to the Exited event of the Process object to receive notification from a process when it exits.

APPLY YOUR KNOWLEDGE

The default value of the EnableRaisingEvents property is False, so the Exited event is not raised. You should set this property to True so that you get event notification when the process is closed.

11. **B.** You should always retrieve the modules used by an application when it is completely loaded. You can ensure that an application is loaded and is ready to start by calling the WaitForInputIdle method on its Process object.

12. **C.** Using the IncrementBy method is the most efficient method to increase or decrease the value of a counter by the specified unit.

13. **A.** The easiest and the most efficient way to find out whether a log exists on a local or a remote machine is to use the static Exists method of the EventLog class.

14. **C.** Answer **C** will give the best performance because it specifies the destination size of the image, thereby avoid any auto-scaling of the image.

15. **D.** The throw statement has the maximum performance penalty and should be used cautiously.

Suggested Readings and Resources

1. Visual Studio .NET Combined Help Collection:

   • Managing Processes

   • Logging Application, Server, and Security Events

   • Monitoring Performance Thresholds

   • Performance Tips and Tricks in .NET Applications

   • Performance Considerations for Run-Time Technologies in the .NET Framework

2. Burton, Kevin. *.NET Common Language Runtime Unleashed.* Sams Publishing, 2002.

This chapter covers the following Microsoft-specified objective for the Creating User Services section of the Visual Basic .NET Windows-Based Applications exam:

Add controls to a Windows Form.

- **Configure control licensing.**

▶ In previous versions of Visual Studio, control licensing was a sometimes difficult subject requiring custom configuration. This objective requires you to understand the way in which Visual Studio .NET handles control licensing. The new method is almost completely transparent to the developer.

This chapter also covers the following Microsoft-specified objectives for the Configuring and Securing a Windows-Based Application section of the Visual Basic .NET Windows-Based Applications exam:

Configure a Windows-based application.

▶ This objective deals with runtime configuration using dynamic properties stored in configuration files. The .NET Framework offers good support for changing the behavior of your applications at runtime by editing XML configuration files.

Configure security for a Windows-based application.

- **Select and configure authentication type. Authentication types include Windows Authentication, None, forms-based, Microsoft Passport, and custom authentication.**

- **Specify the security level for an application.**

- **Use custom attributes to configure security.**

▶ This objective deals with code access security. By configuring security, you can control which applications are allowed to run on the computer and what privileges they have while running. The .NET Framework offers a comprehensive set of classes and attributes to manage code access security.

CHAPTER 15

Configuring a Windows Application

Configure authorization.

- **Configure role-based authorization.**

- **Implement identity management.**

▶ This objective is concerned with authorization and role-based security. With role-based security, you can tie a program's privileges to the identity of the user who is running the program. This identity management lets you assign different levels of functionality to a program depending on the identity of the user who is currently logged on.

INTRODUCTION

As a developer, your job does not end when you deliver an application to the end user. Users expect a well-designed Windows application to be configurable with little trouble and without needing to rewrite code. As a simple example, if your application retrieves data from a database, you should provide some way for the end user to configure the name of the database server.

Administrators, too, will want to configure applications. Administrative configuration often takes the form of setting up security. In some cases, this will be computer security, designed to keep untrusted applications from harming the operating system or the user's critical data files. In others, this will be user security, designed to control who can use a particular application.

The .NET Framework offers substantial control of these and other types of configuration. Dynamic properties and configuration files make most runtime configuration tasks a simple matter of editing XML files. The .NET Framework also includes a complete security system that supports both code access and role-based security.

In this chapter, you'll learn how to design and code your applications to take advantage of these configuration features and how to use these features to configure .NET applications at runtime.

CONFIGURING CONTROL LICENSING

Add controls to a Windows Form

- **Configure control licensing.**

Before looking at areas in which .NET applications are designed to be configured, I should mention one area in which configuration is almost never necessary: control licensing. The .NET Framework provides complete support for licensing of controls (and other classes), but this support is designed to be completely unobtrusive and transparent at runtime.

When you purchase a custom control for use in applications, it typically comes with a design-time license good for a limited number of computers and a runtime license to allow end users to use applications that utilize the control without allowing them to embed the control in new applications. The .NET Framework handles this by using a LicenseProvider object. The default LicenseProvider checks at design time for the presence of a particular text file. If the text file is present, you can insert the control on a form; if it's not present, you cannot insert the control.

Assuming you do have the design-time license, everything else is automatic. When you compile an application, the .NET Framework automatically converts the corresponding runtime license into a binary resource and embeds it into the executable. This resource is available to the Common Language Runtime at runtime. There's nothing to configure and nothing for the administrator to do. The control just works.

However, as with so much of the .NET Framework, this licensing structure is only the default. It's perfectly possible for a control author to implement her own custom LicenseProvider class to handle things in some fashion other than the default. A control might, for example, look for a particular registry key, a hardware dongle, a Web Service, or even a configuration file before it will run. If you run across runtime licensing errors, they almost certainly came from such a custom licensing scheme. In such a case, your best course of action is to contact the control vendor directly for assistance.

CONFIGURING A WINDOWS-BASED APPLICATION

Configure a Windows-based application.

Sometimes you want to leave some options in your program open until runtime. This might be something as central as the name of a database server or something as frivolous as the background color for a form. .NET lets you manage these options with dynamic properties. *Dynamic properties* let you store some of an application's property values to an external file, from which they are retrieved at runtime. The .NET Framework provides all the infrastructure you need to accomplish this, and Visual Studio .NET offers built-in support for dynamic properties. With dynamic properties, you can make changes to an application's configuration without recompiling the application.

Using Dynamic Properties

Dynamic properties are managed by the System.Configuration.AppSettingsReader class at runtime, but seldom must you work with this class directly. Instead, you can use the Visual Studio .NET IDE to define dynamic properties for your applications (see Step By Step 15.1).

STEP BY STEP

15.1 Using Dynamic Properties

1. Create a new Visual Basic .NET Windows application named 306C15. Add a form to the application.

2. Set the Text property of the form to StepByStep15-1. Set the ShowInTaskbar property of the form to False.

3. In the form's Properties window, click the + sign next to the Dynamic Properties entry. Click in the Advanced section and then click the Build button to open the Dynamic Properties dialog box.

4. In the Properties list, check the check boxes for the ShowInTaskbar and Text properties. Accept the default key mapping for each of these properties. Figure 15.1 shows the Dynamic Properties dialog box. Click OK to close the dialog box.

5. Set the form as the startup object for the project.

6. Run the project. The form will appear with the Text property you set and will not be displayed in the taskbar.

7. Stop the project. Double-click the app.config file in the Solution Explorer. Edit the contents of the file as follows:

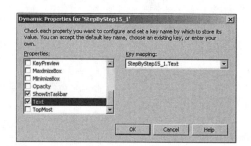

FIGURE 15.1
The Dynamic Properties dialog box.

```xml
<?xml version="1.0" encoding="Windows-1252"?>
<configuration>
  <appSettings>
    <!--  User application and configured _
    property settings go here.-->
    <!--  Example: <add key="settingName" _
    value="settingValue"/> -->
    <add key="StepByStep15_1.ShowInTaskbar" _
    value="True" />
```

```
    <add key="StepByStep15_1.Text" value="Set at _
    Runtime" />
  </appSettings>
</configuration>
```

8. Run the project again. The form will have the text "Set at Runtime" and will appear in the taskbar.

9. Stop the project. Compile the project.

10. Run the compiled project by browsing to the bin directory of the project in Windows Explorer and double-clicking on the project's executable file, 306C15.exe. It will open with the text "Set at Runtime" and will appear in the taskbar.

11. Open the 306C15.exe.config file, which you'll find in the project's bin directory, in a text editor. Edit this file as follows:

```
<?xml version="1.0" encoding="Windows-1252"?>
<configuration>
  <appSettings>
    <!--   User application and configured
property settings go here.-->
    <!--   Example: <add key="settingName"
value="settingValue"/> -->
    <add key="StepByStep15_1.ShowInTaskbar" value="False" />
    <add key="StepByStep15_1.Text"
value="Compiled version" />
  </appSettings>
</configuration>
```

12. Run the compiled project again. It will open with the text "Compiled version" and will not appear in the taskbar.

This example demonstrates the key points about using dynamic properties for components on Windows Forms:

◆ You can set any simple property (that is, any property whose value is not an instance of a class) to be a dynamic property by using the Advanced section of the Dynamic Properties section of the Properties window.

◆ You can use the Properties window to edit dynamic properties, just as you can use it for other properties.

FIGURE 15.2
Default dynamic property for an OleDbConnection component.

◆ When your application is running inside the IDE, the file app.config at the top level of the application will hold the values for the dynamic properties.

◆ When you compile your application, a configuration file with the extension config and the same name as the application's executable file will hold the values for the dynamic properties.

Some components come with default dynamic properties. For example, if you drag an Access database from Server Explorer to a Windows Form, creating an OleDbConnection component, it automatically makes an entry in the Dynamic Properties section of the Properties window for the connection string, as shown in Figure 15.2.

All the forms, controls, and components in a project use a single configuration file. You can't change configuration files from their default name or use multiple configuration files in a single application.

If you change your mind and remove a property from the dynamic properties list for a component, that property's key and last value will remain in the configuration file. The configuration file does not retain any link back to the application, it cannot determine that a particular key and value pair is no longer needed. This will not cause any problem for your applications, though you should keep it in mind. For example, if you use a dynamic property to store a password during development and remove that property to ship your application, your last password will remain in the configuration file. You can edit the configuration file by hand to remove this key and value.

Machine and Application Configuration Files

In addition to dynamic properties, the .NET Framework also supports runtime configuration through machine and application configuration files. For example, these files can direct the Common Language Runtime, decide which version of a particular assembly to load, or enable just-in-time debugging for Windows Forms. These configuration files are XML files whose schema is fully documented in the .NET Framework Developer's Guide. Most of the settings within these files are specific to ASP.NET applications, but some affect Windows applications as well.

Generally, application configuration files override the machine configuration file for those applications. However, the machine configuration file can include settings that direct it not to allow application settings. For example, an attempt to redefine the location of the Common Language Runtime libraries on an application basis won't work, because the machine.config file contains a section that prohibits this from being set at the application level. Of course, you could edit the machine.config file to remove this section, although that would be a very bad idea from the security point of view!

The main use of machine and application configuration files for Windows applications is to specify the version of assemblies that a particular application should use. By default, a .NET application will only load the exact version of an assembly that it was created with, but you can change that at the machine level or at the assembly level. Suppose, for example, that your application uses version 1.0.0.0 of an assembly whose name is CoolCode and whose strong name public key token is 6577fd6241e80701. You've tested your application and you're satisfied that it works with this version of CoolCode. If the user installs version 1.1.0.0 of CoolCode on his computer, it does not affect your application at all. Your application will continue to use version 1.0.0.0.

However, you can use an application or machine configuration file to override this default by specifying a *configured assembly*. A configured assembly is a mapping from one version to another version. You could do this with a section in the configuration file:

```
<runtime>
<assemblyBinding xmlns="urn:schemas-microsoft-com:asm.v1">
  <dependentAssembly>
    <assemblyIdentity name="CoolCode"
     publicKeyToken="6577fd6241e80701" />
    <bindingRedirect oldVersion="1.0.0.0"
     newVersion="1.1.0.0" />
  </dependentAssembly>
</assemblyBinding>
</runtime>
```

If you add this section to the configuration file for an application, then the substitution will be made for the application. If you add this section to the configuration file for the machine (found by default in C:\WINNT\Microsoft.NET\Framework\v1.0.3705\ CONFIG\machine.config), the specified version substitution will be made for any application that uses this assembly.

Using the .NET Framework Configuration Tool

For the most part, you needn't alter .NET configuration files by hand because installing the .NET Framework gives you the .NET Framework Configuration tool (shown in Figure 15.3), which provides a Microsoft Management Console (MMC)-based way to edit the files. You can perform these tasks with the .NET Framework Configuration tool:

◆ Manage the contents of the Global Assembly Cache, which provides assemblies for use by all applications on the computer.

◆ Manage machinewide configured assemblies.

◆ Manage remoting channels, which allow communication with objects on remote computers.

◆ Manage security policy. (You'll learn more about .NET security in the rest of this chapter.)

◆ Manage application settings. Applications can have their own remoting and configured assemblies rules.

Step by Step 15.2 demonstrates the use of this tool to create a configured assembly.

FIGURE 15.3
The .NET Framework Configuration tool.

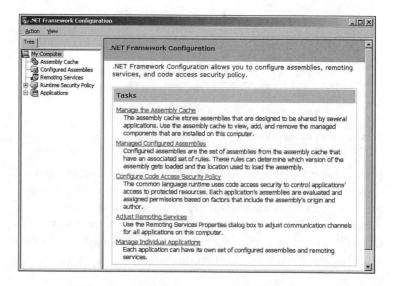

STEP BY STEP

15.2 Creating a Configured Assembly

1. Select Start, Programs, Administrative Tools, Microsoft .NET Framework Configuration.

2. Click the Application node in the treeview.

3. Click the Add an Application To Configure link.

4. In the Configure an Application dialog box, scroll down the list until you find 306C15.exe. Select this application and click OK.

5. Expand the New node in the treeview and click the Configured Assemblies child node.

6. Click the Configure an Assembly link.

7. In the Configure an Assembly dialog box, click the Option button to select an assembly from the list of assemblies this application uses. Click the Choose Assembly button. Select the System.Xml assembly and click Select, Finish.

8. In the System.Xml Properties dialog box, select the Binding Policies tab. Enter `1.0.3300.0` as the Requested Version, and `2.0.0.0` as the New Version, as shown in Figure 15.4.

9. Click OK to save the configured assembly information.

10. Double-click the 306C15.exe file in Windows Explorer. You'll get a just-in-time debugging error, as shown in Figure 15.5, because the specified version of the System.xml assembly doesn't actually exist.

11. Click No to dismiss the Debugging dialog box. Open the 306C15.exe.config file. You'll find these contents if you've followed both Step By Steps in this chapter:

```
<?xml version="1.0" encoding="Windows-1252"?>
<configuration>
 <appSettings>
   <!--  User application and configured
property settings go here.-->
```

continues

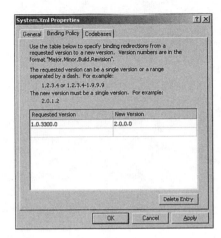

FIGURE 15.4
Creating a configured assembly.

> **WARNING**
>
> **No Validation** As you can see in this example, the Configuration tool performs no validation to determine whether the specified new version of the assembly even exists.

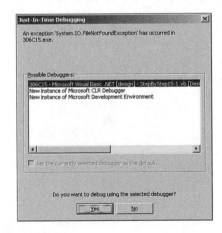

FIGURE 15.5
Attempt to load a nonexistent assembly.

continued

```
    <!--   Example: <add key="settingName"
value="settingValue"/> -->
    <add key="StepByStep15_1.ShowInTaskbar"
value="False" />
    <add key="StepByStep15_1.Text"
value="Compiled version" />
  </appSettings>
  <runtime>
    <assemblyBinding
xmlns="urn:schemas-microsoft-com:asm.v1">
      <dependentAssembly>
        <assemblyIdentity name="System.Xml"
publicKeyToken="b77a5c561934e089" />
        <bindingRedirect oldVersion="1.0.3300.0"
newVersion="2.0.0.0" />
      </dependentAssembly>
    </assemblyBinding>
  </runtime>
</configuration>
```

12. Delete the entire <runtime> section of the configuration file. Save the file. Double-click the executable again. Now that you've removed the configured assembly, the application will once again launch.

REVIEW BREAK

▶ The .NET Framework stores runtime configuration information in XML files that can be edited without recompiling the application.

▶ Dynamic properties provide a built-in mechanism to let you store component properties in runtime configuration files.

▶ Machine and application configuration files hold administrative settings, such as information on configured assemblies and remoting channels.

▶ The .NET Framework Configuration Editor provides a GUI for editing runtime configuration files.

CONFIGURING SECURITY

The .NET Framework offers a wide variety of security features. You can choose to run your machine in wide-open mode, with every user allowed to execute any .NET code, or you can lock down things selectively. You can control which programs have access to which resources, or which users have the right to execute which programs.

Broadly speaking, .NET security breaks down into two separate areas:

◆ Code access security manages the security of .NET source code itself. You can tell the .NET Framework the resources your code needs to execute properly, and the .NET Framework will check for permission to access those resources on the machine at runtime. Code access security is very flexible, including the capability to define your own sets of necessary permissions. Code access security can also be used by administrators to ensure that undesired code never gets the chance to run on a system.

◆ Role-based security manages the user rather than the code. Using role-based security allows you to provide (or deny) access to resources based on an identity provided by the user running the code. In practical terms, this means you can limit program execution to particular users or groups on the computer.

I'll cover both these types of security in this chapter, beginning with code-based security. The .NET Framework also includes other security features, notably public-key and private-key encryption, which are not a part of the 70-306 exam.

Understanding Code Access Security

Configure security for a Windows-based application

- **Specify the security level for an application.**

Code access security controls what code can do on your computer. Code access security is centered around permissions to use resources. The .NET Framework has an entire object-oriented system for managing code access security and the associated permissions.

In the following sections, you'll learn about concepts involved in code access security:

◆ Permissions

◆ Code groups

◆ Permission sets

You'll also learn how to manage code access security. In particular, code can request permissions on a very fine-grained scale, and the administrator can choose to allow permissions on an equally fine-grained scale.

Understanding Permissions

Code access security is based on specific permissions that the Common Language Runtime can grant to or deny from code. For example, the authorization to read or write information in the Windows Registry requires the Registry permission on the part of your code. As you'll see later in the chapter, code can make four different types of permission requests:

◆ It can request the minimum permissions that it requires to run.

◆ It can request optional permissions that it would like but does not require.

◆ It can refuse permissions to ensure that it does not have access to particular resources.

◆ It can demand permissions on the part of calling code.

The Common Language Runtime decides, based on a variety of factors (including the origin of the code and information in the machine and application configuration files), whether a particular permission will be granted. If a piece of code is unable to obtain the minimum permissions that it requires, that piece of code won't execute. The security settings of the computer determine the maximum permissions that code can be granted, but code is allowed to request (and receive) fewer permissions than the maximum.

The .NET Framework groups permissions into three types. Code access permissions represent access to a protected resource or the authorization to perform a protected operation. Identity permissions represent access based on credentials that are a part of the code itself.

Role-based permissions represent access based on the user who is running the code. Each permission in the .NET Framework is represented by a particular class that derives from System.Security.CodeAccessPermission. Table 15.1 lists these permissions.

TABLE 15.1

PERMISSIONS IN THE .NET FRAMEWORK

Permission	Type	Explanation
DirectoryServicesPermission	Code Access	Controls access to the System.DirectoryServices namespace.
DnsPermission	Code Access	Controls access to domain name system (DNS) services.
EnvironmentPermission	Code Access	Controls access to environment variables.
EventLogPermission	Code Access	Controls access to the Windows event log.
FileDialogPermission	Code Access	Controls access to files selected from the Open dialog box.
FileIoPermission	Code Access	Controls access to reading and writing files and directories.
IsolatedStorageFilePermission	Code Access	Controls access to private virtual file systems.
IsolatedStoragePermission	Code Access	Controls access to isolated storage.
MessageQueuePermission	Code Access	Controls access to message queuing via MSMQ.
OleDbPermission	Code Access	Controls access to data via the System.Data.OleDb namespace.
PerformanceCounterPermission	Code Access	Controls access to performance counters.
PrintingPermission	Code Access	Controls access to printers.
ReflectionPermission	Code Access	Controls access to the reflection features of .NET.
RegistryPermission	Code Access	Controls access to the Windows Registry.
SecurityPermission	Code Access	Controls access to unmanaged code.
ServiceControllerPermission	Code Access	Controls access to starting and stopping services.
SocketPermission	Code Access	Controls access to Windows sockets.
SqlClientPermission	Code Access	Controls access to data via the System.Data.SqlClient namespace.
UiPermission	Code Access	Controls access to the user interface.
WebPermission	Code Access	Controls access to making Web connections.
PublisherIdentityPermission	Identity	Represents the identity of the publisher, as determined by the code's digital signature.
SiteIdentityPermission	Identity	Represents the wWeb site from which the code was downloaded.
StrongNameIdentityPermission	Identity	Represents the strong name of the assembly.
URLIdentityPermission	Identity	Represents the exact Uuniform Rresource Llocator (URL) where the code originated.

continues

TABLE 15.1	*continued*

PERMISSIONS IN THE .NET FRAMEWORK

Permission	Type	Explanation
ZoneIdentityPermission	Identity	Represents the security zone where the code originated. You can view security zones on the Security tab of the Internet Explorer Options dialog box.
PrincipalPermission	Role-based	Represents the credentials of the user.

> **NOTE**
>
> **Custom Permissions** If none of these permissions are quite right for your application, you can also define custom permissions. I'll talk about custom permissions later in the chapter.

Requesting Minimum Permissions

To start working in the .NET security framework, your code should request the minimum permissions it needs to function correctly (see Step By Step 15.3).

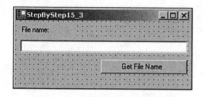

FIGURE 15.6
Form for testing security.

STEP BY STEP

15.3 Requesting Minimum Permissions

1. Add a new form to your Visual Basic .NET application.

2. Place a Label control, a TextBox control named txtFileName, and a Button control named btnGetFile on the form. Add an OpenFileDialog component named dlgOpen. Figure 15.6 shows a design for this form.

3. Double-click the Button control to open the form's module. Add these statements to the top of the module:

```
Imports System.Security.Permissions
<Assembly: FileDialogPermissionAttribute( _
 SecurityAction.RequestMinimum, _
 Unrestricted:=True)>
```

4. Add this code to allow the user to browse for a file name when they click the button:

```
Private Sub btnGetName_Click( _
 ByVal sender As System.Object, _
 ByVal e As System.EventArgs) Handles btnGetName.Click
    Try
        If dlgOpen.ShowDialog = DialogResult.OK Then
            txtFileName.Text = dlgOpen.FileName
        End If
    Catch ex As Exception
        MessageBox.Show("Exception: " & ex.Message)
    End Try
End Sub
```

5. Set the form as the startup object for the project.

6. Compile the project. Launch the executable file from Windows Explorer and verify that you can browse for a file.

This sample requests permissions by applying an attribute to the assembly. The FileDialogPermissionAttribute allows the assembly to request the FileDialogPermission, which in turn allows access to the system's file dialogs. In this particular case, the code runs without any problem, which means it was granted the requested permission. That's because by default you have full permissions to run any code that originates on your own computer. To see code access security in action, you must learn to manage the permissions granted to code on your computer, but first, you must understand the concepts of code groups and permission sets.

Code Groups and Permission Sets

A code group is a set of assemblies that share a security context. You define a code group by specifying the membership condition for the group. Every assembly in a code group receives the same permissions from that group; however, because assemblies can be members of multiple code groups, two assemblies in the same group might end up with different permissions in the end.

The .NET Framework supports seven different membership conditions for code groups:

◆ **The application directory membership condition**—Selects all code in the installation directory of the running application.

◆ **The cryptographic hash membership condition**—Selects all code matching a specified cryptographic hash. Practically speaking, this is a way to define a code group that consists of a single assembly.

◆ **The software publisher membership condition**—Selects all code from a specified publisher, as verified by Authenticode signing.

◆ **The site membership condition**—Selects all code from a particular Internet domain.

◆ **The strong name membership condition**—Selects all code with a specified strong name.

◆ **The URL membership condition**—Selects all code from a specified URL.

◆ **The zone membership condition**—Selects all code from a specified security zone (Internet, Local Intranet, Trusted Sites, My Computer, or Untrusted Sites).

Permissions are granted in permission sets. A permission set is a set of one or more code access permissions that are granted as a unit. If you only want to grant a single permission, you must constuct a permission set containing only that single permission: You can't grant permissions directly. The .NET Framework supplies seven built-in permission sets:

◆ **The Nothing permission set**—Grants no permissions.

◆ **The Execution permission set**—Grants permission to run but not to access protected resources.

◆ **The Internet permission set**—Grants limited permissions designed for code of unknown origin.

◆ **The LocalIntranet permission set**—Grants high permissions designed for code within an enterprise.

◆ **The Everything permission set**—Grants all permissions except for the permission to skip verification.

◆ **The SkipVerification permission set**—Grants the permission to skip security checks.

◆ **The FullTrust permission set**—Grants full access to all resources. This permission set includes all permissions.

You can also create your own custom permission sets, as you'll see in the next section.

Granting Permission

The easiest way to grant or deny permissions in the .NET Framework is to use the Microsoft .NET Framework Configuration tool, as in Step By Step 15.4.

STEP BY STEP

15.4 Granting Permissions

1. Select Start, Programs, Administrative Tools, Microsoft .NET Framework Configuration.

2. Expand the Runtime Security node, then the User node, then the Permission Sets node to see the built-in .NET permission sets.

3. Right-click the Everything permission set and select Duplicate to create a new permission set named Copy of Everything.

4. Right-click the Copy of Everything permission set and select Rename. Rename the permission set `No FileDialog`.

5. With the `No FileDialog` permission set selected, click the Change Permissions link in the right panel of the Configuration tool. In the Create Permission Set dialog box, select File Dialog and click Remove. Click Finish to save your changes.

6. Expand the Code Groups node and click on the default All Code code group. Click the Add a Child Code Group link in the right panel of the Configuration tool.

7. In the Create Code Group dialog box, name the new group `Chapter15`. Enter a description and click Next.

8. Select the Hash condition. Click the Import button and browse to 306C15.exe. Click Open to calculate the hash for this file. Click Next.

9. Select the `No FileDialog` permission set and click Next. Click Finish to create the new code group.

10. Right-click the `Chapter15` code group and select Properties. Check the box to make this code group exclusive, as shown in Figure 15.7. Click OK.

11. Run the 306C15.exe application by double-clicking it in Windows Explorer. You'll receive a policy exception error box indicating that the code cannot be run. Click No to dismiss the error.

FIGURE 15.7
Setting properties for a code group.

In Step By Step 15.4, you first created a permission set that included every permission except for the permission to use the file dialog boxes. You then created a code group that contained the executable file for this chapter's examples and assigned the `No FileDialog` permission set to this code group. The result is that the code cannot run, because it requires at a minimum the one permission that the new security policy will not grant to it.

Imperative Security

Requesting permissions through the use of attributes is known as *declarative security*. A second method to request permissions is known as imperative security. With *imperative security*, you create objects to represent the permissions that your code requires (see Step By Step 15.5). Guided Practice Exercise 15.1 will give you additional practice with imperative security.

STEP BY STEP

15.5 Imperative Security

1. Add a new form to your Visual Basic .NET application.

2. Place a Label control, a TextBox control named `txtFileName`, and a Button control named `btnGetFile` on the form. Add an OpenFileDialog component named `dlgOpen`. You can reuse the design from Figure 15.6 for this form.

3. Double-click the Button control to open the form's module. Add this statement to the top of the module:

```
Imports System.Security.Permissions
```

4. Add this code to allow the user to browse for a file name when she clicks the button:

```
Private Sub btnGetName_Click( _
 ByVal sender As System.Object, _
 ByVal e As System.EventArgs) Handles btnGetName.Click
    Try
        Dim fdp As FileDialogPermission = _
         New FileDialogPermission( _
         PermissionState.Unrestricted)
        ' Check to see whether the code
        ' has the specified permission
        fdp.Demand()
```

```
        If dlgOpen.ShowDialog = DialogResult.OK Then
            txtFileName.Text = dlgOpen.FileName
        End If
    Catch ex As Exception
        MessageBox.Show("Exception: " & ex.Message)
    End Try
End Sub
```

5. Comment out the `FileDialogPermissionAttribute` attribute in the code for Step By Step 15.3, which would otherwise apply to the entire assembly.

6. Set the form as the startup object for the project.

7. Compile the project. Launch the executable file from Windows Explorer and verify that you can browse for a file.

8. Run the Microsoft .NET Framework Configuration tool and locate the node for the `Chapter15` code group. Right-click the code group and select Properties. On the Membership Condition tab, select Import. Browse to the 306C15.exe file and click Open. Click OK to dismiss the dialog box.

9. Launch the 306C15.exe file from Windows Explorer again. Click the Get File button. You'll see the security exception shown in Figure 15.8.

FIGURE 15.8
Exception from imperative security.

Step By Step 15.4 constructed a `FileDialogPermission` object representing unrestricted access to the file dialogs. It then called the demand method of that object to demand the permission from the operating system. When the security policy was such that the permission could not be granted, the code threw an exception.

You might be confused about why the hash for the assembly had to be recalculated to have the proper code group apply. That's because the hash value is calculated by applying a mathematical formula to all the code of the compiled program. When you make any change to an application, its hash code will also change.

> **EXAM TIP**
>
> **Imperative Versus Declarative Security** The only time that you absolutely must use imperative security is when you must make security decisions based on factors only known at runtime, such as the name of a particular file. In many other cases you'll find that declarative security is easier to use.

Computing Permissions

Determining the actual permissions applied to any given piece of code is a complex process. To begin the process, think about permissions at the Enterprise level only. The CLR starts by examining the evidence a particular piece of code presents to determine its membership in code groups at that level. Evidence is just an overall term for the various identity permissions (publisher, strong name, hash, and so on) that can go into code group membership.

Code groups are organized into a hierarchy; in Step By Step 15.3 you created the Chapter15 code group as a child of the All Code code group. In general, the CLR will examine all the code groups in the hierarchy to determine membership. However, any code group in the hierarchy can be marked as Exclusive (the effect of the check box you checked when creating the Chapter15 code group). The CLR stops checking for group membership if code is found to be a member of an Exclusive code group. Either way, code will be determined to be a member of zero or more code groups as a first step.

Next, the CLR retrieves the permission set for each code group that contains the code. If the code is a member of an Exclusive code group, only the permission set of that code group is taken into account. If the code is a member of more than one code group and none of them is an Exclusive code group, all the permission sets of those code groups are taken into account. The permission set for the code is the *union* of the permission sets of all relevant code groups. That is, if code is a member of two code groups, and one code group grants FileDialog permission, but the other does not, the code will have FileDialog permission from this step

That accounts for the permissions at one level (the Enterprise level). But there are actually four levels of permissions: Enterprise, Machine, User, and Application Domain. Only the first three levels can be managed within the .NET Framework Configuration tool, but if you need specific security checking within an application domain, you can do this in code. (Roughly speaking, an *application domain* is a session in which code runs.) An application domain can reduce the permissions granted to code within that application domain, but it cannot expand them.

The CLR determines which of the four levels are relevant by starting at the top (the Enterprise level) and working down. Any given code group can have the LevelFinal property, in which case the examination stops there. For example, if code is a member of a code group on the Machine level, and that group has the LevelFinal property, only the Enterprise and Machine levels are considered in assigning security. The CLR computes the permissions for each level separately and then assigns the code the *intersection* of the permissions of all relevant levels. That is, if code is granted FileDialog permission on the Enterprise and Machine levels but is not granted FileDialog permission on the User level, the code will not have FileDialog permission.

At this point, the CLR knows what permissions should be granted to the code in question, considered in isolation, but code does not run in isolation; it runs as part of an application. The final step of evaluating code access permissions is to perform a stack walk. In a *stack walk*, the CLR examines all code in the calling chain from the original application to the code being evaluated. The final permission set for the code is the *intersection* of the permission sets of all code in the calling chain. That is, if code is granted FileDialog permission but the code that called it was not, the code will not be granted FileDialog permission.

> **EXAM TIP**
>
> **Determining Permissions** The Microsoft .NET Framework Configuration tool can help you determine the effective permissions for a piece of code. Right-click the Runtime Security Policy node and select Evaluate Assembly to do so. You can see the effective permissions for an assembly here or get a list of all the code groups that contribute to the assembly's permissions.

Requesting Other Types of Permissions

Sometimes, you might want to request a particular permission even though your application doesn't absolutely require that permission to proceed. That's the purpose of optional permissions. If you refer back to the code in Step By Step 15.3, you'll see that part of the permission attribute is the SecurityAction.RequestMinimum flag. To request optional permissions, use the SecurityAction.RequestOptional flag.

To use optional permissions in Visual Basic .NET, your code must have a Sub Main starting point with a Try...Catch block. If optional permissions for the assembly can't be granted, this block will catch the exception. If minimum permissions can't be granted, the program will be shut down whether or not this block is present.

You can also tell the CLR about permissions that you do not wish your code to have. This can be useful if the code is potentially available to untrusted callers (for example, users who invoke the code over the Internet), and you want to limit the potential harm they can do. The flag for this is SecurityAction.RequestRefuse.

Finally, you might wish to ensure that all the code that calls your code has a particular permission. For example, you might want to raise an exception if any code in the calling stack doesn't have Registry permissions. You can do this by specifying SecurityAction.Demand in the declaration of the security attribute.

GUIDED PRACTICE
EXERCISE 15.1

One reason you might choose to use imperative security rather than declarative security is to be able to easily catch security violations and respond to them automatically. In this exercise, use imperative security to selectively disable part of a user interface that the user isn't able to activate under the current security policy. You can start with the simple "browse for file" example from Step By Step 15.3 or invent your own problem.

Try this on your own first. If you get stuck or want to see one possible solution, follow these steps:

1. Create a new Visual Basic .NET Windows application. Rename the default form GuidedPracticeExercise15-1.

2. Place two Label controls, a TextBox control named txtFileName, and a Button control named btnGetFile on the form. Name one of the Label controls lblMessage and remove its Text. Add an OpenFileDialog component named dlgOpen.

3. Double-click the Button control to open the form's module. Add this statement to the top of the module:

```
Imports System.Security.Permissions
```

4. Add this code to check security at load time, and to allow the user to browse for a file name when he clicks the button:

```
Private Sub Form1_Load(ByVal sender As System.Object, _
 ByVal e As System.EventArgs) Handles MyBase.Load
   Try
       Dim fdp As FileDialogPermission = _
        New FileDialogPermission( _
        PermissionState.Unrestricted)
       ' Check to see whether the code
       ' has the specified permission
```

```
            fdp.Demand()
        Catch ex As Exception
            btnGetFile.Enabled = False
            lblMessage.Text = _
    "You do not have permission to browse for file names"
        End Try
    End Sub

    Private Sub btnGetFile_Click( _
     ByVal sender As System.Object, _
     ByVal e As System.EventArgs) Handles btnGetFile.Click
        Try
            If dlgOpen.ShowDialog = DialogResult.OK Then
                txtFilename.Text = dlgOpen.FileName
            End If
        Catch ex As Exception
            MessageBox.Show("Exception: " & ex.Message)
        End Try
    End Sub
```

5. Set the form as the startup object for the project.

6. Compile the project. Run the compiled project from Windows Explorer. You should find it possible to browse for a file by clicking the button.

7. Select Start, Programs, Administrative Tools, Microsoft .NET Framework Configuration.

8. Expand the Code Groups node and click the default All Code code group. Click the Add a Child Code Group link in the right panel of the Configuration tool.

9. In the Create Code Group dialog box, name the new group Chapter15GPE. Enter a description and click Next.

10. Select the Hash condition. Click the Import button and browse to the executable file from this exercise. Click Open to calculate the hash for this file. Click Next.

11. Select the No FileDialog permission set and click Next. Click Finish to create the new code group.

12. Right-click the Chapter15GPE code group and select Properties. Check the box to make this code group exclusive. Click OK.

13. Run the program from Windows Explorer again. The Button control should be disabled, and the message should appear, as shown in Figure 15.9.

continues

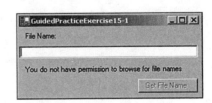

FIGURE 15.9
User interface modified by security settings.

continued

In Guided Practice Exercise 15.1, the imperative security object is used to check the permissions that the application has as soon as the form is loaded. If the call to the Demand method fails, you know the user won't be able to invoke the file dialog. In that case, the code disables the button that would otherwise launch the file dialog and puts up a warning message instead.

Using Custom Security Attributes

Configure security for a Windows-based application

- **Use custom attributes to configure security.**

In some cases, the built-in security permissions might not fit your needs. For example, you might have designed a custom class that retrieves confidential information from your company's database, and you want to restrict permission on it by a more specific means than limiting SQL permissions.

In such cases, you can create your own custom permissions and add them to the .NET security framework. This requires quite a bit of code, and most developers will never need to perform this task. But just in case you do, I'll outline the process. You'll find more in-depth information, including all the code for a simple custom permission, in the Securing Applications section of the .NET Framework Combined Help Collection.

To implement a custom permission, you must create a class that inherits from the CodeAccessPermission class. Your new class must override five key methods to provide its own interfaces to the security system:

- ◆ **Copy**—Creates an exact copy of the current instance
- ◆ **Intersect**—Returns the intersection of permissions between the current instance and a passed-in instance of the class
- ◆ **IsSubsetOf**—Returns True if a passed instance includes everything allowed by the current instance.

◆ **FromXML**—Decodes an XML representation of the permission

◆ **ToXml**—Encodes the current instance as XML

Your class must support a constructor that accepts an instance of the PermissionState enumeration (which has a value of Unrestricted or None). You might also want to implement custom constructors related to your particular business needs. For example, a database-related permission might require a constructor that accepts a server name, if permissions should be handled differently on test and development servers.

Although it's not strictly required, your code should also implement a method named IsUnrestricted, which returns True if this particular instance represents unrestricted access to the resource. This will make your custom permission more compatible with the built-in permissions in the .NET Framework.

To support declarative security, you should also implement an attribute class for your permission. This attribute class should derive from CodeAccessSecurityAttribute (which in turn derives from SecurityAttribute). The class should override the CreatePermission member of the IPermission interface. Within this function, you should create an instance of your base custom permission class and set its properties according to the parameters from the declarative security invocation. Any attribute class must be marked with the Serializable attribute so that it can be serialized into metadata along with the class to which it is applied.

For your custom permission to actually protect the intended resource, you must make changes to both the resource and to the .NET Framework on the computers where the permission will be used. The changes to the resource are simple: Whenever an operation protected by the custom permission is about to be performed, the code should demand an instance of the permission. If the calling code can't deliver the permission, your class should refuse to perform the operation.

The changes to the .NET Framework are somewhat more complex. First, you must create an XML representation of your custom permission in the format expected by the Code Access Security Policy tool, caspol.exe. You can create this XML representation by instantiating your permission and calling its ToXml method.

Given this XML representation, caspol.exe can add a permission set to the .NET Framework that contains your custom permission. It will also add the assembly that implements the custom permission to the list of trusted assemblies on the computer. You must perform this step on every computer where your custom permission will be used.

REVIEW BREAK

- ▶ Permissions control access to resources.

- ▶ Code can request the minimum permissions that it needs to run and optional permissions that it would like to have. It can also refuse permissions and demand permissions on the part of calling code.

- ▶ Code access permissions represent access to resources, while identity permissions represent things that the .NET Framework knows about code.

- ▶ The .NET Framework supplies both attribute-based declarative security and class-based imperative security.

- ▶ Code groups are sets of assemblies that share a security context.

- ▶ Permission sets are sets of permissions that can be granted as a unit.

- ▶ The CLR computes actual permissions at runtime based on code group membership and the calling chain of the code.

- ▶ Custom permissions allow you to create your own permissions to protect particular resources.

CONFIGURING AUTHORIZATION

Configure security for a Windows-based application

- • **Select and configure authentication type. Authentication types include Windows Authentication, None, forms-based, Microsoft Passport, and custom authentication.**

Configure authorization

- **Configure role-based authorization.**

- **Implement identity management.**

The final set of exam objectives for this chapter cover the closely intertwined subjects of authentication and authorization. Authentication refers to the process of obtaining credentials from a user and verifying her identity. Once an identity has been authenticated, it can be authorized to use various resources.

In the Windows application world, authentication is simple: You're authenticated by Windows when you log on. That identity is available to .NET applications to use in making security decisions. Those decisions are handled by the role-based security scheme that you'll read about in the remaining sections of the chapter.

Other authentication methods are available in the larger .NET Framework. These authentication methods only apply to ASP.NET applications, so you're unlikely to see them in conjunction with Windows applications. You should know about the available choices, however, because it's possible for an ASP.NET application to invoke a Windows component (though it will do so using a Windows identity). These methods of authentication include:

- ◆ **None**—In many cases, users of an ASP.NET application needn't be authenticated at all. Pages can simply be delivered to all comers.

- ◆ **Forms-based**—This form of authentication uses an HTML form to request credentials from the user. If the credentials are acceptable, the application sends back an identity key.

- ◆ **Windows**—ASP.NET applications can use the Windows authentication methods built into IIS to authenticate users in a Windows domain.

- ◆ **Passport**—Microsoft Passport provides a centralized authentication and profile service for member sites.

- ◆ **Custom**—You can develop your own custom authentication scheme if you like. You should be aware, though, that it is difficult to design a secure authentication scheme.

NOTE **More on Authentication** For more details on the ASP.NET authentication methods, refer to *MCSD Training Guide: Visual Basic .NET Web-based Applications.*

NOTE

Custom Authorization If for some reason you want to develop a custom authorization scheme, you can implement IIdentity and IPrincipal in your own classes. In use, these classes will function very much like the Windows-based classes that I'll demonstrate in the remainder of this chapter.

Identity and Principal Objects

Within a Visual Basic .NET Windows application, authorization is handled by the role-based security system. Role-based security revolves around two interfaces: IIdentity and IPrincipal. For applications that use Windows accounts in role-based security, these interfaces are implemented by the WindowsIdentity and WindowsPrincipal objects, respectively.

The WindowsIdentity object represents the Windows user who is running the current code. The properties of this object allow you to retrieve such information as the username and authentication method.

The WindowsPrincipal object adds functionality to the WindowsIdentity object. The WindowsPrincipal object represents the entire security context of the user who is running the current code, including any roles to which they belong. When the CLR decides which role-based permissions to assign to your code, it inspects the WindowsPrincipal object (see Step By Step 15.6).

STEP BY STEP

15.6 WindowsIdentity and WindowsPrincipal

1. Add a new form to your Visual Basic .NET application.

2. Place a ListBox control named lbProperties and a Button control named btnGetProperties on the form.

3. Double-click the Button control to open the form's module. Add this statement to the top of the module:

```
Imports System.Security.Principal
```

4. Add this code to retrieve properties when you click the Button control:

```
Private Sub btnGetProperties_Click( _
 ByVal sender As System.Object, _
 ByVal e As System.EventArgs) Handles btnGetProperties.Click
    ' Tell the CLR which principal policy is in use
    AppDomain.CurrentDomain.SetPrincipalPolicy( _
    PrincipalPolicy.WindowsPrincipal)
    lbProperties.Items.Clear()
```

```
' Get the current identity
Dim wi As WindowsIdentity = WindowsIdentity.GetCurrent()
' Dump its properties to the listbox
With lbProperties.Items
    .Add("WindowsIdentity:")
    .Add("  Authentication type: " & _
    wi.AuthenticationType)
    .Add("  Is Anonymous: " & wi.IsAnonymous)
    .Add("  Is Authenticated: " & wi.IsAuthenticated)
    .Add("  Is Guest: " & wi.IsGuest)
    .Add("  Is System: " & wi.IsSystem)
    .Add("  Name: " & wi.Name)
    .Add("  Token: " & wi.Token.ToString)
End With

' Get the current principal
Dim prin As WindowsPrincipal = New WindowsPrincipal(wi)
' Dump its properties to the listbox
With lbProperties.Items
    .Add("  Authentication Type: " & _
    prin.Identity.AuthenticationType)
    .Add("  Is Authenticated: " & _
    prin.Identity.IsAuthenticated)
    .Add("  Name: " & prin.Identity.Name)
    .Add("  Member of Domain Users: " & _
    prin.IsInRole("LARKGROUP\Domain Users"))
End With

End Sub
```

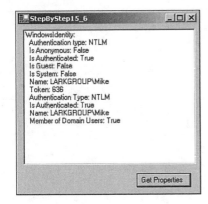

5. Set the form as the startup object for the project.

6. Run the project and click the button. You'll see output similar to that in Figure 15.10.

FIGURE 15.10
WindowsIdentity and WindowsPrincipal properties.

This code first tells the CLR that you're using the standard Windows authentication method by calling the SetPrincipalPolicy method of the current AppDomain. It then retrieves the WindowsIdentity of the current user through the static GetCurrent method of the WindowsIdentity object. After displaying some of the properties of the WindowsIdentity object, it gets the corresponding WindowsPrincipal object by passing the WindowsIdentity object to the constructor of the WindowsPrincipal class.

WARNING

Modify the Domain Name This code contains a reference to a specific domain named LARKGROUP in its call to the IsInRole method. You should change that to the name of your own domain to test this code.

Note that the properties of the WindowsIdentity object are somewhat richer than those of the WindowsPrincipal object, but that the WindowsPrincipal object lets you evaluate role membership for the current user. If you only want to work with the WindowsPrincipal object, you can also retrieve it from the Thread.CurrentPrincipal static method.

Verifying Role Membership

One way to manage role-based security is to use the IsInRole method of the WindowsPrincipal object to determine whether the current user is in a specific Windows group (see Step By Step 15.7). The results of this method call can be used to modify your application's user interface or to perform other tasks.

STEP BY STEP

15.7 Verifying Role Membership

1. Add a new form to your Visual Basic .NET application.

2. Place a Label control named lblMembership on the form.

3. Double-click the form to open its module. Add these statements to the top of the module:

```
Imports System.Security.Principal
Imports System.Threading
```

4. Add this code to run when you load the form:

```
Private Sub StepByStep15_7_Load( _
 ByVal sender As System.Object, _
 ByVal e As System.EventArgs) Handles MyBase.Load
    ' Tell the CLR to use Windows security
    AppDomain.CurrentDomain.SetPrincipalPolicy( _
     PrincipalPolicy.WindowsPrincipal)
    ' Get the current principal object
    Dim prin As WindowsPrincipal = Thread.CurrentPrincipal
    ' Determine whether the user is an admin
    Dim fAdmin As Boolean = prin.IsInRole( _
     WindowsBuiltInRole.Administrator)
    ' Display the results on the UI
    If fAdmin Then
        lblMembership.Text = _
         "You are in the Administrators group"
    Else
```

```
        lblMembership.Text = _
            "You are not in the Administrators group"
    End If
End Sub
```

5. Set the form as the startup object for the project.

6. Run the project. The form will tell you whether you're in the Administrators group.

Three overloaded forms of the IsInRole method are available:

◆ **IsInRole(WindowsBuiltInRole)**—Uses one of the WindowsBuiltInRole constants to check for membership in the standard Windows groups.

◆ **IsInRole(String)**—Checks for membership in a group with the specified name.

◆ **IsInRole(Integer)**—Checks for membership in a group with the specified Role Identifier (RID). RIDs are assigned by the operating system and provide a language-independent way to identify groups.

Using the PrincipalPermission Class

An alternative way to manage identities is to perform imperative or declarative security checking with role-based security by using the PrincipalPermission class, as in Step By Step 15.8, or the PrincipalPermissionAttribute attribute.

STEP BY STEP

15.8 Using the PrincipalPermission Class

1. Add a new form to your Visual Basic .NET application.

2. Double-click the form to open its module. Add these statements to the top of the module:

```
Imports System
Imports System.Security.Permissions
Imports System.Security.Principal
```

continues

continued

3. Add this code to run when you load the form:

```
Private Sub StepByStep15_8_Load( _
 ByVal sender As System.Object, _
 ByVal e As System.EventArgs) Handles MyBase.Load
    ' Tell the CLR to use Windows security
    AppDomain.CurrentDomain.SetPrincipalPolicy( _
    PrincipalPolicy.WindowsPrincipal)
    ' Create a new PrincipalPermission object
    ' This object matches any user
    ' in a group named Developers
    Dim pp As PrincipalPermission = _
    New PrincipalPermission( _
    Nothing, "Developers")
    ' See if the user is in the group
    Try
        pp.Demand()
        MessageBox.Show("You are in the Developers
        group")
    Catch ex As Exception
        MessageBox.Show("Exception: " & ex.Message)
    End Try
End Sub
```

4. Set the form as the startup object for the project.

5. Run the project. If you're a member of a group named Developers, you'll see a message box telling you so. If not, you'll see a Security Exception message from the `PrincipalPermission` class.

Checking permissions with role-based security is similar to checking permissions with code access security. The difference lies in what you are checking. The constructor for the PrincipalPermission class accepts both a name and a group name, so you can also use it to check whether a specific user is running the code.

REVIEW BREAK

▶ The .NET Framework supports both authentication and authorization. Authentication refers to verifying a user's identity. Authorization refers to granting rights based on that identity.

▶ The WindowsPrincipal and WindowsIdentity classes let you check the authentication status of the current user.

▶ You can use the IsInRole method of the WindowsPrincipal object to check for membership in Windows groups.

▶ The PrincipalPermission class allows you to perform declarative or imperative role-based security operations.

CHAPTER SUMMARY

After you've finished writing an application, you might still need to configure it. In this chapter, you learned about several broad areas of configurability that are supported by the .NET Framework.

Dynamic properties allow you to set properties of forms, controls, and other components at runtime by editing XML files. Each assembly can have its own configuration file. You can also edit a master machine configuration file to make systemwide changes.

The .NET Framework also includes two complete security systems configurable by administrators. Code access security controls the access of code to sensitive resources. Code can determine exactly which resources it requires or would like, and administrators can determine exactly which resources to make available. The CLR checks to see whether the requested resources are available before it lets your code run.

Role-based security allows you to make decisions in your code based on the user who is currently logged on. You can check for a particular username or for membership in a built-in or custom Windows group, and make decisions accordingly.

KEY TERMS

- Authentication
- Authorization
- Code access security
- Code group
- Configured assembly
- Declarative security
- Imperative security
- Permission
- Permission set
- Role-based security

APPLY YOUR KNOWLEDGE

Exercises

15.1 Sharing Dynamic Properties

When assigning dynamic properties to the components of a Windows application, you might want to use the same value for more than one property. You can do this by reusing the keys assigned to dynamic properties.

Estimated Time: 15 minutes.

1. Open a Visual Basic .NET Windows Application in the Visual Studio .NET IDE. Add a new form to the application.

2. Place three Button controls on the form.

3. Select the first Button control. In the Button's Properties window, click the + sign next to the Dynamic Properties entry. Click in the Advanced section and click the Build button to open the Dynamic Properties dialog box.

4. In the Dynamic Properties dialog box, check the Enabled property. Change its Key Mapping value to `Button.Enabled`. Click OK.

5. Select the second Button control and repeat the preceding steps. Use the same name, `Button.Enabled`, for the Key Mapping property.

6. Select the third Button control and repeat the preceding steps. Use the same name, `Button.Enabled`, for the Key Mapping property.

7. Set the form as the startup object for the project.

8. Run the project to see that all three buttons are enabled.

9. Stop the project. Open the project's app.config file. Edit this file to change the stored value for

`Button.Enabled` to False:

```
<configuration>
    <appSettings>
        <add key="Button.Enabled"
value="False" />
    </appSettings>
</configuration>
```

10. Run the project. All three buttons will be disabled.

Any time you want two dynamic properties in the same project to stay synchronized, use the same key for each of the properties. The original value of the property will be the value from the first control to which you assigned the key mapping. It doesn't matter whether the components are on the same form or different forms. For example, you might use a shared dynamic property to ensure that every form in your database-backed application gets the same connection string.

15.2 Declarative Role-Based Security

Just like code access security, role-based security can be declarative or imperative. This exercise shows how to use declarative role-based security to cause an exception if the user is not in a specified group.

Estimated Time: 15 minutes.

1. Add a new form to your Visual Basic .NET application.

2. Double-click the form to open the form's module. Add this code to the top of the module:

```
Imports System
Imports System.Security.Permissions
Imports System.Security.Principal
```

APPLY YOUR KNOWLEDGE

3. Modify the class declaration for the form to include a declarative security line with the `PrincipalPermissionAttribute`:

```
<PrincipalPermissionAttribute( _
SecurityAction.Demand, _
 Role:="Administrators")> _
Public Class Exercise15_2
```

4. Add code to run when you open the form:

```
Private Sub Exercise15_2_Load( _
 ByVal sender As System.Object, _
 ByVal e As System.EventArgs) _
 Handles MyBase.Load
    MessageBox.Show( _
      "You are a member of the " & _
      "Administrators group")
End Sub
```

5. Set the form as the startup object for the project.

6. Run the project. If you're not in the local Administrators group, you should see a security exception.

Review Questions

1. What types of projects can use dynamic properties?

2. What types of properties can you set to be dynamic properties?

3. What file contains the values assigned to dynamic properties?

4. How many configuration files can you have in a single application?

5. What tasks can you perform with the .NET Framework Configuration tool?

6. What is the purpose of a configured assembly?

7. What types of permission requests can an application make?

8. What are the three types of permission objects?

9. What is the difference between declarative and imperative security?

10. What do the WindowsIdentity and WindowsPrincipal objects represent?

Exam Questions

1. You developed a database application that stored a connection string as a dynamic property. You finished testing the application and are ready to switch to using the production server. You edit the connection string in the application's configuration file. What must you do to make the application use the new connection string?

   A. Nothing; the application will automatically use the new connection string.

   B. Restart the application.

   C. Recompile the application.

   D. Reboot Windows

2. Users of your application have requested the capability to customize the main form of the application. Which of these form properties can you allow them to set in a config file with dynamic property support?

   A. BackColor

   B. BackgroundImage

   C. Text

   D. Font

APPLY YOUR KNOWLEDGE

3. You are using a .NET application from MegaSloth. This application uses a component from MiniControl to handle file browsing. MiniControl has released a new version of their component with enhanced capabilities for browsing files over the Internet. You want the MegaSloth application to use the new version of MiniControl. What should you do?

   A. Make a configured assembly entry in the MegaSloth application's configuration file to tell it to use the new version of the MiniControl component.

   B. Contact MegaSloth and ask them to compile a new version of their application that incorporates the new MiniControl component.

   C. Contact MiniControl and ask them to compile a new version of the MegaSloth application that incorporates the updated component.

   D. Just install the new version of the MiniControl component on your computer. All applications will automatically use the new version.

4. Your application requires permission to read and write to the Windows Registry to function properly. Which .NET security features should you use to ensure that your code has this capability?

   A. Code access security

   B. Role-based security

   C. Encryption

   D. Type safety

5. Your application requires the user to be in the Domain Admins group to activate certain functions. Which .NET security feature should you use to ensure that the user is in this group?

   A. Code access security

   B. Role-based security

   C. Encryption

   D. Type safety

6. You are using code access security to verify that your application has permission to perform file I/O operations. As part of your testing procedure, you created a permission set that denies file I/O permissions. You also created a code group that uses a hash code membership condition to select your application's executable assembly, and you assigned the permission set to this code group. You set this code group to be an exclusive code group and verified that your program is unable to obtain file I/O permissions.

   To continue development, you change the code group to use the Everything permission set and continue adding new code to your application. When you're ready to test the security features, you change back to the permission set without file I/O permissions. However, you find that your application is able to access files, even though you have not changed the declarative security within the application.

   Why is your code able to perform file I/O even though the code group denies file I/O permissions?

   A. Changing code within your application changes its hash code, so it is no longer a member of the code group.

APPLY YOUR KNOWLEDGE

B. After you've assigned the Everything permission set to a code group, the code group ignores attempts to set more restrictive permissions.

C. The Exclusive property on a code group only applies when the code group is first created.

D. You must reboot your development computer to update the membership records of the code group.

7. Assembly A is a member of the code groups in Table 1 below (and only the those code groups):

What permission does the CLR assign to Assembly A?

A. Everything

B. LocalIntranet

C. Internet

D. Nothing

8. Assembly B is a member of the code groups in Table 2 below (and only the those code groups):

What permission does the CLR assign to Assembly B?

A. Everything

B. LocalIntranet

C. Internet

D. Nothing

TABLE 1

Level	Code Group	Permission Set	Exclusive	LevelFinal
Enterprise	All Code	Everything	No	No
Enterprise	Company Code	LocalIntranet	No	No
Enterprise	Restricted Code	Internet	No	No
Enterprise	Restricted Components	Nothing	No	No

TABLE 2

Level	Code Group	Permission Set	Exclusive	LevelFinal
Enterprise	All Code	Everything	No	No
Enterprise	Company Code	LocalIntranet	No	No
Machine	Restricted Code	Internet	No	No
User	Restricted Components	Nothing	No	No

APPLY YOUR KNOWLEDGE

9. Assembly C is a member of the code groups in Table 1 below (and only those code groups):

   What permission does the CLR assign to Assembly C?

   A. Everything

   B. LocalIntranet

   C. Internet

   D. Nothing

10. Assembly D is a member of the code groups in Table 2 below (and only those code groups):

    What permission does the CLR assign to Assembly D?

    A. Everything

    B. LocalIntranet

    C. Internet

    D. Nothing

11. Your code will be called from the Internet and you want to minimize the chance that it can do unintentional damage to the local computer. As a result, you want to ensure that your code is not granted File I/O permissions. Which SecurityAction flag should you use with the FileIoPermissionAttribute declaration?

    A. SecurityAction.Minimum

    B. SecurityAction.Optional

    C. SecurityAction.Demand

    D. SecurityAction.RequestRefuse

12. Your code wants to ensure that all code in the calling chain has File I/O permissions. Which SecurityAction flag should you use with the FileIoPermission object?

    A. SecurityAction.Minimum

    B. SecurityAction.Optional

    C. SecurityAction.Demand

    D. SecurityAction.RequestRefuse

TABLE 1

Level	Code Group	Permission Set	Exclusive	LevelFinal
Enterprise	All Code	Everything	No	No
Enterprise	Company Code	LocalIntranet	Yes	No
Machine	Restricted Code	Internet	No	No
User	Restricted Components	Nothing	No	No

TABLE 2

Level	Code Group	Permission Set	Exclusive	LevelFinal
Enterprise	All Code	Everything	No	No
Enterprise	Company Code	LocalIntranet	No	No
Machine	Restricted Code	Internet	No	Yes
User	Restricted Components	Nothing	No	No

APPLY YOUR KNOWLEDGE

13. Which of these tasks requires you to use imperative security rather than declarative security?

    A. Ensuring that your application has access to a specific key in the Windows Registry

    B. Ensuring that your application can open a particular file whose name is specified by the user

    C. Ensuring that your application has access to a specific environment variable

    D. Ensuring that your application has access to SQL Server databases

14. Your application uses this code to check for membership in the Developers group:

```
Private Sub frmSecure_Load( _
 ByVal sender As System.Object, _
 ByVal e As System.EventArgs) _
 Handles MyBase.Load
    ' Get the current principal object
    Dim prin As WindowsPrincipal = _
     Thread.CurrentPrincipal
    ' Determine whether the user is an admin
    Dim fAdmin As Boolean = _
     prin.IsInRole("Developers")
    ' Display the results on the UI
    If fAdmin Then
        lblMembership.Text = _
         "You are in the Developers group"
    Else
        lblMembership.Text = _
         "You are not in the " & _
         "Developers group"
    End If
End Sub
```

Users report that the code claims they are not in the Developers group even when they are. What must you do to fix this problem?

    A. Use imperative security to ensure that your code has access to the Windows environment variables.

    B. Create a WindowsIdentity object by using WindowsIdentity.GetCurrent and use this object to construct the WindowsPrincipal object.

    C. Use the WindowsPrincipal.Name property to retrieve the user's name, and use that name to the call to the IsInRole method.

    D. Call AppDomain.CurrentDomain. SetPrincipalPolicy (PrincipalPolicy. WindowsPrincipal) to specify the authentication mode.

15. Your application uses the same OLE DB connection string on OleDbConnection objects on five different forms. You want to allow the user to set this connection string by editing the application's configuration file. What should you do to allow this with minimum effort?

    A. Make the connection string a dynamic property of each OleDbConnection object. Use the same Key Mapping for all five connection strings.

    B. Make the connection string a dynamic property of each OleDbConnection object. Use a different Key Mapping for each connection string.

    C. Make the connection string a dynamic property of the OleDbConnection object on one form. Use code to copy this string to each of the other forms at runtime.

    D. Make the connection string a dynamic property of the OleDbConnection object on one form. Open all connections from this same object.

APPLY YOUR KNOWLEDGE

Answers to Review Questions

1. You can use dynamic properties in any project that compiles to an EXE file. Dynamic properties cannot be used in DLL files.

2. You can set any simple property (that is, any property whose value is not an instance of a class) to be a dynamic property.

3. In the IDE, the app.config file contains the values assigned to dynamic properties. After your project is compiled, the configuration file has the same name as the project's executable file with the added extension .config.

4. An application can only have a single configuration file, though it can also be affected by settings in the machine configuration file.

5. Manage the contents of the Global Assembly Cache, manage configured assemblies, manage remoting channels, manage security policy, and manage application settings.

6. The purpose of a configured assembly is to allow you to change the version of a library used by a particular .NET application.

7. An application can request minimum or optional permissions, refuse permissions, or demand permissions of its callers.

8. Code-based, Identity, and Role-based.

9. Declarative security works by assigning attributes to assemblies; imperative security works by instantiating the various security classes and using them directly.

10. The WindowsIdentity object represents a logged-on user; the WindowsPrincipal object represents the entire security context of the logged-on user.

Answers to Exam Questions

1. **B.** Dynamic properties are only applied when a component is initialized. If your application is already running, you must restart the application (or somehow reload the applicable component) before it will see the changes in the configuration file.

2. **C.** Only simple (nonobject) properties can be handled by automatic dynamic properties.

3. **A.** By using a configured assembly, you can use the new component in an existing application without recompiling anything and without affecting other applications on the computer. .NET applications deliberately do not use new versions of components unless told to do so explicitly; automatically picking up new versions led to "DLL Hell" in previous versions of Windows.

4. **A.** Checking whether code has a particular privilege is the function of code access security.

5. **B.** Role-based security allows you to check whether a user is in a particular group.

6. **A.** Hash codes are calculated from the MSIL code of an assembly, so changing the assembly's contents changes its hash code.

7. **A.** Within a level, the permission set granted to an assembly is the union of all the permission sets of code groups on that level to which the assembly belongs.

8. **D.** Across levels, the permission set granted to an assembly is the intersection of all the permission sets of the levels. Because the user level grants no permissions to Assembly B, Assembly B gets no permissions from the CLR.

APPLY YOUR KNOWLEDGE

9. **B.** The Company Code code group is marked as an exclusive code group, so only its permission set is taken into account when determining the permission set for the assembly.

10. **C.** Because the code group on the Machine level is marked with the LevelFinal property, the code group on the user level is not taken into account when determining the permission set for this assembly.

11. **D.** SecurityAction.RequestRefuse tells the CLR that your assembly does not want to be granted the specified permission.

12. **C.** SecurityAction.Demand demands the specified permission of the calling code.

13. **B.** You must use imperative security to check access to resources whose names are not known until runtime.

14. **D.** You must tell the CLR how users are authenticated, even when you're using a Windows application that automatically employs Windows authentication.

15. **A.** By using the same key mapping on each of the five objects, you allow the user to change all five by changing a single entry in the configuration file.

Suggested Readings and Resources

1. LaMacchia, Brian A., et al. *.NET Framework Security.* Addison-Wesley, 2002.

2. Visual Studio .NET Combined Help Collection

   • Configuring Applications

   • Configuring Applications Using Dynamic Properties

   • Securing Applications

PART II

FINAL REVIEW

Fast Facts

Practice Exam

Now that you've read this book, worked through the exercises, Guided Practice Exercises, and Step By Steps, and acquired as much hands-on experience using Visual Basic .NET as you could, you are ready for the exam. This final review section is designed as a "final cram in the parking lot" before you walk in to the testing center. You can't reread the whole book in an hour, but you will be able to read this section in that time.

This chapter is organized by objective category, giving you not just a summary, but a review of the most important points from the book. Remember, this is just a review, not a replacement for the actual study material! It's meant to be a review of concepts and a trigger for you to remember useful bits of information you will need when taking the exam. If you know the information in here and the concepts that stand behind it, chances are good that the exam will be a snap.

CREATING USER SERVICES

Create a Windows Form by using the Windows Forms Designer.

Add and set properties on a Windows Form.

◆ Properties let you customize the appearance and behavior of a Windows Form.

◆ The Windows Forms Designer lets you define a form based on the properties available in its base class (which is usually the Form class).

Fast Facts

70-306

◆ You can add custom properties to a form.

◆ Attributes let you define the runtime behavior of a property.

Create a Windows Form by using visual inheritance.

◆ Form inheritance allows you to create a new form by inheriting it from a base form. This allows you to reuse and extend the coding that you've already finished.

◆ The Windows Forms Designer lets you inherit a form visually from an existing form through the inheritance picker. You can also visually manipulate inherited properties through the Properties window.

Build graphical interface elements by using the System.Drawing namespace.

◆ Windows Forms follow a two-dimensional coordinate system. A point is an addressable location in this coordinate system.

◆ The Graphics object gives you access to a drawing surface. It can be used to draw lines, text, curves, and a variety of shapes.

◆ The ResizeRedraw property, when set to True, instructs the form to redraw itself when it is resized. It's a good programming practice to design forms that resize their contents based on the form's size. The Resize event of a form can be also used to program the resizing logic.

◆ The Graphics class provides a set of Draw methods that can be use to draw shapes such as rectangles, ellipses, curves, and so on on a drawing surface. The Graphics class also provides a set of Fill methods that are used to create solid shapes.

◆ You can use an object of the Bitmap class to manipulate images. The System.Drawing namespace classes can work with a variety of image formats.

Add controls to a Windows Form.

Set properties on controls.

◆ You can add controls to a form in two ways: You can use the Windows Forms Designer or create them in code.

◆ The Windows Forms Designer in the Microsoft Visual Studio .NET IDE allows you to add controls to a form and manipulate them very easily.

◆ The Visual Studio .NET toolbox provides a variety of controls and components you can use to create common Windows GUI elements.

◆ You can set the properties of controls at design time by using the Properties window or at runtime by accessing them as *ControlName.PropertyName* in code.

◆ Some of the important properties of controls—such as Anchor, Dock, Enabled, Font, Location, Name, Size, TabIndex, TabStop, and Visible—are shared by most common Windows Forms controls.

◆ A dialog box is used to prompt users for input. A few built-in dialog boxes are available, such as ColorDialog, FontDialog, OpenFileDialog, and SaveFileDialog. These function just like the Windows operating system's dialog boxes.

◆ You can build custom dialog boxes to meet custom requirements. You can create custom dialog boxes by first creating a form and setting a few properties of the form to enable the form to behave like a dialog box.

◆ Dialog boxes can be of two types: modal and modeless. You can call the ShowDialog or Show methods of the Form class to create modal and modeless dialog boxes, respectively.

◆ The LinkLabel control is derived from the Label control. The LinkLabel control allows you to add links to the control. The Links property of the LinkLabel control contains a collection of all the links referred to by the control.

◆ The TextBox control can be displayed as an ordinary textbox, a password textbox (where each character is masked by the character provided in the PasswordChar property), or as a multiline textbox (by setting its MultiLine property to True). The RichTextBox control provides richer formatting capabilities than a TextBox control. It can also be drawn as a single-line or multiline text box. By default, the RichTextBox control has its MultiLine property set to True.

◆ GroupBox and Panel controls are container controls. They can be used to group other controls. The Controls property of these controls contains a collection of their child controls.

◆ In a group of CheckBox controls, you can check multiple checkboxes. In a group of RadioButton controls, you can select only a single radio button at a time.

◆ The CheckBox control allows you to set three check states (Checked, Unchecked, and Indeterminate) if the ThreeState property is set to True.

◆ The ComboBox control allows you to select a value from a predefined list of values. You can also enter a value in the ComboBox control. The ListBox control only allows you to select a value from the list of values displayed.

◆ The CheckedListBox control derives from the ListBox control and inherits its functionality. However, a CheckedListBox control displays a CheckBox control along with each item in the list of items to be checked. The CheckedListBox control allows only two selection modes: None (no selection) or One (allows multiple selections).

◆ The DomainUpDown and NumericUpDown controls allow you to select from a list of defined values by clicking up and down buttons. You can also enter values in the controls unless their ReadOnly properties are set to True.

◆ The DateTimePicker control allows you to select a date and time, and the MonthCalendar control allows you to select a date or range of dates. The SelectionStart, SelectionEnd, and SelectionRange properties return the start date, end date, and range of dates selected.

◆ The TreeView control is used to display data in a hierarchical collection of nodes. Each node is represented by a TreeNode object. The AfterSelect event of the TreeView control occurs when a node is selected and the SelectedNode property is set with the new selection.

◆ The ListView control is used to display items in different views—such as List, Details, SmallIcon, and LargeIcon—like the view options of Windows Explorer.

◆ Scrollbars can be associated with controls to provide scrolling functionality.

◆ The TabControl control provides a user interface that can be used to save space as well as to organize large numbers of controls. You usually see TabControl controls used in wizards.

Load controls dynamically.

◆ Adding controls dynamically is a three-step process:

1. Create a private variable to represent each of the controls you want to place on a form.

2. In the form's constructor, place code to instantiate each control and to customize each control, using its properties, methods, or events.

3. Add each control to the form's control collection.

◆ While creating controls programmatically, be sure to add them to their parent container's Controls collection.

Write code to handle control events and add the code to a control.

◆ Control programming is event driven. Events are fired when a user interacts with a control. To take specific action when an event occurs, you write an event handler method and attach it to the event of a control via its delegate.

◆ You can attach an event handler to an event by using the AddHandler statement.

Instantiate and invoke an ActiveX control.

◆ You can use the Windows Forms ActiveX Control Importer to create wrapper classes. Wrapper classes let you host an ActiveX control on a .NET Windows form.

◆ You can import an ActiveX control to a Visual Studio .NET project by adding it to the toolbox.

◆ After they're imported, ActiveX controls can be used just like native .NET controls.

◆ ActiveX controls impose a performance penalty and have other drawbacks.

Configure control licensing.

◆ The default control licensing structure in the .NET Framework requires no configuration by either developers or administrators. If you encounter runtime licensing errors, they are almost certainly coming from a custom licensing scheme. In such a case, the best course of action is to contact the control vendor directly for assistance.

Create menus and menu items.

◆ There are two types of menus in Windows applications. A main menu is used to group all the available commands and option, in a Windows application. A context menu is used to specify a relatively small list of option that applies to a control, depending on the application's current context.

◆ You can make keyboard navigation between menu items possible by including keyboard access keys in the Text properties of menu items. You can also associate shortcut keys with a menu. Pressing a shortcut key directly invokes a command.

Implement navigation for the user interface (UI).

Configure the order of tabs.

◆ All controls with TabStop properties set to True appear in the tab order for a form. The order in which the Tab key moves the cursor to the controls is dictated by the TabOrder properties of the controls.

◆ The Tab Order Wizard provides a convenient way to set the TabIndex properties of controls to implement logical keyboard-based navigation in the form by using the Tab key.

Validate user input.

◆ It is generally a good practice to validate user input at the time of data entry. Thoroughly validated data results in consistent and correct data being stored by the application.

◆ When a user presses a key, three events are generated: KeyDown, KeyPress, and KeyUp, in that order.

◆ The Validating event is the ideal place for storing the field-level validation logic for a control.

◆ The CausesValidation property specifies whether validation should be performed. If it is False, the Validating and Validated events are suppressed.

◆ The ErrorProvider component in the Visual Studio .NET toolbox is used to show validation-related error messages to the user.

◆ A control cannot receive the focus and appears grayed out if its Enabled property is set to False.

Validate non-Latin user input.

◆ The String.Compare method compares strings according to the rules of the CultureInfo object referenced by the CurrentCulture property.

◆ The CultureInfo.CompareInfo object can search for substrings according to the comparison rules of the current culture.

◆ The Array.Sort method sorts the members of an array by the alphabetical order rules of the current culture.

◆ The SortKey.Compare method compares strings according to the rules of the current culture.

Implement error handling in the UI.

Create and implement custom error messages.

◆ If the existing exception classes do not satisfy your exception handling requirements, you can create new exception classes, and they can be specific to your application. Custom exceptions should be derived from the ApplicationException class.

◆ You can use the UnhandledException event of the AppDomain class to manage unhandled exceptions.

◆ You can use the EventLog class to log events to the Windows event log.

Create and implement custom error handlers.

◆ The try block consists of code that may raise an exception. A try block cannot exist on its own. It should be immediately followed by one or more catch blocks or a finally block.

◆ The catch block handles any exception raised by the code in the try block. The Common Language Runtime looks for a matching catch block to handle the exception, which is the first catch block with either exactly the same exception or any of the exception's base classes.

◆ If multiple catch blocks are associated with a try block, the catch blocks should be arranged in top-to-bottom order of specific to general exception types.

◆ The finally block is used to enclose the code that needs to be run, regardless of whether the exception is raised.

Raise and handle errors.

◆ An exception occurs when a program encounters any unexpected problem during normal execution.

◆ The Framework Class Library (FCL) provides two main types of exceptions: SystemException and ApplicationException exceptions. SystemException represents the exceptions thrown by the Common Language Runtime, and ApplicationException represents the exceptions thrown by the user programs.

◆ The System.Exception class represents the base class for all CLR-compliant exceptions and provides the common functionality for exception handling.

◆ The throw statement is used to raise an exception.

Implement online user assistance.

◆ Visual Studio .NET includes the HTML Help SDK for the creation of HTML Help files.

◆ HTML Help files are composed of multiple HTML source files that are compiled into a single .CHM file.

◆ You can create HTML Help topics with any HTML authoring tool. HTML Help Workshop provides a convenient way to organize help projects.

◆ An HTML Help file can include navigation aids such as a table of contents and an index.

◆ HTML Help 2 is Microsoft's latest standard for help files.

◆ The Visual Studio Help Integration Kit includes the tools necessary to build HTML Help 2 files, including Microsoft Help Workshop.

◆ The HelpProvider component is the bridge between a .NET Windows application and an HTML Help file.

◆ You can use HelpProvider to display topics from a help file, Web pages, or pop-up help strings.

◆ Pop-up help is appropriate for dialog boxes, where you don't want the users to switch focus to another task.

◆ ToolTips let you provide quick help for individual controls.

Incorporate existing code into a Microsoft Windows-based application.

◆ You can incorporate existing code into a .NET application by using platform invoke (PInvoke) to execute 32-bit Windows API calls.

◆ You can incorporate existing code into a .NET application by creating a runtime-callable wrapper (RCW) to wrap around COM components.

Display and update data.

Transform and filter data.

◆ The Server Explorer window is a powerful tool for working with SQL Server data.

◆ You can edit and design SQL Server objects directly within Visual Studio .NET.

◆ The DataView object offers client-side sorting and filtering capabilities for data-bound objects.

◆ Using views on a server can be an efficient way to filter or transform data.

Bind data to the UI.

◆ Simple data binding refers to connecting a single entity in the data model to a single property of a control on the user interface.

◆ Any class that implements the IBindingList, ITypedList, or IList interface can deliver data via simple data binding.

◆ You can bind to almost any property of any control.

◆ A form uses CurrencyManager and BindingContext objects to keep track of data binding.

◆ Complex data binding binds a user interface control to an entire collection of data.

◆ To use complex data binding with a ListBox or ComboBox control, you set the control's DataSource and DisplayMember properties.

◆ A ListBox control or a ComboBox control can pull values from one data source and place them in another.

◆ You can cause a ListBox control or a ComboBox control to display one value while binding another by using the DisplayMember and ValueMember properties of the control.

◆ The DataGrid control displays an entire array of data in rows and columns. You specify the data to display by setting the DataSource property of the DataGrid control.

◆ The properties of the DataGrid control include many flexible formatting options.

◆ In one-way data binding, data from the data model is displayed on the form, but changes to the form do not affect the data model.

◆ In two-way data binding, data from the data model is displayed on the form, and changes to the form are also written back to the database.

◆ The .NET Framework uses BindingContext and CurrencyManager objects to manage data binding.

◆ You can use events of the CurrencyManager object to help react to changes in bound data.

◆ The Data Form Wizard helps you create data-bound forms, both simple and complex, quickly. These forms draw their data from relational databases such as SQL Server databases.

Instantiate and invoke a Web service or component.

Instantiate and invoke a Web service.

◆ Web services provide you with the means to create objects and invoke their methods, even though your only connection to the server is via the Internet.

◆ Communication with Web services occurs via XML messages transported by HTTP.

◆ Because they communicate over HTTP, Web services are typically not blocked by firewalls.

◆ The Simple Object Access Protocol (SOAP) encapsulates object-oriented messages between Web service clients and servers.

◆ The Universal Description, Discovery, and Integration protocol (UDDI) allows you to find Web services by connecting to a directory.

◆ The Web Services Description Language (WSDL) lets you retrieve information about the classes and methods that are supported by a particular Web service.

◆ Disco is Microsoft's standard format for discovery documents, which contain information on Web services.

◆ UDDI is a multivendor standard for discovering online resources, including Web services.

◆ The Web Services Discovery Tool, disco.exe, can retrieve discovery information from a server that exposes a Web service.

◆ You can generate proxy classes for a Web service manually by using the Web Services Description Language tool.

◆ You can generate proxy classes for a Web service automatically by setting a Web reference to point to the Web service.

◆ You can test and debug a Web service without a client application by using one of several SOAP proxy tools.

Instantiate and invoke a COM or COM+ component.

◆ Using COM or COM+ components from .NET managed code requires the creation of an RCW.

◆ You can create an RCW for a COM component by using the Type Library Importer or by directly referencing the COM component from your .NET code.

◆ To use COM components that you did not create, you should obtain a Primary Interop Assembly (PIA) from the creator of the component.

◆ RCWs impose a performance penalty on COM code.

Instantiate and invoke a .NET component.

◆ .NET components are classes that implement the IComponent interface.

◆ You can add .NET components to the Visual Studio .NET toolbox. They support the Visual Studio .NET interface with drag-and-drop functionality and the use of the Properties window.

◆ You can instantiate a .NET component by dragging it from the toolbox to a form or by declaring a new instance of the component's class in your code.

Call native functions by using platform invoke.

◆ You can use the .NET PInvoke facility to call functions from Windows libraries, including the Windows API.

Implement globalization.

Implement localizability for the UI.

◆ Localization is a three-step process that consists of globalization (identifying resources), localizability (verifying separation of resources from code), and localization (translating resources).

◆ Many resources may need to be localized, including user interface text, dates, times, currency amounts, and calendars.

◆ Cultures are identified by culture codes. A neutral culture code specifies only a location and cannot be used for localization. A specific culture code specifies both a location and a language, and it provides enough information for localization.

◆ The CultureInfo object represents a culture in the .NET Framework.

Convert existing encodings.

◆ Internally, .NET applications use 16-bit Unicode (UTF-16) as their preferred character encoding.

◆ The System.Text.Encoding class and its subclasses allow you to convert text from one encoding to another.

Implement right-to-left and left-to-right mirroring.

◆ In some languages, the user interface is read from right to left instead of from left to right. Converting a form for one of these languages is referred to as mirroring.

◆ The .NET Framework provides partial support for mirroring through the RightToLeft property on forms and controls.

Prepare culture-specific formatting.

◆ To iterate through the elements of a string in a world-ready application, you should use the GetTextElementEnumerator method of the StringInfo class.

◆ Searching, sorting, and comparing strings in a world-ready application requires you to use standard objects and methods rather than clever programming tricks.

Create, implement, and handle events.

◆ Events allow a program to respond to the changes in the code's environment.

◆ You can cause custom code to be executed when an event fires by registering the code with the event. These pieces of code that respond to an event are called event handlers.

◆ Event handlers are registered with events through Delegate objects.

◆ It is possible to respond to event by using the Handles keyword as a shortcut to creating a delegate.

◆ A delegate can store a reference to a method that has a specific signature. Events are objects whose type is Delegate.

◆ To create and implement an event, you need to take care of the following steps:

 1. Define the EventArgs class that will contain the event-related data. This is required only if you want to pass specific event-related information to the event handlers.

 2. Create a Delegate object that can store a reference to the event handler.

 3. Define the event itself as an object of delegate type.

 4. Define a method that notifies the registered objects of the event. Usually this method has a name such as OnChanged, where Changed is the event name.

 5. Call the method defined in step 4 whenever the event occurs.

Implement print capability.

◆ Printing in .NET is managed by the PrintDocument class. The PrintDocument class exposes a Graphics object that you can draw or write to with any of the System.Drawing methods.

◆ When you're ready to print, you call the Print method of a PrintDocument object. This raises the PrintPage event, in which you can use the System.Drawing methods to construct your printout.

◆ If there is more to be printed when you are done constructing a page in the PrintPage method, set e.HasMorePages to True to tell the CLR to trigger the event again for another page.

◆ The PrintDocument class also supports BeginPrint, EndPrint, and QueryPageSettings events.

◆ The PageSetupDialog component displays a dialog box that allows the user to set page-related printing properties.

◆ The PrintPreviewDialog component displays a preview of the document before it is printed.

◆ The PrintPreviewControl control lets you embed a print preview in a Windows form.

◆ The PrintDialog component allows the user to set printer-related printing properties.

Implement accessibility features.

◆ The .NET Framework supports the five basic principles of accessible design:

 • **Flexibility**—The user interface should be flexibile and customizable, so that users can adjust it to their own individual needs and preferences.

 • **Choice of input methods**—Different users have different abilities and preferences when it comes to using the mouse or keyboard to perform tasks. All operations in your application should be accessible to the keyboard, and basic operations should be available via the mouse as well. In the future, voice and other types of input may also be considered as input methods.

 • **Choice of output methods**—You should not depend on a single method of output (such as sound, color, or text) for important information.

- **Consistency**—Your application should be consistent with the Windows operating system and other applications in order to minimize difficulties in learning and using new interfaces.

- **Compatibility with accessibility aids**—Windows includes a number of accessibility aids, such as the Magnifier (which can blow up text or graphics to a larger size) and the Onscreen Keyboard (which enables keyboard input via the mouse). Your applications should not circumvent these accessibility aids.

◆ Control properties that you should set to ensure accessibility include AccessibleDescription, AccessibleName, AccessibleRole, BackColor, ForeColor, FontSize, BackgroundImage, TabIndex, and Text.

◆ You can support high-contrast mode by checking the value of the Boolean SystemInformation. HighContrast property. The SystemEvents. UserPreferenceChanged event is raised whenever the HighContrast property changes.

CREATING AND MANAGING COMPONENTS AND .NET ASSEMBLIES

Create and modify a .NET assembly.

◆ Assemblies are the basic unit for reuse, versioning, security, and deployment of components that are created by using the .NET Framework. Each assembly includes an Assembly Manifest that stores the assembly's metadata.

◆ Depending on the number of files that make up an assembly, it is called a single-file or a multifile assembly.

◆ A private assembly is an assembly that is available only to clients in the same directory structure as the assembly, and a shared assembly can be referenced by more than one application and is stored in the machinewide Global Assembly Cache (GAC). A shared assembly must be assigned a cryptographically strong name.

Create and implement satellite assemblies.

◆ Satellite assemblies are assemblies that store culture-specific information for use in localizing an application.

Create resource-only assemblies.

◆ Resource-only assemblies are assemblies that contain just resources and no code. Resource-only assemblies may be satellite assemblies, or they may hold the default resources for all or part of an application.

Create a Windows control.

◆ The Microsoft .NET Framework allows programmers to create reusable code components. You can create a Windows component for use on forms by deriving from Component, Control, UserControl, or any of their derived classes.

◆ If you want to create a control by assembling existing controls and you want to add custom-defined functionality to them, you should inherit from the UserControl class. You should create a Windows Control Library template to create a user control.

- You can drag and drop a custom component from the toolbox to a form's surface and set its properties just as you can with any standard Windows component.

- When you create a control by extending it from the Control class, the control does not have any default user interface. You need to handle the control's Paint event to render its user interface.

- When you don't need any visual representation for components, you can extend them from the Component class. This class does not have any user interface to show on a form, but it does provide useful properties and events that can be used by its container to customize and control its behavior.

Create a Windows control by using visual inheritance.

- The technique of inheriting one visual object from another visual object is known as visual inheritance. When you inherit from a control by using visual inheritance, you inherit the functionality and user interface of the base control. This allows you to reuse code.

Host a Windows control inside Microsoft Internet Explorer.

- When a control is hosted inside Internet Explorer, it is rendered as an object element that does not require any registration, unlike an ActiveX objcct. The ClassID of the control within HTML code is composed of the assembly DLL name and the control name, separated with a pound sign.

- Controls can be hosted inside Internet Explorer if the assemblies exist in the same virtual directories where the Web page resides or in the Global Assembly Cache.

CONSUMING AND MANIPULATING DATA

Access and manipulate data from a Microsoft SQL Server database by creating and using ad hoc queries and stored procedures.

- Transact-SQL is the Microsoft SQL Server dialect of the ANSI SQL-92 standard query language.

- You can execute T-SQL statements from a variety of interfaces, including the Visual Studio .NET IDE, osql, SQL Query Analyzer, and custom applications.

- SELECT statements retrieve data from tables in a database.

- INSERT statements add new data to tables in a database.

- UPDATE statements modify existing data in tables in a database.

- DELETE statements remove data from tables in a database.

- You can create new stored procedures from Server Explorer and design them directly in Visual Studio .NET.

- To execute a query or stored procedure, you assign the text of the query or the name of the stored procedure to the CommandText property of a SqlCommand object. You use the Execute, ExecuteReader, ExecuteScalar, ExecuteNonQuery method to execute the command. The Execute method returns a DataSet object. The ExecuteReader method returns a SqlDataReader object.

The ExecuteScalar method returns a single value. The ExecuteNonQuery method does not return a result.

Access and manipulate data from a data store. Data stores include relational databases, XML documents, and flat files. Methods include XML techniques and ADO.NET.

◆ The ADO.NET object model includes both database-specific data provider classes and database-independent DataSet classes.

◆ Data providers contain implementations of the Connection, Command, Parameter, DataReader, and DataAdapter objects that are optimized for a particular database product.

◆ The SqlConnection object represents a connection to a database.

◆ The SqlCommand object represents a command that can be executed.

◆ The SqlParameter object represents a parameter of a stored procedure.

◆ The SqlDataReader object provides a fast way to retrieve a resultset from a command.

◆ The SqlDataAdapter object implements a two-way pipeline between a database and the data model.

◆ The DataSet object represents an entire relational database in memory. It is composed of DataTable, DataRelation, DataRow, and DataColumn objects.

◆ The DataView object provides a filtered row of the data from a DataTable object.

◆ You can change data in a DataSet object by treating the items in the DataSet object like any other variables.

◆ To persist changes from the data model to the underlying database, you must call the Update method of the SqlDataAdapter object.

◆ The UpdateCommand property of the SqlDataAdapter object specifies a SqlCommand object that is to be executed for all changed rows.

◆ The InsertCommand property of the SqlDataAdapter object specifies a SqlCommand object that is to be executed for all new rows.

◆ The DeleteCommand property of the SqlDataAdapter object specifies a SqlCommand object that is to be executed for all deleted rows.

◆ The DataGrid control can provide a convenient way to handle data changes on the user interface.

◆ To retrieve data from disk files as raw bytes, you use the FileStream object.

◆ To retrieve data from disk files in a line-oriented fashion, you use the StreamReader object.

◆ To retrieve data from disk files that are formatted for binary storage, you use the BinaryReader object.

◆ To retrieve data from XML files, you use the XmlDocument object.

Handle data errors.

◆ Every real-world application should include error trapping. Data manipulation adds some special requirements to error trapping code.

◆ The SqlException and SqlError objects provide you with the means to retrieve SQL Server–specific error information.

◆ When you're designing update commands, you can choose between optimistic concurrency and "last one wins" concurrency.

TESTING AND DEBUGGING

Create a unit test plan.

◆ Testing is the process of executing a program with the intention of finding errors. You should design an effective test plan to ensure that your application is free from all detectable defects and errors.

◆ Unit testing ensures that each unit of an application functions as desired. It is the lowest level of testing.

◆ Integration testing ensures that different units of an application function as expected by the test plan after they are integrated.

Implement tracing.

Add trace listeners and trace switches to an application.

◆ Debug and Trace objects share the same Listeners collection. Therefore, any listener added to the Trace.Listeners collection will also be added to the Debug.Listeners collection.

◆ Trace switches provides a mechanism that allows you to change the type of messages traced by a program, depending on a value stored in the XML configuration file. You need not recompile the application for this change to take effect; you just restart it. You need to implement code to display messages, depending on the value of the switch.

Display trace output.

◆ The Trace and Debug classes can be used to display informative messages in an application when the DEBUG and TRACE symbols are defined, respectively, at the time of compilation.

◆ By default, both the TRACE and DEBUG symbols are defined in the Debug configuration for compilation, and only the TRACE symbol is defined for the Release configuration for compilation.

◆ Listeners are objects that receive trace and debug output. By default, there is one listener, DefaultTraceListener, attached to the Trace and Debug classes. This listener displays the messages in the Output window.

◆ Visual Basic .NET preprocessor directives allow you to define symbols in an application, mark regions of code, and conditionally skip code for compilation.

◆ The Conditional attribute allows you to conditionally add or skip a method for compilation, depending up on the value of the symbol passed as a parameter to the attribute.

Debug, rework, and resolve defects in code.

Configure the debugging environment.

◆ Debugging is the process of finding the causes of errors in a program, locating the lines of code causing the errors, and then fixing those errors.

◆ The three options available while performing step-by-step execution are Step Into, Step Over, and Step Out.

◆ Breakpoints allow you to mark code that signals the debugger to pause execution. You can choose to continue step-by-step execution or resume normal execution by pressing F5 or clicking the Resume button.

◆ The various tool windows, such as Me, Locals, Autos, Watch, and Call Stack, can be of great help in tracking the execution path and the status of variables in the process of debugging an application in Visual Studio .NET.

Create and apply debugging code to components and applications.

◆ When an exception is thrown by an application, you can either choose to continue execution or break into the debugger (that is, start debugging operations such as step-by-step execution). You can customize this behavior for each exception object by using the Exceptions dialog box.

◆ You can attach a debugger to a running process (local or remote) with the help of the Processes dialog box.

Provide multicultural test data to components and applications.

◆ When an application is localized for multiple cultures, you should test the application's execution by using test data from each culture. You should use this test data both with the localized version of the application and with the default version of the application.

Execute tests.

◆ To test an application by using debugging features such as breakpoints, you need to be sure to execute the application by using the default Debug configuration. Debugging features are disabled under the default Release configuration.

Resolve errors and rework code.

◆ Whenever code is modified or a new feature is added in an application, you should run all the existing test cases, along with a new set of test cases, to check the new feature. This regression testing helps in developing robust applications.

DEPLOYING A WINDOWS-BASED APPLICATION

Plan the deployment of a Windows-based application.

◆ Although .NET supports XCOPY deployment, XCOPY is not sufficient for advanced deployment requirements. For advanced requirements, you should instead use the Microsoft Windows Installer installation package to deploy applications.

- Microsoft Windows Installer 2.0 is a built-in installation and configuration service of the Windows operating system. It addition to several advanced installation features, it also provides the ability to roll back the installation process, to uninstall an application, and to repair a component or an application.

- Visual Studio .NET provides four types of deployment templates: Setup Project (for Windows-based applications), Web Setup Project (for Web-based applications), Merge Module Project (for shared components and assemblies), and CAB Project (for ActiveX components to be downloaded over the Internet). It also provides the Setup Wizard, which helps you create installation packages for any of these deployment projects.

Plan a deployment that uses removable media.

- Deployment via removable media is the "lowest common denominator" solution and covers the maximum number of users.

- To create a setup project for removable media, you create a setup project, right-click the project in the Solution Explorer window, and select Properties from the context menu. In the Properties window, change Package Files to In Cabinet File(s). This enables the CAB size option. Set the CAB size to Custom and set the size depending on your media size.

Plan a Web-based deployment.

- Web-based deployment reduces the costs of media, replication, and distribution. It also makes the management of software updates simple.

- Creating a setup package for Web-based deployment is similar to doing so for network-based deployment. After the setup files are created, rather than copying them to a network share, you copy them to a virtual directory on a Web server. You might also want to password-protect the deployment Web site so that only authorized users are able to download the application.

Plan a network-based deployment.

- Network-based installation is useful in a scenario in which multiple users are sharing a common network. In such a case, the applications can be installed via a shared network folder. This kind of deployment method is very common in corporate environments.

- While creating a setup project for a network-based deployment, you would create a single setup package rather than create multiple CAB file. After you have built the setup project, you copy all the setup files to a shared folder on the network and publish the address of the network to the users.

Ensure that the application conforms to Windows Installer requirements and Windows logo program requirements.

- Microsoft provides a logo program to ensure the compatibility of applications with the Microsoft operating systems. The logo program provides guidelines to developers for writing applications that interoperate properly with Windows, providing greater stability, better maintenance, and improved management features.

◆ To earn a logo, an application must meet predefined specifications, and an independent lab must test the application to confirm its compliance with the specification.

◆ The "Certified for Windows" logo program certifies compliance with Windows 2000.

◆ The "Designed for Microsoft Windows XP" logo program certifies compliance with Windows XP.

◆ The Windows Installer SDK contains requirements for the Windows Installer. If you build Windows Installer packages by using Visual Studio .NET, they automatically meet these requirements.

Create a setup program that installs an application and allows for the application to be uninstalled.

Register components and assemblies.

◆ When you include a component in a Visual Studio .NET Setup project, the Installer automatically handles component and assembly registration.

◆ For shared components, you should create a merge module rather than a full installer package.

◆ The System.Configuration.Install.Installer class works as a base class for all the custom installers in the .NET Framework.

◆ The Installer class method Install() is called when the application is installed, and Uninstall() is called when the application is uninstalled. The Commit() method is executed if the Install() method executes successfully, and the Rollback() method is executed if the Install() method is not executed successfully.

◆ If you add predefined installation components (for example, a PerformanceCounter installation component) to the Setup project, they are all added to the Installers collection of the ProjectInstaller class.

◆ You can add your own custom Installer classes to a project to perform custom actions through the Custom Actions Editor during installation, such as compiling the code to a native image or creating a database on a target computer.

Perform an install-time compilation of a Windows-based application.

◆ MSIL can be compiled to native code via the Native Image Generator tool (ngen.exe). The assemblies that are compiled into machine-specific native code are placed in the Native Image Cache.

Deploy a Windows-based application.

Use setup and deployment projects.

◆ The File System Editor provides mapping of a file system on a target machine. The folders are referred to by special names that during the installation process are converted to represent the folder as it is named on the file system on the target machine.

◆ The Registry Editor allows you to specify Registry keys, subkeys, and values that are added to the Registry in the target machine during installation.

◆ The File Types Editor allows you to register a file extension with a Windows application.

◆ The User Interface Editor allows you to customize the user interface that is provided to the user during the installation process. Different types of user interfaces are available for end-user installation and administrative installation.

◆ The User Interface Editor and the Launch Conditions Editor for Search Elements provide special properties (such as Property and ButtonProperty) whose value can be evaluated to perform the installation according to the end user's choice.

◆ The Custom Actions Editor allows you to add custom actions that are to be performed during the installation process. It allows you to run DLL, EXE, assembly, and scripts files. There are four phases during which custom actions can be performed: Install, commit, rollback, and uninstall.

◆ The Launch Conditions Editor allows you to set conditions that are to be evaluated when the installation begins on the target machine. If the conditions are not met, the installation stops.

Add assemblies to the Global Assembly Cache.

◆ Shared assemblies are used by multiple applications on a machine. They are placed in the GAC and enjoy special privileges, such as file security (because they are placed in the System folder), shared location, and side-by-side versioning.

◆ Public/private key pairs are generated by using the Strong Name tool (sn.exe). These pairs can be used to digitally sign an assembly.

◆ You can add a shared assembly to the GAC by using Windows Explorer, the .NET Framework Configuration tool, the Global Assembly Cache Tool (gacutil.exe), and the Installer tool.

◆ The best way to add an assembly during deployment is by using Microsoft Windows Installer. The Windows Installer uses reference counting with assemblies, which means that an assembly will be removed at uninstallation time only if it is not being used by any other applications.

◆ When the Assembly Cache folder in the System folder is viewed in Windows Explorer, it displays assemblies from the GAC and Native Image Cache.

◆ The Common Language Runtime searches the GAC to locate assemblies before it looks in the files and folders where the assembly is installed. Therefore, shared assemblies placed in the GAC are efficient because the Common Language Runtime does not have to look in the <codebase> and <probing> elements of the applicable configuration files.

◆ Delay signing allows a shared assembly to be placed in the GAC by just having the assembly signed with the public key. This allows the assembly to be signed with the private key at a later stage, when the development process is complete and the component or assembly is ready to be deployed. This process allows developers to work with shared assemblies as if they were strongly named and yet also secure the private key of the signature from being accessed at different stages of development.

◆ Merge modules allow you to create reusable components that help in deploying shared components. Merge modules cannot be directly installed. When an application uses a component for which you have developed a merge module, you can include that merge module as part of the application's setup.

Verify security policies for a deployed application.

◆ Code Access Security allows code to be trusted to varying degrees, depending on where the code originates, the publisher, the strong name, and the security zone.

◆ If the AllowPartiallyTrustedCallersAttribute is associated with a strong named assembly, even partially trusted assemblies are allowed to call it.

◆ The .NET Framework Configuration Tool can be used to configure the runtime security policy for an assembly or a zone.

Launch a remote application (URL remoting).

◆ URL remoting provides a zero deployment model for deploying a Windows application. The code and configuration files reside on a Web server, and you can execute the application by just pointing to the URL of the EXE file from Internet Explorer on the end user's computer.

◆ The code downloaded from a URL is cached in a central location called the download cache. When the request to the same content is made a second time, the download cache checks the timestamp of the requested assemblies on the server and downloads the file from the server only if its timestamp is changed. Otherwise, it displays the cached copy to the user.

MAINTAINING AND SUPPORTING A WINDOWS-BASED APPLICATION

Optimize the performance of a Windows-based application.

◆ You should avoid boxing and unboxing operations.

◆ You should use the StringBuilder class for strings that will be changed during the course of a program. The StringBuilder class can be changed in place, unlike the String class, which must be destroyed and re-created.

◆ You should use AddRange to add multiple objects to collections in a single operation.

◆ You should use native compilation to reduce startup time. Native images load faster than MSIL code the first time the code is used.

◆ You should throw exceptions only when necessary. Exceptions are time-consuming and should not be used for normal program flow.

◆ You should minimize calls to unmanaged code and use a chunky interface rather than a chatty one. The fewer calls to unmanaged code, the faster an application will run.

◆ You should minimize calls across processes. Cross-process calls are slower than in-process calls.

◆ You should compile an application by using the Release configuration. This removes unnecessary debugging code that can slow down an application.

◆ You should avoid scaling images and performing other advanced graphics operations.

- You should use data source–specific managed providers for data access. These providers (such as the SqlClient classes) are more efficient than the OleDb classes for their specific databases.

- You should use stored procedures instead of SQL statements. Stored procedures can be precompiled on the database server for speed of execution.

- You should use the DataReader classes for sequential table reading.

- You should use connection pooling for faster database connections. Connection pooling avoids the time-consuming process of creating a new connection for each database operation.

- You should avoid using auto-generated commands. Such commands are convenient but impose additional runtime overhead.

- You should avoid distributed transactions.

Diagnose and resolve errors and issues.

- A process is an application that is being executed. Each running process is uniquely identified on a computer via a process identifier (PID).

- The Process class provides a large set of properties to get information about running processes on a local machine or a remote machine.

- The event log provides a central repository for various issues that an application may encounter while it is executing. Use of an event log to record such messages not only makes the job of system administrator easier, but it also allows other applications to take appropriate action when an entry is written to a log.

- Multiple event sources can write to an event log. However, an event source can be used to write to only one event log.

- By default, events of the Process and EventLog class are not enabled. You can set the EnableRaisingEvents property to True in order to instruct these classes to raise events.

- Performance counters are organized in categories that define specific sets of performance counters.

- The process of reading a performance counter value is called sampling the performance counter. The process of updating a performance counter value is called publishing a performance counter.

CONFIGURING AND SECURING A WINDOWS-BASED APPLICATION

Configure a Windows-based application.

- The .NET Framework stores runtime configuration information in XML files that can be edited without the application being recompiled.

- Dynamic properties enable you to store component properties in runtime configuration files.

- Machine and application configuration files hold administrative settings such as information about configured assemblies and remoting channels.

- The .NET Framework Configuration Editor provides a GUI interface for editing runtime configuration files.

Configure security for a Windows-based application.

Select and configure authentication type. Authentication types include Windows Authentication, None, forms-based, Microsoft Passport, and custom authentication.

◆ Windows-based applications use Windows authentication to determine role membership. You can also implement custom authentication schemes if the Windows user identity is not sufficient for your purposes.

Specify the security level for an application.

◆ Permissions control access to resources.

◆ Code can request the minimum permissions that it needs to run and optional permissions that it would like to have. It can also refuse permissions and demand permissions on the part of calling code.

◆ Code access permissions represent access to resources, and identity permissions represent things that the .NET Framework knows about code.

◆ The .NET Framework supplies both attribute-based declarative security and class-based imperative security.

◆ A code group is a set of assemblies that shares a security context.

◆ A permission set is a set of permissions that can be granted as a unit.

◆ The Common Language Runtime computes actual permissions at runtime based on code group membership and the calling chain of the code.

Use custom attributes to configure security.

◆ To implement a custom permission, you must create a class that inherits from the CodeAccessPermission class.

◆ Custom permissions allow you to create your own permissions, to protect particular resources.

Configure authorization.

Configure role-based authorization.

◆ The .NET Framework supports both authentication and authorization. Authentication involves verifying a user's identity. Authorization involves granting rights based on that identity.

◆ Windows applications constructed with the .NET Framework automatically use Windows authentication.

◆ You can use the IsInRole method of the WindowsPrincipal object to check for membership in Windows groups.

Implement identity management.

◆ The WindowsPrincipal and WindowsIdentity classes let you check the authentication status of the current user.

◆ The PrincipalPermission class allows you to perform declarative or imperative role-based security operations.

This practice exam contains 75 questions that are representative of what you should expect on the actual exam "Developing and Implementing Windows-Based Applications with Microsoft Visual Basic .NET and Microsoft Visual Studio .NET" (exam 70-306). The answers appear at the end of this practice exam. I strongly suggest that when you take this practice exam, you treat it just as you would the actual exam at the test center. Time yourself, read carefully, don't use any reference materials, and answer all the questions as best you can.

Some of the questions may be vague and require you to make deductions to come up with the best possible answer from the possibilities given. Others may be verbose, requiring you to read and process a lot of information before you reach the actual question. These are skills that you should acquire before attempting to take the actual exam. Take this practice exam, and if you miss more than 18 questions, try rereading the chapters that contain information on the subjects in which you were weak. You can use the index to find keywords to point you to the appropriate locations.

Practice Exam

EXAM QUESTIONS

1. You have used Visual Basic .NET to develop a process monitor application. Your application can identify any process on the system that has a user interface, and it allows you to collect information about the process. Now you want to add code that can shut down the identified process as well. Which method should you use to shut down these processes?

    A. Process.Kill

    B. Process.WaitForExit

    C. Process.CloseMainWindow

    D. Process.WaitForInputIdle

2. You would like to give the user the ability to customize your application so that it fits in better with his or her company's corporate look and feel. In particular, you want to let the user specify text to appear in the title bar of the main menu form. How should you add this ability to your application?

    A. Supply full source code with your application and tell users that they can edit the text and rebuild the application.

    B. Let the user edit the text in the Registry and use the Microsoft.Win32.Registry class to retrieve the value that the user saves.

    C. Make the Text property of the form a dynamic property and provide an XML file that the user can edit to set the value of the property.

    D. Run code in the form's Load event to retrieve the form's text from a text file by using a FileStream object.

3. You are distributing a .NET component to target computers. This component must be installed in the Global Assembly Cache so that it can be shared by every application on the target computer. In addition, you want to allow clients to check the identity of your company via a certificate from a third-party authority. How should you sign this component's code?

    A. Use sn.exe to sign the assembly.

    B. Use signcode.exe to sign the assembly.

    C. Use signcode.exe followed by sn.exe to sign the assembly.

    D. Use sn.exe followed by signcode.exe to sign the assembly.

4. Your application is failing when a particular variable equals 17. Unfortunately, you cannot predict when this will happen. Which debugging tool would you use to investigate the problem?

    A. Locals Window

    B. Output Window

    C. Immediate Window

    D. Conditional Breakpoint

5. Your graphics application creates and displays a PrintPreviewControl control at runtime. Users complain that the preview image is not sufficiently detailed for them to tell whether the job should be printed. What should you do?

    A. Set the UseAntiAlias property to True.

    B. Set the UseAntiAlias property to False.

    C. Set the AutoZoom property to True.

    D. Set the AutoZoom property to False.

6. Your application is split into two parts. The server is implemented as a Web service, and the client is implemented as a Windows Forms application. The server is still under active development, even though you are already shipping the client application. You anticipate that the data returned by the server will continue to change in the near future and that clients will need to adjust their means of working with the Web service to account for these changes. How should you provide user assistance for the client application?

A. Ship an HTML Help file with the application and use a HelpProvider component to display the information. Ship periodic updates of the help file to the users.

B. Include a readme file, with instructions for running the application, and email updates to the users.

C. Place instructions in ToolTips and ship a new client application when the instructions change.

D. Place the help file on an Internet server that is under your direct control and use a HelpProvider component to display the information.

7. Your application uses the GetSystemDirectory API function, which exists in kernel32.dll in both ANSI and Unicode versions. Your declaration is as follows:

```
Declare Function GetSystemDirectory _
Lib "kernel32" ( _
 ByVal lpBuffer As String, _
    ByRef nSize As Integer) As Integer
```

Your code is failing, with a System.EntryPointNotFoundException exception, whenever you call this function. What should you do to fix the failure?

A. Supply the full path for kernel32.dll.

B. Declare the function as GetSystemDirectoryA instead of GetSystemDirectory.

C. Declare the function as GetSystemDirectoryW instead of GetSystemDirectory.

D. Add the Auto modifier to the declaration.

8. You are moving an existing COM-based application to .NET. Part of your existing application depends on a third-party COM-based library to which you do not have the source code. The library is implemented as a set of objects with no user interface. How should you proceed?

A. Use the ActiveX Control Importer to import the library.

B. Build a COM Callable Wrapper for the library.

C. Build a Runtime Callable Wrapper for the library.

D. Rewrite the library into managed code.

9. Your form allows the user to enter a telephone number into a TextBox control named txtPhone. You use the Validating event of this control to check that the phone number is in the correct format. If the phone number is in an incorrect format, you do not allow the focus to leave the txtPhone TextBox control.

The form also includes a Button control, btnCancel, to cancel the data entry action. The user should be able to click this button any time, even when there is invalid data in the text box. What should you do to ensure that this is the case?

A. Set the CausesValidation property of the TextBox control to True.

B. Set the CausesValidation property of the Button control to True.

C. Set the CausesValidation property of the TextBox control to False.

D. Set the CausesValidation property of the Button control to False.

10. The main menu form of your application uses the System.Drawing objects to draw your company's logo on the background of the form. You want to redraw the logo whenever the form is resized, so that it always fills the entire form. What should you do?

A. Use a Timer control to call the Invalidate method periodically.

B. Call the Invalidate method within an event handler for the form's Resize event.

C. Call the Invalidate method within an event handler for the form's Paint event.

D. Set the form's ResizeRedraw property to True.

11. You are designing a Windows application with a variety of controls on its user interface. Some controls will be infrequently used. For those controls, you do not want the user to be able to tab into the control, but the user should still be able to activate the control by clicking it. Which of the following options should you use?

A. Set the control's TabIndex property to 0.

B. Set the control's TabIndex property to –1.

C. Set the control's TabStop property to False.

D. Set the control's Enabled property to False.

12. How can you generate client-side proxy classes for a Web service? (Select two.)

A. Use a proxy tool such as the .NET WebService Studio tool.

B. Use the Web Services Description Language tool.

C. Use the Web Services Discovery tool.

D. Set a Web reference to point to the Web service.

13. You are designing a Windows service that will be used by computers in many countries. The service stores information related to computer uptime and page faults. When storing this information for future analysis, which culture should you use?

A. The invariant culture

B. The en-US culture

C. The culture specified by Thread.CurrentThread.CurrentCulture

D. A culture selected by the user

14. Your form uses Label controls to convey information. When the text in a label represents a higher-than-average value, you want to display it in bold type; when the text in the Label represents a value that requires the user's attention, you want to display it in italic type. If both conditions are true, you want to display the text in bold italic type. How should you set the Italic FontStyle property for the control when the value requires attention so that it adds italic, whether or not the font is already bold?

A.
```
lblSampleText.Font.Style And _
  FontStyle.Italic
```

B.
```
lblSampleText.Font.Style Xor _
  FontStyle.Italic
```

C.
```
lblSampleText.Font.Style Or _
  FontStyle.Italic
```

D.

```
lblSampleText.Font.Style Or ( _
 FontStyle.Underline And FontStyle.Bold)
```

15. Your application contains the following resource files that contain string resources:

```
AppStrings.resx
AppStrings.fr.resx
AppStrings.fr-FR.resx
AppStrings.en.resx
AppStrings.en-US.resx
```

The user executes the application on a computer that is running French (Canadian) software, so the CurrentUICulture property is set to fr-CA. What is the result?

A. The resources from AppStrings.fr.resx are used.

B. The resources from AppStrings.fr-FR.resx are used.

C. The resources from AppStrings.en-US.resx are used.

D. An exception is thrown.

16. You have created an array of Project objects named aProjects. Each Project object has a Name property and a DateDue property. You want to display all the Name values in a ListBox control named lbProjects. Which code snippet should you use for this purpose?

A.

```
With lbProjects
    .DataSource = aProjects
    .ValueMember = Name
End With
```

B.

```
With lbProjects
    .DataSource = aProjects
    .DisplayMember = Name
End With
```

C.

```
With lbProjects
    .DataSource = aProjects
    .ValueMember = "Name"
End With
```

D.

```
With lbProjects
    .DataSource = aProjects
    .DisplayMember = "Name"
End With
```

17. You are creating a graphics application that will manipulate a variety of image formats. You have created an OpenFileDialog object in your program and have set its Filter property as follows:

```
ofdPicture.Filter="All Image Files|" & _
 "*.bmp;*.gif;*.jpg;*.jpeg;*.png;*.tif;" & _
 "*.tiff|BMP Files (*.bmp)|*.bmp|" & _
 "GIF Files (*.gif)|*.gif|JPEG Files " & _
 "(*.jpg;*.jpeg)|*.jpg;*.jpeg|" & _
 "PNG Files (*.png)|*.png|TIF Files " & _
 "(*.tif;*.tiff)|*.tif;*.tiff|" & _
 "All Files (*.*)|*.*"
```

You have created a Button control with its Text property set to Open Image.... When you click this button, you display the OpenFileDialog control to allow a selection. You want BMP files to be the default choice in the dialog box. Which of the following values for the FilterIndex property must you choose to achieve this in the event handler of the Button control's Click event?

A. 0

B. 1

C. 2

D. 3

18. Your application uses a graphics library from a third-party developer. This library is implemented as a COM component. You are migrating your application to .NET. What should you do to continue to use the classes and methods within the graphics library?

    A. Use the Type Library Importer to create a signed Runtime Callable Wrapper for the library. Install the RCW in the Global Assembly Cache.

    B. Use the Type Library Importer to create an unsigned Runtime Callable Wrapper for the library. Install the RCW in the Global Assembly Cache.

    C. Create wrapper code that uses PInvoke to call functions from the library. Import this wrapper code into your application.

    D. Obtain a Primary Interop Assembly (PIA) from the developer of the library. Install the PIA in the Global Assembly Cache.

19. You are using the PrintDocument class to print a graphical banner that should span multiple printed pages. However, only the first page of the banner prints. What is the most likely cause of this problem?

    A. You have neglected to set e.HasMorePages to True when more than one page should be printed.

    B. You have neglected to set a sufficiently large value for e.MarginBounds.Height.

    C. You have neglected to set a sufficiently large value for e.PageBounds.Height.

    D. You have called the Print method only once rather than once per page.

20. You have created an ASP.NET Web service project that includes a class named RefLibrary. The RefLibrary class contains this method:

```
Public Function Version() As String
    Version = "1.0.0.8"
End Function
```

You are able to instantiate the RefLibrary class from a Web service client project, but the Version method is not available. What could be the problem?

    A. Only Sub procedures can be part of the public interface of a Web service.

    B. You must mark the method with the WebService method.

    C. The methods of a Web service can return only Object data.

    D. You must mark the method with the WebMethod attribute.

21. You are planning to deploy an assembly into the Global Assembly Cache so that it can be used by any application on the target computer. What must you do?

    A. Sign the assembly with a strong name.

    B. Sign the assembly with an Authenticode certificate.

    C. Compile the assembly with the default Release configuration.

    D. Use RegEdit to add a key to the AssemblyFolders key in the Registry.

22. Your application contains the following code:

```
Private Sub Form1_Load( _
 ByVal sender As System.Object, _
 ByVal e As System.EventArgs) _
 Handles MyBase.Load
    Dim el As EventLog = New EventLog( _
     "Application", ".")
    ' Add an event handler for
    ' the EntryWritten event
    AddHandler el.EntryWritten, _
      AddressOf EventLog_EntryWritten
End Sub

Private Sub EventLog_EntryWritten( _
 ByVal source As Object, _
 ByVal e As EntryWrittenEventArgs)
    Debug.WriteLine(e.Entry.Message.Trim)
End Sub
```

After you run this code, no event messages are written to the Output window. You have verified that events are being posted to the Application event log. What could be the problem?

A. Event logs do not by default raise events.

B. You can monitor events only from the System event log.

C. The text of the event log entry is in the EventLogEntry.Source property.

D. You are not a member of the local Administrators group.

23. You wrote a COM component to accept data from an analog-to-digital converter card and made it available to your analysis program. Now you're moving that analysis program to .NET. The COM component is used nowhere else, and you have not shipped copies of it to anyone else. You want to call the objects in the COM server from your new .NET client. How should you proceed?

A. Use the Type Library Importer to create an unsigned RCW for the COM component.

B. Use the Type Library Importer to create a signed RCW for the COM component.

C. Set a direct reference from your .NET client to the COM server.

D. Use PInvoke to instantiate classes from the COM component.

24. Users of your application want to be able to set all properties of their printers, such as device settings and printer security, from within your application. Which component should you add to your form to easily enable this?

A. PrintDocument

B. PrintDialog

C. PrintPreviewDialog

D. PageSetupDialog

25. You are shipping a text-editing application to a variety of locales, including the United States, France, Israel, China, and Japan. One of the features of the application is that the user can use it to search for text within long text passages. What should you use to perform this search?

A. CultureInfo.CompareInfo

B. InStr

C. IndexOf

D. Array.Sort

26. You are invoking a Web service that returns a StreamReader object. Which project requires a reference to the System.IO namespace, where this object is defined?

A. The client project

B. Both the client project and the Web service project

C. The Web service project

D. Neither project

27. You have created a DataSet object that contains a single DataTable object named Customers. The Customers DataTable object has all the rows and columns from the Customers table in your database. Now you would like to bind only selected columns from the Customers table to a DataGrid control. How should you proceed?

    A. Create a second DataTable object in the DataSet object. Copy the desired data to the second DataTable object. Bind the second DataTable object to the DataGrid control.

    B. Create a Command object to retrieve the desired columns from the DataTable object. Bind the Command object to the DataGrid control.

    C. Bind the DataGrid control to the entire DataTable object. Use the Width property of the columns in the DataGrid control to hide the columns that are not desired, by setting them to zero width.

    D. Create a DataView object that retrieves only the desired tables from the DataTable object. Bind the DataGrid control to the DataView object.

28. You plan to use objects from the System.Drawing namespace to draw shapes on a form at runtime. You have already determined that you will draw these shapes during the form's Paint event. How should you create the Graphics object required by the System.Drawing classes?

    A. Call the CreateGraphics method of the form.

    B. Retrieve the Graphics property of the PaintEventArgs object that is passed to the event.

    C. Pass the handle of the form to the Graphics.FromHwnd method.

    D. Call the CreateGraphics method of the control that has the focus.

29. Your application calls a Web service that retrieves and compares traceroute timing information from multiple servers around the world. Users complain that the user interface of the application is unresponsive while this information is being retrieved. What can you do to fix this problem?

    A. Move the application to a faster computer.

    B. Install a faster link to the Internet.

    C. Install more memory in the computer.

    D. Use asynchronous calls to invoke the Web service.

30. Your application includes a SqlDataAdapter object named SqlDataAdapter1 that was created by dragging and dropping the Customers table from a database to your form. Your application also includes a DataSet object named dsCustomers1, based on this SqlDataAdapter object. What line of code should you use to load the data from the database into the DataSet object?

    A.
    ```
    dsCustomers1= SqlDataAdapter1.Fill( _
    "Customers")
    ```

    B.
    ```
    SqlDataAdapter1.Fill("dsCustomers1", _
    "Customers")
    ```

    C.
    ```
    SqlDataAdapter1.Fill(dsCustomers1, _
    "Customers")
    ```

    D.
    ```
    SqlDataAdapter1.Fill(dsCustomers1)
    ```

31. You are developing an accounting application that includes a class named Transaction. Subclasses such as DepositTransaction and PaymentTransaction inherit from the Transaction class. The Transaction class includes a method named VerifyChecksum that should be available to the Transaction class and to all classes derived from the Transaction class, but not to any other classes in the application. Which access modifier should you use in the declaration of the VerifyChecksum method?

    A. Protected

    B. Public

    C. Private

    D. Friend

32. A TextBox control on your form should accept no more than three characters from the user. However, your code may need to place the value Invalid in the TextBox control. What value should you use for the MaxLength property of this control?

    A. 3

    B. 4

    C. 7

    D. 8

33. Your application contains a form, Form1, with its BackColor property set to Red. You add a new form, Form2, to the application by using visual inheritance to derive the new form from Form1. You set Form2 to be the startup object for the application, and you set its BackColor property to be Blue. Next, you change the BackColor property of Form1 to Yellow. When you run the application, what is the background color of Form2?

A. Blue

B. Red

C. Yellow

D. Control

34. You have purchased a library of shared communications routines that is delivered as a .NET assembly. You want to make the classes in this assembly available to all your .NET applications. Where should you install the assembly?

    A. In the Global Assembly Cache

    B. In C:\WINNT\System32

    C. In each application's private directory

    D. In the directory specified by the ASSEMBLY environment variable

35. Your department is responsible for maintaining a variety of accounting applications. You've been assigned the task of creating a standard control to represent credit and debit accounts. The control will be made up of a collection of TextBox and ComboBox controls. On which class should you base this control?

    A. Control

    B. UserControl

    C. Form

    D. Component

36. Your application includes a ListBox control named lbCourses that displays a list of college courses. The DisplayMember property of the ListBox control is bound to the CourseName column of the Courses database table. The ValueMember property of the ListBox control is bound to the CourseNumber column of the Courses database table.

Your form also contains a TextBox control named txtCourseNumber. This control uses simple data binding to display the CourseNumber column from the StudentSchedules table in your database.

When the user selects a course name in the ListBox control, you want to display the corresponding CourseNumber value in the txtCourseNumber control. What should you do?

A. Use simple data binding to bind the SelectedValue property of the ListBox control to the CourseNumber column of the StudentSchedules table.

B. Use simple data binding to bind the ValueMember property of the ListBox control to the Text property of the TextBox control.

C. Use the SelectedIndexChanged event of the ListBox control to copy the data from the ListBox control to the TextBox control.

D. Use simple data binding to bind the SelectedValue property of the ListBox control to the CourseNumber column of the Courses table.

37. You are planning to display invoices on a DataGrid control. The user will specify a customer, and then you'll retrieve from the database all the invoices for that customer. Which database object should you use to retrieve these invoices?

A. A table

B. A view

C. An index

D. A stored procedure

38. Your application's main form contains two Button controls named btnA and btnB. When the user clicks on either of these controls, or when the user moves the mouse over either of these controls, you want to run code to display a message on the form. The message is identical in all cases. How should you structure your code to fulfill this requirement?

A. Write four separate event procedures, one each for the Click event of btnA, the MouseOver event of btnA, the Click event of btnB, and the MouseOver event of btnB.

B. Write two event procedures, the first to handle both Click events and the second to handle both MouseOver events.

C. Write two event procedures, the first to handle the Click and MouseOver events for btnA and the second to handle the Click and MouseOver events for btnB.

D. Write a single event procedure to handle the Click and MouseOver events of both controls.

39. Your application contains Unicode strings encoded in the UTF-16 format. You'd like to save a copy of those strings to disk in the UTF-7 format. What should you do?

A. Use the Unicode.GetChars method to perform the conversion.

B. Use the Unicode.GetBytes method to perform the conversion.

C. Use the UTF7Encoding.GetChars method to perform the conversion.

D. Use the UTF7Encoding.GetBytes method to perform the conversion.

40. Your code uses the Trace class to produce debugging output. In which configuration(s) will this output be enabled?

    A. In the default Release configuration only

    B. In the default Debug configuration only

    C. In both the default Release configuration and the default Debug configuration

    D. In neither the default Release configuration nor the default Debug configuration

41. Your application executes the following code:

```
Trace.Listeners.Add( _
   New TextWriterTraceListener("TraceLog.txt"))
```

    When your application is running in the default Release configuration, where will messages from the Trace class appear?

    A. They will appear in the Output window and in the TraceLog.txt file.

    B. They will appear in the Output window only.

    C. They will appear in the TraceLog.txt file only.

    D. No trace messages will appear in this configuration.

42. You want your application to monitor for changes to the HighContrast setting at runtime, so that it can remove a background image from a form if necessary. Which event must you trap?

    A. SystemEvents.UserPreferenceChanged

    B. Me.Paint

    C. SystemEvents.PaletteChanged

    D. Me.Load

43. Your application allows users to choose between two different sizes of text when printing reports. Users complain that when they choose the small font, there is excessive space between each line of the report. What should you do to fix this problem?

    A. Call the Graphics.MeasureString method to get the width of the text before it is printed.

    B. Call the Font.GetHeight method to determine the vertical size of the font.

    C. Set the AutoZoom property of the associated PrintPreviewDialog component to True.

    D. Force the users to use the larger font.

44. You are supplying both an application and a help file for the application to your users. The help file is in HTML Help 1.3 format. You have a button on your form that you would like to use to display the table of contents of the help file. What should you use for this task?

    A. HelpProvider component

    B. HelpProvider class

    C. Help.ShowHelp method

    D. ToolTip component

45. Your application displays the distance to various planets in a variety of units. You are beginning to sell this application in multiple countries. How should you ensure that the correct numeric formatting is used in all cases?

    A. Allow the user to select a culture from a list. Create a CultureInfo object based on the user's selection and assign it to the Thread.CurrentThread.CurrentCulture property. Use the ToString method to format numeric amounts.

B. Accept the Thread.CurrentThread.CurrentCulture property as it is set when you run your application. Use the ToString method to format numeric amounts.

C. Prompt the user for a numeric format and store it in the Registry.

D. Allow the user to select a numeric format from a list of supported formats.

46. Your application uses a SqlDataReader object to retrieve patient information from a medical records database. When you find a patient who is currently hospitalized, you want to read the names of the patient's caregivers from the same database. You have created a second SqlDataReader object, based on a second SqlCommand object, to retrieve the caregiver information. Calling the ExecuteReader method of the SqlCommand object is causing an error. What is the most likely cause of this error?

A. You are using the same SqlConnection object for both of the SqlDataReader objects, and the first SqlDataReader object is still open when you try to execute the SqlCommand object.

B. You must use a SqlDataAdapter object to retrieve the caregiver information.

C. You must use the OleDbDataReader object to retrieve information from the SQL Server database.

D. You are using the ExecuteReader method of the SqlCommand object, but you should be using the ExecuteScalar method instead.

47. You want to use a Web service that supplies travel weather information in your application. You know the URL of the .asmx file published by the Web service, but you do not know any details of the Web service's interface. What action should you take first?

A. Run the Web Services Discovery tool.

B. Open the .asmx file in a Web browser.

C. Run the XML Schema Definition tool

D. Copy the .asmx file to your client project.

48. Your application retrieves data from the Customers and Orders tables in a database by using a view named vwCustOrders. This view is used as the CommandText property for the SelectCommand property of a DataAdapter object. The application uses the Fill method of this DataAdapter control to fill a DataSet control. The DataSet control is bound to a DataGrid control.

Users report that changes they make to data displayed on the DataGrid control are not saved to the database. What could be the problem?

A. The DataGrid control does not support editing data from a database.

B. You cannot update a DataSet control that is based on a view.

C. The DataGrid control does not support two-way data binding.

D. Your application does not call the Update method of the DataAdapter object.

49. Your application needs to store a large amount of data in a disk file between program runs. You'd like to store this information without wasting space. The disk file does not need to be easily readable by human beings. Which class should you use to accomplish this task?

A. StreamWriter

B. FileStream

C. BinaryWriter

D. StringWriter

50. You are designing a file-analysis application that will use heuristic methods to find information in arbitrary files. When the user specifies a disk file, you want to open that file and read it 1 byte at a time. Which .NET class can you use to accomplish this task?

    A. BinaryReader

    B. StreamReader

    C. FileStream

    D. StringReader

51. You have created a custom component for your application that monitors a bidirectional parallel port for error messages. This component raises an event named PortError whenever an error message is detected. At that point, you must make the error code available to the control container. How should you do this?

    A. Place the error code in a property of the component for the container to retrieve.

    B. Pass the error code as a parameter of the PortError event.

    C. Define a global variable in a separate module and place the value in that variable.

    D. Define a custom PortErrorEventArgs class that inherits from the EventArgs class and pass an instance of the class as a parameter of the PortError event.

52. You are responsible for maintaining a COM component that is used by numerous applications throughout your company. You are not yet ready to migrate this COM component to .NET managed code, but you need to make it available to an increasing number of other projects that are being developed under the .NET Framework. What should you do?

    A. Set a direct reference to the existing COM component from each .NET project.

    B. Use the Type Library Importer to create and sign an assembly that will use the COM component. Place the COM component in the Global Assembly Cache.

    C. Obtain a Primary Interop Assembly for the COM component.

    D. Set a direct reference from a single .NET project to the COM component. Include this project in each solution that must make use of the component.

53. Which of these applications cannot be deployed by the simple XCOPY method?

    A. An application that must deploy assemblies to the Global Assembly Cache

    B. An application that makes use of private assemblies

    C. An application that requires a configuration file

    D. An application that is compiled in debug mode

54. You are using the Installer tool (installutil.exe) to install a set of components. You issue the following command to do so:

```
installutil Assembly1.exe Assembly2.exe
Assembly3.exe
```

Assembly2 fails to install properly on the target computer. Which assemblies will be installed by the command?

    A. None of the assemblies will be installed.

    B. Only Assembly1.exe will be installed.

    C. Only Assembly3.exe will be installed.

    D. Both Assembly1.exe and Assembly3.exe will be installed.

55. You need to retrieve data from a SQL Server database. Which connection class should you use for maximum performance?

    A. System.Data.SqlClient.SqlConnection

    B. System.Data.OleDb.OleDbConnection

    C. System.Data.ConnectionState

    D. System.Data.Odbc.OdbcConnection

56. Your application depends on an assembly from another developer. This assembly isn't signed with an Authenticode key or a strong name, but you have determined that it can be trusted. You want to grant this code permissions by using the .NET Framework Configuration tool. Which type of membership condition should you choose to create a code group that contains only this assembly?

    A. Software publisher

    B. Cryptographic hash

    C. Strong name

    D. URL

57. Your corporate counsel insists that the documents generated by your program be printed on legal-sized paper. Unfortunately, users sometimes use the Printer Setup dialog box to switch to letter-sized paper for their own convenience. Which event of the PrintDocument class can you use to check and (if necessary) change the paper tray?

    A. BeginPrint

    B. EndPrint

    C. PrintPage

    D. QueryPageSettings

58. Form1 contains a TextBox control named TextBox1. The KeyPreview property of Form1 is set to True. The code for this form includes the following event handlers:

```
Private Sub Form3_KeyPress( _
 ByVal sender As Object, _
 ByVal e As System.Windows. _
 Forms.KeyPressEventArgs) _
 Handles MyBase.KeyPress
    If e.KeyChar = "a" Then
        Debug.WriteLine("Handled by form")
        e.Handled = True
    End If
End Sub

Private Sub TextBox1_KeyPress( _
 ByVal sender As Object, _
 ByVal e As System.Windows._
 Forms.KeyPressEventArgs) _
 Handles TextBox1.KeyPress
    If e.KeyChar = "a" Then
        Debug.WriteLine( _
         "Handled by textbox")
    End If
End Sub

Private Sub TextBox1_KeyDown( _
 ByVal sender As Object, _
 ByVal e As System.Windows. _
 Forms.KeyEventArgs) _
 Handles TextBox1.KeyDown
    If e.KeyCode = Keys.A Then
        Debug.WriteLine( _
         "Handled by textbox")
    End If
End Sub
```

The user presses the A key with the focus in TextBox1. What is the output from these procedures?

    A.
```
Handled by form
```

    B.
```
Handled by textbox
Handled by form
Handled by textbox
```

C.

```
Handled by textbox
Handled by form
```

D.

```
Handled by textbox
```

59. You want to display a Help button on the title bar of your Windows Form. Which property settings should you make?

A. HelpButton = True, MinButton = True, MaxButton = True

B. HelpButton = True, MinButton = True, MaxButton = False

C. HelpButton = True, MinButton = False, MaxButton = False

D. HelpButton = True, MinButton = False, MaxButton = True

60. Your application allows you to select any event log on the local computer and monitor the event log for new entries. When a new entry is made to the event log, the application displays the text of the entry. You can then enter an explanatory note, if you like, which is posted back to the event log as another entry.

Now you are adding the capability to work with remote computers as well as the local computer. Which functionality must you disable for remote computers?

A. Select an event log to monitor.

B. Monitor the event log for new entries.

C. Display the text of new entries.

D. Post notes back to the event log.

61. Your application will be used by people who depend on accessibility aids such as screen readers. Which properties should you explicitly set for every control? (Select two.)

A. ForeColor

B. AccessibleName

C. AccessibleRole

D. AccessibleDescription

62. You are creating a custom exception named BusinessException for your application. Which constructors should you implement for this class? (Select three.)

A.

```
Public Sub New()
```

B.

```
Public Sub New(ByVal inner As Exception)
```

C.

```
Public Sub New(ByVal message As String)
```

D.

```
Public Sub New(ByVal message As String, _
    ByVal inner As Exception)
```

63. Your application requires the ability to access OLE DB data sources in order to function properly. Which .NET security feature should you use to ensure that your code has this ability?

A. Role-based security

B. Encryption

C. Code access security

D. Type safety

64. Your application connects to a SQL Server database by using the System.Data.SqlClient.SqlConnection object. It then runs a stored procedure by using a System.Data.SqlClient.SqlCommand object and retrieves the results into a System.Data.SqlClient.SqlDataReader object. The application reads two fields from each row of data and concatenates their values into a string variable. What can you do to optimize this application?

    A. Replace the SqlConnection object with an OleDbConnection object.

    B. Replace the stored procedure with a SQL statement.

    C. Replace the SqlDataReader object with a DataSet object.

    D. Replace the string variable with a StringBuilder object.

65. You are performing final acceptance testing on your application prior to shipping it. You have set a breakpoint inside the SelectedIndexChanged event handler for a combo box. However, when you select a new value in this combo box, the code does not stop at the breakpoint. What could be the problem?

    A. Selecting a value in a combo box does not fire the SelectedIndexChanged event.

    B. You are executing the project by using the default Release configuration.

    C. You have neglected to add the <Conditional("DEBUG")> attribute to the event procedure.

    D. You have neglected to add #Const DEBUGGING = 1 to the code.

66. Assembly A is a member of the code groups in Table 1 (and only these code groups):

    What permission does the Common Language Runtime assign to Assembly A?

    A. Everything

    B. LocalIntranet

    C. Internet

    D. Nothing

TABLE 1

Level	Code Group	Permission Set	Exclusive	LevelFinal
Enterprise	All Code	Everything	No	No
Enterprise	Special Code	LocalIntranet	No	No
Enterprise	Restricted Code	Nothing	No	No
Enterprise	Restricted Components	Nothing	No	No

67. Your application includes a procedure that deletes many records from a database. When this procedure is invoked, you want the user to explicitly confirm his or her intention to delete the records. You have developed a form named frmConfirm to perform the confirmation. This form includes two Button controls, btnOK and btnCancel. The DialogResult property of btnOK is set to OK, and the DialogResult property of btnCancel is set to Cancel.

Which code snippet should you use to display frmConfirm and process the user's choice?

A.

```
Dim frm As New frmConfirm()
frm.ShowDialog()
If frm.DialogResult = DialogResult.OK Then
    ' Delete the records
End If
```

B.

```
Dim frm As New frmConfirm()
frm.Show()
If frm.DialogResult = DialogResult.OK Then
    ' Delete the records
End If
```

C.

```
Dim frm As New frmConfirm()
frm.ShowDialog()
If frm.btnOK.DialogResult = DialogResult.OK
Then
    ' Delete the records
End If
```

D.

```
Dim frm As New frmConfirm()
frm.Show()
If frm.btnOK.DialogResult = DialogResult.OK
Then
    ' Delete the records
End If
```

68. You have deployed your .NET application to several computers in the SALES domain that are not used for development. Your own computer is in the DEVELOPMENT domain. There is a two-way trust relationship established between the SALES domain and the DEVELOPMENT domain. Users report problems with the running application. You want to attach to the remote process for debugging, but you are unable to do so. What could be the problem?

A. The Machine Debug Manager (mdm.exe) is not installed on the computers in the SALES domain.

B. Visual Studio .NET does not support cross-domain debugging.

C. You cannot attach to a remote process that was compiled in the default Release configuration.

D. You must add a switch to the application's configuration file to enable remote debugging.

69. You are designing a custom control for use in industrial automation. This control will monitor a serial port and raise events based on data sent in through the serial port. This control will be hosted on forms, but it does not require any visual representation at runtime. From which class should you derive this control?

A. Control

B. UserControl

C. Form

D. Component

70. Your application includes a CheckBox control with its ThreeState property set to True. Your form displays this control in the indeterminate state. You want to take an action only if the user checks the CheckBox control. Which code snippet should you use?

A.

```
If chkTriState.CheckState =
CheckState.Checked Then
    ' Take action
End If
```

B.

```
If chkTriState.Checked Then
    ' Take action
End If
```

C.

```
If chkTriState.CheckState =
CheckState.Indeterminate Then
    ' Take action
End If
```

D.

```
If Not chkTriState.CheckState =
CheckState.Unchhecked Then
    ' Take action
End If
```

71. Your form requires a control that behaves exactly like a TextBox control, except that for certain values you want to display the text in red. From which class should you derive this control?

    A. UserControl

    B. TextBox

    C. Control

    D. Component

72. You have created a .NET component that will be used by multiple applications from your company. You want to be sure that this component is always installed in the same place with the same Registry settings. What type of installation should you create for the component?

    A. XCOPY installation

    B. Windows Installer merge module

    C. Windows Installer transform

    D. Windows Installer package

73. Your code would like file I/O permission, but it can run without this permission. You plan to request the permission and trap the error that occurs if the permission is not granted. Which SecurityAction flag should you use with the FileIoPermission object?

    A. SecurityAction.Minimum

    B. SecurityAction.Optional

    C. SecurityAction.Demand

    D. SecurityAction.RequestRefuse

74. The following code handles the Click event of Button1:

```
Private Sub Button1_Click( _
 ByVal sender As System.Object, _
 ByVal e As System.EventArgs) _
 Handles Button1.Click
    Dim i, j As Integer
    Try
        i = 0
        j = 5 / i
        Debug.WriteLine( _
          "Result = " & CStr(j))
    Catch aex As ArithmeticException
        Debug.WriteLine( _
          "Arithmetic Exception")
        GoTo EndIt
    Catch ex As Exception
        Debug.WriteLine( _
          "Unknown Exception")
        GoTo EndIt
    Finally
        Debug.WriteLine( _
          "Cleaning up")
        i = 0
        j = 0
    End Try
EndIt:
    End Sub
```

What is the output when you click the button?

    A.

```
ArithmeticException
UnknownExcaption
```

    B.

```
ArithmeticException
```

    C.

```
Result =
ArithmeticException
Cleaning Up
```

    D.

```
ArithmeticException
CleaningUp
```

75. Your application will use SqlCommand objects to directly manipulate the data in a SQL Server database. One of the tasks that you need to perform is add a new row to a table in the database. Which SQL keyword should you use for this task?

    A. SELECT

    B. UPDATE

    C. UNION

    D. INSERT

Answers to Exam Questions

1. **C.** You should use Process.CloseMainWindow to shut down any application that has a user interface. This method gives the application a chance to clean up resources. Process.Kill also shuts down the application, but it does not let normal cleanup processing proceed.

2. **C.** Dynamic properties provide a built-in mechanism to set properties at runtime without requiring you to write any code.

3. **D.** You need to sign the code with sn.exe to give it a strong name so that it can be stored in the GAC, and you need to sign it with signcode.exe to give the code an Authenticode signature. The two tools should always be used in that order.

4. **D.** A conditional breakpoint lets you pause code only when a particular condition is True. In the case of this scenario, you can use that capability to break into the code when the variable has the value 17.

5. **A.** Setting the PrintPreviewControl.UseAntiAlias property to True gives you a higher-quality print preview. The tradeoff is longer rendering times.

6. **D.** Because the application uses a Web service, you're assured that users have Internet access. Placing the help file on an Internet server allows you to display it on the form like any other help file but to change it quickly in one central location when it needs to be updated.

7. **D.** Using the Auto modifier ensures that the PInvoke call will work properly on both ANSI and Unicode platforms.

8. **C.** Runtime Callable Wrappers let you call existing COM components from .NET code without requiring a code rewrite.

9. **D.** Setting the CausesValidation property of a control to False causes the Validating events of other controls to be ignored when the focus is shifted to the specified control.

10. **D.** The Invalidate method triggers the Paint event, so calling it within the Paint event leads to an infinite regress. You could call the Invalidate method periodically or in response to a Resize event, but using the ResizeRedraw property requires less code and is thus a preferable solution.

11. **C.** Setting the control's TabStop property to False removes the control from the tab order. If you set the control's Enabled property to False, the control cannot get the focus under any circumstances.

12. **B, D.** The .NET WebService Studio tool is used to invoke a Web service for testing. The Web Services Discovery tool can locate files related to a Web service, but it does not build any code. The other two methods can generate proxy classes for use in a client application.

13. **A.** For information that will not be directly displayed to an end user but that may need to be used from many different locales, the invariant culture provides a culture-neutral storage format.

14. **C.** Using the Or operator sets the proper bit to represent the Italic FontStyle property without altering any other bits that may already be set.

15. **A.** If resources from a specific culture are not found, the .NET Framework falls back to using resources from the appropriate neutral culture, in this case the fr culture.

16. **D.** To display values from an array in a ListBox control or a ComboBox control, you set the DisplayMember property of the control to a string that contains the name of the field.

17. **C.** The filters in the OpenFileDialog control are numbered, starting at 1.

18. **D.** Because the COM library comes from a third-party company, the only proper way to proceed is to obtain a PIA from that company. You should not import and sign code that you did not write yourself.

19. **A.** You need to set e.HasMorePages to True in the PrintPage event when more than one page needs to be printed in the current print job.

20. **D.** The public, remotely accessible methods of a Web service are the methods that are marked with the WebMethod attribute.

21. **A.** Only assemblies with strong names can be installed in the GAC. This allows the Common Language Runtime to ensure that the assembly has not been tampered with, and it prevents naming collisions with assemblies from other developers.

22. **A.** You must set the EventLog.EnableRaisingEvents property to True to handle events from an event log in your code

23. **C.** Because the COM component is used in only one project, there is no penalty for using the easy direct reference method to use the objects in the COM component.

24. **B.** The PrintDialog component displays the standard Windows Print dialog box.

25. **A.** Array.Sort does not locate substrings. The Instr() method is obsolete and works only in Visual Basic 6 or earlier versions. IndexOf can find substrings, but it is not culture aware. Only the CompareInfo object can correctly handle the search in all character sets, including those that use 2 bytes per character.

26. **B.** The original object on the server and the proxy object on the client are instances of the same class, so both projects need a reference to the namespace that defines the class.

27. **D.** The DataView object provides a customized, bindable view of a DataTable object.

28. **B.** Because the Graphics object is so frequently needed during the Paint event, it is automatically passed to that event's handler.

29. **D.** Calls to a Web service will block other processing unless you use asynchronous calls to invoke the Web service.

30. **C.** To fill a DataSet object, you pass both the DataSet object and the name of the DataTable object to be created to the Fill method of an appropriate DataAdapter object.

31. **A.** The Protected modifier limits member access to the class that contains the member and to subclasses of that class. Public allows any class to call the member. Private limits access to the defining class only. Friend limits access to classes within the same project, whether they are derived from the defining class or not.

32. **A.** The MaxLength property has an effect only on user input. It is not checked when you programmatically set the value of a control.

33. **A.** When you assign a value directly to the BackColor property of Form2, it overrides the inheritance from Form1. Further changes to the same property on Form1 do not have any effect on Form2.

34. **A.** Assemblies installed in the Global Assembly Cache are available to all .NET code on the computer.

35. **B.** The UserControl class provides a design surface on which you can assemble constituent controls to create a custom control.

36. **A.** Simple data binding is the easiest way to move values from one database table to another via controls on a Windows Form.

37. **D.** A parameterized stored procedure allows you to pass in a parameter (in this case, the identifier for the customer) and use the parameter to limit the data returned.

38. **D.** You should avoid duplicating code if you don't have to. Visual Basic .NET allows you to use the AddHandler statement to associate a single event procedure with as many events as you like.

39. **D.** The GetBytes method of any encoding translates from Unicode characters to bytes that are appropriate for the Encoding object that is in use.

40. **C.** The TRACE symbol is defined in both the default Debug configuration and the default Release configuration. The DEBUG symbol is defined only in the default Debug configuration.

41. **A.** By default, Windows displays all Trace messages in the Output window. If you add another TraceListener object to the Listeners collection of the Trace object, then messages is sent to the new listener and to the Output window.

42. **A.** The UserPreferenceChanged event is raised whenever the user changes display properties. You can check the SystemInformation.HighContrast property in this event to determine whether the user has entered high-contrast mode.

43. **B.** The Font.GetHeight method allows you to determine the vertical size of the font so you can adjust the printing position of lines on the page.

44. **C.** The Help.ShowHelp method displays the contents of a specified help file, without requiring a keyword or topic name.

45. **A.** Allowing the user to choose a culture is better than accepting the existing culture of the application because the user might be running on a version of Windows that's not appropriate for his or her culture. There's no need to prompt for or store a numeric format because all necessary formats are stored in the .NET Framework.

46. **A.** You can have only a single SqlDataReader object open on a single SqlConnection object. If you need a second SqlDataReader object, you need to open a second SqlConnection object.

47. **A.** The Web Services Discovery tool uses the information in the .asmx file to locate the other important files for the Web service, including the WSDL file that specifies the Web service's interface.

48. **D.** Changes made to a DataGrid control bound to a DataSet control are automatically saved to the DataSet control. However, they are not persisted to the underlying data source until you call the Update method of the DataAdapter object that was used to fill the DataSet control.

49. **C.** The BinaryReader class uses an efficient encoding method to write data to disk, but the results are not human readable.

50. **C.** The FileStream class is designed for byte-by-byte input and output. The other classes add additional functionality, but they require you to have prior knowledge of the structure of the file that you're reading.

51. **D.** Using a class derived from EventArgs to pass event parameters is preferable to using individual arguments because it's more readily extended in case you need to pass additional parameters in the future.

52. **B.** Using the Type Library Importer allows you to place the RCW assembly in the GAC so that it can be shared by all projects on the computer. A Primary Interop Assembly is for code from other vendors, not for your own code.

53. **A.** An application that must deploy assemblies to the GAC should be deployed by using the Windows Installer Service.

54. **A.** The installutil.exe tool treats each command line as a single transaction. If any of the assemblies listed in the command fail to install, the entire installation is rolled back.

55. **A.** System.Data.SqlClient.SqlConnection offers the best possible performance for SQL Server data sources because it talks directly to SQL Server, using the native TDS protocol.

56. **B.** A cryptographic hash uniquely identifies a particular version of a particular assembly. You can't use a software publisher membership condition because the code does not have an Authenticode signature.

57. **D.** The QueryPageSettings event fires before each page is printed, allowing you to check and change page settings. Page settings cannot be changed in the PrintPage event.

58. **C.** The KeyDown event occurs before the KeyPress events. Setting the Handled property to True in the form's KeyPress event prevents the control's KeyPress event from firing.

59. **C.** The Help button will be displayed on the title bar only if both the MinButton and MaxButton properties are set to False.

60. **D.** You can enumerate and monitor remote event logs, and you can retrieve entries from them. But you can only post new entries to event logs on the local computer.

61. **B, D.** The AccessibleName and AccessbleDescription properties provide information directly to screen reader programs.

62. **A, C, D.** These are the three constructors that any Exception class should implement. Custom Exception classes require the same three constructors that are defined in the base System.Exception class.

63. **C.** With code access security, you can use OleDbPermission to grant permission to use OLE DB data sources.

64. **D.** Strings in Visual Basic .NET are immutable, so concatenating multiple values into a string requires you to delete and re-create the string many times. The StringBuilder object is optimized for changing textual data.

65. **B.** Breakpoints and other debugging features are not enabled in the default Release configuration.

66. **A.** Within a level, the permission set granted to an assembly is the union of all the permission sets of code groups on that level to which the assembly belongs.

67. **A.** To pause the rest of the application while the user makes a choice, you should use the ShowDialog method rather than the Show method to display the form. When the user clicks a button on the form, the value of the DialogResult property of that button is assigned to the DialogResult property of the form.

68. **A.** To enable remote debugging on a computer, the Machine Debug Manager must be installed. You can install this software by installing Visual Studio .NET on the remote machine or by installing Remote Components Setup on the remote machine.

69. **D.** When a custom control does not require a runtime user interface, the Component class provides the lowest overhead.

70. **A.** If a CheckBox control has its ThreeState property set to True, its Checked property returns True even if the check box is in the indeterminate state. You must evaluate the CheckState property to determine whether the check box is actually checked.

71. **B.** The easiest way to get a control to behave precisely like a TextBox control is to inherit from the TextBox class.

72. **B.** A Windows Installer merge module allows you to include the component in any Installer package, and the merge module will have identical settings in every package. You can't use XCOPY deployment to meet these requirements because the component requires Registry settings.

73. **B.** With an Optional request, you can trap the error if the permission is not granted.

74. **D.** An exception is handled by the most specific applicable Catch block. A transfer-of-control statement (such as GoTo) does not skip a Finally block.

75. **C.** The INSERT statement adds a new row to a SQL Server (or other ANSI-compliant database) table.

PART

APPENDIXES

Glossary

A

accessibility   The process of making an application more readily available to users who have disabilities that interfere with their use of computer hardware or software.

ad hoc query   A set of SQL statements that are executed immediately.

Application   The Application class provides a set of static methods and properties to manage an application.

assembly   A logical unit of functionality that can contain one or more files. Every type loaded in the Common Language Runtime belongs to precisely one assembly.

assembly manifest   Stores the assembly's metadata. The metadata provides self-describing information such as the name and version of the assembly, the files that are part of the assembly and their hash values and dependencies on other assemblies, and so on. This subset of information in the manifest makes assemblies self-sufficient.

assembly metadata   Provides the assembly's self-describing information such as the name and version of the assembly, the files that are part of the assembly and their hash values and dependencies on other assemblies, and so on.

attribute   XML attributes are properties of an XML object.

attributes   Visual Basic .NET attributes are Declarative tags that can be placed with certain code elements. Attributes provide additional information about the corresponding code element at runtime.

authentication   Determining the identity of a user from his credentials.

authorization   Allowing a user to use specific resources based on her authenticated identity.

B

backing store   A place to store a file.

boxing   The process of converting a value type to a reference type. The value in the stack is copied into the heap by creating a new instance of object to hold its data.

C

CDATA section   Raw data within an XML file.

class   A reference type that encapsulates its data (constants and fields) and behavior (methods, properties, indexers, events, operators, instance constructors, static constructors, and destructors).

Clipboard   The Windows Clipboard provides a way to transfer data between and within various Windows applications.

code access security   Security based on permission requests made by running code.

code group   A group of zero or more modules that share a common security policy.

column   All the values for one particular property in a table.

Common Language Runtime (CLR)   Executes all managed code and provides code with various services at runtime such as automatic memory management, cross-language integration, code access security, and debugging and profiling support.

complex data binding   Connecting a user interface control to an entire collection of data, rather than to a single data item.

component   The basic unit of code reuse.

configured assembly   An assembly for which you have specified a runtime version substitution.

constructor   A special method that allows control over initialization of a type. It is executed when an instance of a type is created.

context menu   Displays a small list of menu items that depend on your current context of working. A context menu is associated with a control and will be shown when the control is right-clicked by the user.

culture   A combination of language and location sufficient to dictate the formatting of resources.

culture code   An abbreviation that identifies a particular culture.

custom control   A control that is created by deriving directly or indirectly from the System.WindowsForms.Control class and that renders its own user interface in its Paint event handler.

D

data binding   The process of linking controls on the user interface and data stored in the data model.

data provider   The server-specific ADO.NET classes that supply data.

DataSet   A server-independent store that can hold multiple tables and their relations.

debugging   The process of locating logical or runtime errors in an application. It involves finding the cause of the errors and fixing them.

declarative security   Security based on attributes that declare the desired permissions.

delay signing   A technique that allows a shared assembly to be placed in the GAC by just signing the assembly with the public key. This allows the assembly to be signed with the private key at a later stage, when the development process is complete and the component or assembly is ready to be deployed. This process allows developers to work with shared assemblies as if they are strongly named and yet also keeps the private key of the company more secret and secure.

delegate   A special reference type that can store references to both static and instance methods. It can be used to invoke a method dynamically at runtime.

deployment   A process by which a Windows application or component is distributed in the form of installation package files to be installed on other computers.

disco   A Microsoft standard for Web service discovery.

E

element   An XML tag together with its contents.

encoding   A scheme for representing textual characters as numeric codes.

enumeration   The Enum keyword creates an enumerated value type to provide a type-safe way to work with constants.

event   A message sent by an object to signal an action. The action can be a result of user interaction, such as a mouse click, or it can be triggered by any other program.

event handling   The act of responding to an event. This is done by writing special methods called event handlers that are invoked as a response to an event.

exception   Indicates a problem that occurred during normal execution of the program.

exception handling   The process of handling exceptions that are raised when the program executes.

F

field   A variable associated with an object or class.

foreign key   The foreign key in a database table stores values from the primary key in another table. These values indicate which row in the primary table each row in the other table is related to.

Framework Class Library   The .NET Framework Class Library, or FCL, a library of classes, interfaces, and value types included in the Microsoft .NET Framework. This library provides access to system functionality and is designed to be the foundation on which .NET Framework applications, components, and controls are built.

G

garbage collection   A process of reclaiming all unused memory and returning it to the heap of available memory. The Common Language Runtime garbage collector might invoke when your application goes low on memory resources. It also compacts the memory in use to reduce the working space needed for the heap.

GDI+   A modern implementation of Windows Graphical Device Interface. It allows you to create graphics, draw text, and manipulate graphical images.

Global Assembly Cache (GAC)   A cache of assemblies that can be shared by many applications on the computer.

globalization   The process of identifying the resources to be localized in a particular application.

H, I

imperative security   Security based on instantiated classes.

identity   A column whose value is automatically assigned by the server when a new row is entered.

inheritance   Allows you to create a new type based on an existing type. In this inheritance relationship the existing type is called the base type and the new type is called the derived type. When you use inheritance the derived type gets all functionality of the base type without any extra coding.

input validation   A process by which an application examines the user input to determine whether it is acceptable to the application.

intermediate language   The language compilers supporting .NET Framework compile the program in an intermediate language (IL). IL has been ratified as an ECMA standard, and the standard calls it common Intermediate Language (CIL). The Microsoft implementation of CIL is called Microsoft Intermediate Language (MSIL).

J

JIT compilation   Just-in-time compilation is the process of converting the IL (intermediate language) code into machine code at runtime, just when it is required.

K, L

"Last one wins" concurrency control   With "last one wins" concurrency control, an update to a row always succeeds, whether another user has edited the row or not (as long as the row still exists).

localizability   The process of verifying that all localizable resources have been separated from code.

localization   The process of translating resources for another culture.

M

main menu   Groups various commands available in a Windows application. The main menu is displayed at the top of a form just below its title bar and can have several top-level menus. Each top-level menu can have a hierarchy of menu items within itself. A Windows application can have just one main menu. In the case of an MDI application consisting of multiple forms, the menus of the child windows will be merged in the MDI container's main menu.

Managed Code   The code that runs under the services provided by Common Language Runtime. Managed code must expose necessary metadata information to the CLR to enjoy these services (see Common Language Runtime).

MDI Form   A Multiple-Document Interface (MDI) Application allows you to display multiple documents simultaneously. Each document is displayed in its own window. You can recognize an MDI application by the inclusion of a Window menu containing commands for switching between windows or documents.

merge module   Allows you to create reusable components that can be deployed by the Windows Installer. A merge module cannot be directly installed. It must be merged with installers of applications that use the component packed into a merge module.

metadata   Information about elements such as assembly, type, method, and so on that helps the CLR manage garbage collection, object lifetime management, code access security, debugging, and other services.

N

namespace   Provides a way to logically group related types. Namespace benefits are twofold: They help avoid naming conflicts and make it easier to browse and locate classes.

native compilation   The process of precompiling assemblies in the processor-specific machine code. This can be done with the help of the Native Image Generator tool (ngen.exe).

native image cache   A cache that contains precompiled assemblies.

.NET Framework   A platform for building, deploying, and running XML Web services and applications. The .NET Framework consists of three main parts: the Common Language Runtime, the Framework Class Libraries, and a set of language compilers.

O

one-way data binding   In one-way data binding, the bound property of the control reflects changes to the data model, but changes to the control are not written back to the data model.

optimistic concurrency control   With optimistic concurrency control, an update to a row will succeed only if no one else has changed that row after it was loaded into the DataSet.

OSQL   A SQL Server command-line tool for executing queries.

override   An override method or property provides a new implementation of a member that is inherited from a base class.

P

parameter   A piece of information passed to a stored procedure at runtime.

performance counter   The Windows way of publishing performance-related data for applications and their components.

permission   In .NET, controls access to a resource.

permission set   A set of one or more permissions that can be granted or denied as a unit.

platform invoke   The feature of the .NET Framework that allows you to call Windows API and other DLL procedures from managed code.

pop-up help   Help displayed in a pop-up window after the user has clicked the Help button on a control.

primary key   The unique identifier for a row in a database table.

PrintDocument   The PrintDocument class provides object-oriented access to all the features you need to print either text or graphics.

private assembly   An assembly available only to clients in the same directory structure as the assembly.

process   An application under execution.

property   A property is like a public field, but it can also encapsulate additional logic within its Get and Set accessor methods.

Q, R

relation   A connection between two tables in a database.

relational database   Stores multiple tables and the relations between them.

resource file   A file containing string, bitmap, or other resources that can differ between cultures.

resource-only assembly   An assembly that only contains resources and no executable code.

result set   A collection of data arranged in rows and columns.

role-based security   Security based on the identity of the current user.

row   All the values in a table that describe one instance of an entity.

runtime callable wrapper   A proxy that allows .NET code to make use of COM classes and members.

S

satellite assembly   A resource-only assembly that contains culture-specific information.

schema   The structure of a database or XML file.

SDI Form   A single-document interface (SDI) application allows you to work on a single document or form (for an alternative, see MDI Form). Common examples of an SDI application are Windows Notepad and Wordpad applications.

shared assembly   An assembly that can be referenced by more than one application. An assembly must be explicitly built to be shared by giving it a cryptographically strong name. Shared assemblies are stored in the machinewide Global Assembly Cache.

simple data binding   Connecting a single value from the data model to a single property of a control.

SOAP   The Simple Object Access Protocol, a standard for transmitting objects as XML over HTTP.

SQL-92   The official ANSI specification for Structured Query Language.

SQL Query Analyzer   A SQL Server graphical tool for executing queries.

stored procedure   A set of SQL statements stored on the server for later execution.

stream   A file viewed as a stream of bytes.

strong name   A name that identifies an assembly globally. It consists of a simple text name, a version number, and culture information (if provided) that is signed by a digital signature and contains a public key of the assembly. If the assembly contains more than one file, it is sufficient to generate a digital signature just for the file that contains the assembly manifest.

structure   A user-defined value type. Just like a class it has constructors, fields, methods, properties, and so forth; however, structures do not support inheritance.

T

tab order   The order in which controls will receive focus when users navigate on a form using the Tab key on the keyboard.

table   A collection of data about instances of a single entity.

testing   The process of executing programs and determining whether they worked as expected. It is the process of revealing errors by executing programs with various test cases and test data.

ToolTip   A small pop-up window that displays a brief description of a control's purpose when the mouse hovers over the control.

tracing   The process of displaying informative messages in an application at the time of execution. These messages can be helpful in checking the health of the program or finding out errors even though the program is in the production environment as well.

Transact-SQL   Also called T-SQL, the SQL-92 dialect used in Microsoft SQL Server.

two-way data binding   In two-way data binding, changes to the control are written back to the data model.

U

UDDI   Universal Description, Discovery, and Integration, a standard for discovering details of Web services and other business services available via the Internet.

unboxing   The process of converting a reference type to a value type. The value from the heap is copied back into the stack.

Unicode   A universal character set that can represent over a million characters. Unicode is the default internal language of .NET.

unmanaged code Code written in a non-.NET environment that does not benefit from the services of the CLR.

URL remoting The process of launching an application from a remote location.

user assistance Any means of providing information about your application to the user.

user control A control that is created by deriving directly or indirectly from the System.WindowsForms.UserControl class and is created by combining existing controls.

V

Visual Inheritance The process that lets you inherit a visual element, such as a form or a control, based on an already existing element. Visual Inheritance helps you reuse existing code and maintain consistency between visual elements.

W

Web method A method of a Web service that can be invoked by client applications.

Web reference Information in a Visual Studio .NET project that allows you to use objects supplied by a Web service.

Web service A Web service allows you to instantiate and invoke objects over the Internet.

Windows Forms Designer The rich visual environment provided by Visual Studio .NET that allows you to create Windows-based applications.

WSDL Web Services Description Language, an XML language that describes the interface of a Web service.

X

XML Extensible Markup Language

XML declaration The line in an XML file that identifies the file as XML.

XML namespace A set of XML tags private to an application.

Y, Z

z-order Specifies the visual layering of controls on a form along the form's z-axis. The visual layering controls in turn specify the form's depth. A control at the top of the z-order overlaps other controls, whereas other controls overlap a control that is at the bottom of the z-order.

Overview of the Certification Process

You must pass rigorous certification exams to become a Microsoft Certified Professional. These closed-book exams provide a valid and reliable measure of your technical proficiency and expertise. Developed in consultation with computer industry professionals who have experience with Microsoft products in the workplace, the exams are conducted by two independent organizations. Prometric offers the exams at more than 3,500 Authorized Prometric Testing Centers around the world. Virtual University Enterprises (VUE) testing centers offer exams at more than 3,000 locations.

To schedule an exam, call Prometric Testing Centers at 800-755-EXAM (3926) or VUE at 800-TEST-REG (837-8734) (or register online with Prometric at http://www.2test.com/index.jsp or with VUE at http://www.vue.com/ms/). Currently, Microsoft offers seven types of certification, based on specific areas of expertise.

TYPES OF CERTIFICATION

◆ **Microsoft Certified Professional (MCP)**—Qualified to provide installation, configuration, and support for users of at least one Microsoft product or technology. Candidates can take elective exams to develop areas of specialization. MCP is the base level of expertise.

◆ **Microsoft Certified Systems Administrator (MCSA)**—Qualified to implement, manage, and troubleshoot existing network and system environments based on the Microsoft Windows 2000 and Windows .NET Server platforms.

◆ **Microsoft Certified Systems Engineer (MCSE)**—Qualified to analyze business requirements and design and implement the infrastructure for business solutions based on the Microsoft Windows 2000 platform and Microsoft server software. The MCSE credential is the next step up from the MCSA.

◆ **Microsoft Certified Application Developer (MCAD)**—Qualified to use Microsoft technologies to develop and maintain department level applications, components, Web or desktop clients, or back-end data services. This is the entry-level developer certification.

◆ **Microsoft Certified Solution Developer (MCSD)**—Qualified to design and develop leading-edge business solutions by using Microsoft development tools, technologies, and platforms, including Microsoft Office and Microsoft BackOffice. MCSD is the highest level of expertise with a focus on software development.

◆ **Microsoft Certified Database Administrator (MCDBA)**—Qualified to implement and administer Microsoft SQL Server databases.

❖ **Microsoft Certified Trainer (MCT)**—
Instructionally and technically qualified by
Microsoft to deliver Microsoft Education Courses
at Microsoft-authorized sites. An MCT must be
employed by a Microsoft Solution Provider
Authorized Technical Education Center or a
Microsoft Authorized Academic Training site.

> **NOTE**
>
> Microsoft's certifications and the
> exams that lead to them are under
> constant revision. For up-to-date infor-
> mation about each type of certifica-
> tion, visit the Microsoft Training and
> Certification World Wide Web site at
> http://www.microsoft.com/
> traincert/. You must have an
> Internet account and a Web browser
> to access this information. You also
> can contact the following sources:
>
> · Microsoft Regional Education
>   Service Center for North America:
>   800-635-7544.
>
> · MCPHelp@Microsoft.com

CERTIFICATION REQUIREMENTS

An asterisk following an exam in any of the lists that
follow means that it is slated for retirement.

How to Become a Microsoft Certified Professional

Passing any Microsoft exam (with the exception of
exam 70-058, Networking Essentials) is all you need to
do to become certified as an MCP.

How to Become a Microsoft Certified Systems Administrator

You must pass three core exams and one elective exam
to become an MCSA. The following lists show both
the core requirements and the electives you can take to
earn this certification.

Core Exams

The core exams required are as follows:

❖ Installing, Configuring, and Administering
Microsoft Windows 2000 Professional, #70-210

OR Installing, Configuring, and Administering
Microsoft Windows XP Professional, #70-270

❖ Installing, Configuring, and Administering
Microsoft Windows 2000 Server, #70-215

OR Installing, Configuring, and Administering
Microsoft Windows .NET Server, #70-275

❖ Managing a Microsoft Windows 2000 Network
Environment, #70-218

Elective Exams

You must pass any one of the exams from the following
list:

❖ Administering Microsoft SQL Server 7.0,
#70-028

❖ Implementing and Supporting Microsoft
Exchange Server 5.5, #70-081*

❖ Implementing and Supporting Microsoft Systems
Management Server 2.0, #70-086

❖ Implementing and Supporting Microsoft Proxy
Server 2.-, #70-088*

◆ Implementing and Administering Security in a Microsoft Windows 2000 Network, #70-214

◆ Implementing and Administering a Microsoft Windows 2000 Network Infrastructure, #70-216

◆ Installing, Configuring, and Administering Microsoft Exchange 2000 Server, #70-224

◆ Installing, Configuring, and Administering Microsoft Internet Security and Acceleration (ISA) Server 2000, Enterprise Edition, #70-227

◆ Installing, Configuring, and Administering Microsoft SQL Server 2000 Enterprise Edition, #70-228

◆ Supporting and Maintaining a Microsoft Windows NT Server 4.0 Network, #70-244

◆ A+ and Network+, CompTIA exams

◆ A+ and Server+, CompTIA exams

The MCSA is the first Microsoft certification to recognize some third-party certification exams as electives. Two particular combinations of exams from CompTIA qualify as MCSA objectives.

How to Become a Microsoft Certified Systems Engineer

You must pass five core exams (four operating system exams and one design exam) and two elective exams to become a MCSE.

The following lists show the core requirements and the electives you can take to earn the MCSE certification.

Operating System Exams

The four core requirements for MCSE certification are as follows:

◆ Installing, Configuring, and Administering Microsoft Windows 2000 Professional, #70-210

OR Installing, Configuring, and Administering Microsoft Windows XP Professional, #70-270

◆ Installing, Configuring, and Administering Microsoft Windows 2000 Server, #70-215

OR Installing, Configuring, and Administering Microsoft Windows .NET Server, #70-275

◆ Implementing and Administering a Microsoft Windows 2000 Network Infrastructure, #70-216

OR Implementing and Administering a Microsoft Windows .NET Server Network Infrastructure, #70-276

◆ Implementing and Administering a Microsoft Windows 2000 Directory Services Infrastructure, #70-217

OR Implementing and Administering a Microsoft Windows .NET Server Directory Services Infrastructure, #70-277

Design Exam

You must pass one of the design electives on this list:

◆ Designing a Microsoft Windows 2000 Directory Services Infrastructure, #70-219

◆ Designing Security for a Microsoft Windows 2000 Network, #70-220

◆ Designing a Microsoft Windows 2000 Network Infrastructure, #70-221

◆ Designing Highly Available Web Solutions with Microsoft Windows 2000 Server Technologies, #70-226

Elective Exams

You must pass two of the following elective exams for MCSE certification:

◆ Designing and Implementing Data Warehouses with Microsoft SQL Server 7.0, #70-019

◆ Administering Microsoft SQL Server 7.0, #70-028

◆ Designing and Implementing Databases with Microsoft SQL Server 7.0, #70-029

◆ Implementing and Supporting Web Sites Using Microsoft Site Server 3.0, #70-056*

◆ Implementing and Supporting Microsoft Internet Explorer 5.0 by Using the Microsoft Internet Explorer Administration Kit, #70-080*

◆ Implementing and Supporting Microsoft Exchange Server 5.5, #70-081*

◆ Implementing and Supporting Microsoft SNA Server 4.0, #70-085*

◆ Implementing and Supporting Microsoft Systems Management Server 2.0, #70-086

◆ Implementing and Supporting Microsoft Proxy Server 2.0, #70-088*

◆ Implementing and Administering Security in a Microsoft Windows 2000 Network, #70-214

◆ Managing a Microsoft Windows 2000 Network Environment, #70-218

◆ Designing a Microsoft Windows 2000 Directory Services Infrastructure, #70-219

◆ Designing Security for a Microsoft Windows 2000 Network, #70-220

◆ Designing a Microsoft Windows 2000 Network Infrastructure, #70-221

◆ Migrating from Microsoft Windows NT 4.0 to Microsoft Windows 2000, #70-222

◆ Installing, Configuring, and Administering Microsoft Clustering Services by Using Microsoft Windows 2000 Advanced Server, #70-223

◆ Installing, Configuring, and Administering Microsoft Exchange 2000 Server, #70-224

◆ Designing and Deploying a Messaging Infrastructure with Microsoft Exchange 2000 Server, #70-225

◆ Designing Highly Available Web Solutions with Microsoft Windows 2000 Server Technologies, #70-226

◆ Installing, Configuring, and Administering Microsoft Internet Security and Acceleration (ISA) Server 2000 Enterprise Edition, #70-227

◆ Installing, Configuring, and Administering Microsoft SQL Server 2000 Enterprise Edition, #70-228

◆ Designing and Implementing Databases with Microsoft SQL Server 2000 Enterprise Edition, #70-229

◆ Designing and Implementing Solutions with Microsoft BizTalk Server 2000 Enterprise Edition, #70-230

◆ Implementing and Maintaining Highly Available Web Solutions with Microsoft Windows 2000 Server Technologies and Microsoft Application Center 2000, #70-232

◆ Designing and Implementing Solutions with Microsoft Commerce Server 2000, #70-234

◆ Supporting and Maintaining a Microsoft Windows NT Server 4.0 Network, #70-244

You cannot count the same exam as both a core exam and an elective exam for the MCSE.

How to Become a Microsoft Certified Application Developer

You must pass two core exams and one elective exam to earn the MCAD certification.

The following lists show the core requirements and the electives that you can take to earn the MCAD certification.

Core Exams

The two core requirements for MCAD certification are as follows:

- ◆ Developing and Implementing Web Applications with Microsoft Visual Basic .NET and Microsoft Visual Studio .NET, #70-305

  OR Developing and Implementing Windows-based Applications with Microsoft Visual Basic .NET and Microsoft Visual Studio .NET, #70-306

  OR Developing and Implementing Web Applications with Microsoft Visual C# .NET and Microsoft Visual Studio .NET, #70-315

  OR Developing and Implementing Windows-based Applications with Microsoft Visual Basic .NET and Microsoft Visual C# .NET, #70-316

- ◆ Designing XML Web Services and Server Components with Microsoft Visual Basic .NET and the Microsoft .NET Framework, #70-310

  OR Designing XML Web Services and Server Components with Microsoft Visual C# .NET and the Microsoft .NET Framework, #70-320

Elective Exams

You must pass one of the following elective exams for MCAD certification:

- ◆ Designing and Implementing Databases with Microsoft SQL Server 2000 Enterprise Edition, #70-229

- ◆ Designing and Implementing Solutions with Microsoft BizTalk Server 2000 Enterprise Edition, #70-230

- ◆ Designing and Implementing Solutions with Microsoft Commerce Server 2000, #70-234

You can also count as elective one of the four core exams (70-305, 70-306, 70-315, and 70-316). The one you can count as an elective is the exam from the opposite technology and language as the exam that you counted for core. For example, if you take the VB Windows-based Applications exam (70-306) as a core exam, you can take the C# Web Applications exam (70-315) as an elective.

How to Become a Microsoft Certified Solution Developer

The MCSD certification has two different tracks. The new track is for the MCSD for Microsoft .NET certification, whereas the old track covers the previous round of Microsoft technologies. The requirements for both tracks are listed here.

New Track

For the new track, you must pass four core exams and one elective exam. Both the core and elective exams are listed here.

Core Exams
- ◆ Developing and Implementing Web Applications with Microsoft Visual Basic .NET and Microsoft Visual Studio .NET, #70-305

OR Developing and Implementing Web Applications with Microsoft Visual C# .NET and Microsoft Visual Studio .NET, #70-315

❖ Developing and Implementing Windows-based Applications with Microsoft Visual Basic .NET and Microsoft Visual Studio .NET, #70-306

OR Developing and Implementing Windows-based Applications with Microsoft Visual Basic .NET and Microsoft Visual C# .NET, #70-316

❖ Designing XML Web Services and Server Components with Microsoft Visual Basic .NET and the Microsoft .NET Framework, #70-310

OR Designing XML Web Services and Server Components with Microsoft Visual C# .NET and the Microsoft .NET Framework, #70-320

❖ Analyzing Requirements and Defining .NET Solution Architectures, #70-300

Elective Exams

You must pass one of the following elective exams:

❖ Designing and Implementing Databases with Microsoft SQL Server 2000 Enterprise Edition, #70-229

❖ Designing and Implementing Solutions with Microsoft BizTalk Server 2000 Enterprise Edition, #70-230

❖ Designing and Implementing Solutions with Microsoft Commerce Server 2000, #70-234

Old Track

For the old track, you must pass three core exams and one elective exam. Both the core and elective exams are listed here.

Core Exams

❖ Designing and Implementing Desktop Applications with Microsoft Visual C++ 6.0, #70-016

OR Designing and Implementing Desktop Applications with Microsoft Visual FoxPro 6.0, #70-156

OR Designing and Implementing Desktop Applications with Microsoft Visual Basic 6.0, #70-176

❖ Designing and Implementing Distributed Applications with Microsoft Visual C++ 6.0, #70-015

OR Designing and Implementing Distributed Applications with Microsoft Visual FoxPro 6.0, #70-155

OR Designing and Implementing Distributed Applications with Microsoft Visual Basic 6.0, #70-175

❖ Analyzing Requirements and Defining Solution Architectures, #70-100

Elective Exams

You must pass one of the following elective exams:

❖ Designing and Implementing Distributed Applications with Microsoft Visual C++ 6.0, #70-015

❖ Designing and Implementing Desktop Applications with Microsoft Visual C++ 6.0, #70-016

❖ Designing and Implementing Data Warehouses with Microsoft SQL Server 7.0, #70-019

❖ Implementing a Database Design on Microsoft SQL Server 7.0, #70-029

◆ Designing and Implementing Commerce Solutions with Microsoft Site Server 3.0, Commerce Edition, #70-057*

◆ Designing and Implementing Solutions with Microsoft Office 2000 and Microsoft Visual Basic for Applications, #70-091*

◆ Designing and Implementing Collaborative Solutions with Microsoft Outlook 2000 and Microsoft Exchange Server 5.5, #70-105

◆ Designing and Implementing Web Solutions with Microsoft Visual InterDev 6.0, #70-152

◆ Designing and Implementing Distributed Applications with Microsoft Visual FoxPro 6.0, #70-155

◆ Designing and Implementing Desktop Applications with Microsoft Visual FoxPro 6.0, #70-156

◆ Designing and Implementing Distributed Applications with Microsoft Visual Basic 6.0, #70-175

◆ Designing and Implementing Desktop Applications with Microsoft Visual Basic 6.0, #70-176

◆ Designing and Implementing Databases with Microsoft SQL Server 2000 Enterprise Edition, #70-229

◆ Designing and Implementing Solutions with Microsoft BizTalk Server 2000 Enterprise Edition, #70-230

◆ Designing and Implementing Solutions with Microsoft Commerce Server 2000, #70-234

You cannot count the same exam as both a core exam and an elective exam.

How to Become a Microsoft Certified Database Administrator

You must pass three core exams and one elective exam to earn the MCDBA certification.

The following lists show the core requirements and electives that you can take to earn the MCDBA certification.

Core Exams

The three core requirements for MCDBA certification are as follows:

◆ Administering SQL Server 7.0, #70-028

OR Installing, Configuring, and Administering Microsoft SQL Server 2000 Enterprise Edition, #70-228

◆ Designing and Implementing Databases with Microsoft SQL Server 7.0, #70-029

OR Designing and Implementing Databases with Microsoft SQL Server 2000 Enterprise Edition, #70-229

◆ Installing, Configuring, and Administering Microsoft Windows 2000 Server, #70-215

OR Installing, Configuring, and Administering Microsoft Windows .NET Enterprise Server, #70-2715

Elective Exams

You must pass one of these elective exams:

◆ Designing and Implementing Distributed Applications with Microsoft Visual C++ 6.0, #70-015

◆ Designing and Implementing Data Warehouses with Microsoft SQL Server 7.0, #70-019

◆ Designing and Implementing Distributed Applications with Microsoft Visual FoxPro 6.0, #70-155

◆ Designing and Implementing Distributed Applications with Microsoft Visual Basic 6.0, #70-175

◆ Implementing and Administering a Microsoft Windows 2000 Network Infrastructure, #70-216

◆ Implementing and Administering a Microsoft .NET Server Network Infrastructure, #70-276

4. Complete the MCT application, which you can fill out on the MCT Web site.

> **WARNING**
>
> **Things Change** Please consider this appendix to be a general overview of the Microsoft certification process. You'll find much more detailed information, as well as the latest program changes, on the Microsoft Training and Certification Web site mentioned earlier in the appendix.

How to Become a Microsoft Certified Trainer

To understand the requirements and process for becoming an MCT, you must obtain the Microsoft Certified Trainer Program Guide document from the following Web site:

```
http://www.microsoft.com/traincert/mcp/mct/
guides.asp
```

The MCT Program Guide explains the four-step process of becoming an MCT. The general steps for the MCT certification are as follows:

1. Obtain one of the Microsoft premier certifications: MCSE, MCSD, or MCDBA.

2. Attend a classroom presentation of a Microsoft course taught by a Microsoft Certified Trainer at a Microsoft Certified Technical Education Center (CTEC).

3. Demonstrate instructional presentation skills by attending a Train-the-Trainer course or providing proof of experience in technical training.

What's On the CD-ROM

This appendix provides a brief summary of what you'll find on the CD-ROM that accompanies this book. For a more detailed description of the *PrepLogic Practice Tests, Preview Edition* exam simulation software, see Appendix D, "Using *PrepLogic, Preview Edition* Software." In addition to PrepLogic Practice Tests, Preview Edition, the CD-ROM includes an electronic version of the book in Portable Document Format (PDF) and the source code used in the book as well.

PREPLOGIC PRACTICE TESTS, PREVIEW EDITION

PrepLogic is a leading provider of certification training tools. Trusted by certification students worldwide, we believe PrepLogic is the best practice exam software available. In addition to providing a means of evaluating your knowledge of the Training Guide material, *PrepLogic Practice Tests, Preview Edition* features several innovations to help you improve your mastery of the subject matter.

For example, the practice tests allow you to check your score by exam area or domain to determine which topics you need to study more. Another feature allows you to obtain immediate feedback on your responses in the form of explanations for the correct and incorrect answers.

PrepLogic Practice Tests, Preview Edition exhibits most of the full functionality of the Premium Edition but offers only a fraction of the total questions. To get the complete set of practice questions and exam functionality, visit PrepLogic.com and order the Premium Edition for this and other challenging exam titles.

Again, for a more detailed description of the *PrepLogic Practice Tests, Preview Edition* features, see Appendix D.

EXCLUSIVE ELECTRONIC VERSION OF THE TEXT

The CD-ROM also contains the electronic version of this book in PDF. This electronic version comes complete with all figures as they appear in the book. You will find the search capability of the reader handy for study and review purposes.

COMPLETE CODE SAMPLES

You'll find the complete source code for every Step By Step, Guided Practice Exercise, and Exercise for the book on the CD as well. Just open any of the solution files in your copy of Visual Studio .NET, and you'll be ready to follow along with the text.

Using *PrepLogic, Preview Edition* Software

This Training Guide includes a special version of PrepLogic Practice Tests—a revolutionary test engine designed to give you the best in certification exam preparation. PrepLogic offers sample and practice exams for many of today's most in-demand and challenging technical certifications. This special Preview Edition is included with this book as a tool for assessing your knowledge of the Training Guide material while also providing you with the experience of taking an electronic exam.

This appendix describes in detail what *PrepLogic Practice Tests, Preview Edition* is, how it works, and what it can do to help you prepare for the exam. Note that although the Preview Edition includes all the test simulation functions of the complete, retail version, it contains only a single practice test. The Premium Edition, available at `PrepLogic.com`, contains the complete set of challenging practice exams designed to optimize your learning experience.

EXAM SIMULATION

One of the main functions of *PrepLogic Practice Tests, Preview Edition* is exam simulation. To prepare you to take the actual vendor certification exam, PrepLogic offers the most effective exam simulation available.

QUESTION QUALITY

The questions provided in the *PrepLogic Practice Tests, Preview Edition* are written to highest standards of technical accuracy. The questions tap the content of the Training Guide chapters and help you review and assess your knowledge before you take the actual exam.

INTERFACE DESIGN

The *PrepLogic Practice Tests, Preview Edition* exam simulation interface provides the experience of taking an electronic exam. This enables you to effectively prepare for taking the actual exam by making the test experience a familiar one. Using this test simulation can help eliminate the sense of surprise or anxiety you might experience in the testing center because you will already be acquainted with computerized testing.

EFFECTIVE LEARNING ENVIRONMENT

The *PrepLogic Practice Tests, Preview Edition* interface provides a learning environment that not only tests you but teaches the material you must know to pass the certification exam. Each question comes with a detailed explanation of the correct answer that often provides reasons the other options are incorrect.

This information helps reinforce the knowledge you already have and also provides practical information you can us on the job.

SOFTWARE REQUIREMENTS

PrepLogic Practice Tests requires a computer with the following:

◆ Microsoft Windows 98, Windows Me, Windows NT 4.0, Windows 2000, or Windows XP.

◆ A 166MHz or faster processor is recommended.

◆ A minimum of 32MB of RAM. As with any Windows application, the more memory, the better your performance.

◆ 10MB of hard drive space.

INSTALLING *PREPLOGIC PRACTICE TESTS, PREVIEW EDITION*

Install *PrepLogic Practice Tests, Preview Edition* by running the setup program on the *PrepLogic Practice Tests, Preview Edition* CD. Follow these instructions to install the software on your computer.

1. Insert the CD into your CD-ROM drive. The Autorun feature of Windows should launch the software. If you have Autorun disabled, click Start and select Run. Go to the root directory of the CD and select setup.exe. Click Open, OK.

2. The Installation Wizard copies the *PrepLogic Practice Tests, Preview Edition* files to your hard drive; adds *PrepLogic Practice Tests, Preview Edition* to your Desktop and to your Program menu; and installs test engine components to the appropriate system folders.

REMOVING *PREPLOGIC PRACTICE TESTS, PREVIEW EDITION* FROM YOUR COMPUTER

If you elect to remove the *PrepLogic Practice Tests, Preview Edition* product from your computer, an uninstall process has been included to ensure that it is removed from your system safely and completely. Follow these instructions to remove *PrepLogic Practice Tests, Preview Edition* from your computer:

1. Select Start, Settings, Control Panel.

2. Double-click the Add/Remove Programs icon.

3. You are presented with a list of software installed on your computer. Select the *PrepLogic Practice Tests, Preview Edition* title you want to remove. Click the Add/Remove button. The software is then removed from your computer.

USING *PREPLOGIC PRACTICE TESTS, PREVIEW EDITION*

PrepLogic is designed to be user friendly and intuitive. Because the software has a smooth learning curve, your time is maximized because you start practicing almost immediately. *PrepLogic Practice Tests, Preview Edition* has two major modes of study: Practice Test and Flash Review.

◆ Using Practice Test mode, you can develop your test-taking abilities as well as your knowledge with the Show Answer option. While taking the test, you can expose the answers along with a detailed explanation of why the given answers are right or wrong. This gives you the ability to better understand the material presented.

◆ Flash Review is designed to reinforce exam topics rather than quiz you. In this mode, you will be shown a series of questions but no answer choices. Instead, a button reveals the correct answer to the question and a full explanation for that answer.

Starting a Practice Test Mode Session

Practice Test mode enables you to control the exam experience in ways that actual certification exams do not allow:

◆ **Enable Show Answer Button**—Activates the Show Answer button allowing you to view the correct answer(s) and a full explanation for each question during the exam. When the feature is disabled, you must wait until after your exam has been graded to view the correct answer(s) and explanation.

◆ **Enable Item Review Button**—Activates the Item Review button, allowing you to view your answer choices, marked questions, and to facilitate navigation between questions.

◆ **Randomize Choices**—Randomize answer choices from one exam session to the next. Makes memorizing question choices more difficult therefore keeps questions fresh and challenging for longer.

To begin studying in Practice Test mode, click the Practice Test radio button from the main exam customization screen to enable the options detailed previously.

To your left, you are presented with the option of selecting the preconfigured practice test or creating your own custom test. The preconfigured test has a fixed time limit and fixed number of questions.

Custom tests allow you to configure the time limit and the number of questions in your exam.

The Preview Edition included with this book includes a single preconfigured practice test. Get the compete set of challenging PrepLogic practice tests at PrepLogic.com to make certain you're ready for the big exam.

Click the Begin Exam button to begin your exam.

Starting a Flash Review Mode Session

Flash Review mode provides an easy way to reinforce topics covered in the practice questions. To begin studying in Flash Review mode, click the Flash Review radio button from the main exam customization screen. Select either the preconfigured practice test or create your own custom test.

Click the Best Exam button to begin your Flash Review of the exam questions.

STANDARD *PREPLOGIC PRACTICE TESTS, PREVIEW EDITION* OPTIONS

The following list describes the function of each of the buttons you see. Depending on the options, some of the buttons will be grayed out and inaccessible or missing completely. Buttons that are appropriate are active. The buttons are as follows:

◆ **Exhibit**—This button is visible if an exhibit is provided to support the question. An exhibit is an image that provides supplemental information necessary to answer the question.

◆ **Item Review**—This button leaves the question window and opens the Item Review screen.

From this screen you will see all questions, your answers, and your marked items. You will also see correct answers listed here when appropriate.

◆ **Show Answer**—This option displays the correct answer with an explanation of why it is correct. If you select this option, the current question is not scored.

◆ **Mark Item**—Check this box to tag a question you want to review further. You can view and navigate your marked items by clicking the Item Review button (if enabled). When grading your exam, you will be notified if you have marked items remaining.

◆ **Previous Item**—View the previous question.

◆ **Next Item**—View the next question.

◆ **Grade Exam**—When you have completed your exam, click to end your exam and view your detailed score report. If you have unanswered or marked items remaining, you will be asked if you would like to continue taking your exam or if you want to view your exam report.

TIME REMAINING

If the test is timed, the time remaining is displayed on the upper-right corner of the application screen. It counts down minutes and seconds remaining to complete the test. If you run out of time, you will be asked if you want to continue taking the test or if you want to end your exam.

YOUR EXAMINATION SCORE REPORT

The Examination Score Report screen appears when the Practice Test mode ends as the result of time expiration, completion of all questions, or your decision to terminate early.

This screen provides a graphical display of your test score with a breakdown of scores by topic domain. The graphical display at the top of the screen compares your overall score with the PrepLogic Exam Competency Score.

The PrepLogic Exam Competency Score reflects the level of subject competency required to pass the vendor's exam. While this score does not directly translate to a passing score, consistently matching or exceeding this score does suggest you possess the knowledge to pass the actual vendor exam.

REVIEW YOUR EXAM

From Your Score Report screen, you can review the exam you just completed by clicking the View Items button. Navigate through the items, viewing the questions, your answers, the correct answers, and the explanations for the questions. You can return to your score report by clicking the View Items button.

GET MORE EXAMS

Each *PrepLogic Practice Tests, Preview Edition* that accompanies your Training Guide contains a single PrepLogic practice test. Certification students worldwide trust PrepLogic Practice Tests to help them pass their IT certification exams the first time.

Purchase the Premium Edition of PrepLogic Practice Tests and get the entire set of new, challenging practice tests for this exam. PrepLogic Practice Tests - Because You Want to Pass the First Time.

CONTACTING PREPLOGIC

If you want to contact PrepLogic for any reason, including information about our extensive line of certification practice tests, we invite you to do so. Please contact us online at www.preplogic.com.

CUSTOMER SERVICE

If you have a damaged product and need a replacement or refund, please call 800-858-7674.

PRODUCT SUGGESTIONS AND COMMENTS

We value your input! Please email your suggestions and comments to feedback@preplogic.com.

LICENSE AGREEMENT

YOU MUST AGREE TO THE TERMS AND CONDITIONS OUTLINED IN THE END USER LICENSE AGREEMENT (EULA) PRESENTED TO YOU DURING THE INSTALLATION PROCESS. IF YOU DO NOT AGREE TO THESE TERMS, DO NOT INSTALL THE SOFTWARE.

Suggested Readings and Resources

.NET USER ASSISTANCE

Your first source for help with any aspect of Visual Basic .NET should be the user assistance resources that Microsoft ships with their .NET products. These include

◆ **.NET Framework Documentation**--All the classes, methods, properties, and other members of the .NET Framework Base Class Library are documented in this help file. This file is installed by the .NET Software Development Kit (SDK) and is also integrated into the Visual Studio .NET help file.

◆ **Visual Studio .NET help file**--This file includes help on all aspects of the Visual Studio interface, as well as a series of walkthroughs and samples to refer to for examples of using particular pieces of code.

◆ **Samples and QuickStart Tutorials**--These are installed by the .NET Framework SDK and are available through Start, Programs, Microsoft .NET Framework SDK, Samples and QuickStart Tutorials. This set of HTML pages shows examples of many aspects of the .NET Framework in both Visual Basic .NET and C# and includes links to both working copies and source code for each example.

BOOKS

◆ Reynolds, Matthew, et al. *Professional VB .NET 2nd Edition.* Wrox, 2002.

◆ Basiura, Russ, et al. *Professional ASP.NET Web Services.* Wrox, 2001.

◆ Box, Don. *Essential .NET Volume I: The Common Language Runtime.* Addison Wesley, 2002.

◆ Burton, Kevin. *.NET Common Language Runtime Unleashed.* Sams Publising, 2002.

◆ Cerami, Ethan. *Web Services Essentials.* O'Reilly, 2002.

◆ Chappell, David. *Understanding .NET.* Addison Wesley, 2001.

◆ Cisco, Steve. *Migrating to Visual Basic .NET.* M&T Books, 2002.

◆ Cornell, Gary and Jonathan Morrison. *Programming VB .NET: A Guide for Experienced Programmers.* Apress, 2002.

◆ Delaney, Kalen. *Inside SQL Server 2000.* Microsoft Press, 2000.

◆ Grimes, Richard. *Developing Applications with Visual Studio .NET.* Addison Wesley, 2002.

◆ Grundgeiger, Dave. *Programming Visual Basic .NET.* O'Reilly, 2002.

◆ Gunderloy, Mike. *ADO and ADO.NET Programming*. Sybex, 2002.

◆ LaMacchia, Brian A., et al. *.NET Framework Security*. Addison Wesley, 2002.

◆ Nathan, Adam. *.NET and COM: The Complete Interoperability Guide*. Sams Publishing, 2002.

◆ Richter, Jeffery. *Applied Microsoft .NET Framework Programming*. Microsoft Press, 2001.

◆ Scribner, Kenn and Mark C. Stiver. *Applied SOAP: Implementing .NET XML Web Services*. Sams Publishing, 2001.

◆ Short, Scott. *Building XML Web Services for the Microsoft .NET Platform*. Microsoft Press, 2000.

◆ Siler, Brian and Jeff Spotts. *Special Edition Using Microsoft Visual Basic .NET*. Que Publishing, 2002.

◆ Symmonds, Nick. *Internationalization and Localization Using Microsoft .NET*. Apress, 2001.

◆ Troelsen, Andrew. *Visual Basic .NET and the .NET Platform*. Apress, 2001.

◆ Vaughn, Bill. *ADO.NET and ADO Examples and Best Practices for VB Programmers*. Apress, 2002.

WEB SITES

◆ `http://msdn.microsoft.com/library/ default.asp?url=/nhp/ Default.asp?contentid=28000519`. The MSDN Web site contains extensive technical documentation on all aspects of .NET development.

◆ `http://www.gotdotnet.com/`. The GotDotNet site is a Microsoft-sponsored community Web site that includes downloads, tools, samples, and user-contributed code.

◆ `http://msdn.microsoft.com/vstudio/ default.asp`. The Visual Studio home page will keep you up-to-date on new versions and fixes for all the Visual Studio .NET applications.

◆ `http://msdn.microsoft.com/architecture/`. The .NET Architecture Center contains a wealth of information on best practices for designing distributed .NET applications.

Index

C

F

Factorial Calculator, 751
  EventLogTraceListener object, 765-766
FCL (.NET Framework Class Library), 25
  exceptions, 221
  VB .NET, 28-29
field-level validation, 245
  CausesValidation property, 246
  ErrorProvider class, 247-250
  Validating event, 246
fields, database tables, 346
File Signing tool, 846
File System Editor, 815-819
File Types Editor, 815, 820-821
FileName property, 127
files
  disco.exe , 550-551
  disk
    locating, 445-446
    transferring data to, 520-522
  DLL, debugging, 782-783
  editing, dialog boxes, 127
  HTML Help, 642
    compiling, 654-656
    contents, 652-654
    creating, 645
    index, 652-654
    links, 651-652
    testing, 654-656
    topic files, 646-651
  HTML Help 1.3, user assistance, 667
  HTML Help 2, 657-658
    compiling, 665-666
    HelpProvider component, 667-669
    index, 663-665
    links, 662

    pop-up help dialog boxes, 670
    table of contents, 663-665
    testing, 665-666
    ToolTip component, 671-672
    topic files, 659-661
    user assistance, 667
  HTML Help SDK, 644
  library, 38
  localization resources, 578-583
    runtime user interface resources, 583-586
  streams, 446-456
  Web references, proxy classes, 555
  WSDL, Web services, 539
  wsdl.exe, command-line options, 553-554
  wsdl.exe , 551-553
FileStream class, 446-450
  code, 449
  members, 448
FileStream.Read method, 448-450
Fill methods, 79-84
filter expressions, 483
Filter property, 127
FilterIndex property, 126
filtering data, 373, 380, 1001
  DataGrid, 396-397
  DataView object, 381-382
  Server Explorer, 373-374
  through servers, 383-385
Finally block, 223, 228-230
Finally statement, 230
FlashWindowEx API, 682-683
Font property, 111
FontDialog components, 125-127
fonts, locating, 92-93
Form class, 26
  inheritance hierarchy, 29-31
  members, 200

heap, defined, 27

HelpButton property, 670

HelpNameSpace property, 669

HelpNavigator property, 669

HelpProvider component, 667-669

hierarchies, 29-31

High Contrast mode, 677

HScrollBar class, 168-170

HTML Help, 642. *See also* HTML Help 1.3; HTML
 Help 2
  files, 642
    compiling, 654-656
    contents, 652-654
    creating, 645
    index, 652-654
    links, 651-652
    testing, 654-656
  topic files, creating, 646-651

HTML Help 1.3, 642
  creating, 643
  user assistance, 667

HTML Help 2, 643
  compiling, 665-666
  creating, 656
    files, 657-658
    links, 662
    projects, 658-659
    topic files, 659-661
    VSHIK, 657
  HelpProvider component, 667-669
  index, 663-665
  pop-up help dialog boxes, 670
  table of contents, 663-665
  testing, 665-666
  ToolTip component, 671-672
  user assistance, 667

HTML Help SDK, 643-644

HTML Help Workshop, 645

I

ICAO airport codes, Web services, 539

ICAO airport codes Web site, 539

Icon dialog box, 817

IDE (integrated development environment), 25-26

Identity interface, 978

images, Graphics class, 84-88

Immediate window, 777

imperative security, 968-969

incremental testing, 743-755

index
  HTML Help 2, creating, 663-665
  HTML Help files, 652-654

inheritance
  defined, 28
  Visual, 55-57
  Windows Forms Designer, 996

Inheritance dialog box, 55

inheritance hierarchy, 29-31

InitializeComponent method, 36, 48

INNER JOIN keyword, 421

input
  dialog boxes, 123-124
  keyboards, 91-92
  users
    enabling controls, 250-251
    validating, 257-259

INSERT statement, 412, 427-428

InsertCommand property, 491

installation
  network-based deployment, 880
  Windows XP Logo Program requirements, 886

J-K

L

Q

R

root elements, 500

running processes, 780-781

runtime callable wrappers (RCW), 616-617

runtime errors, 767

runtime user interface resources, localizing, 583-586

S

sampling, 926-928

satellite assemblies, 315-323

   creating, 1005

SaveFileDialog components, 125-127

schemes, encodings, 586

scripts, database, 890-891

ScrollBar class, members, 169

SDK (Software Development Kit), 643

security

   .NET Framework, 961

     authorization, 976-977

     code access security, 962-974

     custom attributes, 974-976

     declarative security, 968-969

     imperative security, 968-969

     objects, 978-980

     PrincipalPermission class, 981-982

     role memberships, 980-981

   applications, 1015

   assembly runtime policy, 873-875

     zones, 876-877

   code access, 961-962

     permissions, 962-974

   configuring Windows applications

     authorization, 976-977

     objects, 978-980

     PrincipalPermission class, 981-982

     role memberships, 980-981

   custom attributes, configuring Windows applications, 974-976

   declarative, permissions, 968-969

   downloading code from remote sources, 868-871

     zones, 869

   imperative, permissions, 968-969

   role-based, 961

     declarative, 984-985

     IIdentity interface, 978

     IPrincipal interface, 978

security logs, 920

SELECT clause, 419

SELECT statement, 412, 419-427

SelectedIndex property, 149

sending queries to SQL Server databases, 412

   Osql, 414-415

   SQL Query Analyzer, 415-417

   Visual Basic .NET forms, 417-419

   Visual Studio .NET IDE, 412-413

separators, adding to menus, 179

Server Explorer, 373-374

   data connections, 374-375

   object design, 375-377

   objects, drag-and-drop operations, 377-380

   resources, 374

servers

   filtering data through, 383-385

   Web, creating Web services, 542

services

   COM+ components, 621, 623-625

   Web, platform invoke, 625-628. *See also* Web services

Setup Project templates, 808-814

   configuration properties, 813

   customizing, 815

     editors, 815-829

topic files
  HTML Help, 646-651
  HTML Help 2, creating, 659-661
Trace class, 748-750
  members, 749-750
  trace listeners, 754-757
  trace output, 750-754
    code, 751-752
trace listeners, 754-757
  adding to applications, 1008
Trace object, 1008
trace switches, 758
  adding to applications, 1008
  BooleanSwitch class, 758-759
  customizing, 785-786
  TraceSwitch class, 758-762
    code, 760-761
    properties, 759
TRACE symbol, 765
TraceListener class, 755-757
TraceSwitch class, 758-762
  code, 760-761
  properties, 759
tracing
  defined, 742
  programs, 747
    Debug class, 748-754
    Trace class, 748-754
    trace listeners, 754-757
    trace switches, 758-762
TrackBar class, 165-168
  methods, 166
transforming data, 373, 1001
  lookups, 385-390
  Server Explorer, 373-374
TreeView class, 160-165
  members, 160-161

troubleshooting Windows applications, 1014
Trust an Assembly Wizard, 874
Try blocks, 223
  executing with Final block, 230
tuples, database tables, 346
two-way data binding, 359
Type Library Importer, 617-619
types
  assemblies, 326
  Brush objects, 81-84
  certification (Microsoft), 1051-1052
  dialog boxes, 124
  event logs, 915
  HTML links, 652

U

UDDI (Universal Description, Discovery, and Integration), 549
  Web services, 537
UDDI Web site, 549
UI (user interface), 999
  binding data to, 1001
  Certified for Windows Logo Program, 884
  error handling, 999-1000
  localization, 571, 1003
  non-Latin user input, validating, 999
  reading, 1003
  tabs, configuring, 999
  user input, validating, 999
Unable to Apply Changes dialog box, 777
unhandled exceptions, 220-221, 238-241
  Catch blocks, 224
  EventLog class, 239
  UnhandledExceptionEventArgs class, 238

X-Z